DRAMA
CRITICISM

Guide to Gale Literary Criticism Series

For criticism on	Consult these Gale series
Authors now living or who died after December 31, 1959	*CONTEMPORARY LITERARY CRITICISM (CLC)*
Authors who died between 1900 and 1959	*TWENTIETH-CENTURY LITERARY CRITICISM (TCLC)*
Authors who died between 1800 and 1899	*NINETEENTH-CENTURY LITERATURE CRITICISM (NCLC)*
Authors who died between 1400 and 1799	*LITERATURE CRITICISM FROM 1400 TO 1800 (LC)* *SHAKESPEAREAN CRITICISM (SC)*
Authors who died before 1400	*CLASSICAL AND MEDIEVAL LITERATURE CRITICISM (CMLC)*
Black writers of the past two hundred years	*BLACK LITERATURE CRITICISM (BLC)*
Authors of books for children and young adults	*CHILDREN'S LITERATURE REVIEW (CLR)*
Dramatists	*DRAMA CRITICISM (DC)*
Hispanic writers of the late nineteenth and twentieth centuries	*HISPANIC LITERATURE CRITICISM (HLC)*
Native North American writers and orators of the eighteenth, nineteenth, and twentieth centuries	*NATIVE NORTH AMERICAN LITERATURE (NNAL)*
Poets	*POETRY CRITICISM (PC)*
Short story writers	*SHORT STORY CRITICISM (SSC)*
Major authors from the Renaissance to the present	*WORLD LITERATURE CRITICISM, 1500 TO THE PRESENT (WLC)*

ISSN 1056-4349

DRAMA CRITICISM

Criticism of the Most Significant and Widely Studied
Dramatic Works from All the World's Literatures

VOLUME 7

Lawrence J. Trudeau, Editor

GALE

DETROIT · NEW YORK · TORONTO · LONDON

STAFF

Lawrence J. Trudeau, *Editor*

Kathy D. Darrow, Debra A. Wells, *Assistant Editors*

Susan Trosky, *Permissions Manager*

Kimberly F. Smilay, *Permissions Specialist*
Sarah Chesney, *Permissions Associate*
Stephen Cusack, Kelly Quin, *Permissions Assistants*

Victoria B. Cariappa, *Research Manager*

Michele P. LaMeau, *Research Specialist*
Julie C. Daniel, Tamara C. Nott, Tracie A. Richardson,
Norma Sawaya, Cheryl L. Warnock,
Research Associates

Mary Beth Trimper, *Production Director*
Deborah Milliken, *Production Assistant*

C.J. Jonik, *Desktop Publisher*
Randy Bassett, *Image Database Supervisor*
Michael Ansari, Robert Duncan, *Scanner Operator*
Pamela Reed, *Photography Coordinator*

Library of Congress Catalog Card Number 92-648805
ISBN 0-8103-5532-9
ISSN 1056-4349

10 9 8 7 6 5 4 3 2 1

Contents

Preface

*D*rama Criticism (*DC*) is principally intended for beginning students of literature and theater as well as the average playgoer. The series is therefore designed to introduce readers to the most frequently studied playwrights of all time periods and nationalities and to present discerning commentary on dramatic works of enduring interest. Furthermore, *DC* seeks to acquaint the reader with the uses and functions of criticism itself. Selected from a diverse body of commentary, the essays in *DC* offer insights into the authors and their works but do not require that the reader possess a wide background in literary studies. Where appropriate, reviews of important productions of the plays discussed are also included to give students a heightened awareness of drama as a dynamic art form, one that many claim is fully realized only in performance.

DC was created in response to suggestions by the staffs of high school, college, and public libraries. These librarians observed a need for a series that assembles critical commentary on the world's most renowned dramatists in the same manner as Gale's *Short Story Criticism* (*SSC*) and *Poetry Criticism* (*PC*), which present material on writers of short fiction and poetry. Although playwrights are covered in such Gale literary criticism series as *Contemporary Literary Criticism* (*CLC*), *Twentieth-Century Literary Criticism* (*TCLC*), *Nineteenth-Century Literature Criticism* (*NCLC*), *Literature Criticism from 1400 to 1800* (*LC*), and *Classical and Medieval Literature Criticism* (*CMLC*), *Drama Criticism* directs more concentrated attention on individual dramatists than is possible in the broader, survey-oriented entries in these Gale series. Commentary on the works of William Shakespeare may be found in *Shakespearean Criticism* (*SC*).

Scope of the Series

By collecting and organizing commentary on dramatists, *DC* assists students in their efforts to gain insight into literature, achieve better understanding of the texts, and formulate ideas for papers and assignments. A variety of interpretations and assessments is offered, allowing students to pursue their own interests and promoting awareness that literature is dynamic and responsive to many different opinions.

Each volume of *DC* presents:

- 8-10 entries

- authors and works representing a wide range of nationalities and time periods

- a diversity of viewpoints and critical opinions.

Organization of an Author Entry

Each author entry consists of some or all of the following elements, depending on the scope and complexity of the criticism:

- The **author heading** consists of the playwright's most commonly used name, followed by birth and death dates. If an author consistently wrote under a pseudonym, the pseudonym is listed in the author heading and the real name given in parentheses on the first line of the introduction. Also located at the beginning of the introduction are any name variations under which the dramatist wrote, including transliterated forms of the names of authors whose languages use nonroman alphabets.

- A **portrait** of the author is included when available. Most entries also feature illustrations of people, places, and events pertinent to a study of the playwright and his or her works. When appropriate, photographs of the plays in performance are also presented.

- The **biographical and critical introduction** contains background information that familiarizes the reader with the author and the critical debates surrounding his or her works.

- The list of **principal works** is divided into two sections, each of which is organized chronologically by date of first performance. If this has not been conclusively determined, the composition or publication date is used. The first section of the principal works list contains the author's dramatic pieces. The second section provides information on the author's major works in other genres.

- Whenever available, **author commentary** is provided. This section consists of essays or interviews in which the dramatist discusses his or her own work or the art of playwriting in general.

- Essays offering **overviews and general studies of the dramatist's entire literary career** give the student broad perspectives on the writer's artistic development, themes and concerns that recur in several of his or her works, the author's place in literary history, and other wide-ranging topics.

- **Criticism of individual plays** offers the reader in-depth discussions of a select number of the author's most important works. In some cases, the criticism is divided into two sections, each arranged chronologically. When a significant performance of a play can be identified (typically, the premier of a twentieth-century work), the first section of criticism will feature **production reviews** of this staging. Most entries include sections devoted to **critical commentary** that assesses the literary merit of the selected plays. When necessary, essays are carefully excerpted to focus on the work under consideration; often, however, essays and reviews are reprinted in their entirety.

- As an additional aid to students, the critical essays and excerpts are often prefaced by **explanatory annotations**. These notes provide several types of useful information, including the critic's reputation and approach to literary studies as well as the scope and significance of the criticism that follows.

- A complete **bibliographic citation**, designed to help the interested reader locate the original essay or book, precedes each piece of criticism.

- The **further reading list** at the end of each entry comprises additional studies of the dramatist. It is divided into sections that help students quickly locate the specific information they need.

Other Features

- A **cumulative author index** lists all the authors who have appeared in *DC* and Gale's other Literature Criticism Series, as well as cross-references to related titles published by Gale, including *Contemporary Authors* and *Dictionary of Literary Biography*. A complete listing of the series included appears at the beginning of the index.

- A **cumulative nationality index** lists each author featured in *DC* by nationality, followed by the number of the *DC* volume in which the author appears.

- A **cumulative title index** lists in alphabetical order the individual plays discussed in the criticism contained in *DC*. Each title is followed by the author's name and the corresponding volume and page number(s) where commentary on the work may be located. Translations and variant titles are cross-referenced to the title of the play in its original language so that all references to the work are combined in one listing.

A Note to the Reader

When writing papers, students who quote directly from any volume in *Drama Criticism* may use the following general formats to footnote reprinted criticism. The first example pertains to material drawn from periodicals, the second to materials reprinted from books.

[1]Susan Sontag, "Going to the Theater, Etc.," *Partisan Review* XXXI, No. 3 (Summer 1964), 389-94; excerpted and reprinted in *Drama Criticism,* Vol. 1, ed. Lawrence J. Trudeau (Detroit: Gale Research, 1991), pp. 17-20.

[2]Eugene M. Waith, *The Herculean Hero in Marlowe, Chapman, Shakespeare and Dryden* (Chatto & Windus, 1962); excerpted and reprinted in *Drama Criticism,* Vol. 1, ed. Lawrence J. Trudeau (Detroit: Gale Research, 1991), pp. 237-47.

Suggestions are Welcome

Readers who wish to suggest authors to appear in future volumes of *DC,* or who have other suggestions, are cordially invited to contact the editor.

Acknowledgments

The editors wish to thank the copyright holders of the excerpted criticism included in this volume and the permissions managers of many book and magazine publishing companies for assisting us in securing reproduction rights. We are also grateful to the staffs of the Detroit Public Library, the Library of Congress, the University of Detroit Mercy Library, Wayne State University Purdy/Kresge Library Complex, and the University of Michigan Libraries for making their resources available to us. Following is a list of the copyright holders who have granted us permission to reproduce material in this volume of *DC*. Every effort has been made to trace copyright, but if omissions have been made, please let us know.

COPYRIGHTED EXCERPTS IN *DC*, VOLUME 7, WERE REPRODUCED FROM THE FOLLOWING PERIODICALS:

American Journal of Philology, v. 107, Spring, 1986; v. 166, Summer, 1995. Copyright © 1986, 1995 by The Johns Hopkins University Press. All rights reserved. Both reproduced by permission. —*Artforum,* v. XXIII, March, 1985 for a review of "Swimming to Cambodia" by John Howell. © 1985 Artforum International Magazine, Inc. Reproduced by permission of the publisher and the author.—*Australian Journal of French Studies,* v. XXI, January-April, 1984 for "Marivaux's 'Jeu de l'amour et 'de la raison'" by Thomas M. Carr. Copyright © 1984 by *Australian Journal of French Studies.* Reproduced by permission of the publisher and the author.—*California Studies in Classical Antiquity,* v. 1, 1968. Reproduced by permission.—*CLA Journal,* v. XXXII, December, 1988. Copyright, 1988 by The College Language Association. Used by permission of The College Language Association.—*The Classical Journal,* v. 62, October, 1966. © Classical Association of the Middle West and South, Inc., 1966. Reproduced by permission.—*The Classical World,* v. 70, January, 1977; v. 73, December, 1979-January, 1980. Copyright © 1977, 1980 by The Classical Association of The Atlantic States, Inc. Both reproduced by permission. —*Drama and Theatre,* v. 12, Spring, 1975 for "'Equus': Modern Myth in the Making" by Russell Vandenbroucke. Copyright 1975 by the State University of New York. Reproduced by permission of the author.—*Drama: The Quarterly Theatre Review,* n. 135, January, 1980 for a review of "Amadeus," by John Russell Taylor. Reprinted by permission of the Peters, Fraser & Dunlop Group Ltd.—*Educational Theatre Journal,* v. 25, December, 1973. © 1973 University College Theatre Association of the American Theatre Association. Reproduced by permission.—*ELH,* v. 23, March, 1956. Copyright © 1956 by The Johns Hopkins University Press. All rights reserved. Reproduced by permission.—*Financial Times,* November 5, 1979. © Financial Times Limited 1979. Reproduced by permission.—*Greek, Roman, and Byzantine Studies,* v. 9, 1968. Reproduced by permission.—*The Hudson Review,* v. XXXIV, Summer, 1981. Copyright © 1981 by The Hudson Review, Inc. Reproduced by permission.—*The Journal of Commonwealth Literature,* v. XVII, 1982 for "Big Night Music: Derek Walcott's *Dream on Monkey Mountain* and the 'Splendours of Imagination'" by Robert Elliott Fox. Copyright by the author. Reprinted with the kind permission of Bowker-Saur, a division of Reed-Elsevier (UK) Ltd.—*MLN,* v. 82, May, 1967. © copyright 1967 by The Johns Hopkins University Press. All rights reserved. Reproduced by permission.—*The New Republic,* v. 184, March 28, 1981. Copyright © 1981 The New Republic, Inc. Reproduced by permission of The New Republic./ v. LXII, April 16, 1930. Copyright 1930, renewed 1956 The New Republic, Inc. Reproduced by permission of The New Republic.—*The New Statesman,* v. 86, August 3, 1973; v. 98, November 9, 1979. © 1973, 1979 The Statesman & Nation Publishing Co. Ltd. Both reproduced by permission.—*Newsweek,* v. LXXIX, June 19, 1972; v. LXXXIII, June 10, 1974. Copyright © 1972, 1974, Newsweek, Inc. All rights reserved. Both reproduced by permission.—*New York Magazine,* v. 5, June 26, 1972; v. 7, June 17, 1974; v. 14, March 2, 1981; v. 19, March 24, 1986. Copyright © 1997 K-III Corporation. All rights reserved. All Reproduced with the permission of New York Magazine.—*The New York Times,* March 15, 1971; March 21, 1971; April 4, 1971; June 18, 1972; September 3, 1973; June 3, 1974; November 16, 1984; March 9, 1986. Copyright © 1971, 1972, 1973, 1974, 1984, 1986 by The New York Times Company. All reproduced by permission.—*The New York Times Magazine,* March, 8, 1987. Copyright © 1987 by The New York Times Company. Reproduced by permission.—*The New Yorker,* v. XLVII, March 27, 1971; v. XLVII, June 21, 1971; v. XLVIII, June 24, 1972; v. L, June 10, 1974; v. LXII. Copyright © 1971, 1972, 1974 by The New Yorker Magazine, Inc. All reproduced by permission./ March 24, 1986 for "Murder Most Foul" by Brendan Gill. Copyright © 1986 by the author. Reproduced by permission.—*Performing Arts Journal,*

COPYRIGHTED EXCERPTS IN *DC,* VOLUME 7, WERE REPRODUCED FROM THE FOLLOWING BOOKS:

List of Playwrights Covered in *DC*

Frank Chin
1940-

(Full name Frank Chew Chin, Jr.)

INTRODUCTION

Chin has played an important role in the development of Asian American literature. In his plays and other works, Chin has sought to overthrow the demeaning stereotypes imposed on Chinese Americans by white society. In *The Chickencoop Chinaman* and *The Year of the Dragon* he presents characters who struggle with the history (written from the perspective of white culture) of Asians in the United States, and who strive to forge an essentially American identity that nevertheless recognizes their cultural roots.

BIOGRAPHICAL INFORMATION

Chin was born in Berkeley, California, and was raised in the Chinatowns of Oakland and San Francisco. He attended the University of California at Berkeley and won a fellowship to the Writer's Workshop at the University of Iowa before receiving his bachelor's degree from the University of California at Santa Barbara in 1965. After graduation, he took a job with the Southern Pacific Railroad, becoming the first Chinese American brakeman in the company's history. Chin left the railroad in 1966 and began writing and producing documentaries for KING-TV in Seattle, Washington. Chin began his dramatic career in the early 1970s, staging *The Chickencoop Chinaman* in 1972 and *The Year of the Dragon* two years later. Both plays were produced off-Broadway by the American Place Theatre, making Chin the first Asian American to have work presented on a mainstream New York stage. In 1973 Chin formed the Asian American Theatre Workshop in San Francisco, and he remained its director until 1977. Since the 1980s Chin has had little involvement with theater, preferring to write fiction and essays on Chinese and Japanese history, culture, and literature. He has taught courses on Asian American subjects at San Francisco State University, the University of California at Berkeley, Davis, and Santa Barbara, and at the University of Oklahoma at Norman. He has also received a number of awards and fellowships throughout his career.

MAJOR WORKS

Chin's best-known plays, *The Chickencoop Chinaman* and *The Year of the Dragon,* were staged early 1970s, and the latter was aired on PBS television in 1975. *The Chicken-coop Chinaman* concerns Tam Lum, a documentary filmmaker in search of his own identity as a Chinese American. Tam feels alienated from both Chinese and American cultures: American born, he knows Chinese culture only indirectly, and can speak little of the language; being of Chinese ancestry, however, he is isolated from and stereotyped by white American society. In the course of the play he lashes out verbally with wit and anger, rejecting the myths surrounding Asian Americans but finding nothing to replace them. However, as the play ends, Tam is shown preparing Chinese food and reminiscing about the Iron Moonhunter, a train in Chinese American legend, built from materials stolen from the railroad companies. Thus Chin suggests Tam's first efforts toward building an identity based on elements of the Chinese American experience. *The Year of the Dragon* also focuses on the search for identity but does so in the context of a Chinese American family. In this play Fred Eng, as a tour guide to San Francisco's Chinatown, panders to stereotypes of Chinese Americans. He also plays the role of dutiful son to his father, Pa Eng, a domineering figure who is now dying. Fred longs to leave Chinatown but has sacrificed his desires in order to earn money to pay college expenses for his sister, who has moved to Boston and married a white man. Fred's younger brother Johnny, meanwhile, is descending to a life of crime. Fred wants his brother to get away from Chinatown, but Pa Eng opposes the idea. In a confrontation between Fred and his father on this issue, Pa Eng dies, never having publicly acknowledged his son's worth. The play closes with Fred still in Chinatown, continuing to play the hated role of Chinatown tour guide.

CRITICAL RECEPTION

Chin is recognized as an important voice in Asian American drama, even though he has withdrawn from active participation in the theater. Regarding his rejection of the contemporary theatrical scene, Chin has remarked, "Asian American theatre is dead without ever having been born, and American theatre, like American writing has found and nurtured willing Gunga Dins, happy white racist tokens, with which to pay their lip service to yellows and call it dues. . . . I am out of theatre. I will not work with any theatre, producer, writer, director, or actor who has played and lives the stereotype." Such views, expressed within his plays as well as in essays and interviews, have made Chin a controversial figure. Some reviewers have been put off by the bitterness of Chin's outlook and have criticized his plays as strident. John Simon has likened Chin's plays to soap opera and censured his "tendency to attitudinize." Elaine H. Kim has detected an ambivalence on Chin's part toward his characters. In his plays, she states, "Chin flails out at the emasculating effects of oppression, but he accepts his oppressors' definition of 'masculinity.' The result is unresolved tension between contempt and desire to fight for his Asian American characters." David Hsin-Fu Wand, on the other hand, has interpreted this ambivalence as reflective of Chin's own internal conflicts: "The voices of his characters in the plays are basically the conflicting voices of his Chinese and American identities." Dorothy Ritsuko McDonald has placed this division within the context of the playwright's concern with history; Chin, she argues, possesses a "sense of Chinese American history as a valiant, vital part of the history of the American West, a history he believes his own people, under the stress of white racism, have forgotten or wish to forget in their eagerness to be assimilated into the majority culture." Chin's work, then, attempts to reverse this process, rejecting assimilation and recuperating what historically was cast off by Asian Americans: their differences from the dominant culture.

PRINCIPAL WORKS

PLAYS

The Chickencoop Chinaman 1972
The Year of the Dragon 1974
Gee, Pop! . . . A Real Cartoon 1974
America More or Less [with Amiri Baraka and Leslie Marmon Silko] 1976
Lullaby [with Silko] 1976
American Peek-a-Boo Kabuki, World War II and Me 1985
Flood of Blood: A Fairy Tale 1988

OTHER MAJOR WORKS

Seattle Repertory Theatre: Act Two (television documentary) 1966
The Bel Canto Carols (television documentary) 1966
A Man and His Music (television documentary) 1967
Ed Sierer's New Zealand (television documentary) 1967
Seafair Preview (television documentary) 1967
The Year of the Ram (television documentary) 1967
And Still Champion . . . ! The Story of Archie Moore (television documentary) 1967
Mary (television documentary) 1969
Rainlight Rainvision (television documentary) 1969
Chinaman's Chance (television documentary) 1971
Aiiieeeee! An Anthology of Asian American Writers [editor, with others] (anthology) 1974
Yardbird Reader, Volume 3 [editor, with Shawn Wong] (anthology) 1974
The Chinaman Pacific & Frisco R.R. Co. (short stories) 1988
Rescue at Wild Boar Forest (comic book) 1988
The Water Margin, or Shui Hu (comic book) 1989
Lin Chong's Revenge (comic book) 1989
Donald Duk (novel) 1991

The Big Aiiieeeee! An Anthology of Chinese American and Japanese American Literature [editor, with others] (anthology) 1991
Gunga Din Highway (novel) 1994

OVERVIEWS AND GENERAL STUDIES

David Hsin-Fu Wand (essay date 1978)

SOURCE: "The Chinese-American Literary Scene: A Galaxy of Poets and a Lone Playwright," in *Proceedings of the Comparative Literature Symposium,* Vol. IX, 1978, pp. 121-46.

[*In the excerpt below, Wand asserts that in his plays Chin has "projected onto the stage his own internal conflicts."*]

Although Frank Chin has written prose-fiction and some occasional poems, he is first and foremost a dramatist. Like the protagonists (or heroes), Tam Lum in *The Chickencoop Chinaman* and Fred Eng in *The Year of the Dragon,* "his own 'normal' speech jumps between black and white rhythms and accents." Sometimes, he probably feels like Tam Lum that he has "no real language of my own to make sense with, so out comes everybody else's trash that don't conceive." The protagonists of his two plays are both in conflict, obsessed with the problem of identity. Tam (short for Tampax) Lum in *The Chickencoop Chinaman,* who has been victimized by the white world that surrounds him, is ambivalent toward the Chinese, as characterized by the following dialogue couched in irony:

> *Robbie*: You're Chinese aren't you? I like Chinese people.
>
> *Tam*: Me too. They're nice and quiet aren't they?

This ambivalence is further shown by Tam Lum's acceptance of the Lone Ranger as a hero. In his list of characters, Frank Chin describes the Lone Ranger as follows:

> A legendary white racist with the funk of the West mouldering in his blood. In his senility, he still loves racistly, blesses racistly, shoots straight and is coocoo with the notion that white folks are not white folks but just plain folks.

In the action of the play, the Lone Ranger not only gets away with shooting a silver bullet into Tam Lum's hand, but also lectures him, as he rides away:

> China boys, you be legendary obeyers of the law, legendary humble, legendary passive. Thank me now and I'll let you get back to Chinatown preservin your culture.

He further insults Tam Lum by making him a "honorary white" and relegates him to the company of Pearl Buck, Charlie Chan, and Helen Keller. To Frank Chin, Helen Keller, who lacks a voice of her own, is the image of a passive Oriental. Early in *The Chickencoop Chinaman*, Tam Lum has remarked about Helen Keller ironically:

> Helen Keller overcame her handicaps without riot! She overcame handicaps without looting! She overcame handicaps without violence! And you Chinks and Japs can too.

Not contented with being an "honorary white" or whitemen's pet Chinaman, Tam Lum tries to find a voice of his own to articulate his own consciousness. He lashes out at the synthetic Chinamen, "who are made, not born—out of junk imports, lies, railroad scrap iron, dirty jokes, broken bottles, cigar smoke, Cosquilla Indian blood, wino spit, and lots of milk of amnesia." He articulates his own agony by shouting:

> [I was] no more born than nylon or acrylic. For I am a Chinaman! A miracle synthetic. Drip dry and machine washable.

In *The Chickencoop Chinaman,* Tam Lum has only one close friend, Kenji, a Japanese-American "research dentist" who lives in the depth of Pittsburgh's black slum called "Oakland." Kenji, who gathers around him some bizarre characters living at his expense, shares with Tam Lum the problem of identity. Nicknamed "BlackJap Kenji," the dentist denies that he is a "copycat," that he is imitating black people:

> I know I live with 'em, I talk like 'em, I dress . . . maybe even eat what they eat and don't mess with, so what if I don't mess with other Orientals . . . Asians, whatever, blah, blah, blah . . .

He also goes on to state:

> I'm not Japanese! Tam ain't no Chinese! And don't give me any of that "If-you-don't-have-that-Oriental-culture, -baby, -all-you've-got-is-the-color-of-your-skin," bullshit. . . .

Living in a black ghetto and going to a school where the majority were black, Kenji had to adapt in order to survive:

> Schools was all blacks and Mexicans. We [Kenji and Tam Lum] were kids in school, and you either walked and talked right in the yard, or got the shit beat outa you every day, ya understand? But that Tam was always what you might say . . . "The Pacesetter." Whatever was happenin with hair, or the latest color, man—Sometimes he looked pretty exotic, you know, shades, high greasy hair, spitcurls, purple shiney shirt, with skull cufflinks and Frisko jeans worn like they was fallin off his ass. "BlackJap Kenji" I used to be called and hated yellow-people. You look around and see where I'm livin . . . and it looks like I still do, Pittsburgh ain't exactly famous for no Chinatown or Li'l Tokyo, you know.

Here Kenji has given a brilliant explanation of his strange identity. Having lived as a minority in the heart of a black ghetto, he has adopted the values and *mores* of his immediate environment. From the psychological point of view, introjection is what made him more black than Japanese in behavior.

The plot of *The Chickencoop Chinaman* revolves around Tam Lum's coming to Pittsburgh to make a documentary film about a black boxer and to interview Charley Popcorn, whom the boxer has claimed to be his real father. But Charley Popcorn, who runs a pornographic movie house in Pittsburgh, denies that he is the father and claims that he was only the boxer's manager. Here we find another case of the problem of identity. Perhaps the boxer has chosen to live with the myth, just as Tam Lum, since his childhood, has chosen the Lone Ranger as his cultural hero and expected to find Chinese eyes behind his mask. The problem of identity is never resolved for either Tam Lum or Kenji in the course of the play, but in the last scene Tam Lum ends up in the kitchen, whetting his meat cleaver. This meat cleaver, like Frank Chin's own pen, may chop away much nonsense about white America's stereotyped images of the silent and docile Orientals.

As compared with *The Chickencoop Chinaman*, Chin's second play, *The Year of the Dragon,* has more recognizable Chinese characters, because all the conflicts and headaches take place in an old apartment located in San Francisco's Chinatown. Fred Eng, the protagonist of the play, shares with Tam Lum his eloquence and he uses it to "badmouth" tourists who come to gawk at Chinatown. Making his living as a Chinatown tour guide, he still lives at the Chinatown apartment of his parents. Although he is already in his forties, he cannot get away from his parents, partly because of the antiquated Chinese tradition of filial duty and partly because of self-doubts and internal conflicts. Fred finds his antagonist in his father, who rules the family with an iron hand. The family affair is further complicated by the arrival of "China Mama," the first wife Pa left behind in China in 1935. Ma Eng, American-born and raised, tries hard to be a peacemaker in the family, but it is a thankless task because there is a real conflict of three cultures. The three cultures are represented by the traditional Chinese ways of Pa Eng and "China Mama," the Chinese-American ways of herself and Fred, and the assimilated American ways of Sissy and Johnny, Fred's younger sister and brother. Sissy manages to escape from the problem of identity by marrying a white American and living away in Boston. But when she visits her parents in San Francisco, she finds herself caught in the storm of the conflict. Johnny, who can hardly speak a word of Chinese, has become a tough street kid, plagued by a sense of displacement. Fred Eng, born in China but raised in America, tries to help his younger brother and urges him to move away from home. Torn by filial piety for his parents on the one hand and hatred for the iron-clad Chinese tradition on the other, he lashes out at Pa Eng, the family patriarch, who retaliates by threatening to die. The generation gap or lack of communication between the generations may remind some

Chinese readers of that in Pa Chin's novel, *Family* (1931). The protagonist in *Family* tries to discover his identity and chart a new course for his own generation. He rejects the tradition of the past as irrelevant to his time.

As Bernard Shaw once said, "Without conflict there is no drama," Frank Chin has projected onto the stage his own internal conflicts in the two plays, *The Chickencoop Chinaman* and *The Year of the Dragon.* The voices of his characters in the plays are basically the conflicting voices of his Chinese and his American identities. . . . Frank Chin shows a sense of humor. His humor is shown through the dialogue and the characterization in his plays. . . . His humor is mordant and bitter. In this respect, he might be more American than Chinese, an heir of Mark Twain, who wrote such dark tales as "The Man that Corrupted Hadleyburg" and "The Mysterious Stranger," rather than a literary descendant of Chuang Tzu and the classical Chinese poet-drunkards. But his contribution to the stage is substantial: for the first time in the theater there is an authentic Chinese-American voice. He has demolished the stage Chinaman with his plays and succeeded in articulating his own consciousness. In a strange but different way, Frank Chin's work in the theater reminds us of the effort of that Irish genius, James Joyce, who tries to "forge in the smithy of my soul the uncreated conscience of my race," and, in Frank Chin's case, "the race" is neither the Chinese of the distant land nor the American of the white establishment, but the hitherto unheard and unsung world of the Chinese-Americans.

Dorothy Ritsuko McDonald (essay date 1981)

SOURCE: An introduction to *"The Chickencoop Chinaman"* and *"The Year of the Dragon": Two Plays by Frank Chin,* University of Washington Press, 1981, pp. ix-xxix.

[*In the essay below, McDonald analyzes Chin's treatment of Chinese American history in his plays.*]

1. THE AUTHOR'S SENSE OF HISTORY

"I was born in Berkeley, California in 1940, far from Oakland's Chinatown where my parents lived and worked," begins Frank Chin in his own profile. "I was sent away to the Motherlode country where I was raised through the War. Then back to Chinatowns Oakland and San Francisco. . . ." When offered a fellowship in 1961 for the State University of Iowa's Writer's Workshop, Chin accepted, but soon he was back in the West. "I was the first Chinese-American brakeman on the Southern Pacific Railroad, the first Chinaman to ride the engines. . . . fine riding but I left the rails."

Chinatown, Motherlode country (the Sierra Nevadas), railroads, Chinaman—these are key words for Frank Chin, for they denote his sense of Chinese American history as a valiant, vital part of the history of the American West, a history he believes his own people, under the stress of white racism, have forgotten or wish to forget in their eagerness to be assimilated into the majority culture. But the cost of acceptance has been great, especially for the Chinese male, who finds himself trapped by a stereotype: supposedly lacking in assertiveness, creativity, and aggressiveness, he is characterized as passive, obedient, humble, and effeminate.

For Chin, however, the Chinese men ("Chinamans" as distinguished from assimilated Chinese Americans) who left their families for the New World in the nineteenth century were masculine and heroic, like other "explorers of the unknown—seekers after gold, the big break, the new country . . ." ["Back Talk," *News of the American Place Theatre* 3 May 1972]. But the Chinese pioneers encountered a systematic and violent racism which by now has been well documented. Even Mark Twain, who harbored his own prejudice against the Indians of the West, remarked [in *Roughing It*] on the unjust treatment of the Chinese:

> Any white man can swear a Chinaman's life away in the courts, but no Chinaman can testify against a white man. Ours is the "land of the free"—nobody denies that—nobody challenges it. (Maybe it is be-cause we won't let other people testify.) As I write, news comes that in broad daylight in San Francisco, some boys have stoned an inoffensive Chinaman to death and although a large crowd witnessed the shame-ful deed, no one interfered.

To Chin, Chinatowns were also the products of racism. That the Chinese themselves clustered together to preserve their alien culture is for him a myth: "The railroads created a detention camp and called it 'Chinatown.' The details of that creation have been conveniently forgotten or euphemized into a state of sweet confusion. The men who lived through the creation are dying out, unheard and ignored. When they die, no one will know it was not us that created a game preserve for Chinese and called it 'Chinatown'" ["Confessions of the Chinatown Cowboy," *Bulletin of Concerned Asian Scholars* 4, Fall 1972].

Given this historical perspective, is it any wonder that echoes of the West would resound in the work of this fifth-generation American, imbued with the aborted dreams of the hardworking, manly goldminers and railroad builders of his past? In Chin's first play, *The Chickencoop Chinaman,* the hero, Tam Lum, tells his children of the pioneers' old American dream:

> Grandmaw heard thunder in the Sierra hundreds of miles away and listened for the Chinaman-known Iron Moonhunter, that train built by Chinamans who knew they'd never be given passes to ride the rails they laid. So of all American railroaders, only they sung no songs, told no jokes, drank no toasts to the ol'

iron horse, but stole themselves some iron on the way, slowly stole up a pile of steel, children, and hid there in the granite face of the Sierra and builded themselves a wild engine to take them home. Every night, children, grandmaw listened in the kitchen, waiting, til the day she died.

The Iron Moonhunter, that seeker after the dream, carries the memories and hopes of the proud Chinamen who laid rails across the West.

Chin's grandfather worked as a steward on the Southern Pacific and owned a watch with a train engraved upon it. "I took my grandfather's watch and worked on the Southern Pacific," says Chin. "I rode in the engines up front. . . . I rode in the cabooses where no Chinaman had ever ridden before. I was hired with the first batch of blacks to go braking for the SP, in the 60s when the fair employment legislation went into effect. (Ride with me grandpa, at least it's not the steward service. You get home more often now.)"

In his essay "Confessions of the Chinatown Cowboy," from which the previous quote was taken, Chin describes that rare Western breed, the modern-day Chinaman, in poet and labor-organizer Ben Fee: "a word of mouth legend, a bare knuckled unmasked man, a Chinaman loner out of the old West, a character out of Chinese swordslingers, a fighter. The kind of Chinaman we've been taught to ignore, and forget if we didn't want America to drive Chinatown out of town."

It was Ben Fee who called Chin the "Chinatown Cowboy" for the dramatic black outfit he wore during their first meeting. "A Chinaman dressed for a barndance," says Chin of his younger self, "solid affectation."

Despite the self-irony displayed here, the black-garbed, two-fang-buckled Chin is obviously no assimilated Chinese; he is declaring his aggressive masculinity and claiming the history of the American West as his own. For the unwary reader, then, who rigidly associates Asian Americans with Asian culture and not American history or culture, some passages in Chin's plays can be disconcerting if not downright incomprehensible or offensive. To such a reader, the meaning of Tam's lyrical monologue on the Iron Moonhunter would be lost. And what of the Lone Ranger metaphor that dominates the balance of the play? Aware that Asians were excluded from American heroism, Tam Lum during his boyhood had idolized the black-haired Lone Ranger, whose mask, he thought, hid his "slanty" eyes. But in a farcical scene the Ranger is revealed to be a broken-down white racist. A train whistle is heard, and the young Tam recognizes it as that of the Iron Moonhunter. But the Ranger cautions Tam and his friend: "Hear no evil, ya hear me? China boys, you be legendary obeyers of the law, legendary humble, legendary passive. Thank me now and I'll let ya get back to Chinatown preservin your culture!"

Chin's historical perspective is similarly found in his next play, *The Year of the Dragon,* set in San Francisco's Chinatown. The theme of the West is sounded by the family in various ways, especially in the climactic last scene when Pa Eng dies suddenly while struggling with Fred, who later says, "I woulda like to have packed him up into the Sierras and buried him by the railroad . . . I was saving that one for last. . . ."

2. An Endangered Species

If Chin seeks to preserve the history of the first pioneering Chinamen, he nonetheless looks forward in time and sees—as does Fred Eng in *The Year of the Dragon*—the Chinese Americans as an "endangered species." Not only are the Chinese women like Mattie marrying out white at a rapidly increasing rate, in part no doubt due to the present "sissy" image of the Chinese male, but women have always been outnumbered by men. Historically, the series of discriminatory exclusion laws (1882-1924) made it difficult, then impossible, for both alien and American Chinese to bring their wives from China. Chinatown was therefore essentially a bachelor society. In addition, an American-born woman lost her citizenship when she married a person ineligible for citizenship; and by the Exclusion Act of 1882, immigrant Chinese could not be naturalized. These laws were repealed in 1943 during the Second World War when China was an ally of the United States.

In *The Year of the Dragon,* it is mainly through the American-born Ma Eng that the reader discerns this historical discrimination. She tells Ross: "My grandmother, Ross . . . she used to tell me she used to come home oh, crying like a sieve cuz all she saw was blocks and blocks of just men. No girls at all. She was very lonely." Moreover, she says of her daughter: "You know . . . my Sissy is a very limited edition. Only twenty Chinese babies born in San Francisco in 1938." When she discovers that the mysterious visitor in her home is her husband's first wife, who had to be left in China because of the Exclusion Act of 1924 and now could enter America because of its repeal, she says: "I coulda been deported just for marrying your pa. The law scared me to death but it make your pa so thrilling to me. I'm American of Chinese descent. . . ."

However, had Ma Eng, by some stretch of imagination, desired to marry a white American, it would have been illegal at that time, for in California such an intermarriage was forbidden in 1906 by a law which was not nullified until 1948. But at the time of the play not only are the Matties marrying out white, so are the males. Thus, Fred tells Ross, "it's a rule not the exception for us to marry out white. Out in Boston, I might even marry me a blonde." Later, while urging his juvenile-delinquent brother, Johnny, to leave Chinatown for Boston and college, he adds, "Get a white girl while you're young. You'll never regret it."

This urge toward assimilation and extinction is similarly found in *The Chickencoop Chinaman* when Tam Lum, though a loner in the play, is revealed to have been previously married to a white woman who had deserted him, leaving with his two children to take a white husband. During Tam's subsequent effort to restore his dignity, a member of the aging bachelor society advised him about survival in a hostile America: destroy and forget the past; get along with the "Americans."

In an essay entitled "Yellow Seattle" [in *The Weekly: Seattle's Newsmagazine,* 1 February 1976], Chin repeats his conviction that not only Chinese America but Japanese America is historically doomed, a prediction also made by UCLA sociologist Harry Kitano [in *Pacific Citizen,* 25 February 1977]. "Nationally," says Chin, "between 60 and 70 percent of Japanese Americas are marrying out white. They're abandoning the race, giving up on a people they feel has no history, identity, culture, or art. Chinese Americans aren't far behind. . . . The process of marrying out faster than we can reproduce seems irreversible."

This conviction casts a veil of tragedy over his work, despite its frequently humorous tone. One can see chronologically in his plays an increasing disintegration of both family and self. His heroes, like so many other American heroes, are isolated and wounded. They are articulate but incapable of the action necessary to fulfill the hope and promise of the past.

3. *The Chickencoop Chinaman*: THE SEARCH FOR THE IDEAL FATHER

Chin is a developing artist, and his first play, which won the East West Players playwriting contest in 1971 and was produced by the American Place Theatre of New York in 1972, is a feast of ideas, a sourcebook of themes and concerns that would be developed in his later work and which, in turn, would influence other Asian American writers. It is a difficult, allusive play. One must be aware of Chin's particular vision of history—his researches into a shrouded past—to understand his elliptical references. Like many other artists, he does not believe that he is constrained to explain his work. Therefore, some readers may be confounded when they do not find here the exotic, standardized comfort, say, of a *Flower Drum Song.*

Critical reaction to the stage production of **The Chickencoop Chinaman** was mixed. Clive Barnes of *The New York Times* (14 June 1972) found it "interesting" because of its ethnic content but did not much like the play. Edith Oliver, writing in *The New Yorker,* was delighted by what she saw, describing the play as "theatrical and inventive" and Tam Lum's speeches as a "dazzling eruption of verbal legerdemain" (24 June 1972). Jack Kroll of *Newsweek* found "real vitality, humor and pain on Chin's stage," and said he would "remember Tam Lum long after I've forgotten most of this season's other plays." He thought Chin a "natural writer; his language has the beat and brass, the runs and rim-shots of jazz" (19 June 1972).

Michael Feingold of *The Village Voice* (15 June 1972), who noted that the play was "blossoming all over with good writing, well-caught characters, and sharply noted situations," nevertheless said that when Tam launched into his monologues, "hot air, disguised as Poetry, flies in." Even less complimentary was Julius Novick, also of *The New York Times,* who concluded that while John Osborne was a "master rhetorician," Frank Chin was not.

Given the difficulty of the play, one wonders at the sympathic perception of a Jack Kroll or an Edith Oliver. Betty Lee Sung, author of *Mountain of Gold,* who publicly admits that she and Chin have been "friendly enemies" for years, expressed in *East/West* (3 July 1974) her opinion of **Chickencoop Chinaman**: "I agreed with the drama critics [which ones she does not specify]. I simply did not like the play, nor did the audience, which kept dwindling act after act. My comments: [It]was an outpouring of bitterness and hatred mouthed through lengthy monologue after monologue. Not that it was Randy Kim's fault (the main character actor) but it was Frank Chin showing through." Previously, Chin had publicly declared Sung to be an assimilationist—one who is willing to pay through subservience the "price of acceptance."

In **Chickencoop Chinaman,** Tam Lum epitomizes the cultural and historical dilemma of the incipient Asian American writer. The editors of *Aiiieeeee!* describe him as "the comic embodiment of Asian-American manhood, rooted in neither Asia nor white America" and thus "forced to invent a past, mythology, and traditions from the antiques and curios of his immediate experience."

What is interesting for the American scholar is that Tam's speeches in the first scene deny the stereotype of the Asian American dual personality—he is neither Chinese nor assimilated American, but a new breed of man created by the American experience. Thus he declares to the Dream Girl:

> My dear in the beginning there was the Word! Then there was me! And the Word was CHINAMAN. And there was me. . . . I lived the Word! The Word is my heritage. . . . Born? No! . . . Created! Not born. No more born than heaven and earth. No more born than nylon or acrylic. For I am a Chinaman! A miracle synthetic!

But it is soon apparent that these words are sheer bravado, for even the name of the Dream Girl shows Tam to be enmeshed in history. She is described as a "dream monster from a popular American song of the twenties," a song which parodies the womanless bachelor society.

The ensuing scenes reveal, moreover, that Tam has a deep sense of his own emasculation, his inability to achieve. This is symbolically revealed when the Lone Ranger, whom he had once idolized, unaccountably shoots the innocent youth—the future writer—in the hand. Tam also rejects his own father (whom he nonetheless loves), a dishwasher in a home for the aged, who used to bathe with his shorts on for fear of being peeked at by old white ladies. "Chinamans do make lousy fathers," Tam says later, "I know, I have one." He similarly rejects himself. He had tried to obliterate his Chinese American identity by marrying out white and forgetting the history of his people. And he says of his children: "I don't want 'em to be anything like me or know me, or remember me. This guy they're calling 'daddy' . . . I hear he's even a better writer than me."

For all his self-rejection, however, Tam wishes to discover a more heroic past and identity, and believes his destiny as a writer is "to talk to the Chinaman sons of Chinamans, children of the dead." But the problem of an appropriate language to represent their experience disturbs him. In fact, during the opening scene, the stage directions note that "his own 'normal' speech jumps between black and white rhythms and accents." Ironically Tam says: "I speak nothing but the mother tongues bein' born to none of my own, I talk the talk of orphans." In an interview ["Back Talk"] Chin explains:

> Our condition is more delicate than that of the blacks because, unlike the blacks, we have neither an articulated organic sense of our American identity nor the verbal confidence and self-esteem to talk one up from our experience. As a people, we are pre-verbal, preliterate—afraid of language as the instrument through which the monster takes possession of us. For us American born, both the Asian languages and the English language are foreign. We are a people without a native tongue. To whites, we're all foreigners, still learning English. . . . And to Asians born to Asian culture—Asian by birth and experience and American by choice—our Chinese and Japanese is a fake.

In this context, Tam's self-characterization as a linguistic orphan is made understandable. As the editors of *Aiiieeeee!* point out, "the literary establishment has never considered the fact that a new folk in a strange land would experience the land and develop a new language out of old words."

Conscious of his own emasculation, Tam admires boxers and still hopes he can somehow gain the respect of his children by filming a documentary of the hero of his youth, a black fighter named Ovaltine Jack Dancer, a former light-heavyweight champ. Tam's purpose in flying from California to Pittsburgh is to meet Charley Popcorn, the Dancer's ostensible father, whom the boxer has described in heroic terms. Tam stays at the home of a childhood friend, "Blackjap" Kenji, a research dentist who lives by choice in the black ghetto. Tam enthusiastically looks forward to meeting Charley: "This trip's going to make me well. I'm going to see again, and talk and hear. . . ." Kenji himself is eager: "Father of a champion, man."

Chin's own sympathy for blacks and his acknowledgment of their pioneering efforts in civil rights are revealed in the encounter between the two Asian Americans and Charley, who is puzzled by the appearance of Chinaman Tam after hearing a black voice over the telephone. Charley denies that he is Ovaltine's father and asserts that the Dancer's wonderful tales of an ideal father-son relation are pure fabrications—assertions that the hero- and father-seeking Tam almost hysterically cannot accept. Charley becomes sympathetic, although he confesses that blacks "don't particularly favor Chinese." He also chastises Tam for rejecting his own father: "I just know it's wrong to turn your back on your father however old you be."

The next scene finds Tam in "Limbo," symbolically on the black man's back. But later Charley is on Tam's back as Tam staggeringly reenters Kenji's apartment and meets "Tom," an assimilated Chinese who appropriately plays Tonto in the Lone Ranger scene. Tam arouses Kenji's anger by being extremely rude to Tom. Chastised by Kenji, Tam says he will make a straight, professional fight film without a fake father in it, and, accepting his aloneness, retreats to the kitchen to cook dinner for all.

Disappointed in his search for ideality, Tam recalls the family's dream of the Iron Moonhunter:

> Now and then, I feel them old days, children, the way I feel the prowl of the dogs in the night and the bugs in the leaves and the thunder in the Sierra Nevadas however far that are. The way my grandmother had an ear for trains. Listen, children. I gotta go. Ride Buck Buck Bagaw with me . . . Listen in the kitchen for the Chickencoop Chinaman slowin on home.

4. LANGUAGE AS A MEDIUM OF CULTURE

Before we proceed to *The Year of the Dragon,* a brief comment on Chin's use of language may be helpful. Chin confronts the linguistic problem that Tam faces in a bold, revolutionary manner. Some readers may consequently be daunted by his deliberately unconventional style. His language abounds with slang, obscenities, and unusual grammar. The Cantonese terms may also make for difficult reading. But Chin would argue that he has captured the rhythms and accents of Chinese America without which its culture cannot truly be represented. This philosophical position is perhaps most clearly stated in the introduction to *Aiiieeeee!*:

> Language is the medium of culture and the people's sensibility, including the style of manhood. Language coheres the people into a community by organizing and codifying the symbols of the people's common experience. Stunt the tongue and you have lopped off the culture and sensibility. On the simplest level, a man in any culture speaks for himself. Without a language of his own, he no longer is a man. The concept of the dual personality deprives the Chinese-American and Japanese-American of the means to develop their own terms. The tyranny of language has been used by white culture to suppress Asian-American culture and exclude it from operating in the mainstream of American consciousness.

So influential have been the editors of *Aiiieeeee!* (Chin, Jeffery Chan, Lawson Inada, and Shawn Wong) in defining the white cultural oppression of Asian American writers that they have, curiously, freed these writers and initiated a literary movement. In fact, the preface and introduction to *Aiiieeeee!* can be likened to Emerson's "American Scholar," written at a critical time in our national history when our fledgling republic, though politically free, struggled under England's cultural dominion. Similarly, *Aiiieeeee!* is a declaration of intellectual and linguistic independence, and an assertion of Asian American manhood.

Recent Asian American writers' conferences at the Oakland Museum, the University of Washington, and the Mid-Pacific Institute in Hawaii also give testimony that the linguistic experiments urged by the editors are being more widely accepted. For instance, at the 1978 "Talk Story" conference in Hawaii, pidgin English—once thought to be reprehensible and shameful—was considered a valid medium of communication and poetic expression. Indeed, pidgin, a spoken language, was challenging linguists with the problems of codification. *Aiiieeeee!*'s diction and argumentative pattern have further influenced some autobiographical accounts of self-discovery.

Yet the highly-assertive preface and introduction remain controversial, as do the plays of Frank Chin. He has said [in a letter to the editor of *The Drama Review*, 22 October-23 November 1976] that he was "chosen to write theater like making war," and this is an apt description. Always in the vanguard, he is an outspoken, articulate, funny writer, unconstrained by literary and stylistic conventions.

5. *The Year of the Dragon*:
THE DISINTEGRATION OF THE CHINESE AMERICAN FAMILY

The Year of the Dragon was first produced in 1974 by the American Place Theatre in New York. More traditionally structured than **Chickencoop,** it received generally good notices except from Douglas Watt of *The New York Daily News* (3 June 1974) and Yoshio Kishi of the *New York Nichibei* (6 June 1974), who both found the play incomprehensible. However, a more sympathetic Genny Lim, writing in *East/West* (5 June 1974), found the family drama gripping and the culture and psychological conflicts so realistic that "we are, oftentimes, tempted to watch with our faces averted."

A PBS version for *Theatre in America* was videotaped in 1975. During a 1977 San Francisco production, in which Chin starred, he wrote to a newspaper critic: "The play is set in Frisco, because this city is known as the place our history began. Frisco is the soul of Chinese America. The play is set in the Year of the Dragon because the Dragon was the Bicentennial year. The play sums up where I see Chinese America in the Year of the Dragon: 1976."

To Chin, Chinese America has lost its "soul," or integrity, along with its past. Chinatown is a Shangri-La, a Hollywood set, run by Christian converts. The mission schools first undertook the education of Chinese Americans because of continuing public efforts to segregate or ignore them. The missions nonetheless became political instruments by fostering the ideal of the passive, nonaggressive male who recognizes the superiority of whites, and by eradicating the memory of the bold, pioneering Chinamen of old. The schools also denied other aspects of Chinese American history—the massacres, for instance. Chin observes that "we were indoctrinated into forgetting the names of every burned down or wiped out Chinatown [and became] gah gah for the little town of Bethlehem instead." But despite this indoctrination, Chinese Americans remained tacitly aware of their alien identity. Thus, the Chinatown of **The Year of the Dragon** is not what is seen by the thousands of tourists during the New Year's parade, but the psychological "deathcamp" that is "in the blood of all *juk sing.*" In a moment of compounding frustrations, the hero, Fred Eng, cries out: "I am shit. This family is shit. Chinatown's shit. You can't love each other around here without hating yourself."

The play, with its theme of disintegration, begins with the imminent death of the father. Having lived in America since 1935, he is now the respected "Mayor" of Chinatown, probably by virtue of his presidency of the Christian-dominated Chinese Benevolent Society. Realizing death is near, he is anxious about the future of his family outside Chinatown's confines, because of his dislike and suspicion of whites. Though at times brutally autocratic and selfish, he is loved by his children and wife; and the family thus has a semblance of unity.

He married Ma Eng when she was but fifteen. Through her carefully recited clichés, she shows that she has been mission-educated: "I always told you to be proud to be the best of the East, the best of the West." "Miss Thompson, she said, 'Talking two completely incompatible languages is a great asset.'" Unconsciously, Ma Eng sings repeatedly the American-written *Chinese Lullabye,* which tells of the selling of "slave girls" (purportedly saved by the missions). She loves her home and family, and fears change. She is nonetheless aware of the slow disintegration of her family (her husband is dying; her forty-year-old, still unmarried son, Fred, rarely sleeps at home; Johnny is on probation for carrying a gun; Mattie has married out white and has only returned to Chinatown at her father's request); and she attempts to escape moments of stress by going to the bathroom or bursting into song. But she spiritedly objects to the unexpected appearance of Pa Eng's first wife, brought over from China so that he would be surrounded by "happy families when I die. . . ." Nevertheless, in the uproar that follows, she accepts China Mama's presence to preserve as best she can the family integrity. She even adheres to Pa's request that she instruct China Mama in some English by teaching her the *Chinese Lullabye.*

Unlike her mother, Mattie has escaped entirely. She hates Chinatown and asserts that her home is now in Boston with her white husband, Ross. Years ago, she made clear her intention to leave forever, noting that "it didn't matter where I was born or what color I was . . . especially being a Chinese girl." She was obviously aware of her desirability to white men.

Her brother Johnny brings forth the undercurrent of violence in Chinatown which destroys the image of the strong, law-abiding Chinese American family. Before his appearance, we are informed that his friend has been shot and killed that day. Vigorously hostile to Ross, Johnny is an alienated youth, preferring his criminal escapades with immigrant hoodlums—whose language he cannot understand—to college and Boston and the world his sister has chosen. When Mattie urges that they all leave for Boston after Pa Eng's death ("Out there we'll be able to forget we're Chinamen, just forget all this and just be people . . ."), Johnny replies coldly, "You have to forget you're a Chinatown girl to be just people, sis?"

His older brother, Fred, the head of Eng's Chinatown Tour 'n Travel, hates Chinatown for being the whites' "private preserve for an endangered species." But as Chinatown's top guide with an inimitable spiel, Fred hates himself even more. He knows that he has lost sight of his dream of being a writer and, moreover, his job forces him to conform to the American stereotype of Chinese Americans. According to Chin, a tourist guide is by definition "a Chinaman, playing a white man playing Chinese. . . . A minstrel show. The tourist guides of Chinatown are traditionally the despised and perverted."

Thus Fred's spiels to the tourists are given in a language and manner expected by them. The model on which these expectations are based is Charlie Chan, a character invented by a white man in 1925 and invariably played by white men in the movies and on television. Though intelligent, Chan has the expected Asian American qualities: he is humble, passive, polite, self-effacing, and effeminate, and has difficulties with English. Ross, Mattie's white husband, shows his acceptance of the Chan stereotype by reciting Confucianisms and suggesting that Pa Eng, as Mayor of Chinatown, add a Charlie Chan joke to his speech to be given after the parade. Therefore, before Pa leaves for the occasion, he greets Fred with "You got dah case solve yet?" and insists that Fred, his "Number One Son," call him "Pop": "Gosh, Pop!" "Gee, Pop!"

Fred's own perception of Chan is found earlier in a scene with China Mama, his real mother recently from China. He responds to her question, given, of course, in Chinese:

> You want me to be Chinese too, huh? Everybody does . . . You know how the tourists tell I'm Chinese? No first person pronouns. No "I," "Me" or "We." I talk like that lovable sissy, Charlie Chan, no first person personal pronouns, and instant Chinese culture . . . ha, ha, ha. . . .

Continuing to speak to her uncomprehending ears, Fred declares himself to be a Chinaman:

Chin's impact on Asian American theater:

Asian-American playwriting got its real jumpstart in 1973, when Frank Chin, Janis Chan, Jeffrey Chin and others founded the Asian American Theatre Workshop in San Francisco. Helped by donations of space and acting training from the American Conservatory Theatre, this exciting laboratory yielded the first major play by an Asian-American author: Frank Chin's *Chickencoop Chinaman.*

Incisive, irreverent and raunchy, *Chickencoop Chinaman* was for and about a restive young generation of Asian Americans. Audiences responded to its lampooning of both racist media stereotyping and self-stereotyping, and to characters shaped more by the gritty reality of multiracial America than by the distant culture of their ancestors.

Chin's play toured college campuses for over a year, bringing media attention and new recruits to the Asian American Theatre Workshop. National interest in Chin's work intensified after the American Place Theatre mounted his *The Year of the Dragon* in 1977, billing it as the first Asian-American drama ever produced in New York.

Misha Berson, "Between Worlds," in American Theatre, *Vol. 6, No. 2, March, 1990.*

> I'm not Chinese. This ain't China. Your language is foreign and ugly to me so how come you're my mother? . . . I mean, I don't think I'm quite your idea of a son, either . . . You hear all my first person pronouns, China Mama. . . . Just because we're born here don't mean we're nobody and gotta go away to another language to talk. I think Chinatown Buck Buck Bagaw is beautiful.

The use of the first person pronouns is for Fred the declaration of his American individualism and individual rights. He had wanted to become a writer and be "something special," not just his father's son. But having been born in China and having entered America illegally as an infant, he is torn between his desire for his own life and his responsibilities to his family. The mixture of the old and the new may be seen in some of Fred's small gestures. Twice he lights incense for the ancestral shrine before lighting up a "joint." More importantly, ten years earlier, while yet in college pursuing his dream of being a writer, he was called home by his father, who was dying from a lung complaint. As the eldest son, Fred was expected to be obedient, to earn money for the family, and to be responsible for his younger siblings. In fact, Fred is chastised by his father for Johnny's delinquency, and Sis recalls that in the past it was Fred who was beaten for her misbehavior.

Despite his hatred for his job, Fred is proud of his successful shouldering of family responsibilities. He has enabled Mattie to go away to college and, upon her arrival, gives her the traditional New Year's monetary envelope to present to Pa Eng. He talks of Boston, where her Mama Fu Fu business is prospering, as a place for the revivification of the family. Almost nightly he attends his sick father in the bathroom. But for all his fidelity and success, Fred expects some gratitude and respect from his father. Consequently he is enraged when Pa imports China Mama without consulting him and when Pa declares him to be a "flop," unable to care for the family outside Chinatown's confines.

But Pa, for all his Chinese roots, has taken on the values of this American Chinatown. Though demanding unquestioning obedience from Fred, he ironically selected a tourist guide business for him, a business despised by Chinatown. Thereafter, Pa has never acknowledged his children in print, and once, while lunching with Fred, he did not even bother to introduce his son when other Chinatown dignitaries approached. Although it was Pa who removed Fred from college, he disdains Fred's ambition to be a writer, valuing only the more lucrative and traditional professions—which require a college degree. In preparing his New Year's speech, Pa hurts Fred by asking Ross, a "real" American, for help; but in his own insecurity with English he asks Fred privately to edit the first draft so that Ross will not discover his ineptness.

Since China Mama was brought to America so that Pa could die "Chinese," Fred asks him why he did not return to China instead. Pa replies that he regards Chinatown in America as his home. This for Chin is significant, as he believes most Chinese came here not as sojourners who would eventually return to China but as immigrants, like their European counterparts, with their own vision of America.

Pa, in this bathroom scene, is aware that the family line has probably come to an end and attempts to exact from Fred a promise that he will always remain in Chinatown. Of Mattie, Pa says: "Sissy go colleges and what happening? Bok gwai low! [White devil!] And no more blood. No more Chinese babies born in family. No Merican Chinese babies, nutting doing and flop." Fred is forty, balding, single, and unlikely to marry. Johnny's criminal escapades will probably kill him eventually.

During the last scene of the play, as the festive sounds of the parade float into the room, Fred asks his father to look at him for once as an individual and not just as a son. Aware of his father's power over Ma and Johnny, who are rapidly deteriorating, Fred promises to remain in Chinatown if Pa will tell Ma and Johnny to leave for Boston. But Pa refuses adamantly, and dies during their physical struggle. At the beginning of his aborted speech, Pa was to have introduced Fred as his heir: "dah one who're teck obber solve dah case. My's Number One Son, allaw time, saying 'Gee, Pop!' Fred Eng!"

At first fearing to leave Chinatown to become a "nobody" or discover that his writing ability has died, Fred is further crippled by his father's inability to the very end to see him as an individual. As the lights fade before his final spiel, Fred—his father's heir—is "dressed in solid white, puts on a white slightly oversized jacket, and appears to be a shrunken Charlie Chan, an image of death. He becomes the tourist guide."

6. KWAN KUNG: THE IDEAL DISCOVERED

The masculine ideal that Tam Lum sought and the bold individualism that Fred Eng desired, Chin would eventually find in Kwan Kung, a popular folk hero revered throughout the centuries as a god who had, according to Henri Doré, S. J. [in *Researches into Chinese Superstitions*], "fought many battles, was brave, generous, loyal to the Han dynasty. . . . He was a powerful giant, nine feet tall according to one legend, with a beard two feet long. His features 'were of a swarthy colour, and his lips of a bright rosy hue. His eyebrows resembling those of the phoenix. His whole appearance inspired a feeling of terror.'" Kwan is said to have told his new friend, Liupei, that he had wandered over the country for five years as a fugitive from justice and a champion of the oppressed, "for I have killed a prominent man, who oppressed the people of my native place. I have heard that men are being recruited to repress brigandage, and I wish to join the expedition."

Because of his skill in battle, Kwan came to be deified as the god of war, and his virtues inspired writers and scholars, whom he protected. Characteristically, statues of Kwan show him in both a scholar's robes and a general's uniform. Chin, naturally enough, interrelates these two aspects. In a letter to Michael Kirby, editor of *The Drama Review,* he says that Kwan was "the god of war to soldiers, the god of plunder to soldiers and other arrogant takers, the god of literature to fighters who soldier with words, and the god patron protector of actors and anyone who plays him on stage."

Though revered by the Cantonese—who became the first "Chinamans"—the red-faced Kwan was never as "heavy" as the Christian God, according to Chin. Besides being militant, loyal, and vengeful, Kwan was also selfish and individualistic. This, in Chin's eyes, restored the image of the integrated self that he saw historically disintegrating: "The Chinese used to say the Cantonese were so individualistic, they didn't get along with or trust anyone, not even each other. You could never get close to a Cantonese cuz he either told you everything endlessly and entertainingly and you couldn't sort our what counts—or he told you nothing. EVERY CANTONESE IS WHOLE UNTO HIMSELF AS A PLANET and trusts no other living thing."

Kwan Kung traveled to America with the Cantonese immigrants through the national epic *The Romance of the Three Kingdoms* in the forms of both novel and opera.

Sprawling and complex in structure, the *Romance* even in its condensed version reads like Malory's *Works*. The most popular of Cantonese operas, for Chin it seems "a collection of documents, various story tellers' cheat sheets, doggerel and repeats of folk hearsay by different people writing at different times about the same historical event." It disdains the Western neoclassical unities and is the result "of thousands of years of literate storytelling wordhappy culture." More importantly, both novel and opera "pose as raw documentary history. The form contains the notion of destroying a people by destroying their history. . . ."

The opera also contains the famed fraternal Oath in the Peach Garden sworn by the three heroes: Liu-pei, Kwan Kung, and Chang-fei. They declare their "everlasting friendship" and pledge mutual assistance in all dangers. "It's a soldier's blood oath of loyalty and revenge," says Chin:

> Nothing charitable, necessarily honorable, in any Western sense, passive or timid about it. . . . It encouraged an aggressive self-reliance and trust nobody, watch out killer's sense of individuality that reached a peak in China with the Cantonese, took to the image of what the Chinamans scratching out mountains for gold thought of themselves, grew roots in California and sprouted a Kwan Kung happy race of people who wanted to hear, read, and rewrite, only one story, and sing and sit through and pass with one opera only.

But, says Chin, the imported Cantonese opera became "purely Chinaman" in expression "as it adjusted language, style, detail, event, and setting to the changing world of the Chinamans at work on a new experience, making new language to define the experience, and make new history." Such were the changes made that for "Chinamans in mining and railroad camps and Chinatown," the opera became "a one man medicine show done by traveling kung fu fighters selling their personal kung fu brew. . . ." Whole families of such fighters "traveled by wagon from camp to camp selling tonic, breaking chains, and doing flash versions of *Three Kingdoms.*"

It is to this Chinaman version of Cantonese opera that Chin owes his artistic origins: "I write from links with the original whoremothers of our people and through my mother, ties to the most popular hero of the most popular novel and opera living with me. The Kwan blood from my mother meant I was chosen to write theater like making war, throw everything away and get even."

Chin therefore says: "I am not any white writer. I'm Frank Chin, Chinaman writer. White reviewers like Julius Novick and Clive Barnes stuck in their Christian esthetic of one god, one good, one voice, one thing happening, one talk at a time get so dizzy in the atmosphere of Chinaman word strategy they gotta cancel out every white writer they know to make sense of my simple Chinaman back-

scratch." He believes that an artist should be judged on his own terms, and that to apply the traditional Western criteria to his work is irrelevant and unfair.

Yet, in his conception of a New Man (a Chinaman) and a new language wrought out of the new American experience, Chin shows his awareness of the early nineteenth-century American struggle for cultural and linguistic freedom from Britain. Moreover, to counter the effeminate, Christianized Charlie Chan image of the post-1925 era, he has restored the immensely masculine Kwan Kung, whose strength of mind and body, individuality and loyalty, capacity for revenge, and essential aloneness are reminiscent of the rugged Western hero of American myth. The interested reader might wish to contrast this rugged individualism with the perception of Chinese character in Francis L. K. Hsu's *The Challenge of the American Dream: The Chinese in the United States.* Professor Hsu is an immigrant Chinese.

Kwan Kung's opera also contains an idea that haunts Chin's work: the destruction of a people by destroying their history. Chin is well aware of white fears in this vein; one of his more amusing insights is of James Hilton's Shangri-La as a place designed for the preservation of white culture, where whites with low self-esteem can be worshipped and serviced by yellows. He is regretful, on the other hand, that his own generation has forgotten their past and their old hero:

> "There was a statue of Kwan Kung in every Chinese American home I was ever in," he says, "til my generation moved into houses of their own, and hadn't known 'Chinaman' is what we called ourselves in the English we spoke and made our own for three generations now."

Though acknowledging the eventual extinction of Asian America, Chin in his own life and work has maintained the heroic stance of the old Chinaman god. Recently in a restaurant in Seattle, Chin (who avows he dislikes broken men) was revolted by an aging, embittered No-No Boy of the Second World War who felt his life had been ruined by his imprisonment. "He'd lost all sense of Seattle as a Japanese-American city, all sense of vision," said Chin:

> "You say the Chinese came here with a vision too?" he whined, and I had to move or melt into a pool of boo-hoo and booze and give up with the old man.

> "Get up! Come with me right now!" I said and was walking to the front of the restaurant.

> If he had caught up with me, I'd have collared him and dragged him to the poster of Kwan Kung sitting on his tiger throne with his squire at his right hand, holding Kwan's seal. Kwan's left side robed him like a scholar and his right side armored him like a soldier. "That's the vision of ourselves when we first came over," I said.

THE CHICKENCOOP CHINAMAN

PRODUCTION REVIEWS

Michael Feingold (review date 15 June 1972)

SOURCE: "Portnoy's Chinese Complaint," in *The Village Voice,* 15 June 1972, p. 56.

[*Feingold offers a mixed assessment of* The Chickencoop Chinaman, *arguing that, "though blossoming all over with good writing, well-caught characters, and sharply noted situations, [it] is only about three-quarters finished as a play."*]

The Chickencoop Chinaman will not be serving your shrimp Szechuan in a family restaurant, nor is he likely to be the one demanding a tickee when you go to pick up your shirts at the laundry. Tam Lum, the title character of Frank Chin's first produced play, is a young filmmaker, a resolutely monologizing surrogate for the playwright, who is deeply involved in extricating himself from his ethnic background: not in repudiating it, but coming to terms with it. And, of course, the more he tries to get out from under, the more entangled he gets. Which is how America works on all its minorities, and which is why Chin's play, potentially, could touch a tender spot in the makeup of every ethnic group, and is in no way a mere piece of sweet and sour tokenism.

"Potentially" is the word because **The Chickencoop Chinaman,** though blossoming all over with good writing, well-caught characters, and sharply noted situations is only about three-quarters finished as a play. It has a dramatic, or anyway anecdotal, structure: Tam has been hired to do a documentary film on the life of his childhood idol, the black boxing champion Ovaltine Jack Dancer; he comes east to visit his co-worker and old friend Kenji, and interview the man who is ostensibly Dancer's beloved father and trainer, an old black moviehouse operator named Charley Popcorn. In the evening the play covers, Tam receives, via these two characters, a series of disillusionments (all nonschematic and fairly complex), and has to start coming to terms with both reality and himself.

This very traditional structure for a naturalistic play can result in either boredom or delight, strictly depending on the quality of the writer's perception and inventiveness; Chin scores high on both. What he hasn't done is objectified his autobiographical (I assume) central character fully into the otherwise solid action: Tam is prone to long speeches alone in a spotlight, always a dangerous habit for a hero, and at these moments, as often in young writers' plays, good writing goes out the window and hot air, disguised as Poetry, flies in.

Chin is conscious enough of this lapse to have replaced one of his arias with a juicy dream-memory sequence, of Chinese boys idolizing the radio version of the Lone Ranger. Here, as often, the play summons up Alexander Portnoy [in Philip Roth's novel *Portnoy's Complaint*]: the comparison is not meant to be reductive; what the parallel does suggest is that Roth solved some of the problems in the material (and in himself?) through a primarily comic strategy, a retreat into the self-lacerating humor common to ethnic subgroups. Chin, a younger man less submissive to WASP-induced minority masochism, hasn't fully decided that his hero is comic; the monologues are a way of extricating Tam from the comic-pathetic New Yorker-story predicament of the plot. What they do instead, because they are acts of will and not of feeling, is nullify the naturalism rather than enriching it. Tam is still caught, our attention a bit less so.

Withal, the play is a debut (though who knows if an autobiographic playwright will ever come calling again?) and an enjoyable one. The chief obstacle to perceiving it is not Chin's occasional lapse into gas-poem, but Jack Gelber's smooth, unvariedly-paced, and utterly gelid production, in which a number of good actors stand or lope around, seemingly disconnected from each other, their own feelings, or the texture and point of the writing. Chief offender Randy Kim, in the arduous lead role, is full of technical proficiency but never once manages to suggest that all those ornate phrases are coming out of his being, rather than his mouth. Sally Kirkland has rather perfectly caught the exterior of Kenji's minority-groupie white housemate, but so grievously mislays her feelings that she is onstage for half an hour before the text, rather than her acting, informs us she is under strain. Even the always-dependable Leonard Jackson, as Charley, has afflicted an otherwise fine characterization with overslow timing and half-projection. Roger Morgan's lighting is good, and Willa Kim's costumes as interesting as everyday clothes can be in a naturalistic play, but Gelber has conned talented John Wulp into designing a fatally awkward set, and then used it even more awkwardly.

Julius Novick (review date 18 June 1972)

SOURCE: "No Cheers for the 'Chinaman'," in *The New York Times,* 18 June 1972, Section 2, p. 3.

[*In the following negative review of* The Chickencoop Chinaman, *Novick asserts: "There is the material for a play here, but not much of a play."*]

If John Osborne had been a young Chinese-American playwright of mediocre attainments, he might conceivably have written a play very much like **The Chickencoop Chinaman,** which is the season's final offering at the American Place Theater.

The hero of **The Chickencoop Chinaman,** like Mr. Osborne's most famous hero, is loquacious, disaffected, excitable, sarcastic, angry and young; both heroes, moreover, are hung up about wives, fathers, and (especially) social injustice. And, like some of Mr. Osborne's plays, *The Chickencoop Chinaman* often looks like an ill-concealed pretext for a series of lengthy monologues by the protagonist. But Mr. Osborne is a master rhetorician, and Frank Chin, the author of *The Chickencoop Chinaman,* is not.

Mr. Chin's hero, a documentary filmmaker named Tam Lum, doesn't talk or dress or act like an Oriental. In many respects, he is strikingly like any other bright, neurotic, wise-ass American kid; you don't have to be Chinese to do his Helen Keller imitations. But he has evidently been very deeply marked by the experience of growing up yellow in a white society. Like certain characters in black drama, he constantly makes jokes about racial stereotypes. He seems fascinated by the blackness of blacks, by the ways they have worked out for asserting a prideful non-white identity. He and his friend Kenji (a hip young Japanese-American dentist) call each other "man" a lot, and generally spend a good deal of time half-pretending that they themselves are black. And Tam is intrigued to discover that somebody is writing a study of Chinese-American identity to be called *Soul on Rice.*

There is the material for a play here, but not much of a play. The plotting is fuzzy and unproductive. Tam is making a movie about a black fighter named Ovaltine Jack Dancer, with whom he once shared a moment of mystic brotherhood urinating in the bushes. He comes to Pittsburgh to interview one Charley Popcorn, who is supposed to be the fighter's father. When Charlie Popcorn insists that he is *not* the father of Ovaltine Jack Dancer, Tam seems to undergo some sort of crisis, but it is never entirely clear why he should care so much one way or the other. There is also a white girl named Lee, who gets involved in various ways with no less than three Oriental men, Tam included, but it is hard to see what her emotional life has to do with anything.

When Mr. Chin does have a good idea, he tends to lean on it very hard. It seems, for instance, that Tam used to fantasize that the Lone Ranger wears a black mask to conceal his slanted Oriental eyes. Good: a fine metaphor for an outsider's yearning to possess a share in our national myths. But Mr. Chin drags it out into a long, dull fantasy sequence featuring the Lone Ranger in person. Even the wonderful *Soul on Rice* joke is repeated far past the point of diminishing returns.

But the main problem with *The Chickencoop Chinaman* is that Tam Lum is never interesting enough to justify the attention that is lavished on him. "You have a way with words," he is told, but this is true more in terms of quantity than of quality. A character like this must dramatize himself through language. But Tam Lum's language, while emphatic enough, is never as sharp, bold or vivid as it is obviously supposed to be. It is not written right for the theater; somewhere between the speaker and the audience, it tends somehow to blow away.

Tam is played at the American Place by a young actor named Randy Kim, whose relentlessly exuberant energy sometimes becomes a bit of a nuisance. But it is something to be capable of all that exuberance; and Mr. Kim is quite acceptable when events overtake him and he stops spouting. Sally Kirkland, as Lee, plays much of her part with a memorably sluttish sort of sour, hillbilly weariness; it's monotonous and not very attractive, but it has a very authentic feeling about it. Willa Kim's costumes say more about the characters who wear them than stage costumes usually do; Jack Gelber's direction is unobtrusive.

The Chickencoop Chinaman is a thoroughly conventional play in both form and content—like most black plays, and, of course, most white ones. It seems that American writers of all shades have to draw from the same stock of models, techniques and themes. And why not? We are all, however loudly some of us may try to deny it, Americans—that is one of the implications of *The Chickencoop Chinaman*—and, as such, all inextricably members of European/Western Civilization (as black American intellectuals tend to discover by visiting Africa).

Furthermore, as Treplev says in *The Seagull.* "It's not a question of old and new forms"; we can use unconventional playwrights, but what we need most of all are good playwrights, however we can get them. Our familiar stock of methods and themes is capable of infinite variations and evolutions; new vitality is frequently discovered in the oldest of them, when a playwright appears who is capable of re-energizing them. Mr. Chin—to return from the general to the particular—is evidently a clever and potentially interesting writer; not just anybody could make up a fighter named Ovaltine Jack Dancer. But, in the theater at least, Mr. Chin is not up to much re-energizing at the moment.

Jack Kroll (review date 19 June 1972)

SOURCE: "Primary Color," in *Newsweek,* Vol. 79, No. 25, 19 June 1972, p. 55.

[*In the generally favorable review below, Kroll notes that* The Chickencoop Chinaman "*needs more work— the basic emotional tone of hysteria is too unmodulated, the action is too thin, an awkward structure wrenches the play in and out of fantasy. But there is real vitality, humor and pain on Chin's stage.*"]

In the current orgy of consciousness-raising and identity-searching more and more unmelted ingredients in the American melting pot are crawling out of that cooling crucible and shaking themselves dry. And now we have a new playwright, Frank Chin, reminding us in *The Chickencoop Chinaman* that yellow is a primary color. His play adds a new character to the roster of alienation coming out of our theater and fiction: for Tam Lum the facts of race, culture and psyche compose a nightmare from which he cannot awake. We meet him on a plane to Pittsburgh, where the sexy presence of the stewardess has triggered a fantasy Dream Girl, a strutting Chinese parody of the American majorette, to whom he pours out his rogue poetry of deracination.

"Where were you born?" asks twirling, teasing Dream Girl. "Chinamen are made, not born," Tam tells her. "Out of junk-imports, lies, railroad scrap iron, dirty jokes, broken bottles, cigar smoke, wino spit and milk of amnesia. I am the natural born ragmouth speaking the motherless bloody tongue. I talk the talk of orphans. I am the result of a pile of pork chop suey thrown up into the chickencoop in the dead of night and the riot of dark birds, night cocks and insomniac nympho hens running after strange food that followed. I am the notorious one and only Chickencoop Chinaman himself that talks in the dark heavy midnight. I was no more born than nylon or acrylic. For I am a Chinaman, a miracle synthetic, drip dry and machine washable."

This play is a Chinese *Look Back in Anger,* and Tam is like John Osborne's Jimmy Porter, or like J.P. Donleavy's Ginger Man (Cantonese ginger), or like Lenny Bruce—pop hipsters pouring out a nonstop "ragmouth" stream of rococo riffs, invective and fantasy, a dragnet of words in which to catch their elusive identities. Dressed like Jimi Hendrix, sticking like a Catskill comic, spewing bits and lines and voices from old movies, old radio shows. Tam's real self comes from the glory-trash mélange of American pop culture. "Nothing but outtakes in my head," says Tam. Two sounds express the tension between his stubborn pride of heritage and his self-loathing: the remembered sound of the railroad, built by Chinese sweat, and "Buck Buck Bagaw," the chickencoop cackle with which he puts himself down.

Like the new black playwrights, Chin shows how race permeates the whole of life for someone like Tam, whose mother had told him: "Don't wear green—it makes you look yellow. And don't be seen with no blacks." His best friend, Kenji, is a Japanese-American trying to find himself without the advantage—and disadvantage—of Tam's mad imagination. Kenji is living with Lee, a white girl who specializes in non-white men, and whom Tam accuses of hiding her Chinese blood. Lee's Chinese ex-husband is writing a book about Chinese-American identity called *Soul on Rice.* Tam is making a documentary movie about a black boxer, Ovaltine Dancer, and he has come to see the fighter's legendary father, Charley Popcorn, who runs a porno movie house. The revelation that Charley is not Dancer's father, that the heroic Dancer is just another colored man who makes up fantasies about who he is, is the last straw for Tam, who himself has identified with everyone from Helen Keller to the Lone Ranger.

Thirty-two-year-old Frank Chin is a natural writer; his language has the beat and brass, the runs and rim-shots of jazz. This first play needs more work—the basic emotional tone of hysteria is too unmodulated, the action is too thin, an awkward structure wrenches the play in and

out of fantasy. But there is real vitality, humor and pain on Chin's stage; I will remember Tam Lum long after I've forgotten most of this season's other plays. Under Jack Gelber's direction Randy Kim is very good as Tam: he traps a lot of nuances—he is funny, crazy, smart, dopey, frightened, manly, childish, shrewdly together and hopelessly lost. Sally Kirkland plays Lee; she is one of the most touching and appealing young actresses in theater and her new adeptness at Yoga makes her even lovelier to watch. Despite its weaknesses. *Chickencoop Chinaman* is the most interesting play of the American Place Theatre's first season in their splendid new house.

Edith Oliver   (review date 24 June 1972)

SOURCE: A review of *The Chickencoop Chinaman,* in *The New Yorker,* Vol. XL VIII, No. 18, 24 June 1972, p. 46.

[*Oliver offers a positive evaluation of* The Chickencoop Chinaman, *judging it a "moving, funny, pain-filled, sarcastic, bitter, ironic play."*]

Frank Chin, a poet and dramatist, brings us the first news (theatrically speaking) of the Chinese Americans in our midst in a moving, funny, pain-filled, sarcastic, bitter, ironic play called *The Chickencoop Chinaman,* which almost bursts its seams with passion and energy. It will be playing for the lucky subscribers to the American Place only until June 24th. Mr. Chin's hero, Tam Lum, was born in California. He is, by trade, a documentary-movie maker, and he talks and talks in a furious and dazzling eruption of verbal legerdemain ("I'm tired of talking, but when I stop it's so goddam awful") that reveals, as if in a blaze of Fourth of July fireworks, himself and his parents and his grandmother and his other relatives and his anonymous ancestors who were brought into this country to build the Union Pacific Railroad. The play is no monologue, though. There is action, and there are a lot of other people. It opens with Tam Lum sitting in a plane that is about to land in Pittsburgh, and having some sort of wild daydream about a Chinese drum majorette. He has flown in from Los Angeles, where he has been making a movie about a black boxer, and he intends to film a segment of it in Pittsburgh, where an old black man whom he supposes to be the fighter's father is working as an exhibitor of pornographic movies. While Tam Lum is in Pittsburgh, he stays with a Japanese-American boyhood friend, a dentist, who appears to be completely acclimated to America, and who is living with a pregnant young white woman—a needling, contrary snubber and charmer (Sally Kirkland has never been better or better cast)—and her little boy, the child of a previous marriage or association. The action is complex, and flashbacks and dramatized fantasies abound, but it is the dentist's household that is the focus of it all—the place where most of the characters eventually end up, and where surface frictions mask a kind of love and peace. The young woman senses that Tam Lum is a disturber of the peace the moment he sets foot in the door, and her needling and put-downs are the weapons she uses against him.

I'm afraid that I have made *The Chickencoop Chinaman* sound more exclusively verbal than it is. The words are what count, but the play is theatrical and inventive, and Jack Gelber, who directed it, has let no opportunity for stage life get by him. He is rewarded by fine performances. Besides the indelible Miss Kirkland, Randy Kim is remarkable as the anguished, self-hating, witty hero; and Sab Shimono as his dentist friend, Leonard Jackson as the pornographic-movie man, Calvin Jung as another Chinese, more comfortable in his skin, and Anthony Marciona as the little boy are very good, too. A few of the scenes seem a bit foolish, and others run on beyond their natural breaking point, but there is so much that is right with the play that the few paltry things that are wrong hardly matter.

John Simon (review date 26 June 1972)

SOURCE: "Hardly Worth the Bother," in *New York* Magazine 5, No. 26, 26 June 1972, p. 54.

[*In the following review, Simon gives a negative appraisal of* The Chickencoop Chinaman, *declaring that it is "a loose aggregate of untheatrical surfaces with no real center, no dramatic propulsion and urgency."*]

The Chickencoop Chinaman introduces another minority to our stage, the Chinese-Americans (and also, incidentally, the Japanese-Americans), whose problems seem to be even greater than those of the blacks because, apparently, they not only have to compete against the whites, but must also compete with the blacks in competing against the whites. Frank Chin's play at the American Place Theater has one good scene at the opening of Act II, pointed and funny, and some well-turned lines scattered throughout; but it is a loose aggregate of untheatrical surfaces with no real center, no dramatic propulsion and urgency. Emotions wax and wane quite arbitrarily; small things are made much of and large ones thrown away; and what little shape there is to the play is imposed awkwardly from without.

We are treated pell-mell to the petty misadventures, wistful reminiscences and wishful fantasies of Tam Lum, a young documentary filmmaker—one of those playwright's alter egos on whom their authors lavish much more empathy than a mere spectator can muster. The tone is magniloquent poeticism ("spending your whole time running out of your life into everybody's distance") when it is not mocking self-pity which, in the end, is more enervating than prophylactic. Still, a playwright who can have an adult say to an officious child, "Do you want to be old all your life? Talk like a kid while you are a kid, even if you have to fake it," is not to be dismissed out of hand.

Matters, unfortunately, are not helped by the three principal performances. Randy Kim makes the hero unduly mannered and charmless; Sab Shimono plays his Japanese-American dentist friend with not enough force to extract a wobbly milk tooth; and Sally Kirkland, as the dentist's Platonic concubine (a part that makes even less sense than most), plays with a mumbling, lethargic autism that shows Method acting to be still as deadeningly alive as ever. Jack Gelber's staging is flatfooted and John Wulp's scenery barely adequate, but Willa Kim's costumes are appropriate and Roger Morgan's lighting is to the point. "I'm tired of talking, really tired," says Tam, "but every time I stop it's so goddamn awful." And he doesn't stop, thus refusing to subordinate private interest to the common good.

CRITICAL COMMENTARY

Elaine H. Kim (essay date 1982)

SOURCE: "Chinatown Cowboys and Warrior Women: Searching for a New Self-Image," in *Asian American Literature: an Introduction to the Writings and Their Social context,* Temple University Press, 1982, pp. 173-213.

[*In the following excerpt, Kim examines Chin's depiction of the struggle to define a uniquely Asian American male identity in* The Chickencoop Chinaman *and other works.*]

Chin views Chinese American history as a wholesale and systematic attempt to emasculate the Chinese American male. Racist laws "warred against us . . . to deny our manhood, to drive us out of the country, to kill us. . . . [T]wenty to thirty men for every woman. . . . Chinese-America was rigged to be a race of males going extinct without women." Chinese Americans were deprived of a knowledge of their history, according to Chin and the other editors of *Aiiieeeee!*, and forbidden a "legitimate mother tongue" because they were viewed as foreigners who cannot speak English:

> Only Asian-Americans are driven out of their tongues and expected to be at home in a language they never use and a culture they encounter only in books written in English. This piracy of our native tongues by white culture amounts to the eradication of a recog-nizable Asian-American culture here.
>
> [Frank Chin, Jeffery Paul Chan, Lawson Fusao Inada, and Shawn Hsu Wong, eds., *Aiiieeeee! An Anthology of Asian-American Writers,* 1974]

"The deprivation of language," is part of the castration process:

> [It has] contributed to the lack of a recognized Asian-American cultural integrity . . . and the lack of a

recognized style of Asian-American manhood. . . . Language is the medium of culture and the people's sensibility, including the style of manhood. . . . Stunt the tongue and you have lopped off the culture and sensibility. On the simplest level, a man in any culture speaks for himself. Without a language of his own, he is no longer a man.

> [Frank Chin and Jeffery Paul Chan, "Racist Love," in *Seeing through Shuck*, ed. Richard Kostelanetz, 1972]

The castration that Chin says Asian American males have suffered through history is also reflected, he contends, in culture, so that Chinese American males have not been permitted to speak in American literature: "Our white-dream identity being feminine, the carriers of our strength, the power of the race belongs to our women. The dream women of this dream minority naturally prefer white men to our own. . . . Four of the five American-born Chinese Americans to publish serious literary efforts are women." Chin criticizes Jade Snow Wong, Betty Lee Sung, and Virginia Lee for accommodating the stereotypes of an exoticized Chinese heritage and of the Chinese as a model minority. But he also asserts that the fact that there are more published Chinese American women than men writers emasculates Chinese American men because literary creativity is the proper domain of men: "[I]n this culture [manliness means] aggressiveness, creativity, individuality, just being taken seriously" ["Confessions of the Chinatown Cowboy," *Bulletin of Concerned Asian Scholars*, Fall 1972].

In **"Song of the Monogram Warner Bros. Chink: News To Raise the Dead"** (1971), the first step in reclaiming the manhood of the Chinese American is to gang-rape Joy, who represents the indifferent white majority:

> I've been yellow on the lawn of your keep off the grass grass
> Small and stooped, stupid and small tearing your daisies apart
> Standing around, yelling yellow stillness all over your green grass lawn.
> You yawned in the morning, Joy, bobbed a boob, made my bird fly,
> Called me our Japanese gardener and shut me up.
>
> Because I feared losing my hardon and wanted to please.

The narrator takes revenge for this castrating indifference on behalf of the "twenty thousand bleeding finger-bones" of his yellow forefathers, who carved through granite and ice in the desert darkness to build the American railroad. Those silent men were

> . . . men not I, nor my father,
> Nor you, especially you, dear gollygosh you,
> Ever heard sing of the railroad, of the winds that killed them,
> Of the trains they never rode.

> My faceless grandfathers, men we never heard sing,
> All gone, with their laughable names, all gone.
> The Chinese American is vindicated when
> A hundred years of Chinamen
> In public
> Took turns
> At a piece of
> White ass.

The new Asian American identity, according to Chin, must be built around the Asian American man's being accepted as American. To gain this acceptance, it is necessary to challenge the stereotype of quaint foreigners, to reject the notion of the passive, quiet Asian American, and to move away from the stultifying limitations of the glittering Chinatown ghetto. Three of Chin's pieces of short fiction, **"Food for All His Dead"** (1962), **"Yes Young Daddy"** (1970), and **"Goong Hai Fot Choy"** (1970), from an unpublished manuscript title *A Chinese Lady Dies*, are organized around the theme of Chinatown as decaying beneath an exotic facade. The central character of each work is a young Chinese American male who must come to terms with the absence of a suitable Chinese American male legacy and the stifling decay and futility of life in the Chinese American community. Ultimately, to survive and try to affirm his own manhood, he must leave Chinatown and everything it stands for behind.

The central characters of the three stories are essentially the same: Johnny and Fred, of the former two stories, are sensitive young artists who are outgrowing their families, Chinatown, and particularly Chinese American women. But they are not sure they can survive outside the Chinese American community. In the last story, Johnny and Fred have evolved into the character Dirigible, who is frozen into inaction as he waits for his mother, and by extension Chinatown, to die so that he can be free. Ultimately, Dirigible is developed into the main figure in the play *Chickencoop Chinaman*, Tampax Lum, the Chinese American who searches for a new identity beyond the narrow confines of the Chinatown world from which he has recently escaped.

Chin's Chinatown is a barren, corrupt, and declining place where mothers and fathers are dying of wasting diseases, and their children are crippled, weary, and stifled by boredom. The Chinese people are portrayed as bugs, spiders, frogs, tipped-over mechanical toys, and oily fish gasping on dry land. The community itself is likened to a funeral parlor, an obsolete carnival, or a pathetic minstrel show. . . .

Johnny, Fred, and Dirigible are too good for Chinatown and also too powerless to do anything but watch it die. They detest the self-deception of the people of Chinatown, who unlike them cannot see or refuse to see the dying. Johnny's father continues to rant about the Chinese Revolution of 1911, Aunt Dee insists on powdering her face into a mask and thinking dirty thoughts, and Dirigible's mother observes the Chinese New Year even as she is falling into crumbling decay. Chin's young male protagonists must leave Chinatown because there are no examples of "manhood" there for them to follow. Johnny's father is immersed in an impossible self-deception, knowing less, Johnny thinks, than his son does; Dirigible participated in deceiving his father with his mother when he was a boy. Besides the ineffectual fathers, there are only the shopkeepers, grinning and nodding over the produce in Chinatown vegetable stores.

All three protagonists are embodied in Tampax Lum, the main character in the play *Chickencoop Chinaman,* which is a forum for Chin's ideas on Chinese American culture, identity, and manhood. The play contains a series of lessons for Chinese Americans: that Asian American culture can be found neither by imitating whites nor by imitating Blacks; that Asian Americans should not be forced into either an "American" or a "Chinese" mold; that Asian Americans should not allow themselves to be used as a "model minority." Chin's opinions, as expressed elsewhere in essays, are presented through the characters and situations in the play. But instead of building a new manhood and a new culture to replace the bankrupt Chinatown culture through his imaginative writing, Chin creates an overriding sense of the utter futility of the male protagonist's efforts to redefine himself.

In *Chickencoop Chinaman,* Chinese American identity has been manufactured in a chickencoop by racism: it is "nylon and acrylic. . . . A miracle synthetic! Drip dry and machine washable." Chinese Americans are "children of the dead," their language the "talk of orphans." The legacy of Chinese American manhood is recalled only in vague references to a "Chinatown Kid" who used to frequent boxing matches and whose name no one can quite remember. Tam and his best friend, Blackjap Kenji, get together to sing a song imitating Helen Keller, who symbolizes Asian Americans, since she overcame her "birth defects" and can now see, hear, and speak no evil.

At first, when Tam speaks aggressively and with wit, it seems that he will be the embodiment of the new Chinese American man. But the play ends with Tam, "like a mad elephant, blowing his nose in the dark," chopping green onions with a Chinese cleaver. He has rejected the "petrified cheerios," the Aunt Jemima pancakes, and the "Chun King chopped phooey" of race stereotyping. He has also rejected the myth that Asians could be like Blacks, but he has as yet found nothing to replace the stereotypes and false directions. There are no new mythical heroes; the Chinatown Kid is not his father but a nameless dishwasher who was afraid of old white ladies peeking at him through keyholes.

Tam, the central character who might have embodied a new Asian American male identity, backs down when the half-Chinese girl attacks him, saying, "Everything you say is right. I'm a good loser. I give up." When he tries to fight, he misses the punch and falls flat on his face: "I'm the Chickencoop Chinaman. My punch won't crack an egg, but I'll never fall down." Until he can regain his

true heritage, his identity, and his masculinity, he is good mostly for talk, which he hopes to inject with "some flow, some pop, some rhythm." He tries to seduce the Hong Kong Girl with his talk:

> *Hong Kong Dream Girl*: You sure have a way with words, but I'd like it better if you'd speak the mother tongue.

> *Tam*: I speak nothing but the mother tongue. . . . But I got a tongue for you baby. And maybe you could handmake my bone China.

But she giggles and runs off. When the half-Chinese girl attacks him, he retorts the only way he can, answering, "Wanna fuck?" The play ends with Tam as a midget like Dirigible—a frozen, hopeful midget, but a midget all the same. Although he is eager to find his own history, style, language, and masculine identity now that he has shed self-deception and false heroes, he is not complete. He is still experimenting.

Chin calls Lum a "comic embodiment of Asian-American manhood." Although Chin contends that Tam Lum is a comic figure and the play a comedy, beneath the wit of his verbal jousts peer some of the images of death, decay, and impotence of the earlier stories, in scenes totally devoid of beauty or the possibility of love. The worlds Chin has created are peopled by repulsive cripples and synthetic orphans. One is never quite sure whether or not to laugh at the "comic manifestations of Asian-American manhood"; we are carried forward on clever metaphors and images until we are faced with the Asian American male protagonist squirming helplessly, pinpointed by his own verbal barbs.

Chin says that he wants to promote the creation of an Asian American mythology and language that is not alien or hostile to the Asian American sensibility. The task of the Asian American writer, he asserts, is "to legitimize the language, style, and syntax of his people's experience, to codify the experiences common to his people into symbols, cliches, linguistic mannerisms, and a sense of humor that emerges from an organic familiarity with the experience."

But Chin's protagonists are alienated characters. Their language is often witty and ornate but it is seldom the "backtalking, muscular, singing stomping full-blooded language" Chin believes should express the "Asian American sensibility." Tam Lum's "backtalk" emerges as "outtalk." His characters are used as mouthpieces for thinly disguised lectures on Chinese American history, identity, and manhood, as in the following unbalanced dialogue:

> *Tam*: I mean, we grow up bustin our asses to be white anyway. . . . [W]hat made the folks happiest was for some asshole, some white off the wall J. C. Penney's clerk type with his crispy suit to say I spoke English well—

> *Lee*: You're talking too fast for me. I can't . . .

Tam: (Continuing through Lee's interruption). And praisin me for being "Americanized" and no juvenile delinquency. "The strong Chinese family . . . Chinese culture." And the folks just smiled. The reason there was no juvenile delinquency was because there were no kids! The laws didn't let our women in . . .

Lee: What's this got to do with anything?

Tam: . . . and our women born here lost their citizenship if they married a man from China. And all our men here, no women, stayed here, burned all their diaries, their letters, everything with their names on it . . . threw the ashes into the sea . . . hoping that that much of themselves could find someplace friendly. I asked an old man if that was so. He told me it wasn't good for me to know such things, to let all that stuff die with the old.

Lee: You taking me to school?

Tam: He told me to forget it . . . to get along with "Americans." Well, they're all dead now. We laugh at 'em with the "Americans," talk about them saying "Buck Buck bagaw" instead of "giddyup" to their horses and get along real nice here now, don't we?

Lee: Oh, Tam, I don't know.

In **"Food for All His Dead,"** Johnny suspects the problem: "I hear myself talking all this stupid stuff, it's sort of great, you know? Because I have to listen to what I'm saying or I'll miss it." In **"Goong Hai Fot Choy,"** Dirigible says, "I'm constantly surprised at what I have to say when no one is listening to me in the same room," and Tam Lum in **Chickencoop Chinaman** keeps talking, even though he is tired of talking, because "everytime I stop it's so goddamned awful!"

The Chinese American identity Chin forges through the language and characterization of Fred, Dirigible, Johnny, and Tampax Lum is incomplete. The characters are alienated adolescents, incapacitated by the sense of their own impotence. But they are the only characters in Chin's stories and plays that emerge clearly. All the other characters are mere types. Johnny's parents are not developed; Dirigible's mother is a symbol; in fact, the women in Chin's writings belong to one of two types—dumb broads or castrators. In **Chickencoop Chinaman,** the half-Chinese woman is a castrating bitch and the "Hong Kong dream girl" in her "super no-knock, rust-proof, tit-stiffening bra" and bouffant hairdo is simply a stereotype.

Frank Chin has delineated some of the factors that have suppressed the Asian American male, but a new identity has yet to be forged. It seems obvious that as long as the Asian American male is depicted as a victim of his community, his family, and women in general, the portrayal will be incomplete. Chin's basic contempt for his characters, a contempt that is mixed with compassion for Tampax Lum and his kindred heroes, leaves the reader with the impression of futility and bored misanthropy. Chin flails out at the emasculating effects of oppression,

but he accepts his oppressors' definition of "masculinity." The result is unresolved tension between contempt and desire to fight for his Asian American characters.

The battle against this oppression is individualized in the stories and plays; that the main characters are afflicted with metaphysical *angst* and elitist fantasies is no wonder, since they are drawn large and detailed compared to the mechanical toys and insects that people their world. Chin's preoccupation with death and decay, his sexism, cynicism, and sense of alienation have prevented him from creating protagonists who can overcome the devastating effects of racism on Chinese American men.

THE YEAR OF THE DRAGON

PRODUCTION REVIEWS

Clive Barnes (review date 3 June 1974)

SOURCE: "Culture Study," in *The New York Times*, 3 June 1974, p. 39.

[*In the following mixed review of the New York production of* The Year of the Dragon, *Barnes finds the play's "insights into the Chinese community" "absolutely fascinating" but also judges it lacking in energy.*]

We have a great deal of theater in black and white but not too much in yellow. The American Place Theater, and its director, Wynn Handman, have been encouraging the Chinese-American writer Frank Chin. Last season Mr. Chin gave us **The Chickencoop Chinaman,** and this season the American Place Theater is rounding off its subscription series with his latest play. **The Year of the Dragon,** which officially opened Saturday night.

As in his earlier play, Mr. Chin is concerned primarily with the American Chinese in American society. The position of the Asian in America is very important and interesting. The black, much larger, and therefore more powerful, minority, has pretty much broken away from stereotyped images—indeed society wouldn't like me to say a black dancer had natural rhythm even if he had. But for the Chinese, or Japanese, the situation is more difficult. Laundries, tourism and restaurants, a Chinese writer might well believe that even his plays should come with an egg roll.

The Year of the Dragon is set in San Francisco's Chinatown, now. The hero is Fred Eng, a tourist guide, a travel agent, a man who can collaborate with his Boston-based sister on a best-selling *Mama Fufu's Cookbook,* but can also worry about a kid brother on probation with a gun in his pocket.

As in his earlier play, although even more directly. Mr. Chin is questioning identity—how Chinese or how American is the Chinese-American? And you don't get the answer in a fortune cookie.

Mattie (the Boston sister of Mama Fufu fame) has come home on a visit with her new Caucasian husband. The father of the family is dying, and to be with him in this final rite he brought home his first wife from China, Fred's mother. Now the family, including Ma, who is the father's American-born Chinese wife and mother of two of his children, is gathered around on Chinese New Year for the end. Pa, though near death, is far from the coffin—he still runs his house, and intends to make a public speech with a little joke about Charlie Chan in it.

The Year of the Dragon is an interesting play, but it has a lot of gaps in it. It lacks energy at times. What I found absolutely fascinating was its insights into the Chinese community, and this really held my attention. But as a play its discursiveness is something of a liability. Mr. Chin wants us to feel, but we end up thinking. No harm.

The play has been directed by Russell Treyz with a good eye for incidental detail but insufficient pace. The author needed a little more gusto, I thought. Leo Yoshimura's scenery had the proper Sino-American air to it, and the performances were excellent.

Randy Kim (who according to the program is now styling himself Randall (Duk) Kim) is an excellent actor with a quite individual tautness to his performances. He here conveys a peculiar but endearing mixture of toughness and vulnerability ringed round with cynicism. Tina Chen, with a long-suffering good nature, made an attractive sister. Pat Suzuki was fine as the all-American Chinese mother who ran to the bathroom in times of stress, and Conrad Yama nicely showed absurdity and patriarchalism as a first-generation Chinese father.

First generation and second generation, China and America, this is what fascinates Mr. Chin. It is a fascination that we can intermittently share, especially if we think of his play in the terms of that American melting pot that never seems to be properly heated and never seems to be properly stirred.

Jack Kroll (review date 10 June 1974)

SOURCE: "Sweet and Sour," in *Newsweek,* Vol. LXXXII, No. 23, 10 June 1974, p. 84.

[*In the following evaluation, Kroll admires the "strong emotional writing, sweet and sour comedy and . . . real anguish" in* The Year of the Dragon.]

A couple of seasons ago Frank Chin singlehandedly established the Chinese branch of the new American ethnic theater with his play, *The Chickencoop Chinaman.* He now provides that school its second work, *The Year of the Dragon.* Chin's new play again pivots about a character largely himself, here called Fred Eng, an angry not-quite-young man caught in the limbo between yellow and white, Chinese and American. Fred's dilemma reflects the dilemma of Chin as an artist. A gifted writer and electric sensibility, he is part Chinese Lenny Bruce, "spritzing" a comedy of bitter alienation, and part Number One Son, drawn to the traditional Chinese values—family, duty—which have been diluted by American culture.

Chin's problem is fitting the hip into the square. His new play attempts to solve this by a miscegenation of the Bruce spritz with the Arthur Miller family-problem play, in which Fred is torn between his father, a little big man in San Francisco's Chinatown, and his sister, who has married a white man with whom she runs a Chinese restaurant in Boston. There's also Fred's gun-toting, semi-delinquent younger brother, his stepmother who hides from life in the bathroom, and his "China Mama," his real mother whom his father has suddenly imported from the old country. You can diagram the tensions and flip-flops for yourself, and it's to Chin's credit that he escapes as often as he does from cliché and banality by strong emotional writing, sweet and sour comedy and a real anguish.

Under Russell Treyz's direction the cast at the American Place Theater is strong, especially Conrad Yama as the father, the epitome of impossible autocratic love; and the extraordinary Randall Kim, who plays Fred like a trapped animal, prowling and hissing in the cage of his constricted identity.

Edith Oliver (review date 10 June 1974)

SOURCE: "Reunion," in *The New Yorker,* Vol. L, No. 16, 10 June 1974, p. 64.

[*In the review below, Oliver expresses some reservations about* The Year of the Dragon *but declares that the characters in the drama "are playable, complex, and always convincing."*]

Frank Chin, whose first play, *The Chickencoop Chinaman,* of a couple of years ago, instantly launched him as a dramatist, and launched his leading man, that magnetic marvel Randy Kim, as a potential star, has now done a second play. *The Year of the Dragon,* again presented under the auspices of the American Place (subscribers only), again has Mr. Kim as spokesman and pivotal character. The setting is an apartment in San Francisco's Chinatown, the time is just before and during the celebration of the Chinese New Year, and the people under consideration are the family who live in the apartment. The father, born in China and now the mayor of his community, is dying and knows it; he is the absolute ruler of his household, insistent upon filial obedience. The mother, much younger and born in this country, jokes and grins a good deal, and tends to escape all domestic tensions and blowups (of which there are many) by ducking into the bathroom with a good book. The older son—Mr. Kim, as Fred Eng—is a man of forty who works as a tourist guide. (Stepping in and out of the action, he is also our guide to the family.) The daughter has lived for many years in Boston, where she runs a string of successful Chinese restaurants; she has just returned to San Francisco with her white American husband to promote a cookbook ("Mama Fufu's") that she and Fred have written. And there are others, in the family and out of it.

The plot is filled with incidents, entertaining distractions, and a couple of revelations, but at its core is a struggle for power between the father, who is the embodiment of tradition and is determined to keep the family together, and in that house, after he is dead, and Fred, just as determined to leave and pursue his career as a writer and to set the others free as well. The play, which could be loosely compared to Odets' *Awake and Sing,* is absorbing, and only partly because of its unfamiliar subject matter. Still, it is not yet as strong as it could be. There are moments when the action seems to get out of hand, and too many essential scenes are introduced by such feeble, transparent lines as "I want to have a talk with you." Also, I think it may have been a mistake to make Fred a writer, forcing the audience to autobiographical conclusions. There can be no question, though, about the ability of the gifted, passionate, funny Mr. Chin; his characters are playable, complex, and always convincing, and the words they speak are theirs and theirs alone. The acting, under the direction of Russell Treyz, is very good. Pat Suzuki, delightful as the mother, always makes clear the panic and sadness under the chuckles and snatches of songs and jaunty airs. Conrad Yama is perfect as the stubborn, dying old autocrat, and so, for that matter, are beautiful Tina Chen, as the tender, loyal, but somewhat alienated daughter; Doug Higgins, as her husband, whose every joke misfires or peters out, and whose earnest camaraderie cannot conceal his bewilderment at the squabbles that go off like fire-crackers around him; Keenan Shimizu, as a rebellious younger brother; and Lilah Kan, as a mysterious outsider—an older woman known as China Mama. As for Mr. Kim, he is the indelible Chickencoop Chinaman come to life again, unpacking his soul in one blistering, sarcastic monologue after another, flinging every cliché about the Chinese into the face of the audience and boiling over with rage and love and temperament. Mr. Kim makes the play into a vehicle for Fred every time he opens his mouth—but then, earlier this season, he even made "The Tempest" into a

(sporadic) vehicle for Trinculo. Admirable scenery, lighting, and costumes by Leo Yoshimura, Victor En Yu Tan, and Susan Hum Buck, respectively.

John Simon (review date 17 June 1974)

SOURCE: "Now You See It—Now You Don't," in *New York* Magazine, Vol. 7, No. 24, 17 June 1974, p. 76.

[*In the following negative assessment of* The Year of the Dragon, *Simon contends that Chin "exhibits a lack of discipline and tendency to attitudinize" in the play.*]

"Coming of age" is the basic subject of two essentially realistic new plays, the splashier but also more irritating of which is Frank Chin's **The Year of the Dragon** at the American Place Theater. The Chinese-American author has flashes of wit and flights of anger, a felicitous mordancy here, a bit of a genuine ache there. But, as in his first play, **The Chickencoop Chinaman,** he again exhibits a lack of discipline and tendency to attitudinize; this domestic tragicomedy finally differs from soap opera only in its ethnic coloration and greater vagueness—incidents and people remaining unclarified out of sheer dramaturgic irresponsibility. The themes are noncommunication between parents and children, strife between spouses, centrifugal pull away from Chinatown and centripetal pull back, self-realization through becoming an American college student or writer vs. self-realization through remaining a defiantly yellow tourist guide, or even hoodlum.

Russell Treyz has directed rather too laxly, allowing such cunning scene stealers as Randy Kim—now upstaging his colleagues even with his new name, Randall "Duk" Kim—to introduce enough rubatos and pauses to permit a consultation of the *I Ching* between, or during, many of the lines delivered. Still, we can bask in a handful of personable performances, among which Keenan Shimizu's seems most promising, and Conrad Yama's most accomplished. Tina Chen is a delight to eye and ear, and the others will do. But Kim, playing the hero who, upon his father's death, must rule the family only to disband it, should beware: clever as he is, his mannerisms are becoming disruptive; the *Book of Changes,* under the hexagram K'un, warns: "The superior man is yellow and moderate . . ." And I wonder: was Chinatown as much of a ghetto as Chin would have it? Was it really as hard for yellow persons to make it as for blacks? Was there as much honky-hating among San Francisco's Chinese as he implies, or is the play a bit of a tempest in a teapot?

Additional coverage of Chin's life and career is contained in the following source published by Gale Research: *Contemporary Authors,* Vols. 33-36, rev. ed.

Spalding Gray
1941-

INTRODUCTION

Gray has won critical acclaim for his autobiographical monologues, in which he transforms the banalities and sometimes embarrassing intimacies of his personal life into larger reflections on contemporary society. Described by Don Shewey as "a hybrid of performance artist and stand-up comedian," Gray sits at a desk on a barren stage and improvises from a prepared outline. His performances have elicited comparisons to the work of such contemporary comedians as Woody Allen and Lily Tomlin and to the writings of Mark Twain. While some critics view Gray's monologues as self-indulgent and superficial, many applaud his insights and storytelling expertise. David Hirson has observed that "Gray's revelations tap into a collective worship of the mundane self: he titillates our narcissistic impulses by a titanic display of his own."

BIOGRAPHICAL INFORMATION

Born in Rhode Island to middle-class parents, Gray became interested in theater as a teenager. He studied acting at Emerson College, and after his graduation in 1965 he performed for two years in summer stock theater in New England and New York state. In 1967 Gray traveled to Texas and Mexico; upon his return several months later he learned that his mother had committed suicide. This loss and the consequent family trauma caused him to suffer a prolonged depression that resulted in a nervous breakdown nine years later. In the late 1960s Gray moved to New York City, where he joined the Performance Group, an experimental Off-Broadway theater company. There he composed his first autobiographical dramatic works. In 1977 he founded the Wooster Group with Elizabeth Le-Compte, with whom he wrote *Sakonnet Point* and *Rumstick Road,* two experimental dramas that explored his mother's mental illness and suicide and their effects on his youth and his family. Gray and LeCompte also composed *Nayatt School,* a satire of T. S. Eliot's play *The Cocktail Party.* These three plays made up a trilogy called *Three Places in Rhode Island,* which Gray produced collectively in 1979.

Gray became interested in the possibilities of the dramatic monologue during his tenure as a summer workshop instructor at the University of California, Santa Cruz, in 1978. The following year he performed his first monologue, *Sex and Death to the Age 14,* at the Performing Garage in New York. In the 1980s Gray continued to produce and perform monologues, and publicity from his performances resulted in his being cast as an American ambassador's aide in the 1983 film *The Killing Fields.*

The two months Gray spent filming on location in Thailand became the subject of *Swimming to Cambodia,* considered by many to be his masterpiece. Gray has followed *Swimming to Cambodia* with several more monologues, including *Monster in a Box, Gray's Anatomy,* and *It's a Slippery Slope.* He has also created film versions of *Swimming to Cambodia* and *Monster in a Box* and a television adaptation of *Terrors of Pleasure.*

MAJOR WORKS

Swimming to Cambodia is Gray's best-known monologue and is widely regarded as his finest work. The piece premiered in 1985 and evolved improvisationally at the Performing Garage. Gray, who performed the monologue sitting at a desk with only a glass of water, a notebook, and two maps of Southeast Asia as props, narrated anecdotes and observations from several levels of his own experience—as an individual coping with personal problems, as a professional actor in a large-scale movie production, as an American facing the aftermath of U.S. policy in Cambodia since the Vietnam War, and as a human being learning of the atrocities committed by the Khmer Rouge, a guerilla group that terrorized Cambodia in 1975. The title is taken from Gray's remark that explaining the tragedy of Cambodia "would be a task equal to swimming there from New York." Gray's success with the stage version of *Swimming to Cambodia* inspired him to collaborate with his girlfriend Renée Shafransky on a movie version of the monologue. The film was produced by Shafransky, directed by Jonathan Demme, and released in 1987 to critical acclaim.

CRITICAL RECEPTION

Swimming to Cambodia met with an enthusiastic reception. Critics admired the pace and fluidity of Gray's narrative, the numerous descriptive details in his recollections, and the honesty with which he presented his stories. Elinor Fuchs praised Gray's blending of personal and social events in the play, describing *Swimming to Cambodia* as "an artistic culmination for Gray as well as an impressive political breakthrough." Lydia Alix Gerson admired the way the piece creates "parallels between domestic and international outrage," viewing *Swimming to Cambodia* as a meditation on living in the modern world, which is "without moral compass." Other critics, including William W. Demastes and Jessica Prinz, have focused on Gray's roots in avant-garde theater. Summarizing Gray's unique position as an experimental playwright who has achieved commercial and popular success, Demastes has observed: "Gray's work appeals to middle America, but for those who can see more than vicarious experiences in the works, the pieces take on an ironic significance, revealing fragmentation and uprootedness that is a first step to political awakening."

PRINCIPAL WORKS

PLAYS

Scales 1966
Sakonnet Point [with Elizabeth LeCompte] 1975
Rumstick Road [with LeCompte] 1977
Nayatt School [with LeCompte] 1978
Three Places in Rhode Island [comprising *Sakonnet Point, Rumstick Road,* and *Nayatt School;* with LeCompte] 1978
Point Judith: An Epilog [with LeCompte] 1979
Sex and Death to the Age 14 1979
Booze, Cars, and College Girls 1979
India and After (America) 1979
Nobody Wanted to Sit Behind a Desk 1980
A Personal History of the American Theater 1980
47 Beds 1981
Interviewing the Audience 1981
8 x Gray 1982

In Search of the Monkey Girl [with Randal Levenson] 1982
Swimming to Cambodia 1984
Travels through New England 1984
Rivkala's Ring [adaptor; from a story by Anton Chekhov] 1985
Terrors of Pleasure: The House 1985; as *Terrors of Pleasure: The Uncut Version,* 1989
Sex and Death to the Age 14 (collection) 1986
Swimming to Cambodia: The Collected Works 1987
Monster in a Box 1990
Gray's Anatomy 1993
It's a Slippery Slope 1996

OTHER MAJOR WORKS

Bedtime Story [with Renée Shafransky] (television play) 1987
Swimming to Cambodia (screenplay) 1987
Terrors of Pleasure (television adaptation) 1987
Impossible Vacation (novel) 1992
Monster in a Box (screenplay) 1992

AUTHOR COMMENTARY

Perpetual Saturdays (1981)

SOURCE: Spalding Gray, "Perpetual Saturdays," in *Performing Arts Journal,* Vol. 6, No. 1, 1981, pp. 46-9.

[*In the essay below, Gray offers his observations on performance and on experimental theater, which he calls "backyard theater."*]

I never could relate to the term "avant-garde." When I see a term like that I automatically want to make my own American translation. I want to translate it into, "The Theatre of the Backyard," or even more American, "backyard theatre."

As a boy, growing up in America, I loved Saturdays. Saturday was my favorite day of the week and my secret ambition was to make every day into Saturday. With this attitude, it took me fifteen years, instead of twelve, to get out of school but I did get out and I did eventually find Elizabeth LeCompte, Richard Schechner, the Performing Garage and the whole group. I found them. They found me. We found each other.

To make a long story (*The Drama Review,* Autoperformance Issue, T81) short, I found my backyard. I found my perpetual Saturdays.

Other than being a part of the human race, I have never been aware of being a part of any movement. The radical child in me searched for a place to play. I call it "radical" because the pursuit of play in our culture is a radical act. It is also a very political act as everything we do with any kind of full commitment is political. And by "play," I don't mean weekend leisure activity, I mean viewing one's life as a total act of constructive play. The abolition of weekend consciousness. The decline and downfall of Saturdays.

Backyard theatre is an impossible kind of theatre to make without a backyard and the Wooster Group/Performance Group only grew up because it had the Performing Garage as its backyard. Also, the group grew up realizing how fragile a thing real adult "playing" is. We needed a special time and place in which to play and soon realized we had to work to preserve that place and time. So, Saturdays blended into Mondays and the whole thing took off into a really creative balance of work and play.

Liz LeCompte and I first began *Sakonnet Point* by playing with flashlights. Nothing more, nothing less. If we had any idea of being a part of the "avant-garde" we were not conscious of it. What we were conscious of was that we were inspired by, and wanted to imitate, some of the best American backyard theatre in the world. We saw the groups that Richard mentioned in his article. It was a wonderful experience for Liz and me. Before we came to New York, we never dreamed such things existed or could exist. Seeing it gave us the courage to do our own work. We quickly realized that when you do not make much money for what you do, you better be sure that you're doing what you want to do. In fact, that is the most positive aspect of a lack of funds. It makes you question yourself down to the bone. What is it we want? We kept asking and we made one piece that turned into four. We struck a rich well of personal imagery. We spread seeds. We got fruit but the seeds we spread were not in marked packages and that was all the better because the fruit was such a surprise.

I can't imagine wanting to work if I knew what it was I wanted to make before I made it. I can't imagine stopping a productive process in order to develop a system about a past part of that process in order to teach it. Try to develop a system about American backyards? Try it. Maybe a system about English, French or Dutch backyards but American?

I don't want to slow down or stop in order to teach and yet I am teaching a course in autobiographic composition at New York University's Experimental Theatre Wing this fall. What I do when I "teach" is to bring in present work/play problems. I take what's on my desk or in my head or body and bring it into class. It's about what's going on for me now. It's not about specific significant knowledge of the past. It's about giving energy and presence to the class with the hope that one student might be lucky enough to find a backyard.

Because theatre is a temporal art, you've got to be there for it. No amount of reading Artaud can tell you what he did. His works are not literature. They are descriptions

and scenarios of temporal events. Events that needed to have their being in time. Theatre is about presence = Life = Death. The Wooster Group/Performance Group has played, over the years, to large audiences. People came. People saw. They can't say they didn't. If there is a future for the world there is a future for backyard theatre. There is no more a system to this theatre than there was a system to my Saturdays. They were random and chaotic.

Also, there is hope for passing it all down. It's one that Richard doesn't mention. A few weeks ago I was in a bookstore and a man who worked there came up to me and began to tell me how much he had loved the Wooster Group's production of *Nayatt School*. His description was so intense and so vivid that he began to turn me on to the piece. He brought tears to my eyes and I wanted not only to be doing it again but I could also see it from his outside view as he told it. It was at this point that I realized that his way of transmitting dramatic knowledge was orally. Like the Irish before the English and Tibetans before the Chinese, he was employing the old oral tradition. I like that. It's a fresh breath in these high tech times and it was there, present with all its human energy and vividness.

For me there is nothing larger than the personal when it is communicated well. The very act of communication takes it into a "larger vein" and brings it back to the community. The personal confessional, stripped of its grand theatrical metaphors, is what matters to me now. I am trying to redefine what is significant for me. I am trying to write and speak from my heart, or as my lines from *Walden* went in *Commune*: "I want to speak somewhere with out bounds, a man in his waking moment to men in their waking moments." (Of course, I have to, and want to add, "women in their waking moments.") This personal exploration has made me more politically aware because now that I've come to myself as authority I have found that I still feel repressed and because of this feeling of repression I am forced to look further into the outside world for its source.

After ten years of working in that windowless hothouse, art house, backyard of a Performing Garage, I began to wonder what was outside. What about "the people?" I longed to be with them. I longed to do what they did and feel what they felt. I thought the group was an artificial "polis" and I wanted out. And at last, when I did get out, I found myself in another group. It was the downtown community of New York and I looked around for "the people" and instead I saw a group trying to survive in a corrupt world that contained a corrupt country that contained a corrupt "City" that was controlled by the rich and I realized that all of us, not just Robert Wilson, but all of us in the "arts," are pets of the rich. We may be different breeds, some mutts some pedigrees, but we are all pets of the rich.

Often I have the fantasy that my work will lead me back full circle to where I started and I will know the place for the first time. I fantasize that if I am true to art it will be the graceful vehicle which will return me to life. Oh, what longings; I will move to Oregon. I will teach sixth grade. I will fall in love. I will marry. I will have three children and I will not reflect. I will die when I die. It will go on without me and without my endless commentary.

I know it's a fantasy because I know I have lost my innocence. Somewhere along the line, every action became for me a piece of theatre. At first it was a protection against the deep and painful realization that every act is a futile act. Every act is a ridiculous dance on the toothy edge of the jaws of time. Then it became more studied. It became art. It became the crazy guy who waves goodbye just before he goes down into the jaws.

Finally, for me, the whole issue is not about choice. I never felt I had a choice. Theatre has been my affliction and my salvation. I do it because I have to and I can clearly say this need, this affliction, this salvation, is neither declining, nor is it falling.

Author's Note to *Swimming to Cambodia* (1985)

SOURCE: "Author's Note," in *Swimming to Cambodia,* Theatre Communications Group, Inc., 1985, pp. xv-xviii.

[*The following essay prefaced the published version of* Swimming to Cambodia. *Gray characterizes himself as a "poetic reporter" who, unlike traditional journalists, prefers to "give the facts a chance to settle down until at last they blend, bubble and mix in the swamp of dream, memory and reflection."*]

In *Conversations with Jorge Luis Borges* the author relates, "I remember my father said to me something about memory. He said, 'I thought I could recall my childhood when we first came to Buenos Aires, but now I know that I can't. . . . Every time I recall something I'm not recalling it really, I'm recalling the last time I recalled it, I'm recalling my last memory of it.'"

Swimming to Cambodia evolved over two years and almost two hundred performances. It was constructed by recalling the first image in my memory of each previous performance, so it evolved almost like a children's "Round Robin" game in which a phrase is whispered around and around a circle until the new phrase is stated aloud and compared with the original. The finished product is a result of a series of organic, creative mistakes—perception itself becoming the editor of the final report.

It is this subconscious way of working, rather than any conscious contrivance or manipulation, that captures my imagination. I am interested in what happens to the so-called facts after they have passed through performance and registered on my memory. Each performance becomes like another person whispering a slightly altered phrase. My job is then to let my intuitive side make choices—and there is never a lack of material, because

all human culture is art. It is all a conscious contrivance for the purpose of survival. All I have to do is look at what's around me.

So I like to think of myself as a kind of "poetic reporter," more like an impressionist painter than a photographer. Most reporters get the facts out as quickly as possible—fresh news is the best news. I do just the opposite. I give the facts a chance to settle down until at last they blend, bubble and mix in the swamp of dream, memory and reflection.

It was almost six months after the filming of *The Killing Fields* that I began my first reports, and more than two years passed before I made my last adjustments. Over that time, *Swimming to Cambodia* evolved into a very personal work in which I made the experience my own. Life made a theme of itself and finally transformed itself into a work of fiction.

I titled this work *Swimming to Cambodia* when I realized that to try to imagine what went on in that country during the gruesome period from 1966 to the present would be a task equal to swimming there from New York. Still, in spite of how horrible it seems to allow entire nations to be wiped out, I opted for tolerance, and beneath tolerance, my bottom line, humor. If ever I thought that God could understand American, I would pray and the prayer would go, "Dear God, please, please let us keep our sense of humor." I still understand and love America, precisely for its sense of humor.

When, in Woody Allen's film *Stardust Memories,* a group of extra-terrestrials lands in his proximity, Woody hopes to get some answers. He asks, "Shouldn't I stop making movies and do something that counts, like helping blind people or becoming a missionary or something?" The otherworldly reply: "You want to do mankind a *real* service? Tell funnier jokes." Humor. The bottom line.

I'm convinced that all meaning is to be found only in reflection. *Swimming to Cambodia* is an attempt at that kind of reflection.

OVERVIEWS AND GENERAL STUDIES

Ron Jenkins (essay date 1988)

SOURCE: "Spalding Gray," in *Acrobats of the Soul: Comedy and Virtuosity in Contemporary American Theatre,* Theatre Communications Group, 1988, pp. 123-41.

[*Focusing particularly on* Swimming to Cambodia, *Jenkins emphasizes the importance of memory in Gray's work. "Memory is a recurring character in every one of his performances," Jenkins states. "It is pitted against the dangerous human tendency to forget the past without reflecting on its meaning."*]

> I like to think of myself as a kind of 'poetic reporter,' more like an impressionist painter than a photographer. Most reporters get the facts out as quickly as possible—fresh news is the best news. I do just the opposite. I give the facts a chance to settle down until at last they blend, bubble and mix in the swamp of dream, memory and reflection.
>
> —SPALDING GRAY

Spalding Gray is a virtuoso rememberer. He takes raw memory and sculpts it into finely wrought performances of epic autobiography. Sitting at a table and talking directly to the audience, Gray performs feats of poetic recall that are remarkable in their clarity, resonance and wit. In a culture where collective memory has atrophied and been replaced by a television tube, audiences respond with rapt attention to the simple authenticity of Gray's personal chronicles.

There are moments in Gray's low-keyed monologues when he seems to be caught in the act of remembering. His voice and gestures create the impression that he is conjuring up the past as he speaks, as if his memory were leaving tangible traces of its efforts. The rhythm of his delivery is peppered with hesitations. The lines in his face wrinkle with concentration. His hands move out in front of him as if they are reaching for images on the verge of being forgotten. Although it all appears spontaneous and casual, each nuance is artfully crafted. Gray has mastered the art of self-performance so completely that even his stammers are planned.

In the process of giving his memories a physical shape, Gray sifts them through the filters of contemporary culture. His stories reach the audience through a series of prisms. Gray performs himself remembering himself, as if he were seeing himself in a movie or reading about himself in a newspaper or watching himself on television. His exercises in hyperautobiography are shaped by the popular media that dominate American society. Gray's stories reflect collective as well as personal anxieties. He remembers his past in terms of his relationships with other people and those relationships are mediated by the demands of their shared culture. Gray's stories are full of vivid portraits of people he has met, and each of those portraits is conveyed in a narrative style rooted in the rhetoric of mass communications. Gray is a one-man newspaper reporter, cinematic auteur and television talk-show host. His multiple roles give even his most intimate memories a sense of ironic detachment. He narrates his past like a man who has difficulty believing it, but is determined to re-play it in an effort to make sense of his era.

Gray began performing his autobiographical monologues as an outgrowth of his work with the Wooster Group at New York's Performing Garage. In 1975 the company began work on a trilogy of plays based on Gray's recol-lections of growing up in Rhode Island. The success of these ensemble productions led Gray to investigate the possibilities of performing his past as a sit-down monologist. The first of these efforts, *Sex and Death to the Age 14,* was presented at the Performing Garage in 1979. Since then he has performed the collected chronicles of his life in theatres all over the country. *A Personal History of the American Theatre* was broadcast on the PBS *Alive from Off Center* series. *Terrors of Pleasure* appeared on HBO. And *Swimming to Cambodia* was released in movie theatres as a feature film directed by Jonathan Demme.

The stories in Gray's monologues are always centered around his personal experiences, but he places them in the context of characters and events that mirror the rich landscape of American dreams and nightmares. *A Personal History of the American Theatre* is as much about the success ethic of American artists as it is about Gray's own life as an actor. Gray simply recounts stories about the plays in which he has performed, but he has worked in enough different settings to make his oral memoirs representative of the profession. He moves deftly from the excesses of Stanislavsky-styled realism in Texas regional theatre to avant-garde experiments with grunting and groping disciples of Grotowski in Manhattan, providing oblique insights into the state of the arts in America at the same time that he casts light on the origins of his own storytelling impulses. He says that as a child he discovered that acting things out was "a kind of ontological state. . . . Life was kind of boring for me in Barrington, Rhode Island, and I would dramatize it by taking any cue from life and blowing it up a bit, theatricalizing it." Theatricalization of his experiences includes putting them in a social and historical perspective. His childhood memories as retold in *Sex and Death to the Age 14* are framed by the atomic explosion at Hiroshima and the first test of the hydrogen bomb.

Swimming to Cambodia (1984) is an example of Gray's multileveled narrative style at its most complex. It began as a monologue about his involvement in *The Killing Fields,* a movie based on a magazine article about a war that most people saw only on television. Gray's performance technique is as densely textured as the layers of media memory in which the story has been wrapped. With a few maps and a pointer as his only props, Gray never moves from his chair, but he presents his tale in a style that subtly incorporates elements of each media through which the incidents have been recalled.

Gray opens the theatre version of his piece with a journalistic dateline: "Saturday, June 18, 1983. Gulf of Siam. Thailand." Then he fleshes out the details with verbal and gestural imagery that is cinematically arresting in its specificity. The colored maps he uses enable Gray to convey history and background information with the entertaining ease of a Sunday newspaper magazine supplement. And all the way through he cuts from one story fragment to another with the startling velocity of a television newsreel montage. Having assimilated the rhetorical devices of mass culture without losing the intimacy of old-fashioned storytelling, Spalding Gray transforms personal memory into a miniature spectacle with epic overtones.

While many performers have been reduced by entertainment technology into shells of vapid personality, Gray uses his understanding of mass media to sharpen his senses of perception and heighten his performance of the things he perceives. His gestures and vocal intonations are deeply influenced by the media through which his memories are filtered. Recounting the filming of a helicopter scene in *The Killing Fields,* Gray visually creates the sense of leaving the ground by tilting his head and torso. The illusion of television immediacy is furthered when he begins to shout as if his voice had to carry over the sound of the spinning copter blades. Shifting perspectives quickly, he paints word pictures of the jungle stretching out below him that are the equivalent of a cinematic long shot.

Gray's seemingly random jump cuts are carefully spliced into his monologues to provide the story with texture and resonance that transcend the cross-media grab-bag effect of the story's surface. A poetic writer with a vibrant sense of language, Gray creates cross references that are novelistic as well as cinematic. The tragicomic portrait of Thai peasants hired to imitate the Cambodian dead by smearing chicken blood on their bodies echoes an episode Gray spoke about a few minutes earlier. To pacify Cambodian villagers who had been accidentally bombed by American B-52s, U.S. Embassy officials gave out hundred-dollar bills to families of the dead and fifties to people who had lost arms or legs. Gray's deadpan juxtaposition of these two events satirizes the absurdity of equating the loss of limbs with a cash bonus. Linking the callous values of the filmmakers with those of the American government, Gray's disarmingly simple storytelling begins to assume the dimension of a spoken epic novel.

Gray's oral epic is full of sophisticated literary devices, but his performance language is informed with implicit references to modern media. The filmic quality of *Swimming to Cambodia* was established before Gray ever considered making a movie of the piece. Crosscutting, montage and closeups are embedded in the structure of Gray's visual memory and have nothing to do with Demme's camera work, which is notable primarily in the way it enhances the cinematic qualities that Gray had already built into his stage performance. In the part of *Swimming to Cambodia* where Gray mocks the parallels between movie production and government policy, he makes his points with acting techniques that demonstrate the blurred boundaries between the realms of film and politics. Gray combines the cool detachment of a politician working a crowd with the emotional intensity of a director zooming in for a closeup.

Making a movie about the bombing of Cambodia reminds Gray of demonstrations against the war in Washington and Kent State. He interrupts his description of the movie shoot to remind us that Nixon watched reruns of *Patton* while students demonstrated outside the White House. Gray flashes Nixon's famous double-V sign with upraised arms as he describes the President's midnight visit with the protesters. In a rapid succession of words and gestures, Gray creates a montage of images that recreate that moment in history as if it were a TV movie. Nixon on the phone asking advice from Norman Vincent Peale and Henry Kissinger. Pol Pot and the Khmer Rouge eating nuts and berries in the countryside outside Phnom Penh. General Alexander Haig declaring Cambodian President Lon Nol to be mentally unstable because he wept openly when he saw that his nation's downfall was at hand.

Gray presents this potpourri of past events with a vocal tone that suggests the objectivity of documentary realism at the same time that it hints at irony. The rhythmic pace of his story builds to a series of urgent crescendos. Every so often he stops unexpectedly, as if to reflect on the outrageous incongruities inherent in what he has just reported. The pauses encourage us to reexamine the implications of the particular image that has just passed before us, as if it were being singled out for an instant replay. Nixon, for example, inanely asking one of the student demonstrators, "How's your team doing?"

Like a good journalist, Gray uses direct quotes to help dramatize his story, but his objectivity is only an illusion. His information is factual, but his opinions seep through in the editorial shifts of his intonation and facial expression. With subdued tones of empathy and respect, Gray reads a letter from a Cambodian prince to the American ambassador refusing the offer of safe passage when the American troops withdraw from Phnom Penh. "I cannot, alas, leave in such a cowardly fashion," writes Sirik Matak. Gray dutifully reports that five days later the prince's liver was carried through the streets on a stick. Choosing that moment to take a sip of water, Gray creates a silence in which to begin his account of the Cambodian genocide. Detailing the nightmares of the "worst autogenocide in modern history," Gray hypothesizes a cloud of evil that comes down on the earth and drives men to unthinkable actions: ". . . babies torn apart like fresh bread in front of their mothers." His voice seems muted by the horror of what he describes, as if the same dark cloud were muffling his words.

Next, in an artful cinematic cut that hints at the connections between the Cambodian atrocities and the anti-Communist prejudices of individual Americans, Gray moves from the killing fields of Cambodia to an Amtrak lounge car. There he meets a Navy man who tells Gray he spends most of his time chained to a chair in a waterproof missile silo waiting for orders to push a green button that will launch a nuclear attack. Recreating his conversation with the man, Gray turns his head from side to side as he switches from the booming certainty of the sailor's militaristic anti-Russian prejudices to the incredulous confusion of Gray's stammering responses. The dialogue plays like a television talk show with Gray as the befuddled host.

Audiences accustomed to perceiving experience in electronically condensed bits of packaged information are fascinated by the compelling power of Gray's artistry. The public's interest in his technique becomes apparent when Gray performs a piece entitled ***Interviewing the Audience***. He invites members of the audience onto the stage to talk about their own lives, but when they are given a chance to ask questions, they want Gray to tell them how he makes his stories so intriguing. "How do you make your life sound so interesting?" "How do you get people to say such funny things?" "How do you get people to pay attention to you for so long?" These are some of the questions Gray is asked one evening at the Brattle Theatre in Cambridge, Massachusetts.

The concerns of the audience are symptomatic of a society that has surrendered its communication skills to its television sets. Everyone wants to learn how to make their own life as funny and appealing as the monologues of their favorite celebrity talk-show host. They feel insecure about their abilities to reach out to one another through the simple exchange of conversation, and Gray offers them a model of a man talking about himself with a grace, charm and humor that draws people close to him. His style of storytelling satisfies the part of their nature that hungers for direct human contact, unmediated by technological intervention.

One of Gray's interviewees that Cambridge evening is a reporter for the *Boston Globe*. She laments the fact that she can never get people to say interesting things when she interviews them for her articles. Furthermore, she fears that she herself has nothing very interesting to say and wonders aloud whether anyone in the audience has really had a good conversation lately. A few people claim to have had satisfying discussions about movies or politics. One man said he had a good talk about reincarnation after reading about it in the *National Enquirer*. But most people seemed to agree that conversations in their personal lives left much to be desired. For both the reporter who wants to get more informative details from her interviews and average people who want more spice in their private gossip, Gray is a source of envy and inspiration.

His answers to the audience's questions are enlightening. He tells them that he develops his monologues by listening to them over and over again on tape. Each night he tapes his show, and tries to improve it, basing each new performance not on the original monologue, but on the most recent version of it. Eventually he dispenses with the tape recorder and constructs each new performance on the memory of the one that has preceded it. Ultimately his show becomes a memory of a memory of a memory of a story that has been distilled down to its essence through the process of continually being retold. Gray appears so natural on stage not because he is just being himself, but because he is so well practiced at impersonating himself as he remembers himself performing himself. This is similar to what politicians do when they make public appearances impersonating the images they have carefully cultivated to win the approval of voters.

But while politicians play their roles in earnest, Gray impersonates himself with a clearly self-deprecating sense of ironic detachment.

This self-reflexive irony is the key to Gray's keen sense of humor. While the humor of a master self-performer like Ronald Reagan is calculated to lull the listeners into a reassuring state of acceptance, Gray's ironic humor is designed to encourage thoughtful reflection and critical questioning. He makes things funny by asking us to examine their credibility. In ***Terrors of Pleasure*** Gray plays a tape recording of a message left on his answering machine by an unscrupulous real estate salesman. The tone of Gray's voice when he introduces the recording and the expressions that pass across his face as he listens to it generate a mood of comic skepticism that makes the man's declarations of trustworthiness howlingly funny. Even more ludicrous, Gray makes clear, is the fact that he actually bought property from this man. Gray is so skilled at conveying this sense of self-mocking irony that he often casts a comic sense of doubt on his own words as he speaks them. A perfect example of a Brechtian actor, Gray has mastered the art of speaking in the first and third person simultaneously. He projects a sense of thinking about the significance of what he says, even as he is in the process of saying it.

The quality of thoughtfulness at the heart of Gray's ironic acting style makes him an undesirable candidate for typical commercial acting roles. In ***Terrors of Pleasure*** Gray tells the story of auditioning for a part in a television movie opposite Farrah Fawcett. The director liked him but was disturbed by something he noticed about Gray's acting in the screen test. A quality that he could only describe as "thinking" seemed to pass across Gray's face whenever he was supposed to make romantic advances towards Fawcett. That reflective quality prevented Gray from projecting the all-American "go-for-it spirit" the director was looking for, so he didn't get the role. Apparently Gray's thoughtfulness created the appearance of doubt, hesitation and ambivalence, tones that are not conducive to selling the products advertised on television, but are essential for generating the kind of disturbingly ironic humor at which Gray excels.

Gray's tones of human ambivalence are what distinguishes his memories from the mass media's versions of the past. There is an illusory objectivity to cameras and newsprint that Gray's style avoids. He may borrow the jumpcuts of cinema or the direct quotes of journalism, but he never pretends to be certain about anything. His stance is one of perpetual doubt. In ***Swimming to Cambodia*** he approaches the Vietnam War with a questioning tone that penetrates past the video pictures of network news and the deceptive myths of Hollywood war films. He uses these common images as a starting point, but transforms them into a kind of personalized multimedia narrative about the awakening of a political conscience. As he talks about flying up in the helicopter on location in Thailand, and describes the film producer's re-creation of dead bodies and burning villages below him, the cadences of his story accelerate markedly. His gestures pulse with the chaotic urgency of battle. There is no door on the helicopter and he is dangerously high above the ground, but he isn't afraid because he's in a movie and is comforted by the camera's power to eroticize the space it aims at. "Like Colgate Gard-All," he blurts out ridiculously, invoking the protection of an old television-commercial toothpaste shield.

Gray speaks and moves with an even greater velocity as he realizes that the movie version of the war is almost as terrifying as the real event. In a flash of intuition he comes up with the idea of "War Therapy." Countries could heal the traumas of war by reenacting it in fictional form. Gray describes his newly invented form of social healing as if it were a demented version of *The Dating Game*. Gray has lost the ability to distinguish history from the image of history he remembers in the media. He remembers seeing B-52s in the television coverage of Vietnam in the sixties but when he tries to imagine a connection between himself and the real war, Gray can only think of himself as riding a helicopter in *Apocalypse Now*. The closest association he can make to the real war is a scene from another movie.

Gray's portrayal of his frenzied condition in the helicopter gathers a breathless momentum. It is full of irony, ambivalence and mental doubletakes. The producer hopes his experience in the film will teach Gray that "morality is not a movable feast," but Gray maintains that he "sees it moving all the time." In the swirling complexity of his imagery Gray makes his audience see morality move as well. He generates a whirlwind of cross-media references that dizzy our senses. His arms move back and forth as if he is literally trying to maintain his moral equilibrium in the blur of game shows, TV commercials, film and history. His awakening conscience has to contend with a media blitz that dulls his senses into forgetting that actions have consequences that outlast the closing credits.

In *Swimming to Cambodia,* as in Gray's other monologues, there does not seem to be any source for the kind of conflict found in traditional drama. Gray's theatre is fueled by a different kind of conflict: the conflict between memory and forgetting. Remembering the real implications of war as distinct from the media's manufactured implications is crucial to Gray's awakening conscience in *Swimming to Cambodia*. The interdependence of memory and morality is central to all his work. Gray's portrayal of the struggle between individual memory and the forgetfulness induced by mass media is a potent dramatization of one of our era's most troubling dilemmas. Gray enacts this struggle each time he pulls a surprising detail out of the past and makes us believe it has just occurred to him at that moment. His stammers, his pauses, and the visible traces of thinking that pass over his face are the tangible manifestations of his unwillingness to let history slip away from him undigested. Memory is a recurring character in every one of his performances. It is pitted against the dangerous human tendency to forget the past without reflecting on its meaning.

The drama in Gray's monologues is not born out of emotional clashes. It comes from the excitement of watching him analyze, question, ridicule and embrace the details of the incidents he so artfully recalls. The audience is witnessing an intimate act in the mind of a rememberer, made visible by the power of Gray's extraordinary performance skills. They are enraptured, not because they necessarily identify with the story he is telling, but because they identify with his need to tell it. Responding to a society in which the individual is bombarded with so many images that he runs the risk of forgetting their significance, Gray stages modern morality plays, with memory as the self-reflexive hero slashing away at the dragon of mass-media oblivion. Appealing to his audience's deep collective need to remember, Gray's performance suggests the possibility of salvaging the past simply by caring enough to think about it.

SWIMMING TO CAMBODIA

PRODUCTION REVIEWS

Mel Gussow (review date 16 November 1984)

SOURCE: "Spalding Gray as Storyteller," in *The New York Times,* 16 November 1984, p. C 3.

[*In the following review of the premiere production of* Swimming to Cambodia *at the Performing Garage in New York, Gussow characterizes the play "a virtuosic evening of autobiographical storytelling."*]

Were it not for the absolute simplicity of the presentation, one might be tempted to say that Spalding Gray has invented a performance art form. Sitting at a card table and talking to the audience, he offers a virtuosic evening of autobiographic storytelling. With the perspicacity of a master travel writer, he acts as reporter, comic and playwright of his own life.

His latest and best work is called *Swimming to Cambodia,* presented in two parts, in repertory, at the Performing Garage. The double-barreled dose of Spalding Gray was inspired by his experiences as an actor in the movie *The Killing Fields.* The film is a screen adaptation of a magazine article by Sydney H. Schanberg, the *New York Times* correspondent, concerning his friendship with his assistant Dith Pran while covering the war in Cambodia. Mr. Gray played the small role of an assistant to the American ambassador, and from that vantage point was able to see the movie, whole, and—using his own reading and research—also to comprehend the military and political complexity of our Cambodian involvement.

On the one hand, *Swimming to Cambodia* is an informative supplement to the heat and fire of *The Killing Fields.* On the other hand, it is a close-up, on-location analysis of the monumental absurdities of movie-making, of people and places in Thailand (where the movie was shot) and of the interpersonal relationships of men and women in film combat. One of Mr. Gray's several provocative theories is his concept of "war therapy." He suggests that every country should work out its militaristic aggressions by making "a major war film once a year." He also believes in "displacement of anxiety"—a small worry substituting for a great pain.

Mr. Gray's stream of experience has the zestful, first-hand quality of a letter home from the front. One could enjoy his narrative in print, but it gains enormously from the fact that he is recounting it in person, acting it out and commenting—with a quizzical look as he tells us about a particularly grotesque Asian sexual practice. In performance, Mr. Gray is a one-man theatrical equivalent of the movie, *My Dinner with Andre.*

Most of his previous monologues have been drawn directly from his personal life. With **Swimming to Cambodia,** he expands his world view. He observes a panoply of others as well as himself, bringing back pithy commentary on his producer, his director (a combination of "Zorro, Jesus and Rasputin"), his fellow actors (Haing S. Ngor, John Malkovich) and the lesser known people on the project, who walk around, at least in Mr. Gray's mind's-eye, wearing T-shirts that say, "Skip the dialogue, let's blow something up."

He weaves his observations with aspects of his inner life—as an insecure actor with a "very confrontational" girlfriend and as a man who has two desperate, equally important wishes. He wants to get an agent and to experience a perfect moment. In the second part of his monologue, Mr. Gray embraces the mystical; he is a Holden Caulfield seeking nirvana on a Thai beach, while never losing his self-mocking sense of humor or his gift for telling a shaggy story.

Some of the reportage is so bizarre, it must be fantasy—or is it? In any case, acting in a war movie was clearly a mind-expanding time for this impressionable actor. Completing his brief role in *The Killing Fields,* Mr. Gray remains land-locked on location—in contrast to his colleagues who fly home at the first opportunity. He feels like a poor relation who has stayed too long as a house guest, but he cannot help himself. He is obsessed by the filming, and he transmits his fascination to the audience.

Elinor Fuchs (review date 27 November 1984)

SOURCE: "With the Stream," in *The Village Voice,* Vol. XXXIX, No. 48, 27 November 1984, p. 123.

[*In the review below, Fuchs considers* Swimming to Cambodia *"an artistic culmination for Gray as well as an impressive political breakthrough."*]

Spalding Gray has created eight autobiographical monologues since 1979. Initially charming in their intimacy, they later wearied as we followed Gray into various formal experiments, such as selecting words randomly in a dictionary (**India (and After)**) or holding up cue cards (**A Personal History of the American Theatre**) to generate memories. The last few seemed so slight that one wondered whether the vein had run out. One longed for the Spalding Gray of **Three Places in Rhode Island,** the performance-art trilogy created with Liz LeCompte and the Wooster Group, in which his autobiographical self somehow became the material of an entire dramatic universe. It seems now that Gray was in practice all these years to create in the monologue form the capaciousness of the earlier ensemble work. **Swimming to Cambodia,** especially Part I, represents an artistic culmination for Gray as well as an impressive political breakthrough.

Gray plays a small role in *The Killing Fields,* the ponderous recent film that attempts to tell the story of the Cambodian genocide. Despite its feints at documentary, the film is really—horrible to say—a soap opera. **Swimming to Cambodia,** built around the making of the film, and thus another layer of artifice removed from Cambodia's death agony, is nonetheless more serious politically, and more artistically shaped as well. Like several of Gray's earlier monologues, it tells the story of a journey, but moves beyond anecdote. Here the journey to Thailand to shoot the film is simultaneously Gray's awakening to personal responsibility in a grotesque political world. Gray doesn't announce his consciousness raising, but rather enacts it.

We first learn of Cambodia distantly, through the character of film producer Roland Joffé, whose words summon up a Shangri-la so joyful "they had lost track of evil." Later we learn in Gray's own blunt account how the Khmer Rouge cut out the livers of countrymen who worked with the Americans, gouged out eyes, disemboweled pregnant women. This horrific awakening is echoed moment to moment, as in the opening of Part I, where a glorious marijuana drug flight into a gold-leaf tunnel turns suddenly ominous as Gray gets sick on the beach creating "a death mask of my own vomit."

Throughout, Gray's story proceeds by daring "leaps and circlings," as my companion remarked, as if his perceptions of reality now imitated his earlier Cage-ean experiments. A documentary level, complete with maps, traces the rise and fall of Cambodian governments, the involvement of the Viet Cong, U.S. military policy in Southeast Asia and the Khmer Rouge whirlwind. A powerful story in its own right is the exploitation of Thai women, as bought "wives," ordinary prostitutes, and burlesque performers who cannonade bananas from their vaginas. It is an inspired stroke—in what would be Act Three if this were, as it often seems to be, a five-act play with dozens of characters—to bring in an apparently unrelated drunken encounter on a train with a U.S. Navy man who spends eight hours a day in a waterproof chamber of a nuclear submarine chained to a panel that controls a doomsday rocket. Gray couples this with a digression on his personal difficulties in handling anger. ("How can I think about the Russians if I can't solve a problem with a woman at Greenwich and North Moore?")

In such a tapestry, the actual story of the making of the film becomes a hallucinogenic recapitulation not only of the tragedy in Cambodia but of the universal torment by those who wield power of those who don't. Film itself is not merely a reflector but a performer in this dance of death, as when the crew of *The Killing Field* is greeted at a San Diego military base by overjoyed marines (is this Gray's fantasy?) "singing the 'tune' from *Apocalypse Now*."

The projection of Gray's dislocated WASP *persona* (the kind who has friends named 'Puffy') onto the world scene makes his black humor funnier than ever. Part II stays closer to the conflicts and anxieties of this familiar Spalding Gray, but portrays him as an Everyman in comic moral anguish. Should he stay on the film set long after his part is done, maintaining a kind of crazed witness to the world's suffering—though even here he writhes in what he takes to be unequal competition with film star John Malkovich—or should he return to the land of oblivion and get a West Coast agent? After all, says Gray, the Cambodian refugees blown by history to Long Beach want agents too. He is tortured by missiles and starving Ethiopians; the bluefish at a fancy party in the Hamptons is cooked with napalm. But there is Alan Watts's soothing echo in his ear, "Life is a party. So you happened to come in at the end of it," Gray's search for a "perfect moment"—a theme floating through both parts—could be an escape from reality or an ultimate reconciliation with it.

Swimming to Cambodia is shot with dreams and visions. Part II ends with the most powerful of these, Gray's dream in which a Cambodian boy, perhaps a straw effigy, burns from the legs up. As his smile is consumed by flames the room is filled with an "intelligent joy," but now he is gone forever, and Gray realizes that he will never be able to tell the boy's story. This disappearance even in the moment of greatest intensity grasps in an image the artist's shamanistic powers and pitiable frailty, a fitting end for a conflagration of ideas, characters, and motives pouring through a single performer seated at a wooden table with a glass of water.

John Howell (review date March 1985)

SOURCE: A review of *Swimming to Cambodia*, in *Artforum*, Vol. XXIII, No. 7, March, 1985, p. 99.

[*In the following evaluation of the Performing Garage production of* Swimming to Cambodia, *Howell admires Gray's "deceptively simple storytelling."*]

For nearly ten years Spalding Gray has been performing autobiographical monologues as an adjunct to his activity with the Wooster Group, the seminal experimental theater troupe. Unlike the work of that ensemble, which is multilayered, emotionally distanced, and relentlessly deconstructive, these solos are informal, vernacular, and, in form, an admiring direct quote of a basic storytelling mode. Wearing L.L. Bean-ish street clothes Gray appears as "Spalding Gray," seats himself at a nondescript table, and reels off a picaresque monologue which has been rehearsed into a script. Within this stripped-down format he weaves tales with considerable skill, combining raconteurial expertise, comic shticking, and elements of cosmic teaching, autotherapy, and the confession.

Over time the monologues have become more elaborate— less monothematic bead strings and more interwoven and associative—and Gray's performance of them has become more varied, more animated. He has an unusually broad theatrical background, from classic '60s Off Broadway to cutting-edge experimental theater, and his considerable training, apparently discarded for these "modest" efforts, in fact permeates his deceptively simple storytelling. In fact, it now seems that the monologues are less a low-keyed alternative to the Wooster Group productions than a parallel search for similar dramatic truths on an individual scale.

In *Swimming to Cambodia, Parts I and II,* 1984, two related tales broken apart for convenience, Gray tells about his experiences as an actor in *The Killing Fields,* the recent movie about a *New York Times* correspondent's friendship with a Cambodian colleague caught in the genocidal madness that swept the country under the Khmer Rouge. Gray's part as a State Department assistant was small, allowing both an entrée to big-time moviemaking and plenty of time to observe its inevitable zaniness. Throughout *Swimming to Cambodia* Gray uses a persona carefully cultivated since his earliest solos, that of the astonished, bewildered man-child trying to understand the "real" world. The pose lends itself well to the old tradition of the comedian as a fumbling schlemiel, and in fact these monologues are screamingly funny, as Gray outlines all kinds of misunderstandings, mixed motives, crazed conduct, and confusion at every turn, not least in his own behavior and in his reactions to the antics of others. Gray's existential ironies emerge easily from the particular to the general—in the contradictions between sex-drenched Thailand and the ravaged Cambodia for which it stood in as a movie set, between courage and death-wish patriotism, between anesthetized Long Island suburbia and exotic Indochina. His conclusion: the "real" world isn't more real, it's just bigger.

A unifying thread through both monologues is Gray's search for "the perfect moment," the instant of oneness with self and universe that would put a spiritual gloss on the animal absurdities he finds saturating himself and every situation. Like a great comic, he lays out some avenues for real thought between his black-humor gags— and through them too, as when he describes the appalling damage done to Western "civilization" by its interventions in the Far East, or the craziness of life imitating art imitating life (styling themselves after Francis Coppola's *Apocalypse Now!,* real Marines used as extras sing "The Ride of the Valkyries" when helicopters zoom in to film an action scene). Later, Gray tells of a ridiculous encounter with TV Land in which he was sent to audition for a sitcom that had already been canceled (of course he didn't get the part—his reading of the banal dialogue had "too much edge"). Strangely enough, some of the characteristics of Gray's experimental-theater background—absorption with self, a distanced approach to role-playing, a humorous skepticism—would seem the ideal qualities for a television actor. Such ironies will no doubt remain grist for the finely tuned, engaging, and often mocking stories of this character "Gray," who reports from the front lines of the search for self in such a selfless way.

Mona Simpson (review date 8 March 1987)

SOURCE: "Somebody to Talk About," in *The New York Times Magazine,* 8 March 1987, pp. 40, 92-4.

[*In the following article, Simpson contends that "most of all,"* Swimming to Cambodia *"is about what it's like to be Spalding Gray." She also discusses with Gray the making of the film version of the piece.*]

As the movie opens, a middle-aged man in an unimpressive coat walks through New York traffic, hands jammed in his pockets. He enters a street-level door below a small sign that says "The Performing Garage." Inside, at one end of a large room, an old wooden table holds a pitcher and glass of water. The man, now in a plaid shirt, minus the coat, sits down, places a Ronald McDonald spiral notebook on the table, takes a sip of water, faces the camera and begins to speak:

"Saturday, June 18, 1983, Hua Hin, Gulf of Siam, Thailand. It was the first day off in a long time, and about 130 of us were trying to get a little rest and relaxation out by the pool in this very modern hotel that looked kind of like a prison. If I had to call it anything I would call it a 'pleasure prison.' It was the kind of place you might come to on a package tour out of Bangkok."

The man is Spalding Gray, a 45-year-old performance artist whose name—which is, by the way, real; Spalding has a brother named Channing—has been known for a decade among followers of experimental theater. The film, *Swimming to Cambodia,* which consists almost entirely of Gray sitting at the table and talking, brings to the screen for the first time a theatrical form that Gray has created—the epic monologue. For an hour and 28 minutes, Gray expatiates on the subject, more or less, of his involvement as a bit player in the production of the 1984 Roland Joffe film *The Killing Fields.* Shot in Thailand, *The Killing Fields,* based on an article that appeared in this magazine by a former Times reporter, Sydney H. Schanberg, focused on the genocidal aftermath of the occupation of Phnom Penh, Cambodia, in 1975 by the brutal guerrilla group, Khmer Rouge. But Spalding Gray's monologue, with its elements of standup comedy, psychoanalytic free association and old-fashioned wrestling with conscience, ends up revealing its subject to be the monologist himself.

Directed by Jonathan Demme, who made *Melvin and Howard,* the Talking Heads rock-concert film *Stop Making Sense* and, most recently, *Something Wild,* and with a score by Laurie Anderson, *Swimming to Cambodia* will open Friday in New York and in at least 20 other cities within the next few weeks.

A critic for The Boston Phoenix once described Spalding Gray as "a Wasp Woody Allen, a spaced-out Norman Rockwell, a male Lily Tomlin," and The Minneapolis Star called him the "new wave Mark Twain." What makes Gray different from all of these figures is that he swears everything he says is true. "I'm interested in creative confession," he says. "I would have made a great Catholic."

Gray has been performing monologues since 1979, and a collection of them, reworked for print, *Sex and Death to the Age 14,* has been published in paperback by Vintage. But by almost all accounts, including his own, *Swimming to Cambodia* (also available in paperback, from Theater Communications Group) is his masterpiece. For more than two years, he has performed the piece around the country, including a three-month run at the Mitzi E. Newhouse Theater at Lincoln Center. "I was spreading the word," he says. "The only way I could do it was me doing it. It's like a Johnny Appleseed thing. I went out across America and every place I made friends."

An associational, looping narrative that skips back and forth in time, *Swimming to Cambodia* is the story of one man learning to see himself in a larger context. Gray's subjects include and somehow connect the invasion of Cambodia, fights with his girlfriend Renée, the history and tradition of prostitution in Thailand, the killings at Kent State, disastrous Hollywood auditions, the American support of the former Khmer Rouge leader Pol Pot and the nature and depth of liberal ideology. But most of all, the monologue is about what it's like to be Spalding Gray, a struggling New York actor affected both by the content of *The Killing Fields* and the glamour of being a pampered actor. His developing social conscience battles his career aspirations as he tries to decide, as he puts it, "whether to become a social worker for the Cambodians or to get a Hollywood agent."

As Gray tells it in the monologue, before *The Killing Fields,* he was fundamentally uninformed about recent history in Southeast Asia. "I'm not very political," he admits. "In fact, I've never even voted in my life." But being in the middle of a war movie forces Gray to bone up on the region's history; and he shares what he learns, in his quirky, pedantic way, with his audience. The film could be thought of as a whimsical high-school history class geared for adults, a session with Dear Spalding about America's relationship to Cambodia.

Gray owns up not only to high moral feelings, but also to the seductions of glamour and good food on the set. For Gray, there was more to Thailand than moral consciousness. When his stint on the film is complete, he ponders what he'll miss: "Farewell to the incredible free lunches under the circus tent with fresh meat flown in from America every day . . . Farewell to the Thai maid and the fresh, clean cotton sheets on the king-size bed. Farewell to the cakes and teas and ices at 4. Farewell to the single fresh rose in a vase on my bureau every morning in my hotel."

With its limited cast, essentially theatrical nature and Gray's penchant for digression, *Swimming to Cambodia* may evoke memories of director Louis Malle's 1982 film, *My Dinner With Andre,* or the 1961 screen version of Jack Gelber's play, *The Connection.* Yet it stands a chance of gaining a larger audience. The humor of the piece, Gray's stance as a willing innocent, struggling with a nascent social consciousness in the face of Hollywood's temptations, may, in fact, make the film closer to Richard Pryor's concert work.

Like Pryor, Gray introduce's odd, resonant characters, and through his canny ventriloquism, they seem to come more alive than if they were played by actors on the screen. We meet, for example, a young, hysterically bigoted Navy man named Jack Daniels, whom Gray once encountered on a train to Chicago. "He was cute enough," Gray says. "He was in his civvies, not his Navy outfit. The only kind of weird, demented thing about him was that his ears hadn't grown. They were like those little pasta shells. It was as if his body had grown but his ears hadn't caught up yet."

Then, red-faced and several keys lower, Gray *does* Jack Daniels, yelling his American jingoism in all its vivid profanity, and concluding, "I love the Navy, though. . . . I get to travel everywhere. I've been to India, Africa, Sweden. I . . . didn't like Africa, though. I don't know why, but black women just don't turn me on."

"Now here's a guy," Gray says, back in the narrator's voice, "if the women in the country don't turn him on, he misses the entire landscape."

"You won't believe this," Spalding-as-Jack confides, "The Russians don't even have electrical intercoms on their ships. They still speak through tubes!"

Spalding-as-narrator concludes: "Suddenly I had this enormous fondness for the Russian Navy, for the whole of Mother Russia. The thought of them speaking, like innocent children, through empty toilet-paper rolls, empty paper-towel rolls, where you could still hear confusion, doubt, envy, brotherly love, ambivalence. . . ."

Throughout, *Swimming to Cambodia* is political in just this way. Gray makes grand, inductive leaps to social and moral philosophy from isolated, personal experience. But if this sort of emotional testimony resonates with naïvete and even sentimentality, there is, nonetheless,

considerable dramatic power in the monologue, which comes from Gray's seamless transitions between the ridiculous and the tragic. We are not far removed from the self-important Jack Daniels when suddenly we're hearing the beautifully simple and forthright words of Cambodia's Prince Sisowath Sirik Matak, the text of a letter informing the American Ambassador in Phnom Penh that he will stay with his countrymen and not leave Cambodia with the Americans:

"You have refused us your protection and we can do nothing about it," it says in part. "You leave and it is my wish that you and your country will find happiness under the sky. But mark it well, that if I shall die here on the spot, and in the country that I love, it is too bad because we are all born and must one day die. I have only committed this mistake of believing in you, the Americans. Please accept, Excellency, my dear friend, my faithful and friendly sentiments."

"Five days later," Spalding-as-narrator says, plainly, "their livers were carried through the streets on sticks."

I've never been one to look out for the star role," Spalding Gray says. "I've always been a great supporting actor." He is sitting in the small communal dressing room at The Performing Garage, a theater space in the SoHo section of Manhattan that has been his home as an actor since 1970. The dressing room is dark, cluttered with old furniture. On the wall is a framed letter from Jacqueline Onassis to Gregory Mosher, the director of the Lincoln Center Theater, about Spalding Gray: "What a genius he is!"

Gray says he is happy with any role, however small, providing it furnishes sufficient inspiration to write about later. The monologues, he says, are the product of what he's always doing anyway, "reporting on my personal experiences. Journalism, I call it." Indeed, he seems extremely economical, using most of his professional and personal experiences twice, so to speak. He recently wrote a piece about his Christmas vacation in Miami. "Of course, that's my hope for dying," he says, "that I'll find the right medium and come back and write about it."

Gray's first monologues were created here, improvised in front of audiences at The Performing Garage. He still works improvisationally, starting with notes, talking his stories through and responding to the audience. Later, he'll use a tape recorder to refine and revise them. People who have seen *Swimming to Cambodia* on stage will find subtle changes in the film's text. No two performances have been duplicated. "Spontaneity and serendipity are the guiding principles of my life," Gray says.

If it weren't for the plaid shirt and sneakers and his somehow Balinese-like hand movements, Gray, who is tall, with patrician, silvering hair and balding a little in the back, would look like a middle-aged businessman in, say, insurance. He is a storyteller even when not on stage. Questions such as "What was your childhood like?" elicit long, spiraling answers, punctuated with actorlike pauses for laughter.

"I was born in Barrington, R.I.," Gray says quickly, "I was a quiet child, as my father said recently in an interview. It was very interesting because when they asked him was he surprised to see what I'd become, he said, 'Very! He was a quiet, backward boy!' He kept referring to me as a 'backward boy.'

"My mother has told me that when my cocker spaniel died, I stopped talking for months. They thought of taking me to a psychiatrist. I wouldn't push ahead in lines. I was dyslexic, didn't know it. Oh, everything was fine up until I was moved to the junior high school, and I think at that point I was overwhelmed by the 'others'— the kids from the other side of the tracks, the Italians, and by the fact that there were so many people in the world. I didn't have any girlfriends in high school and I was doing bad and I was a juvenile delinquent and I was failing everything and they sent me away to boarding school and that's when I got interested in theater. It was the only interest I ever had."

A graduate of Emerson College in Boston, Gray first got his Actors Equity card at the Alley Theater in Houston. But he felt disillusioned by the limitations of traditional theater. In the summer of 1967, he went off to live in Mexico. "I was really despondent because I wasn't facing the fact that my mother was breaking down for two years in Rhode Island," he says. "I'd been there for part of it, but I'd fled a good part of it to go to Houston. So that was a dreadful summer—I came back to find she had committed suicide without them being able to notify me. And then I moved to New York and tried to get back on the track."

During his first years in New York, Gray lived with the actress and director Elizabeth LeCompte, her sister and her sister's roommate on 6th Street and Avenue D. "I would spend the days, all day, walking New York, getting to know it," he says, and it's clear that he's talking about the birth of the monologist in him. "I'd come back at the end of the day and I'd fix dinner for them. I remember particularly chicken hearts and cheap red wine, that Spanish burgundy you could buy for 99 cents. And while I was fixing dinner I would just tell my whole day and they were a great audience."

Gray remembers that time as "turbulent. All that stuff was going on in the counter-culture, and I just felt like the real fear of insanity was upon me. I needed a haven." He found it at The Performing Garage, the home of The Performance Group, a theater collective that included many of the seminal forces in the experimental theater, including its founding director Richard Schechner and the actor Willem Dafoe, currently featured in Oliver Stone's film *Platoon*. Among other projects there, Gray played Hoss, the lead in the 1973 New York premiere production of Sam Shepard's play, *Tooth of Crime.*

"Talk about rhythms," Gray says. "That for me was one of the last operatic plays of Sam's, one of the last great ones, in which I'd step into that thing and never stop talking. It was the rhythms that carried me through. And I think that really opened me up and gave me this operatic sense of rhythm that I carry through into my own work."

Gray now lives with Renée Shafransky, a 33-year-old screenwriter and journalist whom he met in 1979 at the then-fashionable late-night club, Studio 54. Ms. Shafransky has been a major character in many of Gray's monologues; in *Swimming to Cambodia,* she is presented as something of a nag, trying to persuade Spalding to leave his paradise in Thailand and return to their house in the unfortunately named town of Krumville, N.Y. "She gave me an ultimatum," Gray says in the monologue. "'Either give me a date when you're coming home—or marry me.'"

Ms. Shafransky doesn't mind. "I know the truth behind the truth," she says. She signed release forms so her real name could be invoked in the film. And it was she who helped Gray trim the original monologue down to its filmable shape. (Gray remembers, "She would say, 'Lengthwise, I think the whorehouse scene is too long.'") But then, Ms. Shafransky, an animated, dark, Jewish beauty, sometimes returns the favor, as in the piece she wrote for *The Village Voice* about living with a Wasp, headlined "The Goy of Sex."

"My fantasy," says Ms. Shafransky, "is that our life is like Nick and Nora Charles, or Dashiell Hammett and Lillian Hellman—all the great romantic sparring partners."

Not incidentally, Ms. Shafransky is also the producer of the film of *Swimming to Cambodia.* In the fall of 1984, Gray was approached by someone who called himself a fan and a producer. "I sort of trusted him because he wore L.L. Bean boots," Gray says. "But I did not trust his partner. We went to this restaurant. And his partner kept jumping up to go to another table."

The alleged producer kept calling. "But it didn't feel right," Gray continues. "And Renée said, 'If there's going to be a film made of this, why don't *you* choose the director and producer? Or *I'll* produce it. You choose the director.'"

Gray had just seen *Stop Making Sense,* the Talking Heads film that Jonathan Demme had directed. "I thought it was a good example of a director's ego being very much out of the material," he says. "And I'd been acquainted with Jonathan, too, socially. So I called him and he had seen the monologue and he was immediately responsive. That was over two years ago. It's taken that long to get the money and the distributor balanced. We'd get a distributor, we'd lose the money. Renée could do a whole monologue on the money that has come and gone. One of the most ridiculous stories was why we went to Florida for Christmas—to meet with a guy who had washing machines in Miami, laundromats."

In the end, it was independent producers Lewis Allen and Peter Newman—"my white knights," Ms. Shafransky says—who provided initial funds for preproduction, and then secured a deal with Cinecom, a film distribution company, for full financing. **Swimming to Cambodia** was made for $400,000, a very low budget, by any standards. Allen and Newman receive screen credit as executive producers.

Already, Gray and Demme had mutual friends. Each had worked closely with the leader of the Talking Heads, David Byrne, Demme in *Stop Making Sense,* Gray as an actor in *True Stories,* the feature film Byrne wrote and directed. Both had been involved with the music of the performance artist Laurie Anderson.

Demme had first seen Gray perform years earlier, at a reading at the Public Theater in New York. "I thought he was fantastic," Demme says. He was "deeply flattered" to be asked to direct **Swimming to Cambodia**.

Demme's directorial vision in **Swimming to Cambodia** is oddly subdued. In feature films like *Melvin and Howard* and *Something Wild,* his style had been markedly idiosyncratic. But this show is always Spalding's. There are few cuts or oblique angles; the camera tends to view Spalding straightforwardly, face front. Even short inserts of footage from *The Killing Fields,* and Laurie Anderson's percussive, beautiful score with its hints of Asian melodies and some briefly emphatic visual effects, don't seriously diminish the camera's apparent reverence for the monologist. In fact, the most identifiable touch of pure Demme can be seen in the syncopated, hip, color credits. Of his plain style, Demme says, simply: "It's a perfect collaboration. A love affair."

"It's a documentary of me," Gray says, in a low voice, with some conscious irony. Though the film will bring his work to a larger audience than it's ever had, he still considers it a byproduct of his live monologues. In them, he says: "I am always working my audience. I am working to keep them attentive and awake, just like a good minister would do in a Puritan church in a long Sunday session. If I see someone nodding, dozing, I will begin to address them to energize them with my voice and presence. I've had very few walkouts ever—maybe there was one at Lincoln Center. Someone gets up and it's the most obscene gesture possible. It almost makes me not able to go on."

At a French restaurant a few blocks from The Performing Garage, Spalding and Renée order steaks and joke about making a film called *The Big Break,* a spoof on the mythology of luck and success. In a low, husky voice, Renée intones, "The chances were one in a million, but through hard, hard work and a combination of luck, circumstance and . . ."

Much of Spalding's work has been about missed chances, the underside of the Horatio Alger story, but these days plenty of opportunities are turning up.

"Lincoln Center made enormous changes in my life," Gray says.

"It's only in the past two years that he's been able to make a real living doing what he wants," says Renée.

Currently, Gray is filming a second movie monologue, this time for Home Box Office, a version of his **Terrors of Pleasure,** about the disasters attendant to his purchase of a house in the country. The working title for his next major project is *L.A.—The Other.* Gray will go into Los Angeles ghettos—the barrio, Watts, one Asian community and the San Fernando Valley ("a ghetto of sorts," Gray says)—and try to discover and work with local storytellers. The results—"I was going to call it a talent show, but I just want people to tell their own stories"—will be staged next fall at the Taper, Too, a satellite facility of the Mark Taper Forum in Los Angeles.

As Renée borrows his knife, Spalding takes out a package of The Three Castles, a mild Virginian tobacco. He rolls himself a cigarette and confides his real wish, which is to work with that other quintessential monologist, Woody Allen. "It's the only project I'm *really* interested in," Gray says. "I met him once in an audition for 'The Happy-Sad Train'"—a reference to a scene from Allen's film, *Stardust Memories.*

He lights up, inhales. "I smoke one a day," he says. "I love Woody Allen."

Finally, Gray is also writing, for print, not performance. "I'm working on what looks like my autobiography," he says. "And I'm determined that it's not to be spoken. It's based, really, on how I've theatricalized my life. I thought it was about my mother's suicide but the suicide seems to be like Brueghel's Icarus. Icarus is falling into the water, everyone's going on doing their tasks around him and it's one incident in the landscape."

Much of the book-in-progress is, apparently, about sex. It has been the subject of some debate at home. Renée would like to see him begin to fictionalize. "So far," she reports, "he's holding out. He feels he has to write what he needs to write. So I'm going to let him write it, and then we'll see."

The two have found a buyer for the troublesome **Terrors of Pleasure** house and bought another one in upstate New York. They plan to live and work there part of every year. "Sane comfort," Gray says. "Something that's not provocative on an absurdist level. The final house, a real house. There won't be any story in it."

"It's the first normal thing we've ever done," Ms. Shafransky says.

Marriage does not seem to be an issue for them. When the subject of children comes up, however, a loud squabble breaks out. Shortly, though, the disagreement subsides, and Renée kisses him on the ear.

"I always figured I could do a great monologue about having a kid," Gray concedes.

Lydia Alix Gerson (review date March 1987)

SOURCE: A review of *Swimming to Cambodia,* in *Theatre Journal,* Vol. 39, No. 1, March, 1987, pp. 96-7.

[*In the following assessment of a performance of* Swimming to Cambodia, *Gerson interprets the piece as a meditation on the loss of shared morality in the modern world:* "We live in a world without moral compass, a world in which small outrages rank with large ones simply because we have lost all sense of scale in evaluating human affairs."]

Swimming To Cambodia, a monologue written and performed by Spalding Gray is the last of a series of three such works offered by the Mitzi Neuhaus Theatre at Lincoln Center. Ostensibly, the piece is a fever chart of Gray's work on the film, *The Killing Fields,* and as such is an impressionistic, introspective revelation. Yet in interweaving his experience from his film work in contemporary Cambodia, his knowledge of the genocide that took place under Pol Pot, and his understanding of life in contemporary America, Gray outlines a continuum of atrocity between the American and Asian continents.

The monologue, ranging freely in time and space, is comprised of fractured, discontinuous episodes. The several stories do not seem to be moral equivalents, moving as they do from urban nuisance to Cambodian genocide. Yet this technique serves to force parallels between domestic and international outrage—and, perhaps more importantly, to point up their connection. Within the same hour and a quarter, the audience is treated to a numbing span of contemporary and historical events: a Nazi mass execution; a verbal portrait of the savagery unleashed by the Khmer Rouge; an offensive upstairs neighbor in New York City; mass prostitution in Bangkok; the prolonged United States' bombing of Cambodia. Gray reports all noncommittally; none of his tones trill in outrage. Nor does he state any of the obvious conclusions. The positioning of the pieces makes the historical point.

Although the moral issues raised in ***Swimming to Cambodia*** are of global significance, somewhere embedded in all this narration is a specific indictment of the United States for creating the requisite conditions for atrocity in Cambodia. The unspoken question in the piece seems to be: what kind of nation have we become to bestow automatic moral probity upon a Pol Pot simply because he answers to the tag of non-Communist?

By way of an answer, we are offered an episode concerning a young naval recruit named Jim. Gray meets him aboard a train bound for Pittsburgh. En route, Jim expounds on the special dynamics of his existence. He explains his predilection for threesomes, domination, submission, that whole "power thing." Spouting a Cold War litany, he tells Gray of his firm commitment to stop the Russians. His job is ideally suited to this imperative: he is tied to a wall in a nuclear battleship, his finger on a green button, just waiting to launch Armageddon. When Gray points out that Jim could easily destroy the whole world, the latter reveals that the Navy has provided him with a list of places that will be safe from radiation in the event of a blast. As Gray dourly notes, Jim will be safe while the rest of us are vaporized. Jim feels no compunction over the many millions that will die in a nuclear exchange; we must prevail over Communism. We leave him contemplating megadeath.

The monologue also focuses on the expendability of human life in a more quotidian context. Gray's upstairs neighbor makes incessant noise into the wee hours. Neither civility nor threat has dampened her enthusiasm for nocturnal riot. Over the course of time, the woman has become, in fact, progressively more offensive. Frustrated, Gray heaves an empty beer bottle through the offender's window. The action nearly precipitates a battle to the death with the woman's allies.

The unifying theme of the piece seems to be the relative value assigned to human life. In Pol Pot's Cambodia, there was no value assigned at all. In Pat Pong, Bangkok, bodies are fractionalized according to a schedule of escalating fees for prostitution. In New York City, human life may well be worth the price of a beer bottle.

This disparity confuses Gray, and it is at this juncture that sociological comment becomes ontological reflection in his piece. What has become of the cultural fraternity that existed in Gray's native Boston where a phone call appealing to mutual civility could accomplish détente? With the lack of a consensually defined humanism, we have lost a common notion of humanity and with it, all sense of proportion. We live in a world without moral compass, a world in which small outrages rank with large ones simply because we have lost all sense of scale in evaluating human affairs.

As usual, Gray's set is a black backdrop and some simple furniture: a desk, a chair, a couple of maps. He relies on himself and is, for the most part, riveting. If at times he lapses into the routine of a stand-up comic, it is because such *kitsch* is the only relief to the anomie which ***Swimming to Cambodia*** relentlessly expounds.

CRITICAL COMMENTARY

William W. Demastes (essay date 1989)

SOURCE: "Spalding Gray's *Swimming to Cambodia* and the Evolution of an Ironic Presence," in *Theatre Journal* Vol. 41, No. 1, March, 1989, pp. 75-94.

[*In the following essay, Demastes argues that while* Swimming to Cambodia *is rooted in the principles of experimental theater, it undermines and transcends those principles.*]

Spalding Gray's career in the theatre has encompassed a variety of theories and practices. He was educated in traditional forms, then moved to Richard Schechner's Performance Group, and later worked with the Wooster Group. Gray's current involvement in auto-performance shows a tremendous debt to these earlier affiliations, yet many critics seem to have dismissed Gray's current work as indulgent, dilettantish, and no longer part of the serious avant-garde experimentalist's concern. He has, after all, been co-opted into mainstream American culture, as his critics are quick to note. This easy dismissal of Gray, however, seems premature. In fact, many of the reasons Gray is dismissed are exactly the reasons Gray should be reconsidered.

This essay is an effort to place Gray's work more clearly into a performance genre context by first outlining the general critical assessment that avant-garde theatre in the 1980s is dying, then considering Gray's debt to Richard Schechner and the Performance Group, evaluating Gray's affiliation with Wooster Group members, and then demonstrating how this rich background is evident in Gray's current auto-performance pieces. In these works Gray creates a sophisticated theatrical persona, who himself reenacts an awakening onstage designed to sensitize the audience to its own awareness. The awakening comes over the persona onstage, and the enactment undermines comforting surfaces, forcing the audience to face realities—political and others—that it perhaps would prefer to ignore. In *Swimming to Cambodia* in particular, Gray has singularly succeeded in bringing to life on the stage a political agenda similar to that demanded by experimentalists of an earlier epoch—the 1960s and 1970s—but in a manner that assures a 1980s reception.

Critical Concern for the Loss of a Political Avant-Garde Agenda

Richard Schechner's 1982 work, *The End of Humanism,* echoes the pain many practitioners and theorists have felt about the recent work of avant-garde American theatre, a theatre whose early vitality promised much but unfortunately soon dissipated. Schechner notes that this vitality centered around a political agenda, one particularly focused on the Peace Movement of the 1960s and opposition to the Vietnam War. But, as Schechner argues,

> Once the war ended and the recession of the mid-seventies hit, artists fell into a formalist deep freeze. Great work was done, but it was cut off: it did not manifest significant content. Instead a certain kind of "high art obscurity" took over.

Moving away from efforts to produce a politically conscious, culturally uniting forum, avant-garde theatre turned isolationist and narcissistic.

In *The Eye of Prey,* Herbert Blau similarly notes the turn toward isolationist undertakings. Reflecting on his own work in the theatre, Blau describes this transformation from the 1960s to current practices

as a deviation from Brecht through Beckett into a highly allusive, refractory, intensely self-reflexive, ideographically charged process in which we were trying to understand, *to think through,* at the very quick of thought—words, words, unspeakably in the body—the metabolism of perception in the (de)materialization of the text.

Though Blau's style is (intentionally) oblique, he seems to be arguing that earlier efforts to fathom broader issues of community have been replaced by the pursuit of understanding individual means of perception. Blau adds, "As with the Conceptual Art of the late sixties—particularly that strain of it which jeopardized the body in the self-reflexive activity of thought—the subject of our work, and the danger of its becoming, was *solipsism.*"

But where Schechner saw vitality and "community" in the 1960s, Blau goes so far as to argue that the activist work of that decade itself was solipsistic in that its dream of paradise was naive and little more than an enfeebled attempt at political and idealistic awakening. The theatrical "recession" of the 1970s and 1980s merely brought greater attention to the fundamental flaws of the ideologies of the previous decade. Whatever their assessments of the 1960s, however, the two critics would agree on one matter. As Blau notes, "What seemed to be left in the recession, along with the new conservatism, was the dispossessed *subject* of the postmodern, reviewing the disenchantments, as if through the solipsistic orifice of a needle's eye." For both Schechner and Blau the unfortunate result of this "high art obscurity" with its attendant "dispossessed *subject*" was that avant-garde theatre lost its cultural base.

The results have become manifest in what Blau observed in *Blooded Thought* as a sort of "advocacy of confession in acting," of which "[t]here is also the offshoot of explicit autobiography, more or less disciplined, more or less confessed." Interestingly, at this point, Blau notes that the best of the genre are Gray's Rhode Island trilogy (formally entitled *Three Places in Rhode Island*) and Lee Breuer's *Animations,* but he adds, "Originally, the impulse had something devout about it, a kind of penance, as in the monastic period of Grotowski. . . ." Though he acknowledged that self-exposure is essential to powerful theatre, Blau insists that "[i]t is not mere authenticity we're talking about . . . , the self-indulgent spillover of existential sincerity"; rather it must be "a *critical* act as well, *exegetical,* an urgency in the mode of performance . . . , part of its *meaning,* that the Text be *understood,* though the meaning be ever deferred." Blau complains that too much of such work has thus far failed to go beyond documenting "authenticity." Exegesis of such events, or of the *presentations* of the events, has yet to be pursued to Blau's satisfaction.

The disenchantment that Schechner and Blau feel, however, is not shared by C. W. E. Bigsby. Bigsby does agree that the American avant-garde "became an expression of intensely private experience, moving from the gnomic tableau of Robert Wilson and Richard Foreman to the heavily autobiographical pieces of the Wooster Group (the Rhode Island trilogy) and the monologues of Spalding Gray" [*A Critical Introduction to Twentieth Century Drama. Volume Three: Beyond Broadway,* 1985]. Bigsby agrees that the work of the isolated subject often "concern[s] itself with the nature of perception and consciousness," which on the surface may do little to establish community and more to increase isolation. But though the works may turn inwardly rather than reach outwardly, Bigsby points out that

> it may well be that in requiring audiences to offer their own completions, in provoking a degree of aesthetic complicity and imaginative collaboration, such theatre practitioners may be reminding them [audiences] of their capacity to act and to imagine a world beyond the banality of appearance.

Such art subtly requires an audience involvement, an "imaginative collaboration," that may ultimately establish a bond more true than any tangible "hand-holding" could strive for. Overt physical involvement has been replaced by a more subtle imaginative involvement, and the substitution, says Bigsby, may in fact be for the better. That such a *possibility* for bonding even exists under these circumstances is something Schechner clearly ignores and Blau seems skeptical that he has ever witnessed—at least he has not seen it in the efforts of performers like Gray and Breuer. For Bigsby, however, not only does the possibility exist, but in rare moments, so does the reality.

Gray's Wooster Agenda: The Rhode Island Trilogy

What Schechner particularly confronts in his *End of Humanism* assault on the "lost" theatre is the work of the auto-performers, which has dominated theatre recently. Schechner argues that the work is "brilliant, but not enough; personalistic rather than concerned with the *polis,* the life of the City, the life of the people." He concludes: "With this personalism comes a passivity, an acceptance of the City, the outer world, the world of social relations, economics, and politics, as it is." In his book, Schechner focuses on the evolution of his own splintered Performance Group, now called the Wooster Group, and the further splintering of that group by the individual efforts of Spalding Gray. Ironically, it was Schechner's own liberating teachings that caused the split and led Gray eventually to work on his own.

Gray explains [in "About Three Places in Rhode Island," *The Drama Review,* No. 1, 1979] the process of overturning his dependency on written texts and directorial leadership, a dependency he had grown accustomed to in his earlier, more traditional training:

> Richard Schechner reversed this process for me. He emphasized the performer, making him more than, or as important as, the text. . . . [H]e was a liberator from assembly line acting techniques. The way that I

interpreted Schechner's theories was that I was free to do what I wanted, be who I was, and trust that the text would give this freedom a structure.

Gray agrees with Blau's assessment, noted earlier, that his early effort after he separated from Schechner, the Rhode Island trilogy, was narcissistically confessional, noting, "I am by nature extremely narcissistic and reflective. For as long as I can remember, I have always been self-conscious and aware of my everyday actions." Gray adds, "I began my own work out of a desire to be both active and reflective at the same time before an audience." This process, however, extended beyond self-conscious presentation of his private life, becoming, in addition, a therapeutic endeavor. For example, Gray describes one of the trilogy pieces, **Sakonnet Point,** as a

> series of simple actions . . . that created a series of images like personal, living Rorschachs. These images were not unlike the blank, white wall in Zen meditations, nor were they unlike the mirror reflection of a good therapist.

Given this personal bent and its therapeutic design, such work could very easily be construed as isolationist. As Bigsby notes, "[F]or Richard Schechner this work [Gray's] and that of others implied a regrettable shift not merely from a public to a private art but from a concern with subject to a concern with subjectivity." In fact, Bigsby notes the obvious conclusion to such thoughts when he observes of Schechner, "As the title of his book, *The End of Humanism,* seems to imply, he [Schechner] saw this as in some sense a betrayal." Gray, however, disagrees that any betrayal occurred, arguing in his own defense: "Often, what the audience saw was the reflection of their own minds, their own projections." In other words, the private art reached the public, though in subtler ways than Schechner might have advocated. Instead of direct surface confrontation, undercurrents began to play a central role.

One of the central reasons Schechner fails to see—or acknowledge—this approach as promoting audience involvement is that Gray and the Wooster Group abandoned Schechner's more overt practice of environmental participation between audience and performer and returned to a clear distinction between performance space and audience space. Bigsby reports the shift that Schechner bemoans:

> Where in the 1960s and early 1970s Off and Off-Off Broadway avant-garde theatre has seen itself as essentially a public art inviting the full physical participation of the audience, either as a gesture of solidarity with its political objectives or as evidence of a refusal of all restraints (including the special framing of the theatrical event), . . . the audience found itself excluded from the stage onto which it had once been invited and increasingly denied access to meaning.

The overall result, claims Schechner, is that "[w]ithout meaning to be, such productions became elitist: not necessarily for the economic elite . . . but for the artistically 'in.'" For Schechner, both the subject and the presentational methods have reduced the audience to coterie size instead of expanding it to build a larger sense of community.

That Gray's work is intensely personal is, of course, a given. But that it is more than just personal therapy is often overlooked, as is the fact that it does strive to embrace more than a coterie following. First of all, the techniques Gray used in the Rhode Island trilogy incorporate elements learned from Schechner, and they helped Gray overcome some of his intensely personal focus. Says Gray:

> Through being part of this [earlier] process, I developed an integrated understanding of how a group could collaborate in the creation of a mise-en-scène. This led directly to being able to work with some Group members and some people outside The Group on my own work. The source of the work was myself, but the final product was a result of the collective conceptual actions of all involved. Thus, in the end, it is a group autobiography.

The "work was myself" idea escaped extreme solipsism since the work was reflected off of other "selves," such as Elizabeth LeCompte, Gray's confidante and directorial advisor. In that regard, at least, there was a nominal sense of community.

But the product was more than merely a blend and modification of selves isolated in a small group, as some would see it. It clearly entered the more universal realm of art in that it confronted aesthetic issues as traditional art did, though in a much more "open-nerved" manner. Says Gray:

> [I]t became not the art of pretending I was someone else but an art that began to approach the idea that I was someone else. I wanted to give up the names, to close the gaps. It was no longer to be the "Stanley Kowalski self" or the "Hamlet self," but now it was a play of moods, energies, aspects of self. It became the many-in-the-one that had its source in the archetype of the performer, not in the text.

The connection between performance in life and in art became a central concern, but it extended beyond Gray's own isolated self. Again, this aspect of Gray's style is one he learned from Schechner. It allowed him to discover "self," but in this presentation and discovery of self, he discovered "other" as well.

> By chance, I might suddenly find myself performing an action that was an aspect of me, and, upon reflection see it as an action belonging to Orpheus. Then, for that moment, I would be both Spalding and Orpheus. I was never one or the other and could be someone or something completely different for each audience member because they also live with their "names" and associations. It is their story as well as mine.

If the trilogy succeeds as intended, the piece should build foundations for community in the manner Bigsby describes, with results Schechner and Blau probably would finally approve. In requiring audiences to exact their own completions, as Bigsby describes it, Gray enables the audience to make contact with "self" and to communicate with "other" as well.

There is yet another aspect of Gray's trilogy work that could lead to charges of solipsism. Gray notes that "[a]ll of *Sakonnet Point* was built from free associations within the performing space. There were no 'ideas' about how it should be, nor was there any attempt to tell a meaningful story." James Bierman [in "Three Places in Rhode Island," *The Drama Review* 19, No. 4, 1975] notes that the piece "is more evocative in style than expositional," and Arnold Aronson [in "Sakonnet Point," *The Drama Review* 19, No. 4, 1975] concludes that the play's "value lay not in any informational structure but in their capacity for evoking further images and moods. The creators did not intend to provoke thought but rather an inward contemplation." The result could very well be solipsistic.

The actors, of course, develop this inward contemplation, but communication transferral occurs when the audience feels the urge toward a similar development. According to Gray, "Often, what the audience saw was the reflection of their own minds, their own projections." But the process clearly requires an active desire on the part of the audience. Gray is aware of the need for active desire, having "desired" it himself while he viewed the works of other artists who strove to achieve the same subtle end. In fact, Gray identifies with a growing avant-garde tradition concerned with such involvement:

> I think *Sakonnet Point* was like the work of Robert Wilson and Meredith Monk. I had found that while watching their work my mind was left free to associate and my eye was grounded in watching the execution of their chosen actions. It was this grounding of my eye that gave my mind a quality of freedom I'd not experienced in theatre before. For me, the work of Wilson and Monk was dealing with the use of, and investigation into the nature of, mind projections. This seemed to be getting to the roots of what theatre and life are about. It is a kind of therapeutic lesson about how we create our own world through our projections.

Gray concludes his observations with a performer's perspective by noting that *Sakonnet Point* "was very involving and seemed therapeutic for the audience as well as the performer." In this regard, Schechner's advocacy of physical involvement of the audience has been replaced by a perceptual, conceptual, emotional, and mental involvement of the audience.

Another part of the trilogy, *Rumstick Road,* focused on Gray's mother's suicide, but as Gray notes, "Although the basis of the piece was the voices and pictures of my family, the other performers were free to take off from this material and develop their own scores." He admits that the piece was "confessional," but asserts "[i]t was also an act of distancing." Through distancing, Gray became, to use Blau's term, exegetical. Gray observes,

> Finally, if it is therapeutic, it is not so much so in the fact that it is confessional but in the fact that it is ART. The historic event of my mother's suicide is only a part of the fabric of that ART. Finally, the piece is not about suicide; it is about making ART.

Perhaps the clearest expression of analysis and exegesis is in the trilogy's final piece, *Nayatt School,* which concentrates on the effects of being introduced to Freudian psychology. Gray argues that despite its distorted perspective on the world in general and language in particular, Freudian psychology is quite "real" nonetheless. Says Gray, "I felt and believed this at the time and wanted to make a theatre piece that was not only a reflection of that strange world, but the world itself."

Considering the trilogy as a unit, Gray states that he has moved beyond therapy and mere presentation of personal events to a realm of philosophical analysis of a more universal condition. His trilogy, he says,

> reflect[s] upon themes of loss. They are not just about the loss of my mother but about the feeling of loss itself. I have had this feeling for as long as I can remember. It is the feeling that the "I" that I call "me" is only a visitor here. No, not even a visitor because a visitor goes elsewhere after he visits. I have no word for it, and the work is the attempt at giving expression to that absent word.

If Gray begins with personal experience, he moves with that experience to a plane that reflects more than just his own condition. Gray admits [in "Perpetual Saturdays," *Performing Arts Journal* 6, No. 1, 1981], "I fantasize that if I am true to art it will be the graceful vehicle which will return me to life." But in this process something more than personal therapy occurs, for "[t]he very act of communication takes it into a 'larger vein' and brings it back to community."

Gray's transition from Group assisted work to performing monologues recounting his life stemmed from a double realization, one part taken from the Group, that "[s]omewhere along the line, every action became for me a piece of theatre" and the other a new one that saw" employing the old oral tradition [as] a fresh breath in these high tech times . . . with all its human energy and vividness." Gray's work has simply developed from an age-old observation that life is performance coupled with a new realization that life's tools, therefore, are performer's tools as well and are complete in themselves.

Gray notes, in a pattern similar to Richard Schechner's, that "Theatre is about presence = Life = Death" and asserts that reviving an oral tradition is his new "hope for passing it all down." With this new realization about performance/presence came a new outlook on theatre: "The personal confessional, stripped of its grand theatrical metaphors, is what matters to me now." Past avant-garde efforts to create a new theatrical "language"—his own efforts or others'—have consumed energy that otherwise could have been utilized for more substantial ends. Perhaps using current tools will be sufficient, and perhaps even returning to simple monologue will be the most effective means of all. In one regard, at least, the return is fortunate. Being unable to establish a way to pass down the lessons and experiences of avant-garde theatre was one of Schechner's incidental concerns in *The End of Humanism.* Gray notes that an answer as simple as "oral tradition" was "one that Richard didn't mention." Since Gray's discovery of the potential of the oral tradition, it has been the avenue he has pursued.

The Wooster's L.S.D. Agenda

Returning to this traditional means of communication in avant-garde art, however, can hinder efforts to challenge the status quo. In particular, problems arise when an art form empowers a lone presence and when it empowers a tool—language—that has acquired a social or political tyranny over any liberating potential in that art. In this regard, Philip Auslander [in "Toward a Concept of the Political in Postmodern Theatre," *Theatre Journal* 39, 1987] joins Blau and Schechner, expressing general concern that recent avant-garde theatre has turned apolitical or, even worse, reactionary. The concept of presence, and therefore of authority, according to Auslander, "is the specific problematic theatre theorists and practitioners must confront in reexamining our assumptions about political theatre and its function." He argues that "the theatre is precisely a locus at which critical/aesthetic and social practices intersect." The aesthetic of presence is necessarily entwined with the social, and therefore political, reality of presence, according to Auslander.

In addressing these issues, Auslander examines the work of the Wooster Group (without Gray) and in particular the piece *L.S.D. (. . . Just the High Points . . .),* arguing that the Group's efforts epitomize the as yet incomplete political efforts of the recent avant-garde to challenge authority as a socially/culturally entrenched power tool. The strategy the Group utilizes involves irony, in a manner that another critic, Elinor Fuchs, has described [in "Performance Notes," *Performing Arts Journal* 23, 1984]: "In the past, the Wooster Group's undercutting of one text by another, of one reading by another, and of both by the incisive use of segments of film, resulted in an almost wholly ironic dramaturgy." In the case of *L.S.D.,* the text of Miller's *The Crucible* is undermined. Although Fuchs concludes of this recent work that Wooster's "irony now seems unclear," Auslander asserts that the Group's efforts are moving in the right direction. He notes with approval the fact that Wooster entangled itself in the well-documented debate over its own right to manipulate Miller's text versus Miller's right to control performance of his work: "LeCompte [the Group's director] correctly describes the conflict with Miller as 'an inevitable outcome of our working process' and as a part of the Group's 'necessary relationship to authority.'"

But Auslander adds that LeCompte has failed to realize fully that "confrontation with authority is a *result* but not the *object* of the Group's process," noting that "[t]he Group seems blithely, perhaps utopianly, to proceed as if the poststructuralist critical/theoretical concept of text as 'a tissue of quotations' belonging more to a culture than an individual were already in place as part of the social hegemony." The Group confronts the text as a product of a social/cultural power structure rather than the product of an individual "author," but before Wooster can attack the text as a social/cultural manifestation, it must first rigorously confront the authority of the individual—Miller—in its art rather than incidentally through outside litigation. So, rather irregularly,

> The effect of the Group's action is not so much to question Miller's rights over his text as to show what would be possible in the realm of cultural production if those rights were not in force, thus emphasizing the importance of the connection between the cultural and the social/political.

According to Auslander, this assumption that as a text *The Crucible* asserts a social/cultural authority is accurate, but it needs further development, given the Group's naively utopian perspective on the issue.

As the Group undermines "authority" as a social/cultural manifestation, so must it strive to undermine "presence" itself—in this case presence of the author—since suspicion has been cast upon presence. According to Auslander, the suspicion "derives from the apparent collusion between political structures of authority and the pervasive power of presence." The Wooster Group needs to continue its "transgressive" behavior in order to overcome the

> obvious inappropriateness of the political art strategies left over from the historical avant-garde of the early 20th century and from the 1960s, and by a widespread critical inability to conceive of aesthetic/political *praxis* in terms other than these inherited ones.

Continuing to refine means of undermining both authority and presence should remain part of the essential political avant-garde agenda.

A major problem arises, however, in the effort to realize that objective, and that has to do with the tool that conveys authority and confirms presence—language. Ideally, a new "language" needs to be constructed in order to free society from an old language rife with empowering prejudices. In response to Auslander's article, Schechner makes the following important concession: "Once I considered the Wooster Group nihilistic, and apolitical, but I was wrong" ["Ways of Speaking, Loci of Recognition," *The Drama Review* 31, No. 3, 1987]. Though Schechner does not specify why he has changed his opinion, it can be assumed that he accepts Auslander's perspective on the Wooster Group, that the politics of *L.S.D.* pulls Wooster out of the depths of nihilism and empty aesthetics. However, Schechner calls attention to a central problem inherent in Auslander's progressive goal of undermining presence and authority in the theatre. Moving away from theatre in particular and seeing what he calls "several kinds of 'progressive' thinking going on simultaneously" in the world at large, Schechner identifies "the problem's nub: translation is impossible; meaning is not separate from or prior to expression."

By translation, Schechner means transferring meaning from one cultural (or professional) idiom to another. He concludes that "[t]he problem today is that ways of speaking are mutually untranslatable." Idioms themselves have become isolated in their very efforts to undermine the old and create new systems. In this regard Schechner notes that even a possible dialogue between a "progressive" artist (LeCompte), theorist (Auslander), and politician (he uses Jesse Jackson) would be difficult, if not impossible, because their languages are so self-confined and so untranslatable into the others' idioms. The solipsistic dilemma arises again, this time out of a progressive agenda that strives to challenge power itself, which entails challenging the language that enforces that power. For even those who have actually tried to challenge the power (LeCompte, Auslander, Jackson) have difficulty uniting under one flag, given the particular sources of power (and language) they are working to challenge. So, if in undermining current language and current cultural power in general these groups cannot unite and make significant contact *during* the struggle, what is the hope for more general cultural unity if such a progressive "revolution" succeeds?

Simply put, since language *is* a source of cultural/social power, any direct efforts at substantively changing the culture's/society's power structure entails reevaluating and "re-creating" language itself. The efforts that Auslander and other similar thinkers espouse seem fated to lead to an impossible cultural/social order, since without communication there can be no community and since the lines of communication have already been severed in the very attempt to communicate this challenge of power. And in regard to art, such efforts can lead only to an impossible theatre. Finally, efforts such as those espoused by Auslander at creating a new cohesion lead to greater solipsism. Schechner seems quite rightly to concede that his earlier "environmental" efforts could be replaced by more subtle means of presentation, but he also quite accurately observes that the idealistic goals of this new generation of theorists/practitioners may ultimately be unattainable. Spalding Gray, however, provides an alternative.

Gray's Auto-Performance Agenda

Gray left Schechner's Performance Group at about the same time Schechner himself left, and the Performance Group re-formed as the Wooster Group. Gray then separately collaborated with Elizabeth LeCompte, the current director of Wooster. The Rhode Island trilogy bears many marks of both groups' ensemble styles and can be considered one of many predecessors of the Wooster Group's later works, which culminated in *L.S.D. (. . . Just the High Points . . .)*. But on a superficial level, at least, Gray's unscripted monologues bear little if any resemblance to the Group's work, since he relies almost completely on a single "presence" seated at a table *verbally* communicating to an audience, instead of opting for a more nondiscursive style that relied less heavily on an empowered language. As Don Shewey notes [in "The Year of Spalding Famously," *Village Voice,* 13 November 1984], "Unlike his colleagues in the Wooster Group and Mabou Mines, whose experimentation took them further into high-tech performance, Gray reclaimed the ancient art of story-telling, simply sitting at a desk and addressing an attentive audience in the intimacy of the Performance Garage." In fact, Vincent Canby notes [in "Soloists on the Big Screen," *The New York Times,* 22 March 1987] that Gray's reliance on language has eliminated virtually any other form of communication, noting that "it would be a coup de theatre if he [Gray] just stood up." Ostensibly, Gray has given up on any idea of creating an alternative form of language for the theatre—technology assisted or otherwise—turning as he does to oral tradition as his means of communication.

This difference between Gray and his former colleagues, however, is more apparent than real. Though Gray is literally "telling" his story, there are indications that he is carrying on the Wooster tradition, utilizing a different approach to achieve virtually the same end. Reviews regularly have made note of Gray's WASP background, and Gray himself openly acknowledges in his monologues his comfortable middle-class, New England heritage. Given his privileged upbringing, it would seem that Gray had two options in pursuing an avant-garde, political agenda. He could reject his personal history and join the ranks of those out of power in an effort to enact change from without, and thus come to the theatre as less than a historically genuine spokesperson—a "have" joining in with the "have-nots." Or he could accept his personal history of privilege and work from within, accepting, at least for rhetorical purposes, his position of authority—"to the manor born"—complete with the empowering tools of that system, language certainly included. This second option, at first glance hardly a position for an avant-garde performer, is the option Gray has chosen. Choosing that option, it seems, was the cause for his split with his former colleagues.

If nothing else, Gray's separation from the Wooster Group and acceptance of his position of privilege circumvents one criticism Auslander advances concerning members of the Group who have been lured, however temporarily, away from the political/aesthetic theatre of the Group and into various commercial media. Such shifting, according to Auslander, "was not considered a worthy objective by the sixties generation," and now that it has occurred, "it could be seen as implying an alarming lack of integrity on the part of young experimental artists." Lack of integrity is, of course, a serious charge. Given Gray's decision to remain in the realm of the empow-

ered, however, he *can* move from one format to another, and this mobility is the basis of his dramatic method.

In this method, several Spalding Grays are at work. First, the "observer-of-events," Spalding Gray the private citizen, works in a nearly reportorial fashion to uncover the system's shortcomings as he lives the life of a privileged middle-class male. The results of this espionage, in turn, are handed over to Gray the artist to create a work offering a critical perspective on the system. The piece is presented by Gray the *naive* performer, who appears fully incorporated into the system and is unaware of the ironies introduced into his presentation by the artist Gray, who shaped the material reported by the observer Gray. Who is the actual Spalding Gray? As far as his Wooster-rooted agenda is concerned, such a question is irrelevant. Gray's onstage work finally presents material, *seemingly* without comment, in an ironic manner that confronts the same power structure exposed by Wooster's *L.S.D.* Thus while Gray's work may *appear* supportive of the status quo, it presents a persona who ironically utilizes an empowered naivety to undermine itself and the authority it seems to uphold.

Gray's ironic approach apparently owes something to his association with Wooster. In fact, as Wooster's irony attempts to do, Gray's ironic posturing confronts both authority and presence, as Auslander hoped the avant-garde in general would do. But given the potential power of "presence" in performance in general and in Gray's work in particular, it would seem that auto-performance—especially monologues—would strengthen the hold of presence rather than weaken it. However, Fuchs has observed [in "Presence and the Revenge of Writing," *Performing Arts Journal* 26/27, 1985] a kind of "revenge of writing," as she calls it, in many recent works of the avant-garde, a revenge whose aim, it seems, "is the undermining of theatrical Presence." Though she does not discuss Gray, Gray's performance "text" seeks just that end—the undermining of the performer's presence. Then what of Gray the behind-the-scenes author? The authority of Gray the author would be expected to assert itself. One must look back at the actual performance to understand how the text in turn undermines Gray the author's authority. One must realize that the performer has "misread" the text as he presents it, thereby undermining any of its discursive "meaning" in favor of a meaning that works to undermine textuality itself. For the audience, there may be—and usually is—a "pleasure in the text," but there is little real didactic substance that ultimately demands attention, and so there is even less attention paid to the authority of the text. Reaching beyond both written authority and physical presence is the design of Gray's works. Each consumes the other, leaving a void that forces the audience to doubt the power of either and search within itself for a replacement, empowering the audience, then, in the process.

In one regard, Gray's work can be seen, superficially, as an unconventional affirmation of the "conventional" itself. But going beneath surfaces, it becomes evident that the work is an attack on empowering convention in general, effected by highlighting the ultimate empowering convention—language. The possibility for confusion is fortunate, for it has allowed Gray to enter the mainstream of popular culture, since his "hidden" agenda has been misread by the mass of socially/politically empowered literalists who have been unable to penetrate beneath Gray's surfaces. As a result Gray has been able to influence the order's very consciousness.

In **"Rivkala's Ring,"** his adaptation of a Chekhov story for the collection of short dramatic works entitled *Orchards,* Gray offers advice to others on how to perform the piece, advice that sums up his view of his own persona on stage:

> I see the character [in "Rivkala's Ring"] as a manic-y paranoid person who's spinning off these kind of paranoid delusions, trying to make order out of a very frightening and chaotic existence. So I see it fashioned after my character, the character of Spalding Gray that I do in the monologues.

The passage both acknowledges Gray's awareness of at least two Spalding Grays and outlines the personality of the stage persona Gray. Frank Rich [in "To Play Oneself May Be The Greatest Illusion of All," *The New York Times,* 29 June 1986] sees the same split and notes,

> What makes Spalding Gray so theatrical in his seemingly nontheatrical way is not only his talent as a storyteller and social observer but also his ability to deepen the mystery of the demarcation line between performer and role.

Thus, although it may at times be difficult to distinguish Gray the private citizen from Gray the performer, Gray himself insists on drawing the distinction.

The "manic-y paranoia" is a deliberately manufactured characteristic. It renders the persona harmless and disarming, enabling him to draw the audience into the monologue, overcoming the defenses with which it would resist a political manifesto on the stage. As Novick notes, "Although he [Gray] was artistically nurtured by that company of screaming meemies, the Wooster Group, his art as a monologuist is the art of understatement" [Julius Novick, "A Lighter Shade of Gray," *Village Voice,* 27 May 1986]. Gussow adds, speaking of the difference between the Rhode Island trilogy in general and a monologue like Gray's *47 Beds* in particular, that "[w]hile the performance pieces often sacrifice intelligibility in the interest of visual and aural stimulation, the solo work is as entertaining as it is eccentric" [Mel Gussow, "Stage: Spalding Gray as Storyteller," *The New York Times,* 16 November 1984].

The strategy is subtle yet effective in evoking the audience involvement Gray desired in his more frenetic Rhode Island trilogy but attained in a different manner. The audience is drawn in with entertaining twists, and the pleasure and attendant complacency are undermined through the same entertainingly palatable means. The man/

presence who has charmed the audience onstage often is also drawn into the process of realization that the audience eventually experiences. It must be emphasized, however, that the language itself undermines, not any empowered presence. As Maslin notes, Gray the performer is "never inclined to talk with ironic detachment, no matter how absurd or strange or painful the circumstances he describes" [Janet Maslin, "Film: Spalding Gray's 'Swimming to Cambodia',", *The New York Times,* 13 March 1987]. Gray the performer is immersed; it is the behind-the-scenes artist Gray who is ironically detached and subtly confrontational. But that is not clearly seen in the performing area. Rather, since the persona onstage is guileless, it is left to the audience to deduce the ironies. Signals from either an empowered physical presence or from an unseen authority are virtually nonexistent.

The above analysis applies best to *Swimming to Cambodia,* but to a lesser degree it applies to most of Gray's monologues. David Guy notes that the collection of early auto-performance pieces (polished transcriptions of his stage work) entitled *Sex and Death to the Age 14* reveals a "belief on Mr. Gray's part . . . that there is more substance in the simple telling of stories than in more self-conscious art forms" [David Guy, "From the Heart: *Sex and Death To The Age 14.* By Spalding Gray," *The New York Times,* 4 May 1986]. Guy adds, "There is also a belief that the real truth in life lies in its most banal and embarrassing moments, that to pretty things up is to falsify them." The pieces go beyond mere documentation. Such works as *Interviewing the Audience,* for example, reveal an underlying motive even in Gray's most purely and simply confessional pieces of the period. Namely, they work, as Shewey notes, at "drawing others into his philosophical obsessions (is there a heaven? does true love exist?) and imparting to unbelievers the rewards of the examined life." As with Gray's trilogy agenda, "self-examination" is the essential point Gray tries to put across in these performance pieces. But here he has shifted approaches, presenting an insubstantial substance that works as bait to draw in his audience. Says Gray [in Don Shewey, "A Spinner Of Tales Moves Into the Mainstream," *The New York Times,* 11 May 1986],

> There are two audiences for my work . . . There are people who live in the kind of life I have. They're very unrooted, they do a lot of different things, and they experience the world as fragmented. The other extreme is the householder who is my age now . . . who's right in the midst of raising two or three children, who's keeping down a job, and who's able to enjoy the stories vicariously, the same way he would Kerouac's *On the Road.*

Gray's work appeals to middle America, but for those who can see more than vicarious experiences in the works, the pieces take on an ironic significance, revealing fragmentation and unrootedness that is a first step to a political awakening.

Having truly made the leap into mainstream American culture with his *Swimming to Cambodia*—first for the stage and recently as a screenplay—Gray has contributed to the postmodern blurring of high art and popular culture that Auslander discusses. But that is only an incidental result of his work. What is central is that the piece clearly moves toward a political agenda in a manner more obvious, it seems, than his earlier work. In this piece Gray clearly observes that he has moved beyond simple narcissism, if ever he were merely narcissistic. With *Swimming to Cambodia,* Gray reports he found an objective situation that freed him from any narcissistic spell: "People writing reviews have called me a narcissist, and I would certainly admit to that. . . . But with *Swimming to Cambodia* I found a larger issue outside of my personal neuroses [Deborah Mason, "New Wave Confidence," *Vogue,* May, 1986]. Concerning this move to a "larger issue," Fuchs remarks, "*Swimming to Cambodia,* especially Part I, represents an artistic culmination for Gray as well as an impressive political breakthrough." [Elinor Fuchs, "With the Stream," *Village Voice,* 27 November 1984]. Gray's method of presentation has finally found matter that allows him to exhibit his form's ironic agenda fully.

The work, in fact, succeeds in a way that led Fuchs to make the following comment: "Throughout, Gray's story proceeds by daring 'leaps and circles' . . . as if his perceptions of reality now imitated his earlier Cage-ean experiments." For Fuchs, Gray's presentation of multiple levels in the work clearly demonstrates the fruits of his "Cage-ean" Rhode Island, Wooster, and Performance Group exercises. It acknowledges processes that go beyond chronological construction and reflect psychological emphases expressed in apparently chaotic ramblings. In truth, however, the apparent rambling reflects a unity: A surface—and narcissistic—goal of finding a "perfect moment" is pursued—while a deeper underlying "moment of understanding" is exposed, and the critical instincts of the audience are required to discern the revelation beneath the naive presentation of Gray the stage persona. It is what Fuchs calls a "projection of Gray's WASP *persona . . .* onto the world scene" in an ironic manner that not only contributes to the piece's humor but also allows it to present historic and political verities without smelling of didacticism.

Looking for a "perfect moment" is one of the central pursuits in *Swimming to Cambodia.* In the tale Gray recounts, he refuses to leave Thailand because, as he says, "I hadn't had a Perfect Moment yet, and I always like to have one before I leave an exotic place." Amidst all the revelations of suffering and death Gray experiences while in Thailand, looking for a perfect moment remains his central obsession. This self-indulgent (or perhaps "therapeutic") end prevents the performer from becoming a reliable political spokesman; in fact, it positions Gray in the role of mindless American oppressor, a part of the problem rather than part of a cure. Gray can even happily report in performance, "I'm not very political," which obviously undermines his authority. But one sees even more than Gray's undermining of himself when he turns into an American "Everyman" in the story by Roland Joffe, director of *The Killing Fields,* who hires

Gray for the movie *because* of this comment: "Perfect! We're looking for the American ambassador's aide."

The event that triggered *Swimming to Cambodia* was the filming of *The Killing Fields,* in which Gray had a small part. The film, shot in Thailand, documents the holocaust in Cambodia under Pol Pot. Gray's participation in the film provided the opportunity for Gray the artist/reporter to present Gray the performer in circumstances that allow that persona unwittingly to present material transcending both his personal narcissism and the narcissism of the filming group, all egocentric artists and craftsmen whose work is undermined by Gray's artistic response. Even though he is a minor figure in the movie, Gray is pampered and coddled during production, given the impression that he is important, while he lacks any sense of awareness whatsoever.

But some of Gray the reporter/author infuses itself. For example, Gray the performer reports about when he learned of American involvement in Cambodia, first observing, "leave it to a Brit [Roland Joffe] to tell you your own history," and then tellingly adding, "as Roland reminded me, we're not living in a democracy." Messages from Gray the author slip through, but ever so subtly, and never supported by the authority of Gray the performer. The comment seems offered as little more than a curious bit of information for the audience to react to. As another example, when discussing the possibility of nuclear holocaust, Gray drops a line reminiscent of something Schechner himself would say: "Mother Earth needs a long, long rest." But the point is not developed any further; it is merely tossed out for the audience to consider.

Gray even directly addresses the issue of language and power that so concerns Auslander, through an anecdote set in New York in which he cannot communicate with his disorderly neighbors, observing: "I don't know the language. I knew the language when I was with my people in Boston in 1962, in whitebread homogeneous Boston, brick-wall Boston." He lifts this personal dilemma to a larger question when he concludes:

> I wonder how do we begin to approach the so-called Cold War (or Now-Heating-Up War) between Russia and America if I can't even begin to resolve the Hot War down on Northmoor and Greenwich in Lower Manhattan?

To a point Gray the performer seems to grow up, becoming more aware of the world around him. But the moments when he "pronounces" judgment on the world are relatively rare, and even those are regularly undermined by his continual return to the narcissistic search for the "perfect moment." So too is any possible authority undermined, since the moments of awakening are little more than subplot *behind* the obsession about the "perfect moment." And Gray the performer loves that search for the "perfect moment," hungers for it.

Fuchs notes that "the actual story of the making of the film becomes a hallucinogenic recapitulation not only of the tragedy in Cambodia but of the universal torment by those who wield power over those who don't." Maslin notes, "What elevates this [monologue] above the realm of small talk is Mr. Gray's round-about—and peculiarly suspenseful—way of dramatizing the episode's [filming's] moral and political repercussions." These go beyond demonstrating the political power of some abstract government force over the oppressed in general to include the "innocent" abuses of the power-wielding camera crews, directors, and actors who manipulate the local inhabitants of the various film sites.

This control is illustrated by an innocent observation by Gray the performer. Recalling an ascent in a helicopter, he states, "I saw, my God, how much area the film covered!" In fact, the film controlled *more* than the physical territory Gray observed from above; there was economic and from that psychological and ethical control as well. As Gussow notes, among other things, *Swimming to Cambodia* "is a close-up, on-location analysis of the monumental absurdities of movie-making." In making this point, Gray the artist has moved from a narcissistic and subjective perspective. He reveals the outside, well-intentioned efforts to portray the monumental destruction of war and revolution upon a culture as an invasion of that same oppressed culture. The effort to document the cruelties of oppression also is oppression.

Though the Gray persona's narcissistic shell hides overt commentary, Gray the artist clearly has abandoned narcissism. The piece makes the point that oppression is endemic to American culture, whether or not it is intentional. It is multi-layered, even in the performance, for *Swimming to Cambodia* challenges the oppression of *The Killing Fields* even as *The Killing Fields* documents the oppression of Pol Pot. Dika comments on this effect in *Swimming to Cambodia*: "What in *The Killing Fields* had seemed a complete, integrated rendition of reality is now disrupted. Gray's words serve to break the seamless flow of images, cracking them open like eggshells" [Vera Dika, "Cinema: Critical/Mass," *Art in America,* January, 1988]. The authority of *The Killing Fields* itself is undermined, very much the same way Wooster's *L.S.D.* worked to undermine *The Crucible*. The result is what Lisa Zeidner calls "a hall of mirrors because nothing is quite real" ["*Swimming to Cambodia.* By Spalding Gray," *The New York Times Sunday Magazine,* 12 January 1986]. Determining the route through this hall of mirrors, ultimately, is left up to the audience.

Finally, at the end of the shorter version recorded as the movie, Gray makes a cryptic observation about the dangerous indulgences he has been part of when he pronounces, without further explanation: "And just as I was dozing off in the Pleasure Prison [what he calls the cast's hotel], I had a flash. An inkling. I suddenly thought I knew what it was that killed Marilyn Monroe." Gray the performer momentarily cracks here to reveal Gray the reporter (or maybe Gray the reintegrated self). The insider's view that Gray the artist has experienced has revealed exactly how destructive/oppressive the indulgences of the power elite can be, even/especially within their ranks.

An even more compelling tale concludes the transcription of the longer stage version. It is of a dream Gray has in which he witnesses a straw boy consumed by flame. The dream takes place in Hollywood, where Gray wanders the streets trying to tell the event to anyone who will listen, including several members of the Wooster Group. Gray concludes both the dream anecdote and the entire piece, with:

> And I knew all the time I was telling this story that it was a cover for the real story, the Straw Boy Story, which, for some reason, I found impossible to tell.

The text, finally, avoids the central issue, never even announces the issue, and thus the validity of the performer's presence is undermined, as is the entire text itself. Finally, *Swimming to Cambodia* strives to ground itself in some "other" that it cannot present because it *cannot* be presented. To fill the void, Gray has presented exactly what is *not* to be valued, which impacts on the audience all the more, since it *has* been valued, to some degree, throughout the performance. It is now all shown to be the very thing that destroys. In some ways what really needs to be told is too horrible to tell except by indirection, even if there were a language to tell it.

Gray has undermined a great many of the cultural icons that Wooster and many other more confrontational groups strive to undermine, but Gray clearly avoids doing so with any alienating revolutionary contempt; rather he employs a disarming process that works its way into establishment sensibilities with an alarming allure that charms as it undermines. But Gray goes even farther, having his own stage presence mesmerized as it mesmerizes the audience. The effect is that audiences are left not with a sense of betrayal, but with a sense that they have developed even as the onstage presence has developed; something of a community has been achieved.

The fact that Gray's work is *art* prevents it from exhibiting no authorial or presence power whatsoever. However, *Swimming to Cambodia* succeeds in minimizing that power in performance while, more importantly, it points out exactly how dangerously engulfing that power is. It critiques *The Killing Fields* and simultaneously undermines the perceived power of its own presence, whose spell has temporarily controlled the audience. Gray observes that we've all been consumed; in fact, he *demonstrates* it by "leading" with his own presence. Though Auslander's wish to see a movement toward no "power" at all seems fated never to occur, minimizing "power," undermining it, and demonstrating its danger seem to be the next best set of options, real options substituting for unreachable idealities.

The directly confrontational political agenda that many have looked for—and perhaps found elsewhere—does not exist in Gray. It is an agenda that owes a debt to the efforts of the 1960s and early 1970s but has indeed moved beyond those efforts. It is indebted to Schechner and the Performance Group, to Elizabeth LeCompte and the Wooster Group, and, though execution and performance does redirect itself, Gray's agenda follows directly, if sometimes obliquely, from the efforts of his predecessors.

FURTHER READING

AUTHOR COMMENTARY

Gray, Spalding. "About *Three Places in Rhode Island*." *The Drama Review* 23, No. 1 (March 1979): 31-42.
>   Recollection by Gray of his early experiences in the theater and the development of *Sakonnet Point, Rumstick Road,* and *Nayatt School.*

OVERVIEWS AND GENERAL STUDIES

Dace, Tish. "Monologues in the Making." *Plays and Players,* No. 389 (February 1986): 16-17.
>   Admiring profile that praises Gray's style: "his phraseology, his structure, his relatively uninflected voice and relaxed face, a tempo of rapid patter punctuated by purposeful pauses."

D'Erasmo, Stacey. "Gray Matters." *Harper's Bazaar,* No. 3365 (May 1992): 46, 135.
>   General appreciation of Gray and his work. D'Erasmo states, "Gray deserves an award for making the spoken word terrifying and spectacular to a mass audience."

Gentile, John S. "Spalding Gray." In his *Cast of One: One-Person Shows from the Chatauqua Platform to the Broadway Stage,* pp. 148-52. Urbana: University of Illinois Press.
>   Links Gray to the solo performance tradition "that is rooted in the art of storytelling and the basic human need to hear and to tell stories."

McGuigan, Cathleen. "Gray's Eminence." *Newsweek* CVIII, No. 4 (28 July 1986): 69.
>   Declares that Gray "has reinvented the oral tradition."

Shank, Theodore. "Spalding Gray and Elizabeth LeCompte: The Wooster Group." In his *American Alternative Theater,* pp. 170-79. New York: Grove Press, 1982.
>   Focuses on the autobiographical content of Gray's work, particularly *Three Places in Rhode Island.*

Shewey, Don. "The Year of Spalding Famously." *Village Voice* XXIX, No. 46 (13 November 1984): 99, 107.
>   Profile of Gray that stresses his status as an "underground celebrity."

Siegle, Robert. "Spalding Gray and the Colorful Quilt of Culture." In his *Suburban Ambush: Downtown Writing and the Fiction of Insurgency,* pp. 252-59. Baltimore: The Johns Hopkins University Press, 1989.

Examines the ways in which Gray's works "disrupt the traditional relationship between a passive audience and method actors preserving the illusion of reality on a raised stage."

THREE PLACES IN RHODE ISLAND

Aronson, Arnold. "*Sakonnet Point.*" *The Drama Review* 19, No. 4 (December 1975): 27-35.
>   Examination of the structure, images, action, and other performance-related elements of *Sakonnet Point.*

Bierman, James. "*Three Places in Rhode Island.*" *The Drama Review* 23, No. 1 (March 1979): 13-30.
>   Detailed analysis of the dramaturgy of Gray's trilogy.

SEX AND DEATH TO AGE 14

Brustein, Robert. Review of *Sex and Death to Age 14. The New Republic* 195, No. 1 (July 7, 1986): 36-7.
>   Favorable evaluation that claims "Gray creates an erotic history of early adolescence that does for New England Protestants what Lenny Bruce and Philip Roth did for New York and New Jersey Jews."

SWIMMING TO CAMBODIA

Canby, Vincent. "Soloists on the Big Screen." *The New York Times* (22 March 1987): II, 19.
>   Review of the movie version of *Swimming to Cambodia* that places it in the genre of "concert film."

Carr, Cindy. "Spalding Gray." *American Film* XII, No. 7 (May 1987): 62.
>   Profile of Gray and an appreciation of the film version of *Swimming to Cambodia* that declares it "an epic meditation on illusion and reality."

Dika, Vera. "Critical/Mass." *Art in America* 76, No. 1 (January 1988): 37-40.
>   Argues that the film version of *Swimming to Cambodia* is not "a mere recording of a previously staged event but a new work, one that actually extends and completes the original aspirations of the performance piece."

Maslin, Janet. Review of *Swimming to Cambodia. The New York Times* (13 March 1987): C 8.
>   Describes the film of *Swimming to Cambodia* as "a two-man undertaking, one that shows off both Mr. Gray's storytelling talents and [director] Jonathan Demme's ability to frame them."

Prinz, Jessica. "Spalding Gray's *Swimming to Cambodia*: A Performance Gesture," in *Staging the Impossible: The Fantastic Mode in Modern Drama,* edited by Patrick D. Murphy, pp. 156-68. New York: Greenwood Press, 1992, pp. 156-68.

Argues that in its attempt to come to terms with the horrors that took place in Cambodia, *Swimming to Cambodia* represents "a reaction to or defense mechanism against the fantastic and seemingly impossible facts of history."

Rich, Frank. "To Play Oneself May Be the Greatest Illusion of All." *The New York Times* (29 June 1986): 3, 25.

Includes a review of *Swimming to Cambodia,* in which Rich observes: "What makes Spalding Gray so theatrical in his seemingly nontheatrical way is not only his talent as a storyteller and social observer but also his ability to deepen the mystery of the demarcation line between performer and role."

MONSTER IN A BOX

Leslie, Guy. Review of *Monster in a Box. Theater Week* 4, No. 16 (26 November 1990): 34.

Finds Gray's storytelling in *Monster in a Box* "highly entertaining" but observes that "some indication that storytelling cannot neatly tie a ribbon around all of life's experiences is called for."

Simon, John. Review of *Monster in a Box. New York* Magazine 23, No. 48 (10 December 1990): 109.

Very mixed assessment asserting that some of *Monster in a Box* "has a fey, off-the-wall charm, [but] some of it is just self-indulgent blather."

Additional coverage of Gray's life and career is contained in the following sources published by Gale Research: *Contemporary Authors,* **Vol. 128;** *Contemporary Literary Criticism,* **Vol. 49;** *DISCovering Authors: Modules— Popular Fiction and Genre Authors Module.*

John Lyly
c. 1554-1606

INTRODUCTION

Lyly was an Elizabethan dramatist and prose writer who composed witty and highly polished works aimed at a sophisticated audience. His earliest works, the treatises *Euphues: The Anatomy of Wit* and *Euphues and His England,* gave the name to the highly elaborate prose style known as euphuism and inaugurated a short-lived but influential vogue for writings in this mode. His dramas, like his prose works, are characterized by rich rhetorical ornamentation and complex structures of balanced antitheses, images, and allusions.

BIOGRAPHICAL INFORMATION

The exact date of Lyly's birth is unknown. The statement by the seventeenth-century writer Anthony à Wood that Lyly entered Oxford in 1569, together with Lyly's application for a bachelor's degree in 1573, suggest that he was born in 1552. However, his name appears on the 1571 entrance list for Magdalen College, Oxford, which points to 1554 as the year of his birth. Since it is known that Lyly's brothers attended the King's School at Canterbury, it is likely that he too received his early education there. He appears to have been a serious student at Oxford but also seems to have gained a reputation as a wit and a carouser. He received a master's degree from Oxford in 1575 and three years later published *Euphues: The Anatomy of Wit.* This and its sequel were hugely successful and in the years following appeared in over thirty editions. Around 1580 Lyly entered the service of the Earl of Oxford, the Lord Great Chamberlain. This connection was highly advantageous for Lyly, and his career flourished. He became a partner in the Blackfriars theater, and in 1583 he married Beatrice Browne, a member of an influential family. Lyly's first plays, *Campaspe* and *Sappho and Phao,* were both produced at the Blackfriars in 1583-1584. *Gallathea* was also composed for performance at Blackfriars, but the playhouse closed in 1584, and the play did not receive its first staging until 1588. By this time Lyly seems to have lost Oxford's patronage and to have become associated with the Children of St. Paul's, a troupe of professional boy actors. This company produced four additional plays by Lyly: *Endimion, Love's Metamorphosis, Midas,* and *Mother Bombie.* Lyly was elected to Parliament several times, the first in 1589. It was around this time that he composed his last dramatic work, *The Woman in the Moon,* which was presented at the royal Court. In the 1590s Lyly hoped to receive the Court appointment of Master of Revels, but he appears to have fallen out of favor and did not get the position. From this time on his finances were in a state of decline. He wrote several petitions to Queen Elizabeth in the 1590s and 1600s, asking for a reward for his services, but she died in 1603 without having shown him any preferment. Lyly himself died in 1606.

MAJOR WORKS

In keeping with the euphuistic mode, Lyly's plays feature highly stylized scenes organized as series of debates between antitheses. *Campaspe* examines the problem of the individual in the state, as Alexander, the conqueror of Thebes, falls in love with Campaspe, one of his prisoners. Alexander is torn between his love and his duty to his country. This is allied in the play to a number of related questions, such as the nature of the king's private and public selves, the relationship between monarch and subject, and the individual's responsibility to obey authority. *Sappho and Phao* similarly revolves around a love between a person of high rank and one of low status. In this drama Queen Sappho falls in love with the beautiful ferryman Phao. The play opposes chastity and eroticism, simplicity and complexity, and life at court versus both an intellectual life and a humble existence. In *Endimion* Lyly again focuses on love and passion, but this play, perhaps the author's most complex, presents a number of pairs of lovers. Endimion is loved by the earth goddess Tellus, but he is enamored of the moon goddess Cynthia who scorns him. The jealous Tellus casts Endimion into a forty-year sleep. Endimion's friend Eumenides learns that he can be awakened by a kiss from Cynthia, and he persuades her to do so. Eumenides himself is in love with the disdainful Semele. Other relationships include the jailor Corsites' love for Tellus (who loves Endimion) and Sir Tophas' passion for Dipsas. Within this framework Lyly explores a variety of oppositions, including love versus friendship and art against nature. *Endimion* is also noteworthy among Lyly's plays for its more involved action and greater depth of characterization.

CRITICAL RECEPTION

The vogue of euphuism passed quickly, and even within Lyly's own lifetime it became the object of satire. His influence on his fellow dramatists, however, was significant. Robert Greene adapted *Campaspe*—which had been written for an aristocratic audience—for the popular stage. Ben Jonson admired Lyly's work, and William Shakespeare incorporated elements of his plays into such comedies as *As You Like It, Love's Labour's Lost,* and *Twelfth Night.* Nevertheless, by the middle of seventeenth century Lyly's plays fell into complete neglect. It was not until

1962, with the publication of G. K. Hunter's *John Lyly: The Humanist as Courtier,* that significant interest in his work was revived. Critics since that time have seen Lyly's plays not merely as assemblages of brilliant images and rhetorical flourishes, but as carefully elaborated demonstrations of a world view based on paradox, opposition, and duality.

PRINCIPAL WORKS

PLAYS

A Moste Excellent Comedie of Alexander, Campaspe, and Diogenes [*Campaspe*] 1583-84
Sapho and Phao 1583-84
Gallathea c. 1585-88
Endimion, The Man in the Moone 1588
Love's Metamorphosis c. 1588-90
Mother Bombie c. 1588-90
Midas 1589-90
The Woman in the Moone c. 1591-94

OTHER MAJOR WORKS

Euphues. The Anatomy of Wyt (prose romance) 1578
Euphues and His England. Containing His Voyage and Adventures (prose romance) 1580
Pappe with an Hatchet. Alias, A Figge for My God Sonne (prose pamphlet) 1589

OVERVIEWS AND GENERAL STUDIES

David Lloyd Stevenson (essay date 1946)

SOURCE: "Lyly's Quarreling Lovers," in *The Love-Game Comedy,* Columbia University Press, 1946, pp. 148-73.

[*In the following excerpt, Stevenson examines Lyly's comedies in relation to the "sixteenth-century rebellion of common sense against the attenuated sentiments of romantic tradition."*]

Romance had been rejected by [Michael] Drayton and [John] Marston; it had been idealized beyond contamination from real life by Spenser and Cardinal Bembo; it had been described by John Donne as the spiritual half of love, which in normal experience exists on both spiritual and physical levels. John Lyly was the first Elizabethan writer to perceive that the opposed attitudes in this quarrel over romance could be used for another purpose. They could be embodied in a series of characters whose conflicts could be used as the basis of a sustained narrative and at the same time illustrate one of the significant problems of the day. Lyly explores the possi-

bilities of his discovery in the two parts of his novel *Euphues, the Anatomy of Wit* (1578) and *Euphues and His England* (1580). He turns his back on the bucolic enchantments which sustain Sidney's *Arcadia,* for example. There is no escaping the realities of the actual world in *Euphues*; its main concern is to exhibit the perplexities of love as they appeared to the ladies and gentlemen of the sixteenth century.

The plot of *Euphues* concerns three lovers, each of whom fails in his attempt to experience traditional romantic passion. The most realistic of the three, the one least subservient to the despairing ritual of adoration which convention decreed, is Euphues. This is not to say that he escapes romance. Love enters his heart through the eye and at his first sight of his lady. He is seated opposite her at dinner, and he "fed of one dish which ever stoode before him, the beautie of Lucilla. Heere Euphues at first sight was so kyndled with desyre, that almost he was lyke to burn to coales." He also endures the customary love-sickness for his mistress, crying out in his pain, "can men by no hearb, by no art, by no way procure a remedye for the impatient disease of love?"

But the goal of Euphues's desire is far less exalted than that stipulated by courtly or Petrarchan ideals. He is indifferent to the ennobling power of love and to lovers' spiritual ecstasies. His wooing seeks only sexual union. He presents his suit to Lucilla, after the fashion of Drayton and Donne, by urging the very perishable nature of love. Of obdurate mistresses he says:

> When the blacke crowes foote shall appeare in theyr eye, or the blacke Oxe treade on their foote, when their beautie shall be lyke the blasted Rose, theyr wealth wasted, their bodies worne, theyr faces wrinckled, their fyngers crooked, who will lyke of them in their age, who loved none in their youth?

Furthermore, Euphues woos the lady already supposedly won by his friend Philautus, and he justifies his treachery by mocking the idea that love is the one supreme, inviolable emotional experience; "he that cannot dissemble in love, is not worthy to live. I am of this minde, that both might and mallice, deceite and treacherie, all perjurie, anye impietie may lawfully be committed in love, which is lawlesse."

When Euphues finds that Lucilla has forsaken him, even as she did Philautus, he repudiates romance, much as Sidney had done, by crying out against his own practices.

> What greater infamye, then to conferre the sharpe wit to the making of lewde Sonnets, to the idolatrous worshipping of . . . Ladies, to the vaine delights of fancie, to all kinde of vice as it were against kinde & course of nature?

Henceforth he becomes a critic of the very ideals of love to which, despite his sense of reality, he had paid allegiance. On the one hand, he generalizes skeptically from his own experience, finding that the ideals common to his age are remote from actual life. He attacks the principle of love at first sight by pointing out that "Love which should continue for ever, should not be begon in an houre, but slowly be taken in hande." On the other hand, he cannot rid himself of the lingering conviction that all human love is wrong because it is basically carnal. We need not then be surprised that Euphues's advice to Philautus turns into a rehearsal of a kind of dismal, worldly wisdom, a Puritan's cry to avoid the snares of courtly romance: "if thou canst not live chastly, chuse such an one, as maye be more commended for humilitie than beautie . . . Fond lust, causeth drye bones: and lewd pastimes, naked pursses."

The second lover in Lyly's novel, Philautus, is less concerned than Euphues had been with the physical side of love. He seeks quite candidly the experience that had been described in twelfth-century romance. But Philautus is too ingenuous in his attempt, as his remarks to Euphues indicate:

> . . . let us goe devoutly to the shrine of our Saincts there to offer our devotion, for my books teach me, that such a wound must be healed wher it was first hurt, and for this disease we will use a common remedie . . . The eye that blinded thee, shall make thee see . . .

The first woman to receive his attentions, Lucilla, leaves him for Euphues. Her infidelity, however, far from making him skeptical, acts as a spur to send him on still further quests for an earthly ambassadress from the medieval Garden of Love. And he enters England, so Lyly tells us, "carying the Image of Love, engraven in the bottome of his hart, & the picture of courtesie, imprinted in his face." A man under the dominance of such an ideal is immediately re-entangled in the same despair over the witty Camilla that he had already suffered for Lucilla. Following his lack of success with Camilla, he proceeds to woo and to wed Frauncis.

He represents the Renaissance in its absurdly determined effort to actualize an inherited theory of love. He is a follower of troubadour ideals, however, rather than Petrarchan, and shows the futility of most attempts to spiritualize passion. In reply to Euphues's philosophy, after the latter's reformation, that "the effect of love is faith, not luste, delightfull conference, not detestable concupiscence," Philautus denies ascetic ideals a place in courtship.

> . . . it would doe me no more good, to see my Lady and not embrace hir, in the heate of my desire, then to see fire, and not warme me in the extremitie of my colde. No, no, Euphues, thou makest Love nothing but a continuall wooing, if thou barre it of the effect, and then is it infinite, or if thou allow it, and yet forbid it, a perpetuall warfare, and then is it intollerable.

The third of these lovers to personify an aspect of the amorous conflict of the Renaissance, Fidus, is the least realistic and the most courtly. In his wooing of Iffida as

if she were a lady out of medieval romance he shows that his bondage to idyllic love is almost complete. Of the three, only for Fidus the "measure of love is to have no meane, the end to be everlasting." His final loss of his lady and his discovery that love is subject to the changes of time are not enough to make him disavow it, like Euphues, or to pursue it farther, like Philautus. He retreats from the world of experience and becomes a hermit in order to preserve his illusions. Fidus is not unaware of reality. Like Philautus he wishes the fruition of his idealized conception of love. Fidus is singular only in that he can be content with no less than such ideal fruition. Hence, though he has become one of love's anchorites, he realizes that he cannot escape the penalties of clinging to illusion. For all his fidelity, he concludes that love has "so many inconveniences hanging upon it, as to recken them all were infinite, and to taste but one of them, intollerable."

By means of these three characters in **Euphues** Lyly suggests some of the difficulties which beset young men seeking the ideals of romance in the real world. Furthermore, here and there in his narrative Lyly anticipates the pattern of the love-game comedy by presenting the quarrel over the nature of love as a witty duel between the lovers and their ladies. Euphues and Lucilla, for example, come to accept each other (and romance of a sort) only after a sharp verbal skirmish concerning current and inconsistent attitudes toward love. Fidus, in his duels of wit with Iffida, defends the ritual of courtesy, while she advocates a realistic contempt of it. He is appalled by her refusal to accept either the idealized sentiment of love or the adoration of a would-be suitor and pours scorn upon her skepticism:

> Is this the guerdon for good wil, is this the courtesie of Ladies, the lyfe of Courtiers, the foode of lovers? Ah Iffida, little dost thou know the force of affection, & therefore thou rewardest it lightly, neither shewing curtesie lyke a Lover, nor giving thankes lyke a Ladye.

But Iffida is moved only to derision. She mocks Fidus by suggesting: "And to the ende I might stoope to your lure, I pray begin to hate me, that I may love you."

Philautus quarrels with Camilla in a different fashion. Although suffering all the required despair of the aspiring lover, he lets his own common sense triumph. He approaches his lady, not protesting humility and adoration, but, like Berowne and Benedick, almost denouncing that for which he sues. Ladies pretend, he says, "a great skyrmishe at the first, yet are boorded willinglye at the last. I meane therefore to tell you this which is all, that I love you." But he concludes this speech, belying himself, "wringing hir by the hand," and Camilla turns upon him for his lack of romantic pretense, crying, "You fall from one thing to an other, using no decorum, except this, that you study to have your discourse as farre voyde of sence, as your face is of favor."

In these lovers' skirmishes is found a sophisticated banter between courtier and lady like that in Castiglione's treatise [*The Courtier*]. It was this sort of dialogue, expressing inconsistencies in love, that was elaborated to carry the burden of lovers' quarrels in Shakespeare's comedies. Lyly, both as a stylist and as a Renaissance psychologist, was quite aware that this method of presenting men and women in love was new to his age. He comments that the amorous language of Henry VIII's time is now considered "barbarous": "in tymes past they used to wooe in playne tearmes, now in piked sentences. . . . And to that passe it is come, that they make an arte of that, which was woont to be thought naturall." Even the despairing Fidus confesses that the one attribute in a woman that most sets his "fancies on edge" is her wit. When he is driven by Iffida's raillery to make a theoretical choice among three possibilities—a witty wanton, a fair fool, and an ugly saint—he chooses the one with wit, because "by hir wit she will ever conceale whom she loves, & to weare a horne and not knowe it, will do me no more harme then to eate a flye, and not see it."

Pairs of contending lovers, as they emerge occasionally from *The Courtier* or from Elizabethan poetry, have been shown neither to solve their own conflict nor suggest a generally acceptable solution. In *Euphues,* however, wholly imaginary characters are involved in an imaginary narrative. They are free from the restrictions imposed by reality. Therefore Lyly is free, as neither Castiglione nor Sidney was, to harmonize these discordant concepts of love by the final union of the lovers who represent the conflict. He is free to present his characters as concluding their sex duels by accepting each other and therewith the natural paradoxes of idyllic love in a skeptical world. But Lyly, at least in *Euphues,* only partially realized the dramatic and comic potentialities of this acceptance. The contentions in the two parts of *Euphues* give dramatic force to the amorous problem they present. But the lovers' quarrels, with the exception of that between Philautus and Frauncis, serve rather to separate the contestants and the attitudes they embody than to bring them together in any kind of harmony (as is done in *Much Ado*). Fidus accurately summarizes all their sex duels when he describes his own battle of wits with Iffida: "Many nips were returned that time betweene us, and some so bitter, that I thought them to proceede rather of mallice, to worke dispite, then of mirth to showe disporte."

In *Euphues,* even when diverse opinions are reconciled by the marriage of the two contestants, comedy is not evoked. The ultimate surrender of Camilla to Surius is merely noted by Lyly in passing. It is highly anticlimactic, breaks no tension, comes almost as an afterthought. "By the preamble, you may gesse to what purpose the drift tended," he says. He draws a moral out of that which to be most effective dramatically should be immediately understood by the audience. There should be no such pointed comment as "This I note, that they that are most wise, most vertuous, most beautiful, are not free from the impressions of Fancy: For who would have thought that Camilla, who seemed to disdaine love, should so soone be entangled." The final solution to the difficulties which have beset Philautus in his effort to find an ac-

ceptable mistress is presented in a similar manner. Lyly breaks the news of Philautus's successful pursuit of Frauncis in an exchange of letters (between Philautus and Euphues) which are mainly concerned with the lady's dowry and with the requisites of a successful married life.

In *Euphues* Lyly presents the fact, of which his age was well aware, that men and women in love do not follow any rigidly prescribed code of behavior. The witty, consciously rhetorical dialogues between lovers show Lyly putting legs to a quarrel over romance and making it walk. His lovers' predicaments are not merely the hazards set up by the improbable events found, for example, in Sidney's Arcadian romance. The characters in *Euphues* dramatize the gulf between the effects of an actual love affair and the supposed effects prescribed by genteel tradition. But Lyly's lovers fail to create the illusion that they have solved the problems which beset them. They illustrate no dramatic and concerted reconciliation, as do the contestants in Shakespeare's *Much Ado*. For this reason, in Lyly's novel the pattern of the love-game comedy remains incomplete.

Contending Attitudes in Lyly's Comedies

In most of Lyly's comedies (as in *Euphues*) he creates a series of lovers whose difficulties are the result of the sixteenth-century rebellion of common sense against the attenuated sentiments of romantic tradition. Lyly's presentation of this conflict in his dramas, however, is complicated by the fact that his characters are usually thought to reflect the ever changing infatuations of the queen and her courtiers. Indeed, the allegorical significance of these characters may well have been Lyly's chief personal interest in them, since he hoped to make them appeal eloquently for his own preferment. For example, in Lyly's first comedy, *Alexander and Campaspe,* Alexander was no doubt meant to be in part a flattering portrait of Elizabeth complacently conquering her desire for an unworthy lover. But he also exists to voice an impersonal protest against those who allow themselves to be overwhelmed by romantic passion. Lyly's prudence, as well as his artistry, dictated that the allegorical meanings of these plays be kept imprecise and the import of their love conflicts general. Although the allusions to specific men and women of his time are too amorphous to make his comedies accurate social history, his presentation of attitudes of actual Elizabethans is important because it emphasizes the very real nature of the sixteenth-century quarrel over romance.

In *Campaspe* Lyly presents love as a quarrel of impulses within the mind of the protagonist, Alexander, who suffers for his Theban captive the languishing despairs of the courtly lover. His problem is whether he shall possess her against her will and be recreant to all the ideals of romantic love or conquer his passion and so deny love itself. Hephestion, who acts as Alexander's moral counselor, insists that romance is mutable and merely a delusion arising from sexual desires. He cautions Alexander that "time must weare out that love hath wrought, and reason weane what appetite noursed." He defines love as "a word by superstition thought a god, by use turned to an humour, by selfwil made a flattering madnesse." Lays, the courtesan, acts as Alexander's realistic counselor. She suggests ironically that the achievement of worldly ambition is for Alexander more important than his realization of a romantic idyl: "You may talk of warre, speak bigge, conquer worldes with great wordes: but stay at home, where in steede of Alarums you shall have daunces, for hot battelles with fierce menne, gentle Skirmishes with fayre womenne."

Alexander finally extricates himself from his entanglement in about the same manner as did Euphues, by accepting asceticism as "reasonable." He is thus enabled to contradict in jocular fashion conventional descriptions of love. Henceforth, he concludes, he will use "fancy as a foole to make his sport, or a minstrell to make him mery. It is not the amorous glaunce of an eie can settle an idle thought in the heart; no, no, it is childrens game, a life for . . . scholers (who) picking fancies out of books, have little els to mervaile at." Alexander does not come to terms with romance, but eludes it, as his final comment illustrates: "It were a shame Alexander should desire to commaund the world, if he could not commaund himselfe . . . good Hephestion, when al the world is woone, and every country is thine and mine, either find me out an other to subdue, or of my word I wil fall in love."

In *Sapho and Phao,* Lyly's second play, Phao, the humble lover of Sapho, was probably meant to suggest the Duc d'Alençon, in whom Elizabeth pretended a teasing sort of interest. Phao also represents the naïve lover, unaware of the actual nature of the world in which he is seeking romance. His love for Sapho follows courtly tradition. He is stricken nearly speechless at his first sight of her, finally declaring: "Madame, I crave pardon, I am spurblinde [i.e., purblind] I could scarse see." He exhibits all the physical anguish that was part of the pattern, only to be refused by Sapho at the end of his wooing. Then he turns from her court back to his ferrying, to endeavor, as he says, "with mine oare to gette a fare, not with my penne to write a fancie." Yet like Fidus, Phao can neither reject romance nor accept a less ideal reality. He finally admits that "loves are but smokes, which vanish in the seeing, and yet hurte whilest they are seene." But he remains faithful to his ideal: "This shal be my resolution, where ever I wander to be as I were ever kneeling before Sapho, my loyalty unspotted, though unrewarded."

Mileta of this play, the lady-in-waiting to Sapho, represents (in contrast to Phao) the unadulterated skepticism of the Renaissance. To her feminine companions she cries out her protests against the courtly tradition which Phao dramatizes: "I laugh at that you all call love, and judge it onely a worde called love. Me thinks lyking, a curtesie, a smile, a beck, and such like, are the very Quintessence of love." She finds the sighs and sonnets of a lover

quite as ridiculous as, a decade later, did such satirists as Marston and Donne. She assumes the regular anti-Petrarchan attitude when she describes these conventional courtiers as "wearing our hands out with courtly kissings, when their wits faile in courtly discourses. Now rufling their haires, now setting their ruffes, then gazing with their eies, then sighing with a privie wring by the hand, thinking us like to be wowed by signes and ceremonies."

In Lyly's third play, *Endimion,* as Bond suggests, "the allegory *is* the plot." Indeed, the Elizabethan audience could scarcely have failed to look for hidden significances in *Endimion,* since it was warned not to do so by the author in his prologue. Again the characters reflect both court intrigues and the more general conflict of Renaissance attitudes toward love. Endimion, whose name gives title to the play, is probably meant to be Leicester, languishingly but ascetically devoted to Cynthia, or Elizabeth, "the Ladie that hee delightes in, and dotes on every day, and dies for ten thousand times a day." He is also the perfect Petrarchan lover; all his amorous thoughts "are stitched to the starres." Eumenides, his friend and rescuer, seems to be something like Sir Philip Sidney. The sharp-tongued Semele, whom he woos, may very well have suggested Penelope Devereux, or "Stella." But these contrasting pairs of lovers also dramatize the general difference between a Platonic respect for one's mistress and a courtly solicitation of her favors.

Endimion, in his absolute devotion to Cynthia, is the romantic lover incarnate. To him love is the only significant human experience. He cries:

> There is no Mountain so steepe that I will not climbe, no monster so cruell that I will not tame, no action so desperate that I will not attempt . . . Beholde my sad teares, my deepe sighes, my hollowe eyes, my broken sleepes, my heavie countenaunce. . . . Have I not spent my golden yeeres in hopes, waxing old with wishing, yet wishing nothing but thy love.

Like Fidus, like Phao, Endimion becomes one of love's anchorites, "divorsing himselfe from the amiablenes of all Ladies, the braverie of all Courts, the companie of al men . . . accounting in the worlde (but Cynthia) nothing excellent." And like Phao, Endimion is untouched by skepticism, although his only reward for his fidelity to Cynthia has been a single kiss.

The attitude of Eumenides, on the other hand, is that of a matter-of-fact lover who is content to have his fortunes "creepe on the earth." He lightly mocks the Petrarchan amorist when he warns Endimion that sleep will do him more good than his ecstatic reverie. Eumenides, like Philautus, seeks a substantial reward for his wooing. To him the goal of courtesy is the yielding by a virtuous lady to her lover. Indeed, he is so much a virtuoso in sensuality that his imagined delight at Semele's final surrender almost overcomes him. He cries out, "I pray thee, fortune, when I shall first meete with fayre Semele, dash my delight with some light disgrace, least imbracing sweetnesse beyond measure, I take surfit without recure. . . ." His only difficulty is that the object of his devotion, like Sidney's "Stella," refuses to conform to his realistic conception of love.

In portraying the character Sir Tophas in this play, Lyly goes beyond a commonsense realism and actually derides romantic ideals. Sir Tophas is a braggart, a pedant, a social climber, and a foolish amorist. His courtship of the old hag Dipsas is a gross parody of the proper ritual of adoration. It may have been meant merely to ridicule some unlucky Elizabethan would-be courtier. But the conduct of Sir Tophas is also a violent caricature of the lover's pageant of woes. Like the neophyte in a twelfth-century romance, Sir Tophas first scorns love before he is caught by it. He ridicules passion by a foolish quarrel with his servant over the physiological origin of love. His servant suggests, "love, sir, may lye in your lunges, and I think it doth, and that is the cause you blow, and are so pursie." Tophas replies, mocking the Elizabethan complimentary sonneteer, "Tush boy! I thinke it but some devise of the Poet to get money." But the caricature goes deeper, and Lyly seems to anticipate for a moment the satiric view of Marston. Conventional conceits of the Petrarchan, or the Provençal lover are burlesqued in Sir Tophas's description of his passion for Dipsas:

I feele all Ovid "de arte amandi" lie as heavie at my heart as a loade of logges. O what a fine thin hayre hath Dipsas! What a prettie low forehead! What a tall & statlie nose! What little hollowe eyes! What great and goodly lypes! Howe harmlesse shee is beeing toothlesse! her fingers fatte and short, adorned with long nayles like a Bytter! In howe sweete a proportion her cheekes hang downe to her brests like dugges, and her pappes to her waste like bagges! What a lowe stature shee is, and yet what a great foote shee carryeth!

The Woman in the Moone, the last but one of Lyly's comedies which treat the Renaissance complexities of love, has been called "a mirthless and bitter denunciation of woman" [by Violet Jeffery, in *John Lyly And the Italian Renaissance*]. Possibly it portrays Lyly's conception of the fickleness of a specific woman, Elizabeth, Indeed, as Feuillerat has pointed out [in *John Lyly*], its original audience could scarcely have failed to think of the queen even if Lyly had conceived the central character in this drama, Pandora, impersonally. Whatever the implied meanings, the import of the play is not limited to them. It contains a somewhat sardonic presentation of lovers' perplexities, which had already been dramatized in Lyly's other plays. The only difference is that here a conflict of attitudes is dramatized as moral allegory. A single woman, Pandora, is sent to Utopia to become the lady of one of the four shepherds who live there in rustic peace. Her response to her wooers is controlled in turn by each of the seven planets. Therefore she represents all the variations of temperament of an actual person in conflict with the shepherds, who voice the sentiments of confirmed idealists. Gunophilus, her servant, makes this clear when he describes his passion in terms of the time-

worn idea that the first glance of the mistress pierced the heart of the recipient through his eye.

As I beheld the glory of thy face
My feeble eyes admiring majestie
Did sinke into my heart such holly feare
That very feare amazing every sence,
Withheld my tongue from saying what I would.

Stesias, whom Pandora under the influence of Sol has chosen as her husband, represents the lover who thinks for a moment that he has realized his idyllic desires. When he has first won Pandora, he cries out:

O Stesias, what a heavenly love hast thou!
A love as chaste as is Apolloes tree:
As modest as a vestall Virgins eye,
And yet as bright as Glow wormes in the night,
With which the morning decks her lovers hayre
O fayre Pandora, blessed Stesias.

Pandora, who has been alternately melancholy, disdainful, raging, chastely coy, is seen in clearest conflict with the romantic ideal envisaged by the shepherds when she is under the influence of Venus. The scorn of this goddess for Pandora's proposed union with Stesias, expressed somewhat in the spirit of the "ars amatoria," is in defiance of all conventional conceits:

Away with chastity and modest thoughts
'Quo mihi fortunam si non conceditur uti?'
Is she not young? then let her to the world:
All those are strumpets that are over chaste,
Defying such as keepe their company.
Tis not the touching of a womans hand,
Kissing her lips, hanging about her neck . . .
That men expect . . .

And Pandora solicits successfully, in turn, the three shepherds she had dismissed to marry Stesias, crying:

A husband? What a folish word is that!
Give me a lover, let the husband goe.

This is no misogynic tract (as Violet Jeffery, for one, would have it), since the shepherds are as willing to play traitor to Stesias as is Pandora. Like the other comedies, this is a study of the contrasts between the idealized pretensions of lovers' desires and the dismal realizations.

Lyly's Resolution of Controversy

Alexander and Hephestion, Sapho and Mileta, Endimion and Eumenides show how Lyly turns to dramatic use incompatible attitudes toward love already established for Elizabethan thought. But Lyly goes farther in the direction of "love-game comedy." Pairs of lovers in some of his comedies dramatize the intellectual conflict between different ideas of love as a witty duel between a courtier and his lady. In **Campaspe,** for example, there is a mild skirmish of wits between Alexander's successful rival, the painter Apelles, and Campaspe. Apelles is traditionally correct when he suggests to Campaspe that the source of his desire for her is in the glance of her eyes. As a romantic lover, he believes that she is to be won by a ritual of humble adoration, by "praier, sacrifice and bribes," at the shrine of Venus. But he is also sufficiently realistic to wish to possess his lady. In his quarrel with Campaspe he represents the Renaissance attempt to possess its ideal woman, and she represents the attempt to keep love an untouchable ideal. They quarrel first because Campaspe has scornfully rejected Apelles, romantically prostrate before her beauty. He then mocks *her,* suggesting that she is both coy and lustful.

> Mistresse, you neither differ from your selfe nor your sex: for knowing your owne perfection you seeme to dispraise that which men most commend, drawing them by that meane into an admiration, where feeding them selves they fall into an extasie; your modestie being the cause of the one, and of the other, your affections.

In their second duel of wits Apelles is finally driven to teasing protest that the real Campaspe is incredibly hard to bend to his preconceived ideal: "It is not possible that a face so faire, & a wit so sharpe, both without comparison, should not be apt to love."

Their skirmish has an air of reality. It is presented as if it had arisen from the lovers' desires and had been mutually contrived. It actually draws the lovers together instead of separating them (as such duels had done in *Euphues* and in *The Courtier*). Out of their final witty game of disagreement comes Campaspe's confession of surrender, though she quibbles with Apelles even as he swears the eternal nature of his passion, mocking him with, "That is, neither to have beginning nor ending." But she immediately relents and admits, "but this assure your self, that I had rather bee in thy shop grinding colours, then in Alexanders court, following higher fortunes." Thus these lovers, like Berowne and Rosalind, like Beatrice and Benedick, do work out their conflict of attitudes after a fashion.

But neither Apelles nor Campaspe is the subtle creature of later comedy, neither one personifies an aspect of the quarrel over love with sufficient clarity to make his compromise or betrayal of his point of view dramatically effective. Each acknowledges his acceptance of the other too soon. Furthermore, narrative events impede the climax to their verbal combats. It is Alexander who finally decides their fate, not they themselves. Their union signalizes less an accommodation of common sense to romantic theory than, like the marriages in pastoral romance, an escape into an unashamedly idyllic world. The benediction pronounced over them by Alexander does not settle their quarrel in a way to satisfy either dramatic or comic considerations: "Two loving wormes, Hephestion! I perceive Alexander cannot subdue the affections of men, though he conquer their countries . . . Well, enjoy one another, I give her thee franckly, Apelles."

In *Sapho and Phao* there is a fragmentary appearance of a sex duel, but it bears no integral relation to the play. Mileta, the vitriolic denouncer of all manifestations of love, falls its momentary victim in the presence of the amorously chivalric Phao. She suggests to him, as she summons him to the bed of Sapho, "Were I sicke, the verye sight of thy faire face would drive me into a sound sleepe." To which Phao replies, in ironic dismissal, "Indeede Gentlewomen are so drowsie in their desires, that they can scarce hold up their eyes for love." She continues to woo him by praising his extreme beauty; to which he retorts, in derision, "Lady, I forgot to commend you first, and leaste I shoulde have over slipped to praise you at all, you have brought in my bewtie, which is simple, that in curtisie I might remember yours, which is singular."

In this exchange of wit Mileta not only repudiates her own convictions, but woos Phao. Their union, however, is never further suggested by Lyly. Like the contention between Fidus and Iffida, this skirmish between Phao and Mileta parts the two antagonists. The suggested solution to the difficulties experienced by the characters in this play does not come from this minor sex duel at all. It is made by Sybilla, whose dramatic purpose is to comment on the nature of love. She cautions Phao, who has asked her advice on the ways of courtesy, not to miss the possession of his lady by following too closely the romantic conventions of courtship. She emphasizes the mutability of that charm which creates love. Her suggestion is to observe in detail the courtly ritual of adoration as a mere means, to the end that he may achieve the less ideal rewards of sensual pleasure. "Love, faire child, is to be governed by arte . . . Looke pale and learne to be leane, that who so seeth thee, may say, the Gentleman is in love." Rosalind was to give Orlando the same advice, but not in shrewd earnest.

In *Endimion* Lyly gives the quarreling lovers a more important role in the dramatic action than they had had in either *Campaspe* or in *Sapho and Phao*. The participants, Eumenides and Semele (the one guided by the ideals of romance, the other controlled by an unyielding sense of reality), never meet, but like Beatrice and Benedick they exchange "unseemely and male-part overthwarts" (i.e., repartee). As in *Campaspe,* the lovers' quarrels in *Endimion* bring about no dramatically effective reconciliation. By his fidelity to Semele "the very waspe of all women, whose tongue stingeth as much as an Adders tooth," Eumenides receives a single wish from a fountain for faithful lovers. At the precise moment when he is given opportunity to ask possession of his lady, however, he reverses his attitude and becomes suddenly skeptical of the entire tradition of romance. He becomes acutely aware that Semele is "of all creatures the most froward" and that he has been "of all creatures the most fond." Like the sardonic Fulke Greville, Eumenides (or Sidney) suddenly sees his love as an illusion, as a mere "golden dreame." Therefore he chooses to release Endimion from his spell, and he lets a cynical sense of fact and his affection for his friend triumph over his romantic desires. Benedick, in Shakespeare's *Much Ado,* forced by Beatrice to make a similar choice, turns against his friend. Benedick thus helps to contrive his ultimate union with Beatrice. Eumenides's decision, on the contrary, turns Semele completely against him. The comic delight of a sudden concord of lovers' wills is therefore impossible to achieve in this play. It is by the command of Cynthia that Semele grudgingly accepts Eumenides. In this fashion Lyly destroys the dramatic effect of the long anticipated surrender of his lovers.

In Lyly's *The Woman in the Moone* no sex duel appears. This play is far too didactic an allegory for witty repartee to reconcile the inconstant Pandora and the faithful shepherds. Stesias, the courtly bucolic lover whom Pandora has agreed to marry, comes to scorn her when he finds how far she is from his exalted conception of woman. He wishes to destroy Utopia, his rustic garden of love, crying:

> Curst be Utopia for Pandoraes sake!
> Let wilde bores with their tuskes plow up my
>   lawnes,
> Devouring Wolves come shake my tender lambes,
> Drive up my goates unto some steepy rocke,
> And let them fall downe headlong in the sea.
> She shall not live . . .

But Stesias is not allowed to flee Pandora, who represents the reality of passion, or to possess her. He is translated to the moon, where he is destined to follow her always, however repulsive she has become to him as a caricature of the mistress of romance. Shakespeare did better in *As You Like It,* presenting a less bitter, a kindlier, acceptance of the conventional illusions of love.

Only in Lyly's final play, *Love's Metamorphosis,* is the conflict over the nature of love dramatized solely by pairs of quarreling lovers. The foresters in this comedy defend romance and the nymphs treat it with derision. Moreover, Lyly creates the impression that the battle of wits is mutually contrived. Both his lovers and their ladies are presented as if they were conscious that they are playing parts in a game in which neither the pretensions nor the denunciations of love are fully justified. Thus, when alone the foresters Ramis, Silvestris, and Montanus are themselves somewhat skeptical. They are willing to follow the ritual of the enamored courtier, to play at being in love, in order to gain their ladies. They do not disavow the precepts of formalized passion, they merely wish to apply them, somewhat crassly, for their own purposes. As Silvestris states it,

> I doe not thinke Love hath any sparke of Divinitie in him; since the end of his being is earthly. In the bloud he is begot by the fraile fires of the eye, & quencht by the frayler shadowes of thought. What reason have we then to soothe his humor with such zeale, and follow his fading delights with such passion?

And Ramis replies that romance should be accepted with a great deal of reservation, "since it will aske longer labour and studie to subdue the powers of our bloud to the rule of the soule, then to satisfie them with the fru-

ition of our loves, let us bee constant in the worlds errours, and seeke our owne torments."

When their ladies, Nisa, Celia, Niobe, are alone, they spend no time analyzing romance. Nisa is the most scornful of the three in her ridicule of Cupid: "What should he doe with wings that knowes not where to flie? Or what with arrowes, that sees not how to ayme? The heart is a narrow marke to hit, and rather requireth Argus eyes to take level, then a blind boy to shoote at random." These nymphs are scornfully amused by their wooers' attempts to play the role of lover in the traditional drama of courtship. They read the poems which the foresters have hung on trees, and Nisa comments on their assertions that they suffer the usual physical languishings of love: "they have eaten so much wake-Robin, that they cannot sleepe for love." Niobe indicates the nymphs' share in the contrived, witty sex duels to come, when she argues, "Give them leave to love, since we have libertie to chuse, for as great sport doe I take in coursing their tame hearts, as they doe paines in hunting their wilde Harts."

When these three sets of lovers meet, it is to release the antagonism that has been carefully built up by the foresters' pretense of accepting idyllic romance and the nymphs' pretense of complete skepticism. Each set of lovers quarrels, in turn, and each of the foresters retires, vanquished in wit, but not in impulse to love. Ramis maintains the immutability of his passion, despite Nisa's scorn, crying after her that he will "practice by denials to bee patient, or by disdaining die, and so be happie." Montanus stresses both his fidelity to Celia and his languishing grief in his petitions to her to "yeelde to love, sweete love." She tempts him into rebuking her for her obdurate pride, and then reduces him to a greater confusion of self-contradiction. He suddenly ceases to be the humble prostrate lover and asserts his independence. But it is only for a moment, and he returns to his pretended humility. Celia dismisses him, crying, "You want wit, that you can be content to be patient." Silvestris, reversing the order of procedure in his conflict with Niobe, begins by suggesting that she is not qualified to play the lady of amorous courtesy. But she soon brings him to despair by her mocking. He begs off, suggesting that when he has but heard her sing he will be content to die, and she replies, "I will sing to content thee."

Even in this final play of Lyly's, however, the lovers do not quite solve their own destinies. Despite their nimble fencing, these characters never come to full dramatic realization. Once more Lyly contrives his denouement by using the device of divine intervention. His foresters are allowed to reach an agreement with the nymphs only by an appeal to Cupid. They offer at his shrine, in evidence of their plight, all the courtier's symbols and symptoms of love. They prevail upon the god to force the nymphs to yield, and therefore the story ends in no swift surrender, in no sudden concord of lovers' conflicting wills to give a comic release to the built-up tension. Lyly himself was aware of this lack, for he makes Silvestris cry, "what joye can there be in our lives . . . when every kisse shall bee sealed with a curse . . . enforcement is worse than enchantment."

There is little comic triumph here, because the play ends in a forced compromise between an idealistic and a realistic attitude. Ramis expresses this play's equivocal conclusion when he suggests that the delights of actual possession will mitigate some of the unpleasant consequences of an inharmonious and forced love. "Let them curse all day," he says, "so I may have but one kisse at night." And to his lady he cries, "O, my sweete Nisa! bee what thou wilt, and let all thy imperfections bee excused by me, so thou but say thou lovest me." But such a terminus does not carry any illusion of momentary belief. Rather it suggests that Lyly regarded the two worlds of romance and real life as irreconcilable. As such, it is more ironic than comic. It may be a revelation of his acute pessimism, but not of his sense of comedy.

In his novel and in his comedies, the play of ideas is like that found in Elizabethan poetry. These comedies represent something new in literature. Lyly did what had not been done before, he brought to the stage the complexities of Elizabethan amorous thought. But even more important than this, Lyly depicts a kind of miraculous adjustment of contradictory theories of love, by a final union of warring lovers. Aesthetically this advances him at once beyond the mere presentation of unsolved dilemma in *The Courtier,* and in Elizabethan poetry. Lyly, however, failed to see all of the comic implications to be derived from a dramatized conflict of attitudes. Drama could do more than relate romantic pretensions to less exalted fact in an incredible and magical fashion. It might lend belief to the resolution that serves to bring the play to an end. Lyly's dramas, therefore, are but a link in the series of literary expressions of the Renaissance love dilemma. They stand somewhere between the recognition and analysis of the problems found in *The Courtier* and the comic solution of the problem portrayed in Shakespeare's love-game comedies.

R. Warwick Bond, in his essay on Lyly as a playwright [in *The Complete Works*], states that Lyly's importance lies in the fact that he wrote a kind of comedy which Shakespeare imitated. Bond remarks,

> Lyly's farcical scenes are undoubtedly the model for the similar scenes in Shakespeare's early work . . . for the wit contests between Boyet and the French ladies, the Two Gentlemen, Romeo and Mercutio; while he is indebted also to Lyly's example of graceful and witty interchange between ladies and courtiers, nymphs and foresters, for many a gentle and pretty scene between Julia and Lucetta, Portia and Nerissa, Rosalind and Celia, Hero and Ursula, and for the witty war between Benedick and Beatrice, and others.

This is all true, but one must add that what Shakespeare borrowed from Lyly's comedies was not only a method of characterization. Shakespeare also borrowed a method of reducing an intellectual conflict between different ideas of love to the form of a witty verbal combat. In the antagonisms that Lyly dramatizes, the lovers never come completely to life. His characters merely voice current attitudes toward love, whereas Shakespeare's characters express these ideas as if they were their own. It is something, no doubt, that Lyly was able to present in dramatic form the complex love dilemma of which ladies and gentlemen of his age were acutely aware. He developed comedy to the stage where its characters exist not merely to relate a story but also to act out the Elizabethan critical revolt from romance. Yet Lyly never turns these intellectual materials into high comedy, because his characterization does not entirely grow out of them. Lyly's characters remain strictly under his control, Shakespeare's characters seem to create their own destiny.

Jonas A. Barish (essay date 1956)

SOURCE: "The Prose Style of John Lyly," in *ELH*, Vol. 23, No. 1, March, 1956, pp. 14-35.

[*In the following essay, Barish comments on Lyly's employment of the techniques of euphuism in his prose romances and demonstrates their use in his plays as well.*]

Lyly's prose style, especially that of **Euphues,** has been studied so often and so exhaustively in the past that further observations on it are likely to appear impertinent, especially if they attempt no radical reformulation. However, the major work of description has been complete for some decades now, and little has been added except for occasional further explorations into the literary origins of Euphuism. It may, therefore, be useful to glance once again at this familiar territory, with two objects in view: first, to try to correlate certain categories of Lyly's style with categories of meaning, and second, to restate some general principles governing all of his prose which may help to erase the sharp line customarily drawn between the style of **Euphues** and that of the plays.

Clarence Child and Morris Croll, whose studies of Lyly [in their editions of *Euphues: The Anatomy of Wit* and *Euphues and His England*] climaxed those of nineteenth century investigators like Landmann, defined Euphuism primarily as an ornamental verbal pattern, characterized by the use of the so-called "figures of sound" rather than by "figures of thought." Croll's description may serve as a basis for comment:

> Euphuism is a style characterized by the figures known in ancient and medieval rhetoric as *schemes (schemata),* and more specifically by the word-schemes (*schemata verborum*), in contrast with those known as *tropes;* that is to say, in effect, by the figures of sound, or vocal ornament. The most important of these figures are three which can be used, and in Euphuism are often and characteristically used, in combination in the same form of words: first, isocolon, or equality

of members (successive phrases or clauses of about the same *length*); secondly, parison, or equality of sound (successive or corresponding members of the same *form,* so that word corresponds to word, adjective to adjective, noun to noun, verb to verb, etc.); thirdly, paromoion, similarity of sound between words or syllables, usually occurring between words in the same positions in parisonic members, and having the form either of *alliteration,* similarity at the beginning, or *homoioteleuton (similiter cadentes* or *desinentes),* similarity at the end, or, as often in Euphuism, of both of these at once. Other *schemata* are also frequently and characteristically used, such as simple *word-repetition,* and *polyptoton* (the repetition of the same stem two or more times within the same clause or sentence, each time with a different inflectional ending); but these need not be detailed. The essential feature of the style—to repeat—is a vocal, or oral, pattern, and all its other characteristics, such as the use of antithesis, and the constant use of simile, are only means by which the Euphuist effects his various devices of sound-design.

This account sums up concisely most of the obvious features of the Euphuistic style. Nevertheless, both its mode of classification and its implied theory of style seem more likely to blur issues for a contemporary reader than to clarify them. It seems peculiar that Croll should have lumped together parison and paromoion as devices of sound-design. Parison, the matching of equivalent parts of speech in parallel clauses, is directly and intimately involved with syntax; it is, indeed, a syntactic procedure, and hence involved with logical structure, at the center of thought. To describe it as "ornamental" is to suggest that thought itself is ornamental. As for paromoion, whether it occurs between words in the same position in parisonic members or not, its effects are primarily alogical, to borrow a term from W. K. Wimsatt [in *The Verbal Icon*], and not directly implicated in logical structure. But even paromoion has its effect on meaning, though the effect be alogical. To regard it as nothing more than vocal ornament *appliqué* may be a convenient way of referring to a psychological fact—that a writer sometimes chooses one word over another for the sake of its sound—but is of little help in determining how such a word functions once it is chosen. On the whole, a contemporary reader is likely to be disturbed by the earnestness with which Croll propounds the Renaissance distinction between "figures of thought" (tropes) and "figures of sound" (schemes). This distinction, which drives a wedge between style and content, and treats them as though they enjoyed separate and independent existence, if it interferes even with objective descriptions of style, interferes still more with any effort to get at the heart of a writer's artistic universe, where style and meaning interpenetrate. The fact is that parison, far from being merely a superficial device of sound-design, is, one might almost say, an instrument of thought whereby Lyly apprehends the world, and from which he cannot escape. It is intimately related, among other things, to his use of antithesis, and since Croll has challenged the validity of the term "antithesis" as applied to Lyly, his caveat must be examined briefly.

To the view that Euphuism is characterized above all by its use of antithesis (a proposition offered by other students of Euphuism), Croll replies by distinguishing between antithesis used as "a figure of words, or sound, on the one hand, and a figure of thought (*figura sententiae*), on the other," and announces his intention to limit the use of the term "antithesis" to those cases where it is a figure of thought and to exclude it from those cases where (as in Lyly) it remains a figure of sound. But, one is obliged to ask, how does one distinguish a "thought" from the "words" in which it is expressed? How separate an idea from the structure which embodies it? Croll's example of a "genuine" antithesis merely intensifies one's distrust of his dichotomy. "In Lyly's use of it . . . antithesis is purely a 'scheme,' that is, a figure of the arrangement of words for an effect of sound. It is not meant to reveal new and striking relations between things; and it is as different as possible, for instance, from such a use of it as in Bacon's saying that 'revenge is a kind of wild justice.'" The implication here appears to be not merely that antithetic schemes of words need not involve any corresponding antithesis of meaning, but that they probably will not, that no self-respecting antithesis would be caught decking itself out in parison or paromoion, and that it ought to be well satisfied if its honesty is glimpsed through its plain clothes. And again, one can only reply that syntactic formulae are not the clothes of thought, they are of its essence; they are not mere schemes imposed on meaning, they are the determinants of meaning. Bacon's statement that "revenge is a kind of wild justice" does indeed reveal a new and striking relation between the concepts of revenge and justice. It does so, however, not by establishing an opposition, but by taking two notions ordinarily felt as contradictory and showing that in fact they are not contradictory at all. By placing the epithet "wild" before the noun "justice," Bacon indicates how the two apparently dissimilar ideas may be thought of as related. The very grammar of the statement, with its linking verb "to be," is an assertion of likeness, of identity, rather than of unlikeness. It might well be regarded as a kind of synthesis. But antithesis necessarily involves unlikeness, the setting of things in opposition to each other, and only by ignoring the basic sense of the term as established by etymology and custom can one apply it to Bacon's aphorism. In Lyly, on the other hand, oppositions of every sort play a paramount role. The soundest approach to a study of Euphuism remains Feuillerat's remark [in his *John Lyly*] that Lyly "ne peut concevoir ses idées qu'au choc de deux oppositions; il ne les associe qu'au travers de contrastes," and his further statement that **Euphues,** in aim and in structure, "n'est en somme qu'une antithèse longuement prolongée." Even the false antitheses that abound in **Euphues** (of which Croll was surely thinking) only testify further to Lyly's pursuit of antithetic meaning, since they exhibit him in the act of forcing two ideas not in themselves necessarily antithetical into a syntactic arrangement which implies that they are. A final objection to Croll's criterion—that antithesis should reveal new and striking relations between things—is that it introduces normative considerations into what has always been a descriptive term. We cannot, that is, refuse to call a trite antithesis an antithesis simply because it is trite, any more than we can refuse to call a mediocre play a play just because it is mediocre.

For purposes of discussion Lyly's antitheses may be broken down roughly into three types, according to the force of mutual attraction and repulsion between the terms. This is relatively weak in the first type, stronger in the second, and decidedly potent in the third. Antithetic terms thus considered resemble atomic particles or heavenly bodies: the gravitational pull between them varies inversely as the square of the distance. The simplest type occurs when a thing is defined by its opposite, or when the mention of a thing evokes the mention of its opposite. This is the case with figures constructed on the model "more *x* than *y*," or "rather *a* than *b*," where in the process of making an affirmation about something, one simultaneously makes a denial of its opposite. The walls and windows of Naples, for example, demonstrate that town "rather to bee the Tabernacle of *Venus,* then the Temple of *Vesta*," and its court is "more meete for an *Atheyst,* then for one of *Athens,* for *Ouid* then for *Aristotle,* for a gracelesse louer then for a godly lyuer: more fitter for *Paris* then *Hector,* and meeter for *Flora* then *Diana*." Such a description emphasizes at least as strongly what Naples ought to be but is not as that which it actually is. The procedure conforms to that recommended by contemporary rhetoricians, who urged the use of opposing terms to intensify the terms under consideration. If one wished to depict chastity, one did so by contrasting it with foul harlotry; if one wished to praise liberality, one might do so by disparaging misers. To know a thing fully, in short, was to know its opposite. And in the power to recognize opposites lay the power to make discriminations. "Hee coulde easily discerne *Appollos* Musicke, from *Pan* his Pype, and *Venus* beautie from *Iunos* brauerye, and the faith of *Laelius,* from the flattery of *Aristippus*."

However, to say that a thing is "more *x* than *y*" or "rather *a* than *b*" is to imply that it might have been otherwise. The description of Naples intimates that the city preferred its own mode of existence to another. Callimachus, entering the hermit's cave, thrusts in his head "more bolde then wise," and proceeds to show himself "delyghted more then abashed at this straunge sight." By using the antithetic pair "more bolde then wise" instead of the simple adverb "boldly," Lyly underscores the fact that Callimachus might have behaved otherwise than he did, that the situation contained equivocal possibilities. Similarly, Euphues, choosing to speak to the ladies of love rather than of learning, declares, "I had rather for this tyme be deemed an vnthrift in reiecting profit, then a *Stoicke* in renouncing pleasure," where he signifies his awareness that to accept one alternative means to decline its opposite.

The elements of choice submerged in such a formula as "rather *a* than *b*" becomes explicit in the second type of antithesis, which proposes alternatives but does not resolve them. Here, instead of one term being asserted and the other denied ("*rather* a *than* b," "*more* x *than* y"),

the two are held in equilibrium: "*either* x *or* y," "*whether* a *or* b." Eubulus, meditating on the ambiguous potentialities of Euphues' talents, "well knewe that so rare a wytte woulde in tyme eyther breede an intollerable trouble, or bringe an incomperable Treasure to the common weale: at the one hee greatly pittied, at the other he reioysed." He not only envisages two possible futures for Euphues, he indulges simultaneously in the emotions appropriate to both. Similarly, he speculates on the possible causes for Euphues' present disordered existence: "I am enforced to thincke that either thou dyddest want one to giue thee good instructions, or that thy parentes made thee a wanton wyth to much cockeringe, either they were too foolishe in vsinge no discipline, or thou too frowarde in reiecting their doctrine, eyther they willinge to haue thee idle, or thou wylfull to bee ill employed." Not each of these pairs is strictly antithetical, but Eubulus treats them as though they are, proposing alternative explanations but according no preference to one over another.

Lyly, in his capacity as author, sometimes hesitates between two interpretations of one event. The friendship between Euphues and Philautus is noncommittally ascribed either to Philautus's courtesy or to the workings of fate, "I know not for certeyntie," and when Euphues visits Lucilla for the first time, "The Gentlewoman, whether it were for nycenesse or for niggardnesse of curtesie, gaue hym suche a colde welcome that he repented that he was come." Thus this second type of antithesis tends to reflect an awareness of ambiguity of interpretation, of potential doubleness of cause or effect. A thing not merely suggests its opposite, but may be traced to one or another contrary origin, may entail one or another consequence or corollary.

The third kind of antithesis asserts the actual co-existence of contrary properties in one phenomenon. A great many of Lyly's celebrated similitudes fall into this category, and perhaps they are best understood as variations on this theme. The range of syntactic formulae here is wide, but characteristically we find those which emphasize duality: "as well *x* as *y*," "both *a* and *b*." In the following instance, Lyly suppresses the sign "both" and allows the unaided grammar, the linkings of subject, verb, and object, to tell its own story:

> Though all men bee made of one mettall, yet they bee not cast all in one moulde, there is framed of the selfe same clay as well the tile to keepe out water as the potte to containe lycour, the Sunne doth harden the durte & melt the waxe, fire maketh the gold to shine and the straw to smother, perfumes doth refresh *the* Doue & kill *the* Betil . . .

Here the reigning idea is that similar substances may have differing qualities, that the same cause may work not merely varying, but contrary effects. The notion that things contain within them their own contraries, or the power to work contrary effects, occurs so often in *Euphues* and in its sequel that by virtue of sheer frequency of repetition it comes to be felt as a major insight. It is an insight to which Lyly's disjunctive imagination is peculiarly sympathetic, and to which his analytic syntax admrably lends itself. The grammatical subject may be made to govern two verbs, each expressing a contrary action ("the Sunne doth harden the durte & melt the waxe"), or one verb may control two antagonistic object phrases ("fire maketh the gold to shine and the straw to smother"). In each case a thing splits up into its mutually antipathetic halves.

Many of Lyly's antitheses take the form of paradox, either in the sense that they propose an idea repugnant to common sense or in that they point out mutually conflicting properties in the same thing. Such paradoxes range from the banal to the startling. When Euphues tells his companions that "The foule Toade hath a fayre stoane in his head, the fine goulde is founde in the filthy earth, the sweete kernell lyeth in the hard shell," he is uttering commonplaces, but he is also directing our attention to a series of logical incongruities. If one expects like to follow like, similars to accord with similars, if one expects things to be all of a piece, then Lyly's kind of simile tends to deceive normal expectations. You may think that the toad, because it is ugly, is ugly all over, but no, it has a precious stone in its head, or you may think, if you think about it, that what comes from the dirty earth must itself be dirty, or that what comes from a tough shell will itself be tough. But no, things seems to engender their contraries rather than their likenesses. The earth discloses gold, and the tough shell conceals a sweet nut. If they do not actually produce their own contraries, they co-exist with them, like the toad with his jewel. Nothing is uniformly of one property. Everything contains within it the seeds of self-contradiction: "*Venus* had hir Mole in hir cheeke which made hir more amiable: *Helen* hir scarre on hir chinne which *Paris* called *Cos amoris,* the Whetstone of loue. *Aristippus* his wart, *Lycurgus* his wenne."

Lyly, who is fascinated by this elementary paradox, is at pains to make it as extreme, as *outré,* as possible. Grammatically, he does so by making his antitheses sharp, by pitting every term as rigidly as possible against its mate. Two comparatives are better than two positive adjectives, because they double the distance between the antithetic terms, and superlatives are best of all, since they drive the terms as far apart as they will go:

> The fine christall is sooner crazed then the harde marble, the greenest Beeche burneth faster then the dryest Oke, the fairest silke is soonest soyled, and the sweetest wine tourneth to the sharpest vineger, the pestilence doth most ryfest infect the cleerest complection, and the Caterpiller cleaueth vnto the ripest fruite . . .

Here, underneath the not necessarily in itself paradoxical idea that the most precious things are also the most perishable, lies Lyly's paradoxical principle that like engenders unlike: the fairest silk lends itself more quickly to soiling, the sweetest wine is ready at a moment's notice to become the sharpest vinegar, and the greenest beech

defies all natural law by burning faster than the driest oak, because in Lyly's world if things do not already defy the proprieties they must be made to do so. The precarious closeness of extremes must be constantly stressed, and it does not much matter whether the illustrative instance conforms to everyday experience or violates it. Both kinds of instance, in fact, are necessary in order to establish precedents on a sufficiently massive scale. If we recognize the illustration as a commonplace, we are being reminded that even humdrum things contains the principle of self-contradiction within them. If the example strikes us as exotic, we are being reminded of the extremes to which nature will go in the propagation of paradoxes.

Such paradoxes often turn on the antagonism between substance and appearance. A recurrent figure is the one contrasting an ugly exterior with a precious interior or the reverse, a fair face with a vile heart, an outer semblance belied by an inner essence, as in the cases of the gold, the kernel, and the toad. The moral is always the same: that the more absolute of its kind a thing may appear to be, the more certain it is that somewhere within it lies its own antithesis, its anti-self.

> Doe we not commonly see that in paynted pottes is hidden the deadlyest poyson? that in the greenest grasse is the greatest Serpent? in the cleerest water the vglyest Toade? Doth not experience teach vs that in the most curious Sepulchre are enclosed rotten bones? That the Cypresse tree beareth a fayre leafe but no fruite? That the Estridge carryeth fayre fethers, but rancke flesh?

Bond [in *The Complete Works of John Lyly*] points out that the analogy of the serpent comes from Pettie, "'vnder most greene grasse, lye most great Snakes, and vnder entising baytes, intanglyng hookes,' which means no more than that snakes are found in grass. There is no authority for Lyly's perversion." Lyly's perversion, of course, lies in his having taken Pettie's general intensives, "most greene grasse" and "most great Snakes," and turned them into real superlatives. Instead of telling us, as Pettie does, that snakes are found in grass, he tells us that the "greenest grasse" conceals the "greatest Serpent," a characteristically drastic antithesis, where the very intense greenness of the grass, its apparently supreme innocence, becomes the guarantee that it conceals the profoundest corruption.

To say this much is not, of course, to say that Lyly ignores the more straightforward relations between things. The interpretations of nature on which he drew—encyclopedic, or fabulous, or occult—all emphasized the multitudes of correspondences that were supposed to govern the natural world, the mysterious sympathies as well as the mysterious antipathies between things. But where his predecessors had aimed at exposing a hidden consistency in the workings of nature, Lyly ranged the affinities and the antipathies side by side so as to unveil the contradictions in nature, the infinite inconsistency of the world. Such glimpses as he does provide of the direct correspondences between things tend again to emphasize their paradoxical character. They reveal a nature who is as resourceful in effecting affinities between dissimilar things as she is in engendering disaffinities between similar things. "The filthy Sow when she is sicke, eateth the Sea Crabbe and is immediately recured: the Torteyse hauing tasted the Uiper, sucketh *Origanum* and is quickly reuiued: the Beare readye to pine, lycketh vpp the Ants and is recouered." Such correspondences are in themselves a defiance of the expected order.

It remains only to mention the thing to which Lyly's *exempla* always return, that for which they exist, their application to human conduct. G. Wilson Knight [in "Lyly," *Review of English Studies* XV, April 1939] has described their function as the attempt "to read the human mind in terms of the living physical universe, and see that universe and its properties—including inorganic matter . . . as a vital extension of the human mind." Lyly peoples creation with bizarre phenomena in order to provide a system of analogies for human behavior. When he does not find the analogy he needs in Pliny the Younger or in Erasmus, he improvises for himself, and his improvisations, like his borrowings, tend to perpetuate contraries and paradoxes, like the "riuer in Arabia which turneth golde to drosse & dust to siluer," where contradictory effects proceed from the same cause, or like the magic herb Araxa and the magic stone Tmolus, the one protective of chastity, the other destructive of it.

To repeat, Lyly prefers the kind of natural curiosity that challenges common sense. The contradictions in human feeling must be illuminated by reference to a universe which displays its own kinds of contradictions. "For neyther is ther any thing, but *that* hath his contraries." And part of the effect of Lyly's instances depends on one's starting with a differing set of assumptions: that like follows like, that predictable correspondences exist between shape and function, appearance and essence, part and whole. Lyly's favorite procedure is to overthrow such assumptions. The result of overthrowing it so many scores of times is to establish a new assumption, a kind of grand paradox emerging from the countless minor ones: that things are *not* what they seem, that like allies itself with unlike, that fair and foul, precious and worthless, hurtful and beneficent co-exit in perpetual and inseparable intimacy. And this whole system of contradictions is Lyly's way of expressing the perpetual ambiguities of human sentiment, and above all, of the most ambiguous of all human sentiments, love. Lyly turns the well-worn Petrarchan paradox into the capstone of a whole view of life. The lover, freezing in flames and burning in ice, joyful in grief and grievous in joy, becomes merely *e pluribus unus,* the final and most perfect expression of a universal paradox. This commanding insight is perhaps the chief thing that distinguishes Lyly from his predecessors in Euphuism, and one of the chief things he passed on to his imitators. Pettie's *Petite Pallace of Pettie his Pleasure,* whose style contains so many elements otherwise Euphuistic, uses this figure only tentatively, and couples it with others of a quite different character. The

early romances of Robert Greene, on the other hand, which owe their existence to the success of *Euphues,* swarm throughout with similes exactly in Lyly's manner, some pilfered from *Euphues* and others improvising on Lyly's master principle of contraries.

The device of the soliloquy, of course, has a closely related function. What the simile does obliquely, by way of poetic analogy, the soliloquy does more discursively. It permits the examination of a single mind possessed by contrary passions, the contrary passions sharpening each other by their proximity to one another. Lucilla, when she retires to lament her infatuation for Euphues, enters into "termes and contrarieties" with herself, expressing the "doubtfull fight" in her heart "betwixt faith and fancie . . . hope & feare . . . conscience and concupiscence." And so with Euphues, in his turn, torn by "extremityes betweene hope and feare." In Lyly's monologues, every claim begets its counterclaim, every argument breeds its counterargument, and every "ay" produces its "but." The nature that decrees that "daunger and delight growe bothe vponn one stalke, the Rose and the Canker in one bud, white and blacke . . . in one border" decrees that this universal law shall prevail in the microcosm of man. The soliloquy then becomes the instrument for dissecting the paradoxes of the mind.

One would scarcely need to go further for the moral of *Euphues* than the style, which offers for our inspection the world as antithesis. Contraries, potential or realized, lurk everywhere in nature and in human nature. Right action consists in the power to perceive them and to choose the worthier alternative: "If witte be employed in the honest study of learning what thing so pretious as witte? if in the idle trade of loue what thing more pestilent then witte?" The two halves of the story unfold before us these ambivalent possibilities: we observe wit's pestilence in the first or narrative part, where Euphues plays the wastrel; we discover its preciousness in the tracts and letters of the second part, where Euphues turns sermoneer.

But antithesis, habitual and even obsessive as it is in Lyly's thought, may be regarded as simply one aspect of a more comprehensive stylistic phenomenon, logicality. Scrutiny of the world may disclose contraries, but it may also disclose component elements that differ without being mutually exclusive. Parts of a whole may complement each other as well as conflict. Motivation may be composite as well as contradictory, and so may consequences. Some of the excerpts already quoted tend to approach simple parallel rather than strict antithesis; it is only Lyly's zeal for antithetic structure that has disguised them as antitheses. When Lucilla dismisses Euphues with the announcement that "fancie giueth no reason of his chaunge neither wil be *con*trolled for any choice, this is therefore to warne you, *that* from hencefoorth you neither sollicite this suite neither offer any way your seruice," the correlatives "neither . . . neither" would seem to imply an antithesis which the explicit meanings do not at all support; indeed, the terms come close to a tautology, differing from each other by scarcely a hair.

Non-antithetic parallels find less eccentric embodiment in such formulae as "the one . . . the other," "as well *x* as *y*," and the like. Cassander has amassed wealth "aswell by his being a long gatherer, as his trad being a lewd vsurer"; the two explanations for his wealth complement each other without conflicting. Euphues acknowledges that Fidus has placed him and Philautus under a "double chaine" of obligation: "the one in pardoning our presumption, the other in graunting our peticion." Here Fidus's bounty analyzed into two stages, the second of which depends on the first.

Once the analytic mind has started decomposing its material and distributing it in series, as the logicians and rhetoricians of the period tirelessly recommended it should be, and as grammar-school training had taught writers to do, there is no necessary limit to the number of subdivisions that may be found in any phenomenon. Fidus explains to Euphues and Philautus that he has spoken harshly "not, that either I mistrust you (for your reply hath fully resoued *that* feare), or *that* I malice you (for my good will may cleare me of *that* fault), or that I dread your might (for your smal power cannot bring me into such a folly), but that I haue learned by experience, etc."—thus examining in turn three possible grounds for his own behavior, rejecting each in turn, and settling on a fourth and correct explanation. It is scarcely necessary to insist on the tendency of this kind of logical subdivision to promote exact correspondence of parts. Each of Fidus' three tentative reasons observes the same grammatical form, as does each of his parenthetical explanations.

Iffida's discourse on the composite nature of love provides a more extended example:

> . . . in perfect loue the eye must be pleased, the eare delighted, the heart comforted: beautie causeth the one, wit the other, wealth the third.

> To loue onely for comelynesse, were lust: to lyke for wit onely, madnesse: to desire chiefly for goods, couetousnesse: and yet can there be no loue with-out beautie, but we loath it: nor with-out wit, but wee scorne it: nor with-out riches, but we repent it. Euery floure hath his blossome, his sauour, his sappe: and euery desire should haue to feede the eye, to please the wit, to maintaine the roote.

Iffida rings the changes on the triple power of love over eye, ear, and heart. Each effect is traced back to its cause in some quality and then considered in itself apart from the other two. All three are finally brought together again in the analogy of the flower. The exactness of correspondence between the parts approaches the diagrammatic.

As Lyly uses antithesis to show the contradictory nature of experience, so he makes use of this more general logicality to express the composite nature of experience. His syntax aims at unravelling the complexities that inhere even in apparently simple things. And if such complexity seems more than a little schematic, it may be recalled that for the first time, in the sixteenth century,

native prose was shouldering the burden formerly carried by the learned languages. The excessive logicality of Lyly's style is merely one issue of a process that had been going on for decades: the search for a structural principle in English which would enable the language to deal adequately and in an ordered fashion with complex material, and thus do the work formerly done by the inflected endings of Latin.

If this logicality is once recognized as the basic principle of Lyly's style, the old difficulty of viewing the plays and the novels as part of a single stylistic system vanishes. Nothing has been said up to this point of the style of **Euphues** and **Euphues and his England** that could not be said with equal justice of the style of the plays. The older generation of critics, exemplified by Croll, defined Lyly's prose chiefly in terms of its devices of sound-design. Quite naturally, when they observed the gradual disappearance of these devices in the prose of the comedies, they tended to think of the later manner as drastically different in kind. So did Lyly's own contemporary, John Hoskins [in *Directions for Speech and Style*], and so does a more recent student of prose style, George Williamson, who [in *The Senecan Amble*] posits for Lyly two separate (though related) styles: the "schematic," an antithetic style heavily encrusted with devices of vocal ornament, and the "pointed," an antithetic style which has discarded such "superficial symmetries" in quest of directness and intensity of utterance. One may, however, take full account of the greater fluidity and informality of the dramatic prose and still feel that Lyly here remains essentially himself, and that to emphasize the evolution from "schematic" to "pointed" is to stress a superficial discontinuity at the expense of a more basic continuity.

A logical style, to say it summarily, is one that marks out divisions of thought, that inspects things in order to classify and subdivide them either into antithetic or into complementary components, which strives for clarity of syntax by opposing clause to clause, phrase to phrase, and word to word (here is where most of the smaller symmetries, the paromoionic devices, come in); and which, furthermore, tends to develop its ideas in terms of some of the traditional topics of logic still felt as logical today: definition, cause and effect, antecedent and consequent, alternative hypotheses, and the like. And such logicality, except for the thinning out of the sound patterns and some loosening of interior symmetry, continues to play as conspicuous a role in the dramatic prose as it did in the novels. The debate remains the characteristic structural device. Now, however, it has extended its range to include not only the antiphonal love laments of nymphs and shepherds and mythological personages, but the mock logic of the page-boys complaining of empty purses, empty stomachs, or the toothache.

Child [in *John Lyly and Euphuism*] quotes the following passage from **Gallathea** as "not only non-Euphuistic, but distinctly poetic in its inspiration":

> CUPID. What is that *Diana*? a goddesse? what her Nimphes? virgins? what her pastimes? hunting?

NYMPH. A goddesse? who knowes it not? Virgins? who thinkes it not? Hunting? who loues it not?

CUPID. I pray thee sweete wench, amongst all your sweete troope, is there not one that followeth the sweetest thing, sweetc louc?

NYMPH. Loue good sir, what meane you by it? or what doe you call it?

CUPID. A heate full of coldnesse, a sweet full of bitternesse, a paine ful of pleasantnesse; which maketh thoughts haue eyes, and harts eares; bred by desire, nursed by delight, weaned by ielousie, kild by dissembling, buried by ingratitude; and this is loue! fayre Lady, wil you any?

(I. ii. 8-20)

Setting aside Child's quaint dichotomy between "Euphuistic" and "poetic," one may ask whether this passage does not seem wholly characteristic of Lyly? If the answer is yes, one may further ask why? The answer would seem to lie in the strict logicality of the language, in the way Cupid propounds his three questions and prompts three answers; in the nymph's reply, which seizes the elements in the given order and turns each question into an answer by way of a fresh question; in Cupid's definition of love, which ponders first the contradictory properties of the sentiment, then its effects on "thoughts" and "harts," and lastly its genesis, chronologically plotted. It may be observed, also, how Lyly's passion for logical structure has in the nymph's reply led to the chief vice of his style: a correspondence between two or more elements implied by their syntactic relationship but denied by their explicit meanings, since for the nymph to ask "A goddesse? who knowes it not?" is logical, and "Virgins? who thinkes it not?" also logical, if more tenuous, but "Hunting? who loues it not?" utterly illogical, and disconcertingly remote from the main level of discourse.

Concerning Act II of **Gallathea,** Child remarks that except for five Euphuistic soliloquies, "the dialogue is practically non-Euphuistic; only five pointed antitheses are discoverable." By pointed antitheses, Child means those reinforced by paromoion. In the following passage, despite its total lack of "pointed antitheses," we recognize the logical tactics habitual in Lyly. Gallathea and Phillida, both disguised as boys, have met in the woods and are smitten by mutual attraction. Their first meeting consists of a series of asides:

GALLA. (*aside*). I perceiue that boyes are in as great disliking of themselues as maides, therefore though I weare the apparell, I am glad I am not the person.

PHIL. (*aside*). It is a pretty boy and a faire, hee might well haue beene a woman; but because he is not, I am glad I am, for nowe vnder the colour of my coate, I shall decipher the follies of their kind.

GALLA. (*aside*). I would salute him, but I feare I should make a curtsie in steed of a legge.

PHIL. (*aside*). If I durst trust my face as well as I doe my habite, I would spend some time to make pastime: for saie what they will of a mans wit, it is no seconde thing to be a woman.

GALLA. (*aside*). All the blood in my bodie would be in in my face, if he should aske me (as the question among men is common) are you a maide?

PHIL. (*aside*). Why stande I still? Boyes shoulde be bolde; but heere commeth a braue traine that will spill all our talke.

(II. i. 16-32)

Symmetry here is striking only by its absence. Elements in correspondence ("though I weare the apparell, I am glad I am not the person") flirt lightly with paromoion or ignore it entirely. But logicality prevails. Each aside resolves itself into an argument, a dispute between would and should, as the speaker debates herself to a standstill between conflicting impulses. The situation permits Lyly to capitalize on his favorite theme, the deceptiveness of appearances. Each girl ponders the discrepancy between her male clothes and her feminine feelings, between the kind of behavior prompted by her attire and that prompted by her state of mind. Each feels the discrepancy with increasing acuteness as a result of the other's presence. And each offers hypotheses of action for herself, only to reject them through fear of consequences. The asides thus preserve in concentrated form much of the logical maneuvering and antithetic vacillation of the soliloquies in **Euphues**. The free use of explicit logical connectives like *for, because,* and *therefore* enables Lyly to compress material which formerly he would have treated at greater leisure, by mere juxtaposition of congruent elements.

Child says of **Midas** that "while the parallelistic and antithetical forms are preserved, there is a manifest decrease in the use of mechanical devices"—or in other words, that Lyly's persistent habit of dividing and subdividing his material logically continues to produce his characteristic effects of neatness and precision, despite the decline in the smaller symmetries. The *dramatis personae* of **Midas** include three bad counsellors to the king, one warlike, one amorous, and one avaricious, whose three ruling humours create constant triplicities in the language as they advance one by one their advice or are rebuked in turn for their folly or wrangle among each other for preëminence. Dramatically, the three may be said to symbolize conflicting bad motives within Midas himself, among which he at first must choose, only later learning to repudiate all in favor of worthier motives. The interior psychology proper to the novel is thus externalized in the fashion peculiar to the theatre. In each sequence of debate, the three prime motives of love, war, and gold are methodically ticked off, isolated with their appropriate epithets or illustrations, and brought to some formal cadence. The princess, for example, rebukes all three counsellors for their baneful influence on the kingdom:

I woulde the Gods would remoue this punishment, so that *Mydas* would be penitent. Let him thrust thee,

Eristus with thy loue, into Italie, where they honour lust for a God, as the Ægyptians did dogs: thee, *Mellacrites* with thy greedines of gold, to the vtmost partes of the West, where all the guts of the earth are gold: and thee, *Martius,* that soundest but bloud and terror, into those barbarous Nations, where nothing is to be found but bloud and terror. Let Phrygia be an example of chastitie, not luste; liberalitie, not couetousnes; valor, not tyrannie.

(II. i. 97-105)

The concluding sentence here observes exact parison, by way of a succinct recapitulation, but in the preceding sentence the three major members differ from each other in numerous details, the inexactness of symmetry, however, being insufficient to blur the hard logical outlines of the syntax. Interestingly enough, the princess is defending what earlier might have been thought of as an unLylyan proposition: that each counsellor ought to be exiled to the country with which he has the closest temperamental affinity. Exact correspondence between human disposition and geography is thought of as an ideal, and no-one steps forward to assert that the coldest climate breeds the hottest lovers, or that the most languid climate begets he fiercest warriors, or that the countries rich in mineral wealth produce a race scornful of gold. A significant hint, if only a negative one, of the extent to which Lyly has relented in his appetite for paradoxes.

Mother Bombie is usually spoken of as Lyly's least Euphuistic play. Here, according to Child, "Lyly well nigh abandons his Euphuism,—not that we do not find the use of parallelism and antithesis, but that they rarely take accurately Euphistic form." In the action of this play, of course, there are more symmetrical configurations than ever, and the strictness of its symmetry dictates a prose which is no whit less logical than that of its predecessors, even though the tightly symmetrical arrangements of sound have been discarded. The first scene opens with a colloquy between Memphio and his page Dromio.

> MEMPHIO. BOY, there are three thinges that make my life miserable; a threed bare purse, a curst wife, & a foole to my heire.
>
> DRO. Why then, sir, there are three medicines for these three maladies; a pike-staffe to take a purse on the high way, a holly wand to brush cholar fro*m* my mistres tong, and a young wench for my yong master: so that as your Worship being wise begot a foole, so he beeing a foole may tread out a wise man.
>
> MEMPHIO. I, but, *Dromio,* these medicines bite hot on great mischiefs; for so might I haue a rope about my necke, hornes vpon my head, and in my house a litter of fooles.

(I. i. 1-8)

Here appears in unusually strict form the kind of logical division we have already observed. Memphio commences by dividing his general misery into three causes and enumerating them. Dromio in turn prescribes three rem-edies correspondent to the three miseries, adhering to the same order in which Memphio described the miseries, and pausing only to draw an extra conclusion from his last remedy. Memphio responds by considering the three medicines as causes in themselves, and predicting the ruinous effects attendant on each. A formal debate could scarcely proceed in more exact fashion. It is worth noting that Lyly's inveterate insistence on logical division, while it lends clarity to the language, may be dramatically misleading. Here, of the three things that make Memphio's life miserable, only one, the foolish son, is strictly necessary to the development of the plot. The threadbare purse plays only a remote and secondary role, while the curst wife plays none at all: she never appears on the stage nor does she affect the action in any way. She disappears even from the language after this scene, but during this scene, as a handy foil to the idiot son, she provides the basis for a whole series of aimless antitheses, none of which bears on the story, and the failure seems clearly traceable to the opening speech, where Lyly could not content himself with giving the one or two dramatically important reasons for Memphio's melancholy, but had to analyze it into three parts, had to deploy his triple categories even where it was necessary to haul in irrelevant material to do so.

One other vice peculiar to Lyly's logical style may be mentioned. The analytic imagination leads to successes of exposition; it enables Lyly to pit character against character and motive against motive with great skill, but it leaves him helpless to cope with the very different requirements of denouement. The force that has disjoined character or analyzed feeling to create dramatic conflict can do little to fuse or recombine them. As a result, certain of the plays—***Campaspe, Gallathea, Sapho and Phao***—suffer from weak or inconclusive endings. Where the ending is not perfunctory, it is likely to bc laborious, as in ***Endimion,*** where it involves lengthy recapitulations of previous matter and prolonged wrangling among the *dramatis personae.* Only in ***Love's Metamorphosis*** does Lyly manage to achieve a genuine reconciliation of conflicting elements, a poetic blending of opposed forces, wherein neither party is wholly victorious or wholly vanquished, but where a fresh equation emerges from the clash of antitheses.

Much more would need to be said in order to describe Lyly's style fully. One would need to discuss, among other things, his predominantly native vocabulary, which contributes its own flavor, and his preference for a resolved rather than a suspended syntax. But perhaps this much suffices to suggest once again his chief virtues and his characteristic weaknesses. Whatever the drawbacks of his method, he effected a revolution in the language of comedy as significant as Marlowe's was for tragedy. Lyly invented, virtually single-handed, a viable comic prose for the English stage, something which could replace the clumsy, uncertain medium of Gascoigne's *Supposes,* the shambling, invertebrate language of *The Famous Victories of Henry V,* and the varieties of broken-down tumbling verse that did duty for prose in the popular theatre. For the first time, dramatic prose rested on an adequate structural foundation; for the first time, it was able to support an intricate plot without confusion and without prolixity. Lyly's techniques of marking out divisions of thought and subdividing his material in parallel sequences not only contribute to clarity of outline, they affect gesture and delivery, dictating stage motion, enforcing pauses and accents, enabling a speech to be heard slowly without fatigue or swiftly without bewilderment. If, in his passion for logicality, he evolved a style too rigid, too removed from common speech to lend itself easily to a wide range of effects, it was at the same time a style that needed only the further flexibility and modulation brought to it by Shakespeare to become an ideal dramatic prose.

Marco Mincoff   (essay date 1961)

SOURCE: "Shakespeare and Lyly," in *Shakespeare Survey: An Annual Survey of Shakespearian Study and Production,* Vol. 14, 1961, pp. 15-24.

[*In the essay below, Mincoff analyzes Lyly's depiction of love and courtship in his plays and assesses their influence on the comedies of Shakespeare.*]

Shakespeare's debt to Lyly has never been denied, and it might well seem that any attempt to resurvey the subject could be no more than the gleaning of an already well-harvested field. Yet in fact much more than the gleaning of a few stray ears of corn has been left for those who would apply themselves to the task of making a fresh study of the relationship between these two authors. In particular, it may be said at once that, in the earlier investigations of the theme, there has been a definite tendency to concentrate rather on concrete parallels than on fundamental principles, and thus to forget how far-reaching the effect of the Lylian formula was upon Shakespeare, how it dominated most of his comedies, overpowering even the Jonsonian humour of *Twelfth Night* and mingling with the Beaumontesque-D'Urfeian romanticism of *The Tempest.* Furthermore, it may be suggested that Lyly's example was of no less importance to Shakespeare for what it gave him positively than for its negative effect in raising in him a spirit of opposition.

Naturally, to speak of a Lylian formula or type of comedy is not altogether correct. If that particular sort of comedy should bear the name of any one man, it might rather have been that of Edwardes, who had given an excellent example of the type nearly twenty years before Lyly; and its roots reach back much further—to that extremely interesting, indeed almost seminal playlet *Fulgens and Lucrece.* But the fact is that Lyly represents for us a genre of which otherwise we should know extremely little; and though it is possible that much of what we may call the Lylian elements in Shakespeare derived either directly or through Lyly from other sources, we are justified in giving his name to English court comedy in

---

Lyly's place in Elizabethan drama:

In Lyly, it is worth noticing, England has her first professional dramatist. Unlike those who had gone before him he was no amateur, he wrote for his living, and he wrote as one interested in the technical side of the theatre. . . . Next to Jonson, the most learned of all the dramatists, yet possessing little of their poetical capacity, he set them the most conspicuous example in technique and stage-craft, in the science of play-writing, which they would probably have been far too busy to acquire for themselves. Lyly's eight dramas formed the rough-hewn but indispensable foundation-stone of the Elizabethan edifice. Spenser has been called the poet's poet, Lyly was in his own days the playwright's dramatist.

John Dover Wilson, in his John Lyly, *1905.*
Reprint. Haskell House Publishers, 1970,
pp. 119-20.

---

general. And there is at least one feature of Lyly's comedies (perhaps the most important of all) that does not occur in *Damon and Pythias*—they are for the most part love-comedies, in which the mainspring of the comedy itself is love. And that was in those days something practically unique; nor has it been very frequent since then. A love interest had, of course, been a standing ingredient of comedy since Greek and Roman times; it had even provided the motive of the action. The scapegrace son of Roman comedy was generally in love with a courtesan, but there was nothing comic in that, it was part of the data. The comedy was provided by his attempts, or rather those of the wily slave, to hoodwink the father—it was essentially a comedy of intrigue. And if occasionally the infatuation of an old man who ought to know better, or of a boastful Thraso, comes up as a subject for satirical treatment, it is still only the inappropriateness of the passion, or the self-love of the character, that rouses laughter, and the nearest we get to the comic treatment of love itself is in a chance remark like Terence's, 'Heu, universum triduum', making fun of the lover's impatience. But with Lyly it is the way in which love cuts across our little plans and makes fools of us all that is the most constant theme—the mere fact of being in love almost is treated as a comic situation.

The attitude of a given society to love depends on so many factors that it is extremely difficult, if not impossible, for another age to recapture it. And Lyly's concept of love is something to which one can only adjust oneself with difficulty, if at all. It was also little likely to appeal to Shakespeare, who had grown up among very different traditions. For Shakespeare's class, love was an easy and simple relation, the natural prelude to marriage, and marriage, as the later Puritans, rooted in the same tradition as Shakespeare, saw it, meant mutual solace and mutual support—a true companionship, in fact. But for Lyly love is above all the love of the courtier, and the main business of the courtier is, as he himself constantly proclaims, love—we should call it flirtation. In a very narrow society of men and women with a great deal of leisure on their hands, of waiting about in anterooms, and boring court functions, the game of flirtation is bound to develop, and it had developed, and had been elaborated into a complicated set of rules centuries before at the courts of Provence. Those rules had naturally undergone changes in the course of time: the rule, for instance, that love must and can only be adulterous was no longer insisted on in theory, although in practice it must still have been in force to a considerable extent, enough at least to put love and marriage into separate compartments. And the court of the Tudors had still enough of the Middle Ages clinging to it for the medieval love of strict symbolical ceremony, so fully described by Huizinga, to determine the behaviour of the lover. He had above all to be wondrous melancholy, to sigh and go without his meals, to affect a foppish slovenliness in his dress, to compose Petrarchistic love songs—in short, to cut every kind of caper and make it abundantly clear that he was in love so that his mistress could triumph in her conquest. And though Lyly still insists, like the trouvères, on secrecy, these flirtations must have been a very open secret. How many fingers were burnt in the game, in how far the convention that everything was strictly Platonic and Petrarchistic was maintained in practice, how far the emotions were engaged at all in the whole affair, we have no real means of knowing. Clearly, it would have been felt as bad taste for any third person to regard the matter in a serious light; but even so, admitted that the conventionality of the flirtation was itself a convention, one finds a difficulty in entering into the mood of Elizabeth's courtiers, or in understanding the public celebrations of *Astrophel* or **Endimion,** or in appreciating why Elizabeth should have wanted to see herself reflected in the love-sick Sapho.

Whatever the reality behind these conventions may have been, the whole concept was at once something highly serious and extremely frivolous. Love was the centre of existence, it was to be 'all made of sighs and tears, of faith and service', but also it was an elaborate game, not only between the protagonists, but one in which the whole court must have taken part, discussing who was paired with whom, and making fun of the lovers' antics. To some extent that is so all the world over: love is the subject of jokes of every kind, and the soft impeachment that Tom is in love with Sue will mostly be met with smiles, sniggers, or laughter, and most of all where there is a romantic tradition to give the joke a point. And the two aspects can seldom have been pushed to such extremes as in the atmosphere of a court when Petrarchism held sway. And it was this ambivalence, complicated by the Platonic doctrine that sexual love is after all the lowest in the scale, and by the necessity for compliments to the Virgin Queen, that provided the soil for a new comic idea.

Thus by introducing love and courtship not as a mere incident but as a theme of comedy, Lyly was opening up new and fruitful ground, and creating, as far as we can tell, an entirely new type. And his awareness of this is to be seen in his well-known assertion:

> Our intent was at this time to moue inward delight, not outward lightnesse, and to breede (if it might bee) soft smiling, not loude laughing: knowing it to the wise to be as great pleasure to heare counsell mixed with witte, as to the foolish to haue sporte mingled with rudenesse.

The mingling of pleasure and counsel had, of course, been the expressed aim of Lyly's fore-runners too; but they had been content to mingle them. What Lyly did in this play was to run them together and to achieve what Sidney was, at about the same time, though his book was not published till much later, suggesting as a possibility—that 'the whole tract of a comedy should be full of delight'. For though, as Sidney explains, laughter and delight are almost opposed to one another in their sources, 'well may one thing breed both together', and he gives as an example:

> in Hercules painted with his great beard and furious countenance, in a woman's attire, spinning at Omphale's commandment, it breeds both delight and laughter; for the representing of so strange a power in love procures delight, and the scornfulness of the action stirreth laughter.

That was certainly the sort of effect Lyly was striving after, and by poking gentle fun at love and its waywardness, by taking the sighs, the tears and the predicaments of lovers as fair game for smiles, while yet subscribing to the Petrarchistic doctrine, he was moving towards a deeper form of comedy, which, like Terence's, but in quite other ways, raises a sigh, half sympathetic, half acquiescent, over human nature itself. Not that he moved very far in that way—it remained for Shakespeare to achieve real depths, and even he did so, as we shall see, by invoking yet another principle; nor yet can one say that all Lyly's comedies are of this kind. Of his eight plays only five can lay any claim to be such comedies of courtship, and perhaps only two—**Sapho** and **Gallathea**—can really substantiate that claim. But he did make a very definite move in a new direction, and for that reason one may be justified in regarding those comedies in which that move is made to be most truly typical of him.

In what is probably his first play, **Campaspe,** there are already elements of this half-humorous, half-serious attitude of gentle laughter at love's foolishness, though the general effect of the main plot is, for us at least, romantic and serious, except for the reflected light it gets from the comic by-work. It is possible, however, that for an age unaffected by certain later romantic sentimentalities, an age that distinguished very pointedly between *amor rationalis* and *amor sensualis,* there was less need to underline the humour inherent in the situation of Campaspe, with the world conqueror at her feet, falling in love with the mere painter Apelles, and of the all-powerful Alexander caught in the toils of a love that is no more rational than hers. And there is, even apart from that, some comedy in the treatment too—in the lovers' secretly pining for each other and too terribly unhappy and earnest over it to take in each other's hints and innuendos; or in Apelles trying to hide his love from Alexander and betraying it by the sighs and melancholy with which he regards Campaspe's portrait; and in the trick by which he is at last compelled to confess; or in the final summing-up, which in the same sentence both glorifies and belittles the power of love—that 'Alexander cannot subdue the affections of men, though he conquer their countries'.

Elements like these are, however, much more heavily underlined in the two succeeding comedies, which, as we said, represent the highest development of the comedy of courtship—chiefly because the introduction of the mischievous boy Cupid as an actual character in the play lends greater immediacy to the theme of love's waywardness. And Cupid, once having been introduced, needs more victims on whom to play his pranks, so that the theme is treated contrapuntally in a way already adumbrated by *Fulgens and Lucrece*. And that in its turn gives scope for the development of the love game in all its artificial conventionality, with its sighs and tears and the publishment of the obdurate beauties who refuse to play it. Here one might draw special attention to Sapho's love-sickness, her feverish tossings in bed, pretending that she is ill with a cold, the perversely coquettish hesitation with which she will and will not have Phao called in to bring simples, and the conversation of misunderstood innuendos in which the one complains that heart's ease grows too high to reach, the other that it grows too low, and both are too self-absorbed to grasp the other's meaning. That is all high comedy of a delicate and subtle kind. And in *Gallathea* there is the wooing by innuendo of two girls disguised as boys, each half divining the true meaning behind the other's words and partly suspecting that she is a girl like herself, and the scene in which Diana's nymphs one after the other confess their love for the disguised girls and their broken vows, a scene which Shakespeare was to take as the foundation of a whole play. But the fact that the two plays have essentially the same framework—the pranks of Cupid and, as a compliment to Elizabeth, his capture and punishment by the Virgin ruler or deity—probably shows why the vein was carried no further. Lyly seemed to have reached the utmost of which it was capable, and in the succeeding comedies that half-humorous treatment of love is pushed into the background—confined to the sub-plots or dropped altogether. In *Love's Metamorphoses* he introduced Cupid once more, no longer as a mischievous boy but as a supreme and ireful godhead punishing any infringement of his code, while in *The Woman in the Moon* the comedy of the shepherds devoting their Petrarchistic service to a woman incapable of valuing it at its worth pales before the satire on woman's capriciousness.

It was thus left to Shakespeare to carry on from the point reached in *Gallathea*. And this he was able to do not only because of his greater genius, but because he was *not* a court poet and was *not* drawn to the artificial code of love that ruled at court, a code which had been fruitful in creating the theme, but was powerless to carry it to any real heights. Indeed it must have taken Shakespeare some time to pierce through the artificialities of

court comedy to the solid core of humanity that it did, after all, contain. At least there is something like definite hostility towards Lyly in his choice of models for his two earliest comedies *The Taming of the Shrew* and *The Comedy of Errors*—and that *The Taming of the Shrew* with its decorative classical imagery, the most Marlovian and at the same time the flattest in style of all his plays was his first attempt, I am firmly convinced. Lyly was, after all, the most prominent comic writer among his predecessors, and, given Shakespeare's obvious taste for romance, one would have expected him to turn to Lyly like the needle of the compass. But there is nothing of the Lylian mode in these plays, and if, as Warwick Bond suggests, Katharine's raillery and the Dromios' quibbles owe anything to Lyly, Shakespeare must have studied him for his wit, but not for his comedy. Italian and Roman comedy could not satisfy Shakespeare however; intrigue did not suffice him as a basis for comedy—it is characteristic, I think, that he took as his model the one Roman comedy in which misunderstandings are due to circumstances and not deliberate hoodwinking. Probably the fundamental reason was that they offered too little 'delight', or poetry, and too little variety of mood. And yet the work on these comedies was perhaps of immense importance, for though he did not actually work it out much in them, they already offered him what was to be the mainspring of his comedies—not actually courtship itself, though that was to be an important theme, but man's lack of knowledge of himself and others, the clash between appearance and reality, something that approaches the Terentian mood, without, however, reaching Terence's denial of the possibility of knowledge.

Then, with *Love's Labour's Lost,* Shakespeare submitted to the inevitable and turned at last to Lyly—and with a will. The very nucleus of the play, the scene in which the courtiers one by one come down the garden path and declare themselves foresworn, is taken from Lyly, as are the characters, and the contrapuntal structure, and the static scenes of wit. And yet it is Lyly with a difference. By comparison with Shakespeare's other comedies, *Love's Labour's Lost* may seem insubstantial and artificial, by the side of Lyly it is like a slice of life itself. Yet, even apart from the power and artistry of his language and character-drawing, Shakespeare introduced certain fundamental alterations in the Lylian formula, alterations so obvious that it is almost a truism to mention them, except that they probably show why it was he withstood Lyly's influence so long. In the first place he gave to Lyly's airy nothings a local habitation and anchored them firmly to the earth. No mythology, no nymphs and goddesses, no mischievous Cupid, but only men and women, though, like most of Lyly's characters, courtiers and sovereigns. And in the second, the love that he depicts is no flirtatious game, no Petrarchistic sentimentalizing, though, to its cost, it assumes the outer forms of both, but a normal, healthy, human love with marriage in view. Not that Lyly had altogether eschewed the treatment of such a love, but he had reserved it mostly for lesser mortals. What Shakespeare retains from Lyly and develops to the utmost, though with a certain satirical twist at the end, is the comedy of courtship—the capers of the men as they strut and preen themselves, the coquetry of the girls, who pretend they will not when they would and plague their lovers and tyrannize over them as hard-heartedly as any Petrarchistic beauty. There is in fact a sort of inversion of the Lylian formula, or a part of it. With Lyly the comedy of love's foolishness lies mainly in the desperate earnestness with which the lovers pursue what is mostly a very unsuitable affair. They are at bottom only playing a game, though compelled to it by Cupid, and they are as miserable over it as any tragic hero. Shakespeare's lovers are following their natural instincts, and in earnest, but their earnestness assumes the forms of a game. They enter into it with gusto, but they are more or less aware—even the men—that it is a game they are playing and that the natural thing would be to do their wooing as simply and directly as Costard; and it is because they have treated it as a game that they are punished in the end. And, furthermore, the very mechanism of the plot, the borrowing of Lyly's theatrical effect without its mythological machinery, almost imposes of itself another comic theme which Shakespeare is quick to seize on, and which he develops even more strongly than the first. In foreswearing love the young men have overestimated their strength of will; their position is very different from that of Diana's nymphs, they have set themselves through lack of self-knowledge in deliberate opposition to nature, and they continue up to the end to let their self-confidence lead them into failure after failure, till they are at last shown a glimpse of themselves as others see them. It is in fact an aspect of that clash between appearance and reality that ordinating Shakespeare had already treated in his earliest comedies, and was to treat again and again, subordinating to it as a rule the comedy of courtship and often fusing the two together.

But the final deflation of masculine complacence with the punishments it imposes brings a strangely harsh splash of colour into the Watteauesque picture. It is as if Shakespeare had suddenly lost patience with the very conventions he had been exploiting. Some new event, some sort of definite finish was needed to round the play off; the women could not just glide softly into their lovers' arms; the death of the king was prepared for, and no doubt intended from the first as a breath of stark reality against which to measure the artificiality of the courtly game of love. Actually the change of mood comes slightly earlier, before the arrival of Marcade, when Holofernes turns on his tormentors and shows them up for a set of conceited ruffians revenging themselves for the ill-success of their own masque on humble folk who cannot retaliate: 'This is not generous, not gentle, not humble.' It comes like a rebuke to the reader too, if he has been merely passively following the jokes, and puts him out of conceit with himself. The punishment of the courtiers is a sort of poetic justice—or so one feels it now—for their cruelty and obtuseness towards others, rather than for their 'taffeta phrases, silken terms precise' through which they had dragged honest love down to the level of courtly flirtation.

By comparison with *Love's Labour's Lost, The Two Gentlemen of Verona* seems like an attempt, and not a very successful one, to throw Lyly off once more—or possibly it is the earlier play, and represents a first half-hearted approach. It begins spiritedly enough with the comedy of love's foolishness—Julia's destruction of her lover's letter, which repeats the mood of Sapho's perverseness, the capitulation of the staunch infidel Valentine before the power of love, and Speed's diagnosis of his complaint or his blindness to Sylvia's hints. But these are, after all, only subsidiary touches; the groundwork of the play is pure sentimental romance, with only the by-work to provide the comedy as in **Endimion**—or *Mucedorus,* or *Sir Clyomon and Sir Clamydes.*

With *A Midsummer Night's Dream* comes a new advance towards Lyly, and further concessions. Shakespeare is now a fully matured dramatist, conscious of his powers and able to treat his material with an ease and freedom that seem to belie its origin. This play is, with the exception of *The Tempest,* his only comedy in which the supernatural plays a part, and with the exception of *The Comedy of Errors,* the only one with a classical background. Probably both these features are due to its having been planned as a wedding entertainment for an audience accustomed to Lylian comedy. And probably too the acceptance of these Lylian conventions again raised in Shakespeare a spirit of deliberate opposition, though mellower and less waspish than in the coda to *Love's Labour's Lost.* Instead of attacking and dealing out punishments he sets up a positive alternative to the Lylian viewpoint. Like Lyly he worked in his famous allegorical compliment to Elizabeth, but he refused to place her and her ideal of virginity and platonic flirtation in the centre. Of course in what seems to have been intended as a kind of prothalamion such a theme would have been out of place, but he not only avoids it, he rather pointedly disavows Lyly's contention that great minds stand superior to love by placing as a frame to the whole play and a standard by which love is to be measured, the mature, rational, unswerving love of Theseus and Hippolyta. Love is for Theseus the fitting crown of his achievements, not as for Alexander an aberration to be ashamed of. And, given the structural position of Theseus in the play, I think we must take his pronouncements on love as more than subjective, dramatic opinions. He is a chorus figure expounding objective values. Judged by the standard of Theseus' ideal love—a love, it must be stressed, in which mind and body are both given their full rights—that of the young people appears as heady, flighty, irrational; it is, in fact, *amor sensualis*; and as such Theseus cannot fully approve of it, though he understands human nature too well, and is too wise and magnanimous in his judgements, to condemn it altogether. He can even sympathize with Hermia almost as obviously as Shakespeare himself, who while representing her love as unreasonable, in defiance of all dramatic tradition, makes her father equally unreasonable in his preference for Demetrius, no better a match from a worldly point of view than Lysander; but he cannot set aside the natural rights of the parent and the laws of his country by openly favouring her. Love, the love of ordinary people at least, is like the wind, it bloweth as it listeth, it is often inconveninent in its waywardness, and so a fit subject for comic treatment, for a comedy that will rouse soft smiles and not rude laughter. And Shakespeare's ambivalent attitude is reflected in the comments of the immortals—in Oberon's ready sympathy with distress and Puck's contemptuous, 'What fools these mortals be!' and the humorous, homespun spell with which he solves the lovers' O so heart-rending problems and dismisses them:

> Jack shall have Jill,
> Nought shall go ill,
> The man shall have his mare again,
> And all shall be well.

As the love that Shakespeare treats is not Lyly's love, so also is he unable to use Lyly's mythology of love. It is well known that Shakespeare's fairies are not the normal fairies of English folklore, though his picture of tiny gossamer spirits has by now entirely replaced the true one. Generally, however, it is tacitly assumed that his invention of these new spirits was an act of creation needing no other explanation than the beauty of the result: Shakespeare, it is thought, was impelled only by sheer delight in creation. Naturally, this creative urge must have played a part, but I imagine that Shakespeare was fully aware of what he was doing in dethroning the mischievous Cupid and putting in his place a friendly, benevolent power that watches over lovers, and, although its performance does not always correspond to its intentions, leads, or tries to lead, them to happiness in spite of themselves and their foolishness. To a certain extent the fairies of folklore were capable of filling that role, for they were the guardians of hearth and home, punishing adultery and promiscuity, as they also punished sluttishness and laziness. But the good-folk were also feared for their love of mischief; they were, indeed more mischievous and unreliable than Cupid himself. Also their associations were too homely and countrified for the new role they were to perform. Shakespeare preserved those associations in his Puck, but he had to etherialize his fairies. And in introducing these new guardian spirits of love, and introducing them too in classical Athens, the home of the classical Cupid, Shakespeare was, I am convinced, offering a deliberate challenge to Lyly and what Lyly stood for. Thus, in fact, his debt to Lyly was as great, or even greater, when he opposed him as when he followed him.

And did the events in the wood really take place? Theseus is convinced they did not, and Theseus' opinion cannot be dismissed out of hand; Shakespeare actually bears him out in the title of his play. And even if Theseus is wrong in this special case, he is right in the abstract; love is a very irrational, heady affair. And one thing is certain—in the moonlit woods the lovers have completely lost their bearings, and the actual comedy there rests on their inability to realize what is happening to themselves and to others: Lysander proclaims his love as the true *amor rationalis* when he has never been so fast in the grip of unreason before; Helena, like Campaspe or Sapho, is unable to realize her happiness when it is offered her, Hermia in her jealousy takes offence where none is meant—they are all at cross-purposes,

floundering, like Terence's characters, in their own particular bog of misapprehensions. But unlike Terence's characters, they are in error as to emotions—including their own—not to facts; and they are watched over by a kindly power that will set them right. Moreover, they are contrasted with a pair of mortals who are above such errors. Error and incomprehension are not the inevitable lot of humanity, we may rise above them; but, after all, most of us are more like Lysander and Hermia than we are like Theseus and Hippolyta, and our laughter at the all-too-human pair is tinged with a realization that but for the grace of God there go we, and we despise them only at our peril. This particular effect, which lies I think at the bottom of the highest types of comedy, and which I believe breaks through in English comedy for the first time definitely here, might owe something to Terence, but it is almost bound to arise when we have a comedy based on inner misapprehensions and when we are in sympathy with the characters involved.

In the structure of his comedy Shakespeare continues to build on Lyly, no less than in his themes, but again he transmutes his material into something new. Counterpoint had, as we saw, long been an element in English comedy. Medwall had opposed the wooing of his heroes with that of the pages, Edwardes had contrasted the true friendship of Damon and Pythias with the selfish alliance of the philosophers; Lyly had employed a more fugal method in which whole groups of characters had been developed in parallel lines, their speeches and reactions chasing one another up and down the scale. In *Love's Labour's Lost* Shakespeare had taken over this method unaltered. Now in *A Midsummer Night's Dream* he has as many pairs of lovers as in *Love's Labour's Lost,* but they are not treated parallelly, there is no hint of a fugue (a form to which he reverted in a single scene of *As You Like It*), and the circumstances are all different for each pair. In the two pairs of young Athenians nearly all the possible permutations that Heywood had given in his *Play of Love* are represented. Pyramus and Thisbe, flying to the woods by night, re-echo the situation of Lysander and Hermia, and their love-making provides an ironic comment on the inflation of the lovers' speeches, just as Titania and Bottom give a farcical comment on the unreason of love, while Theseus and Hippolyta serve as a more serious, measured comment, and Oberon and Titania remind us that, after all, love's problems are not all solved with a Jack shall have Jill. The play is a veritable *tour de force* of construction with its interwoven strains of action and of theme producing a scintillating variety in which the colours blend and reflect on one another. Shakespeare never attempted quite so complex a structural pattern again—not even in *As You Like It,* which with its multiple pairs of lovers approaches it most closely, and where, besides the other permutations we even have Not-loved-nor-loving, but where the pairs are all kept strictly separate, not intercrossed as here. Still, a complexity of interwoven strains, contrasts of high romance, low comedy and scenes of verbal wit were to remain with him as a permanent legacy from Lyly in his formula for comedy.

In the themes of his later comedies, the Lylian strains die gradually away. Beatrice and Benedick still owe everything, if not to Lyly himself, at least to the direction indicated by him; and the comedy of courtship, of love's perversity and of the infidel caught, has never been treated with such gaiety, humour and depth as here. But contrasting with the lightheartedness of this plot is another, nearly tragic, strain. The two plots are brought together by the theme of appearance and reality, and even appearance here is imposed from outside. One pair of lovers is separated by inability to assess the truth, the other united; Dogberry's 'It is proved already you are false knaves, and it will go near to be thought so shortly' sums up the importance of opinion with unintentional irony. The Petrarchistic basis of Lylian comedy has been here overthrown. It is not darts from a beauty's eyes that engender love at first sight in Benedick, nor even in the more romantic Claudio; and the gradual love that grows up between the bickering pair promises a far better companionship than the more conventional pattern followed by the others. Placed before the Petrarchistic problem of love or friendship, Benedick (in contrast with Lyly's Eumenides) decides realistically for love.

In *As You Like It* the Petrarchistic love of the shepherd is openly ridiculed; Phoebe very neatly shows up the emptiness of his romantic imagery, and the utter selflessness of his moving appeal to Rosalind in Lodge, that she should have pity on Phoebe and love her, has been turned into an intrigue situation in which he is made the foolish and unwitting opponent of his own interests; while the sudden awakening of love in Phoebe has been transformed into a hilarious comedy of courtship in which love is awakened through round abuse and expressed in Phoebe's shilly-shallying discourse on the supposed boy's charms. In fact Lodge's Lylianism has been desentimentalized throughout. Orlando is still conventional enough to plaster the woods with despairing sonnets, but he is much too healthy and sensible an animal to forego a meal for love's sake. And while he is willing to play at Petrarchism in other respects too, both he and Rosalind, who has a lot of trouble to keep him up to the mark, are no longer playing it even half in earnest, as at the court of Navarre, but frankly with tongue in cheek, though Rosalind is woman enough to hanker after the privileges of the Petrarchistic beauty.

Even in *Twelfth Night* the ghost of Lyly continues to flicker in Viola's wooing of the Duke by innuendo. But the actual comedy again lies chiefly in Olivia's lack of self-knowledge and the mistaken estimates of the situation by nearly all the characters—the question of appearance and reality again. And indeed *Twelfth Night*, the swan song of Shakespearian comedy, as has often been pointed out, seems to sum up the situations of all the preceding comedies, and with them the comic principle behind them. At the same time a new principle appears—social satire.

Twelfth Night was to remain the last of Shakespeare's true comedies. The tide of fashion had set towards intrigue and satire, and he did not follow it. He had already, in response to Porter's success, tried his hand at intrigue once again in *The Merry Wives,* just as in *The Merchant of Venice* he had in response to a special demand departed, though less markedly, from his basic type, and again apparently it had not satisfied him. Now, since romantic comedy was no longer in demand, he turned instead to tragicomedy in the mode of *The Malcontent, The Dutch Courtesan* and *The Honest Whore,* producing his so-called problem plays, and the Lylian formula was shelved.

In this necessarily very summary survey of the field it will have been seen that the stress has been laid chiefly on the comic principle behind what one may call the main plot of the early comedies. This has of necessity involved a certain amount of what might be taken as interpretation of the comedies as a whole. It was not intended as such. The total meaning of a comedy, especially of so mixed a type as was practised on the Elizabethan stage, is not necessarily to be summed up in an analysis—even a very much fuller analysis than could be attempted here—of its comic situations and the sort of laughter they arouse; though I would suggest that the questions, 'by virtue of what is a given comedy truly comic', and 'what is the author laughing at and how', are essential to any interpretation of its meaning. And I think it is in this extremely important point, involving his very concept of comedy itself, that Shakespeare's greatest and most lasting debt to Lyly lies. In that and in the structural pattern, that peculiar blend of a romantic comedy of courtship with a strain of low-comedy genre scenes, and yet another strain of witty repartee: a blend which, repeated again and again in Shakespeare's comedies, had already been mixed to a nicety in *Gallathea,* and less perfectly in other comedies of Lyly's, but in no other of Shakespeare's forerunners. Shakespeare's comic principle cannot be summed up in the phrase 'comedy of courtship', it has been enriched with another principle, the discrepancy between appearance and reality. At least one aspect of that complex derives from Lyly. One may say, of course, that Shakespeare was perfectly capable of hitting on such points for himself, and so no doubt he was. But even a genius will not break down the wall to enter a room when there is an already open door waiting for him; and his impression of that room will not unnaturally be coloured thereafter by his first glimpse of it through the open door. It was Lyly who opened the door for Shakespeare, and when he was forced to abandon the Lylian view he abandoned comedy.

G. K. Hunter   (essay date 1962)

SOURCE: "The Plays," in *John Lyly: The Humanist as Courtier,* Routledge & Kegan Paul, 1962, pp. 159-256.

[In the following excerpt, Hunter investigates the "debate-theme" of Midas, Endimion, *and* Gallathea.]

Midas

The basic plot of *Midas* is taken from Lyly's favourite classical authority, Ovid, who tells two stories of Midas: first, how he desired the gift of the golden touch, how he came to repent it and was absolved; and, second, how Midas was fitted with asses ears for preferring the music of Pan to that of Apollo. Lyly . . . places this story inside a debate structure. He shows that Midas' judgment that gold is the best of gifts results from a dispute between War (Martius), Wealth (Mellacrites) and Love (Eristus), here presented as the counsellors of their monarch. These three appear throughout the play as the modes of temptation to which a sovereign is most subject, and serve to give a philosophic and even political tinge to activities which, in Ovid, are merely part of the arbitrary and inexplicable relationship of gods and men. In each case the end proposed to Midas is improper: war is desired to give Midas power over neighbouring states; love is to be pursued for the end of 'such a tender wantonness that nothing is thought of but love, a passion proceeding of beastly lust, and coloured with a courtly name of love' (II.i. 61-3); gold is sought because it can buy love, monarchy and even justice:

> Justice herself that sitteth wimpled about the eyes doth it not because she will take no gold, but that she would not be seen blushing when she takes it; the balance she holdeth are not to weigh the right of the cause but the weight of the bribe. She will put up her naked sword if thou offer her a golden scabbard.
>
> (I. i. 90-94)

The story of Midas' golden gift shows how gold leads to sterility. The ills attendant on the other advices are also illustrated in the course of the play, though less fully and less coherently. A point of view opposite to that of the three counsellors is also indicated, by the person of the king's daughter, Sophronia (her name is meant to be indicative of her wisdom); it is she who speaks the clearest denunciation of the different advices and their effects on Midas:

> The love he hath followed—I fear unnatural—the riches he hath got—I know unmeasurable—the wars he hath levied—I doubt unlawful—hath drawn his body with grey hairs to the grave's mouth, and his mind with eating cares to desperate determinations . . . Let Phrygia be an example of chastity, not lust; liberality, not covetousness; valour, not tyranny. I wish not your bodies banished, but your minds, that my father and your king may be our honour and the world's wonder.
>
> (II. i. 88-107)

At the end of the play when Midas comes to self-knowledge, having learned humility and discretion as a result of his double misfortune (and this final episode is, of course, added to Ovid) it is in precisely these terms that his palinode is expressed:

> I will therefore yield myself to Bacchus and acknowledge my wish to be vanity; to Apollo and confess my judgment to be foolish; to Mars and say my wars are unjust; to Diana and tell my affection hath been unnatural.
>
> (V. iii. 58 61)

This framework of moral debate enables the play to make topical reference of a fairly obvious kind without disrupting the structure of the entertainment; where there is already a moral pattern worked into the play, the localization of some of the terms does not require much readjustment of focus. The assimilation of Midas to Philip II of Spain occurs in one of the spaces left open by the framework of debate—the temptation to war, for which Ovid supplies no material. The use of a contemporary reference at this point may sharpen our apprehension of ambition and ill-judgment, but the place of these qualities in the general scheme would still be clear to a reader who had not made the equation between the moral and the political aspects.

In fact, there is nothing to make the equation even plausible till we get to Act III. There, in the long complaint by Midas, which fills the greater part of scene i, we hear, among other confessions:

> Have not I made the sea to groan under the number of my ships; and have they not perished that there was not two left to make a number? . . . Have not I enticed the subjects of my neighbour princes to destroy their natural kings? . . . A bridge of gold did I mean to make in that island where all my navy could not make a breach. Those islands did I long to touch, that I might turn them to gold, and myself to glory. But unhappy Midas . . . being now become a shame to the world, a scorn to that petty prince and to thyself a consumption. A petty prince, Midas? no, a prince protected by the gods, by nature, by his own virtue and his subjects' obedience. Have not all treasons been discovered by miracle, not counsel? that do the gods challenge. Is not the country walled with huge waves? that doth nature claim. Is he not through the whole world a wonder for wisdom and temperance? that is his own strength. Do not all his subjects (like bees) swarm to preserve the king of bees? that their loyalty maintaineth.
>
> (III. i. 31-60)

In the period of the Armada it would be hard to hear of a great fleet miraculously frustrated 'that there was not two to make a number' without thinking of Philip II, and there is nothing in the context to contradict the thought. Again, the unqualified praise of a monarch in Elizabethan court entertainment always requires us to glance towards Elizabeth, and when we hear of Midas' enemy as a paragon, whom he seeks to destroy by plots, by invasion and by lavish expenditure, it is natural to extend the meaning to cover the general opposition between Spain and England. Further, Lyly had already identified Elizabeth with Sapho, and Sapho appears in Ovid as the Queen of Lesbos. Here the ruler of Lesbos is

Midas' enemy. Identification cannot be resisted when all the evidence points one way.

But the identification of Midas with Philip of Spain does not take us very far into the play or require us to interpret every scene allegorically. It does not affect the sub-plot; the scene of Sophronia and her ladies-in-waiting, engaged in a choice between story-telling, song and dancing obviously parodies the original choice between Wealth, War and Love, but it does not follow it down into its political implications. Its point would seem to be made if we accept it as a vignette of courtly grace, otherwise absent from the play.

Halpin and Bond [in *Oberon's Vision* and the *Complete Works,* of Lyly, respectively] wish to extend the allegory to figures other than Midas. They would see Martius, for example, as a pseudonym for the Duke of Alva; the argument against this is simply that it seems an unnecessary restriction of the range of reference that the name and the attitude implies; but I would not deny that the persons of Alva could have occurred to Elizabethans as well as moderns as a local representative of the ambitious bloodthirstiness which Martius represents in general.

The golden gift has an obvious and utilized congruity with the treasure which Spain extracted from the Indies—'the utmost parts of the West, where all the guts of the earth are gold' (II. i. 101)—but we need not seek for political meaning in the fact that this is the gift of Bacchus nor in the bathing in Pactolus which removes the curse. These belong to the source, and it is sufficient for court allegory if the play at some points makes clear the relevance of the modern parallel.

The second story which Ovid tells about Midas starts from his false judgment in the case of Apollo *v.* Pan, and proceeds through his sentence to wear asses ears to the final episode of the blabbing reeds—the means by which the world learns about his deformity. Lyly presents all these without notable alteration, and adds a final scene in which Midas repents of his misjudgment (and of his inordinate ambitions) and is restored to human shape. The addition of this second story does not, however, add anything to the dramatic impact of the play; can it have been intended to add to the allegorical import? Halpin wished to identify the contest between the gods with the Reformation and supposed that Midas' mistaken preference for the music of Pan stood for Philip's adherence to the Roman Catholic church. This is attractive on *a priori* grounds, since *pan* (=all) and *catholic* are cognate terms. But no one at all sensitive to literary atmosphere could read the scene of the contest and suppose that it was intended allegorically; there is nothing in the scene which is not perfectly explicable in terms of the literal meaning. Moreover Pan appears too often in Elizabethan pastoral allegory to represent approved English figures to make the identification at all provable. Pan is here, as there, the representative of rustic poetry, and the qualities ascribed to him bear only a converse relation to those ascribed in this period to Roman Catholicism: subtlety,

treachery, pride, empty ostentation (Spenser's Archimago, Duessa and Orgoglio).

Indeed the figure and song of Pan (as we have it) may seem to readers less asinine than Midas to be as good (in its own way) as that of Apollo, though lacking the music we cannot be confident—and we cannot even be sure that the songs we possess mirror Lyly's intention. The 'low' rustic style has its own charm here in the vein of

> When the merry bells ring round,
> And the jocund rebecks sound
> To many a youth and many a maid
> Dancing in the chequer'd shade.

It is certainly not true that 'Pan [hath showed] himself a rude satyr, neither keeping measure nor time' in lines like

> Cross-gartered swains and dairy-girls
> With faces smug and round as pearls
> When Pan's shrill pipe begins to play
> With dancing wear out night and day.

It would be a curious malformation of intention if Lyly's supposed satire on the Roman Catholic church ended by appearing admirable for the very qualities that Protestants thought of as their own peculiars—homely honesty and downrightness. It seems wisest to drop the whole idea of allegorical intention in this episode and view the musical contest as just another example of Midas' instability of judgment, put in to give added weight to his repentance, and providing the audience with an opportunity to call Philip of Spain an ass.

I have discussed the temptation to wealth, where Ovid supplied the material, and that to war, where contemporary history seems to be the primary source; what of the third temptation, that of Eristus or Love? Sophronia says that Midas' love is 'unnatural' (II. i. 88) and Midas repeats the word in his palinode. On the other hand, the only love mentioned in the play is that of Midas for Celia, whose conquest is anticipated in Act I ('Celia, chaste Celia shall yield'), but who remains chaste in Act II, her words being as follows:

> if gold could have allured mine eyes, thou knowest Midas that commandeth all things to be gold had conquered; if threats might have feared my heart, Midas, being a king, might have commanded my affections; if love, gold or authority might have enchanted me, Midas had obtained by love, gold and authority.
>
> (II. i. 20-25)

The rebuttal of the three temptations of gold, love and force by Celia (the name is no doubt intended to be significant) aligns her clearly with Sophronia as representing the virtue in the play, but does not in the least explain Midas' unnatural love. Bond says that Celia is the daughter of Mellacrites—on the evidence I suppose of I. ii. 1 f., where Licio says to Petulus: 'Thou servest

Mellacrites, and I his daughter'; but there is nothing to suggest that the daughter is Celia. What is clear is that she is also beloved of Eristus, 'whose eyes are stitched on Celia's face, and thoughts gyved to her beauty' (II. i. 60 f.); it is also clear that she does not return any of this love, since she says of herself, 'I am free from love, and unfortunate to be beloved'. There is no evidence in the play of a mode of relationship which would make Midas' love 'unnatural', and I suspect that the pursuit of the question along these lines is misguided anyway. Eristus is nothing but the type of the lover and so Celia, I suspect, is only the object of love in general, a heaven of beauty that it is 'unnatural' to attempt by earthly love:

> Celia hath sealed her face in my heart, which I am no more ashamed to confess than thou that Mars hath made a scar in thy face, Martius.
>
> (II. ii. 81-3)

There is a case here for regarding the difficulty as likely to have arisen from too precise a conceptual framework and too slight a dramatic interest.

This play is also remarkable (and the unusualness may be related to the difficulties I have just discussed) for the lack of interest in courtly love. All Lyly's plays, except this one, turn on the emotion of love, seen as the main motive for human activities. Love shows court life at its most intense, and moves gods or sovereigns to descend into human life and reveal their powers in a context of human passion. The absence of this favourite theme in *Midas* is all the more remarkable in that the framework of debate allows for it so clearly. Martius and Mellacrites have their attitudes exposed at length, but Eristus is confined to a few undeveloped statements. Bond's suggestion that the 'unnatural' love of Midas is meant to be filled out by knowledge of contemporary scandal is completely unconvincing. It might be supposed that the topical allusions to Philip of Spain took up so much space (*Midas* is the second longest of Lyly's plays) that there was no room left for a developed image of love, natural or unnatural. On the other hand, however, one must note that the subject on which the play is centred could never have been intended for a purpose other than that of exposing foolish monarchy. Lyly's other plays of courtly intrigue centre on a divinely good monarch, but here this Alexander-Sapho-Cynthia figure has to be deduced from her opposite, Midas.

Endimion

No one could accuse *Endimion,* Lyly's other play supposedly devoted to court allegory, of lacking the dimension of love; for this is the element in which the whole play moves. The use of the legend of Endimion, about the hopeless love adventures of a shepherd and the moon, is a fairly obvious case of adapting the feelings of love to shadow forth the complex of fear, ambition, admiration that real courtiers felt about their real sovereign; for there can be little doubt that the Cynthia of the play is the Cynthia of Ralegh and Ben Jonson—Queen Eliza-

beth herself. The play uses a strain of high-flown adoration towards Cynthia, which seems to be unnaturally intense if Cynthia is only the moon. Take the oracle that Eumenides sees in the magic well:

> When she whose figure of all is the perfectest, and never to be measured—always one, yet never the same—still inconstant, yet never wavering—shall come and kiss Endimion in his sleep, he shall then rise; else never.
>
> (III. iv. 155-58)

This mood of abject admiration falls on every character when Cynthia is mentioned. Lyly nowhere gives evidence of attachment of this kind to ideal concepts, whether of Love or Truth or Heavenly Beauty or what-you-will; but this is precisely the attitude to Elizabeth that *Sapho and Phao* and *Midas* have prepared us for.

The outline of the plot certainly renders an image which Elizabeth could take as a graceful compliment to her virtue and attractiveness, and which it is hard not to see as a general image of court life . . . [In] *Sapho and Phao* . . . Sapho the queen is left constantly but hopelessly loved by the hero, who is in his turn constantly but hopelessly pursued by another lady with a strong claim on the affections. Lyly uses the same formula here, but makes it more integral to the plot. A noble gentleman hopelessly adoring, from the distance of humility, a goddess-queen who reigns over a 'court' of ladies, is betrayed by his very faithfulness and high-minded constancy to the forces of ingratitude, treachery and envy which lurk unseen around the throne. Evil spells cast him into a perpetual sleep; only the faithfulness of a friend breaks the dark night of disfavour, and reveals to Cynthia the true natures of the faithful and the unfaithful. Cynthia, ever gracious though ever distant, is willing to end the spell by her redeeming kiss. Virtue is rewarded by royal condescension and the corrupters and deceivers are known for what they are. The story reads, as I say, like a generalized transcript of court intrigue, written from the point of view of one who has an axe to grind about unfair disgrace and a hope of reaching favour again by means of judicious flattery.

Moreover, the details of the particular vision that Endimion relates when he is recovered from his sleep are strongly reminiscent of the dream of Sapho which we have already considered as possible allegory, and would seem to derive (as does the other) from an image of court-intrigue and corruption obscuring the true merit of the speaker, and carrying aloft the opportunists and the time-servers:

> There, portrayed to life, with a cold quaking in every joint I beheld many wolves barking at thee, Cynthia, who having ground their teeth to bite, did with striving bleed themselves to death. There might I see ingratitude with an hundred eyes, gazing for benefits, and with a thousand teeth gnawing on the bowels wherein she was bred. Treachery stood all clothed in white, with a smiling countenance, but both her hands bathed

in blood. Envy, with a pale and meagre face (whose body was so lean that one might tell all her bones, and whose garment was so tottered that it was easy to number every thread) stood shooting at stars, whose darts fell down again on her own face. There might I behold drones or beetles I know not how to term them, creeping under the wings of a princely eagle, who, being carried into her nest, sought there to suck that vein that would have killed the Eagle. I mused that things so base should attempt a fact so barbarous or durst imagine a thing so bloody.

(V. i. 119-34)

The 'drones and beetles' here, which suck the life-blood of the Eagle, closely correspond to the 'ants . . . and caterpillers' which suck away the life of the royal cedar in *Sapho*. What is lacking here is a figure equivalent to that of the loyal stockdove, whose guilelessness destroyed his hope of favour; but this is supplied by the whole history of Endimion, and more particularly by the passage immediately preceding, where he refuses 'counsels and policies' when they are offered to him and has to content himself in consequence with 'pictures'. I take this to mean that Endimion could have given Cynthia political advice or counsel which would have protected her; but he refrained out of humility and now has to content himself with a knowledge (? and literary portrait) of the falsehood at court.

Perhaps we should connect with these passages part of the Epilogue to *Endimion,* spoken at court presumably by one of the actors:

Dread Sovereign, the malicious that seek to overthrow us with threats do but stiffen our thoughts and make them sturdier in storms; but if your Highness vouchsafe with your favourable beams to glance upon us, we shall not only stoop but with all humility lay both our hands and hearts at your Majesty's feet.

The use of 'we' here suggests that the aggrieved party can be represented by the Pauls' boys. If this is the same grievance as is represented in the play itself (and why should we multiply grievances without necessity?) then the relationship with Cynthia expressed in the vision must refer to Lyly and his theatrical enterprise. This would be a rather unexciting truth, and would require us to dismiss the charge that 'the malicious' 'would have killed the Eagle' as rhetorical exaggeration. Certainly, for whatever reason, the notion has found no favour with commentators, who have preferred, now for over a hundred years, to brave illogicality in the pursuit of more romantic truths.

The first in this field was the Rev. N. J. Halpin, who published in 1843 a treatise called *Oberon's Vision*; in this (among other implausibilities) he identified Endimion with Leicester and suggested that the sleep in the play figured the disgrace which followed the discovery of his (third) marriage in 1579. This view, with minor modifications, has been accepted by G. P. Baker, in his edition of the play (1894), by Bond in the *Complete Works,* by Schelling in his *Elizabethan Drama* and most recently by F. S. Boas in his *Queen Elizabeth in Drama* (1950).

But powerfully backed though the case for Leicester may have been, it does not seem to have had much except human credulity to support it. There is no evidence that plays were ever performed before Elizabeth to support Leicester or any other faction in the court. Even if such plays existed, it seems highly improbable that Lyly should write one in support of Leicester. He was never a member of Leicester's faction; he was the servant of the Earl of Oxford, who belonged to the opposite party. Again, it is clear that Halpin was ignorant of dates, and that Bond (and Feuillerat for the sake of his own theory [in his *John Lyly*]) distort the external evidence. The title-page tells us that the play was performed at Candlemas before Elizabeth when she was at Greenwich; there is only one Candlemas in our period which the records say was spent at Greenwich—2nd February 1588—and we must give this as the date of the play. This is too late, however, to give any relation to Leicester's disgrace, or to the affairs of James VI that Feuillerat thinks relevant [Albert Feuillerat, *John Lyly,* 1910].

If we must find, in the plot of *Endimion,* any reference to the court affairs of the time, it seems better to retire altogether from the state affairs and to look at the more private intrigues of the court. From this point of view the theory of Professor Josephine Waters Bennett has much to recommend it ["Oxford and Endimion," *PMLA* LVII, 1942]. Mrs Bennett accepts the 1588 dating and remains inside the framework of Lyly's known allegiance to Oxford. . . . Oxford quarrelled in 1580 with associates whom he accused of secret Papism. As a result he was entered into temporary custody and disfavour. In the following year he was accused of adultery with Anne Vavasour, one of the Queen's ladies, and this time the disfavour was more lasting. It was not until 1583 that the Queen consented to receive him again. Anne Vavasour had also been imprisoned, and in the Tower she may have been in the custody of Sir Henry Lee, who had apartments there. Certainly she later became Lee's mistress. In the Woodstock or Ditchley Entertainment in 1592 Lee refers to a long sleep with which the Fairy Queen had punished him for not guarding the pictures left in his care, pictures first seen at the Woodstock Entertainment of 1575. Lee failed in his duty, because

lo, unhappy I was overtaken,
By fortune forced, a stranger lady's thrall,
Whom when I saw, all former care forsaken,
To find her out I lost myself and all,
Through which neglect of duty 'gan my fall.

The 'stranger lady' would seem to be Anne Vavasour, and Mrs Bennett supposes that the sleep refers to a disgrace which she conjectures to have been suffered by Lee after the seduction of his fair captive. If *Endimion* is taken to refer to this affair, viewing it from the side of Oxford, then Tellus who casts Endimion into an enchanted sleep must be Anne Vavasour, who accused Oxford of being the father of her child and so cast him into the dark night of royal disfavour; and Corsites the 'captain' who guards Tellus in her imprisonment must be Sir Henry Lee. Mrs Bennett supposes that the 'kiss' which restores

Endimion is the pension of one thousand pounds per annum which the Queen granted to Oxford in 1586.

As I have stated, Mrs Bennett's interpretation of the play has many advantages; but it also contains some improbabilities. If the play was performed in 1588, the matters it refers to were finished and done with. Mrs Bennett thinks that it *commemorates* the granting of the pension, and gives Oxford's side of the earlier difficulties. On the face of it this seems unlikely. We do not know that the pension and the disgrace were in any way connected, and it would seem impolitic to rake up the disgrace in order to commemorate the pension. But even if we were to grant the possibility of such a play, we should still have to prove that the play as we have it lives up to the intention, and this is not clear at all points. Oxford's apologia would, presumably, move along the following lines: Oxford was innocent of the accusations that Anne Vavasour levelled against him; she on the other hand was not innocent, witness her seduction by Sir Henry Lee. If this was Lyly's brief, the play mismanages it grossly. Mrs Bennett supposes the 'picture of Endimion' which Tellus weaves in her imprisonment, and which she is allowed to keep at the end of the play (V. iii. 251-5) is the child born to Anne Vavasour. But Oxford denied paternity, and it would have been indiscreet of Lyly to suggest that the child was his. Again, the play makes nothing of Anne Vavasour's promiscuity; Tellus loves only Endimion; she answers Corsites' love with deceit, and accepts him at the end only because Cynthia commands it. The play does not, in fact, come anywhere near a competent defence of Oxford, and this must make us doubtful that the play was ever intended for this purpose.

But quite apart from the plausibility or implausibility of these different identifications, is there not an assumption shared by them all which runs counter to the nature of courtly art as we have described it? The argument that it is so has been put persuasively by J. A. Bryant Jnr. in a paper read before the Southeastern States Renaissance Conference in 1956 ["The Nature of the Allegory in Lyly's *Endimion,*" *Renaissance Papers 1956*]. Professor Bryant starts from the point of Lyly's alteration in the classical myth. The myth told of the moon's love for a shepherd; Lyly alters this to one more flattering to the English Cynthia—the moon herself must be loved but cannot be treated as the victim of love. But the alteration involves Lyly in difficulties: in order to show the virtue of the goddess he has to depict an alternative love (to play the Venus to her Sapho, so to speak) and this produces the central design of Endimion between the moon and the earth, Cynthia and Tellus, his higher and lower destinies. Further, if he is to show Tellus as worthy of love, though unequal to Cynthia, he has to counter Endimion's rejection by another man's zealous pursuit, and this introduces Corsites. The whole play can be built up in this way as a functional development of a desire to flatter the Queen. Given Lyly's taste for symmetry and fondness for the conventions of courtly love (the conventions of his art) nothing else need be imported to explain the general structure of the play, with its final

pairing-off of couples—Corsites and Tellus, Geron and Dipsas, Sir Tophas and Bagoa.

The perception that Lyly's play grows naturally out of the conjunction of the myth and the desire to flatter Elizabeth does not, of course, explain away any of the particular elaborations, which appear most obviously in the vision of Endimion, twice presented, and which strongly suggest particular reference to a contemporary situation, which may (as we have seen above) be Lyly's own situation. But does remove the necessity to suppose that Lyly began with a contemporary event, and then set about dramatizing it, finding equivalents in myth and story which would clothe his meanings. I have argued already that the search for point-by-point correspondences in courtly allegory is a vain one and I rejoice to find Mr Bryant writing in a similar vein: 'such academic attempts at explanation usually proceed upon the assumption that the subject at hand is a dead fact, to be dissected, described, tabulated and provided with an index . . . But . . . the assumption is wrong'. This objection applies to those who have supposed *Endimion* to clothe a philosophic scheme, no less than to those who have seen it as a description of history. In either case the form of the play, as we have it, is judged incompetent and unsuccessful, except as a means—and even as a means it is rather inefficient (Bond has to suppose that Lyly did not know enough to get his facts right)—a means to convey a hidden truth, which will then pay back some of its own coherence and importance to the action that Bond and others suppose to be (in itself) 'incoherent and purposeless'.

Yet *Endimion* has often been reprinted, and students are invited to read it on what are, I suppose, literary grounds; moreover the play has been performed on the modern stage with some degree of success. This would seem to argue that Lyly gave his play some measure of literary coherence, and that the 'meaning' that emerges need be no more than an audience can deduce from any myth-like or archetypal situation. The historical critics seem to begin with the perfectly legitimate observation that this situation is *like* court life, and that Cynthia must reflect Queen Elizabeth. Their next assumption is, however, that the coherence of the play must then be pursued at the historical not at the literary level. Halpin and Bond ask, 'if Cynthia is the Queen, who is Endimion her suitor?' and come to the conclusion, very proper in its terms, that Leicester is the obvious suitor. Feuillerat and Bond ask, 'if Cynthia is the Queen, who is Tellus her rival?' and reach the conclusion, very proper in its terms, that Mary, Queen of Scots is the obvious rival. None of these critics has asked, 'is the relationship between Cynthia, Endimion and Tellus one that has any dramatic or artistic justification?' Concentration on this question would at least avoid methods of argument such as are provided (*inter alia*) by Bond's mode of identifying Eumenides with Sir Philip Sidney:

> There is one name that rises instinctively to the lips when acts that are lovely and noble and of good report are mentioned—one that still falls upon the ear like refreshing music in this hard heart-wearying age of

brass, even as its bearer softens and shames with his mild lustre the coarser fames and gaudier heroics of that iron time—the name of

> that pensive Hesper light
> O'er Chivalry's departed sun,

Sir Philip Sidney. Can the relations of Eumenides in the play be made to square with him?

(III. 95)

The method being used here is one which relies on stiffening the play with romantic responses to history and so by-passing the appeal of the play as a play. If Eumenides fulfils the role of a friend, we look for an historical 'friend' to make the play more real to us instead of looking for an artistic pattern that justifies the role.

If we look in the play for artistic pattern we find quite enough to stimulate discussion and response: we can find in it the major elements which appear everywhere in Lyly's plays—debate, mythology, romantic love, symmetrical arrangement—but ordered in a new and individual sequence. The play certainly contains a debate-theme—the old favourite of love *versus* friendship—which is announced unequivocally. Eumenides the faithful friend and lover is entitled to any one wish he may ask for; he is then faced with the problem of having to prefer either friendship or love:

> Why do I trifle the time in words? The least minute being spent in the getting of Semele is more worth than the whole world: therefore let me ask . . . What now, Eumenides? Whither art thou drawn? Hast thou forgotten both friendship and duty? Care of Endimion and the commandment of Cynthia? Shall he die in a leaden sleep because thou sleepest in a golden dream? Ay, let him sleep ever, so I slumber but one minute with Semele. Love knoweth neither friendship nor kindred.

> Shall I not hazard the loss of a friend for the obtaining of her for whom I would often lose myself? Fond Eumenides, shall the enticing beauty of a most disdainful lady be of more force than the rare fidelity of a tried friend? The love of men to women is a thing common and of course; the friendship of man to man infinite and immortal. Tush! Semele doth possess my love. Ay, but Endimion hath deserved it. I will help Endimion. I found Endimion unspotted in his truth. Ay, but I shall find Semele constant in her love. I will have Semele. What shall I do?

(III. iv. 103-19)

We can see the relevance of this conflict to that between the higher love that Endimion feels for Cynthia and the lower love he is offered by Tellus, but there is no explicit conflict in Endimion's situation, and the debate frames the action much less than it does in *Campaspe* or *Sapho and Phao*. In both these plays the different emotional states of the central characters are arranged in a static pattern which allows them to be debated; Alexander debates magnanimity against love, and the play contrasts magnanimity in Alexander against love in Apelles; so Sapho debates love against chastity, and the play con-

trasts chastity in Sapho against love in Venus. But Cynthia is *semper eadem,* and the play studiously refuses to debate the issue between her and Tellus. The contrasted emotional states in this play are treated as developing out of one another in a narrative sequence, rather than as existing in a static design.

It follows that as the debate is less important so the narrative is more elaborate. Of all Lyly's plays, *Endimion* is the one which is nearest to medieval romance. The succumbing of the hero to an enchanted sleep, specially devised for him by a malignant witch, and the adventures of his friend while pursuing a remedy, the encounter with the lover-hermit Geron, the enchanted fountain, only useful to the pure in heart—all this reads like a survey of romance motifs.

Given the story, it is not surprising that *Endimion* is the longest of Lyly's plays, and that in which the symmetries of treatment are most developed towards the Shakespearian mode of parallel human instances—it is also the play which seems to have influenced Shakespeare most directly. The adoration of Cynthia by Endimion is paralleled by the courtship of Semele by Eumenides, by Corsites' pursuit of Tellus, and (in the sub-plot) by Sir Tophas' pursuit of Dipsas. The cruelty of Tellus to Endimion is paralleled by the cruelty of Dipsas to Geron; the sublime chastity of Cynthia is parodied by the merely coquettish chastity of Semele. The denouement, in consequence, works out a broad survey of reconciliations:

> Well, Endimion, . . . thou hast my favour, Tellus her friend, Eumenides in paradise with his Semele, Geron contented with Dipsas.

(V. iii 271-3)

The function of this denouement is no doubt the same as that of *Sapho and Phao*—to highlight the wisdom and sympathy of the Queen—but the effect is very different. In *Sapho* the focus is on the mind of the Queen; Phao is a poor shadow. In *Endimion* the hopeless love of the hero has its own vein of madly poetic appeal:

> Tell me, Eumenides, what is he that having a mistress of ripe years, and infinite virtues, great honours and unspeakable beauty, but would wish that she might grow tender again? getting youth by years and never-decaying beauty by time; whose fair face neither the summer's blaze can scorch nor winter's blast chap, nor the numb'ring of years breed altering of colours. Such is my sweet Cynthia whom time cannot touch because she is divine nor will offend because she is delicate. O Cynthia, if thou shouldest always continue at thy fulness, both gods and men would conspire to ravish thee. But thou to abate the pride of our affections dost detract from thy perfections, thinking it sufficient if once in a month we enjoy a glimpse of thy majesty, and then, to increase our griefs, thou dost decrease thy gleams, coming out of thy royal robes wherewith thou dazzlest our eyes down into thy swath clouts beguiling our eyes.

(I. i. 50-65)

As the love of the subject has come into focus, so the mind of the sovereign has retreated to an altitude out of descriptive range. Cynthia is different in kind from the other characters in the play, and though the action takes place under her benign influence she is not part of it. The contrasts made by the different modes of love reconciled at the end of the play do not affect our conception of Cynthia, even by a process of contrast, for she cannot be conceived to have been tempted to any of these attitudes. In *Endimion,* in fact, we can see the goddess-sovereign figure, who has dominated Lyly's drama up to this point, retreating into a state of aloofness where she ceases to have much effect on the conduct of the play.

HARMONIOUS VARIETY

We have seen the debate-theme 'What is true royalty?' controlling the form of *Campaspe* and *Sapho and Phao,* and we have seen the same formal method applied in a more negative way in *Midas*: 'What interests ought a true monarch to avoid?' We have also seen *Endimion* developing the world of *Sapho and Phao* in a rather different direction. The desire to compliment the Queen does not here involve a contrast of her royalty with other emotional states, but rather requires a demonstration of her influence on the world of courtiers beneath her. As a result, most of *Endimion* is concerned with the interlocking intrigues of a spectrum of characters, all held together in a single situation.

In this respect *Endimion* reaches out to the mode of play construction we are to discuss in this section, where the interest is no longer centred on a single royal figure, Alexander-Sapho-Cynthia-Midas, but is diffused among many parallel instances, these being so organized that they complete a recognizable range of cases. Take away Cynthia, or replace her by a force about which the play has no particular feeling, and the construction of *Endimion* begins to resemble very clearly that which Lyly had first essayed in *Gallathea*.

Gallathea

The only approach to pastoral we have met so far in Lyly's plays is the rather thin wash of rusticity to be found in *Sapho and Phao,* serving there to start off the praise of courtliness when such a one as Sapho is queen; to this we may add the isolated scene of the shepherds in *Midas* (Act IV, scene ii) in which we meet 'we poor commons (who tasting war, are made to relish nothing but taxes)'; but this is proletarian rather than truly pastoral in function. It is clear enough, however, from the opening words of *Gallathea* that this is to be a deliberate exercise in the pastoral mode:

> The sun doth beat upon the plain fields; wherefore let
> us sit down, Gallathea, under this fair oak, by whose

broad leaves being defended from the warm beams we may enjoy the fresh air which softly breathes from Humber floods.

It might be objected that the desire to escape from the warm sun into the shade is not one that characteristically affects the shepherds or other swains on the banks of Humber. As Warton pointed out, 'complaints of immoderate heat, and wishes to be conveyed to a cooling cavern, when uttered by the inhabitants of Greece have a propriety which they totally lose in the character of a British shepherd'. But the objection is irrelevant to the banks of Lyly's Humber. The lines translate and are, I presume, meant to recall words that have universally been allowed to stand for the pastoral world in general—

> Tityre tu patulae recubans sub tegmine fagi

—the opening line of Virgil's eclogues. And as Virgil is recalled in the opening lines of the play, so the title itself and the main motif of the plot is probably intended to recall the other prime pastoral authority, Theocritus, whose sixth idyll tells of the unwelcome attentions that the nymph Galatea has to endure from the monster Polyphemus, and whose eleventh idyll gives the song with which the monster wooed the shrinking nymph. The monster that is due to prey upon Lyly's Gallathea is not a cyclops, however; for, like Hesione and Andromeda and Ariosto's Angelica she is likely to form the virgin-tribute paid to a sea-monster. The name of this monster—the Agar—Lyly seems to have taken from the *eagre* or tidal-wave of the Humber estuary, but for the attendant circumstances he seems to have gone back to the story of Neptune and Hesione, derived it would seem through Natalis Comes, the famous Renaissance mythographer.

The pastoral setting, which the opening of the play establishes, is one that is preserved throughout. No courtiers or royal persons appear. The gain in homogeneousness (as against *Sapho and Phao*) is very great. And the appearance and intervention of the gods does not really affect this. For the pastoral world here presented is one where man and nature interact continuously. The gods act like the forces of nature pressing on man: Cupid pressing him into love, Diana into chastity, Neptune into fear and obedience. And this is indeed what the play is about—the interrelation of gods and men, obedience and deceit. The motto of the play might be taken from what Gallathea says to her father in the first scene: 'Destiny may be deferred, not prevented' which finds a more particular application to the facts of the play in Tyterus' 'dissemble you may with men, deceive the gods you cannot', and this Neptune in his turn takes up and repeats, as if summarizing his whole intention in the play—which is to pay out those who seek to circumvent the destiny he imposes: 'their slights may blear men, deceive me they cannot'. The narrative with which the play opens mirrors in little this theme which pervades the action:

> In times past, where thou seest a heap of small pebble,
> stood a stately temple of white marble, which was

dedicated to the god of the sea—and in right, being so near the sea; hither came all such as either ventured by long travel to see countries, or by great traffic to use merchandise, offering sacrifice by fire to get safety by water; yielding thanks for perils past and making prayers for good success to come. But Fortune, constant in nothing but inconstancy, did change her copy, as the people their custom; for the land being oppressed by Danes, who instead of sacrifice, committed sacrilege, instead of religion, rebellion; and made a prey of that in which they should have made their prayers, tearing down the temple even with the earth, being almost equal with the skies; enraged so the god who binds the winds in the hollows of the earth that he caused the seas to break their bounds, sith men had broke their vows, and to swell as far above their reach as men had swerved beyond their reason. Then might you see ships sail where sheep fed, anchors cast where ploughs go, fishermen throw their nets where husbandmen sow their corn, and fishes throw their scales where fowls do breed their quills. Then might you gather froth where now is dew, rotten weeds for sweet roses, and take view of monstrous mermaids instead of passing fair maids.

(I. i. 13-34)

This story might serve as a natural introduction to a play in which men once again seek to evade the wrath of the gods, though this time there is no element of terror involved.

It will be seen even from the little that has been said so far that the unity and construction of *Gallathea* is very different from that of the plays which have been discussed. A greater homogeneousness is achieved by removing direct reference to the world of courtly manners, but is achieved only at the cost of losing direct comment on formulated ideals of living. To illustrate this point we may compare the debate structure here with that in *Sapho and Phao*: both plays deal with the conflict between Venus and Diana or Love and Chastity. When we compare them in this way it is immediately apparent that the debate matters much less in *Gallathea* than in *Sapho and Phao*. The pressure on the earlier play was to convey the nature of the excellence which cancels any natural opposition between love and chastity, by taking the best things out of both positions

> [so] that your Dian
> Was both herself and Love.

In the earlier play the opposition between the two sides in the debate had to be sharpened in order that the nature of this excellence should emerge, showing Sapho to possess both the humanity to feel love and the magnanimity to conquer it. In *Gallathea* no one is really shown to suffer by the opposition between Cupid and Diana. It is true that the Nymphs of Diana, wounded by Cupid, utter plaints of love not unlike those we have met in the earlier plays:

Can Cupid's brands quench Vesta's flames, and his feeble shafts headed with feathers pierce deeper than Diana's arrows headed with steel? Break thy bow,

Telusa, that seekest to break thy vow and let those hands that aimed to hit the wild hart scratch out those eyes that have wounded thy tame heart. O vain and only naked name of chastity, that is made eternal and perisheth by time, holy and is infected by fancy, divine and is made mortal by folly!

(III. i. 10-17)

But the focus of the play does not rest on the pathos of such a plaint. Sapho's sufferings in love have a central interest, for Sapho (like Alexander) is the obvious centre of the plot; and the whole force of its intellectual discriminations press down on her situation. In so far as the plot has weight, the weight lies here. But in *Gallathea* the love-plaints of the various nymphs are so laid together that we do not rest our interest on any single one of them. The tension between the mortals who hope to deceive both men and gods, and the gods who are lurking in the very same woods, determined not to be outdone in deception—this tension is conveyed by means of a whole series of interrelated episodes which illustrate and make general their points by their very variousness and not by their capacity to be brought to bear on a single situation. We have said that *Campaspe* and *Sapho and Phao* ask and seek to answer in their various ways the question, 'Where lies true royalty?' But no question of this kind will serve to focus the meaning of *Gallathea*. Instead, a whole series of cross-intrigues is used to present a vision of pretensions and limitations, self-will and destiny which is reminiscent of both Greek Romance and Shakespeare's last comedies.

In handling this new technique in *Gallathea,* Lyly produces one of the most beautifully articulated plays in the period. Almost all the plot material is made out of one motif—the attempt to deceive destiny by means of disguise. From this starting-point one can see the play being built up by methods almost exactly analogous to those of fugue in music. The first statement of the *subject* shows Tyterus disguising Gallathea in order to deceive Neptune. The second entry shows Cupid disguising himself to deceive Diana. In the third entry Melebeus disguises Phillida, again in order to deceive Neptune. Finally, in a fourth entry Neptune declares that he will disguise himself as a shepherd, to deceive all the other deceivers. The *exposition,* mathematically exact, is complete. Next, the play moves on to development of this material; by a dramatic equivalent to the contrapuntal texture of a fugue we sound together the themes of Phillida's disguise and Gallathea's disguise, and so arrive at the developing love-plot of these two nymphs, each knowing herself to be a woman and hoping that the other is a man. Add to this the voices of the second entry and one finds the nymphs of Diana, also inflamed, some for Gallathea and some for Phillida—again supposing that they are as male in fact as they are in attire. The re-entry of the fourth voice is delayed to its most dramatic moment. Neptune reiterates the 'subject' in a thunderous bass:

And do men begin to be equal with gods, seeking by craft to overreach them that by power oversee them? Do they dote so much on their daughters that they stick not to dally with our deities? Well shall the inhabitants see that destiny cannot be prevented by craft nor my anger be appeased by submission. I will make havoc of Diana's nymphs, my temples shall be dyed with maidens' blood, and there shall be nothing more vile than to be a virgin. To be young and fair shall be accounted shame and punishment, in so much as it shall be thought as dishonourable to be honest as fortunate to be deformed.

(V. iii. 10-19)

By now, however, the tangle of mistaken loves, of nymphs in love with one another, and of supernatural powers promoting one side or another, is sufficiently complex to take the bite out of Neptune's threat. Diana and Venus enter in what in music would be called 'close imitation' after him. In a *stretto* of all the gods on the stage at one time, the discordant self-deceptions that have resulted from the attempt to deceive others are resolved into concord.

It is tempting to carry the fugal analogies to the structure of *Gallathea* still further, and talk of entries inverted or *cancrizans* (as when the gods invert the human point of view) but probably to take them further would be to reduce their usefulness, which is, of course, only that of analogy. But the analogy is worth using, if only to counteract complaints like that of Feuillerat, '*Gallathea,* de toutes les productions lyliennes . . . c'est . . . une de celles dont la composition est le plus hétérogène' and to show that the 'lack of development' is not due to lack of formal control. By using a critical vocabulary which does not import assumptions that the end of drama is to develop characters, organize intrigue and show personality at work, we take ourselves a little nearer the true excellencies of Lyly's plays.

For the 'dispersed' interest of *Gallathea* does not, for the sympathetic reader, lower the dramatic temperature or cause his attention to wander before the next appearance of these same characters. Where all the characters are arranged to imitate one another, and where the focus of interest is on the repetition and modification and rearrangement of a basic pattern of persons, we do not ask how the persons will develop individually, but how the situation can be further manipulated. Having seen Tyterus disguise Gallathea and hide her in the woods, then Melebeus disguise Phillida and dispose of her in the same way, we are then anxious to hear the two disguises chiming together. Having heard that, we then wonder how the pursuit of the other nymphs by Cupid will affect the first situation; for his threat to 'use some tyranny in these woods' and 'confound their loves in their own sex' is expressed in terms that bring Gallathea and Phillida within its compass. The process is one of agglomeration, by which similar experiences are continually being added together to produce new and piquant situations. As the wheel turns and the same episode comes round again, it is never quite the same, for new confusions and accompaniments are always being added or taken away.

This formal unity is not, however, so oppressive that no space is left for that delicate observation of manners and

witty evocation of refined attitudes that gives Lyly's comedy its characteristic charm. The comedy of errors between the two nymphs is handled without ever invoking the slapstick of Plautus or Shakespeare—people punished or abused for things they never did—but produces instead the 'soft smiling, not loud laughing' over human capacity for self-deception. Each maiden retreats into herself in order to imitate the signs of maleness she finds in the other:

> GALLATHEA. . . . . But whist! here cometh a lad; I will learn of him how to behave myself.
>
> *Enter* Phillida *in man's attire.*
>
> PHIL. I neither like my gait nor my garments; the one untoward, the other unfit, both unseemly. O Phillida! But yonder stayeth one, and therefore say nothing. But O Phillida!
>
> GALLA. I perceive that boys are in as great disliking of themselves as maids; therefore though I wear the apparel, I am glad I am not the person.
>
> PHIL. It is a pretty boy and a fair; he might well have been a woman; but because he is not I am glad I am, for now under the colour of my coat I shall decipher the follies of their kind.
>
> GALLA. I would salute him, but I fear I should make a curtsey instead of a leg.
>
> PHIL. If I durst trust my face as well as I do my habit, I would spend some time to make pastime; for say what they will of a man's wit, it is no second thing to be a woman.
>
> GALLA. All the blood in my body would be in my face if he should ask me (as the question among men is common), 'are you a maid?'
>
> (II. i. 10-30)

It is characteristic of Lyly to organize a situation where we in the audience can watch his characters failing to understand one another. We alone are given the total understanding that is required. Lyly offers us the pleasure of a smiling superiority to and enjoyment of the accidents and misunderstandings that affect others in their lives and (more especially) loves. He repeats the method a little later in the same play. We watch the plaints of love following one another in a regular order, and then witness what follows when each nymph attempts to disguise her feelings from the others

> EUROTA. . . . . why blushest thou, Telusa?
>
> TEL. To hear thee in reckoning my pains to recite thine own. I saw, Eurota, how amorously you glanced your eye on the fair boy in the white coat, and how cunningly (now that you would have some talk of love) you hit me in the teeth with love.

EUR. I confess that I am in love, and yet swear that I know not what it is. I feel my thoughts unknit, mine eyes unstayed, my heart I know not how affected or infected, my sleeps broken and full of dreams, my wakeness sad and full of sighs, myself in all things unlike myself. If this be love, I would it had never been devised.

TEL. Thou hast told what I am in uttering what thy self is. These are my passions, Eurota, my unbridled passions, my intolerable passions, which I were as good acknowledge and crave counsel as to deny and endure peril.

. . .

But soft, here cometh Ramia; but let her not hear us talk.
We will withdraw ourselves and hear her talk.

Enter Ramia.

RAMIA. I am sent to seek others, that have lost myself.

. . .

EUR. . . . Ah, would I were no woman!

RAMIA. Would Tyterus were no boy!

TEL. Would Telusa were nobody!

(III. i. 39-111)

The play is, of course, basically a play about love, and of the three gods who appear on the stage (I take Venus to be a mere extension of Cupid) only Cupid seems willing to do more than preserve the *status quo*. He is the only agent of change, for love is the only emotion in the play which involves the interaction of people and allows their natures to move forward. This remains true even though love here is only the courtly and witty game which is all that Lyly ever touches on, and probably all that his instruments were capable of expressing. I have spoken of the play as lacking direct reference to the court; this is true, in that it is totally unconcerned with magnanimity or honour, but in another sense the play is courtly enough, the loves of the nymphs reflecting the love ideals of refined ladies—ideals which can be indulged here with complete impunity, since there are no male suitors within sight. Here is the supreme example in Lyly of the delicate precision of his style, used to discover in wit-combat the delicacy of virginal sensations about love.

PHILLIDA. It is a pity that Nature framed you not a woman, having a face so fair, so lovely a countenance, so modest a behaviour.

GALLATHEA. There is a tree in Tylos whose nuts have shells like fire, and being cracked, the kernel is but water.

PHIL. What a toy is it to tell me of that tree, being nothing to the purpose. I say it is pity you are not a woman.

GALLA. I would not wish to be a woman unless it were because thou art a man.

PHIL. Nay, do not wish to be a woman, for then I should not love thee, for I have sworn never to love a woman.

GALLA. A strange humour in so pretty a youth, and according to mine, for myself will never love a woman.

PHIL. It were a shame if a maiden should be a suitor (a thing hated in that sex) that thou shouldest deny to be her servant.

GALLA. If it be a shame in me, it can be no commendation in you, for yourself is of that mind.

PHIL. Suppose I were a virgin (I blush in supposing myself one) and that under the habit of a boy were the person of a maid; if I should utter my affection with sighs, manifest my sweet love by my salt tears, and prove my loyalty unspotted, and my griefs intol-erable, would not then that fair face pity this true heart?

GALLA. Admit that I were as you would have me suppose that you are, and that I should with entreaties, prayers, oaths, bribes and whatever can be invented in love desire your favour, would you not yield?

PHIL. Tush, you come in with 'admit'.

GALLA. And you with 'suppose'.

PHIL. What doubtful speeches be these? I fear me he is as I am, a maiden.

GALLA. What dread riseth in my mind! I fear the boy to be as I am, a maiden.

PHIL. Tush, it cannot be, his voice shows the contrary.

GALLA. Yet I do not think it, for he would then have blushed.

PHIL. Have you ever a sister?

GALLA. If I had but one, my brother must needs have two; but I pray have you ever a one?

PHIL. My father had but one daughter, and therefore I could have no sister.

GALLA. Ay me, he is as I am, for his speeches be as mine are.

PHIL. What shall I do? Either he is subtle or my sex simple.

. . .

PHIL. Come let us into the grove, and make much one of another, that cannot tell what to think one of another.

(III. ii. 1-59)

In the discovery of this vein of delicate innuendo, Lyly does more than anticipate Shakespeare; he advances his own art. It is well worth pausing to notice the skill with which he orchestrates (so to speak) the advance and retreat of the two maidens, the desire to speak out and the fear of being understood. The passage is made up entirely of repetitions, but the formality does not in the least impede the movement round a circuit of maidenly daring; so that we end the scene knowing better what sensitivity and delicacy are like. Small wonder that Shakespeare should have remembered the scene, and tried to transplant its easy control of verbal ballet, advance and retreat, into his own richer idiom.

The play thus uses the somewhat savage story of Neptune's anger, and the annual sacrifice of virgins exacted to appease him, to frame a world of exquisite refinement in the emotions. The evocation of the tenderness of virginal feelings acts as a foil to the dangerous and bitter state of virginity most feelingly evoked in Hebe's speech of farewell when she is due to be devoured by the Agar:

> Farewell the sweet delights of life and welcome now the bitter pangs of death. Farewell you chaste virgins, whose thoughts are divine, whose faces fair, whose fortunes are agreeable to your affections, enjoy and long enjoy the pleasure of your curled locks, the amiableness of your wished looks, the sweetness of your tuned voices, the content of your inward thoughts, the pomp of your outward shows; only Haebe biddeth farewell to all the joys that she conceived and you hope for, that she possessed and you shall; farewell the pomp of princes' courts, whose roofs are embossed with gold and whose pavements are decked with fair ladies, where the days are spent in sweet delights, the nights in pleasant dreams, where chastity honoureth affections and commandeth, yieldeth to desire and conquereth.
>
> . . .
>
> Come, Agar, thou unsatiable monster of maiden's blood and devourer of beauty's bowels, glut thyself till thou surfeit and let my life end thine. Tear these tender joints with thy greedy jaws, these yellow locks with thy black feet, this fair face with thy foul teeth. Why abatest thou thy wonted swiftness? I am fair, I am a virgin, I am ready. Come Agar, thou horrible monster, and farewell world thou viler monster.
>
> (V. ii. 25-55)

What would have been rather cloying without the spice of danger, what would have been rather heartless without these hints of flowery tenderness, becomes by the combination of the two a more affecting and effective image.

The loves of the all-female cast are brought to a happy conclusion in the only way possible—by sex-change or metamorphosis. It is often supposed, with Dr Johnson, that 'a new metamorphosis is a ready and puerile expedient'; and the onset of this trick for ending the play may be seen as marking a decline in Lyly's dramatic art. Actually, Lyly's adoption of this mode of denouement coincides with his adoption of the whole mode of play

construction which I have called 'harmonious variety', and can be seen as an integral part of its method. The plays I have dealt with as debates showed a controlling royal figure, who could end the play by rejecting the errors and re-establishing the right. But in *Gallathea* and the other plays of my second group the cast is not controlled from the centre in this way; the cast is grouped in such a way that there is a state of permanent unbalance, keeping the action in movement; balance can be restored at the end only by some *fiat* from outside. It may be that this is a poor thing beside a logical development based on character, but the latter is not possible within the terms of Lyly's art; the interest is focussed on the groups, and the individuals inside the groups are arranged to complement one another, not to establish separate individualities.

CAMPASPE

G. K. Hunter (essay date 1991)

SOURCE: "An Introduction to *Campaspe*," in *"Campaspe": "Sappho and Phao,"* by John Lyly, edited by G. K. Hunter and David Bevington, Manchester University Press, 1991, pp. 1-43.

[In the following excerpt, Hunter examines the source materials and traditions Lyly utilized in Campaspe.*]*

The historical occasion for the action of *Campaspe* was found by Lyly most probably in a source he employed several times in his play: Plutarch's life of Alexander, used apparently in the translation by Sir Thomas North. Plutarch tells us of Alexander's savage destruction of the city of Thebes and of the shock waves this event sent through the Greek world, felt particularly strongly in Athens. In this aftermath, we are told:

> Then the Grecians having assembled a general council of all the states of Greece within the straits of Peloponnesus, there it was determined that they would make war with the Persians. Whereupon they chose Alexander general for all Greece. Then divers men coming to visit Alexander, as well philosophers as governors of states, to congratulate with him for his election, he looked that Diogenes Sinopian (who dwelt at Corinth) would likewise come as the rest had done; but when he saw he made no reckoning of him, and that he kept still in the suburbs of Corinth at a place called Cranium, he went himself unto him . . .

The occasion of the play is thus set in a moment of peace between two destructive wars—Theban and Persian. Of the fear or the political calculation that may have driven the Greek city-states into this improbable harmony Lyly betrays no consciousness. The antithesis between peace and war, arts and arms, is central to Lyly's presentation; but he declines to consider the political na-

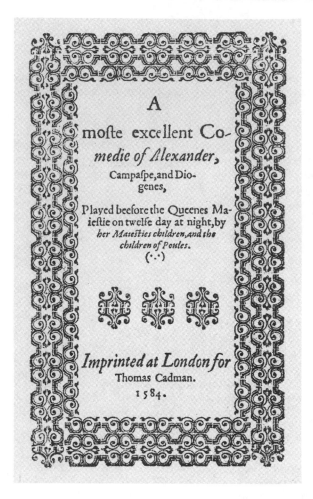

Title page of the 1584 edition of Campaspe.

ture of their interaction. The moment of peace is a moment when power relaxes and warriors play games—whether these be the 'authentic' Greek games of philosophy and art or the more modern diversions of courtly (or at least gentlemanly) love.

The love story that Lyly used was one that was already well known in art as in literature. By 1565/6 it had reached far enough down through the social classes to be entered in the Stationers' Register as the subject of a ballad: the 'history of Alexander, Campaspe, and Apelles, and of the faithful friendship between them'. The ballad itself, like most of its fellows, has not survived. One must assume, however, that it was not the vernacular spread of the story that attracted Lyly. On the contrary it was rather the fact that the story and its environment allowed him to draw (as he did) on a wide range of classical sources.

The thirty-fifth and thirty-sixth books of the *Natural History* of Pliny the Elder are concerned with the methods and personalities of the great Greek painters—Zeuxis, Parrhasius, Protogenes, etc.—among whom, says Pliny,

'Apelles surmounted all that either were before, or came after.' Within his elaborate and detailed account of Apelles, Pliny devotes two paragraphs to his relationship to Alexander the Great. He tells us of Apelles: 'Very courteous he was and fair spoken, in which regard King Alexander the Great accepted the better of him, and much frequented his shop in his own person.' In my book on Lyly [*John Lyly: The Humanist as Courtier*] I have tried to elaborate on the general problem for Renaissance artists (like Lyly) writing primarily for the world of court manners (or 'courtesy'). I suppose that Lyly saw the reported interchange between the 'king' (as he is called in Philemon Holland's translation of 1600) and the courteous artist by the light of this general problem. Pliny describes Apelles as a royal favourite: 'he [Alexander] gave straight commandment that no painter should be so hardy to make his picture but only Apelles'; and his story may be taken as a model of the constraints and opportunities afforded by such a role. Against the strain of sycophancy that might be expected to attach to Apelles' being so 'courteous and fair spoken', Pliny allows a certain freedom or capacity to assert oneself that attaches to the artist as a craftsman professing his own 'mystery'. When Alexander 'being in [Apelles'] shop would seem to talk much and reason about his art, and many times let fall some words to little purpose, bewraying his ignorance, Apelles after his mild manner would desire his grace to hold his peace, and said, "Sir, no more words, for fear the prentice boys there, that are grinding of colours, do laugh you to scorn"'. The key phrase here, for the court artist, is probably 'after his mild manner' (translating Pliny's *comitas,* the actual word that Lyly read). Apelles is said to have been able to exert his own sovereignty, in the area of his special expertise, without giving offence to his prince: 'So reverently thought the king of him, that being otherwise a choleric prince yet he would take any word at his hands in that familiar sort spoken in the best part, and be never offended.' The dangers of being a prince's favourite artist are not concealed here. In his reference to 'choleric prince' Pliny was no doubt remembering the murders of Philotas, Clitus and Parmenio, and especially that of Callisthenes—a case raised by Lyly himself (I.iii.79ff.)—who gave his prince wholesome philosophic advice, but not with the accomplished courtier's mild manner or familiar wit, and suffered torture and death as a consequence. The dangers for the Elizabethan artist were usually less drastic; but Pliny's emphasis on the manner or rhetoric by which a court artist can succeed must have seemed exemplary.

Pliny's next paragraph gives a specific instance of the reward that may come to a court artist whose independence is rendered tolerable by courtesy and fair language. Alexander, 'having among his concubines one named Campaspe whom he fancied especially above the rest . . . he gave commandment to Apelles for to draw her picture all naked: but perceiving Apelles at the same time to be wounded with the like dart of love as well as himself, he bestowed her upon him most frankly'. Pliny is, of course, making a point about the magnanimity of Alexander: 'In this act of his he won as much honour and glory as by any victory over his enemies, for now he had conquered himself.' But Pliny is also indicating the means by which Alexander, however 'great a commander and high-minded a prince he was otherwise', has been eased into acting magnanimously to a commoner; both prince and commoner have learned by the methods of 'courtesy' to allow the space occupied by the other. This is certainly the moral that Castiglione takes from the story:

> I believe Apelles conceived a far greater joy in beholding the beauty of Campaspes than did Alexander, for a man may easily believe that the love of them both proceeded of that beauty, and perhaps also for this respect Alexander determined to bestow her upon him that (in his mind) could know her more perfectly than he did. . . . And let them think that do enjoy and view the beauty of a woman so thoroughly that they think themselves in Paradise, and yet have not the feat of painting: the which if they had, they would conceive a far greater contentation, for then should they more perfectly understand the beauty that in their breast engendereth such heart's ease.
>
> [*The Courtier*]

Lyly stays close to the story that Pliny tells; but the difference that time and temperament have imposed on the meaning of the story is equally obvious. Campaspe is not, in Lyly's play, one of Alexander's favourite concubines (*'dilectam sibi ex pallacis suis praecipue'*); for an Elizabethan audience the love story could not be allowed to conform too closely to these antique manners. What is interesting here is less, however, the revision itself than the method by which Lyly throws his revisionary light on to the material. By a technique which recurs in his work— I shall discuss below its further use in the presentation of Diogenes and Apelles—Lyly brings into close proximity different aspects of behaviour, not so much, however, to achieve contrast as to suggest more central though paradoxical positions. We first meet Campaspe not as a concubine but as a humble Theban captive (and so likely enough to become a concubine). But she is not alone when we meet her: she is in the company of another lady whose condition she seems to share. This is Timoclea, the sister of Theagenes, the Theban general. It is she who does all the talking, while Campaspe stands by. And the talk of this formidable *grande dame* displays her military/aristocratic background. Timoclea's confrontation with Alexander is not that of captive with captor, but closer to that of Porus, the defeated Indian king, who told Alexander that he expected to be treated 'princely': for '"I comprehend all", said he, "in this word princely"'. Lyly here is obviously compressing into a few sentences the whole ethical import of the story Plutarch tells about Timoclea's conduct during the destruction of Thebes. A certain Thracian company, Plutarch tells us, 'spoiled and defaced the house of Timoclea, a virtuous lady of noble parentage'. Their captain, having raped Timoclea, demanded to know where he could find whatever gold and silver she had hidden. Timoclea pretended compliance and took the captain to a well where she said her treasure was stored. But when 'the barbarous Thracian stooped to look into the well she standing behind him thrust him in, and then threw stones on him and so killed him'. For this crime Timoclea was carried before Alex-

ander; he was so impressed by her 'noble answer and courageous deed' that he set her free. Timoclea had appeared at the English court in her own play ten years before *Campaspe*; presumably Lyly could draw on residual memories of this earlier and fuller presentation.

But his purpose here is not to revive admiration for the paragon; Timoclea is in this play only to affect our attitude to Campaspe. When Alexander has heard and admired Timoclea he turns to his second captive: 'But what are you, fair lady, another sister to Theagenes?' Campaspe denies that she is a duplicate Timoclea: 'No sister to Theagenes, but an humble handmaid to Alexander, born of a mean parentage but to extreme fortune' (I.i.81-5). Campaspe's humility and disposability take her close to the concubine status that Pliny describes; but the twinning with Timoclea in this scene (Timoclea never appears again) is sufficient to guarantee her a share of dignity. Lyly is in search of a paradoxical effect compounded of compliance and independence. The story requires Campaspe to appear both as a chattel and as an honourable individual with freedom of choice; and so Alexander responds immediately to Campaspe's statement of humility by conflating her status with that of Timoclea; both are equally 'ladies' in terms of 'virtues', 'whatsoever your births be' (II. 86-7).

I have already spoken about the relationship between Alexander and Apelles as a balance between freedom and constraint. Here again the achievement of the paradoxical balance arises from the combination of divergent sources. Pliny's account of Apelles' freedom of speech could hardly be reproduced by Lyly in the form in which he found it. Pliny speaks of Apelles' 'courtesy' and of his 'mild manner', as I have noted, but his account of Apelles' 'mild' rebuke to Alexander in the paint shop strikes the modern reader as something short of total complaisance. Certainly it is hard to imagine any such exchange between Elizabeth and a Tudor artist. And so Lyly's version of the scene places a further limitation on the artist's freedom of speech. There is now no reference to the paint boys laughing at the prince. Instead, we are given criticism which is evasive by its very brevity. When Lyly's Alexander tries to paint and then says to Apelles, 'But how have I done here?' Apelles is tight-lipped enough to reply only 'Like a king', leaving it for the magnanimous Alexander to turn the point against himself explicitly: 'but nothing more unlike a painter' (III.iv.126-8).

In taking away some of Apelles' freedom of speech Lyly might seem to have unsettled the balance between independence and duty which elsewhere he takes as his central point. It is perhaps with the aim of restoring this balance that he introduces into Pliny's story another figure, whose well-documented dealings with Alexander illustrate independence and freedom of speech with a total absence of awe—Diogenes. Diogenes of Sinope is probably the most famous free-speaker of antiquity, and the accounts of his sharp refusals to compromise with authority came to Lyly from every side of the Humanist tradition. The fullest list is in the *Lives of Eminent Phi-*

losophers by Diogenes Laertius, the source of most subsequent material. Laertius' biographies are more gossipy than analytic, at least as much concerned with smart sayings as with deep thoughts. And so the Life of Diogenes rivals that of Plato in length, but is little more than a string of epigrams, of sharp and unpalatable exposures of social custom and social hypocrisy, setting the sufficiency of self-denial against the greed, pride and ambition of the social world: 'He was great at pouring scorn on his contemporaries. The school of Euclides he called bilious, and Plato's lectures a waste of time, the performances at the Dionysia great peep-shows for fools, the demagogues the mob's lackeys.' His home in a tub, his one cloak folded for a bed, his lamp held up by daylight to look for an honest man—these famous characteristics or eccentricities have kept Diogenes in the sights of anecdotists and collectors of apophthegms, as in the medieval *Dictes and Sayings of the Philosophers* (among the earliest books printed in English) and in the widely read collections of Erasmus.

Erasmus's *Apophthegmata,* whence Lyly derived most of his Diogenes material, was careful in the dedication of the first edition to stress the morality of the form of the apophthegm, as one which (as it were) set a perpetual Diogenes against a perpetual Alexander, philosophic independence against the assumptions of authority. The one-liner is seen, that is, as having a necessary political function, 'none other kind of argument or matter [being] found more fit for a prince, especially being a young man, not yet broken in the experience of the world'. And again:

> The principal best sort of Apophthegms is that saying which in few words doth rather by a colour signify than plainly express a sense not common for every wit to pick out, and such a saying as no man could lightly feign by study and which the longer ye do consider it in your mind, the more and more it doth still delight you . . . most fit for princes and noble men, who for the urgent causes and busy matters of the commonwealth have not leisure to spend any great part of their life in study or in reading of books . . . no men's sayings are more taken up and used than those which be sauced with a certain grace of pleasant mirth[;] undoubtedly Socrates, Diogenes and Aristippus would serve better for teaching and training young children than either Xenocrates or else Zeno.

Erasmus gives more space to Diogenes than to any other philosopher, and the social situation which recurs most often is that in which Diogenes' quick answers denote his fearless independence of Alexander. The situation is given plausibility by revealing at the same time the other side of this Humanist ideal: Alexander's magnanimous allowance of Diogenes' refusal to conform. In this case the king's magnanimity cannot be explained by the courtesy and fair speaking of the interlocutor, since these are the qualities Diogenes is most resolute not to possess.

It is not difficult to understand the element of wish-fulfilment in this image of the glory that was Greece. The Humanists (and particularly the northern Humanists) were anxious to assert the importance of education in Greek texts and imitation of Greek culture as routes to a morality that was free of superstition and illiberal obedience. But the world in which they lived was a world of jealous warring principalities and nascent nation states. The histories of the Greek sophists, the orators and the paradoxical sages showed, though with a teasing fragmentariness, the possibility of a social role for learning and wisdom which was not simply to be absorbed into the life of the court but to be held in tension against it. Lyly's Diogenes is presented, of course, with all the comic exaggeration of an extreme instance, but that left aside, he represents well enough one side of the Humanist dream. Erasmus, with different rhetoric but similar aims, spent much of his life avoiding, eluding and declining the stultifying commitments of court or curial honour. The life of his coadjutor, Sir Thomas More, revealed the other side of the coin: commitment killed him.

The literary consequence of these attitudes also points towards Diogenes. Erasmus and More began their literary collaboration with translations and imitations of Lucian, and Lucian seemed in this period an obvious twin to Diogenes. Like Lucian and Diogenes, Erasmus and More chose, in their major literary works—the *Utopia* and *The Praise of Folly*—to use forms that combined philosophy and comedy, to 'play the fool', as it were, with matters too serious to be allowed a straightforward statement. Lyly's Diogenes likewise lives on the knife-edge of the same paradox. Clearly he pays his way theatrically by the knockabout farce he provides in his encounters with a series of low-life characters. In this sense he is the Clown of the piece. But the Athenian context frees the 'allowed fool' from the nervous jokiness of a household entertainer who can be whipped into obedience. In the Greek context his not belonging can be given the full force of a rational choice. It is a choice whose natural consequence is poverty and contempt, just as the natural consequence of Apelles' choice lies in the uneasy compromise he has to maintain between the hope of pleasing and the fear of falling. Lyly is not concerned to indicate a preference between these alternatives but rather, it would seem, to stress their co-existence as inevitable elements in court culture.

The use of Apelles and Diogenes to embody complementary alternative responses to princely authority (leaving the mid-point between them to appear equally desirable and unrealisable) imposes certain features on the conduct of the play. As alternatives they are normally presented alternately. Several scenes (II.ii; III.iii; V.iv) show Alexander dealing first with one and then the other, so that their different attitudes to the same royal power are brought into an obvious comparative relationship; but, understandably enough, they are never allowed to meet—what would they speak about? The artist's love of beauty places him in the direct line of court tastes and court rivalries, giving him immediate access to the centre of power but rendering him vulnerable to military and aristocratic contempt. The thinker or scholar, on the other hand, may claim exemption from such involvement. His pursuit should render him free from flattery or fashion; but his freedom is bought by the sacrifice of comfort and approval. Within the fiction of the play the magnanimity of Alexander allows both responses to achieve success. In the end the 'king' takes up his true role as a military leader; with careless generosity he simply abandons the effort to make Diogenes a court philosopher and, condemning love as unfit for princes, he abandons Campaspe to Apelles. The very arbitrariness of these decisions reminds us, however, that magnanimity cannot be relied on and that the dilemmas of the court artist may then have a crueler conclusion.

In his presentation of Diogenes and the other philosophers Lyly was following the example set by one of his predecessors as a court entertainer and entrepreneur of child acting, Richard Edwards. Edwards's one surviving play, *Damon and Pithias,* of 1565, takes us to the court of Dionysius the tyrant of Syracuse. We are introduced to this world by Diogenes' fellow-philosopher, Aristippus, here the resident court philosopher and favourite. But Dionysius is no Alexander and so Aristippus can have no space to act like Diogenes. Aristippus makes the difference between them quite explicit in his opening speech:

> Some philosophers in the street go ragged and torn
> And feeds on vile roots whom boys laugh to scorn;
> But I in fine silks haunt Dionysius' palace
> Wherein with dainty fare myself I do solace.
> . . . I profess now the courtly philosophy,
> To crouch, to speak fair, myself I apply,
> To feed the king's humour with pleasant devices,
> For which I am called *Regius canis.*
> But wot ye who named me first the king's dog?
> It was that rogue Diogenes, that vile grunting hog.
> Let him roll in his tub to win a vain praise.

The course of the play reveals the limitations on this 'courtly philosophy'. Aristippus wishes to differentiate himself from the rogue Diogenes at one end of the scale; he hopes equally to differentiate himself from mere parasites and flatterers at the other end. And that, as it turns out, is where the shoe really pinches. The court's ethical standards serve the whims of the tyrant, and the philosopher can maintain his balance only as long as he is permitted to do so. Aristippus is caught between his knowledge that Dionysius is wrong (and Damon and Pithias right) and the need to keep up with his principal rival for favour, the total flatterer Carisophus. And so Aristippus can neither speak out nor act well. True ethical standards have to be carried by the Athenian tourists, Damon and Pithias, who, though 'addicted to philosophy' (l. 444), offer no theories, proffer no advice, but act with such transparent virtue and unflinching self-sacrifice that the cruelty of the tyrant is at last overcome. As each of them in turn claims the right to die for his friend, Dionysius' 'spirits are suddenly appalled' (l. 1651). Even the executioner feels the effect: 'My hand with sudden fear quivereth' (l. 1660). These extraordinary effects, comparable to those that Plato describes as a consequence of the vision of The Good, show us that kings, though not amenable to philosophic instruction, may be changed by a real-life experience similar to

Christian conversion. Aristippus seems to be in the play principally to reveal the dilemma of courtly philosophy, and once he has done so he is allowed to vanish. His false theory makes him useless in practice; the summing-up devolves upon a less contaminated figure, Eubulus, the king's chief counsellor, who can take the practical steps to rescue Damon and Pithias as soon as the king's conversion allows it. In his mouth the doctrine that ideal friendship is a guiding star for kings' courts is plausible as it would not have been if spoken by the self-interested professional philosopher, Aristippus.

A comparison of Lyly's handling of this theme with Edwards's allows us to calculate the degree of indirection that Lyly employs. Lyly does not offer us anything as drastic as a threat of death or a religious conversion. Nevertheless, the strange and apparently dead-end scene of the philosophers' feast (I.iii) provides a cameo view of some of the harsher realities which, though evaded by Apelles and Diogenes, are undoubtedly part of the world in which they live. The scene should also be appreciated as a typical courtly 'show' of famous figures from the past. The 'Seven Sages' are represented here by philosophers from the various Greek schools (spread across several centuries) who engage in philosophic conversation of the type found in Cicero's *De Natura Deorum,* a principal source of the matter discussed. At the same time the context seems also designed to show up a natural contradiction between authority and thought, military obedience and freedom of speculation.

The scene begins with the summoning of the seven philosophers to attend their ruler. At the end of Alexander's previous appearance he had been hailed as Plato's ideal philosopher-king. Yet in this scene the attempt to realise the ideal is shown to be fraught with difficulties. Chrysippus is the first person invited; but he is too caught up in his thoughts to even notice the messenger, and this summoning has to be reported as a failure: as the messenger says, 'seeing bookish men are so blockish and so great clerks such simple courtiers, I will neither be partaker of their commons nor their commendations' (I.iii.10-12). Chrysippus' failure to notice the invitation (in fact he turns up later in the scene as a member of Alexander's 'academy') is only a preparative for the more self-conscious and principled refusal of 'an old obscure fellow who, sitting in a tub turned towards the sun, read Greek to a young boy' (ll. 14-16), a 'fellow' we are expected to recognise as Diogenes.

All the philosophers save only he—Aristotle, Plato, Cleanthes, Crates, Anaxarchus, Chrysippus—do what they are told and perform as they are instructed. 'They were not philosophers', says Hephestion in his blunt soldierly way, 'if they knew not their duties.' This is an interpretation of *de officiis* which reduces philosophy to panegyric. 'My court shall be a school wherein I will have used as great doctrine in peace as I did in war discipline', announces Alexander, though the very next point he makes shows how far soldierly discipline continues to dominate peace no less than war. The case of Callisthenes is raised, 'whose treasons against his prince shall not be borne out with the reasons of his philosophy'. This is a reply to Aristotle's flattering account of what 'literature' (books, reading, knowledge) can do to exalt a king. Alexander points to Callisthenes, Aristotle's relative, a philosopher-courtier whose love of truth did not (or rather will not) lead him to exalt the king but to 'seek to destroy' him. Such truth is not permissible, for 'in kings' causes I will not stand to scholars' arguments' (ll. 89-90). The philosophers have been summoned to court to speak acceptable truths or they may suffer punishment:

> 'This meeting shall be for a commandment that you all frequent my court, instruct the young with rules, confirm the old with reasons. Let your lives be answerable to your learnings, lest my proceedings be contrary to my promises.'

> (I.iii.90-4)

To illustrate what he means Alexander then makes the philosophers jump through the hoops of 'philosophic questions', one snappy question to each philosopher to be followed by an equally snappy answer. Lyly took this royal quiz-show from Plutarch's account of Alexander's dealings with his enemies the Gymnosophistae of India, where the questions were in fact court-martial issues of life and death: 'He did put them (as he thought) many hard questions, and told them he would put the first man to death that answered him worst, and so the rest in order.' In the event he spared them all; and in any case Lyly makes no reference to the life and death issue. But the example of Callisthenes, inserted into the dialogue, keeps something of the flavour of answering for dear life rather than for truth, as an important ingredient of this as of all court performances.

The absorption of the philosophers into court entertainment and their acceptance of this absorption make a point about the moral integrity of these sages, but it does not devalue philosophy itself. The sages enter discussing a central Humanist issue: the relationship between the philosophical conception of a First Mover and the religious conception of a personal God. This is a subject more Oxfordian than Athenian, but still indicative (and surely meant to seem so) of their concern with serious intellectual issues. Their subsequent decline into quiz-show contestants points up by contrast the philosophic integrity of the sage who is not present, Diogenes. The other philosophers visit Diogenes immediately after their interview with Alexander, and Lyly treats us then to a debate where the problem is very clearly set out. The duty of citizen Diogenes is to obey Alexander as the properly constituted authority (I accept without comment Lyly's quite un-Hellenic idea of the political arrangements), and this is what the other philosophers tell him. The duty of Diogenes as a seeker after truth and goodness is, however (as his answer indicates), quite separate: the role of the philosopher is to be on guard against courtly flattery and to protect the integrity of virtue by clowning and scorn and plain rudeness when required. And yet this unrelenting posture of rejection is shown to drive Diogenes into a narrow and even mechanistic response to the world. It is characteristic of Lyly's method that integrity here is

balanced against a concomitant rigidity of attitude, whether the conversation be with Chrysus, the rival Cynic (III.iv), the performing family of Sylvius (V.i), the courtesan Laïs and her bullies (V.iii), the assembled philosophers (I.iii), or Alexander himself (II.ii; V.iv). In these terms we can see integrity as not the good alternative to courtly flattery but only as an antithetical kind of limitation.

In *Campaspe* Lyly shows us the contrasting problems of painting and philosophy, art and thought, in the context of the court. He does not speak about literature. Still, it is easy to see that literary art straddles the two difficulties he does talk about. Literature involves conceptual thinking, like philosophy, while the social responsiveness of its content draws it into the orbit of court entertainment and so of royal flattery, like painting. The writer is thus involved in a search for both the independence of thinking and the intimacy of shared cultural communication. Are these compatible? As a court artist Lyly had to hope they were; but *Campaspe* shows his powerful awareness that only exceptional circumstances could make them so.

SAPPHO AND PHAO

David Bevington (essay date 1991)

SOURCE: "An Introduction to *Sappho and Phao*," in *"Campaspe": "Sappho and Phao,"* by John Lyly, edited by G. K. Hunter and David Bevington, Manchester University Press, 1991, pp. 141-95.

[*In the excerpt below, Bevington discusses Lyly's employment of allegory and the tradition of the comedy of courtship in* Sappho and Phao, *as well as his use of language in the play.*]

ALLEGORY

Lyly plainly intended his dramatic portrait of Sappho as a compliment to Queen Elizabeth, before whom the play was presented at court; although the play has other interests as well, Lyly's dramatic retelling of his many sources keeps this overriding consideration in mind. May he not then have used contemporary history as his most important source, relating through allegory an actual courtship in which Elizabeth triumphed over the entanglements of love? Sappho's obscure dream (IV.iii), like that of Cynthia in *Endymion,* seems to beg its audience to discern topical application; Sibylla enigmatically warns Phao against courtly aspiration and intrigue (II.I.140-57) in terms that seem to go beyond Phao's own situation; the observations of Trachinus and Pandion about a princely tree attacked by blasts, worms and caterpillars (I.ii.37-53) are plainly critical of flattery and suspicion in the

Sapho and Phao,

Played beefore the
Queenes Maieftie on Shroue-
tewfday, by her Maiefties
Children, and the Boyes
of Paules.

By *John Lilly*

Imprinted at London
for Thomas Cadman,
1584.

Title page of the 1584 edition of Sappho and Phao.

courts of princes; and the play's Epilogue expresses concern lest the auditors, entangled in a 'labyrinth of conceits', might misconstrue what they have seen through 'rash oversights'.

Historical criticism has indeed proposed an answer for these apparent puzzles: if Sappho is Elizabeth, then Phao must be the Duc d'Alençon, younger brother of the Duc d'Anjou who had wooed Elizabeth before. Alençon's suit, seriously renewed in 1578 at the instigation of Catherine de' Medici, served as the focus of delicate and prolonged negotiations between France and England. These negotiations were clearly designed by Elizabeth as a counterweight to her struggles with Philip of Spain, with whom also she had entertained the possibility of marriage. Whether serious or not in personal terms, the proposed match with Alençon had the status of state business and was much talked about at court. Alençon, the little 'Monsieur', was far from handsome, but Elizabeth had deigned to say in 1579 that 'she had never seen a man who pleased her so well, never one whom she could so willingly make her husband'. Nothing came of it, and on 6 February 1582 Alençon left England for good to assume the nominal sovereignty of the United Provinces in the Nether-

lands offered him by the Prince of Orange. He died on 9 June 1584, after an unsuccessful military attempt on the liberties of Antwerp in June of 1583.

To Bond, following up on Fleay's suggestion, the identification with Alençon explains a number of the play's most arresting features: the cautions of Prologue and Epilogue against overinterpretation; Sappho's dream; Sibylla's warning to Phao against ambition, which is 'appropriate only to Alençon's career at Court, and is not fulfilled in the play'; Trachinus' and Pandion's animadversions against worms and caterpillars attacking a princely tree; Sibylla's closing observation to Phao that 'destiny calleth thee as well from Sicily as from love', in which there is presumably an allusion to Alençon's installation as Duke of Brabant and his oath of allegiance as sovereign of the United Provinces; Lyly's suppression of what he learned from his sources (especially Ovid) about Sappho's poetic fame, her shortness of stature and her dark features; conversely Lyly's emphatic portrayal of Sappho as a queen surrounded by her court; and of course the story of Phao's invitation to court, Sappho's struggle with her emotions, and her conclusive victory over eros [R. Warwick Bond, ed., *The Complete Works of John Lyly,* 1902; Frederick Gard Fleay, *A Biographical Chronicle of the English Drama,* 1891]. The reading has been endorsed by Felix Schelling, Albert Feuillerat, Tucker Brooke, Evelyn May Albright and others [Schelling, *Elizabethan Drama, 1558-1642,* 1908; Feuillerat, *John Lyly,* 1910; Brooke, *The Tudor Drama,* 1911; Albright, *Dramatic Publication in England, 1580-1640*]. Frederick Boas wonders if the play does not serve the interests of one of Elizabeth's English suitors, such as Leicester, and Gertrude Reese similarly proposes that Lyly is expressing resentment of a French match and joy at Alençon's departure. Bond speculates that Catherine de' Medici may stand behind the figure of Sibylla, and supposes it likely that an original once existed for the witty Mileta and her flirtatiousness with Phao. Fleay . . . identifies Pandion with Lyly himself.

Despite this unanimity of opinion among many historical critics, and the absence of any rival topical interpretation, the Alençon claim seems impossible. A topical theory of dating has to suppose a court performance on 27 February in 1582, a scant three weeks after Alençon's departure from England, and must therefore argue that writing, theatrical preparation, and perhaps even performances at Blackfriars took place while the affair of Alençon had not yet ended. If Lyly's intent was to capitalise on feelings against the proposed French match, he has made Phao surprisingly sympathetic. Whatever Elizabeth may have said about Alençon, Phao's gift of extraordinary beauty would seem oddly and even ludicrously out of place in view of Alençon's ugliness. No historical person has been proposed for Venus as Sappho's rival, whereas for an audience interested in guessing at the meaning of a *roman à clef* this sort of rivalry would be a prime matter of titillation.

Most tellingly, perhaps, the portrait of Sappho in love is hardly flattering if applied to any particular incident. Sappho must compensate for Phao's reticence by a barely disguised hinting at her own passionate feeling (III.iv.42-88). With her women she is moody, restless, demanding; in soliloquy and song she is frantic and desperate (III.iii). Even though Sappho eventually conquers love's tyranny, like Alexander, the suggestion that Elizabeth went through this kind of lovesickness for Alençon would be tactless and inappropriate. Nor could England's queen be supposed to have suffered clinically thus for any of her other wooers, English or otherwise. Elizabeth's reluctance to accept advice on the marriage question, and indeed her readiness to interrupt or abruptly leave any sermon or other utterances deemed offensive, were well enough known to deter even her most intrepid critics, let alone those like Lyly who sought her support.

If on the other hand we view Lyly's play as an allegory of love, these difficulties begin to disappear. Lyly's alteration of his sources requires nothing more topical than to say, as we must, that Sappho is intended to flatter Elizabeth. The portrait is scarcely more personal than that of Alexander in *Campaspe*. A monarch, adored by her subjects and drawn briefly into a strong affection for one of them, chooses singleness of life as best befitting her responsibilities to the entire kingdom. Sappho is portrayed as queen rather than as poet to accentuate her royal function, and the enhancement of her beauty as compared with Ovid's portrait is part of the conventional and outrageous flattery Elizabeth came to expect everywhere. Phao is beautiful to make him worthy of love by so excellent a queen. Phao's ultimate destiny, that of worshipping Sappho from a distance, 'my loyalty unspotted though unrewarded' (V.iii.22), justly portrays the kind of acquiescing and self-abnegating loyalty Elizabeth encouraged in those who served her; it is the kind of Platonic love between grateful subject and graceful ruler we find again in Endymion's selfless service to Cynthia. As in *Endymion,* the political nature of the allegory of love acts to discourage rather than to encourage particular claims on Elizabeth's affection. Lyly's portrait centres on Elizabeth but is generic.

The role of Venus in *Sappho and Phao,* for which the proposed historical equation offers no key, is essential to an understanding of the play's allegory of love. Venus' role is complex, perhaps even inconsistent: she acts at times like an emotional woman, at times like the classical deity, at times like the allegorical figure of the Queen of Love. Nevertheless, as Bernard Huppé argues, [in "Allegory of Love in Lyly's Court Comedies," *ELH* 14, No. 2, June 1947], the allegorical meaning of her unsuccessful attempt to ensnare Sappho is clear enough: it is 'the story of the conquest by a great queen of the urgings of passionate love, her steadfast refusal to accept anything but true spiritual love, a marriage of true minds'. As in all allegories, Venus is a fictional representation of an idea or emotion, not an external foe who may be blamed for failure but a distillation of the power of love as it operates in the human heart. The allegorist invents visible things to express immaterial fact. If Sappho were to be conquered by Venus, the meaning would be that Sappho has succumbed to her own passion.

Lyly's portrayal of Venus embodies the misogynistic proposition, often stated in the play, that any woman will yield in time, and that if Phao uses the arts of seduction set forth in Ovid's *Ars Amatoria* and urged on him by Sibylla he is sure to succeed. Yet Phao is in no way Sappho's equal; if she were to accept his love, she would be succumbing passionately to outward beauty only. Clearly she must hold to the ideal of a marriage of true minds and must therefore heroically resolve not to yield; it would shame her to 'embrace one so mean' (IV.i.18-19). Her incomparable superiority to Venus is in affirming a virtue without which true love is impossible. The affirmation is crucial for Lyly, not merely as flattery to Elizabeth but more broadly as a way of idealising love and womanhood, of countering the seductive image of woman (and of man's basely passionate nature as well) with a spiritualised vision of woman as deserving of man's worship.

Lyly's problem as allegorical dramatist was to devise forms of expression in drama through which he might convey the complex emotions of love. Drama relies on external and visible behaviour; love is pre-eminently internal and intimate. Lyly did of course have numerous models for the application of allegory to the experience of love. He knew the medieval and Renaissance traditions of allegorising Ovid, as in Arthur Golding's Preface to his sixteenth-century translation of *Metamorphoses,* where Phaeton is equated with 'the nature of blind ambition', Daphne with 'the mirror of chastity', and the like. For Golding, the pagan deities (including Venus and Cupid) are not gods but rather symbols of 'Some further things and purposes by those devices meant'. Lyly knew pageants, royal entries and other public entertainments that ceaselessly glorified the Tudor monarchy in the person of Arthur or apostrophised Elizabeth as Truth or Astraea. Allegorical poems like *Le Chasteau d'Amour* created elaborate external forms for the vicissitudes of courtship, and morality drama brought such figures as Contrition and Lust-in-Liking onstage to externalise the states of mind of the protagonist. The popular literary genre of dream allegory gave Lyly a precedent and model not only for his symbolic dreams but also for his conceiving the whole of *Sappho and Phao* as though it were Queen Elizabeth's own dream allegory: 'I on knee for all, entreat that your Highness imagine yourself to be in a deep dream that, staying the conclusion, in your rising your Majesty vouchsafe but to say, "And so you awaked"' (Prologue at Court). Still, the devices of allegory available to Lyly in this manifold tradition were more proficient in symbolising conflict between rival ideologies than in capturing the feeling of what it is like to be in love. As Robert Y. Turner rightly insists, [in "Some Dialogues of Love in Lyly's Comedies," *ELH* XXIX, 1962], English comedy did not really dramatise love in any psychological sense before Lyly began writing plays.

Given the kinds of allegory he knew, what means were at Lyly's disposal to express through outward gesture and dialogue what the heart feels? The available solutions, according to Turner, were not quite satisfactory; characters might simply assert their significance in the conventional language of allegory, or conversely the action might take on a momentum of its own essentially devoid of inward illumination. The latter danger is evident in comedies of romantic adventure in the 1570s, such as *Clyomon and Clamydes* or *Common Conditions,* with their tales of separation and hair's-breadth escape. Lyly's art is seemingly closer to the former model, that of didactic allegorical instruction, as when, in *Sappho and Phao,* the court ladies suggest through their various dreams their varying and typical attitudes towards romantic love (IV.iii), or when Venus explains to Cupid the allegorical significance of six arrows made in Vulcan's forge (V.i). Sibylla uses all the Ovidian commonplaces of advice in love when she warns Phao against ambition or coaches him in the rules of courtly wooing and gamesmanship. Yet Lyly's use of schematic dialogue of this kind, more literary than dramatic, is seemingly part of a conscious strategy on his part to go beyond such traditional allegory; he presents to us the highly formal and emblematic world of allegorical representation that he knew so well in order that we can measure by contrast the real innovation of his more successful love dialogue.

In other words, even while *Sappho and Phao* remains a love allegory in which characters like Venus and Cupid abstractly represent states of mind in the play's central figures, this comedy manages for the first time on the English stage to crystallise into outward gestures what is felt deeply within, in the experience of love. It does so, as Turner explains, by exploring tension, misunderstandings and the limiting qualities of ambiguous language. When Sappho and Phao meet, the social barrier between them causes them to speak enigmatically, partly from fear and partly from a sensitivity to love's delicacy. The tension between unfavourable circumstance and the lovers' unspoken desire 'creates dialogue in which each assertion is tentative and each response quivering'; though love is never mentioned directly, their conversation both poignantly and wittily 'captures an unmistakable sense of what it is like to be in love'. We as audience understand more than the lovers can communicate to one another and are thus privileged by a kind of dramatic irony or discrepant awareness that at once detaches our feelings through knowledge of the situation and intensifies our perception of poignancy in a love that is so nearly successful and yet so impossible.

The tension between desire and prohibition generates as well a series of dramatic situations in which the limitations of language express the predicament of love. Sappho and Phao, unable to speak of love directly, must turn to the language of medicine and sickness, or speak in parables of Jason and Medea, or pun on the word *yew* (you); among her women, Sappho's talk of her discomfort repeatedly suggests hidden meaning (III.iv; III.iii). Inhibited from saying what they feel, the lovers 'dramatize by their oblique expressions both their trapped situation and the desire to break out of it'.

That Lyly is able to convey this insight into love through stage action and dialogue, while still retaining in his play the symbolic language of formal love allegory and the conventional allegorical mode of externalised personification, is an index of the play's innovation. It is well summed up in G. Wilson Knight's tribute to Lyly as one who, with love as his whole theme, is as aware as is Spenser of its complexities, yet 'is more aware than Spenser of its inward contradictions' ["John Lyly," *R.E.S.* XV, 1939]. The interplay of innovation and convention is also suggested in Paul Olsen's comparison of Lyly and Jonson as dramatists writing for a court 'consistently interested in that art which builds its meaning from the materials of traditional emblems and allegories' ["*A Midsummer Night's Dream* and the Meaning of Court Marriage," *ELH* XXIV, 1957].

With this perspective on Lyly's reshaping of allegorical tradition, we are perhaps in a position to measure the import of dreams and other enigmatic statements in the play that seem to invite topical interpretation. Sappho's dream (IV.iii) pictures a stock-dove nesting in a tall cedar only to lose its feathers and fall to the ground, while ants and caterpillars attack the tree and strip away many of its leaves. The dreamer pities both, and takes heart at the bird's attempt to fly up again; the dreamer in fact wishes that the tree might bow to assist the bird, but wakens before this can happen. In this dream ants and caterpillars certainly suggest parasitism and factionalism at court, as do the drones or beetles creeping under the wings of the princely eagle in Cynthia's dream in *Endymion* (V.i), and Lyly's audience might well posit a criticism of those who competed for Elizabeth's favour while preying upon the commonwealth like the 'caterpillars' of *Richard II*.

Such an identification militates against any interpretation that seeks to align Lyly with any particular claim to Elizabeth's favour. On the other hand, the dream is generally consistent with the love allegory in that it invites sympathy for a royal figure drawn to the love of a commoner and expresses an emotional wish that such a union were possible while insisting finally on its impossibility. Phao, like the stock-dove, is beautiful, but his very beauty is disfigured by an unwarranted ambition; his rising again is possible only when he learns, like Endymion, to worship platonically from afar. On a dramatic level the dream is expressive of Sappho's own flickering hope and final resolution; like other allegories in the play, it provides a language of indirection through which she may safely externalise inner conflict.

In a similar way, Sibylla's warnings to Phao against ambition (II.i.140 ff.) have a topical cast without requiring any more detailed hypothesis than a love allegory shaped for the queen's benefit. The imagery is close to that in Sappho's dream, for Phao is cautioned not to keep company with ants that have wings. He is to avoid talk of eclipses of the sun and other such omens of royal catastrophe. He is to gaze upward in worship rather than downward in envy, and is to avoid the ambitious gesture of pointing above him. Naturally he is to expect hatred if he is favoured by a prince's affection. These prophetic utterances do exceed the nature of Phao's own thoughts at the moment he hears them, for he is not yet in love with

Sappho or moved by any desire to leave his life as a ferryman. The generic character of the advice certainly invites allegorical interpretation, but not to the extent of invoking Alençon's suit, since, like Sappho's dream, the delphic wisdom has application to all princes, including Elizabeth and any or all of her courtiers. The advice is dramatically expressive of Phao's emotional situation even if he is unaware of the applicability, for the audience knows already of Venus' designs on him.

So too with delphic passages elsewhere in the play. The disapproval of Trachinus and Pandion for 'blasts and water boughs, worms and caterpillars' brought by eastern wind to attack the princely tree (I.ii) is unambiguously about flattery and deception at court, but is justified by the debate of courtier and philosopher over the merits of their respective ways of life. Phao's call to destiny at the end of the play is in keeping with Sibylla's penchant for prophetic statement and with our sense that Phao, like Endymion, is no ordinary courtier but rather the embodiment of those who will continue to worship Elizabeth even as they carry out in far-flung realms her royal commands. Even Tucker Brooke, while accepting the outline of the Alençon reading, wisely concludes as follows: 'Altogether, it seems clear that the story of the play, instead of reflecting in detail the real incidents of contemporary history, is rather a tissue of harmlessly imaginary pictures shot through with idealized references to such actual happenings as the poet might feel to be wholly devoid of offence to his royal auditress.'

THE COMEDY OF COURTSHIP

Along with their achievement of being the first comedies in English to evoke, beneath externally allegorised action, a deeply felt inner emotion of love, Lyly's comedies are also the first English plays in which love itself provides the mainspring of the comedy. In this latter regard, **Sappho and Phao** has a particular claim to priority, since even more than **Campaspe** it gives us a courtly world in which love is, as Marco Mincoff says, 'at once something highly serious and extremely frivolous' ["Shakespeare and Lyly," *Shakespeare Survey* 14, 1961]. Love is the 'centre of existence' both for the wooers themselves and for the courtiers who amuse themselves with gossip about the emotional entanglements of great persons. Mincoff's point is that in Lyly 'the mere fact of being in love almost is treated as a comic situation', as indeed it is for Ovid in his *Ars Amatoria*. Lyly's theme is the way in which love 'cuts across our little plans and makes fools of us'. Love is also for him an elaborate game, something to occupy the time of a leisured but narrowly circumscribed world at court in which the attentions paid to women are an essential part of the courtier's self-image.

This 'love-game comedy', as David Stevenson terms it [in his *The Love-Game Comedy,* 1946], is first developed by Lyly in the ritualistic love-encounters of **Euphues,** where we find the customary lovesickness, the stark contrast between exalted Petrarchan ideals and sexual desire, the self-abasement and betrayal, the witty duels between lovers and their ladies, the amorous skirmishes expressed in sophisticated banter. **Sappho and Phao** makes considerable use of this tradition. Phao is nearly speechless at his first sight of Sappho; both he and Sappho suffer the physical anguish of lovers. Sibylla advises Phao in Ovidian fashion that love is to be 'governed by art', that 'women desire nothing more than to have their servants officious', that he must 'be prodigal in praises and promises', and that he would be well advised to 'look pale and learn to be lean, that whoso seeth thee may say the gentleman is in love' (II.iv.61-113). The chief love relationship in **Sappho and Phao** is set in comic perspective by our awareness of the elaborate rules supposed to govern courtship.

At the same time, Lyly constantly undercuts the artifice of such courtly codes by the refreshingly irreverent insights of those who find love amusing. Sappho's lady-in-waiting, Mileta, professes to 'laugh at that you all call love, and judge it only a word called love' (I.iv.16-17). To her it is 'good sport' to see men vacuously falling back on what they call good manners, 'having nothing in their mouths but "Sweet mistress", wearing our hands out with courtly kissings when their wits fail in courtly discourses—now ruffling their hairs, now setting their ruffs, then gazing with their eyes, then sighing with a privy wring by the hand, thinking us like to be wooed by signs and ceremonies' (I.iv.38-45). She makes a blatant attempt to woo Phao (III.iv) and is understandably affronted when he adopts a chivalrous line with her. Sappho's other ladies-in-waiting all have their different experiences and attitudes in the relations of the sexes. The play offers us multiple points of view about the game of love, distancing us from it, encouraging an Ovidian comic view of its folly by means of a diverse perspective. Shakespeare's *As You Like It,* with its various views on love propounded by Orlando, Rosalind, Touchstone, Jaques and the rest, uses a similar dramatic technique.

The multiple perspective serves chiefly, through contrast, as a means of our understanding the love relationship of Sappho and Phao. They are not coy and flirtatious, like Mileta, nor driven to cynicism by hard experience like Sibylla (or Euphues). Any love affair of a monarch, reflecting as it does on Elizabeth, is necessarily of a higher order. Nonetheless their love affair is essentially comic too in Mincoff's terms; even without strutting, preening and coquetry, the comedy of their love 'lies mainly in the desperate earnestness with which the lovers pursue what is mostly a very unsuitable affair. They are at bottom only playing a game, though compelled to it by Cupid, and they are as miserable over it as any tragic hero'. Their conversation of 'misunderstood innuendos' is enriched and complicated in comic fashion by the fact that both are 'too self-absorbed to grasp the other's meaning'. Sappho, sustained throughout her tribulations by her dignity as queen, sees at last (though only when hit by Cupid's leaden shaft) what is ridiculous in her own behaviour. Lyly's comedy of courtship, then, points to its own solution: if erotic love is ridiculous, it must be renounced by those who cannot afford to be ridiculous and who cannot also find perfect equality in love. The ending not only flatters Elizabeth but more broadly expresses a judgement about love that is inherent in Lyly's conception of its frivolous and yet serious nature.

Comedy of this delicate sort represents a departure from the farce and slapstick characteristic of much earlier English comedy. Lyly's awareness of innovation is evident in his Blackfriars Prologue, where he speaks of an intent to 'move inward delight, not outward lightness, and to breed (if it might be) soft smiling, not loud laughing, knowing it to the wise to be as great pleasure to hear counsel mixed with wit as to the foolish to have sport mingled with rudeness' (quoted in Mincoff). Lyly allies himself with those who banished 'apish actions' and 'immodest words' from the Roman and Greek stages, and promises in his own art to be 'far from unseemly speeches to make your ears glow'. An appeal to a sophisticated courtly audience combines here with veneration for classical art and humanistic ideals to produce a kind of literary manifesto. It proclaims what Hunter [In *John Lyly: The Humanist as Courtier,* 1962], employing a phrase of George Meredith's, terms 'high comedy', fulfilling as it does Sir Philip Sidney's wish to see in England a 'right comedy' free of scurrility and doltishness fit only for loud laughter.

Indeed, *Sappho and Phao* nicely illustrates the marriage of 'delight' and 'laughter' called for in *The Defence of Poesy* (1595), one in which laughter is mixed with 'delightful teaching'. Sidney offers the subject of Hercules in woman's attire and spinning at Omphale's commandment as an example of what can breed delight and laughter together, 'for the representing of so strange a power in love procures delight, and the scornfulness of the action stirreth laughter'. Lyly is surely aiming at a similar effect. By poking fun at love in all its delightful follies, by inviting smiles at the familiar martyrdom of lovers and the scorn of witty court ladies while insisting at the same time on love's idealism, Lyly moves towards a more rarefied and elegant comedy than the English stage had known, one that (in Mincoff's terms) 'raises a sigh, half sympathetic, half acquiescent, over human nature itself'. To this comedy of courtship Shakespeare is particularly indebted, even though his independence of courtly rules and his freer acceptance of courtship as a prelude to marriage enables him to move well beyond his predecessors (Lyly among them) towards comic resolutions that are satisfactory in purely human terms.

The failure of *Sappho and Phao* to acclaim sexual love or to resolve the difficulties of its protagonists in celebratory marriage, so typical of Lylyan comedy, raises questions of attitude on the part of the dramatist and his courtly audience that go well beyond the particular need to flatter Elizabeth. Mary Beth Rose [in "Moral Conceptions of Sexual Love in Elizabethan Comedy," *Renaissance Drama* n.s. XV, 1984] examines the issue in the context of Elizabethan attitudes towards marriage. For the upper classes in particular, marriage was the basis of property settlement and alliance between powerful fam-

ilies, and in such a case sexual love was not only an improper basis of union but also all too apt to be in conflict with overriding economic and dynastic considerations. Although the Renaissance saw conjugal loyalty and affection replace celibacy as the more socially sanctioned pattern of sexual conduct, erotic love was still often viewed as essentially incompatible with marriage. Neoplatonism, associated in the English mind with Petrarchism, encouraged (as did Christianity) a mistrust of erotic desire as incommensurate with higher idealism in love. Attempts to reconcile these divergent impulses were at times notably successful, as in Spenser's *Four Hymns* and Donne's 'The Extasie', but the conflict remained. It took the form of a polarising consciousness in which women were alternately idealised and debased.

Lyly's art represents, for Rose, an encounter between 'the dualizing, idealizing Petrarchan sensibility to which he was heir' and a newer, more pragmatic view of marriage to which Shakespeare had greater access. The polarising consciousness is everywhere apparent in the idealising raptures men make about women in *Euphues* and the blatant misogyny to which the men eventually succumb. With worship or lust as the sole alternatives available, Lyly's protagonist in *Euphues* can see love only as a compulsive, impersonal and ridiculous passion. In these same terms, *Sappho and Phao* is dominated by an uneasy mixture of cynical statements about the availability of women and idealisation of the play's central figure. The conflict of Venus and Sappho is rooted in this polarising antipathy. Small wonder then that the play ends in a victory over base desire by a woman who thereby earns the everlasting Platonic devotion of her male worshipper. However powerful and unavoidable sexual desire may be, it can form no part of the play's resolution. Only with the wider acknowledgement of moral prestige in love and marriage, and greater acceptance of a kind of equality in the marital relationship (though still within the limits of a patriarchal structure), is English drama capable of the romantic comedy produced by Shakespeare in the 1590s. If one is tempted to conclude, with Hereward Price, that 'Lyly does not like women', the reasons may have something to do with Lyly's courtly world and its ambivalent view of sex and marriage [Price, "Shakespeare and His Young Contemporaries," *Philological Quarterly* XL1, 1962].

The Language of Play

Lyly was once regarded [by John Addington Symonds, in *Shakespeare's Predecessors,* 1884] as a writer whose 'Dresden china style of antiquated compliment', no matter how prettily turned and no matter how influential in the development of English prose in the 1580s and '90s, was ornament divorced from substance and so unvaried in its exotic mannerisms as to be unsuited for true dramatic dialogue. His imagery, in the view of Frederic Ives Carpenter [in *Metaphor and Simile in the Minor Elizabethan Drama,* 1895], is 'entirely ornamental', is 'adventitious, not a part of the thought', and is 'largely imitative of foreign models'. The distinguishing features of Euphuism—its isocolon (the even balancing of parallel clauses of equal length), its paramoion (the even balancing in parallel clauses of recurrent sounds), its parison (the even balancing in parallel clauses of grammatical parts of speech), its use of alliteration (similar sound at the beginning of parallel words or phrases) and *similiter cadens* (similarity at the end), its word-repetitions and polyptoton (the repetition of one stem with different inflectional endings), its use of analogy from fabulous natural history, its apostrophes and set pieces of declamation—were widely regarded as 'figures of sound' rather than 'figures of thought'.

To accentuate this seeming contrast between style and substance is to miss the importance of antithetical structure in Lyly's way of thinking and in his play construction. As Jonas Barish points out [in "The Prose Style of John Lyly," *ELH* 23, No. 1, March 1956], parison is not simply a figure of sound, though it is frequently paired with sound effects; the arrangement of grammatical parts of speech in parallel phrases is a syntactic procedure implying its own logical structure. Parison is antithetical in its expression and in its content, and, as Albert Feuillerat observes [in his *John Lyly*]. Lyly is unable to conceive his ideas other than through the encounter of two opposing things; he makes associations in terms of antithetical contrasts. Lyly's antitheses, according to Barish, either define one thing by its opposite, or hold two possibilities in equilibrium, or assert the paradoxical coexistence of contending properties in a single phenomenon. Each kind of antithesis has its consequences; especially in the third or paradoxical kind of antithesis, we see that like engenders unlike and that inner self-contradiction is an essential condition of human nature.

This self-contradiction regularly takes the form of antagonism between substance and appearance: 'the more absolute of its kind a thing may appear to be, the more certain it is that somewhere within it lies its own antithesis, its anti-self' (Barish). The correspondences and the antipathies are ranged side by side in Lyly so as to unveil 'the contradictions in nature, the infinite inconsistency of the world'. Lyly's examples from fabulous natural history are always applied to human conduct, enabling us, as G. Wilson Knight puts it, 'to read the human mind in terms of the living physical universe'. Human feelings and the universe alike display contradiction. At the same time Lyly's antithetical thought is deeply logical, seeking to show the composite nature of experience as well as its contradictory nature, and using the debate as its most characteristic structural device.

The merger of antithetical style and thought, so admirably suited to the long declamations of *Euphues*, is no less expressive of dramatic conflict in *Sappho and Phao*. The characters are arranged in a series of overlapping antithetical pairs: Vulcan and Venus, Venus and Sappho, Sappho and Phao, Cupid in relation to all these, Phao and Mileta, Trachinus and Pandion, Criticus and Molus, Molus and Callipho. Each of these pairings gives rise to verbal antitheses employing all the sound-repeating de-

vices of Euphuism, as for instance when Venus says of her unlikely liaison with Vulcan: 'It is no less unseemly than unwholesome for Venus, who is most honoured in princes' courts, to sojourn with Vulcan in a smith's forge, where bellows blow instead of sighs, dark smokes rise for sweet perfumes, and for the panting of loving hearts is only heard the beating of steeled hammers' (I.i.21-6).

In the soliloquies of Phao and Sappho, similarly, the mind at debate with itself generates for every claim a counterclaim. Phao rehearses the arguments against his ambition even in the midst of his longing for Sappho (II.iv). The queen expresses her dilemma in a series of natural analogies: the sun shines all day only to dip its head in the ocean, certain herbs are saltier the further they grow from the sea, and the like (III.iii). The logic of antithesis provides both lovers with a means of gaining perspective on the inherent contradiction in their behaviour and hence of attempting to control that behaviour. It provides the audience with sympathy and distance through which the inevitability of the play's unromantic conclusion can be grasped.

One way to measure the pervasive presence of antithesis in the content as well as in the form of **Sappho and Phao** is to consider the many topics that are more or less formally debated, either in soliloquy or, more often, between rival speakers. The topics are at once numerous and interrelated. The focus of Phao's deliberations when we first meet him is the contrast between riches and the simple life, between ambition and contentment with one's lot (I.i; II.i). This debate takes on particularity in the contrast of court and countryside, or the pen (with which to write love sonnets) and the oar (V.iii.12-13). A related antithesis pits the court versus the university, good manners versus learning, and the enjoyment of power and influence versus the poverty of scholars; these matters are seriously discussed by Trachinus and Pandion (I.ii) and more lightheartedly by their pages, Criticus and Molus (I.iii; II.iii; III.ii). The pages also have fun with the supposed merits and demerits of logical reasoning, in a *jeu d'esprit* that seems irrelevant to the play until one considers what has already been said here about the importance of logic in coming to terms with contradictory thought.

The play's etiquette-book survey of the correct way for men and women to behave in love is a debate with major implications for the central figures. Should Phao follow Sibylla's Ovidian advice and play the cynical game of courtship for all it is worth? Will all women eventually succumb to male stratagems? May women take the initiative in wooing? Is chaste affection superior to erotic love? What is the nature of sovereignty, the right relation of sovereign to subject, the suitable place of love in the sovereign's life? The antithetical pairing of Venus and Sappho is, in these terms, a stating of alternative positions about the essential nature of women (especially royal women) and hence of men's relationship to women. Other debates in the play stem from those already mentioned: the relationship of spiritual to physical sickness (III.iii), the nature of dreams (IV.iii), the right use of clothes or of making of oaths by one in love (I.iv), the right way to conduct a duel (II.iii), the use or abuse of cosmetics (II.i), proper and improper table manners (III.ii). The emphasis on manners is not, as it frequently seems, merely superficial, in that the antithetical possibilities offer particular means of evaluating the major choices available to the play's central characters.

Word-play in Lyly is highly antithetical, and as such offers yet another opportunity for the characters to explore the inherent contradictions they face. 'Thou art a *ferry*-man, Phao, yet a *free* man,' Phao begins the play, expressing in the similarity of sound the paradox of servitude to labour and freedom from ambition. 'Thou *farest* delicately if thou have a *fare* to buy anything.' As Geoffrey Tillotson demonstrates, [in "The Prose of Lyly's Comedies," *Essays on Criticism and Research,* 1942], *Sappho and Phao* is (like all of Lyly's writing) remarkably self-conscious about words and their meanings. 'Thou dost not flatter thyself, Phao, thou art fair,' says Phao to himself after receiving Venus' gift of beauty. 'Fair? I fear me "fair" be a word too foul for a face so passing fair' (II.i.6-8). Ismena similarly looks askance at verbal signs and what they signify: 'I laugh at that you all call love, and judge it only a word called love' (I.iv.16-17).

The scepticism is understandable in a play that deals so often, and with such evident cynicism, in the rhetoric of persuasion. Sibylla plies Phao with Ovidian advice on the uses of language and gesture to woo a lady (II.i, iv), Cupid counsels Venus to beg of Vulcan the arrows that can turn Sappho's heart to disdain, and Venus uses her most flattering wiles to obtain her will from Vulcan, who knows well enough that he is being manipulated: 'Because you have made mine eyes drunk with fair looks, you will set mine ears on edge with sweet words' (IV.iv.21-3). The central proposition tested in this play, that all women or men can sooner or later be seduced, is essentially a proposition about language. It is answered at last by Sappho's persuasive wooing of Cupid to the cause of virtue, and by the dramatist's own metaphors of disentanglement of meaning in his Epilogue, but not before the power of language to do good has been called into question.

As a consequence of this testing of the validity of language, words often contain within them the paradoxes and contradictions characteristic of the Lylyan style as a whole; despite their seeming absoluteness, words too reveal an inner antithesis or anti-self. Words are repeated often in *Sappho and Phao,* and almost invariably with a change of meaning suggestive of the contrast between physical substance and a hidden inner truth. Sappho in bed has no recourse to expression other than to play on the medical terms being used by her anxious ladies-in-waiting (III.iii). When they urge her to have more bedclothes and 'sweat it out', that is, sweat out the fever, she replies that her best ease is to 'sigh it out'. *Disease* to them means 'illness' and to her 'absence of ease', *desire* is both 'request' and 'passionate craving', *feel* is 'perceive physically' and 'experience mentally', *burning* means 'feverish' and 'inflamed with passion'.

The entire extended dialogue up to l. 24 is a tour de force of such changes and witty demonstrations of the author's verbal pyrotechnics, and yet it is also a poignant way of showing Sappho's frustrated ability only to hint at what may not be openly said. The technique is strikingly anticipatory of Shakespeare's use of double entendre to reflect conflict that cannot be stated openly, as when Juliet parries her mother's invective against Romeo with double-edged comments—'Would none but I might venge my cousin's death', III.iv.86—or when Hamlet similarly answers his uncle and mother: 'Ay, madam, it is common' (I.ii.74).

Other characters in *Sappho and Phao* make similar use of wordplay. Mileta and Pandion employ medical parlance in their verbal encounter at III.i: *cold* means variously 'a respiratory illness', 'the opposite of heat', and (as an adjective) 'dispirited', while *physic* means 'medical knowledge' or 'a purge'. *Male-content* is used as a form of 'malcontent' to make explicit the contrast with 'female content'. The witty word games and logical demonstrations of the pages often turn absurdly on word definitions: 'Thou art a smith, therefore thou art a smith.' Language seems in fact to be capable of proving anything: 'as sure as he is a smith', says Criticus to Callipho, 'thou art a devil' (II.iii.87-94). Word-play is an essential element not simply of Lyly's style but of his antithetical vision of the hard search for truth.

Along with this seriousness of word-play, we do of course find distinctively playful aspects in Lyly's language. Euphuism can in fact be viewed as a kind of game, even if, as Jocelyn Powell argues [in "John Lyly and the Language of Play," in *Elizabethan Theatre,* ed. John Russell Brown and Bernard Harris, 1966], it is no less essential for being so. Recreation has its own function, one that depends on its being, in Johan Huizinga's terms [in *Homo Ludens,* 1944], 'different from ordinary life'. Games mattered in Renaissance courtly life. Castiglione's *The Courtier* views expertise in games as an important accomplishment for its ideal type; Sir John Davies's *Orchestra* offers courtly dance as an expression of patterned movement and order in the very cosmos as well as at court. Lyly's plays, says Powell, 'organise into an elaborate aesthetic game the exploratory, recreational activities of the court for which they were written'. The debate, of which Lyly makes such extensive use, was a well-established game of court entertainment related to mummings and other seasonal festivities. Court revels lent themselves to repartee and other game-playing with words in order to express both temporary release from social constraint and eventual acceptance of form.

Lyly's acquaintance with this tradition of courtly pastime is evident everywhere in his writing. The atmosphere of purposeful play in his drama enhances stylistic novelty, exuberance, inventiveness and a witty facility for seeing similitude in things apparently different (such as Sappho of Lesbos and Queen Elizabeth of England). Fancy and learning are deployed around a frame of logic, encouraging a play of sound and of meaning in a way that is distinctively self-aware. Allegory and its witty similitudes invite playful cross-reference of idea to fact through which manifold possibilities of meaning emerge, and urge us to welcome his play world and acrobatics of the mind in all their extravagant fantasy.

Lyly's playfulness with language is illustrative of what Joel Altman calls the 'Tudor play of mind' ["Quaestiones Copiosae: Pastoral and Courtly in John Lyly," *The Tudor Play of Mind,* 1978]. Lyly's is a style of inquiry and analysis, through which he 'examines experience as a dialectical rhetorician, always holding any given perception up to the light of other possibilities'. Altman sees the method as originating in the *quaestio* or hypothesised question argued from both sides (*in utramque partem*), a technique that is common in sixteenth-century fiction and notably so in *Euphues.* Although Altman does not analyse *Sappho and Phao,* we can see that the hypothesised question constitutes the basic scenic unit of this play, as it does in *Campaspe* and *Gallathea,* and that flytings, amorous play of wit, and commentary on the main action are the substance of the connecting scenes. Elizabethan courtiers were familiar from their schooling with hypothetical situations posed to train the mind in thinking pluralistically and problematically about characters and ideas. What would it be like if a female sovereign were to fall in love with a male commoner? As in *Campaspe,* concerned as it is with a similar hypothetical situation, the play invites the audience 'to weigh the alternative meanings and values discovered through analysis, and to reassemble the distinctive—if sometimes antithetical—qualities perceived into some kind of harmonious order'. In this way 'the play functions . . . as an exercise in invention', which in Ciceronian rhetorical tradition 'was considered the most important of the five skills of the orator, since it supplied matter for discourse'.

The allegory of *Sappho and Phao* provides an advantage, less evident in *Campaspe,* of exploring the question in greater vividness and with more demands on the audience's inventive faculty. A play designed to 'stimulate the wit to new inferences and more complex perceptions' must of necessity use its images and analogies functionally, not ornamentally, in order to reveal duality and paradox inherent in the natural world and in human relationship to that world. Allegory itself is a form of wit, compelling the audience by its enigmas and dense correspondences (as Erasmus put it) 'to investigate certain things, and learn'. Lyly's plot, says Altman, arising from a *quaestio,* 'is often really a pair of *theses* argued copiously, now through one order of the cosmos, now through another, until the whole universe seems caught up in the strife'. Such an interpretation finds meaning not only in Lyly's use of allegory but also in the bringing together of mortals and immortals in one play, the range of social differentiation, the shifts in style from argumentative to lyric to bantering to chop-logic, the duality in which most characters are both objectively dramatic and emblematic, and the omnipresence of paradox. Along with the obvious flattery of Elizabeth, the play's inquiring mode yields a subtle critique of court life in which general harmony is achieved only at the expense of real personal loss.

ENDIMION

Joseph W. Houppert (essay date 1975)

SOURCE: "Middle Plays," in *John Lyly,* Twayne Publishers, 1975, pp. 84-113.

[*In the excerpt below, Houppert provides a structural and thematic overview of* Endimion.]

Endimion is Lyly's comedy of ideas. Except for some antics, the play offers little action: Dipsas casts a spell, Eumenides journeys to a strange land, Endimion falls asleep, and Corsites is pinched black-and-blue by fairies. There is some slapstick and horseplay, but the comedy is basically an abstract drama which explores the relationships of five different groups of characters. The effect of love on human character provides the stimulus, and the analysis of love in five of its many faces forms the substance of the comedy. *Endimion* is by far the most leisurely examination of love that the drama of the 1580's produced.

Endimion, a courtly lover, loves Cynthia, the Moon Goddess; Tellus, the Earth Goddess, loves Endimion; and Corsites, a plain soldier, loves Tellus. Around this network Lyly weaves a complex tale of magic and folklore. Tellus, in revenge for being spurned by Endimion, arranges for the sorceress Dipsas to place a spell on Endimion which causes him to sleep eternally. Cynthia dispatches messengers to various exotic lands to find a cure, but only Endimion's friend Eumenides is successful in finding one. A magic fountain, to which he is permitted access because of his friendship with Endimion, reveals that Endimion can be awakened by a kiss from Cynthia. A parodic subplot exists in the person of Sir Tophas, a foolish knight, whose actions parallel those of Endimion.

Unfortunately, this play has attracted critics who delight in predicating topical parallels between the characters in the play and real personages in the court of Queen Elizabeth. From N. J. Halpin's *Oberon's Vision* in 1843 to J. W. Bennett's "Oxford and Endimion" in 1942 [*PMLA* LVII] one learned conjecture after another has been entertained. For Halpin, Endimion and Corsites represent the Earl of Leicester and Sir Edward Stafford; for Bennett, they stand for the Earl of Oxford and Sir Henry Lee. Fortunately, recent criticism has shied away from historical allegory in favor of more literary types. Bernard Huppé, for example, argues [in "Allegory of Love in Lyly's Court Comedies," *ELH* 14, No. 2, June 1947] that if *Endimion* is an allegory, "it deals with the mental and psychological world of being: relations in it are relations of ideas and states." For Huppé, Cynthia represents not Queen Elizabeth, but Virtuous Love; Tellus represents not Mary Queen of Scots, but Earthly Passion.

Endimion is the most frequently anthologized of Lyly's plays, and therefore the one most familiar to students of Elizabethan drama. It is, however, atypical. With the exception of *Mother Bombie,* also atypical, *Endimion* is approximately twenty-five percent longer than Lyly's other plays; and it is more complex, especially more complex than the comedies which precede it. *Alexander and Campaspe* and *Sapho and Phao* are basically single-plot dramas, even though Diogenes's story in *Campaspe* tends toward independent coexistence; *Gallathea* has a clearly developed subplot, but one which is relegated to the background (the three brothers appear in five of the twenty scenes). Not only is the main plot in *Endimion* more complex but the subplots are also more heavily stressed (Sir Tophas alone appears in six of the seventeen scenes).

Endimion has a dramatic structure that is extremely balanced. The supernatural sleep of Endimion and his subsequent awakening are used by Lyly as focal points for the action. Endimion falls asleep at the end of the second act and awakens at the end of the fourth. The period before his sleep consists of two acts of seven scenes, five of which are devoted to Endimion and two to Sir Tophas; the period during his sleep consists of two acts of seven scenes, two of which are devoted to Endimion and five to the subplots (actually there is some overlapping here, but the scheme remains valid). The second division, with its emphasis on the subplots, thus inverts the first division, as indeed it must since Endimion is asleep through most of the third and fourth acts. The final division, after Endimion awakens, consists of one act of three scenes: the first is devoted to Endimion; the second, to Sir Tophas; the third, to a denouement which unifies all of the stories.

Endimion is Lyly's *Hamlet.* No historical or allegorical approach satisfies more than a few critics; the ending shrouds the play in ambiguity; and there are so many fashionable topics that every man finds something of interest. Always quick to capitalize on current interests, Lyly outdoes himself in *Endimion* by fastening upon themes and topics that were the rage in fashionable society, such as mutability (I.i), art versus nature (I.iv, II.iii), black versus white magic (II.iii, V.i). The two controlling themes, however, reach back in history, one to Classical antiquity and the other to the late Middle Ages: friendship and romantic love are what *Endimion* is all about.

In the Prologue to *Endimion,* Lyly appears to be establishing a critical principle when he writes: "Wee present neither Comedie, nor Tragedie, nor storie, nor anie thing, but that whosoever heareth may say this, Why heere is a tale of the Man in the Moone" (8-10). That *Endimion* is not a tragedy is obvious; no one dies, and death is essential to Elizabethan tragedy. That it is not a comedy is not so obvious. Perhaps Lyly has in mind the ending, which, far from bestowing blessings in true comic fashion, is a mixed bag of responses. Although Endimion regains his youth, he does not get Cynthia—and to serve by standing and waiting is an uncomfortable position for a lover. Eumenides gets his heart's desire—Semele, a sharp-tongued, shrewish female who will make the connubial bed a noisy place indeed. Corsites gets Tellus, the pro-

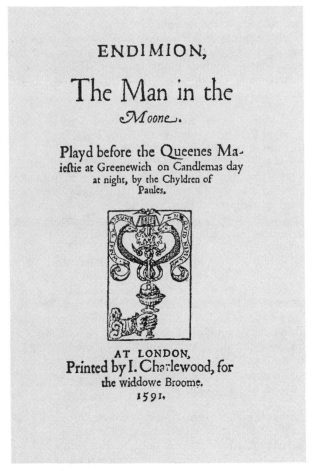

ENDIMION,

The Man in the *Moone.*

Playd before the Queenes Maieftie at Greenewich on Candlemas day at night, by the Chyldren of Paules.

AT LONDON,
Printed by I. Charlewood, for
the widdowe Broome.
1591.

Title page of the 1591 edition of Endimion.

fessional troublemaker. Dipsas and Bagoa are reunited, but far too late, for life has already passed them by. Perhaps of all the lovers, only Sir Tophas will not be disenchanted with his bargain. He asks for little, and little is what he gets. The irony which undercuts the love sentiment in the play is summarized in Sir Tophas's description of his ideal woman: "Turne her to a true loue or false, so shee be a wench I care not" (V.iii. 279-280). Behind Sir Tophas's nonchalance lies a cynical antidote to the various love theories which appear, however diluted, in *Endimion*—God made them male and female, and *vive la différence!*

The ending, then, does not conform to expectation. Although wedding bells ring, their sound is muted. A new society is formed, but there is some doubt that it will be superior to the old. J. W. H. Atkins argues [in *English Literary Criticism: The Renascence,* 1947] that Lyly, although indebted to Roman comedy, rejects the rigidity of Classical drama; and Lyly, in refusing to classify his plays as comedies or tragedies, denies that the boundaries of dramatic form have been permanently fixed. It is possible that Lyly thought of himself as a reformer, but to credit Atkins's argument is to posit a dramatic form more rigidly established than the one that in fact existed in the Elizabethan era. The whole history of the period is one of experimentation and change, from the early rhymed couplets of Nicholas Udall to the finely chiseled prose of Ben Jonson, from the heavy prosody of Robert Greene to the exquisite blank verse of Shakespeare. From *Ralph Roister Doister* to *The Winter's Tale* is a long journey indeed.

The principal theme in **Endimion** concerns the convention of male friendship. It not only serves as a framework, much as Shakespeare uses it in *The Merchant of Venice,* but also links together many of the diverse plot elements, such as Endimion's sleep and Eumenides's excursion into the desert. This theme is revealed through action as well as through dialogue; for example, Eumenides apparently sacrifices his own happiness for the sake of his friend Endimion when he encounters the magic fountain in Act III, Scene iv. Generally, however, themes and issues are revealed through debate; and action is sacrificed to witty exchanges of dialogue. The wit, however, is non-dramatic; for no change in character or situation results. In Act I, Scene i, for example, the confrontation between Endimion and Eumenides is non-dramatic. Nothing that Eumenides says in any way changes Endimion; in fact, all of Eumenides's objections could have been anticipated by Endimion in a soliloquy. Lyly does reveal a sense for the dramatic, however, by presenting the exposition in dialogue form.

The opening scene establishes premises upon which the drama is built. The stage is set for comedy as Endimion's romantic inclinations have been thwarted: boy has met girl, boy wants girl, but boy cannot have girl. There is, in **Endimion,** an even greater obstacle than is found in previous plays. In **Campaspe,** the obstacle was a wealthier suitor, Alexander the Great; in **Sapho and Phao,** the obstacle was social—queens do not marry ferrymen, however attractive they might be; in **Gallathea,** the obstacle was sexual—both lovers were girls; in **Endimion,** the obstacle is celestial—Endimion is literally in love with the moon!

The conflict which evolves from Act I, Scene i, is between what is desirable and what is possible—between the aspirations of Endimion, which are "stitched to the starres" (5), and those of Eumenides, "which creepe on the earth" (73-74). Eumenides's function in this scene is to serve as commentator on the impossibility of Endimion's quest. Such absolutes as Endimion seeks are unattainable in life, says Eumenides—man must compromise. Unable to understand or appreciate Endimion's longing, Eumenides believes that he has fallen prey either to moon madness or to melancholy.

Repetition with variation characterizes Act I, Scene ii. The non-dramatic debate technique is again employed as Tellus and Floscula take the places of Endimion and Eumenides. Just as is the case with Eumenides earlier in the play, Floscula is present for convenience's sake; her criticisms, like those of Eumenides, could have been anticipated by Tellus in a soliloquy. Furthermore, the second scene opens with the speech of a lover and ends with the

speech of a critic, just as did the first scene. Finally, both scenes present identical situations in which a character, lamenting an unrequited love, is criticized by a confidant. Although the situations are identical, the tone is sharply differentiated: Endimion will be satisfied with nothing less than possession of the goddess herself, but Tellus will settle for the appearance of love—"It shall suffice me if the world talke that I am fauoured of **Endimion**" (73-74).

Superficially, Act I, Scene ii, presents a situation common in a love triangle when the jilted female plots revenge. But Tellus is not an ordinary female—she is, in fact, the earth goddess: "No comparison *Floscula*? and why so? is not my beauty diuine, whose body is decked with faire flowers, and vaines are Vines, yeelding sweet liquor to the dullest spirits, whose eares are Corne, to bring strength, and whose heares are grasse, to bring abundance? Doth not Frankinsence & Myrrhe breath out of my nostrils, and all the sacrifice of the Gods breede in my bowels? Infinite are my creatures, without which neyther thou, nor *Endimion,* nor any could loue, or liue" (19-26).

But Tellus wants to play the part of a Petrarchan heroine: "His sharp wit . . . shall hee vse, in flattering of my face, and deuising Sonnets in my fauour" (56-58). Her concluding speech reinforces the passionate craving of love already implied: "*Floscula,* they that be so poore that they haue neyther nette nor hooke, will rather poyson dowe then pyne with hunger: and she that is so opprest with loue, that shee is neyther able with beauty nor wit to obtaine her freende, wyll rather vse vnlawfull meanes, then try vntollerable paines" (78-82).

There is a nice irony in the opening two scenes. As Endimion plots his attack on Cynthia, Tellus plots her counterattack on Endimion. Furthermore, just as Endimion's desire to possess Cynthia is to be frustrated, so is Tellus's desire to possess Endimion. Both attempt to upset the natural order of the universe—Endimion by aspiring beyond his station; Tellus by employing Floscula to destroy a normal human inclination, love. Finally, Tellus's solution to the paradox she formulates—"Loth I am *Endimion* thou shouldest die, because I loue thee well; and that thou shouldest liue it greeueth mee, because thou louest *Cynthia* too well. In these extremities what shall I doe?" (35-38)—is itself an unnatural solution: "He shall neyther liue, nor die" (39). This unnaturalness is made explicit by Floscula's reaction to it: "A reuenge incredible, and if it may be, vnnatural" (52).

To this point in the drama, the situation has been serious, even grim. But now (I.iii) Lyly introduces burlesque in the form of Sir Tophas, originally Pyrgopolynices in Plautus's *Miles Gloriosus* and more recently Ralph in *Ralph Roister Doister.* (Lyly's braggart soldier differs from these predecessors in that he does not profess to be a great lover; in this respect, his literary precedent is Chaucer's Sir Thopas.) The true wit of the pages, Dares and Samias, is contrasted with the false wit of Tophas. The debate technique of the first two scenes is dropped in favor of a mock-heroic approach characterized by a great disparity between words and situation. Tophas's ridiculousness is quickly established by his handling of the fine art of definition. Asked to define a poet, Tophas replies, "Why foole, a Poet is as much as one shoulde say, a Poet" (17). As a university man, Tophas serves as a target for the barbs of not only Dares and Samias but every other intelligent being as well. There is unquestionably much of Lyly's own anti-academic prejudice incorporated in this play. His own dissatisfaction with the curriculum at Oxford was well known and probably had some bearing on the academic satire in *Endimion*.

More important than his inability to define intelligently is Tophas's inability to distinguish between appearance and reality. He imagines that wrens are as dangerous as eagles and would hunt them with a blunderbuss. Like his successor, Sir John Falstaff, Tophas reacts to situations in an exaggerated and absurd fashion. But whereas Falstaff frequently exaggerates for effect, Tophas does it naturally.

Although not himself a lover, Tophas's opening line—"I brooke not thys idle humor of loue, it tickleth not my lyuer, . . ." (7-8)—mocks the earlier love themes and prepares for the retribution that love later exacts from Tophas. In this way, as well as by paralleling the careers of Tophas and Endimion, Lyly unifies the two stories. The Tophas story, however, does function as an independent unit until the end of the play when it is integrated with the main story. For the sake of psychological plausibility, Lyly has to keep the Tophas story separate, since its mock-heroic tone of absurdity and ridiculousness does not harmonize with the grim seriousness that characterizes the Endimion story.

A new danger to Endimion is introduced in Act I, Scene iv, in the form of the sorceress Dipsas. Her magical powers are clearly spelled out—she can darken the sun and remove the moon from its course (20-21). The one thing she cannot do, however, is control love. Although she can weaken its force, she cannot destroy it; and, perhaps more importantly, she cannot rule hearts—she cannot make Endimion love Tellus. The debate technique is used more dramatically here than earlier; characters change under the force of opposing ideas, and stubbornness yields to cooperation as, for the first time in the comedy, one character consents to act on behalf of another.

Act II marks a turning point in the action when Endimion and Tellus are brought together in a face-to-face encounter. The conflict, which until now has been abstract, is made concrete as it is embedded in the clash of human personalities. Endimion's opening soliloquy (II.i), although far too long to be dramatically effective, develops his role as lover. Complaining that for seven long years he has played the role to the hilt, he enumerates his symptoms: "Beholde my sad teares, my deepe sighes, my hollowe eyes, my broken sleepes, my heauie countenaunce" (11-12). Endimion has been suffering as every Courtly lover ought to suffer: "Every lover regularly turns pale in the presence of his beloved. . . . When a lover

---

Endimion as an allegory of Queen Elizabeth's court:

Lyly's plays more precisely than any others reflect the court of Elizabeth; our interest is closely involved in this; his pregnant love-analyses come hot, as it were, from knowledge of court-flirtations; and we rather like to feel there are points in the dialogue and sometimes the whole structure to which we cannot respond as directly as his first audience. The very flavour, as it were, of the plays would be different were he always transmuting, instead of reflecting, his day. Lyly is not, and is not wanted to be, Shakespeare. The conventional choice of *Endimion* as Lyly's most representative play is probably fortunate enough. It distils and intensifies his general qualities. Its various allegories are of shifting importance. There is Cynthia = Elizabeth, Tellus = Mary Queen of Scots, and the otherwise-to-be-interpreted other persons; parallel with this, and of changing importance, is Cynthia = the Moon and Tellus = the Earth, without further correspondences; and last, the more generalized sense of a hero set between a high and divine love and earthy and unscrupulous passions. Cynthia rules the action from the start and statuesquely takes charge at the close. That Cynthia-Elizabeth should so dominate Lyly's most dense and weighty single play is apt, since the Queen is necessarily the focal point of all that courtly eroticism at the back of his work. The imaginative and factual coalesce. The Queen is close-involved in the mysterious dream allegories at the play's heart; so that Lyly's most deeply imaginative, even mystic, apprehension is appropriately locked, as by a navel-string, to the age of its birth. Cynthia's particularity as Elizabeth becomes itself a universal.

G. Wilson Knight, "Lyly," in Review of English Studies, *Vol. 15, No. 58, April, 1939,*
pp. 146-63.

---

suddenly catches sight of his beloved his heart palpitates. . . . He whom the thought of love vexes, eats and sleeps very little" [Andreas Capellanus, *The Art of Courtly Love,* 1957].

The encounter between Endimion and Tellus is dramatic—she lays a trap; he falls into it, thus confirming her suspicions that he only pretends to love her. The trap itself depends on two factors for success, verbal wit and urgency. Lyly employs the rhetorical device of stichomythia (dialogue delivered in alternating lines) effectively as Tellus leads Endimion into making admissions against his will simply because the cut and thrust of the dialogue do not give him time to compose his thoughts. In revealing his affection for Cynthia, Endimion violates the code of secrecy, an integral part of the Courtly Love tradition; and for this violation he pays dearly.

Act II, Scene ii, is divided into two parts: (1) a quarrel between Scintilla and Favilla, and (2) the gulling of Sir Tophas. The quarrel, which has little relevance to the play as a whole, may simply reflect an actual quarrel between two of Elizabeth's ladies-in-waiting. Dares, however, provides a unifying link, however tenuous, with his realistic remarks about love: "How say you *Fauilla,* is not loue a lurcher, that taketh mens stomacks away that they cannot eate, their spleene that they cannot laugh, their harts that they cannot fight, theyr eyes that they cannot sleepe, and leaueth nothing but lyuers to make nothing but Louers?" (9-13).

The second part of this scene (57-156) repeats ideas and attitudes introduced earlier, especially in Act I, Scene iii, but Lyly handles them more dramatically by embodying them in the two ladies-in-waiting. Sir Tophas's anti-romantic tendencies now appear in a concrete situation, and they have as their object the ladies whose business is to be expert in affairs of the heart. In its entirety, Act II, Scene ii, also serves to create tension by delaying the revenge of Tellus.

The first part of Act II, Scene iii (1-23), repeats the opening of Act II, Scene i, and culminates in the symbolic death of Endimion, a motif adopted by Lyly from Udall's *Ralph Roister Doister,* when he falls asleep on a lunary bank. The revenge of Tellus completed, the last part of Act II, Scene iii, recapitulates arguments directed against the unnaturalness of the revenge. In short, magic is being used for improper ends!

Endimion's sleep concludes the first major movement in the play. During the two acts that Endimion sleeps, the dramatic focus shifts to the search for a remedy for his illness. Here, at what is roughly the middle of the play, the hero's fortunes are at their nadir, as they generally are at this point in most comedies. What follows in the last three acts provides a partial restoration. Actually, the first movement concludes with a dumb show, a visual representation of the dream which Endimion explicates upon awakening in the last act.

The new movement initiated in Act III, Scene i, is signaled by the appearance of new characters—Cynthia, Semele, Corsites, Panelion, and Zontes. The initial exchange between Semele and Eumenides follows:

> SEM. It were good *Eumenides* that you tooke a nappe with your friend, for your speech beginneth to be heauy.
>
> EUM. Contrarie to your nature, *Semele,* which hath beene alwaies accounted light.
>
> (12-15)

This exchange contains just enough wit to annoy Cynthia, who orders its immediate cessation. However, a more serious breach of decorum is occasioned by Tellus's tactlessness in suggesting that Cynthia's judgment of Endimion falls somewhat short of the mark. This imprudent remark results in Tellus's exile and prepares for the subsequent scene (III.ii). One's initial view of Cynthia confirms what one has already learned about her in the first two acts: she is dignified, orderly, compassionate, but, when aroused, authoritarian in the extreme. The scene closes with Eumenides being dispatched to Thessaly, Zontes to Greece, and Panelion to Egypt, to find a rem-

edy for Endimion's sleeping sickness. In order to make credible the time required for such journeys, Lyly now devotes his attention to Tellus and Tophas.

Since Cynthia can do little besides await the news from her messengers, since Endimion can do nothing at all, and since the Sir Tophas story will not bear much weight, Lyly introduces a new complication in Act III, Scene ii—the love of Corsites for Tellus. Corsites, a soldier who is aware of the tender side of life, now emerges as an obvious contrast to Sir Tophas; he also emerges, less obviously perhaps, as a parallel to Endimion, for both men pursue one-sided love affairs. Tellus's character continues to degenerate. Like Milton's Satan, she would rather reign in Hell than serve in Heaven: "*Corsites,* there is no sweeter musicke to the miserable then dispayre; and therefore the more bitternesse I feele, the more sweetnes I find; for so vaine were liberty, and so vnwelcome the following of higher fortune, that I chuse rather to pine in this Castle, then to be a Prince in any other Court." (11-15). Both Sir Tophas and Tellus suffer from overweening pride; but, whereas he exemplifies its ridiculousness, she exemplifies its viciousness.

In Act III, Scene iii, Sir Tophas joins the growing list of unrequited lovers, now consisting of Endimion, Eumenides, and Corsites, not to mention Tellus. Love's revenge is complete when Tophas succumbs to the dubious charms of Dipsas. His description of her ought to remind one of Endimion's description of Cynthia, not, of course, in its physical details but in the awe and enthusiasm with which it is delivered:

> O what a fine thin hayre hath *Dispsas*! What a prettie low forehead! What a tall & statelie nose! What little hollowe eyes! What great and goodly lypes! Howe harmlesse shee is beeing toothlesse! Her fingers fatte and short, adorned with long nayles like a Bytter! In howe sweete a proportion her cheekes hang downe to her brests like dugges, and her pappes to her waste like bagges! What a lowe stature shee is, and yet what a great foote shee carryeth! Howe thrifty must she be in whom there is no waste! Howe vertuous is shee like to be, ouer whom no man can be ielous!
>
> (52-60).

That the description is meant to be humorous is obvious; that it is meant to parody sixteenth-century ideas about feminine beauty is equally obvious.

Further parallelism between Tophas and Endimion is reinforced when Tophas falls asleep (67). Not only is the sleep itself an obvious similarity, but so also is the arrival of three pages who attempt to awaken Tophas, just as three messengers try to awaken Endimion. Finally, Tophas, after awakening, reveals a dream, just as does Endimion.

Having diverted the audience's attention with the antics of Sir Tophas, Lyly returns, in Act III, Scene iv, to the main thread of the story. With motifs adopted from folklore, this scene contrasts sharply with the preceding ones as it theorizes about love. There is here no Platonic ladder of love; rather, a dichotomy is created between love and friendship, with the latter clearly in the ascendancy. As a dramatic convention, friendship between men was never stronger than in the sixteenth century (friendship between women never seems to have had much force). One can, in fact, almost measure the development of English comedy by the degree to which conventions are sacrificed to reality.

Until now Eumenides has played a very poor role as Endimion's confidant, but in Act III, Scene iv, he assumes a character and succumbs to the Endimion syndrome—he, too, falls in love with an unwilling female, and this parallelism once again imposes unity on the plot. The last part of the scene achieves additional structural unity through two devices: first, the notion of unity in variety introduced in Act I, Scene i, forms the basis of Geron's philosophy—"Is shee not alwaies *Cynthia,* yet seldome in the same bignesse; alwaies wauering in her waxing or wayning, that our bodies might the better bee gouerned, our seasons the daylier giue their increase; yet neuer to bee remooued from her course, as long as the heauens continue theirs? (174-178). Second, only Cynthia's kiss will release Endimion from the spell placed on him by Dipsas.

There is a natural division between the third and fourth acts. Eumenides has discovered the remedy, but he must be allowed time to return from his journey. Lyly thus repeats the pattern he employed in Act III—he focuses attention on Tellus (Scenes i and iii) and Sir Tophas (Scene ii). And as Lyly began with Tellus and Corsites in the third act, so he begins with them in the fourth. This time Tellus plays a silly trick on Corsites which accomplishes two ends: it further reveals Tellus's frivolous character; more importantly, it brings Tellus and Corsites back into the mainstream of the action. When Corsites, at Tellus's urging, tries to hide Endimion's body in a cave, two lines of action converge.

Act IV, Scene ii, begins by stressing the parallelism in the situation involving Endimion and Sir Tophas, and then exploits the comic potential in the similarity. But the scene degenerates toward the end into an irrelevant discussion about masterless men. With the appearance of the Master Constable and the Watch (line 73), all semblance of relevance disappears; the scene dissolves into a moment's fun, complete with a song.

In Act IV, Scene iii, Corsites joins Endimion and Tophas as sleeping lovers. His love for the whimsical Tellus has led him to violate Cynthia's command and as punishment the fairies have put him to sleep. At this point (IV.iii.42), Cynthia begins to distribute rewards and punishments. Semele is punished for her shrewishness, Corsites is forgiven for his offense, and Tellus is censured for her tricks. Cynthia thus displays her benevolence by dispensing justice combined with mercy.

By Act V, Scene i, the second major movement is almost completed. The curse on Endimion has been lifted, but his restoration is not complete—he has yet to regain his lost youth. Arising from the grave, as it were, Endimion explains his dream: " Methought I sawe a Ladie passing faire, but verie mischeeuous; who in the one hande carryed a knife with which shee offered to cut my throte, and in the other a looking-glasse, wherein seeing how ill anger became Ladies, shee refrained from intended violence" (81-85). The two ladies, anger and mercy, are followed by an old man who offers Endimion a book with three leaves containing counsels, policies, and pictures. Endimion twice refuses the book, and the old man twice tears a leaf in half. Finally, Endimion takes the book and the old man vanishes.

The crux of the dream lies, of course, in the last leaf; and Cynthia requests clarification of its significance, to which Endimion replies,

> There portraid to life, with a colde quaking in euery ioynt, I behelde many wolues barking at thee *Cynthia,* who hauing ground their teeth to bite, did with striuing bleede themselues to death. There might I see ingratitude with an hundred eyes, gazing for benefites, and with a thousand teeth, gnawing on the bowelles wherein shee was bred. Trecherie stoode all cloathed in white . . . her handes bathed in blood. Enuye with a pale and megar face . . . stood shooting at starres. . . . There might I beholde Drones, or Beetles, . . . creeping vnder the winges of a princely Eagle, who being carried into her nest, sought there to sucke that veine, that woulde haue killed the Eagle.
>
> (119-132)

Promising to tell Cynthia more later, Endimion concludes his explication involving the dangers that await a monarch.

Besides creating suspense by holding back the finale, Act V, Scene ii, serves little purpose; moreover, the gulling of Sir Tophas has, by now, become shopworn. As the final scene begins (V.iii), Cynthia is again praised for her justice and mercy, qualities evident in the second round of rewards and punishments she distributes. After Tellus confesses her trickery and begs Cynthia's forgiveness, the men and women are paired off: Endimion with Cynthia, Eumenides with Semele, Corsites with Tellus, Geron with Dipsas, and Tophas with Bagoa. The play thus ends with wedding bells, as a good comedy should. It is doubtful, however, that the couples will live happily ever after. In the Prologue, Lyly warned his audience that **Endimion** was "neither Comedie nor Tragedie," a warning that is realized in what should be the comic denouement. Lyly's comic universe is too complicated and sophisticated to entertain unadulterated bliss.

Lyly captures the spirit of love in a net of skepticism. Celestial love leads not to perfect union with the divine but to partial fulfillment, as Endimion's frustrated desire to possess Cynthia is modulated into a graceful acceptance of his renewed youth. Romantic love finds its fulfillment in two tense alliances between romantically inclined men and sharp-tongued females. The aged Geron is reunited with Dipsas, but much too late; for love—and life—have passed them by. Perhaps in the final analysis only the naturalistic—or biological—love of Sir Tophas achieves complete fulfillment. He asks for little, and little is what he gets, but he registers no complaints. After his fashion, he is no worse off than the rest. Love may be the mysterious force of which poets sing, but its lovely promise does not come true for the characters in *Endimion*.

FURTHER READING

BIBLIOGRAPHY

Tannenbaum, Samuel A. *John Lyly: A Concise Bibliography.* New York: S. A. Tannenbaum, 1940, 38 p.

CRITICISM

Best, Michael R. "Lyly's Static Drama." *Renaissance Drama* n.s. I (1968): 75-86.
    Argues that Lyly's plays characteristically contain, "seemingly arbitrarily," both "complex motivation leading to nothing and action without apparent or adequate motivation."

Hunter, G. K. *Lyly and Peele.* London: Longmans, Green & Co., 1968, 52 p.
    Studies the influence of Humanism on the work of Lyly and one of his fellow "University Wits."

Huppé, Bernard. "Allegory of Love in Lyly's Court Comedies." *ELH* 14, No. 2 (June 1947): 93-113.
    Examines Lyly's allegorical presentation of love in *Sappho and Phao, Endimion, Love's Metamorphosis,* and *The Woman in the Moon.*

Jeffery, Violet M. *John Lyly and the Italian Renaissance.* Paris: Librarie Ancienne Honoré Champion, 1928, 147 p.
    Traces the influence of Italian literature on Lyly's works.

Additional coverage of Lyly's life and career is contained in the following source published by Gale Research: *Dictionary of Literary Biography,* **Vol. 62.**

Emily Mann
1952-

INTRODUCTION

Mann is an award-winning playwright and director whose
works often take a documentary approach to such social
and political events as World War II, the Vietnam War,
and the 1978 murder of two San Francisco politicians. In
Still Life, Execution of Justice, and other plays, Mann
creates what she calls a "theater of testimony" in which
she provokes and challenges audiences to confront often
painful and divisive subjects.

BIOGRAPHICAL INFORMATION

Mann was born in Boston on 12 April 1952. Her parents
were both educators, her father a history professor and her
mother a reading specialist. Mann's family moved to Chicago in 1966, when her father received a position at the
University of Chicago. Mann subsequently attended Chicago Laboratory High School, an experimental school
where a teacher engaged her interest in theater. She went
on to Harvard University and Radcliffe College, receiving
her bachelor's degree in 1974. Mann won a directing fellowship to the Guthrie Theater in Minneapolis and attended the University of Minnesota. In 1976 she received a
Master of Fine Arts degree in directing. The following
year she directed a production of her first play, *Annulla
Allen: The Autobiography of a Survivor,* at the Guthrie
Theater. In 1983 Mann received a Guggenheim fellowship, which she used to do research for her next play,
Execution of Justice. This work was a co-winner of the
Actors Theatre of Louisville's Great American Play Contest in 1983. Mann has won numerous other awards and
honors, and has directed productions of her own plays and
those of others at theaters across the country, including
the Goodman Theatre in Chicago and the American Place
Theatre in New York. She is currently the artistic director
of the McCarter Theatre in Princeton, New Jersey.

MAJOR WORKS

Among Mann's best-known works are *Still Life* and *Execution of Justice.* In *Still Life,* which won five Off-Broadway (Obie) awards, Mann examines the Vietnam War's
toll on the lives of a veteran, his wife, and his mistress.
The veteran, who discovered a taste for killing during the
war, struggles with rage, guilt, and pleasurable feelings
regarding his past. His wife, whom he periodically abuses,
would like to get on with raising their children. His mistress steps lightly over all problems without letting any of
them truly touch her. Staged as a dialogue among the three
characters seated at a table facing the audience, the play
illustrates their failure to communicate and their inability
to deal effectively with the past. *Execution of Justice*
concerns the 1978 murder of San Francisco mayor George

Moscone and gay city supervisor Harvey Milk by city
employee Dan White. Set in the courtroom where White
was convicted of two counts of manslaughter and sentenced to less than eight years in prison, the play reveals
the uproar the "gay murder" sparked among San Francisco's gay community and more conservative citizens. In
this work Mann quotes the official trial transcripts and
news coverage along with the statements of various people whose lives were affected by the event. *Execution of
Justice* received several awards, including the Bay Area
Critics Award. Mann also wrote and directed *Having Our
Say—The Delaney Sisters' First 100 Years,* which was
nominated for an Antoinette Perry (Tony) Award in 1995.
This play is based on the memoirs of black centenarians
Bessie and Sarah Delaney and recounts their lives and
struggles before, during, and after the Civil Rights Move-
ment.

CRITICAL RECEPTION

Mann's critics have focused on her use of interviews, transcripts, and other historical materials, judging her documentary style particularly effective and forceful. Michael
Feingold, for example, likened *Still Life* to "a jagged and

arresting chunk of dramatic shrapnel that is now lodged permanently in my brain." In his review of *Execution of Justice,* Richard Hummler noted that the play "succeeds to a remarkable degree in the theatrically tricky task of putting a complex actual event into dramatic focus." Mann's technique does have its detractors, however. Robert Brustein judged *Still Life* monotonous and little more than a "succession of monologues" in which "the characters rarely engage each other," making it "hard for them to engage us." Similarly, John Simon argued that *Execution of Justice* is "underwritten and overdirected, so that much that should be in clear focus remains fuzzy, and much that should be simply stated and directed is gussied and gimmicked up into shrillness and garishness." Despite such criticisms, many consider Mann's documentary technique a significant contribution to American theater.

PRINCIPAL WORKS

PLAYS

Annulla Allen: The Autobiography of a Survivor 1977; revised as *Annulla, An Autobiography,* 1985
Still Life: A Documentary 1980
Execution of Justice 1984
Nights and Days [adaptor; from a play by Pierre Laville] 1984
Betsey Brown: A Rhythm and Blues Musical [adaptor with Baikida Carroll and Ntozake Shange; from a novel by Shange] 1989
Having Our Say [adaptor; from a memoir by Sarah Delaney and Elizabeth Delaney with Amy Hill Hearth] 1995
Greensboro: A Requiem 1995

AUTHOR COMMENTARY

Interview with Mann (1987)

SOURCE: An interview with Emily Mann, in *Interviews with Contemporary Women Playwrights,* by Kathleen Betsko and Rachel Koenig, Beech Tree Books, 1987, pp. 274-87.

[*In the following conversation with Betsko and Koenig, Mann discusses her use of interviews and transcripts in the creation of* Still Life, Execution of Justice, *and* Annulla Allen.]

[Betsko and Koenig]: *You often utilize performance elements in your plays: recorded dialogue, repetitions, slides.*

[Mann]: I'm fascinated with live performance aspects of theater. It enables you to add another layer of perception to what you are presenting and gives you alternative ways to tell your story. You can stylize without being linear, without the traditional rising and falling action, where you watch one protagonist. The play can then be seen from different angles simultaneously. I did use some performance elements in the writing of **Execution of Justice** [which premiered at the Eureka Theatre in 1982], and I like that aesthetic. Some people called **Still Life** [premiered at the Goodman Theatre in 1980] a performance piece. I don't know if I would or not. But there are certainly performance elements in it.

Simultaneity seems important to you as a playwright, and as a director.

Yes. Incredibly so. For example, when I was working on **Execution of Justice,** I kept telling the dramaturg, Oskar Eustis at the Eureka Theatre [in San Francisco], that I was hearing all this emotional *noise* throughout the play. I wanted to hear both the trial and the community breaking down . . . at the same time. It has to do with content dictating form. The sobs from the community had to be heard. I had been in many living rooms, offices, kitchens in that city hearing people's stories and I knew the people I'd been talking to had to have an opportunity to give testimony. In the theater you can hear many voices at once; it is a wonderful aspect of live theater that can't actually be reproduced in film.

At what point, during the creation of **Still Life,** *did you realize that you were not using standard dialogue?*

When I realized that the dialogue I'd written, which I'd liked by itself, didn't have the muscle I wanted. It became a way to get information across, and the play began to seem like educational theater. The piece seemed very leaden; it didn't have any poetry, it didn't have any drive or electricity or tension in it. And it didn't have the traumatic element.

How did you get the invented dialogue and the material from the transcripts down to the "muscle," the "poetry"?

First, I became obsessed with the material, the story, and with what needed to be said. Then I found the form. For example, when I was editing the court transcript of the Dan White trial for **Execution of Justice,** I knew this was the spine of the play. I felt that I had to get the material in the right order, so that the audience would understand the trial. But that was only one layer, and I didn't know what the next layer would be. I'd edited the trial down well but that was just the first step. The rest came to me when I went to San Francisco for a full month. Once I was there, I heard the community story, breathed it and lived it. When I went back to the raw material of that first draft, voices started to come at me. That's when I discovered that emotional noise and began to let it be words and responses and needs.

How did the structure of **Still Life** *evolve?*

It's not mystical at all. The first draft was a series of monologues in a particular sequence for each of the three characters [distilled from taped conversations with a Vietnam veteran, his wife and his mistress]. Everyone who read the first draft loved it, then I had a reading and it was dead as a doornail. I didn't know why. I talked to my husband, Gerry [Bamman, actor] about it, and he said that he felt each monologue in its distinct form was fantastic, but he was curious as to why I had put the monologues in that particular order. I said, "Don't you see the connections between this moment and this one? Or this and this?" I indicated points in each monologue and how they related to points in others placed close to them in the text. He said, "Why don't you put the connections closer together?" Then he literally handed me scissors and tape. That was the beginning. Then all of my personal connections became so trippy and ultraclear that it was like I was on speed. A whole different part of my brain was working. I didn't sleep or eat for five full days. Before that, each monologue was about ten pages long. When I read a monologue I would *hear* the response in my brain, but it wasn't on the page. Now the response was there as I heard it. It was the beginning of my work with simultaneity, juxtaposition.

What about the line breaks in the monologues? Were the original monologues in poetic form, as they are in the published version [T.C.G. New Plays U.S.A., Volume I, ed. James Leverett, 1982]?

Yes. Those monologues were distilled down to ninety pages from the eight hundred pages of interview transcript. Obviously, when I began to narrow them down, they found their own rhythm, which was, in fact, iambic pentameter. I never had any fat in those monologues, even in first draft. There was never a wasted word. I wanted to retain the actual rhythms of the way each person spoke, in real language, during the interviews. That came from my training in literature and from my work with Shakespearean texts with director Michael Langham. So much of Shakespeare's poetry is in the rhythms of real speech; that's what iambic pentameter actually is! Many powerful moments emerge when speech rhythms change, for example, the witches in *Macbeth,* or the songs in Shakespeare's plays. I also learned about soliloquy from working with Shakespearean texts—they are, after all, conversations between the protagonist and the audience. I know from coaching actors the power of direct address, and so it became clear to me that I wanted to use it in *Still Life.*

Did you realize the power and the poetry of everyday American speech while you were conducting the interviews for **Still Life,** *or did that occur later during the writing process?*

I realized it during the interview process. So many surprising moments occurred. I had expected combat imagery from the marine, but when I heard combat imagery from the two women, I realized that they had shared imagery, concerns, and common language. When Nadine said to me, "I've been in the jungle so long that even

with intimates I protect myself," I thought, "What war were *you* in?" The language they spoke was an inspiration to me.

Edward Albee says that each play has its own musical architecture. Is this true of your writing?

Yes. A Washington reviewer understood that element of *Still Life* and talked about the play as a fugue. I'm very aware of the music and rhythmic structure as I'm writing; it's not just instinct. Before I went into theater, I had to choose between music and the theater. I used to play three instruments, though I don't anymore.

Why did you choose theater over music?

I knew I could never compose. I didn't have the skill. I felt I could become a better technician, but never master the creative side.

Has working with transcripts, for example, the interviews you conducted and edited for **Still Life** *and* **Annula Allen** *[which premiered at the Goodman Theatre, 1978], as well as the court trial you utilized in* **Execution of Justice,** *helped you to develop your extraordinary skill with dramatic exposition?*

Yes. But the skill has partly come out of my experience as a director. I have directed many so-called well-made plays. I loathed having to do Ibsen first acts, because you have to make that exposition seem like it's *not* exposition, and it so baldly is. You must make it seem as if it is all coming out of character. That is hard work for directors and actors. Exposition is THE hardest thing to write. You must get the story out without being heavy-handed. The audience needs the exposition, they need information in order to make judgments and to be able to fully experience the piece. You cannot make judgments without that information. And my plays are *about* asking the audience to face that information, and to actively question it. That is the form and content of *Execution of Justice.* It is a trial. The audience is the jury. The audience must have the information. But finally, the audience must have a visceral reaction to the *play.* All of this information, this exposition has to be made theatrical, rather than expositional. You could write a whole book about this! But I do want to say that you've got to make it *theater.* And that means you've got to make the play an active, live, gripping, in-the-moment event for people. From beginning to end, the audience must experience the information in a visceral way so that they don't notice they are using their intellect; they must be sucked in by their emotions and love for story, and then they must use both intellect and feeling to sort out what they've learned. It's very complex. Given that we're in a world where there is film and television where exposition is sometimes over by the end of the opening credits, anything that smacks of old-fashioned exposition always makes me uncomfortable. I hate it. From that hatred, I think, came a drive to get at it in my own way. A way that satisfied me.

How did you become interested in the Dan White trial [Execution of Justice]? [On November 27, 1978, Dan White—former policeman, former member of the Board of Supervisors of the city of San Francisco—shot and killed San Francisco Mayor George Moscone and City Supervisor Harvey Milk, a liberal, outspoken homosexual. Many believed the murders were politically motivated. White was tried and convicted of voluntary manslaughter. His relatively light sentence touched off serious riots in San Francisco's homosexual community. After his release from prison, White committed suicide.—Ed.]

I went to California to see the Eureka Theatre Company's production of *Still Life,* which was brilliant. They are a political theater, and they had been producing mainly English plays; until *Still Life,* they didn't feel that they had really seen a political playwright in America. They loved working on the play and said it was the most important show they had done with their company. The artistic director, Tony Taecone, said, "We love your work, and whatever you write, we'll produce. Why don't you write something for our company?" That was a fantasy come true. There were several things I was interested in writing, but I felt if I was going to write for a company, I should write something that was specific to their group or to their community. Then Tony quoted British playwright Barry Keefe, who said, "What about the Dan White trial? My God, if this had happened in England there would be ten plays about it." I vaguely knew about the trial, but I didn't know the details. That week I read Randy Shilt's book, *The Mayor of Castro Street,* about Harvey Milk, and I was astonished. The Eureka put together material for me. I read everything I could about the trial, made notes, and asked to get hold of the court transcript. When I returned in May, the people at the Eureka had the transcripts as well as ten weeks of newspaper coverage. During the next fourteen months (I was working outside of New York) I lugged it around in two suitcases. The month my husband and I were in Thailand working on David Hare's movie *Saigon,* I edited the trial, and decided who I needed to interview. There were many possibilities of approach to this material: I could have done the life of Harvey Milk, I could have made a murder mystery; instead I chose to use the trial transcripts and interview the community.

Would you describe the function of the uncalled witnesses in Execution of Justice? Were they based on actual people?

I did interview many people in San Francisco, but the uncalled witnesses are an amalgamation of people, real and imaginary. *Execution,* like *Still Life,* is theater of testimony. I wanted to find out what would happen if you took away the old Perry Mason Fifties realism idea of the courtroom drama. I wanted to show people giving testimony, people on trial, a community on trial *and a* nation on trial. I also wanted to show the people who were *not allowed* to give testimony, and that's where the uncalled witnesses came in. I wanted to find a way to visually break down the walls of a courtroom, and I also

wanted to show that in a trial of national significance, the community *must* be heard from.

Was there ever a temptation to slip into the conventional use of dialogue and of scenes?

Yes. You should see the outs. It was so hard to keep to the form I had chosen because much of the information could have been relayed in half the time and written in half the time if I had written scenes. I had to constantly reinvent the wheel and find new techniques. In fact, the chorus of uncalled witnesses came in late. I don't think I would have come to that breakthrough if I had not recently directed *Oedipus.* I realized that the chorus was the community that had been affected by the characters and their actions.

What is the significance of the sound motif of high heels throughout Execution of Justice?

The high heels are the sound that I always hear when I think of Mary Anne White running to meet her husband in the cathedral. I knew he was alone there, waiting for her. I knew he must have heard her running to him, and I heard that sound in my sleep. It's a sound image that provoked a visual for me of that wife running to her husband who had just committed murder. Her life is shattered in that moment of his confession; his life is shattered; he destroyed an entire community and he destroyed a movement.

The word homophobic is never used in the play. . . .

It did not come up in the trial either, but I would hope it is a word which rings in your brain as you experience the play. I had a whole speech about it in an earlier draft, but I felt it was agitprop and decided to try to say something about it without naming it. That was a challenge I gave myself and I think the point is made stronger. . . .

As a director, do you often have to deal with emotional explosions during rehearsal?

I expect them. Especially from the actors because we are often doing deep emotional work. You have to judge whether the outbursts are healthy or destructive. If someone had walked into a *Still Life* rehearsal, they'd have thought they walked into a looney bin! But the work was fantastic, these actors knew exactly what they were doing. The explosions were about the work. However, when anger surfaces on a personal level, and does not relate to the work, I stop it. Cold. It is destructive and must not be allowed. By anyone. The work is at stake. If the writer is going to explode, I make sure it is outside of rehearsal, and with me. If there is validity in the writer's dissatisfaction we can talk about it. Hopefully, fix it.

Would you tell us what a brain specialist once pointed out to you about the structure of Still Life?

Yes. It had to do with traumatic memory. She said that the juxtapositions, the form of *Still Life,* reminded her of the way the brain works when you are remembering a trauma. She said the play not only mirrored that brain function in the sense that the characters are in the process of remembering traumatic events, but also, the play itself seemed to her to be *my* traumatic memory of hearing their stories during the interview sessions. ***Execution of Justice*** also contains that element—it is an exploration of a community which has been traumatized by an event.

Maybe part of my attraction to and discovery of that form has to do with being female. Women sit around and talk to each other about their memories of traumatic, devastating events in their lives. Even women who don't know each other well! Sometimes, perfect strangers will sit and talk like other people talking about the weather or sports, except that it's about their divorce. You know? We often see the pain in one another and then we talk about it (I want to write a play about this, called *Talking Shop*). Most of what I know about human experience comes from listening. That's why it's very natural for me to believe in direct address in the theater. It is an extension of listening: I hear the stories, then I let *you,* the audience, have the same experience I had as a listener. I don't actually reenact these stories, I let you hear them. Hearing is very powerful for me. When I put these stories on stage, the audience experiences a direct interaction which is in the moment.

It's interesting that the critics in New York responded by directly addressing you. Several even used your name, as if they were having a conversation with you, or writing you an open letter. Do you think this direct response from the critics was a repercussion of the form, the direct address you used in **Still Life***? For example, one critic contemptuously speculated, "O my dear, liberal, radical, feminist, juvenile Emily Mann! These people [the true-life characters] would be just as dreary and hopeless if there had been no Vietnam" [John Simon: "Still Life," New York, March 2, 1981].*

Yes. We hit a *nerve* with **Still Life.** I stand by that. With three years' distance, I can understand why the play received that response and I can feel that it was, as I said, because we hit a nerve. But when I got the "direct" attack, I was devastated, depressed, enraged. Looking back, knowing what I know—that it went on to twenty productions and rave reviews both here and in Europe—I do believe it was a tribute to the work. In hindsight only, though. We got people very angry *and* very moved—the positive and the negative. We disturbed them; that's the goal. You can't write a play like **Still Life** and expect to be loved. . . .

In **Still Life,** *you explored domestic violence between men and women, and drew parallels to the international violence of the Vietnam War. The characters tell the audience about their savage experiences—what led you to the artistic decision to have the violence spoken, rather than dramatized?*

I wanted to show the *effect* of the violence rather than stage it. While I was writing the play I saw *The Godfa-*

ther again on television and during the scene where Gianni Russo beats up his wife, Talia Shire, I realized that it had been staged as a turn-on. I knew, then, that I did not want to perpetrate the myth that violence is sexy, I did not want to be a party to it. That's why when you see **Still Life,** you see a battered woman, not a woman *being* battered. You see what this brutality has done to both the husband and the wife, and it's not sexy, and it's not fun. It's rare to see violence between men and women onstage or in film which is not somehow erotic. I want to break down those clichés.

What is it in our culture that perpetuates this false depiction of violence as erotic?

I'm not sure; all I know is that I want to keep addressing the problem in my work.

Have we cultivated a taste for violence?

We have a lust for it in this society.

Was there something about the subject matter of **Still Life** *that caused it to be turned down at many theaters before it gained the sanction of the Obies? Is there, perhaps, a subtle censorship of women's plays going on at the literary manager level, especially those that link domestic and international violence?*

The literary managers and the artistic directors who are choosing their theater seasons are worried about their subscribers and given the economic times, I understand why. But I feel they are selling their audiences short. If they were willing to put on a good new American play, their subscribers would come to see it. Look at what [artistic director] Jon Jory has succeeded in doing with the New American Play Festival at Actors Theatre of Louisville. That audience has learned how to watch new plays and they are open to different voices, many of which are women's voices. The ability to watch new plays and see new forms can be learned and developed. It's a mistake to rob that subscription audience of a woman's point of view. Certainly the issue of domestic violence in our society, and explorations of the disappointment and rage that men and women feel for each other, are relevant to audiences in any part of the country. I would say that fully half the women I know have experienced physical violence, not just emotional, but physical violence from their lovers at some point in their lives. It's not a pretty subject and there are not many people who want to deal with the anger, the disappointment, and the violence between men and women. But we must make these explorations, so that we can move beyond.

How did you meet the characters of **Still Life***: Mark, the Vietnam veteran, Nadine, his mistress, and Cheryl, his wife?*

A woman friend of mine brought the real Nadine to see my play **Annula Allen** at The Guthrie Theater. Nadine went wild for the play and called me, saying, "I want you to meet a friend of mine who wants to tell you his war story." I said, "No, God, please . . . I don't want to do anything more about war after *Annula*." (*Annula* is based on the life of a central European Jew, 1900-1977, drawn from an oral history I made of her in London, 1974.) Then I found out this person had been in Vietnam. I said to Nadine, "I was in the antiwar movement; that war really chewed up my life, I'm still so confused . . . I can't really deal with it." She said, "Just meet him." I met him, and for three hours he talked in monologue about every atrocity he'd seen in Vietnam. I was so shellshocked by the time I got out of that room, I told him, "I can't handle this." He said, "Well, the real casualty of this war is my wife." That terrified me. I told Nadine I was frightened of Mark and the project. She said, "He's the gentlest man I've ever known." So I met his wife and the first thing she said was, "I'm constantly scared for my life, living with him."

I thought, "Now here's a play: One woman says he's the gentlest man she's ever known, and the other is afraid for her life . . . what is going on here?" It hooked me. But I am telling you, after I went through that series of interviews, and the last meeting where Mark made his confession, I had to get help. I gave the tapes to some volunteers at The Guthrie Theater to transcribe and I didn't look at them for almost a year. I couldn't face what it brought up for me. The most terrifying moment was when he told me how he found out that he loved to kill, that killing was the "best sex [he'd] ever had." I called different veterans' organizations and they said, "Oh, that's very common." [See also: Lt. William Broyles, Jr. (Ret.): "Why Men Love War," *Esquire,* November 1984.] Then a friend sent me a beautiful poem, which goes something like:

> The sad thing is
> When we send our young men to war
> The young men die
> The sad thing is
> When we send the young men to war
> The young men kill
> And the sad thing is that
> When we send our young men to war
> They learn to love to kill.

Greek. Two thousand years old.

STILL LIFE

PRODUCTION REVIEWS

Michael Feingold (review date 25 February-3 March 1981)

SOURCE: "Home Fronts," in *The Village Voice,* 25 February-3 March 1981, pp. 75, 77.

[Still Life *premiered at the Goodman Theatre in Chicago in 1980 and debuted Off-Broadway early the following year at the American Place Theatre. In the following highly favorable review of the latter production, Feingold praises the writing, acting, and staging of the piece.*]

"As incredibly civilized as we are in this room," says the nice young man, "these things go on." The things he is talking about are murder, mutilation, child-killing, schizophrenic breakdowns, battlefield hysteria, and seeing his buddies with their heads blown off. In other words, he is talking about Vietnam. The young man goes on talking. He is such a nice young man—smiling, straight-forward, presentable, aware. We ought to like him, we think. Sure, he did time in jail on a drug rap after serving in Vietnam, but veterans don't have it easy, and drugs are universal. He has a wife and son, and another child on the way. Granted, he takes photographs that tend to feature people smeared with stage blood and stuck with prop weapons; say he's working out his Vietnam trauma, it can't be easy for him. He's still a nice guy. So why does he pound the table that way, and give his wife threatening looks? Why is he getting up menacingly and coming toward us?

The nice young man is the pivotal character of Emily Mann's theatre piece, *Still Life,* a jagged and arresting chunk of dramatic shrapnel that is now lodged permanently in my brain. I recommend it much the same way I would recommend open-heart surgery—the point being that, for the heart of America, such an operation is radically necessary right now. After all, as a nation, we created this nice young man, we sent him to Vietnam, and we caused what he did there. Since he came home, we have been studiously avoiding him; it is the easiest way conceivable of avoiding the part of ourselves that is like him. Under Reagan, we have officially decided that the war in Vietnam was justified and can be forgotten, and if the veterans whom we trained to enjoy killing have come home to kill, that is chiefly a problem for their wives and for the inner cities, which, it seems, are to be officially forgotten too.

The director and compiler of *Still Life* (it is assembled from interviews with three actual people) has of course not omitted dealing with our desire to forget. Lined up next to the vet, along a table which suggests a panel discussion or press conference, are his wife and his mistress. The wife is like a mythological monster composed of elements from different species, a fable-level compendium of compassion, masochism, Medea-like fury and sheer terrified confusion. The mistress, a would-be worldly-wise divorcee, with two adolescent daughters, is one generation off the farm, with a veneer of sophistication so thin it begins to crack and curl almost visibly under the stress of the discussion. The best educated of the three, she is in some ways the most appalling, with her glibly pitying pop-psych, pop-sociology "explanations" of this or that shortcoming in the man; forgiveness was never less divine. But the point which seems to have bypassed some of the daily reviewers is that the two women, like the man, are real people, not dramatic fictions, and the contradictions which Emily Mann has arranged and intercut to such terrifying effect are the contradictions of human beings, not clever little droplets of character writing; the critic who sneers at them—sorry, Frank—is giving a bad review, not to the writer, but to God.

All three, harping obsessively on the blight Vietnam hangs over their lives, trying desperately to analyze it out of existence, are horrible failures, disasters of humanity, but they are horrible in the way in which one's relatives or friends are horrible when they make disastrous mistakes in dealing with life; not accepting them as part of oneself, after getting a chance to look this deeply into their feelings, would be the height of inhumanity.

Mann, in shaping an art object out of her sad human materials, has very wisely kept the whole process cool and understated, making the musical and thematic linkage of these three monologues subtle, never forcing effects or overstressing repetitions, letting the violence and misery in the characters come out naturally at its own rate. The performance-art notion of setting up the evening to look like a flat discussion pays off handsomely: Just as the round-table format starts to lull or bore you, the tensions flare up, so that you are kept in constant expectation of having the whole bland arrangement torn to shreds by some physical outburst. All three actors are excellent; the two women (Timothy Near and Mary McDonnell) occasionally try a shade too hard to seem folksy and normal, a minor blemish on a picture otherwise complete in its horror, which is ours, and irrevocable: *Heart of Darkness,* with apple pie and vanilla ice cream on the side.

John Simon (review date 2 March 1981)

SOURCE: "Various Ways to Lose Your Head," in *New York* Magazine, Vol. 14, No. 9, 2 March 1981, pp. 52-3.

[*In the following harshly negative review of the Off-Broadway production of* Still Life, *Simon describes Mann as "pretentious" and calls the main characters "stupid, crazy, odious, and boring."*]

In *Still Life,* Emily Mann, who wrote and directed, places three people on a platform at a speakers' table. There is Mark, a Vietnam veteran, who seems to be excessively controlled, self-accusing, and at home with his misery; Cheryl, his wife and mother of their small son, who seems insane enough—though calmly, ever so calmly—to be put away; and Nadine, a somewhat older woman—unhappy wife, mother of three girls, photographer, feminist, and Mark's current lover. Mark, apparently, is a photographer too, but he also runs some sort of store; he seems to be separated from Cheryl, though also somehow living with her. They appear to be all right financially, though there often isn't enough to eat. Cheryl, though quite mad, seems to be coping; Nadine, though

quite sensible, is nutty—keeps perceiving herself as a plunger, worries about not being depressed enough, thinks that Mark's having killed a family of five in Vietnam may somehow help her psychic equilibrium.

Where are these people who are often directly addressing us and often merely monologizing into space? Is this a talk show? A symposium? Group therapy? A meeting of Maniacs Anonymous? Beckett's Hell, only with no giant jars encasing the trio? Sometimes the three seem unaware of one another; sometimes they interact. Mark interrupts the proceedings to show some preposterous Vietnam slides, including one of a sweet, well-fed puppy that is supposed to have started devouring its master the moment his head was blown off. Whereupon Mark shot it, incurring guilt feelings maybe worse than from killing that family of five. Nadine tells us how incredibly gentle Mark is; Cheryl, how incredibly violent he is, what with that gun of his. Mark tells us how his mother, the day he came back from the war, told him not to drink so much coffee. And how his parents promptly went off to a party. And how he needs his gun.

One or another character suddenly goes backstage, and may be heard shouting "Wow!" They may be taking in liquids, or letting them out. Mark plays a tape of an anti-genocide song, and everyone strikes suitably distraught poses. Cheryl won't let Mark drive. (How does he get to his store?) He starts getting violent and banging the table. There is much talk about sex, kinky and otherwise. Also drugs. Mark wanted Cheryl to make love to a girl in Hong Kong. Shocking! Yet lesbianism makes sense, given what men are like these days. The war was terrible—people get killed in wars!—and we are all responsible. Also, it seems, for the fact that these three for whom Emily Mann's 28-year-old heart bleeds (the play, it appears, is largely based on their true stories) are so stupid, crazy, odious, and boring.

O my dear, liberal, radical, feminist, juvenile Emily Mann! These people would be just as dreary and hopeless if there had been no Vietnam, and it would be just as much of an imposition to spend 90 minutes in their company—or yours, to the extent that these stories could not be this preposterous historically, clinically, humanly, without your having doctored them. This play is all nostalgia for the sixties, all radical chic: bourgeois radicalism that any true-blue Red—or genuine theater lover—must deplore. The actors—John Spencer, Timothy Near, Mary McDonnell—are convincing enough to make us want to run from them, but not so fast as from their pretentious author.

Richard Hummler (review date 4 March 1981)

SOURCE: A review of *Still Life,* in *Variety,* 4 March 1981, p. 102.

[*In the following assessment of the Off-Broadway production of* Still Life, *Hummler finds the play emotional-*

ly powerful but contends that it "goes too far in rubbing the audience's nose in the brutality of combat."]

Still Life is strong stuff. Emily Mann's three-character documentary drama about the traumatic effects of Vietnam combat on an ex-Marine and the two women in his life is an unflinching and grimly convincing confrontation with the horror of war. It's too long and repetitious, and too much too depressing for popular taste, but it has the ring of truth.

The play is in the fashionable mode of current dramaturgy, in which characters address the audience in monologs and scarcely interact. The psychologically crippled Vietnam vet, his wife and his mistress spend the play's 90 minutes exposing their inner demons while seated at a table. An author's note says most of the dialog was taken verbatim from personal interviews with Vietnam-related Americans.

The veteran suffers from horrendous guilt for surviving the war in which many of his comrades were killed, and from having committed terrible atrocities himself. The My Lai massacre, he insists, wasn't a unique event.

Since his discharge, the former soldier has been a drug trafficker and served time in prison. His marriage is collapsing, and his relationship with another woman isn't too stable either.

It's not a pretty picture, and many may find it tough to sympathize with a character who succumbed to evil tendencies which most Vietnam servicemen resisted. But the pain and reality of the man's plight come across strongly and emphasize the unspeakable nature of war.

The two women, wife and mistress, are also vividly etched. The disillusioned wife, who wasn't aware of the vet's damaged psyche when she married him, is a sadly fascinating character trying vainly to shut out pain. The mistress, an angry feminist, also commands attention with her insistence that hypocritical religious training and social conditioning are to blame for the man's vulnerability to evil behavior.

Still Life goes too far in rubbing the audience's nose in the brutality of combat, it ignores the veteran's obvious need of professional therapy, and it's about 20 minutes too long. But for author-director Emily Mann and the three performers, it's an impressive overall effort.

John Spencer plays the tortured veteran with compelling, indeed scary, intensity, and Mary McDonnell adds another strong credit to a quickly-developing career with a subtle and precisely calibrated performance. Timothy Near is also first-rate as the masochistic mistress. *Still Life* isn't for the squeamish, but in its insistence that the reverberations of Vietnam not be forgotten, it's a valuable piece of theatre.

Robert Brustein (review date 28 March 1981)

SOURCE: "A Theater Marking Time," in *The New Republic,* Vol. 184, No. 13, 28 March 1981, pp. 23-4.

[*In this review, Brustein admires Mann's intentions in* Still Life, *but contends that since "the characters are essentially self-involved, their perceptions never seem to rise much above domestic homilies, as if the major significance of the greatest tragedy in America's recent history was its impact on sex and marriage."*]

Emily Mann's *Still Life* (American Place Theater) is a serious effort to involve us with a searing contemporary issue—namely, the impact of the Vietnam War on the personal and domestic lives of the Americans involved in it. Out of a series of interviews with a Vietnam veteran, his wife, and his mistress, Miss Mann has carved a succession of monologues. All three characters sit facing us at a table, pouring out confessions. The evening has the ring of unadorned truth—also, unfortunately, its monotony. Miss Mann seems less concerned with the war than with how it has influenced personal relations, how the imperatives of government poison the lives of men, and how these poisons in turn infect the lives of women. Barely conscious of each other, the two women nevertheless share a morose perception of masculine failure. "You wonder why there's so much lesbianism around these days, look at the men." "I'm worried about men. . . . They're not coming through somehow." "They were programed to fuck, and now we want them to make love." Since the characters are essentially self-involved, their perceptions never seem to rise much above domestic homilies, as if the major significance of the greatest tragedy in America's recent history was its impact on sex and marriage.

Well, that's a little unfair; the play is not entirely dominated by feminist issues. Some slides are shown, for example, demonstrating the havoc wrought on the Vietnamese people, and Mark, the veteran, occasionally tries to face the enormity of the war, and the question of his own complicity. Even this effort, however, is limited by the characters' narrow range of understanding. I respect the seriousness of this production, which is acted with considerable intensity by John Spencer, Mary McDonnell, and Timothy Near, but I left the theater peculiarly untouched. Speaking monologues, the characters rarely engage each other, and that makes it hard for them to engage us. The single emotion one brings away is guilt—less over the war than over one's failure to sympathize with the sufferers.

CRITICAL COMMENTARY

Kate Beaird Meyers (essay date 1990)

SOURCE: "Bottles of Violence: Fragments of Vietnam in Emily Mann's *Still Life,*" in *America Rediscovered: Critical Essays on Literature and Film of the Vietnam*

War, edited by Owen W. Gilman, Jr. and Lorrie Smith, Garland Publishing, Inc., 1990, pp. 238-55.

[*In the essay below, Meyers examines Mann's depiction of the violence underlying American myths regarding manhood, male/female relations, and heroism in* Still Life.]

Emily Mann's **Still Life** is important to the canon of literature about the Vietnam War not only because it dramatizes the plight of the veteran and his family, who are also "veterans" of the war, but because it examines the basic dichotomies of American culture: "American Myths" are brought into direct confrontation with the realities of the aftermath of Vietnam. The unusual structure of **Still Life** makes it a classic example of a form Philip Beidler finds characteristic of Vietnam literature written since 1975, in which the age's "need to examine the nature of its own myth-making processes" is the central focus. According to Beidler, "even as the shapes of art begin to transform experience into a new medium of signification, experience itself begins to generate new shapes of art in its own image as well" [*American Literature and the Experience of Vietnam,* 1986]. The play, somewhat reminiscent of Jean Paul Sartre's *No Exit,* consists of a long conversation between three characters, each of whom is a metonymic representation of some aspect of the Vietnam generation. Although they are not literally confined together, as are Sartre's, Mann's characters are figuratively bound by their involvement with each other and with the Vietnam War. The characters analyze their own interrelationships, but only superficially. They talk about the war but do not analyze it in terms of its being "right" or "wrong." The real question they address is how to recover from a war that brought an entire nation into conflict with itself and exposed some of the basic conflicts found in American culture: America is both a nation of peace, love, and freedom and a nation with an inherent tendency toward what Richard Slotkin [in his *Regeneration Through Violence: The Mythology of the American Frontier, 1600-1860,* 1973] has called "regeneration through violence"; America is a nation in which both sexes are conditioned to accept the phallocentric myths of the "American Adam" and the "angel of the house" but where the reality of Sartrean "facticity" makes belief in such myths both foolish and dangerous. It is the dialogue between these dichotomies that creates the tension of Mann's play.

The story of **Still Life** is deceptively simple. Mark is a Vietnam veteran, a former Marine. Haunted by the guilt of having killed a Vietnamese family (mother, father, children), angry at the contradictions of the war itself and at the treatment of returning veterans, Mark has difficulty communicating with anyone. He was convicted of selling drugs and served a term in prison; he became an alcoholic but has not had a drink for nearly a year. He has started a career as an artist, creating scenes inside bottles and jars using fragments of memorabilia from Vietnam; he is also an amateur photographer. Cheryl, Mark's wife, is a former "flower child" who spent much of the sixties on drugs. She is now aged beyond her years by her struggles with Mark. She has a young son and is noticeably pregnant again. Mark has beaten her severely several times, for which they both blame the war and Mark's inability to recover from it. Cheryl will not discuss the war; she prefers to think of it as a past event, refusing to acknowledge the fact that Mark still fights it every day. The third character is Nadine, a woman ten years older than Mark and Cheryl. She has several children and is divorced from an alcoholic husband. She has befriended Mark, who has confided in her some of his feelings about the war, which she professes to understand. Nadine was involved in the anti-war movement during the sixties and is now completely disillusioned with the American Dream.

These simple characterizations are in actuality highly complex. Each of them functions as a metonym for a large portion of the generation of Americans to which they belong. Mark represents Vietnam veterans who are confused and angry about the war and its aftermath:

> My unit got blown up. It was a high contact. We got hit very, very hard. [. . .] What can I say? I am still alive—my friends aren't.

Cheryl is both the wife/victim and the voice of a nation that does not want to know about the unpleasantness of the war. If it is not discussed, perhaps it will go away:

> I can't deal with that at all. But I find that if I can at least put it out of my mind it's easier. If I had to think about what he's done to me, I'd have been gone a long time ago.

And Nadine speaks for those members of the sixties generation who no longer believe that "all you need is love":

> God, we hated those vets. [. . .] All that nonsense about long hair, flowers and love. [. . .] I think I knew then what I know now. [. . .] The problem now is knowing what to do with what we know.

Although she is disillusioned, Nadine remains hopeful that if America remembers the lessons of Vietnam, "maybe we can protect ourselves and come out on the other side." Like the larger groups of which they are emblematic, the three characters do not communicate well with each other. During their conversation, they never really connect with each other; in fact, the last words of the script, before "END OF PLAY," are: *"The WOMEN's eyes meet for the first time as lights go down."* They talk about themselves and about each other but always to the audience, which serves as a therapist, watching and listening as Mark, Cheryl, and Nadine work through their problems. The characters do have one concern in common, however—concern for their own futures in an American society that remains unable to come to terms with the Vietnam War.

I

America's involvement in the Vietnam War may be a natural result of a dichotomy that has long existed in the

American psyche between two epistemologies Richard Slotkin equates with the mythical archetypes "hunter" or "warrior" and "shaman." The (masculine) hunter follows a code of "war and killing"; the (feminine) shaman follows a moral code of "self-abnegation, kindness, and peace." The law of the hunter clearly resembles the "entrepreneurial spirit" of the colonists and frontiersmen, and of their modern counterpart the "military-industrial complex," while the laws of the shaman are closely akin to those of Christianity, especially the Quakers. Among the Puritan settlers of America,

> the lifeway represented by the shaman came to be thought of as the way of the victim, the sufferer, the captive. In situations of extreme fear and insecurity . . . the balance between the shaman and hunter as equal symbols of value is destroyed. The shaman then becomes symbolic of weakness in man, the hunter symbolic of strength. . . . The consequences of such a dichotomy are severe: the natures of shaman and hunter become intensified, and the warrior feels driven to prove his strength and power through acts of incredible cruelty, which is exacerbated by his fear of being at one with the totally helpless victim he destroys.

The Puritans synthesized the hunter and the shaman as a means of rationalizing their violence toward the Indians, even though such a rationalization is in direct conflict with the Christian ethics on which the colonies were founded. They created the "errand into the wilderness" as a means of making their followers believe that destroying the Indians and taking their land was a religious duty. Through this synthesis, the voice of the shaman, the peace-maker who spoke against murdering Indians and usurping their land, was silenced.

The Puritans believed that they were the "Chosen People," sent to the New World to build a "City upon a Hill" from which God's light would shine perpetually, a "light whose radiance would keep Christian voyagers from crashing on the rocks, a light that could brighten the world" [Loren Baritz, *Backfire: A History of How American Culture Led Us into Vietnam and Made Us Fight The Way We Did,* 1985]. However, creating that city presented the Puritans with major problems. In order to "civilize" the wilderness, it was necessary to make violence a corollary to their "Christian" mission. The Indian was an obstacle that had to be removed. The Indian wars were an "acceptable metaphor for the American experience," since the Puritans "could pit their own philosophy, doctrine, culture, and race against their cultural opposites and could illustrate God's favor to their way of life in recounting their triumph and the discomfiture of both the heathen enemy and those of their own people who had been less than rigorous in their faith" (Slotkin). The Indian was transformed into evil incarnate, an emissary of the Devil, sent to torment and to test the Puritans.

But this acceptance of violence brought the Puritans face to face with their fear of the wilderness, as represented by the "savage." In his likeness to "primitive inner man" the Indian "was a threat to the Puritan's soul," and many feared that too much contact with Indians might cause even the best of Christians to revert to savage ways. The Puritans were frightened by the fact that their own soldiers "behaved precisely like their Indian enemies—burning the villages of their enemies, slaughtering not only the warriors but also the wounded, the women, and the children." Ministers and historians, attempting to ease the situation, told their listeners and readers that such violence was "divinely sanctioned." Three centuries later, the American government used the same rhetoric to justify sending troops on another "errand." As Frances FitzGerald explains [in *Fire in the Lake: The Vietnamese and the Americans in Vietnam,* 1972]:

> American officers liked to call the area outside GVN control "Indian country." It was a joke, of course, but it put the Vietnam War into a definite historical and mythological perspective: the Americans were once again embarked upon a heroic and (for themselves) almost painless conquest of an inferior race.

It was an American soldier's moral duty to go to Vietnam to kill the "godless Communists," and, as in earlier times, the reversion of some soldiers to a "savage state" was an issue of much concern to the military and to the nation at large. Soldiers in Vietnam created "fantasies of exactly the same sort that the Americans had created about the Indians"; they "stripped the Vietnamese of their humanity in order to deliver themselves of their guilty desires," and, ultimately, the war "brought out their latent sadism, as perhaps all wars between races . . . have brought it out of all armies." One important aspect of the hunter/shaman dichotomy that cannot be ignored is the role of gender. Originally, both the hunter and the shaman were male, but, as the myths became Europeanized, the hunter became associated with qualities traditionally seen as "male" and the shaman with those qualities seen as "female." The active male/hunter figure was valued by society far more than the passive female/shaman. As European civilization increased its territorial holdings, the male/hunter came to see his divine task as settlement of the frontier, penetrating as deeply as possible into the "virgin" wilderness. Through violence against the land and its native population (a figurative rape), he could regenerate himself and his people. The violence he perpetrated against the wilderness, stripping the land in order to plant his seed, provided him, and the society that lived vicariously through his exploits, with a kind of sexual release. The female land, and the females of the land, were there to receive his assaults and provide relief for his pent-up energies. Because Indians were not considered "human," violation of Indian women was not considered criminal behavior. At least indirectly, this same "macho" ideology may be to blame for the rape and murder of Vietnamese women and children during the war and for much of the domestic violence still suffered by American women and children.

II

In Vietnam Mark was forced to confront his own desire for "regeneration through violence," as well as the Puritan fear of the effects of the wilderness on "civilized" man. He was intoxicated by the violence he found in the jungle, by the power it gave him: "At night, you could do anything . . . It was free-fire zones. It was dark, then all of a sudden, everything would just burn loose. It was beautiful. . . . You were given all this power to work outside the law. We all dug it." His gun became a figurative penis; each time he killed, he experienced a pleasure akin to orgasm: "It's like the best dope you ever had, the best sex you've ever had." When he returned home, Mark could not control the savage impulses unleashed by his experience in Vietnam. Now, he is unable to resolve the contradictions he finds in a society that tells him to kill one day, then expects him to be "civilized" the next: "This country had all these rules and regulations and then all of a sudden they removed these things. Then you came back and try to make your life in that society where you had to deal with them. You find that if you violate them, which I found, you go to jail, which I did." He went through a period of needing inordinately frequent sexual orgasm as a means of reaching the same "high" he got from killing Vietnamese: "I wanted to fuck my brains out." Finally, Mark's anger and guilt exploded into violence against his wife and son.

When he first returned from Vietnam, Mark tried to communicate with his family but found it impossible. Even while he was in Vietnam, he tried to convey to his parents and brother the horror of his experience. He sent them a bone from the body of someone he killed—as a warning not to let his brother go to war. But they refused to acknowledge the gesture. Mark's mother was "upset," and his father, a veteran of World War II, had no comment. On his first day home, when he hoped to talk to his parents about the war, they preferred to act as though he had not been gone rather than listening to his pain: "I came home from a war, walked in the door, they don't say anything. I asked for a cup of coffee, and my mother starts bitching at me about drinking coffee"; "I still want to tell my folks. I need to tell them what I did." Initially, Mark saw Cheryl as a means of reconnecting with "the world": "Cheryl is amazing. Cheryl has always been like chief surgeon. When the shrapnel came out of my head, she would be the one to take it out." But Cheryl, too, refused to listen. Finally, Mark turned to alcohol and the violence it released as a form of consolation. Unfortunately, most of the violence was released on Cheryl. After one especially violent episode in which Mark severely injured her (he pushed her down a flight of stairs), he began to see Cheryl as a comrade, a fellow casualty of Vietnam: "See, I see the war now through my wife. She's a casualty too. She doesn't get benefits for combat duties. The war busted me up, I busted up my wife."

Mark has quit drinking and turned to art as a means of expressing his guilt and anger. He collects gruesome photographs of the war dead, some of which he shows as slides during Act II: "(*Snaps on pictures of mass graves, people half blown apart, gruesome pictures of this particular war) [. . .] (Five slides. Last picture comes on of a man, eyes towards us, the bones of his arm exposed, the flesh torn, eaten away. It is too horrible to look at)."*

He uses other photographs to make his "jars." Mark puts little pieces of Vietnam into bottles—photographs, bullets, broken glass, jagged pieces of metal. He bottles up pieces of violence, just as the fragments of war are bottled up inside him.

Cheryl represents certain aspects of the "shaman." She does not understand Mark's violence or his inability to put the war out of his mind. Cheryl "did a lot of speed" in the sixties, but now she wants to put all that behind her. She sees the sixties and the war as part of a past she can only dimly recall: "[T]here's a lot of things, weird things, that happened to us, and I just generally put them under the title of weird things . . . and try to forget it. And to be specific, I'm real vague on a lot of things." She would prefer to shut her eyes to the past, especially Mark's past: it's over, so why remember it? Cheryl is ready for the future. She is concerned about her own and her children's futures. She wants to move on with her life, and Mark's problems are holding her back: "I got a kid and another one on the way. And I'm thinking of climbing the social ladder. I've got to start thinking about schools for them, and I mean this, it's a completely different life, and I've had to . . . I've WANTED to change anyway." Most of all, she wants to return to the Catholic Church: "I mean, when there's no father around, the Church shows some order, you know." She is at a turning point in her life but does not know which way to turn.

Nadine is a personification of the modern shaman/hunter dichotomy. In the sixties, she was totally opposed to the war, abhorred violence, and hated the men who fought in Vietnam. She believed that the violence was not only wrong but could be avoided; then she became a victim of domestic violence. Her ex-husband, an alcoholic, abused her frequently, until one day her own suppressed violence erupted and she fought back: "Okay—I really was drunk, really mad. And I beat him up and do you know what he said to me? He turned to me after he took it and he said: I didn't know you cared that much." Suddenly Nadine understood that everyone is capable of violence; that everyone can feel hatred; and, worst of all, that it is possible to enjoy the kind of release violence can bring: "I was 'anti-war', I marched, I was 'non-violent'. (Laughs) [. . .] But I'm capable of it. [. . .] We all are." She considers herself Mark's "best friend." She does not flinch when Mark tells her about his experience in Vietnam or when she looks at his photographs of mutilated bodies; she wants to hear the stories Cheryl will not listen to: "I'm not moved by anything he tells me. I'm not changed. I'm not shocked. I'm not offended. And he must see that."

Like Cheryl, Nadine also fears for the future, but her reasons are quite different—and more alarming. Nadine's fears are not just personal; they are fears for the future of America:

> You know, all Mark did was—he brought the war back home and none of us could look at it. [. . .] We couldn't look at ourselves. We still can't. [. . .]

Oh, God. I'm worried about us. I keep this quiet little knowledge with me every day. I don't tell my husband about it. I don't tell my kids, or Mark. Or anyone. But something has fallen apart. [. . .] I worry I have these three beautiful daughters (pieces of life) who I have devoted my whole life to, who I've put all my energy into [. . .] then somebody up there goes crazy one day and pushes the "go" button and phew! bang, finished, the end.

She sees the shallowness, or naivete, of those protestors of the sixties who did not understand the tendency toward violence they shared with the soldiers they condemned. Many anti-war demonstrations ended in violence. Whether the police or the protestors instigated the violence is not so important as the fact that violence, used as force or as resistance, existed on both sides of the confrontation. The point is not that those who protested the war were wrong, but that they did not recognize the potential for violence inherent in all Americans—even themselves: "I only hope I would have done exactly what Mark did. [. . .] I think he survived because he became an animal. I hope I would have wanted to live that bad. [. . .] We just can't face that in ourselves." It is this knowledge that frightens Nadine: even the peaceful shaman is susceptible to the intoxicating effects of violence.

III

In American culture, gender relations have operated traditionally on the basis of two equally phallocentric myths: the male myth of the American Adam—the existential hero who is responsible for the security and preservation of the "promised land," during peace and war, and the equally male-centered myth of the "angel of the house"—woman as mother, homemaker, and stoker of home fires. Mark and Cheryl's wrecked marriage is the result of their failure to recognize and deal with the conflicts those myths create for both men and women living in post-Vietnam America. The situation is further complicated by Mark's use of violence as a means of preserving his role as dominant partner and by Cheryl's acceptance, early in their relationship, of Mark's behavior. Mark has been trained to believe that "real men" are obligated to fight wars, to be the sole support their families, to protect and control their women. He has read Hemingway; he has seen John Wayne movies. He is a victim of Americans' tendency to ignore what Sartre called the "facticity" of their lives and create a living history in accordance with what they want to believe about themselves and the past. Rather than dying a quiet death at the end of the nineteenth century, the frontier mentality that created the myth of the existential hero has been perpetuated in American culture in books and movies, especially Westerns, in which the "hero commits murder, usually multiple murders, in the name of making his town/ranch/mining claim safe for women and children" [Jane Tompkins, "West of Everything," *South Atlantic Quarterly* 86, No. 4, Fall 1987]. Movie characters like those played by John Wayne have kept the image of the hunter/warrior alive in American culture, and boys like Mark are still taught to idolize "the cowboy," "the gunfighter," and "the soldier." Lloyd B. Lewis, in a section of *The Tainted War: Culture and Identity in Vietnam War Narratives* called "The 'John Wayne Wet Dream'," discusses the extent to which "The Vietnam War was, at least for some of the soldiers who fought it, *The Vietnam War Movie,* replete with a cast of characters that miraculously included them." War, according to the John Wayne mythos,

> is a test of manhood. It is the ultimate test of the capacity to endure not just fear but also any form of travail from minor irritation to imminent death and disfigurement. Moreover, one is not only required to submit to hardship but also actively to seek it in order that certification be made. . . . As a proving ground for this kind of endurance, Vietnam offered ample opportunity to display "manhood." War, in this view, had been romanticized for Americans into a kind of "placement test," the results of which determined who would wear the social identity of "man" and who would be stigmatized by the label "coward."

Movies like John Wayne's *The Green Berets,* to name only the most glaring example, depicted war as a means of determining who was a *real* man.

At one point in **Still Life** Mark wonders why the soldiers in Vietnam, who knew that the war was out of control, did not just stop fighting: "I could have got out. Everybody could've. If EVERYBODY had said no, it couldn't have happened. There were times we'd say: let's pack up and go, let's quit. But jokingly. We knew we were there. But I think I knew then we could have got out of it." They could not go because the myth is too deeply engrained. Like Huck Finn, the quintessential American Adam, they were forced to choose between the evil of killing and the evil of seeming to be un-American. But Huck Finn was not in a firefight; he had not seen fellow soldiers castrated or decapitated. For Mark and his comrades there was no new territory to "light out" to. They stayed and fought knowing that turning their backs would be suicidal. When they came home, however, the same country whose myths they were fighting to preserve turned against them, on the one hand calling them murderers and on the other completely ignoring them. They were "social outcasts to be ignored or reviled":

> The world's initial response serving to confirm this identity was a deafening silence—the absence of recognitions with which the warriors were met. . . . The Vietnam warriors, returning one by one or in shifts over the span of almost a dozen years, drew no dramatic public acclaim to mark the end of sacrifice for God and country. The most wrenching experience of their young lives went un-remarked, a rite-of-passage aborted (Lewis).

The reality is not the myth; the reality is that America does not like to face unpleasantness, particularly if it requires an admission of guilt or recognition of the potential for violence among its own native sons and daughters.

Cheryl is a product of the myth of the "angel of the house"—a myth that continues to influence the upbringing of both boys and girls in America. The woman's role is to be the homemaker and mother; the man's is to be a good provider and devoted father. The woman cooks and cleans; the man works outside the home. But Cheryl's marriage to Mark does not go according to the myth, because the myth fails to take into account the realities of life lived in the aftermath of the Vietnam War, realities that Cheryl did not anticipate: "It was my naiveté. I was so naive to the whole thing, that his craziness had anything to do with where he'd been. [. . .] I was naive to the whole world let alone somebody who had just come back from there." Mark is abusive, unfaithful, a poor provider. Not only has he has forced Cheryl to have sexual relations with him ("I've exploited Cheryl as a person, sexually . . . it wasn't exactly rape, but . . .") but with other couples and other women as well: "[He] brought this woman into our room. He wanted me to play with her. He wanted me to get it on with her, too. It just blew my mind." He has made her pose for obscene photographs:

> Mark's got this series of blood photographs. He made me pose for them. There's a kitchen knife sticking into me, but all you can see is reddish-purplish blood. It's about five feet high. He had it hanging in the shop! In the street! Boy, did I make him take it out of there. [. . .] You just don't show people those things.

Worst of all, at least from Cheryl's perspective, is the fact that Mark makes so little money, and what money he does make goes to his dog first and his family second: "I run out of dogfood, Mark sends me right up to the store. But I run out of milk I can always give [my son] Kool-Aid for two or three days. [. . .] We haven't been to the grocery store in six months for anything over ten dollars worth of groceries at a time."

Cheryl was raised to believe that marriage is the solution to life's problems; her Catholic upbringing has taught her that divorce is not an option: "Divorce means a lot of nasty things like it's over. It says a lot like Oh yeah. I been there. I'm a divorcee. . . . Geez. You could go on forever about that thing. I gave up on it." Rather than the "angel in the house," Cheryl is a captive in one of Mark's jars—a photograph placed amid scraps of violence:

> I came across this jar . . . [. . .] He had a naked picture of me in there, cut out to the form, tied to a stake with a string. And there was all this broken glass, and I know Mark. Broken glass is a symbol of fire. [. . .] there was a razor blade in there and some old negatives of the blood stuff, I think. I mean that was so violent. That jar to me, scared me. That jar to me said: Mark wants to kill me. Literally kill me. [. . .] He's burning me at the stake like Joan of Arc.

Cheryl knows she should leave Mark, but to do so would be to admit the failure of her own American Dream. So she stays, living in fear of the very person who should make her feel safe:

If I ever told him I was scared for my life, he'd freak out. [. . .] I got too much to lose. [. . .] I have a little boy here. And if I ever caught Mark hurting me or that little boy again, I'd kill him. And I don't wanna be up for manslaughter. [. . .] God, I'm scared. I don't wanna be alone for the rest of my life with two kids. And I can't rob my children of what little father they could have.

Once again, Nadine provides a synthesis between Mark and Cheryl. She also shared the idea of traditional roles. She believed that her husband would provide money, love, and security, and she would be the homemaker. But her husband began to drink, to hit her, to gamble away large amounts of money, eventually leaving her $45,000 in debt. She would be a mother, but she had difficulty with childbearing: "When the labor started, we merrily got in the car and went to the hospital. They put me immediately into an operating room. I didn't even know what dilation meant. And I couldn't. I could not dilate. [. . .] I was in agony, they knocked me out. [. . .] They gave me a C-section. I don't remember anything else."

Although she loves her children, Nadine dislikes the duties of mothering, and sometimes her frustration shows: "Just to keep my kids going. I don't sleep at all. When my kids complain about supper. I just say: I know it's crappy food. Well, go upstairs and throw it up." Still, she does not hate men. In fact, she understands the pressures many men feel:

> What's a man? Where's the model? All they had left was being Provider. And now with the economics they're losing it all. [. . .] We don't want them to be the Provider, because we want to do that ourselves. We don't want them to be heroes, and we don't want them to be knights in shining armor, John Wayne—so what's left for them to be, huh? Oh, I'm worried about men. They're not coming through. [. . .] They were programmed to fuck, now they have to make love. And they can't do it. It all comes down to fucking versus loving. We don't like them in the old way anymore. And I don't think they like us, much.

Placed in the position of "head of household," Nadine can empathize with Mark's frustration (and his bursts of violence) as well as with Cheryl's disappointments and fears. She sees all three of them as victims of America: "Christ, I hate this country. I can remember everything. Back to being two years old, and all these terrible things they taught us. I can't believe we obeyed them all." When the two women finally acknowledge one another at the end of the play, there is an unspoken link between them, as casualties of violence, that resembles the link Mark describes between himself and another veteran, his cousin who also served in Vietnam: "He and I never talked. Ever. Someone else communicated his story to me, and I know he knows my story. [. . .] I saw my cousin at his dad's funeral last December. [. . .] Wherever we moved, we knew where the other was. Something radiates between us. [. . .] Our eyes will meet, but we can't touch."

IV

Two aspects of the narrative strategy Mann uses in *Still Life* enhance the viewer/reader's understanding of the subject (the human cost of the Vietnam War) and intensify the emotional impact of the play. First, the flow of the dialogue imitates the chaotic pattern of the veteran's experience during and after the war. Act I, like the war itself, is fast-paced, confused. Act II is slower, more thoughtful, a little like the first relief of coming home, when the combat veteran tries to describe his experience to friends and family. Act III is filled with confessions, with soul-searching by each character, similar to the kind of analysis many veterans and their families must go through in order to deal with PTSD. And, second, Mann skillfully uses the motif of "still life" throughout the play as both a play on words to illustrate the misery of her characters' lives and as a means of replicating Mark's fragmented artistic vision of the war. The first act of *Still Life* is intentionally fragmented, confused. The characters talk but not to each other. They speak randomly to themselves and to the audience:

> *Cheryl*: He keeps telling me: He's a murderer. I gotta believe he can be a husband. *Mark*: The truth of it is, it's different from what we've heard about war before. *Nadine*: He's just more angry than any of us. He's been fighting for years. Fighting the priests, fighting all of them. *Mark*: I don't want this to come off as a combat story. *Cheryl*: Well, a lot of things happened that I couldn't handle. *Mark*: It's a tragedy is what it is. It happened to a lot of people.

Fragments of their stories pour out but without background or apparent order. Mark rages about the war; Cheryl complains about Mark; Nadine rambles about her relationship with Mark and criticizes Cheryl. Occasionally, the characters interrupt one another to make statements totally unrelated to the subject at hand. At other times, one of them picks up a topic that another brought up and dropped several pages before. At one point, Nadine and Cheryl speak simultaneously. The tempo of the act is rapid, much of it resembling a firefight. The characters are engaged in battle with each other and with the memory of the Vietnam War. Their words are like bullets fired across the stage; a few hit their targets but most miss. Like soldiers in battle, each of them has a position to defend and little sympathy for the enemy.

In Act Two the pace slows. The tiny fragments of stories mentioned in the first act are filled out. Some evolve into whole stories; some remain fragmented but with enough additional detail to allow the audience better insight into the characters. Mark's anger is more focused, and it becomes clear that a dark secret exists at the root of his anguish: "I did a really bad number . . . It went contrary, I think, to everything I knew. I'm not ready to talk about that yet." Cheryl explains her feelings about Mark. She is both afraid of him and extremely angry with him. She was first attracted by the "power" of Mark's "imagination" but came to fear it when she discovered his "art," the gruesome photographs and frightening jars,

and realized that his imagination is "usually sexually orientated." In fact, she says, "Everything he's done, everything is sexually orientated in some way. Whether it's nakedness or violence—it's all sexually orientated." Still buying into the American Dream, she is furious about Mark's inability, or perhaps unwillingness, to provide a real home for his family. Mostly, she wants a house of their own: "Now, if [the rental house] were mine I'd be busy at work. [. . .] I'd be painting the walls, I would be wallpapering the bedroom. I would be making improvements. [. . .] I can't do it because it's not mine. [. . .] And Mark will never be ready to have the responsibility of his own home. Never. Never." Nadine tries to sort out Mark's and Cheryl's problems while sorting out her own. She encourages Mark to keep working at his marriage: "I tried to explain to Mark that Cheryl may not always want from him what she wants right now: looking for him to provide, looking for status." But, though she appreciates Cheryl's position, she cannot understand why a woman living in America in the 1980's does not take control of her own life:

> [B]etween us, I can't understand why a woman her age, an intelligent woman, who's lived through the sixties and the seventies, who's living now in a society where women have finally been given permission to drive and progress and do what they're entitled to do . . . I mean, how can she think that way?

She is especially upset by Cheryl's decision to become pregnant a second time, knowing how troubled her marriage is: "She decided to have that child. [. . .] It's madness. Everyone was against it." Toward the end of the act, Nadine begins to repeat the phrase, "Christ, I hate this country!" like a refrain. It is not really the country she hates as much as the refusal of people to learn from the mistakes of the past.

The final act mirrors the aftermath of the war for many veterans. The voices are calmer, the comments more pointed and coherent. Mark discusses his father, his anger over the treatment of returning veterans, and his own fears about the future, with or without Cheryl. He confesses the truth about his "war crime" and worries about the extent to which it has affected his relationship with his own son:

> I killed three children, a mother and father in cold blood. (Crying) [. . .] I killed them with a pistol in front of a lot of people. [. . .] I have a son . . . He's going to die for what I've done. This is what I'm carrying around; that's what this logic is about with my children. A friend hit a booby-trap. And these people knew about it. I knew they knew. I knew that they were working with the VC infrastructure. I demanded that they tell me. They wouldn't say anything. I just wanted them to confess before I killed them. And they wouldn't. So I killed their children and then I killed them.

His guilt has not been lessened by the fact that the military knew what he did and did not punish him:

It was all rationalized, that there was a logic behind it. But they knew. And everybody who knew had a part in it. There was enough evidence, but it wasn't a very good image to put out in terms of . . . the marines overseas, so nothing happened. [. . .] All that a person can do is try and find words to try and excuse me, but I know it's the same damn thing as lining Jews up. It's no different than what the Nazis did. It's the same thing. I know that I'm not alone. I know that other people did it, too.

Most of all, Mark is confused by the anger he cannot control. Like other veterans suffering the effects of PTSD, Mark is both a victim of the war and of a society that has stereotyped him as potentially dangerous. In many cases, the veteran's "'unprovoked' anger" is actually a result of "justifiable outrage at historical events" rather than a "psychological aberration." Asking the returnees to "bottle up" their anger is the easy answer for society, but it has been devastating for veterans who have no outlet for their rage. Some internalize their distress, harming themselves; some externalize it, harming others. Many, like Mark, do both.

In the penultimate scene, Mark reads a roll call of his friends who died in the war or as a result of it. Nadine fades into the background, but Cheryl continues to talk. Her sermon about male/female relationships, the futility of discussing the war, and the necessity of a future in which everything goes "back the way it was" before the war is interrupted every few lines by the name of a dead soldier. This scene effectively mirrors the veteran's position in post-Vietnam America. The voices of protest have faded, and the nation struggles to forget—to pretend that Vietnam did not happen or that it is best left in the past. But the voice of the veteran remains loud, a constant reminder of those who died and those who are living a "still life":

> *Mark*: Spaulding, Henry. *Cheryl*: You'll look, you'll go in college campuses now and it's completely back the way it was . . . and it should stay there. *Mark*: Stanton, Ray. *Cheryl*: I don't wanna see that shit come back. I didn't even get that involved in it. I got involved in it in my own little niche. [. . .] *Mark*: Vechhio, Michael. *Cheryl*: I'm a happy-go-lucky person. I used to be anyway, before I met Mark, where you couldn't depress me on the worst day. And I had a good day every day of my life. *Mark*: Walker, (*Pause*) *Cheryl*: And that is the way life was gonna be for me. *Mark*: R. J.

Throughout *Still Life,* Mark shows slides, placing a second narrative layer on top of the drama itself. The first slide is a picture of Cheryl as she used to be; the next is a photo of a Marine boot and leg below the knee (Mark wanted to remember his foot in case he lost it). He shows a slide of himself in full Marine dress, wearing his Purple Heart. This is followed by pictures of children, American and Vietnamese. The slideshow turns ugly as Mark begins to show pictures of the war, "mass graves, people half blown apart." As the second act ends, Mark turns off the slide machine and turns on a tape recording of

Holly Near's "No More Genocide," adding a musical component to his already multimedia presentation. Act Three opens with a slide of Mark and his best friend R. J., followed by a picture of a boy whose head was blown off by a rocket. Mark starts to cry and exits the stage. He returns with slides of wounded Vietnamese children, the discussion of which leads to his "confession."

The last slide is a photograph of "two grapefruits, an orange, a broken egg, with a grenade in the center on a dark background"; there is also "some fresh bread, a fly on the fruit." From far away, however, it appears to be an "ordinary still life." The double entendre of the title becomes clear. Mark is "still alive" while his friends are dead. He now leads a "still life," suspended forever in these fragments of war—momentary glimpses of children and mutilated bodies, bits and pieces of glass and bullets and metal. In the photographic "still life" lies Mann's final comment on America: those people who prefer not to look too closely will continue to see America as a nation of plenty, filled with bread and fruit; but up close the picture is not so pretty. At the center of American culture is a penchant for violence, a grenade ready to explode, or perhaps implode, a nation that refuses to look into its own heart of darkness.

EXECUTION OF JUSTICE

PRODUCTION REVIEWS

Leslie Bennetts (review date 9 March 1986)

SOURCE: "When Reality Takes to the Stage," in *The New York Times,* 9 March 1986, Section 2, pp. 1, 4.

[*Execution of Justice received its Broadway debut on 13 March 1986 at the Virginia Theatre. In the following piece, which appeared just prior to the premiere, Bennetts provides background on the genesis of the play, its staging, and its author.*]

If someone had invented the plot, it might seem too incredible: a straight-arrow city official resigns from his post, then changes his mind and requests his job back—but the mayor has already decided to appoint someone else. In a rage, the official—a former policeman and fireman—shoots the mayor and another city official, a prominent homosexual activist.

There is no question he committed the murders, but when the case comes to trial the defense claims, among other assertions, that the accused had been binging on junk food with a high sugar content, which may have precipitated violent behavior—a theory soon immortalized as "the Twinkle defense." The jury declines to convict the assassin of first or second degree murder, passing only a verdict of voluntary manslaughter—which carries a maximum penalty of seven years in jail.

The outraged community riots, with thousands of people storming City Hall and setting fire to police cars. The murderer is paroled after five years in prison, but he has polarized the city and left a legacy of bitterness and anger that will last for years. Long before the wounds fade, the murderer commits suicide in his garage, running a rubber hose into his car to pipe in carbon monoxide and create his own personal gas chamber.

As fantastical as it might sound to one unacquainted with recent American history, Emily Mann didn't have to invent that plot, the story of her new play, *Execution of Justice.* All of it actually happened when Dan White, a former San Francisco City Supervisor, shot Mayor George Moscone and another City Supervisor, Harvey Milk, in 1978. At the time, Miss Mann, a rising young director and playwright whose career had primarily focused on regional theater, paid little attention. Later, however, on a visit to San Francisco to see a production of one of her plays. Miss Mann was shocked by the lasting damage caused by the incident, and she began to explore the subject.

The result was a play based on the Dan White case that has already had seven productions in regional theaters around the country. When a new production opens here at the Virginia Theater this Thursday, it will mark Miss Mann's Broadway debut as both playwright and director.

The work is nothing if not ambitious: using a cast of 23 playing a total of 44 different roles, it re-creates not only the murders and the trial but also a community in turmoil, with a diverse chorus of voices adding their own testimony to official transcripts and recorded facts. The characters range from a young mother of three to a black lesbian leader, from psychiatrists and lawyers to riot police, from Dan White's jailer to Sister Boom Boom, a flamboyanat homosexual in drag as a nun. The production features a large video screen and music that includes Steve Reich, heavy rock, Gregorian chants and Maria Callas. The rich variety of that canvas is essential to the work's larger goal, for in Miss Mann's eyes the Dan White case represents far more than an isolated event.

She began to understand its resonance when she went to San Francisco four years ago to see a production of her earlier play, *Still Life,* at the Eureka Theater. "I found such incredible reactions to the White case, and I realized it was still an open wound," she says. "It surprised me that people who were not necessarily politically oriented found it so shameful and upsetting. The city was still reeling, no matter what people's point of view. What surprised me most was that people who had nothing to do with Harvey Milk, personally or politically or in terms of their sexual preference, were still walking around shell-shocked from this sequence of events—the assassinations, the trial, the verdict. The wounds were really deep, and they hadn't healed. The more I investigated, the more I realized how important the issues it brought up were— not just to San Francisco, but to America as a whole."

When the Eureka Theater commissioned her to write a play on a socially or politically relevant subject, Miss Mann chose the Dan White saga. For the 33-year-old playwright, the case evoked some of the country's deepest, most controversial divisions. Mr. White, a law-and-order conservative who supported the death penalty, originally gained office as a crusader against what he perceived as the city's growing tolerance for overt homosexuality, crime, prostitution and other symptoms of moral decay. His victims were on the other end of the political spectrum: the mayor, George Moscone, was a longtime liberal, and Harvey Milk—the city's first acknowledged homosexual elected to office—had been instrumental in passing a homosexual rights ordinance considered the most stringent in the nation. The murder trial plunged an already polarized city into turmoil, with law enforcement officials wearing "Free Dan White" T-shirts and establishment heterosexuals joining homosexual activists to protest the leniency of the verdict.

"What was on trial became Dan White's set of values versus Harvey Milk's and George Moscone's set of values—the liberal ethic versus the conservative church, family and bedrock values," Miss Mann explains. "This trial is so emblematic of the co-opting of the moral center of the country by the right. Suddenly liberals looked like they lived in a cesspool. The genius of the defense in this trial was to rob the left of any moral strength and push the buttons of moral bigotry in the jury. The defense lawyer would talk about Dan White as being the perfect American male figure we should all aspire to, with good values—as opposed to the men he killed. The conclusion he built to was that good people don't kill other people—unless in some way they were morally repelled, and therefore somehow justified, as if the pressures of immorality and corruption around him had somehow made a good man crack. The underlying feeling was that on some level Dan White stood for what was right in America, and the others symbolized the decay in our society."

The more she learned about the case, the more appropriate it seemed to Miss Mann as a subject for theater. "There was a very strong emotional defense, as opposed to a prosecution that made a decision that they wanted to get the trial over quickly and just let the facts speak for themselves," she notes. "The more I worked on the play, the more I realized that what the defense and the prosecution were at war about was very complicated, emotionally and intellectually. You walk in with what looks like two clear cases of first-degree murder, and by the end of the play you understand why two counts of voluntary manslaughter came down—and why there was a riot in response to that.

"What we learn in theater is that emotionality is often stronger than rationality and fact, and here you had a prosecution that stuck to the facts and a defense that worked on people's sentimentality and unconscious prejudices. Where the prosecution was tough-minded, the defense was passionate—and passion won out in the courtroom."

The consequences were far-reaching. "What the play has become for me is more than just an examination of this particular event," says Miss Mann. "It's become an American tragedy. This event changed the political makeup of San Francisco, and the number of people who were hurt by it is staggering."

In the play, these range from friends and lovers of the victims to the district attorney whose career was ruined by the uproar. Onstage, the story is not so much re-enacted as told in a kind of oral history pastiche culled from trial transcripts and other documents, reportage and interviews. The testimony is rapid-fire, with different voices speaking their sometimes contradictory versions of the truth in overlapping bursts. Miss Mann says that although a few of the characters are fictional, they are composites of real people, and she has limited her material to words actually spoken.

"There's not a line in this that wasn't in some way said to me," she says of the testimony that departs from official documents. "And all the trial stuff is transcript—boiled down, of course, distilled, but in keeping with what was said and meant. I decided to stick with this pure a form because I wanted the rigor and discipline of keeping to the facts as much as possible."

Miss Mann was exposed early to a passion for history and current events; the daughter of a history professor, she grew up in Massachusetts and Chicago and graduated from Harvard University as an English literature major. She worked for several years at the Guthrie Theater in Minneapolis, where she wrote her first play, a one-woman show called *Annulla Allen: The Autobiography of a Survivor* whose text was drawn entirely from tape recordings of a 76-year-old survivor of the Holocaust. Although Miss Mann has worked primarily as a director in regional theaters around the country, her playwriting credits also include *Still Life,* a drama about the effects of the Vietnam War which won her Obie Awards for playwriting and directing when it was produced here at the American Place Theater. It too was shaped from tape recordings, made with a Minnesota veteran, his wife and his girlfriend. Miss Mann currently lives in Rockland County with her 2-year-old son and her husband, Gerry Bamman, an actor who plays the prosecutor in *Execution of Justice.*

Given her own interest in using real events as the basis for theater, Miss Mann is somewhat disturbed by the tendency of many of her contemporaries to restrict themselves to a smaller scope, focusing on personal events unconnected to a social or political context. "I find it very disappointing that our generation of theater people are not writing significant plays about our society," she says. "I feel like I'm trying to write intelligent plays for intelligent people. We're coming into this theater to look at an event that happened in this country, and to judge it."

Her own judgment is reflected in the play's title. "It means two things: justice was done, and justice was murdered," she observes. "The law was carried out, but

I don't think justice was done; clearly Dan White didn't think justice was done either. I think for most people, common sense tells them that when an elected mayor and city supervisor are killed, execution-style, and the killer walks out of jail five years later without having gone through any kind of rehabilitation—he had no therapy, because they said there were no signs of mental disorder—I think society begins to doubt the system that is doing this."

However, the piece has proved controversial in performance. "The responses from audiences really go across political lines," Miss Mann reports. "People come face to face with what their belief system is: what you believe is right and wrong, what you can excuse and what you can't excuse in people's behavior, what you think should be done. Usually the audiences go out arguing with each other. The emotions are surprising."

Such disputes are exactly what Miss Mann hoped to provoke. "What I've done is to let each point of view have a strong and articulate voice," she says. "You hear from so many sides, from the extreme left to the extreme right, and from so many levels of society; from people's hearts and minds and prejudices and convictions. In the end, you may come out with more questions than answers—which is part of my purpose. I don't think there are easy answers, but I think the questions have to be raised."

Richard Hummler (review date 19 March 1986)

SOURCE: A review of *Execution of Justice,* in *Variety,* 19 March 1986, p. 84.

[*Hummler extols nearly every aspect of* Execution of Justice, *declaring: "It's refreshing finally to encounter a play on a pressing contemporary issue on Broadway, and Mann has packaged the volatile material in an effective, high-tech format."*]

Execution of Justice is both a riveting courtroom drama and a penetrating analysis of the social cost of intolerance. Emily Mann's documentary-style play about the Dan White murder trial in San Francisco, widely produced in the nonprofit legit sector, has been given a superior production for Broadway and stacks up as rattling good theater. But it may have difficulties attracting the challenge-shy Broadway public.

White was the blue collar ex-city supervisor who gunned down the mayor, George Moscone, and the city's first openly gay elected official, Harvey Milk, in 1978. His conviction for manslaughter rather than murder and a light seven-year sentence touched off rioting by Frisco's sizable gay population and was widely perceived as evidence of an official homophobic conspiracy. (White served five years and committed suicide last fall.)

It's refreshing finally to encounter a play on a pressing contemporary issue on Broadway, and Mann has packaged the volatile material in an effective, high-tech format. *Execution* mixes extensive film clips, live video footage and apposite music with the basic courtroom drama structure. The trial testimony and other statements by the cops, city officials and community activists are apparently relayed verbatim.

Although there's never any doubt that the author believes that White's conviction on a lesser charge was a miscarriage of justice, the play pulls the audience forward as a whydunit, an attempt to analyze the social factors, that contributed to the murders. It succeeds to a remarkable degree in the theatrically tricky task of putting a complex actual event into dramatic focus.

The play doesn't treat White as a stock heavy but a pathetic, unstable working class stiff imbued with dubious notions of morality. That he killed Moscone and Milk out of rage over a political reversal is clear. His right wing hatred of homosexuality and "declining moral standards" is also stressed. One character convincingly declares that if White had killed only Moscone and not Milk too, he would not have gotten off so lightly.

The play's selective excerpts from the trial make the "manslaughter" verdict a real head-scratcher. The summary by the prosecutor is infinitely more persuasive than the wheedling plea for mercy by the defense lawyer, and it's safe to say that no member of the audience will ever nod in assent when the verdict comes in. It's a problem of the play, perhaps insoluble, that some profoundly important participants in the story—the members of the jury—are not represented.

The play presents the murdered Milk as a virtual saint by including a long film clip of the candlelight parade of grieving San Francisco gays, by a reading from the will in which he anticipated assassination and by loving recollections by his lover. Moscone gets much smaller billing. Periodic outraged outbursts from a black woman activist are overdone.

In the main, however, *Execution* manages to catch the lightning of complicated actuality in a bottle—and on the stage. It's a satisfying theatrical equivalent of nonfiction literature.

Mann has staged it resourcefully. The tricky interweaving of trial testimony, interviews, and film and video footage is handled with smooth dexterity. More important, the play has been cast superbly with accomplished actors who play it with conviction and tight control.

John Spencer is harrowing as the self-justifying White in the long statement to the police which ends the first act with a bang. Spencer makes it scarily clear that the character had parted company with moral judgment, although he doesn't seem to have been insane in the legal sense.

There are other keenly judged performances by Gerry Bamman as the brisk and businesslike prosecutor, Peter Friedman as the tactically shrewd defense lawyer, Nicholas Hormann as the rueful district attorney who nutshells the issues persuasively, Donal Donnelly as the psychiatrist who proffered the famous "twinkie defense," Adam Redfield as Milk's enraged lover and Marcia Jean Kurtz as a plainspeaking city supervisor. Most of the actors double or triple with admirable versatility.

The talented Ming Cho Lee has provided an appropriate playing space which puts some audience members on upstage bleachers and subtly suggests an ominous official civic environment. A four-sided film screen hangs above the proceedings to reflect the film clips and the live video material which enhance the feeling of actuality.

Execution Of Justice certainly deserves a good Broadway run, and is a likely award contender. But this nonprofit-spawned play, precisely the kind of material that the nonprofit theaters should be doing, may prove too unpleasant a dose of reality for today's increasingly escapist-oriented Broadway public.

Brendan Gill (review date 24 March 1986)

SOURCE: "Murder Most Foul," in *The New Yorker,* Vol. LXII, No. 5, 24 March 1986, p. 108.

[*In this review of the Broadway production of* Execution of Justice, *Gill finds the play incoherent, but he reserves his harshest censure for the bleak set design.*]

The number of cross-purposes at work in a failed melodrama called *Execution of Justice,* at the Virginia Theatre, is made manifest by its setting. Ming Cho Lee, ordinarily one of the most gifted and resourceful of our set designers, has been asked to provide a courtroom—specifically, a courtroom in San Francisco, in which we are to observe the trial of Dan White, the former city employee who, in 1978, shot and killed the mayor of San Francisco, George Moscone, and Harvey Milk, a city supervisor, who was a leading member of the homosexual community in San Francisco. The melodrama is made up of transcripts of testimony given at the trial, excerpts from newspaper, magazine, radio, and TV interviews, and recurrent snippets of a movie documentary of the case called *The Times of Harvey Milk.* Mr. Lee's courtroom is as much a curiosity as the play itself. The audience is presumed to be the jury, seated in a jury box that is in fact the auditorium of the Virginia; surrounding the proscenium arch of the theatre are photographic blowups of the pillared, classical San Francisco City Hall, and we are entitled to expect a similar grandeur in the courtroom itself, but, to our astonishment, this turns out to be a grungy space littered with spidery little chrome and black leather chairs of the sort that one buys at Conran's; the presiding judge's bench is at floor level, scarcely visible amid the courtroom clutter. At the back of the courtroom rise rows of bleachers, filled with members of the audience (a borrowing from *Equus*?), and behind the bleachers we glimpse a shadowy wall in traditional judicial style, with the bleak brick wall of the stagehouse rising behind it. Hanging from the supposed ceiling of the courtroom is an immense white cube, upon which video images are projected from time to time.

The incoherence of the setting is matched by the incoherence of the assignment of roles to various members of a large cast, whose transformations we are able to see through with disconcerting ease. Nor is my list of complaints at an end. The wife of one of the most distinguished of our local drama reviewers has been known to assert that her husband has never actually seen a Broadway play, having been too busy scribbling notes to himself for the purposes of the review he will shortly be writing. I never actually saw much of *Execution of Justice,* but that was because lights of blinding force occasionally flashed on, simulating the high-wattage needs of the TV crews in the courtroom.

The author and director of *Execution of Justice* is Emily Mann, and I am truly at a loss to understand what lies behind her attempt to turn this unsavory episode of American history into a work of art. It is in the nature of the genre that established facts may not be altered, and as far as I could tell no new facts have been introduced; a miserable human being committed a heinous crime, was tried and found guilty of it, received what was generally perceived to be far too light a sentence, served his time, and, a year and a half after his release from prison, committed suicide. More than a nervously hyped-up retelling of the circumstances of the crime is required to raise us to a level loftier than that of some inky, eye-catching tabloid headline. Ms. Mann leaves us irritated and exhausted but unmoved.

The cast, which has been encouraged to shout more often than absolutely necessary, includes Gerry Bamman, Peter Friedman, John Spencer, Adam Redfield, Mary McDonnell, Stanley Tucci, Lisabeth Bartlett, and Nicholas Hormann. The costumes are by Jennifer von Mayrhauser, and the lighting is by Pat Collins.

John Simon (review date 24 March 1986)

SOURCE: A review of *Execution of Justice,* in *New York Magazine,* Vol. 19, No. 12, 24 March 1986, p. 96.

[*In the following evaluation of the New York staging of* Execution of Justice, *Simon judges the play underwritten, overdirected, and overproduced.*]

Much as I would like to like *Execution of Justice*—because it deals with a gross miscarriage of justice, and one, furthermore, for which our glorious jury system and those twelve solid, ordinary, wonderful citizens and peers are largely to blame—it is hard to do so. Emily Mann,

who put together and directed this docudrama, has underwritten and overdirected, so that much that should be in clear focus remains fuzzy, and much that should be simply stated and directed is gussied and gimmicked up into shrillness and garishness.

To be sure, the San Francisco trial of City Supervisor Dan White for the shooting of Mayor George Moscone and Supervisor Harvey Milk is not, in the truest sense, stageworthy. The lawyers were not mental giants giving us a gripping intellectual duel, nor were they great demagogues bringing a host of histrionic emotions into epic play. Of interest here were either tiny technicalities or enormous legal, social, political issues; the former are too small for the stage, the latter too large for a mere documentary play and would require the resources of a major poetic and philosophical dramatist freely interpreting. Yet be it said for Miss Mann that, though a known radical, she has tried to be fair to both sides and all individuals—or at least so it seems to one who hasn't followed the case closely. But much of what she has done is puzzling.

Thus she prominently displays Sister Boom Boom, a San Francisco transvestite who affects nun's garb, whom she identifies as a "political activist." Yet as shown, S.B.B. is a grotesque derived from Genet, occasionally pertinent but mostly campy, outrageous, obfuscatory. He/she can be viewed in various ways, but we get no clues, and since this ambiguous character is not germane to the trial, it all seems so much mystification. Again, the prosecutor is presented as a bit of a buffoon. Was he? Or is the actor overacting? Or overdirected? Or doesn't Miss Mann see the buffoonery? Questions like these beset us all along the way, yet because they are not profound moral or intellectual universals but only footling particulars, they don't make for creative ambiguity, merely for distracting murkiness.

What is certain, however, is that *Execution of Justice* is overdirected and overproduced. There are film projections on an overhanging cube wherein the real-life people alternate with the actors performing them, superimpositions or fancy counterpointings of several sets of unrelated utterances, occasional games with chronology, elaborate choreographies for the attorneys every time they rise and move about, several performances whipped up to fever pitch, photomurals of San Francisco and literal-minded background music, an intrusion into the courtroom of outside events (the candlelight march with added gestures, a police counterattack with deafening explosions and blinding lights), and so on. How I yearned for the simple, bare facts consecutively and clearly enacted! Or even a few judicious comments from experts on jurisprudence, sociology, psychiatry—other than the mostly preposterous psychiatrists giving expert testimony, easy targets for the author's ironies.

As for the acting, it can hardly be judged under the circumstances, though John Spencer (White), Nicholas Hormann (D.A. Freitas), and Adam Redfield (Harvey Milk's lover) seem to be doing the right things, and Marcia Jean

Kurtz and Lisabeth Bartlett seem to be doing the wrong ones, while the rest fall somewhere in between. But it is worrisome when such fine actors as Peter Friedman and Donal Donnelly appear to be overreaching. The White case is so important that the play is not without fascination, but I wonder whether it is a good thing when an audience is impelled to applaud a suicide, even if it is Dan White's?

Langdon Brown (review date December 1986)

SOURCE: A review of *Execution of Justice,* in *Theatre Journal,* Vol. 38, No. 4, December 1986, pp. 476-77.

[*In the evaluation below of* Execution of Justice, *Brown notes that "the weakness of the play lies in its similarity to news and documentary technique," but he concludes favorably: "A serious attempt is being made here to question our legal system and the ethics that underlie it."*]

The sentencing of former San Francisco supervisor Dan White for the 1978 murders of Mayor George Moscone and Supervisor Harvey Milk inspired television and print commentary, a film called *The Times of Harvey Milk,* and a play by Emily Mann. We all remember the murders, the trial of Mr. White, and his use of the "twinkie defense." The Eureka Theatre of San Francisco saw potential in this story and commissioned Ms. Mann to dramatize it in 1982. After eighteen months of collaborative effort a work emerged that was produced in regional theatres (Arena Stage, Guthrie, Alley, among others) before opening in New York. The script was published in the November, 1985, issue of *American Theatre.*

Execution's plot faithfully follows events, employing as dialogue only actual statements from trial transcripts, media interviews, or interviews conducted by Ms. Mann, who terms the play "theatre of testimony." Incidents flash rapidly before the audience on a simple set while a cube suspended above the stage displays news clips, excerpts from the film already mentioned, and simultaneous video images of the on-stage action. Things get a slow start because of necessary but familiar exposition before the trial heightens interest and focuses attention on the opposing camps: the conservative "law and order" sympathizers of White versus the liberal constituency of Moscone and Milk. It is here that the play promises a great deal: dramatizing an underlying clash in social values with both sides claiming the moral high ground. In fact the most intriguing part of the story seems to be the violent aftermath of the trial and the continuing polarization of the city.

Unfortunately, however, when the play gets through the early scenes, it fails to establish a dramatic direction. The possibilities inherent in the willingness of the jury to accept the "diminished capacity" defense are not explored beyond the event itself. The emotional travails of the community, while beautifully portrayed in a candle-light march simultaneously accomplished on film and on stage, proceed no further. Perhaps sensing dramaturgic problems, Ms. Mann (who also directed) resorts to a barrage of technical effects that confuse the issue further. Ming Cho Lee's setting, uprooted from its original home at Arena Stage, loses a good deal of its effectiveness enclosed in the proscenium of the Virginia Theatre.

The playwright has chosen to eschew a point of view. While the *New York Times* found Miss Mann's objectivity courageous, I wonder if this is not exactly the play's problem. Miss Mann began a journey in search of truth, trusting to the facts. But in the end we get a compilation not very different from a news report, with the same dissatisfied sense of incompletion we get from the chaos of life: that there are no answers. Even artists may despair of finding answers, but the art of the drama forms a contract with the audience that promises at least a search for answers, or the derivation of an interesting dramatic form from the patterns of despair (for example, *Waiting for Godot*). Here there is nothing like that. In her quest for fairness Miss Mann has left us with so much balance that we are discouraged from either drawing conclusions or, worse, from finding meaning in the murders of Moscone and Milk or from the suicide of White.

Recently there has been a good deal of talk about the relationship between television news and entertainment. Robert Brustein labeled our window on the world "news theatre," while others have been so unkind as to suggest that the ability of news stories to motivate us to turn on the television may have more to do with what we see than factual importance or relevance to our lives. *Execution of Justice* interests particularly in this regard because of its attempt to mine the drama from facts already exploited by television and its use of the technology of television as part of its production design. The weakness of the play lies in its similarity to news and documentary technique: it fails to move beyond the appeal of the events themselves—in short, to dramatize the events.

There are excellent performances by a solid ensemble of two dozen actors doubling in twice as many roles. We receive a vivid sense of the individual events, from the opening announcement of White's crimes onward, because of the acting. Peter Friedman as the defense attorney and Gerry Bamman as the prosecutor spar and jab in the play's liveliest conflict as they elicit testimony from an intense John De Vries as White's police colleague, and a self-consciously meticulous Donal Donnelly as a coroner and psychiatrist. John Spencer is consistently earnest and confused as White and Mary McDonnell as his wife is moving when she demonstrates the personal cost of White's actions.

Having started with the play's failings, I must emphasize that there remains a good deal to praise. A serious attempt is being made here to question our legal system and the ethics that underlie it. The producers deserve credit for their courage. In the midst of all the wailing and gnashing of teeth expended on the ills of the great white way, someone actually tried to present a play on Broadway with a serious subject, a huge ensemble cast, and all the missing elements so fervently desired by commentators who decry empty theatres and empty-headed offerings. We can all hope for more efforts of this kind by theatre artists of serious purpose.

CRITICAL COMMENTARY

Ellen Schiff (essay date 1989)

SOURCE: "From Black and White to Red and Pink: Political Themes on the American Jewish Stage," in *Studies in American Jewish Literature,* Vol. 8, No. 1, Spring, 1989, pp. 66-76.

[*In the following excerpt, Schiff discusses Mann's indictment of the psychiatric profession and the media in* Execution of Justice.]

[*Execution of Justice*] was commissioned by San Francisco's Eureka Theatre in 1982. The play's subject is the trial of Dan White for the assassination of San Francisco Mayor George Moscone and City Supervisor Harvey Milk, the first avowed homosexual to hold elective office in the United States. The particulars are familiar: in November 1978, White, a former policeman and fireman turned city supervisor, resigned his post, then asked to be reinstated. Learning that the mayor was going to turn him down, he slipped into City Hall and gunned down both Moscone and Milk. He was found guilty only of voluntary manslaughter and sentenced to seven years in prison.

Mann's métier is docudrama. She builds the entire work from court transcripts, documentary footage, newsclips, and interviews. In its objective manner, *Execution of Justice* makes incisive observations about the criminal justice system and contemporary American life, for as Mann's ironic title suggests, it is the system that is on trial. There can be little doubt of the playwright's passion about her subject, a passion she artfully manages by channeling it through the facts of the case, which climaxes in the lesser charge and a sentence that even the judge, sympathetic to White but bound by law, admits he finds "completely inappropriate."

As the play recreates the trial, it vividly delineates the factions in opposition: the conservative middle class, the gay community represented by a black lesbian leader and a nun in drag, and Moscone's liberal associates. These groups are never reduced to simple right and left, or simpler right and wrong. The constituency that elected Dan White to the Board of Supervisors is represented by a cop, the third generation in his family to wear the badge, who says "I got nothin' against people doin' what they want, if I don't see it," but who is patently outraged at the extreme public behavior of the city's homosexuals. Dan White's position is presented in his own words. We hear him campaigning for office, promising to combat the "malignancies of society" making inroads on traditional American values, and we understand where the

pressures came from for him to change his mind about giving up his seat on the board. We hear his conviction, as he testifies in court, that he considered himself a conscientious public servant, "trying to do a good job for the city." The play leaves it to the audience to decide whether White was more strongly motivated by thwarted political ambition or homophobia.

Counterpointed is the fierce desire for justice in the gay community, scandalized at the reduced charges and light sentence. Clips are shown from the Oscar award-winning documentary on Harvey Milk, including Moscone's funeral and the enormous candlelight march, which filled the city streets and which is also recreated on stage. Remarks the lesbian leader, "It was one of the most eloquent expressions of a community's response to violence that I have ever seen. . . ."

Nor is George Moscone put forth as squeaky clean. His less-than-perfect moral character, his marital infidelity, and his possible ties with James Jones are all here. The gamut of emotions and opinions displayed at the trial makes plain that more than the fate of a man or even rival political convictions were at stake. As the district attorney who lost his job as a result of the trial puts it, "The fight was over who controlled the city." "The city" takes on metaphoric resonance, for the play, like the trial, demonstrates that the underlying issues, which certainly extend well beyond San Francisco, are far from resolved.

Mann's work puts the case of the *People v. Dan White* in the larger context of its time and place. The shootings occurred a few days after the Jonestown People's Temple tragedy. As the shocking details accumulated, so did rumors connecting Jones to liberal political elements in San Francisco, where he had been chair of the city Housing Authority, appointed by Moscone. Staggering death toll figures from Guyana and hearsay, cited by the defense attorney, that "hit lists had been placed on public officials in San Francisco" ran rampant in the city during those months in 1978-79, intensifying the climate of fear and the license to kill.

One of the most remarkable things about this play is the way it draws on two cultural forces whose impact on the White case was enormous. The first influence is a crucial element in the plot; the second, by contrast, makes its statement from the staging of the work.

First, both the defense and the prosecution in the trial summoned psychiatrists to assess White's behavior. This scene would be comic were it not so gruesome, so crucial to the verdict—and so emblematic of how science has come to legitimize extremes of antisocial behavior. One of the analysts declares that the loaded gun which White carried because he was experiencing so much anxiety must be viewed symbolically as a "transitional object," analagous to a child's security blanket. That diagnosis is only slightly less amoral than the testimony of the forensic psychiatrist that White's ability to reason was inactivated by his diet of junk food. It was, of course, this finding of "diminished capacity," the Twinkies defense, that turned the case for White.

Second, *Execution of Justice* indicts the power of the media and the use of electronic equipment to shape information and the way we learn it and think about it. The inevitable distortions are brilliantly demonstrated in the staging. Throughout the work on stage, TV cameras record moments of strife or personal grief which are instantly played back on huge screens. Observed the critic who saw the play at the Guthrie in Minneapolis, "The effect is extraordinary, at once a transformation of scale, a heightening of importance and spontaneity, a pinpoint shift in focus that tears a character from context and pushes him, larger than life, into the isolation of the screen, . . . as private thoughts and emotions are violated and made hugely public and the video image confusingly takes over from the real person" [Mike Steele, *Minneapolis Star and Tribune,* 21 October 1985].

Emily Mann's *Execution of Justice,* like Clifford Odets's *Waiting for Lefty,* makes a jury of its audience. We can gauge how far the American Jewish stage has come in depicting political issues by comparing the effects of these two works on theatergoers. At the Williamstown Theatre Festival's 1987 tribute to the Group Theatre, Ruth Nelson, one of the Group's original members, held us breathless as she described the electricity that crackled in the auditorium at the 1935 première of *Lefty.* Having seen a production of the play a few years back, I can understand why it was banned in cities across the nation 50-odd years ago. It is easy to appreciate its capacity to galvanize spectators into joining the actors' final curtain cry, as Harold Clurman put it, to "strike for greater dignity, strike for bolder humanity, strike for the full stature of man" [*The Fervent Years,* 1945].

Audience reaction to *Execution of Justice* is less likely to be as volatile or as well focused. It is not that the playwright, despite her evenhanded presentation, is any less eloquent in communicating her convictions or that her subject is any less energizing than Odets's. Simply, *Execution* puts forth no easily identified wrongs to protest because it makes so clear the complexity of the issues it dramatizes. While the work may well have contributed to the state of California's decision to abolish the legal gimmickry that made the Twinkies defense possible, that cannot have been its raison d'être.

FURTHER READING

BIBLIOGRAPHY

Kolin, Philip C. and LaNelle, Daniel. "Emily Mann: A Classified Bibliography." *Studies in American Drama 1945-Present* 4 (1989): 223-66.
    Includes an exhaustive listing of secondary materials on Mann and an essay surveying her important works.

AUTHOR COMMENTARY

Savran, David. "Emily Mann." In his *In Their Own Words: Contemporary American Playwrights,* pp. 145-60. New York: Theatre Communications Group, 1988.
    Interview with Mann in which she discusses her plays *Annulla* and *Still Life,* the influence of Bertolt Brecht on her work, and other topics.

ANNULLA ALLEN

Gussow, Mel. "Testimony of a Survivor." *The New York Times* (2 November 1988): C 23.
    Mixed review of *Annulla Allen* that contends that as "testimony from an atypical survivor of the Holocaust," the play "has a viability, but as a monodrama it needs additional structuring and clarification."

Hersh, Amy. "A Survivor's Voice." *American Theatre* 5, No. 8 (November 1988): 8-9.
    Discussion of *Annulla Allen* that includes comments by Mann and by Linda Hunt, star of the 1988 New Theatre of Brooklyn production of the play.

Massa, Robert. "Unstill Life." *The Village Voice* 33, No. 45 (8 November 1988): 100.
    Favorable review of the New Theatre of Brooklyn production of *Annulla Allen.* Massa observes: "Mann avoids the obvious dangers of her subject through her talent for detail and rhythm and her trust in Annulla's actual words."

STILL LIFE

Kolin, Philip C. "Mann's *Still Life.*" *Explicator* 48, No. 1 (Fall 1989): 61-4.
    Descriptive survey of *Still Life* that considers it "one of the best plays yet written about the Vietnam War."

Ringnalda, Don. "The Theatre of Doing It Wrong, Getting It Right." In his *Fighting and Writing the Vietnam War,* pp. 172-205. Jackson: University Press of Mississippi, 1994.
    Argues that what Mann achieves with the "contrapuntal voicings" in *Still Life* is that "no single voice can ever build up narrative momentum and stake out a claim for the spectator's sympathy. The content of this play is not any or all of the voices; instead it is the charged, silent spaces between the voices."

HAVING OUR SAY

Franklin, Nancy. "Partners in Time." *The New Yorker* LXXI, No. 9 (24 April 1995): 118-19.
    Laudatory review of *Having Our Say* that admires Mann's "intelligent distillation" of the material from Amy Hill Hearth's book about Sadie and Bessie Delaney.

Istel, John. "Say It, Sisters." *American Theatre* 12, No. 5 (May/June 1995): 6-7.

Favorable assessment of *Having Our Say* that focuses particularly on the "festive perspective" and "infectious humor" of the main characters.

Kanfer, Stefan. "Strong Performers." *The New Leader* LXXVIII, No. 4 (8-22 May 1995): 22-3.

Praises all aspects of *Having Our Say,* including Mann's

script, the set and costume designs, and the performances.

Simon, John. Review of *Having Our Say. New York* Magazine 28, No. 18 (1 May 1995): 67.

Negative evaluation in which Simon asserts: "Even with two outstanding actresses, this shortish but still overlong play stretched beyond endurance by supererogatory ovations and endless intermissions left me restless."

Additional coverage of Mann's life and career is contained in the following source published by Gale Research: *Contemporary Authors,* **Vol. 130.**

Pierre Carlet de Chamblain de Marivaux
1688-1763

INTRODUCTION

Marivaux is recognized as an innovative dramatist who produced masterpieces of French comedy concerned with the discovery and denial of love. His works are characterized by subtle description and keen psychological observation; this penchant for minute analysis is termed "marivaudage." A modern revival of interest in Marivaux's comedies has gained him a preeminent position in the history of eighteenth-century French literature.

BIOGRAPHICAL INFORMATION

Extremely little is known of Marivaux's life. He was born in Paris, and while a child, he moved with his family to Riom, where his father assumed the directorship of the royal mint. In 1710, at the age of twenty-two, Marivaux returned to Paris to study law. He eventually received his degree, but by then he had begun to move in literary circles. His friendship with Bernard LeBovier de Fontenelle and others led Marivaux to join the Moderns, a group of progressive writers led by Houdar de la Motte, who quarreled with the group known as the Ancients over the relative merits of contemporary and classical aesthetic views. Marivaux's earliest known play, *Le Père prudent et equitable* (*The Just and Prudent Father*), is a one-act comedy believed to have been written sometime between 1709 and 1711 and then produced privately. In 1720 Marivaux began a highly successful association with the Théâtre Italien, a popular troupe of Italian actors who performed in France and rivalled the national company, the Théâtre Français. His debut comedy, *Arlequin poli par l'amour* (*Harlequin Refined by Love*), fused the sophistication of the French theater with the imaginative stagecraft of the Italian and garnered widespread popular and critical approval. The play typifies Marivaux's departure from such established forms as the five-act verse drama, which he discarded in favor of one- and three-act plays. Also in 1720 Marivaux produced for the Théâtre Français his only tragedy, *Annibal* (*Hannibal*). This drama failed, as did many of his later comedies performed there, due largely to Marivaux's numerous dramatic innovations and his subtle, multi-layered style, which the French actors found difficult to interpret for performance. Despite a relatively unsuccessful history with the Théâtre Français, Marivaux was elected to the French Academy in 1743. For the rest of his life he continued to write comedies, though with lessening frequency. After suffering a prolonged illness, Marivaux died in Paris in 1763.

MAJOR WORKS

The dominant thematic concern in Marivaux's thirty-odd plays centers on individual sincerity within the social

sphere, particularly as it relates to courtship and love. Nonetheless, he wrote several dramas concerned less with love than with eighteenth-century social and philosophical issues. An enormously popular play during its first run, *L'Île des esclaves* (*The Isle of Slaves*), hypothesizes the eradication of barriers between social classes. A similar play in conception, *L'Île de la raison* (*The Isle of Reason*), juxtaposes humanity's paradoxical potential for displaying both folly and wisdom. Marivaux's first masterpiece, *Le Jeu de l'amour et du hasard* (*The Game of Love and Chance*), was produced by the Théâtre Italien in 1730. This was followed by several other highly acclaimed plays, including *Les Legs* (*The Legacy*), *Les Fausses Confidences* (*False Confidences*), and *L'Épreuve* (*The Test*). The performance of *La Mère confident* (*The Mother as Confidant*) in 1735 marked the birth of the *drame bourgeois,* a form halfway between serious drama and sentimental comedy, which explores the family problems of the middle class.

CRITICAL RECEPTION

Nearly all critics of Marivaux's works discuss in some way "marivaudage," the author's distinctive style. During the eighteenth and most of the nineteenth century, harsh evaluations dominated discussions of his writing. Marivaux's contemporary Jean-François de la Harpe disparagingly defined marivaudage as "an artifice which consists in clothing subtle and alambricated ideas in popular language, a vicious fluency which leads him to examine one thought from every possible angle and which scarcely ever allows him to leave it till he has spoiled it; in short, a precious and far-fetched neologism which shocks both language and good taste." Pejorative definitions such as this prevailed until recent times, when marivaudage became equated with talent rather than tastelessness. Several modern critics have defended Marivaux's style, either by demonstrating its affinity with that of other celebrated writers, such as Fontenelle, Henry James, and Marcel Proust, or by stressing Marivaux's relatively spare use of language and dismissing La Harpe's negative commentary as exaggerated. Criticism of the plays themselves has been closely linked to the evolution of the term marivaudage. Today, although a few of Marivaux's plays are dismissed for their lack of originality, most are judged to display liveliness, a variety of situations and characters, and a modern appeal which elevates them over the works of his contemporaries, including Voltaire. Modern critics point out that Marivaux developed his favorite subject, blossoming love, through many different situations and emotions. Critics emphasize that the comedies reveal universal themes, such as human deception and sincerity. *Amour-propre*, or a form of self-love that Marivaux links with a refusal to remove one's "social mask" and open oneself to romantic love, embodies these themes and is a central element in his dramas. Beginning with *La Surprise de l'amour* (*The Surprise of Love*) in 1722, this element suffused Marivaux's comedies and greatly influenced the treatment of love in the theater, which until then had been preoccupied with stage action rather than involved psychological explorations.

PRINCIPAL WORKS

PLAYS

Le Père prudent et equitable; ou, Crispin l'heureux fourbe [*The Just and Prudent Father; or, Crispin the Jolly Rogue*] 1709-11
L'Amour et la vérité [*Love and Truth*; with Louis Rustaing de Saint-Jorry] 1720
Annibal [*Hannibal*] 1720
Arlequin poli par l'amour [*Harlequin Refined by Love*] 1720
La Surprise de l'amour [*The Surprise of Love*] 1722
La Double Inconstance [*Double Inconstancy*] 1723
Le Dénouement imprévu [*The Unforeseen Ending*] 1724
La Fausse Suivante; ou, Le Fourbe puni [*The False Maid, or, The Rogue Punished*] 1724
Le Prince travesti; ou, L'Illustre aventurier [*The Prince in Disguise; or, The Illustrious Impostor*] 1724
L'Héritier du village [*The Village Heir*] 1725
L'Île des esclaves [*The Isle of Slaves*] 1725

L'Île de la raison; ou, Le Petits Hommes [*The Isle of Reason; or, The Little Men*] 1727
La Seconde Surprise de l'amour 1727
Le Triomphe de Plutus [*The Triumph of Plutus*] 1728
La Colonie; ou, L'homme sans souci [*The Colony; or, The Man without Care*] 1729
Le Jeu de l'amour et du hasard [*The Game of Love and Chance*] 1730
La Réunion des amours [*Loves' Reunion*] 1731
L'École des Mères [*The School for Mothers*] 1732
Les Serments indiscrets [*The Indiscreet Vows*] 1732
Le Triomphe de l'amour [*The Triumph of Love*] 1732
L'Heureux Stratagème [*The Successful Stratagem*] 1733
La Méprise [*The Misunderstanding*] 1734
Le Petit-maître corrigé [*The Fop Corrected*] 1734
La Mère confidente [*The Mother as Confidant*] 1735
Le Legs [*The Legacy*] 1736
Les Fausses Confidences [*False Confidences*] 1737
La Joie imprévue [*Unexpected Joy*] 1738
Les Sincères [*The Sincere Ones*] 1739
L'Épreuve [*The Test*] 1740
La Dispute [*The Dispute*] 1744
La Femme fidèle [*The Faithful Wife*] 1746
Le Préjugé vaincu [*Prejudice Conquered*] 1746
Les Acteurs de bonne foi [*The Actors of Good Faith*] 1757
Félicie 1757
La Provinciale [*The Provincial Lady*] 1761

OTHER MAJOR WORKS

Les Effets surprenants de la sympathie; ou, Les Aventures de *** (novel) 1713-14
*Le Télémaque travesti (novel) 1714
†Pharsamon; ou, Les Nouvelles Folies romanesques (novel) 1715
L'Homère travesti; ou, L'Iliade en vers burlesques (poetry) 1716
L'Indigent Philosophe (journal) 1726-27
La Vie de Marianne; ou, Les Aventures de Mme. la Comtesse de ***. 11 vols. (novel) 1731-42
Le Cabinet du philosophe (journal) 1734
Le Paysan parvenu. 5 vols. (novel) 1734-35
Oeuvres completes de M. de Marivaux. 12 vols. (collected works) 1781

*This work was first published in 1736.

†This work was first published in 1737; also published as *Pharsamon; ou, Le Don Quichotte moderne,* 1739.

OVERVIEWS AND GENERAL STUDIES

Oscar A. Haac (essay date 1956)

SOURCE: "Marivaux and the Human Heart," in *The Emory University Quarterly*, Vol. XII, No. 1, March, 1956, pp. 35-43.

[*In the excerpt below, Haac discusses Marivaux's techniques of characterization, contending that the figures in his plays are "not generalized or abstract symbols" but "highly individual and sensitive."*]

The modern rediscovery of an author like Marivaux is an exciting experience and a key to the literary temper of our generation. For almost two centuries the passionate oratory of Voltaire's plays, with their sweeping moralistic overtones, aroused far greater enthusiasm, but today the subtle and brilliant comedies of Marivaux (1688-1763), in the spirit of the Parisian salon society of the prerevolutionary era, are produced more frequently on the French stage than the works of any other author of the century, including Beaumarchais. In the repertoire of the Comédie Française he yields only to Molière, the patron saint of the company, to Racine and to Corneille. Recently in New York the Comédie Française played *Arlequin poli par l'amour*, and a few years ago Jean Louis Barrault produced *Les fausses confidances* during his brief visit. J. M. Barrie's *The Admirable Crichton*, the baroque theater of Giraudoux, the *"pièces brillantes"* of Jean Anouilh, especially *La répétition,* bear witness to Marivaux's growing influence. Jean Louis Barrault, in *Ma troupe et ses acteurs,* recognizes him as his most important model after Molière as the master of dialogue.

Most of Marivaux' comedies were written for Luigi Riccoboni and his Comédie Italienne. This troupe was continuing an old Italian tradition in which each actor represented a stock character and improvised his speeches during the performance. Riccoboni took the part of the principal lover (Lélio), the leading lady was first his wife, later the younger Silvia Benozzi for whom Marivaux created his major parts. Among the supporting cast Arlequin was most colorful, traditionally naïve, clever, and funny. Riccoboni drew his plots from many sources; some were based on Italian adaptations of Spanish plays. He was a man of wide interests and one of the first in France to express his admiration for Shakespeare.

Marivaux adapted himself admirably to this milieu. His characters bear the standard Italian names or their French equivalents; his subject matter was similar to the standard plots. This was essential, since the Comédie Italienne welcomed his plays less for their quality, which remained often unappreciated (Riccoboni pays no tribute to Marivaux in his writings), but because they helped to recapture an audience unfamiliar with the Italian medium and rapidly losing interest.

A review of Marivaux' sources from Molière to current novels and Riccoboni's repertoire would show that he invented neither plots nor characters. His originality lies in the dialogue, that is, in his style, and in his subtle manner of uncovering ideas and feelings. Unlike Voltaire he formulates neither maxims nor slogans. His characters are not generalized or abstract symbols, but dramatically express their subjective experiences. Lélio and Arlequin have become highly individual and sensitive. We shall examine this technique in some of the plays. . . .

Arlequin poli par l'amour (1720) is his first major achievement on the stage. It is a fantasy about an inexperienced but most attractive Arlequin, loved by a fairy queen who would like to bring him under her power. As soon as Arlequin sees the young shepherdess, Silvia, he is completely overcome. His new love renders him resourceful enough to seize the queen's magic wand and render her impotent. We witness "the surprising results of sympathy" (the subtitle of an early novel), for, in direct contrast to what we often hear about the "age of reason," the French eighteenth century recognized the power of emotion, the primacy of feeling over intellect. Marivaux does not disdain reason. He looks upon it as an ideal which we must superimpose on our emotions to become fit for civilized society. As he put it in *L'île de la raison*: "Love is natural and necessary, only we must regulate its violence." Love is all-powerful and will excuse even wilful deceit in *Les fausses confidances,* one of his best plays. Dorante is so sincere and touching that Araminte must forgive that her affection was won through the tricks of Dubois, a crafty servant and forerunner of Figaro.

The charm of sincere love is so invincible that it triumphs over the plans of a fairy queen and, with even greater ease, over the systems of philosophers. The pedant Hortensius in *La seconde surprise de l'amour* cannot even retain the attention of the Marquise who has resolved to follow him and give up the ways of love; Hermocrate in *Le triomphe de l'amour* is outwitted and doubly shamed when he falls in love and then sees his pupil, whom he tried to protect from such passions, marry this very girl. Marivaux' opposition to the party of the Philosophes seems to combine with his youthful antagonism toward the Ancients in the battle of the books. The Philosophe in *L'île de la raison* is least capable of insight of all the shipwrecked Europeans on an imaginary island, inspired by *Gulliver's Travels,* while his companions are subtly and humorously introduced to wisdom, or rather, come to know themselves.

In *La surprise de l'amour* (1722) Lélio and a Comtesse, both disappointed in love, have forsworn it for ever. Marivaux shows how foolish such a resolution is in the case of young, attractive people nowhere near fifty, the age for retiring to convents and for affected piety. Lélio and the Comtesse gradually realize that they love each other, though they are unwilling to admit it even to themselves. They spend much time discussing the marriage of two tenant farmers. It provides the pretext for frequent meetings, since they dare not mention what is really on their minds. Here Marivaux shows his mastery of dramatic dialogue, or of silence and unexpressed feelings. His lines take on their full meaning only in context. Even the proverbs quoted by Arlequin, *e.g.,* "the scalded cat fears water," are meant as individual reactions, often amusing and grotesque. Marivaux observes man and his motives like La Fontaine and La Rochefoucauld, but he replaces the generalized conclusions of their *Fables* and *Maximes* by subtle dialogue which implies more than is said. It is an excellent method of character analysis on the stage, and a good comic device, since it gives the spectator the joy of knowing more than the characters of the play. These, in turn, take on a new individuality. Unlike the earlier followers of Molière, he does not merely present human types. He does not portray the "chevalier à la mode," like Dancourt, the "joueur," like Regnard, the "méchant" of Gresset. He wants a particular "surprise de l'amour," distinct from the "seconde surprise de l'amour" (1727) and from analogous situations in *Les serments indiscrets* (1734). All these plays deal with persons who are in love but do not express it. However, what matters is not this common theme but the particular "chaos de sensations" produced in each situation. In *La surprise,* Lélio seeks solitude to escape future disillusionment, in *La Seconde surprise* a marquise is equally disillusioned, but the tone is more serious and sentimental, and the pedant Hortensius adds other conflicts and overtones. Both of these plays portray people ignorant of their growing passion, while *Les serments indiscrets* show us Damis and Lucile consciously in love, but pledged not to show it, though they cannot keep their word, and this, according to Marivaux' preface, "is another kind of situation entirely unrelated to that of the lovers in *La surprise de l'amour.*" He may be overemphasizing the difference to defend a rather poor play against its harsh critics, but he is justly proud of having portrayed a variety of emotions, all part of his analysis, his "science of the human heart."

This concept is developed in one of his addresses to the French Academy. He complains that this "science" is unjustly neglected and insufficiently honored because it is so accessible and obvious. He clearly states his epicurean principles, evident in his other works, when he maintains that we are stimulated to learn certain things or to follow principles by the rewards accorded to such behavior by our society, and by the natural joy they procure. He implies that treatises of morality are boring and ineffectual, but recognizes that the need for human understanding and for understanding man is the ultimate inspiration of his theater, as it was that of Corneille and Racine. Marivaux' contribution to psychological analysis is considerable and his theoretical pronouncements to the Academy are too little known.

Let us return once more to *La surprise de l'amour.* Lélio forms a striking contrast with his servant, Arlequin. When Lélio proclaims that thinking of women and their deceits is enough to confirm him in his desire to forsake them, Arlequin cannot help replying: "Imagine, such thoughts have opposite effect on me. It is precisely when I think of them that my resistance wavers." Even the birds making love in the trees disturb poor Arlequin, who would like to think like his master. Marivaux' servants are close to nature; this fact makes them into tools of three basic wants, food, money, and love, but at the same time enables them to admit what their masters try to conceal to others and to themselves. Thus the servants add not only comic relief after the sentimental meanderings of their masters, but perceive their masters' problems and point to their solution. The parallel between master and servant becomes even stronger because they generally love and marry in the same house; the servant marries the

maid of his master's bride. This convention can be found also in Molière, for instance in the *Bourgeois gentilhomme.* Marivaux' original contribution is to have analyzed love on two levels and to have portrayed one as the mirror or parody of the other. He has given the theme of Don Quijote and Sancho new life on the stage. This technique, adopted by Lessing in *Minna von Barnhelm,* is an excellent means of orienting the spectator and leading him to understand more about the hero and heroine than they do themselves. He can derive from the grotesque ramblings of the servants what their masters are unwilling or unable to admit. We might call it a technique of defining characters simultaneously by analogy and contrast.

A superior illustration of the parallel between servants and masters is *Le jeu de l'amour et du hasard* (1730), Marivaux' most famous play. Two young people, who have not met but whose marriage has been arranged by their parents, each decide to exchange rôles with a servant in order to observe and judge the proposed partner objectively. The two couples fall in love, as they should, even in disguise. The servants naturally admit their love long before their masters. There is an admirable contrast, and analogy, between the two "crystallizations of love," to use Stendhal's term, and also between the ways in which the disguises are uncovered. Silvia is close to despair when Dorante tells her who he is. This revelation does not make her reveal who she is; she pushes Dorante on to declare himself in spite of what seem inescapable class differences; she forces him to make an almost tragic and heroic decision. Only then does she explain. Compare this dramatic sequence with the burlesque declaration of Arlequin that, instead of being "captain," he is only the "soldier in his master's dressing room," whereupon Lisette admits to an equivalent rank of "hairdresser of Madame." Each time aspects of pride and self-respect, love and need for affection, are brought out in different light. The picture and its image supplement each other.

When Silvia finds that she loves Dorante, not his servant, she states, "It was indeed important that he be Dorante," and also, "Now I understand my heart." The implication is that she could not really have fallen in love with a person whose thoughts were servile or uncouth. Marivaux does not establish social barriers, but recognizes a hierarchy of sensitive and noble souls. This can also be seen in *La double inconstance* (1723), where the couple, Silvia-Arlequin, is broken up by the prince, carefully disguised so as to conquer by merit alone. While he sends Flaminia to capture the heart of Arlequin, which is done by a show of friendliness and a magnificent meal, the prince can prove to Silvia that she needs a lover as tender and sensitive as she is herself, and not a glutton like Arlequin.

The social problems here implied appear frequently. Just as the prince does not hesitate to marry Silvia, a simple girl from his estates, *Le préjugé vaincu* shows how the aristocratic Angélique finally overcomes her "prejudice" against marrying a worthy bourgeois. In Marivaux' novels, Marianne, a foundling, and Jacob, a simple peasant, frequent circles far above their condition. The island plays, *L'île des esclaves* and *L'île de la raison,* show servants undertaking the reform of their masters, though in the spirit of helpfulness and love. Frank and unrestrained as always, these servants can direct those whose very complexity makes it hard for them to change. There is always hope that faults can be mended. In *Le petit-maître corrigé,* a social butterfly is successfully taught the true value of sentiment and love. Marivaux is no revolutionary; he is too kindhearted to assume that violence can ever be justified; he is too much of a dramatist and novelist to lose himself in social theory. He does not appear, therefore, as a major social thinker, but his keen "sensibility" makes him remarkably aware of these problems. . . .

Marivaux belongs to his period. It could, however, easily be shown that he manifests a considerable range of interests, and that the very moderation in his tone makes possible the modulated analysis that constitutes his greatest merit. Marivaux cultivated the art of finding "the fitting word." His préciosité is intentional. Just as he believed that reason must guide us in expressing our emotions, he felt the need for a polite and cultured tone. He was aware of unpleasant truths and basic drives. These dominate his servant characters and are all too evident in their masters. Yet his "marivaudage," which in the *Petit Larousse* is so unjustly qualified as affected, unnatural, and precious language, presents the medium in which the subtle shadings of the "science of the human heart" can be developed. Marivaux' style creates not merely a poetic illusion but implies that ever-present search for truth and for its adequate expression which, as Marivaux himself put it, is the qualifying mark of all great literature.

Kenneth N. McKee (essay date 1958)

SOURCE: "Conclusion," in *The Theater of Marivaux,* New York University Press, 1958, pp. 255-67.

[*In the essay below, McKee summarizes the innovations Marivaux introduced into French theater and surveys his influence on subsequent dramatists.*]

Marivaux . . . was the most original French dramatist of the eighteenth century. In his theater as a whole and in the details of the individual plays, in experimentation with new themes and in the expression of philosophical ideas, his originality stands out.

Perhaps the most salient feature in Marivaux's complete theater is his break with the classical tradition. Though it cannot be said that Marivaux is entirely free of the influence of inherited dramatic material, still the special flavor he gives old subjects sets him apart from his contemporaries. If he derived an occasional idea from a comedy by Molière, from the *canevas* of the *commedia dell'arte,* or from a seventeenth-century novel, what he borrowed consisted at most of a fragment; he so revitalized the idea that his own contribution became the major element in the play. At the same time his theater is pep-

pered with the *philosophie* of the early eighteenth century. Not only are some of his plays based entirely on a philosophical thesis, but most of his comedies—even those written in a tone of sophisticated badinage—contain stimulating precepts and unexpected bits of philosophizing. His style, too often stigmatized by the epithet *marivaudage,* has a freshness that differentiates it from the uninspired versification and stilted prose of his contemporaries. His own inventiveness led Marivaux into heretofore unexplored realms and placed him outside—perhaps one should say, ahead of—the main current of the evolution of the theater in the eighteenth century.

When one applies these generalizations to the individual plays, the originality in detail is even more evident. Perhaps the best-known trait in Marivaux's theater is his depiction of awakening love—"la surprise de l'amour"—and many of his best and most enduring comedies turn on this theme. He already shows a well-developed conception of the "surprise" in *Arlequin poli par l'amour,* and two years later the conception emerges full-blown in *La Surprise de l'amour*: a new formula of comedy has come into being. From then on each comedy of this type has a mainspring of its own, usually based on the protagonists' resistance to falling in love, and Marivaux creates ingenious ways of probing the hearts of his various personages. In all his "surprises" Marivaux leads his young lovers through the enchanting mysteries of *l'amour naissant,* subjects them to tender and heart-searching trials, and leaves them rapturous on the threshold of avowed love.

Voltaire has said of Marivaux: "Il a connu tous les sentiers du cœur sans trouver la grande route." If Marivaux did not re-tread the broad highways of the heart in the classical tradition—which in his day had fallen to the level of hackneyed sterility—it was not for want of understanding, for on occasion Marivaux could probe to profound depths. It was rather that he found newness in exploring byways of the heart that his predecessors had shunned. With his infinite resources of analysis, Marivaux could have prepared a *carte du tendre* with detailed topography unmatched before his time. In developing "la surprise de l'amour" Marivaux made a distinctive contribution to the *fonds dramatique* of the French theater. He introduced into comedy the type of psychological analysis of love that Racine had achieved in tragedy, and in the realm of comedy Marivaux attained a peak of perfection equal to that of Racine in tragedy.

But "la surprise de l'amour," typifying as it does the special quality associated with Marivaux, represents only one aspect of his theater, only one of the many facets of his originality. From the whimsical fantasy of *Arlequin poli par l'amour,* in which the scene changes four times and thereby breaks the classical unity of place, to the enigmatic conceit of *La Dispute,* a plotless philosophical dialogue with subtle beauties, almost each play contains some new element. The creation of new types of character in comedy (*Le Prince travesti, La Mère confidente*), novelty of staging (*L'Ile de la raison*), the multiplication of disguises into a four-way *travestisse-*

ment (*Le Jeu de l'amour et du hasard*), and the reversal of the usual subplot of the servants (*Les Sincères*) are all departures from the past. While Marivaux's whole theater is imbued with *philosophie,* certain plays give new impetus to the ideas circulating in the *bureaux d'esprit* (*L'Ile des esclaves, L'Ile de la raison,* and *La Colonie*). For the first time in eighteenth-century comedy, Marivaux dares assign royalty a prominent place (*Le Prince travesti*). He also looks forward to the *drame* (*La Mère confidente* and *La Femme fidèle*) and to nineteenth-century drawing-room social drama (*L'Heureux stratagème* and *Les Fausses confidences*). Marivaux's turn of mind rarely permitted him to lag in the area of the commonplace.

One of Marivaux's most obvious qualities is his versatility. He composed comedies of love, philosophical comedies, allegories and fantasies, farces, comedies of manners, *drames,* heroic comedies, and a tragedy—all with equal literary and dramatic skill. Critics have classified his plays according to different systems, but any classification is arbitrary, for so many of the plays contain elements that entitle them to be placed in several categories at once. There is no need to attempt still another classification here. Suffice it to say that no other writer in the French theater has worked successfully in as many genres as Marivaux.

Originality of thought is another of Marivaux's traits. Mostly new on the stage, always sparkling, his ideas give added pungency to a dramatic output already remarkable for its novelty and style. Marivaux did not create a philosophical system; rather, he moralized on diverse subjects without plan. One might say that his predominant theme is the innate goodness of man and the necessity of being kindly disposed toward one's fellows. His whole theater exudes a buoyant optimism that springs from his faith in mankind. The expression "le bon cœur" appears repeatedly; a good heart is what distinguishes one man from another, Marivaux implies. The epitome of the philosophy of goodness is in his famous line: "dans ce monde, il faut être un peu trop bon pour l'être assez." When the theme is not actually developed in a particular play, the spirit of it is usually present.

Man is born naturally good, and character is of more fundamental importance than birth. Throughout his writings (and some twenty-five years before Rousseau popularized the doctrine), Marivaux places greater value on character than on birth. There is no instance in Marivaux's theater where birth triumphs over personal merit.

Making character the basis for evaluating merit implies social equality. Marivaux dwelt at length on this subject and made startling observations thereon. The central theme of *L'Ile des esclaves* is that equality springs from natural goodness and that social injustice is a malady that can be cured. A courageous plea for equality is made in *La Colonie,* in which the aristocratic Arthenice sweeps away social barriers between herself and the bourgeois women. Even if in the end Arthenice's ideas are shown not to work, their mere expression on the stage was bold in the eighteenth century. In the same play Marivaux

broached the still more venturesome topic of women's suffrage. The previous flurries of discussion on the education of girls and the rights of women by Montaigne, Molière, La Bruyère, and Fénelon had not yet touched on that point. Perhaps in Marivaux's day no one took him seriously, but he deserves credit for introducing the subject on the stage. Marivaux extends his thesis of social equality so far as to propose marriages that cut across the usual social lines, a proposal that violates the accepted social code of the eighteenth century. This kind of attitude gives a distinctive touch to Marivaux's theater and places him generations ahead of his fellow dramatists. It is one of the factors that account for Marivaux's popularity in the twentieth century.

Marivaux had advanced ideas for his day on the duties of a monarch. At a time when the theory of the divine right of kings was still accepted in France and when the Regency displayed a callous disregard for the welfare of the people, Marivaux expressed stimulating views on *le métier du roi,* which later in the century became part of the concept of the enlightened despot. His admonitions to monarchs to bestow equal justice on all, to follow the simple habits of their subjects, to show paternal concern for their people, to reject flattery, must have brought a smile to those who still remembered the obsequiousness practiced before Louis XIV.

Altogether, these diverse ideas create an ensemble of *philosophie,* of wholesome moralizing, that had not before been expressed on the stage in such straightforward terms. In the classical theater writers had tended to avoid expounding ideas directly; if they wanted to teach a lesson, they attempted to do so by irony, caricature, and other devices. For example, Molière believed that fathers should not force incompatible marriages on their children, but instead of presenting liberal-minded fathers on the stage, he ridiculed obstinate ones such as M. Orgon in *Tartuffe,* Harpagon in *L'Avare,* and M. Jourdain in *Le Bourgeois gentilhomme.* Marivaux, on the other hand, presented his philosophy with disarming simplicity. If he had a point to make, he went straight to the heart of the matter and expressed his conviction as an integral part of the text without deviousness.

Marivaux did much to create the vogue for *philosophie* in the theater. Even while he was still writing, other dramatists were beginning to insert a bit of *philosophie* in their plays; and by the time he finished his professional career in the 1740's, other dramatists were weighting their plays heavily with *philosophie.* The *comédies larmoyantes* of La Chaussée and the *drames* of Diderot, not to mention the philosophical tragedies of Voltaire, were soon to fill the stage with sententious maxims. But one will look in vain for a writer who before Beaumarchais presents his ideas with such sparkling grace and clarity, and, as has already been shown, Beaumarchais borrowed some of his best ideas from Marivaux.

When one discusses the style of Marivaux, one enters an area of extremes: few techniques have been as thoroughly scrutinized as that of Marivaux, and criticism over the generations has ranged from the highest praise to heated scurrility and back to adulation. It is not that a particular epoch was hostile to Marivaux; rather, all degrees of praise and disfavor have been expressed concurrently.

Marivaux's style has brought into being the term *marivaudage,* commonly used in a derogatory sense to refer to an extreme affectation in phraseology and a fatuous analysis of sentiment. In reality, the question of *marivaudage* scarcely enters into an evaluation of Marivaux himself, for he is less guilty of it than his imitators. When Marivaux uses a precious figure of speech reminiscent of the seventeenth-century novel, when he pursues love into hitherto unexplored regions of the heart, when he dwells on subtle nuances of feeling, or when he enters the realm of elfin gaiety, he does so with complete mastery and without affectation. Yet when his successors during a good part of the eighteenth and nineteenth centuries imitate these same artifices, they drift into the silly verbiage and clumsy hyperbole known as *marivaudage.* Lacking the taste and artistry of Marivaux, these imitators have tended, knowingly or not, to associate their own faults with him and have thereby cast disrepute on his name. But on examining his style objectively, one realizes that his personages speak and act in a manner befitting the powdered elegance and beribboned grace of eighteenth-century drawing rooms. Marivaux fuses style and character into an indissoluble whole with an art that few writers have achieved. Fortunately, recent scholarship has led to a re-evaluation of Marivaux's qualities, and the general trend in the twentieth century is to absolve him from the taint of *marivaudage.*

The most frequent charge against Marivaux during the eighteenth century and since was that he had "trop d'esprit." Most of his comedies are full of scintillating badinage, and often even the servants speak with a polished wit that is indistinguishable from the elegance of their masters. But the overabundance of wit has led some critics to speak disparagingly against Marivaux: Voltaire made sarcastic remarks; Geoffroy deplored Marivaux's influence on young writers; Faguet condemned his dramatic style as leading to *marivaudage*; Lièvre acrimoniously indicted Marivaux for concealing nefarious traits under his exquisite style. But such remarks are in a distinct minority. Most often critics have yielded insensibly to the enchantment of his style and have been effusive in their praise of Marivaux. "Un magique ballet verbal," "la poésie de la première moitié du XVIIIᵉ siècle," "une perfection soutenue," and the like recur ad infinitum in reviews of his plays.

Besides, now that revivals of Marivaux's plays are more and more popular, critics are finding new qualities in his writing. Of particular interest is the revelation of the rhythmic beauty inherent in the words spoken on the stage. Modern actors have rediscovered, and spectators have learned to appreciate, the subtleties and purity of eighteenth-century language. In addition, twentieth-century critics have noted a musical quality in Marivaux that previous generations seem to have missed. They perceive in his phraseology the melodic strain and orchestral variations found in musical compositions.

All these elements of originality in subject matter, thought, and style give Marivaux a modernness that makes his plays as enjoyable today as they were when he wrote them. In the mid-nineteenth century Théophile Gautier, comparing Marivaux's heroines with those of Shakespeare, found that "A travers l'œuvre ancienne, le caractère de l'époque où on la représente se fait jour malgré tout," and since then each generation of critics has drawn attention to the contemporaneous qualities in Marivaux's theater.

In reviewing *Le Jeu de l'amour et du hasard,* Brisson says of Dorante: "Il avance sur son siècle comme la plupart des personnages de Marivaux; il est moderne"; and apropos of the same play, Antoine declares: "on aperçoit qu'aucune comédie du XVIIIᵉ siècle ne fut aussi contemporaine. . . . Silvia domine encore ses sœurs modernes." Truffier feels that "*La Mère confidente* est très près de nous."

Far from being museum pieces like the plays of Destouches, Piron, and La Chaussée, the comedies of Marivaux have something that attracts each generation. His characters have enduring appeal, and his ideas are often more akin to the twentieth century than to the eighteenth. Like the plays of Molière and Racine, those of Marivaux transcend the moment of their conception and by reason of their basic truth and inherent beauty are highly valued in the twentieth century.

The paucity of source material for Marivaux's plays only emphasizes his originality. Marivaux is at his best when he is not burdened with someone else's ideas. The most notable achievements in his theater—*La Double inconstance, La Surprise de l'amour, L'Ile des esclaves, Le Jeu de l'amour et du hasard,* and *La Mère confidente*—are those in which his inspiration stems entirely from within. For the most part, attempts to trace sources for Marivaux's comedies have yielded only wisps of information.

He draws but little from the usual sources. Of classical antiquity, there is almost nothing. To be sure, in his only tragedy, *Annibal,* he uses a historical character, and there is a touch of Petronius in *La Seconde surprise de l'amour* and of Plautus in *La Méprise.* But there the classical influence ends.

The seventeenth-century novel influenced Marivaux to some degree. The liberal father, depicted so often by Marivaux, appears in *L'Astrée,* and the *mère-amie,* in *La Princesse de Clèves.* The pedant Hortensus goes back to *Francion.* The heroics of *Le Triomphe de l'amour* are typical of *Le Grand Cyrus.* At times the detailed discussion of love by Marivaux is reminiscent of d'Urfé, Scudéry, and La Calprenède.

Much as Marivaux disliked Molière, he could not entirely escape his influence. *L'Ecole des mères* is the most noteworthy case in point in that it shows similarities to *L'Ecole des femmes, Les Femmes savantes,* and *L'Avare.* The Lélio-Arlequin dialogue in **La Surprise de l'amour** (I, 2) recalls a similar conversation between Cléonte and Covielle in *Le Bourgeois gentilhomme.* The scene of the portraits in **Les Sincères** echoes Célimène's description of her friends in *Le Misanthrope.* Marivaux would probably have repudiated the charge of borrowing from Molière, but in these few instances the evidence is there. It can be said, however, that Marivaux did not imitate the more typical qualities of Molière's work, he did not use Molière as a standard, and he did not write a *comédie de caractère.*

Marivaux has often been likened to Racine, but their likeness is in natural talent. Both men possessed the gift of analyzing love; they portrayed the inner lives of their characters and reduced exterior events to a minimum. Racine excelled in depicting tragic passion; Marivaux, in revealing the awakening of love. Their works are entirely different, and Marivaux borrowed nothing from Racine.

Likewise, critics have found points of similarity between Shakespeare and Marivaux, but as with Racine the similarity is one of talent. Marivaux did not know Shakespeare's theater; hence there is no precise relationship between the authors. However, in spite of their obvious dissimilarities, both writers possessed a certain elfin gaiety and a lyrical manner of projecting love scenes that are curiously akin.

To what extent Marivaux was influenced by his contemporaries is difficult to estimate. On occasion instances of borrowing can be identified with reasonable certainty, but in each of these instances Marivaux has merely utilized a fragment and has so revitalized it that a charge of plagiarism is unjustified. Scholars have often strained a point in an effort to associate an item in Marivaux with some other work. Borrowings by Marivaux are slight, to say the least.

Perhaps the greatest single source of Marivaux's plays is the most intangible one: the *canevas*—and, even more, the spirit—of the Théâtre Italien. As one reads his plays, one is conscious of a detail reminiscent of some other farce. But since Marivaux had to write for stock characters, he could scarcely avoid using some stock material. Whatever Spanish or Italian elements one notes in Marivaux can be traced to the *canevas* of the Riccoboni troupe.

Viewing Marivaux's complete theater in perspective, one realizes that he is less guilty of borrowing than most writers; the rather nebulous comparisons indicated above reflect only on a minor aspect of his theater.

If Marivaux borrowed sparingly from his predecessors and contemporaries, the same cannot be said of his successors. The names of dramatists who quarried in Marivaux's plays make a rather impressive list in the eighteenth-century theater. Destouches patterned Lisimon of *Le Glorieux* after Plutus of **Le Triomphe de Plutus.** La Chaussée imitated Marivaux in *L'Ecole des mères.* Gres-

set drew on **Le Petitmaître corrigé** for many of the characters and ideas in *Le Méchant.* Voltaire adopted "Le Préjugé vaincu" as a subtitle for *Nanine,* and used the basic idea of Marivaux's comedy for the plot. La Noue copied **L'Heureux stratagème** in *La Coquette corrigée.* Borrowings of lesser importance were made by less well-known writers.

Marivaux is the outstanding precursor of the *drame.* In **La Mère confidente,** especially, and in **La Femme fidèle** he created plays that illustrate the *drame* some twenty years before Diderot enunciated his theory. Although the eighteenth century did not give Marivaux credit for his innovation, the nineteenth and twentieth centuries have recognized his contribution to the evolution of the genre. Diderot himself did not borrow material from Marivaux for his two *drames*—the two men were too far apart in style and thought for that—yet one of Marivaux's claims to fame is that he anticipated Diderot in the writing of a *drame.*

One of the outstanding facts about Marivaux is his influence on Beaumarchais, particularly with respect to the creation of the character of Figaro. Repeatedly in his theater Marivaux injects a strain of aggressiveness in the servants, the sum total of which constitutes the personality of Beaumarchais' famous valet. The Trivelin of **La Fausse suivante** and Cléanthis of **L'Ile des esclaves** contain the very essence of Figaro, even down to certain phrasings; they lack only his revolutionary truculence. Beaumarchais borrowed so thoroughly and minutely from Marivaux that he could not have been unaware that he was indulging in overt plagiarism. It should also be noted that he copied some of the guileless innocence of Chérubin from the Arlequin of **Arlequin poli par l'amour.**

Alfred de Musset is generally considered the lineal descendant of Marivaux, and rightly so, for he seems to have inherited Marivaux's penchant for portraying young love and for contriving witty dialogue. In style and spirit Musset carries on the Marivaux tradition, albeit with the moodiness of the romantic period, which Marivaux himself never had. More specifically, Musset found the inspiration for *La Nuit vénitienne* in **Le Dénouement imprévu**; for *On ne badine pas avec l'amour* in **Les Serments indiscrets**; for *Il ne faut jurer de rien* in **Le Petitmaître corrigé**; and for *L'Ane et le ruisseau* in **Le Legs.** Less precise analogies can be drawn that further associate Musset with Marivaux. Since Musset's time no writer in the French theater has been designated as Marivaux's heir.

Aside from the positive influences just discussed, Marivaux has had intangible influences without number. Critics in the second half of the eighteenth century complained of the *marivaudage* in current dramas, and in 1810 Geoffroy laments Marivaux's dominion over young writers of the day. Even after Musset's time numerous nineteenth-century plays evoke some remembrance of Marivaux. Twentieth-century critics have caught glimpses of Marivaux in Curel, Porto-Riche, and Sartre.

Today Marivaux occupies a position of pre-eminence in the French theater, and not without justice. His contemporaries—Destouches, Piron, La Chaussée, Voltaire, Gresset, Diderot—are all but forgotten figures in the modern theater. The secret of Marivaux's popularity in the twentieth century, like that of Shakespeare and Molière, rests on the simple fact that he faithfully depicted the society in which he lived and at the same time endowed his characters with the universal and enduring truths of human nature. If the area in which he wrote is somewhat narrower than that of Shakespeare and Molière, he is no less a master within his sphere. Perhaps Brisson, in a review of *La Mère confidente* that applies with equal justice to most of Marivaux's plays, gives the best account of his position in the French theater: "L'ouvrage . . . dépasse le temps où il fut écrit; il est de tous les temps, il est du nôtre. Marivaux est l'auteur classique le plus près de nous; son œuvre exhale un extraordinaire parfum de 'modernité'!"

Oscar A. Haac (essay date 1961)

SOURCE: "Humor through Paradox," in *L'Esprit Créateur,* Vol. 1, No. 4, Winter, 1961, pp. 196-202.

[*In the following essay, Haac explores Marivaux's use of paradox in his plays to convey the complexity of human psychology and emotion.*]

In his earliest works Marivaux developed a technique of humorous paradox which he successfully perfected and which can be considered the essence of *marivaudage.* It involves a play with concepts and ideas in such a way as to establish a contrast, of which there are two kinds: that between what a character says and what he means, and between what a character understands and what the audience or reader knows to be true. This interplay of interpretations amuses and stimulates an audience, and at the same time provides the author the opportunity to analyze complex attitudes and feelings. Marivaux reveals himself thus as one of the notable commentators of his time, dedicated to psychological analysis or, rather, to rendering the multiple aspects of the heart. The examples chosen to illustrate and elucidate this technique are but a sampling of the many to be found in each of Marivaux's plays, novels, and essays.

In his first successful comedy, *Arlequin poli par l'amour,* Arlequin, naïvely unconscious of his purposes, loves Silvia on first sight without being able to express his feelings while the Fée, with her armament of intelligence and power, her wand and her prime minister, discurses all too well on her love but is unable to attract Arlequin. Ultimately she is deceived and defeated by him. Her illusions are clear from the start and the spectator is flattered to recognize Arlequin's love long before he does himself and before the Fée is aware of it. The spectator is amused because he can outwit her with Arlequin.

Marivaux soon becomes master in the art of writing dialogue which expresses different things for different persons on the stage and for the audience. In *L'Epreuve,* Angélique appeals to Frontin's *honnêteté* and begs him to leave her; it is a burlesque scene because the gentlemanly suitor is a fraud, a disguised servant obeying his master's orders to test her faithfulness. Only the spectator knows Frontin's identity. Thus the contrast between the meanings for *honnêteté,* encompassing external politeness as well as the ideal of uprightness, leads to humorous paradox; it also leads to a new appreciation of their implications. In the conclusion to his *Marivaux et le marivaudage* (Paris, 1955), Frédéric Deloffre has admirably expressed that this technique portrays not only sentiments but shadings of meaning and concise ideas. He points to Marivaux's need to express new concepts in new terms. It is indicative that Marivaux's early critics blamed him precisely for his neologisms, and that he defended them on several occasions, saying that good style requires *finesse* and exact definition.

In order to examine the method more closely, let us analyze a number of scenes where we find illusions and misconceptions, first among the masters, then among their servants, for each group illustrates a different aspect of the fundamental problem of human understanding. A case of thorough misjudgment can be found in the marriage project of Marianne in the novel that bears her name. But then, who can foresee the future? Who could have foretold that, after Valville's marriage to Marianne was set, all obstacles and prejudices overcome, and formal promises made, a beautiful girl would faint and be unlaced before Valville's very eyes. He revives her with an elixir; she casts significant glances and, in confusion, covers herself. The scene undoes all previous plans to the point where the novel falls into two separate parts and lacks unity. It also expresses Marivaux's fundamental pessimism which makes us wonder how many *heureux stratagèmes* might be needed to revive and salvage love and makes us see that the happy endings of many plays are at best temporary solutions. Thus situations where partners marry and plan to live happily ever after take on paradoxical overtones. Marianne's case is extreme and explicit. We can plan and analyze, we cannot foresee and decide the future: "Il faut avoir bien du jugement pour sentir que nous n'en avons point!"

La Double Inconstance yields other examples. Silvia and Arlequin are convinced they love each other and constantly reaffirm their intentions. Unfortunately they are poor prophets. Their strong protestations against the designs of the prince sound like calls to revolt but take on paradoxical meaning. "Une bourgeoise contente dans un petit village vaut mieux qu'une princesse qui pleure dans un bel appartement," says Silvia who later is quite willing to accept the attractive prince. She will not weep for living in a beautiful apartment but rather will spurn Arlequin who dares break an appointment with her for the sake of an excellent meal with good wine. When Trivelin explains Silvia's original refusal to the prince he adds: "Cela n'est pas naturel." We might well ask what is not natural. Should she have yielded to an uni-

A French production of Les Fausses Confidences.

dentified suitor? It might have been more natural, but far less *honnête* (moral) to accept the handsome man on first sight. In fact, she says so to his face: "Non Seigneur, il faut qu'une honnête femme aime son mari, et je ne pourrais vous aimer." When, later, she retracts the last part of this statement because she is made for the prince just as the Silvia in *Le Jeu de l'amour et du hasard* is made for Dorante, what has been said about natural affection takes on further overtones, for it is natural that people with such superior sensitivity should love another. We find a similar paradox when Trivelin, as the agent of the prince, wants to separate Silvia from Arlequin and tells him: "Il ne faut jamais faire du mal à personne." This is hardly the appropriate maxim to accompany an act of alienation. In the same spirit a nobleman tells Arlequin: "Un gentilhomme doit être généreux"; the context is such that the statement serves to emphasize how frequently the principle is violated. These contradictions are carefully planned; the author is most conscious of his technique.

In neither of the two plays just discussed could Silvia have accepted her lover immediately, for in the society portrayed by Marivaux the truthfulness of pretenders must be tested. His characters must frequently disguise themselves in order to penetrate below the veneer of social behavior. They must be unnatural to find the natural personality of a partner. In this game of love, Silvia, in *Le*

Jeu de l'amour, is justified in prolonging the suffering of Dorante because she can force him to declare his willingness to marry her even as a servant. What more beautiful triumph of love could there be? Does it not justify any amount of suffering? In the same spirit Dorante is forgiven in **Les Fausses Confidences.** In spite of his pretense and false protestations, his love is sincere, or rather, his very pretense helped uncover the love of Araminte and is therefore justified.

We see that there is no direct road to love for these characters; by contrast, the love of servants wastes little time. In almost every play the contrast between servants and masters emphasizes these characteristics. There is an aristocracy of feeling and sensibility among the masters which explains why Silvia, in **Le Jeu de l'amour,** cannot accept Arlequin parading as Dorante, just as Dorante cannot accept Lisette playing the part of Silvia. Marivaux is careful to point to the advantages of each class. He emphasizes that there are fundamental qualities independent of social class. In **La Dispute,** he shows young people brought up in total isolation who soon manifest the same tendencies to self-enjoyment and flirtation as everyone else. The play may not be his best, but the situation is as meaningful, and no more artificial, than Rousseau's *Emile.* No more than Rousseau does Marivaux imply that our civilization should be reduced to a more primitive state or that the more natural or direct ways of the servants are preferable to the qualms and detours of their masters.

This holds true even though there are occasions when the more genuine awareness of the simpler characters is needed to extricate the masters from difficult situations. In **La Surprise de l'amour,** Arlequin is barely able to mimic Lélio's aversion for women, based on a disappointment. Arlequin cannot help exclaiming: "C'est pourtant un joli petit animal que cette femme, un joli petit chat." To please his master he adds: "C'est dommage qu'il ait tant de griffes." Unable to follow Lélio's argumentation, he excuses himself: "Quand on n'a pas étudié, on ne voit pas plus loin que son nez." The audience realizes that Lélio cannot see the forest for the trees and that the proverb expresses the opposite of what it says. Arlequin sees further than his master and without realizing it does more than anyone else to set him straight. Thus the fool (quite literally since he wears a fool's costume) is leading the wise! A few pages further Colombine administers a similar lesson to her mistress, the Comtesse, and ridicules her idea of keeping men and women in separate compartments like East and West. In **L'Ile de la raison,** Blaise and Lisette do their best to help and save their masters from their confused egocentric ramblings. In Marivaux's plays the servants go straight to the point. Jacob, the hero of **Le Paysan parvenu,** is well on the way to losing not only peasant status but also the psychology of servants when he outfits himself as Monsieur de la Vallée; he comes to partake in the masquerade of culture and privilege.

If servants obey their instincts more directly than their masters, food, money, and love can be said to summarize their interests, at least if we discount their fundamental loyalty, good nature, and sympathy. They are so intent on these basic drives that their statements become grotesque in their simplicity. Jacqueline, one of the servants in *La Surprise de l'amour,* compliments Pierre on courting her: "Ça me fait plaisir; mais l'honneur des filles empêche de parler. Après ça, ma tante disait toujours qu'un amant est comme un homme qui a faim; pû il a faim, et pû il a envie de manger." She is stating the obvious, she is funny also because she contradicts herself, since girls, according to her, do not admit what she is in the process of expressing; she is even funnier in view of the fact that the masters in this play dare not admit their love; their inability is the motivating force of the entire plot.

Frontin, in *L'Heureux Stratagème,* is somewhat more complex. He tells the Comtesse, intent on regaining the love of the Chevalier through his jealousy, that the Chevalier cannot be jealous of her affection, for he does not act like an unhappy person: "Le désespoir est connaissable. . . . Les désespérés s'agitent, se trémoussent, ils font du bruit, ils gesticulent; et il n'y a rien de tout cela." Actually the Chevalier is most unhappy, the Comtesse knows it and feels confident that her plan will succeed in arousing his love. Frontin is fooling no one, but he tries to do so out of loyalty for his master. He is both funny and touching. The maxim about unhappy persons is, of course, inapplicable like practically all maxims uttered by the buffoons, the servants.

In *La Surprise de l'amour,* another Frontin exclaims: "La tendresse paternelle est admirable." He means the opposite, for Ergaste is about to disinherit his master, Damis. Like the first Frontin, he realizes the irony of the situation. Servants are never dumb in these plays. Arlequin, in the same play, explains Lélio's resolve to flee all women by the maxim, "chat échaudé craint l'eau froide," but, as we have seen, realizes that Lélio's plan is unrealistic. Let us conclude that the use of maxims on the part of servants is grotesque, that proverbs are never quoted as accepted pearls of wisdom, but rather as trite remarks which become funny because they are inapplicable. Not even the servants are fooled by them, although they suffer from illusions like everyone. Their humor is funny but good natured, even if their masters occasionally become exasperated by it. We can understand the progressive despair of Silvia and Dorante in *Le Jeu de l'amour* at the thought of marrying such buffoons, and Silvia's relief upon discovering Dorante: "Allons, j'avais grand besoin que ce fût là Dorante." Arlequin's joviality was utterly repulsive as long as he appeared as her destined husband.

The methodical use of maxims and general statements in contexts where they do not apply shows the fundamental resistance of Marivaux to the tradition of Descartes, to the *esprit de géometrie* to which he opposes, with Pascal, his own analysis of complex meanings, *l'esprit de finesse.* When we consider that it was Voltaire's object, and supreme ability, to reduce complex ideas to simple slogans, we come to understand the gulf that separates the two men. It is no coincidence that, intellectual as

might be his orientation and his humor, Marivaux never misses an opportunity to ridicule the presumptuous *philosophes.* The Philosophe in *L'Ile de la raison* is the only character never to attain reason which, for Marivaux, means the realization of human needs and of one's own shortcomings. The learned Hortensius in *La Seconde Surprise de l'amour,* a teacher of "la morale et la philosophie, sans préjudice des autres sciences" would "purger l'âme de toutes les passions" but is defeated as easily as the Fée in *Arlequin poli par l'amour.* In *Le Triomphe de l'amour,* Hermocrate and Léontine are deceived in similar ways. Marianne, who well deserves the appellation of a flirt, asserts: "Si on savait ce qui se passe dans la tête d'une coquette, Aristote ne paraîtrait qu'un petit garçon." Thus, for Marivaux, philosophy, reason, and *philosophes* have parted company. His ideal of reason implies sensitivity and humility, the attitudes which Rosimond attains in *Le Petit-Maître corrigé,* and which originally he had spurned because "parmi les jeunes gens du bel air, il n'y a rien de si bourgeois que d'être raisonnable." By implication, *philosophes* avid for publicity are included among the fops and are derided.

If sympathy and understanding are the essence not only of honnêteté, the attitude befitting gentlemen, but also the very meaning of reason and object of philosophy, the primacy of sentiment over logic is definitely established. As Marianne says: "Il n'y a que le sentiment qui puisse nous donner des nouvelles un peu sûres de nous." Indeed, Marivaux prefers kindness to intelligence and comes close to feeling that they are mutually exclusive. In *Marianne* he draws two portraits of particular interest since they render his impressions of Mme de Lambert and Mme de Tencin. The first, pictured as Mme de Miran, appears as "une femme d'un esprit ordinaire, de ces esprits qu'on ne loue ni qu'on ne méprise," but she has a heart of gold. The second, Mme Dorsin, is far more brilliant and "aimait mieux qu'on pensât bien de sa raison que de ses charmes." Both portraits are extensive and kindly, but the preference for Mme de Lambert is evident. Marivaux adds: "Supposons la plus généreuse et la meilleure personne du monde, et avec cela la plus spirituelle, et l'esprit le plus délié. Je soutiens que cette personne ne paraîtra jamais si bonne (car il faut que je répète les mots) que le paraîtra une autre personne qui, avec ce même degré de bonté, n'aura qu'un esprit médiocre."

Thus kindness outweighs logic and education. The simple intuition of Arlequin defeats the Fée. The naïve Blaise, in *L'Ile de la raison,* is first to reach human stature because he is first to know his limitations. Frontin in *Les Serments indiscrets* explains about his master: "C'est un garçon qui a de l'esprit; cela fait qu'il subtilise, que son cerveau travaille; et dans de certains embarras, sais-tu bien qu'il n'appartient qu'aux gens d'esprit de n'avoir pas le sens commun?" Thus the simple status of servants and their direct approach to problems may well be an advantage.

Let us note that the author hardly ever speaks for himself. Every line expresses the feeling or impression of a character. This is the note of good theater, for dramatic

Valentini Papadopoulou Brady on the psychology of Marivaux's characters:

The psychology of [Marivaux's] theatre is not the relatively static psychology of crisis, as in the classical theatre, but the dynamic psychology of development. The result is a dilution of the concept of fixed psychological identity, and a demonstration of the metamorphoses through which a character passes. The use of deceit introduces complexity into the psychological presentation of the characters through the resulting interplay between a developmental individual identity and a static mask or a static individual and a developmental mask. For example, when Dorante and Silvia in *Le Jeu* decide to appear as servants, they superimpose upon their own identity, their own fluid psychological continuum, a static mask. On the other hand, the psychology of Silvia ("Le Chevalier") in *La fausse Suivante* does not change, whereas the mask she adopts appears developmental to the Countess, who believes she is witnessing the Chevalier's falling in love with her.

Valentini Papadopoulou Brady, in Love in the Theatre of Marivaux, *Librairie Droz, 1970.*

tension arises between the views expressed and their diverse interpretations. It is also indicative of a categorical opposition to generalization and platitude. In one of his essays Marivaux explains: "Je me moque des règles." He implies that general rules of conduct are false and largely inapplicable. What then are we to do with his contradictory interpretations? We must accept them all, understand that life is complexity and antithesis. Like Diderot, in *Le Neveu de Rameau* or in *Jacques le fataliste,* the objective is not the golden rule, the reconciliation of paradox, never the *juste milieu,* but the acceptance of irreconcilable paradox, with all interpretations worthy of consideration and irreducible by logical argument. Mutual understanding must be reached on another level.

If there is any conclusion, it is that diverse interpretations rest on our inability to express our thoughts, on our basic difficulty to communicate. As Colombine puts it in *La Surprise de l'amour*: "Le chemin de tout le monde, quand on a affaire aux gens, c'est d'aller leur parler, mais cela n'est pas commode." When at a later time, she asks Lélio whether she might convey his respects to her mistress, the Comtesse, Arlequin advises Lélio to send his greetings and best wishes: "Cela serait honnête!" Lélio, however, has no such inclination: "Et moi je ne suis point aujourd'hui dans le goût d'être honnête; je suis las de la bagatelle." He may be amusing, but touches on that *bagatelle,* that little thing which happens to be the key to human relations, the willingness to communicate and to understand. Marivaux touches here on a key theme of our contemporary theater and seems quite modern. We are concerned, as he was, about the abundance of words that fails to lead to communication. He would,

however, never have expressed this "lesson" in so many words. He is convinced that literature cannot and should not attempt to teach and moralize. It should not preach morality, but analyze in the tradition of the *moralistes* like La Fontaine and La Rochefoucauld. There is no rule for overcoming passion, the irrational, and what separates us from another, but to accept the advice: "Réfléchissez sur vos folies pour en guérir" and this principle, contained in the advice of the wise islanders of *L'Ile de la raison* to the shipwrecked Europeans, becomes the very justification of the author's literary enterprise. What better contribution could he make than portray life and stimulate reflection. At that, he takes account of the tremendous difficulty of devising an accurate portrayal: "Le détailler c'est un ouvrage sans fin." Marivaux defends his use of paradox, in particular humorous paradox, since literature must entertain and amuse, but, above all, he stands for *l'esprit de finesse,* and wants to present in man's diversity the best means to initiate "la science du coeur humain."

William S. Rogers (essay date 1961)

SOURCE: "Marivaux: The Mirror and the Mask," in *L'Esprit Créateur,* Vol. 1, No. 4, Winter, 1961, pp. 167-77.

[*In the excerpt below, Rogers argues that Marivaux uses images of mirrors and masks to "probe the reality that lies behind appearances."*]

In the first number of **Le Spectateur français,** Marivaux recounts an incident supposedly drawn from his own life. The passage, perhaps more frequently quoted than any other in Marivaux's prose writings, tells how, at the age of seventeen, he fell in love with a charming and beautiful young lady whose principal attraction for him resided in her indifference to her own beauty, her lack of coquetry, her complete naturalness. One day, after leaving her presence, he discovered that he had left behind a glove which he returned to retrieve. Unnoticed, he came upon his lady-love studying herself in her mirror. She was rehearsing all the facial expressions, all the side glances, all the gestures which had so bewitched him during their conversation. She was, so to speak, practicing her scales. For her, it was a moment of mild embarrassment; for the youthful Marivaux, it was a moment of frightening lucidity.

"Ah! mademoiselle, je vous demande pardon, lui dis-je, d'avoir mis jusqu'ici sur le compte de la nature des appas dont tout l'honneur n'est dû qu'à votre industrie.

—Qu'est-ce que signifie ce discours? me répondit-elle.

—Vous parlerai-je plus franchement, lui dis-je. Je viens de voir les machines de l'Opéra. Il me divertira toujours, mais il me touchera moins." Je sortis là-dessus, et c'est de cette aventure que naquit en moi cette misanthropie qui ne m'a point quittée [*sic*], et qui m'a fait passer ma vie à examiner les hommes, et à m'amuser de mes réflexions.

Marivaux for the rest of his life would experience an unholy joy in catching people unawares, mask off, or mirror in hand.

The mirror and the mask: these two themes recur with such frequency in the writings of Marivaux and represent so vividly his close observation of the human comedy, his desire to probe the reality that lies behind appearances, that an examination of them may serve as a useful approach to his world. Recent critics such as Claude Roy, Jean Rousset and Mario Matucci have briefly treated these themes, which, however, can be profitably amplified.

The mirror is a magnificent instrument of self-awareness. Marianne, at the age of sixteen, tries on the first fine clothes she has ever owned before the mirror of her humble room above the mercer's shop. She sees herself as it were for the first time, and is naïvely enchanted with what she sees. In *La Seconde Surprise de l'amour*, Lisette attempts to revive her mistress' interest in her appearance, in men and in life generally, by forcing her to look at herself in a mirror. In the five *Lettres contenant une aventure*, the heroine, her self-confidence shaken by the neglect of her first suitor, is elated at the realization that she has attracted the attention of not one, but two other eligible young men. She can scarcely wait for the last guest to leave so that she can rush to her room to be alone with her mirror, to reassess her charms, to practice her scales. In one of his late plays, *La Dispute* (1744), Marivaux invents a delightful fantasy in which a prince and his fiancée Hermiane argue as to whether the first example of inconstancy in love was set by a man or a woman. It would seem difficult, to an imagination less fertile than Marivaux's, to adduce adequate evidence to settle the dispute. It so happens that the same argument had arisen at the court of the prince's father, eighteen or nineteen years before. The king conducted an experiment. He selected four infants, two girls and two boys, to be brought up, isolated from one another and from the world, in the care of two aged servants, Mesrou and Carise. The experiment has now reached the stage where results can be observed. The prince and Hermiane will watch, from a hiding-place, what happens when these young people re-enact for them, as it were, the first days of creation. The young maiden Eglé glimpses her own image for the first time in a stream. She calls to Carise, her elderly companion:

> EGLE, *regardant.*—Ah! Carise, approchez, venez voir; il y a quelque chose qui habite dans le ruisseau qui est fait comme une personne, et elle paraît aussi étonnée de moi que je le suis d'elle.

> CARISE, *riant.*—Eh! non, c'est vous que vous y voyez; tous les ruisseaux font cet effet-là.

EGLE.—Quoi! c'est là moi, c'est mon visage?

CARISE.—Sans doute.

EGLE.—Mais savez-vous bien que cela est très beau, que cela fait un objet charmant? Quel dommage de ne l'avoir pas su plus tôt!

CARISE.—Il est vrai que vous êtes belle.

EGLE.—Comment "belle"? admirable! cette découverte-là m'enchante (*Elle se regarde encore!*) Le ruisseau fait toutes mes mines, et toutes me plaisent. Vous devez avoir eu bien du plaisir à me regarder, Mesrou et vous. Je passerai ma vie à me contempler; que je vais m'aimer à présent!

Does the mirror merely express for Marivaux a type of Narcissism? It is true that it affords self-awareness, reassurance, delight, and a practice-keyboard for many of his heroines. For them, however, as for the innocent Eglé, awareness of self is rapidly followed by awareness of others. As we shall see, inevitable comparisons result.

The problem is complex. The reflection in the mirror, although it represents objective reality, is nonetheless viewed by a purely subjective beholder who is, in a sense, a distorting mirror herself. Marivaux imagines the plight of an ill-favoured woman, with a misshapen nose, as she places herself before her mirror. Her nose remains misshapen, says Marivaux, but she takes good care not to concentrate on that. Her eye will fall on other features which, all taken together, will bring the nose into focus as an asset rather than a liability. If all the features are unfortunate, she will create of them in her own mental image, through art or vanity, or both, a harmonious whole more attractive than regular beauty itself, and satisfying to her, if not to others.

For Marivaux, each person is a mirror, receiving and distorting the reflections of others, and at the same time a mask, trying to achieve the most flattering possible picture in the mirrors of others. This explains his passion for scrutinizing closely the reactions of people on people. The image in the mirror is sometimes beclouded by the breath of passion, distorted by jealousy, embellished by the wishful thinking of vanity. Marivaux's role is to polish the surface, to smooth out the deforming concavities and convexities, and to present to his audience both the distortion and the reality. Once the distortion has been rectified by the objective observer, the quality of the mirror, and of the reality which it reflects, can be assessed properly.

Several examples have already been given of Marivaux's use of the mirror or its equivalent as a sort of stage-prop. We may now examine some of the more subtle uses of the mirror technique as an artistic device, most evident in the plays, and of such frequent occurrence as to become almost a trademark.

The two chief protagonists in a Marivaux play usually reflect, like mirrors placed on opposite sides of a room, each other's outlook on life. In *La Seconde Surprise de l'amour,* La Marquise and Le Chevalier mirror each other's sorrow for a lost love. In *La Double Inconstance,* Silvia and Arlequin reflect each other's attempt to remain faithful to their first love in spite of the involuntary formation of new attachments. In *Le Jeu de l'amour et du hasard,* Silvia and Dorante are such exact mirrors of each other that they adopt the same expedient (that of disguising themselves as servants) for the same purpose (that of examining closely the person they may be called upon to marry). In *Les Sincères,* Ergaste and La Marquise reflect each other's passion for complete and outspoken honesty in social intercourse. Here the mirrors crack under the strain. In *Les Serments indiscrets,* Lucile and Damis share a common disinclination for the ties of matrimony which is gradually dispelled as they come to know each other better.

A second mirror device occurs in most of Marivaux's plays. The servants, who advise, cajole, mimic, follow and lead their masters and mistresses, provide a laughing gallery of distortion. This is achieved in a variety of ways. The servants fall in and out of love according to the vicissitudes of their masters' love affairs. Sometimes they take the initiative and see to it that the mistress and master fall in love to protect their own interests; sometimes they follow, taking their cue from their betters. There is, of course, nothing new or original in this device, a classic example of which is found in Molière's *Le Bourgeois Gentilhomme.* But no playwright has used it more persistently and effectively than Marivaux. The love scenes between Lisette and Arlequin in *Le Jeu de l'amour et du hasard,* skillfully placed at appropriate moments in the development of the love between Silvia and Dorante, are masterpieces of comic distortion.

Moreover, in Marivaux, the servants represent, on their own level, the same traits of character, foibles or prejudices, as the master or mistress. If the mistress is overly proud of her rank in society, so is the maid: Angélique and Lisette in *Le Préjugé vaincu.* If she is fickle and inconstant, so is the maid: La Comtesse and Lisette in *L'Heureux Stratagème.* If the master is a gay young man-about-town, needing to be taken down a peg, so is the valet: Rosimond and Frontin, in *Le Petit-Maître corrigé.* . . .

The mirror calls forth the mask. According to Marivaux, one must fit into that vast category of *porteurs de visages* in order to move in society. The mirror of self-awareness and the mirror of other human beings as they reflect ourselves help us to prepare a mask necessary for participation in the mime of the human comedy.

What forms does the mask assume? As in the case of the mirror, the actual object is used at times as a stage-prop. In *La Méprise,* for instance, the masks carried, and worn at appropriate moments in the action by two sisters, Hortense and Clarice, provide the source of the comic misunderstanding which so bewilders the hero, Ergaste.

When the masks are removed in the final act, true identities are established, and the misunderstanding is cleared up.

The most common form of the mask in Marivaux is that of the disguise. Here he had an abundance of models to choose from in the traditions of the Italian and French theatres. He used the device of disguise purely as a source of comedy in *Le Père prudent et équitable.* In one of his last plays, *La Femme fidèle* (1755), preserved only in fragmentary form, the disguise is used as a source of pathos. The Marquis, supposedly killed in a foreign land, reappears disguised as a friend bearing a message for the widowed Marquise about to marry again much against her will. The disguise enables him to see the true sorrow and fidelity of his wife. When he reveals his identity, the recognition scene is one of genuine emotion.

The period of nearly five decades which separate *Le Père prudent et équitable* from *La Femme fidèle* shows such frequent and varied use of Marivaux's device of the disguise that a complete analysis would be impossible here. One of the most successful examples for straight comic effect is the disguise of Eraste in *L'Ecole des meres.* For sheer virtuosity, the use of disguise in *Le Triomphe de l'amour* could scarcely be rivalled. Here it produces, not comic scenes, but scenes of disturbing and equivocal subtlety.

Marivaux's heroes and heroines often adopt the mask of disguise in order to view more clearly the person whom they are to marry. This is the starting-point for the adventures of *Le Jeu de l'amour et du hasard,* in which the disguise becomes the instrument for delicate psychological analysis. When we witness the unsuccessful inner struggle of Silvia, disguised as the servant Lisette, to resist the attractions of Dorante, disguised as the valet Bourgignon, we share with her that delicious moment of lucidity when he drops his mask and she sees that her instinct has guided her correctly: "Je vois clair dans mon coeur."

The mask and its counterpart, the disguise, are merely visible signs of the barriers which man erects between himself and society . . .

Marivaux's magic is performed with mirrors and masks. The aim of this magician, however, is not to conjure up a world of illusion, but to disclose the world of reality. Holding up to nature the crystal-clear mirror of observation, removing the mask by his insight and penetration, Marivaux leaves his attentive reader with a new desire to see clearly—*voir clair*—and to avoid being taken in—*ne pas être dupe.*

Lionel Gossman (essay date 1967)

SOURCE: "Literature and Society in the Early Enlightenment: The Case of Marivaux," in *MLN,* Vol. 82, No. 3, May, 1967, pp. 306-33.

[*In the essay below, Gossman delineates the relations of Marivaux's plays to the social and philosophical views of his day.*]

In the last few years there has been a revival of interest in Marivaux, touched off perhaps by Gabriel Marcel's introduction to a 1947 edition of a selection of the comedies. Not much of the new criticism, on the whole, has been concerned with the relation between Marivaux's work and the society in and for which it was written. It is this relation which I should like to explore. Marivaux wrote both plays and novels, but as a novelist he may well have entered into a different relation to his public from that in which he stood to the public of the plays. It seemed prudent, therefore, to approach the plays and the novels separately and I have made no attempt to deal with the latter here.

* * * *

The son of an undistinguished provincial administrator with aspirations to nobility, Marivaux was one of a large number of young men who climbed on to the band waggon of the *Modernes* in the early years of the Regency. He became a disciple and friend of Fontenelle and found his way to the headquarters of the *Moderne* movement in the salons of Madame de Lambert and Madame de Tencin. Although there has been no full study, as yet, of the social significance of the *Querelle des Anciens et des Modernes,* it does seem, as of now, that the *Anciens* were in the main those who, while often less than satisfied with existing arrangements, were even more apprehensive of change. They included some members of the old nobility, certain religious groups and above all *robins* and bourgeois living on *rentes.* The *Modernes,* on the other hand, expressed the ideas and sentiments of the most active and advanced section of French society in the early eighteenth century, notably the rich and increasingly influential financiers and *fermiers-généraux,* who sought to elevate themselves and gain power, not as the *robins* had done at an earlier stage by purchasing offices and constituting themselves a special privileged class, but by infiltrating the aristocracy, the court and the royal administration. The wealthy bourgeoisie of the first half of the eighteenth century was thus extremely close to and indeed barely distinguishable from the aristocracy, which accepted the influx of new blood and new money with little resistance and in the process adopted many of the ideas and attitudes of its powerful partner. This society of bourgeois aristocrats and aristocratic bourgeois was cultured and generous. It would be hard to exaggerate the cultural role of the *fermiers-généraux,* for instance, throughout the eighteenth century. Marivaux himself was in receipt of a pension from Helvétius.

The *Modernes* embraced many new ideas. They set out to free themselves and France from old tyrannies, to explode old myths that they had been taught to take for granted and to reveal the material and conventional nature of all human arrangements and institutions, political, religious and social. Every realm of human thought and activity was de-sacramentalized: in philosophy essentialist doctrines were rejected, in religion the natural origin of all mysteries (the Christian ones being prudently excepted, of course) was exposed, in literature the classics, and even the classics of the age of absolutism, were toppled from their pedestals, in art academicism came under increasing attack.

Nothing was taken for granted by these early enlighteners. They no longer believed, for instance, that reality is immediately accessible to the intelligence and their work is a constant interrogation not only of our total conceptions of reality but of the apparently solid bricks out of which these conceptions are constructed. Social reality was questioned no less eagerly than physical reality and here too not only society as a whole but the individual self was found to be problematic, for how did a series of discontinuous moments of experience constitute a self? Literature itself was thought of as a means of de-mystification and an exercise in reflection and self-awareness. It no longer presented itself to the reader in analogy with a natural object, the meaning of which is immediately apprehensible, since natural objects themselves could no longer be thought of in this way, but as an artefact designed by an author, the meaning of which is uncertain and requires to be prised out of it, or given to it, by the reader. The style of the *Modernes* is atomic. Causal conjunctions, in particular, are rare with them, and their prose has not the highly articulated architectural quality of their seventeenth century predecessors. They do not construct chains of reasoning. They lay out the observed "facts" and leave it to the reader to evaluate them and put them together as he judges best.

Given their rejection of essentialism in all domains, it is not surprising that the *Modernes* had an image of society as a comedy in which each man plays out his role before others. "Ce monde est un grand bal où des fous déguisés / Sous les risibles noms d'Eminence et d'Altesse / Pensent enfler leur être et hausser leur bassesse," Voltaire declared in his *Discours en vers sur l'homme.* The wise man stands back and recognizes the human comedy for what it is: "Les mortels sont égaux: leur masque est différent." Obviously, the acquisition of such lucidity can serve different ends. The *Anciens* also thought of social life as a theatrical performance and the lines quoted from Voltaire could be matched with similar passages in Pascal, La Bruyère or Boileau. Indeed, this view of social life goes back to Montaigne, and even further. But whereas the *Anciens* took the masquerade of society as an invitation to seek elsewhere for man's "true" nature, the *Modernes* denied that there was any "true" nature of man in a religious or metaphysical sense. For the *Anciens* social life was emptied of significance by the discovery of its inessentiality, for the *Modernes* on the other hand—since they believed in nothing else—it had to be accepted and grasped in its inessentiality.

For those of them, in particular, who, like Marivaux, lived in close proximity to the wealthy bourgeoisie and the aristocracy and shared in their way of life, irreverence with regard to existing institutions and, in particular, to the social order of the ancien regime in no way implied a radical critique of it. It produced instead a quite distinctive outlook in which intellectual audacity was combined with social conservatism and rationalism with respect for irrational forms. It would probably be vain to look for any revolutionary critique of social institutions in the first half of the eighteenth century—with the possible exception of the late seventeenth century *Testament* of Jean Meslier, which was much sought after by amateurs of clandestine literature. The financiers themselves had no thought of attacking the social order at its roots; they owed their fortunes to their skilful exploitation of the fiscal and commercial arrangements of the state. The *Modernes* did not, therefore, wish to destroy the forms of society. On the contrary, they desired to maintain them; but they wished them to be recognized as forms, so that they might then be opened, without the usual tiresome protests, to new content. Whereas the *Anciens* opposed all social change on the grounds that social order depends on the respect accorded to age-old customs, the *Modernes* tended to emphasize the positive value of social arrangements and to justify a certain measure of social change. They admitted that the forms of society do not reflect an essential "nature of things," but since they considered such a "nature" mythical anyway, they could not consider it a useful criterion for judging social forms. The criterion by which they judged was empirical, the correspondence of social forms not to some essential "nature" but to nature as it was observed to be in fact in the world. The *Modernes* thus rejected the either-or way of thinking which allowed the *Anciens* to make a blanket condemnation of society while at the same time insisting that all social change be avoided.

The social thinking of the *Modernes* suited various social groups in the ancien regime rather well. It suited ennobled financiers who wished to base their right to nobility not on their money but on their distinction as human beings and, paradoxically, it also suited the proud aristocracy of the blood which could claim, as Vauvenargues was to do, that its right to nobility rested on its inherent superiority, as a *noblesse de race,* to other men. "J'appelle peuple tout ce qui pense bassement et communément," declared Madame de Lambert, the patroness of the *Modernes*; "la cour en est remplie." The refined, cultivated and magnificently married daughters of the Crozats and the Bernards, the financial wizards of the day, could not but have been pleased by this consecration of their newly acquired nobility. But in fact it is not at all clear that Madame de Lambert's barbs were not directed at them. It is never sure in her writings whether it is a certain refinement of sensibility, a certain distinction of soul, that ensures nobility, or whether it is nobility that ensures distinction of soul. Does a person who has the "style" of nobility deserve to be "noble"—that is, to be recognized as noble—or is this style itself a proof of noble blood? Admittedly there are no essential "natures," but is what man is perhaps biologically determined and if so, is the furthest reality to which we can penetrate not race rather than merit? By depriving social

forms—institutions, ranks, language, etc.—of any necessary or "natural" relation to "reality," by affirming moreover that "reality" was, if not mythical, then at least unknowable and irrelevant to life, the *Modernes* had cleared a way for the simultaneous co-existence of various interpretations of the meanings of social forms. The truly enlightened man, of course, was not the dupe of any of these meanings. Knowing that there was no necessary connection between social forms and an "objective" world of things, he bracketed entirely the question of those objective things to which the forms supposedly referred. To him the forms signified by themselves, independently of any reference to an "objective"—that is, socially undetermined—reality.

This way of thinking is nicely illustrated by the mystery shrouding the birth of the heroine of Marivaux's novel *La Vie de Marianne.* Is Marianne a noble soul because she is in reality the daughter of noble parents, or does she deserve to be treated as a gentlewoman—that is to be one—on account of her delicacy of soul? The answer is never given and never could be, because Marianne's "nobility" is precisely what each must be free to interpret as he chooses, while the truly enlightened will bracket the question of the "reality" on which it is grounded altogether. Such a way of thinking could hardly fail to find favor with a society composed of aristocrats eager to sell their "blood" and of bourgeois eager to be counted on their "merit," that is, ultimately, their wealth. Indeed it is very likely that the phenomenalism of the *Moderne* movement was essential to its success and its historical role.

* * * *

Marivaux's work, like that of all the *Modernes,* is destructive of traditional myths and ideas about literature, about society, about man. Moreover, Marivaux was quite conscious of what, as a writer, he was about. The Prefaces to his plays together with the observations on style in his undeservedly neglected essays—*Le Spectateur français, Le Cabinet du philosophe, L'indigent Philosophe*—reveal what he thought of literature in general, of his own work in particular and of that of his immediate predecessors.

Just as he rejected the pompous acting style of the Comédie Française and insisted that his actors use a "natural" style, Marivaux saw no sense in continuing academic traditions in literature. These traditions, in his view, were connected with the essentialist way of thinking which, as a *Moderne,* he also rejected. Neither man himself, nor his passions, nor natural objects can be apprehended as universals or forms, he held, but only in their qualities, as they are observed and experienced. Many of his shorter allegorical plays in particular turn on the contrast between love-passion as it is supposed to be and love as it can be observed in actual social life—and this contrast between Amour and Cupidon was also for him a contrast of styles, as the short comedy *La Réunion des Amours* makes clear, the style of Amour being pompous, long-winded and cliche-ridden, while that of Cupidon is agile, witty and realistic. Similarly, Marivaux no longer believed in the myth of the hero—one of the favorite whipping horses of the *Modernes.* "Il n'y a ni petit, ni grand homme pour le Philosophe," he declared. ". . . Il y a des hommes ordinaires . . . médiocres, qui valent bien leur prix, et dont la médiocrité a ses avantages. . . ." The authors of the past have put together words and images which on inspection have turned out to be fraudulent or mythical. There is no point, therefore, Marivaux held, in continuing to string together these meaningless words and images. Only the professional author will do that, because he is paid by some king or court to do so.

Marivaux's unrelenting critique of the status of *author* is part of his struggle to impose a modern style in place of the semi-official style of classicism. He never tired of emphasizing that he did not want to be thought of as an author. The **Spectateur français** opens with the statement "Ce n'est point un auteur que vous allez lire ici" and follows it up with a definition of the author as someone who writes about empty ideas. "Un auteur est un homme à qui, dans son loisir, il prend une envie vague de penser sur une ou plusieurs matières: et l'on pourroit appeler cela, réfléchir à propos de rien." As he satirized the "Auteur méthodique" with his "demi-douzaine de pensées dans la tête sur laquelle il fonde tout l'ouvrage." Marivaux was doing for literature what other enlighteners had done for philosophy when they mocked the metaphysicians of the previous century for having drawn out of their heads "le roman de la philosophie," as they liked to put it. Instead of writing as an author, Marivaux proposed to write as a man. "Je veux être un homme et non pas un Auteur."

At the same time as he rejected an earlier notion of the author, Marivaux also rejected an earlier notion of literature. Literature, as he saw it, is not an incarnation of eternal truths and ideal beauty but part of a secular and temporal culture. Marivaux could say in the same breath that he did not write his essays for the "public" in the manner of the classical "author" and that he cannot conceive why he should have written them except for other men to read them: "Cependant pourquoi les ai-je écrits? Est-ce pour moi seul? Mais écrit-on pour soi? J'ai de la peine à le croire. Quel est l'homme qui écriroit ses pensées, s'il ne vivoit pas avec d'autres hommes." To write as a man, in short, means to stop writing as an "author" and to accept willingly the social and historical nature of literature. Literature, for Marivaux, is not made in heaven; it is made by men who do not wish to pronounce as divines or oracles but to communicate with their fellows in their own language, and its subject matter is human experience, not eternal essences. The great writers of the Enlightenment found glory in the humble function they assigned to literature. One recalls Sidrac's words to Goudman as he invites him to dinner in Voltaire's *Les Oreilles du Comte de Chesterfield*: "Votre faculté pensante aura le plaisir de se communiquer à la mienne par le moyen de la parole: ce qui est une chose merveilleuse que les hommes n'admirent pas assez."

As a writer, the *Moderne* will not, therefore, withdraw behind his creation but reveal his presence in it; on the other hand, he will not sit down to write on traditional themes, but will wait until some event, some experience or some striking observation goads him to action. About the ideas he used in his works Marivaux declared: "Je n'examine pas si celle-ci est plus fine, si celle-là l'est moins; car mon dessein n'est de penser ni bien ni mal, mais seulement de recueillir fidèlement ce qui me vient d'après le tour d'imagination que me donnent les choses que je vois ou que j'entends." The writer will not invent, in other words, out of his head, or by elaborating some worn literary theme. A picturesque comment by Montesquieu on the Regent reveals how essential the contact with others was held to be for the artist of the period: "Les paroles qu'il a si admirablement dites sont toujours des reparties, comme s'il s'était refusé toutes les choses charmantes qui ne naissent point de l'occasion." It is no accident that the age of Marivaux was also the age of the art of conversation and of those correspondences—Walpole, Madame du Deffand, Voltaire—of which it is impossible to say whether they are documents of social communication or works of art.

Imitation of other writers obviously had no place among those who had denounced the myth of Parnassus and chosen temporality rather than eternity. Marivaux condemns it out of hand. "L'imitation . . . ne fera qu'un singe." The author Marivaux most admired, if d'Alembert is to be believed, was Montaigne, because his personal style did not lend itself to imitation. Sometimes Marivaux's emphasis on originality strikes a remarkably modern note. "Ecrire naturellement," he declares in the *Spectateur,* "n'est pas écrire dans le goût de tel Ancien, ni de tel Moderne, n'est pas se mouler sur personne quant à la forme de ses idées; mais au contraire, se ressembler fidèlement à soi-même." "Jusqu'ici," he adds later in the *Cabinet du philosophe,* "vous ne connoissez presque que des Auteurs qui songent à vous quand ils écrivent, et qui, à cause de vous, tâchent d'avoir un certain style. Je ne dis pas que ce soit mal fait; mais vous ne voyez pas là l'homme qu'il est."

This critique of the classical concept of the author and of literature is surely not fortuitous. It fits too well with the character, the position and the outlook of the social group with which Marivaux and his fellow *Modernes* were closely associated. Similarly, the new idea of the author and of his relation to society which begins to emerge from the essays reflects the ambiguities of this social group.

The classical idea of the artist rested on the assumption that he shared with the public and, indeed, with reasonable men in all ages certain fundamental principles and values which were true for all time and which could not be changed or improved upon. As a matter of fact, since men in their folly tended, if anything, to be distracted from truth by the flattering images of illusion, innovation was as likely as not to mean degeneration. This view usually went hand in hand, not unexpectedly, with a fairly conservative view of society, for if the ideal of an intimate and secure relation between artist and public was to be maintained, the public of taste and judgment had itself to be maintained. But even in the seventeenth century social change was already undermining the "public" of the classical artists. Boileau and La Bruyère never tire of railing against the financiers and *traitants* who were upsetting the order of things and taking over positions once occupied by persons of sense and discrimination. By Marivaux's time the author could no longer imagine that there was a homogeneous public in which he was but a special voice. Moreover, many of the newer writers themselves came from less solidly established families than their classical predecessors. The eighteenth century writer was thus less conscious and sure of his relation to society than the classical writer had been and for this very reason he became more aware of and interested in his own individuality. Similarly, what he had to say and how he should say it no longer seemed self-evident to him. Nor could he accept the assent of the "public" as the measure of his success.

Marivaux's refusal of the category of "author" is thus a response to a truly altered social situation. No longer enjoying the independence provided by a private income and the feeling of writing for a public of friends and equals, he and his contemporaries were in fact becoming increasingly alienated from the "public" and the latter was already coming to resemble the *market,* as the modern writer knows it. They were thereby assuming some of the essential traits of the bourgeois. But they did not clearly recognize or accept this fact, and in this they resembled a large part of the public for which they wrote. It is characteristic of the whole *Moderne* movement that even in the essays, where he speaks most daringly and provocatively of his relation to the public, Marivaux did not clearly avow—or perhaps fully grasp—the reality of the writer's changed situation and that he expressed it instead in an ambiguous form. The bourgeois author first affirmed his independence by assuming, ironically, the mask of a *grand seigneur* of letters and his cavalier rejection of the models of antiquity and of the classical relation of artist and public, summarized in the formula *instruire et plaire,* has an air of aristocratic dilettantism. "Je ne vous promets rien," Marivaux tells his readers, ". . . Je ne jure de rien; et si je vous ennuie, je ne vous ai pas dit que cela n'arriveroit pas; si je vous amuse, je n'y suis pas obligé, je ne vous dois rien: ainsi le plaisir que je vous donne est un présent que je vous fais; et si par hasard je vous instruis, je suis un homme magnifique, et vous voilà comblé de mes grâces." The acceptance of a traditional form to convey and simultaneously to conceal a new meaning is, as we shall see, characteristic not only of Marivaux's reflections on literature and writers but of his own literary work itself.

Marivaux's insistence on the social nature of literature and on the role of the author's subjectivity in the process of literary creation necessarily excluded the classical ideal of objectivity. While the writer has to write about something, in short, that something, Marivaux held, is not a pure object or essence, but something as the writer sees it or experiences it. Every subject implies an object and every object implies a subject. Man cannot think, feel, indeed he cannot exist, without the world to awaken him and galvanize his faculties into action. "Nous restons là

comme des eaux dormantes qui attendent qu'on les remue, pour se remuer," remarks Lélio in the first *Surprise de l'amour.* The world, on the other hand, can be apprehended only by our reflection upon our experience of it. In a way it too only comes into existence through us. *Esse est percipi* is a radical formulation of a common attitude. Nothing is for us but what is observed. In all the literature and art of the eighteenth century—in content and in form as well—the point of view plays a crucial role. The epistolary novel presents the point of view of the writer of each letter, the novel in the form of mémoires stresses that it is the work of the hero recalling and interpreting his past in later life, the *conte,* the fantasy tale and the third person novel have their auctorial interventions, the theatre has the play within the play, the painting viewers and paintings within the painting. The work of art comes to the public openly as a contrivance, pointing to itself by these various devices and saying or asking what it is. And this is one of its most pertinent comments upon reality itself.

The variety of points of view and the absence of any absolute standard are essential elements of Marivaux's work. While others continued to use the stock characters of courtly comedy—the financier, the fop, etc.—as comic heroes, Marivaux recognized that the norm of nature or reason supporting this kind of comedy is simply the expression of a point of view, that of *la cour et la ville,* which is unaware of itself as a point of view, and that the comic type himself reflects a view of man out of tune with contemporary experience and contemporary thought. Marivaux was conscious of his esthetics. "Il avoit le malheur de ne pas estimer beaucoup Molière," d'Alembert relates. In effect, a good deal of his work is a response to Molière's. *Les Sincères,* as has been frequently pointed out, is Marivaux's answer to *Le Misanthrope.* (The point of the play is that all social behavior is behavior for others, so that sincerity is itself a mask, and a more dishonest mask than most, since it refuses to accept its own nature.) So too the first scene of *La Double Inconstance,* one of the earliest comedies, should probably be read with Molière in mind. "Ne faut-il pas être raisonnable," Trivelin enjoins Silvia, who has been abducted by the Prince from her village and brought to the court. "Non, il ne faut point l'être et je ne le serai point," Silvia answers, overturning what Marivaux took to be Molière's fixed categories of nature and reason. Reason in this scene is simply the perspective of the court, and Silvia has her own reason. "Moi, je hais la santé et je suis bien aise d'être malade," she cries, again pointing up against the author of *Le Malade Imaginaire* that the norm of so-called health is simply that of a social group unaware of the relativity of its own position. "Je ne veux qu'être fâchée," she adds in the next sentence, and the audience must certainly have recalled Alceste's "Moi, je veux me fâcher."

While Marivaux wished to give his audiences a point of view—that of servants, rustics, etc.—from which they could grasp their own conventionality he did not, however, intend them to settle down into this point of view. The point of the comedy would be lost if it were not grasped that all forms are conventional and that none, therefore, not that of *urbs* but not that of *rus* either, can be taken as absolute. What we have to do, Marivaux implies, is to assume this conventionality with complete lucidity, to play out our part as prince, duke or valet, remembering that it is only a part and that as wearers of the mask to which history or accident has assigned us, we are all equal. There is, in Marivaux's view, no escape from this situation. Those who are unaware of it are nevertheless in it. They may not think they are actors—like the children raised in isolation in **La Dispute** and then thrown together by the Prince—but they are actors even if they do not know it: the Court is present watching the so-called children of nature as they awaken to themselves and to each other—and we, of course, are present as spectators watching the play. "Nous sommes tous des tableaux, les uns pour les autres," in the words of the **Spectateur Français.** Everyone is always an actor for someone. Madame Argante in **Les Acteurs de Bonne Foi** will not give her consent to a play, and she is punished for her refusal by being made an unconscious actress in a dramatic situation devised by her friend Madame Amelin. If she will not assume the comedy, she will not escape it. Ergaste and La Marquise in **Les Sincères,** who reject social forms as false, are the most vain, hypocritical and deceitful of all the characters in that play. Let us recall once more the words of the Indigent Philosophe. He likes best, he tells us, those who "ne portent point leur masque; ils ne l'ont qu'à la main, et vous disent: tenez, le voilà, et cela est charmant. J'aime tout à fait cette manière-là d'être ridicule; car enfin, il faut l'être et de toutes les manières de l'être, celle qui mérite le moins à mon gré, c'est celle qui ne trompe point les autres, qui ne les induit pas à erreur sur notre compte." The only honesty and the only freedom, in short, lie in a willing assumption of our social condition and of the conventionality of social arrangements.

The meaning of Marivaux's plays is conveyed not only at the level of dramatic action, but at the level of the very material with which the writer works, at the level of language. Marivaux was acutely conscious of the social nature of language, and a great deal of the apparently innocent word play in the comedies is designed to emphasize it. Again there is an unreflecting realist stage at which words are assumed to be, as if by some divine or natural institution, the direct images of things. Arlequin the rustic in **La Double Inconstance** who is unaware of himself as an actor is also unaware of the nature of language. "A vrai dire, Seigneur," Flaminia reports to the Prince about him, "je le crois tout à fait amoureux de moi, mais il n'en sait rien. Comme il ne m'*appelle* encore que sa chère amie, il vit *sur la bonne foi de ce nom qu'il me donne,* et prend toujours de l'amour à bon compte" (III, 1). It is the writer's aim to give the audience a perspective on this realist view of language and thus to lead it to the second stage, at which it becomes aware that words are no more made in heaven than literature itself is, that they are not images of things but signs which depend for their meaning on a code and that the code itself is conventional. "Eh bien! Infidèle soit, puisque tu veux que je le sois," exclaims the Countess in **L'Heureux Stratagème** to her servant Lisette. "Crois-tu

A 1955 production of Arlequin poli par l'amour *at the Comédie Française.*

me faire peur avec ce grand mot-là? Infidèle! ne dirait-on pas que ce soit une grande injure? Il y a comme cela des mots dont on épouvante les esprits faibles qu'on a mis en crédit, faute de réflexion, et qui ne sont pourtant rien" (I, 4).

Marivaux's word play, like all word-play, is an interrogation of language and meaning. The simple characters in **La Double Inconstance,** Silvia and Arlequin, constantly question the words and phrases used by the courtly characters. Expressions like *honnête homme, votre grandeur* are revealed for what they are. But the rustics are not *right*. We are not intended to identify ourselves with their position which, in the end, is as realist as that of the courtly characters. Quite simply their questioning shows that words are used in social contexts and that they are meaningful only within the social group that uses them. Again folly does not lie in speaking the language of the Court but in imagining that it is the language of universal reason. Significantly the Prince himself does not make that mistake, only his creatures do. Arlequin unnerves Lisette, the servant of the Court, by turning her conventional flatteries into nonsense (**Double Inconstance,** I, 6), but she is unnerved only because she fails to realize that language does not signify to those outside the group using it. Trivelin is similarly nonplussed when he finds that he cannot justify the Prince's abduction of Silvia. "C'est votre souverain qui vous aime," he tells the young peasant girl. But to somebody who is not used to the language of the Court and who does not share the values it conveys this explanation is meaningless. "Je ne l'empêche pas," Silvia retorts. "Mais faut-il que je l'aime, moi? Non . . . un enfant le verroit et vous ne le voyez pas." Trivelin tries again: "Songez que c'est sur vous qu'il fait tomber le choix qu'il doit faire d'une épouse entre ses sujettes." Again Silvia demurs: "Qui est-ce qui lui a dit de me choisir? M'a-t-il demandé mon avis . . . Point du tout, il m'aime, crac, il m'enlève, sans me demander si je le trouverai bon." Trivelin tries to justify the Prince's abduction on the grounds that "il ne vous cnlève que pour vous donner la main." But he continues to use phrases that are meaningful within his own courtly context only. "Eh que veut-il que je fasse de cette main," Silvia retorts, "si je n'ai pas envie d'avancer la mienne pour la prendre?" In a society where the Prince's absoluteness is accepted, "donner la main" is doubtless explanation enough. The other party to the act is presumed to have no independent will, but to Silvia it is not an explanation. She and Trivelin simply do not speak the same language, and like those comedians who play their parts without realizing that they are doing so, Trivelin uses language without understanding what he is doing.

Occasionally in Marivaux's work there occurs a kind of flight or absence even of the self-conscious actor, who refuses temporarily to accept his role and tries to imply that he is a "natural." This "bad faith" has a linguistic corollary which takes the form of an attempt to act as if words naturally signified, so that instead of presenting them explicitly as taking their meaning from a code, the character acts as if they were the transparent reflection of some state of mind or soul. This is what happens in **Les Serments Indiscrets** (II, 5) when Lucile tries to stop the marriage to which she herself in pride has pushed her lover, on the grounds that she would feel eternally guilty for having caused the unhappiness of two people. Lucile believes her own story, she takes her meaning from her mask and her language, denying their true nature.

If language is a cultural phenomenon, as Marivaux's plays urge, no language, not even the language of the great writers of the *grand siècle,* is sacrosanct. Marivaux did in fact take "liberties" with what had become standard literary language. In the milieux he frequented the language of the seventeenth century had given way to one that, within set limits, was adventurous, experimental, attuned to novel and striking configurations, one in which the individual had or felt he had a greater degree of freedom. Marivaux introduced this language into literature, for which the rearguard of the Classical Establishment understandably never forgave him. For the *Anciens* styles, genres and languages were as fixed as the meanings they convey: for each subject matter there was always an appropriate language, an appropriate genre, an appropriate style. Marivaux tried to free the writer and, indeed, the individual from this tyranny of universal laws supposedly inherent in the nature of things. But he did not imagine that freedom was possible except within fairly clearly defined limits. He would probably have agreed with those present-day writers who hold that man can be himself only through language, that is, by appropriating a linguistic system which he did not himself create or will and by participating in social life. Man, in this view of him, has no identity until he has learned to speak. He becomes himself through society, through others, and his being is one with its social and linguistic expression. "Hors de la parole," as one writer puts it, "la subjectivité

reste ineffable." There is likewise for Marivaux no escape from linguistic systems or social forms and we achieve our identity as human beings not by discovering our absolute "nature" but by assuming a mask and accepting the rules of the game. Marivaux did not question the rules of thc game, however, or indicate that they might be changed. Rather he believed that social life brings out certain characteristics of human beings—vanity, competitiveness, dependence on others and desire to make others dependent on us—and that any social institution reflects these "natural"—in the sense of empirically observed—characteristics. The distinction of ranks is thus, in a sense, "natural." Nevertheless Marivaux held, along with many of his contemporaries, that in the very understanding of this situation the enlightened man or woman achieves a limited freedom. We are never free, in short, of the rules imposed by linguistic systems or by social forms or, indeed, by our own natural constitution, but we are, to some degree, free *within* them and *among* them. The actor, for instance, as he renews and improvizes his parts—and we should not overlook Marivaux's long association with the Italian players who were accustomed to improvizing within the framework of their scenario—using now the language of the valet, now the language of the master, now that of the pedant, now that of the fop, combines in the highest degree the two conditions of freedom and identity or social and historical existence.

In the figure of the actor, therefore, the enlightened men and women of Marivaux's world discovered what they thought they were. The actor, as they understood him, is not identical with a role or a language, but he is inconceivable without a role and words to speak; he is at once distinct from his part, creating it in accordance with the rules of the social game and observing and guiding his performance of it, and at the same time he is it, so that the mask is the man himself and the individual is identical with his language. In a somewhat similar way, the enlightened aristocrat or bourgeois of the early eighteenth century transcended on one level the social conventions of his time, since he recognized them as social conventions, while on another level he accepted them, not too unwillingly, one may surmise, as an inevitable condition of human existence. It is not surprising that the upper classes of eighteenth century society were mad about the theatre—or that Rousseau defended the ban on it in Geneva. Moreover, the theatre provided an occasion for reconciling "bourgeois" humanitarianism and sentiment with acceptance of the existing social order. By essaying the role of valets, one could, as it were, experience in play what it was like to be one and this, it was thought, should teach one to be kinder to one's servants in that other play in which one happened to perform the role of the master. Besides his best known play, **Le Jeu de l'Amour et du Hasard,** several short works by Marivaux, well adapted to performance in private theatres (**L'Ile des Esclaves, L'Ile de la Raison, La Colonie**), turn on this theme of the interchange of roles by masters and servants.

Marivaux expressed in his novels and his comedies, as in his reflections on literature, not only the self-awareness of his society but its ambiguities and its hesitancies. He himself seems to have shared both the nostalgia of his audiences for a no-longer believed-in age of innocence and noble virtues (one might call it the golden age myth of the nobility) before the social comedy (that is, the court) began and their presentiment of a new world of individual experience. His parodies of the heroic love-passions of old may well have been the more cutting as he had not completely stifled within himself a certain longing for the immediate, the generous, the "natural." Nor should we forget his youthful fondness for Corneille and his own early attempts at romance writing. But this nostalgia for the past was closely allied in his thought and feeling to the modern experience of a private individual self with its own particular desires and longings and to the modern "bourgeois" dream of intimate and inward communication. In the circle of Madame de Lambert, as among earlier *précieux,* it was not uncommon to believe in elective affinities, in the possibility of immediate communication between persons of delicate sensibility. "Il y a des amitiés d'étoile et de sympathie," Madame de Lambert declared, "des liens inconnus qui nous unissent et qui nous serrent; nous n'avons besoin ni de protestation, ni de serment: la confiance va au-devant des paroles." Marivaux's heroine Marianne also believes in this immediate communication: "Les âmes se répondent," she declares. Almost all Marivaux's comedies close with a "marriage" which puts an end to the play not only for the spectators but also for the actors, as though the world of words had been transcended in a higher and more immediate communication. This evasion from the social comedy, from the world of words, can be viewed as the attainment of genuine love, a meeting of hearts. Alternatively, however, the embarcation for Cythera can be viewed as the culmination of an erotic adventure, a meeting of bodies, though no one to my mind has yet offered this rather obvious reading. But neither interpretation would be adequate on its own. If we are to probe the ambiguity of Marivaux's plays further we must recognize that his heroes are not only actors in their mode of being but—whether masculine or feminine in gender—women; and we must inquire into the significance of this concrete reality lurking behind the abstract figure of the actor-character.

* * * *

Already in the late seventeenth century a code of behavior had begun to evolve for life at court with the purpose of maintaining smooth social relations and a semblance of order and harmony among people who were no longer inwardly convinced that there was a natural order and who were, indeed, in constant competition with each other. The newness of this code is brought out—despite Marivaux!—in Molière's *Le Misanthrope,* where the court no longer stands as an absolute order but is itself shown in its relativity. Alceste, the champion of an earlier and more heroic age protests at the perversion of language by his courtly friends. The latter, however, are not all deceived by the deceits Alceste complains of. They understand their language very well. Alceste, in short, takes

the old language of pre-courtly days to be "natural" and cannot adapt to the new one. Molière also shows how the new language works to maintain both social order and individual freedom by disposing of the myth that words signify "naturally" and by making explicit the role of all parties in communication. In certain extremely favorable circumstances, indeed, the language allows communication to occur without reference to anything outside of the communication itself. The object of the communication seems identical with the act. There is communication and interrelation, in other words, but as there are no solid bodies, so to speak, there is no problem of friction. This is the language spoken by Philinte and Oronte in the first act of *Le Misanthrope.* Philinte praises Oronte's sonnet. Oronte answers: "Vous me flattez." Philinte protests: "Non, je ne flatte point." But neither party communicates anything in this exchange except a general readiness to abide by common rules, while avoiding any open confrontation of the desire, the being, the language of the one with the desire, the being, the language of the other. This is likewise the language that Célimène claims to speak when she protests to Alceste that it is not her fault if different men sometimes think she favors them: she favors all equally and she is not responsible for the interpretations that can be put on her behavior. Signs are only signs and the reading of them, the constituting of a message, as well as all suppositions about the intentionality of the subject behind them are, she claims, the responsibility of the interlocutor. There are phenomena, in other words, but what "reality" they point to, if any, the see-er decides for himself.

Yet Célimène recognizes that pure communication is achieved only in rare circumstances. The needs and desires of individuals have not been cancelled out, and below the level of polite conversation about nothing there are often real struggles of power between individuals, as Célimène's own lawsuit indicates. Célimène herself explains that she seeks to maintain Clitandre's interest in her because of his influence in high places and his usefulness to her. While it may still be true, therefore, that there is no particular intentionality in her words and gestures, Célimène admits that there is a general one.

Far from being pure and an end in itself—a mere sociableness—communication here has a practical purpose for the individual in that through it he avoids making enemies and seeks the goodwill of others. For women in particular it is important to have powerful protectors. Like several of Marivaux's heroines, Célimène is a *veuve,* which is to say that she is equally free from the tutelage of her family and from the tyranny of a husband. As her freedom is limited, however, by the social code, no matter how clearly conventional the latter is recognized to be, she must find gentlemen willing to take up her defense on those occasions when she needs help. In the end, her freedom rests entirely on the goodwill of men. She is not, therefore, without responsibility for her suitors' persistent hopes. Yet she does not deceive them. On the contrary, she is contrasted with Arsinoë who does. In Molière's vision all those who oppose the court and the code on which it is based are either dupes who do not

DRAMA CRITICISM, Vol. 7

understand social rules (Orgon, Alceste) or hypocrites who understand them but refuse to play according to them (Tartuffe, Arsinoë). The hypocrite is thus by definition anti-social and it is, indeed, Arsinoë who destroys the fragile balance in which Célimène has reconciled the goals of individuals and the general requirements of social harmony. In many ways, therefore, Célimène represents the ideal order of courtly society. In her the positive content of particular needs and desires is brought into harmony with the code on which the very possibility of society is based.

Marivaux also sees woman as the characteristic figure of the social order of his time. Like Célimène many of his heroines are "widows," free agents, yet free only on condition that they observe the social code in all its aspects. For them too the only source of strength and influence lies in making themselves attractive to men. "Nous nous entêtons du vil honneur de leur plaire," Arthenice, the leader of the women's revolt in *La Colonie,* charges. "Est-ce notre faute?" the women answer. "Nous n'avons que cela à faire" (Sc. 9). Not surprisingly, vanity plays a predominant role in Marivaux. "Notre vanité et notre coquetterie, voilà la plus grande source de nos passions," Lucile muses, as she discovers her interest in Damis growing in proportion as his in her is, as she believes, declining (*Les Serments Indiscrets,* V, 2). The vanity of woman is one of the great themes of Marivaux and is intimately related to his interpretation of her social condition. ". . . Voir sans cesse qu'on est aimable: "ah! que cela est doux à voir! Le charmant point de vue pour une femme! En vérité, tout est perdu quand vous perdez cela," Hortense confesses in *Le Prince Travesti* (I, 2). In a much discussed second stage of *Le Jeu de l'Amour et du Hasard,* which prolongs the play by an act, Silvia, not content with extracting a declaration of love from Dorante while the latter still believes she is a servant, announces to her family that she will not be satisfied until he has asked for her hand in marriage. Although, of course, Silvia and Dorante are socially compatible, Silvia's enterprise underlines the social significance of female vanity. In the man's pursuit of her, Silvia is saying, woman reverses the position to which she is assigned in social life.

In Marivaux's world, however, general triumphs are no longer enough. Desire has become more pressing, more individual, less easily contained and controlled than it was in the world of *Le Misanthrope.* It is Arsinoë the hypocrite, as we mentioned, who disrupts Célimène's universe; Célimène herself suffers, apparently, from no inner conflicts. The heroines of Marivaux's world, on the other hand, have to struggle hard to maintain that identity of person and persona which Célimène achieves so effortlessly. This struggle is, indeed, one of the principal motifs of his comedies. Characteristically, his heroines are not, like Célimène, engaged only in a kind of generalized coquetterie. The action of Marivaux's comedies concerns usually two lovers, not a court; the problem is not how to harmonize different personae, but how

to harmonize the person and the persona; and the happy denouement, together with the consequent release of dramatic tension, is achieved when this problem is resolved.

At no point, however, whatever the mental anguish of the hero or heroine, is the persona, or the social code, actually abandoned. "Assurément," the Marquise declares in the second *Surprise de l'Amour,* "ce n'est pas que je me soucie de ce qu'on appelle la gloire d'une femme, gloire sotte, ridicule, mais reçue, mais établie, qu'il faut soutenir, et qui nous pare; les hommes pensent cela, il faut penser comme les hommes ou ne pas vivre avec eux" (II, 6). Rather than face a break between the person and the persona, rather than confront their own desire, Marivaux's characters will resort to mental breakdown—whence the frequently heard cry: "Je ne sais où je suis" (first *Surprise de l'Amour,* III, 4)—and they will recover as soon as they discover a means of reconciling their desire with their social role—the occasion of the equally characteristic: "Ah! je vois clair dans mon coeur" (*Jeu de l'Amour et du Hasard,* II, 12). In the last resort, therefore, their own desire is subordinated to the maintenance of the social order. There is a point beyond which they cannot go, most amusingly presented perhaps in Act III, scene 8 of *Le Jeu de l'Amour et du Hasard.*

At the same time, the bare fact that woman does feel and pursue desire, however deviously, is not without significant consequences. To the degree that men recognize her as a creature of desire, they are inevitably prepared to interpret her words and gestures as covert expressions of desire. The code to which these words and gestures refer thus becomes ambiguous—and highly flexible. A word or gesture can be interpreted with reference to the original code by which women were protected from the advances of enterprising males or it can be interpreted according to another code in which desire is only formally denied. In either case the vocabulary remains the same and the burden of interpretation is on the interlocutor. The interlocutor is not always willing to assume this responsibility, however. Whence the exasperation of the Countess in *La Fausse Suivante.* "Il n'y a rien de plus désagréable que votre obstination à me croire polie," she tells the Chevalier; "car il faudra, malgré moi, que je le sois . . . Y a-t-il rien de plus haïssable qu'un homme qui ne saurait deviner" (II, 8). The reticence of the interlocutor indicates a further consequence of woman's pursuit of desire. As a protective device the code of modesty and gallantry had a proper place in a world in which each social group—class or sex—had or was supposed to have its own particular nature. There was a way of being for men, and a way of being for women, as there was a way of being for barons and a way of being for serfs. In Marivaux's world the difference between the sexes, like all other social hierarchies, has become blurred and remains only in form. The behavior of many of his male characters is scarcely different from that of his female ones. Almost all are women in these plays. Rosimond, the hero of *Le Petit-Maître Corrigé,* is only the most explicitly designated of a gallery of similar figures. We need merely think of some of the scenes in which the lovers try to bring their enterprises to a successful conclusion to realize that male and female no longer have their respective roles but behave in exactly the same manner.

Generations of critics have thus done well to emphasize the central role of woman in Marivaux. But Marivaux's theatre is not only predominantly about women, it is also, despite its exposure of her wiles and her vanity, a glorification of woman, and not of the free woman Laclos was to evoke at the end of the century in his book *De l'Education des femmes,* but of the very woman whose secret humiliations Marivaux understood so well.

Woman, as Marivaux presents her, incarnates the highest qualities of civilized life—charm, wit, taste, intelligence, sensibility—and these qualities are the result of a combination in her of desire and inferiority. Where there is only need, there is, in Marivaux's view, no refinement or delicacy of sentiment. The Countess in *Le Legs* is shocked on discovering the naked selfishness of her maid, but the valet Lepine tells her a few simple truths: "Cette prudence ne vous rit pas; elle vous répugne; votre belle âme de Comtesse s'en scandalise; mais tout le monde n'est pas comtesse . . . la médiocrité de l'état fait que les pensées sont médiocres. Lisette n'a point de bien, et c'est avec de petits sentiments qu'on en amasse" (Sc. 21). It is only when need is transformed into desire, when necessity becomes luxury, that refinement of manners and feelings is possible, for desire, unlike need, is itself a social phenomenon, not an individual one, and it brings with it a heightened awareness of others. The less need and the more desire, the more refinement there will be. At the same time, desire destroys all "objective" values. Desirability becomes the sole measure of everything and all traditional values are gathered up in the all-embracing web of exchange value. Sometimes this situation is presented explicitly, as in those comedies where money plays a central role, but it is manifested in all of them by the women characters as they measure themselves exclusively and explicitly in terms of their desirability. The traditional essentialist order of things is thus deeply undermined by a rival order, entirely man-made and without any transcendental foundation.

Nevertheless, the attempt to counter the authority of men, which has produced the characteristic qualities of women, stops short at revolt. The established order of male or parental authority is not to be overturned. Angélique in Marivaux's *Ecole des Mères* differs from her predecessor in *L'Ecole des Femmes* in that she does not reject her mother. The latter is not reasonable; "je ne l'en aime pourtant pas moins," says Angélique (Sc. 18). There is an attempted revolt of the women in *La Colonie,* but it fails because, as Marivaux presents it, it is the "nature" of women, the ruled, to rule by charm and guile, while it is the "nature" of men, the rulers, to be ruled by

their inferiors. Civilization, in other words, is a humanly contrived space of freedom and equality, which the inferiors carve out within a structure of inequality that is thereby softened or even suspended, but neither denied nor abolished. Some lines which are recited in the Divertissement at the beginning of *La Colonie* to console the women for the failure of their revolt sum up this position, though they are probably not from Marivaux's own pen:

> Si les lois des hommes dépendent,
> Ne vous plaignez pas, trop aimables objets:
> Vous imposez des fers à ceux qui vous
>   commandent,
>   Et vos maîtres sont vos sujets.

Marivaux had not lived through the Law affair and burned his own fingers in it without learning anything. The scope of desire, as he saw it, was expanding and possession could not still it. On the contrary, it was among those who already possessed much that it was strongest. The entire social order was thus being reduced to a shadow by the growing intensity of individual desire as it levelled all traditional distinctions before it and reduced them to measurable quantities. Yet there seems to have been no question in Marivaux's mind that the social order might actually be overturned in favor of another, just as in the minds of his heroines there is no question of abandoning the formal social code. Even when he argues against "prejudice" Marivaux does so with respect for traditional forms. Angélique in *Le Préjugé Vaincu* must overcome her distaste for the "bourgeois" Dorante, but Dorante, we are reassured, "n'a pas fait sa fortune; il l'a trouvée toute faite" (Sc. 8). Although he is "sans noblesse," in other words, he lives "nobly."

Perhaps Marivaux's unwillingness to draw the revolutionary consequences of widespread individual desire, as he revealed it in his comedies, can be understood if we recall the peculiar balance which sustained the society he lived in and wrote for. The activities of the bourgeoisie in the early eighteenth century were still intimately bound up with the structure of the feudal-absolutist state, the whole order of which these very activities contradicted. Similarly, the power, wealth and market value of the aristocracy were entirely dependent on a hierarchical order which was flatly contradicted by the outlook and by the behavior of the aristocracy. Bourgeoisie and aristocracy alike, therefore, had an interest in upholding the existing order and seeking the satisfaction of their desires within it, for if the social order and the rules that sustained it were obstacles to individual desire, they were also the conditions of its fulfilment. Desire, in short, could not be avowed; it could be pursued only within the space that could be won for it from a code that officially ignored its existence. Similarly, equality could not be avowed; it could only be realized inside a framework which officially denied it. The celebration of woman by Marivaux is thus a celebration of the whole mode of life of the aristocracy and the wealthy bourgeoisie of his time.

If desire itself is unavowable in Marivaux's work, the nature of desire is shrouded in ambiguity by his art, and this ambiguity is also socially significant. Old-fashioned seduction gives way, as we saw, in many of the comedies to the *aventure galante,* in which both partners seduce and are seduced according to a loosely prescribed ritual. But this ritual is not easily interpreted. The mystery of Watteau's fêtes galantes—uncertainly sentimental and erotic at the same time—should be enough to give us pause. It is not in fact at the level of their content that we can best interpret Marivaux's comedies. To say that they are about "l'amour naissant," the traditional view of them, is to say something of what they are about, but not, perhaps, enough. Just as the words and gestures of Marivaux's heroines do not signify directly in the plays but are offered deliberately as a set of signifiers which the interlocutor has to interpret, so the plays themselves do not signify directly but offer a coherent structure which can be diversely interpreted according to the audience's wish. We can see them as configurations of erotic adventures or as configurations of sentimental ones; the initial desire may be the anonymous desire of a body or it may be "l'amour naissant," the desire of a real individual; the marriages at the end may be taken as the culmination of erotic encounters or as the true meeting of subjects in love. The "aristocratic" reading and the "bourgeois" one both fit. Yet many of the plays would be destroyed if we plumped for one or the other, for they depend on nothing so much as the bracketing of any single "real" meaning. This is not to say that they have no meaning, but that ambiguity is built into their structure, so that their lack of precise meaning becomes itself part of their meaning. Even the most "bourgeois" of the comedies participates in this ambiguity. The problem in **La Mère Confidente,** according to all commentators the most *larmoyante* of Marivaux's comedies, is a typical bourgeois one: firstly, how to be sure of the love of a young man, and secondly, how to marry him with the consent of a parent who is afraid of penniless adventurers and eager to see her child make a solid and appropriate match. The problem is fully resolved at the end, when Ergaste makes Dorante, the young man, his heir—"Ne vous ai-je pas promis qu'Angélique n'épouserait point un homme sans bien." But Marivaux's audiences could, if they liked, view the play as an unusual variation on the familiar theme of the woman who wishes to live *la vie galante* without sacrificing her reputation or flouting social conventions. From this point of view the bourgeois of the comedy are like the shepherds and shepherdesses of the pastoral, and the bourgeois background and sentiments serve only to give a new and piquant flavor to a ritual that otherwise tends to become tedious. One recalls how a sentimental intrigue revived the flagging erotic interest of Laclos' hero at the end of the century. Marivaux does not suggest that the second reading is the "correct" one, but knowing his audiences as he did, he knew that it was possible, and the special charm even of his most "bourgeois" comedy resides in his willingness to leave the interpretation open, so that the audience can move back and forth at its pleasure, allowing itself to be absorbed by the action at one moment, and seeing it as a masquerade at the next.

* * * * *

Along with many of his contemporaries, Marivaux held that whatever might be imagined about a nature of things behind the world of phenomena, the only nature which men could study usefully was the order of the observable world itself. In many respects this was a liberating attitude. Montesquieu's politics and the economics of Galiani and the Physiocrats are but two of the new sciences that rest on it. But there was a danger that the observed order of things might itself be naturalized, so that it became identified as the fundamental and ineluctable order of the world, a second nature as potent as the first had been to those who had believed in it. This is in fact what happened. Human nature and the fundamental structures of human relations as they could be observed in the world of the ancien regime were taken by Marivaux and by many of the *Modernes* to be fixed and unchanging. Time, indeed, they conceived of as no more than a succession of discontinuous instants constantly vanishing and being renewed, while novelty was simply the repetition in different instants of time of age-old rituals. "Toutes les âmes sont du même age," Phocion tells Leontine in **Le Triomphe de l'Amour** (I, 6). Not change, then, but only variety was real, and indeed variety is a key word in the esthetics of the *Modernes.* By change the *Modernes* could mean no more than a constant re-shuffling of roles, an eternal passing back and forth between fixed categories of masters and servants, of mistresses and soubrettes.

Marivaux's comedies, inevitably, are repetitious, variations on a few simple themes, and this repetitiousness is as appropriate to the view of the world that underlies them as that of Lancret is, for instance, in painting. What Marivaux explores in play after play is the relation between the actor and the role, between the performance and the scenario, what he celebrates is the peculiar freedom which the skilful and self-conscious performer finds in it. It is a freedom in many ways similar to that which Montesquieu was to celebrate when he turned *L'Esprit des Lois* into a eulogy of the "temperate monarchy."

But this conception of freedom as something to be realized within a given framework of relations and rules rather than as a condition of action prior to these relations and rules is not, surely, fortuitous. It is too well suited to the situation and the needs of the society with which Marivaux was intimately associated, allowing as it did both for aristocratic libertinage and for bourgeois individualism, on condition that neither upset the apple-cart. A different conception of freedom, turned toward making the future rather than transfiguring the past, is not to be found in Marivaux's comedies, or, if found, turns out to be a vain and in the end playful gesture, such as the women's revolt in **La Colonie.** We shall not find such a conception of freedom in literature until the second half of the century. Significantly, both Rousseau and Laclos, however differently they portray the ideal woman, agree in their disparagement of the type of woman who is the heroine under a multitude of names and guises of almost every one of Marivaux's comedies.

Oscar Mandel (essay date 1968)

SOURCE: An introduction to *Seven Comedies by Marivaux,* edited by Oscar Mandel, translated by Oscar Mandel and Adrienne S. Mandel, University Press of America, 1984, pp. 1-15.

[*In the essay below, which was first published in 1968, Mandel presents a general survey of Marivaux's career, touching on such aspects of his comedies as characterization, situation and plot, mood and tone, and relation to French and Italian theatrical conventions.*]

"Marivaux comes after Molière and Racine as Menander follows Aristophanes and Euripides." Thus Lucien Dubech in his classic *Histoire générale illustrée du théâtre.* At the Comédie-Française, where the thousandth performance of *Le Jeu de l'amour et du hasard* was celebrated in 1948, Marivaux is now the most frequently performed comic playwright after Molière. Since the Second World War, directors like Barrault, Vilar, and Planchon have mounted highly acclaimed productions at the Odéon, the Vieux Colombier, and the Théâtre National Populaire. Quite regularly, the dust is blown off a half-forgotten piece and a "new" work by Marivaux is staged, whether in Paris or in the provinces. Even the working classes are treated to these patrician follies: in the spring of 1965 I saw *La Surprise de l'amour* shiver in a tent in Nanterre, an industrial suburb of Paris.

In their tours outside of France, French theatrical companies often present the best-known of Marivaux's comedies. We might note the highly successful production of *Les Fausses confidences* by the Renaud-Barrault troupe in New York in 1952, and of *Le Jeu de l'amour et du hasard* by the Comédie-Française in London in 1967. But there is scarcely a country, from Latin America to the Soviet Union, in which a French company has not performed one or another of Marivaux's plays.

In France itself, to cite precise figures, nineteen of Marivaux's comedies have been produced at the Comédie-Française between 1901 and 1963, some many times and some only a few. Seven more have been staged in other French theatres in the same period; so that of the thirty comedies which Marivaux wrote for performance, twenty-six can be called "living theatre"—no mean achievement for any writer. Beyond this, the plays continue to be reprinted in all forms, from cheap single school-text editions to luxurious book club collections. And a vast scholarly and critical literature concerning Marivaux keeps pace with editions and productions.

But in spite of occasional visits by French companies, very little of this interest has crossed either the Channel or the Atlantic. In over two centuries, only five of Marivaux's plays have been translated into English. The translations which do exist have all appeared singly; it has never been possible for a British or American reader who knows no French to browse through a volume of these standard plays. He has had to look for them one by one, now in an obscure eighteenth-century tome, now in a defunct magazine, now in a collection alongside other authors. And with one minor exception in 1761, it would seem that Marivaux has not been professionally performed in the English language at all—at least until the summer of 1965, when *La double inconstance* was given in English at the Pitlochry Festival in Scotland.

As for the literature concerning Marivaux, the first English book ever written about him—a specialized study of his novels—was published in 1941, one hundred and seventy-eight years after his death. The first English work dealing with his plays was a handbook published in 1958. It is fair to say therefore that while a rudimentary path to this classic has been beaten, Marivaux is still, for us, the most unavailable of all the great French playwrights.

The young man who chose to make his way in the worlds of literature and fashion as Monsieur de Marivaux was born in 1688 plain Pierre Carlet, the son of a finance official in Riom, a small town in the Auvergne. Nothing precise is known of Marivaux's early experiences, or even of his whereabouts, but in 1710 we find him in Paris, ostensibly to study law, actually to establish himself as a writer. Presently he contrived to be at home among authors like Fontenelle and la Motte, and to be received in several of the best salons; but when and how this son of the provincial bourgeoisie made his useful contacts we again do not know. Before long, however, he was breaking into print, battling at the side of his friends for the Moderns in that famous quarrel, and writing a parody of Homer which did nothing to advance the good cause. He was more successful with fashionable "letters," essays, and stories. To read these is to understand that Marivaux is from the start a man at ease in his times; he breathes and exhales the lucid air of Regency France; he enjoys—he loves—the salons where, according to a witness, he watches for his turn to toss off the aphorism he has been grooming in his mind.

We do not hear of any period of callow apprenticeship which he had to serve at the gatherings of Mme de Lambert or Mme de Tencin. It is as though he had been born full-grown in these drawing rooms; and his work was to remain a perfect formulation of their ideas. We can speak here of "natural elegance" as though the expression were not self-contradictory. Questions of love, the arts, justice, government, politics, religion; observations on mankind; news of the world—every concern was brought to these assemblies, where the rich, the intelligent, and the merely well-connected met. Everything could be said or at least suggested here, provided it was said or suggested with grace. To put it most broadly, this was a society in which a finish of beauty was placed on every activity of man for the last time in the history of the West. Whatever was spoken, conceived, and manufactured was spoken, conceived, and manufactured as beautifully as possible: down to the very weapons which killed other men.

Marivaux had taken his place in this world more as a man of talent than as a man of means. He had, however, means enough to dress well, and a judicious marriage—

whether it was also a marriage of love we do not know—brought him a dowry. But Marivaux was affable and careless; a friend persuaded him to invest his funds in Law's enterprises; and he was nearly ruined in the debacle of 1720. As it happens, he had begun his theatrical career a few months before the disaster; but there is no evidence that he ever sought to make money through his plays: they brought him little, and he wrote nothing to make them bring more.

Marivaux had made the acquaintance of a hack writer named Rustaing de Saint-Jory, with whom he collaborated on a comedy for the Théâtre Italien in March of 1720. The play promptly failed, but we can surmise that it gave Marivaux the introduction he needed. The Italians had reappeared in Paris in 1716 after an enforced exile of nineteen years. They were still newcomers; in serious financial trouble; and casting about for advice, help, and new plays in French. Half a year after his first failure, Marivaux gave them his most Italianate work, *Arlequin poli par l'amour,* a genuine offspring of the *commedia dell'arte.* The public applauded. Marivaux and the Italians were undoubtedly pleased with each other. For twenty years, from 1720 to 1740, Marivaux was to supply them with his best work, eighteen comedies in all. But in 1742 the Academy made him a fellow-Immortal, and this uncomic honor all but closed his career. Unlike Molière, Marivaux had never become a professional man of the theatre. He never acted, never directed, and never produced a play. Novelist and essayist as much as dramatist, and man of the world as much as any of these, he clearly did not dream at any time in his life of becoming a trouper.

Ten of his plays, including his one tragedy, went to the Comédie-Française, but only one of them, *Le Préjugé vaincu,* was really well received by the public. The lightness of his prose, and his unusual talent for shades of feeling, half-differences, and tenuous gradations seem to have been too much—or too little!—for the French actors, who liked alexandrines, oratory, bold effects, and idiosyncratic characters. Though he kept trying to establish himself at the more respectable Théâtre Français, Marivaux had found his true home at the Hôtel de Bourgogne among the Italians, whose gracefulness matched his own; and in Giovanna Benozzi a Sylvia so excellent that many of his contemporaries thought she would take his plays to the grave with her.

As it turned out, the Italians were enriched more in reputation than hard cash during the twenty years in which they faithfully produced Marivaux's plays. The comedies sometimes gave a good account of themselves, but even at best they could not compete with the ballets, fireworks, and musicals to which the Italians had to resort in order to survive. And as often as not, the players performed to nearly empty houses. Marivaux was not a bad commercial risk, but he broke no records and made no impresario rich.

So it was, too, with his literary standing. True, his reputation should not be underrated, as it often is, for romantic effect. He had many devoted admirers who made

no noise, his plays were performed by noble amateurs in several French chateaux, the Italian and French companies took his new work year after year, and he lived to see four collected editions of his plays through the presses. This was a substantial accomplishment, and it would be absurd to think of Marivaux as a neglected author because he was not singled out as the greatest of his time. Still, when the *Mercure Galant* calls him as late as 1747 "a famous Academician, accustomed to deserve the applause [*les suffrages*] of the public," we hardly know whether we should rejoice over his fame, or ruefully observe that he was accustomed to *deserve,* not to *obtain,* his due.

Voltaire and a crowd of lesser wits were hostile to him. They objected to what was immediately and has ever since been called "marivaudage," that is to say a delicate and exquisite banter about details of feeling. Voltaire accused Marivaux of "weighing flies' eggs in scales of gossamer." The great man was obviously put out by a writer who trifled full-time without participating in the epic battles of the day. Pedants, on the other hand, were appalled by audacities and impurities in Marivaux's language which the modern ear is unable to detect. The Academician whose duty it was to welcome the new member in 1743 insulted him instead. Another was heard to say, "Our task at the Academy is to build up the language, while that of M. de Marivaux is to tear it down." In sum, Marivaux was what is called a name, but there is no record of anyone pointing a finger at him to prophesy his permanence.

From a small bundle of anecdotes, from post-mortem *Eloges* and reports, and from the negative evidence of his own reticences, we gather that Marivaux was a quiet, witty, dapper, pleasant, and obliging man, rather more fastidious than most, not victimized by passions, not given to roaring, unwilling to quarrel with the world, and quite unable to beat his own drum. He was not indifferent to criticism—several stories concur as to his touchiness—but his response was to withdraw, not to counterattack, and then to forgive and forget at the first explanation. He wrote only one Preface for a play—a miracle of restraint for his times (or ours)—and engaged in no personal controversies. Nor was he a learned man. And despite his sympathy for the social views of the *philosophes,* he disliked their attacks on Christianity, a religion he respected and perhaps practiced to the end, though he did not allow it to interfere in his work.

He remained poor all his life. His wife had died in 1723, leaving him a daughter who eventually took the veil. As Marivaux could not pay for her annuity, the Duke of Orleans supplied the required funds. From the 1740's to his death in 1763, Marivaux cohabited with a certain Mlle de Saint-Jean, who was a little less poor than he, who supported him, and with whom we can suppose that he lived in quiet concord. There is little enough material for a life of Marivaux even in his best years. He was not the sort of man whose words are set down by eager Boswells, or over whom ladies gossip in their letters. For the autumnal years we have almost nothing. We get an impression of solitude without unhappiness; a corner kept for him in the salons; a tell-tale preoccupation with minor Academic duties. At his death (which was hardly noticed) he left an uncommon amount of fine linen.

The plays showed every sign of falling to dust. And yet in the years of the Revolution, of all times, Marivaux was rediscovered. The Comédie-Française inherited the plays which had been written for the now vanished Italians. And the nineteenth century gave him the absolute renown which had eluded him by a hair's breadth in his own lifetime. As a classic he was allowed to badger students at examinations, while in the theatres he simply managed to keep being amusing and interesting in ways which could neither be imitated nor superseded. Voltaire, it turned out, had chosen to forget that flies' eggs are worth weighing too, that weighing them is no easy matter, and that few artists are dextrous enough to make scales, or anything else, of gossamer. While Voltaire's own plays are shelved, while the tough Regnard is eclipsed, and while even Beaumarchais must be propped up by Mozart and Rossini, Marivaux seems as firmly settled in the French pantheon, a place of no easy admission, as Molière himself. This is, with a vengeance, the Triumph of Gossamer.

Who are the people in Marivaux's typical plays? One or two pairs of lovers at cross-purposes with each other; an occasional rival who leaves empty-handed; the servants, busy with their own love-knots while they are tying or untying their masters'; a father, a mother, an uncle, or a brother; and now and then a loquacious farmer.

Sometimes the principals are nameless; they are called simply la Comtesse, la Marquise, le Chevalier, le Comte: a broad hint that Marivaux is not primarily concerned with the delineation of peculiar characters. He is not, as he himself insisted, and as all critics agree, in Molière's school. Early in life he had determined to be original, by which he meant that he would not be overwhelmed by the presence of Molière. He preferred, says d'Alembert, to sit in the last rank of original writers than in the first row of imitators.

Now the tradition of comedy which Molière had bequeathed required the strong picture of a specific folly or vice. This was comedy of "humour" laced with social satire. Molière painted the miser, the misanthrope, the social climber, the hypochondriac, the religious hypocrite, even the atheist. His followers added the gambler, the married philosopher, the backbiter, the babbler, the stubborn man, the impertinent, the ambitious, the distracted man, and so on. The Comédie-Française looked upon itself as the temple of this drama of types.

In contrast to this genre, the *commedia dell'arte* was non-psychological and non-polemical. It drew on a small set of permanent types—the romantic lovers, the comic servants, the mean father, the dotty rival—and proceeded to embroil them in the most extravagant adventures, from robbed cradles to the revealing mark on the left ankle, through mistaken identities, meetings with mon-

sters or pirates, shipwrecks, visits of the gods, disguises, duels, and other afflictions, all interrupted by the farcical capers—the *lazzi*—of Arlecchino, Brighella, Pedrolino, or any of the other zany servants. The world of the *commedia* was a madcap world of boisterous whimsy. The scenarios (it will be remembered that the actors usually relied on sketches of the action rather than written plays) had no philosophical, moral, or social pretensions of any kind. True, the comedians shot satirical gags in every direction—against lawyers, doctors, pedants, and especially loose wives and cuckolded husbands—but this was satire by the way, and uncontroversial satire at that. These gags peppered the plays; the plays were not acted out for their sake.

While his claim to originality was well-founded, Marivaux nevertheless shared with Molière a deep indebtedness to the *commedia*. The two men merely developed different sides of the Italian drama. Molière took as his province the old men of the *commedia*: the types of the Dottore and Pantalone. He gave them a character and an obsession. They were still grouchy fathers or tottering wooers, but now they were also misers or social climbers, and their activities in character (say the miser ordering a miserly dinner) overshadowed their role as fathers, and even relegated to the margin the intrigue by which the lovers had to be married.

Marivaux, perhaps because of his experience of the salons and his early intention of becoming a novelist, took up what Molière had neglected, and brought the lovers to the fore. The older men and women with their follies and vices recede or even disappear. Before us stand the young romantic principals, whom we immediately recognize as the lovers of the *commedia*. But Marivaux does not treat them in the Moliéresque manner; he does not give them "humours," peculiarities, obsessions—they are not gamblers or liars or prudes or slanderers who parade these shortcomings before us. Marivaux is interested in the normal emotion of love itself (which the *commedia* had accepted as a simple fact requiring no analysis); he watches it appearing in a corner of the mind, then hiding, sometimes vanishing, aroused again, piqued, irritated, held back, offered to the wrong person, and finally settled where it belongs. He tells us how any normal girl feels when she believes she has fallen in love with a social inferior, or how she reacts when she learns by accident that an attractive man is insanely in love with her.

Usually, we might add, his young ladies are more sprightly, more attractive, and better observed than their suitors. Now we see a girl waiting and trembling for a declaration; now a coquette who jilts a man, only to long for him again when he neglects her; now a young widow resolved never to marry again, who struggles against her growing inclination to fall in love; now a flirtatious thing who swears fidelity to one man only to fall in love with another; now a girl so embarrassed by her own emotion that she "represses" it into unconsciousness; and now a girl who avenges herself on a fickle suitor. Marivaux observes his young men, too, but here he tends to repeat himself, and his markedly feminine genius cannot impart the toughness or the vigor we want in them. They do not swoon or weep, thank heaven, but they do sigh and implore too ardently, bashfulness makes them blind and deaf to the most obvious advances, and they have no sense of humor. Sometimes, I am afraid, we feel like kicking them. If all must be said, even Marivaux's young women come in second-best to Molière's, whenever the master applies his mind to them. Marivaux has nothing quite so good as Célimène or Agnès, because he is too reticent, almost too hesitant. Molière is roast beef to his lemon soufflé. He is a miniaturist of genius; and nothing more, but also nothing less, should be claimed for him.

While Molière gave a new dimension to the characters of Pantalone and "il Dottore," and Marivaux explored the romantic lovers of the *commedia,* both joyously adopted Arlecchino and Colombina. These servants—and their French siblings—lead their masters' game, but they also divert us with troubles and wisdom of their own. They make an earthy rejoinder to the lofty sentiments of their superiors. In his plays of social commentary, Marivaux sometimes uses them to convey his cautiously egalitarian views. Elsewhere, with the traditional freedom of the king's fool, they comment acidulously on the mismanaged affairs of society. Marivaux obviously delighted in the speech and the attitudes of the "lower orders." These inferiors are usually the most intelligent characters in the plays. At the same time, along with Arlequin, Lisette, Trivelin, Frontin, and Spinette, Marivaux put shrewd or naïve farmers on stage—Blaise, Claudine, Dimas, and others, probably derived from Molière and the French tradition of popular comedy, and all of them as lovable as Shakespeare's best clods.

Critics of Molière and Marivaux usually fall into the error of giving these servants their secondary attention, because they seem to play secondary roles. Of Marivaux, at any rate, it must be said that he is never more gay and more brilliant than in the so-called subordinate episodes in which his little people appear. In *La double inconstance,* fortunately, they are full-fledged protagonists, a fact which makes this the most effervescent of all his longer plays.

Now and then a rather wicked person makes an appearance on Marivaux's stage, but wicked persons somehow get themselves forgiven (or forgotten) before the curtain falls. Marivaux does not hoot and hound them off the scene as the cruel Shakespeare does with Malvolio and the indignant Molière with Tartuffe. Besides, when all is said and done, they are not so wicked after all. Next to the cynical ferocity of Lesage, Regnard, Dancourt, and other wits of his day (or that of the Restoration dramatists of England), Marivaux's amiability and indulgence are altogether startling. In the work of his contemporaries, all the comic characters are irredeemable scoundrels, down to the ingénue; in his, none. And yet, by a miracle, he remains free of "larmoyance" and "attendrissement," if we accept one or two mediocre attempts in the new bourgeois genre. For while his plays have no real villains, his slyness toward his heroes and heroines keeps our eyes—like their own—thoroughly dry.

Marivaux's success owes much to his control of the half-tone and the trembling uncertainty. Having few characters on stage, and only a short journey to go with them—say, from the birth to the declaration of love—Marivaux is able to *stay with them,* minute step by minute step. He is, in a word, an intimate writer. And in this he breaks with the past, for up to his time both French and Italian comedy had always bustled with activity: a mad crisscross of thwarted lovers, a rich gallery of characters, or a fantastic whirl of events. There had been no time in these plays for psychological details. Marivaux was the first playwright of Western Europe to reduce a comic action to a Racinian minimum in order to make time for the close inspection of love.

When we say "close inspection of love," however, certain limitations must be understood. Marivaux is happier with his "escrime de sentiments" (the phrase belongs to Xavier de Courville) than with expressions of passion or scenes of intimate tenderness. His genius may be feminine, but it is also cool. In fact, it resembles nothing so much as the genius of Jane Austen. As soon as love has been confessed, in Marivaux as in Austen, the story is over; and it declares itself in a single sentence, or even by a gesture.

There are many other points of resemblance between Marivaux and Austen. Among them is their essential concern, not so much with love in general, as with the specific matter of love's relation to vanity—*amour-propre*—the ego's self-esteem. Marivaux is as preoccupied with the ego as La Rochefoucauld had been. This above all is what keeps his plays from sentimentality. Through the flattered or wounded ego Arlequin is won in *La Double inconstance,* the Comtesse in *L'Heureux Stratagème,* Sylvia in *Les Fausses confidences,* and Lucidor in *L'Epreuve.* A shattered ego prevents Sylvia in *Le Jeu de l'amour et du hasard* from acknowledging to herself and others that she is in love with a servant. Not to mention Marivaux's other plays, including the two *Surprise de l'amour,* in which the satisfaction of the ego is represented again and again as the necessary prelude to love. The critical coolness of this view is complemented by Marivaux's easy tolerance of vanity. He smiles at this human weakness; he is not appalled by it. He seems to feel that satisfied vanity, like a sound income, is a natural ingredient in marriage.

It is not easy to decide how "French" or how "Italian" Marivaux really is. A play like *Arlequin poli par l'amour* is obviously in the Italian spirit. But it is his first work of any note, and he did not do another similar fairy tale until he wrote *La Dispute,* twenty-four years later—for the Comédie-Française! A few other plays show unmistakable Italian tendencies: thus the fanciful and "romantic" settings of *La double inconstance, Le Prince travesti,* and *Le Triomphe de l'amour.* The marriage plot is of course common property of the French and the Italian traditions. So is the ubiquitous trick. Or the use of prose. Undoubtedly, the naïve characters whom Marivaux draws so well have a distinctly Italian flavor. And in writing comedies without sharp "humours" Marivaux was again tending toward the Italian rather than the French method. But he is perhaps most distinctly Italian in his use of travesty. Travesty was not unknown at the Comédie-Française; Molière had been fond of it; but it remained a distinctly un-French device. Thus, while Marivaux uses physical disguise in thirteen of his plays, not one of them was meant for the Théâtre Français.

But if Marivaux owed much to the Italian tradition, he continued and accelerated the gallicizing of the Italians. His language and its allusions are of a perfect purity which contrasts with the Italian repertory even of his own day. While Autreau could still write in 1720, "Long live a bright lover and a stupid husband," or call a girl "a skittish and capricious chicken out to get a dumb husband," and have a wedding performed by a notary named Cornelio Cornetto; and while Deportes could refer in 1721 to the scarf that hides a girl's breasts, and write, "One might as well not have . . . something, as not be proud of them"—license, in short, without coarseness of expression—Marivaux excluded every indecorous reference, to say nothing of coarse and indelicate words, from the comedies he wrote after 1720. His indulgent cynicism was untouched, but it was expressed in a language of extraordinary refinement, a pole away from the rough old *commedia.*

Marivaux is unmistakably French in other ways. He obeys the unities of time, place, and action with the rigor of a man determined from his cradle to take his place in the Academy. Far more important, he suppresses every trace of the visual gag, remorselessly snuffing out the *lazzi* and verbalizing his Arlequin, at any rate after his two early successes, ***Arlequin poli par l'amour*** and ***La double inconstance.*** He uses no machines, no spectacle, no music, no songs (except in ***Arlequin poli par l'amour***). He throws out the entire romantic baggage of the *commedia,* banishing apparitions, shipwrecks, kidnapings, duels, corsairs, changelings, and all the other adventures beloved of the *commedia.* He psychologizes and internalizes the action, so that, even though the plays abound in trickery, our awareness is focused on the real persons rather than on the artificial tricks. And he radically simplifies and unifies the intrigue. In sum, favorable as the terrain was to Marivaux at the Hôtel de Bourgogne (where the Italians performed), and much as he learned from the *commedia,* our playwright's gossamer remained firmly French.

"To give us light is only to embrace half of what we are, and indeed the half toward which we are more indifferent; we are much less concerned to know than to enjoy; and the soul enjoys when it feels." Marivaux wrote this in 1755, but the cult of feeling had begun to spread in Europe before 1720, when Marivaux was beginning his career, and even then he did not remain aloof from it. His novels are full of sensibility; the plays are at least touched by it. I have mentioned a "comédie larmoyante" which Marivaux committed to the stage. But in most of his comedies, this new emotionalism manifests itself only as a mellow kindliness, an amiable tolerance which stops short of effusiveness—stops short, that is, of ruining his

work. Marivaux's outlook on life is that of an Epicurean, willing to allow men, and especially women, the weaknesses from which he himself is not exempt. As he does not make the mistake of worshiping Man, he does not sit in ashes when people misbehave. Sensibility, in short, leads him to forgiveness, not to "larmoyance" or to false optimism. He sheds no tears over virtue.

In a word, he stays tough; his gossamer is made of steel. He gives us, though never in anger, representations of spite, vanity, cunning, envy, trickery, betrayal, ruthlessness, avarice, social climbing and snobbery, alongside his pictures of tenderness, affability, generosity, and intelligence. Nor are these vices reserved for his antagonists; he shows, and sometimes accepts them in his principals. What happens when sensibility meets cynicism head-on, and neither will yield its place? The two wed, and what is born of them is the Marivaldian quality I have mentioned before: slyness. Slyness is compatible with benevolence, and it is compatible with cynicism. But it precludes passion of any sort—torment or ecstasy. Marivaux's slyness is equidistant from the brutality of Lesage and Regnard and the sentimentality of Nivelle de la Chaussée and Diderot. Larroumet sums up Marivaux's equilibrium when he speaks of "this irony tempered by goodness, amiable and caressing even in its chaffing, this mild gayness, . . . this orderly, self-controlled verve, this flower of elegance and courtesy."

I look upon Marivaux as the literary master of the rococo, or decorative classicism. I have not seen this term applied to Marivaux's art, perhaps because it carries injurious connotations for us. But rococo art, which is the *idealized* expression of the last great patrician epoch of Europe, is also the last art which frankly makes what Thomas Mann calls "pretense and play" out of human experience. These are the last years in which serious artists will be able to look upon their work as decoration, diversion, the high sport of the intellect, rather than as revelation, commination, and prophecy. When I suggest for Marivaux the title of literary master of the rococo, I do so with nostalgic respect and admiration.

Marivaux is rococo in his transparence and mobility (a mobility without violence); in the come-and-go of moods, actions, decisions, which we can take as the literary equivalents of curls and garlands; in his sanity, his gayety, his unbelievable happiness, his light roses and blues which only a darker rose and blue can threaten; in his unfaltering grace.

For gracefulness is his overriding law, just as wit is the absolute law of Restoration comedy. Marivaux will be witty too, but only as far as gracefulness allows; he will be satirical, but only as far as gracefulness allows; realistic, moralizing, philosophical, tender, or sensual, but only as far as gracefulness allows. This is making a world that never was out of the world that is. In the mirror which Marivaux holds up to us, we do recognize ourselves (otherwise we would lose interest), but radiant and light as we could wish to be in a dream of ourselves. Considering how subversively mild Marivaux is, and how

Oscar A. Haac on love and reason in Marivaux:

Marivaux' appeal remains twofold, to the emotions and to intelligence. This leads him before Rousseau to the concept of "the reason of the heart." His characters act, then seek to discover their motives; often they possess, in addition, an intuitive awareness of the truth, as, for instance, Madame de Miran [in **La Vie de Marianne**]; she understands Marianne's despair immediately. In a different context, the contrast between feeling and thinking produces comic paradox. The girl who uses her mind to "catch up with her heart," i.e., trying to understand what she has done, comically restates a basic mode of action of many characters. Such a technique saved Marivaux from bombastic restatement of the commonplace or evident principle, the great fault of Voltaire's tragedies. Rational analysis in Marivaux serves not popular edification, but illustrates the assumptions, or delusions, of the particular speaker in each case. Marivaux aims to amuse while flattering the reader's, or spectator's understanding; he believes that wisdom, pedantically proclaimed, is ineffective. He underlines this point by presenting a number of intolerable pedants in his plays, representatives of the Ancients and their unrealistic world-view.

Oscar A. Haac, in his Marivaux, *Twayne Publishers, 1973.*

violent and "uncompromising" (dreaded word) we expect even our comedies to be nowadays, one cannot easily say that Marivaux is "our contemporary." But one can utter a prayer, preferably to the accompaniment of a minuet, that a corner may be preserved in our lives, and possibly even enlarged, for a literature which takes gracefulness to heart.

Alfred Cismaru (essay date 1977)

SOURCE: "Introduction" and "Conclusion," in *Marivaux and Molière: A Comparison*, Texas Tech Press, 1977, pp. 3-12, 130-32.

[*In the following excerpts, Cismaru evaluates Marivaux's debt to Molière, and concludes that "Marivaux went beyond* moliéresque *limits, and broadened the playwright's scope into areas heretofore largely ignored by writers of comedies and only touched on by composers of tragedies."*]

In the enormous bibliography devoted to Marivaux, there are far fewer studies of his theater than of other aspects of the writer and his work. Many commentators have written about Marivaux the man, the novelist, the moralist, the philosopher, but relatively fewer have discussed thoroughly his theater. The first English popularization of the plays of the eighteenth-century dramatist was that of Kenneth N. McKee, *The Theater of Marivaux* [1958], which treated each play as a unit and studied the playwright's entire theater in chronological order. A later, more complete work going deeper into the historical and biographical background of each comedy [*Marivaux,* 1965] appeared in Canada and was authored by F. J. H. Greene.

French literary historians have touched often on Marivaux's theater: Gustave Larroumet's book, a good source on Marivaux, dates back, however, to 1881; Emile Gossot, in his *Marivaux moraliste,* is more interested in Marivaux's moralizing, the theater being discussed as only one facet of the writer; Jean Fleury's *Marivaux et le marivaudage* is concerned with Marivaux's work as a whole, and with the meaning of the second noun in its title; the same is true of Frédéric Deloffre's *Marivaux et le marivaudage,* although the book does contain one of the most complete bibliographies to date on Marivaux; Gaston Deschamps' *Marivaux* and Eugene Meyer's work of the same title are not concerned primarily with the writer's comedies; nor is Marcel Arland's *Marivaux,* which devotes only one third of its pages to the author's plays.

Most of the above books mention some of the sources of Marivaux. None, however, treats the subject of sources in detail, and none has analyzed systematically the relationship between Molière's theater and that of Marivaux. This lacuna appears to be in dire need of filling, especially in view of the contradictory statements, and of the affirmations and denials that have been advanced with respect to the influence of the seventeenth-century writer on Marivaux. It would be cumbersome to enumerate all of these, but a few are representative and will be cited below.

The opening sentences of Kenneth N. McKee's book state: "Marivaux was the most original French dramatist of the eighteenth century. In an age when leading dramatists, writing for the Théâtre Français, blindly followed the Molière tradition, Marivaux, writing principally for the Théâtre Italien and sometimes for the Théâtre Français, dared to be different. In fact, he repudiated Molière so openly that he drew the wrath of critics and public alike." This is, of course, in line with what D'Alembert had reported of Marivaux. "'J'aime mieux, disait Marivaux, être humblement assis sur le dernier banc dans la petite troupe des auteurs originaux, qu'orgueilleusement placé à la première ligne dans le nombreux bétail des singes littéraires.'" And D'Alembert commented: "Il avait le malheur de ne pas estimer beaucoup Molière, et le malheur plus grand de ne pas s'en cacher. Il ne craignait pas même, quand on le mettait à son aise sur cet article, d'avouer naivement qu'il ne se croyait pas inférieur à ce grand peintre de la nature." And, as a matter of fact, the critics for *Le Mercure de France,* when reviewing the plays of Marivaux in the 1720's and 1730's, made no mention of any possible *moliéresque* influence. It is curious that, close as they were to the theater of Molière, they failed to indicate any relationship between the seventeenth-century writer and Marivaux.

On the other hand, Molière specialists have made sweeping and even derogatory statements concerning the extended influence of Molière on Marivaux. Ferdinand Brunetière wrote, "Marivaux a voulu refaire telles et telles pièces de Molière, et non pas *Le Sicilien* ou *Le Mariage forcé,* mais **L'Ecole des femmes** dans son **Ecole des mères** et *Le Misanthrope* dans **Les Sincères.**" Other critics of Molière have expressed similar comments. For example, in speaking of the *surprise* plays of Marivaux, Maurice Donnay asserted, "Marivaux n'a fait que répéter, avec mille variantes, détours et subtilités, des situations sentimentales qui sont plus sobrement traitées, et avec moins de marivaudage, c'est certain, dans *La Princesse d'Elide.*" This statement is particularly important because Marivaux is credited with having written a number of *surprise* plays.

More recent Marivaux specialists have admitted, in part, that Marivaux owes a certain amount of inspiration to Molière. Gustave Larroumet declared: "Avec Marivaux, la comédie entre dans une période nouvelle. Il ne se rattachait directement à aucun de ses devanciers. [Il était] Très désireux de ne pas les imiter, même les plus illustres," and in a footnote Larroumet commented, "Telle était du moins son intention; en réalité il n'a pu se garder complètement de réminiscences de détail." Marcel Arland, however, developed the question more explicitly, although in too general a tone and without having recourse to textual examples.

> Qu'il n'ait aimé Molière, c'est possible. . . . Peut-être aussi, à l'antipathie déclarée de Marivaux à l'égard de Molière, faut-il voir la réaction naturelle d'un génie qui veut se préserver d'une redoutable influence. . . . Il lui arrive d'ailleurs de trouver un appui chez son grand aîné, là où coincident leurs natures, par exemple pour certaines querelles d'amoureux, certains traits de moeurs, de caractère, ou telle satire de l'éducation; là aussi où s'imposent, hors de toute nature particulière, les exigences fondamentales de la scène. Au demeurant, il existe entre eux un lien plus profond.

The extent and nature of this *lien* has not been defined yet because "so little scholarship has been devoted to Marivaux's theater that the subject is fraught with unresolved literary problems, such as the exact extent of Molière's influence on Marivaux." And, as a matter of fact, this *lien* still gives birth to what might appear as contradictory statements: for despite the opening sentences of his introduction, and having fully developed his subject, Kenneth N. McKee agrees that "much as Marivaux disliked Molière, he could not entirely escape his influence."

Yet E. J. H. Greene went so far as to call the entire vogue of the *rapprochement* of the two playwrights as nothing but "a red herring, one that should be thrown out." This, in spite of the fact that throughout his book he perceives frequent similarities, not only worth noting but also giving rise to rather detailed, lengthy discussions. Like many Marivaux *aficionados,* the commentator, pleased by the current popular revival of the seventeenth-century playwright, bestows on the latter qualities of extreme inventiveness, which he need not have had in order to explain his successes. If, as one shall see, Marivaux recalled

Molière persistently in about one-half of his total theatrical production, and less often in his novels, he did so almost always without falling into the trap of plagiarism: that is, his imitation of Molière adhered to the age-old tradition followed by the best of writers who compose in approximately the same way, and who express approximately the same feelings and preoccupations that a masterful predecessor would have, had he been alive and active at the same time. This is how Corneille and Racine, for example, have imitated the ancients.

That, outside of his recollections of Molière, Marivaux's multifaceted originality appears indisputable is not a point that needs to be belabored long. However, equally beyond question is the fact that the seventeenth-century playwright had bequeathed such a strong tradition of the comedy of *humour* laced with social satire and had depicted so many "types" (the social climber, the hypochondriac, the religious hypocrite, the atheist, the misanthrope, the impertinent, the ambitious, the babbler, and so on) that early eighteenth-century playwrights found the field severely circumscribed. There was, of course, the *commedia dell'-arte,* the premises of which were less psychological and less polemical, and on which a writer intent on avoiding being overwhelmed by the *moliéresque* tradition could draw more freely. Moreover, the Italian imports and the French popularization of them had their own set of permanent types: the bigot, the lover, the comic, impudent servant, the authoritarian father, the dotty rival, and others, all embroiled in true-to-life and not so true-to-life adventures interspersed with farcical *lazzi* of assorted zany personages. But the world of the *commedia,* whimsical as it was, and in spite of the fact that it had very few philosophical, moral, or social pretentions of any kind, had appealed also to Molière. The latter's digs against doctors, cuckolded husbands, pedantic women, and other controversial personages, were modeled at least partly on the peppered sketches (it will be recalled that the presentations of the *commedia* were based on sketches, not on written plays) that the Italians had introduced. Therefore, the heritage left by Molière was so all-encompassing that, whether Marivaux chose to compose formal or informal comedies, it was still difficult to steer clear of *moliéresque* detail. Besides, his wish to remain original notwithstanding, full-fledged efforts to ignore entirely the typical *moliéresque* ingredients that had survived would have been, from the point of view of the dramatist who wished success, unwarranted and unwise.

The great difference between Marivaux and Molière appears to reside in the former's ability to express that which the latter had thought of minor importance and preferred to leave in the background. Love, for Molière, was what tottering wooers or grouchy old men talked about. Love was not a serious preoccupation, and hardly ever was it an obsession. Obsessions there were, but with other concerns: money, social climbing, religious devotion, relationship with one's doctors, and so on. A miser ordering a miserly dinner or a doctor's prescription of medicine, for example, provided for scenes that surpassed in importance any love plot or subplot that might otherwise be present. On the contrary, Marivaux relegated peculiarities, follies, and vices to a minor role in order to bring to the fore the lovers themselves. These are sometimes young, and often adults, but their chronological age, like their social status, makes very little difference. For them, love is always an emotion requiring analysis, dissection even. Thus Marivaux's personages engage in a dual role: that of loving and that of watching, as a spectator might, the birth and growth of love. The first part needed to be played still in accordance with prescribed social decorum; after all, in the early eighteenth century, family considerations, as in the century of Molière, limited one's exuberance and paled one's overtness. On the contrary, there is much more freedom in acting out the second part. In fulfilling it, the lover-examiner-of-love watches it emerge unexpectedly, states his or her surprise, hides it at times and causes it to become unmasked at others, alternatively observing it vanish and surge aroused again, piqued, irritated, held back, offered to the wrong person, and finally settled where it belongs. Such subtle analysis of tender moods brings out the infinite variety of little conflicts that pride and vanity, and caprice and misunderstanding may produce before the certainty of love is finally attained. In addition, the personages' sudden realization of what love means, their attempt to struggle against it, to make certain of their feelings, and to assure themselves of the genuineness of another's devotion, to detect the motives and to distinguish between shades of difference, required that Marivaux supply all the verbal quibbles in the battle of wits between his contending men and women. The exchanges needed a special vocabulary within an arsenal of ingenious plays on words and refinements of thought, which gave to his style a flavor all its own. This style, which is a combination of the casuistry of love and witty dialog in delicate, figurative language, is what critics have called *marivaudage,* a quality lacking entirely in the theater of Molière. Whereas Marivaux's minor characters chose, in part, the speech characteristics of his more robust predecessor, most of his other personages opted instead for a certain finesse of language in their efforts to penetrate more deeply the intricate pathways of the heart. It is not quite without reason, therefore, that one commentator made the following unexpected remark: "Molière is roast beef to his [Marivaux's] lemon soufflé" [Oscar Mandel, *Seven Comedies by Marivaux,* 1968].

A more frequent comparison has been made with the painter Watteau, who did many portraits of various actors of the Comédie Italienne. The resemblance between the two artists bears on the scenes and figures presented by them in different media, but each interpreting and supplementing the other. Often Marivaux's themes may be likened to some kind of *Embarquement pour Cythère,* although his groups are not so numerous as in Watteau's paintings. For both, however, the final destination is almost always matrimony, in which state we may assume that the well-matched pairs will live happily ever after. In fact, the happy ending of Marivaux's comedies contrasts pointedly with the often sad and unsure dénouements of those of Molière. Morever, in the case of the seventeenth-century playwright, the spectator could be distracted from the less felicitous episodes (whether occurring before or at the end of a play) by the buffoonery and slapstick farce that the author had inherited from the *commedia.* On the contrary, no such distraction was necessary for the viewer or reader of Marivaux's comedies since the playwright could anticipate the happy endings he was going to present. Thus, while his plays are nevertheless lively, the tone remains almost always decent, whether it be expressed in the humor of masters or in that of servants. Delicacy and refinement of language prevail, no easy task when one has to vary the form of expression in order to suit the personage and his station in life. Marivaux excels in this undertaking by utilizing always a different choice of words or turns of phrases to distinguish the master from the valet and the mistress from the soubrette.

The almost total decency and moral tone of his comedies are in sharp contrast with those of Molière and with the manners of the Regency that influenced the followers of Molière in the early eighteenth century. Although Marivaux retains clever servants and numerous intrigues, the latter are far different from the unscrupulous designs and frequently immoral deeds of Molière's Sganarelles, of the Crispins, and the Frontins of Regnard or Lesage, for example. A certain undertone of innocence is maintained, and this, in turn, leads to a reduction of external action in general and of violence in particular. The forces within dominate, and the inner struggles of the personages often are likened to those of the characters of Racine's theater. As in the case of the seventeenth-century tragedy writer, Marivaux's comedies are marked by the supremacy of love, by the author's penetrating psychology of this sentiment, studied, however, in its lighter moods, and by the playwright's predilection for emphasizing feminine parts, which are predominant in most of his plays. Like Racine, also, Marivaux is skillful in maintaining the interest of the spectator with a minimum of plot (plots were often complex in Molière's theater), and he moves easily within the three unities required by classical decorum. Having fewer characters on the stage and only a short journey to go with them (usually from the birth to the declaration of love), Marivaux is able to stick with his personages minute step by minute step. In this, he breaks not only with Molière but with the entire tradition of the French and Italian comedy, which always bustled with much activity, was mad crisscross with thwarted lovers, and contained a rich gallery of characters moving within a frequently fantastic whirl of events. There was little time in those plays for much control of the half-tone, or for the trembling uncertainty in which Marivaux was interested for the purpose of bringing out psychological detail. Thus, it may be said quite bluntly that the eighteenth-century playwright was the first in Western Europe to reduce a comic action to a Racinian minimum in order to make time for the close inspection of love.

Yet, such inspection must not be understood as signifying the analysis of expressions of passion or of scenes of very intimate tenderness. Marivaux's characters are cool by comparison to those of Molière. A single sentence or a single gesture suffices to confess love, and one never finds the pomposity of an Alceste or a Tartuffe. Love has nothing cynical or ferocious about it. There is only amiability and indulgence, aspects, of course, that the more robust did not appreciate and branded as feminine.

But be that as it may, it is a fact that Marivaux's young ladies are more sprightly, more attractive, and better observed than their suitors. Whereas Molière had depicted his female personages in such a way as to bestow upon them much vigor, at times stubbornness, and often qualities that detracted from their femininity, such as immoderation, extreme shrewdness, contrivance, even dishonesty; Marivaux's girls remain feminine. True, we see now and then a coquette who jilts a man, but she quickly longs for him when he neglects her. Of course, Marivaux does write episodes in which a young, flirtatious thing swears fidelity to one man, only to fall in love with another. Yet frivolity does not degenerate into dishonesty; a certain amount of time passes, and, in addition, in her embarrassment she attempts to suppress into the unconscious the emotion that now is addressed to someone else. More often, however, girls simply wait and tremble before a declaration of love is made by or to them. They sigh, weep, affirm, and believe in their sincerity even if readers and spectators do not. And they always maintain a certain amount of innocence and purity, purging them and providing some relief from the recollection of the more quarrelsome and more pugnacious, if more witty, women of Molière.

Marivaux's young men are delineated less well. Their temperament is, in general, devoid of the virility required to distinguish them beyond any doubt from the maidens whom they court. Their lack of toughness makes them blush often, remain timid, swoon, sometime even weep. At any rate, they sigh and implore too ardently; bashfulness makes them blind and deaf to the most obvious advances; and often one feels like kicking them and telling them what should have been obvious a long time ago. Yet in spite of the tone *larmoyant* and the *attendrissement* that one notes in their character, they do have redeeming qualities, such as their lack of extreme slyness and the fact that they are never real villains. Unlike the personages of the followers of Molière in the 1720's, Marivaux's young men hardly ever use coarse or indelicate words, and they remain free from any indecorous reference. They would never say, for example, like one of Autreau's young wooers, "Vive l'amant habile et le mari stupide," or refer to a girl as "une poule capricieuse et rusée, à la recherche d'un mari idiot." Nor would Marivaux ever have described a wedding performed by a notary public whose name is Cornelio Cornetto. Although the then famous Deportes could have one of his male characters refer in 1721 to a scarf hiding a girl's breasts, and remark: "Mieux vaut ne pas les avoir . . . que de n'en pas être fière," the young men of Marivaux banished from their speech anything that might have detracted from their more placid but less debatable personality.

It can be said that the playwright's treatment of young lovers led him to internalize the action so that, even though the plays contained a certain amount of trickery, the spectators' awareness nevertheless could focus on the real persons rather than on the artificial pranks. What happens, in effect, is that the author does use, although never pompously and never in anger, representations of spite, vanity, cunning, envy, trickery, snobbery, and the like; but he remains nevertheless equidistant from the brutality of Molière in the preceding century, and that of Lesage and Regnard in his own, as he does from the extreme sentimentality of Nivelle de la Chaussée and Diderot. His young men and women may have shortcomings, but they do not have vices. Morover, their faults are placed side by side with mellow kindliness, amiable tolerance, and human sensibility. There is little place in Marivaux's work for Molière's cynicism. Although Marivaux, like his predecessor, is an Epicurian, that is, willing to allow men, and especially women, the weaknesses from which he knows hardly anyone is exempt, he sheds no tears over lost virtue; he appears simply to suggest forgiveness. Tricks and pranks make life more palatable, he suggests, and one ought never worship Man, nor engage in revelation, commination, or prophecy. Molière kept repeating that he only wanted to please, but he got caught, nevertheless, in the trap of his own profundity: he philosophized and he taught frequently explicit lessons. On the contrary, Marivaux was less ambitious and viewed his art as the high sport of the intellect, which results in decoration, diversion, above all in an unfaltering grace. Not that there are no lessons to be derived from his comedies, or that moralizing is totally absent; there are ideas, as there are sensuality, satire, wit, and tenderness, but only as far as gracefulness allows. His transparence and mobility are unlike those of Molière, who had used the come-and-go of moods, actions, and decisions without much concern for grace. Marivaldian realism, however, marries sensibility to Epicurianism, and the result is an equilibrium that Gustave Larroumet had defined when he spoke of "cette ironie assagie par la bonté, aimable et caressante même lorsqu'elle se met en colère, cette douce gaieté . . . cette verve pleine d'ordre et de contrôle, cette fleur d'élégance et de courtoisie."

Marivaux's verve benefited, of course, from the example set by the various salons that he frequented. Although Molière had scorned the salons of his time, being too busy and too independent to see in them anything other than a target of mockery, Marivaux was one of the *habitués* of such celebrated gatherings as those conducted by Madame de Lambert, Madame de Tencin, and Madame du Deffand. The first, from 1720 onward, received every Tuesday and Wednesday, Tuesday being the day for men of letters. Marivaux had occasion to meet in her salon such famous writers as Fontenelle and La Motte, and a few years later even Montesquieu. After Madame de Lambert's death in 1733, it was Madame de Tencin who took over the "Tuesdays," and Fontenelle, La Motte, and Marivaux were among the very few who were privileged to have dinner with the hostess before the arrival of the other guests. It was in her salon that the eighteenth-century playwright was exposed to the aristocratic *femmes galantes* and *femmes d'esprit* of the time. Under their influence, conversation in these salons was remarkable for its wit and grace. Discussion was considered to be a sport of the mind, each participant being very careful to seize upon the right moment for the insertion of his own remark, his story or anecdote, often light and sometimes artificial, yet contributing to the graceful surroundings. It is known that Madame de Tencin admired greatly Marivaux's contributions and made consistent efforts in the course of meetings to make certain that his points of view and the sparkle of his phraseology charm, as it so often did, the hostess and her guests. In fact, it was her admiration of him as a nonpompous discussant that prompted her to engage in untiring efforts to gain for him the necessary votes for election to the Academy. It was she who managed to win for her friend the support of the Duke of Richelieu, for example, who otherwise would have given his vote to Voltaire. Marivaux's belief in *la nécessité d'avoir toujours de l'esprit* fit the requirements of the eighteenth-century salons. According to D'Alembert, who was also an *habitué* of Madame du Deffand, the refinement and sagacity of the conversation that Marivaux practiced in the course of the meetings were transferred by him to the characters of his plays. This is corroborated by Marivaux himself in the preface to **Les Serments indiscrets,** in which he wrote that he tried to reproduce the general tone he encountered in the salons. It is known also that the playwright's famous account of the dinner party at Madame de Dorsin's, in the course of which he has Marianne emphasize that what counted most was the effortlessness and natural ease with which conversation was carried on, is modeled after Madame de Tencin's own dinner parties, and that the latter furnished the model for Madame de Dorsin. It is no surprise, then, that Marivaux's comedies should differ from those of Molière with respect to the importance of subtlety, sympathetic affability, and grace. Because he was schooled by the salons, where he found a natural complement to his own personality, it was impossible for him not to reproduce their ambiance and manner of expression.

Having said all of the above, it appears, nevertheless, that after Molière, it was very difficult to continue to invent. Marivaux's predecessor had inserted into comedy the image of human nature, with most of its eternal traits, as well as the image of French society, with its particular characteristics. Molière's ability to summarize in several personages the quintessence of numberless models, his exhaustion, over a long period of time, of great comical plots, resulted in a certain limitation that Marivaux, no matter how much he wanted to diminish, was unable to obliterate. If the eighteenth-century playwright succeeded, however, in extending and altering somewhat the *moliéresque* domains, as was pointed out above, his recollections of the famous predecessor go beyond the mere coincidental.

. . . . .

It probably would be pointless to evaluate Marivaux's efforts on the basis of degree of *moliéresque* influence. This influence was extensive in **La Surprise de l'amour** and in **Les Fausses confidences,** for example, yet (or perhaps because of it) these comedies generally are considered among the best in Marivaux's repertory. The num-

ber of *reprises* and critical approvals bears witness to their quality. On the other hand, Molière's influence was rather minor, by comparison, in **Le Triomphe de Plutus** and in **Félicie,** yet (or perhaps because of it) these comedies are inconsequential: the author refused to sign the first, and the second was performed on the stage only as a ballet. It is also true that other plays, such as **L'Hériter du village** and **Les Serments indiscrets,** in which the *moliéresque* influence appears prominently, generally are considered poor plays, both by audiences and critics. Conversely, **Arlequin poli par l'amour** and **L'Epreuve,** for example, in which the *moliéresque* source of inspiration is only minor, are considered successful theater in the eighteenth and twentieth centuries. From all this, it is difficult to reach conclusions, and unnecessary as well. What matters more than anything else is to begin to disregard d'Alembert's reports concerning Marivaux's alleged dislike for the theater of Molière, and to stop ignoring the presence of the seventeenth-century master, variable as it is, in the comedies of Marivaux.

This presence, of course, points only to the fact that either D'Alembert's reports are erroneous, or simply that Marivaux did not wish to acknowledge his debt to Molière. If it detracts at all from the value of his comedies, it does so to a degree only: the playwright's inventiveness suffers. The individual plays in which the *moliéresque* recollections occur at times profit from, at others are diminished by the measure of remembrance. But if there is one thing that Marivaux did not manage to extract from Molière, it is his predecessor's ability to philosophize by means of irony, caricature, and ridicule. In this connection, Kenneth N. McKee observes:

> For example, Molière believed that fathers should not force incompatible marriages on their children, but instead of presenting liberal-minded fathers on the stage, he ridiculed obstinate ones such as M. Orgon in *Le Tartuffe,* Harpagon in *L'Avare,* and M. Jourdain in *Le Bourgeois gentilhomme.* Marivaux, on the other hand, presented his philosophy with disarming simplicity. If he had a point to make, he went straight to the heart of the matter and expressed his conviction as an integral part of the text without deviousness.

But what is missing from such comments is recognition that one of the reasons Molière's comedies [are] superior resides precisely in the *deviousness* of his approach: it is one that is much more bound to make for laughter than *disarming simplicity.* One might add that preachers make a point, writers of comedies go around it, suggest it, but are never any more presumptuous than that.

All this is not to say that Marivaux knowingly preaches, or even that he does so frequently. The fact remains, nevertheless, that he is much less able than was his predecessor to cause heartfelt, loud laughter. When he does show such a capability, more often than not it is a peasant or a servant who makes one laugh. Most of his other characters are simply content to bring a smile to the spectator's lips, and even the origin of that is intellectual only. If Marivaux may be praised for having abandoned most of the post-Molière crude language and abuse of farcical situations as a means to comicality, it also must be acknowledged that his comedies are less apt to induce that purging, cathartic result that a buoyant, uninhibited mirth produces.

From the point of view of content, Marivaux's inventiveness resides in his depiction of the topography of the heart. In the more classical plays of Molière, love always played a diminished role: it was usually born before the initial curtain and, once acknowledged, it did not constitute the plot of the comedy, rather it served the loftier ends of the author, who laughed, ridiculed, or attacked various human shortcomings. Love rarely came to the forefront and hardly ever was traced, analyzed, or judged either by the lovers themselves or those around them (the comments on love by parents and/or tutors were not designed to explain the feeling, rather to obliterate it). On the contrary, love is a map, Marivaux appears to imply, and he becomes its geographer. He points to the source, to its growing pains as it struggles through mountainous detours and dangerous pits, to the roads it must cross, and the inroads attempted by timidity, parental opposition, financial or social considerations, and other such obstacles. But the stream eventually flows into the ocean, much as the shepherdess is able, ultimately, to join the shepherd in the *Carte du tendre*. What one misses in the way of sparkling jocularity and ensuing catharsis resulting from Molière's plays is made up, to an extent, by Marivaux's explanations of the casuistry of gallantry and coquetry. The analyst of sentiment and dissector of the heart that he was, Marivaux went beyond *moliéresque* limits, and broadened the playwright's scope into areas heretofore largely ignored by writers of comedies and only touched upon by composers of tragedies.

From the point of view of style, the originality of the eighteenth-century playwright consists, even in those plays that show a *moliéresque* inspiration, in his ability to use a form of expression suitable to the depiction of shades and nuances of feeling. The accusation of *marivaudage,* which was brought against such a style, . . . is only partly valid. Monotonous though the frequently long speeches of Marivaux's characters may be at times, detailed explanations and summaries add to the reader's comprehension. This makes up somewhat for the liveliness and brio of Molière's language, which Marivaux, for the most part, was incapable of or found impractical to emulate. This is also one of the reasons why some of the comedies of the eighteenth-century playwright provide for more pleasurable reading than for successful stage presentations.

One need not push the comparison any further. Next to the vigor of Molière one might be tempted to see only the pallor of Marivaux. Yet that probably would be the case in a comparison between most playwrights and the seventeenth-century master. Marivaux can and does stand on his own feet. But in spite of what he is reported to have said and thought of Molière, in many of his plays he relied upon episodes and themes made famous by his predecessor.

H. T. Mason (essay date 1979)

SOURCE: "Women in Marivaux: Journalist to Dramatist," in *Women and Society in Eighteenth-Century France,* edited by Eva Jacobs and others, The Athlone Press, 1979, pp. 42-54.

[*In the excerpt below, Mason investigates the depiction of women in Marivaux's plays. The critic concludes that "Marivaux can scarcely be termed a leading feminist of his day. He is alive to feminine inequality, but he deals relatively little with the disabilities facing eighteenth-century women."*]

It is possible to trace, in Marivaux's plays . . . a steadily growing concern about feminine inequality; in the space of this article, however, one can do no more than touch on some of the more significant plays in this regard. *L'Ile des esclaves* (1725) addresses itself essentially to class differences between masters and servants; but the dramatist does not fail to comment on the caprices of 'femmes de qualité'. On this island, slaves and servants (no clear distinction is made) wish to destroy the barbarism in their masters' hearts and restore them to the ranks of humanity. Candour being one means to this end, Arlequin and Cléanthis recount their masters' faults with great enthusiasm and no small penetration. Cléanthis reminds her mistress Euphrosine of an evening when the latter had used all the tricks of coquetry to conquer her *cavalier*. Having damned a rival with faint praise, Euphrosine had pretended not to notice when her lover 'offrit son cœur'. 'Continuez, folâtre, continuez, dites-vous, en ôtant vos gants sous prétexte de m'en demander d'autres. Mais vous avez la main belle; il la vit, il la prit, il la baisa . . .' (Sc. 3). This picture, . . . strikingly resembles one of Sartre's most famous examples of *mauvaise foi* in *L'Etre et le néant,* . . . In the same scene Euphrosine reiterates Marivaux's views on the *négligé*: 'Regardez mes grâces, elles sont à moi, celles-là. . . . Voyez comme je m'habille, quelle simplicité! il n'y a point de coquetterie dans mon fait.' But before the play is over Euphrosine, her pretensions now shattered, wins Arlequin's pity by her heartfelt cry for mercy. The servants' revolt is not pushed to the point of total ascendancy. The radicalism of the play is moral and religious rather than social and political. Once the masters have acquired a degree of self-knowledge and contrition it is time to call a halt. The attitude which emerges is that of a Christian moralist. Feminine vanity, like human vanity in general, can never be erased but only, at best, abated through the workings of charity and greater understanding.

L'Ile de la raison (1727) dwells too on the marvels of coquetry (II, 6), but adds a different aspect of the feminine situation: on the Island of Reason only women may make declarations of love. Men become the passive element, sought out only when the women want them, and obliged to play the reluctant role until the alliance is assumed. Blectrue, one of the islanders, is horrified at European courtship customs (II, 3: 'Que deviendra la faiblesse si la force l'attaque') which he argues are the consequence of men's vicious inclinations. By contrast, on the Island of Reason men help to save women from themselves. 'L'homme ici, c'est le garde-fou de la femme' (II, 7). This feminist paradox presumably owes something to Mme de Lambert's *Réflexions sur les femmes* (1727), but probably represents too the dramatist's desire to see what the 'pure' woman is like when the need for coquetry is removed.

If so, the exploration of woman *in esse* is more arrestingly carried out in *La Dispute* (1744). Marivaux organises an enquiry into which of the sexes first proved unfaithful, and in typical eighteenth-century manner constructs a situation where two boys and two girls are brought up in isolation from the world. The first heterosexual encounters are idyllic; each looks on the other and loves. The first meeting between the two girls is quite other. The mental universe is Hobbesian; jealousy, suspicion, hostility are the instinctive reactions on each side. By contrast, the two men are initially well-disposed towards each other, so long as no sexual conflict comes between them. Why this essential difference? Because, in Marivaux's view women, being obliged to please others, are immediately moved to jealousy in the presence of another attractive member of their sex. So it is that the girls take the first step in arranging infidelities; it springs almost simultaneously from the inclination in each to prove that she can assert her superiority by winning the other's lover. As Deloffre points out in his 'Notice' to the play [in *Théâtre complet*, 1968], if it were transposed into a tone less naïve and more libertine, these attitudes would be appropriate to *Les Liaisons dangereuses*.

Significantly, the dramatist presents the meeting of the two girls before that of their lovers; their reactions are so much richer for psychological portraiture. Whereas the men drift along more amiably, but also duller of sense, the girls' state of mind is complex to the point of being incomprehensible even to themselves. Eglé, for instance, is upset with herself, upset with her lover Azor: 'je ne sais ce qui m'arrive . . . je ne sais à qui j'en ai'. The real reason for her discontent emerges: she has found Mesrin to be more attractive than Azor. But Mesrin's only advantage is novelty—'d'être nouveau venu'. Even so, Eglé is unhappily divided within herself: 'Je ne suis contente de rien, d'un côté, le changement me fait peine, de l'autre, il me fait plaisir' (Sc. 15). She is able to resolve the dilemma only when she learns that Mesrin is the lover of the other girl, Adine; at that point jealousy impels swift action.

The conclusions of *La Dispute* are therefore sombre ones. Inconstancy, it would appear, is well-nigh inevitable; woman designs, man consents. Though one should not interpret a fable such as this with undue literalism, it seems that for Marivaux the urge to please is deeply ingrained in womankind. Social conditions may, as he shows in the essays, confirm this inclination, but in the uncorrupted environment of *La Dispute* the female sex is just as bent on ruthless demonstration of its capacity to attract the male.

But the women do not emerge as villains from the play. The judicious conclusion of the Prince, who had arranged the whole experiment, is that virtues and vices are equal between the two sexes. Hermiane protests at this: 'votre sexe est d'une perfidie horrible, il change à propos de rien, sans chercher même de prétexte'. The Prince agrees: 'Le procédé du vôtre est du moins plus hypocrite, et par là plus décent, il fait plus de façon avec sa conscience que le nôtre' (Sc. 20). This observation, striking in its disillusioned detachment, seems to sum up Marivaux's whole attitude to women. They are more 'civilized'. More complex psychologically, more committed to the desire they feel to attract the opposite sex, they are more alive in their sensibilities, more aware of a moral order; they do not drift into falsity as do men. Paradox though it is, they show greater integrity in coming to terms with the human predicament.

These attitudes are therefore probably more far-reaching than those emerging from the comedy which one immediately thinks of as most involved with the female question, *La Colonie* (1750). In this play Marivaux's views are sharply developed and dramatically rich; but the subject is narrower. Here the dramatist is mainly concerned with the social question. In *La Colonie* the feminist leaders seek for equality with men, and especially within the state of marriage. Men, however, treat women as 'à n'être . . . que la première de toutes les bagatelles' (Sc. 9). As in the 5e feuille of the *Cabinet du philosophe,* coquetry is a response to male domination, in a world where, says Arthénice to the men, 'c'est votre justice et non pas la nôtre' (Sc. 13). Women are brainwashed into submission and self-denigration. Madame Sorbin finds herself unconsciously saying 'je ne suis qu'une femme' until Arthénice points out to her how deep the conditioning has gone (Sc. 9). Coquetry therefore becomes the only answer. But what a waste of talent and energy go into it; 'plus de profondeur d'esprit qu'il n'en faudrait pour gouverner deux mondes comme le nôtre, et tant d'esprit est en pure perte' (*ibid.*).

The women ask for equality in all realms: finance, judiciary, the army. The claims seem utopian, and besides there is near-revolt in the ranks when the leaders urge their followers to make themselves ugly; in addition, young lovers like Lina will always follow the spontaneous promptings of the heart. So it is hardly a surprise when the feminist cause collapses at the end. Marivaux's attitude towards the women protagonists appears sympathetic; but it is also equivocal.

In *La Colonie* and elsewhere Marivaux seems concerned about the rights of women. But though he indicts men for their tyrannous ways, he feels that the problem goes to the roots of human nature and is not to be solved by social reform. Improvements are however possible. One of the pleas most eloquently expressed in *La Colonie* harks back to the *Cabinet du philosophe*. Both of the women leaders want equality between husband and wife: 'le mariage qui se fait entre les hommes et nous', says Arthénice, 'devrait aussi se faire entre leurs pensées et les nôtres' (Sc. 13). Here at least is a practical way forward, though it depends more on improving the moral climate than on the institution of new laws.

In Marivaux subsists a deep-rooted pessimism about ever effecting wholesale changes in man's, and therefore woman's, lot. The picture is however not black. The essayist, like the dramatist, is presenting a human comedy. Women suffer many disadvantages, but they have consolations. Not only are they prettier, they are more interesting. Besides, if men rule the earth, women rule men:

> Si les lois des hommes dépendent,
> Ne vous en plaignez pas, trop aimables objets:
> Vous imposez des fers à ceux qui vous
> commandent,
> Et vos maîtres sont vos sujets.
> ('Divertissement', *La Nouvelle Colonie*)

Marivaux can scarcely be termed a leading feminist of his day. He is alive to feminine inequality, but he deals relatively little with the disabilities facing eighteenth-century women: the economic and legal limitations, the right to divorce, educational reform. Not that he was unaware of these problems. By choosing for instance a widow as heroine of *Les Fausses Confidences* he recognized the greater degree of liberty she enjoyed as compared with a single girl. But these details were of interest to him in serving the ends of psychological enquiry. If Marivaux can be termed a feminist at all, it is surely in his acceptance, as in *La Colonie*, that women are men's equals intellectually. Indeed, as we have seen and as almost any one of his comedies makes clear, women's minds are far more interesting. They are the more colourful part of the species. Ultimately, they are of value for what they tell us about the human race as a whole; for they are the quintessence of humanity. When in *La Dispute* Adine, who has never seen another young girl, meets Eglé she asks ingenuously: 'Etes-vous une personne?' Eglé retorts: 'Oui assurément, et très personne' (Sc. 9). It is the reply that, about womankind, Marivaux himself might have made.

Derek F. Connon (essay date 1993)

SOURCE: "The Servant as Master: Disguise, Role-Reversal, and Social Comment in Three Plays of Marivaux," in *Studies in the Commedia dell'Arte,* edited by David J. George and Christopher J. Gossip, University of Wales Press, 1993, pp. 121-37.

[*In the follwing essay, Connon explores differing uses of the devices of role reversal and disguise in* L'Ile des esclaves, Le Jeu de l'amour et du hasard, *and* L'Epreuve. *The critic argues that these variations reflect Marivaux's movement away from the conventions of* commedia dell'arte *and towards a more realistic theater.*]

As is pointed out by Norbert Jonard in his study of the *commedia dell'arte,* [*La Commedia dell'arte,* 1982], dis-

guise is one of the principal devices employed in the scenarios of the form. Mel Gordon, in his study of *lazzi,* [*Lazzi: The Comic Routines of the 'Commedia dell'Arte,'* 1983], draws attention to a more specific use of disguise, one which involves not only pretence about the character's identity, but also about his social class: 'Often, the humour grows out of a class reversal, the servant acts like a master and the master becomes confused.' Given the importance of the *théâtre italien* in Marivaux's career, the frequency of his use of the topos of disguise in his plays is hardly surprising, but in only one does he relate it specifically to the notion of social role- or class-reversal, doing so in a context where the device is clearly underlined by the stylized symmetry of the plot: that is to say *Le Jeu de l'amour et du hasard* (1730), where the duplication of the reversal in both male and female characters produces a quarter of individuals all parodying with more or less success their social opposites. Although there is no true use of disguise in the earlier play *L'Ile des esclaves* (1725), since the identity of the various characters is never in doubt either for the audience or for each other, a similarly symmetrical use of role-reversal backed up by costume changes relates it strongly to *Le Jeu,* and in this briefer play the social burden of the device is much more clearly underlined.

Although these are the only plays to use such a symmetrical structure, in a number of others one or other side of the equation is found in isolation. She (or he) stoops to conquer in works like *La Double Inconstance* (1723), *Le Prince travesti* (1724) and *Le Triomphe de l'amour* (1732), and in *La Fausse Suivante* (1724) the result of the trial is the more surprising rejection of the original beloved. But in only one other is there an important use of the situation described by Gordon, in which it is the servant who pretends to be of the class of his master: that is *L'Epreuve* (1740). It is this depiction of the servant as master in these three plays, *L'Ile des esclaves, Le Jeu de l'amour et du hasard* and *L'Epreuve* that it is my intention to examine here. Whilst there seems little doubt that the Italian theatre was a fundamental influence in Marivaux's frequent use of disguise in his plays, it is a device which is by no means unique to that tradition. By focusing on this one particular aspect, on the other hand, we will be led to a consideration of a much more specifically Italianate aspect of Marivaux's theatre, the development of one facet of his treatment of his most persistently archetypal character, Arlequin.

That costume is an important icon of social status in these plays is in no doubt, otherwise there would be no point in the swapping of clothing specified in *L'Ile des esclaves* when the nobles are cast down to servitude and the servants (or, even more pointedly for the philosophical message, slaves, as they are here) are elevated to higher rank, for here there is no deception involved. Even on this island, where the slaves have realized the injustice and artificiality of social inequality, the symbol of the outward trappings of costume will be one of the most important indicators of the masters' fall from grace and the slaves' elevation.

One anomaly should, however, be noted: the swapping of costumes is specified by Trivelin for both couples: '(*Aux esclaves*) Quant à vous, mes enfants, qui devenez libres et citoyens, Iphicrate habitera cette case avec le nouvel Arlequin, et cette belle fille demeurera dans l'autre; vous aurez soin de changer d'habit ensemble, c'est l'ordre' ('[*To the slaves*] As for you, my children, who are now free citizens, Iphicrate will live in this cabin with the new Arlequin, and this beautiful young lady will live in the other; you will make sure to exchange clothing, that is the rule.') Arlequin and Iphicrate exit immediately after this, and at their subsequent re-entry the scene heading specifies 'ARLEQUIN, IPHICRATE, *qui ont changé d'habits*' ('ARLEQUIN, IPHICRATE, *who have exchanged clothing*'). The absence of any similar indication with regard to the female characters, the fact that the continuity of the action prevents them from leaving the stage until after Cléanthis's denunciation of Euphrosine, by which time the exchange has become almost redundant, and the absence of any opportunity for them to resume their original costumes before the final reinstatement of the status quo all point to the fact that Marivaux did not actually envisage any exchange taking place between them in performance. The scene in which the men resume their original clothing (scene ix) is one of the emotional high-points of the play, and, although the fact that this latter exchange takes place in full view of the audience suggests that it was only some sort of over-costume which was exchanged, with Arlequin retaining his traditional motley, it seems fair to assume that much comic effect would be derived from his inappropriate dress. A remark by Silvia in *Le Jeu de l'amour et du hasard* concerning her disguise as a servant—'Il ne me faut presque qu'un tablier' ('Virtually all I need is an apron')—suggests that, on the other hand, as a result of the habitual over-dressing of actors of the time, the costumes of Euphrosine and Cléanthis would have been so similar that the exchange would have made little visual impact; accordingly Marivaux sacrifices it to the fluency of his action. This suggests that, even in *Le Jeu de l'amour et du hasard,* where the women clearly do adopt disguises, the sartorial impression given by Lisette will be both less striking and less inappropriate than that of Arlequin.

The characters' behaviour, though, does not always live up to the costume, and so, in its superficiality, the disguise is shown to have no profound effect on their essence, and it is in the case of Arlequin, where the visual disguise is at its least effective, undermined as it would have been by his traditional trappings of mask and slapstick as well as clear evidence of his suit of shreds and patches under his assumed garb, that the character also proves least able effectively to fulfil his new role. For if we compare him not only with his female counterparts, but also with Frontin his successor in *L'Epreuve,* who, unencumbered by Arlequin's traditional acessories, would have cut a much more dashing figure in his disguise as master, we will find that it is Arlequin who is least able to provide a convincing impersonation of the ruling classes, and who is in consequence the source of the most broadly parodic humour.

Cléanthis, for example, although not totally devoid of vulgarity—even Trivelin becomes exasperated by her inability to know when to stop at the end of scene iii of *L'Ile des esclaves*—displays a rather subtle sense of satire and observation; indeed, as Haydn Mason has shown, [in 'Women in Marivaux: Journalist to Dramatist,' in *Women and Society in Eighteenth-Century France,* ed. E. Jacobs, et al, 1979], her satirical *tour de force* of scene iii is very closely related to a passage which appears later in *Le Cabinet du philosophe* (1734). And it is she who becomes most obviously exasperated by Arlequin's inability to adjust his behaviour to either his new role or costume:

> CLEANTHIS Il fait le plus beau temps du monde; on appelle cela un jour tendre.
>
> ARLEQUIN Un jour tendre? Je ressemble donc au jour, Madame.
>
> CLEANTHIS Comment! vous lui ressemblez?
>
> ARLEQUIN Eh palsambleu! le moyen de n'être pas tendre, quand on se trouve tête à tête avec vos grâces? (*A ce mot il saute de joie.*) Oh! oh! oh! oh!
>
> CLEANTHIS Qu'avez-vous donc? vous défigurez notre conversation!
>
> ARLEQUIN Oh! ce n'est rien; c'est que je m'applaudis.
>
> CLEANTIIIS Rayez ces applaudissements, ils nous dérangent.
>
> CLEANTHIS The weather is as beautiful as can be; people call this a tender [i.e. gentle] day.
>
> ARLEQUIN A tender day? In that case I am like the day, Madam.
>
> CLEANTHIS What do you mean, you are like the day?
>
> ARLEQUIN Sblood! how could I not be tender [i.e. loving], when I am in the company of your charms? (*At this witticism he jumps for joy.*) Ho! ho! ho! ho!
>
> CLEANTHIS What is the matter? you are spoiling our conversation!
>
> ARLEQUIN Oh! it is nothing; I am just applauding myself.
>
> CLEANTHIS Cut the applause, it disturbs us.

It is true that the parody of the poetic lover's conceit at the beginning of this extract is almost subtle, but it is clearly only present to permit the inappropriate oath and the naively childlike ebullience, which are much more typical both of the humour produced by Arlequin elsewhere in this particular play and of his usual archetypal self.

Such internal commentaries by the characters on their own and each other's actions as that found in the above extract are of course impossible in *Le Jeu de l'amour et du hasard,* where the disguises must be sustained, but the comedy of Arlequin's role still resides in the inappropriateness of his behaviour:

> ARLEQUIN Un domestique là-bas m'a dit d'entrer ici, et qu'on allait avertir mon beau-père qui était avec ma femme.

> SILVIA Vous voulez dire Monsieur Orgon et sa fille, sans doute, Monsieur!

> ARLEQUIN Eh! oui, mon beau-père et ma femme, autant vaut; je viens pour épouser, et ils m'attendent pour être mariés; cela est convenu; il ne manque plus que la cérémonie, qui est une bagatelle.

> SILVIA C'est une bagatelle qui vaut bien la peine qu'on y pense.

> ARLEQUIN Oui; mais quand on y a pensé, on n'y pense plus.

> ARLEQUIN A servant down there told me to come in here, and that my father-in-law would be informed that I was with my wife.

> SILVIA No doubt you mean Monsieur Orgon and his daughter, Monsieur!

> ARLEQUIN Yes, my father-in-law and my wife, same difference; marriage is what I am here for, and what they are waiting for; it is all agreed; all we need now is the ceremony, which is a mere trifle.

> SILVIA It is a trifle which it is worth making the effort to remember.

> ARLEQUIN Yes; but once you have remembered it, you do not give it another thought.

Lisette, on the other hand, is used so much by Marivaux as a sort of 'straight-man' for Arlequin's excesses that she provides little humour of her own. As with Cléanthis, her sense of *savoir faire* is sufficiently superior to that of Arlequin for her to react with surprise at his excessive behaviour, as the following extract shows, but it is not developed enough for her ultimately to see through his disguise.

> MONSIEUR ORGON Adieu, mes enfants: je vous laisse ensemble; il est bon que vous vous aimiez un peu avant que de vous marier.

> ARLEQUIN Je ferais bien ces deux besognes-là à la fois, moi.

> MONSIEUR ORGON Point d'impatience; adieu. [*Il sort.*]

> ARLEQUIN Madame, il dit que je ne m'impatiente pas; il en parle bien à son aise, le bonhomme!

> LISETTE J'ai de la peine à croire qu'il vous en coûte tant d'attendre, Monsieur; c'est par galanterie que vous faites l'impatient: à peine êtes-vous arrivé! Votre amour ne saurait être bien fort; ce n'est tout au plus qu'un amour naissant.

> MONSIEUR ORGON Goodbye my children: I will leave you together; it is right that you should have the chance to fall in love a little before you get married.

> ARLEQUIN I would just as soon do the two things at the same time.

> MONSIEUR ORGON Be patient; goodbye. [*He leaves.*]

> ARLEQUIN Madam, he tells me to be patient; it is all very well for him to say that, the old dodderer!

> LISETTE It is hard to believe that you find it quite so difficult to wait, Monsieur; it is through pure gallantry that you pretend to be impatient: you have only just arrived! Your love cannot really be very strong; it is no more than beginning.

And again, in the Frontin of *L'Epreuve,* we find that we have almost left the ineptitude of Arlequin behind. True, there is enough Arlequinesque conceit and whimsicality to give away his origins in a comment like 'On s'accoutume aisément à me voir, j'en ai l'expérience' ('I know from experience that people very easily get used to seeing me'), and his silencing of Madame Argante is much too peremptory to be that of the true master: 'Point de ton d'autorité, sinon je reprends mes bottes et monte à cheval' ('Do not take that authoritarian tone or I will put my boots back on and get back on my horse'). In general though, Marivaux allows his servant character in this play to achieve an impersonation which is almost credible.

So the costume changes nothing: Silvia and Dorante, Lisette and Arlequin are instinctively drawn to their social equals despite the multiple disguises. Convincing as Frontin's acting may be, he still lacks the nobility which will cause Angélique to love him instead of Lucidor (although in this late play Marivaux again weakens the case against Frontin by the strength of Angélique's fidelity: even a real master, he suggests, would still have failed to win her from Lucidor). Perhaps most interesting is the situation presented in *L'Ile des esclaves,* in which the two slaves, rather than being attracted to each other, are unable to resist the attraction of the nobles, despite the fact that on the island of slaves the latter have become technically their social inferiors. The slaves' sense of their masters' superiority will not easily be modified by mere changes in clothing or arbitrary reversals of the power structure.

The social comment in *L'Ile des esclaves* is quite explicit, although critics who have compared Arlequin's remarks to those of Figaro are perhaps underestimating the significant extent to which the subversive character of comments like the following is mitigated by the tone of reconciliation in which they are spoken: 'Tu veux que je partage ton affliction, et jamais tu n'as partagé la mienne. Eh bien! va, je dois avoir le cœur meilleur que toi; car il y a plus longtemps que je souffre, et que je sais ce que c'est que la peine. Tu m'as battu par amitié: puisque tu le dis, je te le pardonne; je t'ai raillé par bonne humeur, prends-le en bonne part, et fais-en ton profit' ('You want me to share your affliction, and you have never shared mine. Go on then! I must be softer-hearted than you, for I have suffered for longer, and I know what pain is. You beat me out of friendship: because you say so, I forgive you; I mocked you out of good humour, take it in the way it was intended, and learn from it'). Ultimately the play calls for humanity rather than social upheaval.

Similarly, although we may be led by the plight of Silvia and Dorante in *Le Jeu de l'amour et du hasard,* in the most emotional moments of the struggle between love and the reason which tells them they cannot cross the social divide, to question the humanity of a society in which Silvia the mistress would not be allowed to wed Dorante if he really were Bourguignon, and although we may have an amused sympathy for the fact that the plans of Lisette and Arlequin to better themselves socially by marriage are doomed to failure, the play leaves us in no doubt that the mutual attraction of the characters comes not from costume, but from a deeper inherent sense of class and the different outlook on life and love which goes with it, neither of which can be so easily donned or doffed. I have discussed elsewhere, in relation to *La Colonie,* the fact that this situation may be more complex than Marivaux's merely negating his social comment by stressing stereotype and reasserting the status quo, and that the traditional elements provide for the audience a familiar framework through which the philosophical point can be made the more effectively ['Old Dogs and New Tricks: Tradition and Revolt in Marivaux's *La Colonie,' The British Journal for Eighteenth-Century Studies* XI, 1988]. The main point for the present argument is, however, the way in which all of these plots contain elements of social climbing: the character who assumes the clothing of his social superior begins to think seriously of aspiring to the rank which would usually go with it.

For the two slaves in *L'Ile des esclaves* social elevation is a reality, but only within the mythic confines of the island, a fact which they seem to understand as well as we do, given their disastrous attempts to woo their social superiors from the real world. And, although Cléanthis is admittedly less convinced than Arlequin, their reversion to their original lowly status is self-willed; they realize that their natures are determined by their original roles and that they cannot cope with their new-found responsibility. When Cléanthis asks Arlequin why he has resumed his original costume, the symbol of his servitude, he replies in terms which can be understood on either the literal or the symbolic plane: 'C'est qu'il est trop petit pour mon cher ami, et que le sien est trop grand pour

moi' ('It is because it is too small for my dear friend, and his is too big for me').

The symmetries of *Le Jeu de l'amour et du hasard* make it clear that this is no more an attempt at realistic theatre than *L'Ile des esclaves.* We are a very long way here from the illusionism of Diderot's dramatic theory, or even the specific references to Paris found in *Les Fausses Confidences.* Neither, however, does Marivaux introduce anything like the distancing effect of the Greek setting of *L'Ile des esclaves*: the period is contemporary, and the location sufficiently anonymous to allow Marivaux's audience to identify it with their own milieu. The fact that the costume changes of this play have become true disguise, rather than mere symbolism, means that, despite the title of the play, for Lisette and Arlequin the attempt at social elevation through matrimony is much less of a game than it was for their predecessors in the earlier philosophical piece. Their failure too, although the audience shares with Monsieur Orgon and Mario the knowledge that it is inevitable, is a result of the given circumstances rather than of choice. So in this play we have moved a step closer to social climbing as a true possibility. But only a step: whilst Lisette and Arlequin here lack the self-knowledge of the Arlequin of *L'Ile des esclaves,* which allows him to understand and express the fact that he is happier in his old position, Marivaux shows, through the ease of their acceptance of their disillusionment, that he wishes us to understand that subconsciously they have come to a similar realization, and our sympathy for them is as short-lived as their disappointment:

> LISETTE Venous au fait. M'aimes-tu?
>
> ARLEQUIN Pardi! oui: en changeant de nom tu n'as pas changé de visage, et tu sais bien que nous nous sommes promis fidélité en dépit de toutes les fautes d'orthographe.
>
> LISETTE Va, le mal n'est pas grand, consolons-nous.
>
> LISETTE Get to the point. Do you love me?
>
> ARLEQUIN Good God, yes: by changing your name you have not changed your face, and you know very well that we promised to be faithful to each other despite all spelling mistakes.
>
> LISETTE Come on, it is no great pity, we will get over it together.

By the time Marivaux came to write *L'Epreuve,* he had already completed *Les Fausses Confidences,* a play in which the crossing of the social divide by marriage becomes a reality, for in marrying Dorante, Araminte weds her own servant, as *intendant* a very high-class servant, it is true, but a servant nonetheless. Dorante may have become *intendant* to Araminte as part of Dubois's stratagem to bring about their marriage, but there is no sense in which he has disguised himself as a social inferior, as does the Dorante of *Le Jeu de l'amour et du hasard*: he really has taken the job as Araminte's servant, and such a post is seen to be compatible with the reduced status brought about by the loss of his fortune. His uncle, Monsieur Remy, certainly sees no shame in this position, and even believes the servant Marton to be a fitting bride for his nephew. Araminte, on the other hand, learns from Dubois of Dorante's condition as impoverished son of a good family as early as the first act of the play, but this high social status certainly does not override his position as servant in her house; it is this which makes the psychological struggle so acute as she gradually falls in love with him and is forced to admit her affection both to herself and to her household. And for Madame Argante, her delightfully odious mother, the status of servant negates all other considerations, preventing her ever accepting Dorante as son-in-law; indeed, she is still affirming this at the final curtain: 'Ah! la belle chute! Ah! ce maudit intendant! Qu'il soit votre mari tant qu'il vous plaira; mais il ne sera jamais mon gendre' ('What an unhappy ending! Ah, that confounded steward! He can be your husband as much as you like; but he will never be my son-in-law').

Despite the mitigating factors of Dorante's high status in both social and domestic terms, Araminte has still taken the very significant step of breaking through the barrier separating her from her servants.

From here we move on to *L'Epreuve,* which is full of the crossing of social barriers, although across a social distance less extreme than that dividing master from servant seen in the earlier plays. Angélique is of a lower class than Lucidor, but they wed. Maître Blaise aspires, however half-heartedly, to his social superior Angélique, and his wealth will eventually represent a step up the social ladder to Lisette, who finally accepts his proposal of marriage.

But what of the disguised character Frontin? Given that the whole point of the plot of this play is that Angélique passes the test which is set for her, perhaps the best measure of Marivaux's intentions concerning the competence of Frontin's impersonation is not his rejection by her, but rather the treatment he receives from Lisette. Whilst her namesake in *Le Jeu de l'amour et du hasard,* although convinced of the social superiority of the disguised Arlequin, is still emboldened to woo him, Frontin, despite being both recognized and loved by his Lisette, nonetheless manages not only to convince her that she is mistaken about his true identity, but also to put any notion that he would be accessible to her out of her mind. So Frontin's disguise succeeds, and we are more inclined to believe his warnings that he may win Angélique away from Lucidor than we are that Arlequin could ever win a true member of the ruling class. But if the servant Dorante is able to win his mistress in *Les Fausses Confidences,* the daring of this conclusion is, as we have seen, at least mitigated not only by his being *intendant* rather than valet, but also by the fact that he is a man who has had both rank and fortune and has been

ruined. In *L'Epreuve,* even in a world where both Lucidor and Maître Blaise marry beneath them, the true servant cannot be permitted to find a wife who is of either the nobility or the *haute bourgeoisie*. And the symmetry of the fantasy of the earlier plots has also disappeared, with the result that in this more realistic world there are victims as well as winners: the role he is playing for Lucidor deprives Frontin of Lisette, just as the Marton of *Les Fausses Confidences* is deprived of the servant who, according to traditional plot-structure, is rightfully hers.

There is a clear development here: as Marivaux moves away from the stock characters and symmetries of traditional *commedia* models, social mobility becomes more of a possibility. And this development is even more pronounced if compared with a well-known seventeenth-century model: the nobles in *Le Bourgeois Gentilhomme* are prepared to trick Monsieur Jourdain out of his money by promises of marriage and of favours, but that these should ever actually be granted is never their intention. In Marivaux's *L'Héritier de village,* on the other hand, the nobles are quite prepared to marry Blaise's children in order to get at his money, the follies and dishonesty of such an alliance being avoided only by the revelations of the *dénouement*.

Clearly this modification has its roots in social reality. It seems likely that contemporary audiences would assume that the Dorante of *Les Fausses Confidences* was ruined in exactly the same way as Marivaux himself, that is in the financial crash caused by John Law. John Lough comments as follows [in *An Introduction to Eighteenth-Century France,* 1960]:

> The immediate economic consequences of the *Système* were mixed. On the one hand thousands of people were ruined (it is perhaps to the *Système* that we owe the plays and novels of Marivaux who was driven by his losses in it to seek a living with his pen), and the violent inflation which caused a steep rise in the cost of living brought suffering to the lower classes, especially in the towns. . . . Enormous fortunes were made almost overnight; the lackeys of yesterday became the masters of today.

But such social mobility does not imply that members of the ruling class suddenly beganforming marital alliances with servants: far from it. Elinor Barber [in *The Bourgeoisie in 18th-Century France,* 1955] points out that nobles were only likely to marry beneath their status for considerable financial gain, and that even this compromise was far from being universal:

> The poverty-stricken provincial nobility continued to disdain any alliance with the rich bourgeoisie, even though they might be reduced to the status of *hobereaux*. The acceptance by the Court nobility of these marriages may, therefore, be one more indication of its defection from a genuine noble ideology and of its espousal of a way of life no longer congruent with its older functions as a political and military aristocracy.

Les Acteurs de la Comédie Italienne *by Nicolas Lancret.*

So the aspirations of Cléanthis and Arlequin in *L'Ile des esclaves* and of Lisette and Arlequin in *Le Jeu de l'amour et du hasard* are unrealistic, and, whilst rightly belonging to the fantasy worlds of these two plays, are, even in that context, inevitably doomed to failure. The slight social mismatch of the marriage of Lucidor to Angélique, on the other hand, may lack some of the fairy-tale extravagance of the earlier plays, but it is perfectly justified in the more realistic atmosphere of *L'Epreuve,* since in terms of contemporary social reality it was actually possible. It is for the same reason that Lisette, although attracted to Frontin, makes no attempt to aspire to the conquest of the master she thinks him to be. Unlike her namesake in *Le Jeu de l'amour et du hasard,* she knows the attempt to be pointless, for she, like the play in which she figures, is more in touch with social reality.

Lionel Gossman comments, however: 'The plain truth seems to be that works of literature do not "reflect" social reality, at least not immediately, so that the relation between the social background and the work of literature is never a simple causal one' [*French Society and Culture: Background for 18th-Century Literature,* 1972]. This is certainly true of *Le Jeu de l'amour et du hasard*: there is a degree of reflection of the increased social mobility of the period in the servants' attempts to marry above themselves, but whilst they are not unaware of the difficulty of the attempt, in the real world of the time it would surely have been impossible. Similarly in relation to the masters: although much of the emotional tension of their roles comes from their reluctance even to con-

sider a *mésalliance,* Silvia's eventual manipulation of Dorante to the point that he proposes marriage to a girl whom he believes to be a servant is again the stuff on which dreams and romantic comedies are made, but is not representative of contemporary reality. It is not just, therefore, the symmetricality of this play or the tidiness of its *dénouement* which have an almost fairy-tale quality; the exaggerated aspirations of the servant characters and the extent to which Dorante's love triumphs over the demands of commonsense and social reality come into a similar category. The characters themselves may not feel that they are involved in a game, but through his title Marivaux signals to his audience that the content of this play should be taken none too seriously.

By the time we reach *Les Fausses Confidences* we are in much more plausible territory, for, despite the daring conclusion in which mistress marries not only a servant, but actually her own servant, we can see that the situation is much more closely analogous to that described by Lough and Barber: Araminte is the rich bourgeoise, and Dorante, although ruined, has a social rank which makes him an acceptable partner; Marton too, is quite justified in seeing Dorante as her legitimate partner, since both belong to the servant class. And then, in Marivaux's final play for the Italians, we move ever further from *commedia dell'arte* fantasy, for, as we have seen, *L'Epreuve* depicts a situation which, on the social level at least, is more or less uncontroversial.

But the collapse of Law's system dates from 1720, *L'Ile des esclaves* from 1725, *Le Jeu de l'amour et du hasard* from 1730, *Les Fausses Confidences* from 1737 and *L'Epreuve* from 1740. The plays certainly inhabit post-Law society, but, given this time-scale, they can scarcely be seen as a specific response to the collapse of the *Système.* Should we seek other reasons for the development in Marivaux's approach seen in these plays?

The naming of the characters is not without significance. In *L'Ile des esclaves* names chosen for their relevance to the Greek setting (Iphicrate, Euphrosine, Cléanthis) rub shoulders with the Italianate (Trivelin and Arlequin). It is, of course, the Arlequin archetype who is the most persistently Italian element of Marivaux's theatre, and we note that when he swaps roles and costumes with Iphicrate, even though, as I have suggested, it seems unlikely that the actor playing the part of the noble took over the traditional elements of the costume (the stylized patchwork suit, the mask and the slap-stick), his master does take over his name. This is part of his humiliation: 'Arlequin', as we are told in this play, is little better as an appellation than 'Hé', and we will learn in *Le Jeu de l'amour et du hasard* that one of its principal features is that it rhymes with 'coquin' ('rascal') and 'faquin' ('wretch'). In *Le Jeu de l'amour et du hasard,* on the other hand, whilst Silvia in her disguise becomes Lisette and Lisette Silvia, Arlequin even becoming Dorante, Dorante is spared not only Arlequin's traditional costume, but also his name: he becomes Bourguignon. In Marivaux's first important play for the Italians, *Arlequin poli par l'amour,* Silvia had been a fitting partner for

Arlequin, but by the time we reach *Le Jeu de l'amour et du hasard* her suitor cannot be expected even to assume his name. Whilst the name Lisette is a traditional enough name for a *soubrette,* it does not have enough archetypal significance to compromise either the dignity or the nature of Silvia's performance as a servant.

Arlequin is another matter: in *L'Ile des esclaves* Iphicrate makes no pretence of actually being Arlequin; all he needs to do is appear offended whenever he is called by this name, and, indeed, the role is so sketchy in the central part of the work that this is virtually all he does do. Dorante, on the other hand, is in disguise, and, in terms of her social status, Silvia has come a long way since her first appearance in a play by Marivaux; there is a sense in which the mere fact of calling himself Arlequin would completely compromise Dorante's wooing of her, for the archetypal force of the name is such that it would be completely inappropriate to the refined servant played by Dorante: 'le galant Bourguignon'. The archetypal force of the name also causes it to demand of the actor playing the part, even in disguise, the *lazzi* which are typical of it, and these were not only counter to Marivaux's purpose, they were also, as it were, the property of Thomassin, who was playing the 'real' Arlequin, and not of Luigi (often known as Louis) Riccoboni, who was in the role of Dorante. So the swapping of names demanded by the role-reversal in *L'Ile des esclaves* has disappeared: here roles are still reversed, master pretends to be servant and servant master, but whilst Arlequin still pretends to be Dorante, Dorante emphatically does not pretend to be Arlequin. Arlequin has, in consequence, been marginalized: in *Arlequin poli par l'amour* he is central to the plot. In *L'Ile des esclaves* the servant characters dominate the action and his presence is also, as it were, duplicated by the fact that Iphicrate is given his name. In *Le Jeu de l'amour et du hasard* it is the action involving the masters which is paramount, and when they are on stage we are not even reminded of Arlequin by the disguised Dorante's using his name. And when we reach *L'Epreuve,* Marivaux's last play for the Italians, he has disappeared completely.

When Marivaux calls his female lead in *Les Fausses Confidences* Araminte and in *L'Epreuve* Angélique, it is true that these changes denote a certain change in the type of character, for the former is a rather more emotionally mature woman than the Silvias of the earlier plays, and the latter a little more modest and passive; but these modifications are subtle, the type remains broadly similar and the parts were still played by the actress Silvia. Much the same is true of Riccoboni's Lélios, Dorantes and Lucidor; and if the Marton of *Les Fausses Confidences* is a slightly more serious character than our two Lisettes, the emphasis is surely on 'slightly'. In the case of Arlequin, however, the situation is completely different, for with the name goes the archetype. Indeed, so strong is the archetypal force of the name, that in the scene in *Le Jeu de l'amour et du hasard* in which Arlequin reveals his true identity to Lisette (III. vii) an interesting situation arises: Arlequin confesses to being the servant of Dorante, but does not give his name.

Logically, given the symmetry of the plot, Lisette should assume that he is called Bourguignon. But no: a few lines further on, without needing to be told, she calls him Arlequin. That this should occur without causing any sense of incongruity, without giving rise to the feeling that here we have an authorial error, is entirely attributable to the impossibility of dissociating the name from the character-type. The one implies the other, so it would be superfluous for the character to identify himself by name. And so the different name given to Frontin implies a significant difference in character: not for him the traditional trappings of Arlequin's costume. Yves Moraud comments, for instance: 'Arlequin est à peu près le seul personnage qui continue, à la fin du XVII siècle, à porter régulièrement le masque' ('Arlequin is virtually the only character who, at the end of the seventeenth century, still regularly wears a mask') [*Masques et jeux dans le théâtre comique en France entre 1685 et 1730,* 1977]. In order to permit the much more convincing portrayal of the master by the disguised Frontin, Marivaux had to make use of such an alternative servant figure: an actor playing Arlequin would have provided the conventional *lazzi,* which the audience would have expected. Not only would the use of the archetypal character without his tomfoolery have disappointed the audience, but the expectations of his name and the conventional trappings of his costume would in any case have ensured that any attempt on Marivaux's part to make the servant's impersonation of the master convincing with him in the role was doomed to failure from the outset.

Kenneth McKee [in *The Theater of Marivaux,* 1958] remarks of *L'Epreuve*:

> With its felicitous role for Silvia, *L'Epreuve* was a fitting climax to Marivaux's career as purveyor to the Italian actors. Yet, strangely, the play shows no trace of the old Italian influences. In the twenty years since Marivaux submitted *Arlequin poli par l'amour* to Riccoboni, he drew less and less on the *commedia dell'arte,* and his writing evolved to such a point that none of his last eight plays, except *Les Fausses Confidences,* contain even a minor part for Arlequin.

And that role in *Les Fausses Confidences* has been even more marginalized than the relegation from central character to servant figure that we noted between *Arlequin poli par l'amour* and *Le Jeu de l'amour et du hasard,* for in this play he has even become a secondary servant, the dolt who amuses us with his *lazzi* in a few cameo-like scenes, and has but minor importance for the plot; the main function is reserved for the Machiavellian first servant and *meneur du jeu,* Dubois.

Arlequin was for Marivaux, to a large extent, not merely an archetype, but an actor: Tommaso Visenti, known as Thomassin. There seems no doubt that, at the height of his powers, he played the part very well, but, in the few years before his death in 1739, 'après une longue maladie' ('after a long illness') as the *Mercure* stated, his failing health must have made him a less acrobatic and lively *zanni* and possibly even a less reliable colleague.

After his death, the Italians replaced him with Carlo Bertaggi, but Marivaux had already written his final Arlequin; his loss of interest in the role coincides with Thomassin's decline. But is the playwright being controlled by the archetype, or the archetype by the playwright? Does Marivaux stop writing roles for Arlequin because he loses Thomassin, or is it through loyalty for the actor that he goes on writing them for as long as he does? Is the development in Marivaux's theatre a result of the disappearance of Arlequin, or is he dropped because he is incompatible with the new direction that Marivaux is pursuing?

There is no clear or certain answer to these questions, and it would be misguided to claim that one alternative were true to the exclusion of the other, but certain trends related to the concerns we have already examined suggest that the second of each pair of alternatives may represent the dominant force in Marivaux's development. We have seen that Arlequin dominates the plot in *Arlequin poli par l'amour*. *La Double Inconstance* (1723) has a similarly artificial symmetricality to our first two comedies of role-reversal, but the work is constructed in such a way that in each part of the plot one of the *commedia* characters (Arlequin and Silvia, who at this point is still seen as his legitimate partner) is paired with one of the courtly characters, thus spreading the *commedia* influence evenly through the texture of the play. By the time of *L'Ile des esclaves* and *Le Jeu de l'amour et du hasard* the servants are paired together as are the masters, but if in the former the servants dominate the plot, in the latter it is the masters who hold centre stage. In *Les Fausses Confidences* and *L'Epreuve* the symmetry has disappeared and it is the masters who are at the centre of the plot-line, the *commedia* archetypes having been first marginalized and then banished. This development marks a gradual abandonment of the *commedia dell'arte* models which Marivaux adopted at the beginning of his career, in favour of a more emotional and sentimental form of drama represented by the dominance of the higher-born characters, a form which is more typical of later currents in eighteenth-century French theatre. And along with this move towards the dominance of a more serious form of comedy we find a tendency for both settings and social attitudes to become more realistic; the latter trend we have already examined, the former can be seen in the move from the fantasy worlds of *Arlequin poli par l'amour* and *L'Ile des esclaves* to the anonymously contemporary setting of *Le Jeu de l'amour et du hasard* and further to the specific references to Paris found in *Les Fausses Confidences* and *L'Epreuve*; the Madame Dorman for whom Frontin has worked, for instance, lives, 'du côcé de la place Maubert, chez un marchand de café, au second' ('by the Place Maubert, at a coffee merchant's, on the second floor'). There are certainly exceptions to this trend, *La Dispute* (1744), for example, which, although written after *L'Epreuve*, inhabits a world every bit as fantastic as the three island comedies, but the general trend seems clear enough. Indeed, *Les Fausses Confidences* and *L'Epreuve* inhabit very similar milieux to Marivaux's two great novels, *La Vie de Marianne* and *Le Paysan parvenu*, both

of which were undertaken during the period between *Le Jeu de l'amour et du hasard* and *Les Fausses Confidences*, and both of which are much concerned with the theme of social climbing which we have alsoobserved in our comedies of disguise and role-reversal.

So the issue of disguise and role-reversal and Arlequin's relationship to this theme turn out to be related to the central development of Marivaux's theatre away from its *commedia dell'arte* origins. Arlequin's inability to change his nature is central to the philosophy of *L'Ile des esclaves*, and adds to the comedy in a play like *Le Jeu de l'amour et du hasard*, where the basic artificiality of the plot structure makes it clear that we should not take lapses in credibility too seriously. A play like *L'Epreuve*, in which our response to Angélique's emotional crisis depends on our ability to believe that she is taken in by Frontin's disguise, would be impossible with Arlequin in the role of disguised servant. For Arlequin cannot ever truly be disguised; Marivaux may polish him, he may become Sauvage, Deucalion or Roi de Serendib, but fundamentally he is always immutably himself.

THE GAME OF LOVE AND CHANCE

E. J. H. Greene (essay date 1965)

SOURCE: "Women and Men," in *Marivaux*, University of Toronto Press, 1965, pp. 124-65.

[*In the following excerpt, Green declares* The Game of Love and Chance *"a masterpiece of comedy" and attempts to identify the sources of its "enduring appeal."*]

The first of Marivaux's works to achieve the status of a classic, *Le Jeu* was not immediately recognized as a masterpiece. Created on January 23, 1730, by the Italians, it had a good first run of fourteen performances, plus two at court and one for the Duchesse du Maine. The *Mercure* termed it a "very great success," but the average box-office receipts at the Hôtel de Bourgogne, 1,200 *livres*, were not outstanding. One must nevertheless conclude that the play made a strong impression on those who attended the first showings, because three months later the *Mercure* printed a long review of it, including a summary of criticisms collected from spectators. A remarkable element in the history of *Le Jeu* is that the *Mercure*'s main criticism has been repeated from age to age, while the play itself has never ceased to show vitality and variety of interest. An early indication of this vitality was the fact that about 1740 it replaced the first *Surprise* as a play in which the Italians tested new actors: Gasparini on May 24, 1740, Francasal on May 18, 1760, made their début as Arlequin, and Mme Durand made hers as Lisette on December 25, 1760.

By its formal perfection, the richness and definitive quality of the text, the complexity and truth of the characters, the variety of the action—alternating emotional tension with exuberance and comic verve, blending the real and the ideal—in almost every way *Le Jeu* has proved itself to be a masterpiece of comedy. A happy fusion of the Italian and French styles, it serves to illustrate the concept of pure theatre, by which term is meant the representation of human action transposed into a world at once close enough to the one we know and far enough removed to permit insights which cannot otherwise be portrayed in such a short length of time. It has proved itself to be a classic in the sense that although it has been enriched by a considerable body of critical comment, no one has yet said the final word about it.

Le Jeu is not included in Lesbros de la Versane's list of the author's favourites among his own plays, whereas the next play in order of composition, *Les Serments indiscrets,* is. The question raised by this distinction is worthy of some attention, and the following observations are advanced as a hypothesis. *Les Serments indiscrets* was accepted by the French comedians on March 9, 1731, but was produced only some fifteen months later, apparently after some prodding by the author. It was his supreme bid to win consecration on the French stage, and it resulted in another failure. In the long *Avertissement* to the published version of the play, he defended it warmly: it is clear that he thought of it, with a certain tenderness, as one of his best and most original comedies. Today it seems rather that he had extended himself to the limit in order to compose a kind of Marivaux superproduction, and that consequently he has given us quantity, not quality; or, to put it another way, that he forced his qualities to the point at which they begin to become defects. In comparison, *Le Jeu,* with a richer human content to begin with, seems natural and spontaneous. A fair guess is that the latter play came easily, and that therefore its author did not himself realize how great was his artistic achievement. Moreover, it is possible that he considered it to be one of his least original, since, of all his comedies, it draws on the largest number of obvious sources and contains the largest number of allusions to well-known works of the preceding hundred years. Today *Le Jeu* appears a classic in the sense also that it is the culmination of a particular theatrical tradition, the work that realizes the possibilities of a cluster of ideas and devices which earlier dramatists had been unable fully to develop. It is a classic in the sense too that Marivaux found in this tradition a perfect vehicle for his own personal vision of human relations.

The particular tradition just referred to is the use of disguises in order to solve problems raised by the marriage customs and class distinctions of the Ancien Régime. It was a favourite dramatic device on both the French and Italian stages, and one for which Marivaux himself had a predilection. It is useful here to distinguish between what one might call its positive and negative uses. The negative aspect is well illustrated in *Le Père prudent,* which follows a standard pattern: disguises are employed to discourage unwelcome suitors so that the field will be left open for the worthy, but penniless, young man of good family. Usually too, and this is true of *Le Père prudent,* the disguises must be backed up by a financial *deus ex machina,* through which it is learned that an uncle has just died, or that a lawsuit has been won, providing the preferred suitor with the money he needs in order to support the young lady in the manner to which she is accustomed, and to win the approval of her father or guardian. In this type of play we see the early, and rather timid, affirmations of the right of the individual to choose his or her mate, and thus to make a *mariage d'inclination.*

In the positive use of the device, these affirmations were even stronger, at least by implication. There were many plays, and indeed novels, such as *Gil Blas,* in which servants masqueraded as masters in order to make love to ladies (real ladies or disguised maids), or in which masters assumed the livery of servants in order to observe, and perhaps test, their beloved or the future spouse proposed by families and guardians. Marivaux was acquainted with a large number of such plays and novels and he drew on several of them. The matter has been well investigated and probably exhausted by now. His initial stroke of genius was to conceive of a quadruple disguise, thus giving himself scope to deal with many facets of the problem in one complex action. He showed no less genius in bestowing upon his principal character a keen consciousness of her individuality: there is little force in a plea for the rights of the individual if no real individuals exist.

The action of the play is so well known that a brief summary will suffice here. Silvia requests permission from her father, M. Orgon, to trade places with her maid, Lisette, so that she may observe, and approve or disapprove of Dorante, the young man he has chosen for her. M. Orgon readily grants the permission because, as he explains to his son Mario a moment later, he has been warned in a letter from the other father that Dorante has been accorded a similar favour; Dorante, who wants a wife suitable to him rather than one merely acceptable to his family, has traded places with his servant, Arlequin. Arlequin and Lisette seize upon the opportunity to try to make what each thinks will be an extremely advantageous marriage; however, since their sense of individuality is limited, they are quite content in the end to accept each other for what they really are. A husband is a husband, says Lisette at the end of the first scene, implying that any one of a thousand men would do. And she is right, for her. But Silvia, a much more highly developed human being, has more exacting standards, as has Dorante; thus these two, after experiencing a mutual first attraction, run headlong into the class question. For each, the idea of marrying beneath one's station in life has the full force of a taboo. Most of Act II is taken up with the conflict in Silvia between her inclination and the taboo. Dorante, under the same strain, yields first, and here Marivaux was being realistic: at this social level a man had more freedom of action, more means at his disposal to combat class prejudice. When Dorante does declare his identity, Silvia feels an immense feeling of relief and utters the famous line: "Ah! je vois clair dans mon cœur." The conflict in her soul has been resolved; but she does not reciprocate with a revelation of her identity. In this situation, all Dorante can think of as a solution is to say that he will never marry, since social considerations will not permit him to be united with a Lisette. Silvia asks him to wait while she finds means to overcome the difficulty. These means, the substance of Act III, consist of machinations which finally bring from Dorante a declaration that he will marry her despite her status as a maid: he is confident that his father will see her through his eyes. When he learns, in the last scene, that his Lisette is really Silvia, he is delighted to know that he has passed the test. For he has proved himself to be the kind of individual Silvia wanted, and not merely the handsome, well-mannered son of Monsieur X (we never do learn his family name).

More than one notable actor has attested to the fact that Dorante is one of the finest and most difficult male roles in all French comedy. Yet it is Silvia who has the principal part in *Le Jeu*: she has 670 lines of text to 332 for Dorante. The play is written from her point of view, and without an understanding of that point of view it is impossible to appreciate or bring out all the facets of her complex personality. It is of course a fact, as the history of the play amply proves, that her character is so rich, so alive, that it is possible to play it in a way quite contrary to the intentions of the author and still make a success of it. For light on these intentions, one should turn not only to the sources of the play but also to the other works written, or being written, by Marivaux at the same period, in particular *L'Indigent philosophe, La Colonie* and *La Vie de Marianne.*

In the two latter works and *Le Jeu* we find the same preoccupation expressed in three different ways. A personal problem may have contributed to this preoccupation: in 1730 Marivaux's daughter had reached eleven or twelve, and because of lack of money her father was probably not going to be able to arrange a decent marriage according to the ideas of the time. However that may be, in *L'Indigent philosophe* we saw him concerned with problems of social status and individual merit, in the broadest terms. In *La Colonie,* he gave women an opportunity to make an organized protest against their social and psychological inferiority, although he turned that play into a satire of political action. It is imprudent to sum up *La Vie de Marianne* in a single sentence, but perhaps one can risk the statement that he conceived that work as a long novel which would deal with the problems of a girl who has all the personal qualities required to be accepted as a "young lady" and yet cannot be so accepted because her social backing—her family—was wiped out in a tragic accident when she was still a babe in arms. The Silvia of *Le Jeu* has all the social, family and material advantages that Marianne lacked, but she is still left to face alone the problems raised by the unequal status of the sexes on the psychological and social level. Thus for *Le Jeu,* Marivaux narrowed down his broad

preoccupation to a theme manageable within the confines of a three-act comedy, and profiting from the experience of his predecessors, treated it so thoroughly that, without realizing it perhaps, he attained the universal.

The *Mercure's* chief criticism, which has been repeated with variations down to the present, recognizes Silvia's central importance but shows a complete failure to understand what it is she wants to accomplish. Briefly, the criticism is that the principal action is really finished at the end of Act II, with Dorante's revelation of his identity. Here she should have told him who she was; instead, she sees the possibility of satisfying her vanity and manages to do so with the help of her brother and indulgent father. In other words, critics who adopt this view see Silvia exactly as do M. Orgon and Mario, and imagine that Marivaux wrote Act III merely in order to give a demonstration of the "insatiable vanité d'amour-propre" of the eternal feminine. Act III appears therefore as anticlimactic and the whole play as poorly constructed: the recognition scene between Arlequin and Lisette, for instance, seems in this view to come *after* the important scenes and so to prolong the action at a lower level of interest (another of the *Mercure's* criticisms). What these critics should add is that Silvia's last long speech, in Act III, scene 8, is pure histrionics; if they do not, it is probably because willy-nilly they feel the emotional power of it: but this speech must be accounted for, if the critic is to be consistent.

We can get at the key points through M. Orgon: was he right? did he understand his daughter or did he not? M. Orgon is by now one of the most celebrated fathers in world literature; his creator has apparently immortalized him by putting into his mouth the line: "va, dans ce monde, il faut être un peu trop bon pour l'être assez" (1, 2). This line has engendered a profusion of nice sentiments from critics who do not seem to have noticed that in the same scene he has just told Silvia that he arranged the marriage with Dorante's father without even having seen the son. It is clear that he has not previously discussed the matter with her. Such behaviour might be construed as a rather casual assumption of parental responsibilities. But perhaps M. Orgon is very wise in playing the probabilities (another sense in which we can take the word *jeu*); the chances are that Dorante, the son of an old and intimate friend, will do, and besides, in giving Silvia the freedom to accept or reject Dorante, M. Orgon has allowed for a margin of error. Whether we judge M. Orgon to be indulgent and wise, or indulgent and lazy, we must agree that he does not see his daughter as the individual she believes herself to be. He sees the problem much as does Lisette: a husband is a husband, the only difference being that the field is narrowed down drastically for Silvia by social considerations. He does not know either what exactly it is that alarms her in the prospect of marriage; it is to Lisette and not to her father that she unburdens herself in the opening scene. It is therefore not surprising that in Act III he should interpret his daughter's action as he does: he thinks in generalities, in terms of set patterns of behaviour. Nor is it surprising that Mario should fall in line with his father's thinking: his conduct is a reflection of the fact that it is possible for a brother to love a little sister without taking the trouble to understand her.

Silvia's sense of individuality is brought out from the start, in one of those arresting opening lines the art of which Marivaux had mastered, and the point is underlined in Lisette's reply:

> SILVIA. Mais encore une fois, de quoi vous mêlez-vous, pourquoi répondre de mes sentiments?
>
> LISETTE. C'est que j'ai cru que, dans cette occasion-ci, vos sentiments ressembleraient à ceux de tout le monde . . .

Later in the scene, the famous portraits are not Marivaux's attempt to rival La Bruyère; they are key speeches in which Silvia explains why the prospect of marriage alarms her. She has observed that men are two-faced, that they have one face for social occasions and another for their wives and children; she has observed too that the handsomer and more intelligent a man is, the more likely he is to multiply his personalities. Once a girl is married, her freedom of action is gone, she is in a helpless and hopeless position; when her husband ceases to respect her, a woman's self-respect disappears too. What Silvia accomplishes in Act III, through the prolonging of her disguise, is to force Dorante to become fully aware of her as a person in her own right, and to decide that as such she is worth more to him than would be a conventional "fille de M. Orgon." Moreover, as Lisette she is able to say things to Dorante which the proprieties would have made impossible for M. Orgon's daughter. Her last long speech is the counterpart of the three portraits of the opening scene; the whole play builds up to it. In it she contrasts the double standard for men with the single standard for women, and makes it clear that the single standard for both for life is what she expects in marriage. She is speaking from the heart for Silvia; fundamentally it makes little difference here whether she is Lisette or Silvia. As Silvia no less than as Lisette she needs to hear Dorante say not only "je t'adore," but also "je te respecte." The significant lines at the end of this scene are not the ones most frequently quoted, Dorante's famous "Mon père me pardonnera dès qu'il vous aura vue, ma fortune nous suffit à tous deux, et le mérite vaut bien la naissance. . . ." The enlightened elements in Marivaux's society were ready to accept the last statement in principle, if reluctant to practise it, as we see in *La Vie de Marianne.* But the quotation always stops there, whereas the passage goes on:

> DORANTE. . . . ne disputons point, car je ne changerai jamais.
>
> SILVIA. Il ne changera jamais! Savez-vous bien que vous me charmez, Dorante?
>
> DORANTE. Ne gênez donc plus votre tendresse, et laissez-la répondre . . .

> SILVIA. Enfin, j'en suis venue à bout; vous . . . vous ne changerez jamais?
>
> DORANTE. Non, ma chère Lisette.
>
> SILVIA. Que d'amour!

It is Silvia's insistence on whether Dorante will change or not which is important and which sends us back to the portraits of Act I. She is finally satisfied ("Enfin, j'en suis venue à bout"), she has obtained the best guarantee she could get, in her situation, that this marriage will be founded on mutual love and respect.

It is perfectly true that, in so doing Silvia has won a very satisfying victory for her *amour-propre.* It is perfectly true also that she has used her weapon, coquetry. "Une femme qui n'est plus coquette, c'est une femme qui a cessé d'être," had written the youthful contributor to the *Mercure,* and Silvia, a spirited girl, at once gay and serious, romantic and realistic, is very much alive. Critics who see only the coquette in her do not see her through the eyes of Dorante, who is attracted to her not only by her physical charms but even more by her quality as a human being. Such critics, to be consistent, must condemn Dorante as something of a nincompoop, and predict for him a future as a henpecked husband. The fact is however that Dorante responds to the challenge which the person of Silvia constitutes. Silvia appeals neither to men who think of a wife as a mirror, a meek helpmate playing the role defined for her by Providence, a domestic convenience, a doormat on which they can wipe their feet, nor to women who are content to play, or pretend to play, these roles. She does appeal to those who think of marriage as a union freely entered into by equals for mutual pleasure and enrichment, to those who seek "un assentiment puissant qui les liera pour une vie commune de levers, de repas et de repos," in Giraudoux's now famous words. Since perhaps most young people nowadays have this ideal, *Le Jeu* is a very satisfying classic to teach, because Marivaux's art permits them to share the hopes, fears and aspirations of both Silvia and Dorante.

The fundamental and enduring appeal of *Le Jeu* is to youth, and it can be most effectively played by young actors for whom the notion of *play* is not too distant a memory. Like Chimène and Rodrigue, Silvia and Dorante enlist the sympathy of the spectator in their struggle to reconcile their self-respect and their love in a world of conventions imposed on them by their elders. It is not that the parents seek to force their personal wishes on them, it is rather that the social status they have achieved places certain obligations on their children. Thus, on a lower plane, Arlequin's observation that "Les pères et mères font tout à leur tête" (11, 5) is no doubt a deliberate, if distant, echo of Rodrigue's "Que de maux et de pleurs nous coûteront nos pères" (*Le Cid,* 111, 4).

In the same way, a number of metaphors used by Arlequin are no doubt deliberate echoes of those of Mascarille. It is to be noted that he plays the part of his master with the same combination of ludicrousness and zest, the same delight in *play;* he well deserves the flattering title of the "Mascarille of the eighteenth century." In making such allusions, Marivaux was utilizing parts of the cultural heritage of his spectators; he was able to draw on both *Le Cid* and *Les Précieuses ridicules* in the same play because the social structure had changed so much in a hundred years.

From Chimène to Silvia, the problem facing a young lady of good family had changed radically, more so than it has since (at least as Marivaux presents it). Silvia has neither to maintain the honour of the family name in terms of the conventions of a late feudal aristocracy nor, like the daughter of a *parvenu,* does she have to prove her right to belong to "the quality" by demonstrating her cultural "accomplishments." Silvia belongs to a family whose social status Marivaux has purposely left rather vague: both M. Orgon and Dorante's father appear to belong to that class which had achieved wealth and had been living nobly, to use the contemporary term, for a generation or more. (The terms have changed since, but not the realities.) The obligations on their children are to conform to the patterns of behaviour appropriate to their class, and to marry at their own social level or higher. But affluence and abundant leisure had produced new problems for the children. On the one hand, in such a favourable milieu, a Silvia can develop into a genuine person of quality (without quotation marks), and be conscious of her individuality; so can a Dorante. The children, when they are as intelligent as these two are, realize that there is likely to be a discrepancy between the individual and the being whose behaviour is, in large part, dictated by his position in society. The problem is more acute for Silvia who, as a young lady, has very limited means of action. In *Le Triomphe de l'Amour,* Marivaux will give another young lady means of action commensurate with her readiness to assume the responsibility for her marriage arrangements, but in order to do so he has to make her an independent reigning princess, in a kingdom out of this world.

There is a play which, from this point of view, marks an intermediate stage between *Le Cid* and *Les Précieuses ridicules* on the one hand, and *Le Jeu* on the other, and which Marivaux had no doubt so thoroughly assimilated that it cannot properly be quoted as a source of the latter play in the sense that *Le Portrait* by Beauchamp is a source. This play, *La Fontaine de Sapience,* by a mysterious M. de B*** (Brugière de Barante?), first performed by the older company of Italians on July 8, 1694, is a *critique,* exploiting the success of *Arlequin Défenseur du beau sexe,* also by M. de B***, a work which seems to have made a lasting impression on Marivaux. In the *critique* we have the reverse of the situation in *Le Jeu*: Lucile knows from the start that Octave is the man for her, but it is her loving father and two maids who multiply the portraits of men who are one thing in public and another at home. Towards the end of the play Lucile has her eyes opened to what men are in general (fortunately

for her Octave is an exception). Arlequin explains that men can be classified according to the characters of comedy:

> ARLEQUIN. . . . ce sont autant de Tartuffes, de Jodelets, ou de Scapins.
>
> LUCILE. Tu as raison. Je vois que je ne connais plus ce que je croyais le mieux connaître. Il y a bien loin de la personne au personnage. Que de Mascarilles!
>
> ARLEQUIN. Du personnage à la personne, il y a loin comme de mon masque à mon visage, et comme de mon habit à ma peau. Vous voyez bien qu'à Paris les comédiens ne sont pas les seuls qui jouent la comédie . . .

This passage might serve as the epigraph to the edition of Marivaux's *œuvres complètes* which we lack today, but an editor who so used it would have to insert somewhere a note to the effect that Marivaux already had some awareness of the distinction between the *personnage* and the *personne* when he wrote his first novel. What he derived from *La Fontaine de Sapience* and the numerous immediate sources of *Le Jeu* was the kind of situation and the types of character he needed to create the synthesis that no one had yet achieved.

His achievement in *Le Jeu,* and the secret of its enduring appeal, is that he gave a definitive dramatic expression to a critical moment in the life of every person, male or female, who aspires to be a *personne,* an individual in his own right. It is a most exciting moment, because the potential individual is threatened by powerful pressures to conform to the role defined for him by his family, his class, his employer (the modern equivalent of *le roi, mon maître*). It is a more difficult moment for a Silvia than it is for a Lisette. How many potential persons, in the upper ranges of society, subside into the social security offered by conformity and let their private lives degenerate into a state of undeclared war, evading the problem of creating an authentic union between two individuals? Despite her inexperience, her impulsiveness, her need to prove to herself that her charms work, Silvia sees the essential question clearly.

As long as there are civilizations in which it is possible for a margin to exist between the *personnage* and the *personne,* a margin created by inequalities of wealth, position and social prestige, there will be an audience for *Le Jeu.* As we have seen, in the opening speech of this marvellously constructed play Marivaux underlines one essential element, Silvia's sense of individuality. In the last speech, Arlequin transposes the solution to her problem into the simplest possible terms:

> ARLEQUIN, *à Lisette.* De la joie, madame! Vous avez perdu votre rang, mais vous n'êtes pas à plaindre, puisque Arlequin vous reste.
>
> LISETTE. Belle consolation! il n'y a que toi qui gagnes à cela.

ARLEQUIN. Je n'y perds pas; avant notre connaissance, votre dot valait mieux que vous; à présent, vous valez mieux que votre dot. Allons, saute, marquis!

Thomas M. Carr (essay date 1984)

SOURCE: "Marivaux's *Jeu de l'amour et 'de la raison'*," in *Australian Journal of French Studies,* Vol. XXI, No. 1, January-April, 1984, pp. 15-25.

[*In the essay below, Carr argues that in* The Game of Love and Chance, *love and reason are not irreconcilably opposed; rather, the apparent opposition is transcended in the play's resolution.*]

At a crucial point in the third act of **Le Jeu de l'amour et du hasard,** Silvia declares that she requires a battle in Dorante between love and reason: "je veux un combat entre l'amour et la raison", a struggle her brother Mario suggests will be to the death. In fact, the work's entire action, not just the last act, can playfully be renamed *Le Jeu de l'amour et "de la raison",* and while it is possible to read Dorante's eventual proposal of marriage as the defeat of reason, in a very real sense such an evaluation must be unanced, if not reversed.

Both as a moralist and a comic writer—two sides of Marivaux's talent which converge in **Le Jeu**—reason serves as a foundation of his enterprise, and although critics of his theatre have touched on the role of reason in his comedies, their primary emphasis has usually been his treatment of love. Approaching **Le Jeu** from the opposite direction by focusing attention of Marivaux's complex notion of reason can serve to highlight his moral preoccupations underlying the play, while elucidating elements of its comic structure common to all his theatre. I will begin by examining how *raison* is treated in his journals and **La Vie de Marianne** and then go on to show how its ethical and social implications underpin **Le Jeu.**

As one element in the broad semantic field of Marivaux's psychological vocabulary, *raison* in its most authentic form is an intellectual lucidity. His most useful description, found in **L'Indigent philosophe,** uses the traditional comparison of reason to sight; it is, he says, "une excellente lunette pour connaitre la valeur des choses." As the intellect's tool for arriving at an adequate appreciation of reality, its function is to see through veneers of sham and pretence, to penetrate from appearances to reality.

This is not to say that all who lay claim to reason attain what Marivaux would consider the most accurate assessment of reality. Two extreme examples of forms of reason he judges to be self-defeating illustrate the pitfalls involved. While he professes on occasion a respect for the seventeenth-century rationalist philosophers, he has little use for *raison* as the speculative faculty which made

possible their elaborate systems. He shared his own century's distrust for "faiseurs de systèmes":

> laissez-leur entasser méthodiquement visions sur visions en raisonnant sur la nature des deux subtances, ou sur choses pareilles.

Frédéric Deloffre has pointed out that the only characters in all of Marivaux's theatre to be ridiculed without mercy are the three professional philosophers—the *philosophe* of **L'Ile de la raison,** Hortensius of **La Seconde surprise,** and Hermocrate of **Le Triomphe de l'amour.** Reason in its purest form is not so much ratiocination, mental agility, or a facility for argumentation, as it is insight, *esprit de finesse,* and intuitive critical vision; it is a quest for objectivity.

As *raison* concerns the will, acting reasonably need not involve extraordinary feats of self-control. Such tension is, in fact, often a sign that the precepts of true reason are being ignored. In **L'Indigent philosophe** there is a lament for the fate of a certain nobleman "qui passait pour un modèle de *raison,* pour un héros de fermeté d'âme, pour un sage." When the man's son died and he lost half his wealth, the strain of keeping up the pretence of calm and serenity, which his reputation seemed to require, caused his death. Rather,

> nous n'avons pas besoin d'un grand effort de l'esprit pour agir *raisonnablement*; la *raison* nous coule de source, quand nous voulons la suivre; je dis la véritable *raison.*

The false reason of both the philosopher and the self-proclaimed stoic is the product of *orgueil*—the ultimate enemy of authentic reason, and it is certainly to counteract pride, which distorts our vision, that the *lunettes* of reason are needed. This point emphasizes the moral content of Marivaux's concept of reason. Any number of partial or defective judgements of reason can be found among his characters, but reason in its highest form is an ethical vision which evaluates a person's worth as a human being, not just wealth, social position, or birth. The journals are tireless in exposing manifestations of *orgueil,* denouncing it in the name of the common humanity all share.

> Grands de ce monde . . . Ces prestiges de vanité qui vous font oublier qui vous êtes, ces prestiges se dissiperaient, et la nature soulevée, en dépit de toutes vos chimères, vous ferait sentir qu'un homme, quel qu'il soit, est votre semblable.

For Marivaux the moralist, to be most truly reasonable is to recognize one's likeness in others; this reasonableness manifests itself in action in the form of an ethic of sympathy, a generous awareness that the needs of others are like one's own:

> Ce que je voudrais *raisonnablement* qu'un autre fit pour moi, ne le fit-il point, m'enseigne ce que je dois faire pour lui.

Orgueil, which is the negation of reason, need not be confused with *fierté,* a legitimate and healthy result of the gaze of reason. *Fierté* involves a knowledge of one's own intrinsic worth; it is more concerned with self-recognition than the recognition of this worth by others. *Orgueil,* on the other hand, cares only about the opinion of others and has no scruple about appearing to have qualities which in fact it lacks:

> L'homme fier veut être intérieurement content de lui. Il suffit au glorieux d'avoir contenté les autres: c'est assez pour lui que ses actions paraissent louables. L'autre veut que les siennes le soient à ses yeux mêmes. En un mot, l'homme fier a du cœur, le glorieux n'a que l'orgueil de persuader qu'il en a. L'un a des vraies vertus dans l'âme; l'autre en joue qu'il n'a pas, et qu'il ne se soucie pas d'avoir.

In the two examples of defective reason examined above, the quest for fame, murtured by *orgueil,* makes the philosopher imagine that by manipulating ideas and concepts he will create the science for human nature, just as the desire for public recognition leads the "martyr de l'orgueil" to feign stoic self-control in the face of personal tragedy.

The ethical implications of Marivaux's concept of reason also inform his view of society. *Orgueil* and its sibling *vanité* are at the root of evil in mankind:

> Les hommes sont plus vains que méchants; mais je dis mal: ils sont tous méchants, parce qu'ils sont tous vains.

But if *vanité,* which is to a large extent the failure to appraise one's worth reasonably, is the cause of evil among men, reason itself provides a remedy by showing the need for a social order to counteract the selfishness of the individual:

> Il est vrai que nous naissons tous méchants, mais cette méchanceté, nous ne l'apportons que comme un monstre qu'il nous faut combattre; nous la connaissons pour monstre dès que nous nous assemblons, nous ne faisons pas plus tôt société que nous sommes frappés de la nécessitéqu'il y a d'observer un certain ordre qui nous mette à l'abri des effets de nos mauvaises dispositions; et la *raison,* qui nous montre cette nécessité, est le correctif de notre iniquité même.

Linking the reason of all humans, and providing the foundation of all social cohesion, there exists a "contrat de justice":

> il faut que mon prochain soit vertueux avec moi, parce qu'il sait qu'il ferait mal s'il ne l'était pas; il faut que je le sois avec lui, parce que je sais la même chose.

This law, which requires us to be just and virtuous, is understood everywhere and is everywhere the same, in contrast to "les usages particuliers des hommes", the products of human invention, which vary from nation to nation.

These particular social arrangements of any given culture, unlike the fundamental moral code, are not necessarily completely in accord with reason; in fact, they well may be "défectueux". One striking example might be "cette inégale distribution de biens", cause of the extremes of poverty and wealth in the France of his day. Happily for the body politic, social and economic inequality produces an "éblouissement de notre *raison*" in the inferiors who are blinded to the failings of their betters by the trappings of power and prestige. While Marivaux recognizes that this indulgence of the weak in regard to the shortcomings of their superiors contributes to social harmony, he would prefer an arrangement in which true reason teaches inferiors to accept their position by being aware that what separates them from their masters is not of any consequence and which teaches the privileged that they are not intrinsically more worthy than their social inferiors whom they must treat with respect and compassion. He does not advocate leveling social ranks any more than economic equality. This is the lesson of plays like **L'Ile de la raison** and **L'Ile des esclaves,** where the moral reform of both masters and servants is presented as the solution to antagonism between classes.

The relation between reason and love is not specifically treated in the journals; however, it does appear in **La Vie de Marianne** where, because of differences in position between Marianne and her suitors, there are parallels with **Le Jeu.** For example, the lecherous old *faux-dévot* M. de Climal appeals to reason in his attempt to obtain Marianne as his mistress:

> Ma fille, je vous parle *raison;* je ne fais ici auprès de vous que le personnage d'un homme de bon sens, qui voit que vous n'avez rien, et qu'il faut pourvoir aux besoins de la vie, à moins que vous ne vous déterminiez à servir.

He argues that in her penniless state the only wise course open to her is to accept his offer to lodge with a woman of his acquaintance who is very "raisonnable." If reason for Marivaux is to see reality clearly, here reality is the hard facts of poverty and lack of protection; and if to act reasonable is to adapt one's behaviour to this perception of reality, reason here dictates a cynical prudence which is concerned with the calculation of self-interest rather than with ethical principle. M. de Climal's version of reason is an ally of his love, but Marianne hesitates before both.

Later in the novel, when the young nobleman Valville falls in love with her, Marianne is calledupon to exercise another form of reason. Mme de Dorsin, one of Marianne's protectresses, who is herself characterized as "raisonnable," suggests that while it may be impossible to cure Valville of this passion, "il suffira de rendre cette passion *raisonnable*," and only Marianne can accomplish this task: "il n'y a qu'elle qui puisse lui faire entendre *raison.*" Here reason implies recognition of the differences of class which forbids a match between a girl of unknown birth and a gentleman of the quality of Valville. Marianne agrees to make him understand that she cannot return his love. This willingness, of course, only raises the esteem her protectresses have for her, and Valville's mother is moved to express reason of the highest sort in Marivaux's eyes. She realizes that only Marianne's unknown parentage and lack of twenty thousand pounds of income stand between the girl and her son's marriage: "La *raison* vous choisirait, la folie des usages vous rejette." And shortly later, upon witnessing further proof of Marianne's merit, Mme de Miran consents to the marriage.

> Je songe que Valville ne blesse point le véritable honneur, qu'il ne s'écarte que des usages établis, qu'il ne fait tort qu'à sa fortune, qu'il peut se passer d'augmenter . . . il n'y aura, dans cette occasion-ci, que les hommes et leurs coutumes de choqués: Dieu ni la *raison* ne le seront pas.

She invokes here much the same contrast between a fundamental moral code established on reason and "les usages particuliers des hommes" which Marivaux had called into doubt as "défectueux" in *Le Spectateur.* Of the two forms of reason in this episode only Mme de Dorsin's presents an obstacle to love; Marivaux does not condemn it, given his acceptance of the contemporary social hierarchy, but he shows Mme de Miran's as superior.

In the light of this interaction of love and reason in *La Vie de Marianne,* we should not expect to find an absolute opposition between the two in *Le Jeu,* as if the triumph of love depended on the utter defeat of reason. Reason, it will be seen, is a fundamental value for both Silvia and Dorante, and although both begin with the assumption that love and reason are mutually exclusive, both eventually are able to reconcile their love and their reason, although the concept holds a different content for each of them.

Silvia announces her allegiance to reason in the opening scene of the play during her discussion with Lisette of marriage. She declares that she is not searching for good looks in a husband, but reason, which she identifies with sound moral character:

> on a plus souvent affaire à l'homme *raisonnable* qu'à l'aimable homme; en un mot, je ne lui demande qu'un bon caractère. . . .

Like Marivaux the moralist, she is preoccupied with the difficulty of distinguishing essential truth about a person from outward appearances. Her first portrait is of a husband who appears reasonable to all the world, but who mistreats his entire household. Thus she proposes her disguise in order to assess better whether her proposed spouse is indeed a man of reason. In her distrust of men, especially handsome ones, she is sure that Dorante will prove as unworthy as the husbands whose portraits she drew in the first scene.

Yet, just four scenes later, this same girl who claimed to prize reason in a husband, declares that she hopes to vanquish the reason of her intended.

> Je ne serai pas fâchée de subjuger sa *raison,* de l'étourdir un peu sur la distance qu'il y aura de lui à moi.

Here reason is the awareness of social rank and obligations to caste which she hopes Dorante will sacrifice. The irony, of course, is that when Dorante finally arrives disguised as Bourguignon, not only is his reason subjected to assault, but her own as well. Both of them find themselves in a position where their "reasonable" perception of social order, where rank and personal merit should correspond, is disturbed. Dorante, struck by Silvia's obvious worth, finds it ridiculous that he wants to treat this servant girl with the respect due to the well-born:

> Enfin j'ai un penchant à te traiter avec des respects qui te feraient rire.

For her part, Silvia accuses Lisette of having lost her senses for not being able to recognize the conspicuous lack of breeding of Arlequin masquerading as his master.

> Etes-vous folle avec votre examen. Est-il nécessaire de le voir deux fois pour juger du peu de convenance?

In both of these comments, the reference to folly points to the implicit norm—reason. Silvia's distress is certainly the greater, so great in fact that her perception of what she owes herself as a member of the privileged order does not allow her to envisage the possibility of loving a servant, no matter what his personal worth. She asserts her indifference, justifying her coldness with a reference to her reason:

> Voilà mes dispositions, ma *raison* ne m'en permet point d'autres, et je devrais me dispenser de te le dire.

Only when the requirements of this notion of reason are satisfied by Dorante's revelation of his identity is the way open for her to admit to herself her love.

When she insists in the third act on a battle in Dorante between love and reason, her father attributes this desire to an "insatiable vanité d'amour-propre." Yet she is not so much motivated by the desire to satisfy her feminine vanity, as her brother insists, as by the instinctive need she feels to expose Dorante's reason to the same distress she had known. The weight of eighteenth-century social proprieties was lighter on a man than a woman; Dorante had been able to verbalize his love in the second act, while Silvia could not even acknowledge it to herself. Pushing him into a proposal of marriage will in a sense equalize their suffering, allowing them to enter marriage on more even terms and making a harmonious union more likely. Her strategy might seem self-defeating, for she refuses to give him the encouragement he seeks—an avowal of her *tendresse* for him. It is a strategy which hardly seems capable of nurturing a love strong enough to overcome his reason, but the clever nature of this tactic becomes clear at the close of her long speech stressing the precariousness of her position:

> L'aveu de mes sentiments pourrait exposer votre *raison,* et vous voyez bien aussi queje vous les cache.

This feigned generosity on her part is exactly what is needed to move Dorante. From the beginning he had been impressed by her *fierté* and her modesty—signs of a nobility of character which sharply contrasted with her servant's costume. Her pretense of concern for his reason is the ultimate proof for him of her worth; it is proof that she is guided by the ethic of sympathy described in *Le Spectateur,* and he submits.

This is not to say, as Silvia would have it, that love wins out over reason. Rather, reason for Dorante is no longer only concerned with his obligation to social rank; he passes to the most authentic level of reason in Marivaux's eyes—that which only looks at individual merit

> il n'est ni rang, ni naissance, ni fortune qui ne disparaisse devant une âme comme la tienne. J'aurai honte que mon orgueil tint encore contre toi, et mon cœur et ma main t'appartiennent.

Renouncing *orgueil,* the enemy of true reason, he accedes, like Mme de Miran, to a perception of reality shared by the finest, most chosen souls in Marivaux's universe. Love does not vanquish reason, but is fulfilled with its aid. If love had won out over Silvia's notion of reason, i.e., if concern for social obligations had been vanquished by love, the implication might not have boded well for their future happiness. After all, if Dorante forgot his duty as a bachelor, what would keep him from doing so again once married? But because he overcomes, not duty, but pride, his decision is based on solid grounds.

Thus we see that love and reason are not necessarily opposed. Thanks to love, Dorante goes beyond reason conceived as self-control and motivated by concern for social rank to a clearer ethical vision. From the outset, Dorante had been more open to this appreciation of personal merit than Silvia. If there is a single point in the play at which it might be said that love vanquishes reason in Dorante, it is II. x. when Dorante comes to grips with his feelings for Silvia. After an indirect avowal of her affection for him, he responds, "si cela est, ma *raison* est perdue." Yet if we compare what it took to bring him to this realization, as against Silvia's comparable "Je vois clair dans mon cœur," we find that, even at this point he is closer to his final emphasis on reason as awareness of personal worth. He required only two motivating elements: the recognition of Silvia's merit, followed by confirmation of her love for him; with her, a third element was necessary: the revelation of Dorante's true status. Fortunately for both of them, Marivaux has contrived a reassuring theatrical universe in which personal merit and social rank correspond.

Going beyond the rule of reason in this one play, we can note its importance in two fundamental components of his dramatic system—*marivaudage* and his comic norm. In terms of *raison, marivaudage* can be seen as the linguistic manifestation of the tension experienced by characters whose notion of what is reasonable is partial or defective. They refuse to see themselves and their situation objectively. In *Le Jeu* it is the refusal of Dorante and Silvia to recognize that they are in love with a person who appears to be out of place socially. Instead, they attempt to talk their way around their predicament without facing it directly. Eventually this circuitous approach does lead to greater insight, and once their vision had been corrected, the tension between theerroneously "reasonable" view they had been trying to maintain and reality disappears, and *marivaudage* ceases. It is no longer needed, for as we have seen "la *raison* coule de source."

This view of *marivaudage* as the process by which characters pass from unreason to reason is further illustrated by *La Seconde Surprise de l'amour,* where the interaction between love and reason is uncomplicated by the social issues found in *Le Jeu.* Both the marquise and the chevalier have recently suffered the loss of a loved one. The marquise only survives the death of her husband *"par un effort de raison,"* and the chevalier, whose beloved Angélique has chosen the convent, finds in the marquise's offer of mutual consolation a remedy against his despair: "Vous me sauvez la *raison,* mon désespoir se calme." The marquise even takes on as her personal reader a stoic "philosopher" Hortensius who preaches that reason is the supreme good to which all the passions, but especially love, must be sacrificed. However, both protagonists instinctively reject such a sweeping condemnation of sentiment for a more moderate, but no less defective version of what is reasonable. They falsely believe that in their grief they will never love again and that they can successfully substitute friendship for love. This belief is inspired less by the *raison* they invoke than by their fear of being rejected, the real cause of their inability to recognize their mutual love. The tension between this unacknowledged love and their outward protestations of friendship is gradually resolved over the course of the play in scenes II, 7, II, 9 and III, 8 where their haggling over terms such as *dédain, injure, amour,* and *amitié* exemplifies Deloffre's description of *marivaudage*: "Chez Marivaux, c'est avant tout sur le mot qu'on réplique, et non plus sur la chose. Mais chaque reprise de mots signifie différence d'interprétation, chicane, discussion, rebondissement imprévu, progression dramatique enfin." Out of this apparent quibbling over words comes their realization that their *amitié* is in fact *amour.* With the chevalier's avowal, "Mon amour pour vous durera autant que ma vie," the *marivaudage* ends. Authentic reason finally triumphs both at the personal level of their new-found insight into their feelings and on the more abstract level where it becomes clear that to attempt to renounce love forever, as the philosopher Hortensius recommends, is vanity.

Finally, just as reason serves as a standard in the ethical realm for Marivaux, it plays a role as his comic norm. In the seventeenth-century *Lettre sur l'imposteur,* which many critics take to be inspired by Molière himself, we find an interpretation of Molière's notion of the comic in which the ridiculous is defined as the contrary of reason. What the spectator perceives as ridiculous is a sensible sign of unreason in the character on stage:

> Le ridicule est donc la forme extérieure et sensible que la providence de la nature a attachée à tout ce qui est déraisonnable, pour nous en faire apercevoir, et nous obliger à le fuir.

Marivaux likewise subscribes to reason as his comic norm, and in *L'Ile de la raison* he went so far as to render the ridiculous "hyper-sensible", as it were, by making the characters shrink and grow before the audience's eyes in proportion to their adherence to reason. Such a visualization of the characters' ridiculousness, while an ingenious device, was perhaps too literal an illustration of Molière's definition of the ridiculous as "la forme extérieure et sensible" of unreason, and the play failed. Just the same, it clearly establishes reason's normative role in Marivaux's comedy.

We have seen that for Marivaux, the true enemy of love is not so much *raison* as the aberrant forms of *amour-propre* such as *orgueil* and *vanité* which invent qualities that do not exist or seek to exalt unduly those that do. *Raison* is the norm of objectivity that allows the manœuvring of *vanité* and *orgueil* to appear comic:

> Quelle misérable espèce d'orgueil . . . aussi n'est-il pas bon qu'à donner la comédie aux gens *raisonnables* qui le voient.

Thus in *Le Jeu* Silvia's somewhat vain confidence in the power of her charms is a chief source of the play's comic vitality. Rather than judge her morally, Marivaux simply manages his plot in such a way that her vanity puts her into comic situations. In the first act she undergoes the same conflict between love and reason that she wanted Dorante to experience, and when she is at the point of seeing the victory of her charms in the last act, Dorante leaves her momentarily alone on stage ready to deny the love she had acknowledged with so much difficulty in the second act. Since Silvia is *vaine* rather than *orgueilleuse,* and since her charms are real, Marivaux treats her with indulgence. However, with a character like Arlequin, who displays a haughtiness that is not merely part of his disguise, more outright ridicule is in store. The gentleness with which Marivaux treats his protagonists hinges, of course, on his realization that neither he, nor his spectators, is without vanity or even *orgueil.* In fact, one critic, sees this indulgence as the basis of a "strategy of identification" by which Marivaux's plays "appear to manipulate on-stage characters in order better to change the perspective on real life of the spectators."

The clear gaze of reason is thus for Marivaux the standard by which the various degrees of the comic are judged, much as it was for Molière. Still, there exists a great difference: while for Molière society's vision of reality was the reasonable norm, Marivaux recognizes a more authentic form of reason which goes beyond society's claims to a vision of human fraternity as the ultimate truth.

Jay L. Caplan (essay date 1991)

SOURCE: "Love on Credit: Marivaux and Law," in *Romance Quarterly,* Vol. 38, No. 3, August, 1991, pp. 289-99.

[*In the following essay, Caplan contends that the value of love in* The Game of Love and Chance *mirrors a growing belief that money has no intrinsic value but is a "pure convention, grounded in nothing more than public belief."*]

In 1716, the French regent, Phillippe d'Orléans chartered John Law's *Banque Générale* (later the *Banque Royale*), and authorized it to issue paper notes. He later placed the Scotsman at the head of the newly consolidated *Compagnie Générale des Indes,* whose notes were guaranteed by the state. The success of these measures was such that in 1720, Law became controller general of finances, and brought the bank and the stock company under his direction. After a frenzied wave of speculation in the so-called "Mississippi bubble," the entire "system" went bankrupt on July 17, 1720.

Law's system was based upon the assumption that the greater the means of payment in a society, the more prosperous that society will become—a position that has been called "Keynesian." He expressed this belief in terms of an analogy with the circulation of the blood, which had been demonstrated in 1628 by William Harvey, in his treatise *Exercitatio anatomica de motu cordis et sanguinis* ["On the Movement of the Heart and Blood in Animals"]. In a 1705 treatise entitled *Money and Trade Considered with a Proposal for Supplying the Nation with Money,* Law asserted that: "When blood does not circulate throughout the body, the body languishes; the same when money does not circulate." Law was doubtless the first influential monetary theorist to think of the economy in terms of physiology and health, and we may owe to him the habit of speaking of a "healthy" or "sick" economy. In order to get money circulating in the Scottish system, Law suggested simply printing it, on paper, while guaranteeing its value in land holdings, rather than in precious metals.

Like many of his contemporaries, Law was an "adventurer," a man who spent his life imagining various schemes in order to become rich or powerful, and yet he never seems to have made any clear distinction between the schemes that had a good chance of working and those that would need a miracle to succeed. For a number of years Law made his living as a gambler, but he was also a rational planner, or "projector." Indeed the first loans and resulting note issued by the "Banque Générale" were

---

Martin Turnell on love as an intellectual game in *Le Jeu de l'amour et du hasard*:

Marivaux's strength and weakness are most apparent in *Le Jeu de l'amour et du hasard*, which is certainly his finest play. Although love is the subject of all his plays, it is not a powerful and dangerous emotion which continually threatens the balance of society as it had done in the previous century. It is an interesting state of mind, a very superior 'game', but a game that you cannot afford to lose. His characters are continually asking themselves not simply: 'What do I feel?' but 'How should I feel in this or that situation?' In other words, the drama does not arise from a clash between two contrary feelings, but from an absence of feeling. . . . Their dissatisfaction leads them to invent artificial situations which will provide them with new and interesting feelings, will enable them to 'see what it feels like'.

Martin Turnell, "Marivaux," in Scrutiny, *Vol. XV, No. 1, December, 1947.*

---

perfectly reasonable moves, and they considerably eased the financial position of the French government. In the judgment of John Kenneth Galbraith, "Had Law stopped at this point, he would be remembered for a modest contribution to the history of banking" [Money: *Whence It Came, Where It Went,* 1975]. Of course, he did not stop there and is now remembered primarily for the panic and bankruptcy that ultimately ensued.

In fact there were two successive, and very different versions of the famous "system." Both versions called for the State-owned Company to purchase the leases on tax farms, and offer to reimburse the entire public debt by buying back its paper obligations (an offer that most *rentiers* would presumably have declined). But while the first version was to rely upon a limited note issue (of "actions rentières"), guaranteed by the land holdings of the company, in the version of the system *that was ultimately adopted* there was no limit (beyond permission of the Regent) to the right of the Banque Royale to issue notes, which were guaranteed only by stock in the Company. Edgar Faure has called the first version "the reasonable plan" ("le plan sage") and the second version, the one finally adopted, "the mad plan" ("le plan fou"). Of course, it certainly remains to be seen whether rational planning and irrational risk-taking are not really two sides of the same coin.

When *Money and Trade* was published in 1705, Law had already been in exile for ten years from Scotland, where he was condemned to death for having killed a man in a duel. Throughout his many adventures in foreign lands, Law, who was the son of a goldsmith, would steadfastly maintain his opposition to the power of gold. As late as 1720, when the System was beginning to un-

ravel, he wrote (this time, in French) that: "Il est de l'intérêt du Roi et de son peuple d'assurer la monnaie de banque et d'abolir la monnaie d'or." By injecting a transfusion of monetary "blood" into the French economic system (that is, by radically increasing the means of payment, while also cutting interest rates drastically), Law's expansionist monetary policy put a temporary end to a prolonged recession. Its long-term effects were less fortunate. According to Charles Kindleberger [in *A Financial History of Western Europe,* 1984], "A traumatic experience with paper money under John Law set back the evolution of bank notes [in France] for a century." By seeking to abolish the use of gold as money, and instead printing guaranteed paper notes (in this case, the notes of Law's bank were guaranteed—temporarily as it turned out—by the reality of the land holdings of the Company in Louisiana, and by the promise of gold that the Louisiana subsoil allegedly contained), Law's system effected a separation between money as substance and money as function. More radically, it had the effect of turning money into a form itself insubstantial, a mere *sign* of real value.

This article argues that, despite the failure of the Banque Royale on July 17, 1720 (after which France would return to the use of precious metals as money), Law's attack on gold money may be viewed as symptomatic of more systematic changes in the status and meaning of signs. In order to suggest the nature of this semiotic shift, I should like to compare *Le Jeu de l'amour et du hasard* (1730) of Marivaux (who was bankrupted by the failure of Law's system) with the play that, in Rousseau's view, most forcefully articulated the corrupt values of the *ancien régime,* Molière's *Le Misanthrope* (1666).

At the beginning of act III of *Le Misanthrope,* the two *petits marquis,* Acaste and Clitandre, argue about which of them has more reason to be satisfied with himself generally, and in particular to believe that the coquettish Célimène loves him. Acaste declares: "Mais le gens de mon air, marquis, ne sont pas faits / Pour *aimer à crédit* et faire tous les frais" (*Le Misanthrope,* III, 1).

What does Acaste mean by "aimer à crédit"? According to Furetière's *Dictionnaire universel* (1690), "crédit" refers to the measure of a person's status within a given community, as in its first definition: "Croyance, estime, qu'on s'acquiert *dans le public* par sa vertu, sa probité . . ." (emphasis added). Credit is a value that one acquires in relationship to a certain *public*; it must be openly, publicly known. It is a value that an individual or groups acquire through action in the public sphere. Although his first definition stresses moral values ("sa vertu, sa probité"), Furetière's first example ("Les Grecs se sont mis en *crédit* par leurs sciences") suggests that the meaning of credit is not limited to the moral sphere. "Crédit" refers more generally to what is publicly believed, or credited, about a person or group. In this sense, credit is the result of previous actions, but it is not itself active; it is the measure ("estime") of what a person or group is believed capable of doing. However, Furetière's second definition of "crédit" has a more active sense, which is retained in modern

French: "CRÉDIT se dit aussi de la puissance de l'autorité, des richesses qu'on acquiert par le moyen de cette réputation qu'on a acquise. Ce ministre a acquis un grand *crédit* à la cour sur l'esprit du Prince." According to this definition, credit is the publicly recognized value or reputation that a community grants a person, on the basis of his or her previous actions, and which allows that person to exert power over the other members of that same community. This sort of credit leads others to pay attention to one's opinions, or to entrust one with money or goods ("richesses"). Since it makes the past actions of a person or group even more valuable within the community, it is active, or productive credit. In both the virtual and active senses recorded by Furetière in 1690, "credit" refers to an interaction between the value or worth of an individual and the beliefs that are publicly held about that individual. Credit, in other words, is based upon an *economy of public belief.*

The third meaning recorded by Furetière locates this credit economy within a specifically commercial context. In business, credit is "ce *prest* naturel qui se fait d'argent & de marchandises, sur la réputation & solvabilité d'un négociant" (emphasis added). Credit is a loan or *prest* and is therefore something that never actually *belongs* to anyone. We may perhaps infer that not only in business, but in all forms of human commerce, credit is always borrowed, and therefore can always be recalled by the lending community. The beliefs on which one's credit is predicated are always subject to revision, as the following ominous example suggests: "Ce banquier a bon *crédit* sur la place, sa banqueroute n'a guère diminué son *crédit.*"

Returning to Acaste's words, "aimer à crédit," we note that the first meaning of "à crédit" ("without paying cash") has also survived in modern French (and English) and is also associated by Furetière with financial ruin: "On dit, Faire *crédit,* vendre *à crédit,* acheter *à crédit* pour dire, ne payer pas comptant ce qu'on achète. C'est le *crédit* que font les Marchands aux Grands Seigneurs qui ruine leur fortune, leur négoce." Like Moliere's Acaste, Furetière does not approve of this sort of credit, although not entirely for the same reasons. From his bourgeois perspective, Furetière implicitly condemns buying or selling "à crédit," since the practice works to the sole advantage of the great noblemen to whom credit is given, while condemning their creditors (such as Mr. Dimanche in Molière's *Dom Juan*) to ultimate ruin. As we shall see, the distaste of a petty court nobleman like Acaste for loving "à crédit" is not related to his desire for immediate "payment." However, Furetière suggests another relevant sense of the term. We read: "A CRÉDIT se dit souvent pour dire, A plaisir, sans utilité, sans fondement. Cet homme s'est ruiné *à crédit,* à plaisir, *sans faire de dépense qui parût*" (emphasis added). In this example, one can still hear the archaic conception of conspicuous, public expenditure ("dépense qui parût") as the measure of a noble's worth. From that perspective, it is useless ("sans utilité") to dilapidate one's resources, unless it is done publicly, in the eyes of the community whose recognition determines an individual's value. A sense of the

contemporary meanings of "crédit" and "à crédit" casts new light upon Acaste's speech, which will be quoted here at greater length:

> *Mais les gens de mon air, marquis, ne sont pas faits*
> *Pour aimer à crédit et faire tous les frais.*
> Quelque rare que soit, le mérite des belles,
> Je pense, Dieu merci, qu'*on vaut son prix* comme elles,
> Que, pour se faire honneur d'un cœur comme le mien,
> Ce n'est pas la raison qu'*il ne leur coûte rein,*
> *Et* qu'*à frais communs* se fassent les avances.
>   (*Le Misanthrope,* III, 1, 815-22; emphasis added)

The meaning of "aimer à crédit" now appears more clearly. In Acaste's social group, "loving" ("aimer") refers to a form of coded public display, and certainly not to one's feelings about another person. According to the conventions of "politeness" ("politesse"), love—like friendship—is a ritualized behavior that is conventionally performed in a certain public situation. It is elicited, not by interior states, but by specific social relations. For example, in the presence of an attractive young widow like Célimène, any gentleman who has an appropriate sense of his own worth ("[quil] vaut son prix") simply must "make love" to her, for the same reason that she must courteously allow those advances to be made. According to the constraints of this code, which would arouse Rousseau's indignation in his famously brilliant misreading of *Le Misanthrope,* a concern with *feelings* (whether one's own or those of other persons) is not only irrelevant but vulgar.

In any case, what Acaste calls "loving" is behavior elicited by an aristocratic form of self-love ("amour-propre"). This behavior is based, first of all, upon an estimation of his position (or "net worth") in a hierarchy of fixed values: rank, wealth, courage (which has become willingness to defend one's "honor" in a duel); it also depends upon an awareness of his audience, and upon the possession of various social graces, all of which are supposedly *inherited,* rather than acquired, and give effortless expressions to a nobleman's social identity. For Acaste and Clitandre, to love is to expect prompt recognition of one's socially recognized worth, and therefore to have only contempt for "loving on credit" (*aimer à crédit*). They know that a gentleman cannot court a lady without declaring his affections, without spending, not just money, but also other tokens of his love. Regardless of his true feelings, he must make considerable symbolic expenditures, to which Acaste refers ("faire tous les frais," "à frais communs," etc.) in his speech. To love costs; it requires making representations of one's love and thereby diminishing, if only temporarily, one's recognized worth. Since it entails offering tokens of love to a woman without rapid repayment in kind, loving on credit ("aimer à crédit")—that is, without the lady's quickly signifying that she loves him, too—is a risky investment for a gentleman like Acaste or Clitandre. The more one spends without being paid back, the more one's worth is visibly diminished in the eyes of one's peers. Since that necessary reevaluation cannot be postponed without a gentleman's devaluation, for him love on credit amounts to love discredited. As a matter of fact, this belief leads the two *marquis* to require from Célimène a public declaration of her preference, and this demand that will precipitate her eventual discreditation.

Louis Marin has argued [in *Le Portrait du roi,* 1981] that portraits of Louis XIV were believed to have the same value as the king himself, in precisely the same sense that the Eucharist was believed to be the body of Christ. Likewise the presence in coins of a certain quantity of precious metal guaranteed their value, and insured that a *louis d'or,* for example, was worth its weight in gold. In the patriarchal hierarchy of this society the value of persons was a treasure, immediately given in their nature. Rank, in turn, was measured by the standard of the Sun-king, just as currency was measured in silver and gold. Yet rank was always subject to rapid and unpredictable turns of fortune, to the sudden devaluation or revaluation that classical theater represented as the *coup de théâtre.*

Whereas in Molière one's worth must always be shown, publicly and theatrically displayed, in order to be effective—a situation that precludes the granting of credit, characters (at least, upper-class characters) in Marivaux refuse to take anyone, especially themselves, at face value, in terms of a public image, and consequently commit themselves to the risks and pleasures of speculation and credit. "Marivaux," whose real name was Pierre Carlet de Chamblain, lost everything in the wake of Law's bankruptcy. It is tempting, and probably not entirely fantastic, to view Marivaux's *Le Jeu de l'amour et du hasard* (1730) as an idealized representation of the experiment in credit whose dramatic failure brought on the ruin of so many speculators. It is also worth noting the biographical fact that, starting in 1698, Marivaux's father was Director of the Royal Mint at Riom, a town in Auvergne. In the ideal, or utopian form of the experiment that *Le Jeu de l'amour et du hasard* can be shown to represent (a form that most resembles the first version of Law's system), credit is granted to "instruments" that are themselves worthless, but whose face value and yield are guaranteed, if the pun can be avoided or pardoned, by Law. In that ideal form, value is no longer fixed in the hierarchical order of the *ancien régime,* but rather is *produced* through the interplay of credit and speculation. The result of this *jeu* will be a new order, based on individual performance rather than inherited social position. The upper-class code of *politesse,* in which Voltaire saw the essence of manners under the *ancien régime,* is replaced by a new code of sincerity. Whereas *politesse* implied an aristocratic subordination of the individual's true thoughts and feelings to the smooth functioning of the social group, the code of sincerity would require a constant effort to express and impose subjective truth. In a world governed by sincerity, "forms" would become synonymous with lack of real meaning, while they had previously been consubstantial with meaning. Forms, and signs in general, would ultimately be

perceived as empty or "rhetorical," irrelevant (if not fundamentally opposed) to the expression of full, interior truth. With this semiotic shift, the status of social behavior and of signs in general would become analogous to that of banknotes in Law's System: insubstantial as paper money, yet guaranteed by something as reputedly solid and reliable as land, gold, . . . or the human heart. This new code of sincerity was perhaps first articulated in France through the exquisite linguistic practice that has come to be known as *marivaudage.*

In Marivaux, love is a *speculative* activity, in several senses of the word: in the etymological sense, it requires looking at a mirror (Latin *speculum*); it entails economic planning, which the eighteenth century called "speculation"; and love is also "speculative" in a more modern sense, that of requiring a high-risk investment. To fall in love is to plan, to gamble, and to mirror (oneself). Falling in love in a Marivaux play entails taking the risk of losing, and perhaps ultimately finding oneself in a *speculum* or mirror image. His most famous play, *Le Jeu de l'amour et du hasard,* opens with a scene in which Silvia, the heroine, expresses her apprehensions about the marriage that her father has arranged for her. Like other leading ladies in Marivaux's *comédies d'amour,* Silvia believes that she and her ideals are unconventional, different from what one might expect to find in young ladies of her social position. She believes, or more precisely, she *feels* herself different from what she appears *at face value.* Behind her conventional appearance, she feels unique, singular, maybe even *originale* (that is, "odd": the word still retains a pejorative value in 1730): "Si elle osait, elle m'appelerait une originale," she says to Lisette in act I, scene 1. She senses that her values are unique, that they cannot be represented or reproduced, and therefore fears that the conventionally attractive young man her father has chosen for her, may not turn out to be her type, that he may not be *unique, like her.* Lisette paints a picture of Dorante as he appears to public opinion (the *on dit*): as an ideal match, a young man who leaves nothing to be desired. His moral qualities are summarized by the term "honnête," which abstractly designates everything that makes Dorante socially desirable; that set of moral qualities that, since the ideal of the *honnête homme* was forged in the early seventeenth century, have depended less and less upon noble birth, and more and more upon that curious form of cultural capital that the English call "breeding." Physically Dorante is *bien fait, de bonne mine,* in short *aimable.* In fact, Lisette adds, no young lady would think twice about marrying this young man: for not only is he attractive ("Aimable, bien fait, voilà de quoi vivre pour l'amour"), but he has all the requisite social graces ("sociable et spirituel, voilà pour l'entretien de la société" (I, 1).) However, Silvia is more concerned with inner worth, or character than she is with appearances, and she is particularly worried about the habit men seem to have of putting on a public face that is very different from their real selves.

It will turn out, of course, that Dorante has the same apprehensions about Silvia, and the same sense of his own uniqueness. In order to negotiate this discrepancy between face value and real worth, between public facade and domestic reality, Silvia and Dorante independently devise (spontaneously, they think) a theatrical strategy as unique (or as conventional) as themselves: with the complicity of Silvia's family and servants, each will trade roles with his or her servant, in order better to observe the other party, before making any rash commitments. Not only does the perfect symmetry of their desires, duplicated by the apparently symmetrical desires of the chamber maid and valet, underline that Silvia and Dorante are meant for each other; but the subsequent interplay of identities leaves Silvia and Dorante apparently defenseless against a development that they fear even more than marriage: love.

Yet that vulnerability may only be apparent. Since neither imagines that the other could remotely resemble her or him, each appears momentarily to take the other at face value, as the valet Arlequin and the chamber maid Lisette respectively, that is, as beings so clearly unlike their masters, so obviously unworthy of their love, that they need not be feared, either. For a moment, Silvia and Dorante appear, to the audience and even to themselves, to have suspended their prejudices against both love and the servant class, long enough for the damage to be done. It remains to be seen however, whether that typical, fatal moment in Marivaux, when the protagonists first lay eyes upon each other, and love is born, whether this is a moment of vulnerability, or of mirroring "speculation." A moment, that is, when each character sees him- or herself in the other, when he or she sees in the other the mirror image of a superior being, who will not take others at face value. Only the servants can really believe that the person with whom they have fallen in love and who has fallen in love with them, is the master or the mistress, and capable of taking her or him for their equal. Precisely because they credit appearances, the servants have no apprehensions about love and marriage either. In that speculative moment, that moment of reciprocal mirroring of one's ideal self, Silvia and Dorante have the impression (that the audience may share) of putting themselves (their ego) at risk: of *speculating,* in another sense. But it is really *speculation without risk*; the masters never have anything to lose (or the servants anything to gain), because the value they will have at the end of the *Jeu*— their *redemption value,* so to speak—is guaranteed (by their fathers, as we shall see). Thus Silvia's brother Mario argues against letting his sister know that Dorante will also be disguised as his servant, because Mario is confident that the two of them will sense what they are worth anyhow: "Voyons si leur cœur ne les avertiraient pas de ce qu'ils valent" (I, 4). A few moments later, the protagonists find themselves alone together for the first time, each pretending to be a servant, and the first thing that the false Arlequin says to the false Lisette is: "[T]a maîtresse te vaut-elle?" (I, 7). The question already contains its own answer: No, the "mistress" is not worth as much as the false Lisette; no, neither of them should be taken at face value. The question already implies what Dorante feels in his heart but does not yet consciously know: namely, that this chamber maid is really worth

more than her mistress, because she really *is* the mistress.

From this speculative moment on, the *Jeu* plays itself out in symmetrical patterns, visibly, in a stylized Italianate performance style, as if to underscore the resemblance of the players to pieces on a game board, as they mirror each other's moves through various stages of amorous development, until a conclusion that was inevitable even before the first exchange of glances. But if the *Jeu* is a game, the ground rules of the game were not written by the young lovers, even though they lay claim to this privilege at the outset of the play. Before the action of the play began, the rules of the game were laid down by M. Orgon and Dorante's (unnamed) father, when they arranged the marriage betwen Silvia and Dorante. But since they are liberal fathers, they have the goodness of heart to allow their children the freedom to choose a partner for themselves. ("[I]l faut être un peu trop bon pour l'être assez," remarks M. Orgon in I, 2.) Of course, their children immediately, spontaneously choose the same person that their fathers had intended for them. In contrast, young lovers in Molière always find themselves in conflict with male authority figures, whether fathers (Argan, the Orgon of *Tartuffe,* et al.) or a guardian like Arnolphe, who always want to marry the poor girl to someone (like themselves) that she is not suited for (because he is too old, too vulgar or both), whom she could not possibly love. In a curious way, as this stock figure of the father who conventionally opposes his children's desires is transformed into a father with a heart of gold, who has only his child's interest at heart, the audience now can notice that even his name ("Orgon") had gold (*or*) in it. Although the name of the father had lost its face value through usage, in Marivaux the play of speculation reinvests "Orgon" with gold, and thereby reaffirms the paternal gold standard.

In Marivaux the obstacle, but also the means, to the realization of the father's desire (the Father's Law) is not another, more appropriate man, but love itself: "love," that is, a determinate form of speculation. In the *Jeu* the well-born heroine does not require any help from the servants to overcome her father's tyrannical desire, since her father is enlightened and good, since he and she ultimately desire the same thing. The strategic objective of the game is to ratify the father's judgment (the "gold standard," speaking anachronistically), to teach the daughter (and the audience) that father (even Marivaux's father, the Director of the Royal Mint) knows best.

In its speculative form then, love is less an obstacle to realization of the father's desire than the ideal means of fulfilling it. As a speculative investment, love is ideal in Marivaux, since it guarantees that everyone (at least everyone "upstairs") will make a profit. M. Orgon gains a worthy son-in-law, while enjoying what for Mario is the sadistic pleasure of staging the *Jeu* ("Je veux me trouver au début et les agacer tous deux," says Mario in I, 4). Silvia and Dorante will not only gain each other, but by overcoming their prejudices they will *prove* themselves worthy of their fathers and transform their trial (*épreuve*) into retrospective pleasure. "Peut-être," suggests Mario, "que Dorante prendra du goût pour ma sœur, toute soubrette qu'elle sera, et cela serait charmant pour elle" (I, 4). Mario does not mean to suggest that his sister will enjoy believing that she has fallen in love with a servant, but that when she learns the truth she will find her error quite *charmant*. At the end of the play, Silvia will look back at herself, and in a final speculative gesture, she will savor the nobility of her real character, of the self that she has revealed to herself.

Dorante, too, has a final moment to discover himself in the speculative mirror. In the very last scene, after having finally become conscious of Silvia's true identity, he exclaims: "[C]e qui m'enchante le plus, ce sont les preuves que je vous ai données de ma tendresse" (V, 9). At the end of the play then, what Dorante finds most delightful is not the girl he loves but the "proof," the image of an ideal self, that he has produced by overcoming social prejudice and proposing marriage to a chamber maid.

For Silvia and Dorante the yield on this speculative investment in love, this *"jeu de l'amour et du hasard,"* is high self-esteem, based on a knowledge of their personal worth that they could only feel or "credit" at the beginning of the play, but which now has acquired full-blown, objective reality. Their initial gesture of investor confidence in speculation has paid off, in self-esteem and pleasure. That is, their initial sense of each other's worth ("de ce qu'ils valent") has now been confirmed by their own *performance,* in all senses of the word, and retrospectively it has been a delightful experience.

Of course the experience, or experiment, was also meant to be "charmant" (and profitable as well) for Mario and his father, the masters of ceremonies. It would perhaps be more accurate to speak of them as the laboratory assistants in a "test" (*épreuve*) called **Le Jeu de l'amour et du hasard,** that they perform for an audience that, like M. Orgon, liked to think of itself as fundamentally good and liberal in the classical sense. The audience was also meant to know the pleasure of seeing an idealized image of itself, of viewing liberal humanity on stage. The importance of these tests or *épreuves* in Marivaux has led critics to emphasize the "scientific" dimension of his theater, its way of constituting the audience as a detached observer of the human heart. But like Silvia and Dorante, the audience sees only its ideal self in the experiment, the intellectual and sentimental *preuves* of its worth.

In this play, value appears in two forms: the real or ideal form, that is, the form in which it appears to the masters, and the illusory, potentially catastrophic form in which it appears to the servants. In the form presented as real or ideal, value is no longer a treasure, determined or guaranteed by the reality of its public representation; it depends instead upon a reality that is hidden from public view (e.g., money depends on land holdings, personal worth on the "heart," etc.). And whereas value in the *ancien régime* depended upon a systematic dilapidation

of resources whose emblem was the Sun, in the utopian economic order of the *Jeu,* the granting of credit ensures a play of speculation, in which the face value at risk is not only realized at the end, but increased. In this theatrical facsimile of Law's system, planning and gambling work together toward the same end.

Servants, however, do not see things this way, and they do not profit from the *Jeu* in the same way, either. Arlequin and Lisette actually believe in the *credibility* of their disguises and that they really can increase their value in a spectacular way, by marrying the master or mistress. For them, the paper is real. Unlike their masters, they *believe* in the bourgeois values of love and marriage. For Lisette and Arlequin, it is as if nothing, no regulation or law, determined their value, or that of paper money, nothing except the willingness of investors to credit it. For them it is as if the paternal gold standard—all the implicit paternal controls over money, persons, language, and love—had magically been abolished, simply by trading roles with their masters. Yet the symmetry between masters and servants is only apparent: for at the end of the play Lisette and Arlequin are worth no more than they were at the beginning. Speculation and *marivaudage* do not concern them, although their labors do make these higher activities possible. Love on credit does not work to the servants' advantage.

Despite the existence of this double standard, both masters and servants in Marivaux repudiate the value of appearances; they all refuse to credit face value or "forms." Either they believe, like the masters, that value is guaranteed by something more substantial than forms or they believe that it is a pure convention, grounded in nothing more than public belief. In Marivaux's play, all of the characters willingly commit themselves to a credit economy that could have been prescribed by Law. Whereas lovers in *Le Misanthrope*—not just Acaste and Clitandre, but also Alceste and Célimène, Philinte and Eliante—refuse to credit anything beyond appearances, and therefore remain alone at the end, in love with their own images. In the credit economy of **Le Jeu de l'amour et du hasard,** love and chance are allowed to interact through speculation, that combination of self-mirroring, planning, and gambling without risk. Thanks to this speculative investment, Silvia and Dorante are saved from emotional bankruptcy.

FURTHER READING

Brereton, Geoffrey. "Marivaux." In *French Comic Drama from the Sixteenth to the Eighteenth Century,* pp. 194-213. London: Methuen & Co., 1977.
   A survey of Marivaux's dramatic works that stresses their depiction of love and the playwright's feminism.

Culpin, D. J. "Marivaux's Apology for Religion." *French Studies* XXXIX, No. 1 (January 1985): 31-42.

Explores Marivaux's religious beliefs as expressed in his works. Culpin argues: "Consciously [Marivaux] was clinging to the faith which around him was disintegrating, but unconsciously he was part of the process which was undermining orthodoxy and substituting natural for revealed religion."

————. *Marivaux and Reason: A Study in Early Enlightenment Thought.* New York: Peter Lang, 1993, 152 p.

Defends Marivaux against charges that his work is intellectually superficial.

Haac, Oscar A. "Marivaux and the *Honnête Homme.*" *The Romanic Review* L, No. 3 (October 1959): 255-67.

Examines Marivaux's use of the term *honnête,* which takes on various meanings, from politeness to "true merit" and becomes imbued with moral and religious significance.

————. "Paradox and Levels of Understanding in Marivaux." *Studies on Voltaire and the Eighteenth Century* CVI (1973): 693-706.

Investigates Marivaux's use of paradox, which, Haac claims, is fundamental to his style, and which "involves a more complex understanding, a more intellectual humour, and a new form of realism."

Howells, Robin. "Structure and Meaning in the *Incipit* of Marivaux's Comedies." *The Modern Language Review* 86, No. 4 (October 1991): 839-51.

Maintains that "a consistent structure and meaning can be identified" in the openings of Marivaux's comedies.

Jamieson, Ruth Kirby. *Marivaux: A Study in Sensibility.* Morningside Heights, N. Y.: King's Crown Press, 1941, 202 p.

Full-length study focusing on Marivaux's depiction of emotional states in his plays.

Papadopoulou, Valentini. "Games People Play in Marivaux's Theatre." *Romance Languages Annual* (1989): 292-99.

Psychological reading of Marivaux's plays that interprets them in terms of Eric Berne's theories of Transactional Analysis.

Poe, George. *The Rococo and Eighteenth-Century French Literature: A Study through Marivaux's Theater.* New York: Peter Lang, 1987.

Likens Marivaux's style to that of rococo in art. Poe asserts: "Visual artists of the rococo period added accessory and ornamental touches to their work, thereby modifying expressional presentation in pleasant and surprising manners all while leaving essence intact. Marivaux did the same in his literary medium."

Poulet, Georges. "Marivaux." In his *The Interior Distance,* translated by Elliott Coleman, pp. 3-28. Baltimore: The Johns Hopkins Press, 1959.

Interprets Marivaux's works as expressions of existential doubt and vacancy.

Tilley, Arthur. "Marivaux." In his *Three French Dramatists: Racine, Marivaux, Musset,* pp. 78-136. New York: Russell & Russell, 1933.

Contends that Marivaux's plays have considerable psychological depth. "The psychological analysis of growing love is the soul of his drama," Tilley declares.

Trapnell, William H. *Eavesdropping in Marivaux.* Geneva: Librairie Droz, 1987, 120 p.

Examines incidents of eavesdropping throughout Marivaux's body of work, finding representations of this situation characteristic of the author.

Additional coverage of Marivaux's life and career is contained in the following source published by Gale Research: *Literature Criticism from 1400 to 1800,* **Vol. 4.**

Peter Shaffer
1926-

(Also collaborated with Anthony Shaffer under joint pseudonym Peter Antony)

INTRODUCTION

Shaffer is a British playwright who has earned a reputation as a preeminent craftsman in several theatrical genres, including psychological drama, historical drama, domestic tragedy, and comedy. He has gained critical and popular acclaim for *Equus, Amadeus,* and other plays which explore themes of idolatry, conflicts between passionate and rational impulses, and the quest for immortality. Shaffer is by his own admission "fascinated by the endless ambiguity of the human situation," and his work is marked by the psychological intricacy of his characterizations.

BIOGRAPHICAL INFORMATION

Shaffer was born in 1926 in Liverpool to Jack and Reka Shaffer, just moments after his twin brother Anthony. In 1936 the family moved to London, where Shaffer attended St. Paul's School. At St. Paul's Shaffer studied piano, giving him a musical background which was integral in the development of *Amadeus.* Between 1944 and 1947 Shaffer worked as a coal miner before enrolling at Trinity College, Cambridge. There, he and his brother co-edited the literary journal *Granta.* Soon after graduation in 1950 Shaffer moved to New York City for four years. Living near New York's theater district afforded Shaffer the opportunity to attend numerous Broadway performances and to learn about American audiences. The difference between English and American audiences would manifest itself later in his career; Shaffer developed a passion for revising, especially when transferring a production overseas. In 1954, after working at a bookstore and the New York Public Library, Shaffer returned to London. There, he worked for a music publisher, served as a literary critic for *Truth* magazine and subsequently as a music critic for *Time and Tide.* After receiving favorable reviews for his television plays *The Salt Land* and *Balance of Terror*, Shaffer decided to pursue his career as a playwright.

MAJOR WORKS

Shaffer's most successful dramas are based in myth and explore the psychological motivations of his characters. His innovative use of masks, music, and dance illuminates thematic concerns, and his conflicts are developed through

characters who function as dramatic foils. His 1964 work, *The Royal Hunt of the Sun,* reenacts the sixteenth-century conquest of Atahualpa's Inca empire by Spanish conquistador Francisco Pizarro. The play focuses on the debased qualities of both characters and the relationship that evolves between them. The psychological drama *Equus,* for which Shaffer received the Antoinette Perry (Tony) Award and the New York Drama Critics Circle Award in 1975, explores the spiritually based motivations of a stable boy who is institutionalized after blinding six horses that he believes are deities. The boy's disillusioned psychiatrist faces his own personal conflict when he questions whether the boy's treatment will strip him of a rare and precious spiritual passion, thus relegating him to a mundane existence. Shaffer's exploration of the human psyche culminates in *Amadeus,* a drama of jealousy and revenge which he has described as "a fantasia on events in Mozart's life." In this play, a successful court composer of moderate ability contemplates with bitter irony why his pious devotion to God has been ignored while the vulgar, self-centered Mozart is blessed with genius. Realizing that God chose to reward him by allowing him to recognize the power of Mozart's genius, the composer takes his ultimate revenge on God and humanity by poisoning his rival. *Amadeus*

won a Tony Award in 1981. Shaffer turned to the genre
of farce with *Lettice and Lovage,* a play which addresses
the decline of modern civilization as symbolized by post-
industrial English architecture. In 1987 *Lettice and Lovage*
was awarded the Evening Standard Drama Award as play
of the year. Shaffer followed this with *Gift of the Gorgon,*
a three-act play examining the conflict between passion
and rationality. Shaffer has also written many screenplays,
including the film adaptation of William Golding's novel
Lord of the Flies, as well as the screen versions of his
own *Equus* and *Amadeus.* This last won an Academy
Award for Best Picture and Shaffer received the Best
Screenplay Adaptation Oscar.

CRITICAL RECEPTION

The use of bold visual emblems—such as the great medallion that transforms into a golden sun in *The Royal Hunt
of the Sun*—as well as elements such as music, dance,
ritual, and mime, is characteristic of Shaffer's dramaturgy,
and critics have often focused on the plays' fusion of such
overtly theatrical devices with realism. *Equus,* for example, mixes naturalistic dialogue and characterization with
a highly abstract presentation of the horses. Shaffer's plays
have also been praised for their brilliant rhetoric and complex characterizations, though his plots have sometimes
been censured as forced and contrived. The subjects of
Shaffer's plays have often stirred debate. Some critics have
charged that *Equus* is little more than a case study in
abnormal psychology; similarly, some reviewers have argued that Shaffer's depiction of Mozart in *Amadeus* as
childish and crude undercuts his effort to examine the
nature of genius. Such criticisms notwithstanding, Shaffer's plays continue to challenge, intrigue, and move audiences and reviewers alike.

PRINCIPAL WORKS

PLAYS

Five Finger Exercise 1958
"The Private Ear" 1962
"The Public Eye" 1962
The Merry Roosters Panto [with Stanley Myers and Steven
    Vinaver] 1963; revised as *It's About Cinderella* 1969
*The Royal Hunt of the Sun: A Play Concerning the Con-
    quest of Peru* 1964
"Black Comedy" 1965
A Warning Game 1967
"White Lies" 1967; revised as "The White Liars," 1968;
    revised again as "White Liars," 1976
The Battle of Shrivings 1970; revised as *Shrivings,* 1974
Equus 1973
Amadeus 1979
Black Mischief 1983
Yonadab: The Watcher 1985

Lettice and Lovage 1987; revised as *Lettice & Lovage,*
    1990
Gift of the Gorgon 1992

RADIO PLAYS

Alexander the Corrector 1946
The Prodigal Father 1957
Whom Do I Have the Honour of Addressing? 1989

TELEVISION PLAYS

The Salt Land 1955
Balance of Terror 1957

SCREENPLAYS

Lord of the Flies [with Peter Brook] 1963
The Pad (And How to Use It) [adaptation of "The Private
    Ear"] 1966
The Public Eye (Follow Me!) 1972
Equus 1977
Amadeus 1984

OTHER MAJOR WORKS

Woman in the Wardrobe [with brother Anthony Shaffer
    under the joint pseudonym Peter Antony] (novel) 1951
How Doth the Little Crocodile? [with Anthony Shaffer as
    Peter Antony] (novel) 1952
Withered Murder [with Anthony Shaffer] (novel) 1955

OVERVIEWS AND GENERAL STUDIES

C. J. Gianakaris (essay date 1991)

SOURCE: "The Artistic Trajectory of Peter Shaffer," in
Peter Shaffer: A Casebook, edited by C. J. Gianakaris,
Garland Publishing, Inc., 1991, pp. 3-23.

[*In the essay below, Gianakaris traces Shaffer's artistic
development throughout his plays, focusing on his "masterful merging of the literalism of realism with the provocative of the abstract pictorial."*]

British playwright Peter Shaffer remains a puzzle today,
particularly for critics and academic scholars. A "moving target" with respect to dramatic styles and thematic
interests, he is difficult to categorize within tidy literary
designations. Is he primarily a realist probing the psychological and social issues facing the modern age? Is he
a somber metaphysician seeking answers to universal

enigmas? Or is he a teasing farceur who targets mundane human follies? Regular theatergoers will recognize elements of all these types in Shaffer. Within the variety of styles evidenced in his many plays, however, stand key technical and conceptual loci which support his work as a whole, no matter what the veneer of the drama.

Those center points—essentially naturalistic in nature—will be taken up later in this discussion. But the puzzle of Peter Shaffer extends beyond mere technique or subject matter. In a larger frame of reference, there is difficulty in isolating the theoretical audience for whom he writes. Shaffer embodies that rare species of writer whose career straddles the worlds both of popular and "serious" drama. Impressive success on commercial stages has brought him enormous worldwide recognition, ready financial backing, and eagerness of top theater artists to work with him. *The Battle of Shrivings* (1970) alone of his dozen plays has failed to win an audience. *Yonadab* (1985), only a modest success, nonetheless ran for a year in repertory at the British National Theatre. All the rest of his works have received strong acclaim whenever they are performed. By most standards, Shaffer enjoys exceptional popularity on world stages and has earned his stature as one of our foremost writers.

Yet by no means does Shaffer pander to mass tastes to gain general audience following. Quite the contrary; his works involve intellectually demanding themes and innovative theatrical staging. Typically, at the center of his plays stands a questioning—or questing—protagonist, obsessed with discerning mankind's true metaphysical status. Shaffer's best known dramas—*The Royal Hunt of the Sun, Equus, Amadeus,* and *Yonadab*—feature heroes such as Pizarro, Dysart, Salieri, and Yonadab who probe their respective universes for answers to philosophical and theological puzzles. Eventually, each protagonist moves toward knowledge of God. At the same time, the hero seeks to discover how far man might assume the powers of God and *become* God—if indeed He exists. More than a hint of Promethian and Faustian hungers exist in his protagonists. Shaffer's underlying thrust in his major dramas resembles that found in ancient classical drama: to define the relationship of mortal man to immortal deity. Simultaneously, Shaffer's dramatic universe infers values mirroring today's God-is-dead intellectual system, thereby allying Shaffer with the existential world view as well. Small wonder that academics find it dicey to pigeonhole Shaffer as a proponent of a single vision. In his wide-ranging and eclectic thinking, he has few peers today, most of whom focus on psychological or social problems.

Nothing in Shaffer's family background mandated a career in the arts. Born in Liverpool on 15 May 1926, Peter Levin Shaffer and his identical twin brother Anthony grew up in a middle-class Jewish household. Jack Shaffer, a property company director, moved his wife Reka and the family to London in 1936. But with the start of the second world war, they moved frequently to evade the German bombers. Despite the ongoing war, Peter and Anthony attended prestigious St. Paul's School

beginning in 1942. Both twins were accepted by Trinity College at Cambridge University; but satisfying their service obligations came first. In their case, they served as Bevin Boys, youths who dug coal in the mines of Kent. In 1947 both Shaffers enrolled in Trinity College where they jointly edited the college paper.

Peter Shaffer came down from Cambridge in 1950 with a specialty in history but no definite career plans. Initially he tried his hand at various jobs until 1951 when he traveled to New York City. There, he worked for a book dealer, retail stores, and the New York Public Library. Shaffer later remarked that this period of his life was bleak and frustrating. But one positive outcome was his frequenting New York theaters. As a result of seeing so much theater, he felt encouraged to try writing plays, his first being *The Salt Land.* Work in the business world provided him little satisfaction, and he returned to London in 1954 to work at a large music publishing house. While holding that position, Shaffer found his initial success in the realm of drama, when *The Salt Land* was telecast over ITV. Paradoxically, during this same period he also was establishing a reputation as a writer of fiction. He published three mystery novels in London and in the United States: *The Woman in the Wardrobe* (1951), *How Doth the Little Crocodile?* (1952), and *Withered Murder* (1955)—the latter two co-authored with his brother Anthony (the Tony-winning writer of *Sleuth*). In 1957, Shaffer had two more broadcast dramas aired—the unpublished radio play *The Prodigal Father* over BBC Radio and *Balance of Terror* (also unpublished) over BBC Television. Once his plays caught on, Shaffer never looked backward. Thereafter, he devoted his entire energies to the theater.

Shaffer's earliest full-length dramas, *Five Finger Exercise* (1958) and *The Royal Hunt of the Sun* (1964), immediately drew applause from critics who recognized a strong new voice in the theater. Awards came swiftly, initially in England and later in the United States, to confirm the importance of his writing to the modern stage. Later, *Equus* (1973) and *Amadeus* (1979) thoroughly won over audiences, earning both critical and popular applause. Both pieces became smash hits on Broadway, and each won a Tony Award as best drama. More recently, *Lettice & Lovage* (1987) received four Tony nominations, including one for best play. (Eventually the comedy won Tonys for Maggie Smith and Margaret Tyzack.) Thus, to this point Shaffer has established an enviable record of successes both commercially and critically.

Nor are Shaffer's plays solely popular on live stages. Movies have been made of nearly all his works to date. Here, the results are very mixed, however. Shaffer far prefers the stage medium to the screen, and readily admits the films of his works to be uneven. Interestingly, the factors that led to success or failure in transferring his plays to the screen—particularly the theatricality of his unique realism—also shed light on the nature of Shaffer's works themselves. Such a topic deserves separate consideration, and only a few points will be touched on here. But one unavoidable conclusion is that his plays, which are "exuberantly and unashamedly theatrical," have proven difficult to reconceive for the large screen. Not surprisingly, the film director's task is easier with those works built on more conventional realism. One example may suffice. An interesting yet ultimately disappointing film of *Five Finger Exercise* was made in 1962. Despite an impressive cast (including Rosalind Russell, Maximilian Schell, and Jack Hawkins) the movie version never attains the psychological richness of the original stage production. However, because of the play's original naturalistic premises, the characterizations of the five principals, along with their fully delineated motivations, translate readily to a movie format.

Just how well *Five Finger Exercise* made the transformation to film—relatively speaking—becomes evident when considering Shaffer's dramas that move beyond realism in their original conception. A disastrous film adaptation of *Royal Hunt* (starring Christopher Plummer and Robert Shaw) followed in 1969, for instance. After viewing the hugely distorted movie made of his noble quest drama, Shaffer knew he no longer could entrust his plays to screen writers. Thereafter, he wrote the film scripts himself for *The Public Eye* (1972), *Equus* (1977), and *Amadeus* (1984). Considering how theater-oriented his pieces are in format and spirit, it is surprising that the movie versions fared as well as they did. There is proof that outstanding results are possible when the play transferences are achieved with imagination and flexibility. An example is Milos Forman's film of *Amadeus* which accumulated eight Academy Awards including Best Film of 1984 and Best Film Adaptation for Shaffer's movie script. Previously, Shaffer received an Oscar nomination for his film script of *Equus*—a movie whose graphic simulations during the horse-blinding scenes fatally compromised it at the box office. As with *Royal Hunt,* the stage script for *Equus* prohibits its being reshaped for film in a literal fashion—a fact the director of the movie, Sidney Lumet, learned at a high price, according to Shaffer. On the more recent front, plans for a movie version of *Lettice & Lovage* are in the works, suggesting that the playwright remains open-minded about filmic versions of his works despite disappointments in the past. Additionally, unlike earlier statements denigrating movies, in a recent interview Shaffer hinted that he might revise *Whom Do I Have the Honour of Addressing?* as a film. He even acknowledges that his most recent radio piece might also be an ideal candidate for a television play. The entire screen issue then remains open where Shaffer is concerned.

But to return to Shaffer's stage dramas, we need to delineate more closely the appeal of his ideas and techniques. Unlike the opaque conundrums underlying plays by certain other twentieth-century theater experimenters (Beckett and Pinter come to mind), Shaffer's dramas have remained accessible to the theater-going public. This fact tends to devalue his plays for politically oriented theorists who esteem a work according to its bewildering effect on audiences. For such detractors, to be "popular" with playgoers becomes an indictment of a play's worthiness. Only the puzzling, uncommercial, radical avant-

garde retains merit for zealots like Brustein and Simon, accounting for their long and active distaste for Shaffer.

Just as his success bridging artistic and popular values elicits mixed reactions, Shaffer evokes ambiguous response and controversy on dramaturgical grounds. If pressed to describe Shaffer's primary writing tools, however, most critics acknowledge the centrality of psychological naturalism. Conventional realism characterizes much of Shaffer's early work, including *Five Finger Exercise,* the one-act comedies, and the ill-fated *Battle of Shrivings* (1970, later rewritten as *Shrivings,* 1974). Although Shaffer temporarily returned to realism with *Lettice & Lovage* (1987) and the radio play *Whom Do I Have the Honour of Addressing?* (1989), naturalism never has been the playwright's favored dramatic approach. The initial draft for *The Royal Hunt of the Sun* already existed when the naturalistic *Five Finger Exercise* launched his career in 1958. His true inclinations lay in "big, sweeping theatre," as he explained to the interviewer D. Zerdin on BBC's "Profile" (11 September 1979). Shaffer elaborates in his Introduction to *The Collected Plays of Peter Shaffer* (New York: Harmony Books, 1982) that the times were not right for the unusual mannerisms of *Royal Hunt*. The tidal wave of realism during the 1950's, he declares, dictated that his early works follow standard conventions: "I became a playwright finally to be part of the grandiloquent and showy world of imaginative reality. It took me some time to acknowledge this to myself. The times, after all, scarcely favored such an ambition. The mid-1950s did not constitute a time when one could admit, with much chance of being sympathetically heard, a purpose to write about gods and grand aspirations, orators and ecstatics. It was a surging time for England, but the cry tended to be for social realism."

Shaffer recognizes the value of representationalism, however. With this first success, he established his ability to write masterfully in the realistic mode. Shaffer states, "On balance, I feel I did crafted work in my first piece. It said what I wanted it to say, and it possessed a shape which made it play easily and finally accumulated its power." Shaffer's next plays—*Shrivings* and the one-act comedies **"The Private Ear," "The Public Eye," "White Lies,"** and **"Black Comedy"**—retained a realistic bias, thereby consolidating popularity with theater audiences. But careful observers of the stage understand that realism alone does not win audience support. His endeavors with realism permitted Shaffer to hone his talent for penetrating dialogue. The occasional intrusion of turgid prose and excessive sentimentality in *Five Finger Exercise* and in *Royal Hunt* largely was refined away in the crucible of this early period. Shaffer thus worked at and mastered dramatic realism with these works. Yet, good as these pieces played on stage, they did not satisfy what Peter Shaffer ultimately intended to achieve. *Five Finger Exercise* proved a valuable base from which he later could launch into more innovative theatrical enterprises.

Most crucial to Shaffer's dramatic style are the imaginative risks exhibited in his masterpieces. *The Royal Hunt of the Sun* (1964), *Equus* (1973), *Amadeus* (1979), and even the revised *Yonadab* (1985) all exhibit the daring theatrical techniques that make up the playwright's imprimatur. What makes the techniques fresh is his brilliant fusion of presentational narrative modes with traditional realism. The four dramas noted convey their respective stories through a system of narrative frameworks. At the outermost perimeter stand the plays' chorus-like narrators serving as moderators or masters of ceremony. Old Martin, Doctor Dysart, Salieri, and Yonadab address the audience from their posts, first as outside observers of the respective story lines; later, they will blend into the inner plot line as active participants. Though not entirely objective, each moderator as watcher enjoys a unique perspective that instantly engages the attention, interest, and curiosity of playgoers, drawing them into the action.

Illustrations from the plays will help. Old Martin, Pizarro's young aide in *Royal Hunt,* quickly gains audience interest when addressing them directly with his opening lines to the play:

> Save you all. My name is Martin. I'm a soldier of Spain and that's it. Most of my life I've spent fighting for land, treasure, and the cross. I'm worth millions. Soon I'll be dead, and they'll bury me out here in Peru, the land I helped ruin as a boy. This story is about ruin. Ruin and gold. . . . I'm going to tell you how one hundred and sixty-seven men conquered an empire of twenty-four million.

Following his tantalizing come-on, Martin conjures flashback scenes through which Pizarro and other characters are introduced.

Parallel opening scenes mark all of Shaffer's finest dramas, whereby a narrator entices the audience into the world of the play. Dr. Dysart in the opening lines from *Equus* speaks directly to the audience while gesturing behind him at a youth, Alan Strang, nuzzling a horse standing next to him. The puzzling tableau is further heightened by the psychiatrist's cryptic words:

> With one particular horse, called Nugget, he embraces. The animal digs its sweaty brow into his cheek, and they stand in the dark for an hour—like a necking couple. And of all the nonsensical things—I keep thinking about the *horse!*

Amadeus opens similarly with a non-realistic invocation. Following an "overture" comprised of stichomythic exposition whispered by two chorus figures, Salieri turns directly to the audience. He then entices his playgoers with an irresistible summons:

> *Vi Saluto! Ombri del Futuro! Antonio Salieri—a vostro servizio!* . . . I can almost see you in your ranks—waiting for your turn to live. Ghosts of the Future! Be visible. I beg you. Be visible. Come to this dusty old room—this time, the smallest hours of dark November, eighteen hundred and twenty-three— and be my Confessors!

Shaffer seems satisfied with the general template laid out here, for he turns again to its use in his most recent serious work, *Yonadab* (1985, heavily revised in 1987). Once he greets the audience at the start of *Yonadab,* the title protagonist begins to spin his web of enticing intrigue:

> This is a singularly unpleasant story. The Rabbis of the Middle Ages omitted it entirely, when they read out the scriptures, to spare the ears of their congregations—and they didn't know the half of it. I alone know it all—and, let me assure you, I don't intend to spare yours.

In the four major plays, once having introduced himself and the general subject of the play, the narrator moves into the play circuitry where he assumes an active role in the enacted scenes of the story. At irregular intervals, the narrator breaks the illusion to comment often to the spectators about the scenic actions. Such "breaks" in the story line allow for clarifying commentary on the plot, just as the omniscient observer in fiction uses stop-action to offer all-knowing remarks on the proceedings. But beyond that useful advantage, the narrator's "interruption" of the tale privileges him to fast-forward to later episodes in the story at will. The narrators—Martin, Dysart, Salieri, and Yonadab—become our guides as we traverse the actions of the plot, moving us faster or slower, directing our attention from one character to another, or from one detail to a second one.

Shaffer did not originate the narrator figure, of course. Witness Shakespeare's Richard the Second and Iago who also plot strategy for the audience before joining in the action. Similarly, tragic heroes in classical Greek drama often speak directly to the spectators. No one, however, develops the narrator character more effectively than Shaffer both as a story-telling device *and* as a fascinating figure unto himself. Use of the narrating "stage manager" also represents a hybrid version of presentational theater. For although the direct address to the audience cannot be considered realistic, the internal scenes introduced by the narrator are staged in what essentially is realism: characters communicate with each other through realistic dialogue, they move about the stage in conventional blocking, and the theatrical illusion is sustained for the duration of the scene being enacted. Shaffer thereby wrings important concessions from the realm of theatrical realism to gain flexibility in the narrative process.

Other non-representational modes emerge in the dramas of Peter Shaffer. Each of his four major works features striking iconographic sets and props to reinforce the substance of his themes. In *Royal Hunt,* the most stunning moments are evoked visually and through sound effects. Shaffer's stage directions to open scene 3 of the first act introduce the audience to the main visual emblem of the play:

> *The stage darkens and the huge medallion high on the back wall begins to glow. Great cries of "Inca!"*

are heard. Slowly the medallion opens outward to form a huge golden sun with twelve great inlaid rays. . . . In the center stands ATAHUALLPA.

Late in the play, that symbol of the sun is burned into the audience's memory during a scene called the Rape of the Sun; there, the greedy Spanish Conquistadors ravage the Incan emblem of gold to obtain its precious treasure. Again, the stage directions describe the non-verbal choreography involved:

> *Above, in the chamber, the treasure is piled up as before.* DIEGO *and the* CHAVEZ *brothers are seen supervising. They begin to explore the sun itself, leaning out of the chamber and prodding at the petals with their halberds. Suddenly* DIEGO *gives a cry of triumph, drives his halberd into a slot in one of the rays, and pulls out the gold inlay. The sun gives a deep groan, like the sound of a great animal being wounded. With greedy yelps, all the soldiers below rush at the sun and start pulling it to bits; they tear out the gold inlays and fling them on the ground, while terrible groans fill the air. In a moment only the great gold frame remains; a broken, blackened sun.*

Other important moments in *Royal Hunt* form indelible imprints by innovatively combining sound with panoramic image. In The Mime of the Great Ascent (scene 8 of Act One), Shaffer conveys the sense of the Spaniards climbing the high, frigid Andes mountains on their way to meet Atahuallpa. Realistic depiction is abandoned for evocative symbols and strange sounds:

> *As* OLD MARTIN *describes their ordeal, the men climb the Andes. It is a terrible progress: a stumbling, torturous climb into the clouds, over the ledges and giant chasms, performed to an eerie, cold music made from the thin whine of huge metal saws.*

Soon, the bloody conjunction of the European and Incan worlds is commemorated in The Mime of the Great Massacre that closes Act One. With no spoken dialogue, Shaffer portrays the horror of the Spaniards' betrayal of the Indians:

> *To a savage music, wave after wave of Indians are slaughtered and rise again to protect their lord, who stands bewildered in their midst. It is all in vain. Relentlessly the Spanish soldiers hew their way through the ranks of feathered attendants toward their quarry. They surround him . . . All the Indians cry out in horror. . . . [D]ragged from the middle of the sun by howling Indians, a vast bloodstained cloth bellies out over the stage. All rush off; their screams fill the theater. The lights fade out slowly on the rippling cloth of blood.*

These illustrative passages only suggest the power of Shaffer's presentational techniques. **The Royal Hunt of the Sun** most fully embodies Shaffer's use of Epic and Total Theaters—modes advanced by Bertolt Brecht and Antonin Artaud.

Analogous scenes of powerful non-verbal theater exist in the remaining serious dramas. Like its predecessor, **Royal Hunt, Equus** constructs its fable with a fusion of highly articulate dialogue in the mode of naturalism, embedded in mind-stretching visual scenes drawing on expressionism. Indeed, the central set utilized in the drama speaks metaphorically to the audience at all times. Shaffer's description of the set starts by calling it *"A square of wood set on a circle of wood."* By requiring that the backdrop for the set consist of tiers of seats on risers with both audience members and cast scated there, Shaffer intends that those persons serve functions in the play as *"Witnesses, assistants—and especially a Chorus."* Shaffer's set instructions further suggest the square set resembles *"A railed boxing ring"* and a *"dissecting theater"* in an operating room. Such images are entirely appropriate for a plot that entails savage battle between the powers of orderly society and the chaotic impulse of instinctual religious worship.

Horses, of course, play a key part in **Equus,** and Shaffer's choice of how to represent them on stage fairly well determines his overall theatrical approach. Shaffer is explicit in his stage directions that the horses only be portrayed abstractly. His descriptions of how actors are to play horses prohibit even the least element of realism. Brown-colored velvet tracksuits are to be worn by the actors, with matching gloves. On their feet are will be four-inch light-weight metal-braced lifts fastened to actual horseshoes. On their heads are large symbolic horse masks constructed of alternating strips of silver wire and leather, with no effort to hide the human head beneath.

Most telling of Shaffer's instructions about the horses is his mandate that *"Any literalism which could suggest the cozy familiarity of a domestic animal—or worse, a pantomime horse—should be avoided. . . . Animal effect must be created entirely mimetically . . . so that the masking has an exact and ceremonial effect."* The ritual base underlying **Equus** requires Alan Strang's orgiastic sessions of worship to be presentationally given. Only symbolic creatures and abstracted movements befit the play's theme. The result theatrically, however, is stunning. At the conclusion of the play's first act, Alan is hypnotized into reenacting his regular worship-rides on the horse Nugget. In Dysart's office, before the mesmerized psychiatrist, the boy activates the half dozen horse figures for his dream ride by calling out, "Equus—son of Fleckwus—son of Neckwus—*Walk.*" The rites which follow are described through stage directions:

> [*A hum from the* CHORUS. *Very slowly the horses standing on the circle begin to turn the square by gently pushing the wooded rail.* ALAN *and his mount start to revolve. The effect, immediately, is of a statue being slowly turned round on a plinth. During the ride, however, the speed increases, and the light decreases until it is only a fierce spotlight on horse and rider, with the overspill glinting on the other masks leaning in toward them.*]

All the while, Alan first croons, then shouts, instructions to the horse, projecting the lad's combined religious and sexual ecstasy that culminates in obvious spiritual and physical orgasm.

Equus contains an equally spectacular finale which relies on symbolic actions using presentationalism. Alan's attempt to make love with Jill at the stables is interrupted by what the boy believes to be Equus' warning from the adjacent stall. His sexual desire totally squelched by religious guilt, Alan brutally dismisses the girl and prepares to answer Equus' demands for obeisance. During this abreacted scene inspired by Dysart's promises for his total recovery, Alan exhibits through his actions why he stabbed out the eyes of six horses: Alan's hopes for a normal sexual life was blocked by his self-designed religion making Equus his personal god. The lad knows of no other choice:

> ALAN [*in terror*]: Eyes! . . . White eyes—never closed! Eyes like flames—coming—coming! . . . God seest! God seest! . . . NO! . . . No more. No more, Equus. . . . Equus . . . Noble Equus . . . Faithful and True . . . God-slave . . . Thou—God—Seest—NOTHING!

> [*He stabs out* NUGGET's *eyes. The horse stamps in agony. A great screaming begins to fill the theater, growing ever louder.* ALAN *dashes at the other two horses and blinds them too, stabbing over the rails. . . . The screams increase. The other horses follow into the square. The whole place is filled with cannoning, blinded horses. . . .*]

As in *Royal Hunt,* Shaffer turns to traditional realism, with its highly explicit and articulate dialogue, to promote plot and characterization for much of *Equus.* But for the climactic moments in the plot, the playwright provides emblematic scenes in which visual and aural effects move audience intellects—and emotions—beyond what is possible through stage literalism. Those remarkable stage images epitomize the glory of Shaffer's playwriting.

Of all that Shaffer has written to date, *Amadeus* elicits the most praise for its dramaturgical strengths. As in *Royal Hunt* and *Equus,* Shaffer punctuates his major scenes in *Amadeus* with haunting theatrical effects to create an unforgettable picture. And as in all his dramas, he consciously designs symbolic moments to conclude each act. Moreover, the epiphanous scenes represent far more than riveting moments appealing to the audience's visual and aural senses. Shaffer in those episodes succeeds brilliantly in embodying crucial truths in a single image. He does so by the imaginative melding of realistic speech with abstract image. The result is the coalescence of previous story understanding into a new, revelatory whole.

The most dazzling scene of enlightenment in *Amadeus* occurs at the close of Act One. By this point in the story, Antonio Salieri, principal musician in Emperor Joseph II's court in Vienna, has come to fear the musical genius of his younger rival Mozart. To measure the threat represented by the upstart newcomer, Salieri coerces Mozart's wife into bringing him Mozart's manuscripts of works-in-progress. Once Salieri begins to read the written musical scores, the sounds of actual music are heard in the theater to designate what he was reading. Shaffer not only has solved the logistics of allowing his audience to share the music Salieri hears in his head; the dramatist also mounts an electric experience on stage to suggest how transcendent the moment stands in musical history.

An analysis of this single scene reflects Shaffer's innovative mind at work. He first needs to have Salieri become aware of the immensity of Mozart's genius. Once that amazing fact has sunk in, Salieri must be made to revolt against God's ordained design. Using a two-part schema, the dramatist first stuns Salieri with Mozart's music itself. The stage directions interweave with Salieri's monologue to forge the climactic moment in his life:

> [. . . *He contemplates the music lying there as if it were a great confection he is dying to eat, but dare not. Then suddenly he snatches at it—tears the ribbon—opens the case and stares greedily at the manuscripts within. Music sounds instantly, faintly, in the theater, as his eye falls on the first page. It is the opening of the* Twenty-Ninth Symphony, *in A Major. Over the music, reading it.*]

> SALIERI: She had said that these were his original scores. First and only drafts of the music. Yet they looked like fair copies. They showed no corrections of any kind. . . . Displace one note and there would be diminishment. Displace one phrase and the structure would fall. [*He resumes reading, and the music also resumes: a ravishing phrase from the slow movement of the* Concerto for Flute and Harp.] . . . The truth was clear. That serenade had been no accident. . . . I was staring through the cage of those meticulous ink strokes at an Absolute Beauty!

To represent how devastating this new understanding is to Salieri, Shaffer instructs the composer to fall into a swoon. The question then arises, what will—or can—Salieri do about the situation with Mozart? With that unspoken query in the audience's collective mind, Shaffer shifts into the scene's second part: Salieri's new resolve. Upon regaining consciousness, lying amidst the fallen manuscripts of Mozart's compositions, Salieri *"addresses his God"*:

> *Capisco!* I know my fate. Now for the first time I feel my emptiness as Adam felt his nakedness . . . *Grazie, Signore!* You gave me the desire to serve you—which most men do not have—then saw to it the service was shameful in the ears of the server. . . . *Why? . . . What is my fault?* . . . I have worked and worked the talent you allowed me. . . . Solely that in the end, in the practice of the art which alone makes the world comprehensible to me, I might hear Your Voice! And now I do hear it—and it says only one name: MOZART! . . . Spiteful, sniggering, conceited, infantine Mozart! . . . [*Savagely.*] *Grazie e grazie ancora!*

[*Pause*] So be it! From this time we are enemies,
You and I! I'll not accept it from You.

And with Salieri's audacious challenge to God, Shaffer closes the first half of his drama. The overall design now is apparent, and the remainder of the play will chronicle Salieri's failed attempt to defeat his deity.

Nothing from the second act achieves quite the equivalent excitement, although the bizarre death scene of Mozart is highly charged as he discovers Salieri's machinations. Salieri's attempted suicide near the end also provides striking visual pictures that reenforce the final frustrated acts of the deranged court composer. Ironically, the emblematic scene which best counterbalances the close of Act One does not appear in Shaffer's play text but rather in his movie script for *Amadeus*. There, a new, important episode is added to depict Mozart—on his deathbed—dictating to Salieri the unfinished score to his *Requiem Mass*. Though the added movie scene attains enormous dramatic power, the actions it proposes are wholly fictitious and incredible. In the stage script proper, the final graphic moment showing Salieri proves powerful enough: he stands before us—an aged, crazed, but still shrewd conniver—arms outspread to welcome us into his brotherhood of Mediocrities.

Shaffer's next drama was *Yonadab* (1985), his fable of human evil and aspirations drawn from Biblical accounts. Given the dark and foreboding tenor of the play, the initial emblematic scene seems entirely suitable. Again, the episode appears near the end of the opening act. Here, another complete scene (scene 8) follows before the act actually concludes. But for all practical purposes, little additional exposition or plot development can occur after the hair-raising events of scene 7.

The plot, in brief, concerns the devilry of King David's errant nephew Yonadab in Jerusalem long before the Christian era. Beginning with facts from Samuel 2 in the Old Testament, Shaffer fashions another god-seeking protagonist. In the case of Yonadab, though he aspires to godhead, he hungers first for finite proof of God's existence. One of his tactics to "flush out God" is to challenge Him on every front. Yonadab gradually convinces his cousin Amnon, heir apparent to David's throne, that Amnon can take whatever he desires and thereby define his godhead. Yonadab, meanwhile, stands on the sideline to watch as those he dupes attempt to become earthly deities through arrogant actions usually reserved for gods alone.

When he confesses to Yonadab that he wants more than anything to sexually possess his half-sister Tamar, Amnon is actively encouraged by Yonadab. Tamar is tricked into going to Amnon's palace and even to his bedroom, under the ruse of his being very ill. Once alone with her, Amnon reveals his true intentions to have her. She remains obdurate to his seduction, and Amnon quickly loses patience and rapes her. Yonadab is the voyeur *par excellence,* and he locates himself near the bed chamber to observe. Unexpectedly, Amnon drops the curtains surrounding the bed, leaving Yonadab the mere watcher of

blurred shadows on the curtains. Shaffer ingeniously constructs a visual version of a momentous event in ancient history—all through a narrated account of shifting shadows. Yonadab is the audience's guide to a deed that ultimately leads to the demise of David's house and unrivalled empire:

> (*With increasing visibility the shadows of their bodies are thrown on to the curtain: immense black shapes enlarged and distorted by the lamps. During the following speech they make a series of abstract and strange shapes: a mysterious procession of glyphs.*)
>
> (*To audience*) All my life I remembered what I saw that night: the shadows!—more terrible than bodies. The limbs thrown up on the curtains like the letters of some grotesque language formed long, long before writing. There on the fall of a Jerusalem drape I saw, writ enormous . . . the archaic alphabet of the Book of Lust.

In *Yonadab* as in the other dramas considered here, the unique achievement of Shaffer's writing involves the surprising merger of realistic and presentational elements that usually remain antithetical to one another. Thus, even as Yonadab narrates the dreadful results of his plottings with Amnon, Tamar, and Absalom, Shaffer knows to insert a visual cameo to underscore the situation emblematically:

> (*Low music sounds. From high above descends the corpse of* ABSALOM *hanging by its long black hair.*)
>
> YONADAB: (*To audience*) Absalom died later—caught in a tree by his famous hair, fleeing the wrath of his father.
>
> (*KING DAVID appears, his head under a prayer shawl. The* HELPERS *depart.*)
>
> The father mourned his eldest son, of course—but the mourning for Absalom far exceeded the mourning for Amnon. It was the hardest pain of his life. . . . I saw all their transports, this royal family, their lusts for transcendence—and I saw nothing. Always the curtain was between us.

Parallel to Shaffer's other dramas, the passage just noted appears at the conclusion of *Yonadab,* serving as a neat sum-up of the entire play, thanks to articulate, realistic narrative joined to an unforgettable visual emblem.

Finally, lest we think Shaffer's patented curtain closers occur only with his serious plays, consider for a moment his comedy *Lettice & Lovage* (1987). Several features are found in *Lettice & Lovage* that resemble those of the more serious drama; but for now we shall focus on the crucial curtain scenes, particularly those ending the first two acts. Act One closes with the tour guide Lettice Douffet fired by her superior at the Preservation Trust, Lotte Schoen. Their "exit interview" had been free-wheeling, and the contrasting views of the two women openly aired. Although she had tried to explain her infelicities with facts concerning the provincial estate of which she was tour guide, Lettice realized in advance that her attempts would be futile. Therefore, when Lotte indeed dismissed her, Lettice was ready. With great august bearing, Lettice likens herself to Queen Mary just before her execution by Elizabeth. Lettice asks her executioner Lotte if she recalled what Queen Mary had worn on that auspicious day:

> LETTICE: Queen Mary appeared in a dress of deepest black. But when her ladies removed this from her—what do you imagine was revealed?
>
> LOTTE: I really can't guess.
>
> . . . . .
>
> LETTICE: . . . A full-length shift was seen. A garment the color of the whoring of which she had been accused! The color of martyrdom—and defiance! *Blood red!*
>
> [*She steps out of her cloak to reveal a brilliant red ankle-length nightdress, embossed all over with little golden crowns . . .*]
>
> Yes—all gasped with the shock of it! All watched with unwilling admiration—that good old word again—all watched with *wonder* as that frail captive, crippled from her long confinement, stepped out of the darkness of her nineteen years' humiliation and walked into eternity—a totally self-justified woman!

The graphic gesture of a doomed woman, metaphorically thumbing her nose at her captors, precisely matches Lettice's circumstances.

Lettice's black cloak figures in the emblem scene closing the play's second act, as well. By now in the plot, Lettice and Lotte are becoming good friends—with the help of "quaff," a strong brew Lettice alleges to be of Renaissance origin. Lotte even reveals that she wears a wig, showing how much a confidante Lettice has become. The women decide to eat out, and Lettice urges her colleague to leave her wig off when they leave to dine. After a hesitation, Lotte agrees:

> LOTTE: Very well . . . I will.
>
> [*They look at each other. Then LETTICE laughs, a clear bright laugh of perception, and walks away across the room. She laughs again.*]
>
> What is it? What are you thinking?
>
> [*But instead of replying, LETTICE takes off her black cloak and lays it ceremoniously at the base of the staircase, in the manner of Sir Walter Raleigh assisting Queen Elizabeth.*]
>
> LETTICE: Come, madame. Your hedgehogs await!

Again, a picture is worth the proverbial thousand words. In both emblem scenes, the logical and literal factors of the moment are fused with an apt pictorial rendition to effect striking theatrical results.

Nowhere among his plays does Peter Shaffer venture far from his personal version of "realism." That fact perhaps should not surprise playgoers, because Shaffer's dialogue stands with the finest written in our times. And articulate language, after all, is "literal" in all senses of that term. But Shaffer is not content with a single dramaturgical strength; his imagination reaches outward to encompass visual displays of literal thought. Nor are the graphic equivalents to realistic details limited to mere symbols on stage. Shaffer, with the help of equally innovative directors such as John Dexter and Peter Hall, stretches to embody spectacular but always intelligent theatrical techniques, as we have seen.

If we seek to isolate one specific attribute that defines Peter Shaffer's genius, then, we could do worse than to choose the methods chronicled here: the masterful merging of the literalism of realism with the provocative of the abstract pictorial. Shaffer's power derives from a type of "trans-literalism" that invites the shorthand of stage emblems. No other playwright today can claim such an achievement.

EQUUS

PRODUCTION REVIEWS

Irving Wardle (review date 27 July 1973)

SOURCE: "Shaffer's Variation on a Theme," in *The Times,* London, 27 July 1973, p. 15.

[Equus *debuted 26 July 1973 in a National Theatre production directed by John Dexter at London's Old Vic Theatre. In the following mixed review of the premiere, Wardle finds the play rather calculated and forced.*]

Peter Shaffer is a writer of formidable intelligence and traditional stage technique whose consistent purpose has been to invoke the primal dramatic forces which would blow his own equipment sky high. In style one can never predict what kind of piece he will write next but his theme remains constant. Whether he is opposing Christian and Aztec culture in **The Royal Hunt of the Sun,** or a philosopher and an anarchist poet in **The Battle of Shrivings** Shaffer is repeatedly mounting a tournament between Apollo and Dionysus under various coats of arms.

The argument of these plays is lacking in sinew; but the really sad thing about them is that while they are intended to celebrate the dark gods, it is always Apollo who wins. Mr Shaffer, a Western intellectual, was born into his service: and when he tries to conjure up Dionysus all he can offer is a projection governed by the Apollonian rules of reason and control.

Equus, although a far better work than *Shrivings,* repeats the same inescapable pattern. It is based on the case of a stable boy, aged 17, who unaccountably put out the eyes of six horses with an iron spike. Why? Mr Shaffer attempts an answer through the authoritarian medium of the institutional psychiatric interview.

Characteristically, the interviewer is the modern equivalent of a spoiled priest, much afflicted by Laingian doubts: but however equal the terms on which they agree to meet (playing a game of mutual interrogation in the early scenes), the fact remains that Dr. Dysart is in charge and can at any minute terminate the session and dispatch Alan back to his solitary nightmares.

Within this framework, taking in discussions with the parents and flashback reenactments with the boy, the play starts unravelling the enigmatic atrocity. Son of a pious mother and atheist father, Alan developed an early obsession with Christian sado-masochism, while a wild ride on the sea coast gave him a parallel fixation on horses. The two obsessions merge in his private cult of "Equus", and on taking a weekend stable job, he consummates his worship in orgiastic night riding. But when a girl takes him back to the stable to make love, he sees this as an act of sacrilege; and, believing that the eyes of Equus will reduce him to permanent impotence, he blinds every horse in the stable.

Clearly the play's main concern is neither with the doctor nor the patient, but with the god-like image of Equus. One senses Mr Shaffer straining to the limit to summon this awful presence. But, not for the first time, he owes whatever numinous results he does achieve to his director, John Dexter.

As with the unearthly masks in *The Royal Hunt,* so with the horses in this play. They are played by standing actors wearing hoof-lifts and wired silver heads through which the performers' own faces remain visible. The effect is totally stylized (while also fitting in with the centaur imagery), but it secures in full the magical transformation which is the special province of the mask. In the night ride on a manhandled revolve, and in the climactic blinding, with silvery muzzles converging questioningly from the shadows of the stable, the play instantly fills the theatre with the sense of a potent and ancient force returning to life.

The text, however, does no such thing. The image of the horse is poetically inexhaustible, and Mr Shaffer draws on its ambiguity (dominion and servitude) to link his pagan and Christian material. But here, as in the surrounding detail, what comes through is not a fiery symbol, but the sense of a painstaking and profoundly dissatisfied intelligence carefully slotting things together. Alan, with his war-horse battle cries against consumer goods, is no less a schematic automaton than his clockwork parents, both wound up to produce a pre-arranged clinical condition and to deliver lines like: "I can't imagine, Doctor, it's unbelievable. He loves animals."

There is very little real dialogue. Even the interviews consist of solo turns introduced with wary parleys on both sides. Peter Firth, a newcomer to the National, brings tremendous nervous energy and lyricism to the part of the boy; the ecstatic tenderness of his stable scenes certainly adds life to the play's calculations. But where Mr Shaffer can take most credit is in the part of the Doctor, played on a knife edge of professional skill and personal disgust by Alec McCowen, who threads his way through the character's confessions (a lover of ancient Greece who is virtually impotent himself) with fully justified trust in the excellence of the writing.

Russell Davies (review date 3 August 1973)

SOURCE: "Horses for Courses," in *New Statesman,* Vol. 86, No. 2211, 3 August 1973, pp. 165-66.

[*In the following review, Davies praises the staging and performances of the London production of* Equus, *but he contends that Shaffer compromised his investigation of "our right to tamper with our fellow-beings in the cause of 'normality'" by focusing on "a bunch of people already far gone in abnormality."*]

Peter Shaffer's new work was greeted with hoots of approval by the first-nighters at the National Theatre, and indeed *Equus* offered much to applaud. A fine central performance by young Peter Firth as the adolescent psycho-patient for whom the horse is the sole fount of passion and focus of worship, was matched by the resourceful daring of author, director and designer in disguising a troupe of young men as two-legged horses. These Mark II centaurs, with beautifully wrought horseheads of shining chrome tubing strapped to their skulls, and matching metal-mesh hooves lashed to their feet in such a way that the human heels stuck out like fetlocks, magnificently brought off the illusion of an animal presence. The bathos of pantomime horseplay never threatened. Mere flicks of the head and flexings of the knee suggested the impatient power of the beasts; and the equine exhalation, half shiver, half snort, that issued from the principal horse centre-stage, as the light died on the first half of the play, was thrillingly done.

Visually, then, John Dexter's production was fine; but the argument of the play was worrying. There is a good deal of argument in *Equus,* for its narrator/chorus, the psychiatrist Dysart, played by Alec McCowen, has a lot of explaining to do. Why did his horsestruck young patient, liberated from an electrical goods shop and working in a stable, suddenly round on the objects of his veneration at dead of night and hideously put out their eyes with a metal spike? What has it got to do with his God-fearing mother, his heavy-footed atheist-socialist Dad? As Dysart gradually works his way past the resentment of his patient, their taut confrontations flare up into dramatic recreations of the lad's formative crises; and these in turn work remorselessly towards the first re-enactment of the grisly, gouging crime.

It's an uncomfortably shaped evening for Dysart. He must hover between the roles of Freudian sleuth and theatrical ringmaster, now goading the boy into further self-revelation, now receiving muted deputations from the anxious parents, now turning to issue a progress report to his on-stage assistants and the audience. And in between times he flogs out of himself a full admission of his own miseries: a dead marriage, low sperm-count, loss of the power to worship, his twee annual pilgrimage to 'primitive' Greece ('sponge bag crammed with Entero-Vioform'), the cold professional smoothness of his days followed at night by violent dreams of ritual human sacrifice. By the time his case is solved, Dysart is wringing his hands at the prospect of applying treatment, for in curing Alan, as he will, he must wipe away from the boy's consciousness all its enviable excesses, all the traces of his unique and irreplaceable passion, making him fit for nothing better than flogging flashlamps again. Thus Dysart arrives, in his breast-beating way, at distinctly Szasz-like conclusions about the nature of mental disturbance, despairingly questioning our right to tamper with our fellow-beings in the cause of 'normality'. The pity is that in constructing a position from which to launch its missiles of doubt, the play must base itself on a bunch of people already far gone in abnormality. Important questions are begged from the start.

Alec McCowen's performance is a noble attempt to make a coherent whole out of a mass of exposition; but vocally he does make things extra-arduous for himself. He herringbones up through some of Mr Shaffer's grittier sentences like a mountaineer speaking in time to the plod of his ill-fitting snow-shoes, flopping back with weary exhaustion on the summit of the final word. Then he returns to the foot of the slope and does it again, always careful, occasionally prim.

Peter Firth is admirable as Alan, whether shrieking with ecstasy during his midnight ride or quaking at the torturing imminence of sexual initiation in his holy of holies, the stable. Clothes are torn off for this climactic seduction scene, and Alan is left naked to face his humiliating failure. Luckily, Mr Firth is a lean, white-fleshed young man upon whose surface muscle and sinew are delineated as in a drawing by Blake; his body sinks impressively from pride to wretchedness. His seductress is played by Doran Godwin, whose flounced and beribboned performance as Jane Austen's Emma has just run its course of TV repeats. Here she appears in a woolly jumper and wellies, yet she brings a little of Emma's challenging archness with her. Possibly this manner is her forte; it has worked very well, at any rate, in both contexts. But

perhaps she should be careful not to stick like that, as scolding mothers used to say.

Walter Kerr (review date 2 September 1973)

SOURCE: "A Psychiatric Detective Story of Infinite Skill," in *The New York Times,* 2 September 1973, Section 2, pp. 1, 3.

[*In this review, Kerr praises nearly every aspect of the National Theatre production of* Equus. *This work, he states, is the "closest I have seen a contemporary play come . . . to reanimating the spirit of mystery that makes the stage a place of breathless discovery."*]

A true myth is a true bind. All the facts are in, and there is no way out. Oedipus, an honorable man, can do whatever he likes to avoid fulfilling the prophecy that he will kill his father and marry his mother, but he will kill his father and marry his mother. We give assent to the unresolvable, see that it is perfectly proportioned, perfectly just, perfectly terrifying.

If there is one thing more than another that a contemporary playwright would like to do, it is to make a myth. We feel a desperate need these days for new icons, images, clothed symbols that will help us come to terms with the "dark cave of the psyche," the cave that thousands of years of reasoning haven't quite lighted after all.

We want a picture of ourselves that renders us whole, with all of the violent contraries and inexplicable self-betrayals locked in. Not an explanation but an intuition become flesh; not thinking, *seeing*. But, it turns out, myths are extraordinarily hard to make, just by the willing of it. We are used to thinking now, used to explaining before we really see, and it's not easy to wheel about and go back to magic.

The closest I have seen a contemporary play come—it is powerfully close—to reanimating the spirit of mystery that makes the stage a place of breathless discovery rather than a classroom for rational demonstration is Peter Shaffer's remarkable *Equus,* now in repertory at the British National Theater. Mr. Shaffer is the author of *The Royal Hunt of the Sun,* and he may have been trying for just such iconography—a portrait of the drives that lead men to crucify themselves—there. Here, I think, he has found it.

He's done it by using reason to despair of reason. We begin in what looks like a lecture lab, a handy enough arena for dissecting the brain: the center space is railed off, some members of the audience are seated above it onstage as though they'd come for a scholarly demonstration. It also looks, vaguely, like a horse-ring in which winners might be put through their paces. Then we notice that there are indeed horses about: from the rungs of steel ladders at both sides of the stage hang the silvered-

A scene from the 1974 production of Equus.

frame skeletons of horses' heads. They are handsome. They are already, as John Napier has exquisitely designed them, in some way haunting.

A doctor is waiting for a patient, one he doesn't want to take on. He is weary and wary of tampering with the psyches of children, though that is his job. The patient is 17, a part-time stable boy. He has rammed a metal spike through the eyes of six horses. It is the gratuitous, unfathomable horror of the act that leads the doctor to accept the charge.

At once we are lured, with infinite skill, into a psychiatric detective story, the tensions of which account for half the evening's force. Clues are grudgingly, suspensefully come by. The defiant boy, blond curls framing a face of stone, won't speak, he will only mockingly hum television commercials when prodded. At last tricked into speech by adroit maneuver, he strikes a sly bargain he means to hold to. For every question of the doctor's that he answers, the doctor must answer one of his. Candor for candor, if we're going to get anywhere.

The process yields tantalizing bits of information. When he was a child his mother read to him—history, the New Testament, stories of horses in which horses spoke and felt. Under his mother's tutelage the boy has become religious enough to tack a cheap lithograph of the suffering Jesus, feet chained, back under the lash, to his wall. His atheist father, enraged, has torn it down and replaced it with the photograph of a horse, head-on, eyes staring.

A suspicion grows that horse and Christ have become one, the chains of the Saviour the bit between the horse's teeth. The boy not only learns to love horses but to adore them: he is caught once by his father with wire forced into his own mouth, slashing at his body with a riding-crop. On dark nights he slips into the stable, strips himself, and goes riding in the fields, sexually excited, joined to his god, self-made centaur.

But all the while that we are fitting bits and pieces together, still far from the sight of any answer, the questioning process has turned up something else: the hopelessly chained soul of the doctor himself. Alec McCowen plays the role: I doubt that he has ever done anything half so brilliant. Tie loose, eyes tired, he is suddenly vulnerable. One of the questions fired at him by the boy, which ought to be answered if the bargain is to be kept, is capable of infuriating him. Does he have any sex with his wife? In an unprofessional temper, he dismisses the boy for the day.

Yet the rage is other than it seems. In point of fact Mr. McCowen has no sex at all, having married an antiseptic Scotch lady dentist: they "briskly wooed, briskly wed, were briskly disappointed, and turned briskly to their respective surgeries." It is his own surgery—his genuine capacity for returning young minds to accepted norms—that frightens him. He dreams, on his unluckier nights, that he is Agamemnon applying the sacrificial scalpel to long lines of children, all waiting to have imagination, passion, individuality taken out of them. He is jealous of the boy he means to cure, jealous of his madness. While he, with his pallid fondness for all things Greek, has leafed drawings of centaurs, the boy has become one. There is a bit between his own teeth that will never come out.

Civilization and its discontents again. Yes. And, as we move into the equally arresting second half of the play, on our way to the metal spike, we are not only aware that the theme is a common enough one in our time, we are also inclined—out of our restless logical impulses—to challenge, or at least think twice about, certain of the icon's ambiguities. Wishing for sex with a girl, the boy is temporarily impotent: "The Lord thy God is a jealous God." Only if the all-seeing god is blinded can the boy take a second step. Questions bother us here: Is it wrong to cure impotence, wrong to kill a false and hurtful equation between one pair of eyes and another? And hasn't the decision to reject his god, to be no longer a centaur, been the boy's rather than the doctor's?

But that is logic at work again—really work for the next day, not while the second act is actually exerting its spell—and it is to be at least temporarily dismissed in view of the fact that the structure, the two terrible tensions pulling in contrary directions, the sense of myth slowly disclosing itself, all do really function in the theater. They function in part because Mr. Shaffer has done his own work with the precision of Agamemnon's scalpel, in part because Mr. McCowen commands us to believe without reserve in the agony and honesty of his man (Peter Firth, as the boy, keeps pace perfectly with his mentor), and in part because director John Dexter has been able to make the experience intensely visual.

There is, for instance, a superb effect at the first act climax, the night-ride of a boy and horse unleashed. We might only have heard of this; it could have been narrated. A film would do it literally and, I think, lose intensity in the doing. Here the boy simply mounts the shoulders of one of the six shadowy figures who have from time to time during the evening slipped beneath the brooding horses' masks. The hooves of the boy's alter ego begin to paw the stage floor: they are spiky silver elevations that look like inverted jeweled crowns.

Then the stage floor itself begins to move, turned on its axis by the nodding, neighing horse-men at hand so that the railings at first slip by, then race by: With the exultation of the boy's passion, the increasing speed of the spinning ground, the rush of air that both seem to generate as track whirls away beneath the silver, we are left not only persuaded but spellbound by the clattering, crying, crop-whipping authenticity of the image.

Over-all, it is the image that stands, and is complete. The boy, with his dangerous creativity, fills one half of it, forever driven, forever blocked. The doctor fills the other, feverishly unwilling to do what he must do, doing it—only to block himself. The two fit together at unpredictable angles, like differently colored pieces in a stained-glass window, but they fit and use up all the space that there is. Any move either makes destroys the other. Locked horns, both right, no escape. The play is perfectly proportioned to its mutual pain.

We have been looking for craftsmanship like this for a long time.

Albert E. Kalson (review date December 1973)

SOURCE: A review of *Equus*, in *Educational Theatre Journal*, Vol. 25, No. 4, December, 1973, pp. 514-15.

[*In the review below, Kalson contends that the character of Dysart, who "embodies the central conflict which affords the play its universality," is insufficiently developed, leaving the doctor's dilemma overshadowed by the psychological "case history."*]

Britain's National Theatre has restored passion to the theatre with what well may be the most controversial production of its first decade—Peter Shaffer's *Equus*. The play marks an auspicious return to the theatre after a three-year hiatus during which the author of *Five Fin-*ger Exercise, The Royal Hunt of the Sun, and *Black Comedy* was frequently referred to as the brother of the author of *Sleuth.*

The new work, concerning the rehabilitation by a psychiatrist of a disturbed stable lad who has blinded six horses, may seem at first a new direction for Shaffer; yet it shares affinities with his earlier plays. Like *Five Finger Exercise,* a youth's total dependence on an older man forces the seemingly stronger to examine the motives of his own actions; like *Royal Hunt,* man creates God in order to enslave him.

Young Alan Strang, seeking someone or something to worship, has entered into an exhilarating relationship, obviously sexual, with a horse he rides at night, a horse who becomes the boy's personal god-slave. His socialist father, an avowed atheist, had forbidden him to keep a picture of a bound and beaten Christ at the foot of his bed, and Alan had replaced it with an hypnotic head-on picture of a horse with staring eyes. Years before he had had one thrilling ride on a horse along the beach, but his father had pulled him from the horse, throwing him to the ground. The intensity of his present relationship with the animal makes him impotent with a girl in the stable while several horses stand nearby. Ashamed and terrified that the horse has witnessed his attempt at what appears to Alan an act of betrayal against his god and his slave, the boy commits the horrible crime of putting out the eyes of all the horses.

The core of the play, however, is not the retelling of this sensational case history. Instead the play examines the relationship in which, subtly, the doctor replaces the horse as the god-slave that the boy creates. But the cure requires the death of the boy's worshipful passion for Equus. The doctor, Martin Dysart, coldly surrounds himself with books on ancient Greece and looks at pictures of centaurs while the boy is himself wildly becoming a centaur in a Hampshire field and reliving the myths which the doctor can only read about. The doctor questions his right to return the boy to a so-called state of normalcy for he comes to envy the passion of which his own life is totally void. By doing what is expected of him as psychiatrist, Dysart symbolically feels the horse's bit clamping his own mouth, and he sees himself picking at children's heads, just as Alan had stabbed the horses' heads.

The question raised by Anthony Burgess in his novels *A Clockwork Orange* and *Enderby*—Has society the right to tamper with what is unique about an individual and remold him into what passes for an acceptable member of the group?—is well dramatized by Shaffer, but perhaps the play's one failing is that the development of the character of the psychiatrist, the character who embodies the central conflict which affords the play its universality, cannot be drawn as vividly as the incidents which lead to the confrontation of doctor and patient. The play's disproportion may be in part a result of the staging by John Dexter, who sets the play in a surgical amphitheatre by seating sixty members of the audience in three steep tiers of seats at the back of a bare stage, thus providing a logical and forcefully symbolic background as Dysart tells the story in which he "murders to dissect." The bare stage nonetheless allows Dexter some moments of directorial over-indulgence as he fluidly stages the scenes on the beach, in the fields, in the stable, the latter scene with performers as bare as the stage itself. The horses are cleverly impersonated by clothed actors who don metal horses' heads through which their own heads can be seen. Dexter has even ingeniously solved the problem of staging a wild ride by the use of a platform which is spun by the actor-horses. The production's imbalance, which centers most of one's attention on the case-history aspects of the piece, is nearly overcome by Alec McCowen's eloquent agony as the troubled doctor. McCowen is magnificently supported by Peter Firth, a young actor whose development will obviously be worth watching.

Equus' imbalance is serious enough to lead some to question if the undoubted passion of the electrifying production has not been misspent. *Equus* does not immediately force its audience to face such overwhelming current problems as political kidnapping and genocide, the subjects of Christopher Hampton's widely acclaimed *Savages*. But perhaps Shaffer's theme is itself finally his play's best defense. *Equus* provides the one evening of *passion* that is currently available to London theatregoers trapped by the late-summer doldrums of the waning season.

CRITICAL COMMENTARY

Russell Vandenbroucke (essay date 1975)

SOURCE: "*Equus:* Modern Myth in the Making," in *Drama and Theatre,* Vol. 12, No. 2, Spring, 1975, pp. 129-33.

[*In the following essay, Vandenbroucke declares that* Equus *is a modern myth that employs "elements of ritual, religion, and ceremony" to "fathom and capture basic truths of man and nature."*]

Camus tells us that myths are made for the imagination to breathe life into them. Peter Shaffer's most recent play, *Equus,* is a myth-like story with the integrity and rich overtones of the finest of artistic works. It is a modern myth, delicately probing a psyche formed by a mingling of modern forces and influences, yet reaching beyond to the concerns and problems of men of all ages. *Equus* is an arresting piece, a vast playground for the imagination.

The story is that of seventeen year old Alan Strang who has blinded six horses in a stable where he works and is placed in a psychiatric hospital under the care of Dr. Martin Dysart. It is clear, from the very beginning, that the play will move inexorably to the abreaction of Alan's outrageous act. In building to this conclusion Mr. Shaffer has created suspense and tension comparable with that of a mystery story. But, unlike the mystery story, the clues into Alan's background and psychology do not fit

into a neat and tidy package. How can they? Mr. Shaffer provides no simple explication or pat lecture but a laboratory for inquiry; he clearly understands the complexities of the mind, understands that the motivation behind complex individual acts cannot be empirically delineated. Rather than providing the sharp lines of simplistic causal relationships, Mr. Shaffer has drawn the curves and parameters within which Alan acts.

The set is a simple wooden square raised a step above the stage proper, surrounded (except downstage) by a railing. Three benches are placed on the platform and others are located downstage right and left and upstage right and left. The simplicity of the set permits it to function as a wide variety of places—Dysart's office, the Strang home, a beach, a shop, a stable, an open field, and a movie theatre. All the actors remain on stage throughout the play, rising and mounting the platform when necessary, then returning to their benches around the perimeter of the platform to act as a Chorus. Upstage right and left are ladders from which are suspended the horse-masks, donned ritualistically at several points in the play by the horse-men. They are fashioned from curved pieces of silvery wire and strips of leather: haunting, masculine, highly suggestive. The horse-men wear platform-like stilts made of the same silvery wire/metal. Wearing their masks, clomping and scraping their hooves on the wooden boards, they evoke not only the sights and sounds of the stable but the very smell of manure.

The play is divided into two acts and thirty-five scenes indicating changes of time, location, or mood. Dysart acts as a narrator at times, explaining himself and the treatment of Alan to the court worker who has seen that Alan is admitted to the hospital rather than imprisoned. At other times Dysart addresses the audience directly—musing about himself or the development and unravelling of Alan's case. As Dysart begins to explain his sessions with Alan the "telling" of the scene shifts smoothly and skillfully to the actual portrayal of it. Similarly, in recounting an incident from his past, Alan may be joined by his parents for the dramatization of that actual moment. Repeated shifts in time are utilized: from present, to past, to further in the past, back to the present and so forth.

Dysart conducts his interviews of Alan methodically—urging, bribing, soothing, or tricking the boy as necessary. Bits and pieces of Alan's family and background are presented, impressed upon the mind, yet uneasily passed over. Each is important. But the way it fits into the puzzle that is Alan is unclear. The audience accompanies Dysart as he searches for clues and assembles them in his attempt to comprehend Alan. Mr. Shaffer starts slowly, using faint pencil marks which gradually become clearer and clearer, collectively creating the firm brush strokes which outline the boy. Each clue is like a pebble dropped into a placid pond: the ripples are visible but require time to make their impact on the shore. At their first interview Alan cannot speak but only sings jingles from advertisements and we learn that Alan's father refuses to allow a television in the home: "It's a dangerous drug. . . . Absolutely fatal mentally." Books, learning, industry, self-improvement are Mr. Strang's values and he is deeply disappointed in his son's lethargy: "It's a disgrace when you come to think of it. You the son of a printer, and never opening a book!" The father is vaguely Marxist and an atheist, much upset at his wife's religiosity and its influence on Alan. He tells Dysart, "If you want my opinion, it's the Bible that's responsible for all this." The remark seems simply reactionary and offhanded but sticks, uneasily, in one's mind. Alan's ex-school teacher mother is fond of reading her son stories from the Bible and stories about horses, "When Christian cavalry first appeared in the New World, the pagans thought horse and rider was one person. . . . It was only when the rider fell off they realized the truth." She allows Alan to visit a neighbor to watch television. Alan claims to know more history than Dysart and asks him a string of questions ending with "Who said 'Religion is the opium of the people'?" Dysart properly answers, "Karl Marx," but Alan says that's the wrong answer. The apothegm is Mr. Strang's?

At the age of six, playing on a beach, Alan is offered a ride by a young horseman. It is gratefully accepted but soon interrupted by the frantic shrieks and protestations of over-protective parents. It appears this is the only time Alan has ridden a horse. This is baffling, for one assumes that a boy who so loves, even adores, horses would like nothing better than to ride them. But no, Alan claims (and is supported by his parents) to have ridden only the one occasion.

Alan once had in his room a picture of Jesus on his way to Calvary, chained and beaten mercilessly. Mr. Strang cannot tolerate the picture and replaces it with one of a horse: "A most remarkable picture, really. You very rarely see a horse taken from that angle—absolutely head-on. . . . It comes out all eyes."

Mr. Strang visits Dysart and tells of a most peculiar rite he has witnessed a year or two previously. Alan, kneeling before the horse picture in his bedroom begins to chant a litany of equine genealogy: "And Legwus begat Neckwus. And Neckwus begat Fleckwus, the King of Spit. And Fleckwus spoke out of his chinkle-chankle! . . . And he said 'Behold—I give you Equus, my only begotten son!'" Alan fashions a bridle from a piece of string, places it over his head, and beats himself with a wooden coat hanger.

From this point the pace quickens and the clues come more easily as Dysart probes deeper and deeper—not blindly now, but with some ideas as to areas for inquiry. Alan recounts the ride on the beach: it was sexy. He looks at the horse and asks if the chain hurts. "Yes."

Alan: It never comes out. They have me in chains.

Dysart: Like Jesus?

Alan: Yes!

Dysart: Only his name isn't Jesus, is it?

Alan: No.

Dysart: What is it?

Alan: No one knows but him and me.

Dysart: You can tell me, Alan. Name him.

Alan: Equus.

Dysart: Thank you. Does he live in all horses or just some?

Alan: All.

Dysart: *(encouragingly)* Go on, then. *(Alan kneels.)* Now tell me. Why is Equus in chains?

Alan: For the sins of the world.

Dysart: What does he say to you?

Alan: "I see you." "I will save you."

Persistently questioned, Alan reveals that he *does* ride horses: furtively, under cover of darkness he makes his secret pilgrimages to the stable-temple. He first puts sandals on the horse's feet/hooves, and then fixes the chinkle-chankle of bridle and bit. He gives the horse a lump of sugar—"His Last Supper." Alan leads the horse into Ha Ha (the open field? the march to Golgotha?) and, stripped of his clothes, mounts the horse-man: "His neck comes out of my body." He begins to ride, slowly at first, and the wooden platform, mounted on a giant ball bearing, is rotated by the attending horsemen: slowly, very slowly, gradually gaining speed as Alan and Equus race through the night, faster and faster as they achieve the most complete of physical, emotional, and sexual unions and Alan shrieks, "Equus, I love you! Now! Bear me away." The ride is over, sexual and spiritual communion achieved. Alan kisses the horse and whispers "Amen!" The first act ends, having achieved one of the most brilliant and arresting visual images ever staged.

On a date, perhaps his first, Alan is talked into seeing a blue movie where, of all people, he meets his father. Everyone has secrets. The girl entices Alan to walk to the stable, near her home. Excited by the movie and attracted by the girl's gentle seductive charm, he attempts to make love but is unable. "When I touched her, I felt *Him*. Under me. . . . His side waiting for my hand . . . His flanks . . . I refused him. I looked. I looked right at her . . . and I couldn't do it. When I shut my eyes, I saw Him at once." Mortified by his failure, he angrily, painfully, dismisses the girl. But Equus remains. "He'd seen everything—he was laughing . . . mocking." Alan reaches for a metal spike and blinds the horses. Shamed by his failure he lashes out, masochistically destroying a part of himself—the epicenter of his life, his god, his lover.

But while much of the focus has been on Alan, Dysart is no shadowy manipulator of the boy—no formal and precise automaton attempting to simply cure Alan. Or is he? Dysart seeks self-knowledge even as he strives to understand Alan. He must confront himself as he confronts Alan, cure his own ills and unhappiness with that of Alan. "The thing is, I'm desperate. You see, I'm wearing that horse's head myself. That's the feeling. All reined up in old language and old assumptions, straining to jump clear-hoofed on to a whole new track of being I only suspect is there. I can't see it, because my educated, average head is being held at the wrong angle. I can't jump because the bit forbids it, and my own basic force—my horsepower, if you like—is too little." He recounts a dream: he is an Hellenic chief priest officiating at the ritual sacrifice of a herd of five hundred children. Armed with a scalpel, he slits the stomachs and disembowels each child in turn. Somewhat nauseated after a time, he nonetheless fulfills his appointed task, fearful that any protest will result in his own sacrifice. Dysart dreams outrageous acts; Alan has committed one.

Dysart is undergoing "professional menopause." He has no children and, asked by Alan if he has sex with his wife, dismisses the boy from his office—obviously upset at Alan's pointed and perceptive question. He has not even kissed his wife in six years. He is sterile. "The lowest sperm count you could find." Is he sexually impotent as well? Perhaps. But is the patient's sexual impotence really any different from the doctor's vapid emotions and helpless inability to effect change in himself?

Dysart spends his evenings at home with his brisk and antiseptic wife, reading art books on Ancient Greece—the joys of which are completely beyond her comprehension. He exclaims, "I sit looking at pages of centaurs trampling the soil of Argos—and outside my window he is trying to *become one*." Dysart is jealous of the boy who has lived and experienced passion, life itself, with a fervor he can never possibly achieve. "That boy has known a passion more ferocious than I have felt in any second of my life. And let me tell you something: I envy it."

What finally are we to make of this collage?

Returning to the idea of *Equus* as myth: a myth may be considered to be a story which addresses basic problems and situations not limited in relevance or interest to one society or era. It fills a need by the presentation of a model which provides an explanation (or at least a delineation) of various human conditions and situations. It is always symbolic of something greater than the characters, incidents, and rhetoric of the story itself. Within such a broad definition, many works seem to aspire to these very ends. Indeed, it is easily argued that all art strives to be larger than the form itself—seeking to fathom and capture basic truths of man and nature. But a myth must also contain elements of ritual, religion, and ceremony. It is in this sense that *Equus* is truly mythical.

In his earlier *The Royal Hunt of the Sun,* Mr. Shaffer sought after the images and ritual to capture the essence of religious conflict, internal strife, and self-crucifixion. In *Equus* he has brilliantly found them, uniting subject and style: Hellenic-high-priest-Dysart's sacrifice of the herd of children, centaur-Alan's worship of his chinkle-chankle lord and ritualistic beating of himself, and, most perfectly of all, the communion of boy, horse, god, and lover in the Field of Ha Ha. Dysart might be speaking for any one of us when he states, "I've stared at such images before—or been stared at *by* them. But this one is the most alarming yet."

The Greek tragedies presented characters of superhuman, regal, stature. But modern would-be egalitarian Western men are bereft of larger-than-life heroes and models to emulate. The modern myth must present its middle-class audiences a hero of its own proportion with which it may identify—a Willy Loman, a Martin Dysart.

The stories of the Greek tragedies were well known to the Hellenic audience and while the story of *Equus* is not well known, its backdrop is. Alan and Dysart have been molded by a search for experience, self-fulfillment, and meaning in their lives, the pressures of sexual performance and its attendant anxieties, the conflicts of religion, and strivings for a greater purpose. Christ, Marx, and Freud stand over their shoulders and these surely are the heroes of the Trojan war and gods of Olympus for Twentieth Century Western man. They are the trinity of contemporary myth-makers, confident in their ability to describe causes, predict results, and provide solutions. They aim to sate man's hunger for coherence and direction, his need to feel secure, and they endeavor to provide relief and comfort. Dysart pleads, "Look! Life is only comprehensible through a thousand local Gods. And not just the old dead ones with names like Zeus—no, but living Geniuses of Place and Person! And not just Greece but modern England." The modern high-priest, exorcist, giver-of-light, knower-of-the-unknowable is the psychiatrist. Is there really any difference between baring one's soul in the confession box or on the analyst's couch? Satan's evil temptations towards impure thoughts, words, and actions have become the murmurings and eruptions of subconscious desires and the struggle between id and ego. Mrs. Strang tells Dysart, "You've got your words, and I've got mine. You call it a complex, I suppose. But if you knew God, Doctor, you would know about the Devil." Yes, *if.*

Dysart has a fantasy of returning to a place by the seas—where gods *used* to live, before they died. "Gods don't die," asserts Alan; but for Dysart they do. We need not take this as a Nietzschean remark. The gods *have* died for Dysart: life itself and meaning have died. Robbed of the center of his life, the giver of meaning, and answerer of questions, Dysart is lost—searching ardently but without direction for order and intelligibility. "I need—more than my children need me—a way of seeing in the dark." Without his gods, his heroes, his pat answers, modern man searches desperately—for meaning, for understanding of the world he would so like to behold as a real home. He longs to be assured of some basic congruence between his aspirations for intelligibility and the essential constitution of reality. "Can you think of anything worse one can do to anybody than take away their worship? . . . it's the core of his life. What else has he got? Think about him. . . . He's a modern citizen for whom society doesn't exist. . . . Without worship you shrink, it's as brutal as that."

Despite his reservations, Dysart *will* effect a cure: the illicit passions will be eliminated—replaced by the socially acceptable but loathsome *ennui* that consumes Dysart. Which is preferable? "My desire might be to make this boy an ardent husband—a caring citizen—a worshiper of an abstract and unifying God. My achievement, however, is more likely to make a ghost! . . . Passion, you see, can be destroyed by a doctor. It cannot be created." Alan will be stripped of that which Dysart so earnestly desires.

The grace, delicacy, and restraint which Mr. Shaffer has called upon to perfect his statement must not be taken lightly. They are the marks of a master craftsman about his trade. *Equus* is an extraordinarily ambitious effort, movingly successful in its total impact. It is a finely wrought statement, redolent with meaning, certain to be performed and remembered for generations to come. *Equus* is the apogee of Mr. Shaffer's work to date. We eagerly await his next attempt to scale even greater heights.

Neil Timm (essay date 1979)

SOURCE: "*Equus* as a Modern Tragedy," in *West Virginia Philological Papers* Vol. 25, 1979, pp. 128-34.

[*In the essay below, Timm compares* Equus *to the classical Greek dramas* Oedipus *and* Antigone *and to Racine's* Phèdre *in an attempt to define a modern version of tragedy.*]

Whether our age is capable of producing real tragedy is a question that has preoccupied critics and philosophers. I would like to pose that question as a basis for discussing Peter Shaffer's *Equus*. I will proceed by comparing the play to several tragedies, *Antigone, Oedipus,* and *Phedre,* in order to evolve a working definition of tragedy. This essay will raise two questions: Is it necessary to have a hero of elevated stature, and can post-Freudian writers find a uniquely "modern" way of approaching tragedy?

Antigone's pattern of oppositions provides a formal paradigm for many of Shaffer's plays: *Shrivings* and *The Royal Hunt of the Sun* in addition in *Equus*. In these plays a person who holds religious or quasi-religious beliefs is violated by a more cynical, more rationalistic outsider. Antigone's religious devotion to the sacred rite of burial brings her into fatal conflict with Creon, who represents (as Hegel suggested) the interests of society,

despite his own blindness. In *Equus* Alan Strang has evolved a personal religion based on the god he sees in all horses. While Creon can literally bury Antigone alive to perpetuate his limited view of the state, Martin Dysart relies on the more subtle instrument of torture, modern psychiatry. There are, of course, important differences between these two young victims. Antigone's act is one of great piety, even socially accepted, while Alan's act of blinding the horses is deviant and repugnant to the audience. In *Equus* what is socially acceptable is opposed to Alan's personal religion. There is also a difference between the tyrant Creon, who himself betrays the public conscience, and Dysart, who serves as the guardian of the Normal. Both Antigone and Alan Strang are pitted against authority figures. Both are consumed by a personal vision that precludes love and marriage. Haimon stabs himself, superfluous next to Antigone's suicide; the girl who tries to seduce Alan, however warm and compassionate, is worse than superfluous. She precipitates Alan's violent attempt at self-punishment and worship: the blinding.

If we assume that a hero must recognize his guilt in order to be tragic, then in both *Antigone* and *Equus* the hero is the persecutor, not the victim. Creon recognizes his tragic error; so too does Martin Dysart. In some ways Dysart is more "tragic" than Creon, for, having realized his error, Dysart will, nonetheless, continue to dispatch his patients to the living death of the Normal through psychiatric cure. Something final has been reached for Creon, who longs for death. There will be no more Antigones. Neither victim is tragic: Antigone has committed no crime, at least against the gods, and Alan will have re-enacted his crime and moved on, not through recognition, but through catharsis.

Oedipus, too, has illuminating similarities to *Equus*. If both Dysart and Oedipus are detectives, they are searching in some sense for different things in bringing the hidden crime to light: Oedipus wants facts and truth; Dysart searches for motives, the why. Yet each becomes the object of his own search through a pattern of reversal. Oedipus is, of course, literally the criminal, while Dysart's guilt is, in some ways, more complex. Dysart is implicated in the murder of the god through Alan's abreaction, but not in the literal murder of a person. Nonetheless, Dysart's guilt is so intense that he becomes the victim, in his own eyes like the boy, with a "sharp chain" in his mouth.

Philosophical questions about the nature of man and his place in the universe are common to all tragedy. In *Equus* the sphinx's riddle appears in terms of the horses. Where does the animal become the man? What is it that makes us uniquely human? As Dysart puts it: "Is it possible . . . a horse can add its sufferings together—the non-stop jerks and jabs that are its daily life—and turn them into *grief?* What use is grief to a horse?" Paradoxically, the horse is both god and animal. There is a strange equation here of the distinction between man and the divine and the distinction between man and the animal. Such is the richness of the horse as a symbol in the play. Grief, or the ability to perceive tragedy, is affirmed as the special realm of the human. As a sex fantasy of an adolescent, the horse god Equus can seem jealous, but only Dysart can experience grief at the loss of a god. As Dysart tells Hesther: ". . . to go through life and call it yours—*your* life—you first have to get your own pain."

In the Oedipus Cycle there is ultimate redemption for suffering, and in most tragedy there is a sense of renewed life after the tragic calamity—a concept which has been associated with fertility myths by such thinkers as Gilbert Murray. The idea of sacrifice is represented in Dysart's dream. He finds himself sacrificing children to an obscure god that we see as the Normal, and he is in danger of being unmasked as a charlatan. Shaffer is showing that the psychiatrist cannot restore fertility through sacrifice. There is no successful transition to heterosexual fulfillment that includes worship. The specific reference to ritual sacrifice is intended, I believe, to make this play an antitragedy, at least in terms of this one approach to tragedy. Re-enactment may bring a catharsis to Alan, exciting his emotions to purge them, but Dysart and the spectator are left with a sense of loss that, if such generalizations make sense, only increases their pity and terror.

A discussion of *Oedipus* in this context would be incomplete without some mention of the rôle of the Oedipus complex in Alan's family life. In an act of symbolic castration, the father drags the boy off the horse in the beach scene, infringing on his ecstatic experience of sex. Alan speculates that his mother denies his father sexually, the father thinks mother and son are "thick as thieves." I believe that the Oedipus complex is a psychiatric cliché and is meant to be seen as such. Freudian analysis alone, no matter how extensively it is developed in the play, is meant to be seen as inadequate. The crime is mysterious and eludes any one rational explanation, including other problems in the boy's life, such as his mother's religious fanaticism, a materialistic culture, and the boy's discovery that his father attends pornographic motion pictures. Even the totality of these negative factors, biological, developmental, and cultural, falls short of explaining the crime. Alan's mother may want to exonerate herself, but she is still speaking for the playwright when she says: "Whatever's happened has happened *because of Alan.* Alan is himself. Every soul is itself. If you added up everything we ever did to him, from his first day on earth to this, you wouldn't find why he did this terrible thing." This is, I think, a central statement about tragedy. The tragic error or crime exceeds any simple explanation, and the tragic hero is more than a victim of circumstances. He manages to find his identity in the very deed that creates his guilt. Alan is not the tragic hero precisely because he becomes or is to become someone else for whom this crime will not have central significance. We should remember that the crime and the boy who committed the crime are central for Dysart and for the audience.

The tragedies of Corneille and Racine focus on a tragic conflict between reason, frequently expressed as duty, and the heart. This pattern works out neatly for Dysart, who listens to Judge Hester remind him of his duty to cure Alan. Dysart experiences the unfulfilled longing of the heart for the ultimate consummation that Alan achieves in the god Equus. (Perhaps this use of Hester is a little too schematic, and the Doctor's wife too stereotypically bland.) The result of these conflicting claims on Dysart is a dilemma: His duty to society and even his compassion for the boy dictate that he effect a cure, while his own repressed instincts tell him of the great wrong he would be committing. Does his choice reflect a passive capitulation? In other words, has he really made a choice?

The central issue here is whether compromise is an acceptable course of action for a tragedy. The tragic hero pursues the consequences of his act to a limit, usually death. Racine's *Phèdre* presents a heroine who, according to Lucien Goldmann in *The Hidden God,* cannot accept the necessary compromise of living in the world. Having lusted after her stepson, Phèdre is caught between this impure desire and her demand for absolute purity. The goddess Venus, representing the ability to attain a pure love, remains hidden. There is a kind of logic in Phèdre's refusal of the world through suicide, and she is clearly tragic. Dysart yearns for a similar kind of absolute that combines illicit sexuality and a hidden god. Dysart imagines an Equus hidden in the "black cave of the Psyche," and he can experience the god only through the reenactment of Alan's immediate or immanent perception of it. Like Phèdre, Dysart has glimpsed the contradiction between truth and his social rôle, between the power of raw emotion and the malaise of a corrupt world. Dysart is not tragic in the sense that Phèdre is because he compromises and survives. But a refusal to be corrupted through actions in the world would condemn Alan to a "superiority based on Alan's sucking of equine perspiration" to quote the critic John Simon ["Hippodrama at the Psychodrome," *The Hudson Review* 28, 1975]. True, the horse may seem like a god, but it is still destroying a human being. There is a logic and inevitability in Dysart's decision to betray the hidden god and act in the world. It may be that this decision to act in the world is tragic in a different sense from Phèdre's decision to refuse to act in the world.

The horses in *Phèdre,* like those in **Equus,** are charged with symbolic meaning. Hippolytus, like Alan Strang, has a private relationship with horses which he has driven "half-deranged along the sand-bars, pulling a foaming chariot . . . tilting and staggering upright through the surf." This image of oneness with the horse is similar to that orgiastic union of Alan and the horse Trojan at the beach. In both plays the turn toward heterosexual love leads to a crisis. Hippolytus is afraid of his love for Aricia, and later of Phèdre's love for him, and tries to flee. Compared to Alan with his "chinkle chankle," Hippolytus is a boy scout in the woods. Still, in both cases the horse represents potentially violent forces of the id, and in *Phèdre,* as in **Equus,** the horse can destroy the man who has failed to find in a woman a successful way to express sexual drives. At the end of *Phèdre* the monster emerges from the ocean, a metaphor for the human psyche, to incite the horses to trample Hippolytus to death.

That which was under control through reason and social decorum (that is, emotions, the id, sex) takes its victims, Phèdre and Hippolytus: ". . . then the horses, terror-struck, stampeded. Their master's whip and shouting went unheeded, they dragged his breathless body to the spray. Their red mouths bit the bloody surf. . . ." This passage from *Phèdre* highlights an important difference in the two authors' approaches to theater. Is it more effective to have an eyewitness describe Hippolytus' death through the medium of poetry than to employ Shaffer's more literal approach in representing horses on stage? It has been argued that Shaffer is too theatrical in exploiting the medium of dance. The scene of the blinding, the nude boy leaping up into the spotlight, is, visually at least, powerful. But the question lingers. Has spectacle been substituted for the power of language or has Shaffer discovered a more elemental language of forms, of the body? Has the play begun to get back to the roots of tragedy in ritual sacrifice? Formally, maybe. Thematically, *Equus* is closer to *Death of a Salesman* than to the Greeks. The Greek chorus, the music of words, has been replaced by the unnerving buzz of the horses, theatrically most effective, and by the bland and unconvincing character of Hester. On the other hand, one could argue that myth precedes language and that Shaffer has fulfilled Thomas Mann's hope that post-Freudian writers may eventually recreate myth ["Freud and the Future," in *Myth and Mythmaking,* ed. Henry A. Murray, 1968]. This would, however, not result in tragedy, which deals with human incompleteness.

Shaffer's more literal approach to theater is also evident in the controversial nude scene. Tragedy frequently involves the progressive stripping away of illusions as, for example, with King Lear, who, it should be noted, does shed clothing, baring his chest, as a metaphor for this process. Lear's nakedness is expressed mainly through language, while Shaffer relies more heavily on literal nudity on stage. In addition to the stripping away of defenses, nudity suggests a sense of indecent exposure in *Equus*. The psychiatrist has violated another individual's integrity, or as Dysart sees it, he has stripped Alan of his religion, his worship. The scene also presents an image of feminine beauty, the heterosexual love that is so violently enticing and threatening to the adolescent boy.

Let us return, at this point, to the questions I raised at the outset. Is *Equus* a tragedy and do we need to revise our definition to accommodate this play? The play does not lead to catharsis, and the action lacks the kind of finality needed to achieve a new order out of tragic disorder. Instead of pursuing his tragic knowledge of his crime, curing the boy, to its limit, Dysart compromises. He does not have the stature of a statesman, someone larger than life. But he does achieve complete recognition of his dilemma, and it may be that there is a kind of transcendence in that recognition. No, he does not transcend himself like Othello, who affirms his personal value in the extremity of guilt before committing suicide. If Dysart does transcend the everyday, it is through his human understanding of and sympathy for Alan Strang.

He tears himself apart in doing what he has to do. Even as he becomes more uncertain of his rôle, more depressed about his own lack of religion, he becomes more intensely involved in the life of his patient. He is by turns clever, wily, cagey, unsparing, sarcastic, sardonic, and ruthless in his quest for a problematic cure that will leave himself exposed and guilty of self-betrayal. Like Oedipus, Dysart knows that he will endanger himself by bringing secrets to light. He lacks Oedipus' faith that the public good, or even the private good, will be served. Dysart is a man of greater courage because he is *not* a man of conviction.

So great is Dysart's insight that, by the end of the play, Dysart knows what Equus will say without the mediation of Alan. In that final brutal cross-examination, Dysart speaks for the god: "And you will fail! . . . You will see ME—and you will FAIL! . . . The Lord thy God is a Jealous God! He sees you." After this moment of great intensity, Dysart cradles the broken Alan in his arms and covers him with a blanket. That gesture speaks with more eloquence than words. Dysart has made his own pain by helping to alleviate Alan's. He has discovered in a personal way his separation from the hidden god that could be described as a kind of worship. He has taken the moral ambiguity of the situation and pursued it to the limit in breaking and thus saving another human being. If he compromises, it is a courageous act in the face of radical doubt.

A definition of modern tragedy would have to allow for a private and incomplete form of transcendence that does not lead to a renewal of community bonds. Whether any public good, social or moral, is affirmed is problematic. But Dysart's honesty in confronting his dilemma and his ability to overcome potential paralysis represent a triumph of imagination and humanity. None of us believes that the boy should be abandoned to a sado-masochistic fantasy. All of us see the loss in Alan's cure through the pain that Dysart, and Peter Shaffer, have made for us.

AMADEUS

PRODUCTION REVIEWS

B. A. Young (review date 5 November 1979)

SOURCE: A review of *Amadeus,* in *Financial Times,* 5 November 1979, p. 15.

[Amadeus *was first staged on 2 November 1979 at London's Olivier Theatre in a National Theatre production directed by Peter Hall. In the following evaluation of that production, Young finds the play "unimaginative" and contends that "there is no life in Mr. Shaffer's sto-*

ry. Salieri recounts it in the manner of an illustrated lecture."]

Peter Shaffer has retold the story of how Antonio Salieri poisoned Mozart, with some romantic decorations of his own. This is how it goes in his version:—

Salieri is Court Composer to the Emperor Joseph II. In 1781 Mozart arrives in the capital, having sacked his Archbishop (or vice versa) and Salieri, overwhelmed by the sounds of the wind serenade K364, begins to see him as a rival. More than that, however: he had dedicated his talent to God, and when he realises that Mozart's talent is greater than his he accuses God of ingratitude and dubs him *nemico eterno*, eternal enemy.

A curious enemy, for Salieri triumphs both at court and in the opera house while Mozart, denied promotion by Salieri's machinations, dwindles into a squalid poverty that his concerts and his exiguous pay as Kapellmeister do little to alleviate. Salieri is not concerned with prosperity but talent. As Mozart struggles to finish his Requiem (and who was the mysterious stranger who commissioned that?) Salieri haunts his lodgings in a black mask and leaves poisoned wine on the doorstep. Mozart goes to his pauper's burial and Salieri progresses to his guilt-ridden old age.

Despite a commanding performance by Paul Scofield as Salieri, on stage for virtually the whole three hours of the play, there is no life in Mr. Shaffer's story. Salieri recounts it in the manner of an illustrated lecture. Discovered in old age in his apartments, crying *"Pietà, Mozart!"* to the world while the world, represented by two "venticelli," little breezes that blow the rumours and look like two Mad Hatters, comment on the tale Salieri is said to have told. Salieri goes to his forte-piano to conjure up an audience (us) and, rejuvenated, recounts the story, occasionally concealing himself in a high-backed chair to accommodate episodes from Mozart's more intimate life.

The decorations of Peter Hall's production do little to invigorate this unimaginative piece. Mozart himself is a macedoine of the qualities we know about—conceited, ambitious, frivolous, given to coprophilous language. Simon Callow gives a birdlike performance of this ultra-lightweight character, adding a high-pitched giggle that I can't take. Was there no more to Mozart? It can be argued that this is Mozart as Salieri saw him, but the point of the play is that Salieri recognised Mozart as a transcendent genius, and Mr. Shaffer might surely have allowed a little more depth.

Other characters are little more than scenery. As the Emperor, John Normington spreads his hands and proclaims "There it is!" when he makes a decision. Andrew Cruickshank as the Director of the Imperial Opera and Nicholas Selby as the Prefect of the Imperial Library, as well as Salieri himself, help him to make the decisions. Constanze Weber (Felicity Kendal) says "Ta very much" to show how common she is. Philip Locke as Salieri's

servant loyally brings him cream cakes at all hours but can't stretch his loyalty so far as to go and haunt Mozart in his lodgings.

The production, as I said, is decorative, and needs to be. John Bury's handsome set, radiant with the cultured elegance of the period, has a proscenium arch at the back and makes me think, not for the first time at the Olivier, that the play is better suited to the Lyttelton. Behind the proscenium a line of Viennese citizens appears now and then to express approval, curiosity, alarm or what have you, a happy extravagance only a large permanent company can afford.

Behind the decorations, both of the text and of the production, I thought the play as hollow as a strip-cartoon. Only once, when Mr. Scofield gave his long speech about the ingratitude of God, did I feel that I was in the presence of masters.

Benedict Nightingale (review date 9 November 1979)

SOURCE: "Obscene Child," in *New Statesman,* Vol. 98, No. 2538, 9 November 1979, p. 735.

[*In this review, Nightingale censures Shaffer's depiction of Mozart in* Amadeus, *maintaining that the playwright's "appreciation of the composer is too vague, general and mindlessly rhapsodic."*]

There was a moment in **Amadeus** that reminded me of the movie in which Beethoven's landlord proclaimed his presence with an ominous rat-tat-tat-TAT on the composer's door. A look of Archimedean discovery flashed across the towering genius's craggy brow, and he dashed to his piano, and then and there began to concoct the Fifth Symphony.

In Peter Shaffer's version, court tunesmith Salieri fêtes the newly-arrived Mozart with a tiny and rather tinny march, upon which the boy-wonder promptly improvises some indolent variations, ending up, believe it or not, with a hit-song from the still-unwritten *Figaro.* Well, perhaps it happened. The programme informs us that Mr. Shaffer was music critic for *Time and Tide* all the way from 1961 to 1962, and he obviously knows his Wolfgang better than most of us. All the same, isn't he inclined to take a romantic, not to say sensational view of composers and composition?

Simon Callow's Mozart is an enterprising piece of acting, but a calculated travesty as biographical. The tactless, mercurial youth, with his well-authenticated weakness for lavatorial banter, is transformed into a spectacularly boorish coprophiliac, with a goofy mule-face and a habit of half-snickering, half-braying, like a castrated donkey. He tumbles clownishly on stage with Felicity Kendal's glad-eyed Constanze—herself apt to signal her less-than-courtly manners with a pert 'ta, very much'—and winsomely promises 'to shit on your nose and watch it run down your chin'. Soon, he is outraging the Hapsburg hierarchy by denouncing his rivals as 'dogshit' or the pre-Mozartian opera as 'boring', leaping onto a chair, tittering and gesticulating as he does so, for all the world like a tarted-up chimp in a Brook Bond ad. Critics apt to take a heady, 19th-century view of 'inspiration' have wondered how a billiard-playing freemason could have composed *Giovanni* or the *Jupiter,* just as they've been shocked at the idea of a money-conscious Stratford burgher writing *Lear.* Shaffer passes the incongruity still further: how could the Mass in C minor conceivably have been penned by an 'obscene child'?

This view of Mozart actually comes from his Salieri, whose 18th-century wig camouflages a far-from-18th-century sensibility. In my experience, musicians tend to discuss their art in technical, downbeat, even banal terms, presumably believing, with Stravinsky, that 'the only true critical comment on a piece of music is another piece of music'; and they would surely have been even more reticent in the rational Austrian 1780's. But Shaffer's Salieri rises to the reverential ecstasies of Emerson, Nietzsche, or the Carlyle who declared that music 'leads us to the edge of the Infinite and lets us for moments gaze into that'. He stumbles from the sound of a Mozart divertimento, deciding he has heard 'the voice of God'; swoons at the very manuscript of the great Mass announcing he's staring through inkpots at 'an absolute beauty'; dubs the late piano concerti 'the finest things made by man in the 18th century'; describes the *Requiem* as 'absolute music'; and proceeds to take monstrous revenge on the divine upstart.

The result is a didactic melodrama, very characteristic of Shaffer. From *Five Finger Exercise* on he has been celebrating the soul of man as it's incarnated in art, and dramatising its battles with philistinism and envy. Indeed, his world has sometimes seemed reducible to an enlightened clique, rapturously crying 'Leonardo', 'Wells Cathedral', 'Peter Grimes' or 'Ingmar Bergman', and a horrid rump, out to deride or destroy such marvels. This play adds Mozart to the cultural treasury, Salieri to the enemies list, but little, I fear, to Shaffer's own reputation as a dramatist. One trouble is that his appreciation of the composer is too vague, general and mindlessly rhapsodic, akin to one of those soaring but unevenly informative travelogues about the beauties of Rome or the wonders of Peking. Where, for instance, is there adequate recognition of the discipline and astringency I hear in my own current obsession, the string quintet K516? The other trouble is the outrageous implausibility of Salieri himself.

The prototype is thought to have schemed to Mozart's disadvantage, and, in his senility, is said to have claimed to have poisoned him. From these hints and rumours Shaffer manufactures a blend of Iago and Faust, much at odds with the historical Salieri, whose conventional efforts were as triumphant as Mozart's musical adventures were neglected, and therefore had no motive for murder. He will ruin the creature who has 'made me feel my emptiness as Adam felt his nakedness'. Doing so he will 'block' God, who has perversely given Mozart the creative genius he prayed for and left him only the agony of perceiving it. He will strike a blow for the world's mediocrities. The tale of the spectral stranger who commissioned what was in effect to be Mozart's own Requiem is well-known. According to Shaffer it was actually a plot devised by the fiendish Salieri. Not content with undermining Mozart's reputation and reducing him to penury, he exploited his Freudian confusions and shattered his damaged morale by confronting him with his dead father in the form of the Stone Guest, a looming shadow who grimly materialises and makes his deadly request to the awesome chords of *Giovanni*: a theatrical moment that Peter Hall, whose production is generally as temperate as hostile circumstances allow, should surely have resisted.

It is a part and a play written for Sir Henry Irving, who unluckily turned out to be indisposed. Paul Scofield is, however, an admirable substitute: not because of any ingenuities of interpretation, though his baleful silence and charged smiles are as eloquent as one would expect; not even for that celebrated voice which ranges from a sepulchral rumble to a quavering squeal, as of Larry the Lamb in second childhood; but because of the effortless power, the brooding charisma, of his mere presence. It is difficult to imagine **Amadeus** with Scofield in command. But that may be because without him to rivet and mesmerise us Mr. Shaffer's lavish argosy would simply sink.

Polly Toynbee   (review date 10 November 1979)

SOURCE: "Slow Motion," in *The Spectator,* Vol. 243, No. 7896, 10 November 1979, pp. 29-30.

[*In the following evaluation, Toynbee faults Shaffer for a lack of character and plot development in* Amadeus.]

Amadeus by Peter Shaffer should have been a musical. The only moments that were really moving were when Mozart's music was played and these, alas, were all too few. More music and less talk would have made a very long evening (three hours) seem a lot shorter.

The first part of the play is crisp and enjoyable, as the dying composer Salieri recounts his relationship with Mozart. Salieri a mediocre court musician, honest, hardworking and virtuous is confronted suddenly with the arrival of the young Mozart at court in Vienna. He has heard of his musical prowess. A wonderful scene shows Salieri, awaiting his meeting with Mozart, in a drawing room hidden from view in a deep arm chair. Mozart cavorts into the room pursuing a pretty girl, and instead of a cultured young genius, Salieri discovers a vulgar foppish near-idiot, shrieking with laughter at kindergarten scatalogical jokes, foul mouthed and ludicrous in an extraordinary blond wig which stands up en brosse.

Later that evening he hears Mozart play, and is agonised and outraged at the exquisite beauty of the music. How could an unworthy, strutting lout be touched with such divine genius, while he, pious, serious and good had never for one moment been granted the gift to lift his music above honest mediocrity? It makes a fine opening to a play, a powerful image of the arbitrariness and injustice of God's grace. But unfortunately, with still another two hours to run, the play has nothing more to say. The story, retold by Salieri, unfolds to the point where Salieri convinces himself of the truth of the rumour that he was responsible for Mozart's death.

Salieri, as a good man dragged down by jealousy, is somewhat two dimensional, but Paul Scofield does the best he can. Simon Callow is a splendid buffoon as Mozart, but again, as the character does not develop, the wretched actor is left repeating himself over and over again in scene after scene. Felicity Kendal—as always exquisitely charming and delicious—is a perfect Constanze, flirtatious but virtuous. We have become used to such beautiful sets in the Olivier that the ugly plastic floor, and curious electric screen—which raises and lowers itself so fussily, is a disappointment.

Modern historical plays, like historical novels, start with many handicaps. They tend to become over-involved in the plot and the history at the expense of having anything to say. Some rather cheap stagy tricks here try to disguise the fact that this is hardly a play at all, but more of a narration.

John Russell Taylor (review date January 1980)

SOURCE: A review of *Amadeus,* in *Drama: The Quarterly Theatre Review,* No. 135, January, 1980, pp. 48-9.

[*In the following evaluation of the London production, Taylor observes that* Amadeus *is a "bit stuffy and old-fashioned, a bit determined to be regarded at all costs as philosophical," but concedes that it succeeds on stage.*]

[Peter Shaffer's *Amadeus* at the Olivier] is a puzzlement. There are big things obviously wrong with it. It takes for ever to get started, as though Shaffer has thought of three or four possible openings and then used all of them. It tends, as is Shaffer's way in his loftier pieces— *Equus, The Royal Hunt of the Sun*—to over-verbalise everything, so that we seldom get a chance to feel his subject-matter in our bones because he is so busy telling us what we ought to be feeling (as if Shakespeare, instead of creating Iago, had written a play explaining him). The two earlier plays had at least, to counter-balance, the vivid theatrical gestures of John Dexter's productions; here Peter Hall is plodding and literal. All the same, it is an interesting subject: Salieri's famous rivalry with Mozart and the legend that he poisoned Mozart are presented in the light of a cosmic battle between Salieri and God, in which Mozart is seen more as a pawn in

God's game than as the direct object of Salieri's hate; indeed, by a sublime irony Salieri, patron saint of mediocrity, is the only man of his age who can wholly, agonisingly appreciate the transcendent genius of the impossible young pup.

So, despite frequent irritations, and strong reservations about Paul Scofield's Old-Mother-Riley impersonation as the aged but not-so-potty Salieri (he is mostly fine when he drops the disguise), I found myself taking more interest in the play than I felt somehow I ought to be: for quite a bit of its length it does, dammit, work. And I kept, fancifully, seeing other allegories in it—one has plenty of time for that sort of thing. For example, the encounter of Salieri and Mozart in terms of a meeting between a Christopher Fry hero and Jimmy Porter somewhere in the West End theatre around the late Fifties. I wish someone had persuaded Shaffer to prune the play and spruce up his dialogue—Salieri's little bits of Italian become rather self-conscious and silly, and I cannot quite see why Constanze should be made to talk like a Thirties barmaid—because he has the core, more than the core, of a very workable play. A bit stuffy and old-fashioned, a bit determined to be regarded at all costs as philosophical, but then that in many ways makes it the perfect new play for a National Theatre audience. But with good acting roles, taken with notable panache by Paul Scofield, Simon Callow as the awful, his-own-worst enemy Mozart and a lot of plotters on the sidelines. Maybe Shaffer can do a *Shrivings* on it for the New York production: then we shall have yet something else to thank the American theatre for.

CRITICAL COMMENTARY

Robert Asahina (essay date 1981)

SOURCE: "Theatre Chronicle," in *The Hudson Review,* Vol. XXXIV, No. 2, Summer, 1981, pp. 263-68.

[*In the essay below, Asahina charges that* Amadeus, *like many of Shaffer's other plays, is inconsistent and self-contradictory.*]

There are two kinds of people, according to a variation on an old joke: those who divide the world into two kinds of people, and those who don't. Peter Shaffer certainly belongs to the first kind. For nearly a quarter-century, he has presented an almost Manichean world-view in one play after another. The characters and settings change: Pizarro and Atahualpa, conquerer and conquered in sixteenth-century Peru; Martin Dysart and Alan Strang, psychiatrist and patient in contemporary England; Antonio Salieri and Wolfgang Amadeus Mozart, *Kapellmeister* and Chamber Composer (and possibly murderer and victim) in eighteenth-century Vienna. But the basic plot— a struggle between two opposing but mutually dependent males—remains the same, whether the play is called *The Royal Hunt of the Sun* (1965), *Equus* (1974), or, most

Tom Hulce as Mozart in a scene from the 1984 film adaptation of Amadeus.

recently, *Amadeus,* the critical and box-office success of the current season.

To be sure, *Amadeus* is much more sophisticated than Shaffer's earlier plays. His first work, *Five Finger Exercise* (1958), was a bourgeois domestic drama, full of recriminations and revelations, conventional in both content and form. And his subsequent one-act plays, **"The Private Ear"** and **"The Public Eye"** (1962) and **"The White Liars"** and **"Black Comedy"** (1968), as well as the full-length *Shrivings* (1970), did not depart from the mundane world that they both portrayed and belonged to. But then Shaffer found God as a theme in *The Royal Hunt of the Sun,* and later discovered psychoanalysis and arena staging in *Equus.* Now, in *Amadeus,* he combines theology and psychoanalysis and presents them along with his latest formal discovery—Brecht's *Verfremdungseffekt.*

The curtain is up; the house and stage lights are on. In the middle of the stage, with his back to the audience, a man is slumped in a wheelchair. All the lights dim; there is a murmur of background voices that grow louder until two characters emerge from the opposite wings and talk

to each other and to the audience. They are the *venticelli*—the "little winds" who carry rumors to their invalid master, Salieri, and to us.

When they began speaking, the stage lights rose, and my spirits sank. "The whole city is talking," the *venticelli* chatter, and in this clumsiest of all possible ways—having them address the audience—Shaffer lays the groundwork for the story that is about to unfold. It is 1823, on the eve of what appears to be the death of Salieri—the First *Kapellmeister* in the court of Emperor Joseph II of Austria, the composer of more than 40 operas as well as various oratorios and vocal and instrumental pieces, and the teacher of Beethoven, Schubert, and Liszt. Thirty-two years earlier, Mozart—born six years after Salieri—had died under uncertain circumstances, and now the older man has decided to confess that he poisoned the younger composer.

Salieri swivels in his wheelchair, stands, and speaks to the audience—"Ghosts of the Future," he calls us—as the house lights grow brighter, supposedly so that the old man can see our faces. In a lengthy monologue that serves as a framing sequence to the play proper, which takes place in a flashback, he confides to us that he had, in his childhood, made a bargain with God. "Let me be a composer," he had asked. "Grant me sufficient fame to enjoy it. In return I will live with virtue. I will strive to better the lot of my fellows. And I will honor You with much music all the days of my life." He then throws off his dressing gown, straightens up, and appears to us as he did when he was thirty-two years younger. "I present to you," he announces, "my last composition, entitled *The Death of Mozart; or, Did I Do It?*" Inviting us along, as the lights dim, he steps back into the 1780s.

Unfortunately, Shaffer's use of this Brechtian staging to invite us to distance ourselves from what will follow means that we cannot totally disregard the playwright's intellectual pretensions. We could ignore the irrelevant staging and even the psychodrama of *Equus,* because the plot was little more than a detective story in sophisticated drag; throughout, like Dr. Dysart, we could chiefly concern ourselves with discovering why Alan Strang blinded all those horses. Likewise, we could watch *The Royal Hunt of the Sun* as nothing but a costume epic about conquistadors and Incas, who just happened to speak a lot of mumbo-jumbo about the supernatural because they both belonged to premodern societies.

But by asking us to regard, as the main character does, the story of *Amadeus* as a "composition"—a play-within-a-play, a drama within quotation marks—Shaffer raises some important questions about the meaning of his work that he then doesn't bother to answer or even to address. How seriously, for instance, are we to take Salieri's claim that he poisoned Mozart? Rumors about the "murder" circulated throughout the nineteenth century; Rimsky-Korsakoff even based an opera, *Mozart and Salieri* (1897), on them. No contemporary authority puts any stock in the stories, however, and Shaffer certainly does not believe, and does not show in his play, that Salieri was literally a murderer.

Yet the playwright obviously believes, or at least dramatizes the belief, that Salieri was in some significant sense indirectly responsible for Mozart's death. Near the end of the play, Salieri announces to the dying composer: "We are both poisoned, Amadeus. I with you: you with me. . . . Ten years of my hate have poisoned you to death." How so? It was a *crime passionnel,* of a sort, although as Shaffer portrays him, Salieri is a man driven by relatively banal passions. Indeed, the character acknowledges himself a "mediocrity." He struck that bargain with God because he "wanted fame," so he could "blaze like a comet across the firmament of Europe." He establishes himself as a court musician in Vienna and then encounters Mozart, who is struggling to make a living. When Salieri first hears the younger man's music, he is consumed with an even baser passion: "I envied Mozart from the depths of my soul."

What particularly infuriates Salieri and stokes the flames of his envy is the disparity he perceives between the beautiful art and the base soul of his rival. "It seemed to me that I had heard a voice of God," Salieri tells us after listening to the *Adagio* from the *Serenade for thirteen wind instruments* (K. 361), "and that it issued from a creature whose own voice I had also heard—and it was the voice of an obscene child!" As Shaffer presents him (based in part on published correspondence), Mozart is a sniggering, truculent case of arrested development, given to foot-stomping, lisping, prancing, mincing, coprophilia, sadomasochism, and possibly homosexuality. And to Salieri, it is an outrage that God has chosen such an unworthy mouthpiece on earth.

In fact, Salieri regards the younger musician's art and very existence as a betrayal of that deal he struck with God so many years before. "The creature's dreadful giggle was the laughter of God," he complains. "You gave me the desire to serve You," he tells the Almighty. "You put into me perception of the Incomparable . . . then ensured that I would know myself forever mediocre. . . . They say the spirit bloweth where it listeth: I tell you NO! It must list to virtue or not blow at all!"

So, in Act Two, Salieri's life acquires "a terrible and thrilling purpose. The blocking of God in one of his purest manifestations. I had the power. God needed Mozart to let himself into the world. And Mozart needed me to get him worldly advancement. So it would be a battle to the end—and Mozart was the battleground." He decides to "reduce the man" to "reduce the God." Occupying the superior position at the court, Salieri is able to thwart Mozart at every stage of his career. As Shaffer tells it, Salieri sabotages *The Marriage of Figaro* by limiting it to merely nine performances; he encourages Mozart to write *The Magic Flute* just so the Masons will cut off their financial aid to the impoverished composer; he offers himself as a father figure to the younger man after the death of Leopold Mozart and then makes sure that the bereaved son is paid only a trifling salary for his services as Chamber Composer; and he finally tries to frighten Mozart to death by disguising himself as the *Commendatore* from *Don Giovanni* and presenting himself to the deranged composer, who is working on the *Requiem Mass* on his deathbed.

Much to his astonishment, Salieri at first finds that he is not punished but apparently rewarded for all these plots against his rival. He is appointed *Kapellmeister* and honored "as infinitely the superior composer. And this despite the fact that these were the . . . years in which Mozart wrote his best keyboard concerti and his string quartets. Each was played once—then totally forgotten!" Yet God eventually makes Salieri pay the price for the fame he had bargained for so many years before: "I was to be bricked up in fame! Embalmed in fame! Buried in fame—but for work I knew to be absolutely worthless! This was my sentence: I must endure thirty years of being called 'Distinguished' by people incapable of distinguishing! . . . And finally—His masterstroke—it would all be taken away from me. Every scrap. I must survive to see myself become extinct!"

So, in the last scene of the play, Salieri returns to 1823 and the framing sequence and resolves to achieve immortality by falsely confessing to Mozart's murder and then killing himself. But God fools him one last time: nobody believes him, and Salieri survives the suicide attempt. Thwarted and resigned to his fate, he then addresses the last line of *Amadeus* to the "Ghosts of the Future" in the audience: "Mediocrities everywhere—now and to come—I absolve you all. Amen."

The least that can be said about this extraordinary conclusion is that it is preposterous. Why should we need absolution? Does Shaffer mean to suggest that, because of our imaginative participation in the play from Salieri's perspective, we are implicated in his crimes? Yet surely it is Salieri, not the audience, who is guilty—of envy, at least, if not of murder. And who is he to call us mediocrities? After all, the only confession that we or any of the characters are expected to believe is Salieri's admission that he is the "Patron Saint of Mediocrity."

But is he? The facts certainly indicate otherwise; Salieri definitely was not in Mozart's league, but he surely is remembered, as hundreds of truly ordinary late-eighteenth- and early-nineteenth-century musicians are not. Still, the question concerns not historical but dramatic truth. And it must be said that *Amadeus* has a hollow ring.

To begin with, as John Simon has noted, it is a mark of the genuine mediocrity not to recognize either his own limitations or the excellence of others. Thus Shaffer sounds a false note when he has Salieri bitterly tell God: "My only reward . . . is to be the sole man alive in this time who shall clearly recognize Your Incarnation." Furthermore, since Shaffer has already asked us to share Salieri's viewpoint, this pronouncement seems like an invitation to the audience to congratulate itself on its superior taste: since all of us recognize Mozart's worth, we can be both sympathetic toward Salieri and condescending toward the other characters, who fail to appreciate the genius in their midst.

Inviting this kind of patronizing historicism raises certain difficulties, however, which are nowhere more apparent than in Shaffer's characterization of Salieri. The mainspring of the plot is the composer's sense of betrayal at God's having chosen as His voice on earth not a virtuous man like himself, but an amoral, if not immoral, "creature" like Mozart. Yet the notion that talent should belong to the virtuous—that geniuses should perforce be moral exemplars or, conversely, that good men deserve to be recognized for their art as well as for their good deeds—is ludicrous, at best. It is also a particularly odd idea for Salieri to have, since we are also supposed to believe that, until the time of his "betrayal," he had been the kind of devout Catholic for whom virtue should have been its own reward. Early in the play, he disparagingly tells us that his parents' "notion of God was a superior Habsburg emperor, inhabiting a Heaven only slightly farther off than Vienna. All they required of Him was to protect commerce, and keep them forever preserved in mediocrity. My own requirements were very different." Of course they were—only someone who believed in God in the first place would make a deal with Him.

So we are presented with a dilemma: either the very idea that animates the plot is ridiculous, or the character whose behavior is motivated by that idea is self-contradictory, and thus equally ridiculous. Neither possibility seems to faze Shaffer, since both flatter the audience's sense of superiority to the past. We "Ghosts of the Future" don't believe in God, so it's all too easy for us to tolerate the contradictory actions of those who do. (Or supposedly do. Chasing after every cheap laugh, Shaffer throws a few crumbs to the secular audience by having Salieri declare in an aside: "Italians are fond of waxworks. . . . Our religion is largely based on them.") On the other hand, thanks to psychoanalysis and the century-and-a-half between the time of the play and today, we are also too sophisticated to be shocked by the revelation of, for instance, Mozart's "true" character—titillated, perhaps, but not shocked, by the idea that virtue and genius do not go hand in hand. In fact, we are entertained.

The problem, of course, is that the formal device Shaffer has chosen—the frank acknowledgement of the presence of the audience by the main character to engender a sense of "alienation"—was never intended by its inventor to entertain. To be sure, there has always been a great gap between Brecht's theory of the role of *"V-effekt"* in "epic theater" and the actual emotional response elicited by his works. Nonetheless, rather than even trying to challenge the audience to be critical of the drama unfolding before it, Shaffer encourages the "Ghosts of the Future" to be complacent by reinforcing a sense of superiority that follows from nothing but their (our) residing in the future (the present), rather than the late-eighteenth or early-nineteenth century.

Shaffer's historicism in *Amadeus* is also worth noting because it apparently reverses the pessimistic attitude regarding the future (the present) that had been a characteristic theme in his earlier works. In *Equus,* Dysart, lost in his picture books, dreams of the gods of ancient Greece. Presented with Alan, an animal-killer seemingly driven to religious fervor by the Furies themselves, the doctor's belief in his ability—nay, his very right—to heal with the modern tool of psychoanalysis is shaken. "That boy has known a passion more ferocious than I have felt in any second of my life," he says of Alan. "And let me tell you something: I envy it. . . . Can you think of anything worse one can do to anybody than take away their worship?" And Dysart's lack of faith in the future is underscored by his loveless and childless marriage, which finds its perfect symbolic expression in his "special dream" about "carving up children."

Likewise, in *The Royal Hunt of the Sun,* Pizarro—a bastard child, unmarried and never a father—muses that "Time cheats us all the way [though] having children goes some steps to defeating it." But the aging conquistador sees something even better in the primitive Atahualpa, also a bastard: he is "an immortal man in whom all his people live completely. He has an answer for time." And in *Shrivings,* the venerable philosopher Gideon Petrie renounces sex and drives away his wife, childless, only to seek as a surrogate child the son of his former disciple.

It should be clear that the homoerotic elements apparent in *Amadeus* have been much more explicit in Shaffer's previous plays. Salieri's love-hate affair with Mozart is seemingly less important to the plot than his relationship with God, or than the competition between Walter and Clive for the affections of Clive's mother was in *Five Finger Exercise,* or the rivalry between Tchaik and Ted over Doreen was in **"The Private Ear,"** or the triangle formed by Julian, Charles and Belinda was in **"The Public Eye,"** or the trio of Frank, Tom and Sue was in **"The White Liars."** There is no important romantic triangle in *Amadeus,* or in *The Royal Hunt of the Sun* or *Equus*; as Shaffer has become more sophisticated, he has stripped his works of such unnecessary elements as women. Which is not to say, however, that they don't continue to figure as significant secondary characters who contribute to the homoerotic tension. Just as Alan refuses Jill Mason after she offers herself, naked, at the climax of *Equus,* Salieri spurns the spread-eagled Constanze Mozart—in the key scene at the beginning of Act Two of *Amadeus,* when the composer renounces God—even though she has decided to accept his offer to secure a court position for her husband in exchange for her favors.

In neither case is the rejection believable, but the latter refusal is particularly astonishing since it was Salieri, after all, who proposed the deal. He first confesses, "I would have liked her . . . then more than ever," but then turns around in the very next line and declares, out of the blue, by way of explaining his inconsistent behavior: "My quarrel now wasn't with Mozart—it was through him! Through him to God." One senses that it is not the character but the playwright who is rejecting the woman.

Thus romantic love—or love between men and women that results in children—has figured less and less in Shaffer's work, and the competition of two males over a female has also gradually ceased to be an important plot mechanism. Instead, Shaffer has dramatized what is, apparently, to him a grander passion: the mutually destructive need of two men for each other. "He has something for me," Pizarro says of Atahualpa—and he doesn't mean the roomful of gold that he has demanded of the Incas as a ransom for their captive ruler. And the noble savage says of his conqueror: "I see my father" in his face. Yet, in the name of a God who no longer commands his belief, the Spaniard kills the Indian, who at first thought that the conquistador was himself a god. Likewise, Dysart "sacrifices [Alan] to the Normal" by curing him and thus robbing him of the passion that the doctor had so envied in the patient who needed him. And, once again, an older man envies and destroys a younger man who depends on him in *Amadeus*—a true *crime passionnel,* though not as the French usually imagine it.

So we can, after all, believe that the *Kapellmeister* is a murderer—of his own humanity. It is not, as he claims, his hate that has poisoned Mozart but his own envy that has poisoned Salieri, just as it did Pizarro and Dysart. And the murderous anger that leads Salieri to "poison" Mozart, Pizarro to kill Atahualpa, and Dysart to destroy Alan's gods is the rage of an aging and bitter man at the

freedom of a younger male who represents all that he is not: a primitive to both the conquistador and the psychoanalyst; a genius to the *Kapellmeister*. Strip away the metaphysics, the accents that thrill the Broadway Anglophiles, the wonderfully versatile and elegant sets by John Bury, and *Amadeus* is really about *amour-propre*—of a particularly twisted kind.

Peter. V. Conroy, Jr. (essay date 1989-90)

SOURCE: "*Amadeus* on Stage and Screen," in *Postscript: Essays in Film and the Humanities,* Vol. 9, Nos. 1-2, Fall, 1989-Winter 1990, pp. 25-37.

[*In the essay below, Conroy assesses the effect of the changes Shaffer made to* Amadeus *in adapting it to film.*]

The transposition of any literary work to the movie screen is an undertaking fraught with danger. This is true even when the literary work in question is a play, that is to say a work that has already been created in the visual and dialogic modes that film shares with drama. Peter Shaffer's *Amadeus* offers a perfect illustration of these difficulties and of how the "same" work can change as it passes from stage to screen. In reformulating his story for the screen Shaffer has rearticulated Salieri's conflict with God, making it more problematic than it was in the play; furthermore, this transposition creates a reflexive text that illuminates a new aspect of Shaffer as an artist.

What strikes me as an initially small but ultimately significant difference between the two *Amadeus*es is a structural pattern that did not exist in the play. Basically the film repeats several times a conversational structure that we can analyze with terms borrowed from Roman Jakobson's communication theory. ["Linguistics and Poetics" in *Style in Language,* 1960]. For Jakobson, any valid communication contains six different elements, each of which is distinct. Here I will use only two of them, the emitting or speaking function (addresser), and the receiving or listening one (addressee). Shaffer's film plays with who is speaking to whom in a way that was not done on stage. Only in its last pages does the play make the point that the film stresses right from the beginning: the importance of listening, of being ears for another's voice. "I was born a pair of ears and nothing else. It is only through hearing music that I know God exists." The series of conversational acts constitutes a pattern, a structure that organizes meaning in ways that distinguish the ultimate significance of the film from that of the play.

The film opens with a framing device that contains information that was given at the end of the play. A new character appears here, the priest to whom old Salieri is telling the story of his crime against Mozart. This priest is confessing Salieri who has already attempted suicide and who is now recuperating from his self-inflicted wounds. He is a special audience, a privileged listener who possesses, by his very identity as a clergyman, the power to forgive. This connection between the listening priest and the speaking Salieri places the film, right from the outset, in the theological context of transgression and absolution, of a sinner demanding pardon from his God.

More important, this confessional frame is not forgotten once we get deeper into Salieri's story (or confession). On stage, Salieri opens and closes each act in 1823, old and infirm. The play is a flashback with Salieri functioning both as a participant in the stage action and as an outside commentator and observer as he moves freely and easily from one role to another. By speaking in asides so as not to destroy dramatic continuity, he can interrupt his dialogue with the characters of the 1780's to address his audience in 1823. He changes costume and voice only at the curtains so that during the acts the Salieri of 1823 merges completely with his younger self. The film, in contrast, maintains the temporal distinction between the two periods. On the screen the young Salieri is sharply differentiated, physically, from the aged penitent. This gap between the young and the old Salieri is emphasized whenever the film cuts back and forth, thus depicting visually the infirm Salieri and the priest and reminding us of their continued presence "in" the film.

What the film visualizes, and what the play passed over, is precisely this confessional scene, this frame of sin and repentance. Although Salieri tells his sin to the priest, he does not in the end really confess. Indeed, he eventually abandons the priest without asking for forgiveness. This question of absolution, or non-absolution, ties into Salieri's blasphemy and his revolt against God.

The sin that Salieri confesses is of course his "crime" against Mozart: his plot to eliminate the bothersome but gifted little Wolfi. On this crime the stage and screen versions are substantially the same. What is different is how this central section echoes and reflects the frame that introduced it: it is a repetition and inversion of that same conversational pattern. First Salieri speaks and the confessor listens; now Mozart and his music speak, and Salieri alone is able to listen. As I mentioned earlier, Salieri characterizes himself as a special ear. According to both of Shaffer's scripts, Salieri is alone in recognizing Mozart's genius. He appreciates the depth and beauty of Mozart's music while everyone else sees him merely as a child prodigy or a "trained monkey." Salieri alone possesses the gift of hearing Mozart's music. He is the only one who knows how to listen:

> My pungent neighbors rolled on their benches at the jokes—And I alone, in their midst, heard—*The Magic Flute.*

> (II, 14)

Both the film and the play contain a poignant scene in which Constanze shows Salieri the music her husband is composing. The sheets drop from Salieri's fingers as he realizes not only how beautiful this music is, but also how effortlessly and flawlessly Mozart wrote it. At this point we hear the music that Salieri is looking at. In a sense we are hearing through Salieri's eyes and ears, through his extraordinary appreciation of Mozart:

> What was evident was that Mozart was simply transcribing music completely finished in his head. And finished as most music is never finished. Displace one note and there would be diminishment. Displace one phrase and the structure would fall. Here again—only now in abundance—were the same sounds I'd heard in the library.

> (I, 12)

Only Salieri knows how great Mozart is. Only Salieri is the perfect listener for Mozart's music, appreciating every subtlety, recognizing the genius behind it.

The film highlights Salieri the exceptional listener who hears what no one else can hear. After Mozart has collapsed at the theater conducting and playing the *Magic Flute*, Salieri brings him home. There, on what turns out to be his deathbed, Mozart dictates the last part of his *Requiem*. Salieri writes down the notes as Mozart creates them. No one else ever gets this close to Mozart's genius as composer. Not only is Salieri present, but he also participates in a moving and miraculous way. As Amadeus speaks the notes, Salieri writes them down and thus allows them to be heard by others, quite literally in fact since we are hearing them on the soundtrack. Salieri's own musical gift is emphasized by this collaboration. Mozart speaks in technical terms that are difficult to understand: "We ended in F major. So now A minor." Not for his fellow musician Salieri, however. Without Salieri to write them down, these notes that were in Amadeus' "noodle" would never be recorded, never passed on to posterity, never available for future appreciation. Salieri is the midwife at the birth of genius. He is the indispensable collaborator without whom this music would be lost forever. Not only does he first hear and appreciate Mozart's music, but he also records and saves that music from death and oblivion. Salieri is therefore Mozart's most avid listener. Salieri listens to Mozart's music just as intently, just as seriously as the priest listens to his confession.

This deathbed scene captures an intimate exchange between two men. With growing excitement and reverent admiration Salieri exclaims, "Yes! Yes!" as he slowly comes to understand how Mozart's music fits together note by inevitable note. This conversation involves no confession, even though Amadeus does ask Salieri's forgiveness for suspecting him as an enemy; rather it records a special state of grace. Precisely because it is touched by grace, the scene is also heavy with tragedy. This Mozart, whom Salieri so loyally serves as amanuensis, is also the man he is planning to betray. On one hand Salieri is giving birth to Mozart's music, on the other he is plotting Amadeus' death. At this climactic point antagonism could give way to intimacy, hatred to love, animosity and rivalry to respect and cooperation. Almost. . . . Nonetheless, the emotion behind Salieri's active listening is powerful. Even as he kills Mozart, he grants him immortality by hearing (and transcribing) the *Requiem*.

More effectively than any other scene in either the play or the film, this deathbed conversation focuses on the speaking-listening relationship between these two men and on the paradoxical motivations of Salieri himself.

If I have accentuated Salieri's role as Mozart's best and most appreciative listener, I must also acknowledge that his acute understanding is limited to musical matters. Salieri correctly evaluates Mozart's music, but he is unreliable as far as Amadeus' life is concerned. Musicologists find it hard to accept Salieri's identification of Frau Weber and the Queen of the Night, for example. By making that marvelous cut from the mother-in-law's jabbering mouth to the Queen trilling her long runs, the film irrevocably connects these figures. That cut creates a continuity of image and sound that is pure film and that requires no justification other than its own doing. It stands apart from logical or historical considerations. Although we cannot change Salieri's version of Amadeus' life, we can note that he is wrong. Mozart wrote this brilliant coloratura aria as a show-stopper to set off the remarkable range and vocal agility of his sister-in-law, Josefa Hefer, who was a member of Schikaneder's company, the impresario who provided the libretto for *The Magic Flute* and who both produced the opera and performed in it.

Critics have been eager to find inaccuracies like this one just as many spectators have been upset by this portrait of Mozart as a spoiled brat and immature adolescent. Later I will argue that these exaggerations serve to sharpen the conflict of talent and genius that lies at the base of his drama. At this point I would simply maintain that, more successfully than the play, the film locates the source of these distortions. They belong to Salieri, that unreliable story-teller and speaker, that fake confessee who at the opening frame was preparing to recount his sin to the priest. The play failed to ground these inaccurate biological details in some meaningful purpose. It did not establish that Salieri was an unreliable source of information about Amadeus while he was the lone appreciator of Mozart's music. Thus the criticisms directed at Shaffer should be laid at Salieri's door. This shift is critical to understanding Salieri's truly paradoxical character and Shaffer's sympathy for and identification with him.

The contrast between the Salieri who appreciates Mozart's music and the Salieri who provides erroneous biographical material echoes the distinction, made earlier, between the old and the young Salieri. That distinction was made most powerfully in the film which visualized both ages. The gap between these two incarnations of the same Salieri (old and crazed, young and cunning; the avid listener and the unreliable story teller) marks the film as truly his story. More than the play the film allows Salieri's character to grow in complexity and in contradictions as it identifies more clearly the dilemma in his heart. Salieri listening in rapt wonder to Mozart's music is not the same Salieri who is confessing murder to the priest.

A third example of the conversational pattern I have been examining includes Salieri again as the speaker and God

as his listener. In an early scene the young Salieri speaks to God and asks him to enter into a bargain, an exchange by which God gives fame and Salieri returns a dutiful life of music and virtue:

> I knelt before the God of Bargains, and I prayed through the moldering plaster with all my soul. "*Signore*, let me be a composer! Grant me sufficient fame to enjoy it. In return, I will live with virtue. I will strive to better the lot of my fellows. And I will honor you with much music all the days of my life!" As I said *Amen*, I saw His eyes flare. (As "God") "*Bene*. Go forth, Antonio. Serve me and mankind, and you will be blessed!" . . . "*Grazie!*" I called back. "I am Your servant for life!"

(I, 2)

In the film there is a scene in which Salieri composes at the keyboard the march that Mozart will shortly transform into his Figaro aria. He looks up at the crucifix and audibly thanks God for "giving" him the note he needs to complete his melody. This almost silent conversation captures his interaction with God: God gives Salieri musical inspiration so that he can give back all his life and all his music. This "bargain" abruptly breaks down when Salieri hears Mozart's music, however. Henceforth he knows that God's gift to him is a paltry one. Amadeus displays none of the virtues at which Salieri has worked so hard. Nonetheless, he writes what can only be divine music.

The episode of the march, just mentioned, illustrates the break-down of Salieri's bargain and conversation with God. Salieri repeats one note several times as he seeks the right harmony, for which he gives thanks to God when he finds it. A similar gesture is repeated later in the Emperor's receiving room when Mozart sits down at the harpsichord and plays Salieri's entire march after just one hearing. He strikes that same note several times, testing, finding Salieri's God-given chord too banal and lifeless, and then inventing a new harmony that brings the whole piece to life. The film greatly expands the stage version, principally by the addition of the part in which Salieri composes his melody. That scene echoes the frame when Salieri plays two of his own pieces for the priest who recognizes neither one. He immediately remembers the third selection, however, humming along even when Salieri stops playing. The only music he recalls is Mozart's *Eine Kleine Nachtmusik*. Without forcing the point, this incident underlines Salieri's fate as a musician abandoned by his listeners. He will be forgotten by posterity even while alive, just as he is being abandoned in the Emperor's receiving room by his Prime Listener, that God with whom he struck his religious and musical bargain.

Salieri's sudden realization that he is a woefully inferior musician informs the theological issue of blasphemy. Up to this point he has considered himself a special vessel of God, a divinely chosen instrument who will reveal God's glory on earth through music. Now his obvious mediocrity is revealed, his mistaken assumption brutally corrected by a Wolfi as immature in behavior as he is gifted in music. Just as he once spoke to the crucifix while composing his march, now he throws that same crucifix into the fire. Salieri is incensed because God is listening to Mozart's music and not to his own. The special conversation or dialogue he carried on with God has now ended; God prefers the libidinous, foulmouthed, and incredibly gauche Wolfi to the dutiful, hardworking, and devoted Antonio. God is no longer listening to him; He has broken their bargain and terminated their conversation. To Mozart He has given a voice that He has denied Salieri. It is to strike back at God that Salieri decides to block Amadeus and provoke his death. Salieri is not merely a jealous competitor or a rival musician. He is doing more than out-maneuvering an adversary in a ruthless game of court politics. His brief against Amadeus proceeds from his revolt against God's will. His decision to "kill Mozart" even if he did not actually do it, constitutes blasphemy because by it he intends to punish God for preferring Mozart to himself. Killing Mozart is his revenge against the God who no longer listens to him.

Although Salieri's blasphemy is articulated both on stage and screen, it is the film which amplifies this theological element through the repetitions of the listening pattern that we have been examining. Salieri's revolt against God echoes his aborted confession to the priest. Salieri is himself depicted as a double, old and young, sick and healthy, a man divided against himself, a schizophrenic who has lost the key to his wholeness. Evil, he glories in the sin he pretends to confess, fabricates a tendentious version of Amadeus' life, and plots to kill him. Warm and sympathetic, he listens to Mozart's music, isolated in his solitary appreciation of its real merits. He approaches tragic stature as he is torn literally in two, Mozart's friend and Amadeus' enemy. He is angelic when he listens in rapture, hidden in a theater box; diabolical when he speaks to commission the fatal *Requiem* or reduce *Amadeus* to penury and despair.

The film's closing scene gathers up the threads of the several conversations we have been discussing. As the frame intrudes back into the film, Salieri breaks off his confession without requesting absolution. His revolt against God, climaxing in his (pseudo-) crime against Amadeus, is repeated in his abuse of the priest and the sacrament of penance. Salieri rejects the listening priest just as God stopped listening to him. His attempted suicide, presented even before the title and credits open the film, places all that follows in the shadow of sin and revolt against God; the suicide attempt does not take place in the play until the penultimate scene. Furthermore, the film belongs within a context of physical and spiritual alienation because of the hospital-madhouse where Salieri is recuperating. Suicide is violence turned against self. It is an extreme gesture but the only one sufficiently powerful to voice Salieri's complaint against the aberrant state of the world in which the right-thinking and the pious are mocked in their devotion while the boorish and the insensitive are rewarded to excess. As desperate as Salieri's attempted suicide is, it is but the inevitable consequence of the mutilation inflicted by his broken bargain-conversation with God.

Located at both ends of the film, the confessional and the madhouse intensify the impact of Salieri's blasphemy. The final travelling shot is especially disturbing. The sight of Salieri, impenitent and aggressive to the end, being wheeled through the madhouse-hospital and its pitiful inmates projects the film into an area of deep emotional frustration that the play did not suggest. More importantly, it prods us to sympathize with Salieri who is simultaneously a sinner and a madman because he suffers from the inequalities and injustices found among men and because he dares to rebel against a Divine Order that is inexplicable and perhaps unjust. We feel offended that he has been brought so low in the end. As he dares to rise up in anger against God, we are not unjustified in feeling that perhaps he is right. His blasphemy is less the result of his evil nature than it is the product of a willful God who has stacked the deck against him.

Our communicative pattern reappears one last time, somewhat outside the film proper but nonetheless closely connected to it. Here Peter Shaffer would be the speaker and we, film spectators, the listeners. What Shaffer is intimating to us touches on the whole question of the real Salieri's "crime" and Shaffer's own distortions of Mozart's juvenile behavior. To what extent does Shaffer want us to believe that Salieri really killed Mozart? I think not at all. I do not think that Shaffer, himself a musician and well versed in musicological matters, is seriously advancing this crime theory. He knows too well that musicologists and historians have long ago debunked this as another one of the many legends that grew up so easily around the incredible genius of Mozart after his premature death. There are, in addition, textual clues that Shaffer does not believe in this crime. The Venticelli repeat the legend that Salieri *poisoned* Mozart. In both the play and the film Shaffer limits Salieri to harassment and mental torture. Finally, Salieri himself reveals the identity of the caped figure who commissioned the *Requiem,* which therefore makes him innocent even of harassment!

> One amazing fact emerged. Mozart did not *imagine* that masked Figure [. . .] It was *real* . . . A certain bizarre nobleman called Count Walsegg had a longing to be thought a composer. He actually sent his steward in disguise to Mozart to commission a piece—secretly, so that he could pass it off as his own work.

Thus the crime is symbolic and we should understand it in its figurative and not its literal sense.

Only because the legend of Salieri's crime had been so thoroughly forgotten could Shaffer succeed in resurrecting it as a valid premise. The whole murder mystery atmosphere which permeated the publicity for both play and film ("Who killed Mozart?") distracted attention from the underlying message of both **Amadeus**es, Shaffer's own reflection on the nature of genius and the value of artistic success. Once we recognize the "crime" for the canard it is, we can look beyond to the more important issue it conceals.

The juxtaposition of Salieri and Mozart as Shaffer has articulated it contrasts the hard-working but not exceptional journeyman from the master, the all-star to whom no rules apply. This is the face-off of talent and genius. It dramatizes the situation of the artist who is extraordinarily successful in his own lifetime but who is drastically diminished by posterity's judgment. The logic of my discussion of conversational patterns and the use of distorted information about Mozart's life point to a profound connection between Salieri and Shaffer. I would argue that Shaffer most resembles Salieri when the latter brags that he has invented this crime and his false confession in order to insure his own immortality:

> All this month I've been shouting about murder. "Have mercy, Mozart! Pardon your Assassin! . . . And now my last move. A false confession—short and convincing! [. . .] For the rest of time whenever men say Mozart with love, they will say Salieri with loathing! . . . *I am going to be immortal after all!* And He is powerless to prevent it.
>
> (II, 18)

Both Shaffer and Salieri are worried by the shaky connection between worldly success and true worth, eager to know if the plaudits of the present will be validated by the future. Both try to deceive their listeners in order to realize a goal of contemporary recognition *and* everlasting appreciation.

Like Salieri in the 1780's, Shaffer is at the top of his profession, generously rewarded for his endeavors, applauded by critics and audiences. But has he written any work that will stand the test of time? Has he produced any real art? I have no answer to this question, but I do think it is a question that informs the structure and the deepest meaning of *Amadeus*. Furthermore, we have to recognize Shaffer's courage in asking it and in envisioning the talented but mediocre Salieri as a possible alter ego. To depict himself as Mozart, misunderstood, an outcast, an outsider (which Mozart never was, but this is one of Shaffer's inaccuracies which helps to articulate his contrast of genius and talent more sharply) would be a flattering, romantic notion but one that has no relationship to his own obvious success, commercial and artistic, as a playwright. However, to imagine himself as Salieri the talented but limited craftsman and not as Mozart, the indisputably immortal genius, gives *Amadeus* especially in its film version, a ring of sobering honesty and of personal soul searching. Identifying Shaffer as Salieri gives *Amadeus* a moving power that recalls the shock of recognition which electrified audiences when in *Equus* the late Richard Burton played the psychiatrist who had wasted his tremendous talent.

Amadeus has been dismissed as a costume piece set in the sumptuous decor of eighteenth-century Prague and, alternatively, as a yuppie dose of "heavy" culture and Music Appreciation. I find, on the contrary, that Shaffer has tried to ask some penetratingly eternal and personal questions about the position of the artist in the world, the relationship of success to true worth, and the vagaries, not to say the inaccuracies, of our artistic judgments.

FURTHER READING

BIBLIOGRAPHY

Thomas, Eberle. *Peter Shaffer: An Annotated Bibliography.* New York: Garland Publishing, 1991, 259 p.
> Annotated bibliography containing sources of discussions of Shaffer's work up to and including *Lettice & Lovage.*

AUTHOR COMMENTARY

Buckley, Tom. "'Write Me,' Said the Play to Peter Shaffer." *The New York Times Magazine* (13 April 1975): 38, 47-50.
> Conversation with Shaffer in which he talks about unfavorable reviews of *Equus,* his personal and collaborative relationship with his brother Anthony Shaffer, and other topics.

Connell, Brian. "Peter Shaffer: The Two Sides of Theatre's Agonised Perfectionist." *The Times,* London (28 April 1980): 18.
> A comprehensive interview with Shaffer in which he discusses his affinity for New York versus London, his early literary development, and the contrast between his existential and farcical plays.

OVERVIEWS AND GENERAL STUDIES

Chambers, Colin. "Psychic Energy." *Plays and Players* 27, No. 5 (February 1980): 11-13.
> Summarizes Shaffer's work from *Five Finger Exercise* to *Amadeus* and includes comments by the playwright.

Cooke, Virginia and Malcolm Page, eds. *File on Shaffer.* London: Metheun, 1987, 88 p.
> A compilation of comments by and about the playwright. Includes a brief chronology of events in Shaffer's life and career as well as a bibliography of primary and secondary sources.

Dean, Joan F. "Peter Shaffer's Recurrent Character Type." *Modern Drama* XXI, No. 3 (September 1978): 297-305.
> An analysis of similar characterization in various Shaffer plays.

Gianakaris, C. J. *Peter Shaffer.* Macmillan Modern Dramatists. Basingstoke, England: Macmillan, 1992, 204 p.
> Traces Shaffer's career and the development of his craft from his early radio plays through *Lettice & Lovage.*

Kerensky, Oleg. "Peter Shaffer." In *The New British Drama: Fourteen Playwrights since Osborne and Pinter,* pp. 31-58. New York: Taplinger Publishing Company, 1977.

> An in-depth analysis of Shaffer's work from *Five Finger Exercise* to *Equus.* Includes a discussion of the playwright's obsession with rewrites.

Klein, Dennis A. *Peter Shaffer: Revised Edition.* Twayne Publishers, 1993, 261 p.

> Comprehensive overview of the themes, characters, structure, and stagecraft of Shaffer's plays.

Stacy, James R. "The Sun and the Horse: Peter Shaffer's Search for Worship." *Educational Theatre Journal* 28, No. 3 (October 1976): 325-37.

> Discusses *The Royal Hunt of the Sun* and *Equus* as works in which Shaffer "enters into the world of magic and ritual, primitivism and religious passion, in search of worship."

Taylor, John Russell. *Peter Shaffer.* Essex, England: Longman Group, 1974, 34 p.

> A critique of Shaffer's plays through *Equus,* giving special consideration to the language in the plays.

EQUUS

Beckerman, Bernard. "The Dynamics of Peter Shaffer's Drama." In *The Play and Its Critic: Essays for Eric Bentley,* edited by Michael Bertin, pp. 199-209. New York: Lanham, 1986.

> An assessment of the structure and stagecraft of *Equus.*

Gifford, Sanford. "'Pop' Psychoanalysis, *Kitsch,* and the 'As If' Theater: Further Notes on Peter Shaffer's *Equus.*" *International Journal of Psychoanalytic Psychotherapy* 5 (1976): 463-71.

> Argues that *Equus* is "kitsch" because "it fails the traditional Aristotelian test of tragic catharsis: purification through pity and terror."

Plunka, Gene A. "The Existential Ritual: Peter Shaffer's *Equus.*" *Kansas Quarterly* 12, No. 4 (Fall 1980): 87-97

> Analyzes the search for identity in *Equus,* finding it a characteristic concern of Shaffer's.

Simon, John. "Hippodrama at the Psychodrome." *The Hudson Review* XXVIII, No. 1 (Spring 1975): 97-106.

> Extremely harsh review of the New York production *Equus* in which Simon declares: "The play pullulates with dishonesty."

Witham, Barry B. "The Anger in *Equus.*" *Modern Drama* XXII, No. 1 (March 1979): 61-6.

> Investigates the theatrical traditions inherent in *Equus,* drawing a comparison to John Osborne's *Look Back in Anger.*

AMADEUS

Gianakaris, C. J. "A Playwright Looks at Mozart: Peter Shaffer's *Amadeus.*" *Comparative Drama* 15, No. 1 (Spring 1981): 37-53.

> An assessment of *Amadeus* based on Shaffer's common themes of conflicting human behavior and humanity's intellectual struggle with the existence of God.

———. "Shaffer's Revisions in *Amadeus.*" *Theatre Journal* 35, No. 1 (March 1983): 88-101.

> Reviews the rewrites of *Amadeus,* and includes a discussion on Shaffer's general tendency toward revising his work.

Huber, Werner and Zapf, Hubert. "On the Structure of Peter Shaffer's *Amadeus.*" *Modern Drama* XXVII, No. 3 (September 1984): 299-313.

> Addresses the "thematic organization, coherence and form" of *Amadeus,* "as well as the complex mechanisms of interaction between stage and audience."

Levin, Bernard. "Clearing Up the Eternal Mystery of Mozart." *The Times,* London (6 December 1979): 14.

> Defends *Amadeus* against its attackers, maintaining that "lovers of Mozart . . . should be profoundly grateful to Peter Shaffer for the courage with which he has faced an eternal mystery, and the humility and grace with which he has offered a tentatively eternal solution to it."

Sullivan, William J. "Peter Shaffer's *Amadeus*: The Making and Un-Making of the Fathers." *American Imago* 45, No. 1 (Spring 1988): 45-60.

> Offers a psychoanalytic interpretation of the play.

Terence

C. 195/185 B.C.–159 B.C.

(Full name Publius Terentius Afer)

INTRODUCTION

Terence is best known for the elegant language, symmetrical plots, and complex, sympathetic characterizations exhibited in his six comedies. Though he has for the most part been viewed as a respected and influential author, Terence has also been criticized by commentators from his own time onward for closely basing his plays on earlier Greek models—a practice some reviewers have interpreted as imitation or even plagiarism. Today most scholars agree that although Terence used the forms and themes of Greek New Comedy, he created a new type of play that transcended its antecedents. Gilbert Norwood, for example, has praised Terence for his "splendid principle of accepting the traditional framework and evolving from it a thoroughly serious, permanently interesting, type of drama."

BIOGRAPHICAL INFORMATION

Most of what is known about Terence's life is very uncertain and comes from a second-century biographical sketch by the Roman imperial biographer Suetonius, preserved in a commentary by Donatus, a fourth-century grammarian. Terence's exact date of birth is not known, but he was probably born in Carthage, North Africa, and brought to Rome as a slave when he was very young. He was then purchased by Terentius Lucanus, a Roman senator, who allowed Terence to be educated and eventually emancipated him: according to custom, Terence took his former owner's name upon being freed. Since Terence reportedly possessed great personal charm and soon demonstrated exceptional dramatic talent, he was quickly accepted into the circle of Scipio Aemilianus—a group of wealthy, well-placed young Roman aristocrats enamored of Greek culture and literature. This circle and their friends comprised Terence's main audience; he never enjoyed the widespread popularity of some of his contemporaries. In fact, a powerful critic of Terence's time, Luscius Lanuvinus, charged that Terence's plays were actually written by Scipio and his friends, and he publicly accused Terence of plagiarizing the Greek dramatist Menander and of "contaminating" his sources by mixing scenes and characters from various plays. In 159 B.C. Terence sailed for Greece, either to escape criticism at home or to become more familiar with the country. Some biographers claim that he was lost at sea on the way back, but the circumstances of his death remain unknown.

MAJOR WORKS

Terence wrote six comedies, all of which have survived, and all of which are close adaptations or translations of Greek plays. Two (*Hecyra*, or *The Mother-in-Law*, and *Phormio*) are derived from works by Apollodorus, and the other four are based on comedies by Menander. The earliest, *Andria* (*The Girl from Andros*), recounts the travails of two young men, both in love and both thwarted by their respective fathers. *The Mother-in-Law*, first produced in 165 B.C., failed three times before it was successfully produced in 160 B.C. *Heautontimorumenos* (*The Self-Tormentor*), like *The Girl from Andros*, treats the problems of two young lovers. Considered Terence's most technically accomplished play, *Eunuchus* (*The Eunuch*), describes the situation of Chaerea, one of Terence's most-discussed characters, who marries a girl he had earlier raped. In *Phormio*, a young husband must contend with a wife whom he erroneously believes to be carrying someone else's child. Terence's last play, *Adelphoe* (*The Brothers*), compares two fathers—one too strict and one too lenient—and their two sons, in an exploration of the merits of different methods of childrearing. Terence's comedies are characterized by his pure, nearly perfect use of the Latin language, and by a sense of realism tempered by urbanity and restraint. Unlike earlier Roman dramatists who rely on raucous humor and vulgar language for comic effect, Terence favors correct, sophisticated speech and a greater use of dialogue than monologue. In characterization Terence also departs from earlier convention: rather than merely relying on stock character types, he makes more use of irony and creates more subtle, less predictable characters. Numerous critics have commented on Terence's humane and objective approach to characters and situations, citing his adherence to his well-known credo, *"homo sum: humani nil a me alienum puto"* ("I am human myself, so I think every human affair is my concern"). Although his models come from Greek New Comedy, Terence depicts a distinctly Roman society, with all its foibles and eccentricities intact. The world of his plays, unlike those of earlier Roman dramas, is an amoral one, however; Terence is more interested in describing and dissecting moral dilemmas than in suggesting the proper ways to solve them. In terms of dramatic structure, Terence's main contribution is his development of the double plot device, which allows for a more balanced and complex development of plot, character, and theme, and which he utilizes in all his plays except *The Mother-in-Law*.

CRITICAL RECEPTION

While in his own time Terence's plays were not popular with audiences, many ancient critics—for example Cicero and Julius Caesar—praised his graceful and correct handling of the Latin language. Caesar tempered his complimentary remarks by calling Terence a "half-Menander" and accusing him of a lack of comic vision. That charge and the question of whether Terence was an original playwright have been the two main areas of critical discussion concerning Terence's comedies. The majority of scholars contend that Terence's sense of comedy was very much intact, but they admit that his plays sometimes strike audiences as somewhat monotonous or over-refined. Terence himself answered the charges of imitation in the prologues to his plays, including himself in the long, honorable tradition of younger writers paying tribute by copying their predecessors. Most critics believe that, while he was not an inherently original author, Terence artfully transformed the situations and themes of Greek New Comedy into a genuinely Roman milieu. In the Middle Ages there was a resurgence of interest in Terence's plays, and their texts served as the basis for Latin language curricula in schools and monasteries. The influence of Terence's comedies has also been traced to works of the Renaissance and the eighteenth century. Today Terence commands admiration for his humanistic approach to his characters, for the new directions he made possible in drama through his introduction of double plots, and for the excellence of his Latin.

PRINCIPAL WORKS

PLAYS

Andria [*The Girl from Andros*] 166 B.C.
Hecyra [*The Mother-in-Law*] 165 B.C.
Heautontimorumenos [*The Self-Tormentor*] 163 B.C.
Eunuchus [*The Eunuch*] 161 B.C.
Phormio 161 B.C.
Adelphoe [*The Brothers*] 160 B.C.

PRINCIPAL ENGLISH TRANSLATIONS

The Comedies of Terence (translated by Sidney G. Ashmore, 2nd ed.) 1910
Terence. 2 vols. (translated by John Sargeaunt) 1912
The Complete Roman Drama, Volume II (translated by George E. Duckworth) 1962
Terence: Comedies (edited by Robert Graves; based on the translation by Lawrence Echard) 1963
Terence: The Comedies (translated by Betty Radice) 1965
The Comedies of Terence (translated by Frank O. Copley) 1967
The Complete Comedies of Terence (translated by Palmer Bovie, Constance Carrier, and Douglass Parker) 1974

OVERVIEWS AND GENERAL STUDIES

Richard Levin (essay date 1966)

SOURCE: "The Double Plots of Terence," in *The Classical Journal,* Vol. 62, No. 1, October, 1966, pp. 301-05.

[*In the essay below, Levin focuses on the two-level plot structure tracing parallel love affairs that is characteristic of several of Terence's plays.*]

Certainly one of the most striking features of Terence's plays is his use of a double-plot structure which combines the stories of two pairs of young lovers. Virtually all the commentators, from Donatus and Evanthius down to the present day, have dealt with this aspect of his dramaturgy, and virtually all of them have found that it contributes materially to his unquestioned artistic achievement. On the nature of that contribution, also, there appears to be quite substantial agreement, for while these discussions have been as various as the points of view which have been brought to bear upon the subject, the specific advantages claimed for the Terentian "duality-method" generally focus around two basic topics: the enrichment of the comic complication that results from the interaction of the two plots, and the illuminating contrasts that this provides between the parallel characters—the two *adulescentes,* the two *senes,* and sometimes others—of these plots. There is, however, yet another dimension to this dual structure which has been neglected in these studies, even though it seems to have figured significantly in Terence's conception of that structure, and in the influence it was to exert upon later drama.

This additional dimension becomes evident as soon as the comparison is extended beyond the individual characters in these two romantic stories to the nature of the two romances themselves. In the four comedies built upon the double-plot structure (this does not include the **Andria,** since Charinus' love for Philumena never leads to any action that might constitute a separate plot), the parallel love affairs have been clearly differentiated along the same lines: in each play one pair of lovers (Clinia and Antiphila in the **Heautontimorumenos,** Chaerea and Pamphila in the **Eunuchus,** Antipho and Phanium in the **Phormio,** Aeschinus and Pamphila in the **Adelphoe**) are eventually united in a legal and socially accepted marriage, while the other pair (Clitipho and Bacchis, Phaedria and Thais, Phaedria and Pamphila, Ctesipho and Bacchis respectively) only form an irregular sexual liaison. From this, moreover, there follows another important difference in the nature of the action appropriate to the two kinds of romance: in the "marriage-plot" the central problem is always the social status of the young woman, which seems to disqualify her as a wife, and the resolution therefore typically turns upon a *cognitio* revealing her true parentage; in the "liaison-plot," on the other hand, the problem is not the status of the woman (which never changes), but the ability of the young man to obtain or to keep possession of her, and this is resolved through some stratagem, usually involving money, initiated by him or his allies to that end. This does not mean, of course, that all four plots in each category are identical, for the pattern admits of considerable variation in detail from play to play, and there are even a few which do not exactly fit it in all respects; thus the marriage in the **Adelphoe** requires no *cognitio,* and the money to maintain the liaison in the **Eunuchus** is not acquired by the usual trickery. But, as a general formula, it does indicate a fundamental contrast between the combined plots which is developed so consistently in this group of plays that it surely must have been the result of Terence's conscious intention, either in his initial choice of Greek models or in the alterations he made in them.

A few modern critics have noted this pattern, without attaching much significance to it; but more often it has simply been ignored, especially by those who attempt to reduce all the products of New Comedy to a single archetypal scheme. Moses Hadas, for example [in his *Roman Drama,* 1965], asserts that in this genre the following story is "repeated with only minor changes from play to play":

> a young man is in love with a girl owned by a white slaver who is about to dispose of her elsewhere; his cunning servant defrauds the young man's father of the necessary sum; the girl is discovered to be of good birth (having been kidnapped or exposed in infancy) and hence an eligible bride.

And Gilbert Norwood [in his *Plautus* and *Terence,* 1932] constructs a similar "composite photograph" of the plots of Plautus and Terence:

> A young Athenian is in love with a charming but friendless girl who is the purchased slave of a *leno* . . . He wishes to purchase her and keep her as his mistress . . . Here intervenes his slave, loyal to his young master but otherwise conscienceless, who saves the situation by an elaborate ruse either to defraud the hero's father of the needed sum or to induce the slave-owner to part with the girl. When discovery of this deception arrives, all is put right by a sudden revelation that the heroine is really of Athenian birth (but kidnapped or lost in babyhood) and can therefore marry the hero.

And another such "conventional" plot, couched in Freudian terms, is presented by Northrop Frye [in his "The Argument of Comedy," *English Institute Essays 1948*]. All formulations of this type, it can be seen, conflate the two distinct kinds of romantic attachment and of dramatic action which Terence has managed to separate by his dual structure, and it is therefore not surprising to find that scholars operating from these reductive schemes will fail to appreciate this aspect of the structure, and may even criticize it unjustly, as when Norwood, for instance, complains of the **Eunuchus** that "the dualism would have been perfect had Thais been legally possible as a wife for Phaedria." But that would have meant a second marriage-plot for this play, with a second *cognitio,* which is just what Terence has always avoided.

One reason for avoiding such duplication seems obvious enough: Terence probably realized that two separate discoveries of long-lost daughters would have been too much for his audience to accept. The use of this same coincidental resolution for each plot would make them both much less "probable." Moreover, it would make them much less interesting, because of the predictable and boring repetition. The sense of fascinated excitement which Terence is able to engender depends in large measure upon the variation of situation and incident provided by his formula, since it brings together two very different kinds of comic action—one presided over by a benevolent Fate, where the principal errors and ironies result from an essential ignorance, shared by all the characters, which is innocent of human contrivance and which is finally dispelled in a happy, and equally uncontrived, revelation of the truth; and the other directed by a shrewd schemer who carefully arranges most of the confusion and invites us to enjoy the cleverness of his deceptions and the ridiculous discomfitures of his victims. In terms, then, of both credibility and variety, it is easy to see the advantages of the special formula adopted by Terence.

This may account for his formula on the level of the contrasted actions combined there, but we have still to consider the effect of the contrast between the two kinds of romance portrayed within these actions. It is not a simple matter, since it involves the emotional and moral coloring of those romances, and that is determined not by the real-life attitudes toward marital and extramarital love to be found in Terence's society in second-century Rome, nor in the fourth-century Athens of his models, but by a dramatic convention which has created an artificial exotic world of its own kept at some distance from the audience, the world of the *palliata*. Some of the nuances of feeling implied in this contrast, therefore, may well be irrecoverable. Because they are defined by the convention, Terence is able to assume these affective values instead of establishing them through his action, which is concerned not so much with the romantic affairs themselves as with the conflicts precipitated by them between the two young men and their fathers (or between the two fathers in the **Adelphoe** and, to a lesser extent, in the **Heauton**). There are very few scenes bringing the young lovers together (indeed, often the girl is never seen); their emotional relationship has usually been formed before the play opens and undergoes no real development, being treated in terms of the convention as a kind of *donnée*. And the attempts to describe the passion of the *adulescens,* either in his own words or indirectly through others, are seldom very helpful in distinguishing these two sorts of love. In the liaison-plot as in the marriage-plot this passion is called *amor,* of course, and in both he typically reacts to the threatened loss of his beloved with the same despairing thoughts of death or exile, and to their prospective union (or reunion) with the same rhapsodic delight.

Nevertheless, Terence seems to have taken some pains to provide his audience with an explicit statement of this crucial distinction. Thus in the **Heauton** Clitipho compares the haughtiness and avarice of the *meretrix* he loves to the virtuous modesty of the *virgo* loved by Clinia (223-7), and in a later scene Bacchis enlarges on this comparison from the woman's point of view (381-95); each young man in the **Phormio** contrasts his plight with his friend's, Phaedria arguing that Antipho is more fortunate in having married a respectable lady (162-72), and Antipho that Phaedria is better off since his problem was solved as soon as he paid the *leno* (820-27); and in the **Adelphoe** a number of persons point out the basic difference between Aeschinus' attachment to Pamphila, whom he had promised to marry, and his supposed infatuation with the slave-girl he bought for Clitipho (326-34, 469-77, 724-5). But it is through the action itself that the distinction emerges most clearly. In the marriage-plots of the **Heauton, Phormio,** and **Adelphoe** the young man has been living with a decent girl, though apparently of humble or foreign birth, whom he already regards as his wife, so that when the climactic discovery occurs it does not alter his attitude toward her, but simply allows their relationship to be regularized. The liaison-plots really involve two different kinds of love-object—in the **Heauton** and **Eunuchus** she is a free woman, a professional courtesan whose favors the youth has been enjoying for some time, while in the **Phormio** and **Adelphoe** she is a music-girl (*citharistria* or *psaltria*) who is owned by a slave-dealer and is at first unattainable—yet the liaisons themselves are akin in that they always require money (to maintain the courtesan or buy the girl) and are always transitory, the thought of marriage never crossing anyone's mind. There also seems to be a calculated effort to debase these affairs even further. In the first two dramas the young man is made to complain of his mistress' infidelity or cupidity, the usual stigmata of the *meretrix,* and his romantic posturings are severely qualified during the final episode by the ease with which he consents to share her in a *ménage à trois,* in the **Heauton,** or, in the **Eunuchus,** to abandon her completely. The other two denouements leave the youth in undisputed possession of the slave-girl, but the carnal basis of his affection is emphasized by his eagerness to rush her off to a drunken bedroom "party," and the closing lines here, too, serve to belittle their relationship, in the condescending permission he is given to take her home, as if she were a new toy or pet puppy that he would soon outgrow.

This would suggest that the contrast between the two kinds of romance in these plays has also been designed as a contrast in emotional tone—that the marriage-plot is meant to be more serious and more elevated (while still remaining, of course, within the bounds of comedy) than the plot with which it is combined. And the difference already noted between the two types of comic action should contribute to this same effect. The seriousness of the liaison-plot is deflated because that plot is resolved through the farcical trickery of a contest of wits and butts, just as the seriousness of the other plot is enhanced by the resolving role of a benign Fortune operating above (and often defeating) the plans of the human intriguers. The most crucial determinant of this difference in tone can be found, however, in the issues upon which each of these resolutions is made to turn. In the liaison-plot this issue—the goal of the scheming and the means of uniting the lovers—is typically *money,* as is pointed out, for instance, in the **Phormio**: *hic simul argentum repperit, cura sese expedivit* (823). This necessarily affects the audience's view of the action, reducing it to a kind of confidence game, and of the romance itself, which becomes a commercial transaction; but, more important, it makes everything less serious precisely because it is an external object, loss or gain of which does not really change the characters or their place in the world. In the marriage-plot, on the other hand, the basic issue is never money, but someone's *identity*. It is not a very profound conception of identity, to be sure, since it is defined in familial and social terms, but it is still much more elevated than money and much more internal, in that it does alter people's lives radically and permanently, the public acceptance of the marriage at the close of these plots being in fact the guarantee of this.

The kind of love depicted in each plot, then, and the kind of action dramatized there, seem to work together in establishing the two distinct emotional effects. Moreover, since the plots interact causally and are juxtaposed through a sequence of alternating episodes, these two effects will tend to reinforce each other by way of contrast, the presence of the more serious marriage-plot making the liaison-plot seem more farcical, and vice versa. Thus it would seem that Terence's duality-method develops a "foil" relationship, not only between parallel characters in the two plots, but also between the plots themselves—or, more strictly, develops the liaison-plot as a foil to the marriage-plot. For the latter action appears to be the more important in each of these dramas (although in some the difference in magnitude is not very great), so that there is a foil arrangement here in the most meaningful sense of that term—a devaluated background fashioned to set off and enhance the superior values, both esthetic and moral, of a more significant centerpiece. This response is not so effectively realized as it might have been, one must admit, since the playwright seldom focuses on the love affairs as such, yet it does provide an artistic rationale for the specific pattern he utilized in all his double plots. (In fact, he may even be striving for this in his two single-plot comedies, both essentially of the "marriage" type, by suggesting a contrast between his chaste heroine and a courtesan—Chrysis, the supposed sister of Glycerium in the **Andria,** and Bacchis, the supposed rival of Philumena in the **Hecyra.**)

It is instructive to find a very similar arrangement in some of the comedies of the Elizabethan period, where a more or less sentimentalized pair of lovers in the main plot is juxtaposed to a much less romantic and much more comic pair in a subplot. The source of these subplots is always traced back to certain episodes in the so-called "native" tradition of the Mystery cycle and Morality play, in which clownish characters, often servants, are shown trying to mimic the deeds of their "betters" in the major action. But there is no valid reason for excluding Terence as a possible source of this structure, especially since his influence upon other aspects of comic theory and practice in the Renaissance has been of such obvious importance. Of course, one must allow for the modification required by a different set of dramatic and social conventions; thus the main action in these comedies is not resolved by a classical *cognitio* but, usually, by some change in the characters' feelings for each other, and the subplot terminates in another wedding rather than in concubinage. Yet, given these necessary translations, the Terentian pattern can be discerned in the treatment of the subplot couple as foils for the more serious lovers of the main action; and the traits they are given for this purpose—earthiness, cynicism, cunning, and the like—often could have been derived from the intriguers of Terence's liaison-plots. Shakespeare was particularly fond of this arrangement, for almost all his romantic comedies contain "anti-romantic" subplots of this general type (Don Armado and Jaquenetta in *Love's Labor's Lost,* Bottom and Titania in *A Midsummer Night's Dream,* Touchstone and Audrey in *As You Like It,* Sir Toby Belch and Maria in *Twelfth Night,* Benedick and Beatrice in *Much Ado about Nothing*), and many other examples could be cited in the works of his contemporaries. In fact, the fundamental scheme reappears in the nearest approach to an indigenous popular drama that our country has yet produced, the musical comedy, which has evolved a definite formula in terms of two parallel courtships contrasted along Terentian lines—a main action where a lyric soprano ingénue finds true love, and a subordinate action where a much more jaded lady, in a husky contralto, settles for considerably less. The line of transmission from Rome to Broadway may be very long and tenuous, but the continued popularity of this same pair

of love stories testifies to the effectiveness of the idea that Terence embodied in his double-plot dramas.

Walther Ludwig   (essay date 1968)

SOURCE: "The Originality of Terence and His Greek Models," in *Greek, Roman, and Byzantine Studies,* Vol. 9, No. 1, 1968, pp. 169-82.

[In the following essay, Ludwig attempts a balanced assessment of the effects of Terence's adaptations and translations of Greek sources. He finds both dramatic gains and losses.]

It is remarkable what different judgements about the poetical achievement of Terence can be found in modern scholarship. One finds him represented sometimes as a mere translator and adapter, sometimes as an original poet worthy to stand beside Menander himself. The best representative of the first view is Jachmann, who saw Terence's independence at work only in *contaminatio*, [See G. Jachmann, *RE* 5A, 1934]. But the main tendency in Terentian scholarship of the last few decades has been to go in the other direction, to emphasize the originality of Terence as a poet and to discover that in remodeling the Greek comedies he created a new kind of drama and that he added important new elements of his own, even when he lost some of the beauties of his Greek sources. Norwood [in *The Art of Terence,* 1923] was the most extreme in this line—he granted Terence the liberties of a Shakespeare using Plutarch—and therefore his views have not been accepted by the majority of scholars. But a considerable number of German and Italian Latinists also depict Terence as a Roman poet in his own right. Some prominent exponents of this view are Erich Reitzenstein, Haffter, Büchner, Paratore and Bianco. There are divergencies, but on the whole they share a view of Terence remodeling and reworking the Greek comedies according to his own artistic ideals. Terence, in their view, aimed at a more realistic drama, avoiding the comedy of typical scenes and characters, eliminating actors' addresses to the public, shortening unrealistic long gnomic reflexions, strengthening the colloquial language and attempting to give his figures individual features. Likewise, according to these critics, he despised coarseness and vulgarity and deepened noble and humane sentiments, trying to show to his audience the right values. I may confess at the outset that I regard this picture in its essential points to be wrong and distorted, although I do not deny that some useful observations have been made; but, in my opinion, they have not been properly evaluated. On the other hand, I am not a close adherent of Jachmann, although there are several points upon which we would agree.

There seem to be three main reasons for this great range of opinion about Terence's originality. First, we lack complete agreement about the nature and extent of Terence's departures from his lost Greek originals, and in some cases it will never be possible to determine them with certainty. Second, even if we agree about a specific alteration made by Terence, it is still often difficult to state its motive. And finally, classical scholars often seem in the case of Terence more emotionally involved than usual. Those who see in him a highly original poet sometimes accuse their opponents of a romantic philhellenism, while they in their turn seem not entirely uninfluenced by a certain determination to vindicate the independence of Latin literature at any price, or even by a nationalistic Italian pride in the Roman past. Nevertheless we should not give up before the problem of the originality of Terence, as scholars like Beare and Duckworth are rather inclined to do [W. Beare, *The Roman Stage,* 1955; G. E. Duckworth, *The Nature of Roman Comedy* 1952]. The problem is and will remain important for the development of Roman literature. It can be solved only by taking into consideration the relation of Terence's plays to his Greek models, and this relation is by no means in every case so impossible to determine objectively that we must restrict ourselves to a neutral *non liquet.* Although we do not have space here to discuss in detail all relevant arguments, I should like to touch on certain points which seem to me of special importance.

It has always been noticed that Terence in choosing his Greek models was influenced by definite characteristics of his own interests and tastes. He limited himself to Menander and his follower Apollodoros of Karystos. He was careful about a certain morality, keeping within the bounds of what the Roman meant by *decorum.* A lovesick old man, who perhaps becomes his son's rival for a *hetaira,* is not to be found in his plays. His *senes* are all quite respectable, well-intentioned and serious fathers, who are as sincerely concerned as their wives for the happiness of their children. His slaves do intrigue, but are not too unscrupulous about it. He did not enjoy presenting frivolous *meretrices.* The respectful prostitute aroused his interest. He avoided the low and the fantastic, putting on stage domestic affairs such as could happen every day. He also preferred an action rich in characters, if possible with two pairs of lovers and a correspondingly double happy ending. There is normally a moving recognition of someone long lost. Finally, he is attracted not least by psychologically subtle delineation of humane and sensitive characters, by the representation of problems of interpersonal relations and of those concerning the proper behavior by the older generation towards the younger.

But it would be rash to suppose not only that these interests determined the choice of his models, but that in adapting the Greek comedies he deliberately emphasized and expanded these elements and thus was working on his own in the direction we have described. It can easily be shown that the opposite was often the case.

For three of his six plays Terence used a second Greek original. As he himself explains in a prologue, he was convinced that it was not enough to translate a good Greek play in order to write a good Latin one, and so took the liberty, where he thought it in place, to work scenes or parts of scenes from a second Greek play into the primary model,

the practice called *contaminatio.* What considerations guided him in the choice of his secondary models?

In the **Adelphoe** he inserted a scene from the *Synapothneskontes* of Diphilos, in which a young man appears who has just stolen a girl out of a brothel and who now has the *leno,* who pursues him with insults, brought to reason by the blows of his slave. In Menander's *Adelphoi* the carrying off of the girl was only narrated, probably by the young man, and the *leno* appeared on stage later to negotiate for the damages. Terence thought it fitting to substitute a lively slapstick scene in place of the narrated event. Thus he strengthened the part of the *leno* and introduced a cudgeling scene, both contrary to the intentions which guided him in the choice of his primary model. He evidently found that thus enlivening the **Adelphoe,** otherwise distinguished by its ethical and psychological interests, would not harm the play. His intentions therefore entail a certain compromise. On the one hand he wanted to get away from the traditional and, in his view, vulgar jokes of a Plautus to the cultivated and meaningful drama of Menander; on the other hand he apparently felt that you could have too much of a good thing. In his opinion the play could only gain by a bit more color. He overlooked or chose to ignore the fact that the omitted narration of Aeschinus contained an indication that Aeschinus was stealing the girl not for himself but for his brother. Such an explanation however was extremely important for the understanding of the speeches of the two fathers, since only thus does a proper judgement of the attitude of the mild Micio and the strict Demea become possible, and this is the whole point of the play.

In the **Eunuchus** we can observe an analogous situation. Here Terence inserted monologues and dialogues from Menander's *Kolax.* The proven sure-fire types of the parasite and the *miles gloriosus* were meant to enliven the action even more (perhaps because the dramatist had indifferent success with the more staid **Hecyra**). In Menander's *Eunuchos* in place of the parasite there stood only a slave, in place of the *miles* a less colorful rival. Both rôles were less prominent there. So in the second act of the **Eunuchus** Terence inserted an effective bravura scene from the *Kolax,* the entrance speech of the parasite Gnatho. But this also shifted the emphasis of the scene. In Menander a slave had brought Pamphila, the girl to whose recognition the play leads, across the stage to the house of the *hetaira* Thais. This an event full of consequence for the whole drama, for it is in the house of Thais that the rape will take place, because of which the happy ending of the play is seriously endangered. Pamphila appears on stage only in this scene. She does not speak a word. But although two slaves carry on the dialogue, she remains by her very silence the center of attention. In Terence the parasite upstages her. For the sake of a momentary comic effect the careful disposition of the action is somewhat obscured.

At the end of the **Eunuchus** the soldier and the young Athenian agree to share the *hetaira* Thais. The parasite draws a commission. Such arrangements occurred in

Menander's Athens. But this can not have been the conclusion of the Menandrian *Eunuchos*. It is in contradiction not only to the goal of the external action of this play, but also to the completion of its inner dramatic development. Thais has revealed herself in the course of the play—contrary to what one would have expected first—as a *bona meretrix*. She has solved all difficulties and behaved in a truly humane fashion. As a reward she has got a rich old Athenian as a patron and is finally united with the young man whom she loves. For her then to be treated as an article of merchandise is irreconcilable with the external and internal structure of the Menandrian *Eunuchos*. Terence's ending seems to have been composed in imitation of the *Kolax*, where the *hetaira* was not free but the property of a *leno*, and where such an arrangement, in which the parasite too gets his cut, suits excellently the young man's repeatedly emphasized lack of money and the wealth of the proud and stupid officer. Terence may have added this conclusion in order to gain one final comic effect. That is, the *miles* is led around by the nose once more through the agreement (his share will consist mostly of paying the bills) and the lucky parasite is the only real winner. For the sake of such effects Terence has destroyed the unity of the play, which he had maintained so far. He has weakened the unconventional theme of the *bona meretrix*, which he had chosen, by adding two traditional comic types.

A quick look to the *Andria*: the origin of the parts which concern Charinus, the second lover of the play, is controversial. I follow the view of those who regard these passages not as an independent addition by Terence but as essentially a borrowing from the *Perinthia*. In any case, Terence preferred in this play too the fuller double plot and chose as primary model not the coarser *Perinthia* but the psychologically refined *Andria*. He took from the *Perinthia* only what seemed to him suitable to enliven and enrich the *Andria*, for instance the motif of the drunken midwife, although this involves a slight inconsistency in her character.

Thus Terence chose in each case a psychologically complex Menander play as his primary model. But he enriched it and strengthened its farcical elements from cruder plays of Menander and Diphilos, doing some damage thereby to the balanced organization of his primary models. If one observes this compromising tendency of Terence, one is in no danger of accepting the widespread idea that he is responsible for a fundamental humanizing and deepening of his models and that his use of *contaminatio* was guided by a humane aesthetic ideal.

Further consideration of the way in which Terence combined parts of a second Greek play with his primary model may save us from another error. It is frequently assumed that *contaminatio* was often in effect a dissolution of the primary model and meant a new conception of the play as a whole. In the *Adelphoe*, to be sure, no one could fail to see that only one or two scenes were replaced by the scene from Diphilos. But in the *Eunuchus* a fundamental remodeling of the middle part has been generally assumed. In my opinion the additions from the *Kolax* are limited to four separate scenes. There are no elements which would give the action an essentially new direction. Only the conclusion, about which we have already spoken, does not fit into this picture. Here Terence actually made a decisive change and destroyed the original conception of the play. But here too he was influenced not by a new conception of the play as a whole, but rather by the desire for an effective conclusion, which led him into the dénouement taken from the *Kolax*. The earliest play of Terence, the *Andria,* is the most deeply affected by *contaminatio*. The working in of the second lover involved a consistent alteration of the whole plot. But an analogous plot with two lovers was probably already to be found in the *Perinthia,* and Terence was generally able to insert scenes from the *Perinthia* at corresponding places in the *Andria* and so had to compose independently only the short final scene, in which Charinus is informed of the happy solution.

In no case was a radical alteration of the construction of the primary model necessary in order to work in the desired parts of the secondary model. Terence was able to get by with a few omissions, the addition of suitable transitions, retouchings to remove obvious contradictions and similar devices; and in this he succeeded quite well. The additions are far more carefully inserted than in Plautus, where marked inconsistencies and contradictions often become apparent.

Terence altered his originals in still other ways. The listing of a few examples suffices to show that it is misguided to explain these alterations, as has been done, from principles such as "progress towards realistic drama," "humanising and ennobling of the characters" or "a will to the universally valid." The desire for comprehensive syntheses and the wish to find deep meanings everywhere have often led to exaggerations and forced interpretations, or to the overlooking of contrary instances.

When Terence omits the name of an Athenian suburb and instead writes *in his regionibus,* it is certainly paying too much honor to this modification to see in such an avoidance of a reference too specifically Greek a search for the universal. Naturally Terence left out Greek place-names and customs which meant nothing to his public, as far as he could do so without harm to the intelligibility of the action. Unlike Plautus he consciously avoided for the most part allusions to anything specifically Roman. It was his principle to keep the Greek milieu of the plays except for certain details which seemed to him pointless and could only make comprehension more difficult.

Thus, for instance, it was a specifically Greek custom to cut one's hair short as a sign of mourning. Apollodoros, the author of the original of the Terentian *Phormio,* had a barber report to the young men waiting in his shop that he had just cut the hair of a poor and beautiful girl who had lost her mother. The young Antipho decides to visit her and falls in love at once with the girl, who at the end of the play is fortunately recognised as the daughter of a well-to-do citizen—and they live happily ever after. In

Terence, too, the young men are sitting in the barber's shop, but the barber as narrator must disappear, to eliminate the non-Roman custom of cutting the hair in mourning. Instead Terence has a weeping young man enter who has just seen the unfortunate girl and describes her with emotion. The barber will probably have told the story without tears. Terence then would have also sentimentalized the scene. But it is certainly out of place to speak on that account of a deepening of emotional and spiritual content. In terms of the rest of the play this change, though it makes the scene itself more moving, creates difficulties later, because the agitation of the weeping young man is more than his merely intermediary role calls for. The spectators' interest in him is aroused and in his further connection with the poor girl, an interest which is not satisfied later on. For the young man immediately disappears into the wings, and, as in Apollodoros, only Antipho matters.

There are other instances of a certain sentimentalizing. This tendency however is not in undisputed command. Thus, to take one example, Terence does not allow an unhappy lover to think, as in Menander, of suicide, but only of emigration. A feeling for the limits of Roman common sense seems to have been at work here.

Still another tendency becomes apparent when we consider the negro slave girl who appears in the ***Eunuchus.*** Terence added her as a mute part, certainly for no other reason than that the audience would like to see this exotic figure. He sometimes kept minor figures on stage longer than in the original, or had them appear earlier. In these cases he gives them a few unimportant lines; otherwise they stand around rather purposelessly. His aim was to enrich the appearance of the stage.

But the playwright gives evidence of a more creative ability when he transforms a narrative monologue into a dialogue by introducing a second person, as he apparently sometimes did. There he enlivened the scene with poetical talent. But once, on the contrary, he eliminated a highly effective dialogue. The case in point is the dialogue of the *matrona* Myrrhina and the *hetaira* Bacchis in the original of the ***Hecyra.*** It was in this dialogue that the decisive recognition took place. The reason for the elimination of this scene and the substitution of a short narration of the event is difficult to see. Scholars have supposed that Terence wanted to avoid recognition on stage as too worn a theatrical motif. But this is improbable. Terence knew very well that comedy to a certain degree consisted of conventional *topoi* and that all depended on their variation in the particular situation. The recognition scene in the ***Hecyra*** was quite unusual. Nevertheless Terence eliminated it. Why has he introduced the parasite and the *miles gloriosus* into the ***Eunuchus,*** why has he added a beating on stage to the ***Adelphoe,*** if he was in principle against typical comic figures and scenes? And why has he, contrary to Plautus, generally chosen recognition plays? One might consider another

motive: perhaps the meeting of the respectable wife of a citizen with a prostitute, who saves the desperate lady, offended Roman morals. Roman *meretrices* seem to have had a worse social reputation than their Athenian counterparts. And it has already been noticed that Terence had a respect for proper behavior. Regard for Roman morality seems to have been at work, too, at the end of the ***Adelphoe,*** where the strict father Demea comes off better than in the original in which the mild and humane Micio apparently was preferred. So in the ***Hecyra*** regard for Roman *decorum* seems to have worked against his general preference for dialogues.

But he was consistent in his refusal of a prologue in the form of a narrative monologue and gave the exposition always in dialogue. Although he could find such a form of exposition already present in Greek plays, he certainly sometimes substituted a dialogue of two persons for a Greek prologue spoken by a god. Expositional material which he could not use here he skillfully distributed later in the play. One reason for avoiding exposition by monologue surely was that after a long personal prologue, which he regularly used for introducing the play, a second long speech could have been boring. Further, the suspense was heightened when the audience was not informed by a god about the final solution (but at the same time certain dramatic ironies were necessarily lost). It is not impossible that the prologue-god was eliminated also to avoid a fantastic and unreal theatrical device.

But other instances which have been adduced to show the greater realism of Terentian drama often need correction. It is true that we have less breaking of the dramatic illusion in Terence than in Plautus (perhaps even less than in Menander), but Terence too kept the unreal convention of the speaking of asides which are not to be heard by the interlocutor but by the audience. And it is surely wrong to see in Terence's treatment of gnomic reflexions an attempt at greater realism. Terence did not at all avoid gnomic sentences; on the contrary he liked them in rhetorically brilliant form. Perhaps he cut off longer reflexions, but obviously not because of an inherent unreality of the scene, but simply because his public would not have favorably accepted too much philosophy.

Let me now remark briefly on the problems of Terence's translating from the Greek. Scholars have often attempted to show the special way Terence translated by a comparison between the few existing Greek fragments and their Terentian counterparts. But one should not try to discover in each slight deviation an important artistic principle, and the wish to balance each loss by an equivalent gain has sometimes prevented a just evaluation. Comparison of one-line fragments needs a cautious critic who does not burden our small material with too heavy deductions. But there is another way to investigate the translating of Terence, not yet adequately applied. Papyrus discoveries have brought rather extensive fragments of Menandrian comedies to our knowledge. Although no play which served Terence as a model has yet been found, a general comparison between Menandrian and Terentian style has become possible. For instance, the relative frequency of colloquial and rhetorical elements, of stereotyped and individual expressions can be observed. It seems that Terence used more rhetorical figures than Menander. With them he aimed at stronger effects, sometimes at the price of specific nuances. He used more interjections; the intent was vivid colloquialism, but the result occasionally yielded a sort of cliché. On the whole we must be careful not to attribute to Terence what should be attributed to differences between Greek and Latin or to the traditional language of the Roman stage. Only from this background can the specific character of the Terentian way of translating be investigated.

But this kind of translating was at any rate a great achievement. It meant the creation of a new literary language in Latin with a purity, refinement and flexibility of diction that had not previously existed and that was capable of expressing complicated psychological processes. Even if Terence was stimulated by the urbane colloquial language of aristocratic Roman circles, the step to definite formation of a literary style was still a major one. It was brought about in the process of dealing with the texts of Menander and attempting to transpose the natural language of the Greek comedies into an appropriate Roman form.

Furthermore, Terence put before the eyes of the Romans in this new literary language subjects which had not been represented in Roman literature before. The psychological subtleties and problematical human situations of Attic comedy were reproduced with an understanding and a sympathy previously unknown. The Terentian conception of *humanum* is in my opinion such a reproduction of an analogous Greek idea. The term has neither been deepened, compared with the meaning of the corresponding Greek words, nor has it been filled with a specifically Roman mentality. But Terence was the first to open Roman comedy to this conception. With all this he helped unlock new realms to the Roman spirit, and this intermediary function is certainly not to be underrated.

Finally, Terence took an independent view of the question how Greek plays should be adapted in detail. On the one hand he strove, in reaction to the liberties taken by Plautus, for a closer imitation of the originals. On the other he kept to his own judgement and considered it his task not only to make the Greek plays accessible to the Roman spirit, but also as far as possible to improve them as stageplays. He worked, however, not by inventing new plot threads, and only occasionally by adding characters or freely rewriting speeches and dialogues. Terence found in the Attic comedies such a completely formed tradition of the well-made play that he knew his own attempts could not, as a rule, compete with it. As long as this reservoir was not exhausted, it probably seemed to him pointless to offer necessarily weaker creations of his own. He was able in general to confine himself to enriching

the plays with additional Greek material where it seemed suitable. He hoped in this way to combine the advantages of two Greek plays. Where he found occasion to alter his models with inventions of his own, the result was normally not an essentially new creation. The changes are mostly of the sort that would be considered today as falling in the province of a director or producer, who does not feel bound to strict adherence to the script.

The tendency of his changes was especially towards a richer visual element, livelier plots and stage business, increase in suspense or emotional effect, regard for Roman morality or even simply consideration for the limited knowledge of his public—tendencies which sometimes worked against each other but to a certain degree converge in the basic aim of adapting the comedies in such a way that, while sticking as closely as possible to the Greek comedies, they might also be more effective on the Roman stage for the Roman public.

It is striking that precisely in his earliest play, the *Andria,* he made his most independent contribution with the invention of the *libertus* Sosia, and that the *contaminatio* is more extensive and more consequential in this play than later. One might imagine that Terence would have proceeded to freer and freer reworking of the originals. The contrary was the case. Terence deliberately bound himself in the course of the six years of his productive career closer to his models, even though he never adopted the principle of the absolute fidelity which his literary opponent Luscius Lanuvinus maintained. While the latter regarded addition from a second Greek play as well as independent interpolations as spoiling and defiling the beauty of the Greek original, Terence allowed himself alterations of this kind. But he willingly limited his liberties in reworking—a fact which can only be explained by his belief in the value of the Greek works which he wanted to bring to the Roman public.

Terence's deliberate adherence to his Greek models is basically different from the way in which Plautus used the Greek originals as raw material for his own creations, as well as from the way later Roman poets emulated the *exemplaria Graeca.* Terence was surely not the Virgil of Roman comedy, as Benedetto Croce has called him [in *La Critica* 34, 1936], and the picture of his literary development is totally distorted if we see him as a Latin poet who used the Menandrian comedies with the same liberty as, for instance, the Greek Apollodoros. The fundamental difference between Terence's achievement and that of a creative poet in the specific sense of the word (who may be very much indebted to literary predecessors) should not be obscured. Of course, we do not deny the kind of creativity which was necessary for the translating itself, nor do we see his activities restricted to the translating. But a warning against common misrepresentations of his poetical achievements may not be useless in order to gain a better view of the kind of originality which he did display.

THE GIRL FROM ANDROS

Terry McGarrity (essay date 1978)

SOURCE: "Thematic Unity in Terence's *Andria*," in *Transactions of the American Philological Association*, Vol. 108, 1978, pp. 103-14.

[*In the essay below, McGarrity examines the father-son relationship between Simo and Pamphilus in* The Girl from Andros.]

Scholarship on the **Andria** has focused primarily on two additions by Terence: first, the freedman Sosia in the opening scene, and then the second young lover Charinus and his slave Byrria. The attention on these two alterations has been directed particularly toward a consideration of Menander's Greek original of the **Andria.** The purpose of this paper, however, is to show that there is a continuing theme in the **Andria** of Terence and that these two changes by Terence develop and support this theme.

The father-son relationship is a favorite theme of Terence, and it appears most fully developed in the **Adelphoe.** The **Andria,** however, offers the first treatment of this theme and in a manner quite different from the later **Heautontimorumenos** and **Adelphoe.** In the **Andria** Terence does not employ two fathers and sons (as in the two later plays mentioned above) to contrast approaches to child rearing and the results of these approaches. Rather, one father and son are shown, and in their ideas and goals there is virtually no area of difference. Pamphilus and his father Simo are not at odds with each other; they are in fact striving for the same end, namely, that Pamphilus assume the duties of a responsible young man. These duties include the taking of an honorable wife and becoming a father. Whatever differences they have arise concerning the path to this end.

Pamphilus makes his first appearance immediately after he has been falsely informed by Simo that a marriage to Chremes' daughter, which Chremes had earlier opposed, has once more been arranged and is to take place that very day. Overwhelmed by this announcement, Pamphilus rushes on stage and cries out: *hoccinest humanum factu aut inceptu? hoccin[est] officium patris?* (236). This concern for proper behavior as a human being and as a father is a statement of the theme and the motive of the play. It is this concern which directs the actions of both Simo and Pamphilus.

The two forms of proper action create a problem for Pamphilus, as he is torn between his love and feeling for his beloved Glycerium and his respect for his father (260-62). Placed in this quandary Pamphilus is uncertain as to what he should do (264), but, when upbraided by Mysis, the *ancilla* to Glycerium (267-70), Pamphilus shows his character by resolving to stand by Glycerium. The bases given for his decision are first his moral responsibility to Glycerium and then his love for her (271-76). Just as

Pamphilus has first cited his obligation as a human and then his personal feelings of affection as the reasons for his decision, so does he again include love as only one element among those traits which will cause him to behave honorably and to accept his obligation.

> adeon me ignavom putas,
> adeon porro ingratum aut inhumanum aut ferum,
> ut neque me consuetudo neque amor neque pudor
> commoveat neque commoneat ut servem fidem?
>
>   (277-80)

This leads to Pamphilus' account of Chrysis' prayer to him as she lay dying. This beautiful and emotional speech answers the questions posed at the beginning of the scene concerning what is *humanum* and what is the *officium patris.*

> O Mysis Mysis etiam nunc mihi
> scripta illa dicta sunt in animo Chrysidis
> de Glycerio. iam ferme moriens me vocat:
> accessi; vos semotae: nos soli: incipit
> "mi Pamphile, huiu' forman atque aetatem vides,
> nec clam te est quam illi nunc utraeque inutiles
> et ad pudicitiam et ad rem tutandam sient.
> quod ego per hanc te dexteram [oro] et genium
>   tuom,
> per tuam fidem perque huiu' solitudinem
> te obtestor ne abs te hanc segreges neu deseras.
> si te in germani fratri' dilexi loco
> sive haec te solum semper fecit maxumi
> seu tibi morigera fuit in rebus omnibus,
> te isti virum do, amicum tutorem patrem;
> bona nostra haec tibi permitto et tuae mando
>   fide[i]."
>
>   (282-96)

Chrysis' first concern is for the physical and financial security of Glycerium, so that she will not be forced into the life of a *meretrix* as had befallen Chrysis earlier. Her own affection and the feeling of Glycerium for Pamphilus are the final points in her argument. She then assigns Pamphilus his responsibilities and rôles: *te isti virum do, amicum tutorem patrem* (295). Sexual love is one function, but the culminating rôle of responsibility is that of *pater.* The constraint assuring this commitment is not Pamphilus' love for Glycerium or affection for Chrysis, but the *fides* which he was eager to protect earlier (280). Chrysis calls upon this *fides* twice (290, 296) as the source of assurance that Pamphilus will honor her request.

Thus the *officium patris* and *humanum factu* are defined in terms of the rôles of *amicus, tutor,* and *pater.* The responsibilities of these rôles are *ad pudicitiam et ad rem tutandam* (288), and the safeguard is *fides.* Pamphilus does not try to avoid this responsibility, but assumes it deliberately and succinctly: *accepi: acceptam servabo* (298). In this way Pamphilus has himself become a *pater.*

Has the portrayal of Pamphilus been sufficiently developed prior to this scene so that his actions here are credible and consistent? What information about Pamphilus has been provided? In considering the evidence it is worthwhile to keep in mind the premise of Ortha Wilner that descriptions of a character are more likely to be true if he is absent and less likely so if he is present [Ortha L. Wilner, "The Technical Device of Direct Description of Character in Roman Comedy," *CP* 33 1938]. Since Pamphilus is not present during the earlier scenes there may be a presumption of truth concerning the remarks about him.

Simo, his father, begins by saying that it is impossible to appraise a young man's character while his age, fear, and his guardian restrain him (53-54). Pamphilus has engaged in the normal activities of horses, hunting, and philosophy, but not in excess, a fact which gives pleasure to Simo (58-60). After Sosia interjects that the golden mean (*nequid nimis,* 61) is the best way of life, Simo continues his description and praise of Pamphilus. He recounts the association of Pamphilus with the suitors of Chrysis, and his concern for his son's well-being is made obvious by his relief at hearing that Pamphilus was not involved romantically with Chrysis (83-91). *Gaudebam* (89) is his reaction here just as it was earlier (60). From this example Simo concluded that Pamphilus' virtue was intact (91-98). This report of Pamphilus' character not only pleased Simo but caused Chremes to arrange the marriage of his daughter to Pamphilus.

At the death of Chrysis, Pamphilus mourned (*nonnumquam conlacrumabat,* 109), and this also pleased his father.

> sic cogitabam "hic parvae consuetudinis
> causa huiu' mortem tam fert familiariter:
> quid si ipse amasset? quid hic mihi faciet patri?"
> haec ego putabam esse omnia humani ingeni
> mansuetique animi officia.
>
> (110-14)

The *officia humani ingeni* are important to Simo, and he takes delight once more in seeing their presence in his son, although he is somewhat mistaken in attributing all of his son's emotions to grief.

Pamphilus, then, has performed according to the expectations which the descriptions of him have created. Here, now, an explanation for the noble character of Pamphilus is suggested. In the second scene Davos sets forth the primary (and only explicitly stated) reason—it is the *lenitas* of Simo (175). Similarly, Pamphilus acknowledges the gentle rearing by Simo as one of the causes of his respect for his father (262-63).

At this point it is essential to deal with the opening scene of Terence's ***Andria.*** Donatus has stated quite clearly that in the Greek *Andria* the *senex* spoke in a monologue and that in the *Perinthia* there was a dialogue between the old man and his wife, but that in Terence's ***Andria*** the old man speaks with his freedman. Critics do not question the testimony of Donatus, but their approaches and explanation for the change vary greatly.

Lefèvre attacks the problem through a consideration of the format of the Greek plays and by detailing the difficulties which retaining the original form would create. He explains the change to a freedman by Terence in terms of the inconsistencies which retaining the wife would intrude. But this is essentially a negative approach, and Lefèvre does not consider the positive reasons for the choice of a freedman rather than a slave. Sosia is not distinguished from a slave except by the speech of Simo and is later dismissed to keep an eye on Davos and Pamphilus (169-70). This is the same task which Charinus later assigns to his slave Byrria (412-15). Furthermore, Sosia is a protatic character, and hence his freedman's status has no further function in the play.

But Simo pointedly states that Sosia is a freedman (37-39), and Sosia is the only freedman in extant Roman comedy. Jacoby suggested that Terence was, in fact, portraying his own situation in order to pay homage to his own master who had freed him. While this is possible, it poses two problems: first, any argument based on Suetonius' life of Terence must be viewed with skepticism since this life admits such great uncertainty; second, the praise is directed toward the freedman rather than toward the master. If Terence had wished to express his personal gratitude, he might have been more generous in his thanks. Furthermore, an explanation derived from the theme of the drama is available.

The substitution of Sosia for the wife of the *Perinthia* allows Terence to introduce the ideas which will suggest the theme of *officium* and of the growth of a young man into a responsible person. The traits of faithfulness and taciturnty in Sosia are praised (34), and he is described as having behaved like a free man (*liberaliter,* 38). These qualities are attributed, to a great extent at least, to the gentle manner with which Simo has treated Sosia. In talking to Sosia Simo first commends these aspects of Sosia's personality and then describes his treatment of Sosia.

> ego postquam te emi, a parvolo ut semper tibi
> apud me iusta et clemens fuerit servitus
> scis. feci ex servo ut esses libertus mihi,
> propterea quod servibas liberaliter:
> quod habui summum pretium persolvi tibi.
>
> (35-39)

Thus the fair and gentle treatment by Simo has resulted in a trustworthy freedman. Just as Sosia has become a free man through his good character and the gentle direction of Simo, so also through the continued mildness of Simo and through Pamphilus' own proper actions will Pamphilus become "free." Throughout the play Pamphilus gradually undergoes a freeing, but it is a freeing which leads not to license but to the acceptance of duty and responsibility.

Simo relates to Sosia the entire situation involving Pamphilus and the supposed marriage. At the opening of this exposition there begins a correspondence between Sosia

Illustration from a twelfth-century edition of The Girl from Andros.

and Pamphilus. The proper behavior of the slave/son is commended and is implied to result from the guidance of the master/father. Sosia's life is described by *liberaliter* (38), and Pamphilus' is called *liberius* (52). Yet Simo recognizes that a man cannot be judged truly while constrained by *aetas metus magister* (54). Thus Sosia must be free for his rôle to have any significance. If he were still a slave, then fear of his master would negate Simo's appraisal of his character and eliminate his usefulness based on his trustworthiness. These same restraints have held Pamphilus up to this point but are now coming loose.

Simo has mentioned Pamphilus' completions of duty as an ephebe (51) which removes age as an obstacle for his freedom. *Metus* will be replaced in Pamphilus' mind by *pudor* as seen in I.v. Any remaining fear is later directly removed by Davos in a scene with Charinus. In this manner two restraints are taken away from Pamphilus, and he begins to be allowed to show his character.

Only the *magister* remains to block Pamphilus' complete emergence as a free man. Simo is, of course, the *magister* for Pamphilus, and he is aware of his son's proper

behavior, as has been indicated earlier. But, Simo does not realize consciously that the actions of Pamphilus are the natural consequences of his teaching. Due to his conscious ignorance, then, Simo becomes a comic figure as he first lurks about the house of Chrysis asking about his son's activities and then contriving a test for Pamphilus. Simo knows the moral damage which a bad teacher can inflict on a student as he indicates by his description of Davos as a *magistrum . . . improbum* (192), but he fails to consider the analog of this: that his good teaching will result in a good product, his son.

The foundation of Pamphilus' character has been well laid, both morally and dramatically. The audience is prepared for a noble youth, and that is what Terence has supplied. The main cause for Pamphilus' nobility is cited as the gentle treatment by his father, first by Davos (*lenitas,* 175), then by Simo himself (*sivi,* 188), and finally by Pamphilus (*leni . . . animo,* 262). Simo connects this thought with the idea of age and maturing.

> dum tempus ad eam rem tulit, sivi animum ut
> expleret suom;

nunc hic dies aliam vitam defert alios mores
postulat:

(188-89)

Pamphilus has acted properly within the limits set for a youth, but now he must leave that behind and become something else. The alternative which Simo is striving to arrange is for Pamphilus to become a husband and father. These are the same rôles which Pamphilus chooses for himself as part of his *officium patris* (295).

Since the character of Pamphilus is dependent on the teaching of Simo, it is necessary to consider the evidence of his instruction. This includes the words of Simo and others but also includes the actions of Simo and Chremes, the other father. Together they show the attitude and actions which exemplify the responsibilities and functions of a father. Simo shows his concern for his rôle as a tolerant father when he explains why he has not approached Pamphilus directly with an accusation concerning his association with Glycerium. He begins his remarks to Davos with the extremely casual *meum gnatum rumor est amare* (185), and follows with an explanation.

sed nunc ea me exquirere
iniqui patris est; nam quod ant(e)hac fecit nil ad
me attinet.

(186-87)

Although Simo has in fact investigated his son's activities, he wishes to avoid the stigma of being an *iniquus pater,* and he is reluctant to tell everything to Davos, whom he mistrusts (159-60). Davos later reveals his understanding of Simo's motives (and confirms Simo's apprehensions) as he tells Pamphilus that Simo would feel unjust if he criticized Pamphilus before any offense was actually committed, and Davos agrees that this would indeed be an injustice (376-78).

The encounters between Simo and Chremes, the father of Philumena, demonstrate the concern each of them has for the welfare of his own child. Simo greets Chremes and begs of him that the marriage be reinstituted. Simo's basis for his request is that the marriage will be good for Pamphilus (538-43). Chremes is hesitant to agree and for the same reason, his concern for the welfare of his daughter. In this regard he asks Simo to examine the situation as if Philumena were his daughter (546-49). The concern for Philumena's well-being is continued in the refusals of Chremes (563-64, 566), as Simo expresses his hopes that the marriage will take Pamphilus away from Glycerium. Finally, Simo sums up his argument by comparing the possible loss to the certain gains from the marriage (567-71).

Thus Chremes and Simo have shown that their concern is to watch over the welfare of their children. This is the specific responsibility which Chrysis had assigned to Pamphilus and which Pamphilus had accepted in his rôle as *tutor* and *pater* (295): *ad pudicitiam et ad rem tutandam* (288). Once more near the end of the play when Chremes has again cancelled the marriage, he expresses his distress for the damage nearly done to his daughter,

not to himself: *dum studeo obsequi tibi, paene inlusi vitam filiam* (822). The well-being of a child and the duty of the father in that regard are the motivation for the actions of Simo and Chremes. Money is never mentioned until all the problems are resolved and Chremes assigns the dowries (950-51).

This overly conscious effort to fulfill his responsibility as a father is, however, the trait which causes Simo to complicate the action and to expose himself to the schemes and tricks of Davos. Duckworth has observed that the typical Terentian *senex* outwits himself by refusing to accept the truth, whereas Plautine *senes* are all too willing to accept falsehoods as truth [George E. Duckworth, *The Nature of Roman Comedy,* 1952]. This is precisely the situation with Simo: he so fears and distrusts Davos that Davos is able to fool him with piety and truth. First Davos convinces Pamphilus to agree to the marriage (418-20). Simo has foreseen this possibility (165-67), but he is taken by surprise at the birth of the child to Glycerium, and he persuades himself that this is a trick of Davos (469-80). Simo's self-satisfaction provides Davos with further opportunity (498), and he seizes upon it to confuse Simo (524-26). Much of the comedy of the play is centered in these scenes, particularly when Mysis and Davos explain the story of the childbirth to Chremes (740-95). Chremes, however, is not self-righteous and does not expose himself to trickery as does Simo. Although Simo's reluctance to believe the truth makes him appear somewhat foolish, it is in no way the cause of the recognition scene; the knowledge revealed by Crito, the kinsman of Chrysis, brings this about.

Criticism has been directed at Terence for his handling of the characters of Charinus and Byrria, and this criticism is, for the most part, deserved. The rôles of Charinus and his slave Byrria are said by Donatus to be the creations of Terence, although they are often believed to be derived from the *Perinthia.* Regardless of their source, Charinus and his love for Philumena do not suit the standards for the dual plot as defined by Norwood and as practiced by Terence in his later plays, particularly the ***Phormio.*** The dual plot is "the method of employing two problems or complications to solve each other. [Gilbert Norwood, *The Art of Terence,* 1923]. Duckworth has modified this definition by saying that the two problems only need affect one another, for in several dramas one love affair complicated the other. The ***Andria*** does fit Duckworth's definition but only with difficulty, for the main love story is that of Pamphilus which is not affected at all by the desires of Charinus. Yet, despite any flaws in the dramatic presentation, Charinus does have a definite function in the play. In addition to providing contrast to Pamphilus, his scenes with Pamphilus accent the theme of responsibility and duty and are closely linked to the idea of freedom.

Charinus differs from Pamphilus particularly in his lack of initiative as he longs for Philumena. His slave Byrria acknowledges this fault in his master by offering this aphoristic advice: *quoniam non potest id fieri quod vis, / id velis quod possit* (305-306). The arrival of Pamphilus spurs Charinus to seek help, but it does not suggest any line of direct action for him. Pamphilus, on the contrary, has chosen his course in his acceptance of Glycerium and is steadfast in his decision. He does seek assistance from Charinus and Byrria here (333-34) and later from Davos (383), but his desire is for them to facilitate the acceptance of his decision by Simo. Charinus twice uses morality as a pretext for his inertia, when Byrria points out to Charinus that his interest in Philumena will imply a possibility that he might become Philumena's lover after her marriage to Pamphilus (315-17), and again when Pamphilus asks if Charinus has been involved prior to this time with Philumena (325). Pamphilus' *quam vellem* (326) sums up his disappointment in Charinus' inactivity. Charinus' only active plan is to remove himself from the sight of the marriage either permanently (322) or at least for a few days (328-29).

Pamphilus shows his consciousness of his growing stature as he disclaims any credit for his effort to forestall the marriage (330-32). The *officium liberi hominis* (330) introduces the arrival of Davos who further amplifies both the idea of freedom and the contrast between Charinus and Pamphilus. After the typical *servus currens* entrance, Pamphilus begs Davos that he free him from his fear, a request which Davos gladly grants (351-52). The freeing of a master by his slave is comical enough to justify its use by Terence, but its greater significance for the drama is shown when Charinus asserts that he too is free (370). Davos immediately rejects this claim as unfounded, for Charinus has not yet earned freedom from his fear. Until Charinus is willing to assume responsibility and to work to achieve his desires, he cannot be free. That a close relationship exists between initiative and success is indicated later by Pamphilus when he blames his misfortune on his own inactivity and his willingness to rely on Davos (607-609). For Pamphilus the lack of resolve is brief, but for Charinus it is a way of life.

Pamphilus is now freed from *aetas* and *metus*, although *metus* is replaced by *pudor*. It is with respect to *pudor* and *fides*, the defined limits for *officium*, that Charinus makes his next appearance. Byrria has overheard Pamphilus agree to the marriage and has informed Charinus of the seeming lack of faith on the part of Pamphilus.

> CH. immo id est genus hominum pessumum in
> denegando modo quis pudor paullum adest;
> post ubi tempu' promissa iam perfici,
> tum coacti necessario se aperiunt,
> et timent et tamen res premit denegare;
> ibi tum eorum inpudentissuma oratiost
> "quis tu es? quis mihi es? quor meam tibi? heus
>   proxumus sum egomet mihi."
> at tamen "ubi fides?" si roges,
> nil pudet hic, ubi opus [est]; illi ubi
>   nil opust, ibi verentur.
>
> (629-38a)

When Pamphilus attempts to explain, Charinus again accuses him of breaking his word (*solvisti fidem,* 643). Pamphilus assigns the major portion of the blame for the

situation to Davos, but he does accept his share of the responsibility because he listened (664).

The criticism of Davos by Pamphilus sets the scene for the removal of the last obstacle to Pamphilus' becoming a man. Davos does not let this criticism pass, but forces Pamphilus to face his new rôle as he becomes aware of his position as *magister.*

> ego, Pamphile, hoc tibi pro servitio debeo,
> conari manibu' pedibu' noctesque et dies,
> capitis periclum adire, dum prosim tibi;
> tuomst, siquid praeter spem evenit, mi ignoscere.
> parum succedit quod ago; at facio sedulo.
> vel meliu' tute reperi, me missum face.
>
> (675-80)

Davos is not displaying disrespect, for he previously had admonished Pamphilus about the respect due Simo (380), but he is reminding Pamphilus of the duty of his position as *magister.* For his part, Davos has long been aware of his duty. He debated to whom he owed the greater obligation (209-14), and he provides a great deal of the humor and action in the drama by striving to fulfill his responsibility. Moreover, he does not seek any personal gain for himself, least of all his freedom.

Pamphilus reacts to the instruction of Davos and then to the concern of Mysis by once again pledging his steadfast devotion to Glycerium (694-97). This proclamation of faith shows that Pamphilus has not changed since his original decision in spite of the difficulties which have arisen.

Simo grudgingly, and at times bitterly, accepts this decision of his son but is not convinced either of the legality or propriety of it. He speaks sarcastically of the *pietatem gnati* (869), and asks Pamphilus if he is not ashamed of himself (871). Simo calls the actions damaging to Pamphilus' reputation and contrary to custom, law, and the will of his father (879-81). The complaint that Pamphilus has acted contrary to the will of his father is clearly the fact which troubles Simo most, for after he gives his sanction to Pamphilus' relationship with Glycerium (886-89), he reacts sharply to Pamphilus' exclamation of joy (*mi pater,* 889).

> quid "mi pater"? quasi tu huius indigeas patris.
> domus uxor liberi inventi invito patre;
> adducti qui illam hinc civem dicant: viceris.
>
> (890-92)

Simo complains that Pamphilus has a home, wife, and children, yet these are exactly what Simo was attempting to arrange for Pamphilus. Simo, however, has been denied his prerogative as a *pater* because Pamphilus has already assumed the duties of a father for himself.

Although Pamphilus has himself become a *pater,* nevertheless he does not forget his responsibility as a son. Pamphilus denies having suborned Crito to support the story that Glycerium is a citizen (899). Pamphilus further offers to abandon Glycerium and marry Chremes' daughter if only Simo will dismiss his suspicion that Pamphilus is responsible for Crito's timely arrival. Simo has pointedly rejected Crito's story because he believes his son has brought about Crito's appearance to establish Glycerium's citizenship (892). Should Simo set aside his only expressed basis for doubt, then his own reasoning will compel him to accept Crito's story as the truth. This is then an arrangement in which Pamphilus cannot lose, for if Simo accepts Crito's testimony that Glycerium is really an Athenian citizen, then Pamphilus will be obliged to marry her. Thus Pamphilus has gambled nothing for everything. Chremes concludes the scene by suggesting to Simo the proper attitude for a father toward his son: *pro peccato magno paullum supplici satis est patri* (903). This scene, then, which marks the final liberation of Pamphilus and reveals his evolution as an adult capable of assuming the *officia patris,* ends with another responsibility included in those *officia.*

If one accepts that the theme of the *officium patris* is present in the **Andria,** then one must also acknowledge that the scenes involving first Sosia and then Charinus and Byrria, far from weakening the play, strengthen the drama both dramatically and thematically.

THE MOTHER-IN-LAW

David Konstan   (essay date 1983)

SOURCE: "*Hecyra*: Ironic Comedy," in *Roman Comedy,* Cornell, 1983, pp. 130-41.

[*In the excerpt below, Konstan contends that* The Mother-in-Law *interrogates the traditional Roman values of* amor *and* pietas *(love and filial duty) and in the process "challenges and confounds their customary meanings."*]

The tension between father and son in new comedy was available . . . as a vehicle for representing issues of caste and class in ancient society. At a certain level, to be sure, these issues manifest themselves as moral conflicts, which we may interpret according to the traditional Roman disjunction of virtue and passion: Modesty and obedience contend with amorous impulses which conventional wisdom regarded as selfish or antisocial. For this reason, moral or psychological interpretations of the plays inevitably come to mind. . . . [Many Roman plays] however, point beyond such abstract values to the matrix of social relations which endows them with content, and the social interest is, accordingly, essential to an adequate exegesis. In certain plays, however, the traditional moral psychology may itself be problematized in ways involving special permutations of the usual narrative formulas. Such works seem to exploit the conventions of new comedy so as to challenge the ideological premises of the genre. In this chapter, I shall take up an ingenious play of this sort by Terence.

Sidney G. Ashmore, in his school edition of Terence's comedies [*The Comedies of Terence*], pronounced that the *Hecyra,* or "Mother-in-Law," was "the one of least merit." He has not been alone in this verdict. At the first two performances of the play, the Roman audience deserted the theater before the show was over. The first time they abandoned it to see a tightrope walker or some boxers, as the prologue indicates, while, at the second performance, they were seduced, soon after the first act, by the report of a sideshow featuring gladiators. Only at the third performance, it appears, the Romans saw it through.

There are exceptions to this general repudiation, of course. The most outstanding, certainly, is Gilbert Norwood, who [in *The Art of Terence,* 1923] described the *Hecyra* as "possibly the finest masterpiece of high comedy in the world." The problem, as Norwood saw it, was to discover why the glories of the play lay unperceived. The reaction of the Romans was easy to explain: "Barbarians," Norwood calls them, who "did not appreciate good art." What then of all those succeeding generations who have failed to appreciate the play? "Tempting as it is," writes Norwood, "to refer these extraordinary criticisms to the Victorian blight which brought both drama and popular taste to the lowest point compatible with civilization, we must remember that all other opinion, tacitly or not, has pointed the same way." Our error, he explains, is to have confused comedy with farce, "to follow Roman tradition, and look upon a markedly unfarcical comedy as no comedy at all." I take it, on the other hand, that this near unanimous sentiment which has persisted over two millennia responds to a reality in the *Hecyra,* which distinguishes this play from others of the genre.

The first scene of Terence's *Hecyra* consists of a very brief exchange between a young courtesan and an old madam or adviser. The old lady counsels the girl to be merciless with her lovers, to make them, take them, and break them, one and all (*spolies, mutiles, laceres quemque nacta sis,* 65), for they seek nothing but their own pleasure at the cheapest price. "But it's wrong," replies the girl, "to treat them all the same." "Wrong to punish the enemy?" the old lady asks; "if only I had your looks or you had my brains," she sighs. This rather cynical piece of dialogue is motivated by the news that Pamphilus, the hero of the play, has reneged on his promise to his mistress Bacchis and taken a wife. Otherwise, it contributes nothing to the plot of the **Hecyra.** The girl and the old woman will remain through the next scene so that they may learn, and the audience with them, something of the background, but after that they will disappear for good, for they are what the ancients called protatic characters, a dramatic device which Terence favored in place of the narrative prologue. I have described the scene rather fully because the egotistical idea of *amor* or love expressed so wittily sets a tone for the play which is out of keeping with the more romantic or passionate moods prevailing in Terence's other comedies. In the **Andria,** the hero, also called Pamphilus, swears to endure anything rather than abandon his beloved, whom he maintains in his heart as his true wife (270ff.). Alternatively, in less pensive, more melodramatic comedies such as the *Eunuch,* love appears as an elemental force that cannot be contained or controlled. The opening scene of the *Hecyra* presents the passion of love as a base and selfish desire and thereby anticipates an important theme in the play.

In the second scene, Parmeno, the slave of Pamphilus, arrives with news of his master's situation. Terence's commentator Donatus exhorts us to "notice the fact that from the beginning of the comedy to the end Parmeno is sent about running and kept in the dark despite his passionate curiosity." Gilbert Norwood observed quite rightly that Parmeno was anything but the usual comic slave:

> Parmeno understands what is expected of him, but he is never given his chance. Never was there a role more desperately devoid of what professional slang calls "fat." Every time this unhappy satellite enters manfully to perform his duty as a *veterator,* a *versutus servus,* and the rest, he is mercilessly ordered off the stage to make room for the play.

It is true: Parmeno, like the two protatic prostitutes, has only a limited part in the play, which will get on without the entertaining wiles of the clever slave. In this reduction of the role of the comic slave, to be sure, Norwood did not find fault. Terence sacrificed the stereotype here, according to Norwood, and in the case of other characters in the play as well, for the sake of truth. In fact, it was just this originality, this realism, which offended the Roman "barbarians." "Terence has failed ignominiously," Norwood wryly complains, "through giving us real people and natural conduct." Parmeno reports that Pamphilus had been in love with the courtesan (*meretrix*) Bacchis, when his father began to urge him to take a wife of his own station. Pamphilus was torn between the *pudor* or modest respect he owed to his father, and the *amor* which he felt for Bacchis. In the end, his father's insistence won out, and Pamphilus married a neighbor's daughter called Philumena. So vexed did he remain, however, that for months he refused to touch his wife, visiting instead with Bacchis. But Bacchis understandably grew cold toward him under the circumstances, and the noble patience of Philumena gradually overcame his disdain, arousing first his pity, and, at last, his love.

Now, a most interesting feature of this play is that it begins where many other ancient comedies leave off—with a legitimate and acknowledged marriage. Here the young hero does not swear loyalty to his beloved in the teeth of his father's opposition, so that the standoff can only be resolved through a recognition scene, revealing that the beloved, after all, is that very daughter of the rich neighbor to whom he had long since been betrothed. The conflict between *amor* and *pietas,* the warring claims of personal passion and obligations to parent and class, all this, it appears, is long since ended, not through comic coincidence, where the tensions of real life find a fictive reconciliation, but through the pragmatic victory of responsibility over passion. This is as it should be, says Donatus. But such a story is not the stuff of comedy.

Impulse has yielded to necessity; we are in the ordinary world. The cynicism of the opening scene seems confirmed: Love is selfish, inconstant, unreliable; authority conquers all. The *Hecyra* reveals at once that the ideal reconciliation between all claims and all parties, between passion and duty, cannot be achieved.

In the meantime, Pamphilus has been obliged to leave Athens on business for several months, and in his absence things have gone badly. ("Good," says the *meretrix,* "if it will help Bacchis!") Philumena appears to have quarreled with Pamphilus's mother, Sostrata, with whom she had been living; in any case, she has returned to her own mother's house. This is the situation to which Pamphilus returns. The audience of the original Greek *Hecyra,* written by Apollodorus of Carystus, was perhaps not so perplexed as readers of Terence are at this point about the reasons for the separation, for Apollodorus may have provided his play with an expository prologue, in which one would have learned that the unlucky Philumena was in fact expecting a baby, and that the child was conceived shortly before her marriage, when she was raped one night by a drunken brawler. Terence abandoned such prologues for his own prefatory monologue, which touches upon literary debates of his own age rather than the plot of the drama. But the effect, in Terence's version, of the drastic delay in exposition is to focus all attention on the background narrative, which no longer appears as a prelude to the chief problem of the play, but is recorded, so far as the audience can tell, for its own interest. What is more, the absence of the prologue gives special emphasis to the first scene, and its cynical view of passion. We are not prepared for a conventional comedy of intrigue and recognition. What we expect is an investigation of a marriage in which passion has been sacrificed to social conformity. There is a morning-after feeling here which may be Terence's own contribution.

The second act of the play dramatizes the suspicions and the growing certainty of Pamphilus's father, Laches, that Sostrata was the cause of the quarrel. Only in the third act does Pamphilus himself appear, with a soulful lament on his ill-starred life in love. Parmeno quite sensibly reminds him that the problem between his wife and his mother will doubtless be easily resolved, now that he is back, but Pamphilus significantly interprets his present situation in terms of his earlier misfortune in his love for Bacchis. This reminder of Bacchis is important for the plot of the play; for Bacchis will later be summoned by Laches on the suspicion that she is still involved with Pamphilus, and, as it will turn out, she bears the clue or token which will undo the comic knot. But however much the audience may have known of these developments in Apollodorus's original, readers of Terence are in the dark about them. What stands out in Pamphilus's speech is that he sees himself involved once more in the conflict between love, which he now bears toward his wife, and the filial piety due his mother. The tension described in the first act seems to be replicated. Pamphilus's lament is interrupted by Philumena's cry—she is suffering the pains of childbirth, but Pamphilus guesses only that she must be severely ill—and the scene draws to a close with Pamphilus's passionate

Wall niche with masks for The Mother-in-Law, *from an early manuscript of the play.*

apostrophe to his wife, "whatever danger you face, it is certain that I shall perish together with you" (326).

Pamphilus rushes into Philumena's house. When he re-emerges, he relates his discovery of Philumena's real situation in a long soliloquy, which was very likely adapted from a dramatic dialogue in Apollodorus's original. Pamphilus deduces that the child is not his own, because he had not lain with his wife during the first months of his marriage. No one but Philumena and her mother share with Pamphilus full knowledge of all the damaging facts. Pamphilus is disconsolate. He relates the prayer of Philumena's mother, Myrrhina, that he keep secret the circumstance of her daughter's dishonor, even if he cannot bring himself to take his wife back again. It is this exchange that was enacted dramatically by Apollodorus, but which Terence has presented, in his preferred way, as a struggle in the soul of Pamphilus. Passion, conjugal affection, even pity bind him to his wife, but taking her back, he declares (403-4), is out of the question. So much for that selfless participation in her trials which he had so recently proclaimed. He concludes his speech with the recollection once more of his former experience in love, which, as he says, makes him a practiced hand at quenching his feelings.

Pamphilus must now justify his decision not to take back his wife to his father and to hers, without revealing, if possible, the matter of the child. For pity inclines him to respect his wife's desire. And so he will, but in such a way as to preserve his filial piety, his *pietas*. For he must obey his parent rather than the claims of love (448-49). We have once again a reminiscence of his earlier experience with Bacchis, but it is not altogether appropriate here. Donatus explains simply that Pamphilus "has recalled the fact that his mother was hurt by his wife." But Ashmore aptly remarks that "Terence would appear to be woolgathering just at this point. Pamphilus," he continues, "is no longer ignorant of the reason why his wife left her mother-in-law's house. We can account for the apparent lapse, however: Pamphilus is speaking *ironically*. The thought has only just struck him, and its source is surely the analogy which Pamphilus has long since perceived between his present situation and his former love for Bacchis. He will yet hesitate for a couple of lines, wondering just what to say, before he announces firmly: "Now I am resolved to follow the path I have decided upon" (454). He will keep up the pretense of a quarrel between his mother and his wife, so that he may extricate himself from the again unwanted marriage by pleading his filial duty. This he does to a father who affirms that he is pleased to have so loyal a son—no Roman father could quarrel with *pietas*—but he at once urges his son to come to his senses, for his conduct is mad.

I like to think that it was at this point that the Roman audience deserted the first performance of the play. Certainly they might well have found themselves uncomfortable at the turn of events here. For Pamphilus has invoked the traditional tension between passion and responsibility, but twisted it in an extraordinary and hypocritical way to serve his own interest in what is now, as Ashmore puts it, "a personal matter only." Take first his love. It is compromised in advance: Pamphilus gave up Bacchis when pressed by his father, a fact which echoed the cynical dialogue on love with which the play began; and here he will give up love again. His protestations that piety obliges him are false, of course. The inhibition is his own. Its source is in conventional values, but of these Pamphilus is now the vehicle, and he is obliged, accordingly, to contain his own passion. His passion is clearly a domitable one—a subtle variation in the comic phenomenology of *amor*. Indeed, when he speaks his mind openly, he speaks of pity (446), not of love, as the bond between himself and Philumena. As for his piety, moreover, it is doubly counterfeit, for it is the pretense of a diminished and hollow version of the virtue. For *pietas* does not mean that one obliges the whims of parents, their inconsequential and personal likes and dislikes. That view involves a contradiction in the idea of piety, reminiscent of the problem in Plato's *Euthyphro,* where obedience toward one of the gods may entail contempt for another. Worse, Pamphilus's mother, Sostrata, will urge him herself, naturally enough, to overlook the alleged quarrel and take back his wife. So Pamphilus must then disobey both his parents, adducing as his reason—filial piety. No, the object of filial piety is not a parent's whim or convenience, what Pamphilus calls *commoda* (481, 495); it is rather a social code which is understood to be objective, to be represented by the parents, chiefly the father. Pamphilus, we might say, exploits the fact that the subjective and objective content of *pietas* are not clearly distinguished, that they dwell undifferentiated under the cover of a single term. Terence has re-created the conventional conflict between *amor* and *pietas*, which he probes in other plays with remarkable psychological insight—an insight, as Peter Flury has shown, distinctly his own—and which he suggests in this play in the background story of Pamphilus and Bacchis; but he has re-created it in a way that appears perverse. *Pietas* is distorted from the idea of obligation to traditional authority to an indulgence of an elder's tastes; *amor* is neither an unquenchable force nor a deep and reasoned affection engaging one's loyalties (*fides*) on the deepest level, but a negotiable feeling which retreats, now all too readily, before more interested concerns. Finally, the entire conflict is a mock-up, pretended by Pamphilus so that he can escape a threat, not to conscience or to passion, but to ego. And escape he does, running off before his father or father-in-law can pursue him with their angry questions.

The appeal to a ternary conception of the psyche, which we today associate, broadly speaking, with the doctrines of Freud, should be explained. Romans did not interpret their own psychology in these terms. We have seen that their own language points rather to a binary division, between *pietas* and associated virtues on the one hand, and *cupidines* or passionate desires such as love (or ambition or avarice) on the other. This dichotomous structure can in general give an account of the kind of situation in which Pamphilus finds himself in this play. Love for Philumena inclines Pamphilus in one direction, while his concern for his status or *dignitas,* which would be compromised if he accepted his violated wife, inclines him in another. Concern for *dignitas* is part of the complex of tradition-regarding virtues which the Romans subsumed under the notion of *boni mores.* In Menander's *Epitrepontes,* which many scholars believe to have been the model for Apollodorus's *Hecyra,* the situation of Charisios is practically the same as that of Pamphilus here, yet his behavior does not appear to challenge the concepts of conventional psychology. The character of Pamphilus seems exceptional, perhaps, because the domain of *pietas* and its cognate virtues is, as it were, preempted by his pretended obligations toward his mother, while his true motives are kept concealed. Thus Pamphilus appears to bear a private responsibility for his behavior, which accordingly seems willful or egotistical. The action of the play so divides the psychological field that neither duty nor passion but selfishness alone is left to account for Pamphilus's choice.

In the fourth act, Philumena's father reasons that his own wife must be the cause of his daughter's estrangement, harboring, he supposes, a resentment about Pamphilus having maintained relations with Bacchis for some time after he was married. His wife does not disabuse him of this suspicion, for otherwise he may press her too closely concerning Philumena's child, whose existence he has just discovered. He, for his part, broadcasts the news of the child, which delights Laches, though both men are perplexed why its birth was concealed. Pamphilus, finding that his argument from *pietas* is beginning to totter, now that his mother is planning to retire to the country with his father, quickly changes strategy, claiming that the concealment of the child shows plainly that Philumena is loath to be his wife (655-60). From here to the end of the play, the developments are rapid, tight, and masterful. Laches perceives his son's tergiversations and accuses him of still harboring a love for Bacchis—untrue, but a natural supposition, resurrecting the original conflict of *amor* and *pietas* in a way that reverses Pamphilus's argument: *Pietas* should induce him to keep his wife, not reject her, while it is *amor* which tears him from her. Laches thus reverts to the standard paradigm of this moral tension. Both old men decide to summon Bacchis for a showdown. She appears, denies any connection now with Pamphilus, and agrees to go in to Philumena to lay to rest any unease which she and her mother may have on that score. This she does because she wishes, contrary to the rule of her profession, to see Pamphilus prosper in marriage. When she emerges, she, like Pamphilus earlier, speaks in a long monologue which we know, from Donatus, was originally a dramatic dialogue at least in part. She tells us how a ring she was wearing, which Pamphilus had given her, was recognized as Philumena's, the very one which had been stolen from her on the night she was raped. Thus, the rapist was none other than Pamphilus himself, and the play ends happily for all, though not in what Northrop Frye [In *Anatomy of Criticism*] calls a scene of "festive ritual." Bacchis and Pamphilus agree to keep the unsavory details of the affair confidential. There is no general participation in the comic revelation, "as happens in comedies" (the phrase

is Pamphilus's, lines 866-67). Dante Nardo has observed that "the expression, *ut in comoediis,* represents the repudiation, conscious and deliberate, of a drama where everything always goes one way, and that not the way of human truth."

Several scholars have suggested that this conclusion, with its humble resignation to the plain demands of common experience, reveals an essentially Terentian humanism at its best. Here is realism rather than stock comic types and scenes, a universalism that derives from fidelity to human truth rather than hackneyed formulas. Certainly the **Hecyra** shows a deep sensitivity to human differences, and portrays especially well a certain nobility of mind in both mothers-in-law, in Bacchis, even in the two fathers, types who are ordinarily imprisoned in their rather rigid and sterile roles. The character of Pamphilus is exceptionally complex.

Much of this was doubtless in the Greek original. Terence's own contribution, perhaps, lies in the emphasis—for, in the end, it is no more than an emphasis—on the formal or conventional opposition between love and filial duty. We should be hard pressed to find a real Greek equivalent for the Latin *pietas*: It is a concept peculiarly Roman, and Terence has, in the **Hecyra,** laid out and drawn taut the structure of this traditional Roman psychology on the rack of Apollodorus's drama. In so doing, he revealed stresses within the concept of *pietas* and the nature of *amor* which put in question the fundamental ideological presuppositions of new comedy as a genre. These tensions are factitiously resolved, of course, through the brilliant recognition scene with which the play concludes. But the resolution fails to dispel the conflict between personal feeling and public forms. Instead of comic relief there is a peculiar sense that familiar moral categories have become opaque or ambivalent, and the hero of the play does not seem to be a comic scoundrel or a mad lover, but a subtle and dubious manipulator of the moral tradition.

The air of secrecy, of conspiracy, at the resolution of the play is an emblem of its dubious propriety. It is also coordinate with the interiorization of social inhibitions within the person of Pamphilus. Indeed, a remarkable feature of the **Hecyra** is that the blocking character is identical with the lover himself—a feature which strangely anticipates some comedies of Shakespeare. Pamphilus for this reason seems a more fully realized individual than is the rule for new comedy, and he has won the praise and sympathy of several critics and commentators, beginning with Donatus. For all that, the interest in Terence is not finally in issues of personal identity and development, but in the operations and tensions of the traditional moral code. The inversions and reversals in the story come near to stripping this code of all normal sense. Remaining within the formal conventions of its genre, the **Hecyra** challenges and confounds their customary meanings. In this respect, it represents the ironic moment in new comedy.

Walter E. Forehand   (essay date 1985)

SOURCE: "The Plays of Terence," in *Terence,* Twayne Publishers, 1985, pp. 37-119.

[*In the following excerpt, Forehand provides an introduction to the plot, themes, and characters of* The Mother-in-Law.]

Plot. The play begins with a conversation between Philotis, a young courtesan, and Syra, an old woman in the household of Bacchis, another courtesan with an establishment in the neighborhood. Syra is advising the young woman against being too soft toward her clients, while Philotis wonders if it is right to treat all men the same. They are met by Parmeno, family slave of Laches, his wife, Sostrata, and their son Pamphilus. Pamphilus was an ardent lover of Bacchis when Philotis left Athens two years before; she is surprised to hear he is now married and coaxes Parmeno to tell her what has happened.

The slave explains that Pamphilus came under heavy pressure from his father to marry. He resisted staunchly, but finally acceded to his father's wishes out of filial duty, and was promptly betrothed to Philumena, daughter of the neighbors, Phidippus and Myrrina. Just before the wedding he came to Parmeno in tears regretting his decision. Though he went through with the marriage, he resolved not to consort with his young wife and tried to continue his liaison with Bacchis. She grew cool toward him, however. He soon began to recognize the fine qualities of his wife who remained devoted to him despite his actions, and after a couple of months their marriage was consummated in mutual affection.

As Parmeno continues his story, however, we learn that trouble has arisen in the marriage: Pamphilus was sent to Imbros by his father to look after the estate of a deceased relative; in his absence some sort of problem arose between Philumena and her mother-in-law, Sostrata; the girl used the occasion of a religious festival to return to her parents' home and has neither come back to Sostrata, complaining now of illness, nor allowed her mother-in-law to visit her, although she has been very solicitous. That is where matters stand, as everyone awaits Pamphilus's return. Philotis leaves for a party at which she is expected, and Parmeno goes to the port to seek word of Pamphilus.

Laches and Sostrata come from their house in an argument. Laches, who spends most of his time at their country estate, has come into Athens because he has heard about the problems in his city household. He is berating Sostrata, accusing her of being a typical mother-in-law and of precipitating an argument with her daughter-in-law. Sostrata maintains her innocence and professes both concern for Philumena and confusion as to why the girl has taken a dislike to her.

At this moment Phidippus, Philumena's father, comes out of his house. The two old men greet each other cordially and express the hope that the problems can be resolved, but Phidippus is apprehensive for his daughter's welfare. They go off together to discuss the situation, leaving Sostrata pitifully lamenting the fact that mothers-in-law are typecast so badly.

After exiting, Parmeno returns from the port with Pamphilus, who has just arrived. Parmeno has been reporting the family problems to him, and Pamphilus is torn with confusion over his devotion to his wife and loyalty to his mother. As they near the houses, they hear Myrrina shout to her daughter, and Pamphilus rushes into his in-laws' house to find out what the problem is with his wife.

Sostrata returns, for she has heard that something has happened next door and is afraid Philumena's condition has worsened. As Parmeno tells her of Pamphilus's return, the latter himself comes out. He tells his mother that Philumena is better; she returns to her house, relieved. He then sends Parmeno to the port for his baggage. After the slave leaves, he muses about what he has discovered inside: Philumena is in childbirth. Myrrina had rushed to meet him to explain the pregnancy, for they have been married only nine months, and the marriage went unconsummated for two months. Shortly before their marriage, however, Philumena was raped by an unknown assailant. She begged Pamphilus not to reveal the details of their first months of marriage. If their early marital problems somehow do become known, she plans to claim that the child is premature. At any rate, she promised to destroy the infant immediately. Pamphilus is crushed by the development. He loves Philumena, but he cannot accept the new situation.

Parmeno returns with another slave, Sosia, bringing the baggage. Pamphilus realizes that he knows about the delay in the marriage's consummation, so he sends him away to the acropolis on pretext of keeping an appointment with a fictitious friend, thereby removing him from the scene of the birth.

The old men, Laches and Phidippus, return eager to find Pamphilus, of whose arrival they have learned. Pamphilus is too confused to deal with them, however, so he merely reports that Philumena seems irreconcilable toward her mother-in-law, and he suggests a divorce. The old men are not willing to accept such a solution, since they feel that the difficulties between the women should be resolved rather than the marriage ended, so they go off to confront their womenfolk.

Soon after, Myrrina rushes from her house excitedly talking about Phidippus's discovering the baby. He follows her full of anger that the pregnancy had been kept secret and orders that the baby not be harmed. He blames the marital problems on Myrrina, whom he accuses of a mother-in-law's jealousies, and goes off to attend the care of the child, leaving her onstage to lament her situation. Before she goes in, she elaborates on the rape of Philumena, mentioning that her attacker pulled a ring from her finger.

Sostrata and Pamphilus return. Sostrata has decided for the sake of her son's marriage to abandon the house in Athens and join her husband in the country. Pamphilus protests, but Laches, who has been listening from the doorway, is pleased with the idea. He sends his wife to pack. He and Pamphilus are met by Phidippus, full of news. Laches learns for the first time about the child, and Phidippus asserts his belief that Myrrina, not Sostrata, has been the instigator of Philumena's behavior. Pamphilus does not accept this information as a basis for reconciliation, of course, and the two old men are frustrated at his reaction. Laches suddenly decides that his obstinacy must be a means to destroy his marriage so that he can return to Bacchis. Without replying to the charge, Pamphilus bolts off in confusion, and the two old men decide to call in Bacchis in order to clear up the matter.

Laches returns with her, and she assures him that since the marriage she had discontinued her affair with his son. He convinces her, against her sense of social decorum, to go inside and tell this to the women.

Parmeno returns from his errand, disgusted that Pamphilus's "friend" never appeared. Bacchis comes from the house and eagerly greets him. She sends him to look for Pamphilus with the message, which she says he will understand, that the ring he gave her belongs to Philumena. While she waits for their return, she reports what transpired within: her ring was recognized as the one taken from Philumena by her assailant; but Pamphilus had given her the ring one evening, arriving unexpected and drunk, with the story, produced after some prodding, that he had just attacked a young woman in the street; thus, Pamphilus is the child's father after all.

Parmeno returns with Pamphilus. The master is overjoyed at the turn of events; Parmeno does not understand what is happening, and it is clear that Pamphilus has not confided in him about the rape. They resolve not to tell the fathers, but let them merely assume that the young couple is reconciled as they wished. And so the play ends happily.

The plot of *The Mother-in-Law* is the slowest of all Terence's plays. Furthermore, it contains several details which might be considered contradictory or confusing. For example, how long after the rape were Pamphilus and Philumena married? We know that the marriage was not consummated until two months after the wedding and that we are in the "seventh month" after Philumena "came to" Pamphilus (cf. 393-94). Does this mean that Philumena came to her wedding fully aware she was pregnant? Or, does "came to" mean her coming to Pamphilus's bed, two months after her wedding and only a little more since the rape? Thus, has Pamphilus been the victim of deception throughout, or did Philumena come to her wedding innocent of any knowledge of her pregnancy, only to be driven to desperate action when she was faced with her prospering womb? We may infer the latter, but the point remains vexed. Also, we might question the discrepancy between Parmeno's report that Pam-

philus visited Bacchis frequently after his marriage until her rapacity cooled his ardor (157 ff.) with her oath to Laches that she broke with him immediately after his marriage (750-52). Here the difficulty is imaginary, for it is part of Parmeno's characterization that he assumes more than he knows, but there remains the possibility of confusing the audience. On the whole, however, the plot moves smoothly and is cleverly constructed, despite the fact that to grasp its subtleties requires extraordinary attention from the audience.

Still, this is Terence's most unusual play, and we cannot fail to note its problems in production. Critics have often cited its unusual plot as the reason: Roman audiences were not ready for something both slow-moving and complicated. It does have its supporters, however, and we should recall that it is by no means certain to what extent problems with production were due to audience disfavor or to the sabotage of Terence's literary rivals.

Structure. As in other respects, so in construction, *The Mother-in-Law* differs from Terence's other plays. Most notably, it does not employ the "duality" method so favored in other pieces. Rather, our attention is focused on one problem alone and on one young man. Of greater significance, the play often teeters, until near its conclusion, on the edge of becoming romantic tragedy rather than New Comedy. Its seriousness of spirit is remarkable. And yet it is assuredly a comedy. Its serious mood is alleviated in part by the careful use of characters in traditionally comic situations interspersed through the play.

The "Prologue Problem.". . . Terence eschewed the use of an expository prologue in all his plays, using the portion of the play usually reserved for the prologue to make statements about his dramatic methods and the criticisms of his enemies. Thus his plays do not rely on audience omniscience but unfold before an audience "in suspense." The opening scenes, therefore, bear especial burden for exposition.

In his other plays the plots are based on such stock situations that the eventual resolutions are obvious enough to the informed play-goer, and the "suspense" lies more in the handling of specifics than in any surprise. *The Mother-in-Law,* however, has an unusual story, and although it employs a stock resolution, the information necessary to recognize it is withheld until late in the play. The effect is radical, especially in view of what we know about the practices of Greek authors. Therefore, critics have examined Terence's structure by speculating on the changes he has made in his model by Apollodorus of Carystus. Principally, they posit that the Greek play contained a prologue, perhaps following the conversation between Philotis and Parmeno. This prologue would have corrected and expanded upon the information just provided by the slave.

Were there a prologue, we would, in fact, be able to evaluate Parmeno's information early on, instead of being surprised later by contradictory revelations; we would be better informed about the relationship between the rape and the wedding; we would know in advance the reason for Philumena's leaving Sostrata; and we would know what sort of resolution to expect. In Terence's play, whether or not his original had a prologue, the exposition leads to a different state of audience awareness. The tension created by the characters' interactions is not lessened by an underlying surety of how the happy ending will be achieved. We must instead go with the play as it unfolds and change with it as it changes, evaluating events on the information at hand until rather late in the play.

The Protatic Character Philotis. The opening scenes, as we have noted, are quite important to Terence for providing expository information. The use of protatic characters is common as a means of stimulating a dialogue between a principal character and a figure who will command no more of our attention. In *The Mother-in-Law* Terence uses such a scene especially well.

The first characters on stage are Philotis, the young courtesan, and Syra, an old woman in the house of Bacchis. They are discussing the correct attitude of a courtesan toward her clients. Syra argues that every man must be fleeced, and rightly so, for they are all interested only in pleasure gained as cheaply as possible. Philotis thinks this a harsh position: "Should I think no man different?" (66); "But surely it's not right to be the same to everybody" (71).

Their conversation is an example of the technique Terence uses to establish his comic mood. This is a stock situation in which an old woman preaches her jaded philosophy to a more idealistic young woman (another example is found in Plautus's *The Haunted House* [157 ff.], where a courtesan, Philematium, is instructed in the ways of the world by her old maid, Scapha, as she is grooming). Thus Terence begins a rather unconventional play with a quite conventional scene. As we will see, he uses conventional comic motifs at intervals in order to keep the mood from becoming too somber. In addition, Philotis's responses allude, here at the beginning of the play, to its principal theme. Throughout, *The Mother-in-Law* presents the effects of typecasting, just the practice which Philotis is questioning.

The Use of Parmeno. In a play that features sharp conflicts between major figures to such an extent that human sadness seems a likely outcome, Parmeno is just the sort of figure whose presence provides contact with the ordinary comic world.

In the first part of the play we have every reason to expect that the slave will be Pamphilus's advisor and confidant. In his conversation with Philotis he gives the impression that Pamphilus turns to him in need regularly (cf. 130-34), and he talks like an advisor when they enter together from the port at our first view of Pamphilus (281 ff.). But, when Pamphilus learns of the true situation with Philumena, he is eager to get Parmeno out of

the way, a bit embarrassed that the slave knows too much about his early months of marriage (409-14). Thus, if we had thought that Parmeno would be the "clever slave" who would resolve his master's problems, we are surprised.

Parmeno enters (415) in conversation with a fellow slave who has been abroad with Pamphilus. Their conversation, like that between Philotis and Syra, is part of the conventional repertoire of slave scenes, as they complain about their tasks. He meets Pamphilus and is sent off immediately to await a fictitious friend of his master in another part of the city, a "wild goose" chase which was a popular motif of New Comedy.

Parmeno returns (799) just in time to meet Bacchis and deliver the message about the ring to Pamphilus, with whom he soon comes back. He is completely in the dark as to why they are so happy at the discovery of the ring, and so we know that despite Parmeno's self-importance his master has not regularly confided in him at all. In response to Pamphilus's profuse expressions of gratitude he can only say, "I've done more good today without knowing why than I've ever done before when I've tried!" (880). With this line the play ends.

Thus Terence has used Parmeno to provide a conventional comic focus at key points in his play in order to relieve the more serious moments with stock antics. He surprises us in so doing by showing us a slave different from the sort Parmeno had led us to believe he was, and he brings his play to a thoroughly joyous conclusion, which Parmeno's confusion underscores.

Characters. . . . Terence has been praised by critics of many eras for his skill in characterization. *The Mother-in-Law* is his most radical experiment in character. Depth of characterization in New Comedy does not arise from unique creations. In a theater where the stock types are well understood by the audience, however, effective portrayals can be derived from subtle deviations from the norm. In *The Mother-in-Law* we find stock figures common to New Comedy, but they are drawn in an unusual way and interact differently than in most plays of the genre.

[The fourth century A. D. commentator Aelius Donatus] recognized that the play had novel qualities in his commentary. And yet, the richness of the characters may be regarded as more of a liability than an asset, for many have felt that their unusualness, combined with the play's slow pace, yields a dramatic whole which is less satisfactory than Terence's other pieces. It is often suggested that this failing can be cited as the reason behind the problems in production. Much of this sort of criticism is based on taste, though it would be hard on any grounds to rate *The Mother-in-Law* as Terence's best play. Certainly it was not his most popular in antiquity. Yet, a modern audience looking back on New Comedy from a dramatic perspective schooled to accept comedies of quite varied sorts, may well find this play a refreshing variant of a somewhat repetitive tradition.

The Men: Laches, Phidippus, Pamphilus. It is unusual to have a play without an unmarried young man. That is, however, our situation in *The Mother-in-Law.* If one reads the play with a mind too saturated with the stock plots of New Comedy, it is easy to fall unawares into the error of reacting to Pamphilus as the comic young man in love, but, of course, he is a married man, and so has a quite different status in the Roman world. Nor do we find the expected "blocking figure," a father bent on keeping him from his beloved. Instead, Laches works very hard to bring his son and Philumena together. But, as we will see, the characters also exhibit stock traits.

It comes perhaps as a surprise to be reminded by Donatus that Laches is the play's principal character, based on the number of lines assigned to him, to be sure. Pamphilus is second in "volume," Phidippus third.

Laches enters (198) in a stock argument with his wife, Sostrata. He blames her for causing trouble with her daughter-in-law, assuming that she is acting like a typical mother-in-law, for whom no one is good enough for her son. Phidippus's first words (243-45) are to assure his daughter Philumena that he is concerned about her feelings. Such concern for the son's interests on the one hand, the daughter's on the other, is reminiscent of the situation in *The Girl from Andros.* And Phidippus is just as willing as Laches to indict his wife as the malefactor when he learns of the birth of the child (cf. 536 ff.). Laches plays the role of the irascible father well enough when he decides that Pamphilus is being perverse in order to break up his marriage and return to Bacchis (cf. 671 ff.), and he assumes the position of the father working against a profligate son.

But, despite these affinities with stock characters, the situation is such that the old men's actions are not quite those of strictly conventional figures. Laches is driven throughout by concern. His relationship with Sostrata is not terrible, as we see from his general willingness to take her with him to the country when she decides to leave the young people alone. And his efforts are in fact directed not toward depriving Pamphilus of pleasure but toward enhancing his chances for happiness. Phidippus, much like Chremes in *The Girl from Andros,* remains committed to his daughter's happiness, and so any disagreeableness in his character is ameliorated.

Pamphilus acts the part of the young lover with his indecision and confusion. But these traits in him are moving rather than humorous. Based on all that he knows of the situation, he has found himself in dire straits: his mother accused falsely; the young wife, whom he has grown to love, the mother, seemingly, of a child sired by another; and he himself thrust into a quandary between love and duty.

His is an ironic position. Whereas other plays tend to show fathers eager to take their sons away from unacceptable love affairs by binding them to an acceptable marriage, here Pamphilus is on the other side of the process. He has been led away from Bacchis to a successful marriage. But, instead of the happy result one

would expect, Pamphilus finds himself in an unhappy situation indeed. His "off-center" position makes his character quite effective. The adolescent confusion is comic in the young lover, but in the young husband it is touching. The young man is all the more contrasted with the old men who are considerably more jaded in their marital relationships.

The Women: Sostrata, Myrrina, Bacchis. [Gilbert Norwood, in *The Art of Terence,* 1923] has said of *The Mother-in-Law,* "It is a woman's play—not feminist, not expounding any special doctrine, but with women as the chief sufferers, the chief actors, the bearers here of the Terentian *humanitas.*" Thais, of *The Eunuch,* may be Terence's strongest female figure, but surely *The Mother-in-Law* does, in fact, bring women to the forefront of the play's theme in a way not approximated elsewhere.

Neither of the wives in other plays, Sostrata in *The Self-Tormentor* and Nausistrata in *Phormio,* is given the depth of character of the women here. Certainly the other Sostrata and Nausistrata are significant roles, each a notch above the colorless ciphers or the henpecks often found in Plautus, but in *The Mother-in-Law,* especially with the role of Sostrata, we find characters who demand real sympathy.

Terence is careful to give us a positive view of Sostrata from the start, when Parmeno tells Philotis of her efforts to accommodate her daughter-in-law and to bring her home. We are prepared then to be sympathetic to her attempts to acquit herself to Laches when we first see her. Her only negative trait, at least as concerns a conservative Roman audience, is her tendency to prefer the luxury of the city and the company of her friends to Laches' rustic life. But her relationship with Pamphilus is excellent, as attested by his devotion to her. She is, in fact, the victim of stereotyping on Laches' part, and her short monologue (274-80) both establishes this point clearly and expresses well the extent to which she has suffered over the situation.

Unlike the case of other wives, her characterization does not stop with her encounter with Laches. Sostrata's relationship with her son is seen firsthand (336 ff.). Furthermore, the depth of her commitment is shown us when she comes out personally to tell him of her decision to forego the city so that the way will be cleared for Philumena's return:

> This is now my major concern, that my long life not be a burden to anyone and that no one wait eagerly for my death.
>
> (595-96)

She asks of Pamphilus, "Allow me, please, to escape the bad repute people hear of women" (600).

Myrrina is drawn in less depth, but she too is hurt by the stereotyping of women. Our first view of her is from Pamphilus's description of her efforts to protect Philumena's reputation (378 ff.). Her desperation comes through clearly from his report. Thus, as when Laches accused Sostrata, so when Phidippus attacks her for keeping the birth of the child secret, we are prepared to take her side. Her comment aside when he accuses her of trying to undermine the marriage because she had disapproved of Pamphilus's relationship with Bacchis, "I'd rather he suspect any reason than the real one" (540), is indicative of her willingness to shield Philumena by bearing the brunt of accusations herself.

Bacchis stands in obvious contrast to the two matrons, but in an important sense she must be compared with them. Just as Sostrata wants to do the best for Pamphilus, so Bacchis is eager also to help him. And like the two older women she is the object of typecasting (cf. 774-76). But, when Laches suggests that she tell her story directly to the women, she is appropriately concerned that her presence before married women will be an embarrassment. She, like Sostrata, has a monologue (816-40) that does much to express her character. Her distinctiveness is underscored by these lines:

> I'm glad so much happiness has come his [Pamphilus's] way because of me, even if other courtesans don't feel like this. It's not in our professional interest for a lover to be happy in his marriage.

> (833-35)

Theme. We have seen a number of examples of the unusual qualities found in *The Mother-in-Law.* The play is also exceptional in the seriousness of its theme. Terence's plays generally have a coherent message, but never expressed in the severe tone which is assumed for most of this play. Seriousness of theme does not provide automatic access to dramatic success, as the number of critics of this piece will attest, and it may be that the play is more successfully studied than played. The two issues it raises, however, the effects of stereotyping and the position of women, deserve our examination.

Unfair Stereotyping. The plot of *The Mother-in-Law* is constructed throughout on wrong conclusions. Its action is put into motion by Philumena's deceptions which lead to unfair blame on Sostrata. Laches' actions stem first from an unfair assumption that mothers-in-law in general and Sostrata in particular relish the discomfort of their daughters-in-law; he then moves to a wrong conclusion about Pamphilus's motives, based on the notion that young men are overcommitted to their love affairs. Phidippus is no better in that he jumps to the wrong conclusion as to why the baby's existence has been kept secret, accusing Myrrina unjustly and further complicating things.

The effects of this tendency to stereotype go deeper than the level of mere plot. Speeches by various characters show that it is a key issue in the play. Philotis puts it forth at the play's beginning when she disagrees with old Syra that all lover's should be treated alike. Sostrata's concern for Philumena is carefully outlined in Parmeno's description of events before the opening of the play. Thus, we can see the unfairness of typecasting clearly when Laches says in his anger:

> So all mothers-in-law and daughters-in-law dislike each other. They're equally ready to fight their husbands; their stubbornness is just alike. I think they all go to the same school for meanness, and if there is a school, I know for sure she's its principal.

> (201-4)

In her monologue Sostrata cries, "Oh God, we're all hateful to our husbands in the same unjust way because of a few women who act so as to make us all seem to deserve disgrace" (274-75). Finally, Laches quickly typecasts Pamphilus as the unrepentant lover, and Phidippus warns against believing Bacchis, simply because she is a courtesan.

As much as the women suffer from this unfair treatment, it is Pamphilus who illustrates its greatest harm. He is caught squarely between his heart and his sense of duty (cf. 403-8), certainly because of the extraordinary ironies of the plot, but also because he cannot cope with two typical responses. He cannot accept the bastard readily as his son or find a way to forgive Philumena for the situation despite her innocence of intentional wrongdoing, and he feels drawn to his mother against his wife out of filial duty.

In this atmosphere an important irony emerges. Whereas in a less charged setting the fact that Pamphilus is after all the father of the child would be simply an element of the stock plot, here it emphasizes the harm in his making wrong assumptions in the same way as have the older men. He is very much in danger of treating his wife with the same unfairness with which they have treated theirs. Thus, one of the important triumphs of the play's comic spirit is that the young marriage retains more hope than the old ones. The young couple can rise above the behavior of their elders, though, in keeping with the play's mixed tone, it has been a near thing.

The Position of Women. We must avoid the urge to make modern social criticism of *The Mother-in-Law.* In any terms, however, the female characters bear the brunt of the males' ill-conceived accusations. We have seen how the women, Philotis, Sostrata, Bacchis, question the fairness of stereotypical reactions. But they are all, including Myrrina, the victims of this attitude. The slave Parmeno expresses the general attitude well when he is trying to assure Pamphilus that all will be well with his mother and Philumena:

> How is it that little boys get mad over little problems? Why, they have weak self-control. These women are about the same as little boys with their flighty minds.

> (310-12)

Coming from a character such as Parmeno, the gratuitous comparison is especially acrid.

One of the most satisfying outcomes of the play is, as we have just seen, that Pamphilus and Philumena overcome their difficulties. The young man has not resorted to the bickering common to the stock relationship of older couples, but it seems that he too is destined for an unhappy marriage. After his situation is unexpectedly resolved, Pamphilus gives us reason to think about this proposition when he says, alluding to his desire not to tell the old men the details of his reconciliation with Philumena, "I'd rather it not happen in the same way as in the comedies where everybody knows everything" (866-67). The resolution of *The Mother-in-Law,* like so much else in the play, is not in the usual New Comic manner.

THE SELF-TORMENTOR

A. J. Brothers   (essay date 1988)

SOURCE: An introduction to *Terence: The Self-Tormentor,* edited and translated by A. J. Brothers, Aris & Phillips Ltd, 1988, pp. 1-26.

[*In the excerpt below, Brothers provides an overview of* The Self-Tormentor, *discussing its relationship to its Greek source, its plot, and its characterization.*]

It has long been part of scholarly practice to attempt to understand the relationship of the Roman comedies to their lost Greek originals, and to try to pinpoint the additions, omissions and alternations of the Roman dramatists and recover the original Greek form—to play, in fact, 'hunt the New Comedy' with the text of a Terence (or Plautus) play. Though this type of activity has its limitations, particularly if carried out to the exclusion of other studies, it is nevertheless not merely legitimate but interesting and valuable.

Such investigations are always difficult, because we have so little to go on. With [Terence's *The Self-Tormentor*], the problem is perhaps worse than usual, since we do not have Donatus' commentary and so do not possess, as we do for the other five of Terence's plays, the rather sparse information, varying greatly in quality, which he can provide about Terentian workmanship; we do, however, have the less helpful commentary of Eugraphius. We have some fragments of Menander's play, preserved (not as are most of the fragments of the other originals) by Donatus, but by chance quotation elsewhere; however, not all of these obviously match up with the Latin text. We also have the prologue, where lines 4-6 are crucial, but we have seen that that evidence may not be straightforward. Lastly, we have the play itself, which we can examine for internal evidence of change—though . . . "we must at all times beware of assuming that Terence was so unskilled that his points of alteration will always be obvious to us if only we look for them hard enough".

In the prologue (6) Terence says of his version of the play *duplex quae ex argumento facta est simplici* "which from being a single plot has been turned into a double play". The seemingly inescapable interpretation of this

(especially since all of Terence's other plays except *Hecyra* involve the love affairs of two couples) is that the Roman poet has 'doubled' the play by increasing the pairs of lovers from one to two; attempts to interpret the line without assuming that it entails some such 'doubling' do not succeed. However, if one attempts to remove one of the pairs (presumably Clitipho and Bacchis, since Clinia, as son of the self-tormentor of the title, and Antiphila, for whose sake he incurred his father's displeasure, must have been in Menander), the entire fabric of the play falls apart. Two themes in particular, the pretence that Bacchis is Clinia's and not Clitipho's, and the cock-and-bull story that Antiphila is surety for a debt owed to Bacchis, ensure that the affairs of Clitipho and Bacchis are so closely interwoven with those of Clinia and Antiphila that they cannot be divorced from one another without the plot totally disintegrating. And if the plot does disintegrate in this way, it means that all elements involving Bacchis (and possibly Clitipho and Chremes too) would derive from Terence and not Menander's *Heautontimorumenos*; and this in turn means that Terence largely rewrote the play from line 223 onwards (if he introduced Bacchis) or totally (if he introduced the other two as well). Quite apart from the nature of the existing Menander fragments making this extremely unlikely, it would mean that Menander's *Heautontimorumenos,* containing only the Menedemus / Clinia / Antiphila element, would have been dramatically very thin. It is the virtual certainty that this hypothesis of almost total re-writing by Terence is therefore wrong which has led scholars to try to interpret line 6 in such a way that they need not say that Terence has 'doubled' the play. This, as I have said, seems quite impossible, and so the argument returns to its starting point.

However, there is another way of looking at the 'doubling' of a play. It concerns the introduction of extra characters, not into the plot, but into the action of the play as presented on stage. There seems to be good internal evidence for believing that in his adaptation Terence has made Antiphila and Bacchis speaking characters, when in Menander they either did not appear on stage at all or were non-speaking parts. If this is true, then in the Greek original there were two pairs of lovers in the plot, but only the young men were given full roles in the action; Terence, however, for reasons of his own, decided to give the women something to say as well. He therefore took from Menander a single plot in the sense that he only used one play and did not add characters from his own head or from another original; but he 'doubled' the play in the sense that he showed all four lovers with speaking parts, whereas Menander had shown only two. Clearly, this is not 'doubling' in the obvious sense; the additions are to the action only and not to the plot, the chief change is not a second pair of lovers but two women provided for the two men, and the extra writing consists of just two short scenes not half the play. But the statement in line 6 is not absolutely untrue, though it is exaggerated and misleading—perhaps deliberately so. R.C. Flickinger mentions "the deliberate policy of teasing and bewilderment which is pursued throughout the prologue" [*Philological Quarterly* 6, 1927]. Perhaps by saying that he had made a single plot double, Terence was hoping to trap Luscius; he had 'doubled', but not in the way he hoped his critic would think.

Briefly, arguments for suspecting the change are that Bacchis only appears in two short scenes (381ff., 723ff.), Antiphila only in the former, and that there are grounds for thinking that Terence, not Menander, was the author of these.

381ff. divides easily into two (381-97; 398-409). The first part consists largely of a monologue by Bacchis which shows her to be much more respectable and considerate than previous description (223ff.) has led us to expect and than the picture of her given later (455ff.) will show; the second part, where Bacchis makes little contribution, is the reunion of Clinia and Antiphila (awkwardly delayed by Bacchis' speech). It seems that Terence wanted to depict this reunion on stage, and felt that in doing so he could give Bacchis something to say which would reinforce the audience's high opinion of Antiphila—even though what she said was out of keeping with her character. This view of the scene entails that Terence must also have altered the end of the previous scene (376ff.).

In 723ff. nothing essential is done apart from what is said will happen at the end of the previous scene and what we are told has happened at the start of the next—the transfer of Bacchis and her *grex ancillarum* "retinue of maids" from Clitipho's house to Clinia's. The rest is merely a humorous threat by Bacchis to leave, which is immediately averted by Syrus' assurance that he will obtain the money Bacchis wants. The scene is also awkward dramatically, with doubts about Clinia's exit and an impossibly short time allowed for the transfer of the *grex*. If this scene is Terentian, then Terence created Phrygia, Bacchis' maid, who only appears here.

Both scenes involve movements by Bacchis and her *grex*. It is probable that in Menander these movements were 'masked' by choral interludes. When Terence dispensed with the chorus, for two of its four appearances he substituted these scenes.

Other changes have been suspected. If Menander's original had an explanatory prologue, the long exposition scene in Terence (53ff.) may have been expanded with some information originally there. Chremes' supposed exit at 170 to visit his neighbour Phania, where the Oxford Text marks a *saltatio convivarum* "dance of supper-guests", has been thought by some to mark the place of a Greek choral interlude or deferred prologue; his hurried exit to put off some business with neighbours (502) and his rapid return (508) have seemed so odd to others that they have been held to mark Terentian alteration. Another difficulty has been found in the spread of the action over two days with a night interval, which has been though un-Greek and therefore Terentian; and yet another has been the ending, which some have felt too untypical. Other theories about change, based on scenes where in Terence more than three characters speak, are

now seen to have less force than was thought. Finally, the fact that Menedemus, the self-tormentor of the title, is not for long the centre of attention and the focus for intrigue in the play has been taken by some as evidence of wholesale rewriting by Terence of the type already indicated. This has been seen to be unlikely; and the argument from the title of Menander's and Terence's plays is in fact spurious, since in this type of drama titles are not necessarily good guides to content.

. . . . .

In the early part of this century, the attention paid to the relationship of the plays of Terence (and Plautus) to their Greek originals took precedence over appreciation of the plays as they stand. The Roman dramas were regarded merely as pale reflections of their Greek predecessors, useful mainly as a means of learning about Greek New Comedy, and they were not given full consideration as independent art. More recently, however, the emphasis has shifted, and this imbalance is being corrected; no doubt this change has been assisted by the discovery of enough New Comedy to provide a basis for fruitful first-hand study. It has been rightly said that "research could be more profitably directed into what the comedies of Plautus and Terence have themselves to offer than into their uncertain relationships with lost sources." We must always remember that Terence wrote for the Roman stage and that his audience regarded *The Self-Tormentor* as a Roman play.

In the prologue (36) Terence calls his play *stataria,* "containing more talk than action". But, though it does not contain vigorous action like the siege in **Eunuchus** (771ff.) or exaggerated cameos like the pimp or the "running slave" in **Adelphi** (155ff., 299ff.), the "talk" nevertheless produces a fast-moving and complicated play. The twists and turns of the plot, as Syrus proves ever more inventive about getting money for Clitipho's mistress each time he is thwarted, leave the audience (or reader) breathless and perhaps confused. Such confusion is deliberate. The spectator is meant to be amazed by the frequent changes of direction brought about by Syrus' unending ingenuity; he is not necessarily meant to keep up with him every step of the way. One is reminded of Sandbach's comment that "close attention was necessary to follow Menander's dramas"; this is no less true of Terence's adaptation of this Menander play.

The "talk" also produces excellent character-drawing. The chief example is Chremes; but, apart from the interest centred on him, Menedemus, Syrus, Clitipho, Clinia and Sostrata are also characters fully, sensitively and sympathetically drawn.

It is Chremes, rather than the 'self-tormentor' Menedemus, who is the central character of the play and the victim of deception and trickery by Syrus, Clitipho and Clinia for much of its duration. Menedemus' problems begin to be resolved as early as 182, when the audience learns that his son Clinia has returned from abroad; and, but for Chremes' snap decision (199) not to reveal Menedemus' true feelings to his own son Clitipho, who is Clinia's close friend, they would have been swiftly settled. By contrast, Chremes' problems are only just beginning with the first mention of Clitipho's affair with the courtesan Bacchis (223) and Syrus' sudden revelation that Bacchis is on her way to Chremes' house (311). Thereafter the gradual but steady resolution of Menedemus' worries (assisted by the recognition of Clinia's love, Antiphila, as Chremes' daughter) becomes almost a subplot as interest centres on the increasing state of self-deception into which Chremes drifts until he is finally forced to confront the truth about his son's affair (908), and tries to salvage what he can of his self-sought reputation for sound judgement at the end of the play.

There are several ways of looking at Chremes' character. One, now largely discredited, regards him as someone whose genuine interest in and regard for others, typified by the sentiments of 77, is a model of human sympathy. Another sees him as a busybody, too anxious to take a hand in other people's affairs and to preach to them, when he cannot even keep his own house in order. A third sees him as something of both: "inquisitive, opinionated, self-satisfied, and insensitive, yet genuinely moved by the other man's situation and ready to extend his unwanted help".

The first view, at least, cannot be right. It is surely the essence of the comedy that a rather unpleasant man gets his 'comeuppance', not that a good one comes to grief through honest refusal to believe ill of his son. And the whole irony of the situation is that Chremes is too busy intervening in other people's affairs to notice what is going on under his nose, not that his genuine concern for others does not leave him time to see what is happening. The unattractive side to his character is underlined by his treatment of his wife Sostrata, whose words he mockingly imitates (622), and to whom he is rude and overbearing (624, 630, 632ff., 1006ff., 1018ff.). Moreover, his judgement, on which he prides himself, is unsure; his decision to keep Clitipho (199) and Clinia (436) in the dark about Menedemus' feelings is misconceived and prolongs his neighbour's unhappiness, while his encouragement of Syrus' mischief (533ff.) merely rebounds on himself. Only when he has been made to look a complete fool at the end of the play and his moral authority has been seriously impaired, does he allow himself (with rather bad grace, 1053) to be persuaded to forgive his son.

How far one accepts the view which combines both traits depends upon the interpretation put on several passages. For example, are Chremes' words at 159-60 genuine encouragement or empty platitude? Is his dinner invitation (161ff.) anything more than a desire to play Lord Bountiful? Is his expression of sorrow at 167-8 sincere or perhaps a little too perfunctory? Is his wish to be first to tell Menedemus (184ff., 410ff.) prompted by concern for his neighbour or eagerness for credit as a bringer of good news? I tend to take the less charitable, more jaundiced view; but the reader must decide, and even Chremes' sternest critic must accept that the complaints he makes about Clitipho at 1039ff. are fully justified.

Menedemus is altogether more attractive. His vivid accounts of how he drove Clinia away (96ff.) and afterwards in remorse chose a life of hard labour and rejected all pleasure and relaxation (121ff.) combine with the picture of his continued misery (420ff.) to excite our sympathy; his ready acknowledgement of how wrong he was (99ff., 134, 158) arouses respect for his candour and creates an impression of his essential good nature. And towards the end of the play this impression is reinforced by a contrast drawn with Chremes: whereas Menedemus behaved as he did towards Clinia with nobody to advise him otherwise, Chremes acts in precisely the same manner towards Clitipho even though he has the lesson of Menedemus before him and even though Menedemus (932) and Sostrata (1013) warn him of the trouble he will cause. It is only with difficulty that Chremes is persuaded to relent—and it is fair and honest Menedemus, wiser for his recent sufferings, who in his new-found happiness finds time to come outside and reconcile his neighbour with his son (1045ff.). It is small wonder that we earlier shared this appealing character's resentment at Chremes' curiosity (75-6), just as later (897, 914) we felt we could allow him to have a little fun at the expense of his discomfited *adiutor . . . monitor et praemonstrator* "helper, counsellor and guide".

Syrus, one of Chremes' slaves particularly attached to Clitipho, is the next most important figure in the action after Chremes; from him stems all the intrigue aimed at securing for his young master enough money for him to continue to enjoy Bacchis' favours. As in many plays of this type, the young men prove rather unimaginative and helpless when confronted with problems; it is the slaves who make all the running, and Syrus is the *servus callidus* "cunning slave" *par excellence,* quick-witted, bold, full of ideas and never downcast. In this he is contrasted to Clinia's slave Dromo, whom he calls *stolidus* "pretty stupid" (545) and whom earlier Clitipho had felt should be accompanied by Syrus when Clinia sent him to fetch Antiphila (191).

As a schemer, Syrus enjoys freedom of action, not waiting for instructions; it comes as a complete shock to Clitipho (311) that he has taken the amazingly bold step of bringing Bacchis along with Antiphila, intending to pretend to Chremes (332-3) that she is Clinia's. His task is now to find the wherewithal to keep Bacchis there, and this search, which occupies his mind until money is secured at 831, shows his ingenuity at its best. He starts (512-3), as is natural, by planning to get the money out of his own master Chremes, but is deflected from this by a golden opportunity presented by Chremes himself (546-7) into attempting to get it from Menedemus. He pretends (599ff.) that Antiphila is surety for a debt owed to Bacchis, and proposes (608ff.) to tell Menedemus that she is a captive from Caria and to persuade him to buy her from the courtesan. When Chremes tells him that Menedemus will not agree, Syrus replies that there is no need for him to; but, although pressed to explain, he does not (610ff.). This is one of a number of occasions where the exact nature of what Syrus has in mind is not explained. Such instances are devices intended to boost

The characters of The Self-Tormentor, *from a 1503 edition of Terence's works.*

our opinion of the slave's cleverness. There is no need to suppose that Terence (or Menander) worked out what these unexpressed plans were, and the audience had no need to know; it is sufficient to be told that Syrus' fertile brain has produced them.

The discovery that Antiphila is Chremes' daughter ruins Syrus' plan of getting Menedemus to purchase her. We are amused to see his despair as it collapses (659-60, 663) and vastly impressed by the speed with which he thinks up another (668-78). This one, he boasts (709ff.), is his masterpiece, because he will achieve his aim simply by telling the truth. He persuades Clinia to allow Bacchis, still supposedly Clinia's, to transfer to Menedemus' house, and gets him to tell his father the truth—that Bacchis is Clitipho's and that he himself wants to marry Antiphila. When Menedemus later duly tells this to his neighbour (847, 852-3), Chremes does not believe it; he has already been duped by Syrus (767ff.), and thinks it is a ruse for Clinia to get money for Bacchis out of Menedemus under the pretence that it is needed for his wedding. However, Syrus' plan again fails, because Chremes refuses to cooperate (779) in pretending to betroth Antiphila to Clinia. But in an instant the slave comes bouncing back; he returns (790ff.) to the story of the debt and says that Chremes must pay it since his newly-discovered daughter is surety. Without a murmur Chremes agrees; Syrus has at last got money for Clitipho to give to Bacchis, and he has got it from Chremes himself, the person he had originally intended to defraud. And his crowning glory is that he persuades Chremes to let Clitipho take it to Bacchis himself (799-800).

The complexities of all this are enormous, but the plot construction which brings them about is masterly. In the end we have a situation where Chremes is confronted with the truth and refuses to believe it; but when presented with the nonsense about Antiphila and the debt, he swallows it whole and pays up. Syrus' triumph is complete.

When the truth eventually comes out and Chremes' anger erupts, another side to this likeable rascal emerges; he is genuinely sorry for getting Clitipho into such trouble (970), and attempts to take his share of the blame (973-4). When this is brushed aside, there is one more service his cleverness can do for his young master, and his final trick plays a major part in bringing about a reconciliation between father and son. By suggesting to Clitipho that the extent of Chremes' anger is due to the fact that he is not his parents' real son (985ff.), and by prompting him to ask Chremes and Sostrata what his true parentage is (994-6), Syrus ensures that Sostrata will be shocked into helping her son obtain his father's pardon. We have seen that Menedemus is influential in achieving this; but so is Sostrata, and it is Syrus' ingenious move (cf. 996-7) which, though it causes Clitipho some short-term pain, nevertheless helps to ensure that his father does forgive.

Clinia and Clitipho are not so instrumental in the advancement of the plot; young men in this type of comedy tend to protest at the actions or plans of their slaves (Clitipho 311ff., 589, 810ff.; Clinia 699, 713), or be exaggeratedly grateful for them (Clitipho 825), rather than be initiators themselves. Standing in awe of their fathers (Clinia 189, 433-5) and complaining—but not doing much—about them (Clitipho 213ff.), they entrust the resolution of their troubles entirely to their slaves (Clitipho 350-1). Our two young men provide good examples of the extremes of despair and elation between which they can swiftly alternate (Clinia 230ff., 244, 246ff., 308; Clitipho 805ff., 825). They are also appealing characters, particularly in their mutual friendship (182ff.) and support (358-60)—facets upon which Syrus plays (688ff.).

Perhaps the most attractive figure of all, despite her comparatively small role, is Sostrata, who is excellently drawn. Devout (1038), endearingly superstitious (650-2, 1015), self-deprecatory (649-50) and devoted to her family (1029ff., 1060-1), she has to put up with a lot from her husband, but not without protest (1003ff., 1010-1), and she knows how to handle him (623-4, 631-2, 644ff.). And she takes equal credit with Menedemus for reconciling Chremes and Clitipho at the end of the play.

The complexities of the plot, with its frequent changes of direction, make for a fast-moving play, which in turn combines with the skillfully-executed character drawing to produce good theatre. But there are some weaknesses in the construction, many of which have been held, rightly or wrongly, to be evidence of Terential workmanship. . . . Among others which have been identified are the contrast between the two older men's only recent acquaintance (53ff.) and their sons' long friendship (183-4), the awkwardness of the empty stage at 873-4, and the contrast between Chremes' threats against Syrus (950ff.) and his actual words to his face (974ff.). It need hardly be said that such comparatively minor inconsistencies and awkwardnesses, though evident to a careful reader, would have been scarcely noticeable to the audience as it was swept along by the quickly changing pattern of events being enacted on the stage. . . .

Ortwin Knorr (essay date 1995)

SOURCE: "The Character of Bacchis in Terence's *Heautontimorumenos*," in *American Journal of Philology*, Vol. 116, No. 2, Summer, 1995, pp. 221-34.

[*In the excerpt below, Knorr contends that the courtesan Bacchis in* The Self-Tormentor *"actually has a good core below the surface of a grabbing prostitute."*]

Most readers of Terence have viewed the hetaera Bacchis in ***Heautontimorumenos*** as a stereotypical wicked prostitute, a greedy, hardnosed businesswoman, in short, "Terence's only mercenary courtesan" [G. E. Duckworth, *The Nature of Roman Comedy*, 1952]. Yet at least one passage in the play, namely Bacchis' speech in lines 381-95, does not quite fit into this negative picture of her character. Scholars who have noticed this, most recently Lefèvre and Brothers, usually evaluate this alleged inconsistency in her portrayal as a dramaturgical flaw on the part of Terence. Moreover, they assume that the Roman playwright inserted this scene into the original Greek plot.

In this essay I suggest that Bacchis is not the money-grabbing, hardnosed hooker she is usually seen as, although she is clearly a prostitute struggling to make a living. She might even be subsumed under the term "good hetaerae," as defined in a much-discussed passage in Plutarch's *Table Talks* which deals with the suitability of Menander's comedies for recital at symposia:

> There is no pederasty in all these plays, and the rapes of virgins end decently in marriage. Relation-ships with prostitutes . . . , if they are insolent and bold, are broken off by the young men's coming to their senses or changes of heart, whereas for [prostitutes] who are good and love in return, either a legitimate father [who is a citizen] is discovered [which allows them to marry their lover] or out of a humane sense of consideration [for the girls] some extra time is added to their love-affair.

In applying Plutarch's notion of "good" and "bad" courtesans to Bacchis and her colleagues in New Comedy, caution seems appropriate for several reasons. One has to be aware that "good" and "bad" in the context of hetaerae do not so much indicate moral qualities as categories defined by the economic needs of their male paying customers. Accordingly, a hetaera is "good" when she loves her customer in return and "bad" when she drives a hard bargain. In addition, both Menander and Terence often undermine traditional stereotypes, so that we are unlikely to find in their plays pure examples of "good" and "bad" prostitutes. I therefore do not try to prove that Terence's Bacchis in **Heautontimorumenos** is a *bona meretrix*. Instead, I hope to demonstrate that he portrays her consistently throughout the whole play as a good-hearted hetaera, not as a ruthless gold-digger. To do so, I reexamine all of the passages in **Heautontimorumenos** that allow us to infer from them the nature of Bacchis' character.

During the first two acts, until she enters the stage in person, Bacchis indeed seems to be the flagrantly mercenary courtesan most scholars perceive her to be. When Clitipho reveals in his soliloquy (223-29) that he, like his friend Clinia, has been involved with a hetaera for some time without his father's knowledge, he himself calls this liaison a *malum*. He is less concerned, however, about the ethical implications of his conduct than about the inadequacy of his financial means. Full of self-pity, he declares his situation to be far worse than that of his friend Clinia. For Clinia's girl, Antiphila, has been chastely brought up and is still unfamiliar with the tricks of the trade, whereas his own mistress constantly demands gifts and money. Clitipho resorts to empty promises, because he does not dare to confess to her his meager resources lest he lose her. On the other hand, neither

does he want to ask his father, Chremes, for financial support for his erotic adventures. It is thus not surprising that the young man in his despair for money describes his girlfriend rather unfavorably as *potens, procax, magnifica, sumptuosa, nobilis* (227), that is, "imperious, exacting, showy, expensive, and notorious."

This description of a greedy professional who has trapped poor Clitipho with her charms soon gains credibility when Bacchis' entourage is described by Syrus and Dromo, the slaves who lead her to the dinner party at Chremes' home (245-55). The courtesan approaches his house accompanied by a large number of maidservants burdened with her jewelry and dresses, and Syrus gloats about how much it will cost his stingy master to entertain this crowd (254-55).

Bacchis' "bad" character is further emphasized in Syrus' report to his young master Clitipho (364-68). The young man is surprised that the fastidious hetaera so readily agreed to follow his servant. The slave explains that Clitipho's invitation came just in the nick of time for her, allowing her to reject the offer of a soldier, apparently a new customer, to celebrate the Dionysia with him. Thus she would at the same time enhance the soldier's desire for her and make Clitipho feel especially obliged to her. Syrus consciously neglects to tell his master that he has also offered Bacchis ten minae if she would follow him (723-24). This information would have upset Clitipho, who has not been able to contrive a way to pay for Bacchis' favors at all, not to mention a considerable sum like ten minae (223-29). Thus Syrus' biased representation of the facts confirms the impression of Bacchis the audience has won from Clitipho's speech. The clever scheming the slave attributes to the courtesan lets her appear as an experienced professional who plans far in advance and is able to play two customers off against each other in order to keep both of them.

Up to this point in the play, Bacchis looks just like another of the stereotypical avaricious and cold-hearted hetaerae of Greek and Roman New Comedy, whose promiscuity and success is reflected by their wealth and splendid appearance. We have not heard a single nice word about her, and we might even speculate that it is her very viciousness that attracts Clitipho to her, were is not usual in New Comedy that hetaerae are endowed with beauty and sometimes esprit. Hence the next scene (381-409) comes as a surprise, for it displays a Bacchis quite different from the one we have learned about thus far.

In this scene Bacchis and Antiphila are approaching old Chremes' house, followed by the courtesan's *grex ancillarum*. We, like Clinia and Clitipho, overhear the end of their conversation, just as Bacchis is praising Antiphila for striving to have her character match her beauty (381-82). At the same time she tries to justify her own life-style, which is much more open to criticism (387-91). She blames her lovers who force her to drive a hard bargain, since they are only interested in her beauty and will abandon her once it withers. If she does not provide for the future in time, she will suffer a lonely old age in poverty. In contrast, she claims, it pays off for girls like Antiphila to be "good" and to devote themselves to a single customer. For once a man with a similar character chooses them, they will grow old together in lasting mutual love (392-95).

Bacchis' view of life, as expressed in her conversation with Antiphila, seems on the surface less concerned with her reputation in society than determined by practical considerations. However, she clearly acknowledges the moral superiority of the other girl's conduct and, thus, feels the need to defend her own behavior. That her words are to be taken seriously and are a sincere expression of her feelings is clear from the context of the conversation. First of all, the women do not realize that they are overheard by the waiting young men. Secondly, they are professional colleagues, so that there is no need for Bacchis to conceal her true thoughts from Antiphila and to pretend to have a sense of morality which no one expects her to possess. Consequently, Bacchis emerges as a prostitute who has not lost her sense of good and evil. There might even be an undertone of regret in the way she describes the final reward for being a "good," namely, monogamous girl, for she has lost this chance of a long-term relationship long ago.

If we interpret Bacchis' speech in this fashion, it has several important effects on the further development of the plot and our understanding of it. First, the apparently unobserved conversation between the girls removes Clinia's last doubts about the flawlessness of Antiphila's character, as his reaction shows (397-400). Secondly, Bacchis' words also serve to correct the unfavorable picture that Clitipho and Syrus have drawn of her earlier. The audience now might view her more sympathetically, realizing that fastidiousness and driving a hard bargain are the only ways for Bacchis to provide for financial security in her old age.

My thesis here, that Terence deliberately uses Bacchis' speech not only to exonerate Antiphila but also to correct the negative portrait of Bacchis herself that other characters of the play have created before, is supported by the fact that the dramaturgical technique applied in this instance is not unique to *Heautontimorumenos*. In several plays by Terence, most often in their expositions, one or two characters pass on their limited personal knowledge of past events to the audience. Necessarily, their characterization of the persons involved in those reported events is often twisted by personal bias and misinterpretation. The audience, however, usually "buys into" these half-reliable representations of the actual background of the comedy's plot, because they very often confirm prejudices the audience shares (for example, about prostitutes and mothers-in-law). Later in the play, the author supplies additional information which contradicts those initial accounts of the facts, thus introducing dramatic irony. Most frequently, this new information is given in a monologue which marks it as trustworthy according to the conventions of New Comedy. These soliloquies are often delivered by a character who has been previously misrepresented.

One example of this technique of character presentation is Thais, another hetaera, in *Eunuchus,* who assures the spectators of her genuine love for Phaedria (197-206) after her lover himself had expressed doubts. Similarly, Sostrata in *Hecyra* asserts her innocence in a monologue (274-80) after her husband has informed her about his suspicion that she has harassed her daughter-in-law until the girl left her in-laws' house. Not much later in the same play, Myrrina is attacked by her husband, Phidippus, because she concealed from him that her daughter was pregnant by Pamphilus (529-31). Phidippus suspects that she wanted to expose the baby secretly right after its birth, as otherwise it would consolidate the marriage of Philumena and Pamphilus (532-34), which his wife has always opposed because of Pamphilus' liaison with the hetaera Bacchis (536-39). But Myrrina's monologue (566-76) soon makes it clear that Phidippus' allegations are completely false; she had preferred to leave him ignorant because the truth (that Philumena was raped by an unknown offender) is even worse. Micio's soliloquy in *Adelphoe* (141-54) is also comparable, for it shows that he is not as self-confident concerning his pedagogic principles as he pretended to be in the previous scenes. And in *Heautontimorumenos* Clitipho's monologue (213-29) contradicts the positive self-representation of his father, Chremes, in the presence of Menedemus. Clitipho reveals his father as a hypocrite (220-21) who himself should be the first to listen to the advice he gives his neighbor (151-56).

Bacchis' speech in *Heautontimorumenos* (381-95) is exceptional only in that it is directed toward another character, and hence is not a pure soliloquy. It comes very close to monologue, however: the courtesan speaks for fifteen lines before her companion, a mere interlocutor, utters a brief reply of two lines to close the scene.

Terence did not invent the dramatic technique of building up the audience's expectations and then thwarting them by revising earlier representations with a monologue. From the fragments of the first act of Menander's *Epitrepontes* we can still infer that both the conversation between the cook, Karion, and the slave, Onesimos, and Smikrines' speech (134-37) suggest that Charisius, though recently married, is cheating on his wife with the hetaera Habrotonon. In line 430, however, this hetaera angrily rushes out of the house where Charisius is momentarily staying, and reveals in a soliloquy that her customer has not even allowed her to lie on the same couch with him. Another passage which functions somewhat similarly is a short aside by Sostratos in *Dyscolus* (135-39). In this scene the young man suddenly discloses that right from the beginning he has distrusted Chaireas, who up until then appeared to be his confidant. There are many other instances in Menander's plays where later developments shed new light on earlier scenes and the actors' real characters. . . .

The question that arises next is what effect Bacchis' speech (381-95) has on the rest of the play, if it is to be understood as Bacchis' sincere disclosure of her thoughts to Antiphila. It seems to me that the playwright thus grants the audience a knowledge of the facts which is superior to that among the characters onstage, enabling the audience not only to see the previous scenes differently but also to appreciate the dramatic irony of the succeeding scenes.

In lines 439-64 Chremes warns Menedemus about the dangers of overindulging his son Clinia. He maintains that the character of the boy's mistress has substantially deteriorated. Chremes reminds his neighbor that he earlier had forced his son into abandoning his *amica* (104) even though she, then, was modest and grateful for the small contributions Clinia could afford. So, the old man argues (443-49), how can Menedemus tolerate this relationship now that the girl has begun to earn her living as a common prostitute and has developed far more expensive demands? To prove his contention, Chremes then complains that hosting the hetaera and her large entourage the night before almost ruined him financially (450-56). He describes in detail how she acted as if nothing were good enough for her spoiled palate, and it especially upset him that she despised his wine, not to mention that she persisted in calling him *pater* (457-61).

Much of the humor of this scene derives from our knowledge that Chremes is describing not Antiphila, but Bacchis, the mistress of his own son Clitipho. But the new perspective on Bacchis that the spectators have gained from her conversation with Antiphila in 381-97 adds even more comic vigor to it. Now the audience may realize that her fastidiousness and extravagant behavior at Chremes' dinner party were nothing but an act, deliberately performed in order to distress him. Later, her conduct on that evening lends credibility to Syrus' allegation that Bacchis, *pessima meretrix* that she is (599), demands ten minae in exchange for Antiphila. The girl, the slave explains to his master, Chremes, serves the hetaera as security for a debt the girl's mother owed her (600-606).

In lines 723-48 Bacchis makes her final appearance onstage. She is upset and angry because Syrus fooled her by promising her ten minae he did not have. Accordingly she ponders how best to take vengeance on him (724-28). The slave himself, who eavesdrops and overhears her words, takes them quite seriously (729-30). When Bacchis notices Syrus and Clinia standing nearby and watching her, she demonstrates how well versed she is in *ars meretricia* (730-35). She pretends not to see them and recapitulates, together with her servant, Phrygia, the directions to the country house where the rival customer, the soldier (365), is staying at the moment. She pretends that a messenger sent by the soldier has just come by to invite her again. Finally, when she orders Phrygia to run ahead and announce her near arrival, Syrus panics and steps forward begging her to stay (736). Yet Bacchis persists in sending Phrygia on her errand, until Syrus in total despair exclaims that the money is already at hand. Although this offer is as much in vain as the earlier one—

as everybody in the audience knows—Bacchis then gives in with surprising willingness. Almost too quickly, the *meretrix*, who in lines 737-38 is still teasing the slave, seems to lose control of the situation. For even though Syrus persistently dodges her suspicious questions about what exactly he intends with this move (740-41), she nevertheless follows him into Menedemus' house at the end of the scene. She does not push him to explain his scheme, as if she had already decided to go with him anyway.

How is it possible that Bacchis, who earlier convincingly demonstrated her skills as a hard-bargaining prostitute, is so easily and even repeatedly duped by Syrus? The most plausible explanation seems to be that she actually does not want to leave Clitipho, Syrus' master. Even in her plans for revenge (724-28) she does not seriously consider abandoning Clitipho, but simply wants to put him off for a while until Syrus gets whipped. This is even more amazing if we keep in mind that she has not yet seen any money from Clitipho, as he himself reveals (224, 228). This does not quite fit the image of a hetaera who "minds her shop professionally, negotiates her fees aggressively" [Dwora Gilula, "The Concept of the *Bona Meretrix*: A Study of Terence's Courtesans," *RFIC* 108, 1980]. So it might well be that Bacchis feels mutual love for her customer Clitipho and is, therefore, not the stereotypical *pessima meretrix* (599) who consumes young men by the dozen and is only interested in fleecing them.

To sum up: Bacchis is obviously not an innocent lamb, but this is of course to be expected of a prostitute. In both of her appearances onstage, however, she makes a much better impression than the descriptions of her by Syrus, Chremes, and even her lover Clitipho might have indicated. This does not at all mean that Terence sketched her character sloppily or inconsistently. Rather, her personal appearances reveal that she actually has a good core below the surface of a grabbing prostitute. This insight supplies the spectators with a new perspective on the play in general. It intensifies their appreciation of the dramatic irony behind Chremes' warnings to Menedemus (439-64).

If one accepts this interpretation, there is no need to explain alleged inconsistencies in the portrayal of Bacchis' character by assuming that Terence added both scenes in which she speaks to the original plot of Menander's *Heautontimorumenos*. From this perspective it is thus important to counter some points made by Brothers in favor of the hypothesis that Terence inserted lines 381-97 from another play of Menander, *Arrephoros* [A. J. Brothers, "The Construction of Terence's *Heautontimorumenos*," *Classical Quarterly* 74, 1980].

Brothers takes the change of meter after line 397, from trochaic septenarii to iambic octonarii, to indicate an insertion because this change, as he sees it, serves no dramatic function. This argument seems to imply that Terence was such a poor poet that he was not even able to adjust the metrics when he adapted the original Greek verses to Latin for his own play.

I prefer to suggest that Terence had good reason to choose a trochaic meter for lines 381-97. After 41 lines of discussion between Syrus and Clitipho (occasionally joined by Clinia) in iambic senarii, Clitipho leaves the stage at line 380. The entrance of Bacchis and Antiphila from the other side of the stage is marked by a change of the meter to trochaic septenarii (381). They are followed by a *grex ancillarum* consisting of more than ten maids who carry *aurum, vestem* (248) with them. The group resembles a religious procession . . . when it approaches Chremes' house. It thus strikes me as very appropriate that they move onto the stage accompanied by flute music and perhaps dancing among the maidens, as indicated by the underlying trochaic septenarii (381-97).

The ensuing iambic octonarii (398-404) express a considerably higher degree of excitement. They reflect the excitement of Clinia's rejoicing and relief after overhearing the conversation of the girls and thus being reassured of Antiphila's faithfulness. They also fit the storm of emotions that overcomes Antiphila when she suddenly recognizes the waiting Clinia (403-4). When the meter changes again at 405, to iambic senarii, the meter appropriate for conversation, it indicates that both Antiphila and Clinia have calmed down a bit.

Brothers also claims that 381-97 are taken from Menander's *Arrephoros*. He bases this assertion on the Greek verse which the scholiast of the Codex Bembinus quotes on line 384. The attribution of this line to *Arrephoros*, however, is a mere guess, as Brothers himself admits. Most importantly, the verse shows so few similarities to Terence's alleged translation of it that it seems to be quoted rather as a parallel thought than as a model for this line.

In conclusion, I submit that Terence has portrayed Bacchis carefully and consistently throughout the whole play, though neither as *bona* nor as *mala meretrix*. Like his admired predecessor Menander, he has avoided using the stock types of *meretrices* that were traditional in comedy. Instead his Bacchis in *Heautontimorumenos* shows affection towards her customer . . . but also reveals some nasty potential in her conduct at Chremes' house and when she takes her little revenge on Syrus in scene 4.4. Thus it is in accordance with Plutarch's description of poetic justice in Menander that, on the one hand, Bacchis' relationship with Clitipho is abruptly cut short at the end of the play but that, on the other hand, this loss is also sweetened. For Clitipho is, finally, able to bring her the long-promised ten minae (831), and both are allowed to enjoy a last reunion in Menedemus' house (902-6) before the young man is forced by his father, Chremes, to abandon the hetaera and marry a respectable girl.

THE EUNUCH

Douglass Parker (essay date 1974)

SOURCE: An introduction to *The Eunuch* by Terence, translated by Douglass Parker, in *The Complete Comedies of Terence: Modern Verse Translations,* edited by Palmer Bovie, Rutgers University Press, 1974, pp. 147-52.

[*In the essay below, Parker provides a survey of issues relating to* The Eunuch, *focusing especially on the influence of Plautus and Menander on Terence's work.*]

Success dies hard. **The Eunuch** was Terence's most successful play during his lifetime, earning an immediate second production and a considerably increased royalty. It has yet to be forgiven this by critics who, equating excellence with unpopularity, prefer the **Hecyra**'s double failure as an index of attainment. Since this is not a universal standard, they find themselves faced with a thorny problem: **The Eunuch** is fast and funny, and, in fact, an excellent case can be made for its being Terence's best play. How to dispose of it? The answer is simple and somewhat sinister: Call it "Plautine."

The precise meaning of this epithet is not so obvious as might at first appear, but its connotations are clear enough: When used by a pro-Terentian (or pro-Menandrean) critic, it implies that the play is a sort of regrettable mistake, an attempt at pit-pandering by a playwright who should have known better, and usually did. And, when picked up and employed by an anti-Terentian, it passes implicit judgment against his other five plays. Either way the poet loses.

And loses yet another way: In making **The Eunuch,** Terence modified Menander's *Eunouchus* considerably to admit two characters, the soldier Thraso and the parasite Gnatho, from another play by the same Greek author— the *Kolax* ("Today" or "Yes-Man"). Unfortunately, literary politics compelled him to admit this in his prologue. I say "unfortunately," not because this defense of dramatic *contaminatio* failed (it did not), but because, by his rather detailed admission, he supplied critics of two millennia later with their most substantial handle for the reconstruction of lost Greek plays. Thus armed, they have prodded joyously for a century or so, descrying the necessarily seamless excellence of the originals through the gaps they make in the Roman poet's necessarily shoddy composition.

The play, of course, however categorized or tortured, has not changed, and annoyance at its criticism may seem ill-taken. After all, "Plautine" can be a perfectly accurate and unexceptionable, if somewhat otiose, synonym for Donatus' *motoria*: it must be granted that fast and furious fun is not exactly a characteristic Terentian virtue (though the **Phormio** abounds in it). And there is certainly nothing wrong per se with the attempted recovery of Menandrean comedies. But, as it happens, the two practices described above have interacted to form a barrier to the proper understanding of just what Terence has done in this play, "Plautine" becoming a rug under which to sweep, unexamined, any difficulties in taste, *Quellenforschung* a sieve with which **The Eunuch** is axiomatically strained of any real dramatic unity.

To take the first point: Many critics who are not bothered by the hot-blooded rape of Pamphila become quite upset at the play's ending—the projected *ménage à trois* that involves the cold-blooded diddling of Thraso. If this does not signal a blast against the morality of the playwright, it is generally resolved by recourse to the adjective "Plautine." Such a situation obtains at the end of Plautus' *Asinaria* and *Bacchides* and unsettles no one; why should it here? But this begs the question; the unease remains undissolved. And that such a reaction from his audience might have been a reasoned dramatic aim of Terence is an observation that rarely occurs; the poet is evidently the prisoner of the style he has chosen.

Or the second point: Gnatho's bravura disquisition on his new method of coney-catching (Act II, Scene 2) is the longest and most memorable speech in the play; it should logically have something to do with the over-all action. But the seeker after Menander, anxious to pin something down for good, is all too ready to overstate his case for its derivation from the *Kolax* by declaring that the speech's only function is to delineate the character of the parasite.

These are not random points, but both are intimately bound up with the meaning of **The Eunuch,** and the critic neglects them at his peril. The play, whatever its genealogy, is more than farce, more than loose-knit romp; it is a serious dramatic exploration, all of a piece.

Returning to the ending, to call it "Plautine" merely intensifies the problem: Why should critics who are proof against anything written suddenly be found muttering about "the dubious morality of **The Eunuch**'s conclusion"? Why should otherwise hardheaded translators feel impelled to give their readers the perfectly gratuitous (and unfounded) intelligence that, when Gnatho proposes milking Thraso, Phaedria accepts the suggestion "reluctantly"? In sum, why should a phenomenon that passes without objection in a play by Plautus cause unease when it occurs in a play by Terence? Provisionally, the only possible answer would appear to be that Terence has somehow employed it in a different fashion. And he has; he has indulged in one of his most effective practices: Taking a comedic *datum* and, by a change in its context, pushing it beyond the bounds of comfortable acceptability, he has achieved that bite which is distinctly his own.

The change involved is one in "characterization"—a bad word for critics, but no matter. Terence has humanized and deepened the stock *personae* of New Comedy, not greatly, but enough to involve the audience with them at a different level, a level where hackneyed situations acquire a new and distressing reality through their partic-

ipants. Upset at **The Eunuch**'s conclusion arises, not from abstract disapproval of confidence-games or *ménages à trois,* but from a directed feeling that *these* lovers ought not to be doing such a thing to *this* soldier. Therefore Phaedria must be "reluctant." Therefore at least one critic has suggested (I am not making this up) that Terence's ending must derive, not from Menander's *Eunouchos,* but from his *Kolax,* since Thais, taken from the former play, is really too noble to be party to such an arrangement, even in prospect. Ridiculous remedies, arising from misreadings, but they locate the ailments: Phaedria, the lovestruck and ineffectual *adulescens* who possesses enough self-knowledge to see his weakness but not to avoid it; Thais, the whore with, not a heart of gold, but an overlay of altruism—they really should behave better.

For the object of the diddling is to be Thraso, and to dupe him is not to take a deserved revenge on a monster, but to shoot a very sorry fish in a very small barrel. In the abortive siege of Thais's house he has demonstrated his purely military futility, but other deficiencies have emerged as well. It is really ironic that this character should have supplied English with an adjective—*thrasonical*—to describe vaingloriousness; Thraso is the first *miles gloriosus* whose *words* completely fail him. He fumbles for quotations, relies on ludicrously inept repartee, goes gauche at the sight of Thais. He needs only poverty to match the most inept specimen of the breed, Armado in *Love's Labour's Lost*—like him, a would-be Hercules who cannot fight; like him, a hopeless lover who solicits instruction from an unqualified source; like him, total prisoner of a rhetoric that his opponents can use more effectively in fun than he can in earnest. Stupid and defenseless, a man rattling around in a monster's role, he resembles Armado in one more, one most important particular: Sincerely in love, he is the only person in the play actually willing to make a sacrifice for his love. And his sacrifice, to everyone else's profit, constitutes the ending of **The Eunuch.**

To return to the second point raised earlier—Gnatho's speech in Act II, Scene 2—it is certainly obvious that the ending proceeds, logically and inevitably, from the enlightened self-interest set forth in the parasite's *nouom aucupium.* It marks, in fact, the conversion of the principal members of the play's cast to Gnatho's way of life: Thraso, giving in to a hopeless love, will be gulled by almost everyone in sight.

This way of life is itself an answer to Parmeno's sarcastic comment on love's (and life's) vicissitudes in Act I, Scene 1:

> Incerta haec si tu postules
> ratione certa facere, nihilo plus agas
> quam si des operam ut cum ratione insanias.

> No mind can reduce this mess
> To any controllable order; you're better off
> To spend your effort devising a plan to go mad
>   on.

And a method for madness is what Gnatho supplies; more specifically, a blueprint for subservience. All of the principal characters in the play, one way or another, are in search of dependence and its fruits: Chaerea, who puts on the weeds of slavery and unmanliness to gain his beloved; Thais, whose regard for her "sister," however touching, is a means to patronage; Phaedria, whose ideal love can always be altered by practical consideration. Even Parmeno, whose moral disapproval is strongest, is not immune; he may think that the information he gives to Chaerea's father is done in the boy's best interest, but his own admission and Pythias' accusation show the truth. When the crunch comes, try as he will, his guiding impulse is to save himself:

> Huius quidquid factumst, culpa non factumst mea.

> Whatever happened, it wasn't my fault that it happened.

In this play as elsewhere, comic characters are rarely to be taken at their own evaluation.

The Eunuch, then, from Phaedria's initial whines to Thraso's invitation to the slaughter, is a study of the workings of dependency in which all noble motives, except for that of the play's standard butt, shrink alarmingly to one ignoble motive—the one unblushingly practiced and preached by that two-dimensional caricature from the older style of comedy, Gnatho:

> Me huius quidquid facio id facere maxumo causa mea.

> Whatever I do, I do from pure self-interest.

A most unpleasant motif for a cynical sermon—but it is not offered as such. Its effect is to counterpoint and bind together the play's farcical fun, to weave its strands to a not-quite-happy end, to produce in the audience that reasoned confusion of viewpoints, that contradiction in attitudes, that mark the best comedy. And it is in this achievement, proceeding from the play's *Gestalt* rather than from any part of it, that we can see the playwright's excellence: The fun may be Plautine, the characters and plot may be Menandrean, but the totality is Terence's own.

David Konstan (essay date 1986)

SOURCE: "Love in Terence's *Eunuch*: The Origins of Erotic Subjectivity," in *American Journal of Philology,* Vol. 107, No. 1, Spring, 1986, pp. 369-93.

[*In the essay below, Konstan analyzes the complex and contradictory views of love presented in* The Eunuch, *focusing particularly on the unresolved tension between love and commerce inherent in the situation of the courtesan Thais.*]

> Date operam, cum silentio animum attendite,
> ut pernoscati' quid sibi Eunuchus velit.
> —*Eunuch,* Prologue 44-45

Like all but one of Terence's comedies, the *Eunuch* has a double plot. One strand, which serves as the frame story, is based on a rivalry between two lovers: a more or less sympathetic young man, though not, in this case, destitute or subject to the control of a parsimonious father, versus the vainglorious mercenary soldier familiar in the genre (whose role here may derive from Terence himself rather than from Terence's Greek model, a play by Menander also called *Eunuch*). Terence mentions in his preface that he imported the character of the soldier, and also that of a calculating flatterer in the soldier's entourage, from another play by Menander, and it is possible that the rival in the original *Eunuch* was other than a soldier. However this may be, in Terence's version youth and soldier contend for the attentions of a courtesan, who, by the conventions of the genre, which in turn are grounded in Athenian social institutions, is a free woman of non-citizen status, and ineligible for marriage with a citizen. In our play, the courtesan, whose name is Thais, is self-employed, that is, she does not depend upon a procurer.

The competition between the two lovers takes the form of gifts. The soldier, called Thraso, has purchased an attractive and cultivated young maid, whom he sends to Thais in the escort of his hanger-on, Gnatho. Phaedria, as the young inamorato is called, commissions his slave Parmeno to deliver to Thais an Aethiopian slave-woman, who is decrepit and has no importance, and also a eunuch, from whom the play derives its title. The eunuch is, in fact, a poor specimen himself, and at the initial presentation by Parmeno and Gnatho, the soldier's side has the distinct advantage. When the transaction is complete, however, and both the eunuch and the young maid have been admitted into Thais' house, neither will be what they seem. For the maid, whose name is Pamphila, is really a free citizen, as so often proves the case in new comedy, and will, after she is recognized, be restored to her household, over which her elder brother now presides. The role of the eunuch, in turn, will be assumed by Phaedria's younger brother, Chaerea, in order that he may gain entry into Thais' establishment. His motive is an instant passion he conceived for Pamphila when he noticed her en route to Thais' house, and once inside he presses his affections upon her; that is, he rapes her. Later, when Chaerea, the pretended eunuch, is unmasked, and Pamphila's identity is revealed, the way is open to marriage between two citizens, which is duly arranged.

The motif of the gifts, then, which is a mechanism in the rivalry of Phaedria and the soldier Thraso, is the integument, so to speak, for the second strand of the plot, Chaerea's passion for Pamphila, which is resolved by the device of *anagnorisis* or recognition. The gifts have, one may say, a double value: as slaves, the maid and the eunuch have a price, and the competition between Thraso and Phaedria is commercial. The courtesan goes to the highest bidder. As persons, they figure in their own nar-

Illustration from an early manuscript of The Eunuch: Thraso attacks the house of Thais.

rative, but the relations which they bear to other characters impose a special meaning on what Phaedria and the soldier bestow. Pamphila is not only a free citizen. Having lost her parents as a child, she was reared by Thais' mother as a kind of foster-sister to the courtesan. Thais, then, has a personal interest in recovering authority over Pamphila, and this automatically gives Thraso the edge over Phaedria in their competition, irrespective of the market value of their gifts. At the same time, to the extent that Thais' motives are not narrowly avaricious, Phaedria's claims too must exceed mere cash. On his side, he has love, not so much his own love for Thais, since this the soldier can match, but Thais' love for him; or perhaps we can say, their mutual love.

I have been sketching the way the plot of the *Eunuch,* or rather, the juncture between its two plot lines, produces a double aspect to the rivalry between the youth and the soldier. In one way, it appears as a commercial competition between Phaedria and Thraso, to be decided by the exchange value of their gifts. But the gifts have also another value, since by virtue of their hidden identities they are also persons. The position of Thais, in turn,

varies according to the conception we entertain of the gifts she receives. Her role as courtesan corresponds to their material value, the cash interest. Her personal concern for Pamphila, however, opens a moral dimension in which two opposed motives, the need to oblige Thraso, and love for Phaedria, both operate. We may add that Thais' interest in Pamphila is itself a double one. Certainly, there is a sentimental bond, for as girls they had been raised like sisters; but there are also practical considerations, since Thais is a relative stranger in Athens, and has hopes of securing a patron in Pamphila's brother Chremes, who is a young man of breeding. These hopes are dashed by the rape, but all is made good by the proposed marriage with Chaerea. The episodes involving Chaerea and Pamphila, then, react throughout on Thais' fortunes, and on the delicate balance between love and security that the rivalry between her lovers represents.

The tension between love and constraint or interest is inscribed in the *Eunuch* from the very beginning, and in such a way as to oblige love to accommodate necessity. The first two scenes develop, in a remarkably clear and programmatic manner, several different conceptions of erotic passion which served as a source for later writers as different as Cicero and Catullus. What is more, these conceptions have a logic and a progress. They are presented in such a way as to suggest the solution to a dilemma. The solution may be seen, as one might expect in the case of a problem so close to the antinomy of freedom and necessity, as an ideological and overdetermined construct. In any case, it motivates, I believe, the surprising conclusion to the **Eunuch,** which has shocked and offended many readers of the play. It is a harbinger as well of a moment in the history of love that found expression in the elegists of the Augustan principate, and, after another transformation, in the mediaeval tradition of courtly love.

The play begins with the entrance of Phaedria, who is debating with himself whether to respond to a summons from Thais—similar lines survive as a fragment of Menander's *Eunuch,* which evidently opened in the same way. Phaedria resents that on the previous day Thais had barred him from her house. Phaedria's slave, Parmeno, counsels him against a show of independence, which, when he later submits, will only leave him more completely in Thais' power. He goes on to explain Thais' mercurial behavior as follows: "A thing that has neither sense nor measure you cannot control by sense. In love, these are all inbred vices: insults, suspicions, hostilities, truces, war, peace again; when you insist on making such unstable things stable by means of reason, it's exactly like trying to be rationally insane" (57-63). The equation of love with madness was proverbial at Rome, and is captured in a jingle that goes as far back as Plautus: *amans amens.* Nevertheless, it is worth teasing out the precise sense of Parmeno's analysis. If I read him right, Parmeno contrasts the mutability of passion with the fixed and constant nature of reasoned dispositions. Passionate states are unstable, *incerta;* reason cannot endow them with the stability characteristic of its own self-control. Associations based on reason or calculation (*ratio*) are not disrupted by arbitrary quarrels, any more than enmities are abolished by sudden reconciliations. Implicit here is a principle of Roman social morality: *constantia,* or consistency, which Cicero lauded in *De Officiis.* Rational behavior is settled and determinate. Love is in principle the reverse. Fights do not mean that love is over; they are simply part of the syndrome, as much as making up again. It is in just this compatibility of opposites, this collapse of sustained discriminations, that the irrationality of love consists. This is why it is fruitless to resist Thais' call so long as Phaedria is in love.

To this advice, Phaedria replies: "What a shameful business. Now I realize that she's evil and I'm miserable. I'm fed up and yet I'm burning with passion; conscious and aware, alive and alert, I'm dying, and I don't know what I'm doing" (70-73). There is a superficial similarity between Phaedria's outburst and Parmeno's theory, which it would seem to illustrate. But in fact, Phaedria takes rather a different line. His complaint is not about the irrationality of passion as such. What he laments is that his love is abused by a wicked woman, as he imagines Thais to be. Like Parmeno, Phaedria exploits the figure

of oxymoron, but to a different effect. The source of the lover's contradictoriness lies not so much in the volatile nature of passion as in the tension between love and knowledge or moral awareness. To be sure, love will not be dominated, but that is because it is stubborn rather than mutable. While Parmeno identifies an opposition between passion and rationality—his terms are *ratio* and *consilium*—Phaedria sees simply an inconsistency between love and good sense, *prudentia, scientia*—an inconsistency that is problematic when the object of desire is undeserving.

We may call it a debate between an intellectual and an ethical view of love. For Parmeno, Phaedria's indignation is the vestigial scruple of reason that does more harm than good. He counsels his master to buy himself off as cheaply as possible, and adds: "Do not torment yourself" (the Greek original had, "Don't fight the god"—*me theomachei*—but Terence consistently internalizes the source of passion, as Peter Flury has shown). "And don't," Parmeno continues, "add to love's own miseries; those it possesses, bear properly" (76-78). What Phaedria had read as criminal arrogance or *hybris* (surely the Greek behind *contumelia,* 3), Parmeno charges to the essence of *amor.*

At this moment, Thais emerges from her house. Parmeno notes her entrance with a metaphor drawn from agriculture that is very likely Terence's own touch: "There, out she comes, that blight on our property" (*nostri fundi calamitas,* 79). An entire theme is activated here that had been latent in Phaedria's complaint. Thais is, after all, a professional courtesan. Her motive is not passion but business, or, as the lover perceives it, greed. Phaedria is a type familiar in new comedy, the young wastrel who squanders his fortune on a high-class call-girl, like Diniarchus in Plautus' *Truculentus* (Parmeno's image recalls a formulaic phrase in that comedy). Thais' fickleness is not a symptom of love, as Parmeno pretended, nor a change of heart, as Phaedria had perhaps led one to imagine. It is simply a matter of profit and loss, and, on the pattern of the *Truculentus,* one supposes that Phaedria has come near to exhausting his resources, and that another customer, still flush, is on the scene. I do not mean, however, that Parmeno's caustic phrase cancels his little disquisition on love. I have already revealed, what in the Greek original was perhaps disclosed in a prologue, that Thais is not so mercenary. I am remarking rather how Terence, in the thirty-five verses of the opening dialogue, has adumbrated the complex of motives, mercantile and amatory, that we found implicit in the action by which the rivalry between Phaedria and Thraso was dramatized: the presentation of gifts, each of which contained, behind its value as a commodity, a meaning grounded in personal identity.

Thais makes her appearance worrying aloud that Phaedria may have misconstrued his exclusion from her house the previous day. By this, she undercuts the two accounts of her behavior so far proffered: Parmeno's suggestion of love's whimsicality, which derives, on the whole, from the lyric tradition, and Phaedria's intimation of avarice or malice, in the spirit of comic satire. The situation is thus set for the move to a third pattern. Phaedria begins by protesting the inequality of feeling between himself and Thais, such that he is wounded by rejection while she can be indifferent (91-94). Terence will pick up this motif again later, in connection with Thraso's passion for Thais, as we shall see. Thais explains that she did not turn Phaedria out because of love for anyone else, but rather because it had to be done (*faciundum fuit,* 97). We may note how Thais has modified the terms in the discussion of her motives. She allows two possible reasons for having excluded Phaedria: that she might have preferred another lover, which she dismisses, or that she is under compulsion. Constraint and passion form a correlative pair of motives, as opposed to the simple or quantitative character of greed or romantic moodiness. The tension between them gives Thais' character depth or structure. Her object now is to reconcile Phaedria to necessity without offense to his role as lover. Thais proceeds matter-of-factly, by describing Pamphila's history to the time when the soldier acquired possession of her. To recover the girl will be difficult, because Thraso has become suspicious of Phaedria, and may himself have an eye for Pamphila as well. Thais confesses that her interest in Pamphila is both personal, since she is called her sister, and practical, for she hopes to provide herself with useful friends by restoring Pamphila to her family. She asks Phaedria to grant her several days devoted exclusively to the soldier, to insure the transfer of the girl.

Phaedria is outraged. He pretends that the whole story has been fabricated, that Thais loves the soldier and fears Pamphila's charms. There is a momentary standoff, but Phaedria deflects the argument by asking: "Is he the only one who gives?" (163). Here Phaedria mentions his own offering of maid and eunuch, which of course signals the subplot. At the same time, Phaedria has put his case for precedence in terms of cash value—he specifies the cost of the maid and eunuch at twenty minae. The gifts are ambiguously a kind of purchase price and tokens of affection—an ambiguity that will, as we shall see, be exploited throughout the play, and inheres in the role of courtesan. Thais, however, cannot let the charge stand, and makes a bold move: rather than have Phaedria as an enemy (*inimicum,* 174), she will do as he bids, despite her own wishes. To which Phaedria replies: "If only you said that from the heart (*ex animo*) and honestly, 'rather than have you as an enemy'! If I could believe that was sincerely said, I could endure anything" (175-77).

This is the crucial turn in the argument. Phaedria has demanded sincerity. With that, he can allow Thais freedom of action. The language is very careful here, and repays close attention. Phaedria puts his faith in the word: *utinam istuc verbum diceres,* "If you could speak that word (or phrase)," Phaedria says, and the slave Parmeno picks it up with the remark: "How quickly he collapses, conquered by a single word." It is a matter of belief whether Thais' words reveal what is truly in her heart or mind, her *animus.* Phaedria solves the problem of submitting to his rival by opening up a space between act

and desire or feeling. It is the only solution that will preserve both the claims of love and a frank acknowledgment of the rival's power. Precisely this situation is paradigmatic for the notion of true or sincere love. Thais at once assures Phaedria that she is speaking *ex animo,* citing her previous favors toward him as evidence—she does not press an absolute division between deeds and words, or what they signify. Phaedria consents to two days apart, and Thais says: "I love you for good reason, you do me kindness" (186). There is a range of meaning in Thais' phrase, *bene facis,* that is difficult to capture, for it recalls *beneficium,* the kind of service by which one wins friends or supporters. When Thais spoke of providing herself with friends by restoring Pamphila to her family, *beneficium* was the term she employed. With Phaedria it occurs again in the same semantic ambience, since Thais's concern not to have Phaedria as an enemy, *inimicus,* betrays a quite practical interest, however Phaedria may choose to understand her.

"For these two days, Thais," Phaedria says, "good-bye." Thais responds with the coventional Latin interrogative formula of leave-taking, "Want anything else?"—which, like a common expression in Arabic today, requires no answer—but Phaedria responds with a soulful plea: "What do I want? That when you're with that soldier of yours, you not be with him (*praesens absens ut sies*); that day and night you love me, miss me, dream of me, wait for me, think of me, hope for me, rejoice in me, be totally with me—to sum it up, become my soul (*animus*), since I am yours" (191-96).

The idea of love as a communion or exchange of minds or hearts sounds romantic. It conjures up the kind of conceit the metaphysical poets would exploit. The paradox of absence in presence has for us a philosophical ring, and the jingle *praesens absens* appears later in spiritual contexts. These lines, together with his earlier expostulations about mutual and sincere love, establish Phaedria as a figure of deep passion. If we read it as sublime, we may experience some difficulty in reconciling such an emotion with the cross-bidding for Thais' favors represented in the offers of gifts. It has been suggested, for example, that the Roman comedians failed to understand the refined relations that Greeks might enjoy with a courtesan or *hetaira,* for there was no comparable convention or institution at Rome, and the rough Latin equivalent, *meretrix,* always retained the rather base connotation of whore, that is, *scortum* in Latin, or *porne* in Greek—quite a different thing from *hetaira.* Alternatively, the modern reader has been warned against sentimentalizing the courtesan who for Greeks and Romans alike remained a woman for hire. The controversy erupts over the final scenes of the **Eunuch** where Phaedria consents to an arrangement in which he will share Thais with the soldier, on the condition that Thraso foot the bills: a denouement that is startling and, to some scholars, objectionable, not because such arrangements are unheard of in Greece or Rome—for that is not the case— but because it appears degrading to Thais, who is represented as a good-hearted courtesan (*bona meretrix*), and inconsistent with the nature of Phaedria's love, for which our evidence is precisely the passages we have been examining. Phaedria has only a limited part in the rest of the action. He quits the stage to isolate himself in the country for the two-day interval he has pledged to Thais, and while, not surprisingly, he returns almost at once, his hands will be full with the problem caused by his brother Chaerea. He has no further meetings with Thais, and encounters the soldier only in the finale.

We have seen already how the tension between prices and passion is written into the first act of the **Eunuch,** and also how it operates in the structure of the plot, where the two movements, centering on Phaedria and Chaerea respectively, are spliced through the double function of the gifts to Thais. As I shall indicate shortly, Terence keeps both aspects present to the audience in Acts II and III. There is not only tension, however, but also a necessary relation between material constraints and the kind of inward love that Phaedria expresses and demands. The distinction between interior and exterior, between a disposition of the *animus* and behavior conditioned by compulsion, arises out of the interaction between Phaedria and Thais: it enables the simultaneous belief in their love and the propriety of Thais' submission, if only temporary, to the will of Thraso—a submission already enacted the day before. If Phaedria is to believe in Thais' love, he must detach act from feeling. But the reverse is equally the case: the notion of sincerity, of interiority, of the true love of minds and hearts, presupposes a rival whose claims are in some sense acknowledged by the lover himself. Far from being incompatible with concessions to a rival, the conception of love that Phaedria advances with such intensity and sincerity demands them. It is, we may say, the narrative form of true love.

When Phaedria completes his impassioned speech, he leaves the stage, without waiting for a reply from Thais. Thais, with the stage to herself, delivers a brief monologue. "Wretched me," she exclaims, repeating the cry that had escaped her when she first appeared. "Perhaps he has little faith in me and is judging me by the characters of other women. But I am conscious and know for certain that I have not invented any lies and that no one is dearer to my heart (*cordi*) than Phaedria" (197-201).

There is some reason to suppose that this monologue, and even the outburst of Phaedria that immediately precedes it, may have been the work of Terence, though the question cannot be resolved to the satisfaction of all competent scholars. The use of a soliloquy to reveal Thais' true feelings certainly deserves notice. She asserts that she has acted entirely in the interest of the maiden Pamphila, adding also that she is at the very moment expecting the arrival of Pamphila's brother, which would presumably clinch the case for the girl's citizen status. The monologue as a vehicle for inner feelings assumes, by an easy shift, an expository function, such as belonged customarily to Greek prologues. Whether there is evidence here for Terence's workmanship we may leave moot. Thais' brief monologue, in any case, responds formally to Phaedria's demand for sincerity, and the language in

which she expresses her certainty and self-awareness (*certo scio,* 199) appears to answer Parmeno's indictment of love's instability (*incerta,* 61), as well as Phaedria's own contrast between loving and knowing (*scio,* 73), resolving by a kind of verbal closure the doubts about love which they had raised.

Until very near the end of the first act, Parmeno has remained on stage, introducing occasional remarks into the conversation between Phaedria and Thais. The ancient commentator on Terence, Donatus, perceived a difficulty here, since Parmeno can presumably surmise that Pamphila is freeborn, yet later he assists Chaerea in the scheme to gain access to her. Whether Parmeno has dismissed or forgotten the possible identity of Pamphila, or whether he did not imagine that Chaerea would go so far as rape, I shall not conjecture. Karl Büchner inferred that the role of Parmeno in the first act must have been Terence's own contribution, which is why, in Menander's original version, he can have abetted Chaerea's plan without scruple. It is certainly true that Parmeno has, in the second scene of Act I, no very important role. Thais asks Phaedria whether his slave can keep a secret before she proceeds with the facts in the case of Pamphila. Parmeno answers: "Me? Perfectly. But I warn you, this is the rule on which I pledge my good faith to you: whatever I hear that is true, I keep quiet and hold in perfectly; but if it's false or hollow or made up, it's immediately out in the open—I'm full of cracks, and I pour out this way and that" (100-05). Deleuze has mentioned the connection between imagery of perforated bodies and schizophrenia, in which surfaces break down, "the entire body is nothing but depth," and, as a corollary, words lose their meaning, or are experienced as false [Gilles Deleuze, "The Schizophrenic and Language: Surface and Depth in Lewis Carroll and Antonin Artaud," in Josué V. Harari, ed., *Textual Strategies,* 1979]. Parmeno is no schizophrenic. Quite the contrary, he is in perfect command of his own surface, which he can render porous at will. I should like to suggest, however, that his image of container and contained, and the association of truth with things held within, falsehood with the rupture of boundaries, may be a figure for the inwardness or subjectivity that Phaedria looks to in the love of Thais.

There is another exchange, almost certainly and by general consensus an interpolation by Terence himself, where the interpenetration of love and sale is exposed with caustic irony. It occurs between the soldier and his parasite. Thraso's first entrance, at the beginning of Act III, is with customary braggadocio, egged on by Gnatho. Then, with an abrupt change of subject, Thraso inquires whether he ought to clear himself before Thais of the suspicion that he is in love with Pamphila (434-35). Gnatho counsels against it: better to keep Thais jealous in order to have in reserve a weapon against Phaedria. Thraso submits a curiously modest and sober objection: "If she really loved me, then that would help, Gnatho" (446). To this Gnatho replies: "Since she looks forward to and loves what you give her, she has long since loved you, it has long since been easy to hurt her. She's constantly afraid that the profit she now reaps you may angrily bestow elsewhere." Thraso says, "You're right, that hadn't occurred to me." "Ridiculous," answers Gnatho; "you just weren't thinking" (447-52). This blunt equation of avarice and romantic love passes with the *alazon* figure of the soldier, because he is vain and dim enough to miss, or want to miss, the paradox. We have seen, however, that this contradiction is not an accident of the soldier's wealth and gullibility. Phaedria is in precisely the same position. In his case, the contradiction was finessed through artful transitions in the dialogue and by the professed sincerity of the lovers, to be elicited only by critical analysis. But sincerity does not abolish the contradictions of the courtesan's role, it merely contains them. The difference with the parasite and the soldier is that, for the soldier, Gnatho is free to unmask them.

When Thais comes out and greets the soldier, he at once puts Gnatho's theory to work: "My Thais, my pet, what's up? Do you love me on account of that harp-girl?" (455-57). Thraso's formulation is not quite so stark as the parasite's: appreciation of gifts is the cause of love, not love itself. But the coarseness is remarked by Parmeno, who is on hand with the Aethiopian maid and the eunuch, or rather, with his replacement, Chaerea in drag: "How charming! What a start he's off to" (455-58). But such delicacy does not prevent Parmeno from competing on the same terms: "Whenever you're ready, the gifts from Phaedria are here," he puts in (464-65). In an earlier scene, when he still had on his hands the genuine, decrepit eunuch, who was no match for the Pamphila whom Gnatho was bringing to Thais, Parmeno had admitted that the doors were open to the parasite because of the girl (282); but there, however Gnatho might take it, Parmeno had in mind the plot to rescue Pamphila, and even allowed himself to refer cryptically to the two-day period of grace that Phaedria had agreed upon (283-85). With the handsome Chaerea in tow, he is prepared to let gifts speak for themselves, and even to turn Phaedria's absence to advantage, giving it out as a sign of suave superiority that his master makes no exclusive claims upon the courtesan (480-81, 484-85). Phaedria and Thraso are on the same level here. The debonair want of possessiveness on Phaedria's part may seem a ploy of Parmeno's, and difficult to reconcile with the romantic intensity of Phaedria's love, but we may also understand it as an extension of the idea of love inaugurated in the first act, which requires the acknowledgment of the rival.

For all his good intentions, Phaedria does not succeed in retiring for as much as a few hours, and is soon back on the scene, if not to touch, as he says, at least to look (638-40). His return, however, does not precipitate a confrontation with his rival, nor does it, as I have said, discommode the scheme to recover Pamphila. By this time, the girl has been installed in Thais' house and raped by Chaerea into the bargain, and Phaedria, who is hard put to comprehend how a eunuch could have done the damage, has his hands full defending himself against the angry accusations of Thais' servants, who have discovered the deed. An interrogation of the real eunuch soon betrays Chaerea's part in it, despite Phaedria's attempts to corrupt his testimony, once he sees where it is leading. At

this point, Pamphila's brother, Chremes, returns, having already searched for Thais at her house and then at Thraso's, where his arrival caused consternation for the jealous soldier (618, 623).

Chremes' role here provides an interesting indication of how Menander composed his plays. One might have expected that the intervention at the house of the rival—in Menander's *Eunuch* he was not necessarily a soldier—would be the work of Phaedria rather than of Chremes, Pamphila's brother, who has no amorous relation to Thais save in the mind of Thraso. Terence, in the interpolated passage mentioned above, has Gnatho prepare the soldier for just such an encounter—with Phaedria. Günther Jachmann, who, in a brilliant article, opened the whole question of contamination in the **Eunuch,** concluded that in the Menandrian original it must have been Phaedria, or his counterpart, who disrupted the rival's party, and it was Terence who transferred this function to Chremes. But Menander, in fact, chose to make Phaedria as good as his word, and he does not disrupt Thais' efforts to recover Pamphila through an untimely confrontation with Thraso. Thus, Chaerea's rape of Pamphila, which takes on this function, appears, for all the amplitude with which it is developed, as a complication in the story of Phaedria and Thais, as Walther Ludwig incidentally reveals in his masterly analysis of the structure of the **Eunuch**'s plot. But the alternative possibility, that Phaedria himself might have disturbed Thais' scheme by a jealous intervention, while it is excluded from the **Eunuch** by the insertion of the subplot and by the subjective and therefore tolerant character of Phaedria's passion, remains available as a paradigm or scene-type which Menander, or perhaps Terence, adapted to the role of Chremes. The way in which Menander worked with scene-types and could exploit a single pattern in quite different contexts was demonstrated elegantly by Woldemar Görler, in a comparison between a series of scenes in the **Eunuch** and in Menander's *Dyscolus,* shortly after the *Dyscolus* was first published in 1959.

After the episode at the soldier's house, which is reported indirectly rather than enacted on stage, Chremes meets Thais at her own house, where she at last has the opportunity to tell him about Pamphila, and to produce the birth tokens—which Chremes does not recognize. He prepares to summon his old nurse, who will know the trinkets, but is forestalled by the arrival of Thraso and a small army of slaves and cooks. With considerable encouragement from Thais and inspired by the likelihood, at least, that Pamphila is his sister, Chremes faces the soldier down, though he retires to bring on the nurse before Thraso's actual retreat. The frustrated or incomplete recognition of Pamphila here, which will require confirmation in a later episode, may be a stylistic device, if it is true, as Wehrli has suggested, that Menander liked to vary the *anagnorisis* and rarely staged such scenes straightforwardly (the **Andria** is the notable exception), but it also articulates the double movement of the plot, for Thais, still ignorant of the rape of Pamphila, believes that she has now succeeded in establishing the citizenship of the girl. When, after the departure of Chremes and of Thraso with his troops, she discovers what has happened, she will have to adapt her tactics, if not abandon her plan altogether, since Pamphila is no longer an acceptable or eligible woman by the conventions of new comedy, and Chremes will, presumably, have no interest in establishing his connection with her. Only marriage with Chaerea can save her, and this is achieved by the unmasking of Chaerea and the finally corroborated identification of Pamphila, so that all obstacles to the union—Chaerea's father on his side, Chremes and Thraso on Pamphila's—are simultaneously eliminated.

After the revelations about Chaerea and Pamphila and a scene in which Parmeno, through a ruse of Thais' servant, is given a good scare for his part in Chaerea's masquerade, a love-sick and mostly humbled Thraso slips in once more—a bare seventy verses from the end of the play. Two brief scenes more, and he meets Phaedria for the denouement. This is engineered by Gnatho. Thraso has understood that he is defeated. He has lost Pamphila, and learned that Chaerea will marry her with his father's consent; the old man has also agreed to take Thais under his protection, which Terence expresses in terms of the Roman relationship of patron and client (1039-40). Thais is wholly Phaedria's. But Thraso's love increases with his despair (1053), and he appeals, rather pathetically, to Gnatho for help. In exchange for a permanent place at Thraso's table, Gnatho girds himself for action against the now arrogant Phaedria. His strategy is to recommend that Phaedria share Thais with the soldier, to which he persuades him with three arguments: Thraso will cover the expenses for Phaedria's affair; his silly self-importance will be a great source of general amusement; and there is no chance that Thais could fall in love with him. The soldier, at once grateful and harmlessly vain, thanks the parasite and remarks that everyone loves him wherever he goes. "Just what you promised," says Phaedria to Gnatho in the final line of the play.

Such festive inclusiveness is of course compatible with new comedy, but it is by no means demanded by the genre. It is quite conventional to drive out the discomfited rival, and Phaedria's self-regarding magnanimity again may seem at odds with his earlier idealized devotion, if not a downright lapse of taste on the part of Terence. But the point of the final scene is not to reward the soldier for having been a good sport, nor to extract a last bit of humor from his salvaged vanity. For it serves as a solution to the paradox of commercial love that has been in suspense since the beginning of the play—or, if not a solution, then at all events a new and explicit statement of it. The courtesan is in business. But the customer is a lover, and wishes to be loved. We have seen how Phaedria took refuge from this dilemma in the demand for sincerity, which posits a division between one's role and one's true or inner self. Phaedria now has possession of Thais, but this does not alter the contradictory basis of their relation. There can be no question of marriage, both because of her profession and because of her alien status, which absolutely prohibit union with a citizen. The idea of love—Thais' love for Phaedria—is reimported by the cynical Gnatho, however, in order to mark the necessary distinction between Phaedria and Thraso (1080). The opposition between love and sale which Gnatho himself has collapsed in order to reassure the soldier of Thais' favor, is here exploited with comic abandon to undo Phaedria's possessiveness, enabling him to admit and profit from the double relation which had earlier been a cause of anguish. The spirit of elation that attends upon the victory of Phaedria and Chaerea and the humiliation of Thraso, who is a likable ass, make the conclusion palatable, and one might analyze according to a psychological theory of reception how such effects in comedy facilitate ideologically ambiguous resolutions. But the point is that the ambiguity here is, with respect to the plot, gratuitous. Just when the lovers have the power to be united, the rival is welcomed to share. The amatory division of labor which they enjoy rests precisely on the notion of love which Phaedria had raised at the beginning of the play. Love ceases to be a balm for the pain of a compromised allegiance and becomes instead the inspiration or rationalization for it. The hero's complaint about the courtesan's submission to material constraints is transformed into a frank and genial game with them. Sincere love, then, is not only compatible with the life of a courtesan, it is proper to it. The finale of the play is an emblem of this complex.

Before considering some of the implications or meanings of love as it is developed in the relations among Thais, Phaedria and Thraso, we may briefly examine the forms of passion developed in the counterplot of the ***Eunuch***. When Chaerea dashes on stage where Parmeno is loitering, in pursuit of a maiden so beautiful she has driven all others from his mind, Parmeno dryly observes: "Here's the other one" (297). He knows his man. Phaedria had been a serious and sober character before he was transformed by love's disease (*morbi,* 225)—child's play compared to what a rabid Chaera will unleash (200-01). The plan is struck to have Chaerea impersonate his brother's eunuch, who is standing mutely by. Chaerea dismisses Parmeno's misgivings, arguing that it is better to trick a whore, who lives off deceit, than to turn his wiles against his father (382-86). We may fill in the argument implicit in this telegraphic disjunction: love must have its way; it is a matter only of means. Since the lover himself is without resources, comedy affords him two avenues to his object: he may raid his own estate, which is to say, most commonly, his father's; or he may cozen the girl's master or mistress. Here, Thais stands for the latter, as a self-employed courtesan whose house is as good as a brothel (*domum meretriciam,* 382). Hence she herself may be despised as a *lena* or brothel-keeper, fair game for force or fraud, like Sannio in ***The Brothers***. Later, when he emerges from Thais' house, Chaerea exults in his conquest, narrating each step in his escapade to the delight and approbation of his friend Antipho, with whom he has fallen in. He is unashamed of his costume, since passion is sufficient excuse (574-75), and he explains how any scruples that might have lingered were banished by the chance view of a painting of Jupiter's seduction of Danae, which Chaerea, with trite irreverence, interprets as divine sanction for his stratagem.

While all of Menander's plays, as Ovid said, treated love, love was not all of a kind. Chaerea's passion is not an abiding and reciprocal affection such as Phaedria entertains. Indeed rape, while it is often in the background of new comedy—*exŏ tou dramatos,* in Aristotle's phrase—is not normally a part of the action, and the characterization appropriate to such a motive is correspondingly unusual in the repertory of amorous roles. The lovers in new comedy may contemplate less than forever, but rarely only a day. Where a courtesan is involved, a fixed duration, such as a year, may be stipulated; most often, the term of the liaison is unspecified. Chaerea is the exception: his passion simply to possess the virgin, with no thought of consequences, summons up a novel persona. It is certainly a successful one. Chaerea is an engaging scamp, witty, frank, and ebullient, and it is easy to enjoy his ingenuous elation, despite the injustice to Thais, whom we know as sympathetic, and to her innocent ward. An untroubled empathy with the youth is licensed by the holiday mood of comedy, as well as by the custom of the genre, which will require that he accept as wife the citizen whom he has violated. A recognition scene suffices to establish the girl's legitimacy. But transforming Chaerea into a plausible husband will take art, for it involves an alteration of intention and of style.

Chaerea reenters crestfallen in the final act. The parents of Antipho both proved, as Chaerea relates, to be at home, and he was constrained to flee down alley after alley to escape encounters with acquaintances (840-47). His former bravado has deserted him, and when he sees Thais, who is fuming with indignation, he freezes in confusion (848-49). His object attained, the spell is now broken, and Chaerea is again subject to a sense of decorum and shame. This change of heart enables us to bracket his outrageous interlude as a transient impulse or aberration.

When he is charged by Thais and her excitable maid, Pythias, for having assaulted a citizen girl, Chaerea briefly takes refuge in his disguise: "I thought she was a fellow slave" (858). Thais then drops pretenses, addresses Chaerea by his proper name, and reproaches him for his offense against her, whereupon Chaerea takes another tack, intimating that his better acquaintance with the girl may announce a happy conclusion to bad beginnings. At all events, he did it "not for pride's sake, but for love" (877-78). Thais, who professes to understand the power of love, forgives him. "Now I love you too, Thais," he exclaims, which prompts a warning to her mistress from Pythias, and Chaerea's shocked reply, "I wouldn't dare." Chaerea pleads to have Pamphila as wife, on condition that she is a citizen (890; cf. 1036), and, after some further squabbling with the still skeptical Pythias, he is taken into Thais' house, unwilling to be seen in the eunuch's garb. "Ashamed?" asks Thais. "A regular virgin," Pythias puts in, as he and Thais withdraw.

Chaerea's disguise, and his willingness to sport it, are an index of his passion. The return of his sense of decency is coordinate with his intention to marry Pamphila. There is a transition from one mood to another, but no real moral or personal complexity in Chaerea. This is quite

different, for example, from the function of disguises in Shakespeare, which, as Muriel C. Bradbrook explains, "provide a second dramatic identity which is superimposed upon the first, and interlaced with it. When Shakespeare puts his heroines into page's wearing, the two roles are sharply contrasted, giving an effect like shot silk, as the boyish wit or the feminine sensibility predominates. Both must be sustained . . ." [M. C. Bradbrook, *The Growth and Structure of Elizabethan Comedy,* 1973].

It is no occasion for surprise that Pamphila's feelings about the marriage are not consulted. She has, by the conventions of the genre, no other hope of respectability. In any case, marriage is the concern of her guardian, and with Thais' consent, Chremes will pose no objection. It is not a question of options. Sex between citizens is coded as marriage. Without marriage, sex expels Pamphila from the citizen community, precisely as though Chremes had been unable to recognize her (which, prior to Chae-rea's offer of marriage, is exactly the case). The meaning of Chaerea's passion varies with Pamphila's status, and there is no room here for personal conflict, or for the emergence of a subjective voice.

With respect to the status-based polarization of erotic relations on which Chaerea's affair with Pamphila is predicated, Phaedria's association with Thais appears as a third term: a free relation that depends on mutual assent and affection. But, as we have now clearly seen, that relation too has a double aspect in which passion is opposed to necessity, or, stated otherwise, sincere love is set against the courtesan's need to earn her living by the commerce of her body. The four terms suggest the semantic parallelogram designed by A.-J. Greimas, the corners of which we may label as rape, marriage, commercial love, and sincere love. While rape and marriage correspond more or less to the status division between slave and citizen, the tension between personal love and the courtesan's trade is inscribed within the courtesan role itself. It has frequently been observed, of course, that the practice of arranged marriages and the relative seclusion of women in Athens inhibited free romantic attachments among citizens, and that such sentiments found expression in liaisons with *hetaira.* These were not associations among equals, and the image of the courtesan as a professional engaged in business exposes her essential degradation behind the appearance of voluntary association. In the **Eunuch,** the simultaneous acknowledgment of both aspects of the courtesan's role invites a further inflection in the idea of love, which is carried in the notion of sincerity. Love is mutual and by consent, but assent in the lady is etherealized as an inward reflex of the mind, leaving the body in the control of other forces. This conception of love is evolved in the dialogue of the opening act, but the structure of feeling it expresses informs as well the bargain struck in the finale.

In the present state of our knowledge, it is impossible to say how much of the **Eunuch** as we have it is the work of Terence, and what parts derive certainly from his model or models. Opinions differ, for example, on the provenience of the conclusion, though the majority of scholars favor its attribution to Terence himself. I am inclined to believe that the structure of feeling that I have been describing is more Roman than Greek, and the theme we have been pursuing is most in evidence in those passages which may be plausibly assigned to Terence. One may recall once more that Rome had no institution comparable to that of the Greek *hetaira,* nor a status exactly analogous to that of the Athenian *metic* or resident alien—the term *peregrinus,* which Terence applies both to Thais and to Thraso, is a different matter. What was, by custom at least, a natural relationship in Greece may have been for the Romans, or at least for Terence, complex and contradictory.

If it permissible to venture a little further in the airy domain of speculation, we may also remark a difference in the Greek and Roman erotic vocabulary that bears upon our investigation. Samuel Richardson, in the Postscript to *Clarissa,* written when the ideology of love was evolving yet another structure, observed that "what is too generally called *love* ought (perhaps as generally) to be called by another name," and he offered as a substitute "*Cupidity* or a *Paphian stimulus* . . . however grating they may be to delicate ears." Now, Greek terminology for love or passion was rich and nuanced. *Philia* expressed the bond among friends and equals, *storge* that between parents and children, *agape* a strong affection, while *eros* denoted a powerful and ungovernable passion, such as that which inspired Chaerea to rape Pamphila. For all these feelings, or drives, Latin had the single term *amor.* The word called for specification, as fraternal or paternal love, love of country, true love. While in Greek, the expression *alethes eros* would be quite odd, and would certainly not suggest a deep or interior emotion, *verus* or *sincerus amor* is a natural phrase in Latin, discriminating a love that is genuine, in some sense, from a transient or base passion. A fact of vocabulary may inspire distinctions that assume an ideological importance.

In a famous epigram to Lesbia, Catullus imitated Phaedria's appeal to Thais for truth and sincerity. It was a happy inspiration. Catullus, too, was obliged to share the woman he loved with a rival whose claims he had perforce to acknowledge, since his rival was Lesbia's husband. In his frustration, Catullus assailed the motility of passion, as did Parmeno, and the wicked callousness of his beloved. I should propose also to locate in the tradition of the *Eunuch* the complex of themes that constitutes Roman elegy: the ambiguous status of the mistress, who remains aloof from marriage; the problem of greed and gifts; the necessary role of the rival; and the emphasis on sincerity and inner feeling, for which the Roman elegists have been honored as the inventors of subjective love lyric.

If we have rightly discovered in Terence's *Eunuch* an anticipation of elegiac subjectivity, we cannot fail finally to acknowledge its proper character as comedy, a genre whose creative phase at Rome did not outlive the second

century B.C. I believe that it pertains to the essence of new comedy that it always presupposed, even when it was critical of, the recognition of status relations, which the elegists, a century later, could leave blurred or indistinct. Thais is, of course, both resourceful and dignified—Walther Ludwig has insisted that she is the heroine of the drama—and she acts as a kind of patron toward Chaerea and Chremes. Nevertheless, as George Pepe has pointed out in a very perceptive paper ["The Last Scene of Terence's *Eunuchus,*" *The Classical World* 65, 1972], roles are restored when the father of Phaedria and Chaerea is introduced toward the end of the play and accepts Thais as his client or dependent. Pepe adds that "the disharmony of the final scene is that Phaedria's action"—sharing Thais with Thraso and thereby reducing her to the role of a common courtesan—"reasserts [the] pejorative, stereotyped picture of her." Pepe concludes: "If we accept for the purpose of analysis the view that the end of a comedy envisions a new society, we are in a better position to define the dissatisfaction felt at the end of the *Eunuchus.* Instead of a new society it reasserts the old even though that society is deficient in its treatment of Thais."

Yet Pepe's reaction to the conclusion is perhaps too severe. To be sure, Thais does not alter her station, but that is not the form in which comedy puts the challenge to convention. More often, comedy enjoys a confounding of social relations that are affirmed precisely to be cancelled through the evocation of an undifferentiated community—what we may call the saturnalian moment. If we look over the movement of the *Eunuch* as a whole, we may perceive how every character in the play is drawn to the house of Thais. Phaedria and Thraso contend over the right to enter, the latter resorting to an attack under arms; Chaerea and Pamphila gain access in the guise of gifts. Chaerea's father enters to rescue his son, when he learns that Chaerea has raped a free woman. By the end of the play, everyone is inside Thais' place, where all relations appear to coexist (one may compare the conclusion to Plautus' *Bacchides* for another instance of this festive formula). Thais' role as *patrona* and manager of the action, insofar as it reverses conventional status functions, suggests the pattern of inversion that Erich Segal, for example, has identified as characteristic of the Plautine moment in comedy. This inversion is not so much corrected in the finale by Thais' reduction to a common *meretrix* as it is sublimated: all forms meld, and Thais' roles as patron and client coalesce in a comic community characterized by the negation of structured relations. On this level, the subjectivity grounded in rivalry and constraint is dissolved in the very same crucible that distilled it into being, the pleasure-house of courtesan. If Thais nevertheless remains, as she does for many critics, an individual of personal worth who is somehow demeaned by such a merry arrangement, this is perhaps because the contradictions which gave birth to the genre of erotic comedy have not been entirely canceled in the *Eunuch,* but survive its factitious resolution. In the end, it seems, not even sincerity can mask the tensions inherent in relations of social exploitation.

PHORMIO

R. K. Bohm (essay date 1977)

SOURCE: "Money Matters in *Phormio*," *The Classical World,* Vol. 70, No. 4, January, 1977, pp. 267-69.

[*In the essay below, Bohm delineates the differing attitudes toward money held by six characters in* Phormio.]

Terence begins three of his six plays with a protactic character, which Donatus defines as a *persona quae semel inducta in principio fabulae in nullis deinceps fabulae partibus adhibetur* (*ad And. praef.* I, 8). Critics have found fault with Terence for his use of such characters. Ashmore, for example, discusses Terence's change of the opening scene of Menander's *Andria* from a monologue to a dialogue with a protactic character and relates the change to a similar one in *Phormio.* Although Ashmore praises Terence's attempt to avoid the dullness of a monologue, he describes the introduction of a new character as "merely a mechanical device." [S. G. Ashmore, *The Comedies of Terence,* 1908]. Similarly, with a specific citation of Davus in *Phormio,* Duckworth claims

> Terence deserves praise for the laudable desire to substitute dramatic dialogue for the monologue of the Greek original, but he has not been entirely successful with his protactic characters; there is no harm in the fact that they do not appear later in the play; the fault is that they are colorless and have no personality; they contribute nothing to the scene and are, as Donatus says, *extra argumentum.* Such scenes are not really dialogues but monologues which pretend to be dramatic.

> [G. Duckworth, *The Nature of Roman Comedy,* 1952]

In *Phormio* the protactic character is Davus, who has come to pay a debt to Geta. Geta needs the money to provide a wedding gift for his young master, Antipho, and explains to Davus the reason for the wedding. Thus the audience learns the background information necessary to understand the play. The motivation for Davus' appearance is set in the conditions of the play: Antipho's marriage, a center of attention in the play, is the reason for Davus' visit. Davus' departure, however, motivates no further dramatic action.

Another convenient device for the introduction of a protactic character, had Terence chosen to use it, is the arrival of a letter at the port. Geta remarks to Davus, *epistulam ab eo adlatam esse audivi modo / et ad portitores esse delatam* (149-50). Terence could have used a messenger from the port announcing the arrival of a letter as a protactic character instead of Davus returning a debt. News of a letter would provide Geta with an opportunity to voice his fears about the return of Antipho's father. The audience would thus learn the background situation of

the play. In this variation for the opening scene the protactic character motivates continuing action in the play by providing the reason for Geta's departure: the scene ends as Geta leaves to pick up the letter.

Although the scene with Davus does not have any such dramatic consequence, it does serve an important purpose by sounding a note which will echo throughout the play. Davus' opening words call attention to friendship, personal relations, and money, payment of debts: *Amicus summus meus et popularis Geta / heri ad me venit. Erat ei de ratinucula / iam pridem apud me relicuom pauxillulum / nummorum* (35-38). Davus proceeds to complain about the informal 'debts' of friendship, the gifts expected for the subsequent births, birthdays, and initiations of children, for which Geta will have to draw money from his hard earned savings. Davus, sensitive to the value of money, complains that *ei qui minus habent / ut semper aliquid addant ditioribus* (41-42), and wishes that he were rich, *oh, regem me esse oportuit* (70). In contrast to Davus' serious attitude towards money, Geta has a casual attitude. He does not bother to count the coins but accepts Davus' claim *conveniet numerus quantum debui* (53). At the end of the scene he gives the money to a slave with the command *Cape, da hoc Dorcio* (152). Taking and giving money and the interplay of money with personal relationships become recurring themes in *Phormio.*

Money passes among six characters. Nausistrata provides money from her dowry to her husband, Chremes. Chremes gives the money to Demipho. Demipho transfers the money to Phormio. Phormio surrenders it to Phaedria, who uses it to pay the *leno* Dorio, the sixth and last character in the sequence. Terence portrays each of these characters with a different attitude towards money.

Nausistrata expresses concern that her husband, Chremes, has not managed her dowry as wisely as he might have: *quia pol mei patris bene parta indiligenter / tutatur* (788-89). Her husband has wasted money by supporting his former mistress on Lemnos, *haecine erat ea quae nostros minuit fructus vilitas?* (1013). Rather than dwell on the monetary loss, however, she complains that she can no longer trust her husband. Her main concern is that her husband remain faithful, *quid mi hic adfers quam ob rem exspectem aut sperem porro non fore?* (1025).

Chremes himself shows little concern for money, much concern for people. He insists, for example, that Antipho's wife should understand that she is being treated fairly and not being callously sold back to Phormio (719-26). He is concerned enough to continue the monetary support of a woman with whom he had a brief affair fifteen years previously (1017-18). And without hesitation he volunteers his own funds to assist Demipho in paying Phormio (670, 679-81). In these ways Chremes uses money to support friends and friendships.

Demipho, who accepts the money from Chremes, has little interest in personal relationships; acquisition of wealth is his main concern. Although already abundantly wealthy, he has gone on a journey to earn more money (67-70). During his absence his own son can neither draw on his father's funds nor borrow money on the strength of his father's wealth (302). Insensitive to his son's feelings, Demipho objects to his marriage because the bride was poor and lacked a dowry, *qua ratione inopem potius ducebat domum?* (298). Phormio repeats this idea, claiming that Demipho opposed the marriage *quia egens relictast misera, ignoratur parens, / neclegitur ipsa: vide avaritia quid facit!* (357-58). Unlike Chremes, who showed sympathy for the girl's plight, Demipho shows no kindness to her and wants only to be rid of her.

Nausistrata, Chremes, and Demipho are all wealthy; Phormio is not. His poverty, however, is useful: when he plays his roguish tricks none of his victims can hope to gain anything by suing him. By means of clever pranks which help his friends Phormio builds up 'debts of friendship' later paid by invitations to dinner (330-36). As Chremes puts his wealth at Demipho's disposal, so Phormio puts his advantageous poverty at the disposal of both Antipho and Phaedria.

Like Phormio, Phaedria has no money and hence cannot buy his girl friend from the *leno,* Dorio. Instead of solid coins, then, friendship becomes the commodity with which Phaedria tries to bargain with Dorio: *tu mihi cognatus, tu parens, tu amicus* (469). Personal appeals, kindness, and mercy are, however, not currency in which Dorio deals. He insists on cash and affirms a principle of first come, first served, *Mea lege utar, ut potior sit qui prior ad dandumst* (533).

These six characters consequently can be grouped in three pairs. The first pair, Nausistrata and Chremes, are less concerned about money and more concerned about people. Both Demipho and Dorio, the second pair, are interested more in money than in people; people and personal relations are but means of gaining, or losing, money. Finally, both Phaedria and Phormio lack money, but the former's poverty makes him helpless; the latter's poverty enables him to run risks and gain rewards. Money and personal relationships thus form an important motif of the play; Davus' return of a loan in the first scene introduces it.

David Konstan (essay date 1983)

SOURCE: "*Phormio:* Citizen Disorder," in *Roman Comedy,* Cornell, 1983, pp. 115-29.

[*In the excerpt below, Konstan explores the theme of private emotion versus social codes in* Phormio.]

Terence particularly favored such plots as the frame story in [Plautus's] *Cistellaria,* based on the elementary triangle of stubborn father, enamored son, and maiden apparently ineligible for marriage. Thus R. H. Martin remarks, in the introduction to his excellent school edition of the ***Phormio*** [*Terence: Phormio,* 1959]:

The following elements of plot are found in all Terence's plays except the **Hecyra.** Two young men, often brothers, are engaged in love affairs. One of them loves a courtesan, the other wishes to marry a young woman, who is either poor but freeborn, or ostensibly a courtesan. The father opposes his son's marriage or even wants him instead to marry the daughter of a friend or relation. The young woman turns out to be freeborn or the daughter in question, and all ends well.

In a general way, the **Phormio** may be seen to fit this pattern. Antipho is in love with and, in his father's absence, has actually married a poor young woman called Phanium; his father, Demipho, is opposed to the match, because he intends the boy to marry his niece, the daughter of his brother Chremes; by means of a recognition scene, it is discovered that the niece is none other than Phanium, Antipho's bride, thereby bringing about the congruence of the father's wishes with the son's.

A closer look at the structure of the **Phormio,** however, questions the simplicity of this analysis. For the play falls into two distinct parts or movements, each of which appears to have its own theme and resolution. The two parts are joined by an elegant turn of the plot, and in their synthesis the proper significance of the **Phormio** emerges.

From a conversation between two slaves, Geta and Davus, we learn at the beginning of the play that the girl with whom Antipho has become infatuated is an Athenian citizen (114). As a result, he is unable to arrange the kind of irregular liaison that might have been formed with a woman of inferior status. He is obliged, if he will have her, to take her as his wife, but recognizes in her poverty a social barrier his father will not ignore. As Geta says: "Would he give him a maiden dowerless and common? Never!" (*ille indotatam virginem atque ignobilem daret illi? numquam faceret,* 120-21). Since it was scarcely possible for an Athenian youth to marry against the wishes of his father—while at Rome, it was entirely out of the question, since the boy would be *in patria potestate,* in the power of his father, and therefore without the status of a person before the law—it was necessary to devise a stratagem that would prevent Demipho from annulling the arrangement upon his return. This purpose is accomplished according to the advice of Phormio, who plays a role technically known as a parasite, that is, a free man of no property who lives by his wits at the expense of others. Phormio's scheme is to pass himself off as a friend of the girl's father, who had been, he will allege, a relative of Demipho's; according to Attic law, the nearest kin is obliged to marry an orphaned maiden, or provide five hundred drachmae for her dowry.

The action begins when Geta announces to the fainthearted Antipho and his cousin, Phaedria, the imminent arrival of Demipho. Antipho flees in panic, and Geta and Phaedria are left to handle his defense. Their argument is well rehearsed: Antipho's natural modesty tied his tongue in court; Geta, as a slave, was unable to testify;

neither had the resources to raise or borrow the money necessary to provide a dowry and wed the girl to some other suitor. Finally, Demipho demands an interview with Phormio himself. Phormio is in no way daunted by Demipho and the three elders he brings with him as witnesses and counselors; he refuses to discuss the case, reminding Demipho that the law does not allow double jeopardy (403-6). The ruse thus proves entirely successful, and with it the plot is brought to a stalemate. Demipho is trapped, so long as Phormio refuses to negotiate. The action is set in motion again through a subplot involving an affair of Phaedria's with a lute girl called Pamphila. Before examining this transition, we may review the basic elements in the first movement of the comedy.

The issue that divides father and son is one of social class or caste. When Demipho denies any connection or acquaintance with Phanium's father, Phormio rejoins: "Really? Aren't you ashamed? But if he had left an estate of ten talents, you'd promptly summon up your lineage mindfully all the way back to your grandfather and greatgrandfather" (392-95). The theme is familiar in new comedy, and central to such plays as Menander's *Samia* and Terence's **Adelphoe.**

The prejudice of the father and the passion of the son are essentially correlative motives. Demipho endorses a customary exclusiveness; Antipho's desire, like that of young men generally in the comic tradition, is heedless of status and defies the respect for conventional boundaries characteristic of the older generation. The dramatic function of passion is thus determined in relation to the particular norms that contain it, here the restrictions pertaining to class, represented by Demipho. This relationship between the father and son is captured in their names: Demipho suggests something like "voice of the people," Antipho, "voice of the opposition." In general, names with the root *dem,* meaning "the people" or "the community," are reserved for figures of authority. Put another way, we may say that while love is a personal emotion, it acts in tension with a social code, and this polarity of rule and passion constitutes the theme of the play.

Phormio's cunning abuse of the law relating to orphaned women succeeds, as we have seen, in baffling Demipho. In effect, Antipho has triumphed over his father, achieving the union he desires in spite of his father's opposition. But this victory does not furnish a comic closure. Ordinarily, in new comedy, the point is not the mere discomfiture of the paterfamilias and his conservative ideals. Rather, the denouement reestablishes the harmony of the group, reconciling the interests of father and son. Without this harmony, Antipho's success appears not as a resolution of the tension but as a standoff, demanding some further action or revelation to complete the story. Let us consider, moreover, the ways in which the complication might be satisfactorily resolved. We usually think of the recognition scene as the favored device in situations of this sort: Unexpected tokens or testimony reveal the eligibility of the girl. But in fact this means is normal only in questions of citizenship or civic status. Where the obstacle is simply a matter of

wealth, the reconciliation was conventionally achieved through a change of heart or a revelation of true feelings in the blocking character. In Menander's *Samia,* for example, where a young man has had a child by the daughter of a humble neighbor, it turns out that the two fathers had independently decided to arrange the match between them. In Terence's **Adelphoe,** based on a play by Menander, Micio insists that his son meet his responsibilities by marrying the impoverished young woman who has borne his child. The difference in the treatment of themes of class and citizenship reflects the ideology of the classical city-state. The discriminations that separate members of the community from outsiders—whether strangers, slaves, resident aliens, or otherwise illegitimate or disfranchised individuals—were sanctified by law and custom, and their abrogation was a serious matter. Divisions based on wealth, on the other hand, were felt to strike at the solidarity of the community and were therefore regarded as the baleful effects of prejudice and greed. Their proper resolution is thus alteration of character or opinion. To reveal a poor citizen as an heiress or heir would imply that boundaries of class are in principle absolute and unbridgeable, like the boundaries that delimit the community, and this would be incompatible with the spirit of civic unity that reigns in comedy. In the **Phormio,** as we shall see, the problem assumes an entirely different form because of the supervention of the second movement of the play.

The argument we have been analyzing occupies the first two acts into which the **Phormio** is conventionally divided. Geta had indicated, in his conversation with Davus, that Phaedria had conceived a passion for a lute girl while his father, Chremes, the brother of Demipho, was abroad. In the third act we learn that Pamphila's master, Dorio, has sold her to a foreign soldier, but if Phaedria can raise the sum of thirty minae within a day, he can preempt the contract (531-33; 557). In the fourth act, Phormio rises once more to the occasion by pretending that he will marry Phanium himself if Demipho will provide a dowry of thirty minae. This sum he will lend to Phaedria, until the lad can collect the like amount from his friends (703). Then he will return both the money and the girl to Demipho on the pretext that the omens are against the marriage, thereby saving at a single stroke Antipho his bride and Phaedria his concubine. The transfer of the money to Phormio is accomplished by the beginning of Act V.

The second stage of the intrigue occupies a considerable part of the action in the **Phormio** (all of Act III; Act IV except for the first scene; and four scenes—two through five, omitting an intercalary scene following number three—in the final act). Nevertheless, Phaedria's affair remains a subplot rather than a second plot for two reasons. First, it never achieves the confrontation and resolution that occur between Antipho and Demipho. Indeed, after the third act, Phaedria disappears from the play. To be sure, he gets his money and his girl, but the machinations in his behalf on the part of Geta and Phormio occur in the new context that arises with the second movement of the play, in which Phaedria's problem is

An illustration from a manuscript of Phormio: *typical slaves with scarves.*

overshadowed by quite different concerns. The subordination of Phaedria's complication is a good illustration of the essentially correlative nature of passion in new comedy: Without an articulated opposition from Chremes, it recedes to an ancillary status in the drama. The second reason is that the exchange of the thirty minae and the right to wed Phanium serve formally to facilitate the second movement, which requires that Demipho and Chremes work to recover the girl for Antipho. We may now examine this unusual conversion of the plot in detail.

In the first scene of the fourth act, it is disclosed, through a dialogue between Chremes, who has just arrived home, and Demipho, that Chremes has been maintaining on the island of Lemnos the daughter of a bigamous marriage. The purpose of his trip was to fetch the girl, since he and his brother have conspired to marry her to Antipho in order to conceal his conduct from his legitimate wife, Nausistrata, whose dowry is the sole source of his wealth (586-87). With this brief conversation, the entire structure of the plot is transformed. Demipho's objection to Phanium is now revealed as unrelated to her poverty; he

was not motivated by avarice or class feeling, but by his desire to protect his brother's domestic peace and security. The issue of class was only virtual, based on Antipho's natural assumption that this would be the basis of his father's anger. When it emerges that Demipho's opposition stems not from conventional prejudices but from private contingencies, the meaning of Antipho's passion is correspondingly reduced from a challenge, albeit personal and accidental, to public norms to a matter of individual disobedience. Thus the issue shifts from social boundaries, which had been represented by parental authority, to authority itself, without that embeddedness in communal values by which it is legitimized. With the disclosure of Demipho's true motives, the play beings anew, because the obstacle has been altered, and the obstacle is the essence of the comic tension. To be sure, Demipho remains the blocking figure, and this sustains the continuity of the narrative, but here we may see once again and most clearly how the conflict in comedy is located not simply in the struggle between the characters but in the complex of values and impulses which they enact.

For the rest of Act IV, Demipho and Chremes continue their efforts to end the marriage between Antipho and Phanium, and finally accede to Phormio's demand for thirty minae as her dowry. However, the change in focus from class division to domestic imbroglio opens the way to a recognition scene, which comes at the beginning of Act V: Chremes encounters Sophrona, the nurse of his Lemnian daughter, and learns that she is the very girl whom Antipho has taken as his wife. Naturally, the brothers make haste to recover the thirty minae, which have already been transferred to Phormio, but the parasite, informed of the circumstances by Geta, sees a way to press his advantage: He will give up his claim to Phanium only on condition that the dowry remain with him, as compensation for the one he lost when he broke off—he pretends—a previous engagement in their behalf (927-29). Phormio's real purpose, as he reveals in an earlier soliloquy, is to relieve Phaedria once and for all of his financial anxieties and to enjoy the utter duping of the two old men (885-86). When the brothers hesitate to concede, Phormio informs them that he is apprised of their secret, and is prepared to reveal it to Chremes' wife. Chremes is inclined to submit, Demipho to resist the extortion, now that the truth is out in any case and must soon reach the ears of Nausistrata. The plot has here arrived at an ambiguous juncture, at which it might develop in either of two ways, depending on whether Chremes and Demipho can come to terms with Phormio. Here, we may evaluate the significance of both the second movement, and the shift in content from the first part to the second, for in this transformation resides the theme of the play as a whole.

The action following the revelation of Phanium's relationship to Chremes has an unusual twist: Father and uncle striving to recover for the son the object of his enamorment. This situation is contrived by the placement of the recognition scene in the subplot: Had it occurred earlier, Chremes and Demipho would still have been in possession of the girl and their money; later, and Phormio's intention to renounce Phanium would have been realized. This inversion of dramatic vectors, in which the two old men suddenly are made to swing round and contend for the girl they have just contrived to be rid of, may be taken as an image of a deeper reversal of roles on the thematic level. Because Demipho and Chremes are abetting a marriage for private rather than social reasons—reasons which they must conceal, for they have their source in a violation of the conjugal code—they are more in the position customarily occupied by the wayward young lover than that of the stern, old-fashioned paterfamilias. This reversal stands out most clearly when we see the play as a whole, projecting the argument of the second movement upon that of the first.

Let us look once at the characteristic paradigm of ancient new comedy; we have observed that, in the formal pattern of separation and union of lovers structuring virtually every play in the genre, the differentiating principle essentially lies in the nature of the obstacle, and further that this obstacle is best understood as a code of values or motives represented in the blocking character.

The opposition of the father, then, is normally predicated on the status rules of the city-state, and the recognition is designed to remove an apparent violation by bringing the woman into the community. In the ***Phormio,*** however, the discovery of Phanium's identity appears to have the reverse effect. In the first part of the play, where the central issue is class, the citizenship of the girl is not in doubt. But in the second part, when she is revealed as the illegitimate daughter of Chremes' Lemnian mistress, Phanium's civic status would seem most precarious. In real life, of course, her citizenship would be crucial, since she would, at Athens or at Rome, be ineligible for connubial rights as a foreigner. Commentators have therefore been concerned to explain away the contradiction. Thus, Bond and Walpole, in their note to line 114, where Phanium's nurse asserts her citizenship, remark: "The Lemnian mother must have been of genuine Athenian extraction: otherwise Phanium could only have been made legitimate by a vote of the citizens or by proclamation at the meeting of the *phratries.* The penalty for a false claim of citizenship was very heavy" [John Bond and Arthur Sumner Walpole, eds., *The Phormio of Terence,* 3d ed., 1964; orig. 1889]. This kind of solution, I believe, is beside the point. The character Phanium serves different functions in the two parts of the play. In the first, she must be a citizen, since her status is critical to Phormio's scheme of forcing her marriage to Antipho. In the second, where the focus is on Chremes' domestic difficulties, the technical point of citizenship can remain moot. The decision of the court in favor of Phormio's suit may of course be construed as internal evidence in support of Phanium's claims, but her foreign birth, the bigamous marriage of her parents, and the need to preserve secrecy concerning her identity all create an aura of illegitimacy which is both the dominant and relevant aspect for the later developments in the plot. Rather than attend too nicely, therefore, to the legal status of Phanium, we might better consider the implications of the shift in story paradigms from one in which her status is secure and significant to a second in which it is dubious and peripheral.

The plot of the ***Phormio*** advances from the conventional world of comedy, where order and authority are respected, even if in the breach, to a topsy-turvy situation in which everyone is involved in a transgression of the rules. The fathers had been perceived as defenders of the boundaries, but with the revelation of their true motives, the tension between impulse and custom which had informed the first movement gives way to a morally ambiguous opposition, where fathers and sons alike evade the social code and undermine its distinctions. Thus the recognition scene seems perverse: Instead of resolving the issue of class with which the ***Phormio*** began, it merely provides for the convergence of Antipho's and Demipho's private intentions. Since Demipho's reasons for desiring the marriage are if anything more scandalous than Antipho's, Phanium comes off the worse for the revelation of her identity.

That the play displaces rather than mends the violation of convention is thematically significant. In the archetypal story forms of ancient new comedy, the denouement normally accommodated apparent dislocations in the social structure by revealing that the actual state of affairs was as it should be. The principle was not unlike the Persian belief concerning parricide, according to the report of Herodotus: "They say that no one has ever killed his own father or mother, but that every time such things have happened, it is absolutely necessary that upon close examination they would be discovered to involve either supposititious or adulterous children. For they say that it is against reason that a true parent should die at the hands of his own child" (1.137). John K. Davies, in his article "Athenian Citizenship" [*Classical Journal* 73, 1977-78], analyzes this pattern in the plays of Menander:

> If one stands back from the wild complexities of Menandros' plots, they can be seen to share one primary characteristic—an intense, even obsessive awareness of the status boundaries separating citizen from foreigner, citizen from slave, well-born from low-born, legitimate from illegitimate, wife from concubine, wealthy man from poor man from beggar. Plot after plot is exploring this sensitive area and mediating a transition from one status to another— always, of course, in the fantasy, in an upwards direction. For example, the cardinal fact of *Heros* and *Epitrepontes* is that young man rapes girl, and they subsequently marry without knowing that the other was the person involved, while the children born of the rape are exposed. However, they then turn up, to cause embarrassments and suspicions till the heavy use of the *gnorismata* [i.e., recognitions] motif makes everything straightforward again between virtuous wife, mortified and repentant husband, and (after all) legitimate children. Or again the *Sikyonios,* where Stratophanes is in love with Philoumene but (a) he though rich is a Sikyonian and therefore a foreigner, and (b) she, though upperclass Athenian by origin, had been kidnapped and sold as a slave, and though Stratophanes knows her real status it will be hard to get it publicly recognized. Difficulty (a) disappears when it emerges that Stratophanes was 'really' an Athenian all the time: difficulty (b) vanishes when Stratophanes' parasite Theron tries to find someone to impersonate her father and just happens, as it were, to stumble upon the one man, Kichesias, who can perform that role without pretense. Since so much depends on citizenship, while for fifteen years of Menandros' adult lifetime Athens was powerless to determine her own citizenship criteria, his obsession with the theme is understandable: he was dealing with something of crucial contemporary importance. Of course, in his fantasies things come right in the end without the need for action and change, since the plots consist of discovering what is the case, which is what the participants want. In that sense Menandros is deeply escapist, since for the facts once discovered not to be as the participants want them to be would constitute a recipe for neurosis, tragedy, or revolution.

Clearly, the *Phormio* is a different kind of play. The transition of status is not upward but sideways at best. The characters get what they want, but not because they discover what is the case, for what is the case at the end is as incompatible with public norms as it was at the beginning. When Demipho and Chremes learn the identity of Phanium, they are as much at pains as before to keep her real position concealed.

The facts, however, do not remain a secret, since Phormio denounces the whole affair to Nausistrata, just when it seemed that the last loose end of the plot had been tied. Herbert Charles Elmer, in the introduction to his commentary on the play [*P. Terenti Phormio,* 1901], wonders about the reasons for this coda:

> To one feature of the play, critics may, perhaps, take exception. Why does not Phormio, after having sufficiently bantered the old men and compelled them, by threatening to tell Nausistrata of the secret marriage, to give up all claim to the money already paid him,—why does not Phormio content himself with this result? Why does he, by carrying out his threat, again set at stake what he has won? He must indeed have foreseen that he would not be able to carry out his plan without exposing the secret of Phaedria. The play might well have come to a rapid close after vs. 947, when all the complications had come to a happy termination.

To this question, which is plainly an important one for the theme since it touches on the action just where it exceeds the plot, Elmer offers the following series of responses:

> Still, it is quite in harmony with the bold, determined character of Phormio, that he improves the opportunity for the spirited scene which follows; and again the demands of justice, as it were, required that Chremes should be made to pay the penalty of his faithlessness and ill-becoming conduct. For Phaedria there was the prospect of winning his mother as an ally in his love-affair, and for Phormio that of becoming a permanent guest in the house of Chremes.

Elmer does not, however, seem altogether satisfied with his own explanation, for he adds: "Whatever may be said regarding this addition from an artistic point of view, it may at any rate be said that the play is thereby enriched by a very effective scene."

The exposure of Chremes and Demipho forecloses a hypocritical accommodation to public sentiment and obliges the characters to confront openly the improprieties related to Phanium's situation. Chremes and Demipho in other ways have betrayed a concern with appearances. Chremes, for example, was at pains earlier to make the repudiation of Phanium as seemly as possible, both by providing her a dowry and by assuaging her distress through the offices of Nausistrata. When Demipho protests against this officiousness, Chremes replies: "It is not enough to have done your duty if public opinion does not approve it; I want this to happen in accord with her own wishes too, so that she doesn't spread the word that she has been kicked out" (724-25). Later, when the brothers are trying to recover their money from Phormio, Demipho explains his change of heart about Phanium as a scruple for his reputation: "He [i.e. Chremes] convinced me not to give her to you. 'For what will people say,' he said, 'if you do it? Before, when it could have been done honorably, she wasn't given; to drive her out now is foul.' Pretty much the same things which you were accusing me of a while back to my face" (910-14). Demipho is being dishonest here of course, but the excuse reveals what he and his brother think of as a persuasive consideration. In the end, however, the strong-willed Demipho decides to face disclosure rather than endure the mockery of Phormio (955-56), and Chremes reluctantly follows suit.

For all her distress, Nausistrata will finally forgive her husband, in accord with the requirements of the genre. But before she grants her pardon, Phormio slips in a word about Phaedria's affair, and his need for thirty minae (1038-39). Chremes is taken aback, but Nausistrata turns on him at once: "Does it seem so wrong to you that your son, a young man, has one girlfriend, when you have two wives? Shameless! With what countenance will you rebuke him? Answer me!" (1040-42). Chremes meekly submits but Nausistrata goes further, putting the whole matter before the judgment of her son (1045-46); a moment later it is Phormio she elects as arbiter: "Phormio, from now on to the best of my ability I shall do and say whatever you want" (1050-51), and then, at his suggestion, she invites him in to dinner as a final insult to her husband. The play closes with the matron, the youth, and the parasite in command, while the two old men are humbled and obedient.

The *Phormio* began with a son in dread of his father; it ends with a father at the mercy of his son. This reversal mirrors the progression from the first movement of the play to the second, in which the fathers have lost their role as guarantors of social exclusiveness and restraints and are shown themselves to be transgressors. In the ancient city-state, adult propertied males constituted the citizen body. Normally, they are the repository of those values by which distinctions of status are maintained. The lapse in the moral authority of Demipho and Chremes produces a certain blurring of the boundaries, a relaxation in the conventional structures. The old men are obliged to be more tolerant once their own motives are publicly known to be compromised, while Nausistrata, Phaedria, and Phormio—all of them disfranchised in varying degrees—have less of a stake in preserving the traditional social codes. When Nausistrata learns that Chremes has changed his mind about evicting Phanium, though she does not yet know the reasons why, she remarks: "It's much better this way for everybody, I think, than what you started to do—that the girl should stay. For when I saw her, she seemed a thoroughly fine girl (*perliberalis*)" (814-15). Nausistrata judges by her sense of the person and is indifferent to considerations of class. Radical divisions of status are tempered by a spirit of humanity.

This spirit of humanity presides over the opening scenes of the play, where the slaves Geta and Davus are portrayed seriously and sensitively, and endowed with a generosity and good faith, despite their straitened circumstances, which put to shame the greed and casuistry of their masters. But the figure who best incarnates the challenge to the narrow exclusivism of the conservative city-state ideology is the parasite, Phormio himself. Many have acclaimed the subtlety and artistry of the characterization in the *Phormio,* and certainly the personality for whom Terence named the play is done with special brilliance and verve. Phormio is clever, bold, generous, loyal, independent, and ironic. He is, like many another of his métier in comedy, proud of his style of life (see especially lines 326-45). It is not that of a respectable citizen, and Phormio's social status is most dubious. Yet without question he is the hero of the comedy, in whose hands Antipho and Phaedria rest their fate. He manipulates each stage of the action successfully and in the end triumphs personally over Demipho and Chremes. His encouragement of love and disdain for conventional barriers suit perfectly his ambiguous station in society. Phormio's victory is also a victory for his point of view, that of a marginal person who is prepared to improvise with laws and customs in order to facilitate passionate, if not quite socially acceptable, unions. He is fixer, who bends the rules and softens the lines that define the social structure. Each time his work is vindicated: The fathers turn out to desire the marriage he has brought about, although for personal reasons of their own; Phaedria is indulged in his affair by a broad-minded mother and a crestfallen father. Phormio's invitation to dinner and elevation to arbiter of the household's destiny are the confirmation of his wisdom. With the inner dislocation of the old structure, the old men cede place to a new type: Phormio, rootless and humane, is at the moral center of gravity of his play and the society it represents.

THE BROTHERS

W. Ralph Johnson (essay date 1968)

SOURCE: "Micio and the Perils of Perfection," in *California Studies in Classical Antiquity,* Vol. 1, 1968, pp. 171-86.

[*In the following essay, Johnson delineates the defects in the character of Micio in* The Brothers, *flaws which prepare us for his fall at the play's conclusion.*]

In the manner of fine comedy, the *Adelphoe*'s initial snarl is extremely neat: irascible and rigid, Demea has allowed his brother, the affable and marvellously sane Micio, to adopt his elder son, Aeschinus; his young son, Ctesiphon, he keeps with him and rears with the strictness which alone, he feels, will ensure for the young man a life of virtue; Ctesiphon, of course, comes to pine for a music-girl, and Aeschinus, sophisticated, high-spirited, and ingenious by virtue of the liberal upbringing his adoptive father has given him, contrives to steal the girl from the pimp who possesses her and to hand her over to his brother. Throughout four acts of the comedy Micio skates with grand finesse on very thin ice, while Demea flounders from misunderstanding to absurdity to utter humiliation. But in the fifth act, having tactfully and patiently illumined the muddle which Aeschinus' generosity had brought about, Micio, all without warning, takes a pratfall, while Demea prances, grins and chortles.

This sudden reversal, the humiliation of Micio, has made not a few readers nervous. Why has this paradigm of classical humanism been subjected to wild mockery? Why is he given no final chance to defend himself? Has Terence botched his original? Or may we somehow ignore, somehow mitigate, the violence of the denouement? Or does the violence itself establish a satisfying and necessary equilibrium? I join those who find the violence and the final equilibrium it creates aesthetically and psychologically sound; in this paper I want to examine how the violence functions in the hope of defining the nature of this equilibrium. The *Adelphoe* is less concerned with two rival theories of education in conflict or with a confrontation between a gentleman and a boor than it is with two self-satisfied men who are made to collide in order that we may witness the universality of self-satisfaction and its inevitable frustrations. The smugness of Demea is abundantly clear from the moment he opens his mouth, but the smugness of Micio, the poised and gentle humanist, is far from evident and so requires careful probing and forceful revelation: the heart of the comedy is Micio's self-deceptions and self-contradictions.

That Micio's opening soliloquy is marked by immense charm and agreeable wisdom none would deny, yet for all its charm and wisdom there are indications of other aspects of Micio's mind and heart which want scrutiny here at the outset. From the comparisons which he draws between wives whose husbands tend not to come home at night and himself, anxious because Aeschinus has not returned from an evening of partying, it would appear that he has a fair opinion of himself, his sensitivity and his deep concern:

> profecto hoc vere dicunt: si absis uspiam
> aut ibi si cesses, evenire ea satius est
> quae in te uxor dicit et quae in animo cogitat
> irata quam illa quae parentes propitii.
> uxor, si cesses, aut te amare cogitat
> aut tete amari aut potare atque animo obsequi,
> et tibi bene esse soli, sibi quom sit male.
>
> (28-34)

The wives, then, are concerned only for themselves, but the bachelor father is concerned only for the well-being of his son:

> ego quia non rediit filius quae cogito!
> quibus nunc sollicitor rebus! ne aut ille alserit
> aut uspiam ceciderit aut praefregerit
> aliquid. vae, quemquamne hominem in animo
>   instituere aut
> parare quod sit carius quam ipse est sibi!
> atque ex me hic natus non est, sed ex fratre. . . .
>
> (35-40)

Though *vae, quemquamne hominem* defines the genuine concern of *quibus nunc sollicitor rebus,* it also defines the attitude which invites the bachelor father to imagine that his anxieties are unselfish, while the anxieties of real wives are not. For all his sensitivity, his real concern for and generosity to Aeschinus, Micio is rather self-centered, rather used not to having to be concerned for others (*carius quam ipse est sibi* will reappear at the climax of the play). He further reveals this predeliction which has become a lifetime's habit when he blurts out, almost as if taken by surprise, that Aeschinus is not his natural son, that his having taken on this (once) alien worry was a gratuitous (rather generous?) act.

It is this recollection of his brother which brings him composure. For a while he forgets his worries to meditate on the wide differences between his brother and himself (40ff), then passes from this comparison to his justly famous disquisition on humane child-rearing. Since most of what Micio says here is, as usual, admirable, I shall remark only on such passages as suggest that he says more than he is aware of saying. His initial comparison between Demea and himself is quite well-bred; only at *ego hanc clementem vitam urbanam atque otium* (42) and at *(ille) semper parce ac duriter* (45) do we hear tones of righteous superiority. There is no reason to doubt his statement of his deep love for Aeschinus (48-49), but his honest admission that he works hard to ensure that Aeschinus return his love (*ille ut item contra me habeat facio sedulo,* 50ff) yields gradually to meditations on the triumph of his own handling of Aeschinus and on the failures of other fathers in general and of Demea in particular; amid self-congratulations wherein his particular *liberalitas* seems to become universal law the significance of his self-interest, and indeed any awareness of it, gets lost.

> nam qui mentiri aut fallere insuerit patrem aut
> audebit, tanto magis audebit ceteros.
> pudore et liberalitate liberos
> retinere satius esse credo quam metu.
> haec fratri mecum non conveniunt neque placent.
>
> (55-59)

There is no question, of course, of Micio's describing Demea unfairly. The crabby, sour, hectoring speech which Micio imagines for Demea at 60-63 will soon be familiar enough to us; the parody is exact, and if Micio parodies Demea out of irritation with him, we can surely allow that Demea is very irritating. But Micio's great error lies in assuming that his *liberalitas* must necessarily have the overwhelming efficacy he imagines for it:

> ille quem beneficio adiungas ex animo facit,
> studet par referre, praesens absensque idem erit.
>
> (72-73)

Aeschinus is soon to prove him wrong on this point, and though he will complain of the way that Aeschinus behaves, he will not admit that he is wrong until the end of the play, where squeals and mutterings neatly betoken the guilt and the confession of this eloquent, unruffled spirit.

nimium ipse est durus praeter aequomque et
　　bonum;
et errat longe mea quidem sententia. . . .

(64-65)

The doctrine of Micio is, then, for the moment fool-proof; but as he cannot see the virtues of Demea, so he cannot see the defects of his own virtues, virtues on which he preens himself, completely unaware that he is doing so:

hoc patriumst, potius consuefacere filium
sua sponte recte facere quam alieno metu:
hoc pater ac dominus interest. hoc qui nequit,
fateatur nescire imperare liberis.

(74-77)

Fateatur nescire? It is a ruthless judgment and for so accomplished a humanist rather a narrow one. In a short while Micio will be wanting to recant what he has just said, and the fine irony of these verses flares just at the moment when Demea makes his entrance. Demea enters not knowing that he is about to spend hours of weari-ness, ridicule, and anguish, and he now blusters for all he's worth. For the moment, then, the gracious and witty Micio can give a wry smile, lift a suave eyebrow and say: *credo iam, ut solet, iurgabit* (79-80)—for a little while, but not for long.

We have been prepared for Demea's entrance (and to some extent prejudiced against him) by Micio's descrip-tion of him; for the first four acts we see Demea mainly through Micio's eyes, for not only do we accept Micio's initial evaluation of his brother's character, but as we watch Micio exacerbate Demea's worst traits (thereby displaying his own best traits to their best advantage) we come to adopt Micio's attitude to his brother. Indeed, the wrath of Demea increases in proportion as his broth-er's patience, tolerance, and genial resourcefulness in-crease. The wrath is comic, of course, by virtue of De-mea's wildly excessive responses to what he misunder-stands, his unfailing capacity for being victimized, his strength, discipline and purpose mocked and foiled at every turn—there is in this a brilliant handling of a great comic motif: tremendous energy and determination squan-dered on hopeless and trivial obstacles, the fight to get out of the paper bag. Yet towards the end of the comedy, at the very climax of this comic wrath, after a quick poignant moment of grief, his rage, though remaining comic, is changed to extravagant cunning, and it is the turn of patient benevolence to be mocked:

derides? fortunatu's qui isto animo sies.
ego . . .

(852-853)

For what I have to say about the nature of the three encounters between Micio and Demea, I had best begin with the implications of *derides*. (First Confrontation, 1.2, 82ff, where Demea, having heard of Aeschinus and the music-girl, comes to rebuke Micio; Second Confron-tation, IV, 7, 719ff, where Demea returns to rebuke his brother, this time because he has heard that Aeschinus

has seduced Pamphila, and is aghast to hear Micio—who is being rather naughty here, since he amuses himself by not telling all that he might at this point—blandly dis-cussing preparations for the wedding; Third Confronta-tion, V.3, 787ff, where Demea vents his rage, having at last learned the truth about Ctesiphon and the music-girl.) The debonair gentleman, having got a wife for his adoptive son and a concubine for his nephew, allows himself a coarse joke at the expense of his baffled, angry brother (third confrontation). What is to be done with Ctesiphon's girl? Take her out to the farm and make her perform menial chores? Micio lends his support to these suggestions with heavy irony:

nunc mihi videre sapere. atque equidem filium
　　placet:
tum etiam si nolit cogam ut cum illa una cubet.

(849-851)

Never, of course, does Micio descend to the sheer cru-dity of Syrus, but it is worth noticing that he can ridicule Demea rather mercilessly as well as read him lectures. The lectures, like the ridicule, issue from an amour-pro-pre, a belief in his moral and intellectual superiority over Demea which nothing in his life has shaken, which noth-ing in his life will shake, until Demea parodies that su-periority with grand wit and so trims his younger brother down to his proper size.

It is true that Demea lectures Micio on every possible occasion, that his lectures are funny and irritating (funny because irritating) even as his rage and self-pity are fun-ny and irritating. But the wounds he gives are clean, and for all his energy and bluster he is not merely narrow-minded and tough but rather desperate and rather lonely as well. We should expect much more of the self-assured Micio; but with a habit of patronizing and a smugness which has its roots in real arrogance he combines cal-lousness and something very close to sophistry:

homine imperito numquam quicquam iniustiust,
qui nisi quod ipse fecit nil rectum putat.

(98-99)

　　et tu illum tuom, si esses homo,
sineres nunc facere, dum aetatem licet,
potius quam, ubi te expectatum eiecesset foras,
alienore aetate post faceret tamen.

(107-110)

natura tu illi pater es, consiliis ego.

(125)

tamen vix humane patitur; verum si augeam
aut etiam adiutor sim eius iracundiae,
insaniam profecto cum illo.

(145-147)

DE. quid facias? si non ipsa re tibi istuc dolet,
simulare certe est hominis. MI. quin iam virginem
despondi; res compositast; fiunt nuptiae;
dempsi metum omnem: haec magis sunt hominis.

(736-741)

DE. ceterum
placet tibi factum, Micio? MI. non, si queam
mutare. nunc quom non queo, animo aequo fero.
ita vitast hominum quasi quom ludas tesseris:
si illud quod maxime opus est iactu non cadit,
illud quod cedidit forte, id arte ut corrigas.

(736-741)

multa in homine, Demea,
signa insunt ex quibus coniectura facile fit,
duo quom idem faciunt, saepe ut possis dicere
'hoc licet impune facere huic, illi non licet',
non quo dissimilis res sit sed quo is qui facit.

(821-825)

In the first five of these passages (from the first and
second confrontations) Demea is *imperitus* and *insanus,*
and Micio is the champion of *humanitas,* self-assured,
infallible (*si esses homo, vix humane, haec magis sunt
hominis*). In the sixth passage (second confrontation) and
in the seventh (third confrontation) Mico begins to make
excuses, but there is not the least admission of error. *Id
arte ut corrigas*? Here, as always, Micio's theory is unquestionably attractive, for we need to be reminded of
making do, easy go, muddling through, *je me débrouille.*
And yet—how much sloth and irresponsibility and self-
indulgence does this wisdom labor to excuse? So, in the
final passage, the notion is beautiful, and one of the
glories of humanism is its insistence that we consider the
individual, refuse moralities that cannot allow for discriminations; but, again, there lurks here a lazy relativ-
ism which derides (and has no business deriding) another great moral truth: that human beings have to work
very hard merely to become decent and to stay barely
decent. The virtues of Micio, then, exclude the virtues of
Demea utterly, and that is their ruin. But Micio is as
graceful as Demea is clumsy, and for the moment the
ruin is not apparent, and the self-satisfaction which ensures the ruin continues blithely as before. Micio has
some genial remarks to offer his brother on the natural
goodness of some individuals (natural gentlemen of Micio's stamp?) and on the dangers of stinginess in old age
(831ff), but his suavest barb and his crowning sophistry
come when he answers Demea's charge (799ff) that Micio
has interfered with Ctesiphon after having himself suggested that each father tend to his own son (129ff):

nam vetus verbum hoc quidemst,
communia esse amicorum inter se omnia.

(803-804)

In listing the defects of Micio's virtues, I am aware that
it is not fair to snatch them from context, but I can only
hope to dispel Micio's charm by bunching his defects
together in such a way that the seductiveness cannot force
us to mitigate or ignore those defects. Nor would I wish
to pretend that these remarks are unprovoked (it would
be impossible to forget that Demea is also smug, and
rasping in the bargain). What I am concerned to show is
that Micio, for all his equability, can be provoked by
Demea (even as he can provoke Demea), that what Demea succeeds in eliciting from Micio falls far short of
what Micio's own notion of his *humanitas* leads us to
expect from him. If the vitality of Demea and the good
sense of Micio combine to center our attention on the
flaws in Demea's character it is perhaps worth suggesting that our reverence for *liberalitas* and *humanitas* blinds
us to the defects of Micio.

Since we have here to do with a carefully imagined representation of a human being, we ought not to be surprised if his virtues are in large measure connected with
and even dependent on his vices; nor should we fail to
wonder whether playrights who spend their time leafing
through philosophers might be thought to have a poor
understanding of what playwrighting is. Micio is really
generous and really devoted to making and keeping peace?
Yes, but to what extent does this trait arise from a temperament which is essentially lazy and squeamish about
"scenes," the easy way out? To what extent does his
benevolence have its origins in hunger for approval and
delight in controlling others by ensuring their gratitude
and their dependence? Finally, then, to what extent is
this delightful humanist ignorant of his self-contradictions? I feel that it is precisely the disparity between his
ignorance and his smugness on the one hand and his
wisdom and tolerance on the other that will make him at
the end of the play a brilliant and significant figure, and
it is precisely the unexpected reversal, the abruptness
and poetic justice with which his ignorance and self-
contradictions are revealed, which provide the play with
its verve and intellectual sting.

The brothers' third confrontation ends with the triumph
of Micio, and I now turn to Demea in total defeat. Exhausted from running fool's errands, enraged, humiliated, confused, wholly bitter, this whirlwind of bluster and
scorn now sinks down (or so it might be staged) and tries
to understand what has happened to him. His difficulty
and his success in this regard are more interesting than
they are often thought to be. He is not, on the one hand,
suddenly transfigured, nor is it a question of his naively
supposing that, if only he can manage to ape his brother's *Lebensart,* he can trick his sons into loving him. The
opening verses of his soliloquy (855-861) are to be delivered neither pensively (all passion spent, his mind made
up, his personality transformed) nor shrilly; he is thinking, he is upset—there are pauses, changes of mood,
tempo: a living voice.

numquam ita quisquam bene subducta ratione ad
  vitam fuit

quin res, aetas, usus semper aliquid adportet novi,
aliquid moneat: ut illa quae te scisse credas nescias,
et quae tibi putaris prima, in experiundo ut
  repudies.
quod nunc mi evenit; nam ego vitam duram, quam
  vixi usque adhuc,

prope iam excurso spatio omitto. id quam ob rem?
  re ipsa repperi

facilitate nil esse homini melius neque clementia.

What seems to him now the complete reversal of his beliefs, of his very existence, forces him to utter what tragic choruses had been saying for centuries, but from Demea this is not mellow gnomic wisdom; he has been shocked, and he is shocked into bitter irony: *ego vitam duram,* like *facilitate nil esse melius,* expresses terrible self-pity and savage envy. *Omitto?* Does he mean that he will change his way of life? The closing scenes of the play argue against this interpretation as does the bitter reprise of Micio's self-satisfied *ego hanc clementem vitam* (40ff). With *omitto* he does not announce the necessity for (much less the possibility of) changing his life; rather he admits that his life seems suddenly ugly and hopeless, and he himself a failure. *Omitto* is an angry cry of despair, for he sees himself now as Micio and the others see him, though he does not, as the denouement shows, in any way agree with their estimate. But what is more important, he sees Micio as *he* is:

> ille suam egit semper vitam in otio, in conviviis,
> clemens, placidus, nulli laedere os, adridere
>   omnibus;
> sibi vixit, sibi sumptum fecit; omnes bene dicunt,
>   amant.
> ego ille agrestis, saevos, tristis, parcus, truculentus,
>   tenax . . .
>
>   (863-866)

These verses express not self-hate but indignation (what has happened is not fair) and jealousy, and from this combination comes the insight he needs: *sibi vixit! (carius quam ipse est sibi,* 39). He who gives himself to no one may give himself to everyone, and that without cost. Micio's secret is that he is not responsible to or for anyone or anything, he is carefree, *papillon de Parnasse.* The butterfly, then, is adored by one and all, while *paterfamilias* and his paraphernalia are swept to oblivion (*duxi uxorem: quam ibi miseriam vidi! nati filii! / alia cura,* 867-868). A calm philosophical speech that issues in humility and repentance? Here the wrath of Demea hits its stride:

> heia autem, dum studeo illis ut quam plurimum
> facerem, contrivi in quaerundo vitam atque aetatem
>   meam:
>
> nunc exacta aetate hoc fructi pro labore ab eis fero,
> odium: ille alter sine labore patria potitur
>   commoda.
> illum amant, me fugitant; illi credunt consilia
>   omnia,
> illum diligunt, apud illum sunt ambo, ego desertus
>   sum;
> illum ut vivat optant, meam autem mortem expectant
>   scilicet.
>
>   (868-874)

Each *illum* strikes like a hatchet. He is hated and he hates. Rage begets understanding, and it is the climax of the play:

> ita eos meo labore eductos maxumo hic fecit suos
> paulo sumptu: miseriam omnem ego capio, hic
>   potitur gaudia.

He is still concerned with money, to be sure, but beyond that far he is very jealous and very angry. Why should he not be? *Paulo sumptu sibi vixit.* Then a long and fiendish pause, and then, rather slowly, smiling like an Elizabethan villain:

> age age nunciam experiamur contra, acquid ego
>   possiem
> blande dicere aut benigne facere, quando hoc
>   provocat . . .

It is a Revenge Comedy.

The plot, of course, seems taken care of by this point in the play, and everyone (or so it seems) but Demea is happy. But Demea surprises us by securing the happiness of Sostrata, Hegio, Syrus and his wife, and in so doing manages to secure his revenge as well. In the closing scenes of the play, as in the soliloquy which sets them in motion, reprise yields deft and stinging ironies. Demea parodies the *liberalitas* and the *humanitas* of Micio to expose their limitations and preconceptions, and by this parody he takes his revenge, altering Micio's life radically by an ingenious application of Micio's methods to Micio.

At 909-910 (*unam fac domum*; / *traduce et matrem et familiam omnem ad nos*) and at 925-927,

> ego vero iubeo et hac re et aliis omnibus
> quam maxume unam facere nos hanc familiam,
> colere, adiuvare, adiungere . . . ,

there seems to me a witty echo of Micio's joke at 746-748:

>   DE. pro divom fidem,
> meretrix et mater familias una in domo!
> MI. quor non? DE. sanum te credis esse? MI.
>   equidem arbitror.

The bachelor father, who had managed to avoid the responsibilities and annoyances of total domesticity and had therefore been able to joke about large households, a prostitute, a matron and two old gentlemen keeping high holiday in a *ménage à quatre,* suddenly sees the walls that create his solitude and independence totter and fall. *Unam fac domum*: "only connect"—a lovely humanistic idea. But the wise, detached gentleman who had viewed the busy lives of others with amused tolerance is now being swept from the decorous periphery of life into its frenzied center. No sooner has his calm establishment more than tripled itself than he is urged to marry Sostrata. The poise and good humor are strained to the breaking point, break, and we may now speak of the wrath of Micio. Having thus transformed the tranquil philosopher to a petulant bourgeois, Demea quite logically proceeds to tamper with his pocketbook. He who did not *have* to support anyone and could therefore use and abuse his money as he chose is now treated to an exquisite reprise of his last piece of advice. At 832ff Micio had hinted that Demea was stingy and had counselled generosity and a wise unconcern for wealth. The free spirit now sputters as he sinks from easy detachment into human bondage. Hegio, Micio's new relation by marriage, is not very well off, and Demea can quote scripture:

> postremo nunc meum illud verbum facio quod tu, Micio,
> bene et sapienter dixti dudum: 'vitium commune omniumst,
> quod nimium ad rem in senecta attenti sumus': hanc maculam nos de
> cet
> ecfugere; et dictumst vere et reapse fieri oportet.
>
> (952-955)

Wives chattering and scolding, children shrieking, the strange sudden appearance of impecunious relations on the wife's side, china clattering, hungry mouths everywhere, money fluttering away, irritations, near despair: the abyss yawns. Where now are equability, inexhaustible patience, scrupulous impartiality? These luxuries are doomed when Micio becomes a part of humanity (at least, humanity as Demea understands it, and he understands it tolerably well), and here the irony of Demea is superb. When Micio concedes to Demea's demands for Hegio, Demea's reprise of Micio's distinction between kinship by blood and kinship by mind and spirit (126) is flawless:

> nunc tu mihi es germanus frater pariter animo et corpore.
> suo sibi gladio hunc iugulo.
>
> (957-958)

But the manumission of Syrus and his wife is Demea's finest irony. The license of Syrus represents *liberalitas* gone mad, and Syrus, even more than Aeschinus, represents the potential dangers of *liberalitas*. Thus when Demea pleads for Syrus' freedom,

> postremo hodie in psaltria ista emunda hic adiutor fuit,
> hic curavit: prodesse aequomst: alii meliores erunt,

he echoes the indiscriminate tolerance which Micio had propounded:

> ille quem beneficio adiungas ex animo facit,
> studet par referre, praesens absensque idem erit.

Aeschinus hardly lived up to his father's hopes; Syrus overturned them. So Demea: "This man fleeced you of money for the whore; naturally when the other slaves observe how you reward industry and initiative, they'll do their damndest to improve on their model."

When the last shot has been fired, Micio cannot restrain himself:

> quid istuc? quae res tam repente mores mutavit tuos?
> quod prolubium? quae istaec subitast largitas?

Demea's answer,

> ut id ostenderem, quod te isti facilem et festivom putant,
> id non fieri ex vera vita neque adeo ex aequo et bono,
> sed ex adsentando, indulgendo et largiendo, Micio,

is not entirely honest, but Micio's question is not quite precise. Demea has not changed his habits, he has ridiculed Micio's; he has done this not so much to show his sons the truth of the matter as to give Micio a taste of his own medicine, to expose his weaknesses to everyone and so humiliate him as he himself had been humiliated. Demea has not changed (nor, probably, will Micio), but he has glimpsed the essential limitations of his personality (as, probably, has Micio; as, perhaps, have we—that is the point): comedy can do no more.

Hodie modo hilarum fac te. Demea has joyfully taken this advice and so become *pater festivissimus*, and the boisterous ingenuity of his revenge, for all its origins in anger and resentment, yields to a gracious close: Micio's *istuc recte* is at once praise for his brother's virtues and a vindication of his own, for the varieties of arrogance have now been exorcised, and, after a ruthless winnowing, the great virtues of parenthood, firmness and tenderness, are reasserted as grand unity.

For all its emphasis on what is worst in us the play is not ugly. Both heroes are arrogant, lively, and inadequate; neither knows what he is or what he is up against: that is comic enough and human enough. The play's major theme could be the paradox of liberal smugness (its major theme can hardly be the vice of conservative smugness), but the play is not so shaped. It is not a question of Demea's being (finally) right and of Micio's being (finally) wrong, nor is it really a question of both men having some right on their side or of both men having some wrong on their side: both men are victims of their illusions and of the limitations those illusions impose on them.

I would prefer to say that the play is about the illusions of fatherhood, or, more precisely, about the arrogance of adults. Experience and maturity? To be sure. But to believe in one's own seasoned infallibility and to inflict that belief on other human beings is probably never very safe, and it may be that experience and maturity are among our most dangerous illusions; add pure *liberalitas* to such fancies and the dangers are past counting. And here, I think, is the reason for the play's sudden shift in point of view and for its peculiar shape. It is easy enough to demonstrate that Demea is more smug than is good for him, and few of us would wish to be like Demea in any case; but Micio, as Webster and Norwood make all too clear, represents a persistent and somewhat treacherous cultural ideal, and to demonstrate his weakness the play-wright must catch us off our guard, as pleased with our-selves (for we too are convinced that Demea is neither very bright nor very nice) as Micio is with himself. Lulled to a rapture of self-esteem by the familiar pageant of humanism's irresistible triumph, we are suddenly smacked in the face with the truth about the limitations of our favorite *paideia* and about our own chances for perfec-tion. Whether we are Micios by temperament or Demeas by temperament, we need to be reminded that our predi-lections do not constitute eternal law, that few of us will be very close to the ideals we profess. Whether Micios or Demeas, we need all to be reminded how ignorant, droll, and selfish we are. In its universal chastening the *Adelphoe* is a triumph of moral dialectic and of mirth.

Nathan A. Greenberg (essay date 1979-80)

SOURCE: "Success and Failure in the *Adelphoe*," in *The Classical World*, Vol. 73, No. 4, December, 1979-Janu-ary, 1980, pp. 221-36.

[*In the essay below, Greenberg compares the parenting theories of Micio and Demea in* The Brothers.]

The *Adelphoe* of Terence presents an uncomfortable amalgam of the serious and the comic. In one of the most startling comic reversals in ancient comedy, the elder, sterner brother, Demea, achieves a final farcical triumph which is in strong and jarring contrast with the seemingly serious and approving treatment of Micio and Micio's theories on child raising throughout the preced-ing bulk of the play, This contrast has caused such crit-ical discomfort for so long a time that any attempt to explain or soothe it away seems doomed to failure. The issue is further complicated by attempts to connect Ter-ence with his lost originals in Greek New Comedy. In what follows, we shall largely ignore the question of Terence's treatment of Menander and concentrate upon some critical issues present in the play we actually pos-sess.

Any critical reading of the play must somehow come to terms with the final triumph of Demea, and it may well be that no amount of pleading will ease the discomfort felt by all readers as the play abruptly shifts from "high comedy" to "farce." Rather, we shall attempt to show that the discomfort felt is consonant with an important thematic strand of the play. Further, we find it difficult to escape the notion that Demea's victory is meant to be the climax of a kind of joke. If it is the case that we are dealing with a joke of large dimension, then certain crit-ical corollaries follow concerning the nature of comic surprise and suspense. Despite the apparently serious discussion in the play of various modes of child raising, the hypothesis that we are dealing with an essentially comic structure will explain how we are called upon in paradoxical fashion to take and not take these matters seriously. Such theatrical double-think is not really sur-prising or unusual. Given the comic structure of the play, it is perfectly possible and perhaps inevitable that we seriously accept one set of rational and thoughtful mo-tives, while simultaneously some lower inner self em-braces with gleeful malice a radically opposed and de-structive set of views.

There is a long history of reading the *Adelphoe* as a contest between Micio and Demea and their respective theories of child raising or, to be more precise, the prop-er parental management of youths old enough to pursue members of the opposite sex. In this long history, there has been, perhaps understandably, a tendency to associ-ate the fate of the *senes* with an evaluation of the theo-ries they espouse. Critics who approve of Micio's per-missiveness are hard put to explain why Terence has brought about his final defeat, and they tend to be the ones who speculate on how and why Terence has devi-ated from his Menandrian original. Other critics, less impressed by the excellence of Micio's theory, are more intent on finding weaknesses in Micio's character which render him a morally acceptable butt for the comic finale of the play. It will help to consider the success or failure of the theories apart from the fate of the characters who espouse them.

One reasonable way of assessing the relative merits of the competing theories in the play is to look at their results. Aeschinus, the product of Micio's theory, is clear-ly superior to Ctesipho. Even Norwood, who [in *The Art of Terence*, 1923] called Aeschinus an "insolent, fastid-ious, elegant bully," also described Ctesipho as "secre-tive, weak, timid, hysterical, and self-indulgent," and we may gingerly conclude that even here Aeschinus is placed at a higher level of estimation. If the play is to be viewed seriously as a contest between competing theories most would admit that Micio has won, and we would conclude simply: the better theory produces the better son. This would seem to settle the matter, but in fact the general verdict has been rather different, a general verdict which has been sanely expressed by Duckworth [in *The Nature of Roman Comedy*, 1952]:

> Neither system is successful, as Demea proves when he gives up his severity and reveals by a *reductio ad absurdum* how Micio's character has been undermined by his own leniency. Neither Aeschinus nor Ctesipho lived up to his father's expectations. Terence favors neither extreme but a compromise that involves a reasonable amount of restraint and advice (cf. 992 ff.). If the scales seem tipped in favor of discipline, we should recall that throughout most of the comedy Micio is presented far more sympathetically than Demea, and also that Aeschinus proves to be a far more attractive and upright youth than Ctesipho; his regret for his misdeeds and his love and respect for his adoptive father (cf. 681 ff., 707 ff.) indicate that Micio's system (as outlined in 69 ff.) was, in spite of its disadvantages, preferable to Demea's harshness.

The above passage is marred by the usual uneasiness. Both fathers have failed, but Micio has not failed quite so badly. Demea's final triumph simply balances Micio's ascendancy throughout the bulk of the play, and Terence has Demea sponsor a final compromise superior to either theory.

What constitutes success or failure within this context? Agreement as to whether or not a failure has occurred must depend upon some prior agreement concerning goals and standards of social behavior, and we know that such standards are not always stated either explicitly or sincerely. Without belaboring this point, it is not obvious that Micio's theory (or, for that matter, Demea's theory) has failed. Indeed, Micio argues, perhaps speciously, that both methods have succeeded (826-829), and we do not have any difficulty in imagining that Aeschinus and Ctesipho will both turn out to be quite acceptable members of their society.

Even if the idea of failure is rejected, however, we surely recognize differing degrees of success, and it is on this basis, perhaps, that one may hold that while Aeschinus is better than Ctesipho, he is not as good as he could conceivably be nor as good as Micio would like him to be. But such expectations are excessive and insincere, for the perfectly well-behaved young paragon of conventional virtue can and will be castigated for lack of spirit or initiative, while his opposite will be condemned for the lack of that same conventional virtue. To be sure, these are not symmetrically opposed situations. Rather, the criticism aimed at the conventionally well-behaved youth will be of a more covert sort, and we are in the realm of social hypocrisy. It is not new to realize that parents do not and perhaps should not always say exactly what they mean. The theme of social or parental hypocrisy is explicitly recognized in the **Adelphoe**:

> si non ipsa re tibi istuc dolet,
> simulare certe est hominis.
>
> (733-734)

Why, if you are really not put out at this, at any rate it would be your duty to pretend that you are.

It is not unlike the situation in which a parent chastises a child for some misdeed while, at the same time, admiring and approving the aggressive or venturesome aspects of the socially unsanctioned act. It is clear that Aeschinus' youthful misdeeds have been of this sort, the sort which societies and parents condemn on the surface, but which are tacitly condoned and welcomed as evidences of youthful (and perhaps aristocratic) vigor and spirit. Given the conventions of Roman comedy, it is difficult to imagine an *adulescens* who is more praiseworthy than Aeschinus.

The above considerations apply to the one important instance where it may be alleged that Micio's theory has failed:

> postremo, alii clanculum
> patres quae faciunt, quae fert adulescentia,
> ea ne me celet consuefeci filium.
>
> (52-54)

In short, I have accustomed my son not to conceal from me those little extravagances natural to youth, which others are at so much pains to hide from their parents.

It seems clear that by not telling Micio about his love affair, Aeschinus has not complied with the standard of behavior enunciated. But there are other considerations. It is most important to note that in the world of Roman comedy, as the above citation shows, sons ordinarily do not tell their fathers everything. Nor is this an observation confined to the stage. Fathers and sons cannot escape the history of their relationship. The father represents authority, and he is a source of chastisement and correction in a way that a friend is not. Such chastisement need not take the form of blatantly physical punishment, and it can be peculiarly oppressive in that the punished son is called upon to acknowledge that it has all been for his own good. Small wonder then that shame and guilt enter and complicate the relationship. Besides, there are areas, particularly in the realm of sexual behavior, where a degree of reticence is positively, if tacitly, encouraged. Does any father really expect or want his son to tell him everything? Once the son has reached a sufficient level of development, excessive paternal interest in the details of sexual activity is viewed with disapproval, although there may be differences of opinion as to what constitutes an excessive interest. As a result of considerations like these, Micio's desire for openness from his adoptive son arouses some discomfort. In palliation, it can be held that Micio has proposed his openness as a matter of subsidiary importance to what seems rather to be the focal point of his theory:

> hoc patriumst, potius consuefacere filium
> sua sponte recte facere quam alieno metu:
>
> (74-75)

This indeed is the part of a father, to accustom his son to do what is right, more from his own choice than any fear of another.

The development of ethical autonomy is the primary goal, as Micio realizes. Even in the scene of confrontation when Micio taxes Aeschinus with his misbehavior, it is not the breakdown in communication to which Micio objects, but Aeschinus' failure to fulfill his responsibilities. It is only in an aside that Micio first refers to the matter of openness:

> tacet. quor non ludo hunc aliquantisper; melius est,
> quandoquidem hoc numquam mihi ipse uoluit
>   credere.
>
> (639-640)

He doesn't answer. Why shouldn't I play with him for a while? It's right, seeing that he never chose to tell me anything about this.

It is important to note that this is an aside and that the lack of openness does not constitute in and of itself the subject of a reproof addressed directly to Aeschinus. It is only after another fifty verses that Micio speaks directly to Aeschinus on the subject:

> si te mi ipsum puduit proloqui,
> qua rescicerem?
>
> (690-691)

If you were ashamed to confess to me yourself, how was I to find out?

Here the main point is that openness would have enabled Micio to help Aeschinus discharge his obligations. So much then for openness as a primary goal. The overemphasis by critics on openness and frankness approaches a confusion of means with ends, and is largely due to their desire to show that both Demea and Micio have failed in a pleasingly balanced fashion.

In addition, there is a sense in which Aeschinus' failure to communicate is witness to the success of Micio as a father. Affection, generosity, and permissiveness are not the sole ingredients of Micio's theory:

> pudore et liberalitate liberos
> retinere satius esse credo quam metu.
>
> (57-58)

I believe it is better to influence children through modesty and generosity than through fear.

We have already quoted 690 where reference to *pudor* is also made. The other famous passage is:

> erubuit: salua res est.
> He blushes; all is well.
>
> (643)

Micio here reassures himself that *pudor* is still having its effect upon Aeschinus and he appears to take Aeschinus' blush as a sign of success rather than failure. We have already noted the role of shame and guilt in the relationship of father and son. From that point of view, Micio's success in instilling *pudor* in Aeschinus is a measure of his success in taking on the role of father. But it is also clear that *pudor* is not compatible with complete openness. A young man will tell his friend things which he is ashamed to tell his father.

In summary, the proper test of Micio's theory is not whether Aeschinus confides in him, but whether or not Aeschinus is behaving as he should. He does blush, but not because he has shunned his responsibilities. The case of Aeschinus is largely that of a normally energetic upperclass youth in a Roman comedy who has been caught out by circumstance. Like any normal, spirited *adulescens,* Aeschinus has been carrying on:

> quam hic non amauit meretricem? aut quoi non
>   dedit
> aliquid? postremo nuper (credo iam omnium
> taedebat) dixit uelle uxorem ducere.

sperabam iam deferuisse adulescentiam:
gaudebam. ecce autem de integro!

> (149-153)

What courtesan is there in all Athens whom he has not been in love with, or to whom he has not made a present? Last of all, the other day, sick of them all, I believe, he said that he should like to marry. I hoped that he had sown his wild oats, and was glad of it; now, behold he has begun afresh.

As this passage shows explicitly, Aeschinus had begun to lay the groundwork for revealing his serious love affair to Micio. There is no reason to believe that he had been particularly reticent about his previous affairs. Presumably, he picked what he considered the right moment to mention them. Just so, it is fair to conclude that he would have had matters under reasonable control here. But in the interim he has felt obliged to respond nobly to his brother's need for action and for secrecy (283, 623). Micio cannot know this and hence experiences a feeling of disappointment (147-153) which is not justified by the facts. The alternative would be an Aeschinus who came running to Micio for help and direction at every turn. Would this be a more admirable Aeschinus?

To be sure, Aeschinus has seduced a young lady, and this is not quite proper even in Roman comedy, but there is a sense in which it is acceptable. Demea, of course, expresses the proper degree of dismay when he hears of the affair (468), but Hegio, who may be better taken as an interested bystander expressing the conventional view of society in a Roman comedy, condones it (*humdnumst,* 471) especially since Aeschinus has manfully shouldered the responsibility of promising marriage. The marriage is to take place after the birth of the child, since it is Aeschinus' plan to win parental permission by setting the child in his father's lap:

> qui se'in sui gremio positurum puerum dicebat
>   patris,
> ita obsecraturun ut liceret hanc sibi uxorem
>   ducere?
>
> (333-334)

And he promised he would put the baby in its grandfather's arms and beg the old man's leave to marry her!

Hegio is disturbed only because Aeschinus seems to have broken his promise. But of course he has not. His plans have gone awry because of an emergency. He has had to act quickly and without explanation to those deserving one, i.e., Pamphila and her family. When we see him, he is on his way to give them that explanation at the first available opportunity (632). It is unfortunate that Pamphila's family has already heard and, as Aeschinus notes, justifiably misinterpreted the news. It is at this point that Aeschinus ruefully notes:

> haec adeo mea culpa fateor fieri: non me hanc rem
>   patri,

utut erat gesta, indicasse! exorassem ut eam
  ducerem.

(629-630)

I admit that I was wrong in that matter, not to have
told my father the whole story of my love, and wrung
permission from him to marry her.

Let us now subject Aeschinus' behavior to a degree of
analysis not to be imputed to the character himself. The
strategies smacking of cold calculation which follow are
the result of the analytical process; Aeschinus surely picks
his course of action in a more passionate fashion. Within
the conventions of Roman comedy, it is Aeschinus' duty
to ensure as best he can that his marriage with Pamphila
will take place. He has chosen to bring this about by
dropping small hints to Micio about his intention to marry
but otherwise keeping his affair with Pamphila secret.
The plan is to present Micio with a grandson, a *fait
accompli,* and thus overcome the usual father's objection
to a dowerless marriage. The strategic reason for not
telling Micio sooner is that this increases the risk that
Micio will somehow prevent the marriage. Note that such
prevention need not consist of a stern prohibition; it is
also conceivable that Micio's good sense and affection
may persuade Aeschinus not to marry, and this too is an
eventuality which is to be avoided. Of course, the plan
is also attractive because it allows Aeschinus to post-
pone discussion of a matter about which he feels shame.
But the plan is not without cost. It entails keeping Micio
in the dark, in effect deceiving him, but there is no help
for that. It would be unmanly for Aeschinus to do any
less. The other shortcoming of the plan is that it requires
a long period of time within which all sorts of untoward
events may occur, and this, of course, is what has happened. As Aeschinus realizes, his strategy has resulted in
unforeseen anguish for all concerned. He now believes
that a second strategy would have been better wherein he
would have begged Micio much earlier for permission to
marry. That plan would have avoided the need to keep
Micio in the dark and the risk of unforeseen events occurring in the interim, but it would have increased the
risk that Micio might somehow prevent the marriage.
This second strategy, however, is no longer available
and Aeschinus, the noble *adulescens,* is committed to
carrying out as best he can whatever shambles of his
original plan remains. The obvious third course of confessing to Micio now does not occur to him. He is over-
wrought, intent on explaining himself to Pamphila, and
Micio catches him unawares. He could be forgiven for
not thinking of this third course at this point in the plot.
But it is also possible to argue that this course would be
inferior to either of the first two since it would mean
confessing to a Micio now angered at not being informed
earlier and still with some opportunity to forestall the
marriage. So Aeschinus cling to the original plan, although he is now forced into an active lie instead of the
lengthy evasion which was his original intention. Merci-
fully, Micio does not allow Aeschinus to show to what
lengths of deceit his love for Pamphila and his sense of
honor would have driven him.

At this stage, then, we see an Aeschinus manfully prepared to deceive Micio, but it is also clear that he is not
going to be very good at it. He blushes. Both his determination and his incapacity are meant to win our approval. The bond of affection forged between these two is
too strong to allow either to persist in active deception
of the other. Micio's theory has been eminently successful, and it may now be set aside as we move to consider
Micio himself.

While Micio's theory does not fail, it is clear that he
himself experiences disappointment in the play, and we
may well suspect that Micio values frankness and openness from Aeschinus more than his theory demands. Even
though he realizes that ethical autonomy is the primary
goal, there are the revealing passages in the aside at 639-
640 and the following:

in eo me oblecto, solum id est carum mihi.
ille ut item contra me habeat facio sedulo;
do, praetermitto, non necesse habeo omnia
pro meo iure agere;

(49-52)

He has been my joy and sole delight. And I do all I
can to ensure that he returns my affection. I give him
money, turn a blind eye, don't feel called on to
exercise my authority in everything.

These passages, which are not uttered publicly, i.e., to
another character in the play, indicate that within Micio's private world winning and retaining Aeschinus'
affection and confidence are very much primary goals.
Micio wants to be Aeschinus' friend and, as we have
said, this is a goal not completely compatible with inescapable aspects of fatherhood. In designing a permissive
mode of upbringing which is aimed publicly at promoting ethical autonomy and privately at winning affection
and trust, it may be held that Micio is engaged in a sort
of gambling. It is by no means clear that the pursuit of
the latter goal will not interfere with achieving the former.
Micio realizes that there are risks and that he is engaged
in a gamble. He cannot be certain that his approach is
effective, as is revealed by:

nec nil neque omnia haec sunt quae dicit: tamen
non nil molesta haec sunt mihi:

(141-142)

There's something in what he says, but it's not the
whole story. Still I find these reports rather disturbing.

Again, it is with a sigh of relief that he says the famous
erubuit: salua res est (643), indicating that a risky procedure has not succumbed to failure. Indeed, Micio's lack of
assurance in the efficacy of his theory is one of the endearing aspects of his character. To be sure, his relationship with his brother is such that he feels he can reveal
none of his uncertainty publicly. But while Micio's lack
of assurance is a positive quality, the combination of this
lack with his willingness to gamble arouses disquiet. As it
happens, the gamble is successful, but it could conceiv-

ably have failed. If the gamble had been entered upon solely because it would promote Aeschinus' welfare, then, well and good. But to the degree that the gamble is directed at the ulterior goal of winning Aeschinus' affection, it is not justified.

Micio's willingness to gamble is accompanied by a tendency toward manipulating people, i.e., getting them to do what he wants without their being aware of it. It is worth noting that unlike the archetypal comic trickster who gleefully manipulates others without compunction, Micio must find excuses for himself:

> nam itast homo:
> quom placo, aduorsor sedulo et deterreo;
> tamen uix humane patitur; uerum si augeam
> aut etiam adiutor sim eius iracundiae,
> insaniam profecto cum illo.
>
> (143-147)

> He's that sort of man. When I try to placate him, I carefully oppose and dissuade him. Still he's unreasonable, but if I were to add to his fury or even try to share it, I should soon be as crazy as he is.

Just so in the *quor non ludo hunc aliquantisper* (639-640) aside, Micio seeks to justify himself (and is therefore ashamed to some degree of what he is doing) in a way that Syrus never would. In an interesting parallelism, Micio and Aeschinus are both schemers with a conscience who are caught out.

Micio's gambling ethic appears in another passage where he also evinces disappointment:

> *Demea*:   ceterum
> placet tibi factum, Micio? *Micio*: non si queam
> mutare. nunc quom non queo, animo aequo fero.
> ita uitast hominum quasi quom ludas tesseris:
> si illudquod maxume opus est iactu non cadit,
> illud quod cecidit forte, id arte ut corrigas.
>
> (736-741)

> *Demea*: But, Micio, do you approve of what he has done? *Micio*: No, not if I could alter it; but since I can't, I make the best of it. The life of man is like playing with dice: if you don't throw exactly what you want, you must use your wits to make shift with what you have thrown.

Micio's speech is sincere in tone. He is surely more amenable to taking risks than Demea and the speech is not out of character. On the other hand, Micio is not frank with Demea in this scene either before or after this exchange. In a manner both cruel and kind, he does not apprise Demea of mitigating details in Aeschinus' conduct, cruel in that Demea remains the comic butt, but kind in that the truth would reveal Ctesipho's part in the affair. Instead, Micio adopts a pose of permissiveness that goes beyond his true feelings or behavior, and he assumes the caricatured posture of excessive indulgence that Demea has all

along imagined to be the case. It is this same exaggerated posture that Demea will assume in his comic triumph.

The comedy moves on, and Demea learns of Ctesipho's participation very shortly thereafter (778 ff.) This is the scene just before Demea's climactic monologue and the mood to be sustained here is very important. Micio has been caught out:

> dictum hoc inter nos fuit
> (ex te adeo ortumst) ne tu curares meum
> neue ego tuom?
>
> (796-798)

> Was it not arranged between us (you started the arrangement) that you were not to meddle with my son, and I was not to meddle with yours?

At first, Micio continues his exaggerated pose of indulgence and tries to carry it off with a proverbial joke about friends having all things in common (804), but Demea will have none of that. Micio might defend himself by saying that he did not "meddle" with Ctesipho until after Demea had to all intents and purposes lost him. On the other hand, an agreement had clearly been made, and it was Micio's duty not to interfere with the relationship between Demea and Ctesipho, no matter how tenuous that relationship had become. It is clear that an unthinking legalism, fully consonant with his unthinking strictness, will allow Demea to feel righteously angry in the scenes that follow. Given Demea's stance, it would not be helpful for Micio to adopt the defensive position outlined above, nor would it suit the playwright's purpose. Instead, Micio concludes this part of the play by asserting that both sons have turned out all right and hence that both theories have been successful:

> quae ego inesse in illis uideo, ut confidam fore
> ita ut uolumus. uideo sapere intellegere, in loco
> uereri, inter se amare: scire est liberum
> ingenium atque animum:
>
> (826-829)

> Now by what I see of them, I am confidert that they will turn out as we wish. I see that they are sensible, intelligent, highminded, and fond of one another. You can see that they are gentlemen in thought and disposition.

Micio is largely correct and, as noted, we have no difficulty in imagining the sons later turning out to be *senes* not inferior to their fathers. It is an ironic response to the critical tradition which insists that both methods have failed. But once again, Micio is being both kind and less than frank in suggesting that the sons are of equal quality. They are not. Besides, even if the two were of equal worth, it is clear that Demea's method has been more costly. That is the gist of Demea's famous soliloquy. The sons love Micio and they reject Demea (872) and that is somehow unfair, for Demea has been fully as well-intentioned as Micio.

Micio both is and is not a father to Aeschinus, a fact of central import to our understanding, for the play would be somehow less palatable if the roles were reversed, and Demea were the adoptive father and Micio the natural one. In a quite irrational fashion, the artificiality of Micio's position constitutes an offense against the passionate order of nature, and it is this offense which justifies the farcical tone of the closing scenes of the drama when rationality has been abandoned. The impact of the irrational finale is enhanced if we accept the notion that, on a rational level, Micio is for the most part an admirable person. This is not to say that there are no chinks in Micio's armor. He does engage in actions that may be questioned, but as the character in the play most closely approaching the role of the manipulative comic trickster (apart from the minor Syrus), Micio must deviate from some notions of ethical perfection. *Aliter non fit comoedia.* One can also imagine a production of the play in which the potentially unctuous aspects of Micio's role were emphasized or at least not deemphasized. Such a production would have the advantage of reducing the inconcinnity of tone between the bulk of the play and its conclusion, but there are greater advantages in not moving toward this rationalization of the play.

For one, what we would gain in dramatic consistency we would lose in comic surprise and the peculiar consistency entailed in that concept. By surprise is meant not real surprise but the kind to be associated with the conventions of the theater and the conventions of the comic. It is trite but useful to note that what happens on the stage is not to be confused with real life. We know when we enter the theater that we shall be watching an artifact and we have sizable expectations about what we shall see. In much the same way, we ordinarily know beforehand that we are to be introduced to the comic. Our model is the joke with its attendant comic conclusion. It is sometimes possible for us, when we are being told a joke, to anticipate the ending, but whatever sense of accomplishment we have will ordinarily be accompanied by a feeling of disappointment. For, unlike the case of the riddle, we tend to suppress our analytical faculty, and we look forward to the agreeable sensation of being surprised and amused by the conclusion. In a comic version of the willing suspension of disbelief, we make little effort to anticipate and, with our capacity to swallow contradictions, we can be amused and somehow re-surprised by the expert retelling of a joke we have heard before. Further, the anatomy of the joke requires (and our expectations concur) a body of narrative elements so contrived and arranged as to endow the conclusion with maximum comic effect. Within this structure considerations of morality and realism become secondary.

There are difficulties in using the joke as a paradigm for drama. Jokes are usually quite brief, while drama ordinarily demands scope and framework sufficient to allow and perhaps compel the members of the audience to "lose" their sense of identity and to become implicated in the make-believe events taking place on the stage. Breaking the dramatic illusion is a device we associate with comedy and, insofar as it partakes of both the joke and of serious drama, comedy is an uneasy medium. This seems particularly true of Terence who notoriously avoids the more robust comedy of Plautus. To some degree, however, the difficulty exists for all comedies which contain a bid to be taken seriously in whole or in part, or which ask even minimally for the compassionate loss-of-self which characterizes serious drama.

Notwithstanding the above, the farcical finale of the ***Adelphoe,*** beginning with the transformation of Demea, functions rather like the ending of a joke. In retrospect, the earlier parts of the play fall into place, but whereas the paradigm of serious drama requires a Micio whose essential smugness demands retribution, the impact of the comic moment requires a Micio upright enough to exploit our comic surprise. The moral satisfaction we feel at a culpable Micio getting his just punishment is at least matched by our naughty malice when a relatively blameless Micio is made ridiculous. More to the point, if the paradigm of the joke is useful, then it follows that anterior parts of the play need not be taken too seriously, since their major purpose is to enhance the effect of the comic conclusion. In particular, Micio's theories about child-raising need not be taken seriously, or rather one need not conclude that Micio's theories are seriously attacked. By the same token, Demea's statements at the end of the play need not be seriously acclaimed.

We have already considered some sociological and psychological aspects of the relationship between father and son. Micio's views on fatherhood are set forth in the extraordinary opening monologue of the play. While placing himself in the role of anxious father, Micio goes on to rebel against certain aspects of the role. He is to be an unusual character in that he sees the stock role but intends to rise above it. He is not going to make the mistakes his. brother and fathers in general make. He then enunciates his program and concludes as follows:

> hoc patriumst, potius consuefacere filium
> sua sponte recte facere quam alieno metu:
> hoc pater ac dominus interest.
>
> (74-76)

> This, indeed, is the part of a father, to accustom his son to do what is right more from his own choice than any fear of another; and here chiefly lies the difference between a father and a master.

We have already commented upon the first two lines of the above. Our interest is in the nascent sociological analysis in the final line, where Micio explicitly contrasts the role of *pater* and *dominus* and thereby emphasizes both their similarities and their differences. Just a few lines earlier:

> et errat longe mea equidem sententia
> qui imperium credat grauius esse aut stabilius
> ui quod fit quam illud quod amicitia adiungitur.
>
> (65-67)

> And in my judgment he deceives himself greatly to imagine that an authority established by force will be

more lasting or of greater weight than one to which friendship is joined.

Pater and *dominus* both exercise *imperium,* but, says Micio, that of the master is founded upon force, while that of the father is, or should be joined with *amicitia.* The explicit consideration of social roles is compounded by Aeschinus' remarks after Micio has finally resolved his problem:

> quid hoc est negoti? hoc est patrem esse aut hoc
>   est filium esse?
> si frater aut sodalis esset, qui mage morem gereret?
>   (707-708)

> What's this? Is this to be a father or to be a son? What more could he do for me if he were my brother or my bosom friend?

Brothers and friends exercise *amicitia* but they do not have *imperium.* If nothing else, these quotations reveal the uneasy status of the role of father, ranging as it does from "master" to "bosom friend." There are inhibiting factors in the relationship between father and son which are not explicitly recognized, but which have generally remained present in Western society, at least until quite recently. The confrontation between Micio and Aeschinus is preceded by a blush and, as we have seen, it is far too simple to say that Micio has a right to be angry because Aeschinus has not confided in him.

It is important to note that Aeschinus' reticence has to do with a love affair, but further speculation leads us into murky waters and we must tread carefully. Repressions of sexual rivalry between father and son may play a part. These notions come close to the surface in the *Mercator* and *Casina,* but even in these most blatant cases it is glossed over in that the rival son never appears in the former, while in the latter, the father does not realize that it is his son's girl he is after. Again, it seems to be no accident that Roman comedy represents the stabilization of a form of popular entertainment. When plots get reduced to a formula: forbidding father, irresponsible son, wily slave, etc., then one may hold that the form is responding to psychosocial needs as well as to aesthetic demands.

The above is meant to be no more than suggestive; it is not an area amenable to formal demonstration. We can do little more than ask the reader to bring his or her own experience to bear. A father is neither a master nor a bosom friend— but no one else can play the role of father. At the close of the *Adelphoe,* a part of us welcomes the downfall of Micio because he has usurped the role of father. It is not that Micio has made any mistakes in his educational theory. The comic structure of the play allows us to give assent to his ideas. His position is intellectually defensible, but the uncertain limits of his role give rise to disquiet and resentment. Just so, Demea is too honest and too earnest to be a completely satisfying comic butt; there is enough humanity in him to allow a bit of the sympathy coming to the underdog, but that does not mean his theories, even in their final

form, are correct. In all, we sense an uneasiness wonderfully consonant with the uneasiness inherent in the relationship of father and son, and it is to this that we link the unacceptability of reversing the roles of Micio and Demea. As noted above, a Micio as the real father would be psychologically unacceptable, and the discomfort inherent in the role of biological father is illustrated in the play, Demea is the usual comic father, a figure whose authority is ultimately based upon brute biological fact, but his role, in all its variety, can be assumed by no one else. The power of the *Adelphoe* lies in that its comic structure goes to the core of the issue. Sons become fathers in a relentless course of events that can be stemmed by no sexless Micio. In a strange welter of subsurface tensions, Micio can be accepted as correct in his ideas, but he is found wanting and artificial. In the end, we recognize viscerally that our continuation depends upon Demeas and not Micios.

FURTHER READING

OVERVIEWS AND GENERAL STUDIES

Amerasinghe, C. W. "The Part of the Slave in Terence's Drama." *Greece and Rome* XIX, No. 56 (June 1950): 62-72.
> Contends that Terence continually rebelled against the dramatic convention of the wily slave and in so doing, sought "to liberate himself as an artist in such a way that he [could] make human action the significant result of character and situation rather than the mere sport of slaves."

Beare, W. "Terence, an Original Dramatist in Rome." *Hermathena,* No. LXXI (May 1948): 64-82.
> Analyzes Terence's adaptations of Greek plays in his comedies, concluding that it "is not Terence's borrowings but his originality which makes him so significant a figure."

Clifford, Helen Rees. "Dramatic Technique and the Originality of Terence." *The Classical Journal* XXVI, No. 8 (May 1931): 605-18.
> Maintains that Terence's "technical ability is weak in comparison with that of his Greek prototypes. . . . The parts which he himself has created reveal weakness in characterization and aimlessness of movement."

Earl, D. C. "Terence and Roman Politics." *Historia* XI (1962): 469-55.
> Explores Terence's attitudes toward Roman politics as expressed in his plays. Earl concludes that the playwright was largely apolitical.

Flickinger, Roy C. "Terence and Menander." *The Classical Journal* XXVI, No. 9 (June 1931): 676-94.
> Defends Terence against charges that his plays are inferior to their Menandrian models.

Goldberg, Sander M. *Understanding Terence.* Princeton, N. J.: Princeton University Press, 1986, 231 p.

> Proposes to approach Terence "through the Latin tradition of New Comedy and [focus] on his contribution to the Roman's literary development."

Harsh, Philip W. "A Study of Dramatic Technique as a Means of Appreciating the Originality of Terence." *The Classical Weekly* XXVIII, No. 21 (1 April 1935): 161-65.

> Scrutinizes Terence's dramaturgy in an effort to achieve a balanced assessment of him as a playwright. Harsh concludes that he was neither a "clumsy and uninspired" writer, nor an "original genius."

Henry, G. Kenneth G. "The Characters of Terence." *Studies in Philology* 12 (1915): 55-98.

> Close examination of each of Terence's comedies that seeks to "interpret characters of every kind, including mutes and even those characters that do not appear on the stage, in their relation to the story of the play."

Laidlaw, W. A. *The Prosody of Terence: A Relational Study.* London: Oxford University Press, 1938.

> Technical analysis of Terence's use of meter and accent in his poetry.

Norwood, Gilbert. *The Art of Terence.* Oxford: Basil Blackwell, 1923, 156 p.

> Influential study that praises Terence for his "splendid principle of accepting the traditional framework" of comedy "and evolving from it a thoroughly serious, permanently interesting, type of drama."

Post, L. A. "The Art of Terence." *The Classical Weekly* XXIII, No. 16 (3 March 1930): 121-28.

> Declares that "Terence is not concerned with truth. He writes plays, not to present the life of man as he sees it, but as a frame for the sententious remarks which he had the art to remodel to suit the Roman taste."

THE MOTHER-IN-LAW

Carney, T. F. "Notes on the *Hecyra* of Terence." *The Proceedings of the African Classical Associations* 6 (1963): 16-23.

> Addresses two issues in the play: the chronology of Philumena's pregnancy (upon which rests Pamphilus's charge of her infidelity) and the doubling of roles (the performance of two or more roles by a single actor).

McGarrity, Terry. "Reputation vs. Reality in Terence's *Hecyra.*" *Classical Journal* 76, No. 1 (October-November 1980): 149-56.

> Explores the theme of "public image and reputation versus true character" in *The Mother-in-Law.*

THE SELF-TORMENTOR

Brothers, A. J. "The Construction of Terence's *Heautontimorumenos.*" *Classical Quarterly* 30 (1980): 469-85.

> Discusses Terence's dramatic technique in *The Self-Tormentor,* focusing particularly on the play's action and plot construction.

THE EUNUCH

Frangoulidis, S. A. "The Soldier as a Storyteller in Terence's *Eunuchus.*" *Mnemosyne* XLVII, No. 5 (November 1994): 586-95.

> Discusses the two "boastful narratives" told by Thraso and contends that they have "an ironic appropriateness: they resemble the main narrative of the play, and thus point to the soldier's ultimate weakness."

Pepe, George M. "The Last Scene of Terence's *Eunuchus.*" *The Classical World* 65, No. 5 (January 1972): 141-45.

> Examines the disconcerting conclusion of *The Eunuch* in which Thais, Phaedria, and Thraso agree to continue their love triangle. Pepe describes the last scene as "a vignette of cynical realism."

Philippides, Katerina. "Terence's *Eunuchus*: Elements of the Marriage Ritual in the Rape Scene." *Mnemosyne* XLVIII, No. 3 (June 1995): 272-84.

> Investigates the incorporation of the marriage ceremony in the scene in *The Eunuch* in which Chaerea rapes Pamphila. Philippides contends that the violence of Chaerea's action is "significantly mitigated since the rape becomes part of the ritual of the wedding ceremony."

PHORMIO

Arnott, W. Geoffrey. "Phormio Parasitvs: A Study in Dramatic Methods of Characterization." *Greece & Rome* XVII, No. 1 (April 1970): 32-57.

> Detailed analysis of Terence's development of the title character of *Phormio.*

Godsey, Edith R. "Phormio the Magnificent." *The Classical Weekly* XXII, No. 9 (10 December 1928): 65-7.

> Declares that with Phormio, "the type of the daring, clever, unscrupulous slave of the earlier comedies has been brought to fit culmination."

Riedel, Ernest. "The Dramatic Structure of Terence's *Phormio.*" *The Classical Weekly* XI, No. 4 (22 October 1917): 25-8.

> Carefully looks at the setting and the entrances and exits of all the characters in *Phormio.* Riedel observes that "every character, at least every more important one, after he has been introduced, is never lost sight of. . . . We always know where each one is and what he is doing, so that, in reality, the scene of action is no longer the fronts of three houses, but the entire city."

Segal, Erich, and Moulton, Carroll. "*Contortor Legum*: The Hero of the *Phormio.*" *Rheinisches Museum für Philologie* 121, Nos. 3-4 (1978): 276-88.

> Proclaims Phormio "an expert advocate in a play which abounds in legalistic maneuvers, legal language both

straightforward and metaphorical, and which culminates in a transformation of the entire stage into a courtroom."

THE BROTHERS

Enk, P. J. "Terence as an Adapter of Greek Comedies." *Mnemosyne,* third series, XIII, No. II (1947): 81-93.

Evaluates Terence's modifications to Menander's play in *The Brothers.* Enk asserts that Terence improved upon his predecessor's dramatic technique.

Grant, John N. "The Ending of Terence's *Adelphoe* and the Menandrian Original." *American Journal of Philology* 96, No. 1 (Spring 1975): 42-60.

Maintains that Demea's victory at the end of *The Brothers* "indicates that . . . his strictness is preferable to Micio's methods."

Additional coverage of Terence's life and career is contained in the following source published by Gale Research: *Classical and Medieval Literature Criticism,* **Vol. 14.**

Ivan Turgenev
1818-1883

(Full name Ivan Sergeyevich Turgenev)

INTRODUCTION

The first Russian author to achieve widespread international fame, Turgenev was considered his country's premiere novelist by nineteenth-century audiences and is today linked with Fyodor Dostoevsky and Leo Tolstoy as one of the greatest Russian authors of the nineteenth century. As a writer deeply concerned with his country's politics, he vividly documented the tumultuous political environment in Russia from the 1840s to the 1870s. As a literary artist, he created works noted for their psychological truth, descriptive beauty, and haunting pathos.

BIOGRAPHICAL INFORMATION

Turgenev was born into a weathy family in the city of Orel. His father, a charming but ineffectual officer in the cavalry, paid little attention to Turgenev. His childhood on the family estate of Spasskoye was dominated by his eccentric and capricious mother. Her treatment of her son alternated between excessive affection and mental and physical cruelty. She ruled Spasskoye and its 5000 serfs with the same arbitrary power. Biographers have cited his mother's influence to explain much about the development of Turgenev's personality—particularly his horror of violence and his hatred of injustice—as well as his writing, which is populated by strong women and well-meaning but weak-willed men. When Turgenev was nine, the family left the country for Moscow, where he attended boarding schools before entering Moscow University in 1833. The following year Turgenev transferred to the University of St. Petersburg. After graduation, he went abroad to study, and in 1838 he enrolled in the University of Berlin. During the next several years he studied philosophy, but he never finished his degree.

Although Turgenev had begun writing poetry as a student in St. Petersburg, the work that first established his reputation as a writer was the narrative poem *Parasha,* published in 1843. It was highly praised by the influential Vissarion Belinsky, who was associated with the radical journal *Sovremennik* (*The Contemporary*). Between 1847 and 1852 Turgenev published in the *Contemporary* a series of short prose pieces whose common theme is the injustice of Russian serfdom. When these pieces were collected and published in book form as *Zapiski okhotnika* (*A Sportsman's Sketches*) in 1852, they were enormously popular with everyone but government officials.

That same year Turgenev wrote an admiring obituary of Nikolai Gogol which was refused publication by St. Petersburg censors. When he instead published the piece in Moscow, he was arrested and jailed for a month, then placed under house arrest at Spasskoye for nearly two years. Although he was ostensibly arrested for excessive approval of the "suspect" author Gogol, he was more likely detained as the author of the controversial *A Sportsman's Sketches*. When the serfs were finally freed in 1861, many credited the collection with having helped to achieve their emancipation. Turgenev's first novel, *Rudin,* which was published in 1856, introduced several character types and themes that appear in his subsequent work. The title character is a political idealist who combines a genius for words with an inability to act on them. Such "Russian Hamlets" recur frequently in Turgenev's work and were regarded by his contemporaries as insightful personifications of a national malaise of irresolution and indecision.

The Russia of the nineteenth century was a divided and politically troubled country, unsure of its future political course. Tension existed not only between conservatives and liberals but also, in the latter camp, between the radicals, who called for immediate change and economic communism, and the moderates, who favored slow, peaceful reform and free enterprise. Turgenev managed to draw the enmity of nearly every Russian ideologue, from reactionary to revolutionary, with his most famous novel, *Ottsy i deti* (*Fathers and Sons*), published in 1862. Bazarov, the protagonist of the book, is considered Turgenev's most successful and most ambiguous character (alternately attractive and repellent, he aroused ambivalent feelings even in his creator), as well as an intriguing portrayal of a political type just then coming into existence in Russia: the nihilist. Distressed by this unfavorable reaction, Turgenev spent more and more time abroad, and he counted among his friends some of the most illustrious authors of his era, including Gustave Flaubert, Henry James, Emile Zola, Guy de Maupassant, and George Sand. His absence from Russia left him vulnerable to charges, leveled at his subsequent novels, that he was out of touch and out of sympathy with his native land. His remaining works—prose poems and stories—are described by critics as nostalgic, philosophical, and frequently pessimistic, and are often concerned with the occult. After a long and debilitating illness, Turgenev died in Bougival, near Paris, on September 3, 1883. His body was returned to Russia by train. There, despite the unfavorable reception of his later works and the efforts of the Russian government to restrict memorial congregations, Turgenev was widely mourned by his compatriots.

MAJOR DRAMATIC WORKS

Turgenev wrote some dozen plays, but his best-known drama is *Mesiats v derevne* (*A Month in the Country*). This work was completed in 1850 and submitted to the Russian censors for review. They demanded significant changes to the text, which Turgenev made. Ultimately, however, the censors withheld permission to stage the work. The censored version of *A Month in the Country* was published in the *Contemporary* in 1855 and finally received its first performance in 1872. The publication and the performance had equally little impact on audiences and critics of the time. Its first successful staging came in 1879, in a performance by the actress Maria Gavrilovna. After the Moscow Art Theatre in 1909 mounted a brilliant production directed by Konstantin Sergeevich Stanislavsky, it became one of the most famous plays in the Russian repertory. Prior productions stressed the elements of social commentary in *A Month in the Country*, but Stanislavsky's staging emphasized the psychology of the characters, an approach to the play that long remained dominant. *A Month in the Country* continues to be frequently performed, and it is heralded as an important influence on the works of the preeminent Russian playwright, Anton Chekhov.

CRITICAL RECEPTION

Because of the highly political content of most of Turgenev's works, the earliest Russian commentators tended to praise or disparage his writings along partisan lines. Similarly, foreign critics of the nineteenth century were interested in Turgenev's works for the light they shed on the volatile sociopolitical situation in Russia. Early Russian and English-language critics by no means neglected the aesthetic qualities of Turgenev's works, however, recognizing from the start that his writing was more than simply the literal portrayal of the people and concerns of a particular country at a given historical moment.

Turgenev's literary reputation has remained generally stable over the years, with twentieth-century commentators echoing and amplifying the conclusions reached by their nineteenth-century counterparts. Critics agree that Turgenev's work is distinguished by solid literary craftsmanship, especially in the areas of description and characterization. Keenly observant, he infused his work with precise, realistic detail, bringing a natural scene or character into focus through the evocative power of his words. Given Turgenev's slight plots, interest in the works centers largely on the characters. Critics note that his characters—recognized both as unique individuals and as representatives of universal human qualities—are drawn with a psychological penetration. Turgenev was particularly adept, critics contend, at portraying women in love and at creating an atmosphere of pathos but not sentimentality in his unhappy love stories. Fatalism and thwarted desires are hallmarks of Turgenev's work: his characters are generally unable to control their destiny, either because of their own flaws or through the arbitrariness of fate. Scholars suggest that Turgenev's work reveals his own sense of the futility of life, but they add that he tempered his essentially pessimistic outlook with an appreciation of life's beauty. As the author himself remarked, "Everything human is dear to me."

PRINCIPAL WORKS

PLAYS

Styeno 1834

"Neostorozhnost" ["Indiscretion"] 1843

"Bezdenezh'e" ["Penniless"; also translated as "Moneyless," "Insolvency," and "Lack of Funds"] 1845

"Gde tanko, tam i rvetsa" ["Where It Is Thin, There It Breaks"; also translated as "It Breaks Where It's Thin" and "Where the Thread's Weakest, There It Breaks"] 1848

Nakhlebnik [*The Parasite*; also translated as *The Boarder, A Poor Gentleman,* and *The Family Charge*; also published as *Chuzoy khleb* (*Alien Bread*)] 1848

Kholostiak [*The Bachelor*] 1849

"Zavtrak u predvoditelya" ["Lunch with the Marshal of the Nobility"; also translated as "Breakfast at a Nobleman's Home"; also known by its subtitle "An Amicable Settlement" or "An Amicable Division"] 1849

"Provintsialka" ["A Provincial Lady"; also translated as "The Lady from the Provinces"] 1850

Mesiats v derevne [*A Month in the Country*] 1850
"Razgovor na bolshoi doroge" ["A Conversation on the
    Highway"; also translated as "A Colloquy on the High
    Road"] 1850
"Vecher v Sorrente" ["An Evening in Sorrento"] 1852

OTHER MAJOR WORKS

Parasha (poetry) 1843
"Dnevnik lishnego cheloveka" ["The Diary of a Superflu-
    ous Man"] (short story) 1848
Zapiski okhotnika [*A Sportsman's Sketches*] (sketches
    and short stories) 1852
Rudin (novel) 1856
Asya (novella) 1858
Dvoryanskoe gnezdo [*A Nest of the Gentry*] (novel) 1859
Nakanune [*On the Eve*] (novel) 1860
Pervaya lyubov' [*First Love*] (novel) 1860
Ottsy i deti [*Fathers and Sons*] (novel) 1862
Dym [*Smoke*] (novel) 1867
"Stepnoi Korol' Lir" ["A Lear of the Steppes"] (short
    story) 1870
Veshnie vody [*The Torrents of Spring*] (novella) 1872
Nov' [*Virgin Soil*] (novel) 1877
Stikhotvoreniya v proze [*Poems in Prose*] (poetry) 1882
Turgenev's Letters (correspondence) 1983

OVERVIEWS AND GENERAL STUDIES

Oliver M. Sayler (essay date 1921)

SOURCE: "Turgenieff as a Playwright," in *The North
American Review*, Vol. 214, No. 790, September, 1921,
pp. 393-400.

[*In the essay below, Sayler surveys Turgenev's dramatic
output, stressing the realistic aspects of his work.*]

When the art and the literature of two countries are as
widely separated by the barrier of languages expressed
in dissimilar alphabets as those of Russia and America,
it is small wonder that contemporary men and movements are often delayed in transit from one nation to the
other, and that Moscow and Petrograd are as unaware today of the existence of Edgar Lee Masters and Vachel
Lindsay as we are of Igor Severianin and Vassily Kamy-
ensky. It is not so easy, though, to understand how after
years of acquaintance with and admiration for a master
of letters like Ivan Turgenieff, we can still be unconver-
sant with the plays he wrote, and ignorant even of the
fact that he ever turned his hand to the drama.

Turgenieff as playwright is an aspect of the great rival of
Tolstoy and Dostoievsky of which we are almost completely unaware, and yet an aspect which no Russian is

willing for a moment to forget. His contributions to the
theatre were limited in number, in comparison with his
voluminous output of novels and stories, but that is not
a sufficient reason for his biographers and critics and
translators in western lands to pass them by unnoticed,
for some of them are not only the equal in literary power
of his best work in other fields, but they have also won
an enviable place purely as drama on their native stage.
As acted drama on our own stage, they might not measure up to our demand for decisive action, although one
or two of the shorter pieces should fulfil our specifica-
tions in this respect. We may not be ready, either, in our
hasty and slipshod method of mounting plays, to do them
the patient and sympathetic justice which they would
require. But they are so thoroughly in the vein of Turgenieff's narrative manner of depicting the life of his native
country, and so worthy merely in a literary sense to stand
beside his novels and tales, that they should be made
available for the reading public which is attracted to-day
as never before to the art and letters of Russia.

My first impression when I saw on the Moscow Art Theatre bulletin, shortly after the playhouses reopened following the Bolshevik Revolution, the announcement that
the repertory of the following week would include *A
Month in the Country,* a "comedy in five acts by I. S.
Turgenieff", was that someone had made a play out of
one of the novelist's stories. Which one, I could not tell
from the title. It might be *A Sportsman's Notebook*; or
Virgin Soil. The Art Theatre, I knew, had thus brought
effectively to its stage several of the novels of Dostoievsky, such as *The Brothers Karamazoff, Nikolai
Stavrogin* (dramatized from *The Possessed*), and *The
Village Stepantchikovo*, although Dostoievsky had never
written for the stage nor remotely intended his stories to
be used thereon. My next impression, after I was informed that *A Month in the Country* had been composed originally as a play, was that it would prove to be
an inferior *étude* of the author, a typical novelist's play
unsuited for the stage and honored by his compatriots
merely out of respect for his other work; else why had
we never heard of it outside Russia? This second surmise, however, proved to be as groundless as the first,
for in performance at the hands of Stanislavsky's players
it was disclosed as a suave and mannerly transcript of
Russian life,—not so much a drama of action according
to conventional formulas as a rich and illuminating panorama of personalities and incidents on the estate of a
landed proprietor in the days of 1840, brought to vivid
representation as drama on the stage. And for double
proof of Turgenieff's talents as a playwright, the Art
Theatre revived from its storehouse later in the same
season a group of shorter works, including a masterpiece
in droll humor, **"The Lady from the Provinces"**; another glimpse in miniature of the same life which *A Month
in the Country* depicts, **"Where the Thread's Weakest,
There It Breaks"**; and the first act of a longer play in
more sombre mood, ***The Boarder.***

A Month in the Country was written in 1850, at about
the time of the death of the author's mother. Turgenieff
was thirty-two years of age, and had written only occa-

sional poems and sketches, which were later collected under the title, *A Sportsman's Notebook.* Tradition in Russia has it that in the leading character of the play, Rakitin, he drew an autobiographical portrait, and that Rakitin's hopeless love for Madame Islaieva had its counterpart in the author's own life. It is this tradition which has induced Stanislavsky whenever he plays the rôle to make up in the likeness of the Turgenieff of that period.

The curtain rises on a salon done in the grand style of native Russia crossed with imported France, reflection of the same fashion which led the playwright's mother to teach him nothing but French and compelled him to learn his own tongue from the peasant servants. Natalia Petrovna Islaieva and Mihail Alexandrovitch Rakitin form one of two groups in the salon. They are reading to each other, but only fitfully, for their minds wander to Byelaieff, a student who has come to tutor Natalia's son, Kolya. Natalia displays more than a passing interest in the young man with his bold, free and unabashed manner, and proposes completing his education against the advice of Rakitin. Dr. Shpigelsky arrives, ostensibly to tend the coachman but really to press the suit of Bolshintsoff, a neighbor, for the hand of Vyerotchka, Natalia's adopted daughter. The girl comes racing in from a morning at play and Mme. Islaieva's answer to the doctor is, "She is a mere child!" At Islaieff's entrance, his wife departs, unable to endure his blunt, practical ways, but when he takes Rakitin away to view some new improvement on the estate she returns to a confidential scene with the tutor. Envy and suspicion enter her mind, though, when she sees the young man and Vyerotchka talking and laughing together, and on their departure she informs the doctor that she might consider his friend's proposal, after all.

The garden on Islaieff's estate is fitting locale for the growing love of Vyerotchka for Byelaieff, and it serves as well for an amusing scene wherein the doctor coaches the awkward Bolshintsoff for the ordeal of courtship. The third act returns indoors to recount the deepening rivalry between mother and foster-daughter, Byelaieff's shocked denial to Natalia that he loves the girl, and Rakitin's unrequited concern for Natalia. A summer-house on the estate is rendezvous in the fourth act for Vyerotchka and Byelaieff; the girl's dream is shattered, and in her anger and excitement on the appearance of Natalia she accuses her mother of being her rival, and runs away weeping. Natalia and the tutor, thus thrown together, confess their love for each other, only to be surprised in turn by Rakitin. The last act, once more in the great salon, discloses Islaieff and his mother deeply worried over Natalia and the love they think she bears for Rakitin. Islaieff consults with his guest, and Rakitin decides it would be best for him to leave. As he bids them all farewell, Byelaieff suddenly understands that he himself has been the cause of all this tangled web of misdirected affections, and in a rush of remorse such as only a Russian can comprehend, he, too, departs, and life on the estate resumes its monotonous course above the wreckage of unfulfilled passions.

A play of so slender a narrative thread, of course, places a heavy burden on everyone concerned with its production. I know of no other producer except Stanislavsky, no other company except that of the Moscow Art Theatre, which could overcome the obstacle of this element of passivity. Constant training together through years of experiment, however, and a keen, almost intuitive, sense of atmospheric ensemble resulting from this intimate collaboration, have enabled these players not only successfully to master the difficulty inherent in Turgenieff's comedy, but even to capitalize it and make it serve positive ends. On its first inclusion in the repertory of the Art Theatre in the season of 1909-10, critical Moscow was unanimous that Stanislavsky had made the play expressive of all that Turgenieff means to the Russian heart. Here was set forth with unbroken illusion that romantic fineness of feeling and sensitive understanding of character which runs through all of Turgenieff's work; here, too, was a compelling and moving glimpse of that sadness and hopelessness which is so deeply ingrained in the Russian soul. I have maintained elsewhere that the secret of the Moscow Art Theatre's use of realism as a mode of artistic expression is a calculated minimization, a toning down of life to make its portrayal seem more convincing; and it is this minimization, this frank and courageous utilization of subdued tones throughout the performance, which helps Stanislavsky to achieve the emotional effect that Turgenieff intended.

One of Russia's foremost living artists, Mstislaff Dobuzhinsky, collaborated with Stanislavsky as designer of the four settings of the play, contributing through his lighting and his sense of design and locale a sympathetic understanding not only of the playwright's mood but of the grand manner of life under the first Tsar Nicholas. Stanislavsky and Katchaloff alternate in the rôle of Rakitin, but each makes him the model of unruffled gentility. Massalitinoff's Islaieff is in fitting contrast, but as urbane as a courtier when measured by the manners of to-day. Moskvin's Doctor and Luzhsky's Bolshintsoff are admirable examples of the droll humors which high comedy can achieve within the bounds of the strictest realism. Mme. Knipper, Tchehoff's widow, is proof in the rôle of Natalia of the power of repression in the depiction of jealous affection. And Mlle. Korenieva as Vyerotchka supplies an enchanting lyric note to one of Turgenieff's most engaging feminine portraits.

A wholly different aspect of Turgenieff as playwright emerged in the Moscow Art Theatre's programme of short plays from his pen which was first included in the repertory in the season of 1911-12. There is not so great a variation in mood and manner in *The Boarder,* the first act of which was presented as a self-sufficient play, for it is dependent on intimate characterization rather than on incident. Its story deals with that curious phase of the old Russian social and family life which persisted occasionally at least until the time of the Revolution—the presence in the household of landed proprietors, or of well-to-do dwellers in the towns and cities, of an outsider who is blessed with birth or breeding or a fortunate past, but who has been reduced in circumstances to the point where he will accept a living in a strange *menage*. Dostoievsky deals with such a figure in Foma Fomitch Opiskin, the leading character in *The Village Stepantchikovo*, which has just been published in an English translation under the title, *The Friend of the Family*; but Opiskin had so capitalized his fortuitous position that he had become absolute master over the feelings and the finances of his benefactors. Kuzovkin in Turgenieff's play is a less vigorous personality, the butt of everyone's jokes, and almost a tragic figure in his compulsory sufferance of humiliation. *The Boarder* is laid in a country house over a hundred years ago, and the author has made it eloquent of the crudeness, the bluffness, and the lack of refinement which characterized all but the heads of the household in the days before the introduction of western customs brought about the metamorphosis which is evident in the picture presented by *A Month in the Country*. The scenes with the servants are like nothing so much as the corresponding incidents with the awkward attendants in an English country house in Goldsmith's *She Stoops To Conquer*.

There is even less divergence from the style of *A Month in the Country* in another of the short plays, **"Where the Thread's Weakest, There It Breaks,"** a comedy of manners and of finely analyzed affections out of the same life and time as the longer play. In fact, it is almost *A Month in the Country* in miniature, and for it Dobuzhinsky designed and devised a salon setting reminiscent of the grandiose airs of that of the longer play, only more delicately shimmering in its representation of the suave artificiality of the age and the sentimental atmosphere of the Russian countryside under intense summer suns.

Originality, however, comes to the fore in still another of the short plays, **"The Lady from the Provinces."** Here Turgenieff dispensed with his sometimes cloying sentiment and substituted light and engaging and even satiric humors. His attention is no less devoted to the painstaking drawing of character, but he does not rest satisfied with that service alone, for he has built up in this masterly example of the one act play a fabric of plot and incident, slender but amusing, which should make it a pleasant acquaintance on the stage of any country. Alexei Ivanovitch Stupendieff, Daria Ivanovna, his wife, and the Count Valerian Nikolaievitch Lyubin, are the leading characters. Stupendieff is an official in a small district-capital, and the play unfolds in his home in a parlor of mid-Victorian fuss and feathers. He is a blunt but well-meaning fellow; his wife is an amiable and light-hearted, not to say flirtatious, young person who is bored by the hum-drum of life so far from the gayety of the city.

To this quiet but potentially restless scene comes the lackey of the Count Lyubin announcing the approach of his excellency, and wearing his hat in the house in the fulness of his pride. Stupendieff makes him take it off, not once, but numerous times, until the count is heard in the hallway. Everyone disappears unceremoniously, permitting the visitor to enter a vacant room. When the ends of self-importance have been served, Stupendieff returns formally, followed by his wife. The latter and the count

---

Henry James on Turgenev's temperament:

[I first met Turgénieff] in Paris, where he was then living, in 1875. I shall never forget the impression he made upon me at that first interview. I found him adorable; I could scarcely believe that he would prove—that any man could prove—on nearer acquaintance as delightful as that. Nearer acquaintance only confirmed my hope, and he remained the most approachable, the most practicable, the least precarious, man of genius it has been my fortune to meet. He was so simple, so natural, so modest, so destitute of personal pretension and of what is called the consciousness of powers, that one almost doubted at moments whether he were a man of genius, after all. Everything good and fruitful lay near to him; he was interested in everything; and he was absolutely without that eagerness of self-reference which sometimes accompanies great, and even small, reputations. He had not a particle of vanity; nothing whatever of the air of having a part to play, or a reputation to keep up. His humor exercised itself as freely upon himself as upon other subjects, and he told stories at his own expense with a sweetness of hilarity which made his peculiarities really sacred in the eyes of a friend.

Henry James, *"Ivan Turgénieff," in* The Atlantic Monthly, *Vol. 53, No. CCCXV, January, 1884.*

---

exchange a glance of recognition as Stupendieff pleads an engagement elsewhere and leaves them alone together. The two talk of the old and romantic days before she had left the city, and the count, becoming amorous despite his more than middle age, moves closer in recalling the past. Daria Ivanovna finally permits him to kiss her hand, but just for a moment. On his departure to get his music, she reflects lightly on the chances of life which have brought her to this secluded nook of the empire, but her revery is broken by the return of her husband, who requests his dinner at three, and then, on overhearing the count humming a tune outside, pretends to be called away once more. At the piano, the titled visitor, in atrocious voice, and Mme. Stupendieva proceed with their flirtation, but the suspicious husband breaks in upon them, only to find them harmlessly occupied. He extricates himself awkwardly but a moment later returns again, only to find his apprehensions still unfulfilled. He risks a third trial, though, and this time he catches the count on his knees before his wife, unable on account of his age and stiffness to rise gracefully or promptly and the butt of the heartless laughter of the Lady from the Provinces, who has used him to point a needed lesson to her grumbling husband.

In the Moscow Art Theatre's production of this delightful bit of banter, Stanislavsky takes a holiday from his more serious rôles and proves himself master as well of more fleeting and light-fingered fancies in the part of the count. His wife, Mme. Lilina, an expert actress of charming personality, makes a perfect foil for him in the rôle of Daria Ivanovna.

Aside from these four works, Turgenieff is represented in dramatic form by other less known and less regarded compositions which are seldom if ever presented in the theatre. One of them, *The Bachelor,* is a long play in three acts, but it is notably inferior to *A Month in the Country.* "Imprudence" is a comedy in one act, and "Breakfast at a Nobleman's Home" is another of the same type; while there are three sketches that are little more than conversations: "Pennilessness," "A Colloquy on the High Road," and "An Evening at Sorrento." The fate of these lesser *études* probably deserves to be that which thus far has unfortunately been the lot of the major works.

To those who know Turgenieff as novelist, these brief notes will indicate a marked similarity of method and treatment in his plays and his stories. In both *genres* he was concerned primarily with character portrayal and with the half-tones of mood and feeling as a background for these portraits. In both, his method was, on the whole, that of the realist, but the realist as romancer rather than the realist as morbid analyst or propagandist. The nobility of his spirit and the fineness of his imagination, inherent in all his work, justify the consideration of his plays in any study which the western world may make of his genius.

Henry Ten Eyck Perry (essay date 1939)

SOURCE: "Crosscurrents in Russia: Gogol, Turgenev, and Chekhov," in *Masters of Dramatic Comedy and the Social Themes,* Harvard University Press, 1939, pp. 314-58.

[*In the following excerpt, Perry analyzes Turgenev's depiction of love in his plays.*]

Gogol's *Marriage* and *The Gamblers* were published in 1842. The next year marks the beginning of the work of an author more important in the realm of the novel than in that of the theater, Ivan Sergeyevich Turgenev. Turgenev began his literary career as a writer of plays. For nine years, from 1843 to 1852, he devoted his energies chiefly to that form of art. Toward the end of this period he began writing the short stories which compose *A Sportsman's Sketches,* and these proved so successful that they turned his attention away from the drama. His comedies are by no means negligible, however; in his own way he helped to carry on the tradition that had been formulated by Gogol. His admiration for Gogol was very great, as he showed not only by several references in his plays and novels but by an enthusiastic tribute written at the time of Gogol's death in 1852. This obituary notice was displeasing to Nicholas I, who, fearing that Russia might be infected by the revolutionary spirit of 1848 in western Europe and distrusting authors as dangerous Liberals, had Turgenev imprisoned for a month and then exiled to his country estate for a year and a half. It is true that, like Gogol, Turgenev was acutely conscious of the social abuses of his day, but he treated them more in his stories than in his plays. In the drama

he devoted his principal attention to a psychological analysis of human beings, particularly in matters of love.

Turgenev wrote ten plays in all, the greater part of his dramatic work being composed in the three years from 1847 to 1850. One of the ten pieces is "Lack of Caution," a tragedy of intrigue with a Spanish setting. Two of them are mere sketches which do not pretend to do more than outline a situation. "A Conversation on the Highway" contrasts a decadent young landowner, who has lost all his money, and a simple old coachman, who is devoted to his master from habit rather than from conviction; the difference between the cynicism of the one and the superstition of the other is used to illustrate the chasm separating social classes, in morality as well as in economics. "Lack of Funds" pictures another impecunious young aristocrat, who is living beyond his means in St. Petersburg and whose faithful old servant urges him in vain to return to the country home of his mother.

"Lunch with the Marshal of the Nobility" portrays the inefficiency of rural magistrates; "A Provincial Lady" hints at venal corruption in higher governmental circles. In this latter piece the wife of a poor official in a small town is trying to get her husband a more important position in St. Petersburg by flirting with a count, who is an influential old admirer of hers. The wife has just got the count to promise that her husband shall secure the coveted post when the husband returns unexpectedly and finds the count on his knees before the wife. The count is chagrined and feels that he has been duped, but he nobly agrees to carry out his promise. How far the wife has been playing with him is the crucial point of this comedy. After the discovery she continues to hint that her affection for him may be real. "A comedy can be played well only where one feels what he is saying," she maintains, and that statement contains the heart of Turgenev's comic theory. "A Provincial Lady" is partly a comedy of social situation, hinging upon the desire of the lady and her husband to live in the metropolis, and partly a comedy of sentiment, with the lady's feelings perhaps more involved than she has been willing to admit, even to herself.

The same sort of ambiguity created by a conflict between sentiment and comedy pervades Turgenev's two-act drama, *The Parasite.* The heartlessness of an aristocratic husband and the sympathetic nature of his well-to-do wife are brought into opposition when the parasite who has been a hanger-on of the family asserts publicly in a moment of drunkenness that he is the wife's father. The husband refuses to believe the story and succeeds, as he thinks, in buying off the parasite's claims, but the wife feels that the poor man has told the truth and arranges to see him again without her husband's knowledge. The comedy ends with the dramatic irony of a misunderstanding between husband and wife which permits both of them to think that they are in the right. The background of *The Parasite* is a picture of life on a large country estate. As in the work of Gogol, the tendency toward realism fuses to a certain extent the satirical and emotional factors which are in conflict beneath the surface of Turgenev's art.

Another of his longer plays, in which the same fundamental contrast occurs, is *The Bachelor,* a detailed analysis of various kinds of love. The main subject of this drama is the struggle in the heart of an old bachelor between paternal and sexual love for his young protégée. To this principal theme several subsidiary ones are closely related. The heroine's young fiancé is torn between ambition and affection for the girl, whom he considers beneath him in social position; she is attracted at the same time to both her lover and her protector. The girl is so much the most interesting character in the piece that Turgenev might well have developed her part at greater length. He is always extremely successful with his portraits of young women uncertain of their own feelings. The heroine of *The Bachelor* is not a comic figure like her fiancé, who gives her up for worldly considerations, nor a sentimental one like her self-sacrificing guardian, but somewhere between the two extremes. Soon after she loses her young lover, she tells the old bachelor that some day later on she may consent to become his wife.

Turgenev handles with exceptional delicacy love affairs to which there is some obstacle, such as social position, age, or temperament. In **"An Evening in Sorrento"** he shows how a woman of thirty loses a man of twenty-eight, with whom she is in love, to a young girl of eighteen. In **"Where It Is Thin, There It Breaks"** the heroine agrees to marry a dull, phlegmatic man whom she does not love when the volatile and artistic one to whom she is attracted does not propose to her. **"Where It Is Thin, There It Breaks"** is the most effective of Turgenev's minor works for the theater. Of them all it most closely resembles his dramatic masterpiece, *A Month in the Country,* particularly in respect to the background against which the principal intrigue develops. The love affair in the slighter play takes place on a country estate, presided over by a flighty but not altogether impractical woman of the upper middle class. Her complicated household is composed of such diverse characters as an elderly female relative, who hates being compelled to accept the bread of charity, a French governess, who is always sewing and sighing for Paris, and a ruined ex-captain, who looks like a bully but is really a servile flatterer. They drift on and off the stage, exchanging random observations which have little to do with the plot and which intensify the air of casualness that envelops the entire proceedings. These characters are depicted, with a candor that seems almost brutal to an Anglo-Saxon, as futile creatures who discuss eating candy and mushrooms, who play at pool or preference, and who, when it begins to rain, have not the faintest idea of how to amuse themselves. With their cultivation and their incompetence, they are striking examples of the leisureliness and aimlessness of one stratum of social life in Russia during the middle of the nineteenth century.

This same atmosphere of apparent tranquillity and concealed uneasiness pervades Turgenev's one superlative comedy, *A Month in the Country.* The owner of the rural estate on which this play takes place is a stupid, well-intentioned man who cannot become reconciled to the fact that, although the Russian peasants are intelligent, they refuse to work consistently. He knows that they have no patience, but he respects them nevertheless. His establishment consists of his wife, his ten-year-old son, his elderly mother, his mother's companion, his son's two tutors, and a young girl dependent on the family. The life of the mother, her companion, and the German tutor is desultory, unmotivated, and only enlivened by games of preference. At the end of the play they are just where they were when it began, except that the coquettish companion is about to leave to marry a country doctor, who has analyzed for her, with extraordinary detachment, his own assets and liabilities as a husband. This doctor serves as a sardonic chorus throughout the comedy. He describes himself as a jolly but satiric person, not a very good doctor but a successful, self-made man. He is a curious mixture of brutality and honesty, shrewdness and naïve complacency.

The doctor comments slyly on the principal characters in the play, but he does not take an active part in the plot beyond acting as an amateur marriage broker for a rich middle-aged neighbor, who wants to marry Vera, the young girl of seventeen, dependent on the family. Vera finally agrees to marry the shy but kind neighbor after she has discovered that she cannot marry Belyayev, one of the tutors, with whom she has fallen in love during the month that he has been on the country estate. The character of Vera, which Turgenev himself did not consider of first importance, is one of the most finely drawn in the whole piece. The gradual unfolding of her love for Belyayev is indicated with great tenderness. She is so much of an unformed girl that she does not admit her love even to herself, until the avowal is drawn from her by the apparent sympathy of Natalya, the landowner's wife. When Vera has come to understand her own feelings, she also suddenly realizes that Natalya is her successful rival with the tutor, and she finds it hard to forgive the older woman's treachery. Vera is a girl with a straightforward emotional nature, which gradually comes to dominate her and which teaches her the harsh realities of Turgenev's comic world.

Belyayev is a much less fused and admirable human being. A simple young man, neglected by his father, he has managed to get an education and is now supporting himself by being a tutor. Though he is drawn to Vera, who reminds him of his sister, he is much more fascinated by the older and more accomplished Natalya. When he realizes that Natalya loves him, he is flattered and believes for a moment that he loves her, but he soon realizes the absurdity of his position. He falls under the influence of Rakitin, an older man, who is also in love with Natalya and who tells the young tutor with deep sincerity what a painful thing it is to be in love. Rakitin is motivated partly by jealousy and partly by a consideration for Natalya's true welfare. He himself leaves the estate to save her honor, taking the burden of her love affair with Belyayev upon his own shoulders. Rakitin cares for

Natalya profoundly, but by disillusioning the young tutor he brings about the temporary unhappiness of the woman to whom both of them are devoted.

Natalya is the central figure of *A Month in the Country*. Turgenev admits that he was most interested in her, and hers is an effective part, although a somewhat theatrical one. Her character is not altogether persuasive, in spite of the fact that her actions can be partially explained by the lack of a sufficient outlet for her average intelligence and her more than average emotional energy. Turgenev tells us a good deal about Natalya's past history, as if he wished to suggest that her psychology may be largely accounted for by her early environment. She had a stern father, to whom she had always been slavishly obedient and whom she feared even after he became old and blind. Her childhood was a constant series of repressions; she had little real youth of her own. Now that she is a married woman and has reached the dangerous age of twenty-nine she is eager to try to recapture at second hand some of the normal sensations which she had never experienced in her girlhood. She is slow to appreciate the state of her feelings for Belyayev, but when she once does so she is ruthless in attempting to gratify them. After the tutor's departure, she is for the moment completely heartbroken, but one suspects that Rakitin's solution of the difficulty was the best one for her ultimate happiness. Natalya will sooner or later recover from her painful experience. She will be fortunate if, later on, she does not meet another attractive young man, with no Rakitin to give him mature counsel.

A Month in the Country ends without having reached a very decisive conclusion. Natalya, her husband, her husband's mother, her son, and her son's German tutor will continue living on the estate. Life will go on in much the same way as it has done heretofore, and Natalya will no doubt continue to be restless and dissatisfied. She and Belyayev seem to be badly coördinated people by comparison with Rakitin and Vera, both of whom have secured emotional tranquillity at the cost of immediate happiness. No one of the four principal characters in this play has an agreeable prospect for the future. Only Natalya's stupid husband thinks that everything has come out in the best possible way for himself and all the others.

Turgenev's constant preoccupation seems to be with the idea that love is a capricious and unpredictable emotion, strong enough to upset any sensitive human being's equilibrium but not powerful enough to cause him to direct his complete energies into a single concentrated channel. All of the people in *A Month in the Country* have more or less violent passions, but no one of them is able to satisfy his impulses. There is some inhibiting force within them all which makes it impossible for them to express themselves as they would like to do. The practical circumstances of their lives have too much influence over them. They lack the strength of character that they should have if they are to be the masters of their own fates. This weakness provides excellent material for a highly individualized and original type of comedy. A sense of humor becomes identified with a perception of what man would be in contrast to what the innumerable details of life have made him become. A makeshift arrangement is the best outcome that can be hoped for in matters of the heart, which have to be organized according to man-made conventions, of marriage, of property, and of class distinctions. Unless there should be a radical shift of attitude towards these human institutions, there is no possibility that a healthy balance can be established in the unsteady society which is pictured in the comedies of Turgenev.

Maurice Valency (essay date 1966)

SOURCE: "Chekhov's Theatre," in *The Breaking String: The Plays of Anton Chekhov*, Schocken Books, 1983, pp. 3-47.

[*In the following excerpt from a work that was first published in 1966, Valency finds Turgenev's plays a mixture of realism and idealism, noting that they demonstrate "a very different realism from the noncommittal, 'scientific' sort, in which the author pointedly refrains from making judgments and taking sides. Turgenev took sides. He left no doubt as to where his sympathies lay."*]

Turgenev's career in the theatre was relatively short. In 1840, when he was 22, he completed his first serious play, *The Bachelor*. Ten years later, in 1850, he wrote *A Month in the Country*. Both plays were works of genius—the theatrepieces he wrote in the interval seem trivial in comparison. Shchedrin produced *The Bachelor* in 1849. Turgenev followed it up at once with *A Month in the Country*. But the censor handled this play so roughly that a complete text could not be published until 1869, and there was no performance until 1872, ten years after the publication of *Fathers and Sons*. By that time Turgenev had decided he had no talent for the stage, and wrote nothing more for it.

The Bachelor is a comedy. It has to do with the problems of a middle-aged jurist who is charged with the duty of marrying off his young ward, a charming girl. He ends by marrying her himself. The play is said to show the influence of Gogol. The relation seems clearer to Dostoevsky's early novel *Poor Folk* (1845). Gogol's *The Marriage* is a bitter farce; but plays like *The Bachelor* have few sharp edges. They are kindly works which take a relaxed and humane view of human nature; their humor differs widely from the acerbity of the type of social comedy in which the world is seen as a wilderness inhabited by jackals and kites. In Chekhov it is easier to see Turgenev than Gogol.

A consequence of the idea that realism and idealism are contrary attitudes is the expectation that the first will invariably disparage humanity, and the second will flatter it. But there certainly exists a considerable body of idealistic literature which takes society to task, more or less fiercely, for its shortcomings; and many examples come to mind of a type of realism which finds in the limitations of humanity a source of understanding, compassion, and hope. It is to this category that the work of both Turgenev and Chekhov belong. This is obviously a very different realism from the noncommittal, "scientific" sort, in which the author pointedly refrains from making judgments and taking sides. Turgenev took sides. He left no doubt as to where his sympathies lay; but he did not quarrel; he forebore to argue; and this aristocratic posture Chekhov also found congenial to his temper.

In *The Bachelor,* the young clerk Vilitsky, Masha's suitor, is not especially sympathetic. He is evidently a snob, and not overly bright; but Turgenev does not despise him. He understands his psychic predicament, and he sees the comic side of his Hamlet-like state of indecision. The kindly lawyer Moskvin, also, lends himself easily to caricature. A man of fifty who courts a young girl is traditionally out of his depth, but Turgenev's treatment of his middle-aged lover is a miracle of tact and sympathy. Similarly, in *A Month in the Country,* Turgenev tells the truth regarding his characters. None of them is especially admirable. But the author is courteous; there are neither heroes nor villains in his play, only men and women, subject to the impulses of nature, like all living things.

In *A Month in the Country* the portraiture could hardly be more realistic. Islayev is a good-natured man, simple, but no fool. He has long been cuckolded by his best friend; this is, after all, not an unusual state of affairs and, since the matter is never brought to his attention, it does not harm him in the least. Natalya is not only unfaithful to her husband, but also to her lover; when she realizes her passion for the young tutor, Belyayev, she becomes cruelly jealous of her ward, who also loves him, and in general she behaves abominably with respect to everyone. Yet she does not forfeit our sympathy; on the contrary, she arouses compassion. From a moral viewpoint, Rakitin, her lover, is doubtless much to blame, but he preserves his nobility. Even the scoundrelly old doctor Shpigelsky is drawn with understanding. What gives charm and depth to what might be considered a sordid situation is, evidently, the warm and delicate characterization, but there is more than this—it is, above all, a question of tone. The story is told from the viewpoint of one who has no idea of being censorious, but who desires chiefly to demonstrate the intricacy of human character. Unlike Stendhal, whose bitterly indignant novel *Le Rouge et le noir* perhaps suggested the situation in *A Month in the Country,* Turgenev seems to be at peace with the world he created. It makes a difference. The play is warm and wise. It is a comedy which leaves one with a feeling of sadness, but also with a feeling of strength. This was precisely the effect at which Chekhov aimed. Before he achieved it, however, he had to study Turgenev.

Turgenev's plays made use of a mode of characterization which as yet had no great currency in the theatre, and which was not clearly defined until Strindberg gave it memorable formulation in the Author's Foreword to *Miss Julie.* Characterization in the French drama of the period

was generally based on a static concept of personality, vaguely related to the theory of humors and similar physiological notions derived from the ancients. According to these ideas, character was predicated on the *faculté maît-resse,* the dominant trait which shaped the man. All that was necessary to fix a character for stage purposes was to identify this trait; an individual's behavior could then be motivated and justified in whatever circumstances the plot required. This system, which could be referred to such weighty authorities as Aristotle and Theophrastus, had the additional merit of convenience. It vastly simplified the definition of character, and made it possible to differentiate human types quite easily by means of identifying symbols which served the same purpose as the masks of the ancient stage or the *commedia dell'arte.* Moreover, the wealth of information handed down through the centuries with regard to human types distinguished in this manner was always readily available for the guidance of the actor, and, once he was given a clue with regard to the character—often the name was enough—he could invest himself with the role as if it were a costume.

This system, delightfully simple at bottom, was capable of considerable elaboration. It was conceivable that a dominant trait, no matter how masterful, could be nullified or transformed through a sufficiently powerful experience. Characters could thus be "developed" by means of plot, and a play could become an auto-educational experience, an exercise in self-revelation. Thus a coward, under stress, might discover that he was in fact brave, a generous man could be made to see his own stinginess, an ascetic might learn that he was at heart a lecher, or a pirate that he was in reality a sentimentalist. Unmaskings of this sort were, of course, by no means foreign to the classic concept of character. What was involved was a special sort of agnition, the sudden discovery, not of a physical but of a spiritual identity, accompanied by a psychic peripety. This could take place in an instant. It was therefore a very convenient device for the stage, and was in fact a favorite with authors from Farquhar to Shaw.

Turgenev's characterizations are not of this sort. For his people, life is a process of self-realization. They neither know themselves from the start, nor do they stumble upon themselves suddenly in the end. They discover themselves little by little, and are constantly surprised at the things they feel and do. The result is that we gain insight into their natures step by step as they do themselves, and are quite unprepared for the turns and contradictions in their behavior. The effect of this kind of development is extraordinarily lifelike.

Turgenev forebore to analyze. He did no more than to suggest, and since it is not always quite certain what it is that he suggests, the spectator's mind is not trapped in the author's labyrinth, but quite free to consider and to reflect. This technique is one of exploration and not of definition. Each suggestion is offered as temporary and provisional. In the end, the characters retain the enigmatic quality of people. The author makes no attempt to explain them beyond the point where they have explained themselves. This is the technique of impressionism.

In *A Month in the Country,* at the inception of her scene with Vera in act three, Natalya Islayeva has no certainty as to her feelings for the handsome young tutor. At the most she has a vague premonition, and she has no idea of what she is going to do, if anything. It is her behavior that defines her passion in her mind. When she realizes her motives, she is shocked, and still more when she sees how badly she is behaving. But she cannot help herself; it is as if she were possessed, and no one is more astonished than she when she recognizes this trace of evil in a nature that has so far revealed nothing but its kindliness.

In comparison with this sort of characterization, the classic methods are likely to seem summary and unvital. The idea that we do not know ourselves until our behavior forces us to a recognition is by now in the nature of a truism, but no dramatist before Turgenev—save perhaps Shakespeare in *Measure for Measure*—had thought to formulate a character in such terms. This technique, in fact, does not belong to the stage. The characters of drama are traditionally simple and whole, and completely submissive to the exigencies of the plot. Turgenev's methods belong to the novel. It was by way of Pushkin, Stendhal, and Balzac that Turgenev learned how to emancipate his characters from their story. Russian actors, whose ideas of characterization were formed mainly along classical lines, could not be expected to play these "over-delicate" pieces in which characters had no certain outline and quite defied definition; and Turgenev's awareness of the inappropriateness of his method very likely motivated his acceptance of the suggestion that his plays were not suited to the stage but might be read profitably as novels. At any rate, he acquiesced in this view and, after 1850, forebore to trouble the players with his subtleties.

Nick Worrall (essay date 1983)

SOURCE: "Turgenev's Plays 1834-1848" and "Turgenev's Plays 1848-1850," in *Nikolai Gogol and Ivan Turgenev,* Grove Press, Inc., 1983, pp. 116-38, 139-69.

[*In the following excerpt, Worrall analyzes all of Turgenev's plays except* A Month in the Country.]

Turgenev's reputation as a dramatist, in the English-speaking world, rests largely on a single play—*A Month in the Country*—the only one of his plays to be widely available in translation. Yet he was a far more prolific dramatist than Gogol. There are, in fact, five other substantial works which deserve to be considered in the same company: **'Where It's Thin, There It Breaks,'** *The Parasite, The Bachelor,* **'Lunch with the Marshal of the Nobility'** and **'A Provincial Lady'** plus two other shorter, but nonetheless interesting works: **'Indiscretion'** and **'Moneyless'.** This still does not take into account early works such as *Styeno* and the incomplete **'The Temptation of St Antony'** or the minor one-act plays **'Evening in Sorrento'** and **'Conversation on the High Road'.** In addition to the above, there exist titles and planned outlines of several other plays which were abandoned when Turgenev turned permanently to prose writing. His friend, the poet and editor Nekrasov, thought Turgenev as capable a dramatist as he was a short-story writer and novelist, even going so far as to say that it would be an advantage if he turned his hand permanently to the writing of plays.

His best plays were written in France, mostly during the late 1840s, including *The Parasite,* intended for Shchepkin's benefit but banned on the grounds that it was prejudicial to the good name of the landed gentry. *A Month in the Country,* completed in the early 1850s, was also banned, mainly on moral grounds. Nearly all his plays ran into problems of varying degrees of gravity with the censor, ranging from requests for excision and revision to outright bans on publication and performance. Disheartened by official reaction and by public response to his plays generally, disappointed by indifferent performances of his work in the theatre, Turgenev eventually turned his back on playwriting for good. He revised his existing work from time to time but otherwise turned his attention to the creation of novels and short stories. There is little doubt that he wished to make his mark as a dramatist. It was to drama, after all, that he addressed himself in the first instance. Prose writing had been a secondary attraction. There is also little doubt that Turgenev, like Gogol, although severely limited by the conditions of the theatre of his day, sought to reform the art of theatre and to mould a new form of dramatic writing. Instead he learned, if not exactly to despise the theatre, then seriously to underrate his achievement as a dramatist and, in later years, he was painfully dismissive of work which had cost him dearly in terms of patient creative effort.

Styeno

Literary critics and historians had known of the existence of Turgenev's Romantic drama, *Styeno,* written in the 1830s, but for a long time it was considered lost. It was rediscovered by the Turgenev scholar M. O. Gerzhenson and published in the magazine *Voices of the Past* in 1913. The adolescent Turgenev began work on the play in September 1834, and completed it in December the same year. It is a substantial work in terms of scale as well as ambition and runs to fifty pages of the 1970 edition of his poems and verse. The handling of the iambic verse form is rather uneven throughout and there are several inconsistencies of scansion (a point which was made to him at the time). Years later, when writing *Rudin,* Turgenev gave some of his own feelings about *Styeno* to the character Lezhnyov:

> You perhaps think I didn't write verses? I did, sir, even a complete drama in the style of *Manfred.* Among the characters there was a ghost with blood on its breast, and not his own blood mark you, but the blood of mankind in general.

In later life, Turgenev admitted to having worshipped Byron in his youth and *Styeno* certainly bears the marks of this idolatry, with many scenes from *Manfred* finding their way into it in barely concealed form.

'The Temptation of St Antony'

The text of the uncompleted play **'The Temptation of St Antony'**, about which Turgenev had written to A. A. Bakunin in 1842, was eventually located and published in the *Revue des études slaves,* vol. 30 (1953), by the French scholar André Mazon. Work on the play belongs to the spring of 1842 and the date on the first page of the manuscript is 8 March. In a letter to Bakunin, in early April, Turgenev described how he was 'seeing the play in my sleep'. The first three scenes (the largest) were, he said, complete and there was a character, Annunziata, who, although she was the devil's mistress was, nevertheless, 'an extremely amiable [*prelyubeznaya*] girl etc. etc. . . .' (The word suggests a possible pun on the Russian for 'fornicator'—*prelyubodei*.) At the end of April, Turgenev announced that work on the play was proceeding in fits and starts and mostly by night. That is the last that was heard of it, except for the song which Annunziata sings towards the beginning:

> Under the window of the beautiful 'donna'
> For more than an hour, in full moonlight
>   There walks a youth in love
>   Clad in a black velvet cape . . .

which appeared in another play, **'Two Sisters'**, set in Spain, which Turgenev started work on in 1844 and then abandoned. The song took a slightly different form in the second play but what is interesting about both variants is that they prefigure the basic situation in the drama which became **'Indiscretion'**.

The basis of the rather fantastic plot of Turgenev's **'The Temptation of St Antony'** was the original legend, but the subject had been suggested to him by Prosper Mérimée's comedy *The Devil Woman,* or *The Temptation of St Antony*; Mérimée had included this in his volume of plays called *The Theatre of Clara Gazul,* which was a hoax in the form of the works of an imaginary Spanish woman playwright, but which had been taken as a kind of French manifesto of Romanticism. Critics had also detected traces of a new realistic direction in the work, which seems to have appealed to Turgenev who, by 1842, had already shed most of his youthful Romantic leanings. The Romantic style in the manner of *Styeno* is both recalled and made fun of in this play, which is in no sense a mere re-working of the Mérimée original but stands as a totally independent work. It parodies the clichés of the saintly life and contrasts realistic scenes set in the boudoir of the courtesan, Annunziata, with romantically fantastic scenes on the seashore, involving devils, imps, clouds and waves (all with speaking parts). In a seemingly complete overthrow of the values enshrined in *Styeno,* Turgenev appears to exalt the real over the ideal

and 'exposes over-fervid religious ecstasy'. The experimental aspect of the play is important in so far as it shows Turgenev bent on destroying old forms and reaching forward to a dramatic world which anticipates something akin to Strindberg's *A Dream Play.*

The play, as it exists, occupies twenty pages of the 1970 edition of Turgenev's poems and verse and breaks off part way through Scene 3 at a fairly crucial point in the development. The only substantial gaps are in the 'Chorus Of The Waves', in Scene 3, where Turgenev was clearly having problems with the verse and left some of the lines incomplete. Most of the play is in prose dialogue, except for the songs and choruses. One whole scene of reminiscence between the hermit Antony and his former comrade-in-arms, Carlo Spada, is composed in verse form. The title page describes it as a 'drama in one act'.

'Indiscretion'

Turgenev's first published dramatic work, like **'The Temptation of St Antony'**, was a direct result of the influence of Prosper Mérimée's *The Theatre of Clara Gazul.* **'Indiscretion'**, described as a 'comedy in one act', is a typical product of the Spanish theatre with its serenading under balconies, culminating in a bloody drama of jealousy and murder.

The play was first published in 1843 and its only stage production to date was in 1884 when a German company in St Petersburg performed it on two or three occasions in a German version. Belinski recognized a similarity between the 'conversion' of the hero, Victor Alexeyevich (in Turgenev's long poem, *Parasha*) to that of Don Pablo in **'Indiscretion'**. When Victor marries Parasha he changes from a Byronic hero into a conventional landowner, just as the perpetrator of a *crime passionel,* Don Pablo, metamorphoses into a respectable civil servant in the epilogue to **'Indiscretion'**. Just as Belinski saw *Parasha* to be 'full of inner content and distinguished by humour and irony', so the parodistic conjunction of ultra-romantic passion with elements of the comedy of manners was seen to characterize **'Indiscretion'**.

One of the interests of the play is that it works in several different modes at once—farcical, romantic and realistic. There seems a clear debt to Molière in the marriage of a young wife to an old husband and in the depiction of the serenading lover who climbs fences and balconies, is threatened by a drunken gardener with a club and a pack of dogs, who hides behind trees to escape detection and, generally, cuts a fairly undignified figure. In the romantic mode there is the crime of passion commited by Don Pablo, as well as elements of Don Rafael's wooing of Donna Dolores. On the realistic level there is an element which can be seen to underlie Mozart's *Don Giovanni,* and which relates to the contemporary position and treatment of women. In this sense, Donna Dolores occupies a position similar to that of Donna Anna and Donna Elvira in the opera. It is probably true to say that, had **'Indiscretion'** been known to the Feminist Movement, it would not have remained neglected.

Donna Dolores (her name signifies her condition) is twenty-seven and married to a man nearly thirty years her senior. She lives in a house which is guarded like a fortress and which seems to be surrounded by an outer stone wall and an inner picket fence, through which the only access is a gate kept permanently locked and guarded by Pepe, the gardener. Inside the house, Margarita, an old servant, acts as additional guard to Donna Dolores and, when necessary, locks her in her room whenever her husband is away. Dolores has led a permanently sheltered life, having been educated in a convent, and her view of alternatives to her humdrum existence has been gained from romantic novels. It is in this condition, at night on her balcony, that we and the would-be seducer, Don Rafael de-Luna, discover her at the beginning of the play.

The most striking aspect of Donna Dolores is her vulnerability in relation to the predominantly masculine world around her. To Don Rafael she is an innocent fool to be sexually exploited. To her husband (until his feelings of security are undermined) she is an object of consumption, or a fetishist plaything. For Don Pablo Sangre (whose name suggests his bloodiness) she serves as the focus of all his frustrated passions which exist irrespective of their object and which can just as easily turn to mad destructiveness. Even for Margarita, she is the personification of all her class frustrations in a world where the servant sees 'riches' as of prime importance. She

even blames the innocent Donna Dolores for the evil effects of such values on her own daughter. The actual causes of both their sufferings are shown to be the men who control their lives and the male-dominated society which exists to perpetuate these forms of control. The metaphor used to describe the relationship between the male characters in the play and Donna Dolores is that of cat to mouse. Don Balthasar d'Esturiz says, as he contemplates the prospect of Donna Dolores awaiting his return:

> I remember, when a good juicy, ripe pear was given to me, I did not eat it right away like any other foolish boy or scapegrace . . . no, I would sit down, stealthily take the pear out of my pocket, examine it from all sides, kiss it, stroke it, put it to my lips, take it away again—admire it from a distance, admire it close to, then, at last, shut my eyes and bite into it. Ah, I really should have been born a cat.

Later, when Don Pablo is contemplating murder, he describes Donna Dolores as being 'in his claws' and there is a sense in which Don Rafael's playful asides to the audience, as he comments on the naïveté of his victim, also convey a predatory aspect to the seduction.

The men in the play are revealed as inferior, passionately, to Donna Dolores. The double fence which surrounds her is more a barrier to their own male fear of passion than it is a bar to female feeling. The 'weak spot' in the barrier, which has to be built higher and stronger, refers more to their own incarceration in a prison of suppressed emotion than it does to the suppression of women. (Turgenev uses this image of a barrier, or dam, built against the release of emotion in **'Where It's Thin, There It Breaks'** and also in *A Month in the Country.*) Don Pablo's love, which has turned to destructive hate, appears as a direct product of this involuted self-suppression.

The final scene of the play contains the confrontation between the insane Don Pablo and Donna Dolores. He confesses his love and recognizes that she has nothing but contempt for him. The intention to murder her has been there from the outset and the prolongation of the scene becomes a form of perverse luxury. When faced with death, Donna Dolores, who has been conscious of a sense of fate, is superbly and pathetically defiant. A final irony is her declaration of love for the pitiful Don Rafael. In a denouement reminiscent of Lessing's *Emilia Galotti,* the male murderer stands holding the knife over the murdered female but here the real tragedy is obscured by the selfconscious melodramatization of the male protagonists, who experience the situation as an illustration of their own tragic destiny, in a manner which anticipates Ibsen. An epilogue of a few lines, depicting the scene ten years later, sets the seal on the 'comedy':

> *Scene: The Office of an important official. A secretary at the table. Enter Don Pablo Sangre, Count of Torreno.*
>
> COUNT PABLO: (*busily to the secretary*) Are my papers ready? It's time for me to. . . .

SECRETARY: (*respectfully*) Here they are, your Highness. (*Both go out.*)

Not only has the murder gone unpunished but Don Pablo appears to have been elevated to the rank of Count. Aristocratic and bureaucratic life goes on over the corpses of the victims. Commenting on this façade, Don Pablo had earlier remarked:

> True, some eccentric person might think a crime was being committed in the house, or was about to be committed. . . . But that's all nonsense. Here are living modest, quiet, settled people. . . .

'Moneyless'

Nothing appears more surprising than Turgenev's decision in 1845, following the composition of **'Indiscretion'**, to turn his attention to a pure Russian vaudeville. The main influence in his attempt to exploit a debased genre appears to have been the example of Gogol, especially in the choice of milieu and in the conception of the central characters, Zhazikov and Matvyei. Another influence can be seen in the increasing popularity, during the 1840s in Russia, of vignettes of Russian life in prose form, in which the manners and mores of specific classes were depicted with considerable fidelity—the so-called 'physiological sketches' of the Natural School which Russian criticism refers to, and which find a counterpart in the pictorial art of the period. In **'Moneyless'**, however, Turgenev exploits vaudeville only superficially; the play is devoid of the traditional couplets, the conventional love intrigue and only retains one typical device—the string of creditors who call at Zhazikov's apartment, but here each is a carefully delineated social type, not a caricatural mask.

The Russian title **'Bezdenezh'e'** literally means 'one without money' and the play is, indeed, about money and the lack of it. At the same time, it is like a kaleidoscope through which can be observed the changing patterns of a whole social system. Through the close-up technique of the vaudeville-cum-physiological sketch, Turgenev offers a view of a complete social process and a changing society. The play's subtitle is **'Scenes from the Petersburg Life of a Young Nobleman'**. The young nobleman (clearly modelled on Khlestakov [in Gogol's *The Inspector General*]) and his servant (very like Osip) occupy an apartment on an upper (that is, inferior) floor of a St Petersburg tenement house. The life-style of the young man is at odds with his claim to the title of nobleman. He is penniless and the apartment is modest. During the course of the action various representatives of the emerging class of city tradesmen, the petty bourgeoisie, call on him virtually non-stop in an attempt to retrieve debts, while the master feigns absence and leaves his servant to deal with the callers. Finally, an acquaintance from the country appears, who lends him some money, and the play ends with a comment from the servant on how times have changed.

At the centre of the play is Zhazikov. He has left his family estate in the country in charge of his ageing mother and has settled in St Petersburg, the centre of everything epitomizing the truly noble existence in early nineteenth-century Russia. The implication is that the estate is rapidly deteriorating, while Zhazikov squanders family money. He appears to represent the culmination of a process of profligacy and waste, but acts as if no change at all were taking place and the status of the nobility unaffected; as if this concept were in some miraculous fashion separable from the possession of money. The play sets out to demonstrate the vacuousness of the notion of 'the nobleman' once the basis of superiority, in the form of property and wealth, is absent. Zhazikov and Matvyei retain and act out their roles as master and servant in circumstances which are ludicrously inappropriate, and yet their identities depend entirely on this notion of role-playing. The actual reversal of these roles, with the pattern of their necessary maintenance for the parties concerned, is conveyed with superb comic effect. Whenever a creditor calls, this is accompanied by the persistent ringing of a bell. The aristocrat (the conventional ringer of the bell to summon a servant) starts like a frightened hare on each occasion and runs for cover. It has become an almost Pavlovian motif by the end of the play as we observe the nobleman reduced to his reflexes. Meanwhile, Matvyei assumes the role of the master in confronting the creditors, as well as becoming the spokesman for aristocratic values.

The comedy of the piece is skilfully contrived and is mainly based on contradictions and contrasts within what is said and between the various characters who come and go, three of whom are never seen by the audience. Turgenev makes great play with the spectator's imaginative capacity to envisage the character behind the highly flavoured speech patterns and is particularly successful in the case of the invisible merchant—anxious about his money and constantly returning to the topic with mechanical variations on the same phrase: 'There's none lying around by any chance?', and torn between not wishing to appear presumptuous or over-pressing and a natural impulse to lay his hands on what is owed him.

The arrival of Blinov, the acquaintance from the country, highlights a principal social theme of the play—the contrast, but at the same time the fundamental connection, between town and country. The country, for Matvyei the servant, represents tradition and a secure master and serf relationship whose lineage he describes in the family as he remembers it in Zhazikov's grandfather's and in his father's time. 'Things are not what they used to be', says Matvyei; 'Your grandfather, Timofei Lukich, blessed be his memory, was a very tall man', he declares, as if the present were composed of midgets. In fact, the terms of Matvyei's description of the members of the family are reminiscent of the decaying grotesques who populate Gogol's *Dead Souls*. Zhazikov, by contrast, has nothing but contempt for the country, where he sees 'lack of education' and unattractive girls. An ironic point here is that his range of choice in St Petersburg appears to extend all the way from one 'Verochka' to the laundry girl who calls with a bill. Matvyei wants to be a serf, and a serf is not a serf in town. Zhazikov wants to be an aristocrat—and how can one be an aristocrat in the country?

In an extended soliloquy, Zhazikov eventually manages to convince himself that things are not so bad in the country after all—a recognition of the need to return and try to get the estate into some sort of order. But the contemplated return becomes a nostalgic turning-back of the clock, as if the process of superannuation, so obviously present in the context of the city, did not extend to include the landed estates which were now rapidly being engrossed by a new entrepreneurial class with business acumen.

Blinov represents the new type. His description of the prolonged legal wrangling about estate boundaries, which he is disputing with his neighbour, and which he has come to the capital to settle in court, suggests just how closely the apparent opposites of town and country are linked. We also gain an insight into what St Petersburg actually represents for Zhazikov. He shares Blinov's eagerness to combine going to the theatre to see 'a tragedy' with dining out at 'a cafe with an organ' and visiting the circus to watch big fat 'mamzelles' who 'ride standing on horses'. There is an element of condescension in Zhazikov's expression of his willingness to introduce Blinov to these delights, but they appear to represent to him the apotheosis of city culture.

The play ends with Zhazikov and Blinov going off to the tragedy and to the circus. Now that he has been lent some money, the country can 'go to the devil'. Matvyei concludes the action with an ultra-conservative remark addressed at the back of the departing Blinov, whom he recognises as the new breed of master:

> Gone is the Golden Age! How changed is the nobility!

'Where It's Thin, There It Breaks'

In 1847, Turgenev attended a performance of Alfred de Musset's 'proverbe', *Un Caprice* in Paris. The dramatic form of the 'proverbe' was originally that of a charade designed to illustrate the proverbial saying which formed the last line of the play and it was this form which Turgenev adopted for his next comedy, written in 1848, for the St Petersburg actress V. V. Samoilova. The work is conceived in an altogether different style from his previous plays. The emphasis is on the subtle psychological interplay of feeling which underlies the surface of salonplay dialogue. A more genuine level of reality surfaces when the flimsy veil ruptures at its most vulnerable points.

Musset's theatre was very popular in Russia at the time and continued to be so. Later, Tchaikovsky is said to have been wildly enthusiastic about his work. Even plays which were not popular in Paris were highly successful in St Petersburg and, in fact, the triumphant de Musset

revival at the Comédie Française, which really began with the production of *Un Caprice* witnessed by Turgenev, owed much to the championing of his cause by the Russian actress A. M. Karatygina.

'Where It's Thin, There It Breaks' depicts the attempts of Vera Nikolayevna, the daughter of a rich landowning widow, Anna Vasilyevna Libanova, to get Gorski, the son of a female neighbour, to marry her. The action is set against the background of the Libanova country house, a resplendent eighteenth-century edifice of Italian design in the Russian countryside. Vera's romantic view of love and marriage is opposed by Gorski's more cynical realism, and the plot concerns the latter's emotional vacillation—first romantically susceptible and then prosaically disinclined. The action climaxes in Vera's frustrated acceptance of the proposal of the naïve and lovesick Stanitsyn, an action which contains, as part of its intention, an attempt to pierce the protective shell of Gorski's egotism. In the background hover a third suitor, Mukhin, the governess Mlle Bienaimé, a Captain Chukhanov, who is a permanent guest in the Libanova household, and Libanova's companion and relation, Varvara Ivanovna.

The play's first performance was given on 10 December 1851, and was not a success. It was revived at the Alexandrinski Theatre in 1891 and, more successfully, at the Moscow Art Theatre in 1912, with Olga Knipper and Vasili Kachalov. Kachalov acted Gorski as someone whose ideas and desires are weakened by coldness of spirit, exhausted by egotism and fruitless activity of the mind. This view of the character corresponds to a tendency in Russian criticism to see Gorski as one of the first dramatic embodiments of the 'superfluous man'. Typically, he is a scion of the upper class, cut-off intellectually from that class and from society as a whole, doomed to agonize self-obsessively over every action and to sully everything of worth with which he comes into contact, either from a sense of world-weary cynicism or in a spirit of casual destructiveness. The prototype of the species is considered to be Pushkin's Eugene Onegin. Turgenev wrote his own **'Diary of a Superfluous Man'** in 1850 and the type is well described by Alexander Herzen:

> The distinguishing feature of our epoch is *grübeln* [to deliberate]. We do not wish to take a step without first having thought about it; we constantly delay, like Hamlet, and think, think. . . . There is no time to act; we chew interminably over both the past and the present, everything which is happening to us and to others; we seek justification, clarification, enquire into ideas and truths.

The play can be described as Turgenev's version of Gogol's *Marriage*. At one point Gorski declares that he will not, like Podkolyosin, leap out of the window but will leave quietly by the door into the garden. The irony is that he sees this as superior behaviour when, in fact, Turgenev implies that the leap from the window had something to recommend it. It was at least unconventional. Everyone in the play is in the grip of convention. Everything is codified by rules and regulations. The

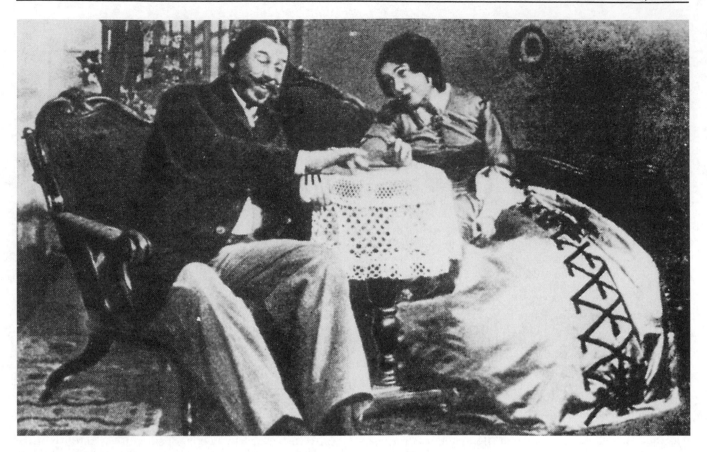

A scene from the 1912 Moscow Art Theatre production of A Provincial Lady.

characters appear to be trapped between two worlds—the world of Nature on the one hand and the world of art and artifice on the other, between romantic ideals and prosaic realities. The only way in which they chart a course between the 'Scylla' of the one and 'Charybdis' of the other (to borrow Gorski's mythological terminology) is through the establishment of civilized rules and conventions. But these merely succeed in parodying the 'higher', more spiritual, sides of the equation while suppressing the connection with the 'lower', more prosaic and physical sides of reality—an aspect of severance from the natural world in general. The characters exist in a kind of limbo, part flesh, part spirit, struggling half-heartedly towards a higher unity of opposites. As in Gogol's play, the symbol of that desired unity is marriage, seen by some as an end in itself, recognized by others as an evasion. Ideal marriage involves the unity of opposites. Actual marriage is a ritualized and conventionalized hollow unity masking an essential separateness.

Critics usually see Vera as in some sense superior to Gorski—she a kind of Don Quixote, he a Hamlet figure. The truth, however, is that Vera's positive, almost Shavian, drive towards improving the species through marriage with Gorski is revealed as a parodied version of natural and instinctive drives, just as his retreat into the

world of the mind in order to counter her assault on his emotions is revealed as a parodied version of the world of intellect and imagination. Both are entirely conventional creatures whose egos just happen to be more strongly developed than others. The desirable conflict, leading to a unity of opposites, is presented as a petty egotistical affair which, instead of leading to a synthesis on a higher plane, leads to a false unity on a lower plane—the marriage between Vera and Stanitsyn.

As well as being a very Gogolian play, we are reminded of Turgenev's interest in the Hegelian dialectic but, in this instance, the conflicts are presented in all their hollowness. There is much talk of winning and losing, which metaphorically links the world of human action with talk of military conflict and with game-playing. Losing and winning have become the human by-products of a petty and meaningless conflict. The recognition of the necessity of battle is implicit within the play, but winning or losing in a conventional sense is shown not to be the point. For the most part, the characters evade the recognition of necessary struggle, or take part in activities which merely parody it. They view life in a petty, individualistic way where there can only be the see-saw oppositions between 'higher' and 'lower', 'winner' and 'loser'. Never, it seems, can the conflict be converted into a higher synthesis through concerted human struggle. The 'break' in the play occurs at the thinnest point between opposites—between winning and losing, between male and female, between the ideal and the real, between art and nature. It is as if the fabric of life were being tugged from opposed ends, destructively, instead of being co-operatively woven into clearer and more durable form. Because there exists no co-ordinated and conscious recognition of the pattern and purpose of struggle, its parodied version takes the form of the love duel and games of chance, where there is opposition but no genuine conflict and the outcome is based on arbitrariness and hazard.

There are two symbolic gestures in the play which appear as intended parallels. Vera plucks a rose to give to Gorski but is then prevented from doing so by the presence of Mukhin. She ends by throwing aside the rose, which Gorski later picks up and puts in his pocket. The parallel is with the action of Captain Chukhanov. He is kept on sufferance in the Libanova household as a permanent guest and to make up a third at card games. He has been picking mushrooms in the garden, which he then offers to Libanova in his hat. Her response is to tell him that a hat is no place for mushrooms; they belong on a plate. The mushrooms have been stooped for at ground level, are then placed in something taken from the head and, in this form, are offered in a gesture of self-effacing generosity. The only dialectic appreciated by Libanova is a connection between mushrooms and plates as an aspect of conventional propriety. Although only a modest moment of synthesis, the significance of Chukhanov's gesture evades her consciousness entirely. Turgenev intends that it should not escape us. By contrast, the rose is offered in a totally different spirit. Vera intends it as a symbol, which implicates her feelings for Gorski and his for her. The presence of Mukhin forces her to lie and say that she picked it for herself. But the lie contains a truth. She did, in fact, pick it for herself, because she is symbolized by it and projects her own feelings into the rose as symbol. It is a gesture of pure egotism. Once its extraneous value is redundant, she casts the rose aside and the original plucking of the flower can now be seen as a wilfully destructive action. Gorski's placing it in his pocket merely compounds the desecration. He will produce the rose at the end of the play, wilted, merely in order to humiliate Vera with a reminder of the evanescence of her feelings for him.

The figure of the captain is allied with that of the companion, Varvara Stepanovna. They are the dialectical opposites of Gorski and Vera but occupy an equivalent position of importance in the play. Varvara Stepanovna appears to count hardly at all in the scheme of things, like Ivanov in *The Parasite.* She and the captain say very little but, in the triangular card game, it is she who appears to deliberately 'lose' in order that the captain should 'win'. Their saying nothing, or next to nothing, becomes the dialectical opposite of the pointless garrulousness of the protagonists. Their possessing nothing is the opposite of the others' possessing everything. They emerge, strangely, as the hero and heroine of the play,

linking arms in military formation at the end when the group prepares to march 'out there', into the forest. The two are linked together by the notion of service. The captain's final words are 'Ready to serve'. Excursions into the outer world appear brief and hazardous. The captain, like Zhevakin in *Marriage,* has made these sorties and knows what it is to 'storm a fortress'—a version of the eternal conflict which has its own lessons to teach about the capacity of humans for violence and suffering. The others venture out timidly in the rain and sun and have to scurry back to the protective confines of their Rastrellian dwelling. What could better exemplify the absurd challenge which one form of art lays before nature than the erection of a Rastrellian mansion in the wilderness of the Russian countryside? The more permanent forms of challenge, or transcendence, are made by poetry and music, the first of which Gorski despises, the second of which Vera merely dabbles in.

Poetry appears to occupy an equivalent position in this play to the rose plucked by Vera. It is only seen to exist as an appendage of the egos of the characters. The most poetic moment is the evocation, by Gorski, of the moonlit night on the lake where he has rowed Vera Nikolayevna and when, as he describes it, he almost lost control of himself under the spell of her physical proximity and the moonlit setting, even going to the lengths of delivering himself of some verses by Lermontov. The first thing to note is that Gorski's recounting of this magical moment is in a mood of cynical disavowal and shame, now that the spell has worn off. It is also a betrayal of Vera's confidence, which he calculates Mukhin will relay to her and so precipitate the untying of the emotional knot he fears has been made by the shared experience. What we also note is another kind of betrayal in the egotistically false note of the poetic evocation. Nature is reduced to a mere theatrical backdrop for the posings of the characters. The lake becomes reduced to a modest-sized pond and the light on the scene comes as much from the candle held by the watchful Mlle Bienaimé on the balcony as it does from any actual moon.

The musical moment comes later, when the two egos of Vera and Gorski clash, again under the watchful eye of Mlle Bienaimé, as Vera accompanies herself on the piano (a Clementi sonata) while carrying on an accusatory conversation with Gorski. The beauty of the music is incidental to her self-expression and she even uses the music, in the manner of the rose, to add symbolic emphasis to what she is saying by 'beating hard on the keys' or 'playing gently' when she is being more seductive. The comic irony here is that she seems to be a merely average dilettante. The tête-à-tête is interrupted by Mlle Bienaimé's dry cough and her pointed remark that the sonata 'sounds difficult to play'.

Gorski turns out to be contemptuous of poetry and poetic natures: 'Long live mockery, hilarity and malice', he declares, 'Now I am again in my element'. (The phrase he uses translates literally as 'on my own plate again'— a conscious echo of the earlier episode with the mushrooms.) In opting out of marriage, he has opted out of the dialectic into singleness and has thrown away the poetic part of himself, just as earlier he had cast aside the novel he was reading, the contents of which seemed to him to be just obvious foolishness. He can only joke at the end of the play. *'Welche Perle warf ich weg!'* (What a pearl I've thrown away!)—the retreat into a foreign language being part of the evasion. He has also thrown the more precious part of himself away but can only melodramatize his situation—the gall and bile which rise in his throat being the consequence of egotistically wounded pride where Vera's sword-thrust (her engagement to Stanitsyn) can be seen to have found its mark. Words are the only protection he has against his own nullity, which he chooses to think of as complexity: 'Don't tear the last decisive word out of me . . .' he begs Vera as he dodges this way and that to escape definition, because in his heart of hearts he suspects that in veering between one state and another he has ended up as nothing.

Gorski is very fond of attributing everything to Fate or Chance and wondering whether Fate is laughing at him or assisting him. He plays a game on his own whereby the chance potting of a billiard ball will be seen to determine his fate. Recognizing this as mere childishness, he throws the cue aside. Yet the tripartite pattern of the game itself is important, although Gorski does not recognize the fact. He has earlier said in conversation with Mukhin that his task was to chart a course between Scylla and Charybdis. The point becomes the active charting of a course and not the leaving of matters to chance, just as the skill in billiards involves a relationship between three elements and maintaining those elements in play.

What, finally, is the implication of the proverb which forms the title to the play? What does Mukhin mean when he quotes it at the end? He would seem to be referring to a 'break' in Gorski's ego which his manifestation of high spirits is not quite managing to disguise. Anyone who attempts to exist through mere singularity (and all are single in this play) constructs the world purely in terms of the self, the most extreme manifestation of which is egotism. The finale produces the harnessing of couples—a realignment of forces within a group—for the march to the forest. However, allying yourself to another, or forming ranks, does not automatically overcome the problem, but can constitute other kinds of weakness, or thinness. The relationship between Vera and Stanitsyn seems especially vulnerable. Between the captain and Varvara Ivanovna there is a kind of unity of relationship, although not a particularly profound one, which is synthesized in a third element—that of 'service'. Anna Vasilyevna simply represents indomitable egotism and it is apt that she joins ranks with Gorski in the finale. The case of Mlle Bienaimé appears to be slightly different. She is not just a governess and watchdog but has something of the spiritual guardian about her as both worker and educator. The most striking images of her presence in the play are when she is seen holding a candle on the balcony, providing a third element in this moment of epiphany, this Moonlight Sonata, and also, when she sits, working a pattern on canvas, during the piano-playing scene. She appears to be a comic version

of a dialectical trinity, the three in one, offering work, service and enlightenment. One of her final actions, in order to 'win' Mukhin, is to engage him in a game of billiards which she 'loses' (we suspect that she ensures that he wins).

As well as the debt to de Musset, we are reminded of how steeped in the work of Shakespeare Turgenev had been since childhood. The subtitle of this, his most Shakespearian, as well as his most de Musset-like play, might well be *Much Ado about a Midsummer Night's Dream of Nothing.*

. . . . .

The Parasite

Turgenev's second major play for the professional theatre, *The Parasite,* was written at the request of Shchepkin and completed, in France, in 1848. Like the pictures in the album which Mukhin contemplates in **'Where It's Thin, There It Breaks'** of 'views from Italy'—with the suggestion of a reciprocal process, both 'views of' and 'views from'—this play is a view of Russia 'from abroad', where one of the characters, Tropachov, always intends going but, instead, has to make do with lithographs in an album. The play was immediately banned, ostensibly because, according to the censor, it presented the Russian nobility in a 'contemptuous light'.

The Parasite circulated in manuscript and achieved quite wide popularity. It was first published in *The Contemporary,* in 1857, under the title **Alien Bread** and the first performance was permitted in 1861. During the nineteenth century and, occasionally since, the two-act play has been presented as a one-acter, leaving out the whole of the second part and concluding with the revelation of Kuzovkin's paternity at the end of Act 1. The actor V. N. Davydov was among the first to appreciate what a travesty this was when he wrote:

> I cannot understand how Russian actors have not been able, and are still unable, to understand the beauty of the second act, finding it faded and pale, even unnecessary. The second act is unconditionally stronger and more artistic than the first. It is full of incomparable psychology.

The parasite in question is Vasili Semyonich Kuzovkin, who has lived on the estate of the Korin family for the past thirty years, fourteen of which have been spent in the company of the daughter of the deceased owners and an aunt who looked after the girl following the death of her mother. Olga Petrovna, the daughter, moved to St Petersburg at the age of fourteen and is now returning to her family estate seven years later in the company of her newly acquired husband, a thirty-two-year-old, town-bred collegiate councillor, Pavel Nikolayevich Yeletski. Kuzovkin still lives on the estate, which continues to be staffed by a retinue of servants, because of a prolonged legal wrangle surrounding the settlement of his own inherited property which has gone on for the past twenty years or so. In Korin's time, Kuzovkin appears to have served as a butt for the cruel humour of a tyrannical master who, as well as being consistently unfaithful to his wife, was an unpredictable and violent man. The memory of Kuzovkin's role as 'estate fool' is revived by the arrival of an old friend of the family, the neighbour Tropachov, who has come to greet the newly-weds. [In this scene, Kuzovkin is] . . . baited into recounting the history of his abortive litigation, mocked at and, finally, crowned with a fool's cap. His response to this revival of earlier humiliations is to declare in the presence of the young husband, and within earshot of the daughter, that he is, in fact, her real father.

The second act deals with the aftermath of this revelation, in which Kuzovkin first declares this admission to have been madness and then, in private conversation with Olga, says it is true. Out of a sense of loyalty to her husband, Olga conveys this to him. He, in turn, seeks to remove Kuzovkin from the house by buying his confession to having told a lie, giving him enough money to purchase his estate from in chancery and over the head of rival claimants—the heirs of a German called Hanginmester. Olga eventually persuades Kuzovkin to accept the money, and his departure is explained by the announcement that he has finally 'come into his estate'. He leaves, having reached an agreement in confidence to have private conference with 'his daughter' whenever he should visit the Yeletski estate in future.

The first production opened on 30 January 1862, at the Bolshoi Theatre, Moscow, for Shchepkin's benefit performance and with a strong cast. The play was revived at the Alexandrinski Theatre in 1889 for V. N. Davydov's benefit, when only the first act was presented, then again in 1916 when it was acted in its entirety. The first act was given as part of the Moscow Art Theatre's *Turgenev Evening,* in 1912. Just before his death, Davydov revived his performance as Kuzovkin during the 1924-25 season at the Maly Theatre, Moscow. In an otherwise lukewarm review in *Pravda,* the critic Pavel Markov described Davydov's performance as:

> . . . material for research not only into the art of the actor, but into the lives of the insulted and the injured such as Davydov shows us in the parasite Kuzovkin.

The reference to the 'insulted and injured' is a common one in Russian criticism of the play which places it, as Marc Slonim has pointed out [in *Russian Theater from the Empire to the Soviets,* 1963], in a line which 'stems from Gogol's "little man", later taken up by Dostoevski', with Akaki Akakyevich, in 'The Overcoat,' as a forerunner.

Davydov was right when he pointed to the wealth of psychological matter in the play. At the same time, most critics would seem to be wrong in regarding it as a defence of the 'little man', in addition to its being a criticism of feudal Russia. English translators tend to evade a recognition in the play's title, **Nakhlebnik,** of a direct

meaning of 'parasite' in favour of the more neutral **The Boarder, A Poor Gentleman,** or **The Family Charge.** Foreign translations opt for the even more neutral **Alien Bread.** However, the true significance of the play needs to be seen to depend upon the recognition that the meanings of *nakhlebnik* are negative. It *is* a Gogolian play, but its roots lie less in 'The Overcoat', as is generally thought, than in the Gogol work which Tropachov refers to indirectly in Act 2 when he speaks of the Emperor or China, namely *The Diary of a Madman.* Seen in this light, the play becomes an altogether different and more original, as well as more profound, artistic work.

The themes of the play can be stated, in general terms, as social breakdown and fragmentation accompanied by loss of meaning and individual identity. The loss of connection in the social world is paralleled in the more intimate world of personal and family relationships. People move and respond to the dictates of natural instinct and appetite, or to the mechanical and tyrannical demands of convention and habit, or out of a grossly distorted sense of their own individual significance—an aspect of an attempt to counter the prevailing sense of a loss of individual meaning. In this situation, those at the bottom of the heap serve to confirm the identity of those at the top. A psychological means of asserting one's own value is to imagine oneself, like Gogol's madman, to be the Emperor of China. Those at the top of the heap can only tolerate this destabilization of hierarchical order by describing the claim as mad. To a certain extent, this is what happens when Kuzovkin makes a claim for his own worth, by asserting a consanguinous relationship with the wife of a 'high Petersburg official'. The complication arises from the fact that, whereas we recognise Poprishchin's claim to be the Emperor of China as 'false', there are less good reasons for doubting Kuzovkin's claim to be Olga's father. Yet, the situation which Turgenev portrays is a form of madness. The division between social and personal worlds is given poignant significance through the *making public* of the claim. To 'go out of one's mind', in this sense, is to make generally public knowledge that which was hitherto personally intimate. The reason Kuzovkin 'goes out of his mind', lies in the fact that the claim to paternity has less to do with the fact of intimate feeling and blood relationship, than with his claim for his own *individual* significance in *this kind of world.* In brilliant fashion, Turgenev dramatizes the claim for, and the attribution of, identity of an inherently false kind, as well as the simultaneous destruction of true identity in the human connection between father and daughter. To declare that Kuzovkin *is* mad, as he frequently describes himself to be, and as he is frequently described by others, flies in the face of generally accepted readings of the play, but madness, social and personal, appears to be its crucial theme.

The opening is almost pure 'theatre of the grotesque' and owes much to Gogol's fragment 'The Servants' Hall'. Presided over by the grotesque *maitre d'hotel,* Trembinski, who is given the physical attributes of a puppet and whose personal existence is merely instrumental to the requirements of a sanctioned hierarchy, the contemporary life of the estate moves to the mechanized rhythms of his motorized responses, seen in contrast to the patterns and rhythms of the past compounded of chaos and inertia. The superficial contrast is between the values of the town and those of the country, between the new values and the old—Trembinski insisting on a strict, mechanized division of labour and organization for their own sake, where the estate managers have been content to let matters go to rack and ruin while lining their own pockets in the absence of authority. The contrast between town and country is intensified by the arrival of the 'new man', the Petersburg councillor Yeletski, the new estate owner, for whom the language of estate management might just as well be Chinese. He too moves in the mechanical grooves carved out by utilitarian principles, conventional procedures and the dictates of social propriety, while emanating the mystifying aura of authority which attaches to his quasiaristocratic background and his hailing from St Petersburg.

Identity becomes a matter of passive submission to a preordained social role, whether that of servant or master, and yet there persist the claims for individual meaning and significance. Turgenev makes great play with people's names, a normal aspect of identity which is here thrown into disarray. 'Who are you?' Trembinski asks the baffled Pyotr and when the latter offers his name is told that his true identity is 'lackey'. The attempt to identify throughout is not to discover an authentic individuality, but to place in a social scale of higher and lower. This is especially true of the men. They deliberately forget each other's names, or get the right first name and the wrong patronymic as part of the pattern of social and self-assertion. All that appears to matter is the pecking order, while human connection is lost in the process. Humanity is commonly seen as being reasserted in the human claims voiced by Kuzovkin, but these are, in fact, part of that same process. A vestigial humanity persists only on the margins—in the person of the young servant, Masha, who laughs at the absurd ritual which welcomes the newlyweds; in Kuzovkin's friend, Ivanov, who is a passive, almost silent witness to the underlying truth; and in Olga Petrovna herself, who is torn apart, finally, by her attempt to reconcile the claims of society, represented by her husband, and the claims of her nature, represented by her daughterhood.

The central character, Kuzovkin, exemplifies the schizophrenic nature of the society and embodies the split within himself. He is both the most self-effacing and the most self-assertive person in the play. He is at the bottom of the social heap, yet possesses the conventionally superior feelings of a nobleman. He is both the most inarticulate and the most rhetorical, the most self-important and the most self-demeaning. His existence is a surrogate existence. He is, in fact, a parasite. Kuzovkin is an integral part of the grotesque elements in the play; his habits of mind are entirely conventional and completely mechanical. His account of the legal proceedings surrounding the inheritance of his estate is presented in a manner which, ironically, justifies the 'cruel' laughter with which it is received. It is manic in its obsessiveness and in its

command of intricate detail, as well as giving the impression of mechanical repetitiveness—in the recurrence of the word *veksel* (a bill of exchange), for example, and in the exhausted repetitions at the end of the long speech towards the end of Act 1 as the machine of his mind winds down. The process of litigation is relayed as a form of madness, a metaphor of breakdown, setting individual members of the same family against each other while dividing the estate 'to the fourteenth part'. The final attribution of blame to the ubiquitous 'Hanginmester', Turgenev asks us to note, actually represents the mechanical principle itself, as Kuzovkin wrestles with his name: 'Han-han-han-gin-mester'.

The irony of this pathetic scene, which culminates in the fool's cap being set on Kuzovkin's head, is that it is simultaneously his humiliation *and* his moment of glory. Being humiliated is an essential aspect of his identity. It is essential to his ultimate feeling of superiority to those who humiliate him. It provides him with opportunities for self-assertion as when, previously, he fathered the illegitimate child and, now, announces the fact. These scenes of abasement are the only moments in his life when his essentially selfconscious and theatrical personality finds itself at the centre of the stage, the focus of attention. This craving for attention might be explicable, even tolerable, in a disturbed child. In a fifty-year-old adult the signs are ominous. It is inevitable that the demand for social recognition cannot satisfy the claims of personal identity. These can only be harboured in the mind, as ideals. Once released into the light of day, the one claim cancels the other. The truth and reality of the father/daughter relationship can only be sustained as an ideal of the mind. Once it becomes instrumental in the claim for social recognition, its inherent quality is destroyed at the moment of its public utterance. Kuzovkin is, indeed, mad to have 'come out of his mind'. The accompanying stage direction is 'Olga disappears'. Yeletski's conventional recognition—'You're mad'—veils a perception at a deeper and more tragic level of this apparent comedy.

As usual, in Turgenev, the victim is a woman. Olga only exists to serve her husband's interests or as an aspect of Kuzovkin's identity. She is neither true wife nor true daughter. She is a victim of this instrumentality just as her dead mother was a victim of her husband's brutality. Olga is further humiliated by her husband in being made instrumental in buying off Kuzovkin. The latter will not accept the 10,000 roubles from Yeletski out of a sense of his dignity as a nobleman (a way of seeking a moral advantage over his ostensible 'superior'). Olga agrees to act as her husband's emissary in a tactical sense, and acknowledge her daughterhood, in order to force Kuzovkin to accept the money. In a brilliant dramatic stroke, Turgenev has Kuzovkin first drop the paper-bill and then accept it when it is physically pressed on him by Olga, who simultaneously says she believes him to be her father. At the point of genuine human contact, the promissory note comes between. The revelation of natural connection involves a simultaneous cancellation of that connection. Olga's recognition of Kuzovkin as a father *in these terms* actually severs her connection with him as a daughter. Because the acceptance of the money sanctions a social lie for propriety's sake, it also makes a lie of the personal relationship. The agreement to carry on an illicit, secret sense of their true kinship, under the umbrella of the social life, becomes both ironic and pathetic. It can possibly satisfy Kuzovkin who has 'come into his estate' as both owner and father. For Olga it can only be sacrifice and loss.

Kuzovkin believes he has gained his identity, when in fact he has lost it. He has 'come into his estate' only in the most meaningless sense. Olga is left to escape alone to her room to weep over her own loss, while Tropachov congratulates Yeletski on his decency and generosity, no doubt harbouring thoughts of seducing his wife at the first opportunity. He and his parasitic double, Karpachov, have already become semi-permanent guests and he will no doubt batten on the family flesh with the same relish with which he tackled the meal in Act 1—a parasite in a world of parasites. 'Nature . . . is the death of me', he announces at one point. Tropachov, is, indeed, symptomatic of dead nature in the debilitated world of the play as a whole.

The Bachelor

The Bachelor is unique among Turgenev's plays in having been written, published and performed all in the same year. It was also the first Turgenev play to be given a public performance. He composed it between January and March 1849 in Paris, from where he sent the manuscript to Shchepkin in Moscow. The play was permitted for the stage in October, although not before the censor had been to work with his blue pencil. A dialogue between Shpundik and Von Fonk about the difficult conditions prevailing in the countryside was excised, as was a speech by Moshkin in which he talked of the freedom and equality of women in marriage. All references to God were eliminated and certain names were changed—Von Fonk to Von Klaks and Belokopytova to Belonogova (literally Whitehoof to Whiteleg). The first performance was given for Shchepkin's benefit, on 14 October, at the Alexandrinski Theatre in St Petersburg with the beneficiary in the role of the minor official, Moshkin. It was a great success.

The basic situation in the three-act play concerns one Moshkin (*moshka* = midge), a fifty-year-old bachelor who has assumed the guardianship, since the death of her mother three years previously, of a nineteen-year-old girl, Masha. For more obscure reasons he has also assumed semi-parental responsibility for another orphan, Pyotr Vilitski, a twenty-three-year-old Petersburg minor official, and has contrived a match between them which is two weeks away from consummation at the opening of the play. During the course of the action Vilitski breaks off the engagement, largely under the influence of the above-mentioned Von Fonk, who appeals to his innate snobbery in suggesting that he could make a better match elsewhere. Dismayed by the outcome, Moshkin himself

proposes marriage to his ward, a proposal which she half accepts, and Moshkin is left at the final curtain deliriously hopeful that something will come of this and that Masha will be happy.

Criticism and performance of *The Bachelor* appear bedevilled by some of the problems which also affect our understanding of *The Parasite*. In fact, the plays have a great deal in common, but not in the way in which these comparisons are traditionally made. The problem with the conventional way of seeing both *The Parasite* and *The Bachelor* seems to be the need to find positive elements in Turgenev's dramatic world with which to identify and sympathize. It has become traditional to see both Kuzovkin and Moshkin as representing a focus of moral opposition to the world around them. However, as in the case of Gogol, this is not the way in which Turgenev works. His method is essentially Gogolian in that the conflict is between negative elements in which the outcome is far from being so easily affirmative as criticism is inclined to suggest. The crucial element which has been missed in both *The Parasite* and *The Bachelor* is the way in which Turgenev has captured the spirit of Gogol's comedy of the grotesque and it is in this light that *The Bachelor,* in particular, needs to be viewed. To suggest that the play concerns another form of parasitism, that it is also about impotence and, again, about madness and that these themes are woven around the 'good' and 'kind-hearted' central character might raise a few eyebrows (possibly Turgenev's own). But this is the play he has demonstrably written and it is a much finer one than the play he is usually credited with being responsible for.

The first act introduces us to the milieu of Petersburg minor officialdom. The setting is Moshkin's apartment and Moshkin is at the centre of the action as he prepares a dinner party for the engaged couple and Vilitski's departmental colleague, Von Fonk. The dominant impression is of weirdness and eccentricity. The presence of both Masha and her aunt in what is a small bachelor apartment emphasizes the overcrowdedness. Moshkin's former sleeping accommodation appears to have been given over permanently to Masha, so that the reception room, where the first act is set, also functions as a bedroom for Moshkin—a corner of which is screened off. There is also a young servant, Stratilat, who, instead of occupying his traditional place in the hallway, appears to spend a good deal of his time lounging on his master's sofa. There is an all-pervading sense of curious incongruity. Under these conditions, cramped and chaotic, the master of the house manages his ménage in a fashion which might be appropriate in a country house, but which appears ludicrously out of place in the flat of a minor official in St Petersburg. The effect is of someone in thrall to the dictates of the values of his masters, whose ideals and codes of conduct he apes and aspires to emulate. The effect is of a *moshka* (midge) imitating a butterfly and the prospect is both absurd and grotesque.

The servant's speech at the opening of the play introduces us to the themes of education and enlightenment, which are referred to in various forms by several of the characters. Stratilat's level of 'enlightenment' consists in his struggling to pronounce that very word, syllable by syllable, in the book he is desperately trying to read, but which is frustrated by his constantly having to answer the bell. Moshkin's friend, Shpundik, is described by Turgenev as having 'pretensions to education'. Moshkin wishes to gain the approval of others by being associated with people of good upbringing and education. He wants Masha to be thought 'a queen' in society, as well as being anxious for Vilitski to work his way up the ladder of promotion in the civil service so that, eventually, Moshkin can claim a vicarious eminence through a form of kinship. Von Fonk represents that world of education and 'breeding'—the entirely false values which terrorize everyone else in the play and before which they pathetically abase themselves. This is represented through the forms of their dress, exaggerated to the point of caricature, their artificially mannered speech and in their sycophantic, intimidated humility in face of Von Fonk and everything he stands for.

The arrival of Shpundik, at the beginning of the play, also introduces the theme of 'Time'. In the world of the first act, everything is seen to move at a breathtaking, unnatural speed, with everybody consulting their watches and wondering what time it is from minute to minute. It all amounts to a portrait of Petersburg bureaucratic life, and its unnatural spirit is proportionately reflected in the artificial behaviour which such consciousness of time imposes on those whose movements are dictated by the tick of the clock. The manic impression is especially noticeable in the behaviour of Moshkin, whose characteristics are distinctly puppet-like. Against this is set the discussion of mortality between Shpundik and Moshkin, in which Turgenev is surely echoing that between Shallow and Silence in Shakespeare's *Henry IV, Part 2.*

In Moshkin's account of how he met Masha and her mother, rendered in comic-grotesque detail and style, complete with clown-like actions, we are introduced to another sense of 'Time'. Moshkin is always referring to himself as 'an old man'. His life is seemingly fixated on his relationship with the young couple and his desire to see them married. Equally, the actual duration of their acquaintance seems to be disproportionately short. Moshkin behaves as if at a crisis point in his own life. Well into middle-age, he appears to be seeking to live out his own unlived life vicariously, through the lives of the young people, and precipitately, because he feels he has not much time left. Time is making itself felt in Moshkin's own life with peculiar force. The childless bachelor, who has been a petty official all his life, suddenly seizes on a chance to live and, in the process, imposes his own necessities on the lives of two orphans who are unable to resist the pressures he exerts. What appears as altruism is, when looked at more closely, a form of parasitism which is entirely, if unconsciously, selfish.

Moshkin is also obsessed with his own inferiority and lack of distinction. This sense stems directly from a total acceptance, even worship, of a false society's evaluation of what constitutes distinction and superiority. Again, he seeks these qualities vicariously through the ambition he has for Vilitski's advancement. 'He will soon be titled', he tells Shpundik in a confidential whisper, 'he has a good and extensive acquaintance' and 'he works alongside the minister himself.' Vilitski's marriage to Masha can be seen as calculated, less to confer status on this girl of 'inferior' birth than to confer potency and social status on Moshkin by proxy through its association with his own surrogate parenthood and tutelage.

The entry of Von Fonk introduces us to the values of that wider external world which exerts such intense pressures and exercizes such power over the interior world of the play. Moshkin is moved to tears for reasons which he cannot explain by the visit of this supercilious and punctilious bureaucrat. The reason is not far to seek. It is as if a monarch had condescended to visit his humble abode. Moshkin is touched for his own sake, not for Masha's. In the pre-lunch conversation, he reveals himself as the perfect would-be bourgeois in his conduct of the deadeningly banal conversation and in his attempts to cover up any hiatus in the flow, while preserving an impression of surface calm. Underneath, a kind of inner panic reigns in the hearts of all as they seek to impress the imperturbable Von Fonk. When the latter actually tells his story, which concludes with the profound observation that 'there are people who look alike', Turgenev reveals him for the superficial fool he is.

The underlying madness comes to the surface when the decorum is threatened by the cook, Malanya, who comes to announce that dinner is ready. The stage directions indicate that Moshkin runs to bar her entrance 'in a frenzy; placing his knee in her stomach' like a mad majordomo. He then turns rapidly to his guests and with sycophantic nicety asks: 'Does anybody require anything else?' as if the breach of etiquette had been a figment of everyone's imagination.

The opening of Act 2 shows us the impoverished conditions in which Vilitski lives and which he clearly wishes to climb out of. Again the sense of grotesque parody is apparent in the incongruity of setting and behaviour. Vilitski orders his pipe to be brought as if he were seigneur of a chateau, while his throwing aside of the book with the words 'upbringing is a very important thing' serves to underline the hypocrisy of his reasons for rejecting Masha, ostensibly on the grounds of *her* lack of education, when his decision is in fact dictated by social snobbery. At the same time, what seems simply affectation can also be seen as a form of resistance to Moshkin's imposition of a match which is not of his own choosing. The values which Vilitski accepts are those of Von Fonk, who is shown to be providing him with an education in these values. The irony is, that in essence, they are indistinguishable from Moshkin's and, in many respects, echo him:

> I have already told you about my rule to avoid getting acquainted with people of the lower classes; from this rule, there naturally follows another, namely: try

as hard as you can to become acquainted with people
of the upper classes

says Von Fonk. And this is the path which Vilitski chooses to follow, a logical extension of Moshkin's own wishes for him, with the exception that Masha will need to be
replaced by someone who will make 'a better marriage'.

In the scene between Masha and Vilitski at the latter's
apartment, in Act 2, Vilitski is more conscious of his
concealed and eavesdropping guests in the adjoining room
than he is of Masha's emotional plea. The scene has a
Dickensian element of caricature which Masha's mispro-
nunciation of the word 'examine' as 'ixamine', followed
by Vilitski's wincing response, emphasizes. Turgenev, to
a degree, invites us to share the laughter of those in the
next room who can scarcely contain themselves. During
the course of the subsequent interview between Vilitski
and Moshkin, it emerges that the latter is less troubled
by whether Vilitski loves her or not, than by whether he
intends going through with the wedding. It is 'what people will think and say' which principally concerns him.

Moshkin's anger, in Act 3, is of a similar order. It is
manifested less for Masha's sake than for his own. It is
his protégé, as he sees it, who has been rejected by society. His decision to challenge Vilitski to a duel is deliberately rendered comic, as well as absurdly inappropriate, by Turgenev. It is interesting that Moshkin's response
is already more like that of a husband than a father, but
this only serves to redouble the irony. His challenge is
only apt if the opponent is seen as a rival in love. In this
case, the rival has *rejected* the loved one. The whole is
a grotesque inversion of any recognizable norm. In this
context, the most grotesque aspect of all is Moshkin's
decision to propose to Masha.

This is the most critical scene in the play. Despite her
rejection, it is clear that Masha still loves Vilitski and
hopes that he will change his mind. At the same time,
she recognizes that there is little hope. She clutches at
his letter like a drowning person. Moshkin already knows
the contents but, in his present state of feeling, wants the
contents to kill off the vestigial love. When she reads the
confirmation of rejection, Masha stifles in that same moment the possibility of ever loving again. There is nothing
left in life to hope for. Yet who is it who is responsible for
evoking this love and inspiring this hope? Who is to blame?
It is not Vilitski, but the man who stands before her offering himself as a substitute marriage partner.

Moshkin describes himself as 'losing his mind' and as 'a
madman' and, indeed, in an important sense he is. It is
plain that Masha has been merely instrumental in fur-
thering his wider claims for recognition and significance.
Now that this possibility no longer exists, the wider social ambition shrinks to the compass of the narrow arena
of the apartment. In fact, fantasy takes over as a substitute for an unattainable 'reality':

> All I want to do is to prove to the world, that to marry
> you is the height of happiness . . . That's what I want

to prove to the world—that is, to Pyotr Ilyich . . . I
offer you, then, peace, quiet, respect, shelter. . . . Here,
you will be a mistress, a madam, a lady. . . .

and he adds, in pathetic acknowledgement of his own
impotence which puts a seal on the barren prospects before her:

> . . . and I . . . the screens, you understand, the
> screens, and nothing further. . . .

Masha does not agree to marry him but agrees to stay for
the time being:

> You will not deceive me: you will not betray me. I
> can depend on you.

And she gives him cause for hope.

Once again, we see the woman as victim. For someone
whose own hope, not to say her whole life, has been
shattered to smithereens, faced with the person who is
the Svengali-like cause of her suffering, Masha's offer to
him of hope in return is fraught with irony. Moshkin's
condition towards the end of the play is surely not the
one traditionally rendered in performance. His manifestation of joy is close to dementia. Pryazhkina clearly
thinks he has had a stroke:

> Why, his face is all twisted, and his lips too. He has
> had a stroke.

He stands as someone condemned to hope and to the
belief that his life may now begin to take on meaning.
But he himself recognizes that ' . . . it's a dream, an
illusion'. His final cry: 'She will be happy! She will be
happy!' is less a cry of joyful determination than an attempt to drown the recognition of hopelessness and despair in the face of the ruin which is his own life, and the
ruin he has brought on the lives of others.

'Lunch with the Marshal of the Nobility'

It is probably true to say that there is little evidence in
his prose work that Turgenev was, potentially, a comic
writer of considerable stature. There is certainly nothing
in his novels or short stories which has the comic liveliness of his play **'Lunch with the Marshal of the
Nobility'**, one of the funniest Russian comedies of the
nineteenth century. Like **'Moneyless'**, it shows evidence
of a strong debt to the techniques of vaudeville as well
as to the plays and short stories of Gogol. In the humour
of the quarrel over estate boundaries, the play anticipates the Chekhov of *The Proposal,* but without ever
becoming quite as farcical.

The action of the one-act play takes place on the estate
of Marshal of the Nobility, Balagalayev, whom the dis-
putants, Bespandin and his widowed sister Kaurova, have
turned to in the hope of a rapid resolution (rather than a

protracted legal wrangle) of a problem over estate division. The marshalship, an honorary post, was subject to election on a short-term basis by the landowners of a specific region. Balagalayev's rival for the marshalship is one Pekhterev, who also becomes involved in the resolution of this particular dispute and introduces a subsidiary theme of the rivalry between the two marshals, incumbent and presumptive. A third theme is introduced in the person of Alupkin, newly arrived in the district from Tambov, who is in dispute with the district inspector, Naglanovich, as to whether it is one of his (Alupkin's) peasants who is responsible for stealing a goat. Beneath the surface of this farcical plot the currents of the play run deep.

It was originally written for Nekrasov's *The Contemporary* but was forbidden publication by the censor. Surprisingly, the play was passed for stage performance and the first production was given at the Alexandrinski Theatre in December 1849. The sub-title of the first performed version was **'An Amicable Division'**, but, despite its success, it was not permitted publication until 1856, by which time Turgenev had revised it and weakened it considerably (this is the version which has come down to us). The first version is said to have been more actable than the final, published version. The original script contained very precise directions from the author as to intonations and group dispositioning on stage—for example at the moments when the map of the estate is consulted. Reference to a 'dumb-scene' (presumably influenced by *The Government Inspector*) is omitted from the published version, as is a story which Mirvoshkin (Mirvolin in the published edition) tells about his wife, and a scene where some of the characters imitate the gobbling of turkeys. Bespandin was depicted in far more grotesque fashion in the original, where he is described as stuffing his mouth with both hands while feeding, and spitting, whistling and so forth.

The background to the play involves last-ditch attempts by the authorities to prop up a collapsing feudal order by clarifying boundary divisions between estates. Where own-ers died intestate and there were several legal claimants to the estate, the resulting litigation as to the precise extent of what each inherited became a legal nightmare. Turgenev focuses the dispute on close relatives in order to reinforce a connection between a process of division and separation in the social sphere and the way in which this is reflected in internecine strife within families. The point which forms the centre of the action, and which is referred to at the end of the play, is not that an amicable 'settlement' has been reached (as M. S. Mandell's translation has it) but, ironically, an amicable 'division' or 'partition'. The agreement is to divide and separate, not to unite. The official appointed by the government to assist in the determination of these disputes appears as a *deus ex machina* at the end of the play but, typically and comically, is unable to resolve the difficulty.

The major theme of the play is division, in society and in the family. Within this sense of division there is also the theme of separation between male and female, as well as that of inheritance. Colouring each strand and interwoven with them is a refrain repeated from *The Parasite* and *The Bachelor*—that of madness. The amiable farce is concerned with disintegration and breakdown in both the social and personal spheres. We are, once again, in territory already made familiar by Gogol. The incipient insanity in the play is an aspect of the obsessiveness of the characters. Balagalayev is obsessed with his status and privately concerned with the personal advantage to be gained from the settlement which he is ostensibly superintending as impartial arbiter. His personality is inherently fragile and the chorus of conflicting demands produces an inner fragmentation in his being. He reaches the point of breakdown near the end:

> I beg of you, my head's swimming . . . Division, a goat, obstinate woman, Tambov landowner, unexpected district inspector, a duel tomorrow, my conscience isn't clear, the estate, cut-price woods, lunch, noise, confusion . . . no, it's too much.

Alupkin is obsessed by four things—the goat which his peasant is supposed to have stolen, his dislike of women revealed through his attitude to Kaurova, his status as 'an old soldier', and the fact that he has managed to father a daughter. Pekhterev is obsessed with the marshalship. His apparent favouritism towards Kaurova has nothing to do with the merits of her case, but is a stance adopted simply in order to upset his rival, Balagalayev. He is also upset because the session has begun without him.

Bespandin is obsessed with winning the quarrel over the division of the estates. His apparent willingness to compromise is because he knows the cards are stacked against his sister as all the arbitrators present are male. He himself is unmarried. The only person who is not obsessed is the one who stands accused of incurable obstinacy, Kaurova. She is the only one who can conceivably be described as 'acting' the part she is playing—of 'stubborn female', 'helpless widow', 'put-upon litigant and *faux-naif* disputant'. The men are as if enclosed in the roles they play and unable to see beyond themselves to the insane ludicrousness of the situation. Kaurova not only understands but wilfully stretches the logic of the general insanity beyond the point where any normal person would go, just for the pleasure of watching the men pass beyond this point. She is far from being stubborn and is, in fact, so flexible that the men are incapable of noticing. There is a key point in the play, half-way through, immediately before the entry of Pekhterev. Up until this point, Bespandin's apparent flexibility has been countered at every turn by the sister's apparent stubbornness. They have reached a point of impasse. At this juncture Kaurova declares: 'I'll agree to anything. Let me have the papers. I'll sign anything you want me to!'—a remark which is completely ignored by all present.

Nearly everybody at some stage is described as 'mad'—Bespandin, his sister, Alupkin, even the aunt who left the will. Bespandin challenges Alupkin to a duel to defend the honour of his family, while simultaneously declaring that he doesn't give 'that much' for his sister. Pekhterev's suggestion that he make sacrifices because his sister is a woman, he answers with: 'That's only in theory'. Alupkin declares that nothing would surprise him any more—even if someone were to announce, 'I have eaten my own father!' Finally the desperate Balagalayev forgives the cause of his despair, Kaurova, *because* she is a woman. In the atmosphere of exaggeration, charge and counter-charge, Kaurova chimes in with an assertion that her brother is a murderer who is prepared to cut her throat and has already tried to poison her several times. As the chorus mounts, the district inspector enters and is immediately assumed by the self-preoccupied Alupkin to be there on account of the goat. This individualistic interpretation signals the point of breakdown for Balagalayev, who lists the fragments of a fragmenting world in the speech already quoted.

A final irony concerns that which remains in dispute, namely the possession of 'waste land', which connects with Alupkin's inheritance of his wife's estate, described as 'absolute rubbish . . . just sand'. The play's last line: 'That's what I call an amicable division! . . .' underwrites the incongruity and absurdity of the action.

'A Provincial Lady'

'A Provincial Lady' was written in 1850 and published in *Notes of the Fatherland* in 1851, an event which had been preceded by public readings of the work given by Turgenev himself, with great success, at various private houses in St Petersburg and Moscow. Described as 'a comedy in one act', **'A Provincial Lady'** looks at first glance, very much like a trivial French-inspired vaudeville.

The plot is certainly typical. Darya Ivanovna, the twenty-eight-year-old wife of Stupendyev, a very conventional district government clerk twenty years her senior, has lived the eight or so years of her married life in a boring provincial town with only a cook, a houseboy and a nineteen-year-old male distant cousin for company, for the last-mentioned of whom she has assumed the role of benefactress. She, in her turn, was reared as a humble ward in the home of *her* benefactress, a local countess, since deceased, and retains memories of other ways of life as well as of her youthful ambitions. These are revived by a return visit to his country estate of the countess's son, Count Lyubin, now an ageing dandy of forty-nine who, some ten years previously, had flirted in a casual fashion with the young ward whilst on leave from the military. His affairs in St Petersburg appear to have taken a turn for the worse and he needs to consult the local district government officer (Darya's husband) about matters concerning his late mother's estate. The young wife exploits this opportunity to remind the count of their erstwhile connection and to exploit her now mature powers of sexual charm to gain for both herself and her husband, as well as her ward, positions in the more glamorous world of St Petersburg. This she manages to do, although her

husband's jealousy (he is not informed of his wife's plot) nearly undoes the whole scheme as well as leading to the count's enlightenment as to the young wife's subterfuge. Despite this, the play concludes on a happy note as the group exits for dinner and the count looks forward to their next meeting—in the capital.

The play is far from being as superficial as the plot outline may make it sound. In it, Turgenev reveals himself to be not only a precursor of a minor revolution in dramatic form, but also a forerunner of the master of domestic drama in the nineteenth century, Henrik Ibsen. Just as, through the surface texture of the domestic drama, Ibsen reaches beyond a surface realism towards something altogether more abstract, so Turgenev manages something very similar in **'A Provincial Lady'**, although the emotional colouring of the drama is much lighter than the darkness which can be detected in the Norwegian dramatist. Another important connection with later drama, and in particular with the Symbolists, lies in Turgenev's recognition of the puppet-show elements which underlie the ostensibly realistic surface of human actions.

There are strong parallels between the domestic worlds of **'A Provincial Lady'** and *A Doll's House, Hedda Gabler* and even *Rosmersholm*. The connecting link is through the remarkable character of Darya Ivanovna. Through her, the play becomes a drama of the phenomenal and thwarted power of woman, but without the serious consequences which this is shown to have in Ibsen's plays. There is a persistent sense, in Ibsen, that the typical nineteenth-century woman sitting at her knitting, or at the embroidery frame, is simultaneously weaving the pattern of fate which will engulf the protagonists at the conclusion. In this respect, Darya Ivanovna possesses some of the power of Rebecca West in *Rosmersholm* and, at the outset, is shown sitting at her embroidery from where she appears to conduct the sequence of events which follows. She assumes the role of the man, just as Hedda and Nora Helmer do, and her relationship with her husband has much in common with that between the women and the conventional, weak men in Ibsen's plays. Everyone who comes within her reach comes under her extraordinary spell and moves in the way she wants them to, prompted by a hand gesture or a nod; or else they come under the magnetic influence of her powerful sexual attraction.

Although the play is a comedy and the resolution appears trivial and rather unsatisfactory, Turgenev manages to convey a sense, if not of tragedy, then of waste of human energy and paucity of ambition. It is stressed that the desire to leave this provincial backwater and move to St Petersburg is merely trivial. It is implied, that in this kind of society, the energy of a Darya Ivanovna either lies dormant or can only be purposeless and without direction, determined, to a large extent, by the ideological ambience of aristocratic taste which nurtures it and in which she has been reared. These values are both subconsciously recognized as worthless and, as if prompted by environmental determinism, simultaneously striven for. The resolution of the problem is not, as in Ibsen, on the level of tragedy but on a level of absurdity. It has the effect of reducing the world, as experienced by the central character, to the proportions of a puppet show in a fairground, a kind of *bouffonade*.

With brilliant originality, Turgenev manages to convert the realistic milieu into a kind of miniature 'theatre of the mind', which is a grotesque reflection of the ostensible normality of everyday appearances. Just as, in *Hedda Gabler,* the inner room with its curtains across it, which separate it from the rest of the setting and in which Hedda commits suicide, represents the theatre of *her* mind, similarly, in **'A Provincial Lady'** everything appears filtered through the consciousness of the central protagonist. In the process, what emerges is a fairly light-hearted puppet show, in which Darya Ivanovna is revealed as the puppet master, while being herself subject to certain manipulative constraints.

Turgenev manages to suggest the reduction in physical scale, reminiscent of a fairground booth, through details of the stage setting, which suggest not only constriction but also diminution. It is the world of the doll's house as seen from the adult height of Darya Ivanovna, but where the rest of the characters are of a size proportionate to the environment. The garden, *sad,* is given in the opening stage directions as a *sadik* (tiny little garden), the table *stol* is described as a *stolik* (tiny little table), the piano is 'small', the screen 'low' and one can imagine the rest of the setting in equivalent terms. The puppet-show element is then carried over into the characterization. The houseboy (named Apollo) is kitted out in light-blue livery which does not fit him. He manifests one permanent emotion, fear, and keeps poking his head round doors, rapidly exiting into adjoining rooms or is seen emerging from them in flight. The count is described in terms of a doll. Not only is his every move dictated by Darya Ivanovna, but his hair is dyed and his face is powdered and rouged, like the painted image of a clown. When he gets down on his knees, it is as if his 'wooden' legs lack the muscle power to get him to his feet again. He eventually leaps up, apparently under his own volition, but the impression is of someone being jerked to his feet on strings. It is a critical moment. Darya Ivanovna's suppressed laughter threatens to make the grotesquerie of the characters permanent. In restoring the count to his feet (seemingly by an act of will on *her* part, not on his) and in laughing openly, demonstratively, Darya Ivanovna restores to some kind of normality the marionette world whose scenario she has written. The puppet-like nature of the husband has characteristics in common with the count. He wears a wig which, when removed, one imagines reveals a perfectly bald head, like that of a wooden doll. At one point he provides us with a glimpse of his marionette-like status when complaining about the cut of his coat: 'I feel as though I were being dragged up on a string'.

Movement in the play, when it is not precipitate, has all the formal characteristics of marionettes. People seem to be constantly propelled to their feet, jerkily bowing, ma-

terializing in doorways, parading up and down on seemingly involuntary impulse. The power of the theatre holds sway over all and the only person who is aware of this power and is consciously exploiting it is Darya Ivanovna. She is congratulated by the count, following the restoration of 'normality', on how well she has 'played her comedy'. People are provided with their roles and told when to make their entrances. At one point, Stupendyev enters before his cue. Darya Ivanovna is like a female Gulliver in Lilliput, pinned to the ground by constraining threads, but maintaining a hold on strings attached to each Lilliputian figure in the drama she has staged and directed.

There is the major problem of Darya Ivanovna's involvement in the world she ridicules. With part of herself she *does* seek to advance her husband's position in the social world of St Petersburg and 'save' him, as Nora does Torvald. In flirting with the count she is also, in a rather trivial way, seeking to confirm a sense of her own attractiveness at twenty-eight (which she sees as more than half-way to the grave). There is also a feeling that, in fairly petty fashion, she is avenging an earlier humiliation when the count appears to have trifled with her affections, evidence of which she retains in the form of a letter he once wrote to her. Her attempt to exercise power over him is experienced as a form of victory, whereas we have learned from a play such as **'Where It's Thin, There It Breaks'** that to win can be, in fact, to lose and that there may be more to be gained from losing than from winning. She becomes part of this reduced world, significantly, when we see her *on her own* and when the stage in the theatre of her mind is occupied by the image of herself, soliloquizing while getting ready for 'battle', or posing before the mirror and dreaming of exchanging her simple dress for something in velvet, more in keeping with St Petersburg. This, of course, is also Hedda Gabler's problem—one of trivially snobbish ambition, and an aspect of the many contradictory sides to her nature which can only find resolution in suicide. There is a suggestion in **'A Provincial Lady'** that the contemplated move to St Petersburg may be a form of suicide or, at least, will certainly end in disillusionment.

The actor at the Moscow Art Theatre who played the part of Darya's ward, Misha, in the 1912 production, A. D. Diki, suggests, in his published account of work on the play, that Stanislavski instinctively felt this sense of *bouffonade* and certainly managed to capture it in his portrayal of Lyubin. It is precisely this element of caricature which was criticized at the time by commentators who had come to expect their Turgenev to be served up in conventionally realistic fashion. It is interesting to note that the designer was M. V. Dobuzhinski who had designed Potyomkin's *Petrushka* for Meyerhold in St Petersburg, in 1908, in the style of a quasi-grotesque puppet show. In *My Life in Art,* Stanislavski suggests that there was a dispute between himself and Dobuzhinski over the kind of image Lyubin was to present, especially in the manner in which his face was to be made up. The implication is that the approach of the actors at this stage was in terms of their preparatory work on *A Month in the Country* (that is, within the psychological realistic framework of Stanislavski's development of the 'system') and that Dobuzhinski's suggestion as to the physical make-up and appearance of the count was altogether more schematic and simplified, based, Stanislavski suggested, on unfamiliarity with the text and on insufficient knowledge of the theatre's working methods. However, that which finally emerged in performance appears to have been something closer to Dobuzhinski's schematicism than a clear product of the 'system'.

It was in a mood of doubt and despair that Stanislavski suggested that the cast put on a special performance for the theatre's other artistic director V. Nemirovich-Danchenko and, as a consequence of this, he was forced to re-think his whole approach to the play, and to move away from the previous style towards something altogether more original. 'Why did Turgenev call the play 'A Provincial Lady' and not "Provincial Life" or "A Provincial Story"? was the question posed by Nemirovich-Danchenko, and it was as a result of this that a shift in emphasis was brought about in the overall conception, more in keeping with the ironical intentions of Turgenev's writing. The theme then became the *contrast* between the provincial surrounding and the ultra-sophistication of the provincial lady herself. From playing Lyubin as an aristocrat, Stanislavski began to convert him into an image of 'provincialism' masquerading as aristocracy. Everything was now framed in contrast to Darya Ivanovna with the result that, although she was not the main focus of the production, the theme of provincialism which the director had wanted to stress all along was thrown into much sharper focus. Even the notion of St Petersburg itself, symbol of nineteenth-century Russia, was drawn into the theme of 'provincialism as a way of life, as a mode of being' with its banality, its lack of vision and its 'profound hostility to any ray of talent'. This was emphasized by the atmosphere of total boredom at the opening of the play and by stressing the clumsy gaucheness of the servants. Dobuzhinski's setting helped to convey the sense of a typically Russian provincial milieu, in which the dominant colour was a rather tasteless yellow with a view through the window of the town beyond, with its naïve-looking church.

Stanislavski's approach to the role of Lyubin gradually developed away from the realistic portrayal of a decayed aristocrat towards the style of the *bouffonade*. Critics who noticed this took him to task for it while others closer to the Art Theatre, such as N. E. Efros, detected these elements in the play itself, quite rightly, and described Stanislavski's creation as a genuine work of art:

> Stanislavski brought out in the character everything which was archetypically comic, everything which is close, namely, to the 'buffo'. . . . The caricature grew to the level of an artistic creation.

A MONTH IN THE COUNTRY

PRODUCTION REVIEWS

Richard Dana Skinner (review date 2 April 1930)

SOURCE: A review of *A Month in the Country,* in *The Commonweal,* Vol. XI, No. 22, 2 April 1930, p. 622.

[*The first American performance of* A Month in the Country *in English was a Theater Guild presentation that premiered on 24 March 1930. In the following assessment, Skinner praises nearly every aspect of that "excellent production."*]

In presenting [*A Month in the Country*] by Turgenev, the Theatre Guild is giving American audiences their first experience of this classic Russian dramatist in English. In fact, only one other play of his, a one-act curtain raiser called **"The Lady from the Provinces,"** has ever seen the New York stage, and that was in Russian during the first visit here of the Moscow Art Theatre.

Turgenev belongs to that general period of Russian literature distinguished by Tolstoy, Gogol and Dostoievsky. He was born shortly after the close of the Napoleonic era and lived until 1883. He was one of the first to introduce into Russian playwriting the "natural" style later adopted, or carried on as a tradition, by Chekov and others. He is, in this sense, the originator of a school. In his general method of displaying character, he is not unlike the modern Spanish school typified by the Quintero brothers. That is, he works along very simple lines, never forcing action, and permitting characters to display themselves through mental or emotional conflict with others rather than by the pulling of the dramatist's strings from without. He is, however, inclined to probe more deeply into the recesses of the mind than his Spanish counterparts of today. He takes rather more complex emotions for his theme, and without using any of the patented jargon of modern psychologists, anticipates frequently many of the problems to which they have given particular attention.

A Month in the Country gives briefly and simply the leading events on a large Russian estate during the visit of a young man named Rakitin. Rakitin is deeply, though honorably, in love with the wife of his host, one Islaev. Natalia reciprocates his love. Their feeling for one another takes itself out entirely in a quiet companionship and understanding during the long hours when Islaev, simple and honest-minded, is absorbed in the management of his estate. But Natalia has engaged a young tutor, Aleksei, for her son, and this Aleksei bit by bit captures her interest—first by his shyness, then by his youth and strength. Further to complicate matters, Natalia's seventeen-year-old ward, Viera, also falls in love with Aleksei. You have then a many-cornered emotional tug of war, with the restless and unstable Natalia at the bottom of all the difficulties. She is one of those types never

The set design for the first act of the 1909 Moscow Art Theatre production of A Month in the Country.

quite ready to relinquish her hold upon anyone, no matter what the cost in misery to the captive. She wants the tranquillity of the life with her husband, the platonic attachment of Rakitin, the devotion of Aleksei, the confidence of Viera. The substance of the play is the manner in which she tries to keep each of them but succeeds only in losing all of them except her docile and patient husband. Rakitin sees the futility of the situation and decides to leave. Aleksei, flattered by the obvious attentions of a great lady, finds his own emotions involved and also decides that his only course is to leave. Viera, whose budding romance with Aleksei has been blasted by Natalia's unscrupulous intrigues, decides in desperation to marry a ridiculous old man who has asked for her hand. Soon the house will be quite empty. Natalia has reaped the harvest of her egotism.

On this well-drawn portrait of a neurotic woman, the Theatre Guild has lavished an excellent production. Special settings have been used, reproducing the original designs of Dobuzinsky for the Moscow Art Theatre. They are singularly effective in the realistic atmosphere they convey of the hot silence of the great Russian estate. Rouben Mamoulian has done the directing, and shows many signs of an increasing sureness in the management of tense but quiet scenes, punctuated subtly by gestures and movement which give an almost orchestral rhythm.

The casting, too, has many excellent points. The play is the occasion for the first appearance with the Guild of Alla Nazimova. She plays Natalia to the hilt, with excellent restraint and much quiet grace, as if in outward contrast to the inner turmoil. Elliot Cabot as Rakitin gives one of the best-modulated and best-poised performances of his career. Alexander Kirkland as the tutor makes good on all the fine promise of his work in Wings Over Europe. Dudley Digges as an intriguing country doctor and Henry Travers as the aged suitor supply delicious comedy, and Eunice Stoddard is a poignant figure as the little niece.

Joseph Wood Krutch (review date 9 April 1930)

SOURCE: "Nosce Te Ipsum," in *The Nation,* New York, Vol. CXXX, No. 3379, 9 April 1930, pp. 430, 432.

[*In the review below of the Theater Guild production of* A Month in the Country, *Krutch extols Turgenev's penetrating psychological portraits of the characters.*]

The Theater Guild's experiments with standard plays have not always been among its happiest efforts, but with *A Month in the Country* (Guild Theater) it has achieved a delightful production of a delightful play. Chekhov himself never imagined a more charming group of people than that which Turgenev has here brought together, and Chekhov himself never scrutinized character with a keener or more tolerant gaze. One will look in vain for that tumultuous despair which is commonly supposed to be inevitably a part of the famous Russian soul, but one will find in its place something which is, perhaps, hardly less characteristic—a gently bubbling gaiety just tinged with melancholy and a quiet, almost elegiac beauty. These people are, to be sure, all idlers; they have eaten of some lotus and they dream their lives away, content to watch the birches grow and to speak of love. But no one ever justified idleness more completely by making it graceful, for they talk divinely about nothing in particular, and they get the full savor of the tiniest, almost non-existent adventure. After two hours in their company it seems that life could not be more profitably spent than in such doings as these.

Natalia Petrovna, married to a gentle, ineffectual country gentleman, has a lover of long standing; but when a young tutor appears in the house she confesses a penchant for him. The tutor is flattered by the favor of the great lady, and the lover, tardily scrupulous now that he has been displaced, persuades him that they should leave together.

They say goodby after some nervous references to the delicacy of their honor, and the lady accepts their farewell with an irony whose delicacy makes its deadliness almost imperceptible: "I am sure that you are both honorable men—very honorable men. In fact, I think that you are the most honorable men I have ever met." And that is all, but it is quite enough. Quite enough because, I think, both the author and his creatures are so exquisitely aware of every value which the situation contains. Turgenev sees through them all. He follows every turn of every individual's psychology. But he does not see through them any more completely than they see through themselves, or know them any better than they know themselves, for it is, indeed, in learning to do just that that they seem to have spent their lives. Self-knowledge, complete in the adults, may be still growing in the youths, but as one watches the keenness with which they note their own emotions, one is sure that their experiment with living will achieve the success at which it aims. Doubtless they will never do anything, and quite probably they will be unhappy. But they will be thoroughly familiar with their own souls, and they will get the full value out of every emotion. They will see it coming, they will know when it is there, and they will reflect upon it after it has passed—even though, perchance, they have never heard of the "hard and gem-like flame."

Turgenev and Chekhov are the only writers I know who have completely justified a pause on the road which leads from tragedy to comedy. Both have reached the detached and critical intelligence which belongs to the latter. Both are completely sophisticated and, in certain senses at least, completely disillusioned. Yet neither has even approached the brittle hardness of pure comedy. Each is knowing without being quite cynical, and though neither has any lingering tendency to find cosmic significance in man or his doings yet both feel with and for him. In them human nature is neither funny nor grand, but somehow, without being either, it is charming. And that perhaps is the secret of their fascination. Here for once one does not have to make one's choice between intelligence and feeling or be put off with comedy tinged with inappropriate sentimentality. The clarity of vision is never clouded; no veils are drawn in order to make people or things seem softer than they are. And yet their little joys and little sorrows take on a significance which is more than comic.

In such a play as this, where everything depends upon the evocation of a mood, it is obvious that only the most expert acting and the most expert direction will do, but the production at the Guild Theater leaves almost nothing to be desired. Nazimova, as Natalia Petrovna, gives a finely modulated performance which seems to me quite the best she has achieved since her return to the stage; Henry Travers and Dudley Digges are very fine in comic roles; and in fact the whole cast, including Eunice Stoddard, who was seen first in "Red Rust," is excellent. Moreover, the settings, modeled by Raymond Sovey upon the designs by M. S. Dobuzhinsky for the Moscow Art Theater production of the same play, contribute much. Perhaps the garden scene reveals the weakness of all attempts to treat outdoor scenes realistically with the aid of paper flowers and poisonous-looking grass, but the empire room, done in blue, is one of the loveliest I have ever seen.

Stark Young (review date 16 April 1930)

SOURCE: "Turgenev and Richard III" in *The New Republic*, Vol. LXII, No. 802, 16 April 1930, pp. 246-47.

[*In this review, Young offers a mixed evaluation of the Theater Guild presentation of* A Month in the Country, *arguing that the actors were unable to fully convey the subtleties of Turgenev's characterizations.*]

A good deal of thinking must have been done by the Theater Guild before it decided finally to chance a production of Turgenev's famous play [*A Month in the Country*]. Technically, this drama prepares the way for Chekhov, but that is likely to be of more interest to Russians than to our public. The tone of the play is somewhat unsettled and, therefore, even more difficult for American actors than it would be in Moscow. The wholeness of this play depends very largely on the undercurrent and *rapport* that the acting gives to it; and in this respect our American acting is not as capable as it might be.

A Month in the Country, as a story, is, we all know, not unrelated to the dramatist's own life. He had for a long time a relation to a household, the wife and the husband combined, that duplicated that of Rakitin to Islaev and Islaev's wife, Natalia Petrovna—a long-continued intimacy, something like a love affair, with the status of the lover somewhat vague. During the four acts of the play we see the wife's boredom with this perfect lover—or at least this complaisant and docile worshiper—that Rakitin is; we see her interest in the new tutor she has engaged for her little son. Islaev's mother has a companion; there is a provincial doctor, full of wiles and resentments and talents for making himself diverting; and between these two a gradual betrothal comes about. There is Islaev's ward, Vera Aleksandrovna, and a musty bachelor, Bolshintsov, whose suit for Vera's hand the doctor, for a price, tries to further. Vera falls in love with the tutor and has her secret pumped out of her by Natalia Petrovna, who is also attracted by him. In the end she gives herself in despair to the foolish Bolshintsov. The husband and his wife's lover have a friendly talk, confusing to them both perhaps; the wife allows the tutor to see her infatuation; and at the very last both the lover and the tutor go away, and the household is left to make what it can out of the rambling and mild routine of its daily existence.

It is worth while setting down so jumbling an account of the situation in *A Month in the Country,* if only to show how much the quality of the play lies in the characters and in the interweaving of the motives that make it up, and to show also what a curiously delicate task the Guild undertook.

For diverse reasons we may be grateful. Turgenev's piece belongs to the middle of the last century. In it we have an opportunity to see the Russian theater moving, as Ibsen did, through the mazes of the Parisian technique of the day and on toward a technique of naturalism as we know it in Chekhov. Just as in *The Doll's House*—up to that last moment when Ibsen begins to inject a moral seriousness into his fluent technical procedure, and attaches a startling moral ending to the spirited piece that he has evolved—the skeleton is French, and the animation of the motives derives from Ibsen's French masters, so in this play of Turgenev's we note the constant winding in and out of familiar themes, more or less hackneyed, or at least business-like. They are old friends, these motivations with which the French playwrights of that time constructed their dramatic houses, houses that were so often of cards, unsteady, tricky, specious and expert. Looking forward, however, instead of backward, from Turgenev's method, we see Chekhov ahead. This technical structure in *A Month in the Country* is based on racial foundations. The emotional variations, the occasional philosophy, the genuineness creeping into that dramatic panorama of personal, living and intimate moods, the blunt impact of personalities, the lack of a certain social masking and suavity—all these are Russian and promise well.

This closeness to the French technique, plus the fact of Turgenev's living so much abroad, away from Russian life, plus the fact also of his being a highly literary talent compared with some of the great Russian geniuses who followed him, will account for a good deal of that sense of uncertainty which we have in *A Month in the Country*. We feel in it a statement that is not compelling, a mildness of accentuation. In a Russian production of the play no little of this elusiveness could be overcome, because of the intensity of temperament brought to the acting, the vivid subtlety and spontaneity of the characters created, and above all, the emotional flow among the persons present on the stage. But this is just the kind of stage necessity that taxes our actors most. It could not be said that the Theater Guild production of this Russian play merges everything into that elusive, unbroken current by which the play comes to life and the characters, emotions and actions reveal themselves and one another. It could not be said that the company plays together. Mr. Elliot Cabot's performance of Rakitin, the friend and lover, sins worst in this matter of *rapport*. The character himself may be reserved or unassertive, perhaps, but Mr. Cabot never seems able to connect with the other players—not even with Madame Nazimova in their closest scenes. Madame Nazimova is at the other extreme; she may not be easy for the other actors to cope with, considering her advantages as a Russian and her vivid presence, but she is always varied, alive and dramatic, and, as matters stand, supplies the thread on which the whole continuity of the drama is strung. Miss Eunice Stoddard, coming from the American Laboratory Theater by way of the Guild Studio, does them both credit in her performance of the young girl. Mr. Dudley Digges and Mr. Henry Travers, as the doctor and the moldy suitor, give

character performances that, if somewhat isolated, are capital.

The handsome settings for *A Month in the Country* are reproduced by Mr. Raymond Sovey from the designs made by Dobuzinsky for the Moscow Art Theater's production of the play, in 1909.

As an artistic venture and as an evening's entertainment, this new offering of the Theater Guild's has no little distinction.

John Hutchens (review date May 1930)

SOURCE: A review of *A Month in the Country,* in *Theatre Arts Monthly,* Vol. XIV, No. 5, May, 1930, pp. 373-75.

[*In the following assessment of* A Month in the Country, *Hutchens argues that the Theater Guild actors significantly enlivened Turgenev's rather diffuse and vague play.*]

To Turgenev's *A Month in the Country,* [a] troupe of Guild actors, under Rouben Mamoulian's direction, brings the flow of ensemble acting effectively orchestrated, spaciously framed in Raymond Sovey's brilliant, old regime settings. They bring, also, the first Turgenev play to be performed in this country in English; a play which, arriving so long after Tchekov's popularity has been established here, is yet curiously prophetic. Like the Tchekov plays which Turgenev's preceded by half a century and unquestionably influenced, *A Month in the Country* has an apparent formlessness, a veiled and moody quiescence. It is less searching, less subtle and moving than any of the Tchekov masterpieces; and, unlike them, it would hardly be endurable were it to be badly played. There is in it no passionate necessity for a statement of human futility and despair. The stature of its characters does not change palpably under the stress of emotion, and its interludes are without the compact and telling strokes that make a Tchekov play close knit for all its seeming languor. But this is to judge competence by genius. *A Month in the Country* does not waste its time. Its leisure is devoted to the creation of an old, rich provincial atmosphere, and its tragi-comedy—as far as it goes—is etched with certainty. One must admit that the certainty does not go far, that Turgenev is excessively gingerly with a theme that asked for sharper treatment even in his time, and is a little mouldy now without it. Natalia, beautiful and mature, loves the tutor Aleksei, who loves her ward Viera but is quickly susceptible to the former when he is awakened to her. The play wanders through its pattern of mild hysteria and passiveness to a final frustration, passively encountered—Aleksei will return to Moscow, and the entire matter will go on from there as best it may. . . . Finally, the structure, as Turgenev shaped it, is only half a play; but a half good play can be immeasurably enlivened, even if it cannot be made important, by the playing that goes into it. To see Nazimova is to know how creative an actress so endowed can be in a mediocre role, and how important are subtle silences and fluent gesture to the fragility and weakness that are the character of Natalia. And in keeping the movement of the play in a state of placidity, Mr. Mamoulian turned from what might have been mere excited absurdity to give full room to the development of the character portraits Dudley Digges, Henry Travers and Douglas Dumbrille have provided. The portraits, like the best moments of the play, exist for their own sake. When they are fitted as well and harmoniously into a gallery as they have been here, the result is justifiable in the theatre whether or not it is dramatic.

Euphemia VanRensselaer Wyatt (review date May 1930)

SOURCE: A review of *A Month in the Country*, in *Catholic World*, Vol. 131, No. 782, May, 1930, p. 215.

[*In the review below, Wyatt declares: "For characterization and acting,* A Month in the Country *is unexcelled."*]

Feeling perhaps that their season so far has lacked luster, the Theater Guild have now consolidated their talent and conciliated their subscribers in this most delectable production of Turgenev's comedy [*A Month in the Country*]. And though laid in the heart of Russia, it really is a comedy. The genius of Turgenev was not oppressed by the spiritual burdens which overlaid the personal tragedies of Dostoievsky; the flaming fanaticism of Tolstoy. He saw his countrymen in kindly, philosophical perspective. One might call him the Slavic Thackeray, though his humor is less robust; his caricature more subtle; his narrative richer in delicate analysis than such sumptuous romance as the *Ball before Waterloo*. When the French stage minced through the artificialities of Scribe to the panting crises of Sardou, and London produced nothing nearer literature than *The Lady of Lyons* and *Richelieu* and Robertson's *School*; while New York laughed for twenty years over *The Loan of a Lover, All That Glitters Is Not Gold,* etc., and succumbed for half a century to *Uncle Tom's Cabin*, Russia was developing modern drama. But while the realism of Chekhov became completely local, Turgenev, in a cosmopolitan life, absorbed a sense of form from the French and made his characters Russian in manner but universal in type.

A Month in the Country is a polished pastoral of the woes of the charming Natalia, whose entertainment, a preoccupied husband has delegated to the polite devotion of his friend, Rakitin. Everyone is satisfied until Natalia engages a bashful but handsome student as her little boy's tutor and the unfortunate young man infects the entire small neighborhood with romance. Natalia loses her pretty head completely—in a ladylike fashion; the old doctor proposes to the companion; the rich farmer to Natalia's ward; the ward sobs for love of the tutor; the husband suddenly realizes he is a husband and Rakitin

discovers that his polite devotion is losing politeness. As they are all honorable and well-bred people, the ending may prove a surprise to audiences used to more modern and less well-bred standards.

For characterization and acting, *A Month in the Country* is unexcelled. Nazimova in the soft silks and swelling skirts of the '40's is delicious. Her grace is so softly subtle that it seems of rare simplicity. Dudley Digges as the country doctor has mellowed his mannerisms to his side whiskers. One short scene is made memorable by Henry Travers as the timid bachelor. Rakitin is Elliot Cabot and the tutor is Kirkland who has been playing the boy inventor in *Wings Over Europe*. Eunice Stoddard, a newcomer to the Guild, is not only exceedingly pretty as the ward but has fresh and genuine emotion. The settings, which were copied from the original Russian designs, are the very best which the Guild or New York has seen for a long time. There is a beautiful sweep to the country seen over the garden's hedge and through the drawing-room window. The clear coloring of the interiors are more Kate Greenaway than Victorian in the graceful but simple formality of their furniture and backgrounds. The clever Mamoulian who directed the production, has preserved throughout the same delicacy of pattern and tone.

FURTHER READING

OVERVIEWS AND GENERAL STUDIES

Gassner, John. "The Russian Dramatists." In *Masters of the Drama*, pp. 495-525. New York: Dover Publications, 1940.
    Discussion of the poetic as well as realistic aspects of Turgenev's plays.

BIOGRAPHY

Magarshak, David. *Turgenev: A Life*. London: Faber and Faber, 1954, 328 p.
    A literary biography that discusses Turgenev's life in terms of his works.

Schapiro, Leonard. *Turgenev: His Life and Times*. New York: Random House, 1978, 382 p.
    Attempts to portray Turgenev's "thought, his actions, and his work, on the basis of the most reliable evidence available."

A MONTH IN THE COUNTRY

Briggs, A. D. P. "Two Months in the Country: Chekhov's Unacknowledged Debt to Turgenev." *New Zealand Slavonic Journal* (1994): 17-32.

Assesses the degree to which Chekhov's *Uncle Vanya* was influenced by *A Month in the Country.*

Franklin, Nancy. "Words of Love." *The New Yorker* 71, No. 11 (8 May 1995): 98-9.

    Review of a recent production at the Roundabout Theater in New York. Franklin finds *A Month in the Country* light and insubstantial: "Chekhov without tears."

Kroll, Jack. "Unhappy in Their Own Way." *Newsweek* CXXV, No. 19 (8 May 1995): 67-8.

    Admiring review of the 1995 Roundabout staging that judges *A Month in the Country* "a wonderfully appealing play."

MacCarthy, Desmond. Review of *A Month in the Country. The New Statesman* XXVII, No. 689 (10 July 1926): 358.

    Assessment of the first British production of the play that urges: "Go and try if this quiet, old-fashioned play, with its asides and slow pace, does not strike you as solid as well as light, human as well as conventional, in short a good work of art."

Simon, John. Review of *A Month in the Country. New York Magazine* 28, No. 19 (8 May 1995): 73-4.

    Censures the Roundabout Theater production for missing the delicacy and subtleties of Turgenev's play.

"Turgenev and George Sand." *The Spectator* 137, No. 5115 (10 July 1926): 46-7.

    Evaluation of the first English-language production of *A Month in the Country* that finds the play sentimental and "interminable." The critic concedes, however, that "there are a few exquisite moments, a few scenes that move us by virtue of the restraint in Turgenev's methods."

Young, Stuart. "*A Month in the Country* in the British Theatre." *New Zealand Slavonic Journal* (1994): 207-27.

    Traces the English stage history of the play, from its first performance in 1926 to the present.

Additional coverage of Turgenev's life and career is contained in the following sources published by Gale Research: *DISCovering Authors*; *DISCovering Authors: British*; *DISCovering Authors: Canadian*; *DISCovering Authors: Modules—Most-Studied Authors Module,* and *Novelists Module*; *Nineteenth-Century Literature Criticism,* Vols. 21, 37; *Short Story Criticism,* Vol. 7; and *World Literature Criticism.*

Derek Walcott
1930-

INTRODUCTION

Walcott is a highly respected dramatist and poet and a leading voice in contemporary West Indian literature. Of mixed African and European heritage, Walcott embodies the cultural division that provides the major tensions in his work. Employing diverse styles, settings, and subject matter, he explores such themes as racism, the injustices of colonialism, the collapse of empires, and the quest for personal, cultural, and political identity. His synthesis of French Creole and West Indian dialect with the formal structures and eloquent language of Elizabethan verse, in addition to his topical imagery and calypso rhythms, creates a hybrid literature that reflects his personal experiences as well as the history and culture of the West Indies.

BIOGRAPHICAL INFORMATION

Walcott was born on St. Lucia, a small island in the West Indies. He has characterized his childhood as "schizophrenic," referring to the divided loyalties associated with his African and English ancestry and to the fact that he grew up in a middle-class, Protestant family in a society that was predominantly Catholic and poor. His mother, a teacher who was actively involved in the local theater, strongly influenced his artistic development. Although his father died when Walcott was still an infant, he drew inspiration from the poems and numerous watercolor paintings he left behind. In an interview Walcott explained: "[My father's paintings] gave me a kind of impetus and a strong sense of continuity. I felt that what had been cut off in him somehow was an extension that I was continuing." Walcott's childhood ambition was to be a painter, but he also developed an affinity for the English literature he read in school. While still a student he began writing poetry, often imitating such writers as W. H. Auden, T. S. Eliot, and Dylan Thomas. At the age of eighteen Walcott financed the publication of *25 Poems,* his first poetry collection. While studying literature at St. Mary's College in St. Lucia and at the University of the West Indies in Jamaica, he completed two more volumes of poetry and composed his first play, *Henri Christophe,* a historical drama written in verse. His play *Drums and Colours* brought Walcott both critical recognition and a Rockefeller Fellowship to study theater in the United States. Upon his return to the Caribbean he became intensely involved in Trinidad's artistic community, writing reviews and organizing the Trinidad Theatre Workshop, where several of his plays were produced during the 1950s and 1960s. Since the 1970s Walcott has divided his time between the West Indies and the United States, where he has taught at Yale, Columbia, and other universities. In 1971 his play *Dream on Monkey*

Mountain won an Obie Award, and in 1992 Walcott received the Nobel Prize for literature.

MAJOR DRAMATIC WORKS

The importance of understanding and preserving West Indian culture is a prominent theme in Walcott's works. Many of his plays, often called "folk dramas," are firmly rooted in the common life and language of the West Indies, and they frequently evoke Caribbean dialect and legends. These folk dramas, including "The Sea at Dauphin," *Ione, Ti-Jean and His Brothers,* and *Dream on Monkey Mountain,* are considered his most effective work for the theater. "The Sea at Dauphin," a tale of the St. Lucian fishing community's struggle to survive the forces of the sea, is derived from West Indian folklore and marks Walcott's first use of the native idiom. *Ti-Jean and His Brothers,* in which a humble, sensible boy named Ti-Jean succeeds in outwitting the Devil, continues the folk tradition by blending a morality play and a West Indian fable. The play celebrates the triumph of native resourcefulness over imperialist power and also comments on racism and the exploitation of the poor by the wealthy. Walcott explained his use of folklore and dialectical speech in this work: "The great challenge for me was to write as powerfully as I could without writing down to the audience, so that the large emotions could be taken in by a fisherman or a guy on the street, even if he didn't understand every line." *Dream on Monkey Mountain* is often considered Walcott's most successful play. It focuses on a charcoal vendor who descends from his mountain home to sell his wares but is jailed for drunkenness. While in jail, he dreams of becoming the king of a united Africa. Walcott has said that *Dream on Monkey Mountain* is about the West Indian search for identity and is concerned with the damage inflicted on the human soul by colonialism. Combining dream and reality in the play, Walcott emphasizes what he perceives to be the dangers of replacing the realities of Caribbean cultural diversity with a romanticized vision of Africa in the hope of reestablishing cultural roots. Instead, Walcott advocates introspection and art as the means to rediscover one's personal and cultural heritage. He continues his search for identity in such later plays as *O Babylon!,* which focuses on the Rastafarian rejection of Western culture, *Remembrance,* and *Pantomime.*

CRITICAL RECEPTION

Critics and reviewers of Walcott's plays have focused on their synthesis of diverse elements—cultural, theatrical, linguistic—as well as their merging of dreams and reality. Lowell Fiet has examined Walcott's use of a variety of theatrical techniques and devices in his plays and has argued that increasingly "the act of performance itself, the play and/or plays within the play, rehearsals, creative processes, theatre settings, and actor/writer/artist characters become increasingly prominent metaphors in [Walcott's] interpretation of Caribbean culture and society." In a consideration of Walcott's use of "contradictory" language in *Dream on Monkey Mountain,* Jan R. Uhrbach has observed that in the play nothing is certain: "Everything constantly changes: the characters' identities; the balance between reality and dream; the meanings of words, phrases, symbols, and images." Robert D. Hamner has underscored the playwright's utilization of a variety of theatrical and cultural material, calling Walcott's work a "theater of assimilation." This drama, he contends, "provides unique evidence in support of Donne's 'No man is an island, entire of itself.' Not only are there elements of poetry, music, dance, narrative, mime; and influences of Eastern, Western, and local folk traditions; but undergirding them all is the personal experience of a comprehending intelligence; the man and the artist in the West Indies, Derek Walcott."

PRINCIPAL WORKS

PLAYS

Henri Christophe: A Chronicle in Seven Scenes 1950
Paolo and Francesca 1951

Harry Dernier: A Play for Radio Production 1951
Wine of the Country 1953
"The Sea at Dauphin: A Play in One Act" 1953
Ione: A Play with Music 1957
Drums and Colours: An Epic Drama 1958
Ti-Jean and His Brothers 1958
"Malcauchon; or, Six in the Rain" 1959
Dream on Monkey Mountain 1967
In a Fine Castle 1970
Franklin 1973
The Charlatan [music by Galt MacDermot] 1974
The Joker of Seville [music by MacDermot] 1974
O Babylon! [music by MacDermot] 1976
Remembrance 1977
Pantomime 1978
Beef, No Chicken 1981
The Isle Full of Noises 1982
The Last Carnival 1982
A Branch of the Blue Nile 1983
Haitian Earth 1984
To Die for Grenada 1986
Steel 1991
The Odyssey 1992

POETRY

25 Poems 1948
Epitaph for the Young: A Poem in XII Cantos 1949
Poems 1951
In a Green Night: Poems, 1948-1960 1962
Selected Poems 1964
The Castaway and Other Poems 1965
The Gulf and Other Poems 1969
Another Life 1973
Sea Grapes 1976
Selected Verse 1976
The Star-Apple Kingdom 1979
The Fortunate Traveller 1981
Selected Poetry 1981
Midsummer 1984
Collected Poems, 1948-1984 1986
The Arkansas Testament 1987
Omeros 1990

*This play is a revised version of *In a Fine Castle.*

AUTHOR COMMENTARY

Interview with Walcott (1971)

SOURCE: An interview in *The New Yorker,* Vol. XLVII, No. 19, 26 June 1971, pp. 30-1.

[*In the following conversation, conducted at the time of the New York production of* Dream on Monkey Mountain, *Walcott elucidates the play's themes and discusses the person who inspired the character Makak.*]

Derek Walcott, author of the Obie Award-winning play *The Dream on Monkey Mountain,* is a tall, lithe West Indian of forty-one who has striking hazel eyes, longish hair (sideburns but no Afro), and a kind of casual, mussed elegance that stamps him as a man of the theatre. He has had two books of poetry published commercially, and one of plays (which includes the text of *Monkey Mountain*), and is the founder-director of the Trinidad Theatre Workshop, a group of twenty-odd actors who travel around the Caribbean presenting plays to audiences that often have very little contact with live drama. We met Mr. Walcott when he was here during *Monkey Mountain*'s successful run at the Negro Ensemble Company Theatre, on Second Avenue, and we arranged to have a talk with him one evening after a performance. We arrived at the apartment of a mutual friend with the sounds of Mr. Walcott's magnificent, almost Shakespearean sentences still ringing in our ears, and immediately asked him to explain some of the thinking behind the plot.

"On the surface, your play is the story of an old and ugly charcoal burner named Makak who comes down from his hut on the mountain to sell his wares, gets drunk, and spends a night in jail, where he has vivid hallucinations about Africa," we said. "But what are you really getting at? There seem to be as many theories as there are critics."

Mr. Walcott smiled gently and lit a cigarette. "*Monkey Mountain* is about many things," he replied, in the lilting cadences of the Caribbean. "It's about the West Indian search for identity, and about the damage that the colonial spirit has done to the soul. Makak and the people he meets in the play are all working out the meaning of their culture; they are going through an upheaval, shaking off concepts that have been imposed on them for centuries. They live in the West Indies because I live in the West Indies, but the basic situation is true of any society where man has been downgraded to a primitive, uninformed, unpurposed existence. Makak is an extreme representation of what colonialism can do to a man—he is reduced to an almost animal-like state of degradation. When he dreams that he is the king of a united Africa, I'm saying that some sort of spiritual return to Africa can be made, but it may not be necessary. The romanticized, pastoral vision of Africa that many black people hold can be an escape from the reality of the world around us. In the West Indies, where all the races live and work together, we have the beginnings of a great and unique society. The problem is to recognize our African origins but not to romanticize them. In the first half of the play, the concept of the beginning of the world and the evolution of man is—shall we say?—basically white. Then, when Corporal Lestrade, the brainwashed colonial servant, retrogresses to become an ape and emerges as a man to walk through the primeval forest, the play swings over to a black Adamic concept of evolution. But the same sins are repeated, and the cycle of violence and cruelty begins again. When the two criminals, who are virtually brothers, fight, that's where the dream breaks for Makak. He thought he was going to an Africa where man would be primal and communal. Instead, it's back to original sin, with the tribes killing one another. He ultimately rejects both insanities—the extremity of contempt for the black and the extremity of hatred for the white. At the end, having made a spiritual trip to Africa and survived the middle passage, he compares himself to a drifting tree that has put down roots in the new world."

"But at the end of the play, when Makak returns to his hut on the mountain, isn't he rejecting both white and black societies?" we said.

"You forget that Makak is a charcoal burner," Mr. Walcott said. "He has to face reality, too. He has to come down to the market every Saturday to make a living."

While we were absorbing this piece of information, Mr. Walcott added, with a grin, that the character of Makak, an elderly, poetic alcoholic, was based on a man he'd known when he was a child in the Windward Islands. "I was born in St. Lucia," he said. "A very green, misty island, which always has a low cloud hanging over the mountaintops. When you come down by plane, you break through the mist, and it's as if you were entering some kind of prehistoric Eden. Monkey Mountain, where Makak lives, is really a peak called La Sorcière, and the town where he is put in jail is Castries, where I grew up. St. Lucia changed hands thirteen times during various wars. The people there speak the same Creole that people do in Haiti; we learn English in school almost as a foreign language, and perhaps that makes us value English the more. Islands are great places to live in, because the sea is close and there is the elemental feeling of things that are bigger than you are. And so, when I started to write this play, I remembered an almost inhuman man named Makak Rougier—I suppose his name meant 'Rougier's monkey,' because he worked for a man named Rougier—who used to come into town and get terrifyingly drunk. He'd roar up and down the main street, fling things around, and get arrested. At the same time, I was influenced by Japanese No plays and the whole Kabuki thing. I thought that I could see in the truly ethnic West Indian dances—some of the surviving celebrating or warrior dances—the same kind of force you get in the Japanese theatre. We have a similar percussive feel—we use flute and drums—and we have a great oral tradition in the islands that gives us a reference for speech. So I tried to combine these elements into a play that could be done on a completely bare stage with just light, because we in the West Indies are also very poor."

"How did you get interested in writing in the first place?" we asked.

"I grew up with a terrific mother in a house full of books," replied Mr. Walcott. "My father died when I was one, and my mother, a schoolteacher, who never remarried, loved to act. I have an older sister, and a twin brother who is also a playwright and lives in Canada."

By the time Mr. Walcott was eighteen, he had written three books of poetry, which he published himself. "Shortly afterward, I got a scholarship to the University of the

West Indies, in Jamaica, where I took a degree in French, Latin, and Spanish," he said. "I taught for a few years in Jamaica and Grenada, and in 1958 I was commissioned to write an epic pageant to celebrate the first meeting of the West Indian Federal Parliament. On the strength of that, I got a Rockefeller grant to study in New York, and it was here, twelve years ago, that I began thinking about St. Lucia and writing *Monkey Mountain.*"

At the present time, Mr. Walcott lives in Port of Spain, Trinidad, with his wife, Margaret, who is a psychiatric social worker, and two young daughters and a son. "Trinidad is a fantastic island," he said. "It's such an amalgam of races that it's perhaps the best place for the development of a genuine West Indian culture. And it's an enormously creative society; if you include all the people who work on Carnival, there are probably seventy thousand artists on the island. I could never become a Trinidadian, though, because there's also a basic irresponsibility in the Trinidadians' nature, which I, with my Methodist, St. Lucia bringing-up, find delightful but immoral. Last year, for example, we had a revolution, and right after it failed everybody said, 'Shoot those criminals! Hang them!' The government held a long, expensive trial, but the final judgment was suspended, because Carnival had begun. By the time it ended, the whole affair had started to bore the Trinidadians so much that public sentiment had changed to 'Well, give the boys a break.' So you have a whole country with not only compassion but a kind of shrug concerning a very serious political matter. In any Latin-American country, those boys would have been shot the next day."

We asked Mr. Walcott if he had ever tried to capture the Trinidadian spirit onstage, and he replied that his latest play, *In a Fine Castle,* is the story of a bourgeois French Creole family who live in one of Port of Spain's elaborate Victorian mansions. "When I began it, I was just interested in the characters," he said. "But the revolution came along, and they got mixed up in it. Now I guess the play deals with the contrast between Carnival and revolution. Trinidad is a society where Carnival is regarded as a serious matter and revolution as fun. It's the ambiguity of this view that makes life there so interesting."

OVERVIEWS AND GENERAL STUDIES

Robert D. Hamner (essay date 1979)

SOURCE: "Derek Walcott's Theater of Assimilation," in *Philological Papers,* Vol. 25, February, 1979, pp. 86-93.

[*In the essay below, Hamner surveys the development of Walcott's drama through* O Babylon! *He underscores the playwright's assimilation of diverse cultural and theatrical influences in his works.*]

When Derek Walcott's earliest poems came out in 1947, when he was only nineteen years old, he was immediately hailed in his native West Indies as a prodigy. His first book of poetry *In a Green Night* (1962) led Robert Graves to proclaim, "Derek Walcott handles English with a closer understanding of its inner magic than most (if not any) of his English-born contemporaries." Today with six published volumes to his credit, and several literary prizes, he is one of the leading poets not only of the West Indies but internationally as well.

At the same time he is also an accomplished dramatist—having formed his own company, the Trinidad Theatre Workshop, in 1959. Four of his best plays have been published together in *Dream on Monkey Mountain and Other Plays.* He won an Obie in 1970 for *Dream on Monkey Mountain*; and in 1974 he was commissioned by the Royal Shakespeare Company of London to write a modern version of Tirso de Molina's seventeenth-century Spanish classic *El burlador de Sevilla* (1618?). On the surface it may seem odd that a writer from the small, distant island of St. Lucia should be honored with such an assignment; and yet, Walcott's entire career makes him particularly well suited to the re-creation of another time and another place, within the eternal present.

Walcott has argued that West Indian writers of his generation are "natural assimilators [in **"What the Twilight Says"** in *Dream on Monkey Mountain and Other Plays,* 1970]. The term is crucial to his dramatic technique, and deserves definition. He uses the adjective "natural" because there are geographical, social, cultural, and economic factors involved which are indigenous to the West Indian situation. History shows the Spanish conquistadors sweeping through the islands in search of treasure. They were joined by English, French, and Dutch adventurers and settlers. When native Indians proved unsatisfactory as agricultural laborers, slavery was instituted to fill the gap.

Thus the Middle Passage, the third side of a triangular trade route, was added to link Europe, Africa, and the Americas. With emancipation in 1834, the negroes deserted the sugar plantations in masses. To supply the needed workers, indentured Chinese and East Indian laborers were brought in.

To say today that the West Indian suffers an identity crisis because of slavery and colonization is to utter a shopworn cliche. The so-called "melting pot" has produced not a blend, but an amalgamated society with strong race, class, and culture differences. The problem is that no one knows where to look for his heritage. There are attempts to copy European patterns, to preserve East Indian customs, or to revert to Africa. Unfortunately, there are large gulfs of space and time between the present-day West Indian and the land of his ancestors. What is needed, according to Walcott, is not a romantic revival of something foreign, but recognition of the authentic heritage at hand: "Pastoralists of the African revival should know that what is needed is not new names for old things, or old names for old things, but the faith of using the old names anew, so that mongrel as I am, something prickles in me when I see the word Ashanti as with the word Warwickshire, both separately intimating my grandfathers' roots, both baptising this neither proud nor ashamed bastard, this hybrid, this West Indian."

There is an admirable quality of hardnosed humility in this concept. It brings us to the second term in Walcott's key phrase "natural assimilators." Walcott has been criticized for being an imitator: and he candidly admits the heavy debt he owes to a number of sources. He does not, however, feel any need to apologize for enjoying the fruits of experiments and discoveries made by poets and dramatists who planted seeds before him. By definition, to assimilate means more than mechanical imitation. Assimilation denotes not only taking something in and thoroughly comprehending it; the term signifies also the incorporation and conversion processes that occur as foreign matter is absorbed and adapted. Fusion takes place and new energy is released. Some of the criticism directed at Walcott's method is obviously motivated chauvinistically. He is guilty of having assimilated only too well Western culture when he should have leaned toward Africa and the "folk." Walcott's career does, indeed, have its apprenticeship phase, but in his maturer works he does not really lean in any direction: he stands erect and uses the various traditions that flow naturally through his multifaceted culture.

There are basically two attitudes to take toward this mixed colonial legacy. One is negative, the popular tendency to denounce imperialism, to decry slavery, and either to idealize poverty and degradation, or escape into metropolitan exile. The positive approach, and Walcott's choice, is to pass judgment on history, but to grow beyond it by building on the foundation that it provides. Walcott responds, for example, to the charge that nothing has been created in the West Indies by stating that everything is yet to be made. To complaints about education imposed by the imperialists he answers: "I think

that . . . our early education must have ranked with the finest in the world. The grounding was rigid—Latin, Greek, and the essential masterpieces . . . and both the patois of the street and the language of the classroom hid the elation of discovery." ["**Meanings,**" *Savacou* 2, 1970]. The creative artist's task is to fuse the old and the new, forge a new creation, and thus lay claim to his birthright.

Walcott's apprenticeship phase runs approximately from 1950 through 1958. *Henri Christophe,* his first play, deals with the Haitian revolution of the 1800's, but by his own admission the play is in the language and style of seventeenth-century Jacobean drama. *Harry Dernier* (1951) is set on an island that resembles T.S. Eliot's wasteland more than any real locale. The poetry, too, is Eliot's in tone, image, and vocabulary. Next, in 1954, there is **"The Sea at Dauphin,"** which Walcott based on John Millington Synge's *Riders to the Sea.* In diction, setting, and character, this is much closer to Walcott's native St. Lucia. **"The Sea at Dauphin"** and *Ione* (1957)—which was inspired by Greek tragedy in general—both belong to the Caribbean and owe nothing more than their conventional structure to Western tradition. The language is English, but it derives from the patois and is in keeping with the type of character and action being portrayed.

Drums and Colours, which rounds off the apprenticeship, is a West Indian historical pageant commissioned for the opening of the First Federal parliament of the West Indies in 1958. Because of the necessity of covering four hundred years of history the play ranges too broadly to be well unified. To aid continuity, however, Walcott introduces for the first time an aspect of West Indian life that does not enter into his earlier plays. He frames the action and provides interludes between scenes with a band of carnival maskers. These celebrants bring along not only song and dance, but also the élan, the flamboyance of West Indian life that parallels the tragic movement of its dark history. By including basic elements of carnival in *Drums and Colours*—music, dance, masks, pageantry, mime, and parody—Walcott moves significantly closer to the kind of drama that can give adequate expression to his cultural experience.

The year 1958 marks a turning point in Walcott's career. With *Drums and Colours* behind him he takes up the study of directing and scene design in New York on a Rockefeller Fellowship. Here several important ideas come into focus and give more purposeful direction to his thinking. The central influence dating from this year is Bertolt Brecht. After Brecht, he is convinced that West Indian audiences will respond to an exciting, highly physical theater. A second Brechtian concept, that of alienation—the distancing of actor from rôle and audience from performance that shifts the audience's concern from the story to the meaning—, also appeals to Walcott. Then, through Brecht, he begins to appreciate the subdued power and beautiful simplicity of Japanese Kabuki and Noh drama. In anticipation of renewed charges that Walcott is again revealing his lack of originality, I should like to point out that analogues to all three of these Brechtian factors already exist in Walcott's earlier plays. Brecht is primarily a catalyst, not a model to be copied but a contributor to the process of evolution.

Whatever the source, Brecht or his own imagination, it did not take Walcott long to put theory into practice. Before the year was out, he wrote and produced *Ti-Jean and His Brothers,* a play based on a St. Lucian folktale. He calls it his first experience at writing a stylized West Indian drama. "For the first time I used songs and dances and a narrator in a text. . . . Out of that play, I knew what I wanted" ["**Meanings**"]. The plot of *Ti-Jean* is very simple. The devil challenges three brothers to a contest of will. If any one of the brothers causes him to experience a human emotion, that brother will be rewarded; but failure means death. The eldest, Gros Jean, relies on brute strength. Mi Jean thinks his bookish wisdom will support him. Ti-Jean succeeds in the end, where his brothers fail, because first, he is humble enough to profit from the advice of friendly creatures and his aged mother; and second, he is wily enough to shift tactics and use clever tricks. He is the deceptively simple man, dangerous because of his apparent innocence, a version of the trickster figure of popular tales.

The story is recounted through animal narrators (another folk element) not only associated with oral tradition but also functioning like a Greek chorus. To be sure that his audience does not miss the Greek connection, Walcott has his frog raise the curtain on the lines "Greek-croak, Greek-croak," sneeze, and then excuse himself with "Aeschylus me!" Such flippant allusions are not likely to be missed by his countrymen, who have been reared on a rich diet of the puns, metaphors, and verbal play of lightning-fast calypsonian rhetoric. The movement is paced with music, dance, emphatic gesture and pause, asides to the audience, and intervals with animals conversing about the human actions. This combining of artifice with elemental simplicity is the kind of assimilated entity that Walcott seeks. It is appropriate to him because of his split family tree; it is appropriate to his society because of its divided heritage. Recognizing this dichotomy, Walcott says that one side pulls him toward the mimetic, the narrative, and the dance; the other inclination is toward the literary, the classical tradition.

Bringing these traditions together, Walcott wishes to impress his audience with a sense of masculine virility, of controlled violence. In part, this results from his preference for color and movement, but it is also a reaction against the heavily psychological and feminized element of much modern Western theater. Sounding more than a bit chauvinistic, Walcott defines the kind of effect he wants: "I think that in a theatre where you have a strong male principle, or where women aren't involved at the beginning, a kind of style will happen; there will be violence, there will be direct conflict, there will be more physical theatre and there will be less interest in sexual psychology" ["**Meanings**"].

In order to achieve this end with any kind of consistency, Walcott realized while he was still in New York in 1958 that he needed a trained company. For this reason, soon after he arrived in Trinidad he founded the Trinidad Theatre Workshop and joined forces with the Little Carib Dance Company. The first requisite was discipline, since Walcott felt that self-indulgent, uncontrolled enthusiasm was the besetting sin of West Indian theater. The Theatre Workshop and Dance Company did not remain together long, but the separation did not affect Walcott's program very greatly. By then, his concern was with actors who could dance, not dancers among the cast of actors. For eight years, until 1966, he kept up a schedule of improvisations and method acting while his company of amateurs and semiprofessionals acquired the kind of skills they needed, and while Walcott developed the elements of his assimilated style.

Kabuki may have inspired Walcott primarily because of the parallels he finds between it and his native culture: in folklore, dance, its primitive mythological figures, its masks. Yet, Kabuki's rigid symbolic structure is not as conducive to improvisation as he desires. Consequently, he resorts to the freer music and dances of the West Indies: the calypso, reggae, shango, and kalenda of African origin. All the while, Walcott's emphasis is on acting. The choreographer designs movement which promotes dramatic exposition. He wants a play that is sparce and essential, as compressed as Oriental drama, so that gesture, the language of the body, does as much as speech. This creation is to be verbally rich literature within a mimetic tradition.

In brief, these are the kinds of ideals Walcott instills in his Company as he prepares them for the play that is presently his best known, *Dream on Monkey Mountain.* This play (first performed in 1967, and awarded an Obie in 1970) culminates Walcott's years of experimentation. It incorporates all the diverse elements he has acquired. No matter how foreign some of the original sources may be, the heart of the play is purely West Indian. Walcott cites precedents for Makak, his protagonist, in African warriors and Japanese Samurai, but Makak is derived as well from his personal childhood memories of an old St. Lucian woodburner whose drunken rampages used to terrify him. Degraded as the old man may have been, he possessed an elemental force worthy of a warrior king.

There are too many complexities within *Dream on Monkey Mountain* to be explicated here. It should be noted, however, that the basic theme is as widely applicable as the sources which feed into it are diverse. Makak has a vision that informs him that he is the descendent of African kings. Guided by his vision, he rejects the abject status he has been accorded by white men and attempts to set up an African kingdom. As the dream progresses, Makak finally comes to know that whether a man is white or black, when he attempts to impose his values and order on others he is paradoxically both a tyrant and a slave. Makak rejects first the white man's established rôle for him and then he rejects the black man's preconceived categories. Only then is he free. He decides in the final scene to be himself, to do his work, to return to the mountain that he now recognizes to be his real home.

Walcott's message, contrary to some interpretations, is not to reject social intercourse, and it is not a call to revert to a primitive state: Makak journeys to ancestral Africa in order to exorcise the history of slavery, and to satisfy the exile's longing for an established heritage. His return to the mountain is not a negative act. He exclaims in benediction: "Lord, I have been washed from shore to shore, as a tree in the ocean. The branches of my fingers, the roots of my feet, could grip nothing, but now, God, they have found ground." Critics who try to make Makak into a revolutionist tend to leave him before the climb back up Monkey Mountain. In so doing they miss the true revolution of his obtaining personal liberty, freedom that goes beyond "the right to be like everybody else."

The Joker of Seville, Walcott's adaptation of Tirso de Molina's Don Juan play provides another instance of his assimilative technique. The fact that it has not yet been published is unfortuante because it is a faithful translation of the poetry and spirit of the original and at the same time it conforms to Walcott's evolving pattern. One experiment in staging that Walcott believes works very well for *The Joker* is using an open arena, like a cockfight pit, with few props. The audience seated around the pit is invited to eat, drink, and participate in the action as interested bystanders might be expected to do. The theme, dramatized in the career of the arch rebel Don Juan, goes another step beyond *Dream on Monkey Mountain.* Ironically, Don Juan, who flouts custom and law and breaks others free from society's imposed restraints, is at last a victim trapped in the very rôle of liberator that he has always played. When the vengeful statue of Don Gonzalo summons him to hell, Juan is ready to go:

> You see here a man born empty,
> with a heart as heavy as yours;
> there's no hell you could offer me,
> sir, that's equal to its horrors.

Yet, as Juan's corpse is borne off in the closing scene to an insistent calypso rhythm, the joker's rôle is transferred to death itself: "If there is resurrection, death is a joker, / sans humanité!?" (II, vii). Juan's reward like Makak's is to become immortalized as a dream figure. Unlike Makak, however, Juan cannot descend from the realm of the ideal to the mundane tasks of daily life.

The significance of this distinction carries over into Walcott's latest play *O Babylon!,* a reggae musical about the Rastafarians in Jamaica. Rufus Johnson is another humble man like Makak whose dream of returning to Africa does not materialize. Johnson recovers from despair and contemplation of suicide to realize that faith is greater than a failed dream. In the end he takes back Priscilla, the woman who had abandoned him while he was in prison, and tells her to begin planting her garden.

Out of endings like these in *Dream on Monkey Mountain, The Joker of Seville,* and *O Babylon!* it is possible for new life to grow. Rastafarians form an esoteric sub-culture, yet their advocacy of spiritual values in opposition to a world mad over materialism strikes a responsive chord in a wide audience, and the reggae rhythm they created is proving to be a powerful force in current music. *The Joker of Seville* originated in a Spain that is long passed; yet it is that very seventeenth-century Spain which another West Indian, V.S. Naipaul, uses to describe the social milieu of the present-day Caribbean [*The Middle Passage,* 1962]. *Dream on Monkey Mountain* treats of an obscure hermit; yet the burdens of seeking authentic roots and of establishing the integrity of the individual apply everywhere.

Walcott's theater of assimilation provides unique evidence in support of Donne's "No man is an island, entire of itself." Not only are there elements of poetry, music, dance, narrative, mime; and influences of Eastern, Western, and local folk traditions; but undergirding them all is the personal experience of a comprehending intelligence: the man and the artist in the West Indies, Derek Walcott.

Erskine Peters (essay date 1988)

SOURCE: "The Theme of Madness in the Plays of Derek Walcott," in *CLA Journal,* Vol. XXXII, No. 2, December, 1988, pp. 148-69.

[*In the essay below, Peters analyzes Walcott's depiction of madness in his characters as a response to the clash between European, African, and New World cultures.*]

Madness in the works of Derek Walcott and most Afro-American writers means freedom from inhibitions resulting from living under cultural, political, economic, social, and philosophical proscription. Those deemed mad usually are able to delineate in the most profound terms how the proscriptive forces operate. In many cases characters like Derek Walcott's Makak, Ralph Ellison's Surgeon Vet, Alice Walker's Meridian Hill, and Ernest Gaines' Copper dare to confront what those who hold to the same norm consider overwhelming and matchless odds. These characters, in contrast to their "normal" counterparts, often wander toward the realm of the absurd. From the perspective of those who hold cautiously to what they think is sanity, the audacious characters already appear to have been overwhelmed by that which needs to be confronted. The desired action of these characters, to put it simply, is deemed dangerously impertinent. In this they differ substantially from the host of mad characters created by white writers and studied by Sander Gilman in his "The Nexus of Madness and Blackness" [in *On Blackness Without Blacks: Essays on the Image of the Black in Germany,* 1982]. Gilman emphasizes the link between madness and disguise, demonstrating that "only in the mask of the ultimate lack of freedom, in madness and in death, can freedom be assured. . . . The mad characters of black writers usually lay themselves bare instead of donning the mask. Gilman argues that often these characters "see the pragmatic value of [the] myth [of blackness and madness] as a manner of manipulating those who believe in it." The mad characters of black writers may certainly exploit the fear of "potential destructiveness [as] . . . a common feature of the nexus of blackness and madness."

Derek Walcott's *Dream on Monkey Mountain* (1967) is a play constructed around the subconscious rumblings and images that emerge from the dream state of the old man Makak, whose name means monkey, and who is said by his friend and business partner Moustique to suffer a slight mental imbalance. The first words of *Dream on Monkey Mountain,* given initially by the Conteur or storyteller and immediately repeated by the Chorus, speak directly to the issue at the heart of Makak's madness:

> Mooma, mooma,
> Your son in de jail a'ready,
> Your son in de jail a'ready,
> Take a towel and
>   band your belly.

Walcott has the major action of the play take place in a jail where Makak is being held for disturbing the peace. Through this introductory chant, Walcott establishes the essential point that the existence of Makak and his people is based on historical imprisonment, a form of proscription in which their bodies, minds, tongues, hearts, and generations are bound. It is a form of existence which seeks to doom them from the outset—even before birth. Thus, the words of the chant are signs or omens for potential bearers of children. The situation of these children is the same doomed encasement symbolized by the rat-terrorized room inhabited by the four people in the opening of Richard Wright's *Native Son* and actualized by Bigger's incarceration at the novel's end. The situation of encasement is the extension of a slave system which never totally ended.

Although he may be called half-mad, Makak's gestures—like those of Walker's Meridian, Ellison's Surgeon Vet, and the ostensibly mad characters of other Afro-American writers—show an effort to break out of the encasements which indeed have driven them, or may drive them, mad. As all these characters demonstrate in one form or another, attempts to escape the existence from behind bars always entail supreme challenges, risks, and dangers. The danger is certainly best and most hauntingly expressed by the Corporal in *Dream on Monkey Mountain.* Upon finding that his prisoners have escaped, the Corporal observes: "Let them run ahead. Then I'll have good reason for shooting them down. . . . . Attempting to escape from the prison of their lives. That's the most dangerous crime." Escaping often involves monkey work, gestures, and antics to misguide and manipulate the guards and the members of society, who are varyingly, consciously or unconsciously, socialized to serve as guards.

Through the surreal life of Makak, we understand the nature of the encasement, and especially of Makak's troubled identity. Makak sometimes forgets his name and is evasive concerning the identity of his race. If Makak forgets his name, he also forgets his essence. If he does not know his true origins, he probably will not know from whence to draw his power for wholeness. If he forgets what power he stands on, he is likely to have trouble maintaining his poise and balance and, consequently, trouble maintaining any definite sense of personal autonomy.

With respect to Makak's identity, the fact that he lives on Monkey Mountain suggests at least two points of significance. First, he is sardonic in the face of the authorities, who deem him as belonging to a biologically inferior race. The second point of significance is that one who suffers from a troubled identity is, like a monkey, inclined toward frivolous, erratic behavior, possessed of an uncentered and dislocated consciousness. This may carry the implication that it is ludicrous to expect to accomplish anything major in a monkey state of mind, although seeing life from Monkey Mountain may have its vantage points. Makak will certainly have to come to an understanding of this if he expects to fulfill his dream of becoming a healer of the historical and symbolic leprosy which has besieged the consciousness of his race. A man is no longer bound to the monkeyism or madness of Makak's kind when he can be decisive, when he can with clarity and courage deracinate and decapitate the beguiling phantoms that have attempted to guide yet destroy him.

Makak's continuous declarations mean little to his associate Moustique, who perceives that both their identities together add up to a virtual nothingness. For it is from the voice of Moustique that we hear: "You is nothing. You black, ugly, poor, so you worse than nothing. You like me. . . . Man together two of us is minus* one." Makak hears in Moustique's voice a collective problem of identity and self-concept. Thus, when called to heal the sick Josephus, Makak sends forth an incantation directed toward the hearing of the entire group: "Like the cedars of Lebanon, / like the plantains of Zions, / the hand of God plant me / on Monkey Mountain. / He calleth to the humble. / And from that height, / like trees without names, / a forest with no roots! / By this coal in my hand, / By this fire in my veins / let my tongue catch fire, / let my body like Moses, / be a blazing bush." Makak ends the incantation with the wish that the race become "brilliant diamonds / In the hand of . . . God."

The collective body cannot be healed unless the members take into their minds Makak's words. Makak calls upon their recognition of this and their ability to put his message into action when the collective healing incantation does not manifest itself through Josephus. In Makak's call for Moustique to make the spiritual journey with him, he both proclaims and further highlights the tragedy of their encasement. This is evident in his saying, "These niggers too tired to believe anything again." But Makak's disparaging words to his group are supplemented by other words of piercing psychological power: "Remember, is you all self that is your own enemy."

In a similar spiritual journey toward regeneration, the character Headeye in Henry Dumas's "Ark of Bones" compares the situation of the Afro-American to that of the Biblical story of the valley of dry bones in the book of Ezekiel. The Afro-American is not in possession of his total self. Someone must make the spiritual journey back through history to the source of his existence to find the answers for wholeness. Headeye answers the call and makes the journey. Upon his return, his disposition is seen by his acquaintances as more mystical or mysterious, and his sanity is held in great suspicion. Nevertheless, Headeye feels that in having made the mystical journey back into the ark or womb of history, and in having been anointed and initiated there, he has a better understanding of what is required to give his racial existence wholeness. Thus, Headeye feels that he has been given the fundamental preparation for leadership and has taken the vows for such. Like Makak, Headeye will hold the formula for the healing ritual of the race.

For Walcott, the true power of the mind is therefore the power to reestablish one's identity, to reestablish one's mental balance. In Makak, the yearning for Africa becomes the symbol for a yearning for the reorientation of one's potential, integrity, and autonomy. A people who do not recognize who they are cannot recognize their true leaders. Consequently, the inmates who share Makak's cell mock him when he declares that he is the King of Africa. Yet Makak yearns to return to Africa to make contact with his submerged autonomous consciousness and to undertake his needed regeneration toward primal strength. Makak declares that he "will ride to the edge of the world . . . walk like he used to in Africa, when his name was lion!" Makak understands that he is a being who has fallen into suffering under "the divine sadness." In Aimé Césaire's *A Season in the Congo,* the character Lumumba believes likewise that the African has been robbed of his *self* and that the only way to withstand the continuing mental onslaught of colonial experience is to plant in the African mind "an invulnerable idea" of its identity. This, he feels, is the only magic or ritual of salvation for a people hungry for themselves.

One may have to risk walking on the borderline of the gulf of insanity in order to avoid insanity. Since so much of the madness is indeed caused by the proscribed value system, and since one's identity is intricately involved with what one values, to escape one must necessarily move into a certain void or a certain dimension of a lack of identity for an existential moment or instant. Making this existential step is often portentous and therefore terrifying. One considers whether there is more security in the existent state than there is in the prospective chasm should one not be successful or not ingenious enough in one's attempt to manage his or her own metamorphosis. For all do not survive the slaying of the dragon: since to slay the dragon often involves to some degree the slaying of the self.

Mad characters like Makak and the Surgeon Vet move beyond the borders of signifying and double-talking. They use these two rhetorical features with such virtuosity that they turn the supposed real or norm on its head to reveal that supposed real or norm as absurd and surreal. The absurd here is the circumstance in which the rational is compelled to reckon with the irrational, whereas the rational is generally predisposed to consider the irrational, the nonsensical, or the utterly stupid as dismissable. The surreal here is the situation or circumstance in which the sense of time, place, action and/or reasoning operates upon or within an apparent illogically constructed consciousness which, however, when examined by its own system, may very well be found to be "logical."

We say Ellison's Surgeon Vet is "mad" not only for what he says but how he says it, that is, the way he engages himself in the speech act itself. He breaks the taboo of appropriate forms prescribed for use in expressing himself as a "Negro" to a white man. Stated more simply though still metaphorically, the Vet engages in cutting, a cutting of the most skillful type. His thoughts are sinister within themselves but are not so much so without his cynical manipulation of the language. Moreover, his language is sweetly or finely styled. Combined with the cutting edge of his daggered tongue, the effect is necessarily somewhat surreal and absurd.

Both Makak's and the Vet's language usage falls under the patterns of "speech behavior and decorum" which Roger Abrahams [in *The Man-of-Words in the West Indies,* 1983] has described as part of the language consciousness of people in the St. Vincentian Afro-community of the Caribbean in their preoccupation with the realm of speech. Writes Abrahams: "These speech acts are often the most ceremonious in tone and manifest what has been the most conscious linguistic ideal of the community. Their salient attributes are in an elevated diction, and elaboration of stylistic features, and an approximation of standard English speech patterns, with an emphasis on the demonstration of fluency and knowledge, both in the form of facts and effective arguments."

In a discussion of Walcott, it is important not to forget the relative nature of madness. One wonders, for example, whether it is a radical or mad act when in Walcott's **Remembrance** Frederick Jordan paints a "mural" on the roof. Indeed the impertinency present in Frederick Jordan's act of art is twofold. First, Frederick has gone beyond general artistic modes as a visual artist by creating what is virtually an invisible visual mode, a rather physically inaccessible mode. Secondly, to achieve the creative, he has by impertinence disordered the object of his art, the American flag. The natural ripples of the corrugated tin roof form the basis for the flag's stripes. The holes worn into the roof form the basis for the stars. Society may be inclined, however, to acquiesce to the satiric implications of the art form and its creator, even though Frederick's parents see his deed as a mad act. Nevertheless, somewhat ironically, radical or impertinent art can be granted the status of appeasing or benign madness by society.

Perhaps the granting of such a status by our individual perceiving consciousnesses allows avoidance of personal conflict. Perhaps it holds the perceiver in the relatively safe realm of ambiguity, allowing one not to have to decide whether the artist's subject is an issue or whether that subject, arguably, might not be aesthetics itself. So the artist's mad act may come off in a more favorable light than the act of Makak in his creation of the new politically apparent role for himself as the healing King of Africa, one who reinstates cultural soundness.

One wonders why Clay's climactic virtuoso performance in Amiri Baraka's *Dutchman* is not thought of as mad. Clay certainly dares to make the delineations which others called mad have made. There is little notable difference in what he says from that of Walcott's Makak and Ellison's Surgeon Vet. Clay's hauntingly impertinent declaration to the white woman Lula that what blues singer Bessie Smith was actually saying to the white power chauvinist structure was, "Kiss my ass, kiss my black unruly ass," and what jazzman Charles Parker was saying is virtually the same as Makak and the Vet, and that neither Bessie Smith nor Charlie Parker would have needed their music had they "killed some white people," had they performed "that simple act. Murder. Just murder!" The answer to this discrepancy lies inevitably in human sanctions. It is these sanctions that set the behavioral norm for what is sane and what is not. Clay happens to be initiating and speaking for an historical moment when blacks feel more collectively empowered to reorder their mental world through public directness rather than indirectness, and at a time when the old power structure is losing its cohesion. Direct delineation of the obscenities of the power structure is no longer so much madness or impertinence but laudable purgation—the ritual matrix of salvation which Makak is also seeking to put into effect.

Mad characters like Makak exhibit the acute need to work to prevent alienation from the self as well as from society. Misappropriation of physical and psychic energy, when ordered around a self-negating value system, fosters the grotesque. It creates the inverse of the psychic clarity, potency, and wholeness which the African ancestors apparently tried to crystallize in thoughts and in various symbologies and rituals emphasizing the primacy of cosmic rhythm and spiritual balance.

Truly, a part of this ostensible madness may originate in the fact that traditional Afro-cultures struggle against the attempts of any epistemology to give extraordinary primacy to the material world. For the African, the world is not first matter but spirit; the action or interaction spirit produces matter. It is therefore illogical in the Afro-worldview to yield to the primacy of matter. It is abusive of the human intellectual complex to analyse and manage existence from a perspective of the primacy of matter. Yet it is so often the characters who do yield to this perspective of the primacy of matter—who wish to condemn this illogicalness—who are perceived as mad or who may in fact be driven mad when they do not possess the requisite internal coherence to resist what they perceive as the larger madness of the material ordering of nature.

Those artists like Walcott who not only depict and document these perverse and mad approaches to reality, but who seem to triumph over them, do so because they, through either their narrators or protagonists, are insightful about both the manner and construction of language and symbols. These narrators and protagonists are artful in the process of demystifying and decoding, as well as artful in the process of reconstructing, coding, and encoding. Walcott understands that demystification and decodification are the true domain of ritual, its priests, and its initiates. One cannot slay the beast, whether it be language or symbol, until the historical or other particular context is demystified or decoded. Any resultant optimism in the mad characters is thus to be linked to their artfulness and artful insight.

The power for getting to Africa, to the locus of reorientation and healing is not through the body but the mind, Makak explains to Souris, one of his cell-mates. Going to Africa, then, is a matter of taking a journey homeward to the self, away from the historical locus of madness. As he and his race presently exist, according to Makak, they "are shadows in the firelight of the white man's mind." One finds the requisite peace in being at home with the racial self even if one is not able to find the way to the entelechal or pure self. Otherwise, one remains bound to his own history's madness.

Walcott's earlier play, *Ti-Jean and His Brothers* (1957), is also a commentary on madness in that it challenges historical victims of violence to counteract the spell of their own rage or madness by making the champion agent of madness himself, the Devil, mad. Walcott's ultimate desire, however, is not so much that the victims simply make the Devil mad but that they will in the process, hopefully, discern the formula which made them rage and, consequently, sometimes mad. As Professor Robert Hamner has pointed out, [in *Derek Walcott*, 1981], "[t]he theme [of *Ti-Jean and His Brothers*] centers on the characters' methods of resisting malignant authority in their struggle to survive and improve their lot."

In *Ti-Jean and His Brothers,* the eldest brother Gros-Jean loses his battle with the devil or white planter as he loses patience with his tedious assignments to count the leaves in the cane field and to collect the fireflies. Most significantly, however, Gros-Jean loses the battle and moves toward rage and madness because the Devil repeatedly forgets or simply will not acknowledge what Gros-Jean considers to be his true name. As with Malak, there is the sense that to eclipse the name is to annihilate the potent self, along with, of course, one's poise and one's mental balance. Yet Walcott is also using this incident in this allegorical play of moral, political, and social implications to present a point of irony. The lesson Walcott would teach, without becoming overly didactic, is that the memory of one's name, one's identity, is sacred foremost to oneself. It is indeed logical for an exploiter not to acknowledge the desired identity of the one exploited. One falls readily into the trap of the Devil's cunning to expect otherwise. Mi-Jean, too, is lured into infuriation and rage and toward madness as he falls prey to the same vain expection that the planter-exploiter will hold sacred his human identity.

In Makak's mad dream-plot we find that the ritualistic steps toward freedom come through movement toward self-examination and a reorientation of one's worldview and action. If Makak is mad, there is certainly much reason in his madness; if he would believe in his reason, he would necessarily have to be impertinent, moving against societal forces as a host of other kindred characters do. In Walcott's *Drums and Colors* (1958), Mano's joke, as told and portrayed to Pompey in the Interlude and Part 7, reflects upon how in history the ostensible joke sometimes becomes the warped reality. The servant or slave may thus outspeak the master in advocating the purported nobleness of hierarchical colonial rule.

Thus we see in Walcott's play about domination, *Pantomime* (1978), a farcical commentary on the "helpless obedience," the shadow-reflector tangledness existing in the master-servant relationship. Being conscious of living the life of a shadow figure is not necessarily the first step toward self-liberation, Walcott implies. Consciousness of the intricate and pervasive life-existence of the shadow as a cultural, social, economic, political, philosophical force may very well lead to madness. This is especially so at the moment the servant perceives that he may very well have inbibed the shadow, that he may very well have become the fortification of his disease. Comments the servant Jackson in *Pantomine*:

> "But after a while the child does get frighten of the shadow he make. He say to himself, That is too much obedience, I better hads stop. But the shadow don't stop, no matter if the child stop playing that pantomine, and the shadow does follow the child everywhere; when he praying, the shadow pray too, when he turn round frighten, the shadow turn round too, when he hide under the sheet, the shadow hiding too. He cannot get rid of it, no matter what, and that is the power and black magic of the shadow, boss . . . until it is the shadow that start dominating the child, it is the servant that start dominating the master."

However, if the servant does manage to reverse the psychohistorical act enabling himself to start dominating the master, giving victory to the shadow, the servant may indeed be freed of his problems to some extent but not necessarily totally freed from a general world of madness. The world order is reversed, but not the order of the world, not the historical tragedy of repetition which interests Walcott very much.

II

Derek Walcott is deeply concerned with the madness of history. To the degree that madness is synonymous with confusion, the character Mano's words at the opening of *Drums and Colours* (1958) reveal the insanity of history. The carnival form occurring in the play pageant is seen as questionable, and Mano suggests that the comic form needs to be changed to that of "War and Rebellion." While the usual functioning of carnival is the revising of the general order, carnival here is indicted also by the character Pompey as a confusion which needs to be changed "to a serious play!" Important here is the concept of masking. We remember Levi-Strauss' words [in *The Way of the Masks,* trans. Sylvia Models, 1982]: "Tragedy and Comedy are both seen as masks, thus therefore neither must be considered the *norm*." The twin faces of time, farce and tragedy, both being extremes, foster duress, even though the former is used generally as a relief from the latter. It is Walcott's suggestion, however, that farcical and comic circumstances as modes of being may not be always so comic as they are tragic.

Walcott allegorizes memory as the mace-bearer or grand marshall in the play *Drums and Colours.* Memory is the leader of the ceremonial procession, representing the progression of history. Memory is also created by Walcott to serve as an instrument against history since the mace is a heavy, disruptive armor-breaking club. Memory is equated with the ceremonial and conventional. It is the symbol of unquestioned authority. But it is not to be forgotten that memory can also push one to madness. Thus, to temper their maddening memories, the carnival population often envelop themselves in the farcical and the comic.

In Walcott's view, history is a quarrelsome, mad force against which one is admonished to move with caution. Thus, in *Drums and Colours* we are to watch the unfolding or the rememberance of history by observing four quarrelsome or litigious men: Christopher Columbus, Sir Walter Raleigh, Toussaint L'Ouverture, and George William Gordon. Although the litigious history will be revealed in harsh light, the Chorus' admonishment against making judgment in favor of remembrance is certainly not to be taken at face value. The warning is not so much against making judgement but rather against becoming mad. To judge this history, already revealed as harsh, would be to thrust oneself into confrontation with it. One could become litigious with it and tragically more vulnerable to it if one's sanity is not correctly forged to make one capable of withstanding or overcoming it. One also hears in the Chorus' voice of admonition that same art of subterfuge, i.e., double-talking, which Paul Laurence Dunbar's preacher uses as an instrument of protection in "An Ante-bellum Sermon," himself admonishing his audience not to tell their masters he is preaching discontent. All of this, however, is not to discount the possibility of Walcott's attempting to pursue in earnest the idea of remembrance as a virtue.

At the outset of *Drums and Colours,* the presumed directors (intercessors in the carnival) are attempting to move from carnival or play to ritual or from a profane activity to a more sacred one. If this is their intention, the intercessors are thereby suggesting that one is near madness not to be aware of this opportunity. Yet periodically, both madness and drunkenness may have the parallel function of sharpening one's vision of the opportunity of taking advantage of the carnival play. Quadrado, an officer of watch overseeing Columbus' return to Spain as prisoner, expresses this parallel function of madness and drunkenness, declaring with a touch of irony to his fellow watchmen seizing the wineskin: "I have forbidden the use of wine till it is issued, / . . . Some get so drunk they have a sense of justice."

The specific madness of history as observed by the ship's watchman, Fernando, is exemplified in the Christian conversion mission. For every Arawak native converted, it is surmised that thousands of others perished from the capitalist exploitation. Nevertheless, the watchmen's wine-inspired vision of the madness of history does not exempt them from moving in its current. The Indian, Paco, who approaches the same watchman and his fellow on deck is regarded essentially as one belonging to a lower species. Thus, Walcott implies early in the play that vision spawned by drunkenness may not lead to the most desired conclusions. The alcoholic vision seems to allow one to observe the world but not the self.

But an element or some possibility of madness does seem inherent to historical and psychological transformation. For in a sense, in order to facilitate movement from one state to another, screws must be loosened, we might say. One risks going on edge. Such is the case of Quadrado in *Drums and Colours* undergoing his transformation of Christian conversion. His increasingly sensitive conscience makes him aware of the madness of history and his participation in it.

As early as *Henri Christophe* (1950), which Walcott refers to as his "first real involvement in theater," Walcott's evolving preoccupation with history's tragic cycles or tragic madness is evident. Robert Hamner so aptly characterizes the motivation of the young author of *Henri Christophe* by pointing out how Walcott chose to focus on Christophe instead of Toussaint L'Ouverture as the protagonist of his play about the Haitian revolution. It is not that Walcott saw a greater heroism in Christophe than in L'Ouverture. It was rather that Walcott was more curious about the factors in Christophe and his erstwhile ally Jean Jacques Dessalines which motivated them to resort "to intrigue and betrayal to remove Toussaint from their path to power." Thus Walcott opens the play by having the second speaker, General Petion, allude to the tragic cycle of history already apparent in the Haitian nation's infancy. The young country with its initial yearning "to greet / The sun of history rising, will have its throat cut. . . ."

In *Henri Christophe,* a profound use of poetic language and a profound understanding of vanity are demonstrated by a young man only nineteen or twenty years old. The young Walcott's vision of the world is already divided into an arena composed of sanity and insanity. Personal vanity is the fundamental factor in the tragic and mad psychology of history. Vanity and desire lead more to the transferral of corruption instead of to its reversal or dissolution. In Walcott's terms, transference of corruption from one power force to another is too

often mistaken as revolution, and vanity and desire draw only from a lexicon necessarily grounded in treacherous thought. It is this, Walcott suggests, that perpetuates the tragic cycle and forms the madness.

For Walcott, surely much of the folly of history is related to human obsession. The obsession with gold, or whatever, as is illustrated in the relationship of the persistent but physically ill Walter Raleigh and his son, blurs one's vision while causing one to value the elusive and to aim for power over a world of illusion. Thus, Raleigh is shown in a mad pursuit not only for fool's gold but also in the mad pursuit to have dominion over it. In his shortsightness and obsession, Raleigh turns the care of his son over to another but does not perceive how he has also set up the structure to bring about his son's death. But Raleigh's allusions to his own madness in the moments before his beheading are consistent with his definition of the madness of his victims. Suggesting that he has made a more sane turn of mind in comprehending the vanity of his obsessive pursuits for wealth and power, Raleigh is apprehensive that those guards and power figures to whom he speaks will think him insane. Ironically, using the imminent manner of his own death in a pun, Raleigh quips about the tragic madness of his life and his death: "If I sound unreasonable sir, it is because again, I have lost my head" (Part 7).

The kernel of Walcott's vision of history's tragic madness is perhaps best expressed in *Drums and Colors* in the words of the young Anton Calixte, half African and half French: "It is sad to see belief contradicted by necessity, / It is sad to see new countries making old mistakes / One could hope from the past the present would be simple, / But it is sad to see only the repetition of desire" (Scenario 9). Undoubtedly the word Walcott wishes to summon into our consciousness at this moment is *cupiditas*. The tragedy of human history is gross desire, made possible by a common human disequilibrium, the striving for sufficiency and the fear of insufficiency.

The tragedy of history is certainly its madness, as Walcott sees it, but the tragedy of man is fundamentally his fear of insufficiency. The jeers of Dessalines at the egotism of Napoleon are criticisms of a mad insufficiency (Scenario 12). Dessalines' criticism of Toussaint L'Ouverture as "power drunk" is a comment not upon intoxication but human disequilibrium pursued in compensation for insufficiency. Walcott brings us back to the heart of the meaning of Greek tragedy, which, as more recent scholars attest, is not so much a matter of hubris or overweening pride but rather a matter of miscalculation of boundaries. For Walcott, homicide represents the horrible miscalculation of boundaries. The observer-critic Dessalines, being human and insufficient, is susceptible as well to the tragic repetitive desires. Finding a feeling of sufficiency in war, he does not escape the historical desire to relish and express the madness of his thoughts, declaring, "It is a new age, the black man's turn to kill" (Scenario 12). Madness is a paradox inherent in the historical choices. The madness of history is in partaking of the pride of history in the Hegelian manner. As character Albert Jordan declares in

Remembrance, "Someday, someday, / We'll have our own flag. Our own wars!"

For Walcott, another type of madness is that of the distortion and arrogance represented in the wanting mentality of the Planter Calixte in *Drums and Colours.* Walcott portrays Calixte as not only mad in the nature of his verbal expression but also as infuriating. So captivated is Calixte by his colonial egotism that in the midst of the bloodshed and chaos he can mourn only the destruction of the symbols of his own power, betraying in his mourning the heart of colonial madness—*cupiditas.* Thus Calixte is capable of the inept lamentation: "I have walked through the smoking field, through the burnt land / that we all loved, destroyed, that was once green, / Racked by a rabble, turned savage as wild pigs" (Scenario 12). The essential *dementia* here is without doubt found in Calixte's use of the phrase "the burnt land / That we all loved." "All" obviously includes the slave here, which makes Calixte's *dementia paradoxia* complete. So excessive are Calixte's self-directed thoughts that one easily begins to perceive that he is mad and to doubt that he can reason. His cry, "What is happening to the world, to Haiti?" (Scenario 12), makes no allowance for what already has happened to the world. It does not acknowledge that he wishes to continue to benefit from so many monstrous things that have already occurred.

The philosophical proposition of the Buddha as expressed in 1833 by the character General Yu in Jamaica in *Drums and Colours* is the unavoidable and logical outcome of Walcott's tacit revolution against revolutions. In the advice of the General, in order to avoid the madness of history it is "better to observe the discretion of Buddha" who "observed that one may conquer a thousand thousand men in battle but he who conquer[s] himself he is the greatest victor" (Scenario 13). The tragic madness of history is further accentuated, however, when we are forced to admit that we are not convinced of General Yu's other proverb that "a smashed head brings wisdom" (Scenario 13).

In the final analysis, Walcott's *Drums and Colours* represents history as a tragic and absurd play of madness for which no one can find the appropriate language of explanation. The natural order and the confused order are difficult to distinguish. In *Remembrance* Albert Jordan suggests that the madness of history is a result of the Christian God's alienation. Jordan implicates the Christian God by declaring to the sky, "We born alone. We suffer alone. We dead alone, Right? / You know, since your own son dead, we ain't been hearing much from you" (Pt. I, sc.i).

For Walcott the true heroes of the New World are those who yield their history, be they victimizer or victim. The true heroes sacrifice or relinquish their egos. Servitude to history produces an anguished present. The servant of the muse of history forgoes the "elemental privilege of naming the new world" [Derek Walcott, **"The Muse of History: An Essay,"** in Orde Coombs, ed., *Is Massa Day Dead?*, 1974]. If one does not take advantage of the

elemental privilege to begin anew, one is robbed of the experience of elation which Walcott feels distinguishes true New World poets like Walt Whitman, St.-John Perse, and Pablo Neruda. When one succumbes to history, explains Walcott,

> [t]he vision of progress is the rational madness of history seen as sequential time, of a dominated future. Its imagery is absurd. In the history books the discoverer sets a shod foot on virgin sand, kneels, and the savage also kneels from his bushes in awe. Such images are stamped on the colonial memory. . . . These blasphemous images fade, because these hieroglyphs of progress are basically comic. And if the idea of the New and the Old becomes increasingly absurd, what must happen to our sense of time, what else can happen to history itself, but that it too is becoming absurd?

For Walcott, "the [Hegelian] process of history" makes the victim "contemplate only the shipwreck" and seeds one with memories "of vines ascending broken columns." One's focus is, then, not spiritual but material, and one becomes enslaved to historical cycles of achievement and despair. Similarly, the victim sets himself up for torture when he focuses on "history as language, when he limits his memory to the suffering of the victim." Obsession with history pushes the slave toward revenge and the master toward remorse. Both lead to anguished existence, foregoing the opportunity to turn loss into rebirth, renewal, or redemption.

Walcott's appeal to the Adamic or Edenic reconstitution of the self does ask a great deal. It perhaps does overlook the fact that some of the historically oriented poets and priests to whom he reacts are indeed caught in a mad obsession. The very architecture of the Old World, with its broken columns and clinging vines, has been transported to the New World with the insistence that it be maintained as the foundation. Indeed, most would hold that the New World accentuates Walcott's idea of the mad, cyclical process of history. As James Baldwin has said [*In The Evidence of Things Not Seen*, 1985], Europeans became white not in Europe but in America. The American Adam accentuated the human polarities. Adam in America was not to be everyman, but the white man. It is the persistence of this historical force that pushes many of Walcott's and other Afro-American writers' victimized characters toward or into madness. Not many who seek spiritual freedom can achieve Walcott's model as represented in the perennial freedom of St.-John Perse. In Walcott's view, Perse's "hero remains the wonderer, the man who moves through the ruins of great civilizations with all his worldly goods by caravan on pack mule, the poet carrying entire cultures in his head, bitter perhaps, but unencumbered. His are poems of massive or solitary migrations through the elements." Neither does one find very much sanity in the senile, colonized Alex Jordan of *Remembrance* who insists that his black schoolboys subscribe to his dictum that "Color don't matter!" (p. I, sc. i). For Jordan the schoolboys must accept this dictum as the universal of social life, poetry, and art. Jordan insists that they overlook the horrid particulars. It does not matter that in subjecting themselves to such internal violence they should run the risk of schizophrenia.

The essential problem with which one is left is creating and supplying a sufficient number of Adams, or, better stated, new or renewed people. Alex Jordan's schoolboys begin to encounter and embrace what Walcott has elaborated as history's tragic cycle of repetition and desire before entering school. By historical, social, and economic circumstances, they, perhaps unavoidably, perceive the world from the point of view of the victim. In doing so, then, they begin early their entrapment in the victim's dilemma with discourse. That is, in perceiving the world as victim, in effect they will have no self-authenticating voice. The schoolchildren will grow up seeing themselves and forming their personalities through the reflections of their victimizers. Without the support of a community of new and renewed people, the historical stage is always set for descent into schizophrenia and, as Walcott emphasizes, into tragic repetition and desire, more than it is set for producing the courageous and nobly impertinent madness of characters like Makak.

Lowel Fiet (essay date 1991)

SOURCE: "Mapping a New Nile: Derek Walcott's Later Plays," in *The Art of Derek Walcott,* edited by Stewart Brown, Seren Books, 1991, pp. 139-53.

[*In the following essay, Fiet provides an overview of Walcott's plays from the mid-1970s to the mid-1980s, stressing their use of theatrical metaphors and settings.*]

> God, I hate actors! They refuse to accept the reality they live in! I pronounce these solemn self-deceivers guilty of doubling the dream that is life.
>
> (*The Joker of Seville*)

> That ain't just a bloody poem. . . .
>
> (*Remembrance*)

> But if you take this thing seriously, we might commit Art, which is a kind of crime in this society.
>
> (*Pantomime*)

> Give art a rest. This ain't theatre, is Carnival, Mas!
>
> (*The Last Carnival*)

> We are not Americans! But give us time . . .
>
> (*Beef, No Chicken*)

> Oh, God, a actor is a holy thing. A sacred thing. . . . And it don't matter where it is: here, New York, London. . . . Do your work.
>
> (*A Branch of the Blue Nile*)

In Walcott's 'later' plays, the act of performance itself, the play and/or plays within the play, rehearsals, creative

processes, theatre settings, and actor/writer/artist characters become increasingly prominent metaphors in the interpretation of Caribbean culture and society. By 'later' I mean the post-Trinidad Theatre Workshop plays, works written and/or staged after 1976: *Remembrance* (first performed 1977) and *Pantomime* (first performed 1978) were published together in 1980; *Beef, No Chicken* (first performed 1981), *The Last Carnival* (based on the earlier *In a Fine Castle* and first performed 1982), and *A Branch of the Blue Nile* (performed 1983) were published together in 1986. (Plays unpublished or not accessible to the general reader are not included in this discussion.) These are the Trinidad plays—Trinidad-Tobago in the case of *Pantomime,* which takes place on 'Crusoe's island'—and form a thematic and stylistic grouping, especially when contrasted with the rather vaguely labelled 'poetic drama' or St. Lucia plays of the earlier—1949-1970—period perhaps best characterized by *Ti-jean and His Brothers* (performed 1958) and *Dream on Monkey Mountain* (performed 1967).

The earlier work concerns themes and formal considerations voiced in **'A Far Cry From Africa'** still probably Walcott's best known poem, and arising from the Afro-Caribbean, French patois and Catholic traditions of the majority population of his native St. Lucia. If *Ti-Jean* is an Aristophanic poetic comedy based on Afro-Caribbean myth, then *Dream on Monkey Mountain* depends on a dream/play-within-a-play structure and becomes Walcott's most fully articulated theatre image illuminating the position of Caliban as the Caribbean issue of Sycorax and colonizer, empire-builder, slaveowner Prospero.

The later plays vary from the early work in their dependence on surface realism. The language remains poetic—and Walcott often writes dialogue in verse—but the mytho-poetic nature of the action changes. These are social plays, plays of commentary and are analytical in form and structure. Ariel's colonial attitude, Crusoe and Friday in a contemporary context, Black Power versus creole aristocracy, modernization, Americanization, government graft, and colonial restraints on creativity assume primary thematic importance. However, a close examination of structural design also reveals the incorporation of dramatic devices that, beneath the surface realism, fragment the action and allow it to double back and comment on itself.

In another sense, these later plays record Walcott's association with foundations, theatre organizations, and universities in the United States, and *Remembrance* and *Pantomime* comply to demands characteristic of U.S. productions: tightly-knit, one-set, small-cast 'realistic' plays that concentrate on conflicts between characters in family, work, and/or social contexts which give them the texture of being more up-to-date, more about real people and possible events.

Between what I'm calling the early St. Lucia plays and the later Trinidad plays two other published works also require mention. They are *The Joker of Seville* (performed 1974), a creolized version of Tirso de Molina's *El burlador de Sevilla,* and *O Babylon!* (performed 1976), a musical evocation of Rastafarianism in Jamaica at the time of Haile Selassie's 1966 visit there, both with original music by Galt MacDermot, and were published together in 1978. (*In a Fine Castle,* performed 1970, *Franklin,* 1973, and *The Charlatan* 1973 as well, none of which has circulated widely, also form part of this transitional period.) *The Joker of Seville* was commissioned by the Royal Shakespeare Company, although not performed by them, whereas *O Babylon!* was one of the last productions of Walcott's years working directly with the Trinidad Theatre Workshop.

With *The Joker of Seville,* Walcott successfully adapted Spanish Golden Age drama to a contemporary idiom. The rhythm of Calypso, the dance of stick fighting, the pageant-like nature of Carnival, and the repartee of Afro-Caribbean oral tradition inform the action. The play begins with "A field, ringed with bleachers, used as a bull ring, a cockpit, or stickfighters' *gayelle,* on a Caribbean estate" as a framing device, and in that setting, Tirso's Don Juan Tenorio comes alive as he probably could not in a standard English translation.

O Babylon! proves less satisfying. The musicalized form captures little of Rasta-based myths and themes that does not find fuller expression in music and lyrics by Marley and the Wailers, Burning Spear, or numerous other Rasta-inspired reggae artists or dub poets, or in Roger Mais' flawed but compelling *Brother Man.* But Walcott's next two plays, *Remembrance* and *Pantomime* represent significant advancements in dramatic form and technique.

I

"*Pre-dawn*" Trinidad, 1977: two men, one old, one young, converse. The older man is a retired schoolteacher, a writer, a known figure in Port of Spain, while the younger, "sitting in the half dark", is the son of a former student and works for *The Belmont Bugle,* a local newspaper edited by the older man's best friend and for which his own son wrote before he was killed seven years before. The younger man holds a tape recorder, it is four o'clock in the morning, and the older, Albert Perez Jordan, is recording "The story of [his] life", "a journey through time", as he calls it.

Jordan's recollections begin with his days as schoolmaster "One Jacket Jordan", "Who taught the wrong things" and continue with "readings" of his two "best-known" stories, one a more recent satire on neo-colonialism, and the other the romance of a failed love affair with an English woman during the Second World War.

At the same time, other characters' versions become intertwined in the events of Jordan's "journey" and provide information not available in the stories. Perhaps most important is Jordan's inability to accept the rebellion and death of his elder son, Albert Junior. He even writes

a poem in which he blames his best friend for betraying him and leading his son astray. Later he tries to relive his own past by convincing his artist son, Frederick, to leave Trinidad with the young American he has cast in the role of Esther Trout Hope, the woman he "lost" 35 years before. At the end, which is really still the beginning, he is left alone with the interviewer to begin, again.

I mistakenly want to call *Remembrance* (first performed 1977) 'Performance', perhaps because it was published with *Pantomime* (also a kind of play within a play), but more I suspect because a 'remembrance' is an already displaced or transformed memory, not so much the memory itself as its staging, its re-enactment. That means that we are all like Brecht's streetcorner actor in the poem 'On Everyday Theatre', giving our versions of facts. But each act of memory, telling, acting, or writing is a displacement, the mediation of a framing device, a means of breaking or segmenting the memory, story, poem, or play from its original context.

Remembrance is memory inside memory, and what is remembered forms an account of 35 years in the life of the writer-character Albert Perez Jordan—a period that corresponds to the modern history of Trinidad and the West Indies: World War II, the fall of empire, emigration, independence, identity crisis, Black Power, and neo-colonialism.

The person who best understands the relation of Jordan's life to his memories and writing is Mabel, his wife. As she prepares to leave him, Mabel asks, "You think I never read 'My War Effort', and realize that if you wasn't such a coward thirty years ago, you would of leave me?" Mabel also seems to understand more about Junior's death, that he was killed by "a frightened policeman in Woodford Square on the day of the riot", and that they both bear some of the responsibility:

> I kill him with hymns and Jesus . . . and maybe he was so ashamed of both of us, all the mockery and the way you talk like a black Englishman, that he had to go out and do something.

When Jordan's friend, Ezra Pilgrim, questions him about the poem 'Remembrance', Jordan squirms and says, "It's just a bloody poem". But the line "when sons have died and friends betray" implies that Pilgrim turned Junior against his father by allowing him to "read Césaire and Marx and Fanon" and publish articles in *The Bugle* that cast Jordan in the role of an Uncle Tom. Jordan says, "Face the truth, Ezra. It's time. We avoid it. . . . That poem is the truth", no longer "just a bloody poem." For Jordan, Pilgrim betrayed not only friendship—"nearly . . . stealing away my son"—but also the "principles we considered sacred"—"you recanted on all the culture we had known". Falling just short of accusing Pilgrim of being his son's "murderer", he ejects,

> They shot him, Ezra. They put a hole in that boy's body, but they've ripped out a hole in my own heart that nothing, nothing can fill.

Where is Albert Perez Jordan in this recounting of his life? Whether his 'My War Effort (1948)' or 'Barrley and the Roof (1971)' the narrative voice rings of self-aggrandizement, rhetorical posing that moves away from the actual conditions of colonialism and neocolonialism, the real bases of his stories, into nostalgic romance or sneering, self-justifying satire. From 'My War Effort', Jordan reads,

> . . . I was not English, but I considered myself to be. I was a colonial, but did not consider myself to be so. . . . I adored England and there was nothing more England to me . . . than the adorable Miss Esther Hope.

After he supposedly "went to the men's room for twenty years"—to marry Mabel, to whom he was already engaged, and not his English Esther—the narrator reflects, "Since then I have been a mind without a country". With the loss of England, he feels that he lost himself. That appears to be the "hole in [his] own heart that nothing, nothing can fill."

Esther's lines:

> Albert, I think you're a silly, affected, but lovely man. You've pestered me relentlessly for three months. It's been worse than the Blitz. I've thought very carefully about this, all the possible complications, but if you want me to, I'll marry you.

—the same words Jordan also puts in the mouth of Anna, the "Pavlova from Rhode Island", 35 years later—serve only to puff up the narrator's self-image. Thus, it is not surprising that Frederick, discussing the story with Anna, asks, "You mean, if [Esther] was real?", because the writing seems more like Mabel's description of the young Jordan:

> . . . splattered with duck shit, but he would hold his nose high, and as he throw crumbs to the ducks in that stinking canal, he would say, "We are feeding the swans of Avon."

'Barrley and the Roof' bears the epigraph, drawn from Blake, "A Man's worst enemies are those of his own House and Family", but in fact, the acted story/play demonstrates the opposite: Frederick feels that his father taught him not to sell out, and Mabel understands and cares for him. The story ends as a comic resistance to neo-colonialism, but not without first projecting the narrator's superiority to his environment and situation.

The second act brings the two earlier stories together. Anna Herschel becomes a reincarnated Esther Trout. But Anna's dancing career—"doing the Funky Chicken at ten in the morning with two stars on your tits under the red lights of an empty bar in Jersey"—bottomed out, and she took a plane "South! The farther the better". By accident, she and her baby arrive on Jordan's doorstep.

Jordan tries to force the romantic relationship between Anna and Frederick to correct what he sees as his past mistakes. He tells Frederick to:

> Leave this place. It dried me up and it will dry you up. You're an artist boy. You're one of God's chosen. That's what that blasted poem [Gray's 'Elegy'] is all about. Don't bury yourself out here. Go on that plane.

When Jordan plays out his memory of 'One Jacket Jordan', teaching Thomas Gray's 'Elegy', hearing the jeers of "*Jordan is a honky-donkey white nigger man!*" and beating his own hand, rather than the imagined boy's, with a ruler as he exclaims that in "what is called poetry, and art, color don't matter! Color don't matter!" the importance of teaching to his concept of self becomes apparent. He says, "I was a schoolmaster. . . . Who taught the wrong things", and at play's end—Mabel has left for Brooklyn, Anna returns to the States, Frederick goes to the country—he again sits with the Interviewer, the tape recorder, his memories, and Gray's 'Elegy'. He tells his remembered class,

> Your body is the earth in which it springs and dies. And it's the humble people of this world, you Junes, you Walcott, and you Brown, and you Fonesca, and you Mango Head, that [Gray] concerned about.

Is there an authentic Albert Perez Jordan behind the posturing, the borrowed values, the compensating, and the colonial self-aggrandizement? He "taught with a passion", but not so much the "wrong things" as only those "things" and not others equally important as well. Walcott permits Albert Perez Jordan to tell his own story and by so doing creates the history of a generation of West Indians who lost themselves when they 'lost' England.

When **Remembrance** works out the position of Ariel in relation to Caliban after Prospero's departure, its companion piece, **Pantomime,** re-creates the story of Robinson Crusoe and his man Friday. The setting is a contemporary Tobago guesthouse run by Harry Trewe, a retired English actor in his mid-forties, and "his factotum" Jackson Phillip, a forty-year-old, retired calypsonian from Trinidad. The central issue is who is to be Crusoe and who Friday in the comedy sketch Harry has conceived to provide guests who will be arriving in less than a week's time with the "nightly entertainment" they have been promised. At first, Jackson refuses to participate, but slowly as the tension ebbs and flows between the white-English-owner-boss and the black-Trinidadian-employee and they rehearse their varying and conflicting social and comic roles, the relationship between them assumes a new dimension. Race, class, culture, and personal differences become obscured. Jackson kills the "Heinegger, Heinegger" parrot, Harry admits his own pretending and accuses Jackson of being "a kind man" who thinks he has "to hide it", and Jackson brings a photo of Harry's ex-wife, Ellen, and plays her role until Harry chases him with an ice pick and confesses, "That's the real reason I wanted to do the panto. To do it better than [Ellen] ever did". Harry was Friday to Ellen's Crusoe. The ending leaves the men in the same but different positions: "An angel passes through a house and leaves no imprint of his shadow on the wall". Harry and Jackson have changed. They now relate to each other face-to-face, man-to-man, friend-to-friend.

Pantomime is a compact and searing play. The two characters share their suspicions, resentments, and scepticism of each other, and the action becomes a process of bonding through which those socially generated feelings are at least partially exorcised. The rehearsal is the play itself, and the characters act out different roles and positions—now Crusoe, now Friday, now servant, now master—dropping as well as assuming different poses until a new social relation forms.

II

Issues of colonial attitudes, politics, and art characterise *The Last Carnival* (first performed 1982), a rewriting of the earlier *In a Fine Castle*. The play covers the years from the post-war period (1948) to Trinidadian independence (1962) to the Black Power uprising in 1970 and focuses on the aristocratic, French-creole De la Fontaine family, owners of both the Santa Rosa estate and the 'Castle' in Port of Spain. The first act is devoted principally to Victor De la Fontaine, would-be 'Impressionist' painter, and the English governess, Agatha Willet, he hires to educate his children. Victor's wife is dead, and his relation with Agatha assumes romantic and sexual overtones. But where he encases himself in his attempt to re-create and paint the past, Agatha comes from a working-class background and begins to teach the estate's children, white and black, egalitarian principles.

Victor's painting is derivative—unfinished copies of Watteau (he cannot paint Agatha's unaristocratic hands)—and he becomes increasingly a temperamental recluse. By the opening of the second act, during the Black Power uprising at Carnival time in 1970, Victor has committed suicide, and the focus of the action shifts to the conflict between the now more conventional and politically powerful Agatha and Victor's daughter, Clodia. Even though faced by rejection in the country she loves, Clodia sides with Sydney, a former groom on the Santa Rosa estate and one of Agatha's pupils, and the Black Power guerrillas. Miss Jean Beauxchamps, formerly a De la Fontaine family maid but now a government minister, is another of Agatha's ex-pupils. Jean argues for crushing the uprising, whereas the reporter Brown (reduced to a minor as opposed to the major role he plays in *In a Fine Castle*), who comes to write about Victor's paintings, remains in the middle, uncommitted.

At the end of the play, when the rebels burn Santa Rosa and the army kills Sydney, the old servant George, Sydney's uncle, remains stoic when confronted with his nephew's death, Agatha, still a British citizen, is warned of her possible evacuation, and as she sits in customs on the docks waiting to sail to England on the *Antilles,* Clodia

retraces for Brown the steps of Agatha's arrival in Trinidad twenty-two years before. In her last speech, Clodia asserts, "I don't want to be like her", and the play leaves a bitter aftertaste, the ambivalent sense that the real tragedy is captured in Brown's question, "All you niggers ain't tired killing your own people?" But the root issue appears better expressed by Walcott in a 1986 *Paris Review* interview:

> The departure of the British required and still requires a great deal of endeavour, of repairing the psychological damage done by their laziness and by their indifference. The desolation of poverty that exists in the Caribbean can be very depressing. The only way that one can look at it and draw anything of value from it is to have a fantastic depth of strength and belief, not in the past but in the immediate future.

The Last Carnival remains problematical: it brings to light the influence still wielded by old wealthy families and makes a striking statement on the economic and political composition of the modern West Indies, but its uneven form makes it less convincing than other later plays.

Beef, No Chicken presents a very different situation. An energetic folk comedy, the play satirizes the neo-colonial Americanization—the McDonaldization—of the Caribbean and the amount of graft, bribery, and swindling the process entails. In that context, progress means fast-food outlets, expressways, shopping malls, credit cards, television commercials, imported consumer goods, and the disappearance of the particular, native character and the products of Caribbean life, economic independence, and political self-reliance.

In *Beef, No Chicken,* Otto Hogan, owner of Otto's Auto Repair and Authentic Roti, and member of the Couva Borough Council, refuses to go along with a highway project that promises to bring profits to fellow Council members. He claims that without his signature the highway is illegal and that he is being harrassed and his business destroyed as a result. But his real reasons for opposing the road seem to be: "Hustle and bribe, run a big racket like the deal between the highway and the Borough Council? My father ain't bring us up so." To retaliate, Otto creates the Mysterious Stranger, a masked woman who haunts the construction area to jinx the highway and publicize his protest.

The tactic brings results: Cedric Hart, American-accented, local television newsman, crashes his car outside the restaurant and begins to recruit the new talent, including Otto's sister, Euphony, courted by schoolmaster Franco but engaged for the past 10 years to the absent boxer and miner Alwyn Davie (alias Cardiff Joe), who returns and threatens to bomb the highway's inaugural ceremony, Calypsonian Limer, Indian *chanteuse* and roti maker Sumintra, a riotous meeting of the corrupt Couva Borough Council, the mysterious appearance ("*A huge shadow crosses the stage*") of "The spirit of the countryside", no longer Otto's creation, and the vagrant Deacon who appears to marry Alwyn and Euphony and functions as a *raisonneur*:

> Pretty soon there'll be no country left. Nowhere to walk, nowhere to sit in the shade, whole place one big concrete suburb. Oh! Yes! It's about McDonaldizing everything, it's Kentucky Frying everything, it's about going modern with a vengeance and televising everything, it's hamming up everything, trafficjamming up everything.

As it becomes increasingly incorporated into First World, United States dominated, economic spheres, the Caribbean more and more comes to resemble the "mini-Miami" of mogul Mongroo's dream of:

> Clover-leaf overpass . . . toll booth, rest area. . . . Beefburgers, cheeseburgers . . . no more roast corn by the side of the road, no more . . . shrimp stands, oysters, all those Third World shacks, but just highway humming south . . .

Beef, No Chicken demonstrates sophistication and poetic ease in a genre more often characterized by slapstick farce, dialect buffoonery, and stereo-typed thinking. It effectively captures and satirizes in human terms what neo-colonial economic and political policy is all about: whether it is International Monetary Fund loans, the Caribbean Basin Initiative, or the Grenada Invasion, the West Indies have passed from one pair of colonial hands to another.

The scene is a theatre, the characters are West Indian actors and their English director, they are rehearsing *Antony and Cleopatra,* and the director asks Cleopatra,

> What's all this sexual hesitation, Sheila? You know how sensual his corpse is to her?

But the actress (Sheila) replies that she is not Cleopatra, that she cannot "play" that, to which the director responds that she should act what she "feels" for another cast member, "Chris, not Antony". She replies, "Just leave my personal life out of this please." Suddenly some of the polarities of formal Caribbean theatre materialize on stage: Shakespeare or more profitable 'dialect' comedies? Euro-American methods and attitudes—Stanislavskian acting and Strasberg's 'Method' adaptation of it, for example—or local production standards and expectations? professionalism or amateurism?, and perhaps, Theatre or Carnival, Poetry or Calypso? The difficulties become personalized in Sheila—full-time typist, part-time actress—when she says,

> I'm not a fucking queen, I'm not a celebrity; when you turn my name into mud it stays mud, and no magic in any theatre in the world can turn that mud into gold . . . this foreign Method shit . . . it's bad Method, anyway, and maybe it doesn't travel.

She understands that Port of Spain is not London or New York, that the anonymity enjoyed by metropolitan artists does not necessarily extend to the Caribbean, where cities often remain small towns in every way except size. She is a convert in search of a 'religion' in the theatre, and her "epiphany" while rehearsing Cleopatra—"The soldier's pole is fall'n . . . / . . . / And there is nothing left remarkable / Beneath the visiting moon."—even though it takes place in the first scene, is perhaps the play's most crucial moment. But when performance demands conflict with her evangelical background, she leaves the theatre group for the revivalist church:

> 'cause the Caroni isn't a branch of the river Nile, and Trinidad isn't Egypt, except at Carnival, so the world sniggers when I speak [Cleopatra's] lines, but not in a concrete church in Barataria.

The other characters cover a range of possibilities: Harvey, the 'professional' director, English background and training, possibly gay and possibly dying of AIDS, his values are metropolitan; Chris, an accountant and successful businessman, the writer of popular 'dialect' plays (one of which is also being rehearsed in the play), married to a white English woman but having an affair with Sheila, and author of the play about the play; Marilyn, pretty, light-skinned, not really talented but willing to let her cleavage help her career—"theatre ain't no religion, it's a whorehouse", she says—and she leaves for New York; and Gavin, the "mercenary"—"a professional sweetheart"—actor, home from battling for parts off- and off-off Broadway to rest up for a while before heading back to New York, where he went "to be an actor and found out that [he] was a nigger . . .", and at play's end he is teaching acting in Jamaica and considering his options. Thus, the group is really a stepping-stone, a means of making it elsewhere in 'real' theatre, of trying to be, as Marilyn puts it, "another Cicely Tyson, or Meryl Streep, but here . . . Here?" Or, to quote from another context, "They [show] that cursed colonial hunger for the metropolis."

In **'What the Twilight Says: An Overture'** [in *Dream on Monkey Mountain and Other Plays,* 1970], Walcott writes that

> When one began twenty years ago it was in the faith that one was creating not merely a play, but a theatre, and not merely a theatre, but its environment.

That sense of personal history and experience is perhaps more central to *A Branch of the Blue Nile* (first performed 1983) than to any other of Walcott's plays. The action seems to restructure the memory of actual events and constitutes, along with **'What the Twilight Says'** (1970), articles in the *Trinidad Guardian* and interviews, a record in play form of the years 1959-1976 when as playwright, director, designer, and critic, Walcott lived in Port of Spain and worked toward the creation of a resident professional company, an ensemble that could equal production standards of non-commercial, regional, state-sponsored and/or subsidized repertory companies and 'art' theatres throughout Europe and the United States.

Set in a theatre, the layered quality of the play of actors rehearsing and performing plays—as well as 'A Branch of the Blue Nile', the play Chris is writing from their experiences—ensures that characters play multiple and overlapping roles. Thus, when theatre should be its most 'realistic', it portrays—or betrays—itself as more steamed, fragmented, and critical than normally assumed.

If Walcott's group portrait does not inspire confidence, it is no doubt because it records a discredited artistic process—a concept outdated even in the First World settings that gave birth to it. Whether in Port of Spain, Trinidad, San Juan, Puerto Rico, Portland, Oregon, Flint, Michigan, Durham, England, or Dijon, France, such semi-professional and community theatres often mistakenly attempt to copy metropolitan production techniques and attempt to make their actors interchangeable with actors in New York, Hollywood, London, or Paris, where 'real' acting happens. The critical tone in *A Branch of the Blue Nile* is harsh, and the play reveals bitterness and loss; perhaps the sense that "In these new nations art is a luxury, and the theatre the most superfluous of amenities" ('Twilight'), and that a different kind of theatre and artist is necessary. The mad, ex-singer Phil describes the difficulties—

> 'Tain't rain they 'fraid, nuh, sister, 'cause if it ain't rain, the sun too hot. People always have a excuse, is natural. Like if it don't rain in London or New York! Rain don't stop white people, snow, tornado, what they have to do they does do. Here, if a butterfly fart, they jump. They would dance in the rain Carnival time, though. They would roll in the mud self. But all you doin' something serious, you see. I was in that scene. Is to go 'way, that is all. Leave them home sheltering, and head for greener pastures. Give up early, or they kill you self in this place, yes. Slow death. Something in them out kill you, dead or alive.

—but also supplies the insight that art can happen:

> Even in this country. Even here . . . And it don't matter where it is: here, New York, London . . . Continue. Do your work.

III

To speak of Walcott's later plays is premature. At least three other, as yet unpublished works have been performed: *The Isle Full of Noises* (1982), *Haitian Earth* (1984), and *To Die For Grenada* (1986)—perhaps there are more, for Walcott's productivity shows no signs of faltering. The early, St. Lucia plays such as *Ti-Jean and His Brothers* and *Dream on Monkey Mountain* established Walcott's reputation as a poetic, West Indian playwright and, no doubt due to the colonial history of his native St. Lucia, resemble the drama of francophone writers—Aimé Césaire, Edouard Glissant, Daniel Boukman, Ina Césaire, and Simone Schwarz-Bart—more than plays by fellow English-language Caribbean dramatists. (And perhaps only Césaire begins to equal Walcott's

overall accomplishment as playwright and poet.) Other West Indians—Dennis Scott and Trevor Rhone (Jamaica) and Errol John, Errol Hill, and Earl Lovelace (Trinidad), to mention only a few—share many of Walcott's concerns but none matches his creativity and critical stature.

The most notable of his post-1970, Trinidad plays—*Remembrance, Pantomime, Beef, No Chicken,* and *A Branch of the Blue Nile*—demonstrate Walcott's versatility and secure his position as a playwright whose works compare favourably to those of international contemporaries such as Dario Fo, Harold Pinter, Wole Soyinka, Heiner Müller, Athol Fugard, Slawomir Mrozek, and Sam Shepard and as well as to major modern figures such as Shaw, O'Neill, Brecht, and Beckett.

The first major dramatist from the anglophone Caribbean, Walcott and his plays hold central positions in the development of the idea of a Caribbean theatre. His work futher distinguishes itself through his practical theatre experience and the effort to establish a professional, regional company. Thus, along with other notable groups such as Cuba's Teatro Escambray, Martinique's Théâtre de la soif nouvelle, and Jamaica's Sistren, the Trinidad Theatre Workshop has contributed to the formation of a genuine and unique theatre aesthetic. If the Trinidad or later plays form a chapter in Walcott's career as playwright, then perhaps the yet-to-be-published works of the 1980's promise another that broadens the focus to reinterpret *The Tempest* for the entire Caribbean region.

DREAM ON MONKEY MOUNTAIN

PRODUCTION REVIEWS

Clive Barnes (review date 15 March 1971)

SOURCE: "Racial Allegory," in *The New York Times,* 15 March 1971, p. 52.

[Dream on Monkey Mountain *received its New York debut on 14 March 1971 in a production by the Negro Ensemble Company (NEC) at the St. Mark's Playhouse. In the following assessment of the premiere performance, Barnes calls the play a "richly flavored phantasmagoria" and stresses its poetic aspects.*]

Derek Walcott's **The Dream on Monkey Mountain,** which the Negro Ensemble Company presented last night at the St. Marks Playhouse, is a beautiful bewildering play by a poet. Mr. Walcott, a black Trinidadian, rightly sees the English language as one of his ethnic inheritances, and he fell in love with it in a way that few people can.

He writes with a mind clarified with the clouds of literature. Even in this play we can see hints of *Don Quixote, Waiting for Godot,* the Bible and a heritageful of Elizabethan and Jacobean playwrights. But if the language is a variation of white, the thought is interestingly black.

The play is a fantasy. An old man is thrown in jail for drunkenness. The play is remembrances of his past and dreams of his future, and the fantasy encroaches into the minds and possibly lives of the jail's two other inmates, Tigre and Souris, and the jail keeper, the mulatto Corporal Lestrade.

It is rich in comic incident, such as when the old man, Makak, tries to revive a man dying from a snakebite, or when his Sancho Panza-like Moustique pretends to be Makak and to sell blessings, only to get beaten up for his pains. But beyond the picaresque incidents there lies some dim poetic allegory about blackness and colonialism—a subject almost as pertinent to the United States as it is to Trinidad.

Makak is given a white vision from the moon and walks down his mountain, Monkey Mountain, in search of Africa. Among the people he finds fools and charlatans, who cannot recognize his saintly idealism and confuse it simply with the madness that, yes, it partly is. Makak is innocent; Moustique, his friend, is practical to the point of venality. But no one is venal in the way that Corporal Lestrade is venal, for he is whiter than coffee-milk at the time of the whites and yet opportunistically blacker than the blackest at the time of the blacks. Lestrade is law and order, and the pistol knows no color.

Through this richly flavored phantasmagoria, Mr. Walcott, with his wry poet's eye, is, I think, trying to place the position of the transferred African into the Western environment of the New World. Should, in an attempt to find Africa, all white civilization be abandoned?

In one amusing scene—when in apotheosis Makak has become King of Africa and Lestrade is his First Minister—the executioner reads off a list of white thinkers and artists—from Aristotle to Shakespeare, from Galileo to Wilberforce—and they are all, with the only possible exceptions of Pushkin and the two Dumases, found guilty of the terrible crime of whiteness. Mr. Walcott sees the irony of this, and he also knows that Africa is a very long way away.

I think that what Mr. Walcott is counseling is a 20th-century black identity rather than any attempt to impose a reversal to a preslave black identity. But much of the play's interest is in its spectacle and poetry.

Makak is ugly, keeps no mirrors and never looks in pools. One day he does look into a water bucket, and later ponders that his image from that water has passed without trace, while even now "the water is licking with its tongue a dead leaf." That mixture of philosophical insight (why should our very own images pass unremembered across promiscuously uncaring reflecting surfaces?) and physical observation (the swaying of the leaf and the capillary attraction of the water is inherent in the phrase) strikes me as the purest of poetry.

Michael A. Schultz has directed **The Dream on Monkey Mountain** with flair and full-blooded vigor. The choreography by Mary Barnett and the setting by Edward Burbridge add to the mystic gallimaufry, and the acting is coherent and contained, the one sure guidepost in the author's mist-racked world.

Roscoe Lee Browne made Makak into a properly puzzled prophet, his face a succession of surprises, his strength coming from his big and stubby body indomitably stomping the landscape of the stage. This big man is given two contrasts in Antonio Fargas's Moustique and Ron O'Neal's Lestrade. Mr. Fargas makes Moustique into a very reasonable insect; a practical man, fearing death and hoping for life and a little profit on the side.

Mr. O'Neal's Lestrade is the play's most subtle portrayal, joking and yet serious, totally self-obsessed; a man who can even turn the conversion of his blood to good account. Then we have the not-too-evil villains, with Lawrence Cook as the hard-skinned Tigre and Afolabi Ajayi as the soft-skinned Souris, and, of course, Basil, the undertaker figure of Death. Despite his voodoo-Baron Samedi make-up, Basil is like the Button-Moulder in *Peer Gynt,* and Robert Jackson plays him with a mocking dignity.

Walter Kerr (review date 21 March 1971)

SOURCE: "How to Discover the Corruption in Honest Men?" in *The New York Times,* 21 March 1971, Section 2, p. 3.

[*In the following evaluation of the New York staging of* Dream on Monkey Mountain, *Kerr judges the play wordy and slow.*]

Derek Walcott's **The Dream on Monkey Mountain,** now being well performed by the Negro Ensemble Company, is a very long time catching up with the precision of its program notes. The notes are from Sartre: "In certain psychoses the hallucinated person, tired of always being insulted by his demon, one fine day starts hearing the voice of an angel who pays him compliments; but the jeers don't stop for all that; only from then on, they alternate with congratulations. This is a defense, but it is also the end of the story. The self is disassociated, and the patient heads for madness."

On stage, Roscoe Lee Browne, his voice rumbling through the St. Marks Playhouse like the underground warnings of a volcano, is the tattered black seer, the mountain mystic who begins to see his salvation in a lady who inhabits the cloud-streaked moon. The lady is white. Spurred on by her image, and carrying a white mask as her symbol and his juju, he begins to practice healing, begins to promise his West Indian fellow blacks a visionary kingdom of his own. But he is already compromised.

His problem is not the colonialized, white-man's black, rigidly and effectively played by Ron O'Neal, spouting admiration for Roman law and all the not truly inherited glories of Western civilization. His problem is that he is trying to heal the black with white magic. But when he has realized this, and when he has rigorously set himself to decapitating his long-beloved lady in the moon, he has still not cut the ultimate knot. For white values are not only *there* to be confronted, they are already to some degree imbedded in the black psyche, however unwelcome they may be there. A man is tearing himself apart, and where is the flagellation to end?

I hope I am not misreading the play. It would be easy to misread, in spite of Michael A. Schultz's admirably composed production (bough-laden women becoming, the night sounds of the forest, brilliantly robed "natives" crowning the old man king while pronouncing anathema everything Western from Aristotle to Al Jolson), because the author has a strong bent toward poetic digression. He is so long over some scenes that the thread of essential meaning is lost altogether; forward movement is clogged by a waterfall of words. At this point in his career Mr. Walcott is not fashioning words riveting enough to hold us through his prolonged investigation of by-ways; perhaps the strongest sense we have is of unprofitable delay.

Certain of the visual effects, however, are in themselves quite beautiful, particularly a passage in which the masked and sinuously twitching bodies of the company suggest not only that a fire is flickering but that, in its leap and crackle, it is also speaking.

Edith Oliver (review date 27 March 1971)

SOURCE: "Once upon a Full Moon," in *The New Yorker,* Vol. XLVII, No. 6, 27 March 1971, pp. 83-5.

[*Oliver declares* Dream on Monkey Mountain *a "masterpiece" and praises its "beauty, imagination, humor, and vigor."*]

The Dream on Monkey Mountain, at the St. Marks, is an enthralling play by the West Indian poet and dramatist Derek Walcott, and the performance of the Negro Ensemble Company, under Michael A. Schultz's clear, inspired direction, matches it in beauty, imagination, humor, and vigor. The Dreamer is an old black charcoal peddler, who thinks himself so ugly that he has not been able to look into a mirror for thirty years. At the beginning of the play, after he has gone into a frenzy and caused considerable damage in a local bar, declaring that God is black, not white, he is thrown into the jail of some West Indian island by a mulatto corporal. He cannot even remember his Christian name—only the name,

Makak, that he has given himself—and we learn that at every full moon this madness descends upon him. His frenzy continues. God, he claims, speaks to him in the guise of a white moon-goddess, who lies in his arms all night and tells him that he, a descendant of African kings and a great healer, must lead his people back to Africa. "I will tell you my dream," he says, standing in his cell with arms outstretched. The white goddess appears, singing, in a huge cutout of the moon, though he is the only one who can see her. Two mocking prisoners in the cell next door roll about with laughter, and the mulatto corporal (who by now has put on a barrister's wig and gown and has been addressing a chorus of islanders in highflown British "my-lord" language) comments drily upon "this rage for whiteness that does drive niggers mad."

In a classic sense, the antagonists of the script (or, more exactly, the two characters in opposition to each other, who hold the script taut) are Makak, the peasant visionary—regal, mysterious, and commanding whether in rags or in African robes (and powerfully played by Roscoe Lee Browne)—and the mulatto corporal, quiet, worldly, complex, and tongue-in-cheek. (Ron O'Neal, who was so wonderful as the poet and dramatist's surrogate in Charles Gordone's *No Place to Be Somebody,* is just as wonderful in a role that has some similarity to that one.) But there are others almost as important. There is Makak's crippled little partner, Moustique, part Sancho Panza to his Don Quixote, part Sparrow to his Liliom (a fine performance by Antonio Fargas). There is Basil, coffin-maker and Spirit of Death, who stalks about in a top hat, half of his face in chalk-white makeup (another good performance, this one by Robert Jackson), and who, toward the end, reads a list of the damned of history, a list that includes Aristotle, Abraham Lincoln, Lorenzo de' Medici, Al Jolson, Mandrake the Magician, and Horatio Nelson, their crime being "that they are indubitably . . . white. . . . A drop of milk is enough to condemn them." ("My hatred," says Makak, "is deep, black, quiet as velvet.") And then there are those two mocking, funny rascals from the adjoining cell (Lawrence Cook and Afolabi Ajayi), who eventually become converts, of a lightly treacherous kind, to the great King Makak. As episode follows episode, the chorus of dancers and singers and minor players becomes, in turn, judges; mourners gathered around the body of a fellow dying of snakebite, who is cured by Makak; and, later, Makak's African warriors and subjects.

By the end of the play, the full moon has sunk into the sea, the night is over, and with it all the frenzy, fever, and hallucination. Makak is back in his cell, and his lines "My name is Felix Hobain. . . . Hobain. I believe in my God. I have never killed a fly" and "Makak lives where he has always lived—in the dreams of his people" are as steady and calm and as moving as Oberon's "And then I will her charmèd eye release / From monster's view, and all things shall be peace." Come to think of it, Peter Brook and his troupe could take a lesson or two in magic from Mr. Schultz and the Negro Ensemble Company. This production is the richest and strongest that the N.E.C. has ever given us, and in the service of a masterpiece. ***The Dream on Monkey Mountain*** is a poem in dramatic form or a drama in poetry, and poetry is rare in the modern theatre. Every line of it plays; there are no verbal decorations. A word, too, must be said for the absolute trust that Mr. Walcott engenders in his audience, convincing us that there is a sound psychological basis for every action and emotion. The setting, choreography, costumes, and lighting, all of which greatly enhance the mood of the production, are the work of Edward Burbridge, Mary Barnett, Lewis Brown, and Ernest Baxter and Oyamo, respectively.

Clayton Riley   (review date 4 April 1971)

SOURCE: "A Black Man's Dream of Personal Freedom," in *The New York Times,* 4 April 1971, Section II, p. 3.

[*In this review of the NEC production, Riley describes* Dream on Monkey Mountain *as a "lush depiction of the many moods implicit in the ritual and realistic aspects of Caribbean Black life" but notes that at times the play does "falter under the weight of its voluminous dialogue."*]

Well, all right. "The Negro Ensemble Company has chosen to devote its entire 1970-71 season to a program of plays centered around a single subject: Themes of Black Struggle.'" A program note. The commitment is substantially realized with NEC's third production of the season, Derek Walcott's brooding allegorical drama, ***The Dream on Monkey Mountain.***

The playwright, a Trinidadian, offers a very extended work, too long and sometimes structurally unsteady. Too many words. Yet an engrossing study, exercising its fascination upon us, designed within a lengthy framework that regularly compels.

On an island in the West Indies, Makak, a Black and ancient visionary, considered mad by most folks, reveals from a jail cell his recent exposure to destiny. To his mountain hovel has come a persistent visitation—Western civilization in the form of a silent White woman Makak has named the Moon Lady.

Her appearances move the Black man to attempt to define who he is, and what he must do to escape the pervasive influence she weaves about him. Escaping from jail with two village layabouts, Makak pursues his vision of an empire, presided over by him, that he will create in Africa. Finally, as a resplendently robed Black chieftain, Makak slays the Moon Lady—and with her, presumably, dies the evil curse of White colonial oppression. Makak has journeyed through a deathless sequence of dreams, arriving, ultimately, at the estate of personal freedom he has sought for so long.

The play is rich and complex; the author's use of fable interwoven with a stark elaboration of historical evidence of oppression illuminates his work, lends it an arresting

weight and texture. Walcott's characters are drawn with bold, sometimes extravagant strokes and, prodded by the author, they have an inclination to talk a bit too much. But the play also achieves a lush depiction of the many moods implicit in the ritual and realistic aspects of Caribbean Black life. In this, Walcott has been ably assisted by director Michael Schultz, who seems most at home when staging the spectacular in dazzling fashion. Schultz explores movement among his players with an almost obsessive precision, combining dance qualities with dashes of pantomimic expressiveness and music to bring sparkle to a play that can, and frequently does, falter under the weight of its voluminous dialogue. Walcott is a writer who obviously loves the sound of the language he uses in his work. This affection is not always requited, the theater being an essentially visual arena. (And anyway, Walcott's ideas seem sturdy enough to reach us in a less verbally overdressed manner.)

But what he has to say is extremely important at a time when, in America, Black people are regularly challenging the more basic concepts' of governmental and cultural "normalcy." The thesis, as proposed in ***The Dream on Monkey Mountain,*** is that the West cannot—nor should it—exist forever, given its deplorable record of racist exploitation and butchery throughout the world.

For this production, the NEC has gathered one of the most distinguished casts ever to perform there. Ron O'Neal offers a brilliant portrait of Makak's jailer, Lestrade, colonialism's perpetually anachronistic figure whose fair complexion is still Black enough to exclude him from any real privilege in a privileged regime. Yet he is "white" enough to understand just how arbitrary that exclusion is. The quality of Lestrade's endless frustration and rage is executed by O'Neal with a splendid combination of subtlety and anguished, muted power.

He would seem the perfect player to complement Roscoe Lee Browne's Makak, but that potentially dynamic combination never really achieves its full flower. Incredibly, Browne, a magnificently gifted performer, is more unconvincing in his role than I would have thought possible. From his strained, rigidly affected vocal selections to the awkward—and largely ineffective—uses of his body. Browne appears to work against his strengths as a player. Perhaps I have become too accustomed to the sound of that stunning voice he ordinarily possesses, a superbly modulated, full-toned instrument that so completely dominated the stage in Genet's *The Blacks* a decade ago.

Walcott's intention with Makak was, I believe, to give us the picture of a failed but majestic figure. It is the majesty that somehow is absent from Roscoe Lee Browne's portrayal, and that absence is both sad and puzzling.

Two of the supporting performers offer notable work. As the coffin-maker and symbolic figure of death, Robert Jackson seizes our attention whenever he appears, slender as a scythe, a grim, dancing collector come to terrify his victims. And in the part of Souris, the loafer and prison mate of Makak, Afolabi Ajayi gives us a total look at the crushed personality of the colonized Brother, Fanon's Wretched One come to life, unshakably devoted to serving the oppressor for as long as they both shall live: Ajayi's nervous wit and hollow laughter echo through all the sound systems society maintains.

We can, we *must* thank the NEC for access to this awesome reality.

CRITICAL COMMENTARY

Robert Elliot Fox (essay date 1982)

SOURCE: "Big Night Music: Derek Walcott's *Dream on Monkey Mountain* and the 'Splendours of Imagination'," in *The Journal of Commonwealth Literature,* Vol. XVII, No. 1, 1982, pp. 16-27.

[*In the essay below, Fox traces the theme of dreams and the imagination in* Dream on Monkey Mountain.]

> —Dream. Ona nonday I sleep. I dreamt of a somday.
> Of a wonday I shall wake.
>
> [James Joyce, Finnegan's Wake]

In Derek Walcott's own words, "The play is a dream, one that exists as much in the given minds of its principal characters as in that of its writer, and as such, it is illogical, derivative, and contradictory. Its source is metaphor . . ." ["**A Note on Production,**" in *Dream on Monkey Mountain and Other Plays,* 1970]. This statement is crucial to any profound understanding of the work [*Dream on Monkey Mountain*], and my purpose in this essay shall be to examine the nature and function of dreams in the play in an effort to elucidate one essential level of meaning in Walcott's *magnum opus.*

I

In the world of the work—that is, within the context of the play itself—we are presented with a dream and a dream-within-a-dream. But in the context of the work within the world—that is, beyond the text or enactment of the drama—we are also confronted with a dream: Walcott's creative vision which informs the play, and which is itself a part of a larger dream in the mind of mankind, an edenic dream of elemental freedom. Beginning on a "realistic" level in the play we move rapidly into the realm of *poetic* reality, spiraling evermore inward toward an essential core of meaning before ascending once more to the "logic" of the waking world. But this essential core of meaning, discoverable by the individual through an internal voyage, exists beyond the individual—or any individual work of art—in a collective consciousness which Art as a spiritual endeavour has always striven to articulate. So, at the play's conclusion,

when we are told that "Makak lives where he has always lived, in the dream of his people," the world within the work and the work within the world merge at the crossroads of the imagination. Makak comes from, and he returns to, the world of myth.

One of the perennial motifs of myth is that of the seeker, the defier of odds and gods, and his redemptive quest; and one of myth's lessons to mankind lies in the articulation of the rhythms of recurrence, the repetitive nature of experience. Walcott grasped these concepts early. He "recalls the familiar scene in his childhood when the story teller would sit by the fire to narrate stories involving a 'hero whose quest in never done', and explains how it became necessary for him to appropriate the image of that hero in his plays." And his brother, Roderick Walcott, has noted that "The legends of Papa Diablo, Mama Glos, lajables, and the sukuya can remain if only we tell them over and over again."

Imagination solidified itself in the ambiguous person of an actual individual whom Walcott vividly remembers. "My Makak comes from my own childhood. I can see him for what he is now, a brawling, ruddy drunk who would come down the street on a Saturday when he got paid and let out an immense roar that would terrify all the children . . . When we heard him coming we all bolted, because he was like a baboon . . . This was a degraded man, but he had some elemental force in him that is still terrifying; in another society he would have been a warrior."

These images from Walcott's past, forkloric and literal, are fused in the character of Felix Hobain, whose metaphoric identity is Makak, the monkey-man, the lion and king. Makak, one of the lowliest of the low, is the one in whom the dream is invested. The dream that transforms Makak is, in a very real sense, Walcott's own dream, his artist's vision which espies the potential for greatness in "a degraded man", which recognizes the raw power behind seeming impotence.

> These dead, these derelicts,
> that alphabet of the emaciated,
> they were the stars of my mythology.
>
> [*Another Life*]

Makak then becomes representative of the downtrodden and impoverished blacks who long to be redeemed, and of the transformation that brings about, or at least prefaces, such redemption.

II

Speaking specifically of the anguish of the West Indian, Walcott says, "we have not wholly sunk into our own landscapes thus," defining an inherent rootlessness. It is a concern that numerous writers share, but Walcott, like Wilson Harris, attempts the absorption into the indigenous landscape along with a corresponding exploration of a mind—or dreamscape: "a country for the journey of the soul," as Walcott calls it. Both of these geographies—the literal and the imaginative—are recreated and fused through *language*.

It is through language, in fact, that Walcott envisions the salvation of "the New World Negro." "What would deliver him from servitude was the forging of a language that went beyond mimicry, a dialect which had the force of revelation as it invented names for things, one which finally settled on its own mode of inflection, and which began to create an oral culture of chants, jokes, folk-songs and fables. . . ." The poet in his primal role as maker is the one who can forge this recreative language that will provide a vehicle for the liberation of consciousness from its colonized state. But it is obvious here that the way forward is the way back: to roots. "For imagination and body to move with original instinct, we must begin again from the bush. That return journey, with all its horror of rediscovery, means the annihilation of what is known . . . On such journeys the mind will discover what it chooses. . . ." But a choice made via the annihilation of the known can only be instinctual, unconscious, intuitive; it will not be *rational*.

The true arena of the drama, then, is that of the mind, of imagination. Its vehicle is dream, which enables Walcott to dispense with normal logic, linearity, literalness, and emphasize instead myth, recurrence, ambiguity. When the cages rise out of sight during Makak's deposition—his first recital of his dream—we have a graphic representation of the liberating power of the imagination. This is Walcott's strategy throughout: to demonstrate the disparities between a consciousness that is creative and metaphoric, and one that is straightforward and imprisoning. Makak, for instance, is said to be in a state of "incomprehensible intoxication." He may literally be drunk, or this could be merely a pejorative characterization of his dream and madness by someone who remains untouched by them. Especially the dream is described as "vile," "obscene" and "ambitious". The charges of being "uppity" and sexually depraved are those traditionally levelled at blacks by racists, and Corporal Lestrade has absorbed this mentality, or rather, he has been possessed by it.

"Incomprehensible intoxication" might be one label a modern, scientific mind would apply to the trance states of mystics, seers and shamans. When Makak declares, "Spirits does talk to me," a "rational" person would perhaps dismiss this as hallucination, but a "primitive" individual would know that Makak is in touch with the traditional world, which encompasses a nonmaterial reality. Makak is a visionary, and the visionary stance is fraught with peril. He is able to exorcise a dying man's sickness when "priest," "white doctor," and "bush medicine" fail, and he tries to do the same with his people, only to be rejected by them because they are incapable of belief. Makak is struggling with a pejorative limitation on his psyche and being which his dream helps him transcend. Failure to "dissolve in his dream" means that one remains imprisoned. Moustique, for example, masters the rhetoric of salvation but he lacks vision; he has

not experienced the power of the dream but merely wishes to exploit it. Hence Basil says of him, when unmasking him in the marketplace, "The tongue is on fire, but the eyes are dead."

In his recital of his dream, Makak describes himself as walking through white mist to the charcoal pit on the mountain. He is ascending the slope of consciousness, journeying through whiteness to blackness, through vagueness toward a solid identity. "Make the web of the spider heavy with diamonds / And when my hand brush it, let the chain break"—that is, the chain of slavery, both psychological and actual. The spider's web represents the entanglements of history, racism, colonialism; the diamonds are the oppressed. In his role as saviour, Makak is able to shatter this evil beauty with an almost casual gesture. The dream transcends time, telescopes spiritual and physical evolution, so that Makak moves, in the infinite space of a poetic moment, from ape to God:

> I have live all my life
> Like a wild beast in hiding. . . .
> And this old man walking, ugly as sin,
> In a confusion of vapour,
> Till I feel I was God self, walking through cloud.

Again, in the healing scene, Makak stands with a burning coal in his palm, chanting a formula for salvation, striving to save the sick man from an actual death and his people from the living death of degradation and despair. "Faith! Faith! / Believe in yourselves." The energy released by the burning charcoal symbolizes the spiritual energy released by Makak's positive confirmation of his blackness. "You are living coals," he tells them, "/ you are trees under pressure, / you are brilliant diamonds. . . ." The decomposed matter from primeval vegetation was transformed into coal, and diamonds are the result of coal under enormous pressure, over great periods of geological time. Burning coal brings light; diamonds reflect and refract light. Hence Moustique's echo, in the marketplace, of Makak's metaphor: "One billion trillion years of pressure bringing light, and is for that I say, Africa shall make light." Here, of course, Moustique is speaking better than he knows. The "revelation of my experience" that he talks of is that of his people, the broader dimensions of which Makak's dream calls back from a darkness of oppression, forgetfulness and ignorance.

The dream which redeems, the imaginative reversal that transforms a poor charcoal burner into royalty, has its roots in historical fact. In his book *The Loss of El Dorado*, V.S. Naipaul relates how the black slaves in Trinidad at the beginning of the nineteenth century created kingdoms of the night, with their own kings, queens and courtiers, elaborate uniforms, and other regal paraphernalia. During the day the blacks laboured and endured the cruelty and contempt of their masters; but beneath the moon these same slaves were for a time themselves metamorphosed into masters, issuing commands and miming splendours, while their white owners became the objects of mockery and fantasies of revenge. One of these nocturnal regiments, led by a King Sampson, was known as the Macacque regiment. In light of the condemnations meted out during the apotheosis scene in *Dream,* it is significant to note as well from Naipaul's account that "the role of the Grand Judge, who punished at night as the overseer punished by day, was important."

This nighttime pageantry was redemptive drama, an elaborate masquerade which enabled the oppressed to vivify their ancestral memories while at the same time reversing, if only momentarily, the bitter realities of the present. Naipaul remarks, "Negro insurrection, which seemed so sudden in its beginnings and so casual in its betrayals, was usually only an aspect of Negro fantasy; but an adequate leader could make it real." It never came to this. In 1805, the imaginary kingdoms were revealed—practically voluntarily, as if the secret were too good to keep—and the slave aristocracy was executed or whipped. Still, until such time as the powers of rebellion proved to be sufficiently substantive, the dream remained as a possible vehicle of escape from despair; and, while they lasted, the kingdoms of the night must have been a positive force, a means of sustaining the slave in what were otherwise intolerable circumstances. There are those who would argue—and indeed the same criticism has been directed against *Dream*—that the blacks would have been better off had they refrained from fantasy and resorted instead to violence. But this is itself a form of romanticism. When you have been reduced to a dehumanized state, you must first regain your dignity; when you have been relegated to physical toil, the mind must sometimes soar above the body. If you are an animal, why not be a lion? If you are a slave, why not dream of being a king (especially when you may be the descendent of kings?). Dreams may be attacked as nothing more than dreams, but in the beautiful words of Delmore Schwartz, "In dreams begin responsibilities."

III

Monkey Mountain is depicted in the Prologue as "volcanic," which suggests unpredictability, slumbering violence, submerged and smouldering energies that will one day demand release. Makak's dream touches and taps these hidden energies and gives them form and substance in a way that the criminality of Tigre or Souris or the oppressive mentality of the corporal (themselves crude manifestations of the need for self-assertion, of a refusal to accept identity-lessness) cannot. Makak repeatedly insists that his dream is not a dream, whereas others characterize it, not only as a dream, but a *bad* one. They are literalists, fatalistic and unimaginative, like the politicians whom Walcott describes as "generation after generation / heaped in a famine of imagination" ["**Party at the Hilton,**" in *Sea Grapes,* 1976]. Even though the charges that the corporal addresses against Makak clearly include incitement to rebellion, even though Makak himself declares that it is "better to die, fighting like men, than to hide in this forest," *Dream on Monkey Mountain* cannot be said to advocate revolution in the

circumscribed political sense. What Walcott thinks about colonialism, racism, oppression—the "dream of milk" as he calls it—ought to be evident from the play; but Walcott is equally clear about an opposite but attendant danger, characterized by him as "Witchdoctors of the new left with imported totems." The solution is not politics. "The future of West Indian militancy lies in art."

One reason why this should be so can be adduced from the tension in the play between a fulfilling, integrative sensibility—represented by Makak and his dream—on the one hand, and divisive, reductionist tendencies—manifested in the likes of the corporal and Moustique—on the other. Plurality of experience is suggested by the number of doublings and pairings we find in the play. Makak and Moustique provide one dual, complementary partnership; Tigre and Souris present another pair who offer a similar contrast. Basil seems sometimes to be paired with the dancer, sometimes with the white apparition. The corporal is really a double in himself: he is both black and white, and shifts from one pole of being to the other partway through the play. The sun and the moon form another pair, the former representing "reality" and the latter "dream." The prevailing tendency—which the play implicitly condemns—is to emphasize *one* aspect of identity or experience at the expense of all others. The corporal tries to be white, then reverses the process and strives to be as black as possible. The pragmatic aspect of Makak, symbolized by Moustique, dies twice. The moon is slain in order to free the sun. White supremacy is established on the myth of black inferiority, then black supremacy asserts itself.

According to Walcott's stage directions, the moon reversed becomes the sun; the two are opposed but joined, Janus-like. Makak "kills" the moon so that the sun can rise and free them all from the dream in which they are locked "and treading their own darkness." Sun and moon each have their particular clarity; it is only that all things appear equal under the sun (Makak, Moustique, the corporal, the thieves are all "imprisoned"). It is the moon and its attendant world of dreams beneath which we experience vital contrasts, revealing differentiations.

In the contradictory dreamworld, these differentiations become ambiguous; distinctions between things keep shifting, altering. But characters with restrictive, "logical" mentalities keep struggling to reduce things to simple black and white, and Corporal Lestrade is perhaps the pre-eminent example of this behaviour. In his role as the upholder of the rules of Her Majesty's government, the corporal functions as Makak's prosecutor. Later, in the important apotheosis scene, where the power of shaping history now lies with Makak and his retinue, the corporal is still functioning as a prosecutor, but this time upholding the law of the tribes against the threat of whiteness. He has changed his allegiance but retains his legalistic devotion, with its logic and rationalism. (When the corporal says of Makak, "I can both accuse and defend this man," he is articulating his ability to switch sides easily, a testimony to his innate opportunism and uncertain sense of identity.) For him, the white goddess, who represents the negative aspect of his own previous possession (by "English" and all that it implies), is much more of a threat than she is to Makak, for whom she functions as muse. The corporal has reduced her to one (especially for him) damaging context: the mother of (Western) civilisation—in other words, Europe. (Eur-opë = "she of the broad face"—that is, the full moon.)

IV

Walcott himself characterizes the apparition as having four roles (or phases): the moon, the muse, the white goddess, a dancer. All of these manifestations coalesce into a simultaneous complex of meaning, splendidly articulated by Robert Graves in *The White Goddess*. He writes, "Her name and titles are innumerable. In ghost stories she often figures as 'The White Lady', and in ancient religions, from the British Isles to the Caucasus, as the 'White Goddess'." She is the Muse, "the Mother of All Living, the ancient power of fright and lust—the female spider or the queen-bee whose embrace is death." The Night Mare is one of her cruellest aspects. But it is she who inspires the magical language of poetic myth which "remains the language of true poetry." Hence the goddess has complementary moods of creation and destruction.

One of the further aspects of the muse is Mnemosyne, "Memory": and this is important for the play in that it is through the dream inspired by the white goddess that Makak journeys back to the roots of his heritage, to the time when he was both "lion and king." Before his inspiration, Makak could declare, like the speaker in Walcott's poem **"Names"**: "I began with no memory. I began with no future." And when he does make a beginning, it is "where Africa began: / in the body's memory."

Since Makak is clearly posited in the play as a kind of Christ-figure, one is likely to question the simultaneous emphasis on the rather pagan white goddess, since, as Graves reminds us, the concept of such a creative anima was banned by Christian theologians nearly two thousand years ago and by Jewish theologians even earlier. But if we move outide the mainstream of orthodoxy, as artists are wont to do, there is no real contradiction or incompatibility, for the ancient Irish and British poets "saw Jesus as the latest theophany of the same suffering sacred king whom they had worshipped under various names from time immemorial." Furthermore, the Gnostics held that Jesus "was conceived in the mind of God's Holy Spirit, who was female in Hebrew"—which is enlightening in view of the fact that Makak refers to himself as "responsible only to God who once speak to me *in the form of a woman* on Monkey Mountain" (my emphasis). Graves goes on to remark that the "male Holy Ghost is a product of Latin grammar—*spiritus* is masculine—and of early Christian distrust of female deities or quasi-deities." The corporal's indictment of the apparition—"She is the wife of the devil, the white witch"—contains strong echoes of this intolerance.

Makak in his role as the King of Africa and the saviour of his people is an image of the Sacred King who is the moon goddess's divine victim, who dies and is reborn in the cycle of perpetual renewal; and, as the madman, the dreamer, the visionary poet, he is also the muse's victim, for the two roles interpenetrate. But Makak refuses to die this death, slaying the white goddess instead, under the pressure of the corporal's vehement prosecution and the collective animosity of the tribes. In doing so he frees himself from the dream, but only on one level—a level on which, as Moustique correctly diagnoses, a betrayal of the true cause is taking place, blindness replacing vision, maleficent madness driving out beneficent madness. It is Moustique who dies, and, in so doing, attains wisdom; he who had himself betrayed the dream by attempting to market it is later able to see that the dream is now being prostituted by others for political ends. And the corporal has to go to the verge of death before he experiences a necessary (but not thoroughgoing) transformation.

Makak has to kill the white goddess for several reasons: one, because he cannot forever go on depending upon his source of inspiration but has to begin to rely upon himself (just as he had earlier insisted that the people have faith in themselves as well as in an outside force); two, he has to come back from the world of visionary truth to the everyday world, in order to translate and transmit the fruits of his experience; and, three, he has to escape from the somewhat perverted role of tyrant which the corporal and others have thrust upon him, as well as from the complementary role of saviour that is so fraught with agony and peril.

When Makak divests himself of his royal robe before he beheads the apparition, he is symbolically freeing himself from the bondage of kingship as well as that of the dream and all externally-imposed definitions of selfhood. Indeed, Makak's real name, Felix ("happy") is only revealed in the Epilogue, after he has finally discovered who he is. It is not quite as simple as waking up, because, paradoxically, on one level the dream continues right to the play's end. What happens is that Makak moves from his personal dream back to the realm of collective dream, where his experience becomes universalized and undifferentiated.

In an early poem by W.B. Yeats ["Fergus and the Druid"], Fergus of the Red Branch tells a druid of his desire to "Be no more a king / But learn the dreaming wisdom that is yours." Taken as an admonition, these words could apply appropriately enough to Makak, who in the apotheosis scene witnesses the clarity of his vision being distorted by the blindness of revenge, the salvational role of leadership reduced to a rallying-point for fanaticism. Just as he must escape from the thrall of the muse, Makak must free himself from the perversions of power. The recognition of kingliness, the possibility of triumph, are sufficient for the satisfaction of the psychic hunger for reinforcement. It is similar to the realization that it is enough to travel to Africa in one's mind; indeed, that such an imaginative journey may be ultimately preferable to an actual one. Ironically, the dream seems to reassert reality once more, though on a higher plane of recognition. Makak, after all, is no king; he is merely himself—but that self is now endowed with dignity and a certain prophetic wisdom. As long as the dream remains a dream, we can awaken from it or dream it again. The danger is when people like Corporal Lestrade try to make the dream literal. Then there is no more imagining and no more awakening; no true freedom, only another confining structure.

FURTHER READING

AUTHOR COMMENTARY

Hamner, Robert D. "Conversation with Derek Walcott." *World Literature in English* 16, No. 2 (November 1977): 409-20.
Interview in which Walcott discusses the influence of William Butler Yeats and John Millington Synge on his drama.

Walcott, Derek. "The Poet in the Theatre." *Poetry Review* 80, No. 4 (Winter 1990-91): 4-8.
Text of a lecture in which Walcott discusses the need for poets to compose drama in order to restore tragedy to contemporary theater.

OVERVIEWS AND GENERAL STUDIES

Breiner, Laurence A. "Walcott's Early Drama," in *The Art of Derek Walcott,* edited by Stewart Brown, pp. 69-81. Chester Springs, Penn.: Dufour Editions, 1991.
Chronicles Walcott's development as a playwright through *Dream on Monkey Mountain.*

Colson, Theodore. "Derek Walcott's Plays: Outrage and Compassion." *World Literature in English* 12, No. 1 (April 1973): 80-96.
Surveys the pieces included in *Dream on Monkey Mountain and Other Plays,* observing that "just because they are so intensely of and about the West Indian people and places, they are intensely for the world."

Hamner, Robert D. "Mythological Aspects of Derek Walcott's Drama." *Ariel* 8, No. 3 (July 1977): 35-58.
Asserts that "Walcott is mythopoetic because there are motifs, characters, actions, and symbols in his poetry and drama that provide coherent patterns of belief, explanations of a way of life."

————. *Derek Walcott.* Boston: Twayne Publishers, 1981.
Full-length study of Walcott and his works. Includes a chronology of major events in the author's career and a bibliography of works by and about Walcott.

————. *Critical Perspectives on Derek Walcott.* Washington, D.C.: Three Continents Press, 1993, 482.
Extensive collection of essays by and about Walcott.

Ismond, Patricia. "Walcott's Later Drama: From *Joker* to *Remembrance.*" *Ariel* 16, No. 3 (July 1985): 90-101.
Perceives a development in Walcott's plays towards presenting "various responses to the post-independence scene, and its increasingly more pressing political and social contexts."

Juneja, Renu. "Derek Walcott." In *Post-Colonial English Drama: Commonwealth Drama since 1960,* edited by Bruce King, pp. 236-66. New York: St. Martin's Press, 1992.
Broad assessment of Walcott's career as a dramatist.

King, Bruce. *Derek Walcott & West Indian Drama.* Oxford: Clarendon Press, 1995, 410 p.
Meticulously researched history of Walcott's involvement with the Trinidad Theatre Workshop. King discusses "Walcott as a theatre director, the influence of dance on the kind of total theatre he wanted, the relationships between his paintings and plays, and the unique acting style he created."

The Literary Half-Yearly 26, No. 1 (January 1985).
Issue devoted entirely to Walcott and his works. Includes several essays on his plays.

Omotoso, Kole. *The Theatrical into Theatre: A Study of the Drama and Theatre of the English-Speaking Caribbean.* London: New Beacon Books, 1982, 173 p.
Includes numerous references to Walcott and his plays.

DREAM ON MONKEY MOUNTAIN

Olaniyan, Tejumola. "Derek Walcott: Islands of History at a Rendezvous with a Muse." In *Scars of Conquest/Masks of Resistance,* pp. 93-115. New York: Oxford University Press, 1995.
Examines *Dream on Monkey Mountain* in the context of Walcott's writings on West Indian cultural history.

Uhrbach, Jan R. "A Note on Language and Naming in *Dream on Monkey Mountain.*" *Callaloo* 9, No. 4 (Fall 1986): 578-82.
Investigates the numerous and changing meanings of various names, words, and phrases in *Dream on Monkey Mountain.*

Willis, Robert J. "*Dream on Monkey Mountain*: Fantasy as Self-Perception." In *Staging the Impossible: The Fantastic Mode in Modern Drama,* edited by Patrick D. Murphy, pp. 150-55. New York: Greenwood Press, 1992.
Delineates the frame structure of *Dream on Monkey Mountain,* in which the prologue and epilogue enclose Makak's elaborate dream of achieving identity and freedom.

THE JOKER OF SEVILLE

Thieme, John. "A Caribbean Don Juan: Derek Walcott's *Joker of Seville.*" *World Literature Written in English* 23, No. 1 (Winter 1984): 62-75.

Argues that in *The Joker of Seville* Walcott "creolized" the Don Juan myth to produce "a metatheatrical piece which investigates the question of tradition in West Indian drama."

PANTOMIME

Taylor, Patrick. "Myth and Reality in Caribbean Narrative: Derek Walcott's *Pantomime*." *World Literature Written in English* 26, No. 1 (Spring 1986): 169-77.

Investigates how Walcott avoids "the pitfalls of ethnic or national chauvinism" while depicting the colonial history of the Caribbean.

A BRANCH OF THE BLUE NILE

Breslow, Stephen P. "Trinidadian Heteroglossia: A Bakhtinian View of Derek Walcott's Play *A Branch of the Blue Nile*." *World Literature Today* 63, No. 1 (Winter 1989): 36-9.

Applies the theories of Mikhail Bakhtin to Walcott's play. Breslow asserts: "Intertextual and intercultural references, woven through much of Walcott's poetry and drama, multiply exponentially in *A Branch of the Blue Nile*."

Additional coverage of Walcott's life and career is contained in the following sources published by Gale Research: *Black Literature Criticism*; *Black Writers*, Vol. 2; *Contemporary Authors*, Vols. 89-92; *Contemporary Authors New Revision Series*, Vols. 26, 47; *Contemporary Literary Criticism*, Vols. 2, 4, 9, 14, 25, 42, 67, 76; *DISCovering Authors*; *DISCovering Authors: British*; *DISCovering Authors: Canadian*; *DISCovering Authors: Modules—Most-Studied Authors Module, Multicultural Module, Poets Module*; *Dictionary of Literary Biography*, Vol. 117; *Dictionary of Literary Biography Yearbook*, 1981, 1992; and *Major Twentieth-Century Writers*.

Zeami
1363-1443

(Full name Zeami Motokiyo)

INTRODUCTION

Zeami is the foremost nō dramatist and theorist, whose plays and treatises are largely responsible for transforming nō from a rustic form of entertainment into a high art. He is credited with having written 240 plays, some 100 of which still survive and are regularly performed. In addition, his treatises are regarded as a significant contribution not only to the dramatic arts but to Japanese aesthetics as a whole.

BIOGRAPHICAL INFORMATION

Zeami was born near Nara, Japan, the son of Kan'ami, an eminent practitioner of the Kanze form of nō drama. As a child Zeami performed in his father's troupe, where he attracted the notice of the Shōgun Ashikaga Yokimitsu and the renowned poet Nijō Yoshimoto. It is believed that through the influence of these two prominent figures Zeami received an excellent education, for his treatises demonstrate a wider knowledge of literature and philosophy than was typical of one who pursued the lowly profession of actor. Kan'ami died when his son was only twenty-two, leaving him responsible for the troupe. At this time Zeami wrote his first treatise, *Fūshikaden* (*Teachings on Style and the Flower*), to preserve and pass on his father's teachings. As they had under his father, Zeami and his troupe received the patronage of Yokumitsu until the shōgun's death in 1408. Yokumitsu's successor, Yoshimochi, seems to have been indifferent to Zeami, but when he died in 1428 and his younger brother, Yoshinori, assumed power, Zeami's fortunes declined sharply. In 1432, when Zeami was seventy, his elder son, Motomasa, died—possibly he was murdered—and the shōgunate authorities made Zeami's cousin, On'ami, head of the family troupe. (Zeami himself had retired from acting a decade earlier to become a Buddhist monk.) Two years later Zeami was exiled to the island of Sado for reasons that remain unclear, but possibly because of his opposition to On'ami. After the death of the Shōgun Yoshinori in 1441, Zeami was pardoned, and he returned to the mainland. He died two years later in Kyoto.

MAJOR WORKS

Of the 100 surviving plays attributed to Zeami, many, such as *Aoi no Ue* (*The Lady Aoi*), *Nishikigi* (*The Brocade Tree*), and *Takasago,* remain essential works in the nō repertory. Nō theater is performed on a bare stage with few props. The actors—all of whom are male—are clothed in splendid costumes and wear elaborate masks to portray an old man, a woman, a supernatural being, or other standard figures. The acting style is formal and stylized and incorporates elements of dance. A small orchestra of drums and flutes provides musical accompaniment. There are typically two acts to each play, and the protagonist (*Shite*) appears in both, depicting different facets of the character. In addition to the *Shite,* characters in a nō play may include the *Waki,* or supporting character, and the *Tsure,* or followers. A chorus often comments on the action. Historically, five nō plays—separated by comic interludes called *Kyūgen*—were performed together in a single program.

CRITICAL RECEPTION

Historians and scholars of nō theater all concur that Zeami, continuing the work begun by his father, developed nō from a low form of popular entertainment into a brilliant art form that seamlessly combines dance, song, mime, and poetry. As demonstrated in his plays and expressed in his treatises, Zeami infused nō with religious significance derived from Zen Buddhism. The concept of *yūgen*—a complex idea that indicates beauty, grace, depth—was particularly important to Zeami. For him, *yūgen* was inseparable from nō and was the wellspring of its spirituality. Makoto Ueda has observed that in Zeami's theories *yūgen* is "the inner beauty of an object outwardly expressed by means of art. It is the manifestation of the 'primary meaning' which lies in the mysterious depth of things. In this sense it is identical with truth—the truth caught by the artist's 'soul'." It is this fusion of art and spirituality, critics agree, that lies at the heart of Zeami's greatness.

---

*PRINCIPAL WORKS

PLAYS

Akoya no Matsu [*The Pine of Akoya*]
Aoi no Ue [*The Lady Aoi*]
Aridōshi
Ashikari [*The Reed Cutter*]
Atsumori
Fujisan
Funabashi [*The Floating Bridge*]
Furu
Fushimi

Hanagatami [The Flower Basket]
Hanjo [Lady Han]
Hatsusei Rokudai [Rokudai at Hatsuse]
Hibariyama [Hibari Mountain]
Higaki
Hōjōgawa [The River for the Hōjōe Ceremony]
Hyakuman
Izutsu [Well Curb]
Kayoi Komachi [Komachi and the Hundred Nights]
Kinuta [The Cloth-Beating Block]
Kiyotsune
Koi no omoni [The Burden of Love]
Kōya monogurui [The Madman at Kōya]
Matsukaze
Michimori
Nishikigi [The Brocade Tree]
Obasute [The Deserted Crone]
Oimatsu [The Aged Crone]
Ōsaka monogurui [Osaka Madman]
Saigyōzakura [Saigyō and the Cherry Tree]
Sakuragawa [Sakura River]
Sanemori
Sekidera Komachi [Komachi at Sekidera]
Semimaru
Suma Genji [Genji at Suma]
Tadanori
Taisan Pakun [The Great Lord of Mount T'ai]
Takasago
Tango monogurui [The Madman at Tango]
Tōru
Tsuchiguruma [The Barrow]
Ukifune
Ukon no baba [The Riding Ground of Ukon]
Yamamba [The Mountain Hag]
Yashima
Yorimasha
Yōrō   [The Care of the Aged]
Yumiyawata [The Bow at Hachiman Shrine]

TREATISES

Fūshikaden [Teachings on Style and the Flower]
Kandensho [Book of Transmission of the Flower]
Kakyō   [A Mirror Held to the Flower]
Kyūi [Notes on the Nine Levels]
*Sandō [also called Nōsakusho] [The Three Elements in
    Composing a Play]*
†*Sarugaku dangi [An Account of Zeami's Reflections
    on Art]*
Shikadō   [The True Path to the Flower]
Shūdōsho [Learning the Way]
*Shūgyoku tokka [also spelled Shūgyoku-Tokuka] [Find-
    ing Gems and Gaining the Flower]*
Yūgaku shūdō fūken [Disciplines for the Joy of Art]

* Given the uncertainties related to establishing the canon of Zeami's
works and their chronology, no attempt has been made here to attach
dates to the works, nor has an attempt been made to determine a
definitive list of his works. Some of the plays included here are
certainly by Zeami, others are his revisions of earlier plays, and still
others have simply been attributed to him.

† These comments by Zeami were written down by Hata No
Motoyoshi.

OVERVIEWS AND GENERAL STUDIES

Makoto Ueda (essay date 1961)

SOURCE: "Zeami on Art: A Chapter for the History of
Japanese Aesthetics," in *The Journal of Aesthetics and
Art Criticism*, Vol. XX, No. 1, Fall, 1961, pp. 73-9.

[*In the following essay, Ueda delineates Zeami's views
on the nature and technique of Nō, particularly the
concept of* yūgen, *or "elegance, calm, profundity, mixed
with the feeling of mutability.*]

Due to the increasing interest in Japanese theater in recent years, Zeami Motokiyo (1363-1443) is now a well-
known figure in the West as a great writer of the *Nō*
drama; yet few people know that he is the author of
some twenty essays which mark one of the highest peaks
in the development of Japanese aesthetics. He was a
most gifted performer of the *Nō* whose fame overwhelmed
the contemporary court circles already early in his career, but he was also a very self-conscious artist who
constantly endeavored to explore and expand the meaning of his art. Those essays, written over a period of
thirty years, consistently reveal his never-failing passion
for the improvement of his art; "a man's life has an
ending," he says, "but there is no ending in the pursuit
of the *Nō*." Although the essays were written primarily
to provide proper guidance for professional *Nō* actors,
they contain a number of interesting comments on the
nature of art in general, as Zeami's keen insight breaks
through the conventional particulars of Japanese theater
and reaches the level of the universal. Roughly speaking, Zeami's concept of art centers upon three basic
principles: imitation, *yūgen,* and sublimity.

Among these three the principle of imitation is the most
elementary one. Anyone who wishes to learn the art of
the *Nō* must start with this principle. "Objects to be
imitated are too many to be enumerated here," Zeami
says. "Yet they have to be thoroughly studied since
imitation is the foremost principle in our art." Then he
adds: "The basic rule is to imitate things as they are,
whatever they may be." A *Nō* actor should carefully
observe the manners and speech of princes, statesmen,
courtiers, and warriors; he might ask such people, when
they are in his audience, whether his performance has
been an acceptable imitation of what they actually say
and do. Zeami especially advises an actor not to become
too intent on producing the effect of forcefulness or
elegance on the stage. When an actor consciously tries
to show forcefulness in his acting, his performance will
appear not forceful but coarse; when he deliberately
attempts to make his acting elegant, his performance will
look not elegant but weak. For, as Zeami remarks:

> Forcefulness or elegance does not exist by itself. It
> lies in the proper imitation of an object. It should be
> known that weakness or coarseness arises when the
> actor does not follow the principle of imitation.

Any act of imitation which distorts nature for the sake of artistic effectiveness will result in coarseness or weakness; it is artifice, and not art. An aesthetic effect like forcefulness or elegance is potential in natural objects themselves. "Therefore," Zeami says, "if an actor gives himself up to this principle and truly becomes one with the object of his imitation, his performance will be neither coarse nor weak."

Basically, then, Zeami's idea of imitation is to imitate natural objects as they are, without distorting them or imposing any artifice upon them. However, when an actor proceeds to a higher stage of training, he should not be satisfied with the mere imitation of outward appearance. In the last-quoted sentence Zeami advocates the identification of the imitator with the thing he imitates; this is not an imitation in its ordinary sense, because an imitation usually requires the imitator's objective awareness of the thing he is imitating. In fact Zeami says: "In the art of imitation there is a stage called non-imitation. If the actor proceeds to the ultimate stage of imitation and entirely enters the thing he is imitating, he will no longer possess a will to imitate." In the highest stage of imitation the actor becomes unconscious of his art; the imitator is united with the imitated. The dualism of man and nature is gone; man and a natural object are the same in their ultimate essence. An artist should nullify his own individual self to express this essence; or, from another point of view, a natural object should be represented in its essence through the transparent soul of the artist. Zeami calls this essence the "primary meaning." A *Nō* performer, in his early stage of training, should try to imitate the patterns of clothes or manners of speech as they are in actual life; but as his training goes on to a more advanced stage he need not be too concerned with the appearance of things but should strive to represent the "primary meaning." In point of fact it is impossible to realistically imitate a demon from Hell, because there is no such thing in our ordinary life. Still, a demon could be convincingly represented if the artist successfully creates the feeling of its "primary meaning." "Nobody has ever seen a demon from Hell," Zeami says. "It is more important, therefore, to act the role in an impressive manner than to attempt to imitate the demon."

What Zeami exactly means by the "primary meaning" is not easy to define, but we may have a general idea of it as we read his comment on the art of acting a frenzied man's role. He writes:

> It is extremely difficult to play the roles of those who are mentally deranged due to various obsessions, such as one would suffer at the parting with one's parent, at the loss of one's child, or at the death of one's wife. Even a fairly good actor does not distinguish these particulars one from another, but portrays all frenzied men in a similar manner; the audience, consequently, is not impressed. A person is frenzied on account of his obsession; therefore, if the actor makes the obsession the primary meaning of his portraiture, and the frenzy the effective expression of it, then his acting will certainly impress the audience and create a breath-taking climax. An actor who

moves the audience to tears by such means is a performer of true greatness.

The "primary meaning" of a person, then, is the inmost nature that constitutes the core of his personality. In a frenzied man mental derangement is merely an outward expression of an inner cause; the deepest truth in this person lies in his obsession, or what has caused the obsession, rather than in his symptoms of madness. The actor who wishes to portray such a man will try to represent the obsession, not merely to copy the features of any madman; he will imitate the characteristics of a frenzied man in such a way that the primary cause of his insanity may be revealed to the audience. A true artist, Zeami implies, pierces through the surface of everyday reality and reaches the hidden truth of things. Only when this is successfully done the characters in the drama will be given life; the supernatural will become natural. Only then the effectiveness, or beauty, of a performance will be fully achieved.

Zeami's idea of beauty is thus closely related to his way of looking at life. *Yūgen,* his ideal beauty, is not only an aesthetic principle but a mode of perception. Zeami remarks:

> An actor should never divert himself from the principle of *yūgen,* irrespective of whatever kind of imitation he is engaged in. This will be like seeing a noble princess, a court lady, a man, a woman, a monk, a peasant, a humble man, a beggar, an outcast, all standing in a line with a spray of blossoms. Although they differ in social status and in outward appearance, they are equally beautiful blossoms insofar as we feel the impact of their beauty. The lovely blossoms are the beauty of human form. The beauty of form is created by the soul.

Yūgen is not a superficial surface beauty; it is a beauty that lies deep in the heart of things. Therefore, even an imitation of something which is not beautiful on the outside may be made beautiful if the inner beauty finds its way out. A withered old man, ugly in appearance, can be made to have a certain beauty: Zeami describes the beauty as "the blossoms blooming on a dead tree." A dreadful demon of Hell can be made beautiful too: Zeami describes the beauty as "the blossoms blooming on a crag." What creates real beauty is the "soul." Zeami uses the term in many different ways, but basically it seems to imply the "soul of art"—a spirit in pursuit of ideal beauty. To learn the "soul" of playwriting, one should study classical poetry; to learn the "soul" of mimicry, one would better start with the imitation of elegant persons. An actor should firmly get hold of what makes a person or a thing beautiful, and should attempt to express that essence of beauty in his performance. Zeami explains this process of artistic transformation with an anatomical metaphor—the bone, the flesh, and the skin. The bone is a spirit which tries to discover and express ideal beauty; it is "pre-art," as it were, and a genius may attain an amazing success even at a very early stage of his training. The flesh stands for that part of art which can be learned by training. The skin signifies artistic effectiveness; it is the visible part of art. A human body consists of the bone, the flesh, and the skin, although our eyes can see nothing but the skin. Similarly, the beauty of the *Nō* is derived from artistic inspiration, conventionalized form, and externalized action, although the audience may see only the last of the three. Zeami emphasizes the importance of the invisible part of artistic creation as essential in producing visible beauty.

Yūgen, then, is the inner beauty of an object outwardly expressed by means of art. It is the manifestation of the "primary meaning" which lies in the mysterious depth of things. In this sense it is identical with truth—the truth caught by the artist's "soul." External reality is only illusory; there is a higher reality lying somewhere beyond the reach of our ordinary senses. The artist, in pursuit of beauty, momentarily penetrates the surface reality and gets hold of hidden truth. Zeami particularly yearns for the romantic world of *The Tale of Genji* wherein life and art, truth and beauty, are one and the same. Characters in this Japanese classic, such as Lady Aoi, Lady Yūgao, and Lady Ukifune, will be the most precious gems if they are made into the protagonists of *Nō* plays, because these ladies, making beauty the basic principle of their life, have the most refined aesthetic sensibility. Thus the imitation of a court lady, as Zeami teaches, is the basis of all the other imitations. When this type of beauty is caught on its highest level, it will give the impression of "a white bird with a flower in its beak." The famous metaphor suggests Zeami's romantic concern with pure and graceful beauty, with a creation of unearthly beauty by means of art.

Yet it is in the very essence of *yūgen* that this elegant beauty is entwined with a tone of sadness. If *yūgen* is also a mode of perception into the hidden nature of things, it cannot but bring out a pessimistic notion of life. For the law of the universe prescribes that even the most beautiful ladies must suffer the tortures of living, that even the loveliest blossoms must fade away. Immediately after stressing the importance of graceful beauty in *Nō performance,* Zeami goes on:

> But there are even more precious materials for producing the visible effect of *yūgen* than the elegant appearance of court ladies I have just referred to. These rare examples are seen in such cases as Lady Aoi cursed by Lady Rokujō's spirit, Lady Yūgao carried away by a ghost, or Lady Ukifune charmed by an unknown being.

Yūgen, then, lies not simply in the refined beauty of a court lady but in such a lady going through an intense suffering—a suffering caused by a power beyond her control, by the law of causation, by the supernatural, or by the unknown force of the universe. Such a suffering naturally leads to sad resignation. A court lady, lacking the masculine courage to heroically fight out her fate, gives herself up to religion when she comes to realize that suffering is the condition of being alive in this world. *Yūgen,* in its final analysis, may be conceived as a com-

bined quality of elegant beauty and sad resignation—the elegant beauty which is the result of man's quest for an ideal life through art and artifice, and the sad resignation which comes from man's recognition of his powerlessness before the great cosmic power ruling over this world. Thus Zeami defines *yūgen* as "elegance, calm, profundity, mixed with the feeling of mutability."

Of these two elements of *yūgen* Zeami stressed the first much more than the second in the earlier part of his career: in those years *yūgen* was almost equivalent to graceful beauty. Yet as he grew old, the emphasis was reversed: he came to admire cold, serene, subdued beauty more and more. Already in one of his early essays there is a suggestion of this when he expresses his preference of a withering flower to a fully blooming one. Later he becomes more explicit: he says that a superb actor, when he comes to an important scene, will "perform chanting, dancing, and mimetic action in an inconspicuous manner, yet in such a way that the audience is somehow deeply moved by the subdued simplicity of the atmosphere." Elegant beauty has given way to the beauty of a calm, serene mind of a man who has perceived the sad truth of life and has finally transcended the sadness through religious resignation. In fact the latter phase of *yūgen* is so much emphasized in his later essays that Zeami uses a different term for it—"sublimity."

Zeami explains the nature of "sublimity" in two of his essays where he classifies plays and performances into five different types. Here the effect of *yūgen* is illustrated by a classical Japanese poem:

> Snowy petals scatter
> At the cherry-blossom hunting
> On the field of Katano:
> Shall I ever see again
> Such a beautiful spring dawn?

The image of cherry-blossoms like snow neatly combines the purity of beautiful whiteness with the sense of life's mutability, adequately introducing the sentiment of the last two lines. "Sublimity," however, is a somewhat different beauty from this. Its mood is comparable to that of this poem:

> Slowly, quietly,
> The spear-shaped cedar-tree
> On Mt. Kagu
> Came to assume an air of austerity,
> With its roots under the moss.

Instead of the gay, colorful loveliness of cherry-blossoms, "sublimity" has the silent, quiet dignity of an old cedar-tree. If *yūgen* is the calm, subdued beauty of youth, "sublimity" is the calm, subdued beauty of old age. *Yūgen* implies a sad awareness of life's change and mutability; "sublimity" transcends such and other sentiments of ordinary life, it implies permanence in nature, like an old cedar-tree standing among non-evergreen plants, or eternity in the cosmos, like the immortal Shinto god residing in Mt. Kagu.

Zeami further clarifies his idea of "sublimity" as he grades the different styles of *Nō* performances into nine ranks. The quality of "sublimity," as he seems to suggest, lies in the highest three ranks: "the Style of Calm Flower," "the Style of Infinitely Deep Flower," and "the Style of Mysterious Flower." "The Style of Calm Flower," the lowest of the three, yields an effect which may be illustrated by an old Zen saying: "Snow is piled in a silver bowl." The style shows the ease and calm of an artist who is confident of his art after mastering all the required stages of training. A silver bowl, a wonder of art, contains snow, a wonder of nature, and both the container and the contained are united in the purity of whiteness. This is a superb beauty, yet still it is surpassed by the beauty of a higher style, called "the Style of Infinitely Deep Flower." Zeami explains this style again by metaphor: "Snow has covered thousands of mountains all in white. Why is it that one solitary peak remains unwhitened?" And he adds later: "The Style of Infinitely Deep Flower is the ultimate form of *yūgen*. It is a style which reveals the middle ground where being and non-being meet." A performer who has the Style of Calm Flower is still in the world of being, the world of empirical reality, even though his art may show the purest beauty of snow in a silver bowl. An actor who has advanced to the Style of Infinitely Deep Flower goes beyond the limitations of ordinary reality; an irrational element, like a black peak towering among snow-covered mountains, may enter the world which his performance creates. His art is beyond our measure; it is like a deep sea whose bottom lies somewhere in the mysterious unknown.

Yet there is still a higher rank, "the Style of Mysterious Flower," the highest of all nine ranks. Zeami explains:

The Style of Mysterious Flower:

"In Silla the sun shines brightly at midnight."

The "mysterious" means something which cannot be explained in words, something which cannot be thought of in human mind. It is like the sun shining at midnight, a phenomenon which transcends the expository capacity of speech. The profound art of a rare master in the *Nō* cannot be adequately described by any word of praise. It leads the audience to a state of trance; it is a styleless style which surpasses any scheme of grading. A style which yields such an impression upon the audience may be called the Style of Mysterious Flower.

A little later Zeami adds that this style covers "an imaginative landscape which is beyond verbal description as it lies in the realm of the absolute." The realm of the absolute, a term from Zen Buddhism, implies a sphere where there is neither good nor evil, neither right nor wrong, neither one nor all. The sun shining at midnight, which is a flat contradiction in ordinary reality, is perfectly acceptable in this realm. Silla, the present Korea, is located to the east of China; the sun is already rising there when it is still night in China. What seems to be a flat contradiction to our ordinary senses may be a profound truth when it is viewed from a point which transcends the limitations of time and space. Above our everyday reality there is a higher reality ordinary human faculties cannot sense. A perfect work of art can lead us into this realm in a trance, where we are made to perceive the invisible and hear the inaudible.

To Zeami, then, art means something which attempts to illuminate what lies in the deepest depth of human mind, what cannot be known through ordinary senses. It is concerned with the realm of the unconscious, with that part of human mind which cannot be reached through intellect, which belongs to the all-pervasive universe. Zeami seems to have believed in some great primal force that flows through life and death, through the conscious and the unconscious—a force which manifests itself in the "primary meaning" of every object in nature. He says that "one contains many while two are just two," referring to the same concept. An artist should try to represent this invisible energy of the cosmos by means of symbolism. Zeami, in one of his most suggestive passages on art, remarks:

> If I may illustrate my purport by the principle of two ways in Buddhism, being and non-being, then the appearance will correspond to being and the vessel to non-being. To take an example, a crystal, although it is a pure, transparent object without color or pattern, produces fire and water. Why is it that two entirely heterogeneous things like fire and water emerge out of one transparent object? A poem says:

> Smash a cherry-tree,
> And you will find no blossom
> In the splinters.
> It is in the sky of spring
> That cherry-blossoms bloom.

The seed for the flower of art is the artist's soul that has a power to feel. As a crystal body produces fire and water or a colorless cherry-tree bears blossoms and fruit, so does a superb artist create a variety of works out of his imaginative scenery. Such a man may be compared to a vessel. Works of art, treating the wind and the moon or flowers and birds, accompanying a festival or a picnic, are many and various. The universe creates thousands of things as the seasons roll on—blossoms and leaves, snow and the moon, mountains and seas, trees and grass, the animate and the inanimate. An artist should try to attain the stage of Mysterious Flower by letting these numerous things be the materials of his art, by making his soul the vessel of the universe, and by setting the vessel in the vast, windless way of emptiness.

Zeami recognizes the existence of two worlds, the world of being and that of non-being. The one is the world we can perceive through our senses, the world of appearance. The other cannot easily be seen because it is hidden beneath the surface; it can be felt only by the sensitive soul of an artist who has a power to feel. An artist creates his work out of his own soul, just as the universe creates thousands of things out of itself; the artist, as well as the universe, is a vessel which contains potential creative energy. The artist's soul gets its expression through the things of the universe; here the human and the cosmic, the microcosm and macrocosm, become one.

Zeami's concept of art, we may conclude, is based on an animistic mode of perception; it presumes a great collective mind running through all the things in the cosmos. Art imitates nature, but it does so in such a way as to reveal the hidden essence of man and things, the "primary meaning" which the sensitivity of the artist alone can feel. Naturally the artist will be concerned not so much with social or ethical problems as with the issues of man's deepest self which lies beyond the realm of the conscious. Inevitably he will approach the issues not through a reasoned analysis or a systematized metaphysics, but through an instantaneous perception, an emotional understanding, which is possible only when he annihilates himself into the things that surround him. He sees life through death, being through non-being, permanence through change. *Yūgen*, Zeami's ideal beauty, can be understood as such a mode of perception; it is not merely inherent in the things observed but lies in the way the observer looks at things. "Sublimity," an emotional impact produced by a supreme work of art, roots in the calm and serenity of mind which the artist attains as he becomes aware of man's mortality, as he recognizes eternity in myriads of changing things in nature.

Here Zeami's aesthetics approaches religion. Medieval Buddhism, particularly the Shingon sect, maintained that eternal truth, while it transcended the natural world, could be understood only through the things of the natural world. The priests expressed their ideas through images and symbols; they were, in a sense, artists who transformed the abstract into the concrete by means of symbolism. Kūkai (774-835), the founder of the Shingon school, openly stated that the essential truths of the esoteric teaching could not be set forth without the means of art, that "art is what reveals to us the state of perfection." The aesthetic qualities of Buddhism were further strengthened as the medieval age advanced and new sects such as Zen and Jōdo grew influential. The "artistic religion" almost became a "religious art." The *Nō* drama was born and developed within this tradition, and Zeami's concept of art, apart from the question of direct influence, got its nourishment from the tradition. His insistence on the imitation of "primary meaning" rather than outward appearance reflects the Buddhist negation of visible reality as temporary and illusory. His concept of *yūgen* as "elegance, calm, profundity, mixed with the feeling of mutability" has an obvious Buddhist tinge. His "sublimity" seems parallel to simple and austere beauty, the highest aim of life as Zen Buddhism conceives it. The Buddhist dialectic permeates his whole aesthetics: in numerous ways he urges an artist to transcend being through non-being, to look at reality through super-reality. In fact the *Nō* itself, as we have it today, is a religious drama: in its final analysis it presents man's original sin and the scheme of salvation by means of symbolic poetry and ritualistic stage-action.

The synthesis of aesthetics and Buddhist philosophy was nothing new. In medieval Japan Buddhism was the very center of life; it was the way in which man moulded chaos into order. Medieval Japanese poetics, which culminated in Fujiwara no Teika (1162-1241), was no exception, and it preceded Zeami's aesthetics by several centuries. The origins of Zeami's ideas on art are easily found in the writings of Teika and his followers: *yūgen* in *aware* ("sensitivity to the sadness of things"), "sublimity" in "chilliness," the imitation of "primary meaning" in the idea of "complete submersion of the self in the thing." If one comes to the question of origins, one will note that a number of ideas external to the *Nō* have gone into Zeami's aesthetics—Shintoism, Confucianism, Chinese poetics, calligraphy, in addition to Buddhism and Japanese poetics. Zeami amalgamated them all into his own theory, with the help of the poets and artists who preceded him. The medieval age was the era of synthesis, as against our modern time which is the age of individualism and specialization. Zeami's concept on the *Nō* shows his remarkable genius as an artist and theorist, but it is, from another point of view, the most beautiful, mature, and sophisticated expression of medieval Japanese aesthetics.

Zeami on the qualities of yūgen (grace):

An actor must come to grasp [the] various types of Grace and absorb them within himself; for no matter what kind of role he may assume, he must never separate himself from the virtue of Grace. No matter what the role—whether the character be of high or low rank, a man, a woman, a priest or lay person, a farmer or country person, even a beggar or an outcast—it should seem as though each were holding a branch of flowers in his hand. In this one respect they exhibit the same appeal, despite whatever differences they may show in their social positions. This Flower represents the beauty of their stance in the *nō* ; and the ability to reveal this kind of stance in performance represents, of course, its spirit. In order to study the Grace of words, the actor must study the art of composing poetry; and to study the Grace of physical appearance, he must study the aesthetic qualities of elegant costume, so that, in every aspect of his art, no matter how the role may change that the actor is playing, he will always maintain one aspect in his performance that shows Grace. Such it is to know the seed of Grace.

Zeami, "The True Path to the Flower (Shikadō)*,"*
in On the Art of the Nō Drama: The Major
Treatises of Zeami, *translated by J. Thomas*
Rimer and Yamazaki Masakazu, Princeton
University Press, 1984.

Makoto Ueda (essay date 1962)

SOURCE: An introduction to *The Old Pine Tree and Other Noh Plays,* translated by Makoto Ueda, University of Nebraska Press, 1962, pp. vii-xxiv.

[*In this essay, Ueda provides a detailed consideration of the conventions of Nō as prescribed by Zeami.*]

The Japanese Noh drama has been attracting increasing interest in the West since it was first introduced early in this century. Ezra Pound was fascinated with it and edited some of its earliest English translations; Yeats wrote at least ten plays using the Noh as a model; and it attained an even greater popularity when Arthur Waley published his superb translations in the early twenties. Today it appears in almost every anthology of world literature that includes any Oriental writings at all.

The Noh's popularity is in large part due to its strange, mysterious outlook. This medieval Japanese drama, subtle, remote, and symbolic, offers something quite foreign to the tradition of Sophocles, Shakespeare, Molière, and Ibsen. The world of the Noh is inhabited by gods, spirits, and monsters; if there are any human beings they are priests, travelers, and children who have scarcely any individuality. By and large it is a timeless, superhuman world where no man of flesh and blood is likely to dwell. It is a world of night rather than of day, of dreams rather than empirical reality, since it deals with issues incapable of solution by a reasoned analysis.

In comparing the Orientals with the Westerners, it is often argued that in their attempts to grasp the truth of life the former are generally intuitive while the latter are discursive. Within its limited validity the generalization seems to be true of the Noh drama: compare the Noh with the works of the four playwrights just mentioned. A Noh play does not try to analyze man's problems; rather, it presents them in a mystical vision, momentary but far-reaching, and the resolution of the problems is left to the individual spectator. The resolution must be sought in the relation between man and the cosmos rather than between man and man; the scheme of salvation the Noh provides is necessarily religious.

The nondramatic nature of the Noh has evoked unfavorable criticism from some Western readers, who regard it as dull, trite, or sentimental. Ezra Pound himself became critical of the Noh in his later years, saying that it was too "soft." (Many present-day Japanese feel the same; they would rather go to see a Western drama, or a modern Japanese drama written in Western style, than sit in the Noh theater.) Since the dawn of dramatic literature in Greece, Westerners have seen the core of tragedy in a clash between all-powerful, ruthless fate and a brave, noble-hearted individual. We are overwhelmed by fear as we watch the black hand of Fate pitilessly destroying good people as well as bad, but we also feel pride as we observe one of our fellow men heroically fighting with a great unknown power; the tragic effect lies in the equilibrium of these two emotions. Such a concept, however, has never existed in the Japanese theater tradition. The Noh drama, in particular, seems to stand at the opposite pole.

The aim of the Noh has been clearly set forth by Zeami Motokiyo (1363-1443), a great Noh writer whose twenty-

odd essays on art mark one of the highest peaks in the history of Japanese aesthetics. The basic principles of the Noh, according to Zeami, are three: imitation, *yūgen,* and the sublime. Anyone who wishes to learn the art of the Noh must first master the principle of imitation. "Objects to be imitated are too many to be enumerated here," Zeami writes. "Yet they have to be thoroughly studied since imitation is the foremost principle in our art." Then he adds: "The basic rule is to imitate things as they are, whatever they may be." If an actor neglects this principle, his acting no longer will be art; it will sink to the level of artifice. At times, for example, an actor is too intent on producing the effect of forcefulness or elegance. The result is that he does not imitate things as they are; he exaggerates their attributes. An artistic effect like forcefulness or elegance is potentially present in natural objects themselves. "Therefore," Zeami remarks, "if an actor gives himself up to this principle and becomes one with the object of his imitation, his performance will look neither coarse nor weak." The artist, in other words, should try to put himself into the heart of natural objects rather than to bring them into the subjective sphere of his mind. He should minimize the activities of his ego; no personal element should intrude on the process by which an object in nature is transformed into its equivalent in art.

"In the art of imitation [Zeami says] there is a stage called 'non-imitation.' If one proceeds to the ultimate of imitation and entirely enters the thing he is imitating, he will possess no will to imitate." In the highest stage of imitation the artist becomes unconscious of his art; the imitator is united with the imitated. He can achieve this union only by projecting himself completely into the essence of the object he is imitating; then the man and the object are one in the essence they share with each other. An artist should dissolve his own individual self to express this essence—or, from another point of view, an object in nature should be represented in its essence through the transparent soul of the artist. Zeami calls this essence the "true intent." At the beginning of his apprenticeship a Noh actor tries to represent an object as it is, but as his art advances to a higher stage he endeavors to express the true intent of a thing rather than to copy its outward appearance. In acting out a madman's role, a mediocre actor merely imitates various symptoms of insanity; he portrays all frenzied men in a similar manner. A good actor heeds the words of Zeami: "A man is frenzied because of an obsession. Therefore, if the actor makes the obsession the true intent of his portraiture, then his acting will certainly impress the audience and create a breathtaking climax." The true intent of a character is the inmost nature of its personality, and in a frenzied man the deepest truth lies in his obsession, or in the cause of his obsession, rather than in the visible symptoms of his madness. Thus, instead of copying the features of a madman, the actor should try to represent the obsession itself. The true intent of a thing is the center of its existence: it is what makes an insane person insane, a forceful thing forceful, an elegant thing elegant. When the artist is perfectly united with the true intent, artistic effectiveness, or beauty, is finally attained.

Yūgen, the second of Zeami's aesthetic principles, can be understood as a type of beauty which results from such an act of imitation. It is not a superficial beauty; it is a beauty which resides in the heart of things. Even the imitation of something crude or ugly on the outside may be made beautiful if its inner beauty is evoked by means of art. A withered-up old man can be made beautiful; Zeami describes such beauty as "blossoms on a dead tree." A dreadful demon of hell can be made beautiful "blossoms on a crag," in Zeami's words. The truth lying deep at the bottom makes the ugliest thing beautiful. Truth is beauty.

It is the artist's obligation to search for truth and beauty which now are hidden beneath the surface but in the olden days were manifest everywhere in life. Zeami sets this golden age of Japanese arts in the tenth and eleventh centuries, a period whose culmination is masterfully described in *The Tale of Genji.* The ladies and gentlemen of the court, possessed of most refined taste in the arts, perpetually sought for ideal beauty; subtle, delicate, elegant beauty was for them the animating force of life. To imitate a court lady of that time an artist has only to copy her as she was in actual life, for she was *yūgen* itself, inside and out. Characters in *The Tale of Genji* such as Lady Aoi, Lady Yūgao, and Lady Ukifune are the most precious heroines of Noh. When their kind of beauty is pursued to its highest level of perfection, it gives the impression of "a white bird with a flower in its beak."

Yet in its very nature *yūgen* has an overtone of sadness. This is inevitable insofar as *yūgen* is the expression of the true intent. Every animate and inanimate object in nature must follow the law of the universe; it is born, grows, matures, declines, dies. Man, seeking permanence, cannot but feel sad confronted with this great law of change and mutability. The ladies in *The Tale of Genji* represent ideal beauty not only because they are lovely in outlook and graceful in behavior but also because they are subject to the universal law. Zeami, having praised the elegant beauty of these ladies, goes on to say:

> But there are even more precious materials for producing the visual effect of *yūgen* than the elegant appearance of the court ladies I have just referred to. These rare examples are seen in such cases as Lady Aoi haunted by Lady Rokujō's spirit, Lady Yūgao carried away by a ghost, or Lady Ukifune possessed by a supernatural being.

Yūgen lies not simply in the graceful beauty of a court lady, but in her experiencing intense suffering caused by a power beyond her knowledge and control. Against such an unknown superhuman power she has neither the ability nor the will to fight. Without fiery courage, superabundant vigor, or revolting spirit to defy heaven and earth, the only way open to her is to submit, to give herself up to religion; in sad resignation she tells herself that suffering is the condition of being alive in this world. Thus *yūgen,* in the final analysis, may be conceived as a combined quality of elegant beauty and sad resignation. Elegant beauty derives from man's quest for ideal beauty hidden beneath the surface reality; sad resignation from his recognition that he is a most fragile existence before the great cosmic power.

Zeami defines *yūgen* as "elegance, calm profundity, mixed with the feelings of mutability." In the earlier part of his career he stressed the first of these elements; to him in those years *yūgen* was almost equivalent to graceful beauty. But as he grew older the emphasis was reversed: calm, subdued, even chilly beauty came to fascinate him. Already in one of his early essays he confesses his preference for a withering flower to one in full bloom. Later, becoming more explicit, he says that a superb actor when he acts an important scene will "perform chanting, dancing, and mimicry in such a manner that the audience may, without knowing it, be deeply impressed by the subdued simplicity of the atmosphere." Zeami calls acting of this kind a "chilled performance" and ranks it the highest of all. The elegant beauty of a young woman who has the most refined taste in the arts has been superseded by the austere beauty of an old man who has experienced all the sad truths of life and finally transcended them with calmness of mind. In his later essays Zeami emphasizes the latter aspect of *yūgen* to such a degree that he gives it a different name: the sublime.

Illustrating the difference between *yūgen* and the sublime, Zeami quotes two classical Japanese poems which he believes represent the two types of beauty. The mood of *yūgen* prevails in the following poem:

> Snowy petals scatter
> At the cherry-blossom hunting
> On the field of Katano.
> Shall I ever see again
> Such a beautiful spring dawn?

The image of cherry blossoms falling like snow neatly combines the beauty of pure whiteness with the feeling of sadness over life's brevity. It is spring, it is dawn, the year and the day are newly born; yet the blossoms are falling in the whiteness of snow and death. The truth in nature holds true for man: *who can assure me that I shall live to see cherry blossoms next year?* The sublime, on the other hand, does not have this colorful elegance and mellow sentimentality. It is illustrated in this poem:

> Slowly, quietly,
> The spear-shaped cedar tree
> On Mount Kagu
> Came to have a venerable air
> With its roots under the moss.

The sublime is a silent, stately, austere beauty. It is not like the bright cherry blossoms which fall in a day or two; it implies permanence in nature, like an old cedar tree standing among annual plants, or eternity in the cosmos, like the immortal Shinto god residing in Mount Kagu.

Zeami uses another series of metaphors to clarify his idea of the sublime. It appears that he thought there were three kinds of sublimity. The first, called the *Style of a Calm Flower,* is like "the snow heaped in a silver bowl." It is pure, chill, and white. A silver bowl, a wonder of art, contains snow, a wonder of nature; the container and the contained are united in the purity of whiteness. But superb though this beauty is, it is surpassed by the second kind, the *Style of an Infinitely Deep Flower.* It may be illustrated by a Buddhist question: "The snow has covered thousands of mountains all in white. Why is it that one solitary peak remains unwhitened?" The silver bowl has disappeared; only snow, the beauty of nature, remains, now on a much larger scale. But natural beauty is not all; there is present also supernatural beauty—the black peak towering among snow-covered mountains, a seemingly discordant note which yet resolves the whole into harmony. This style goes beyond the limits of empirical reality and enters the infinitely deep realm of the mysterious. In turn, however, it is surpassed by the third kind of sublimity and the highest ideal of art, the *Style of a Mysterious Flower.* Zeami explains it by a line from a Chinese monk's saying: "In Silla the sun shines at midnight." This style, he adds, conveys "an imaginative landscape which is beyond verbal description as it lies in the realm of the absolute." The realm of the absolute, a term taken from Zen Buddhism, implies a sphere where there is neither good nor evil, right nor wrong, one nor all. The sun shining at midnight, in ordinary reality a flat contradiction, is perfectly acceptable in this surreal sphere. Silla, the present Korea, is east of China; the sun is shining brightly there when it is still night in China. A statement which appears preposterous to our ordinary senses may be a profound truth when viewed from a point which transcends the limitations of time and space. Far beyond everyday life, far beneath the conscious level of the mind, there is another order of reality of which tangible reality is but a shadow. A great work of art can introduce us into this other world; through it, even though but momentarily, we may touch on the absolute.

Zeami's aesthetics explains why the form of the Noh should be as it is. The essence of things is so deeply hidden that man's faculties barely reach it; its beauty is too beautiful for ordinary human senses to feel or perceive. A Noh writer assumes himself to be a seer; in his mystical experience he touches upon the essence of life and creates a beautiful vision out of it. He wants his audience to feel *yūgen* and the sublime, to see the vision with him.

Such a vision of life is best expressed in poetry. Thus the Noh is primarily poetry rather than drama; or it is poetry acted on the stage. Everything is highly stylized. The dialogue, in large part written in verse, is sung or chanted, accompanied by orchestral music and often by dancing as well. Every play has a musical structure, starting with a slow, regular rhythm and ending with a fast, irregular beat. The language of the Noh is poetic and emotive, making profuse use of allusions, metaphors, and symbols. The Noh stage is almost completely bare; if there is any stage property it has but slight resem-

blance to the actual object that it represents. The principal actor wears a mask, which makes it impossible for him to display his individuality through facial expression. All these artistic devices lead the audience away from reality toward the realm of the absolute where it is not the individual man and human society that matter, but the whole human race and the cosmos.

But what is this realm of the absolute? For the answer we must go to the Noh plays themselves. They were written precisely because the question could not be adequately answered in ordinary speech. Zeami's aesthetics, however, already suggests the direction the answer will take. To recapitulate briefly, his idea of the true intent implies the dual nature of reality: above our ordinary reality is a higher reality which works on man with its great, mysterious power. Before this power man is a tiny, insignificant existence; all he can do is submit himself to it. When he recognizes the universal law and sadly submits himself, there appears the beauty of *yūgen*; when he submits without sadness, there appears the beauty of the sublime. The latter form of submission signifies a state of mind so serene that it can calmly accept nature and art, life and death, time and eternity all as one; it is the perfection not only of art but of life. To attain such a state of mind requires that one be constantly aware there is nothing valuable in life; at all times one's eyes must be kept fixed on death. Yet the fact remains that man is a biological and social creature; in order to live he must fulfil certain physical, social, and moral laws. And here arises the Noh writers' concept that all living things are sinners, that sin is inherent in man.

It is no accident that a great number of Noh protagonists are men and women obsessed with the awareness of their sins. They really are not living persons but departed souls unable to rest in peace because they are so keenly aware of sins committed when they were living. Their sins, which seemingly vary in nature from play to play, are really one—a universal sin, the root of all evil. This fundamental sin stems from man's failure to recognize the great law that governs the universe, the law that rules over him before his birth, during his lifetime, and after his death. Man should conduct his life according to this timeless primary law before he follows manmade secondary laws. If one should see only the laws of the present world and lose sight of the transcendental law, it would be a reversal of values and constitute a fatal sin. The fact that a person has been morally perfect in his lifetime does not guarantee heaven for him after death. Thus we have many Noh plays in which the protagonist—a warrior of courage and loyalty, an artist of rare distinction, a child of great filial piety—suffers the torments of hell apparently without having committed any crime. All the Noh protagonists are, or have been, sinners except in a comparatively small number of plays called God Plays. (These are the exceptions because their heroes are gods who need not follow the ways of man.) Animals and plants too are doomed to suffer in hell; indeed some Noh plays have made this their theme. All living things are sinners; to live is to sin.

How, then, can anyone ever be saved? No man can save his fellow men, since all men are sinners. Salvation must come from a mighty power above men, God—Buddha, in medieval Japan. Thus the Noh drama has a Buddhist priest or monk for its deuteragonist. Since he is merely an agent of Buddha, there is no individuality in his physical and mental make-up; he is even without a name in many plays. Usually it is the priest who first appears on the stage and describes the setting to the audience. His function as a medium between the stage and the audience is indicative of his more important function as a medium between Buddha and man, helping man to perceive the true way of life and saving him from self-made hell. He is the link between a dream-world and the everyday world, the one who dreams and visualizes heaven and hell for us.

Frequently he is a wandering monk; oftentimes he visits Shinto shrines, thereby making himself holy in both the Buddhist and the Shinto sense. On his journey he meets the protagonist, the departed soul of a sinner who has come out of hell to ask for help. In the Noh drama it is always the sinner who brings about the encounter; the monk is a mere passer-by. The sinner, having come to a painful recognition of his sin, transforms himself so that he can come back into the present world and seek a way to salvation. In some plays he may even be engaged in a symbolic act of penance—offering water to a god or sweeping the garden of a shrine every day. When he meets the monk, he is at first too shy to confess his sin; when he tells the story of his sinful life he pretends that it has happened to someone else. Becoming more and more emotional as the story progresses, he asks the monk to pray for him, and disappears. Here the first part of the play ends. When the second part opens we see the monk praying for the peace of the sinner's soul. Thereupon the sinner reappears, no longer in disguise. Now he is not ashamed of revealing his true identity and confessing his sin. He performs a dance, the reenactment of his sin. This frank, bold confession indicates that he is fully aware of his sin, that he has courage enough to face it, and that he is truly repentant.

This ecstatic dance is the climax of the play. The audience as well as the monk now sees the protagonist's sin in its entirety. From the latter's point of view the dance also functions as a means of purgation. The protagonist has hitherto been obsessed with the constant awareness of his sin; now his excessive emotions are purged through this dance of confession. According to Freud, a person who is obsessed with the memory of a painful event tries to overcome his neurosis by going through a similar experience in his dreams. The protagonist of a Noh play does the same thing. He re-creates his past sinful act, experiences it once more, and thereby overcomes his obsession. After the dance we see the sinner attaining serenity of mind, at times even ascending to heaven.

The Noh drama, we may say then, provides a scheme of salvation, after leading the audience to the realization that all men are sinners. This, as we have seen, is done within a play. Yet this is also done within the pattern of a day's performance, on a larger scale. A Noh performance, if orthodox, consists of a sequence of five plays; a Noh play is never performed by itself. All plays in the Noh repertoire are classified into five categories according to the place they occupy in the sequence. The five types are commonly called, in the order of performance, God Plays, Man Plays, Woman Plays, Frenzy Plays, and Demon Plays. Each Noh play, while complete in itself, has a part to perform within the sequence as a whole, and in this larger context takes on greater scope and complexity of meaning.

A Noh performance starts with a God Play. The play prepares the audience for a mystical experience; it is the invocation of a god through a ritual. Since its protagonist is a god, this type of play differs somewhat in mood from those in the other categories. Divine blessing prevails over the world here: the god is exalted as the head of the cosmic hierarchy while the emperor is respected as the protector of social order. The world is devoid of sin; men and gods live in the same sphere. A man can even meet a god, as does the traveler in *The Old Pine Tree*. Moreover, the most virtuous of men can actually become immortal gods; God Tenjin was once a man. A God Play presents the world of innocence and man before his fall.

In the Man Play, the next in the sequence, we see a fallen man. The hero in most Man Plays is a warrior who once distinguished himself in battle but is now dead and suffering in hell. In *The Battle at Yashima,* for example, Yoshitsune is a Hector figure, not only valiant but honorable, the most popular figure in Japanese war-legends. The play portrays him as an ideal warrior fighting among soldiers who are all brave and noble, saving his honor at the risk of his life. Nonetheless, he must suffer the torments of hell after his death, and at the play's end we are still not sure of his salvation. Worldly honor is not condemned, but there is a higher value than that, and Yoshitsune did not recognize it while he was alive. Man has lost his innocence. Even though he has violated no moral law in his lifetime, even though he has done many a meritorious deed on earth, he has to go to hell when he dies. Unlike the peaceful, orderly world of a God Play, violence and chaos prevail over the world of a Man Play. Man's world has turned into a battlefield where the strong prosper and the weak perish.

In contrast to the epic forcefulness of a Man Play, lyrical gracefulness is the mood pervading a Woman Play, the third in the sequence. Just as the hero of a Man Play is a famed warrior perfect in military arts, the protagonist of a Woman Play usually is a lovely court lady most refined in artistic taste. Again the fact that she is an ideal woman measured by the medieval moral standard does not secure heaven for her; she cannot rest in peace after her death, and her soul sorrowfully haunts the present world. Many Woman Plays, however, differ somewhat from the Man Plays in depicting the protagonist not in her days of glory but in her time of penitence. In many Woman Plays the heroine is engaged in acts of penitence. The heroine of *The Woman within the Cypress Fence,* as an outward expression of her inner effort toward redemption, daily offers water to the gods. Water, a nature symbol signifying the source of life, is also a Buddhist symbol of karma, and her salvation is typically Buddhist: she gains calmness of mind through a contemplation of man's mortality. The play's mood approaches the sublime.

The fourth category in the sequence includes various kinds of plays, but the most representative is the so-called Frenzy Play. The world of a Frenzy Play is predominantly human; there is seldom a god, a ghost, or a demon involved. The protagonist is often a mother who has gone insane because her child was kidnaped. She goes on a lonely journey through many provinces in search of the lost little one, and at last by a miraculous coincidence mother and child are reunited. In Man and Woman Plays we have seen people suffering in hell after their death; now we realize that hell exists in our own world. At the same time we are shown that miracles are possible in man's world too, that a soul can be redeemed just as a lost child can be restored—but only if one dedicates oneself to that single purpose with such ardor that people think it madness.

Jinen the Preacher . . . is not a typical Frenzy Play. But in theme it is obviously in line with, or rather extends the line of, an ordinary Frenzy Play. Instead of a protagonist who is struggling for salvation, we have a priest who has already redeemed himself and is now engaged in saving others. The world he lives in is very human, with plenty of sins; in fact, there are even slave merchants transacting their degrading business. Jinen is a man of flesh and blood; he cracks jokes, and he can become a showman if the audience is sleepy. Yet Jinen is able to perform a miracle—he rescues a little girl from the slave merchants. A man, being a sinner, cannot save another; but Jinen is a redeemed man, almost a god.

A Demon Play, which concludes a Noh performance, describes a battle between a man and a demon. The protagonist is usually a terrifying monster or devil, but he is finally killed or forced to flee. In a Frenzy Play man conquers hell on earth; in a Demon Play he is victorious over the inhabitants of the underworld. The victor in this battle need not be an enlightened priest like Jinen. In *The Mirror of Pine Forest,* for example, a simple little country girl, by virtue of the intensity and steadfastness of her devotion to her late mother, is able to drive away a demon from Hades. Despite the supernatural element at the end, the play's world is very human. The father suspects his daughter of calling down curses on her stepmother; and the daughter imagines that her father is suffering pangs of conscience because he took a second wife too soon. It is, as the father says, a degenerate age when no miracle is likely to occur. Yet the playwright asserts that man may become a divine being, that transfiguration is still possible, if only he can devote his whole personality to the single purpose of loving another.

The performance of five Noh plays in orthodox sequence thus delineates man in innocence, fall, repentance, re-demption, and final glory. As the performance completes its cycle, the scheme of redemption is completed. But, as we have seen, the Noh writer's intent lay not so much in presenting Buddhist philosophy as in leading the audience into the mood of *yūgen* or the sublime. The audience would thoroughly enjoy the variety and change of mood from the ritualistic, slow-moving **Old Pine Tree** to the more realistic, quick-paced *Mirror of Pine Forest.*

The mood development throughout the cycle will become apparent if we observe the dance which climaxes each play. The first play has a solemn ritual dance, the second a vehement war dance, the third a graceful court dance, the fourth a suite of popular dances, and the fifth a dreadful demon dance. The structural unity of a Noh play is achieved through its rhythm and tempo rather than through plot or character development. Generally speaking, a Noh play starts with a slow, regular rhythm, often with a succession of alternating five- and seven-syllable lines. As the play proceeds the line length becomes more and more irregular, and the rhythm more and more diversified. Then, as the protagonist reveals himself to be a ghost, the sentences become fragmentary, the tempo quicker, the tone no longer subdued. The main actor's slow movements now turn to a lively dance. The beginning, the middle, and the ending of a Noh play may be compared to movements of a sonata: exposition, development, recapitulation.

The pattern of the Noh drama can be considerably changed within its general framework according to the individual plays chosen for presentation. One director may use for the Woman Play a gay piece with a young girl or a fairy as its protagonist; this will give a lighter tone to the whole sequence. Another director might select for the fourth play a typical Frenzy Play with an insane mother as the protagonist, which would give a grave, pathetic coloration to the cycle. It is a unique feature of the Noh drama that the director can give a different tone and color to the performance by varying his choice of plays. It has been assumed that there were more than two thousand plays in the repertoire in the golden years of the Noh. About eight hundred survive today.

In the Noh drama we see a typical example of medieval Japanese art. Art and religion were united in one, the former giving the form, the latter the content. Medieval Japanese Buddhism maintained that eternal truth, while it transcended the natural world, could be understood only through the objects in the natural world. The priests of the day expressed their ideas through images and symbols; in a sense they were all artists who transformed the invisible into the visible by means of symbolism. The artists, on the other hand, were well aware that true beauty lay hidden in the innermost nature of things, and in their attempt to grasp the buried truth they inevitably adopted a religious approach. The artists were priests who could evoke the spirits of the "other world" in the present life. This point is eloquently set forth by Zeami:

> If I illustrate my purport by the principle of two ways in Buddhism, being and nonbeing, then the appearance

will correspond to being and the vessel to nonbeing. To take an example, a crystal, although it is a pure, transparent object without color or pattern, produces fire and water. Why is it that two entirely heterogeneous things like fire and water emerge out of one transparent object? A poem says:

Smash a cherry tree,
And you will find no blossom
In the splinters.
It is in the sky of spring
That cherry blossoms bloom.

The seed for the flower of art is the artist's soul which has a power to feel. As a crystal body produces fire and water or a colorless cherry tree bears blossoms and fruit, so does a superb artist create a variety of works out of his imaginative scenery. Such a man may be called a vessel. Works of art, treating the wind and the moon or flowers and birds, accompanying a festival or a picnic, are many and various. The universe creates thousands of things as the seasons roll on—blossoms and leaves, the snow and the moon, mountains and seas, trees and grass, the animate and the inanimate. The artist should try to attain the Mysterious Flower by letting these numerous things be the materials of his art, by making his soul the vessel of the universe, and by setting the vessel in the vast, windless way of emptiness.

The passage sums up the aesthetics not alone of the Noh but of all art forms in medieval Japan.

This attitude is essentially different from that of Western dramatists. In the drama of the Hellenic tradition one is always aware of one's identity as different from the others, from the objects in nature, from Fate, from Fortune. Western playwrights thus present a man clashing with Fate or running after Fortune. But classical Japanese dramatists had little objective awareness of external reality, since they thought themselves to be part of nature. In their way of thinking, man had no free will (hence no tragedy); nor was he a social or moral creature (hence no comedy). Their image of an ideal man was a person liberated from the perishable self, a man who would live in the three worlds, past, present, and future, according to the great cosmic law. Naturally all they wrote were religious plays which described the inherent sin in man and suggested a possible way to salvation. The Noh drama shows this tradition in its most beautiful, mature, and sophisticated form.

Donald Keene (essay date 1970)

SOURCE: "The Conventions of the Nō Drama" and introductions to *Komachi at Sekidera* (*Sekidera Komachi*), *The Brocade Tree* (*Nishikigi*), *Semimaru, The Deserted Crone* (*Obasute*), *Lady Han* (*Hanjo*), and *The Reed Cutter* (*Ashikari*), in *Twenty Plays of the Nō Theatre,* edited by Donald Keene with Royall Tyler, Columbia Univer-

sity Press, 1970, pp. 1-15, 66-7, 82-3, 100-01, 116-17, 130-31, 148-49.

[*In the excerpts below, Keene discusses some of the difficulties inherent in establishing a canon of Zeami's works, and he offers brief introductions to six of his plays.*]

The difficulties confronting the would-be critic of Nō are enormous. Not a single play is dated, and all we can infer about even the most famous works is the date before which they must have been composed, information perhaps gleaned from a diary entry mentioning a performance. Some plays can be dated only by century, and others seem to have been rewritten so often that the establishment of a single date of composition would be impossible. Even when we know that a play with a certain title was performed, say, in the fifteenth century, it is by no means clear that this is the same work currently performed with that title. *Dōjōji* was formerly attributed to Kan'ami (1333-1384); it has recently been attributed by careful scholars to Nobumitsu (1435-1516); but other authorities are convinced that in its present form it cannot be older than the late sixteenth century. A few texts have been miraculously preserved in Zeami's own handwriting. Some are of plays no longer performed, but those of plays in the current repertory differ so conspicuously from their present versions as to throw doubt on claims by the schools of Nō that they have preserved unaltered the authentic traditions of the past. The dating of the plays is further complicated by the fact that they were written in an artificial poetic language that only inadvertently reflected current speech; this meant that the differences in language separating, say, Shakespeare and Congreve, do not distinguish a Nō play of the fourteenth century from one of the sixteenth.

The authorship of the plays is almost as perplexing as the dating. Before 1940 scholars generally accepted the traditional attributions that gave credit to Zeami for about half the plays in the repertory of some 240 works. The application of more rigorous standards drastically reduced the number of plays attributed to Zeami, and some scholars now hesitate to allow him more than a dozen or so. Zeami undoubtedly borrowed and modified works by his father Kan'ami and other early dramatists to suit the audiences of his own time, and these revised plays were further modified after his death. The main outlines of the plays and much of the poetry might remain essentially unchanged, but innumerable variants cropped up in the prose sections. The five schools of Nō each insist that their own texts are the only authentic ones, and they sometimes have their own traditions about the authorship as well.

Attributions of the plays were formerly based chiefly on various lists prepared in the sixteenth and seventeenth centuries, but these lists are no longer trusted. Too often they credited plays to Zeami, rather than admit that the author was unknown. Today scholars recognize as genuine works by Zeami only those mentioned by name in his critical writings. Zeami quoted extracts from different plays, and we know that he identified by author only works by other men; an extract not followed by the author's name must therefore have been from a play by Zeami himself. However, the insistence on a mention in Zeami's critical works may be imposing too rigorous a criterion. It is possible that he failed to mention all of his plays in his criticism, and some plays may have been written after the critical works relied on for dating. It is difficult otherwise to imagine who else could have written such masterpieces as *The Shrine in the Fields* (*Nonomiya*) or *Yuya,* works now listed merely as "anonymous" by meticulous scholars.

Attributions on the basis of style have also been attempted. It obviously does not make much sense to speak about a dramatist's style if his works were all revised again and again by later men; nevertheless, critics customarily praise Kan'ami's "strength and simplicity," Zeami's *yūgen* (or style of mystery and depth), Motomasa's pathos, Miyamasu's realism, or Zenchiku's philosophical loftiness. But surely no one reading *Matsukaze,* attributed to Kan'ami, would be struck by its "strength and simplicity"; perhaps his original play was so extensively revised by Zeami and others as to remove any personal imprint. The danger of making attributions on the basis of preconceptions as to a dramatist's distinctive manner is obvious, but some critics feel so sure of their grasp of Zeami's style as to be able to declare, for example, that *The Shrine in the Fields* cannot have been written by Zeami because the last word is a noun (*kataku,* the Burning House) and Zeami always ended his plays with verbs. Certainly the style of a play offers important clues both to the authorship and the date, but as yet it is not possible to do more than suggest with varying degrees of confidence some twenty-five plays that may be by Zeami. Not only do we lack information on the dates of these plays, but we have no way of establishing their relative order. It is as if we were able to decide on the basis of internal and external evidence that both *Romeo and Juliet* and *King Lear* were by Shakespeare, but had no idea which work came earlier in his career or if Shakespeare merely revised the work of a predecessor.

Studies of Nō as a literary form are still in their infancy, though the history of the Nō theatre and the techniques of performance have been investigated with diligence and sometimes with brilliant results. Japanese critics have generally contented themselves with describing the characteristic style of the poetry as a "brocade" consisting of lovely bits and pieces of old poetry. The extensive borrowing from such collections as *Kokinshū* ("Collection of Poems Old and New," 905) and *Wakan Rōei Shū* ("Collection of Japanese and Chinese Poems for Reading Aloud," c. 1010) sometimes does indeed suggest a "brocade" of allusions, but the Nō plays clearly possess a distinctive style of their own. Because drama fell outside the range of interest of traditional scholars of Japanese literature it was left to Yeats to point out the patterns of symbols in the plays, a remark that inspired some Japanese scholars for the first time to examine the recurring imagery that is so characteristic a feature of

Zeami's style [William Butler Yeats, *Certain Noble Plays of Japan*].

The evolving style of the Nō plays can also be traced in terms of the degree of conformity to the "standard" models. Zeami himself cited his work **Yumi Yawata** as a paradigmatic example of Nō, but hardly another play in the repertory conforms exactly to its formulae. It is nonetheless true that plays of Zeami's time tend to follow a set form. With respect to the division into parts, for example, there is little deviation from the established categories: *shite,* the principal character, the only true "person"; *waki,* or secondary actor, whose arrival on the scene introduces the story and who asks the questions the audience itself might ask; and *tsure,* or companion, who may accompany either the *shite* or *waki,* but rarely rises above being a shadow. Some of the older works of the repertory (like *Shōkun*) seem to have been composed before the standard roles (*shite, waki,* and so on) had been evolved, and the present divisions seem arbitrary and unnecessary. Even Zeami's works do not always follow the paradigms of composition: in **Lady Han** (*Hanjo*), for example, the *kyōgen* part is vital to the action and not merely a diversion. But such departures from the standard seem minor when compared to those in pre-Zeami or post-Zeami plays. In **Komachi and the Hundred Nights** (*Ka, i Komachi*), for example, Komachi is the *tsure,* but far from being a mere "companion" to the *shite* is his antagonist. *Hatsuyuki* by Zemp (c. 1474-c. 1520) altogether lacks a *waki* part. The *shite* part in *The Valley Rite* (*Taniko*) is so minor the character does not utter a word. In other late works the distinction between *shite* and *waki* is so vague that the nomenclature differs according to the school.

In terms of the roles, then, one can say that before Zeami the distinctions were probably fluid; with Zeami they attained a "classical" definition; but after Zeami the conventions increasingly tended to break down in face of new demands by the audiences. A similar pattern of development can be described with respect to other aspects of Nō. The art gradually reached maturity late in the fourteenth century, largely thanks to the patronage by the shogun's court. Nō had originally developed as a popular theatre, and its repertory consisted mainly of plays on religious themes presented at Buddhist temples and Shinto shrines throughout the country. But when the shogun Ashikaga Yoshimitsu decided in 1374 to extend his patronage to the art, it changed its character. The texts were embellished with quotations from the poetry and prose of the past, no doubt to please members of the shogun's court who had literary pretensions; but this meant that the illiterate commoners who had formerly supported Nō were gradually forgotten by the playwrights who turned their backs on dramatic or didactic themes in favor of aesthetic excellence. Zeami especially delighted in literary display, even when it led to a static dramatic situation. The speech in **Komachi and the Hundred Nights** in which Komachi describes the fruits and nuts she has gathered, giving a poetic allusion for each, contributes nothing to the action, but it helps create a mood that is associated with Zeami, who added this section to the less ornamented text by Kan'ami.

With Zeami Nō attained its classic form and its highest level of literary distinction. Although Zeami also composed some works in a realistic manner, his plays are known especially for their *yūgen,* a haunting poetic quality both in the language and in the overall effects. ***Komachi at Sekidera (Sekidera Komachi)*** is perhaps the supreme example of *yūgen* in Nō. There is almost no plot to the play—some priests take a young disciple to hear from an old woman the secrets of poetry and gradually become aware she is the celebrated poet Komachi—and the *shite* is virtually immobile during the first hour of the performance, but the poetry and the atmosphere it creates make this play incredibly moving. . . .

. . . The patterns of poetry and prose vary from play to play, but they present as a whole a distinctive literary form. The frequent use of quotations is a literary convention, and a text which made few references to the poetry found in the famous anthologies would seem thin and without overtones. Nō is deeply concerned with Japanese poetic traditions. Not only are many poems embedded in the dialogue, but poetry itself is the subject of such plays as ***Komachi at Sekidera,*** and a principal theme of ***The Reed Cutter (Ashikari).*** It would not be normal for characters in a European drama to relate the principles of the art of poetry and give examples of favorite works, but this is precisely what we find in these plays. In the Nō theatre many different arts—poetry, music, dance, and mime—converge, at a level that does justice to all.

The Nō theatre makes maximum demands on the audience. The texts are difficult and the relatively scant mimetic elements contribute more to establishing the inner tensions of the characters than to clarifying the words or actions. Some plays indeed are so exceedingly slow-moving as to lull a sizable part of the audience to sleep. But precisely because it takes this risk Nō succeeds in its unique domain.

. . . . .

Komachi at Sekidera belongs to the third category. It was probably written by Zeami, though some authorities hesitate to make the attribution. The play is considered to be the loftiest and most difficult of the entire Nō repertory. In the past century only a few great actors at the close of their careers have ventured to perform it. It enjoys its high reputation because it celebrates, with the most exquisite simplicity, the bittersweet delight of being alive. Childhood, maturity, extreme old age, the pleasure and pain of life, are immediately communicated. The play conveys a timeless moment in the brief interval between birth and death. Its subject is poetry. Much of the great poetry in Nō lies somewhat outside the main Japanese poetic traditions, but ***Komachi at Sekidera*** is at once a superb Nō play and a splendid expression of the sources of Japanese poetry. The *shite* role is consid-

ered so difficult because there is little an actor can add to the text unless he is supremely gifted. During the first hour of the performance Komachi hardly stirs.

The setting is wonderfully appropriate. The time is the festival of Tanabata, the seventh night of the seventh month: the one night of the year when the Cowherd star can cross the River of Heaven to join the Weaver-girl star. On earth all are celebrating the lovers' brief reunion. Even at Sekidera, a place of quiet renunciation, the priests and child acolytes are about to observe the festival. But while talking about poetry with the aged woman who lives in a hut nearby, the abbot of the temple discovers she is none other than Ono no Komachi.

Komachi, a woman of great beauty and literary gifts, lived at the Heian court during the ninth century. She became a legend in later times, with many apocryphal stories surrounding the few known biographical facts. Five Nō plays about Komachi are in the present repertory; ***Komachi and the Hundred Nights*** presents another aspect of the Komachi legend, and *Sotoba Komachi* (translated in Keene, *Anthology of Japanese Literature*) ranks nearly on a level with ***Komachi at Sekidera.***

The structure of the play is classic, and remarkable for its economy and simplicity. Nothing jars, nothing is wasted. The moment when Komachi admits her identity to the Abbot is particularly touching because so unaffected.

Sekidera ("The Barrier Temple") still exists at Ōtsu, a city east of Kyoto; its modern name is Chōanji.

Komachi at Sekidera is in the repertory of all schools of Nō.

. . . . .

The Brocade Tree belongs to the fourth category, and is by Zeami. The *Shūchūshō,* a late twelfth-century work, quotes the following verse:

My brocade trees
Number a full thousand;
Now I shall see within
Her chamber forbidden to other men.

It goes on to explain *nishikigi,* "brocade trees," as follows: "When an Ebisu man in the interior of Michinoku wishes to propose to a girl, he does not write her a letter. Instead, he decorates a stick about a foot long with different colors, and sets it in the ground before the girl's gate. If the girl wishes to meet him, she immediately takes it into her house. If she is slow to do so, her suitor plants more. By the time he has planted a thousand, the girl sees that he really is sincere, so she takes them in and the two meet. If she does not take them in, her suitor gives up. The poem just quoted is by a man whose thousand brocade trees have brought him success." The Ebisu were a "barbarian," probably non-Japanese, people. Michinoku is the area at the northern end of Honshu.

On *hosonuno,* the "narrow cloth of Kefu," the same source quotes the poem,

> The narrow kefu cloth of Michinoku
> Is so very narrow
> That it will not meet across my breasts;
> Just so is my unrequited love!

The *Mumyōshō,* also of the late twelfth century, says, "Narrow kefu cloth is a cloth made in Michinoku. It is woven of feathers. Since this material is scarce, a narrow loom is used and only short lengths of cloth are made." In the play, *kefu* is used as a place name. No such village exists, however. *Kefu* is simply the name of the cloth.

Some Japanese critics admit that the happy tone of the ending of **The Brocade Tree** comes as rather a surprise, but they do not feel that this detracts from the play's quality. Good though it is, however, the play is not often performed.

Ezra Pound's version of **The Brocade Tree,** based on an unpublished translation by Ernest Fenollosa, is too far from the original to qualify as a translation. . . . **The Brocade Tree** is performed by all schools of Nō.

. . . . .

Semimaru, a work of the fourth category, was written by Zeami. The story of Semimaru, the blind *biwa* player—the *biwa* is a kind of lute—appears as early as the twelfth-century collection of tales, *Konjaku Monogatari,* but apparently has no historical basis. The *Konjaku Monogatari* version relates that Semimaru lived near the barrier of Ōsaka, between Kyoto and Lake Biwa. Once he had been in the service of a courtier, a famous *biwa* master, and learned to play by listening to his master. Minamoto Hakuga, the son of a prince, heard of Semimaru's skill and wished to bring him to the Capital. Semimaru, however, refused. So eager was he to hear Semimaru's *biwa* that Hakuga journeyed to Mt. Ōsaka, a wild and distant place in those days, though today a half-hour journey from Kyoto.

By the time of the writing of the *Heike Monogatari,* a century later, Semimaru had become known as the fourth son of the Emperor Daigo (r. 897-930). Like the Semimaru of the *Konjaku Monogatari,* he lived by a barrier, but it was the one at Shinomiya Kawara. A man named Hakuga no Sammi was so anxious to hear him play that he visited Semimaru's hut every day, rain or shine, for three years without fail.

Zeami borrowed from various versions of the legend of Semimaru as known in his day, but especially from the *Heike Monogatari.* No previous version of the story, however, mentions Princess Sakagami, who was apparently Zeami's creation. **Semimaru** is one of the rare plays in which the *tsure* (Semimaru) is nearly as important as

the *shite* (Sakagami); another such play is **Komachi and the Hundred Nights**.

Semimaru is perhaps the most tragic play of the entire Nō repertory. Unlike *The Sought-for Grave,* in which Unai returns to earth to tell of her endless torments in hell, the tragedy of **Semimaru** takes place in this world, and involves two human beings who are nearly as real and immediate to us as characters in Western drama.

During the height of the fanatical nationalism of the 1930s and 1940s **Semimaru** was banned from the stage for its alleged disrespect to the Imperial Family, but today it is performed by all schools of Nō.

. . . . .

The Deserted Crone, a play belonging to the third category, seems unmistakably a work by Zeami. Sanari Kentarō, the editor of the great collection of Nō plays *Yōkyoku Taikan,* summed up the play aptly: "An old woman has been abandoned deep in the mountains. Dressed in white robes, she dances a quiet dance in a landscape brightly lit by the moon. She utters hardly a word of complaint but, resigned to the world, confines herself to expounding the Buddhist teaching of nonattachment. . . . This play surely must be close to the apex of Zeami's *yūgen.*"

The source of the legend of the "deserted crone" may be found in an anonymous poem in the *Kokinshū* (no. 878):

> No solace for my heart at Sarashina
> When I see the moon
> Shining down on Mount Obasute.

The tenth-century poem-tale *Yamato Monogatari,* which gives the same poem, explains that it was written by a man who, at the urging of his wife, had carried his aged aunt into the mountains on a moonlit night and abandoned her there. The next day he regretted his action and brought her back home. The mountain became known as Obasute-yama, the Mountain of the Deserted Crone. However, Fujiwara Toshiyori is reported in the thirteenth-century book of criticism *Mumyōshō* to have said that the poem was composed by the old woman herself, as she gazed at the moon from the place where she was abandoned. Zeami followed the latter version.

Evidence in other sources indicates that at certain times and places old people were indeed taken out into the wilderness and left there, probably in order to conserve the limited food supply of a village. A small body of literature exists on this theme, going down to our time.

The moon is prominently mentioned in many Nō plays, often as a symbol of Buddhist enlightenment, but no other play is as filled with moonlight as **The Deserted Crone.** Sarashina, the site of Mount Obasute, was famous for moon-viewing, and the action of the play takes place on the night when the moon is at its brightest, the "famous moon" of the eighth month. The entire fabric of the play is filled with the atmosphere of a longing melancholy under the "pure full disc of light." The moon descends, and as the play concludes the spirit of the old woman remains behind in the thin glow of dawn, a cold and lonely wraith unable to break away from mortal attachments to the world.

The Deserted Crone is performed by all schools except Komparu.

. . . . .

Lady Han, a play of the fourth category, is one of Zeami's most romantic works. In several Nō plays the *shite* goes mad with grief over the loss of her child, but Hanago is one of only two *shite* in plays of the current repertory who goes mad because of love. Even rarer is the completely happy ending.

No source for *Lady Han* has been found. Hanago's nickname, Hanjo or Lady Han, refers to Han Shōyo (Pan Chieh-yü in Chinese), a poetess of the Early Han dynasty. The lady was a favorite of the Emperor Ch'eng Ti (c. 36-32 B.C.), but was eventually replaced in his affections by an even more celebrated beauty. The discarded favorite wrote a poem comparing herself to a fan in autumn. The round, white fan also resembles the moon, a typical sight of autumn. Zeami alludes to this poem again and again in the course of the play. Other allusions to Chinese poems in the collection *Wakan Rōei Shū* ("Collection of Japanese and Chinese Poems for Recitation Aloud") and to Po Chü-i's famous *Everlasting Lament* sustain the Chinese mood of the imagery.

Lady Han begins with a long *kyōgen* passage. This unusual expository device was given special dramatic value by Zeami. The *waki* part is unusual too: Instead of being a priest or a courtier, the *waki* is Hango's lover, Yoshida. Any suggestion of romantic love was generally avoided on the Nō stage, and the part of one of the lovers would be taken by a child in order to remove erotic overtones, but Yoshida is a full romantic character. Some scholars, however, have suggested that the part of Yoshida may originally have been played by a child, and that the *waki* role was assigned to a traveler or some other character not now in the text, but this remains conjectural.

The play is considered to be about a madwoman, a standard variety of fourth-category plays, but Hanago's madness does not express itself in lunatic behavior. She is obsessed with her memories of the lover who failed to return, so much so that she fails to recognize him when at last she sees him again. Her madness seems to express itself also in an exaggerated form of a typical literary device of Nō, the accidental associations of words. Saying the words *itsu made,* "until when," carries her to *itsumadegusa,* the name of a plant; then to the dew that settles on the plant; then to the time it takes for the dew to evaporate; then (from the shortness of that time) to her main theme, her love and its brevity; then to mention of famous lovers of the past; and finally to what

appears to be an attempt to check herself in her rambling, the question as to how we know today what words the lovers of the past exchanged in private. Certainly such chains of associations are not unique to plays describing "madness," but they contribute in *Lady Han* to its atmosphere of distraught love.

Lady Han is performed by all schools of Nō.

. . . . .

The Reed Cutter belongs to the fourth category of plays. It is generally attributed to Zeami, though he may have adapted an older work. The source of the story is the *Shūishū,* an imperial collection of poetry compiled in the late tenth century. Two poems with their prose preface supplied the outlines of the story: "When a certain woman went to Naniwa for a purification ceremony, she met on the way a man who had formerly been her lover. He was now a reed cutter, and presented a most peculiar appearance. Somewhat disconcerted, she remarked that they had not met for a long time. The man replied,

> As I cut reeds without you
> I knew I had been wrong;
> Life here by Naniwa Bay
> Has grown so melancholy.

She answered,

> You did no wrong.
> 'Fare thee well,' we said,
> As our parting words:
> Why should life by Naniwa Bay
> Have grown so melancholy?"

A much fuller account is given in the tenth-century poem-tale *Yamato Monogatari.* A wellborn couple has fallen on hard times. The husband urges the wife to seek employment in the Capital, promising he will join her if his own fortunes improve. The wife succeeds in finding a position in a nobleman's household, and the nobleman eventually marries her when his wife dies. But she continues to worry about her former husband, and goes to Naniwa to look for him. Their old house has vanished, but she finds the husband, attired like a peddler and selling reeds. When she offers to buy his reeds the man recognizes her and, ashamed to be seen in his humble appearance, runs off and hides in a hut. The lady sends a servant after him, but he refuses to come out. Instead he and his wife exchange the poems translated above. She also gives the man her outer cloak before she returns to the Capital alone.

The play modifies the *Yamato Monogatari* story, especially in its ending. It is unusually long, and abounds in plays on words and allusions to old texts. It is notable also for its sympathetic treatment of marital love.

The Reed Cutter is performed by all schools of Nō.

Tatsuro Ishii   (essay date 1983)

SOURCE: "Zeami on Performance," in *Theatre Research International,* n.s. Vol. VIII, No. 3, Autumn, 1983, pp. 190-206.

[*In the essay below, Tatsuro explores Zeami's insistence that performances of Nō must consider such factors as the time, the location, and the audience in order to be successful. According to Zeami, the critic observes, a "good performer . . . is not only sustained by his inborn talent and incessant training but also is the one whose instinctive judgement and creativity harmonize with the mood and atmosphere at the very moment of each performance."*]

Since the survival of Noh theatre at the time of Zeami (1363-1443) and Kanami depended entirely upon the support of its audience, which consisted mainly of laymen, warriors and nobles, it was essential that each presentation had its own unique beauty and power enabling each performance to become an unrepeatable idiosyncratic event. In particular, Zeami demands that each performance will attain the goals of *hana* (the *flower,* i.e. a strangeness and novelty in beauty that will attract the audience) and *yūgen* (a mystic quality of beauty and elegance) on stage. In order to achieve these goals, he provides us with a great deal of suggestive and analytical ideas from various points of view, ranging from precise technical comments to pure metaphysical concepts.

Zeami appears to have been well conscious of the fact that training is one thing and performance quite another. A performance is forced to change because of the many distinctive elements which structure each individual presentation. In **Kadensho,** we first encounter Zeami's thoughts on the singularity of events in a performance when we read of *in* (*yin*) and *yō* (*yang*), a dualistic principle which is considered to permeate the entire space of a performance.

Although the concept of *yin/yang* presents itself in both Taoism and Confucianism, its origin can be traced back to a philosophy which predates both in ancient China. The *yin/yang* doctrine teaches that all phenomena in the universe are brought into being by the interactions of two opposing, yet complementary forces; they are the universal polarities and one cannot stand alone without the other. The *yin* principle symbolizes the negative, centrifugal, passive, dark side of nature, and the *yang* symbolizes the positive, centripetal, active and light side. Evidence of the *yin/yang* principle can be seen everywhere and at every time. Some common examples are cold/hot, winter/summer, water/fire, wet/dry, night/day, repose/movement, etc. Since *yin* and *yang* are reciprocally co-existent, not exclusive, they must be accepted simultaneously.

Zeami takes this principle of *yin* and *yang,* and applies it to Noh performance. He tells us that the accomplishment of a presentation comes about only when all its elements are in harmony with this principle. Zeami goes on to point out that it is of particular significance to be aware of the *yin/yang* concept in which a performance is to be given and that an attempt must be made to balance that context in accordance with this principle.

It is a good policy, for instance, that when a Noh performance is to take place during the day, the mood of the presentation should be that of *yin,* i.e. quiet and restrained, since this would balance the natural daytime spirit of brightness and activity. Conversely it would be quite appropriate for an evening performance to be in the *yang* mood, for then the spirit of the audience would be more subdued and the presentation should be able to balance that with a bright and active performance. However, it should be kept in mind that these are merely examples which are meant to illustrate a more fundamental and flexible principle, which points out that the performers of Noh should constantly be aware of the ever changing mood of the audience and of the variables which go into making up the performance space, and adjust themselves accordingly so as to attain harmonious balance of *yin* and *yang.*

Zeami states quite positively that without this proper harmony of *yin* and *yang,* the performance can neither enhance the audience's interest nor achieve success. The harmony of *yin* and *yang* in his speculations is quite clearly indicated by the conditions in which all the essential elements of a performance, such as actors, audiences, time, space, etc. are coordinated with each other in a complementary symbiotic fashion, which leads to the 'achievement' of a performance.

It is quite natural for us to expect that if the various contributing elements of a performance are in their optimal state, the result should approach excellence. However, Zeami in the latter part of **Kadensho** discusses the possibility of an unsuccessful performance even when the performer and the text are of excellent quality. This question of why a performance based on a good text and executed by an expert performer sometimes fails to achieve success is one which remains unresolved by Zeami throughout his works, and shows up in **Shūgyoku-Tokuka** which is separated by more than twenty years from **Kadensho** where it was first posited. In **Shūgyoku-Tokuka** he states: 'Even though an expert performer gives a superb performance, there may exist a superiority or inferiority in the performance depending upon where or when it takes place. This might be due to the unharmonious balance of *yin* and *yang* between the mood of the performance and the atmosphere of its environment.'

It appears that for Zeami a performance should maintain a fluid quality somewhat like water so that it may be poured into the metaphorical vessels of time and space. A performance of Noh in Zeami's mind, unlike the impression we get from today's Noh performances, must have been much more flexible and spontaneous. There should be a number of indeterminate variables delicately at play even within the context of strictly defined and stylized form. Noh performance must bring to each occasion a developed sense of spontaneity. This idea is made clear in the last section of *Kadensho*:

> The sutra says, 'Good and evil are not dual; right and wrong are one.' How can we fix the essential distinction between good and evil? We can only regard that which satisfies the need of the moment as good and what does not as bad. Also concerning the variety of styles in this art, the style which is selected according to the people and the place and the day and in conformity with general present preference is the Flower for it satisfies the need. While people here appreciate one style, there people enjoy another. This shows that the conception of the Flower varies with the person and the mind. Which of them can we define as being the genuine Flower? Know that only that which satisfies the need of the occasion is the Flower.

The idea of achievement or fulfilment in the performance becomes clearer as we begin to understand the harmonious balance which needs to be attained in the physical and metaphysical dynamics of *yin* and *yang* and the related structural elements of *jo/ha/kyū*. The delicate interaction between the diachronic aspect of *jo/ha/kyū* and the synchronic aspect of *yin* and *yang* is one worthy of a further explanation. *Jo/ha/kyū* (introduction-development-climax), being time based and applied to every aspect of performance, is intended to engender a sense of completion through a development process over a certain period of time, whereas the principle of *yin* and *yang* is more of an atmosphere or mood which allows a performance to materialize.

The element of time in Zeami's writings takes into account the effect on the performance space brought about by chronological changes such as day, night, and the seasons. For example, if we take into consideration the fact that in the era of technological simplicity where lighting effects were realized through the use of torches, it is easy to imagine that a day performance was drastically different from one taking place at night. Climatic conditions would also have affected the mood of a performance since a great number of performances took place outdoors.

The element of space is most elaborated upon in *Kadensho*. It can be divided into two categories, one being the district where a performance takes place, i.e. urban or rural, the other being the actual physical structure of the theatre itself, such as the residence of a noble, a temple or a shrine etc.

Judging from some passages in Zeami's works, it appears that some form of competition among different troupes of performers was occasionally carried out, which may have been somewhat similar to those held in the era of ancient Greek theatre. It is through these competitions that we are introduced to another dualistic concept, *medoki* (female time) and *odoki* (male time), the context of which can be thought of as being close to that of the *yin/yang* principle.

Medoki and *odoki* respectively refer to the bad or good luck which may dominate the time and space of a match or game. When luck is against a particular player and everything he does turns out negatively, he may be in *medoki*. On the other hand, if his luck is favourable and everything turns out positively, he is in *odoki*. Zeami tells us—and it is by and large believed by the Japanese people—that on the occasion of a long contest the *odoki* and *medoki* change sides from time to time. A performer should be moderate and temperate in his performance at the time of Noh competition when he thinks he is faced with *medoki*, and wait patiently for the momentum to shift, at which time *odoki* will return to his side and his performance and choice of plays to be performed will be greatly improved.

Both concepts of *odoki/medoki* and *yin/yang* in Zeami's treatises show us that there is some unseen power of *time* working in this universe, against which man should not struggle. If time functions in accordance with its own laws, a performance of Noh is not so much a creation opposed to time as a delicately evolving process developing in harmony with time. In *Kadensho* Zeami wrote succinctly: 'Be humble in the presence of time.'

The basic purpose of the *yin/yang* principle in his works lies in his desire to keep the performance as flexible as possible so as to guard a performer from becoming completely influenced by his own creative consciousness while ignoring all the other elements that surround him; this power is generated by every element which exists in the space of each performance—the particular season, day or night, locale, theatre, audience and so on.

Although time and discipline are demanded for the acquisition of the various styles and forms and there seems very little room in this mosaic structure for the individual creativity of a performer, it becomes increasingly apparent that the ultimate spirit of Noh theatre consists of a great degree of freedom within the performance. The principle of *yin* and *yang* in Zeami's writings also seems to reveal another lifelong desire, that is, to link the performance of Noh theatre to something beyond the human realm.

One of the characteristics seen in *Kadensho* and later treatises of Zeami is that the art of performing in Noh is examined from the perspective of an audience. It is also interesting to note a subtle change in his notion concerning the relation of performance and audience as he matures. Although the audience is an indispensable component in all styles of theatre, there are very few theoreticians of theatre who take it as seriously as Zeami does, and who are willing to give it the degree of consideration that we find throughout his works.

Zeami insists on the intellectual and emotional balance that must be maintained between the audience and performers. The more profound and internalized a performance becomes, the more narrowly it appeals to the people. The ideal relationship between a performer and his audience is one in which an actor performs from the point of view of the audience, and the audience sees the performance from the standpoint of the performer. Therefore, certain demands are put on the spectator in order that he may gain a profound level of appreciation of Noh theatre.

His first essay, **Kadensho,** can be characterized by the use of frequent references to the audience, and by its emphatic awareness of the audience in the presentation of Noh theatre. We can imagine that Zeami must have hoped a performance would have a mesmerizing effect on an audience much in the same way as an ancient shaman would have on the people around himself. *Hana,* which is the central concept of **Kadensho,** is nothing but this effect which arouses the feelings of novelty, strangeness and interest in the mind of an audience; these are all somewhat similar qualities to those brought about by the actions of a shaman.

The main features of Zeami's ideas on the audience in **Kadensho** can be summarized as follows: (1) it is imperative that Noh theatre gain the support of the masses; (2) a performer should pay particular attention to the nobility; and (3) a definition of the distinction among the various classifications of the audiences.

Zeami presumably inherited the idea that the art of Noh has to be supported by vast public esteem from his father, Kanami, who mainly performed in the rural districts and had to be supported by the general public in these areas. Noh theatre, says Zeami, must impress even the 'foolish eye.'

> In this area, public favour and esteem afford the blessings for the establishment of the company. Therefore, performance exclusively in a style too inaccessible to the ordinary audience will again cause failure to win the public. For this reason, the way of obtaining the blessing is that, bearing in mind your novitiate in the Noh, you perform the Noh in a manner varying with the circumstances, so as to impress even the foolish eye as something indeed interesting.

We have to take into consideration the fact that, in the period of Kanami, when the present form of Noh was gradually taking shape, the performance of Noh theatre was quite free of any style and form. The theatre existed mainly for the entertainment of the general public, not for any privileged sectors of society.

Zeami, on the other hand, had the strong support of the Shogun, Yoshimitsu, the most powerful man of that period, whose attention he gained at the age of twelve. While under his patronage, he began the refinement of the various aspects of Noh theatre by deepening its artistic quality with an added emphasis on the elements of dance and music. Zeami, unlike his father, enhanced his artistic sense in urban aristocratic culture, and it is reasonable to assume that he must have found cognoscenti of his work among the nobility and warriors of the period.

Zeami, then, was faced with the problem of trying to resolve two apparently contradictory ideas, one that the art of Noh must please the masses, the other that somehow it should remain centred on the nobility. This invites a comparison to the idea in *Nātya-Sāstra,* an ancient Indian theory of theatre and dance, that a drama must appeal to all the different elements within a society.

> A drama teaches duty to those who go against duty, love to those who are eager for its fulfilment, and it chastises those who are ill-bred or unruly, promotes self-restraint in those who are undisciplined, gives courage to cowards, energy to heroic persons, enlightens men of poor intellect and gives wisdom to the learned.

However, with the concept of *rasa* we can see the concern that Indian theoreticians had with the problem of mass appeal versus elitist recognition:

> Just as well-disposed persons, while eating food cooked with many kinds of spice, enjoy its tastes, and attain pleasure and satisfaction, so the cultured people taste the Durable Psychological States while they see them represented by an expression of the various Psychological States with Words, Gestures and the Sattva, and derive pleasure and satisfaction.

Although we may feel that it was ambivalent or contradictory for Zeami or Bharata to deal with the problems of elite and mass audiences in the manner we have discussed, we can conclude that it was their sincere desire that a theatre should gain mass favour while at the same time realize that the fullest appreciation could be achieved only by a minority of the spectators. Neither *yūgen* nor *rasa* is a concept that is expected to affect the members of an entire audience. Another significant concept of Zeami, *hana,* may fulfil this function more readily since its emphasis lies primarily in the external visual stage effects.

It is astonishing to notice how Zeami states in **Kadensho** that the mature performer who has acquired a variety of skills should be able to satisfy people whose level of appreciation may vary ranging from the connoisseur to those who entirely lack a sense of appreciation. He is quite emphatic on this point:

> It is difficult for the expert to conform to the mind of the non-critic and for the amateur to please the eye of the critic. It is no wonder that the amateur does not please the eye of the critic. But that the expert does not conform to the mind of the non-critic is because of what is lacking in the eye of the non-critic. Nevertheless an enlightened expert who is an actor of many skills will perform the Noh in such a manner as to be interesting even to the eye of the non-critic.

When **Kadensho** was written, Zeami was at the peak of his career. He had experienced many different facets of Noh theatre as a critic and theoretician as well as performer. Since he realized that the success of each performance totally relied on the reaction of the audience, he was extremely sensitive as to the quality of the spectators and their critical ability. It is worthwhile to be aware of the many delineations of spectators Zeami set forth in *Kadensho*:

1. Spectators who enhance an audience

jōkon jōchi—people who have refined sense and good appreciative ability

mekiki—spectators who have a good critical eye

makoto no mekiki, shinjichi no mekiki—spectators who have an excellent critical eye

2. Spectators whose interest in the theatre is superficial

mekikazu—people who do not have a critical eye

3. Spectators in the countryside (negatively used)

ongoku denja no hito, denja ongoku—people in the suburbs or in the countryside

denja yamazato no katahotori—people in the countryside and in a hamlet among the hills

4. Aristocratic spectators

kinin—nobles

jōhō (sama)—people of the higher class

5. Spectators in general

kenbutsushū —spectators

kenbutsu no jōge—spectators of both higher and lower class

kenjo—(having a dual meaning) spectator's seats or spectators

miru-hito—people who see and hear

shonin—people in general

yosome—other's eye

teki, tekikata—enemy (used as a simile of spectator)

In his later works Zeami was apparently more interested in the degree and profundity of a performance itself with less regard to the reaction of an audience than in the time of *Kadensho*. Such various expressions for the nuances of an audience as we have seen in *Kadensho* disappear, and one begins to notice an emphasis on the inviolability of the art itself.

This does not mean that he had totally abandoned any consideration for the audience. On the contrary, he was just as aware of the audience as he was in *Kadensho*,

but it seems clear that he was no longer concerned that a performance must impress and interest even the eye of a fool. We can catch a glimpse of his state of mind in the following statement in *Kakyō* written in his early sixties, which shows this subtle change: 'Speaking of Noh criticism, people's tastes vary. Therefore it is never easy to please everyone.'

One of the reasons why Zeami underwent this change of attitude is that the critical level of the audience increased as he himself matured. Zeami tells us at the end of *Shikadō,* which was written at the age of fifty-eight, that contemporary audiences of the nobles had so refined their critical abilities that they began to criticize even small defects in the performers, who therefore were unable to satisfy them unless they possessed an equivalently developed sense of *yūgen*.

Generally speaking, the audience in Zeami's later works is not merely there for the performers to impress, but it acts as a guard against the performer becoming self-complacent and not maintaining an objective standpoint. The audience which has the ability to function with good critical sense is somewhat like the chisel of a sculptor acting on the mind and body of the performer rather than on stone. Zeami's most significant concept regarding the consciousness of an audience is that of *riken no ken,* where he maintains that a performer should gain the perspective of the spectator in order to perfect his performance.

In *Sarugaku-Dangi,* which is a collection of Zeami's instructions and remarks on Noh theatre written by his son when Zeami was sixty-eight, we may be surprised at an utterly pessimistic statement of his concerning the audience; that people in the future would be unable to appreciate the profundity of a play like *Kinuta*. The question can be asked as to whether Zeami had entirely lost his trust in the audience after having gone through a difficult period, where he had lost the patronage of the Shogunate and much of his support from the nobility as well. Is it possible that he felt himself to be the only one with qualifications necessary to be a member of a Noh audience, during this period of distrust and disillusionment?

In summation, Zeami's awareness of the audience could be roughly represented in terms of two categories which are the public vs. the nobles, and the critics vs. the noncritics. Although we can perceive a subtle change in his awareness of the audience as he matured (going through difficulties both social and personal as well as experiences as a performer, playwright and thinker) his consistent ideal on the conditions necessary for a good Noh performance throughout his life remained unchanged. It can be best put as follows: a good actor should perform the best play possible for the most appreciative audience that can be found.

The careful consideration and attention which Zeami gives to the classifications of the audience finds its way to his investigation of what he referred to as *toki no chōshi* (the spirit of time). If a performance is to proceed in accordance with the *yin/yang* mood that surrounds the performers, it should not begin merely because of a precise attention to the particular time or because of a one-sided decision on the part of the performers, but the commencement of the performance should be guided by the following suggestions put forth by Zeami in **Kadensho**:

1. It should begin only when the performers have properly grasped the audience's psychology so that they can react to it.

2. For practical reasons, since Noh theatre was supported primarily by the nobility, care should be taken to begin a performance with their arrival whether it was early or late.

3. If it appears that an audience is restless and is not quite ready for a performance, the voice and movement of the actor should be more emphatic than usual so as to calm them down.

4. Only an experienced performer knows whether the audience is alert or inert and is capable of making the decision to initiate the action of the play.

5. The performer should take into account the different moods of day and night.

The first item may be the most interesting of all from the general point of view of the performance: we are told that when the audience is impatient, the performer can take advantage of that opportunity to enter and recite his lines, with the result that the entire audience will be in tune with the 'spirit of time' and the performance stands a better chance of being successful.

The beginning of the performance, or the moment when the *shite* performer begins the chanting in his first appearance, is more elaborately explained in **Kakyō.** When the performer appears and stops on the *hashigakari,* he has to pay attention to the entire audience, and his first words should be uttered right at the moment when all of them are waiting for it on the edges of their seats. Thus the performer penetrates into the tension or expectation in the spectator's mind, and the proper moment of his first utterance is perfectly united with that expectation. The performer must catch this moment instinctively for, if he misses it, he will lose the spectator's attention. It is that point in time where one performer draws the majority of an audience's eyes and minds into himself, and is the most crucial moment of the day.

What then is the 'spirit of time' and how does being in harmony with it aid in leading to a successful performance? The original Japanese phrase for the 'spirit of time,' *toki no chōshi,* can also be rendered as the 'condition of time' or the 'mood of time' or the 'tone of time,' This *toki no chōshi* sounds somewhat mysterious, but it appears that Zeami places much importance on it as an essential element of the performance space. He must have sincerely believed in *toki no chōshi* throughout his life, judging from the fact that this phrase also appears again in some various works of his later period, such as **Kakyō, Shūgyoku-Tokuka,** and **Sarugaku-Dangi.**

In **Kakyō,** Zeami puzzles us with an elaborate explanation of *toki no chōshi* which sounds somewhat pedantic. According to this passage, *toki no chōshi* refers to five different modes in music applied to four seasons and certain hours of the day and night. They are *sojō, ōshiki-chō, ichikotsu-chō, hyō-jō,* and *banshiki-chō* (the ending of each word, *chō* or *jō,* means the mode, which were adopted from the tonal system of *Gagaku,* ancient Japanese court music imported from China). To apply a particular mode of *Gagaku* to a particular time of day or season was then customary as if that period of the day or season had its own tone inseparably related to the mood or atmosphere.

We are also given another rather abstruse explanation on the spirit of time in the same chapter of the book: '*Toki no chōshi* refers to the moment when the tone from heaven reaches the earth and harmonizes with it on the occasion of dance and music performed by heavenly beings.'

Though both explanations are mystic, we can at least say that *toki no chōshi,* like *yin* and *yang,* is the belief that there are certain dynamics beyond human reach working in time and space, and the performance must be in accord with them. It cannot succeed if it ignores those dynamics in nature. In **Shūgyoku-Tokuka,** Zeami repeats that there can be no psychic exchange between a performer and the audience if the tone of the performer's lines is not in accord with *toki no chōshi.* Since nature cannot be expected to adjust itself to the performer, he must adjust the tone of his voice to the dynamics of the various elements of nature in that particular time and that particular space. We see here that what is denoted as *toki no chōshi* is actually close to the spirit of the *yin/yang* concept.

Though the nuance of each term differs, the concepts of *toki no chōshi, yin/yang,* and *odoki/medoki* are basically the same in that these concepts see the existence of unknown natural dynamics that control space and time. The *yin/yang* principle is concerned with both time and space. *Toki no chōshi* and *odoki/medoki* are originally concerned with time, but they also deal with space, since time and space are inseparable. These concepts are the ones which point out the necessity of arriving at a balance whereby one lives with nature, not against it, and which should enable a performance to have within itself an accord with beauty and order of nature.

What has been gained by the constant, rigorous training and discipline is not presented as it was practised but must be adjusted to the time and space of that particular day, since it is only the ultimate event of the performance itself from which the audience will make the final judgement as to its artistic value. A good performer, therefore, is not only sustained by his inborn talent and incessant training but also is the one whose instinctive judgement and creativity harmonize with the mood and atmosphere at the very moment of each performance.

If the form and style of Noh theatre still leaves some indeterminate and flexible elements on the day of the performance in order to create a mysterious tension in the theatrical space, the written text is handled somewhat differently; its content remains exactly the same in the performance as well as in the rehearsal period. The basic presentational style of Noh theatre is through dance and music (*buka*), but the written text is essential. If the text is to be presented to the audience exactly in the same way as the playwright had written it, how is writing a play related to its presentation on stage?

Zeami, as is generally well known, was a genius as a play-playwright as well as a theorist, performer and director. Besides some twenty treatises on the art of Noh theatre, Zeami had written a great number of plays, perhaps as many as two hundred. What totally differs from the present situation is that Zeami seemed to have thought it extremely important for a performer to be a playwright too:

> If the Noh playwright and the actor are different persons, the actor cannot play according to his wishes, however skilful an actor may be, whereas in his own compositions, he can sing and act as he thinks fit. Therefore, one who is capable at all of performing the Noh, if he has literary talent, will be able to compose *Sarugaku* with ease. This is the life of this art. This being the case, however skilful an actor may be, if he has not any Noh of his own composition ready, it is as if a man who is a match for a thousand appears on the battlefield unarmed.

Ideally a Noh performer, therefore, should be one who is capable of verbalizing his poetic image as a playwright and bringing it to a physical realization as an actor.

Zeami's idea on the relationship between playwriting and performance is succinctly expressed in two notions, *kaimon* and *kaigen* in **Nōsakusho (On the Art of Playwriting)**, which was written in his early sixties, and which provides us with deepest insight on playwriting. *Kaimon* is concerned with the auditory function of performance, and *kaigen* with the visual function. Both of them have to do with the conditions necessary to bring about the climactic moment in the performance. These conditions have to be met in either the *ha* or *kyū* section of a play.

Kaimon, which literally means 'to open the auditory function,' 'to open the ear,' is the moment when two different elements of the auditory experience are harmoniously united in the audience's mind. One element is what impresses the audience by the literary or poetic image of the play which conveys the spirit of the original story that the play is based on. Another element is the musical expression by which the words are chanted. In other words, *kaimon* can be interpreted as the climactic moment aroused in the audience's mind when the literary

impression of the play, which is logical, and musical impression of the play, which is emotional, are felt simultaneously.

Kaigen, on the other hand, is the climactic moment which is brought about by the total visual effect of the stage such as dance and vigorous movement of the performers. However, we can be assured here that it does not refer to the mere superficial stage effect at all but to the superb artistic quality achieved by the performer. Since *kaigen* is primarily realized by the actor, not by the playwright, it is not basically related to the text of the play. Nonetheless the effect of *kaigen* should be considered throughout the process of playwriting because it cannot come into effect without certain passages in the text that makes it possible.

Two Kinds of Climactic Moments in Performance

Kaimon:	*Kaigen*:
auditory	visual
literary poetic	artistic
music text	dance movement
logical intellectual	emotional
playwright	performer

Kaimon and *kaigen* are Zeami's analytic tools which he applies to the climactic moment of a performance, and to the way it is created. It is interesting to note that Zeami divides the nature of the climactic moment and the emotional excitement on the part of the audience into two separate aspects, the auditory and the visual. We can easily imagine that at the moment when these two aspects are joined together, there is the capability of imparting the ultimate climactic impression upon the mind of an audience. The climactic moment may be simply a very few seconds in the presentation of one play, nonetheless both a playwright and a performer have to be well conscious of this short period of time, and endeavour to achieve its realization.

Senmon-goken, which appears in **Kakyō,** is another notion having to do with the consideration of a performance from the point of view of the auditory and visual function. It is this concept which advises actors to recite their lines first, then follow with their body movement, so that the audience may *hear* first and then *see*. The physical movement should not come before the words, nor should they come simultaneously. Zeami seems to mean that if the movement comes first it is against the fundamentals of acting, because an audience gains the sense of achievement when the cognitive function is somewhere between the processing of data from these two sensory faculties. Though we wonder whether this *senmon-goken* could be applied to the modern Noh theatre whose theatre space differs from Zeami's period and also where the audiences arc generally much more familiar with each play, the concept which asserts that acting should finish in visuality is worth paying attention to.

The important ideas which show Zeami's concept as regards the relationship between the degree of achievement of a performance and that of the appreciative quality of an audience are the ones called *ken/mon/shin* in **Kakyō** and its related notion, *hi/niku/kotsu* in **Shikadō.** The idea of *ken/mon/shin* is unique and significant since a performance is analysed from the standpoint of a performer and an audience simultaneously with consideration to visual, auditory and psychic performances respectively. *Ken* (to see), *mon* (to hear), and *shin* (heart), each refers to a different quality of a successful performance depending upon whether the performance has appealed to an audience visually, auditorily, or spiritually.

Ken refers to a good performance which is visually various and effective. *Buka* (dance and music) may be particularly impressive in a performance which conforms to requisites of *ken*. In this kind of a performance the spectators' attention is drawn on to the stage soon after the beginning of the show, and they are struck by the richly colourful stage effects. Non-critics as well as connoisseurs are equally capable of appreciating it. However, in a performance which contains this quality of *ken,* everything tends to work out so well and it interests spectators so much that the performance is apt to become flimsy, being in danger of leaving a superficial impression on the audience. A performer, therefore, should restrain his gestures and movements, giving the audience some moment of repose, and trying to show the most interesting scenes in a quiet manner.

Mon, on the other hand, is performance based on the auditory faculty, and has a sober, subtle atmosphere from the very beginning. The chanting and the music with which it harmonizes present the audience with a tranquil atmosphere. *Mon* is also produced when an expert actor creates his own artistic world. An excellent performer is capable of presenting a performance of this kind without any technical endeavour, a variety of effects coming out of his mind naturally. An actor, in playing this Noh of *mon,* should be careful so that the performance will not look downcast and dispirited because of its suppressed quiet beauty. This type of performance can be appreciated only by connoisseurs who have a sophisticated eye, not by self-indulgent critics.

The highest level of performance, *shin,* is still further beyond the sensuality of visual and auditory faculties. A great master can impress upon his audience a mood of lonely desolation without letting the spectators become aware of his strong influence on them. This level of performance can only be mastered when every technique and artifice of Noh have been assimilated into the subconscious of the performer. *Shin* touches the audiences'

heart spiritually and psychically in quiescence and loneliness. It is a performance where a communication from psyche to psyche is possible, but it is only possible by an expert of the highest rank who has acquired the mind of nothingness (*mu*) similar to that spoken of in Zen Buddhism, since he has to be free from any consciousness of his attempts at performing.

Zeami tells us that among even the most experienced connoisseurs there are some who cannot appreciate this highest level of performance. The audience as well as the actors must be sophisticated and appreciative enough to enjoy this level of the performance art. Noh is an art which places demands on an audience to maintain constantly the development of its sensibility to that art. A sophisticated audience sees the performance and senses the heart of the performer much in the same way as a good actor in performance senses the heart of the audience.

In **Shikadō,** we are introduced to another triple concept which is known as *hi/niku/kotsu*. This notion in turn congruently is related to the idea which we saw in **Kakyō** known as *ken/mon/shin*. *Hi, niku* and *kotsu* (literally translated as *skin, flesh,* and *bones*) were originally the terms used in the traditional calligraphy when one's handwriting was likened to the constitution of the human body. Zeami adapted these terms to the three different styles of a performer's art. They are explained as follows:

> The display in this art of the special powers which have enabled one to become a master-actor naturally, by virtue of inborn abilities, may be designated the bones (*kotsu*); the display of the perfect powers which have come from study and experience of dancing and singing (*buka*) may be called flesh (*niku*); and an appearance which exhibits these qualities at their highest pitch, with perfect gentleness and beauty, may be termed the skin (*hi*).

Ken (to see)	*Hi* (skin)
* visual	*beauty and
* richly colourful stage effect	gentleness
* non-critics as well as connoisseurs can appreciate	

Mon (to hear)	*Niku* (flesh)
* auditory	* dance and music
* tranquil	
* an expert performer	
* only connoisseurs can appreciate	

Shin (spirit)	*Kotsu* (bones)
* spiritual	* inborn abilities
* lonely, desolate	
* a superb master	
* can be appreciated by only a select few among the connoisseurs themselves	

In **Shikado,** we are told that there are no contemporary performers who are possessed of these three different levels at the same time, and that some performers are not even cognizant of their existence. Performers may reach the level of *hi* at best, but more often than not it is superficial, not genuine. A performer who has mastered all the levels of *hi/niku/kotsu* is absolutely beyond any technique and artifice, and is able to give a purely enchanting performance quite easily. The audience is endlessly attracted and interested by this type of performance and becomes enraptured.

Both *ken/mon/shin* and *hi/niku/kotsu,* as we have seen, refer to the different levels of quality in a performance. However, unlike the nine rank differentiation system set forth in **Kyūi** which deals with levels of performance both positive and negative, both of the above triple concepts, which are dealt with in the chart, are concerned with only the positive aspects of a successful performance. We can, therefore, assume that *ken/mon/shin* and *hi/niku/kotsu* correspond only to the upper ranks of the nine ranks in **Kyūi.** Even the lowest ranks of those notions, *ken* and *hi* seem to contain a quality of *yūgen* and *hana* in themselves.

We have to recall at this point what Zeami mentioned in **Kadensho**: *shiore* (the *drooping* or *withering* of a flower) is on a higher level than *hana,* though to acquire *hana* is prerequisite in Noh. *Shiore* is a metaphor of a performance which may not be visually as rich and appealing as *hana,* but which is oriented more to an internal, solitary atmosphere. Accordingly we will not find it difficult to notice that what *hana* is to *shiore* is analogous to what *ken* is to *mon* and *shin.*

In other words, Zeami attaches more positive, aesthetic importance to the tranquil, internal feeling of withered trees in winter than gay, flowery ones in spring. A performance which is plain without any kind of ostentation and yet has an internal psychic dynamic is ranked more highly than the one which has external, visual effects that attract every member of an audience.

Here we have to note one other major difference between the nine ranks of **Kyūi** and *ken/mon/shin.* It is the fact that in *ken/mon/shin,* the appreciative ability of an audience and the way in which it is involved with the performance are both taken into account. While *shin,* the highest level of a performance, can be appreciated only by an extremely limited number of spectators in an audience, *ken* is capable of pleasing everyone ranging from connoisseurs to non-critics.

Zeami desires a performer to become deepened and sophisticated by years of training to the point where even some experienced connoisseurs cannot appreciate his performance. However, he, at the same time, never ignores a certain style of performance which is artistically successful and yet which pleases a mass audience. One of the ways to keep having an aesthetic development constantly in the art of Noh performance without losing the interest of the public and non-critics is to possess and perform various styles of acting ranging from the rough to the sophisticated, and from the visual to the psychic, etc. This variety is like the incessantly changing variety of nature. Nature never stays the same. If man is part of nature, a performance created by man is to be in tune with it developing with its infinite diversity and disappears into its eternal rhythm.

Shohei Shimada on Zeami's greatness:

Zeami refined the *Nō* and made it gracefully beautiful, attaching importance to chanting and dancing. He made it more and more artistic, so that it has endured life up to the present. He is the greatest figure in the history of the *Nō*. He was a great dramatist, actor and theorist, which strikes us with admiration. He is as rare as a blue diamond in the theatrical world.

> *Shohei Shimada, in "The Translator to the Reader," in* The Fushikaden, *translated by Shohei Shimada, privately printed, 1975.*

James R. Brandon (essay date 1994)

SOURCE: "Japanese Noh," in *Staging Japanese Theatre: Noh & Kabuki,* edited by John D. Mitchell and Miyoko Wantanabe, Institute for Advanced Studies in the Theatre Arts Press, 1994, pp. i-v.

[*In the following excerpt, Brandon presents a broad overview of the form, content, characters, and staging of Nō plays and discusses Zeami's role in the drama's development.*]

Between the tenth and the thirteenth centuries, performers of a number of Japanese theatre forms vied for audience attention and for the patronage of Buddhist temples and the court in and around the important cities of Nara and Kyoto. Jugglers and acrobats, singers of epic romances, and players of various kinds of short plays and dances especially those known as dengaku, literally field music, and *sarugaku,* monkey music—were part of the theatre scene. Both *dengaku* and *sarugaku* troupes performed sketches, songs, and dances, but as independent pieces. Around the middle of the fourteenth century, the *sarugaku* troupe leader Kannami Kiyotsugu (1333-1384) introduced into his performances a sung dance section, the *kusemai* or *kuse,* thus for the first time giving the dance a genuine dramatic function. In the *kuse* section of a play, a crucial tale of the past is narrated as the protagonist dances out the story. Kannami's new way of performing was called *sarugaku*-noh, and in time this was shortened to Noh.

Kannami's son, the famous Zeami Motokiyo (1363-1444), was twelve years old when he was seen performing Noh by Yoshimitsu, the shogun, or military ruler of Japan. Yoshimitsu was captivated by the boy's beauty and grace, and he brought Zeami to the palace in Kyoto to be his catamite. Zeami spent most of his adult life at the court, even after his patron died. In the sophisticated atmosphere of the shogun's court, he raised Noh from a plebeian, almost rustic, theatrical form to an exceptionally subtle art. Zeami was not only the chief performer of his troupe (inheriting this position from his father) but also the writer of more than one hundred plays. And in a series of treatises on the practice of his art, he established the aesthetic basis of Noh. For four hundred years following Zeami's death, Noh troupes were supported by feudal lords in Kyoto and in the outlying provinces, thus preserving down to the present the texts of Noh and the style of performance as well. About two hundred and forty plays make up the Noh repertory that is performed today. Another two thousand or so plays have been written, but are not performed. Plays are divided into five groups according to subject matter and style: god (*kami*) plays, congratulatory pieces praising the gods; warrior (*shura*) plays, in which the protagonist is usually a slain warrior who appears as a ghost and relives his sufferings; woman (*katsura*) plays, in which the protagonist is a woman; miscellaneous plays—one type concerns a woman driven mad by grief for a lost child or lover, another a character who is obsessed, and a third, known as living person plays, an unmasked male protagonist; and demon (*kiri*) plays, in which the protagonist is a demon, devil, or supernatural figure.

A day's performance in Zeami's time was made up of one play from each group, staged in order, and interspersed with comedies called *kyogen*. A program of five plays was viewed as an artistic entity. Atmosphere, tempo, and tension changed perceptibly from one play to the next. The god play was quiet and dignified, the warrior play active and strong, and the woman play radiated elegant beauty. Increased tempo marked the fourth play, and in the demon play, a furious battle between demon and hero was resolved with the demon being killed or subdued—thus bringing the performance back to a congratulatory mood similar to that of the first play. Zeami wrote that the five-play series should be organized according to the principle of *jo,* or introduction (first play); *ha,* or development (second, third, and fourth plays); and *kyu,* or scattering (fifth play). According to Zeami, also, each play was to be organized into *jo, ha, kyu*—beginning, middle, end—with the same principle of artistic progression in mind. Significantly, the *jo-ha-kyu* concept is derived from *gagaku* court music, and not for literature.

Noh plays are deeply impregnated with the doctrine of Amida Buddhism, according to which human salvation is achieved through prayer and penance. The profoundly pessimistic Buddhist theme of the impermanence of life is common to a number of plays. . . . A noble warrior is slain before achieving his dream of conquest; a beautiful young woman eagerly sought after in her youth wanders alone in her withered old age. In Buddhist thought, the soul that clings to earthly attachments after death dwells in a purgatory of ceaseless torment. Plays of the second and third type concern these tortured souls.

Only a small number of characters appears in most Noh plays. In a text they are designated by their role-type and not by their character's name. The *shite,* or doer, is the central figure, and is usually an aristocrat, a court lady, or a powerful spirit. The *shite* completely dominates a performance; other actors are mere by-players. It is the *shite* who always performs the *kuse* dance and other important dances. Normally the *shite* is masked. The *shite* may have attendant courtiers, retainers, or maids (*tsure*). In the play there may be a noble child role (*kokata*) or roles for other minor characters (*tomo*), all of which are acted by lesser performers associated with the *shite* actor's school. The *waki,* or supporting role, is most often that of a priest who initiates the action or the play. Only rarely is the *waki* an antagonist to the *shite*. The *waki* may have attendants (*wakizure*), acted by performers associated with the *waki*'s school. *Kyogen* actors play roles of villagers or other commoners (*kyogen* actors also perform the *kyogen* farces between two Noh plays).

Plays are presented on a raised stage, about eighteen feet square, with a highly polished Cyprus floor. Scenery is not used, but constructed props and hand props commonly are. A bridgeway (*hashigakari*) about thirty feet long, leading from stage right to the dressing rooms, is used for exits and entrances. The tempo of song and dance is regulated by accompanying music, played by musicians who sit in view of the audience at the rear of the stage. One flute, two hand drums (one large and one small), and in some plays a stick drum compose the small Noh ensemble. A chorus of six to ten actors from the *shite* group sits on the left side of the stage. Several other actors, disciples of the *shite* and sometimes of the *waki,* assist their teachers on the stage. They give and take away hand properties, adjust costumes, and move larger set properties. All performers in Noh are male.

The most important influence on the aesthetics of Noh theatrical art is Zen Buddhism. From austere Zen came the principle that suggestion is preferable to flat statement, that subtlety is preferable to clearness, that the small gesture is preferable to the large, that, in short, the secret of beauty lies in restraint. Beauty in Noh is refined and it is everywhere: in the chaste planes of the masks, in the simplicity of the stage, in the rigor of the line of musicians or chorus on the stage, in the quavering tone of the actor's chanting voice, in the elegant movements of the performers. Zeami described the unique beauty which Noh strives toward in two terms: mysterious and sublime. Mysterious beauty, or *yugen,* is the ephemeral beauty that lies in impermanence. The cherry blossom, delicate and fragile, is touched by the wind and in an instant is scattered and gone. Elegance is tinged with the sadness of passing. The sublime would appear to be Zeami's more mature view. In sections of Noh that suggest the sublime, melancholy over the impermanence of life gives way to serenity and acceptance. The beauty of the sublime is the beauty of old age, restful, at peace with the world. It is silent, austere. That such a theory of beauty was developed for a theatrical art must impress us deeply. Indeed, there is no other form of theatre in the world in which the externals have been more thoroughly abandoned in favor of elliptical, concentrated, austere expression.

Noh is not a storyteller's art; it does not (in most cases) present the unfolding of a human action. Rather, through recollections of the past, it evokes a mood, an emotion, a religious state. Human characters appear on the stage, but they are not three-dimensional figures living the usual round of daily routine. At the most extreme they are quite literally momentary manifestations of the spirit world; at the very least, they exhibit an unworldly degree of composure and restraint. Through the gradual increase in tension created by the steady musical accompaniment, the chanting of the chorus, and the formal movements of the characters, content is subsumed to form, until the knowledgeable spectator perceives the occurrences before him, not as emotionally bound human actions but as elegantly formed patterns of sound and color that impinge on his emotions peripherally if at all. Noh is the purest of the art forms of theatre and consequently makes the most demands on its audience.

FURTHER READING

Hoff, Frank. "Seeing and Being Seen: The Mirror of Performance." In *Flowing Traces: Buddhism in the Literary and Visual Arts of Japan,* edited by James H. Sanford, William R. LaFleur, and Masatoshi Nagatomi, pp. 131-48. Princeton, N. J.: Princeton University Press, 1992.

> Explores Zeami's views on the relationship between actor and audience in performances of Nō.

LaFleur, William R. "Zeami's Buddhism: Cosmology and Dialectic in Nō Drama." In his *The Karma of Words: Buddhism and the Literary Arts in Medieval Japan,* pp. 116-32. Berkeley: University of California Press, 1983.

Traces the influence of Zen Buddhism on Zeami's art and thought.

Rimer, J. Thomas, and Yamazaki Masakazu, trans. *On the Art of Nō Drama: The Major Treatises of Zeami.* Princeton, N. J.: Princeton University Press, 1984, 298 p.

> Includes, in addition to translations of Zeami's treatises, essays on the background of the treatises and on Zeami's artistic theories. Also features English-Japanese and Japanese-English glossaries and a bibliography.

Sata, Megumi. "Aristotle's *Poetics* and Zeami's *Teachings on Style and the Flower.*" *Asian Theatre Journal* 6, No. 1 (Spring 1989): 47-56.

> Compares these two "superb theatrical treatises to which we owe much of our knowledge of tragedy and *nō.*"

Shigenori Nagatomo. "Zeami's Conception of Freedom." *Philosophy East and West* 31, No. 4 (October 1981): 401-16.

> Examines Zeami's theoretical writings to elucidate the playwright's definition of freedom as something that is achieved through artistic training.

Tatsuro Ishii. "Zeami's Mature Thoughts on Acting." *Theatre Research International* 12, No. 2 (Summer 1987): 110-23.

> Scrutinizes Zeami's theoretical essays, which contain "the nucleus of his concepts on acting and performance based on his own experience and deep insights as a thinker, actor, director and playwright."

Ueda, Makoto. "The Implications of the Noh Drama." *Sewanee Review* LXIX, No. 3 (July-September 1961): 367-74.

> Discusses the theme of sin and salvation common to many Nō dramas.

Waley, Arthur. Introduction to *The Nō Plays of Japan,* pp. 15-55. London: George Allen & Unwin, 1921, 319 p.

> Surveys the origin, development, and characteristic features of Nō, with particular reference to Zeami's artistic theories.

CUMULATIVE INDEXES

How to Use This Index

The main references

list all author entries in the following Gale Literary Criticism series:

BLC = *Black Literature Criticism*
CLC = *Contemporary Literary Criticism*
CLR = *Children's Literature Review*
CMLC = *Classical and Medieval Literature Criticism*
DA = *DISCovering Authors*
DAB = *DISCovering Authors: British*
DAC = *DISCovering Authors: Canadian*
DC = *Drama Criticism*
HLC = *Hispanic Literature Criticism*
LC = *Literature Criticism from 1400 to 1800*
NCLC = *Nineteenth-Century Literature Criticism*
PC = *Poetry Criticism*
SSC = *Short Story Criticism*
TCLC = *Twentieth-Century Literary Criticism*
WLC = *World Literature Criticism, 1500 to the Present*

The cross-references

list all author entries in the following Gale biographical and literary sources:

AAYA = *Authors & Artists for Young Adults*
AITN = *Authors in the News*
BEST = *Bestsellers*
BW = *Black Writers*
CA = *Contemporary Authors*
CAAS = *Contemporary Authors Autobiography Series*
CABS = *Contemporary Authors Bibliographical Series*
CANR = *Contemporary Authors New Revision Series*
CAP = *Contemporary Authors Permanent Series*
CDALB = *Concise Dictionary of American Literary Biography*
CDBLB = *Concise Dictionary of British Literary Biography*
DAM = *DISCovering Authors: Modules*
    DRAM: Dramatists Module; MST: Most-Studied Authors Module;
    MULT: Multicultural Authors Module; NOV: Novelists Module;
    POET: Poets Module; POP: Popular Fiction and Genre Authors Module
DLB = *Dictionary of Literary Biography*
DLBD = *Dictionary of Literary Biography Documentary Series*
DLBY = *Dictionary of Literary Biography Yearbook*
HW = *Hispanic Writers*
JRDA = *Junior DISCovering Authors*
MAICYA = *Major Authors and Illustrators for Children and Young Adults*
MTCW = *Major 20th-Century Writers*
NNAL = *Native North American Literature*
SAAS = *Something about the Author Autobiography Series*
SATA = *Something about the Author*
YABC = *Yesterday's Authors of Books for Children*

Literary Criticism Series
Cumulative Author Index

Anderson, Robert (Woodruff)
1917- .... CLC 23; DAM DRAM
See also AITN 1; CA 21-24R; CANR 32;
DLB 7

Anderson, Sherwood
1876-1941 .... TCLC 1, 10, 24; DA;
DAB; DAC; DAM MST, NOV; SSC 1;
WLC
See also CA 104; 121; CDALB 1917-1929;
DLB 4, 9, 86; DLBD 1; MTCW

Andier, Pierre
See Desnos, Robert

Andouard
See Giraudoux, (Hippolyte) Jean

Andrade, Carlos Drummond de ...... CLC 18
See also Drummond de Andrade, Carlos

Andrade, Mario de 1893-1945..... TCLC 43

Andreae, Johann V(alentin)
1586-1654 .... LC 32
See also DLB 164

Andreas-Salome, Lou 1861-1937... TCLC 56
See also DLB 66

Andrewes, Lancelot 1555-1626 .... LC 5
See also DLB 151, 172

Andrews, Cicily Fairfield
See West, Rebecca

Andrews, Elton V.
See Pohl, Frederik

Andreyev, Leonid (Nikolaevich)
1871-1919 .... TCLC 3
See also CA 104

Andric, Ivo 1892-1975 .... CLC 8
See also CA 81-84; 57-60; CANR 43;
DLB 147; MTCW

Angelique, Pierre
See Bataille, Georges

Angell, Roger 1920- .... CLC 26
See also CA 57-60; CANR 13, 44; DLB 171

Angelou, Maya
1928- .... CLC 12, 35, 64, 77; BLC; DA;
DAB; DAC; DAM MST, MULT, POET,
POP
See also AAYA 7, 20; BW 2; CA 65-68;
CANR 19, 42; DLB 38; MTCW;
SATA 49

Annensky, Innokenty (Fyodorovich)
1856-1909 .... TCLC 14
See also CA 110; 155

Annunzio, Gabriele d'
See D'Annunzio, Gabriele

Anon, Charles Robert
See Pessoa, Fernando (Antonio Nogueira)

Anouilh, Jean (Marie Lucien Pierre)
1910-1987 ...... CLC 1, 3, 8, 13, 40, 50;
DAM DRAM
See also CA 17-20R; 123; CANR 32;
MTCW

Anthony, Florence
See Ai

Anthony, John
See Ciardi, John (Anthony)

Anthony, Peter
See Shaffer, Anthony (Joshua); Shaffer,
Peter (Levin)

Anthony, Piers 1934- .. CLC 35; DAM POP
See also AAYA 11; CA 21-24R; CANR 28,
56; DLB 8; MTCW; SAAS 22; SATA 84

Antoine, Marc
See Proust, (Valentin-Louis-George-Eugene-)
Marcel

Antoninus, Brother
See Everson, William (Oliver)

Antonioni, Michelangelo 1912- ..... CLC 20
See also CA 73-76; CANR 45

Antschel, Paul 1920-1970
See Celan, Paul
See also CA 85-88; CANR 33; MTCW

Anwar, Chairil 1922-1949 .... TCLC 22
See also CA 121

Apollinaire, Guillaume
1880-1918 .... TCLC 3, 8, 51;
DAM POET; PC 7
See also Kostrowitzki, Wilhelm Apollinaris
de
See also CA 152

Appelfeld, Aharon 1932- .... CLC 23, 47
See also CA 112; 133

Apple, Max (Isaac) 1941-........ CLC 9, 33
See also CA 81-84; CANR 19, 54; DLB 130

Appleman, Philip (Dean) 1926- ..... CLC 51
See also CA 13-16R; CAAS 18; CANR 6,
29, 56

Appleton, Lawrence
See Lovecraft, H(oward) P(hillips)

Apteryx
See Eliot, T(homas) S(tearns)

Apuleius, (Lucius Madaurensis)
125(?)-175(?) .... CMLC 1

Aquin, Hubert 1929-1977......... CLC 15
See also CA 105; DLB 53

Aragon, Louis
1897-1982 ..... CLC 3, 22; DAM NOV,
POET
See also CA 69-72; 108; CANR 28;
DLB 72; MTCW

Arany, Janos 1817-1882........ NCLC 34

Arbuthnot, John 1667-1735 .... LC 1
See also DLB 101

Archer, Herbert Winslow
See Mencken, H(enry) L(ouis)

Archer, Jeffrey (Howard)
1940- .... CLC 28; DAM POP
See also AAYA 16; BEST 89:3; CA 77-80;
CANR 22, 52; INT CANR-22

Archer, Jules 1915- .... CLC 12
See also CA 9-12R; CANR 6; SAAS 5;
SATA 4, 85

Archer, Lee
See Ellison, Harlan (Jay)

Arden, John
1930- ..... CLC 6, 13, 15; DAM DRAM
See also CA 13-16R; CAAS 4; CANR 31;
DLB 13; MTCW

Arenas, Reinaldo
1943-1990 ...... CLC 41; DAM MULT;
HLC
See also CA 124; 128; 133; DLB 145; HW

Arendt, Hannah 1906-1975 ..... CLC 66, 98
See also CA 17-20R; 61-64; CANR 26;
MTCW

Aretino, Pietro 1492-1556 .... LC 12

Arghezi, Tudor................... CLC 80
See also Theodorescu, Ion N.

Arguedas, Jose Maria
1911-1969 .... CLC 10, 18
See also CA 89-92; DLB 113; HW

Argueta, Manlio 1936-............ CLC 31
See also CA 131; DLB 145; HW

Ariosto, Ludovico 1474-1533........ LC 6

Aristides
See Epstein, Joseph

Aristophanes
450B.C.-385B.C........ CMLC 4; DA;
DAB; DAC; DAM DRAM, MST; DC 2
See also DLB 176

Arlt, Roberto (Godofredo Christophersen)
1900-1942 ..... TCLC 29; DAM MULT;
HLC
See also CA 123; 131; HW

Armah, Ayi Kwei
1939- .... CLC 5, 33; BLC;
DAM MULT, POET
See also BW 1; CA 61-64; CANR 21;
DLB 117; MTCW

Armatrading, Joan 1950-.......... CLC 17
See also CA 114

Arnette, Robert
See Silverberg, Robert

Arnim, Achim von (Ludwig Joachim von
Arnim) 1781-1831 .... NCLC 5
See also DLB 90

Arnim, Bettina von 1785-1859.... NCLC 38
See also DLB 90

Arnold, Matthew
1822-1888 ..... NCLC 6, 29; DA; DAB;
DAC; DAM MST, POET; PC 5; WLC
See also CDBLB 1832-1890; DLB 32, 57

Arnold, Thomas 1795-1842 ...... NCLC 18
See also DLB 55

Arnow, Harriette (Louisa) Simpson
1908-1986 .... CLC 2, 7, 18
See also CA 9-12R; 118; CANR 14; DLB 6;
MTCW; SATA 42; SATA-Obit 47

Arp, Hans
See Arp, Jean

Arp, Jean 1887-1966............... CLC 5
See also CA 81-84; 25-28R; CANR 42

Arrabal
See Arrabal, Fernando

Arrabal, Fernando 1932- ... CLC 2, 9, 18, 58
See also CA 9-12R; CANR 15

Arrick, Fran.................... CLC 30
See also Gaberman, Judie Angell

Artaud, Antonin (Marie Joseph)
1896-1948 ... TCLC 3, 36; DAM DRAM
See also CA 104; 149

Arthur, Ruth M(abel) 1905-1979.... CLC 12
See also CA 9-12R; 85-88; CANR 4;
SATA 7, 26

Artsybashev, Mikhail (Petrovich)
1878-1927 .... TCLC 31

Arundel, Honor (Morfydd)
    1919-1973 .... **CLC 17**
    See also CA 21-22; 41-44R; CAP 2;
    CLR 35; SATA 4; SATA-Obit 24

Arzner, Dorothy 1897-1979 .... **CLC 98**

Asch, Sholem 1880-1957 .... **TCLC 3**
    See also CA 105

Ash, Shalom
    See Asch, Sholem

Ashbery, John (Lawrence)
    1927- ...... **CLC 2, 3, 4, 6, 9, 13, 15, 25,**
                    41, 77; DAM POET
    See also CA 5-8R; CANR 9, 37; DLB 5,
    165; DLBY 81; INT CANR-9; MTCW

Ashdown, Clifford
    See Freeman, R(ichard) Austin

Ashe, Gordon
    See Creasey, John

Ashton-Warner, Sylvia (Constance)
    1908-1984 .... **CLC 19**
    See also CA 69-72; 112; CANR 29; MTCW

Asimov, Isaac
    1920-1992 ...... **CLC 1, 3, 9, 19, 26, 76,**
                    92; DAM POP
    See also AAYA 13; BEST 90:2; CA 1-4R;
    137; CANR 2, 19, 36; CLR 12; DLB 8;
    DLBY 92; INT CANR-19; JRDA;
    MAICYA; MTCW; SATA 1, 26, 74

Assis, Joaquim Maria Machado de
    See Machado de Assis, Joaquim Maria

Astley, Thea (Beatrice May)
    1925- .... **CLC 41**
    See also CA 65-68; CANR 11, 43

Aston, James
    See White, T(erence) H(anbury)

Asturias, Miguel Angel
    1899-1974 .... **CLC 3, 8, 13;**
                    DAM MULT, NOV; HLC
    See also CA 25-28; 49-52; CANR 32;
    CAP 2; DLB 113; HW; MTCW

Atares, Carlos Saura
    See Saura (Atares), Carlos

Atheling, William
    See Pound, Ezra (Weston Loomis)

Atheling, William, Jr.
    See Blish, James (Benjamin)

Atherton, Gertrude (Franklin Horn)
    1857-1948 .... **TCLC 2**
    See also CA 104; 155; DLB 9, 78

Atherton, Lucius
    See Masters, Edgar Lee

Atkins, Jack
    See Harris, Mark

Atkinson, Kate .... **CLC 99**

Attaway, William (Alexander)
    1911-1986 .... **CLC 92; BLC;**
                    DAM MULT
    See also BW 2; CA 143; DLB 76

Atticus
    See Fleming, Ian (Lancaster)

Atwood, Margaret (Eleanor)
    1939- ..... **CLC 2, 3, 4, 8, 13, 15, 25, 44,**
        84; DA; DAB; DAC; DAM MST, NOV,
                    POET; PC 8; SSC 2; WLC
    See also AAYA 12; BEST 89:2; CA 49-52;
    CANR 3, 24, 33; DLB 53;
    INT CANR-24; MTCW; SATA 50

Aubigny, Pierre d'
    See Mencken, H(enry) L(ouis)

Aubin, Penelope 1685-1731(?) .... **LC 9**
    See also DLB 39

Auchincloss, Louis (Stanton)
    1917- .... **CLC 4, 6, 9, 18, 45;**
                    DAM NOV; SSC 22
    See also CA 1-4R; CANR 6, 29, 55; DLB 2;
    DLBY 80; INT CANR-29; MTCW

Auden, W(ystan) H(ugh)
    1907-1973 ...... **CLC 1, 2, 3, 4, 6, 9, 11,**
        14, 43; DA; DAB; DAC; DAM DRAM,
                    MST, POET; PC 1; WLC
    See also AAYA 18; CA 9-12R; 45-48;
    CANR 5; CDBLB 1914-1945; DLB 10,
    20; MTCW

Audiberti, Jacques
    1900-1965 ...... **CLC 38; DAM DRAM**
    See also CA 25-28R

Audubon, John James
    1785-1851 .... **NCLC 47**

Auel, Jean M(arie)
    1936- .... **CLC 31; DAM POP**
    See also AAYA 7; BEST 90:4; CA 103;
    CANR 21; INT CANR-21; SATA 91

Auerbach, Erich 1892-1957 ...... **TCLC 43**
    See also CA 118; 155

Augier, Emile 1820-1889 .... **NCLC 31**

August, John
    See De Voto, Bernard (Augustine)

Augustine, St. 354-430 ..... **CMLC 6; DAB**

Aurelius
    See Bourne, Randolph S(illiman)

Aurobindo, Sri 1872-1950 .... **TCLC 63**

Austen, Jane
    1775-1817 ..... **NCLC 1, 13, 19, 33, 51;**
        DA; DAB; DAC; DAM MST, NOV;
                    WLC
    See also AAYA 19; CDBLB 1789-1832;
    DLB 116

Auster, Paul 1947- .... **CLC 47**
    See also CA 69-72; CANR 23, 52

Austin, Frank
    See Faust, Frederick (Schiller)

Austin, Mary (Hunter)
    1868-1934 .... **TCLC 25**
    See also CA 109; DLB 9, 78

Autran Dourado, Waldomiro
    See Dourado, (Waldomiro Freitas) Autran

Averroes 1126-1198 .... **CMLC 7**
    See also DLB 115

Avicenna 980-1037 .... **CMLC 16**
    See also DLB 115

Avison, Margaret
    1918- .... **CLC 2, 4, 97; DAC;**
                    DAM POET
    See also CA 17-20R; DLB 53; MTCW

Axton, David
    See Koontz, Dean R(ay)

Ayckbourn, Alan
    1939- ...... **CLC 5, 8, 18, 33, 74; DAB;**
                    DAM DRAM
    See also CA 21-24R; CANR 31; DLB 13;
    MTCW

Aydy, Catherine
    See Tennant, Emma (Christina)

Ayme, Marcel (Andre) 1902-1967... **CLC 11**
    See also CA 89-92; CLR 25; DLB 72;
    SATA 91

Ayrton, Michael 1921-1975 .... **CLC 7**
    See also CA 5-8R; 61-64; CANR 9, 21

Azorin .... **CLC 11**
    See also Martinez Ruiz, Jose

Azuela, Mariano
    1873-1952 ..... **TCLC 3; DAM MULT;**
                    HLC
    See also CA 104; 131; HW; MTCW

Baastad, Babbis Friis
    See Friis-Baastad, Babbis Ellinor

Bab
    See Gilbert, W(illiam) S(chwenck)

Babbis, Eleanor
    See Friis-Baastad, Babbis Ellinor

Babel, Isaac
    See Babel, Isaak (Emmanuilovich)

Babel, Isaak (Emmanuilovich)
    1894-1941(?) ...... **TCLC 2, 13; SSC 16**
    See also CA 104; 155

Babits, Mihaly 1883-1941 .... **TCLC 14**
    See also CA 114

Babur 1483-1530 .... **LC 18**

Bacchelli, Riccardo 1891-1985 ..... **CLC 19**
    See also CA 29-32R; 117

Bach, Richard (David)
    1936- ...... **CLC 14; DAM NOV, POP**
    See also AITN 1; BEST 89:2; CA 9-12R;
    CANR 18; MTCW; SATA 13

Bachman, Richard
    See King, Stephen (Edwin)

Bachmann, Ingeborg 1926-1973..... **CLC 69**
    See also CA 93-96; 45-48; DLB 85

Bacon, Francis 1561-1626 .... **LC 18, 32**
    See also CDBLB Before 1660; DLB 151

Bacon, Roger 1214(?)-1292 ...... **CMLC 14**
    See also DLB 115

Bacovia, George .... **TCLC 24**
    See also Vasiliu, Gheorghe

Badanes, Jerome 1937- .... **CLC 59**

Bagehot, Walter 1826-1877 ...... **NCLC 10**
    See also DLB 55

Bagnold, Enid
    1889-1981 ...... **CLC 25; DAM DRAM**
    See also CA 5-8R; 103; CANR 5, 40;
    DLB 13, 160; MAICYA; SATA 1, 25

Bagritsky, Eduard 1895-1934 ..... **TCLC 60**

Bagrjana, Elisaveta
    See Belcheva, Elisaveta

Bagryana, Elisaveta .... **CLC 10**
    See also Belcheva, Elisaveta
    See also DLB 147

Bailey, Paul 1937- .... **CLC 45**
See also CA 21-24R; CANR 16; DLB 14

Baillie, Joanna 1762-1851 .... **NCLC 2**
See also DLB 93

Bainbridge, Beryl (Margaret)
1933- .... **CLC 4, 5, 8, 10, 14, 18, 22, 62;**
DAM NOV
See also CA 21-24R; CANR 24, 55;
DLB 14; MTCW

Baker, Elliott 1922- .... **CLC 8**
See also CA 45-48; CANR 2

Baker, Jean H. .... **TCLC 3, 10**
See also Russell, George William

Baker, Nicholson
1957- .... **CLC 61; DAM POP**
See also CA 135

Baker, Ray Stannard 1870-1946 ... **TCLC 47**
See also CA 118

Baker, Russell (Wayne) 1925- ...... **CLC 31**
See also BEST 89:4; CA 57-60; CANR 11,
41; MTCW

Bakhtin, M.
See Bakhtin, Mikhail Mikhailovich

Bakhtin, M. M.
See Bakhtin, Mikhail Mikhailovich

Bakhtin, Mikhail
See Bakhtin, Mikhail Mikhailovich

Bakhtin, Mikhail Mikhailovich
1895-1975 .... **CLC 83**
See also CA 128; 113

Bakshi, Ralph 1938(?)- .... **CLC 26**
See also CA 112; 138

Bakunin, Mikhail (Alexandrovich)
1814-1876 .... **NCLC 25, 58**

Baldwin, James (Arthur)
1924-1987 ...... **CLC 1, 2, 3, 4, 5, 8, 13,**
15, 17, 42, 50, 67, 90; BLC; DA; DAB;
DAC; DAM MST, MULT, NOV, POP;
DC 1; SSC 10; WLC
See also AAYA 4; BW 1; CA 1-4R; 124;
CABS 1; CANR 3, 24;
CDALB 1941-1968; DLB 2, 7, 33;
DLBY 87; MTCW; SATA 9;
SATA-Obit 54

Ballard, J(ames) G(raham)
1930- .... **CLC 3, 6, 14, 36; DAM NOV,**
POP; SSC 1
See also AAYA 3; CA 5-8R; CANR 15, 39;
DLB 14; MTCW

Balmont, Konstantin (Dmitriyevich)
1867-1943 .... **TCLC 11**
See also CA 109; 155

Balzac, Honore de
1799-1850 .... **NCLC 5, 35, 53; DA;**
DAB; DAC; DAM MST, NOV; SSC 5;
WLC
See also DLB 119

Bambara, Toni Cade
1939-1995 ...... **CLC 19, 88; BLC; DA;**
DAC; DAM MST, MULT
See also AAYA 5; BW 2; CA 29-32R; 150;
CANR 24, 49; DLB 38; MTCW

Bamdad, A.
See Shamlu, Ahmad

Banat, D. R.
See Bradbury, Ray (Douglas)

Bancroft, Laura
See Baum, L(yman) Frank

Banim, John 1798-1842 .... **NCLC 13**
See also DLB 116, 158, 159

Banim, Michael 1796-1874 ...... **NCLC 13**
See also DLB 158, 159

Banjo, The
See Paterson, A(ndrew) B(arton)

Banks, Iain
See Banks, Iain M(enzies)

Banks, Iain M(enzies) 1954- .... **CLC 34**
See also CA 123; 128; INT 128

Banks, Lynne Reid .... **CLC 23**
See also Reid Banks, Lynne
See also AAYA 6

Banks, Russell 1940- .... **CLC 37, 72**
See also CA 65-68; CAAS 15; CANR 19,
52; DLB 130

Banville, John 1945- .... **CLC 46**
See also CA 117; 128; DLB 14; INT 128

Banville, Theodore (Faullain) de
1832-1891 .... **NCLC 9**

Baraka, Amiri
1934- .... **CLC 1, 2, 3, 5, 10, 14, 33;**
BLC; DA; DAC; DAM MST, MULT,
POET, POP; DC 6; PC 4
See also Jones, LeRoi
See also BW 2; CA 21-24R; CABS 3;
CANR 27, 38; CDALB 1941-1968;
DLB 5, 7, 16, 38; DLBD 8; MTCW

Barbauld, Anna Laetitia
1743-1825 .... **NCLC 50**
See also DLB 107, 109, 142, 158

Barbellion, W. N. P. .... **TCLC 24**
See also Cummings, Bruce F(rederick)

Barbera, Jack (Vincent) 1945- ...... **CLC 44**
See also CA 110; CANR 45

Barbey d'Aurevilly, Jules Amedee
1808-1889 .... **NCLC 1; SSC 17**
See also DLB 119

Barbusse, Henri 1873-1935 .... **TCLC 5**
See also CA 105; 154; DLB 65

Barclay, Bill
See Moorcock, Michael (John)

Barclay, William Ewert
See Moorcock, Michael (John)

Barea, Arturo 1897-1957 .... **TCLC 14**
See also CA 111

Barfoot, Joan 1946- .... **CLC 18**
See also CA 105

Baring, Maurice 1874-1945 .... **TCLC 8**
See also CA 105; DLB 34

Barker, Clive 1952- ... **CLC 52; DAM POP**
See also AAYA 10; BEST 90:3; CA 121;
129; INT 129; MTCW

Barker, George Granville
1913-1991 ..... **CLC 8, 48; DAM POET**
See also CA 9-12R; 135; CANR 7, 38;
DLB 20; MTCW

Barker, Harley Granville
See Granville-Barker, Harley
See also DLB 10

Barker, Howard 1946- .... **CLC 37**
See also CA 102; DLB 13

Barker, Pat(ricia) 1943- .... **CLC 32, 94**
See also CA 117; 122; CANR 50; INT 122

Barlow, Joel 1754-1812 .... **NCLC 23**
See also DLB 37

Barnard, Mary (Ethel) 1909- .... **CLC 48**
See also CA 21-22; CAP 2

Barnes, Djuna
1892-1982 ... **CLC 3, 4, 8, 11, 29; SSC 3**
See also CA 9-12R; 107; CANR 16, 55;
DLB 4, 9, 45; MTCW

Barnes, Julian (Patrick)
1946- .... **CLC 42; DAB**
See also CA 102; CANR 19, 54; DLBY 93

Barnes, Peter 1931- .... **CLC 5, 56**
See also CA 65-68; CAAS 12; CANR 33,
34; DLB 13; MTCW

Baroja (y Nessi), Pio
1872-1956 .... **TCLC 8; HLC**
See also CA 104

Baron, David
See Pinter, Harold

Baron Corvo
See Rolfe, Frederick (William Serafino
Austin Lewis Mary)

Barondess, Sue K(aufman)
1926-1977 .... **CLC 8**
See also Kaufman, Sue
See also CA 1-4R; 69-72; CANR 1

Baron de Teive
See Pessoa, Fernando (Antonio Nogueira)

Barres, Maurice 1862-1923 .... **TCLC 47**
See also DLB 123

Barreto, Afonso Henrique de Lima
See Lima Barreto, Afonso Henrique de

Barrett, (Roger) Syd 1946- .... **CLC 35**

Barrett, William (Christopher)
1913-1992 .... **CLC 27**
See also CA 13-16R; 139; CANR 11;
INT CANR-11

Barrie, J(ames) M(atthew)
1860-1937 .... **TCLC 2; DAB;**
DAM DRAM
See also CA 104; 136; CDBLB 1890-1914;
CLR 16; DLB 10, 141, 156; MAICYA;
YABC 1

Barrington, Michael
See Moorcock, Michael (John)

Barrol, Grady
See Bograd, Larry

Barry, Mike
See Malzberg, Barry N(athaniel)

Barry, Philip 1896-1949 .... **TCLC 11**
See also CA 109; DLB 7

Bart, Andre Schwarz
See Schwarz-Bart, Andre

Barth, John (Simmons)
1930- ...... **CLC 1, 2, 3, 5, 7, 9, 10, 14,**
27, 51, 89; DAM NOV; SSC 10
See also AITN 1, 2; CA 1-4R; CABS 1;
CANR 5, 23, 49; DLB 2; MTCW

Belloc, (Joseph) Hilaire (Pierre Sebastien
    Rene Swanton)
    1870-1953 ... **TCLC 7, 18; DAM POET**
    See also CA 106; 152; DLB 19, 100, 141,
    174; YABC 1

Belloc, Joseph Peter Rene Hilaire
    See Belloc, (Joseph) Hilaire (Pierre Sebastien
    Rene Swanton)

Belloc, Joseph Pierre Hilaire
    See Belloc, (Joseph) Hilaire (Pierre Sebastien
    Rene Swanton)

Belloc, M. A.
    See Lowndes, Marie Adelaide (Belloc)

Bellow, Saul
    1915- ...... **CLC 1, 2, 3, 6, 8, 10, 13, 15,
    25, 33, 34, 63, 79; DA; DAB; DAC;
    DAM MST, NOV, POP; SSC 14; WLC**
    See also AITN 2; BEST 89:3; CA 5-8R;
    CABS 1; CANR 29, 53;
    CDALB 1941-1968; DLB 2, 28; DLBD 3;
    DLBY 82; MTCW

Belser, Reimond Karel Maria de 1929-
    See Ruyslinck, Ward
    See also CA 152

Bely, Andrey .... **TCLC 7; PC 11**
    See also Bugayev, Boris Nikolayevich

Benary, Margot
    See Benary-Isbert, Margot

Benary-Isbert, Margot 1889-1979... **CLC 12**
    See also CA 5-8R; 89-92; CANR 4;
    CLR 12; MAICYA; SATA 2;
    SATA-Obit 21

Benavente (y Martinez), Jacinto
    1866-1954 ..... **TCLC 3; DAM DRAM,
    MULT**
    See also CA 106; 131; HW; MTCW

Benchley, Peter (Bradford)
    1940- ..... **CLC 4, 8; DAM NOV, POP**
    See also AAYA 14; AITN 2; CA 17-20R;
    CANR 12, 35; MTCW; SATA 3, 89

Benchley, Robert (Charles)
    1889-1945 .... **TCLC 1, 55**
    See also CA 105; 153; DLB 11

Benda, Julien 1867-1956 .... **TCLC 60**
    See also CA 120; 154

Benedict, Ruth 1887-1948 .... **TCLC 60**

Benedikt, Michael 1935- .... **CLC 4, 14**
    See also CA 13-16R; CANR 7; DLB 5

Benet, Juan 1927-................ **CLC 28**
    See also CA 143

Benet, Stephen Vincent
    1898-1943 ...... **TCLC 7; DAM POET;
    SSC 10**
    See also CA 104; 152; DLB 4, 48, 102;
    YABC 1

Benet, William Rose
    1886-1950 ...... **TCLC 28; DAM POET**
    See also CA 118; 152; DLB 45

Benford, Gregory (Albert) 1941-.... **CLC 52**
    See also CA 69-72; CANR 12, 24, 49;
    DLBY 82

Bengtsson, Frans (Gunnar)
    1894-1954 .... **TCLC 48**

Benjamin, David
    See Slavitt, David R(ytman)

Benjamin, Lois
    See Gould, Lois

Benjamin, Walter 1892-1940 ...... **TCLC 39**

Benn, Gottfried 1886-1956........ **TCLC 3**
    See also CA 106; 153; DLB 56

Bennett, Alan
    1934- ... **CLC 45, 77; DAB; DAM MST**
    See also CA 103; CANR 35, 55; MTCW

Bennett, (Enoch) Arnold
    1867-1931 .... **TCLC 5, 20**
    See also CA 106; 155; CDBLB 1890-1914;
    DLB 10, 34, 98, 135

Bennett, Elizabeth
    See Mitchell, Margaret (Munnerlyn)

Bennett, George Harold 1930-
    See Bennett, Hal
    See also BW 1; CA 97-100

Bennett, Hal .... **CLC 5**
    See also Bennett, George Harold
    See also DLB 33

Bennett, Jay 1912-................ **CLC 35**
    See also AAYA 10; CA 69-72; CANR 11,
    42; JRDA; SAAS 4; SATA 41, 87;
    SATA-Brief 27

Bennett, Louise (Simone)
    1919- ..... **CLC 28; BLC; DAM MULT**
    See also BW 2; CA 151; DLB 117

Benson, E(dward) F(rederic)
    1867-1940 .... **TCLC 27**
    See also CA 114; DLB 135, 153

Benson, Jackson J. 1930-.......... **CLC 34**
    See also CA 25-28R; DLB 111

Benson, Sally 1900-1972 .... **CLC 17**
    See also CA 19-20; 37-40R; CAP 1;
    SATA 1, 35; SATA-Obit 27

Benson, Stella 1892-1933........ **TCLC 17**
    See also CA 117; 155; DLB 36, 162

Bentham, Jeremy 1748-1832 ..... **NCLC 38**
    See also DLB 107, 158

Bentley, E(dmund) C(lerihew)
    1875-1956 .... **TCLC 12**
    See also CA 108; DLB 70

Bentley, Eric (Russell) 1916-....... **CLC 24**
    See also CA 5-8R; CANR 6; INT CANR-6

Beranger, Pierre Jean de
    1780-1857 .... **NCLC 34**

Berdyaev, Nicolas
    See Berdyaev, Nikolai (Aleksandrovich)

Berdyaev, Nikolai (Aleksandrovich)
    1874-1948 .... **TCLC 67**
    See also CA 120

Berendt, John (Lawrence) 1939-.... **CLC 86**
    See also CA 146

Berger, Colonel
    See Malraux, (Georges-)Andre

Berger, John (Peter) 1926- ...... **CLC 2, 19**
    See also CA 81-84; CANR 51; DLB 14

Berger, Melvin H. 1927- .... **CLC 12**
    See also CA 5-8R; CANR 4; CLR 32;
    SAAS 2; SATA 5, 88

Berger, Thomas (Louis)
    1924- .... **CLC 3, 5, 8, 11, 18, 38;
    DAM NOV**
    See also CA 1-4R; CANR 5, 28, 51; DLB 2;
    DLBY 80; INT CANR-28; MTCW

Bergman, (Ernst) Ingmar
    1918- .... **CLC 16, 72**
    See also CA 81-84; CANR 33

Bergson, Henri 1859-1941........ **TCLC 32**

Bergstein, Eleanor 1938-............ **CLC 4**
    See also CA 53-56; CANR 5

Berkoff, Steven 1937-............. **CLC 56**
    See also CA 104

Bermant, Chaim (Icyk) 1929- ...... **CLC 40**
    See also CA 57-60; CANR 6, 31, 57

Bern, Victoria
    See Fisher, M(ary) F(rances) K(ennedy)

Bernanos, (Paul Louis) Georges
    1888-1948 .... **TCLC 3**
    See also CA 104; 130; DLB 72

Bernard, April 1956- .... **CLC 59**
    See also CA 131

Berne, Victoria
    See Fisher, M(ary) F(rances) K(ennedy)

Bernhard, Thomas
    1931-1989 .... **CLC 3, 32, 61**
    See also CA 85-88; 127; CANR 32, 57;
    DLB 85, 124; MTCW

Berriault, Gina 1926- .... **CLC 54**
    See also CA 116; 129; DLB 130

Berrigan, Daniel 1921-............ **CLC 4**
    See also CA 33-36R; CAAS 1; CANR 11,
    43; DLB 5

Berrigan, Edmund Joseph Michael, Jr.
    1934-1983
    See Berrigan, Ted
    See also CA 61-64; 110; CANR 14

Berrigan, Ted..................... **CLC 37**
    See also Berrigan, Edmund Joseph Michael,
    Jr.
    See also DLB 5, 169

Berry, Charles Edward Anderson 1931-
    See Berry, Chuck
    See also CA 115

Berry, Chuck.................... **CLC 17**
    See also Berry, Charles Edward Anderson

Berry, Jonas
    See Ashbery, John (Lawrence)

Berry, Wendell (Erdman)
    1934- .... **CLC 4, 6, 8, 27, 46;
    DAM POET**
    See also AITN 1; CA 73-76; CANR 50;
    DLB 5, 6

Berryman, John
    1914-1972 ...... **CLC 1, 2, 3, 4, 6, 8, 10,
    13, 25, 62; DAM POET**
    See also CA 13-16; 33-36R; CABS 2;
    CANR 35; CAP 1; CDALB 1941-1968;
    DLB 48; MTCW

Bertolucci, Bernardo 1940- .... **CLC 16**
    See also CA 106

Bertrand, Aloysius 1807-1841 .... **NCLC 31**

Bertran de Born c. 1140-1215 ..... **CMLC 5**

Besant, Annie (Wood) 1847-1933 ... **TCLC 9**
    See also CA 105

Bragg, Melvyn 1939- .... **CLC 10**
See also BEST 89:3; CA 57-60; CANR 10,
48; DLB 14

Braine, John (Gerard)
1922-1986 .... **CLC 1, 3, 41**
See also CA 1-4R; 120; CANR 1, 33;
CDBLB 1945-1960; DLB 15; DLBY 86;
MTCW

Brammer, William 1930(?)-1978 .... **CLC 31**
See also CA 77-80

Brancati, Vitaliano 1907-1954..... **TCLC 12**
See also CA 109

Brancato, Robin F(idler) 1936- ..... **CLC 35**
See also AAYA 9; CA 69-72; CANR 11,
45; CLR 32; JRDA; SAAS 9; SATA 23

Brand, Max
See Faust, Frederick (Schiller)

Brand, Millen 1906-1980 .... **CLC 7**
See also CA 21-24R; 97-100

Branden, Barbara .... **CLC 44**
See also CA 148

Brandes, Georg (Morris Cohen)
1842-1927 .... **TCLC 10**
See also CA 105

Brandys, Kazimierz 1916- .... **CLC 62**

Branley, Franklyn M(ansfield)
1915- .... **CLC 21**
See also CA 33-36R; CANR 14, 39;
CLR 13; MAICYA; SAAS 16; SATA 4,
68

Brathwaite, Edward Kamau
1930- .... **CLC 11; DAM POET**
See also BW 2; CA 25-28R; CANR 11, 26,
47; DLB 125

Brautigan, Richard (Gary)
1935-1984 .... **CLC 1, 3, 5, 9, 12, 34, 42;**
DAM NOV
See also CA 53-56; 113; CANR 34; DLB 2,
5; DLBY 80, 84; MTCW; SATA 56

Brave Bird, Mary 1953-
See Crow Dog, Mary (Ellen)
See also NNAL

Braverman, Kate 1950- .... **CLC 67**
See also CA 89-92

Brecht, Bertolt
1898-1956 ...... **TCLC 1, 6, 13, 35; DA;**
DAB; DAC; DAM DRAM, MST; DC 3;
WLC
See also CA 104; 133; DLB 56, 124; MTCW

Brecht, Eugen Berthold Friedrich
See Brecht, Bertolt

Bremer, Fredrika 1801-1865 ..... **NCLC 11**

Brennan, Christopher John
1870-1932 .... **TCLC 17**
See also CA 117

Brennan, Maeve 1917-............. **CLC 5**
See also CA 81-84

Brentano, Clemens (Maria)
1778-1842 .... **NCLC 1**
See also DLB 90

Brent of Bin Bin
See Franklin, (Stella Maraia Sarah) Miles

Brenton, Howard 1942- .... **CLC 31**
See also CA 69-72; CANR 33; DLB 13;
MTCW

Breslin, James 1930-
See Breslin, Jimmy
See also CA 73-76; CANR 31; DAM NOV;
MTCW

Breslin, Jimmy .... **CLC 4, 43**
See also Breslin, James
See also AITN 1

Bresson, Robert 1901- .... **CLC 16**
See also CA 110; CANR 49

Breton, Andre
1896-1966 ..... **CLC 2, 9, 15, 54; PC 15**
See also CA 19-20; 25-28R; CANR 40;
CAP 2; DLB 65; MTCW

Breytenbach, Breyten
1939(?)- ...... **CLC 23, 37; DAM POET**
See also CA 113; 129

Bridgers, Sue Ellen 1942- .... **CLC 26**
See also AAYA 8; CA 65-68; CANR 11,
36; CLR 18; DLB 52; JRDA; MAICYA;
SAAS 1; SATA 22, 90

Bridges, Robert (Seymour)
1844-1930 .... **TCLC 1; DAM POET**
See also CA 104; 152; CDBLB 1890-1914;
DLB 19, 98

Bridie, James..................... **TCLC 3**
See also Mavor, Osborne Henry
See also DLB 10

Brin, David 1950-............... **CLC 34**
See also CA 102; CANR 24;
INT CANR-24; SATA 65

Brink, Andre (Philippus)
1935- .... **CLC 18, 36**
See also CA 104; CANR 39; INT 103;
MTCW

Brinsmead, H(esba) F(ay) 1922- .... **CLC 21**
See also CA 21-24R; CANR 10; MAICYA;
SAAS 5; SATA 18, 78

Brittain, Vera (Mary)
1893(?)-1970 .... **CLC 23**
See also CA 13-16; 25-28R; CAP 1; MTCW

Broch, Hermann 1886-1951....... **TCLC 20**
See also CA 117; DLB 85, 124

Brock, Rose
See Hansen, Joseph

Brodkey, Harold (Roy) 1930-1996 .. **CLC 56**
See also CA 111; 151; DLB 130

Brodsky, Iosif Alexandrovich 1940-1996
See Brodsky, Joseph
See also AITN 1; CA 41-44R; 151;
CANR 37; DAM POET; MTCW

Brodsky, Joseph
1940-1996 .. **CLC 4, 6, 13, 36, 100; PC 9**
See also Brodsky, Iosif Alexandrovich

Brodsky, Michael Mark 1948- ..... **CLC 19**
See also CA 102; CANR 18, 41

Bromell, Henry 1947-.............. **CLC 5**
See also CA 53-56; CANR 9

Bromfield, Louis (Brucker)
1896-1956 .... **TCLC 11**
See also CA 107; 155; DLB 4, 9, 86

Broner, E(sther) M(asserman)
1930- .... **CLC 19**
See also CA 17-20R; CANR 8, 25; DLB 28

Bronk, William 1918-............. **CLC 10**
See also CA 89-92; CANR 23; DLB 165

Bronstein, Lev Davidovich
See Trotsky, Leon

Bronte, Anne 1820-1849.......... **NCLC 4**
See also DLB 21

Bronte, Charlotte
1816-1855 ..... **NCLC 3, 8, 33, 58; DA;**
DAB; DAC; DAM MST, NOV; WLC
See also AAYA 17; CDBLB 1832-1890;
DLB 21, 159

Bronte, Emily (Jane)
1818-1848 .... **NCLC 16, 35; DA; DAB;**
DAC; DAM MST, NOV, POET; PC 8;
WLC
See also AAYA 17; CDBLB 1832-1890;
DLB 21, 32

Brooke, Frances 1724-1789 .... **LC 6**
See also DLB 39, 99

Brooke, Henry 1703(?)-1783 .... **LC 1**
See also DLB 39

Brooke, Rupert (Chawner)
1887-1915 .... **TCLC 2, 7; DA; DAB;**
DAC; DAM MST, POET; WLC
See also CA 104; 132; CDBLB 1914-1945;
DLB 19; MTCW

Brooke-Haven, P.
See Wodehouse, P(elham) G(renville)

Brooke-Rose, Christine 1926- ...... **CLC 40**
See also CA 13-16R; DLB 14

Brookner, Anita
1928- .... **CLC 32, 34, 51; DAB;**
DAM POP
See also CA 114; 120; CANR 37, 56;
DLBY 87; MTCW

Brooks, Cleanth 1906-1994 ..... **CLC 24, 86**
See also CA 17-20R; 145; CANR 33, 35;
DLB 63; DLBY 94; INT CANR-35;
MTCW

Brooks, George
See Baum, L(yman) Frank

Brooks, Gwendolyn
1917- ...... **CLC 1, 2, 4, 5, 15, 49; BLC;**
DA; DAC; DAM MST, MULT, POET;
PC 7; WLC
See also AAYA 20; AITN 1; BW 2;
CA 1-4R; CANR 1, 27, 52;
CDALB 1941-1968; CLR 27; DLB 5, 76,
165; MTCW; SATA 6

Brooks, Mel..................... **CLC 12**
See also Kaminsky, Melvin
See also AAYA 13; DLB 26

Brooks, Peter 1938-.............. **CLC 34**
See also CA 45-48; CANR 1

Brooks, Van Wyck 1886-1963...... **CLC 29**
See also CA 1-4R; CANR 6; DLB 45, 63,
103

Brophy, Brigid (Antonia)
1929-1995 .... **CLC 6, 11, 29**
See also CA 5-8R; 149; CAAS 4; CANR 25,
53; DLB 14; MTCW

Brosman, Catharine Savage 1934-.... **CLC 9**
See also CA 61-64; CANR 21, 46

Brother Antoninus
See Everson, William (Oliver)

Broughton, T(homas) Alan 1936- ... **CLC 19**
See also CA 45-48; CANR 2, 23, 48

Broumas, Olga 1949- .... **CLC 10, 73**
See also CA 85-88; CANR 20

Brown, Alan 1951- .... **CLC 99**

Brown, Charles Brockden
1771-1810 .... **NCLC 22**
See also CDALB 1640-1865; DLB 37, 59, 73

Brown, Christy 1932-1981 .... **CLC 63**
See also CA 105; 104; DLB 14

Brown, Claude
1937- ..... **CLC 30; BLC; DAM MULT**
See also AAYA 7; BW 1; CA 73-76

Brown, Dee (Alexander)
1908- .... **CLC 18, 47; DAM POP**
See also CA 13-16R; CAAS 6; CANR 11, 45; DLBY 80; MTCW; SATA 5

Brown, George
See Wertmueller, Lina

Brown, George Douglas
1869-1902 .... **TCLC 28**

Brown, George Mackay
1921-1996 .... **CLC 5, 48, 100**
See also CA 21-24R; 151; CAAS 6; CANR 12, 37; DLB 14, 27, 139; MTCW; SATA 35

Brown, (William) Larry 1951- ...... **CLC 73**
See also CA 130; 134; INT 133

Brown, Moses
See Barrett, William (Christopher)

Brown, Rita Mae
1944- ..... **CLC 18, 43, 79; DAM NOV, POP**
See also CA 45-48; CANR 2, 11, 35; INT CANR-11; MTCW

Brown, Roderick (Langmere) Haig-
See Haig-Brown, Roderick (Langmere)

Brown, Rosellen 1939- .... **CLC 32**
See also CA 77-80; CAAS 10; CANR 14, 44

Brown, Sterling Allen
1901-1989 .... **CLC 1, 23, 59; BLC; DAM MULT, POET**
See also BW 1; CA 85-88; 127; CANR 26; DLB 48, 51, 63; MTCW

Brown, Will
See Ainsworth, William Harrison

Brown, William Wells
1813-1884 .... **NCLC 2; BLC; DAM MULT; DC 1**
See also DLB 3, 50

Browne, (Clyde) Jackson 1948(?)-... **CLC 21**
See also CA 120

Browning, Elizabeth Barrett
1806-1861 ..... **NCLC 1, 16; DA; DAB; DAC; DAM MST, POET; PC 6; WLC**
See also CDBLB 1832-1890; DLB 32

Browning, Robert
1812-1889 .... **NCLC 19; DA; DAB; DAC; DAM MST, POET; PC 2**
See also CDBLB 1832-1890; DLB 32, 163; YABC 1

Browning, Tod 1882-1962 .... **CLC 16**
See also CA 141; 117

Brownson, Orestes (Augustus)
1803-1876 .... **NCLC 50**

Bruccoli, Matthew J(oseph) 1931- .. **CLC 34**
See also CA 9-12R; CANR 7; DLB 103

Bruce, Lenny .... **CLC 21**
See also Schneider, Leonard Alfred

Bruin, John
See Brutus, Dennis

Brulard, Henri
See Stendhal

Brulls, Christian
See Simenon, Georges (Jacques Christian)

Brunner, John (Kilian Houston)
1934-1995 ...... **CLC 8, 10; DAM POP**
See also CA 1-4R; 149; CAAS 8; CANR 2, 37; MTCW

Bruno, Giordano 1548-1600 .... **LC 27**

Brutus, Dennis
1924- ..... **CLC 43; BLC; DAM MULT, POET**
See also BW 2; CA 49-52; CAAS 14; CANR 2, 27, 42; DLB 117

Bryan, C(ourtlandt) D(ixon) B(arnes)
1936- .... **CLC 29**
See also CA 73-76; CANR 13; INT CANR-13

Bryan, Michael
See Moore, Brian

Bryant, William Cullen
1794-1878 ..... **NCLC 6, 46; DA; DAB; DAC; DAM MST, POET**
See also CDALB 1640-1865; DLB 3, 43, 59

Bryusov, Valery Yakovlevich
1873-1924 .... **TCLC 10**
See also CA 107; 155

Buchan, John
1875-1940 .... **TCLC 41; DAB; DAM POP**
See also CA 108; 145; DLB 34, 70, 156; YABC 2

Buchanan, George 1506-1582 .... **LC 4**

Buchheim, Lothar-Guenther 1918- ... **CLC 6**
See also CA 85-88

Buchner, (Karl) Georg
1813-1837 .... **NCLC 26**

Buchwald, Art(hur) 1925- .... **CLC 33**
See also AITN 1; CA 5-8R; CANR 21; MTCW; SATA 10

Buck, Pearl S(ydenstricker)
1892-1973 .... **CLC 7, 11, 18; DA; DAB; DAC; DAM MST, NOV**
See also AITN 1; CA 1-4R; 41-44R; CANR 1, 34; DLB 9, 102; MTCW; SATA 1, 25

Buckler, Ernest
1908-1984 .. **CLC 13; DAC; DAM MST**
See also CA 11-12; 114; CAP 1; DLB 68; SATA 47

Buckley, Vincent (Thomas)
1925-1988 .... **CLC 57**
See also CA 101

Buckley, William F(rank), Jr.
1925- .... **CLC 7, 18, 37; DAM POP**
See also AITN 1; CA 1-4R; CANR 1, 24, 53; DLB 137; DLBY 80; INT CANR-24; MTCW

Buechner, (Carl) Frederick
1926- ...... **CLC 2, 4, 6, 9; DAM NOV**
See also CA 13-16R; CANR 11, 39; DLBY 80; INT CANR-11; MTCW

Buell, John (Edward) 1927- .... **CLC 10**
See also CA 1-4R; DLB 53

Buero Vallejo, Antonio 1916- ... **CLC 15, 46**
See also CA 106; CANR 24, 49; HW; MTCW

Bufalino, Gesualdo 1920(?)- .... **CLC 74**

Bugayev, Boris Nikolayevich 1880-1934
See Bely, Andrey
See also CA 104

Bukowski, Charles
1920-1994 .... **CLC 2, 5, 9, 41, 82; DAM NOV, POET**
See also CA 17-20R; 144; CANR 40; DLB 5, 130, 169; MTCW

Bulgakov, Mikhail (Afanas'evich)
1891-1940 .... **TCLC 2, 16; DAM DRAM, NOV; SSC 18**
See also CA 105; 152

Bulgya, Alexander Alexandrovich
1901-1956 .... **TCLC 53**
See also Fadeyev, Alexander
See also CA 117

Bullins, Ed
1935- .... **CLC 1, 5, 7; BLC; DAM DRAM, MULT; DC 6**
See also BW 2; CA 49-52; CAAS 16; CANR 24, 46; DLB 7, 38; MTCW

Bulwer-Lytton, Edward (George Earle Lytton)
1803-1873 .... **NCLC 1, 45**
See also DLB 21

Bunin, Ivan Alexeyevich
1870-1953 .... **TCLC 6; SSC 5**
See also CA 104

Bunting, Basil
1900-1985 .... **CLC 10, 39, 47; DAM POET**
See also CA 53-56; 115; CANR 7; DLB 20

Bunuel, Luis
1900-1983 .... **CLC 16, 80; DAM MULT; HLC**
See also CA 101; 110; CANR 32; HW

Bunyan, John
1628-1688 ...... **LC 4; DA; DAB; DAC; DAM MST; WLC**
See also CDBLB 1660-1789; DLB 39

Burckhardt, Jacob (Christoph)
1818-1897 .... **NCLC 49**

Burford, Eleanor
See Hibbert, Eleanor Alice Burford

Burgess, Anthony
. **CLC 1, 2, 4, 5, 8, 10, 13, 15, 22, 40, 62, 81, 94; DAB**
See also Wilson, John (Anthony) Burgess
See also AITN 1; CDBLB 1960 to Present; DLB 14

Burke, Edmund
1729(?)-1797 ...... **LC 7, 36; DA; DAB; DAC; DAM MST; WLC**
See also DLB 104

Burke, Kenneth (Duva)
1897-1993 .... CLC 2, 24
See also CA 5-8R; 143; CANR 39; DLB 45,
63; MTCW

Burke, Leda
See Garnett, David

Burke, Ralph
See Silverberg, Robert

Burke, Thomas 1886-1945 .... TCLC 63
See also CA 113; 155

Burney, Fanny 1752-1840 .... NCLC 12, 54
See also DLB 39

Burns, Robert 1759-1796 .... PC 6
See also CDBLB 1789-1832; DA; DAB;
DAC; DAM MST, POET; DLB 109;
WLC

Burns, Tex
See L'Amour, Louis (Dearborn)

Burnshaw, Stanley 1906- ..... CLC 3, 13, 44
See also CA 9-12R; DLB 48

Burr, Anne 1937- .... CLC 6
See also CA 25-28R

Burroughs, Edgar Rice
1875-1950 .... TCLC 2, 32; DAM NOV
See also AAYA 11; CA 104; 132; DLB 8;
MTCW; SATA 41

Burroughs, William S(eward)
1914- .... CLC 1, 2, 5, 15, 22, 42, 75;
DA; DAB; DAC; DAM MST, NOV,
POP; WLC
See also AITN 2; CA 9-12R; CANR 20, 52;
DLB 2, 8, 16, 152; DLBY 81; MTCW

Burton, Richard F. 1821-1890 .... NCLC 42
See also DLB 55

Busch, Frederick 1941- ... CLC 7, 10, 18, 47
See also CA 33-36R; CAAS 1; CANR 45;
DLB 6

Bush, Ronald 1946- .... CLC 34
See also CA 136

Bustos, F(rancisco)
See Borges, Jorge Luis

Bustos Domecq, H(onorio)
See Bioy Casares, Adolfo; Borges, Jorge
Luis

Butler, Octavia E(stelle)
1947- ..... CLC 38; DAM MULT, POP
See also AAYA 18; BW 2; CA 73-76;
CANR 12, 24, 38; DLB 33; MTCW;
SATA 84

Butler, Robert Olen (Jr.)
1945- .... CLC 81; DAM POP
See also CA 112; DLB 173; INT 112

Butler, Samuel 1612-1680 .... LC 16
See also DLB 101, 126

Butler, Samuel
1835-1902 ...... TCLC 1, 33; DA; DAB;
DAC; DAM MST, NOV; WLC
See also CA 143; CDBLB 1890-1914;
DLB 18, 57, 174

Butler, Walter C.
See Faust, Frederick (Schiller)

Butor, Michel (Marie Francois)
1926- .... CLC 1, 3, 8, 11, 15
See also CA 9-12R; CANR 33; DLB 83;
MTCW

Buzo, Alexander (John) 1944- ...... CLC 61
See also CA 97-100; CANR 17, 39

Buzzati, Dino 1906-1972 .... CLC 36
See also CA 33-36R; DLB 177

Byars, Betsy (Cromer) 1928- .... CLC 35
See also AAYA 19; CA 33-36R; CANR 18,
36, 57; CLR 1, 16; DLB 52;
INT CANR-18; JRDA; MAICYA;
MTCW; SAAS 1; SATA 4, 46, 80

Byatt, A(ntonia) S(usan Drabble)
1936- ... CLC 19, 65; DAM NOV, POP
See also CA 13-16R; CANR 13, 33, 50;
DLB 14; MTCW

Byrne, David 1952- .... CLC 26
See also CA 127

Byrne, John Keyes 1926-
See Leonard, Hugh
See also CA 102; INT 102

Byron, George Gordon (Noel)
1788-1824 ..... NCLC 2, 12; DA; DAB;
DAC; DAM MST, POET; PC 16; WLC
See also CDBLB 1789-1832; DLB 96, 110

Byron, Robert 1905-1941 .... TCLC 67

C. 3. 3.
See Wilde, Oscar (Fingal O'Flahertie Wills)

Caballero, Fernan 1796-1877 ..... NCLC 10

Cabell, Branch
See Cabell, James Branch

Cabell, James Branch 1879-1958 ... TCLC 6
See also CA 105; 152; DLB 9, 78

Cable, George Washington
1844-1925 .... TCLC 4; SSC 4
See also CA 104; 155; DLB 12, 74;
DLBD 13

Cabral de Melo Neto, Joao
1920- .... CLC 76; DAM MULT
See also CA 151

Cabrera Infante, G(uillermo)
1929- ..... CLC 5, 25, 45; DAM MULT;
HLC
See also CA 85-88; CANR 29; DLB 113;
HW; MTCW

Cade, Toni
See Bambara, Toni Cade

Cadmus and Harmonia
See Buchan, John

Caedmon fl. 658-680 .... CMLC 7
See also DLB 146

Caeiro, Alberto
See Pessoa, Fernando (Antonio Nogueira)

Cage, John (Milton, Jr.) 1912- ..... CLC 41
See also CA 13-16R; CANR 9;
INT CANR-9

Cain, G.
See Cabrera Infante, G(uillermo)

Cain, Guillermo
See Cabrera Infante, G(uillermo)

Cain, James M(allahan)
1892-1977 .... CLC 3, 11, 28
See also AITN 1; CA 17-20R; 73-76;
CANR 8, 34; MTCW

Caine, Mark
See Raphael, Frederic (Michael)

Calasso, Roberto 1941- .... CLC 81
See also CA 143

Calderon de la Barca, Pedro
1600-1681 .... LC 23; DC 3

Caldwell, Erskine (Preston)
1903-1987 .... CLC 1, 8, 14, 50, 60;
DAM NOV; SSC 19
See also AITN 1; CA 1-4R; 121; CAAS 1;
CANR 2, 33; DLB 9, 86; MTCW

Caldwell, (Janet Miriam) Taylor (Holland)
1900-1985 .... CLC 2, 28, 39;
DAM NOV, POP
See also CA 5-8R; 116; CANR 5

Calhoun, John Caldwell
1782-1850 .... NCLC 15
See also DLB 3

Calisher, Hortense
1911- ..... CLC 2, 4, 8, 38; DAM NOV;
SSC 15
See also CA 1-4R; CANR 1, 22; DLB 2;
INT CANR-22; MTCW

Callaghan, Morley Edward
1903-1990 ..... CLC 3, 14, 41, 65; DAC;
DAM MST
See also CA 9-12R; 132; CANR 33;
DLB 68; MTCW

Callimachus
c. 305B.C.-c. 240B.C. .... CMLC 18
See also DLB 176

Calvin, John 1509-1564 .... LC 37

Calvino, Italo
1923-1985 ..... CLC 5, 8, 11, 22, 33, 39,
73; DAM NOV; SSC 3
See also CA 85-88; 116; CANR 23; MTCW

Cameron, Carey 1952- .... CLC 59
See also CA 135

Cameron, Peter 1959- .... CLC 44
See also CA 125; CANR 50

Campana, Dino 1885-1932 .... TCLC 20
See also CA 117; DLB 114

Campanella, Tommaso 1568-1639 .... LC 32

Campbell, John W(ood, Jr.)
1910-1971 .... CLC 32
See also CA 21-22; 29-32R; CANR 34;
CAP 2; DLB 8; MTCW

Campbell, Joseph 1904-1987 .... CLC 69
See also AAYA 3; BEST 89:2; CA 1-4R;
124; CANR 3, 28; MTCW

Campbell, Maria 1940- .... CLC 85; DAC
See also CA 102; CANR 54; NNAL

Campbell, (John) Ramsey
1946- .... CLC 42; SSC 19
See also CA 57-60; CANR 7; INT CANR-7

Campbell, (Ignatius) Roy (Dunnachie)
1901-1957 .... TCLC 5
See also CA 104; 155; DLB 20

Campbell, Thomas 1777-1844 .... NCLC 19
See also DLB 93; 144

Campbell, Wilfred .... TCLC 9
See also Campbell, William

Campbell, William 1858(?)-1918
See Campbell, Wilfred
See also CA 106; DLB 92

Campion, Jane .... CLC 95
See also CA 138

Campos, Alvaro de
See Pessoa, Fernando (Antonio Nogueira)

Camus, Albert
1913-1960 .... CLC 1, 2, 4, 9, 11, 14, 32,
63, 69; DA; DAB; DAC; DAM DRAM,
MST, NOV; DC 2; SSC 9; WLC
See also CA 89-92; DLB 72; MTCW

Canby, Vincent 1924-.............. CLC 13
See also CA 81-84

Cancale
See Desnos, Robert

Canetti, Elias
1905-1994 .... CLC 3, 14, 25, 75, 86
See also CA 21-24R; 146; CANR 23;
DLB 85, 124; MTCW

Canin, Ethan 1960-............... CLC 55
See also CA 131; 135

Cannon, Curt
See Hunter, Evan

Cape, Judith
See Page, P(atricia) K(athleen)

Capek, Karel
1890-1938 ...... TCLC 6, 37; DA; DAB;
DAC; DAM DRAM, MST, NOV; DC 1;
WLC
See also CA 104; 140

Capote, Truman
1924-1984 ...... CLC 1, 3, 8, 13, 19, 34,
38, 58; DA; DAB; DAC; DAM MST,
NOV, POP; SSC 2; WLC
See also CA 5-8R; 113; CANR 18;
CDALB 1941-1968; DLB 2; DLBY 80,
84; MTCW; SATA 91

Capra, Frank 1897-1991.......... CLC 16
See also CA 61-64; 135

Caputo, Philip 1941-.............. CLC 32
See also CA 73-76; CANR 40

Card, Orson Scott
1951- ...... CLC 44, 47, 50; DAM POP
See also AAYA 11; CA 102; CANR 27, 47;
INT CANR-27; MTCW; SATA 83

Cardenal, Ernesto
1925- .... CLC 31; DAM MULT,
POET; HLC
See also CA 49-52; CANR 2, 32; HW;
MTCW

Cardozo, Benjamin N(athan)
1870-1938 .... TCLC 65
See also CA 117

Carducci, Giosue 1835-1907...... TCLC 32

Carew, Thomas 1595(?)-1640........ LC 13
See also DLB 126

Carey, Ernestine Gilbreth 1908-.... CLC 17
See also CA 5-8R; SATA 2

Carey, Peter 1943-......... CLC 40, 55, 96
See also CA 123; 127; CANR 53; INT 127;
MTCW

Carleton, William 1794-1869...... NCLC 3
See also DLB 159

Carlisle, Henry (Coffin) 1926-...... CLC 33
See also CA 13-16R; CANR 15

Carlsen, Chris
See Holdstock, Robert P.

Carlson, Ron(ald F.) 1947-........ CLC 54
See also CA 105; CANR 27

Carlyle, Thomas
1795-1881 ...... NCLC 22; DA; DAB;
DAC; DAM MST
See also CDBLB 1789-1832; DLB 55; 144

Carman, (William) Bliss
1861-1929 .... TCLC 7; DAC
See also CA 104; 152; DLB 92

Carnegie, Dale 1888-1955 .... TCLC 53

Carossa, Hans 1878-1956........ TCLC 48
See also DLB 66

Carpenter, Don(ald Richard)
1931-1995 .... CLC 41
See also CA 45-48; 149; CANR 1

Carpentier (y Valmont), Alejo
1904-1980 .... CLC 8, 11, 38;
DAM MULT; HLC
See also CA 65-68; 97-100; CANR 11;
DLB 113; HW

Carr, Caleb 1955(?)-.............. CLC 86
See also CA 147

Carr, Emily 1871-1945........... TCLC 32
See also DLB 68

Carr, John Dickson 1906-1977 ...... CLC 3
See also CA 49-52; 69-72; CANR 3, 33;
MTCW

Carr, Philippa
See Hibbert, Eleanor Alice Burford

Carr, Virginia Spencer 1929-....... CLC 34
See also CA 61-64; DLB 111

Carrere, Emmanuel 1957- .... CLC 89

Carrier, Roch
1937- ... CLC 13, 78; DAC; DAM MST
See also CA 130; DLB 53

Carroll, James P. 1943(?)-......... CLC 38
See also CA 81-84

Carroll, Jim 1951-............... CLC 35
See also AAYA 17; CA 45-48; CANR 42

Carroll, Lewis .... NCLC 2, 53; WLC
See also Dodgson, Charles Lutwidge
See also CDBLB 1832-1890; CLR 2, 18;
DLB 18, 163; JRDA

Carroll, Paul Vincent 1900-1968.... CLC 10
See also CA 9-12R; 25-28R; DLB 10

Carruth, Hayden
1921- ...... CLC 4, 7, 10, 18, 84; PC 10
See also CA 9-12R; CANR 4, 38; DLB 5,
165; INT CANR-4; MTCW; SATA 47

Carson, Rachel Louise
1907-1964 .... CLC 71; DAM POP
See also CA 77-80; CANR 35; MTCW;
SATA 23

Carter, Angela (Olive)
1940-1992 ...... CLC 5, 41, 76; SSC 13
See also CA 53-56; 136; CANR 12, 36;
DLB 14; MTCW; SATA 66;
SATA-Obit 70

Carter, Nick
See Smith, Martin Cruz

Carver, Raymond
1938-1988 .... CLC 22, 36, 53, 55;
DAM NOV; SSC 8
See also CA 33-36R; 126; CANR 17, 34;
DLB 130; DLBY 84, 88; MTCW

Cary, Elizabeth, Lady Falkland
1585-1639 .... LC 30

Cary, (Arthur) Joyce (Lunel)
1888-1957 .... TCLC 1, 29
See also CA 104; CDBLB 1914-1945;
DLB 15, 100

Casanova de Seingalt, Giovanni Jacopo
1725-1798 .... LC 13

Casares, Adolfo Bioy
See Bioy Casares, Adolfo

Casely-Hayford, J(oseph) E(phraim)
1866-1930 .... TCLC 24; BLC;
DAM MULT
See also BW 2; CA 123; 152

Casey, John (Dudley) 1939-....... CLC 59
See also BEST 90:2; CA 69-72; CANR 23

Casey, Michael 1947-............. CLC 2
See also CA 65-68; DLB 5

Casey, Patrick
See Thurman, Wallace (Henry)

Casey, Warren (Peter) 1935-1988... CLC 12
See also CA 101; 127; INT 101

Casona, Alejandro................ CLC 49
See also Alvarez, Alejandro Rodriguez

Cassavetes, John 1929-1989........ CLC 20
See also CA 85-88; 127

Cassian, Nina 1924-............... PC 17

Cassill, R(onald) V(erlin) 1919-... CLC 4, 23
See also CA 9-12R; CAAS 1; CANR 7, 45;
DLB 6

Cassirer, Ernst 1874-1945 .... TCLC 61

Cassity, (Allen) Turner 1929- .... CLC 6, 42
See also CA 17-20R; CAAS 8; CANR 11;
DLB 105

Castaneda, Carlos 1931(?)-......... CLC 12
See also CA 25-28R; CANR 32; HW;
MTCW

Castedo, Elena 1937- .... CLC 65
See also CA 132

Castedo-Ellerman, Elena
See Castedo, Elena

Castellanos, Rosario
1925-1974 ...... CLC 66; DAM MULT;
HLC
See also CA 131; 53-56; DLB 113; HW

Castelvetro, Lodovico 1505-1571..... LC 12

Castiglione, Baldassare 1478-1529 ... LC 12

Castle, Robert
See Hamilton, Edmond

Castro, Guillen de 1569-1631........ LC 19

Castro, Rosalia de
1837-1885 ...... NCLC 3; DAM MULT

Cather, Willa
See Cather, Willa Sibert

Cather, Willa Sibert
1873-1947 .... TCLC 1, 11, 31; DA;
DAB; DAC; DAM MST, NOV; SSC 2;
WLC
See also CA 104; 128; CDALB 1865-1917;
DLB 9, 54, 78; DLBD 1; MTCW;
SATA 30

Cato, Marcus Porcius
234B.C.-149B.C............. CMLC 21

Catton, (Charles) Bruce
1899-1978 . . . . CLC 35
See also AITN 1; CA 5-8R; 81-84;
CANR 7; DLB 17; SATA 2;
SATA-Obit 24

Catullus c. 84B.C.-c. 54B.C. . . . . . CMLC 18

Cauldwell, Frank
See King, Francis (Henry)

Caunitz, William J. 1933-1996 . . . . . CLC 34
See also BEST 89:3; CA 125; 130; 152;
INT 130

Causley, Charles (Stanley) 1917-. . . . . CLC 7
See also CA 9-12R; CANR 5, 35; CLR 30;
DLB 27; MTCW; SATA 3, 66

Caute, David 1936-. . . . CLC 29; DAM NOV
See also CA 1-4R; CAAS 4; CANR 1, 33;
DLB 14

Cavafy, C(onstantine) P(eter)
1863-1933 . . . . TCLC 2, 7; DAM POET
See also Kavafis, Konstantinos Petrou
See also CA 148

Cavallo, Evelyn
See Spark, Muriel (Sarah)

Cavanna, Betty . . . . CLC 12
See also Harrison, Elizabeth Cavanna
See also JRDA; MAICYA; SAAS 4;
SATA 1, 30

Cavendish, Margaret Lucas
1623-1673 . . . . LC 30
See also DLB 131

Caxton, William 1421(?)-1491(?). . . . . LC 17
See also DLB 170

Cayrol, Jean 1911-. . . . . CLC 11
See also CA 89-92; DLB 83

Cela, Camilo Jose
1916- . . . . . CLC 4, 13, 59; DAM MULT;
HLC
See also BEST 90:2; CA 21-24R; CAAS 10;
CANR 21, 32; DLBY 89; HW; MTCW

Celan, Paul . . . . . . CLC 10, 19, 53, 82; PC 10
See also Antschel, Paul
See also DLB 69

Celine, Louis-Ferdinand
. . . . CLC 1, 3, 4, 7, 9, 15, 47
See also Destouches, Louis-Ferdinand
See also DLB 72

Cellini, Benvenuto 1500-1571 . . . . LC 7

Cendrars, Blaise . . . . CLC 18
See also Sauser-Hall, Frederic

Cernuda (y Bidon), Luis
1902-1963 . . . . CLC 54; DAM POET
See also CA 131; 89-92; DLB 134; HW

Cervantes (Saavedra), Miguel de
1547-1616 . . . . LC 6, 23; DA; DAB;
DAC; DAM MST, NOV; SSC 12; WLC

Cesaire, Aime (Fernand)
1913- . . . . CLC 19, 32; BLC;
DAM MULT, POET
See also BW 2; CA 65-68; CANR 24, 43;
MTCW

Chabon, Michael 1963- . . . . CLC 55
See also CA 139; CANR 57

Chabrol, Claude 1930- . . . . CLC 16
See also CA 110

Challans, Mary 1905-1983
See Renault, Mary
See also CA 81-84; 111; SATA 23;
SATA-Obit 36

Challis, George
See Faust, Frederick (Schiller)

Chambers, Aidan 1934- . . . . CLC 35
See also CA 25-28R; CANR 12, 31; JRDA;
MAICYA; SAAS 12; SATA 1, 69

Chambers, James 1948-
See Cliff, Jimmy
See also CA 124

Chambers, Jessie
See Lawrence, D(avid) H(erbert Richards)

Chambers, Robert W. 1865-1933. . . TCLC 41

Chandler, Raymond (Thornton)
1888-1959 . . . . TCLC 1, 7; SSC 23
See also CA 104; 129; CDALB 1929-1941;
DLBD 6; MTCW

Chang, Jung 1952- . . . . CLC 71
See also CA 142

Channing, William Ellery
1780-1842 . . . . NCLC 17
See also DLB 1, 59

Chaplin, Charles Spencer
1889-1977 . . . . CLC 16
See also Chaplin, Charlie
See also CA 81-84; 73-76

Chaplin, Charlie
See Chaplin, Charles Spencer
See also DLB 44

Chapman, George
1559(?)-1634 . . . . . LC 22; DAM DRAM
See also DLB 62, 121

Chapman, Graham 1941-1989 . . . . . . CLC 21
See also Monty Python
See also CA 116; 129; CANR 35

Chapman, John Jay 1862-1933 . . . . . TCLC 7
See also CA 104

Chapman, Lee
See Bradley, Marion Zimmer

Chapman, Walker
See Silverberg, Robert

Chappell, Fred (Davis) 1936-. . . . CLC 40, 78
See also CA 5-8R; CAAS 4; CANR 8, 33;
DLB 6, 105

Char, Rene(-Emile)
1907-1988 . . . . CLC 9, 11, 14, 55;
DAM POET
See also CA 13-16R; 124; CANR 32;
MTCW

Charby, Jay
See Ellison, Harlan (Jay)

Chardin, Pierre Teilhard de
See Teilhard de Chardin, (Marie Joseph)
Pierre

Charles I 1600-1649 . . . . LC 13

Charyn, Jerome 1937- . . . . CLC 5, 8, 18
See also CA 5-8R; CAAS 1; CANR 7;
DLBY 83; MTCW

Chase, Mary (Coyle) 1907-1981 . . . . . . DC 1
See also CA 77-80; 105; SATA 17;
SATA-Obit 29

Chase, Mary Ellen 1887-1973 . . . . CLC 2
See also CA 13-16; 41-44R; CAP 1;
SATA 10

Chase, Nicholas
See Hyde, Anthony

Chateaubriand, Francois Rene de
1768-1848 . . . . NCLC 3
See also DLB 119

Chatterje, Sarat Chandra 1876-1936(?)
See Chatterji, Saratchandra
See also CA 109

Chatterji, Bankim Chandra
1838-1894 . . . . NCLC 19

Chatterji, Saratchandra . . . . TCLC 13
See also Chatterje, Sarat Chandra

Chatterton, Thomas
1752-1770 . . . . LC 3; DAM POET
See also DLB 109

Chatwin, (Charles) Bruce
1940-1989 . . CLC 28, 57, 59; DAM POP
See also AAYA 4; BEST 90:1; CA 85-88;
127

Chaucer, Daniel
See Ford, Ford Madox

Chaucer, Geoffrey
1340(?)-1400 . . . . LC 17; DA; DAB;
DAC; DAM MST, POET
See also CDBLB Before 1660; DLB 146

Chaviaras, Strates 1935-
See Haviaras, Stratis
See also CA 105

Chayefsky, Paddy . . . . CLC 23
See also Chayefsky, Sidney
See also DLB 7, 44; DLBY 81

Chayefsky, Sidney 1923-1981
See Chayefsky, Paddy
See also CA 9-12R; 104; CANR 18;
DAM DRAM

Chedid, Andree 1920-. . . . . CLC 47
See also CA 145

Cheever, John
1912-1982 . . . . . . CLC 3, 7, 8, 11, 15, 25,
64; DA; DAB; DAC; DAM MST, NOV,
POP; SSC 1; WLC
See also CA 5-8R; 106; CABS 1; CANR 5,
27; CDALB 1941-1968; DLB 2, 102;
DLBY 80, 82; INT CANR-5; MTCW

Cheever, Susan 1943-. . . . . CLC 18, 48
See also CA 103; CANR 27, 51; DLBY 82;
INT CANR-27

Chekhonte, Antosha
See Chekhov, Anton (Pavlovich)

Chekhov, Anton (Pavlovich)
1860-1904 . . . . . TCLC 3, 10, 31, 55; DA;
DAB; DAC; DAM DRAM, MST; SSC 2;
WLC
See also CA 104; 124; SATA 90

Chernyshevsky, Nikolay Gavrilovich
1828-1889 . . . . NCLC 1

Cherry, Carolyn Janice 1942-
See Cherryh, C. J.
See also CA 65-68; CANR 10

Cherryh, C. J. . . . . CLC 35
See also Cherry, Carolyn Janice
See also DLBY 80

Chesnutt, Charles W(addell)
1858-1932 . . . . TCLC **5, 39; BLC;**
DAM MULT; SSC 7
See also BW 1; CA 106; 125; DLB 12, 50, 78; MTCW

Chester, Alfred 1929(?)-1971 . . . . . . CLC **49**
See also CA 33-36R; DLB 130

Chesterton, G(ilbert) K(eith)
1874-1936 . . . . TCLC **1, 6, 64;**
DAM NOV, POET; SSC 1
See also CA 104; 132; CDBLB 1914-1945; DLB 10, 19, 34, 70, 98, 149; MTCW; SATA 27

Chiang Pin-chin 1904-1986
See Ding Ling
See also CA 118

Ch'ien Chung-shu 1910- . . . . CLC **22**
See also CA 130; MTCW

Child, L. Maria
See Child, Lydia Maria

Child, Lydia Maria 1802-1880 . . . . NCLC **6**
See also DLB 1, 74; SATA 67

Child, Mrs.
See Child, Lydia Maria

Child, Philip 1898-1978 . . . . CLC **19, 68**
See also CA 13-14; CAP 1; SATA 47

Childers, (Robert) Erskine
1870-1922 . . . . TCLC **65**
See also CA 113; 153; DLB 70

Childress, Alice
1920-1994 . . . . CLC **12, 15, 86, 96; BLC;**
DAM DRAM, MULT, NOV; DC 4
See also AAYA 8; BW 2; CA 45-48; 146; CANR 3, 27, 50; CLR 14; DLB 7, 38; JRDA; MAICYA; MTCW; SATA 7, 48, 81

Chin, Frank (Chew, Jr.) 1940- . . . . DC **7**
See also CA 33-36R; DAM MULT

Chislett, (Margaret) Anne 1943- . . . . CLC **34**
See also CA 151

Chitty, Thomas Willes 1926- . . . . CLC **11**
See also Hinde, Thomas
See also CA 5-8R

Chivers, Thomas Holley
1809-1858 . . . . NCLC **49**
See also DLB 3

Chomette, Rene Lucien 1898-1981
See Clair, Rene
See also CA 103

Chopin, Kate
. . . . TCLC **5, 14; DA; DAB; SSC 8**
See also Chopin, Katherine
See also CDALB 1865-1917; DLB 12, 78

Chopin, Katherine 1851-1904
See Chopin, Kate
See also CA 104; 122; DAC; DAM MST, NOV

Chretien de Troyes
c. 12th cent. - . . . . CMLC **10**

Christie
See Ichikawa, Kon

Christie, Agatha (Mary Clarissa)
1890-1976 . . . . . . CLC **1, 6, 8, 12, 39, 48;**
DAB; DAC; DAM NOV
See also AAYA 9; AITN 1, 2; CA 17-20R; 61-64; CANR 10, 37; CDBLB 1914-1945; DLB 13, 77; MTCW; SATA 36

Christie, (Ann) Philippa
See Pearce, Philippa
See also CA 5-8R; CANR 4

Christine de Pizan 1365(?)-1431(?) . . . . LC **9**

Chubb, Elmer
See Masters, Edgar Lee

Chulkov, Mikhail Dmitrievich
1743-1792 . . . . LC **2**
See also DLB 150

Churchill, Caryl 1938- . . . CLC **31, 55; DC 5**
See also CA 102; CANR 22, 46; DLB 13; MTCW

Churchill, Charles 1731-1764 . . . . LC **3**
See also DLB 109

Chute, Carolyn 1947- . . . . CLC **39**
See also CA 123

Ciardi, John (Anthony)
1916-1986 . . . . CLC **10, 40, 44;**
DAM POET
See also CA 5-8R; 118; CAAS 2; CANR 5, 33; CLR 19; DLB 5; DLBY 86; INT CANR-5; MAICYA; MTCW; SATA 1, 65; SATA-Obit 46

Cicero, Marcus Tullius
106B.C.-43B.C. . . . . CMLC **3**

Cimino, Michael 1943- . . . . CLC **16**
See also CA 105

Cioran, E(mil) M. 1911-1995 . . . . . . CLC **64**
See also CA 25-28R; 149

Cisneros, Sandra
1954- . . . . . CLC **69; DAM MULT; HLC**
See also AAYA 9; CA 131; DLB 122, 152; HW

Cixous, Helene 1937- . . . . CLC **92**
See also CA 126; CANR 55; DLB 83; MTCW

Clair, Rene . . . . CLC **20**
See also Chomette, Rene Lucien

Clampitt, Amy 1920-1994 . . . . CLC **32**
See also CA 110; 146; CANR 29; DLB 105

Clancy, Thomas L., Jr. 1947-
See Clancy, Tom
See also CA 125; 131; INT 131; MTCW

Clancy, Tom . . . . . CLC **45; DAM NOV, POP**
See also Clancy, Thomas L., Jr.
See also AAYA 9; BEST 89:1, 90:1

Clare, John
1793-1864 . . . . NCLC **9; DAB;**
DAM POET
See also DLB 55, 96

Clarin
See Alas (y Urena), Leopoldo (Enrique Garcia)

Clark, Al C.
See Goines, Donald

Clark, (Robert) Brian 1932- . . . . CLC **29**
See also CA 41-44R

Clark, Curt
See Westlake, Donald E(dwin)

Clark, Eleanor 1913-1996 . . . . CLC **5, 19**
See also CA 9-12R; 151; CANR 41; DLB 6

Clark, J. P.
See Clark, John Pepper
See also DLB 117

Clark, John Pepper
1935- . . . . CLC **38; BLC; DAM DRAM,**
MULT; DC 5
See also Clark, J. P.
See also BW 1; CA 65-68; CANR 16

Clark, M. R.
See Clark, Mavis Thorpe

Clark, Mavis Thorpe 1909- . . . . CLC **12**
See also CA 57-60; CANR 8, 37; CLR 30; MAICYA; SAAS 5; SATA 8, 74

Clark, Walter Van Tilburg
1909-1971 . . . . CLC **28**
See also CA 9-12R; 33-36R; DLB 9; SATA 8

Clarke, Arthur C(harles)
1917- . . . . CLC **1, 4, 13, 18, 35;**
DAM POP; SSC 3
See also AAYA 4; CA 1-4R; CANR 2, 28, 55; JRDA; MAICYA; MTCW; SATA 13, 70

Clarke, Austin
1896-1974 . . . . . . CLC **6, 9; DAM POET**
See also CA 29-32; 49-52; CAP 2; DLB 10, 20

Clarke, Austin C(hesterfield)
1934- . . . . CLC **8, 53; BLC; DAC;**
DAM MULT
See also BW 1; CA 25-28R; CAAS 16; CANR 14, 32; DLB 53, 125

Clarke, Gillian 1937- . . . . CLC **61**
See also CA 106; DLB 40

Clarke, Marcus (Andrew Hislop)
1846-1881 . . . . NCLC **19**

Clarke, Shirley 1925- . . . . CLC **16**

Clash, The
See Headon, (Nicky) Topper; Jones, Mick; Simonon, Paul; Strummer, Joe

Claudel, Paul (Louis Charles Marie)
1868-1955 . . . . TCLC **2, 10**
See also CA 104

Clavell, James (duMaresq)
1925-1994 . . . . CLC **6, 25, 87;**
DAM NOV, POP
See also CA 25-28R; 146; CANR 26, 48; MTCW

Cleaver, (Leroy) Eldridge
1935- . . . . . . CLC **30; BLC; DAM MULT**
See also BW 1; CA 21-24R; CANR 16

Cleese, John (Marwood) 1939- . . . . . CLC **21**
See also Monty Python
See also CA 112; 116; CANR 35; MTCW

Cleishbotham, Jebediah
See Scott, Walter

Cleland, John 1710-1789 . . . . LC **2**
See also DLB 39

Clemens, Samuel Langhorne 1835-1910
See Twain, Mark
See also CA 104; 135; CDALB 1865-1917; DA; DAB; DAC; DAM MST, NOV; DLB 11, 12, 23, 64, 74; JRDA; MAICYA; YABC 2

Cleophil
See Congreve, William

Clerihew, E.
See Bentley, E(dmund) C(lerihew)

Clerk, N. W.
See Lewis, C(live) S(taples)

Cliff, Jimmy...................... CLC 21
See also Chambers, James

Clifton, (Thelma) Lucille
1936- .... CLC 19, 66; BLC;
DAM MULT, POET; PC 17
See also BW 2; CA 49-52; CANR 2, 24, 42;
CLR 5; DLB 5, 41; MAICYA; MTCW;
SATA 20, 69

Clinton, Dirk
See Silverberg, Robert

Clough, Arthur Hugh 1819-1861.. NCLC 27
See also DLB 32

Clutha, Janet Paterson Frame 1924-
See Frame, Janet
See also CA 1-4R; CANR 2, 36; MTCW

Clyne, Terence
See Blatty, William Peter

Cobalt, Martin
See Mayne, William (James Carter)

Cobbett, William 1763-1835 ..... NCLC 49
See also DLB 43, 107, 158

Coburn, D(onald) L(ee) 1938- ...... CLC 10
See also CA 89-92

Cocteau, Jean (Maurice Eugene Clement)
1889-1963 .... CLC 1, 8, 15, 16, 43; DA;
DAB; DAC; DAM DRAM, MST, NOV;
WLC
See also CA 25-28; CANR 40; CAP 2;
DLB 65; MTCW

Codrescu, Andrei
1946- .... CLC 46; DAM POET
See also CA 33-36R; CAAS 19; CANR 13,
34, 53

Coe, Max
See Bourne, Randolph S(illiman)

Coe, Tucker
See Westlake, Donald E(dwin)

Coetzee, J(ohn) M(ichael)
1940- ...... CLC 23, 33, 66; DAM NOV
See also CA 77-80; CANR 41, 54; MTCW

Coffey, Brian
See Koontz, Dean R(ay)

Cohan, George M. 1878-1942 ..... TCLC 60

Cohen, Arthur A(llen)
1928-1986 .... CLC 7, 31
See also CA 1-4R; 120; CANR 1, 17, 42;
DLB 28

Cohen, Leonard (Norman)
1934- .... CLC 3, 38; DAC; DAM MST
See also CA 21-24R; CANR 14; DLB 53;
MTCW

Cohen, Matt 1942-.......... CLC 19; DAC
See also CA 61-64; CAAS 18; CANR 40;
DLB 53

Cohen-Solal, Annie 19(?)- .... CLC 50

Colegate, Isabel 1931- .... CLC 36
See also CA 17-20R; CANR 8, 22; DLB 14;
INT CANR-22; MTCW

Coleman, Emmett
See Reed, Ishmael

Coleridge, Samuel Taylor
1772-1834 ..... NCLC 9, 54; DA; DAB;
DAC; DAM MST, POET; PC 11; WLC
See also CDBLB 1789-1832; DLB 93, 107

Coleridge, Sara 1802-1852...... NCLC 31

Coles, Don 1928- .... CLC 46
See also CA 115; CANR 38

Colette, (Sidonie-Gabrielle)
1873-1954 .... TCLC 1, 5, 16;
DAM NOV; SSC 10
See also CA 104; 131; DLB 65; MTCW

Collett, (Jacobine) Camilla (Wergeland)
1813-1895 .... NCLC 22

Collier, Christopher 1930-........ CLC 30
See also AAYA 13; CA 33-36R; CANR 13,
33; JRDA; MAICYA; SATA 16, 70

Collier, James L(incoln)
1928- .... CLC 30; DAM POP
See also AAYA 13; CA 9-12R; CANR 4,
33; CLR 3; JRDA; MAICYA; SAAS 21;
SATA 8, 70

Collier, Jeremy 1650-1726.......... LC 6

Collier, John 1901-1980.......... SSC 19
See also CA 65-68; 97-100; CANR 10;
DLB 77

Collingwood, R(obin) G(eorge)
1889(?)-1943 .... TCLC 67
See also CA 117; 155

Collins, Hunt
See Hunter, Evan

Collins, Linda 1931-............. CLC 44
See also CA 125

Collins, (William) Wilkie
1824-1889 .... NCLC 1, 18
See also CDBLB 1832-1890; DLB 18, 70,
159

Collins, William
1721-1759 .... LC 4; DAM POET
See also DLB 109

Collodi, Carlo 1826-1890........ NCLC 54
See also Lorenzini, Carlo
See also CLR 5

Colman, George
See Glassco, John

Colt, Winchester Remington
See Hubbard, L(afayette) Ron(ald)

Colter, Cyrus 1910- .... CLC 58
See also BW 1; CA 65-68; CANR 10;
DLB 33

Colton, James
See Hansen, Joseph

Colum, Padraic 1881-1972........ CLC 28
See also CA 73-76; 33-36R; CANR 35;
CLR 36; MAICYA; MTCW; SATA 15

Colvin, James
See Moorcock, Michael (John)

Colwin, Laurie (E.)
1944-1992 .... CLC 5, 13, 23, 84
See also CA 89-92; 139; CANR 20, 46;
DLBY 80; MTCW

Comfort, Alex(ander)
1920- .... CLC 7; DAM POP
See also CA 1-4R; CANR 1, 45

Comfort, Montgomery
See Campbell, (John) Ramsey

Compton-Burnett, I(vy)
1884(?)-1969 ...... CLC 1, 3, 10, 15, 34;
DAM NOV
See also CA 1-4R; 25-28R; CANR 4;
DLB 36; MTCW

Comstock, Anthony 1844-1915 .... TCLC 13
See also CA 110

Comte, Auguste 1798-1857....... NCLC 54

Conan Doyle, Arthur
See Doyle, Arthur Conan

Conde, Maryse
1937- .... CLC 52, 92; DAM MULT
See also Boucolon, Maryse
See also BW 2

Condillac, Etienne Bonnot de
1714-1780 .... LC 26

Condon, Richard (Thomas)
1915-1996 ..... CLC 4, 6, 8, 10, 45, 100;
DAM NOV
See also BEST 90:3; CA 1-4R; 151;
CAAS 1; CANR 2, 23; INT CANR-23;
MTCW

Confucius
551B.C.-479B.C........ CMLC 19; DA;
DAB; DAC; DAM MST

Congreve, William
1670-1729 .... LC 5, 21; DA; DAB;
DAC; DAM DRAM, MST, POET;
DC 2; WLC
See also CDBLB 1660-1789; DLB 39, 84

Connell, Evan S(helby), Jr.
1924- .... CLC 4, 6, 45; DAM NOV
See also AAYA 7; CA 1-4R; CAAS 2;
CANR 2, 39; DLB 2; DLBY 81; MTCW

Connelly, Marc(us Cook)
1890-1980 .... CLC 7
See also CA 85-88; 102; CANR 30; DLB 7;
DLBY 80; SATA-Obit 25

Connor, Ralph................... TCLC 31
See also Gordon, Charles William
See also DLB 92

Conrad, Joseph
1857-1924 .... TCLC 1, 6, 13, 25, 43, 57;
DA; DAB; DAC; DAM MST, NOV;
SSC 9; WLC
See also CA 104; 131; CDBLB 1890-1914;
DLB 10, 34, 98, 156; MTCW; SATA 27

Conrad, Robert Arnold
See Hart, Moss

Conroy, Donald Pat(rick)
1945- ... CLC 30, 74; DAM NOV, POP
See also AAYA 8; AITN 1; CA 85-88;
CANR 24, 53; DLB 6; MTCW

Constant (de Rebecque), (Henri) Benjamin
1767-1830 .... NCLC 6
See also DLB 119

Conybeare, Charles Augustus
See Eliot, T(homas) S(tearns)

Cook, Michael 1933- .... CLC 58
See also CA 93-96; DLB 53

Cook, Robin 1940- .... CLC 14; DAM POP
See also BEST 90:2; CA 108; 111;
CANR 41; INT 111

Cook, Roy
See Silverberg, Robert

Cooke, Elizabeth 1948- .... **CLC 55**
See also CA 129

Cooke, John Esten 1830-1886..... **NCLC 5**
See also DLB 3

Cooke, John Estes
See Baum, L(yman) Frank

Cooke, M. E.
See Creasey, John

Cooke, Margaret
See Creasey, John

Cook-Lynn, Elizabeth
1930- .... **CLC 93; DAM MULT**
See also CA 133; DLB 175; NNAL

Cooney, Ray .... **CLC 62**

Cooper, Douglas 1960-........... **CLC 86**

Cooper, Henry St. John
See Creasey, John

Cooper, J(oan) California
.... **CLC 56; DAM MULT**
See also AAYA 12; BW 1; CA 125;
CANR 55

Cooper, James Fenimore
1789-1851 .... **NCLC 1, 27, 54**
See also CDALB 1640-1865; DLB 3;
SATA 19

Coover, Robert (Lowell)
1932- .... **CLC 3, 7, 15, 32, 46, 87;
DAM NOV; SSC 15**
See also CA 45-48; CANR 3, 37; DLB 2;
DLBY 81; MTCW

Copeland, Stewart (Armstrong)
1952- .... **CLC 26**

Coppard, A(lfred) E(dgar)
1878-1957 .... **TCLC 5; SSC 21**
See also CA 114; DLB 162; YABC 1

Coppee, Francois 1842-1908 ...... **TCLC 25**

Coppola, Francis Ford 1939-....... **CLC 16**
See also CA 77-80; CANR 40; DLB 44

Corbiere, Tristan 1845-1875 ..... **NCLC 43**

Corcoran, Barbara 1911-.......... **CLC 17**
See also AAYA 14; CA 21-24R; CAAS 2;
CANR 11, 28, 48; DLB 52; JRDA;
SAAS 20; SATA 3, 77

Cordelier, Maurice
See Giraudoux, (Hippolyte) Jean

Corelli, Marie 1855-1924......... **TCLC 51**
See also Mackay, Mary
See also DLB 34, 156

Corman, Cid..................... **CLC 9**
See also Corman, Sidney
See also CAAS 2; DLB 5

Corman, Sidney 1924-
See Corman, Cid
See also CA 85-88; CANR 44; DAM POET

Cormier, Robert (Edmund)
1925- .... **CLC 12, 30; DA; DAB; DAC;
DAM MST, NOV**
See also AAYA 3, 19; CA 1-4R; CANR 5,
23; CDALB 1968-1988; CLR 12; DLB 52;
INT CANR-23; JRDA; MAICYA;
MTCW; SATA 10, 45, 83

Corn, Alfred (DeWitt III) 1943-.... **CLC 33**
See also CA 104; CAAS 25; CANR 44;
DLB 120; DLBY 80

Corneille, Pierre
1606-1684 .... **LC 28; DAB; DAM MST**

Cornwell, David (John Moore)
1931- .... **CLC 9, 15; DAM POP**
See also le Carre, John
See also CA 5-8R; CANR 13, 33; MTCW

Corso, (Nunzio) Gregory 1930-... **CLC 1, 11**
See also CA 5-8R; CANR 41; DLB 5, 16;
MTCW

Cortazar, Julio
1914-1984 ...... **CLC 2, 3, 5, 10, 13, 15,
33, 34, 92; DAM MULT, NOV; HLC;
SSC 7**
See also CA 21-24R; CANR 12, 32;
DLB 113; HW; MTCW

CORTES, HERNAN 1484-1547..... **LC 31**

Corwin, Cecil
See Kornbluth, C(yril) M.

Cosic, Dobrica 1921- .... **CLC 14**
See also CA 122; 138

Costain, Thomas B(ertram)
1885-1965 .... **CLC 30**
See also CA 5-8R; 25-28R; DLB 9

Costantini, Humberto
1924(?)-1987 .... **CLC 49**
See also CA 131; 122; HW

Costello, Elvis 1955-............. **CLC 21**

Cotter, Joseph Seamon Sr.
1861-1949 .... **TCLC 28; BLC;
DAM MULT**
See also BW 1; CA 124; DLB 50

Couch, Arthur Thomas Quiller
See Quiller-Couch, Arthur Thomas

Coulton, James
See Hansen, Joseph

Couperus, Louis (Marie Anne)
1863-1923 .... **TCLC 15**
See also CA 115

Coupland, Douglas
1961- .... **CLC 85; DAC; DAM POP**
See also CA 142; CANR 57

Court, Wesli
See Turco, Lewis (Putnam)

Courtenay, Bryce 1933-........... **CLC 59**
See also CA 138

Courtney, Robert
See Ellison, Harlan (Jay)

Cousteau, Jacques-Yves 1910-...... **CLC 30**
See also CA 65-68; CANR 15; MTCW;
SATA 38

Coward, Noel (Peirce)
1899-1973 .... **CLC 1, 9, 29, 51;
DAM DRAM**
See also AITN 1; CA 17-18; 41-44R;
CANR 35; CAP 2; CDBLB 1914-1945;
DLB 10; MTCW

Cowley, Malcolm 1898-1989 .... **CLC 39**
See also CA 5-8R; 128; CANR 3, 55;
DLB 4, 48; DLBY 81, 89; MTCW

Cowper, William
1731-1800 ...... **NCLC 8; DAM POET**
See also DLB 104, 109

Cox, William Trevor
1928- .... **CLC 9, 14, 71; DAM NOV**
See also Trevor, William
See also CA 9-12R; CANR 4, 37, 55;
DLB 14; INT CANR-37; MTCW

Coyne, P. J.
See Masters, Hilary

Cozzens, James Gould
1903-1978 .... **CLC 1, 4, 11, 92**
See also CA 9-12R; 81-84; CANR 19;
CDALB 1941-1968; DLB 9; DLBD 2;
DLBY 84; MTCW

Crabbe, George 1754-1832....... **NCLC 26**
See also DLB 93

Craddock, Charles Egbert
See Murfree, Mary Noailles

Craig, A. A.
See Anderson, Poul (William)

Craik, Dinah Maria (Mulock)
1826-1887 .... **NCLC 38**
See also DLB 35, 163; MAICYA; SATA 34

Cram, Ralph Adams 1863-1942.... **TCLC 45**

Crane, (Harold) Hart
1899-1932 .... **TCLC 2, 5; DA; DAB;
DAC; DAM MST, POET; PC 3; WLC**
See also CA 104; 127; CDALB 1917-1929;
DLB 4, 48; MTCW

Crane, R(onald) S(almon)
1886-1967 .... **CLC 27**
See also CA 85-88; DLB 63

Crane, Stephen (Townley)
1871-1900 .... **TCLC 11, 17, 32; DA;
DAB; DAC; DAM MST, NOV, POET;
SSC 7; WLC**
See also CA 109; 140; CDALB 1865-1917;
DLB 12, 54, 78; YABC 2

Crase, Douglas 1944-............. **CLC 58**
See also CA 106

Crashaw, Richard 1612(?)-1649...... **LC 24**
See also DLB 126

Craven, Margaret
1901-1980 .... **CLC 17; DAC**
See also CA 103

Crawford, F(rancis) Marion
1854-1909 .... **TCLC 10**
See also CA 107; DLB 71

Crawford, Isabella Valancy
1850-1887 .... **NCLC 12**
See also DLB 92

Crayon, Geoffrey
See Irving, Washington

Creasey, John 1908-1973.......... **CLC 11**
See also CA 5-8R; 41-44R; CANR 8;
DLB 77; MTCW

Crebillon, Claude Prosper Jolyot de (fils)
1707-1777 .... **LC 28**

Credo
See Creasey, John

Creeley, Robert (White)
1926- ..... **CLC 1, 2, 4, 8, 11, 15, 36, 78;
DAM POET**
See also CA 1-4R; CAAS 10; CANR 23, 43;
DLB 5, 16, 169; MTCW

Daudet, (Louis Marie) Alphonse
1840-1897 .... NCLC 1
See also DLB 123

Daumal, Rene 1908-1944 .... TCLC 14
See also CA 114

Davenport, Guy (Mattison, Jr.)
1927- .... CLC 6, 14, 38; SSC 16
See also CA 33-36R; CANR 23; DLB 130

Davidson, Avram 1923-
See Queen, Ellery
See also CA 101; CANR 26; DLB 8

Davidson, Donald (Grady)
1893-1968 .... CLC 2, 13, 19
See also CA 5-8R; 25-28R; CANR 4;
DLB 45

Davidson, Hugh
See Hamilton, Edmond

Davidson, John 1857-1909 .... TCLC 24
See also CA 118; DLB 19

Davidson, Sara 1943- .... CLC 9
See also CA 81-84; CANR 44

Davie, Donald (Alfred)
1922-1995 .... CLC 5, 8, 10, 31
See also CA 1-4R; 149; CAAS 3; CANR 1,
44; DLB 27; MTCW

Davies, Ray(mond Douglas) 1944- .. CLC 21
See also CA 116; 146

Davies, Rhys 1903-1978 .... CLC 23
See also CA 9-12R; 81-84; CANR 4;
DLB 139

Davies, (William) Robertson
1913-1995 ..... CLC 2, 7, 13, 25, 42, 75,
91; DA; DAB; DAC; DAM MST, NOV,
POP; WLC
See also BEST 89:2; CA 33-36R; 150;
CANR 17, 42; DLB 68; INT CANR-17;
MTCW

Davies, W(illiam) H(enry)
1871-1940 .... TCLC 5
See also CA 104; DLB 19, 174

Davies, Walter C.
See Kornbluth, C(yril) M.

Davis, Angela (Yvonne)
1944- .... CLC 77; DAM MULT
See also BW 2; CA 57-60; CANR 10

Davis, B. Lynch
See Bioy Casares, Adolfo; Borges, Jorge
Luis

Davis, Gordon
See Hunt, E(verette) Howard, (Jr.)

Davis, Harold Lenoir 1896-1960 .... CLC 49
See also CA 89-92; DLB 9

Davis, Rebecca (Blaine) Harding
1831-1910 .... TCLC 6
See also CA 104; DLB 74

Davis, Richard Harding
1864-1916 .... TCLC 24
See also CA 114; DLB 12, 23, 78, 79;
DLBD 13

Davison, Frank Dalby 1893-1970 ... CLC 15
See also CA 116

Davison, Lawrence H.
See Lawrence, D(avid) H(erbert Richards)

Davison, Peter (Hubert) 1928- ..... CLC 28
See also CA 9-12R; CAAS 4; CANR 3, 43;
DLB 5

Davys, Mary 1674-1732 .... LC 1
See also DLB 39

Dawson, Fielding 1930- .... CLC 6
See also CA 85-88; DLB 130

Dawson, Peter
See Faust, Frederick (Schiller)

Day, Clarence (Shepard, Jr.)
1874-1935 .... TCLC 25
See also CA 108; DLB 11

Day, Thomas 1748-1789 .... LC 1
See also DLB 39; YABC 1

Day Lewis, C(ecil)
1904-1972 .... CLC 1, 6, 10;
DAM POET; PC 11
See also Blake, Nicholas
See also CA 13-16; 33-36R; CANR 34;
CAP 1; DLB 15, 20; MTCW

Dazai, Osamu .... TCLC 11
See also Tsushima, Shuji

de Andrade, Carlos Drummond
See Drummond de Andrade, Carlos

Deane, Norman
See Creasey, John

**de Beauvoir, Simone (Lucie Ernestine Marie
Bertrand)**
See Beauvoir, Simone (Lucie Ernestine
Marie Bertrand) de

de Brissac, Malcolm
See Dickinson, Peter (Malcolm)

de Chardin, Pierre Teilhard
See Teilhard de Chardin, (Marie Joseph)
Pierre

Dee, John 1527-1608 .... LC 20

Deer, Sandra 1940- .... CLC 45

De Ferrari, Gabriella 1941- .... CLC 65
See also CA 146

Defoe, Daniel
1660(?)-1731 .... LC 1; DA; DAB; DAC;
DAM MST, NOV; WLC
See also CDBLB 1660-1789; DLB 39, 95,
101; JRDA; MAICYA; SATA 22

de Gourmont, Remy(-Marie-Charles)
See Gourmont, Remy (-Marie-Charles) de

de Hartog, Jan 1914- .... CLC 19
See also CA 1-4R; CANR 1

de Hostos, E. M.
See Hostos (y Bonilla), Eugenio Maria de

de Hostos, Eugenio M.
See Hostos (y Bonilla), Eugenio Maria de

Deighton, Len .... CLC 4, 7, 22, 46
See also Deighton, Leonard Cyril
See also AAYA 6; BEST 89:2;
CDBLB 1960 to Present; DLB 87

Deighton, Leonard Cyril 1929-
See Deighton, Len
See also CA 9-12R; CANR 19, 33;
DAM NOV, POP; MTCW

Dekker, Thomas
1572(?)-1632 ..... LC 22; DAM DRAM
See also CDBLB Before 1660; DLB 62, 172

Delafield, E. M. 1890-1943 .... TCLC 61
See also Dashwood, Edmee Elizabeth
Monica de la Pasture
See also DLB 34

de la Mare, Walter (John)
1873-1956 .... TCLC 4, 53; DAB; DAC;
DAM MST, POET; SSC 14; WLC
See also CDBLB 1914-1945; CLR 23;
DLB 162; SATA 16

Delaney, Franey
See O'Hara, John (Henry)

Delaney, Shelagh
1939- .... CLC 29; DAM DRAM
See also CA 17-20R; CANR 30;
CDBLB 1960 to Present; DLB 13;
MTCW

Delany, Mary (Granville Pendarves)
1700-1788 .... LC 12

Delany, Samuel R(ay, Jr.)
1942- .... CLC 8, 14, 38; BLC;
DAM MULT
See also BW 2; CA 81-84; CANR 27, 43;
DLB 8, 33; MTCW

De La Ramee, (Marie) Louise 1839-1908
See Ouida
See also SATA 20

de la Roche, Mazo 1879-1961 ...... CLC 14
See also CA 85-88; CANR 30; DLB 68;
SATA 64

Delbanco, Nicholas (Franklin)
1942- .... CLC 6, 13
See also CA 17-20R; CAAS 2; CANR 29,
55; DLB 6

del Castillo, Michel 1933- .... CLC 38
See also CA 109

Deledda, Grazia (Cosima)
1875(?)-1936 .... TCLC 23
See also CA 123

Delibes, Miguel .... CLC 8, 18
See also Delibes Setien, Miguel

Delibes Setien, Miguel 1920-
See Delibes, Miguel
See also CA 45-48; CANR 1, 32; HW;
MTCW

DeLillo, Don
1936- ..... CLC 8, 10, 13, 27, 39, 54, 76;
DAM NOV, POP
See also BEST 89:1; CA 81-84; CANR 21;
DLB 6, 173; MTCW

de Lisser, H. G.
See De Lisser, H(erbert) G(eorge)
See also DLB 117

De Lisser, H(erbert) G(eorge)
1878-1944 .... TCLC 12
See also de Lisser, H. G.
See also BW 2; CA 109; 152

Deloria, Vine (Victor), Jr.
1933- .... CLC 21; DAM MULT
See also CA 53-56; CANR 5, 20, 48;
DLB 175; MTCW; NNAL; SATA 21

Del Vecchio, John M(ichael)
1947- .... CLC 29
See also CA 110; DLBD 9

de Man, Paul (Adolph Michel)
1919-1983 .... CLC 55
See also CA 128; 111; DLB 67; MTCW

De Marinis, Rick 1934- . . . . **CLC 54**
See also CA 57-60; CAAS 24; CANR 9, 25, 50

Dembry, R. Emmet
See Murfree, Mary Noailles

Demby, William
1922- . . . . . **CLC 53; BLC; DAM MULT**
See also BW 1; CA 81-84; DLB 33

de Menton, Francisco
See Chin, Frank (Chew, Jr.)

Demijohn, Thom
See Disch, Thomas M(ichael)

de Montherlant, Henry (Milon)
See Montherlant, Henry (Milon) de

Demosthenes 384B.C.-322B.C. . . . **CMLC 13**
See also DLB 176

de Natale, Francine
See Malzberg, Barry N(athaniel)

Denby, Edwin (Orr) 1903-1983 . . . . . **CLC 48**
See also CA 138; 110

Denis, Julio
See Cortazar, Julio

Denmark, Harrison
See Zelazny, Roger (Joseph)

Dennis, John 1658-1734 . . . . **LC 11**
See also DLB 101

Dennis, Nigel (Forbes) 1912-1989 . . . . **CLC 8**
See also CA 25-28R; 129; DLB 13, 15;
MTCW

De Palma, Brian (Russell) 1940- . . . . **CLC 20**
See also CA 109

De Quincey, Thomas 1785-1859 . . . **NCLC 4**
See also CDBLB 1789-1832; DLB 110; 144

Deren, Eleanora 1908(?)-1961
See Deren, Maya
See also CA 111

Deren, Maya . . . . **CLC 16**
See also Deren, Eleanora

Derleth, August (William)
1909-1971 . . . . **CLC 31**
See also CA 1-4R; 29-32R; CANR 4;
DLB 9; SATA 5

Der Nister 1884-1950 . . . . **TCLC 56**

de Routisie, Albert
See Aragon, Louis

Derrida, Jacques 1930- . . . . **CLC 24, 87**
See also CA 124; 127

Derry Down Derry
See Lear, Edward

Dersonnes, Jacques
See Simenon, Georges (Jacques Christian)

Desai, Anita
1937- . . . . **CLC 19, 37, 97; DAB;
DAM NOV**
See also CA 81-84; CANR 33, 53; MTCW;
SATA 63

de Saint-Luc, Jean
See Glassco, John

de Saint Roman, Arnaud
See Aragon, Louis

Descartes, Rene 1596-1650 . . . . . . **LC 20, 35**

De Sica, Vittorio 1901(?)-1974 . . . . . **CLC 20**
See also CA 117

Desnos, Robert 1900-1945 . . . . **TCLC 22**
See also CA 121; 151

Destouches, Louis-Ferdinand
1894-1961 . . . . **CLC 9, 15**
See also Celine, Louis-Ferdinand
See also CA 85-88; CANR 28; MTCW

de Tolignac, Gaston
See Griffith, D(avid Lewelyn) W(ark)

Deutsch, Babette 1895-1982 . . . . **CLC 18**
See also CA 1-4R; 108; CANR 4; DLB 45;
SATA 1; SATA-Obit 33

Devenant, William 1606-1649 . . . . **LC 13**

Devkota, Laxmiprasad
1909-1959 . . . . **TCLC 23**
See also CA 123

De Voto, Bernard (Augustine)
1897-1955 . . . . **TCLC 29**
See also CA 113; DLB 9

De Vries, Peter
1910-1993 . . . . **CLC 1, 2, 3, 7, 10, 28, 46;
DAM NOV**
See also CA 17-20R; 142; CANR 41;
DLB 6; DLBY 82; MTCW

Dexter, John
See Bradley, Marion Zimmer

Dexter, Martin
See Faust, Frederick (Schiller)

Dexter, Pete
1943- . . . . **CLC 34, 55; DAM POP**
See also BEST 89:2; CA 127; 131; INT 131;
MTCW

Diamano, Silmang
See Senghor, Leopold Sedar

Diamond, Neil 1941- . . . . **CLC 30**
See also CA 108

Diaz del Castillo, Bernal 1496-1584 . . **LC 31**

di Bassetto, Corno
See Shaw, George Bernard

Dick, Philip K(indred)
1928-1982 . . . . **CLC 10, 30, 72;
DAM NOV, POP**
See also CA 49-52; 106; CANR 2, 16;
DLB 8; MTCW

Dickens, Charles (John Huffam)
1812-1870 . . . . . . **NCLC 3, 8, 18, 26, 37,
50; DA; DAB; DAC; DAM MST, NOV;
SSC 17; WLC**
See also CDBLB 1832-1890; DLB 21, 55,
70, 159, 166; JRDA; MAICYA; SATA 15

Dickey, James (Lafayette)
1923-1997 . . . . **CLC 1, 2, 4, 7, 10, 15, 47;
DAM NOV, POET, POP**
See also AITN 1, 2; CA 9-12R; 156;
CABS 2; CANR 10, 48;
CDALB 1968-1988; DLB 5; DLBD 7;
DLBY 82, 93; INT CANR-10; MTCW

Dickey, William 1928-1994 . . . . . **CLC 3, 28**
See also CA 9-12R; 145; CANR 24; DLB 5

Dickinson, Charles 1951- . . . . **CLC 49**
See also CA 128

Dickinson, Emily (Elizabeth)
1830-1886 . . . . **NCLC 21; DA; DAB;
DAC; DAM MST, POET; PC 1; WLC**
See also CDALB 1865-1917; DLB 1;
SATA 29

Dickinson, Peter (Malcolm)
1927- . . . . **CLC 12, 35**
See also AAYA 9; CA 41-44R; CANR 31;
CLR 29; DLB 87, 161; JRDA; MAICYA;
SATA 5, 62

Dickson, Carr
See Carr, John Dickson

Dickson, Carter
See Carr, John Dickson

Diderot, Denis 1713-1784 . . . . **LC 26**

Didion, Joan
1934- . . **CLC 1, 3, 8, 14, 32; DAM NOV**
See also AITN 1; CA 5-8R; CANR 14, 52;
CDALB 1968-1988; DLB 2, 173;
DLBY 81, 86; MTCW

Dietrich, Robert
See Hunt, E(verette) Howard, (Jr.)

Dillard, Annie
1945- . . . . **CLC 9, 60; DAM NOV**
See also AAYA 6; CA 49-52; CANR 3, 43;
DLBY 80; MTCW; SATA 10

Dillard, R(ichard) H(enry) W(ilde)
1937- . . . . **CLC 5**
See also CA 21-24R; CAAS 7; CANR 10;
DLB 5

Dillon, Eilis 1920-1994 . . . . **CLC 17**
See also CA 9-12R; 147; CAAS 3; CANR 4,
38; CLR 26; MAICYA; SATA 2, 74;
SATA-Obit 83

Dimont, Penelope
See Mortimer, Penelope (Ruth)

Dinesen, Isak . . . . **CLC 10, 29, 95; SSC 7**
See also Blixen, Karen (Christentze
Dinesen)

Ding Ling . . . . **CLC 68**
See also Chiang Pin-chin

Disch, Thomas M(ichael) 1940- . . . **CLC 7, 36**
See also AAYA 17; CA 21-24R; CAAS 4;
CANR 17, 36, 54; CLR 18; DLB 8;
MAICYA; MTCW; SAAS 15; SATA 92

Disch, Tom
See Disch, Thomas M(ichael)

d'Isly, Georges
See Simenon, Georges (Jacques Christian)

Disraeli, Benjamin 1804-1881 . . **NCLC 2, 39**
See also DLB 21, 55

Ditcum, Steve
See Crumb, R(obert)

Dixon, Paige
See Corcoran, Barbara

Dixon, Stephen 1936- . . . . . **CLC 52; SSC 16**
See also CA 89-92; CANR 17, 40, 54;
DLB 130

Dobell, Sydney Thompson
1824-1874 . . . . **NCLC 43**
See also DLB 32

Doblin, Alfred . . . . **TCLC 13**
See also Doeblin, Alfred

Dobrolyubov, Nikolai Alexandrovich
1836-1861 . . . . **NCLC 5**

Dobyns, Stephen 1941- . . . . **CLC 37**
See also CA 45-48; CANR 2, 18

Doctorow, E(dgar) L(aurence)
1931- . . . . . **CLC 6, 11, 15, 18, 37, 44, 65;**
DAM NOV, POP
See also AITN 2; BEST 89:3; CA 45-48;
CANR 2, 33, 51; CDALB 1968-1988;
DLB 2, 28, 173; DLBY 80; MTCW

Dodgson, Charles Lutwidge 1832-1898
See Carroll, Lewis
See also CLR 2; DA; DAB; DAC;
DAM MST, NOV, POET; MAICYA;
YABC 2

Dodson, Owen (Vincent)
1914-1983 . . . . **CLC 79; BLC;**
DAM MULT
See also BW 1; CA 65-68; 110; CANR 24;
DLB 76

Doeblin, Alfred 1878-1957 . . . . **TCLC 13**
See also Doblin, Alfred
See also CA 110; 141; DLB 66

Doerr, Harriet 1910- . . . . **CLC 34**
See also CA 117; 122; CANR 47; INT 122

Domecq, H(onorio) Bustos
See Bioy Casares, Adolfo; Borges, Jorge
Luis

Domini, Rey
See Lorde, Audre (Geraldine)

Dominique
See Proust, (Valentin-Louis-George-Eugene-)
Marcel

Don, A
See Stephen, Leslie

Donaldson, Stephen R.
1947- . . . . **CLC 46; DAM POP**
See also CA 89-92; CANR 13, 55;
INT CANR-13

Donleavy, J(ames) P(atrick)
1926- . . . . **CLC 1, 4, 6, 10, 45**
See also AITN 2; CA 9-12R; CANR 24, 49;
DLB 6, 173; INT CANR-24; MTCW

Donne, John
1572-1631 . . . . **LC 10, 24; DA; DAB;**
DAC; DAM MST, POET; PC 1
See also CDBLB Before 1660; DLB 121,
151

Donnell, David 1939(?)- . . . . **CLC 34**

Donoghue, P. S.
See Hunt, E(verette) Howard, (Jr.)

Donoso (Yanez), Jose
1924-1996 . . . . **CLC 4, 8, 11, 32, 99;**
DAM MULT; HLC
See also CA 81-84; 155; CANR 32;
DLB 113; HW; MTCW

Donovan, John 1928-1992 . . . . **CLC 35**
See also AAYA 20; CA 97-100; 137;
CLR 3; MAICYA; SATA 72;
SATA-Brief 29

Don Roberto
See Cunninghame Graham, R(obert)
B(ontine)

Doolittle, Hilda
1886-1961 . . . . . **CLC 3, 8, 14, 31, 34, 73;**
DA; DAC; DAM MST, POET; PC 5;
WLC
See also H. D.
See also CA 97-100; CANR 35; DLB 4, 45;
MTCW

Dorfman, Ariel
1942- . . . . **CLC 48, 77; DAM MULT;**
HLC
See also CA 124; 130; HW; INT 130

Dorn, Edward (Merton) 1929- . . . **CLC 10, 18**
See also CA 93-96; CANR 42; DLB 5;
INT 93-96

Dorsan, Luc
See Simenon, Georges (Jacques Christian)

Dorsange, Jean
See Simenon, Georges (Jacques Christian)

Dos Passos, John (Roderigo)
1896-1970 . . . . . . **CLC 1, 4, 8, 11, 15, 25,**
34, 82; DA; DAB; DAC; DAM MST,
NOV; WLC
See also CA 1-4R; 29-32R; CANR 3;
CDALB 1929-1941; DLB 4, 9; DLBD 1;
MTCW

Dossage, Jean
See Simenon, Georges (Jacques Christian)

Dostoevsky, Fedor Mikhailovich
1821-1881 . . . . . . **NCLC 2, 7, 21, 33, 43;**
DA; DAB; DAC; DAM MST, NOV;
SSC 2; WLC

Doughty, Charles M(ontagu)
1843-1926 . . . . **TCLC 27**
See also CA 115; DLB 19, 57, 174

Douglas, Ellen . . . . **CLC 73**
See also Haxton, Josephine Ayres;
Williamson, Ellen Douglas

Douglas, Gavin 1475(?)-1522 . . . . **LC 20**

Douglas, Keith 1920-1944 . . . . **TCLC 40**
See also DLB 27

Douglas, Leonard
See Bradbury, Ray (Douglas)

Douglas, Michael
See Crichton, (John) Michael

Douglas, Norman 1868-1952 . . . . . . **TCLC 68**

Douglass, Frederick
1817(?)-1895 . . . . **NCLC 7, 55; BLC; DA;**
DAC; DAM MST, MULT; WLC
See also CDALB 1640-1865; DLB 1, 43, 50,
79; SATA 29

Dourado, (Waldomiro Freitas) Autran
1926- . . . . **CLC 23, 60**
See also CA 25-28R; CANR 34

Dourado, Waldomiro Autran
See Dourado, (Waldomiro Freitas) Autran

Dove, Rita (Frances)
1952- . . . . **CLC 50, 81; DAM MULT,**
POET; PC 6
See also BW 2; CA 109; CAAS 19;
CANR 27, 42; DLB 120

Dowell, Coleman 1925-1985 . . . . **CLC 60**
See also CA 25-28R; 117; CANR 10;
DLB 130

Dowson, Ernest (Christopher)
1867-1900 . . . . **TCLC 4**
See also CA 105; 150; DLB 19, 135

Doyle, A. Conan
See Doyle, Arthur Conan

Doyle, Arthur Conan
1859-1930 . . . . **TCLC 7; DA; DAB;**
DAC; DAM MST, NOV; SSC 12; WLC
See also AAYA 14; CA 104; 122;
CDBLB 1890-1914; DLB 18, 70, 156;
MTCW; SATA 24

Doyle, Conan
See Doyle, Arthur Conan

Doyle, John
See Graves, Robert (von Ranke)

Doyle, Roddy 1958(?)- . . . . **CLC 81**
See also AAYA 14; CA 143

Doyle, Sir A. Conan
See Doyle, Arthur Conan

Doyle, Sir Arthur Conan
See Doyle, Arthur Conan

Dr. A
See Asimov, Isaac; Silverstein, Alvin

Drabble, Margaret
1939- . . . . **CLC 2, 3, 5, 8, 10, 22, 53;**
DAB; DAC; DAM MST, NOV, POP
See also CA 13-16R; CANR 18, 35;
CDBLB 1960 to Present; DLB 14, 155;
MTCW; SATA 48

Drapier, M. B.
See Swift, Jonathan

Drayham, James
See Mencken, H(enry) L(ouis)

Drayton, Michael 1563-1631 . . . . **LC 8**

Dreadstone, Carl
See Campbell, (John) Ramsey

Dreiser, Theodore (Herman Albert)
1871-1945 . . . . **TCLC 10, 18, 35; DA;**
DAC; DAM MST, NOV; WLC
See also CA 106; 132; CDALB 1865-1917;
DLB 9, 12, 102, 137; DLBD 1; MTCW

Drexler, Rosalyn 1926- . . . . **CLC 2, 6**
See also CA 81-84

Dreyer, Carl Theodor 1889-1968 . . . . **CLC 16**
See also CA 116

Drieu la Rochelle, Pierre(-Eugene)
1893-1945 . . . . **TCLC 21**
See also CA 117; DLB 72

Drinkwater, John 1882-1937 . . . . . . **TCLC 57**
See also CA 109; 149; DLB 10, 19, 149

Drop Shot
See Cable, George Washington

Droste-Hulshoff, Annette Freiin von
1797-1848 . . . . **NCLC 3**
See also DLB 133

Drummond, Walter
See Silverberg, Robert

Drummond, William Henry
1854-1907 . . . . **TCLC 25**
See also DLB 92

Drummond de Andrade, Carlos
1902-1987 . . . . **CLC 18**
See also Andrade, Carlos Drummond de
See also CA 132; 123

Drury, Allen (Stuart) 1918- . . . . **CLC 37**
See also CA 57-60; CANR 18, 52;
INT CANR-18

Dryden, John
1631-1700 . . . . LC **3, 21**; DA; DAB;
DAC; DAM DRAM, MST, POET;
DC **3**; WLC
See also CDBLB 1660-1789; DLB 80, 101,
131

Duberman, Martin 1930- . . . . CLC **8**
See also CA 1-4R; CANR 2

Dubie, Norman (Evans) 1945- . . . . . . CLC **36**
See also CA 69-72; CANR 12; DLB 120

Du Bois, W(illiam) E(dward) B(urghardt)
1868-1963 . . . . CLC **1, 2, 13, 64, 96**;
BLC; DA; DAC; DAM MST, NOV; WLC
See also BW 1; CA 85-88; CANR 34;
CDALB 1865-1917; DLB 47, 50, 91;
MTCW; SATA 42

Dubus, Andre
1936- . . . . CLC **13, 36, 97**; SSC **15**
See also CA 21-24R; CANR 17; DLB 130;
INT CANR-17

Duca Minimo
See D'Annunzio, Gabriele

Ducharme, Rejean 1941- . . . . CLC **74**
See also DLB 60

Duclos, Charles Pinot 1704-1772 . . . . . LC **1**

Dudek, Louis 1918- . . . . CLC **11, 19**
See also CA 45-48; CAAS 14; CANR 1;
DLB 88

Duerrenmatt, Friedrich
1921-1990 . . . . . . CLC **1, 4, 8, 11, 15, 43**;
DAM DRAM
See also CA 17-20R; CANR 33; DLB 69,
124; MTCW

Duffy, Bruce (?)- . . . . CLC **50**

Duffy, Maureen 1933- . . . . CLC **37**
See also CA 25-28R; CANR 33; DLB 14;
MTCW

Dugan, Alan 1923- . . . . CLC **2, 6**
See also CA 81-84; DLB 5

du Gard, Roger Martin
See Martin du Gard, Roger

Duhamel, Georges 1884-1966 . . . . CLC **8**
See also CA 81-84; 25-28R; CANR 35;
DLB 65; MTCW

Dujardin, Edouard (Emile Louis)
1861-1949 . . . . TCLC **13**
See also CA 109; DLB 123

Dumas, Alexandre (Davy de la Pailleterie)
1802-1870 . . . . NCLC **11**; DA; DAB;
DAC; DAM MST, NOV; WLC
See also DLB 119; SATA 18

Dumas, Alexandre
1824-1895 . . . . NCLC **9**; DC **1**

Dumas, Claudine
See Malzberg, Barry N(athaniel)

Dumas, Henry L. 1934-1968 . . . . . CLC **6, 62**
See also BW 1; CA 85-88; DLB 41

du Maurier, Daphne
1907-1989 . . . . CLC **6, 11, 59**; DAB;
DAC; DAM MST, POP; SSC **18**
See also CA 5-8R; 128; CANR 6, 55;
MTCW; SATA 27; SATA-Obit 60

Dunbar, Paul Laurence
1872-1906 . . . . . . TCLC **2, 12**; BLC; DA;
DAC; DAM MST, MULT, POET; PC **5**;
SSC **8**; WLC
See also BW 1; CA 104; 124;
CDALB 1865-1917; DLB 50, 54, 78;
SATA 34

Dunbar, William 1460(?)-1530(?) . . . . LC **20**
See also DLB 132, 146

Duncan, Dora Angela
See Duncan, Isadora

Duncan, Isadora 1877(?)-1927 . . . . . TCLC **68**
See also CA 118; 149

Duncan, Lois 1934- . . . . CLC **26**
See also AAYA 4; CA 1-4R; CANR 2, 23,
36; CLR 29; JRDA; MAICYA; SAAS 2;
SATA 1, 36, 75

Duncan, Robert (Edward)
1919-1988 . . . . CLC **1, 2, 4, 7, 15, 41, 55**;
DAM POET; PC **2**
See also CA 9-12R; 124; CANR 28; DLB 5,
16; MTCW

Duncan, Sara Jeannette
1861-1922 . . . . TCLC **60**
See also DLB 92

Dunlap, William 1766-1839 . . . . NCLC **2**
See also DLB 30, 37, 59

Dunn, Douglas (Eaglesham)
1942- . . . . CLC **6, 40**
See also CA 45-48; CANR 2, 33; DLB 40;
MTCW

Dunn, Katherine (Karen) 1945- . . . . . CLC **71**
See also CA 33-36R

Dunn, Stephen 1939- . . . . CLC **36**
See also CA 33-36R; CANR 12, 48, 53;
DLB 105

Dunne, Finley Peter 1867-1936 . . . . TCLC **28**
See also CA 108; DLB 11, 23

Dunne, John Gregory 1932- . . . . CLC **28**
See also CA 25-28R; CANR 14, 50;
DLBY 80

Dunsany, Edward John Moreton Drax
Plunkett 1878-1957
See Dunsany, Lord
See also CA 104; 148; DLB 10

Dunsany, Lord . . . . TCLC **2, 59**
See also Dunsany, Edward John Moreton
Drax Plunkett
See also DLB 77, 153, 156

du Perry, Jean
See Simenon, Georges (Jacques Christian)

Durang, Christopher (Ferdinand)
1949- . . . . CLC **27, 38**
See also CA 105; CANR 50

Duras, Marguerite
1914-1996 . . . . . CLC **3, 6, 11, 20, 34, 40,**
68, 100
See also CA 25-28R; 151; CANR 50;
DLB 83; MTCW

Durban, (Rosa) Pam 1947- . . . . CLC **39**
See also CA 123

Durcan, Paul
1944- . . . . CLC **43, 70**; DAM POET
See also CA 134

Durkheim, Emile 1858-1917 . . . . . . TCLC **55**

Durrell, Lawrence (George)
1912-1990 . . . . CLC **1, 4, 6, 8, 13, 27, 41**;
DAM NOV
See also CA 9-12R; 132; CANR 40;
CDBLB 1945-1960; DLB 15, 27;
DLBY 90; MTCW

Durrenmatt, Friedrich
See Duerrenmatt, Friedrich

Dutt, Toru 1856-1877 . . . . NCLC **29**

Dwight, Timothy 1752-1817 . . . . . . NCLC **13**
See also DLB 37

Dworkin, Andrea 1946- . . . . CLC **43**
See also CA 77-80; CAAS 21; CANR 16,
39; INT CANR-16; MTCW

Dwyer, Deanna
See Koontz, Dean R(ay)

Dwyer, K. R.
See Koontz, Dean R(ay)

Dylan, Bob 1941- . . . . . . CLC **3, 4, 6, 12, 77**
See also CA 41-44R; DLB 16

Eagleton, Terence (Francis) 1943-
See Eagleton, Terry
See also CA 57-60; CANR 7, 23; MTCW

Eagleton, Terry . . . . CLC **63**
See also Eagleton, Terence (Francis)

Early, Jack
See Scoppettone, Sandra

East, Michael
See West, Morris L(anglo)

Eastaway, Edward
See Thomas, (Philip) Edward

Eastlake, William (Derry) 1917- . . . . . CLC **8**
See also CA 5-8R; CAAS 1; CANR 5;
DLB 6; INT CANR-5

Eastman, Charles A(lexander)
1858-1939 . . . . . TCLC **55**; DAM MULT
See also DLB 175; NNAL; YABC 1

Eberhart, Richard (Ghormley)
1904- . . CLC **3, 11, 19, 56**; DAM POET
See also CA 1-4R; CANR 2;
CDALB 1941-1968; DLB 48; MTCW

Eberstadt, Fernanda 1960- . . . . CLC **39**
See also CA 136

Echegaray (y Eizaguirre), Jose (Maria Waldo)
1832-1916 . . . . TCLC **4**
See also CA 104; CANR 32; HW; MTCW

Echeverria, (Jose) Esteban (Antonino)
1805-1851 . . . . NCLC **18**

Echo
See Proust, (Valentin-Louis-George-Eugene-)
Marcel

Eckert, Allan W. 1931- . . . . CLC **17**
See also AAYA 18; CA 13-16R; CANR 14,
45; INT CANR-14; SAAS 21; SATA 29,
91; SATA-Brief 27

Eckhart, Meister 1260(?)-1328(?) . . CMLC **9**
See also DLB 115

Eckmar, F. R.
See de Hartog, Jan

Eco, Umberto
1932- . . . CLC **28, 60**; DAM NOV, POP
See also BEST 90:1; CA 77-80; CANR 12,
33, 55; MTCW

Farren, Richard M.
See Betjeman, John

Fassbinder, Rainer Werner
1946-1982 . . . . **CLC 20**
See also CA 93-96; 106; CANR 31

Fast, Howard (Melvin)
1914- . . . . **CLC 23; DAM NOV**
See also AAYA 16; CA 1-4R; CAAS 18;
CANR 1, 33, 54; DLB 9; INT CANR-33;
SATA 7

Faulcon, Robert
See Holdstock, Robert P.

Faulkner, William (Cuthbert)
1897-1962 . . . . . **CLC 1, 3, 6, 8, 9, 11, 14,**
18, 28, 52, 68; DA; DAB; DAC;
DAM MST, NOV; SSC 1; WLC
See also AAYA 7; CA 81-84; CANR 33;
CDALB 1929-1941; DLB 9, 11, 44, 102;
DLBD 2; DLBY 86; MTCW

Fauset, Jessie Redmon
1884(?)-1961 . . . . **CLC 19, 54; BLC;**
DAM MULT
See also BW 1; CA 109; DLB 51

Faust, Frederick (Schiller)
1892-1944(?) . . . . . **TCLC 49; DAM POP**
See also CA 108; 152

Faust, Irvin 1924- . . . . **CLC 8**
See also CA 33-36R; CANR 28; DLB 2, 28;
DLBY 80

Fawkes, Guy
See Benchley, Robert (Charles)

Fearing, Kenneth (Flexner)
1902-1961 . . . . **CLC 51**
See also CA 93-96; DLB 9

Fecamps, Elise
See Creasey, John

Federman, Raymond 1928- . . . . . . **CLC 6, 47**
See also CA 17-20R; CAAS 8; CANR 10,
43; DLBY 80

Federspiel, J(uerg) F. 1931- . . . . **CLC 42**
See also CA 146

Feiffer, Jules (Ralph)
1929- . . . . . . **CLC 2, 8, 64; DAM DRAM**
See also AAYA 3; CA 17-20R; CANR 30;
DLB 7, 44; INT CANR-30; MTCW;
SATA 8, 61

Feige, Hermann Albert Otto Maximilian
See Traven, B.

Feinberg, David B. 1956-1994 . . . . . . **CLC 59**
See also CA 135; 147

Feinstein, Elaine 1930- . . . . **CLC 36**
See also CA 69-72; CAAS 1; CANR 31;
DLB 14, 40; MTCW

Feldman, Irving (Mordecai) 1928- . . . . **CLC 7**
See also CA 1-4R; CANR 1; DLB 169

Fellini, Federico 1920-1993 . . . . . **CLC 16, 85**
See also CA 65-68; 143; CANR 33

Felsen, Henry Gregor 1916- . . . . **CLC 17**
See also CA 1-4R; CANR 1; SAAS 2;
SATA 1

Fenton, James Martin 1949- . . . . **CLC 32**
See also CA 102; DLB 40

Ferber, Edna 1887-1968 . . . . **CLC 18, 93**
See also AITN 1; CA 5-8R; 25-28R; DLB 9,
28, 86; MTCW; SATA 7

Ferguson, Helen
See Kavan, Anna

Ferguson, Samuel 1810-1886 . . . . . **NCLC 33**
See also DLB 32

Fergusson, Robert 1750-1774 . . . . **LC 29**
See also DLB 109

Ferling, Lawrence
See Ferlinghetti, Lawrence (Monsanto)

Ferlinghetti, Lawrence (Monsanto)
1919(?)- . . . . **CLC 2, 6, 10, 27;**
DAM POET; PC 1
See also CA 5-8R; CANR 3, 41;
CDALB 1941-1968; DLB 5, 16; MTCW

Fernandez, Vicente Garcia Huidobro
See Huidobro Fernandez, Vicente Garcia

Ferrer, Gabriel (Francisco Victor) Miro
See Miro (Ferrer), Gabriel (Francisco
Victor)

Ferrier, Susan (Edmonstone)
1782-1854 . . . . **NCLC 8**
See also DLB 116

Ferrigno, Robert 1948(?)- . . . . **CLC 65**
See also CA 140

Ferron, Jacques 1921-1985 . . . **CLC 94; DAC**
See also CA 117; 129; DLB 60

Feuchtwanger, Lion 1884-1958 . . . . . **TCLC 3**
See also CA 104; DLB 66

Feuillet, Octave 1821-1890 . . . . . . **NCLC 45**

Feydeau, Georges (Leon Jules Marie)
1862-1921 . . . . . **TCLC 22; DAM DRAM**
See also CA 113; 152

Ficino, Marsilio 1433-1499 . . . . **LC 12**

Fiedeler, Hans
See Doeblin, Alfred

Fiedler, Leslie A(aron)
1917- . . . . **CLC 4, 13, 24**
See also CA 9-12R; CANR 7; DLB 28, 67;
MTCW

Field, Andrew 1938- . . . . **CLC 44**
See also CA 97-100; CANR 25

Field, Eugene 1850-1895 . . . . **NCLC 3**
See also DLB 23, 42, 140; DLBD 13;
MAICYA; SATA 16

Field, Gans T.
See Wellman, Manly Wade

Field, Michael . . . . **TCLC 43**

Field, Peter
See Hobson, Laura Z(ametkin)

Fielding, Henry
1707-1754 . . . . . . **LC 1; DA; DAB; DAC;**
DAM DRAM, MST, NOV; WLC
See also CDBLB 1660-1789; DLB 39, 84,
101

Fielding, Sarah 1710-1768 . . . . **LC 1**
See also DLB 39

Fierstein, Harvey (Forbes)
1954- . . . . . **CLC 33; DAM DRAM, POP**
See also CA 123; 129

Figes, Eva 1932- . . . . **CLC 31**
See also CA 53-56; CANR 4, 44; DLB 14

Finch, Robert (Duer Claydon)
1900- . . . . **CLC 18**
See also CA 57-60; CANR 9, 24, 49;
DLB 88

Findley, Timothy
1930- . . . . . . **CLC 27; DAC; DAM MST**
See also CA 25-28R; CANR 12, 42;
DLB 53

Fink, William
See Mencken, H(enry) L(ouis)

Firbank, Louis 1942-
See Reed, Lou
See also CA 117

Firbank, (Arthur Annesley) Ronald
1886-1926 . . . . **TCLC 1**
See also CA 104; DLB 36

Fisher, M(ary) F(rances) K(ennedy)
1908-1992 . . . . **CLC 76, 87**
See also CA 77-80; 138; CANR 44

Fisher, Roy 1930- . . . . **CLC 25**
See also CA 81-84; CAAS 10; CANR 16;
DLB 40

Fisher, Rudolph
1897-1934 . . . . **TCLC 11; BLC;**
DAM MULT; SSC 25
See also BW 1; CA 107; 124; DLB 51, 102

Fisher, Vardis (Alvero) 1895-1968. . . . **CLC 7**
See also CA 5-8R; 25-28R; DLB 9

Fiske, Tarleton
See Bloch, Robert (Albert)

Fitch, Clarke
See Sinclair, Upton (Beall)

Fitch, John IV
See Cormier, Robert (Edmund)

Fitzgerald, Captain Hugh
See Baum, L(yman) Frank

FitzGerald, Edward 1809-1883 . . . . **NCLC 9**
See also DLB 32

Fitzgerald, F(rancis) Scott (Key)
1896-1940 . . . . **TCLC 1, 6, 14, 28, 55;**
DA; DAB; DAC; DAM MST, NOV;
SSC 6; WLC
See also AITN 1; CA 110; 123;
CDALB 1917-1929; DLB 4, 9, 86;
DLBD 1; DLBY 81; MTCW

Fitzgerald, Penelope 1916-. . . **CLC 19, 51, 61**
See also CA 85-88; CAAS 10; CANR 56;
DLB 14

Fitzgerald, Robert (Stuart)
1910-1985 . . . . **CLC 39**
See also CA 1-4R; 114; CANR 1; DLBY 80

FitzGerald, Robert D(avid)
1902-1987 . . . . **CLC 19**
See also CA 17-20R

Fitzgerald, Zelda (Sayre)
1900-1948 . . . . **TCLC 52**
See also CA 117; 126; DLBY 84

Flanagan, Thomas (James Bonner)
1923- . . . . **CLC 25, 52**
See also CA 108; CANR 55; DLBY 80;
INT 108; MTCW

Flaubert, Gustave
1821-1880 . . . . **NCLC 2, 10, 19; DA;**
DAB; DAC; DAM MST, NOV; SSC 11;
WLC
See also DLB 119

Flecker, Herman Elroy
See Flecker, (Herman) James Elroy

Fredro, Aleksander 1793-1876..... **NCLC 8**

Freeling, Nicolas 1927- .... **CLC 38**
See also CA 49-52; CAAS 12; CANR 1, 17,
50; DLB 87

Freeman, Douglas Southall
1886-1953 .... **TCLC 11**
See also CA 109; DLB 17

Freeman, Judith 1946-............ **CLC 55**
See also CA 148

Freeman, Mary Eleanor Wilkins
1852-1930 .... **TCLC 9; SSC 1**
See also CA 106; DLB 12, 78

Freeman, R(ichard) Austin
1862-1943 .... **TCLC 21**
See also CA 113; DLB 70

French, Albert 1943- .... **CLC 86**

French, Marilyn
1929-................ **CLC 10, 18, 60;
DAM DRAM, NOV, POP**
See also CA 69-72; CANR 3, 31;
INT CANR-31; MTCW

French, Paul
See Asimov, Isaac

Freneau, Philip Morin 1752-1832.. **NCLC 1**
See also DLB 37, 43

Freud, Sigmund 1856-1939 .... **TCLC 52**
See also CA 115; 133; MTCW

Friedan, Betty (Naomi) 1921-...... **CLC 74**
See also CA 65-68; CANR 18, 45; MTCW

Friedlander, Saul 1932-........... **CLC 90**
See also CA 117; 130

Friedman, B(ernard) H(arper)
1926-....................... **CLC 7**
See also CA 1-4R; CANR 3, 48

Friedman, Bruce Jay 1930-.... **CLC 3, 5, 56**
See also CA 9-12R; CANR 25, 52; DLB 2,
28; INT CANR-25

Friel, Brian 1929-........... **CLC 5, 42, 59**
See also CA 21-24R; CANR 33; DLB 13;
MTCW

Friis-Baastad, Babbis Ellinor
1921-1970 .... **CLC 12**
See also CA 17-20R; 134; SATA 7

Frisch, Max (Rudolf)
1911-1991 ..... **CLC 3, 9, 14, 18, 32, 44;
DAM DRAM, NOV**
See also CA 85-88; 134; CANR 32;
DLB 69, 124; MTCW

Fromentin, Eugene (Samuel Auguste)
1820-1876 .... **NCLC 10**
See also DLB 123

Frost, Frederick
See Faust, Frederick (Schiller)

Frost, Robert (Lee)
1874-1963 .... **CLC 1, 3, 4, 9, 10, 13, 15,
26, 34, 44; DA; DAB; DAC; DAM MST,
POET; PC 1; WLC**
See also CA 89-92; CANR 33;
CDALB 1917-1929; DLB 54; DLBD 7;
MTCW; SATA 14

Froude, James Anthony
1818-1894 .... **NCLC 43**
See also DLB 18, 57, 144

Froy, Herald
See Waterhouse, Keith (Spencer)

Fry, Christopher
1907- ..... **CLC 2, 10, 14; DAM DRAM**
See also CA 17-20R; CAAS 23; CANR 9,
30; DLB 13; MTCW; SATA 66

Frye, (Herman) Northrop
1912-1991 .... **CLC 24, 70**
See also CA 5-8R; 133; CANR 8, 37;
DLB 67, 68; MTCW

Fuchs, Daniel 1909-1993 .... **CLC 8, 22**
See also CA 81-84; 142; CAAS 5;
CANR 40; DLB 9, 26, 28; DLBY 93

Fuchs, Daniel 1934-............. **CLC 34**
See also CA 37-40R; CANR 14, 48

Fuentes, Carlos
1928-...... **CLC 3, 8, 10, 13, 22, 41, 60;
DA; DAB; DAC; DAM MST, MULT,
NOV; HLC; SSC 24; WLC**
See also AAYA 4; AITN 2; CA 69-72;
CANR 10, 32; DLB 113; HW; MTCW

Fuentes, Gregorio Lopez y
See Lopez y Fuentes, Gregorio

Fugard, (Harold) Athol
1932- .... **CLC 5, 9, 14, 25, 40, 80;
DAM DRAM; DC 3**
See also AAYA 17; CA 85-88; CANR 32,
54; MTCW

Fugard, Sheila 1932- .... **CLC 48**
See also CA 125

Fuller, Charles (H., Jr.)
1939- .... **CLC 25; BLC; DAM DRAM,
MULT; DC 1**
See also BW 2; CA 108; 112; DLB 38;
INT 112; MTCW

Fuller, John (Leopold) 1937-....... **CLC 62**
See also CA 21-24R; CANR 9, 44; DLB 40

Fuller, Margaret .... **NCLC 5, 50**
See also Ossoli, Sarah Margaret (Fuller
marchesa d')

Fuller, Roy (Broadbent)
1912-1991 .... **CLC 4, 28**
See also CA 5-8R; 135; CAAS 10;
CANR 53; DLB 15, 20; SATA 87

Fulton, Alice 1952-............... **CLC 52**
See also CA 116; CANR 57

Furphy, Joseph 1843-1912....... **TCLC 25**

Fussell, Paul 1924-.............. **CLC 74**
See also BEST 90:1; CA 17-20R; CANR 8,
21, 35; INT CANR-21; MTCW

Futabatei, Shimei 1864-1909..... **TCLC 44**

Futrelle, Jacques 1875-1912 ...... **TCLC 19**
See also CA 113; 155

Gaboriau, Emile 1835-1873 ...... **NCLC 14**

Gadda, Carlo Emilio 1893-1973 .... **CLC 11**
See also CA 89-92; DLB 177

Gaddis, William
1922- ..... **CLC 1, 3, 6, 8, 10, 19, 43, 86**
See also CA 17-20R; CANR 21, 48; DLB 2;
MTCW

Gage, Walter
See Inge, William (Motter)

Gaines, Ernest J(ames)
1933- .... **CLC 3, 11, 18, 86; BLC;
DAM MULT**
See also AAYA 18; AITN 1; BW 2;
CA 9-12R; CANR 6, 24, 42;
CDALB 1968-1988; DLB 2, 33, 152;
DLBY 80; MTCW; SATA 86

Gaitskill, Mary 1954-............. **CLC 69**
See also CA 128

Galdos, Benito Perez
See Perez Galdos, Benito

Gale, Zona
1874-1938 ...... **TCLC 7; DAM DRAM**
See also CA 105; 153; DLB 9, 78

Galeano, Eduardo (Hughes) 1940-... **CLC 72**
See also CA 29-32R; CANR 13, 32; HW

Galiano, Juan Valera y Alcala
See Valera y Alcala-Galiano, Juan

Gallagher, Tess
1943- .. **CLC 18, 63; DAM POET; PC 9**
See also CA 106; DLB 120

Gallant, Mavis
1922- .... **CLC 7, 18, 38; DAC;
DAM MST; SSC 5**
See also CA 69-72; CANR 29; DLB 53;
MTCW

Gallant, Roy A(rthur) 1924- .... **CLC 17**
See also CA 5-8R; CANR 4, 29, 54;
CLR 30; MAICYA; SATA 4, 68

Gallico, Paul (William) 1897-1976 ... **CLC 2**
See also AITN 1; CA 5-8R; 69-72;
CANR 23; DLB 9, 171; MAICYA;
SATA 13

Gallo, Max Louis 1932-........... **CLC 95**
See also CA 85-88

Gallois, Lucien
See Desnos, Robert

Gallup, Ralph
See Whitemore, Hugh (John)

Galsworthy, John
1867-1933 ...... **TCLC 1, 45; DA; DAB;
DAC; DAM DRAM, MST, NOV;
SSC 22; WLC 2**
See also CA 104; 141; CDBLB 1890-1914;
DLB 10, 34, 98, 162

Galt, John 1779-1839............ **NCLC 1**
See also DLB 99, 116, 159

Galvin, James 1951-.............. **CLC 38**
See also CA 108; CANR 26

Gamboa, Federico 1864-1939...... **TCLC 36**

Gandhi, M. K.
See Gandhi, Mohandas Karamchand

Gandhi, Mahatma
See Gandhi, Mohandas Karamchand

Gandhi, Mohandas Karamchand
1869-1948 ..... **TCLC 59; DAM MULT**
See also CA 121; 132; MTCW

Gann, Ernest Kellogg 1910-1991.... **CLC 23**
See also AITN 1; CA 1-4R; 136; CANR 1

Garcia, Cristina 1958- .... **CLC 76**
See also CA 141

Garcia Lorca, Federico
1898-1936 ... **TCLC 1, 7, 49; DA; DAB;**
DAC; DAM DRAM, MST, MULT,
POET; DC 2; HLC; PC 3; WLC
See also CA 104; 131; DLB 108; HW;
MTCW

Garcia Marquez, Gabriel (Jose)
1928- .... **CLC 2, 3, 8, 10, 15, 27, 47, 55,**
68; DA; DAB; DAC; DAM MST,
MULT, NOV, POP; HLC; SSC 8; WLC
See also AAYA 3; BEST 89:1, 90:4;
CA 33-36R; CANR 10, 28, 50; DLB 113;
HW; MTCW

Gard, Janice
See Latham, Jean Lee

Gard, Roger Martin du
See Martin du Gard, Roger

Gardam, Jane 1928- .... **CLC 43**
See also CA 49-52; CANR 2, 18, 33, 54;
CLR 12; DLB 14, 161; MAICYA;
MTCW; SAAS 9; SATA 39, 76;
SATA-Brief 28

Gardner, Herb(ert) 1934- .... **CLC 44**
See also CA 149

Gardner, John (Champlin), Jr.
1933-1982 ..... **CLC 2, 3, 5, 7, 8, 10, 18,**
28, 34; DAM NOV, POP; SSC 7
See also AITN 1; CA 65-68; 107;
CANR 33; DLB 2; DLBY 82; MTCW;
SATA 40; SATA-Obit 31

Gardner, John (Edmund)
1926- .... **CLC 30; DAM POP**
See also CA 103; CANR 15; MTCW

Gardner, Miriam
See Bradley, Marion Zimmer

Gardner, Noel
See Kuttner, Henry

Gardons, S. S.
See Snodgrass, W(illiam) D(e Witt)

Garfield, Leon 1921-1996 .... **CLC 12**
See also AAYA 8; CA 17-20R; 152;
CANR 38, 41; CLR 21; DLB 161; JRDA;
MAICYA; SATA 1, 32, 76;
SATA-Obit 90

Garland, (Hannibal) Hamlin
1860-1940 .... **TCLC 3; SSC 18**
See also CA 104; DLB 12, 71, 78

Garneau, (Hector de) Saint-Denys
1912-1943 .... **TCLC 13**
See also CA 111; DLB 88

Garner, Alan
1934- .... **CLC 17; DAB; DAM POP**
See also AAYA 18; CA 73-76; CANR 15;
CLR 20; DLB 161; MAICYA; MTCW;
SATA 18, 69

Garner, Hugh 1913-1979 .... **CLC 13**
See also CA 69-72; CANR 31; DLB 68

Garnett, David 1892-1981 .... **CLC 3**
See also CA 5-8R; 103; CANR 17; DLB 34

Garos, Stephanie
See Katz, Steve

Garrett, George (Palmer)
1929- .... **CLC 3, 11, 51**
See also CA 1-4R; CAAS 5; CANR 1, 42;
DLB 2, 5, 130, 152; DLBY 83

Garrick, David
1717-1779 ...... **LC 15; DAM DRAM**
See also DLB 84

Garrigue, Jean 1914-1972 .... **CLC 2, 8**
See also CA 5-8R; 37-40R; CANR 20

Garrison, Frederick
See Sinclair, Upton (Beall)

Garth, Will
See Hamilton, Edmond; Kuttner, Henry

Garvey, Marcus (Moziah, Jr.)
1887-1940 .... **TCLC 41; BLC;**
DAM MULT
See also BW 1; CA 120; 124

Gary, Romain .... **CLC 25**
See also Kacew, Romain
See also DLB 83

Gascar, Pierre .... **CLC 11**
See also Fournier, Pierre

Gascoyne, David (Emery) 1916- .... **CLC 45**
See also CA 65-68; CANR 10, 28, 54;
DLB 20; MTCW

Gaskell, Elizabeth Cleghorn
1810-1865 .... **NCLC 5; DAB;**
DAM MST; SSC 25
See also CDBLB 1832-1890; DLB 21, 144,
159

Gass, William H(oward)
1924- ... **CLC 1, 2, 8, 11, 15, 39; SSC 12**
See also CA 17-20R; CANR 30; DLB 2;
MTCW

Gasset, Jose Ortega y
See Ortega y Gasset, Jose

Gates, Henry Louis, Jr.
1950- .... **CLC 65; DAM MULT**
See also BW 2; CA 109; CANR 25, 53;
DLB 67

Gautier, Theophile
1811-1872 .... **NCLC 1, 59;**
DAM POET; SSC 20
See also DLB 119

Gawsworth, John
See Bates, H(erbert) E(rnest)

Gay, Oliver
See Gogarty, Oliver St. John

Gaye, Marvin (Penze) 1939-1984 ... **CLC 26**
See also CA 112

Gebler, Carlo (Ernest) 1954- .... **CLC 39**
See also CA 119; 133

Gee, Maggie (Mary) 1948- .... **CLC 57**
See also CA 130

Gee, Maurice (Gough) 1931- .... **CLC 29**
See also CA 97-100; SATA 46

Gelbart, Larry (Simon) 1923- ... **CLC 21, 61**
See also CA 73-76; CANR 45

Gelber, Jack 1932- .... **CLC 1, 6, 14, 79**
See also CA 1-4R; CANR 2; DLB 7

Gellhorn, Martha (Ellis) 1908- .. **CLC 14, 60**
See also CA 77-80; CANR 44; DLBY 82

Genet, Jean
1910-1986 ...... **CLC 1, 2, 5, 10, 14, 44,**
46; DAM DRAM
See also CA 13-16R; CANR 18; DLB 72;
DLBY 86; MTCW

Gent, Peter 1942- .... **CLC 29**
See also AITN 1; CA 89-92; DLBY 82

Gentlewoman in New England, A
See Bradstreet, Anne

Gentlewoman in Those Parts, A
See Bradstreet, Anne

George, Jean Craighead 1919-...... **CLC 35**
See also AAYA 8; CA 5-8R; CANR 25;
CLR 1; DLB 52; JRDA; MAICYA;
SATA 2, 68

George, Stefan (Anton)
1868-1933 .... **TCLC 2, 14**
See also CA 104

Georges, Georges Martin
See Simenon, Georges (Jacques Christian)

Gerhardi, William Alexander
See Gerhardie, William Alexander

Gerhardie, William Alexander
1895-1977 .... **CLC 5**
See also CA 25-28R; 73-76; CANR 18;
DLB 36

Gerstler, Amy 1956-.............. **CLC 70**
See also CA 146

Gertler, T. .... **CLC 34**
See also CA 116; 121; INT 121

gfgg .... **CLC XvXzc**

Ghalib .... **NCLC 39**
See also Ghalib, Hsadullah Khan

Ghalib, Hsadullah Khan 1797-1869
See Ghalib
See also DAM POET

Ghelderode, Michel de
1898-1962 .... **CLC 6, 11; DAM DRAM**
See also CA 85-88; CANR 40

Ghiselin, Brewster 1903- .... **CLC 23**
See also CA 13-16R; CAAS 10; CANR 13

Ghose, Zulfikar 1935-............. **CLC 42**
See also CA 65-68

Ghosh, Amitav 1956- .... **CLC 44**
See also CA 147

Giacosa, Giuseppe 1847-1906 ...... **TCLC 7**
See also CA 104

Gibb, Lee
See Waterhouse, Keith (Spencer)

Gibbon, Lewis Grassic .... **TCLC 4**
See also Mitchell, James Leslie

Gibbons, Kaye
1960- .... **CLC 50, 88; DAM POP**
See also CA 151

Gibran, Kahlil
1883-1931 .... **TCLC 1, 9; DAM POET,**
POP; PC 9
See also CA 104; 150

Gibran, Khalil
See Gibran, Kahlil

Gibson, William
1914- .... **CLC 23; DA; DAB; DAC;**
DAM DRAM, MST
See also CA 9-12R; CANR 9, 42; DLB 7;
SATA 66

Gibson, William (Ford)
1948- .... **CLC 39, 63; DAM POP**
See also AAYA 12; CA 126; 133; CANR 52

Gide, Andre (Paul Guillaume)
1869-1951 . . . . **TCLC 5, 12, 36; DA;
DAB; DAC; DAM MST, NOV; SSC 13;
WLC**
See also CA 104; 124; DLB 65; MTCW

Gifford, Barry (Colby) 1946- . . . . **CLC 34**
See also CA 65-68; CANR 9, 30, 40

Gilbert, W(illiam) S(chwenck)
1836-1911 . . . . . **TCLC 3; DAM DRAM,
POET**
See also CA 104; SATA 36

Gilbreth, Frank B., Jr. 1911- . . . . **CLC 17**
See also CA 9-12R; SATA 2

Gilchrist, Ellen
1935- . . . . **CLC 34, 48; DAM POP;
SSC 14**
See also CA 113; 116; CANR 41; DLB 130;
MTCW

Giles, Molly 1942- . . . . **CLC 39**
See also CA 126

Gill, Patrick
See Creasey, John

Gilliam, Terry (Vance) 1940- . . . . **CLC 21**
See also Monty Python
See also AAYA 19; CA 108; 113;
CANR 35; INT 113

Gillian, Jerry
See Gilliam, Terry (Vance)

Gilliatt, Penelope (Ann Douglass)
1932-1993 . . . . **CLC 2, 10, 13, 53**
See also AITN 2; CA 13-16R; 141;
CANR 49; DLB 14

Gilman, Charlotte (Anna) Perkins (Stetson)
1860-1935 . . . . **TCLC 9, 37; SSC 13**
See also CA 106; 150

Gilmour, David 1949- . . . . **CLC 35**
See also CA 138, 147

Gilpin, William 1724-1804 . . . . . . **NCLC 30**

Gilray, J. D.
See Mencken, H(enry) L(ouis)

Gilroy, Frank D(aniel) 1925- . . . . **CLC 2**
See also CA 81-84; CANR 32; DLB 7

Gilstrap, John 1957(?)- . . . . **CLC 99**

Ginsberg, Allen
1926- . . . . . . **CLC 1, 2, 3, 4, 6, 13, 36, 69;
DA; DAB; DAC; DAM MST, POET;
PC 4; WLC 3**
See also AITN 1; CA 1-4R; CANR 2, 41;
CDALB 1941-1968; DLB 5, 16, 169;
MTCW

Ginzburg, Natalia
1916-1991 . . . . **CLC 5, 11, 54, 70**
See also CA 85-88; 135; CANR 33;
DLB 177; MTCW

Giono, Jean 1895-1970 . . . . **CLC 4, 11**
See also CA 45-48; 29-32R; CANR 2, 35;
DLB 72; MTCW

Giovanni, Nikki
1943- . . . . . . **CLC 2, 4, 19, 64; BLC; DA;
DAB; DAC; DAM MST, MULT, POET**
See also AITN 1; BW 2; CA 29-32R;
CAAS 6; CANR 18, 41; CLR 6; DLB 5,
41; INT CANR-18; MAICYA; MTCW;
SATA 24

Giovene, Andrea 1904- . . . . **CLC 7**
See also CA 85-88

Gippius, Zinaida (Nikolayevna) 1869-1945
See Hippius, Zinaida
See also CA 106

Giraudoux, (Hippolyte) Jean
1882-1944 . . . . **TCLC 2, 7; DAM DRAM**
See also CA 104; DLB 65

Gironella, Jose Maria 1917- . . . . **CLC 11**
See also CA 101

Gissing, George (Robert)
1857-1903 . . . . **TCLC 3, 24, 47**
See also CA 105; DLB 18, 135

Giurlani, Aldo
See Palazzeschi, Aldo

Gladkov, Fyodor (Vasilyevich)
1883-1958 . . . . **TCLC 27**

Glanville, Brian (Lester) 1931- . . . . . . **CLC 6**
See also CA 5-8R; CAAS 9; CANR 3;
DLB 15, 139; SATA 42

Glasgow, Ellen (Anderson Gholson)
1873(?)-1945 . . . . **TCLC 2, 7**
See also CA 104; DLB 9, 12

Glaspell, Susan 1882(?)-1948 . . . . . . **TCLC 55**
See also CA 110; 154; DLB 7, 9, 78;
YABC 2

Glassco, John 1909-1981 . . . . **CLC 9**
See also CA 13-16R; 102; CANR 15;
DLB 68

Glasscock, Amnesia
See Steinbeck, John (Ernst)

Glasser, Ronald J. 1940(?)- . . . . **CLC 37**

Glassman, Joyce
See Johnson, Joyce

Glendinning, Victoria 1937- . . . . **CLC 50**
See also CA 120; 127; DLB 155

Glissant, Edouard
1928- . . . . **CLC 10, 68; DAM MULT**
See also CA 153

Gloag, Julian 1930- . . . . **CLC 40**
See also AITN 1; CA 65-68; CANR 10

Glowacki, Aleksander
See Prus, Boleslaw

Gluck, Louise (Elisabeth)
1943- . . . . **CLC 7, 22, 44, 81;
DAM POET; PC 16**
See also CA 33-36R; CANR 40; DLB 5

Gobineau, Joseph Arthur (Comte) de
1816-1882 . . . . **NCLC 17**
See also DLB 123

Godard, Jean-Luc 1930- . . . . **CLC 20**
See also CA 93-96

Godden, (Margaret) Rumer 1907- . . . **CLC 53**
See also AAYA 6; CA 5-8R; CANR 4, 27,
36, 55; CLR 20; DLB 161; MAICYA;
SAAS 12; SATA 3, 36

Godoy Alcayaga, Lucila 1889-1957
See Mistral, Gabriela
See also BW 2; CA 104; 131; DAM MULT;
HW; MTCW

Godwin, Gail (Kathleen)
1937- . . . . **CLC 5, 8, 22, 31, 69;
DAM POP**
See also CA 29-32R; CANR 15, 43; DLB 6;
INT CANR-15; MTCW

Godwin, William 1756-1836 . . . . . . **NCLC 14**
See also CDBLB 1789-1832; DLB 39, 104,
142, 158, 163

Goebbels, Josef
See Goebbels, (Paul) Joseph

Goebbels, (Paul) Joseph
1897-1945 . . . . **TCLC 68**
See also CA 115; 148

Goebbels, Joseph Paul
See Goebbels, (Paul) Joseph

Goethe, Johann Wolfgang von
1749-1832 . . . . **NCLC 4, 22, 34; DA;
DAB; DAC; DAM DRAM, MST,
POET; PC 5; WLC 3**
See also DLB 94

Gogarty, Oliver St. John
1878-1957 . . . . **TCLC 15**
See also CA 109; 150; DLB 15, 19

Gogol, Nikolai (Vasilyevich)
1809-1852 . . . . **NCLC 5, 15, 31; DA;
DAB; DAC; DAM DRAM, MST; DC 1;
SSC 4; WLC**

Goines, Donald
1937(?)-1974 . . . . **CLC 80; BLC;
DAM MULT, POP**
See also AITN 1; BW 1; CA 124; 114;
DLB 33

Gold, Herbert 1924- . . . . **CLC 4, 7, 14, 42**
See also CA 9-12R; CANR 17, 45; DLB 2;
DLBY 81

Goldbarth, Albert 1948- . . . . **CLC 5, 38**
See also CA 53-56; CANR 6, 40; DLB 120

Goldberg, Anatol 1910-1982 . . . . **CLC 34**
See also CA 131; 117

Goldemberg, Isaac 1945- . . . . **CLC 52**
See also CA 69-72; CAAS 12; CANR 11,
32; HW

Golding, William (Gerald)
1911-1993 . . . . **CLC 1, 2, 3, 8, 10, 17, 27,
58, 81; DA; DAB; DAC; DAM MST,
NOV; WLC**
See also AAYA 5; CA 5-8R; 141;
CANR 13, 33, 54; CDBLB 1945-1960;
DLB 15, 100; MTCW

Goldman, Emma 1869-1940 . . . . **TCLC 13**
See also CA 110; 150

Goldman, Francisco 1955- . . . . **CLC 76**

Goldman, William (W.) 1931- . . . . **CLC 1, 48**
See also CA 9-12R; CANR 29; DLB 44

Goldmann, Lucien 1913-1970 . . . . . . **CLC 24**
See also CA 25-28; CAP 2

Goldoni, Carlo
1707-1793 . . . . **LC 4; DAM DRAM**

Goldsberry, Steven 1949- . . . . **CLC 34**
See also CA 131

Goldsmith, Oliver
1728-1774 . . . . . . **LC 2; DA; DAB; DAC;
DAM DRAM, MST, NOV, POET;
WLC**
See also CDBLB 1660-1789; DLB 39, 89,
104, 109, 142; SATA 26

Goldsmith, Peter
See Priestley, J(ohn) B(oynton)

Gombrowicz, Witold
1904-1969 . . . . CLC 4, 7, 11, 49;
DAM DRAM
See also CA 19-20; 25-28R; CAP 2

Gomez de la Serna, Ramon
1888-1963 . . . . CLC 9
See also CA 153; 116; HW

Goncharov, Ivan Alexandrovich
1812-1891 . . . . NCLC 1

Goncourt, Edmond (Louis Antoine Huot) de
1822-1896 . . . . NCLC 7
See also DLB 123

Goncourt, Jules (Alfred Huot) de
1830-1870 . . . . NCLC 7
See also DLB 123

Gontier, Fernande 19(?)- . . . . CLC 50

Goodman, Paul 1911-1972 . . . . CLC 1, 2, 4, 7
See also CA 19-20; 37-40R; CANR 34;
CAP 2; DLB 130; MTCW

Gordimer, Nadine
1923- . . . . CLC 3, 5, 7, 10, 18, 33, 51, 70;
DA; DAB; DAC; DAM MST, NOV;
SSC 17
See also CA 5-8R; CANR 3, 28, 56;
INT CANR-28; MTCW

Gordon, Adam Lindsay
1833-1870 . . . . NCLC 21

Gordon, Caroline
1895-1981 . . . CLC 6, 13, 29, 83; SSC 15
See also CA 11-12; 103; CANR 36; CAP 1;
DLB 4, 9, 102; DLBY 81; MTCW

Gordon, Charles William 1860-1937
See Connor, Ralph
See also CA 109

Gordon, Mary (Catherine)
1949- . . . . CLC 13, 22
See also CA 102; CANR 44; DLB 6;
DLBY 81; INT 102; MTCW

Gordon, Sol 1923- . . . . CLC 26
See also CA 53-56; CANR 4; SATA 11

Gordone, Charles
1925-1995 . . . . . CLC 1, 4; DAM DRAM
See also BW 1; CA 93-96; 150; CANR 55;
DLB 7; INT 93-96; MTCW

Gorenko, Anna Andreevna
See Akhmatova, Anna

Gorky, Maxim . . . . TCLC 8; DAB; WLC
See also Peshkov, Alexei Maximovich

Goryan, Sirak
See Saroyan, William

Gosse, Edmund (William)
1849-1928 . . . . TCLC 28
See also CA 117; DLB 57, 144

Gotlieb, Phyllis Fay (Bloom)
1926- . . . . CLC 18
See also CA 13-16R; CANR 7; DLB 88

Gottesman, S. D.
See Kornbluth, C(yril) M.; Pohl, Frederik

Gottfried von Strassburg
fl. c. 1210- . . . . CMLC 10
See also DLB 138

Gould, Lois . . . . CLC 4, 10
See also CA 77-80; CANR 29; MTCW

Gourmont, Remy (-Marie-Charles) de
1858-1915 . . . . TCLC 17
See also CA 109; 150

Govier, Katherine 1948- . . . . CLC 51
See also CA 101; CANR 18, 40

Goyen, (Charles) William
1915-1983 . . . . CLC 5, 8, 14, 40
See also AITN 2; CA 5-8R; 110; CANR 6;
DLB 2; DLBY 83; INT CANR-6

Goytisolo, Juan
1931- . . . . . CLC 5, 10, 23; DAM MULT;
HLC
See also CA 85-88; CANR 32; HW; MTCW

Gozzano, Guido 1883-1916 . . . . PC 10
See also CA 154; DLB 114

Gozzi, (Conte) Carlo 1720-1806 . . NCLC 23

Grabbe, Christian Dietrich
1801-1836 . . . . NCLC 2
See also DLB 133

Grace, Patricia 1937- . . . . CLC 56

Gracian y Morales, Baltasar
1601-1658 . . . . LC 15

Gracq, Julien . . . . CLC 11, 48
See also Poirier, Louis
See also DLB 83

Grade, Chaim 1910-1982 . . . . CLC 10
See also CA 93-96; 107

Graduate of Oxford, A
See Ruskin, John

Graham, John
See Phillips, David Graham

Graham, Jorie 1951- . . . . CLC 48
See also CA 111; DLB 120

Graham, R(obert) B(ontine) Cunninghame
See Cunninghame Graham, R(obert)
B(ontine)
See also DLB 98, 135, 174

Graham, Robert
See Haldeman, Joe (William)

Graham, Tom
See Lewis, (Harry) Sinclair

Graham, W(illiam) S(ydney)
1918-1986 . . . . CLC 29
See also CA 73-76; 118; DLB 20

Graham, Winston (Mawdsley)
1910- . . . . CLC 23
See also CA 49-52; CANR 2, 22, 45;
DLB 77

Grahame, Kenneth
1859-1932 . . . . TCLC 64; DAB
See also CA 108; 136; CLR 5; DLB 34, 141;
MAICYA; YABC 1

Grant, Skeeter
See Spiegelman, Art

Granville-Barker, Harley
1877-1946 . . . . . . TCLC 2; DAM DRAM
See also Barker, Harley Granville
See also CA 104

Grass, Guenter (Wilhelm)
1927- . . . . . CLC 1, 2, 4, 6, 11, 15, 22, 32,
49, 88; DA; DAB; DAC; DAM MST,
NOV; WLC
See also CA 13-16R; CANR 20; DLB 75,
124; MTCW

Gratton, Thomas
See Hulme, T(homas) E(rnest)

Grau, Shirley Ann
1929- . . . . CLC 4, 9; SSC 15
See also CA 89-92; CANR 22; DLB 2;
INT CANR-22; MTCW

Gravel, Fern
See Hall, James Norman

Graver, Elizabeth 1964- . . . . CLC 70
See also CA 135

Graves, Richard Perceval 1945- . . . . CLC 44
See also CA 65-68; CANR 9, 26, 51

Graves, Robert (von Ranke)
1895-1985 . . . . . . CLC 1, 2, 6, 11, 39, 44,
45; DAB; DAC; DAM MST, POET;
PC 6
See also CA 5-8R; 117; CANR 5, 36;
CDBLB 1914-1945; DLB 20, 100;
DLBY 85; MTCW; SATA 45

Graves, Valerie
See Bradley, Marion Zimmer

Gray, Alasdair (James) 1934- . . . . . . CLC 41
See also CA 126; CANR 47; INT 126;
MTCW

Gray, Amlin 1946- . . . . CLC 29
See also CA 138

Gray, Francine du Plessix
1930- . . . . CLC 22; DAM NOV
See also BEST 90:3; CA 61-64; CAAS 2;
CANR 11, 33; INT CANR-11; MTCW

Gray, John (Henry) 1866-1934 . . . . TCLC 19
See also CA 119

Gray, Simon (James Holliday)
1936- . . . . CLC 9, 14, 36
See also AITN 1; CA 21-24R; CAAS 3;
CANR 32; DLB 13; MTCW

Gray, Spalding
1941- . . . . CLC 49; DAM POP; DC 7
See also CA 128

Gray, Thomas
1716-1771 . . . . . . LC 4; DA; DAB; DAC;
DAM MST; PC 2; WLC
See also CDBLB 1660-1789; DLB 109

Grayson, David
See Baker, Ray Stannard

Grayson, Richard (A.) 1951- . . . . CLC 38
See also CA 85-88; CANR 14, 31, 57

Greeley, Andrew M(oran)
1928- . . . . CLC 28; DAM POP
See also CA 5-8R; CAAS 7; CANR 7, 43;
MTCW

Green, Anna Katharine
1846-1935 . . . . TCLC 63
See also CA 112

Green, Brian
See Card, Orson Scott

Green, Hannah
See Greenberg, Joanne (Goldenberg)

Green, Hannah . . . . CLC 3
See also CA 73-76

Green, Henry 1905-1973 . . . . . CLC 2, 13, 97
See also Yorke, Henry Vincent
See also DLB 15

Green, Julian (Hartridge) 1900-
See Green, Julien
See also CA 21-24R; CANR 33; DLB 4, 72;
MTCW

Green, Julien . . . . CLC 3, 11, 77
See also Green, Julian (Hartridge)

Green, Paul (Eliot)
1894-1981 . . . . . . CLC 25; DAM DRAM
See also AITN 1; CA 5-8R; 103; CANR 3;
DLB 7, 9; DLBY 81

Greenberg, Ivan 1908-1973
See Rahv, Philip
See also CA 85-88

Greenberg, Joanne (Goldenberg)
1932- . . . . CLC 7, 30
See also AAYA 12; CA 5-8R; CANR 14,
32; SATA 25

Greenberg, Richard 1959(?)- . . . . . . CLC 57
See also CA 138

Greene, Bette 1934- . . . . CLC 30
See also AAYA 7; CA 53-56; CANR 4;
CLR 2; JRDA; MAICYA; SAAS 16;
SATA 8

Greene, Gael . . . . CLC 8
See also CA 13-16R; CANR 10

Greene, Graham
1904-1991 . . . . CLC 1, 3, 6, 9, 14, 18, 27,
37, 70, 72; DA; DAB; DAC; DAM MST,
NOV; WLC
See also AITN 2; CA 13-16R; 133;
CANR 35; CDBLB 1945-1960; DLB 13,
15, 77, 100, 162; DLBY 91; MTCW;
SATA 20

Greer, Richard
See Silverberg, Robert

Gregor, Arthur 1923- . . . . CLC 9
See also CA 25-28R; CAAS 10; CANR 11;
SATA 36

Gregor, Lee
See Pohl, Frederik

Gregory, Isabella Augusta (Persse)
1852-1932 . . . . TCLC 1
See also CA 104; DLB 10

Gregory, J. Dennis
See Williams, John A(lfred)

Grendon, Stephen
See Derleth, August (William)

Grenville, Kate 1950- . . . . CLC 61
See also CA 118; CANR 53

Grenville, Pelham
See Wodehouse, P(elham) G(renville)

Greve, Felix Paul (Berthold Friedrich)
1879-1948
See Grove, Frederick Philip
See also CA 104; 141; DAC; DAM MST

Grey, Zane
1872-1939 . . . . TCLC 6; DAM POP
See also CA 104; 132; DLB 9; MTCW

Grieg, (Johan) Nordahl (Brun)
1902-1943 . . . . TCLC 10
See also CA 107

Grieve, C(hristopher) M(urray)
1892-1978 . . . . CLC 11, 19; DAM POET
See also MacDiarmid, Hugh; Pteleon
See also CA 5-8R; 85-88; CANR 33;
MTCW

Griffin, Gerald 1803-1840 . . . . NCLC 7
See also DLB 159

Griffin, John Howard 1920-1980 . . . . CLC 68
See also AITN 1; CA 1-4R; 101; CANR 2

Griffin, Peter 1942- . . . . CLC 39
See also CA 136

Griffith, D(avid Lewelyn) W(ark)
1875(?)-1948 . . . . TCLC 68
See also CA 119; 150

Griffith, Lawrence
See Griffith, D(avid Lewelyn) W(ark)

Griffiths, Trevor 1935- . . . . CLC 13, 52
See also CA 97-100; CANR 45; DLB 13

Grigson, Geoffrey (Edward Harvey)
1905-1985 . . . . CLC 7, 39
See also CA 25-28R; 118; CANR 20, 33;
DLB 27; MTCW

Grillparzer, Franz 1791-1872 . . . . . . NCLC 1
See also DLB 133

Grimble, Reverend Charles James
See Eliot, T(homas) S(tearns)

Grimke, Charlotte L(ottie) Forten
1837(?)-1914
See Forten, Charlotte L.
See also BW 1; CA 117; 124; DAM MULT,
POET

Grimm, Jacob Ludwig Karl
1785-1863 . . . . NCLC 3
See also DLB 90; MAICYA; SATA 22

Grimm, Wilhelm Karl 1786-1859 . . NCLC 3
See also DLB 90; MAICYA; SATA 22

Grimmelshausen, Johann Jakob Christoffel
von 1621-1676 . . . . LC 6
See also DLB 168

Grindel, Eugene 1895-1952
See Eluard, Paul
See also CA 104

Grisham, John 1955- . . CLC 84; DAM POP
See also AAYA 14; CA 138; CANR 47

Grossman, David 1954- . . . . CLC 67
See also CA 138

Grossman, Vasily (Semenovich)
1905-1964 . . . . CLC 41
See also CA 124; 130; MTCW

Grove, Frederick Philip . . . . TCLC 4
See also Greve, Felix Paul (Berthold
Friedrich)
See also DLB 92

Grubb
See Crumb, R(obert)

Grumbach, Doris (Isaac)
1918- . . . . CLC 13, 22, 64
See also CA 5-8R; CAAS 2; CANR 9, 42;
INT CANR-9

Grundtvig, Nicolai Frederik Severin
1783-1872 . . . . NCLC 1

Grunge
See Crumb, R(obert)

Grunwald, Lisa 1959- . . . . CLC 44
See also CA 120

Guare, John
1938- . . . . CLC 8, 14, 29, 67;
DAM DRAM
See also CA 73-76; CANR 21; DLB 7;
MTCW

Gudjonsson, Halldor Kiljan 1902-
See Laxness, Halldor
See also CA 103

Guenter, Erich
See Eich, Guenter

Guest, Barbara 1920- . . . . CLC 34
See also CA 25-28R; CANR 11, 44; DLB 5

Guest, Judith (Ann)
1936- . . . . CLC 8, 30; DAM NOV, POP
See also AAYA 7; CA 77-80; CANR 15;
INT CANR-15; MTCW

Guevara, Che . . . . CLC 87; HLC
See also Guevara (Serna), Ernesto

Guevara (Serna), Ernesto 1928-1967
See Guevara, Che
See also CA 127; 111; CANR 56;
DAM MULT; HW

Guild, Nicholas M. 1944- . . . . CLC 33
See also CA 93-96

Guillemin, Jacques
See Sartre, Jean-Paul

Guillen, Jorge
1893-1984 . . . . . . CLC 11; DAM MULT,
POET
See also CA 89-92; 112; DLB 108; HW

Guillen, Nicolas (Cristobal)
1902-1989 . . . . CLC 48, 79; BLC;
DAM MST, MULT, POET; HLC
See also BW 2; CA 116; 125; 129; HW

Guillevic, (Eugene) 1907- . . . . CLC 33
See also CA 93-96

Guillois
See Desnos, Robert

Guillois, Valentin
See Desnos, Robert

Guiney, Louise Imogen
1861-1920 . . . . TCLC 41
See also DLB 54

Guiraldes, Ricardo (Guillermo)
1886-1927 . . . . TCLC 39
See also CA 131; HW; MTCW

Gumilev, Nikolai Stephanovich
1886-1921 . . . . TCLC 60

Gunesekera, Romesh . . . . CLC 91

Gunn, Bill . . . . CLC 5
See also Gunn, William Harrison
See also DLB 38

Gunn, Thom(son William)
1929- . . . . CLC 3, 6, 18, 32, 81;
DAM POET
See also CA 17-20R; CANR 9, 33;
CDBLB 1960 to Present; DLB 27;
INT CANR-33; MTCW

Gunn, William Harrison 1934(?)-1989
See Gunn, Bill
See also AITN 1; BW 1; CA 13-16R; 128;
CANR 12, 25

Gunnars, Kristjana 1948- . . . . CLC 69
See also CA 113; DLB 60

Gurganus, Allan
1947- . . . . CLC 70; DAM POP
See also BEST 90:1; CA 135

Gurney, A(lbert) R(amsdell), Jr.
1930- . . . . CLC 32, 50, 54; DAM DRAM
See also CA 77-80; CANR 32

Gurney, Ivor (Bertie) 1890-1937 . . . **TCLC 33**

Gurney, Peter
  See Gurney, A(lbert) R(amsdell), Jr.

Guro, Elena 1877-1913 . . . . **TCLC 56**

Gustafson, James M(oody) 1925- . . **CLC 100**
  See also CA 25-28R; CANR 37

Gustafson, Ralph (Barker) 1909-. . . . **CLC 36**
  See also CA 21-24R; CANR 8, 45; DLB 88

Gut, Gom
  See Simenon, Georges (Jacques Christian)

Guterson, David 1956-. . . . . **CLC 91**
  See also CA 132

Guthrie, A(lfred) B(ertram), Jr.
  1901-1991 . . . . **CLC 23**
  See also CA 57-60; 134; CANR 24; DLB 6;
  SATA 62; SATA-Obit 67

Guthrie, Isobel
  See Grieve, C(hristopher) M(urray)

Guthrie, Woodrow Wilson 1912-1967
  See Guthrie, Woody
  See also CA 113; 93-96

Guthrie, Woody . . . . **CLC 35**
  See also Guthrie, Woodrow Wilson

Guy, Rosa (Cuthbert) 1928-. . . . . **CLC 26**
  See also AAYA 4; BW 2; CA 17-20R;
  CANR 14, 34; CLR 13; DLB 33; JRDA;
  MAICYA; SATA 14, 62

Gwendolyn
  See Bennett, (Enoch) Arnold

H. D. . . . . **CLC 3, 8, 14, 31, 34, 73; PC 5**
  See also Doolittle, Hilda

H. de V.
  See Buchan, John

Haavikko, Paavo Juhani
  1931- . . . . **CLC 18, 34**
  See also CA 106

Habbema, Koos
  See Heijermans, Herman

Hacker, Marilyn
  1942- . . . . **CLC 5, 9, 23, 72, 91;**
                                          DAM POET
  See also CA 77-80; DLB 120

Haggard, H(enry) Rider
  1856-1925 . . . . **TCLC 11**
  See also CA 108; 148; DLB 70, 156, 174;
  SATA 16

Hagiosy, L.
  See Larbaud, Valery (Nicolas)

Hagiwara Sakutaro 1886-1942 . . . . **TCLC 60**

Haig, Fenil
  See Ford, Ford Madox

Haig-Brown, Roderick (Langmere)
  1908-1976 . . . . **CLC 21**
  See also CA 5-8R; 69-72; CANR 4, 38;
  CLR 31; DLB 88; MAICYA; SATA 12

Hailey, Arthur
  1920- . . . . **CLC 5; DAM NOV, POP**
  See also AITN 2; BEST 90:3; CA 1-4R;
  CANR 2, 36; DLB 88; DLBY 82; MTCW

Hailey, Elizabeth Forsythe 1938-. . . **CLC 40**
  See also CA 93-96; CAAS 1; CANR 15, 48;
  INT CANR-15

Haines, John (Meade) 1924-. . . . . . . **CLC 58**
  See also CA 17-20R; CANR 13, 34; DLB 5

Hakluyt, Richard 1552-1616 . . . . **LC 31**

Haldeman, Joe (William) 1943-. . . . . **CLC 61**
  See also CA 53-56; CAAS 25; CANR 6;
  DLB 8; INT CANR-6

Haley, Alex(ander Murray Palmer)
  1921-1992 . . . . **CLC 8, 12, 76; BLC; DA;**
            DAB; DAC; DAM MST, MULT, POP
  See also BW 2; CA 77-80; 136; DLB 38;
  MTCW

Haliburton, Thomas Chandler
  1796-1865 . . . . **NCLC 15**
  See also DLB 11, 99

Hall, Donald (Andrew, Jr.)
  1928- . . **CLC 1, 13, 37, 59; DAM POET**
  See also CA 5-8R; CAAS 7; CANR 2, 44;
  DLB 5; SATA 23

Hall, Frederic Sauser
  See Sauser-Hall, Frederic

Hall, James
  See Kuttner, Henry

Hall, James Norman 1887-1951 . . . **TCLC 23**
  See also CA 123; SATA 21

Hall, (Marguerite) Radclyffe
  1886-1943 . . . . **TCLC 12**
  See also CA 110; 150

Hall, Rodney 1935- . . . . **CLC 51**
  See also CA 109

Halleck, Fitz-Greene 1790-1867 . . **NCLC 47**
  See also DLB 3

Halliday, Michael
  See Creasey, John

Halpern, Daniel 1945- . . . . **CLC 14**
  See also CA 33-36R

Hamburger, Michael (Peter Leopold)
  1924- . . . . **CLC 5, 14**
  See also CA 5-8R; CAAS 4; CANR 2, 47;
  DLB 27

Hamill, Pete 1935- . . . . **CLC 10**
  See also CA 25-28R; CANR 18

Hamilton, Alexander
  1755(?)-1804 . . . . **NCLC 49**
  See also DLB 37

Hamilton, Clive
  See Lewis, C(live) S(taples)

Hamilton, Edmond 1904-1977 . . . . . . **CLC 1**
  See also CA 1-4R; CANR 3; DLB 8

Hamilton, Eugene (Jacob) Lee
  See Lee-Hamilton, Eugene (Jacob)

Hamilton, Franklin
  See Silverberg, Robert

Hamilton, Gail
  See Corcoran, Barbara

Hamilton, Mollie
  See Kaye, M(ary) M(argaret)

Hamilton, (Anthony Walter) Patrick
  1904-1962 . . . . **CLC 51**
  See also CA 113; DLB 10

Hamilton, Virginia
  1936- . . . . **CLC 26; DAM MULT**
  See also AAYA 2; BW 2; CA 25-28R;
  CANR 20, 37; CLR 1, 11, 40; DLB 33,
  52; INT CANR-20; JRDA; MAICYA;
  MTCW; SATA 4, 56, 79

Hammett, (Samuel) Dashiell
  1894-1961 . . . . **CLC 3, 5, 10, 19, 47;**
                                                    SSC 17
  See also AITN 1; CA 81-84; CANR 42;
  CDALB 1929-1941; DLBD 6; MTCW

Hammon, Jupiter
  1711(?)-1800(?) . . . . **NCLC 5; BLC;**
                        DAM MULT, POET; PC 16
  See also DLB 31, 50

Hammond, Keith
  See Kuttner, Henry

Hamner, Earl (Henry), Jr. 1923- . . . **CLC 12**
  See also AITN 2; CA 73-76; DLB 6

Hampton, Christopher (James)
  1946- . . . . **CLC 4**
  See also CA 25-28R; DLB 13; MTCW

Hamsun, Knut . . . . **TCLC 2, 14, 49**
  See also Pedersen, Knut

Handke, Peter
  1942- . . . . **CLC 5, 8, 10, 15, 38;**
                                  DAM DRAM, NOV
  See also CA 77-80; CANR 33; DLB 85,
  124; MTCW

Hanley, James 1901-1985 . . . **CLC 3, 5, 8, 13**
  See also CA 73-76; 117; CANR 36; MTCW

Hannah, Barry 1942-. . . . . . . **CLC 23, 38, 90**
  See also CA 108; 110; CANR 43; DLB 6;
  INT 110; MTCW

Hannon, Ezra
  See Hunter, Evan

Hansberry, Lorraine (Vivian)
  1930-1965 . . . . . . **CLC 17, 62; BLC; DA;**
            DAB; DAC; DAM DRAM, MST,
                                        MULT; DC 2
  See also BW 1; CA 109; 25-28R; CABS 3;
  CDALB 1941-1968; DLB 7, 38; MTCW

Hansen, Joseph 1923-. . . . . **CLC 38**
  See also CA 29-32R; CAAS 17; CANR 16,
  44; INT CANR-16

Hansen, Martin A. 1909-1955 . . . . . **TCLC 32**

Hanson, Kenneth O(stlin) 1922- . . . . **CLC 13**
  See also CA 53-56; CANR 7

Hardwick, Elizabeth
  1916- . . . . **CLC 13; DAM NOV**
  See also CA 5-8R; CANR 3, 32; DLB 6;
  MTCW

Hardy, Thomas
  1840-1928 . . . . . . **TCLC 4, 10, 18, 32, 48,**
         53; DA; DAB; DAC; DAM MST, NOV,
                     POET; PC 8; SSC 2; WLC
  See also CA 104; 123; CDBLB 1890-1914;
  DLB 18, 19, 135; MTCW

Hare, David 1947- . . . . **CLC 29, 58**
  See also CA 97-100; CANR 39; DLB 13;
  MTCW

Harford, Henry
  See Hudson, W(illiam) H(enry)

Hargrave, Leonie
  See Disch, Thomas M(ichael)

Harjo, Joy 1951- . . . **CLC 83; DAM MULT**
  See also CA 114; CANR 35; DLB 120, 175;
  NNAL

Harlan, Louis R(udolph) 1922-. . . . . **CLC 34**
  See also CA 21-24R; CANR 25, 55

Harling, Robert 1951(?)- .... **CLC 53**
See also CA 147

Harmon, William (Ruth) 1938- ..... **CLC 38**
See also CA 33-36R; CANR 14, 32, 35;
SATA 65

Harper, F. E. W.
See Harper, Frances Ellen Watkins

Harper, Frances E. W.
See Harper, Frances Ellen Watkins

Harper, Frances E. Watkins
See Harper, Frances Ellen Watkins

Harper, Frances Ellen
See Harper, Frances Ellen Watkins

Harper, Frances Ellen Watkins
1825-1911 .... **TCLC 14; BLC;**
DAM MULT, POET
See also BW 1; CA 111; 125; DLB 50

Harper, Michael S(teven) 1938- .. **CLC 7, 22**
See also BW 1; CA 33-36R; CANR 24;
DLB 41

Harper, Mrs. F. E. W.
See Harper, Frances Ellen Watkins

Harris, Christie (Lucy) Irwin
1907- .... **CLC 12**
See also CA 5-8R; CANR 6; DLB 88;
JRDA; MAICYA; SAAS 10; SATA 6, 74

Harris, Frank 1856-1931 .... **TCLC 24**
See also CA 109; 150; DLB 156

Harris, George Washington
1814-1869 .... **NCLC 23**
See also DLB 3, 11

Harris, Joel Chandler
1848-1908 .... **TCLC 2; SSC 19**
See also CA 104; 137; DLB 11, 23, 42, 78,
91; MAICYA; YABC 1

Harris, John (Wyndham Parkes Lucas)
Beynon 1903-1969
See Wyndham, John
See also CA 102; 89-92

Harris, MacDonald .... **CLC 9**
See also Heiney, Donald (William)

Harris, Mark 1922- .... **CLC 19**
See also CA 5-8R; CAAS 3; CANR 2, 55;
DLB 2; DLBY 80

Harris, (Theodore) Wilson 1921-.... **CLC 25**
See also BW 2; CA 65-68; CAAS 16;
CANR 11, 27; DLB 117; MTCW

Harrison, Elizabeth Cavanna 1909-
See Cavanna, Betty
See also CA 9-12R; CANR 6, 27

Harrison, Harry (Max) 1925- ...... **CLC 42**
See also CA 1-4R; CANR 5, 21; DLB 8;
SATA 4

Harrison, James (Thomas)
1937- .... **CLC 6, 14, 33, 66; SSC 19**
See also CA 13-16R; CANR 8, 51;
DLBY 82; INT CANR-8

Harrison, Jim
See Harrison, James (Thomas)

Harrison, Kathryn 1961- .... **CLC 70**
See also CA 144

Harrison, Tony 1937-............. **CLC 43**
See also CA 65-68; CANR 44; DLB 40;
MTCW

Harriss, Will(ard Irvin) 1922-...... **CLC 34**
See also CA 111

Harson, Sley
See Ellison, Harlan (Jay)

Hart, Ellis
See Ellison, Harlan (Jay)

Hart, Josephine
1942(?)- .... **CLC 70; DAM POP**
See also CA 138

Hart, Moss
1904-1961 ...... **CLC 66; DAM DRAM**
See also CA 109; 89-92; DLB 7

Harte, (Francis) Bret(t)
1836(?)-1902 .... **TCLC 1, 25; DA; DAC;**
DAM MST; SSC 8; WLC
See also CA 104; 140; CDALB 1865-1917;
DLB 12, 64, 74, 79; SATA 26

Hartley, L(eslie) P(oles)
1895-1972 .... **CLC 2, 22**
See also CA 45-48; 37-40R; CANR 33;
DLB 15, 139; MTCW

Hartman, Geoffrey H. 1929-....... **CLC 27**
See also CA 117; 125; DLB 67

Hartmann von Aue
c. 1160-c. 1205 .... **CMLC 15**
See also DLB 138

Hartmann von Aue 1170-1210.... **CMLC 15**

Haruf, Kent 1943- .... **CLC 34**
See also CA 149

Harwood, Ronald
1934- .... **CLC 32; DAM DRAM, MST**
See also CA 1-4R; CANR 4, 55; DLB 13

Hasek, Jaroslav (Matej Frantisek)
1883-1923 .... **TCLC 4**
See also CA 104; 129; MTCW

Hass, Robert
1941- .... **CLC 18, 39, 99; PC 16**
See also CA 111; CANR 30, 50; DLB 105

Hastings, Hudson
See Kuttner, Henry

Hastings, Selina................... **CLC 44**

Hatteras, Amelia
See Mencken, H(enry) L(ouis)

Hatteras, Owen................... **TCLC 18**
See also Mencken, H(enry) L(ouis); Nathan,
George Jean

Hauptmann, Gerhart (Johann Robert)
1862-1946 ...... **TCLC 4; DAM DRAM**
See also CA 104; 153; DLB 66, 118

Havel, Vaclav
1936- .... **CLC 25, 58, 65;**
DAM DRAM; DC 6
See also CA 104; CANR 36; MTCW

Haviaras, Stratis.................. **CLC 33**
See also Chaviaras, Strates

Hawes, Stephen 1475(?)-1523(?) ..... **LC 17**

Hawkes, John (Clendennin Burne, Jr.)
1925- ...... **CLC 1, 2, 3, 4, 7, 9, 14, 15,**
27, 49
See also CA 1-4R; CANR 2, 47; DLB 2, 7;
DLBY 80; MTCW

Hawking, S. W.
See Hawking, Stephen W(illiam)

Hawking, Stephen W(illiam)
1942- ....:.... **CLC 63**
See also AAYA 13; BEST 89:1; CA 126;
129; CANR 48

Hawthorne, Julian 1846-1934 ..... **TCLC 25**

Hawthorne, Nathaniel
1804-1864 .... **NCLC 39; DA; DAB;**
DAC; DAM MST, NOV; SSC 3; WLC
See also AAYA 18; CDALB 1640-1865;
DLB 1, 74; YABC 2

Haxton, Josephine Ayres 1921-
See Douglas, Ellen
See also CA 115; CANR 41

Hayaseca y Eizaguirre, Jorge
See Echegaray (y Eizaguirre), Jose (Maria
Waldo)

Hayashi Fumiko 1904-1951....... **TCLC 27**

Haycraft, Anna
See Ellis, Alice Thomas
See also CA 122

Hayden, Robert E(arl)
1913-1980 ...... **CLC 5, 9, 14, 37; BLC;**
DA; DAC; DAM MST, MULT, POET;
PC 6
See also BW 1; CA 69-72; 97-100; CABS 2;
CANR 24; CDALB 1941-1968; DLB 5,
76; MTCW; SATA 19; SATA-Obit 26

Hayford, J(oseph) E(phraim) Casely
See Casely-Hayford, J(oseph) E(phraim)

Hayman, Ronald 1932-........... **CLC 44**
See also CA 25-28R; CANR 18, 50;
DLB 155

Haywood, Eliza (Fowler)
1693(?)-1756 .... **LC 1**

Hazlitt, William 1778-1830...... **NCLC 29**
See also DLB 110, 158

Hazzard, Shirley 1931- .... **CLC 18**
See also CA 9-12R; CANR 4; DLBY 82;
MTCW

Head, Bessie
1937-1986 .... **CLC 25, 67; BLC;**
DAM MULT
See also BW 2; CA 29-32R; 119; CANR 25;
DLB 117; MTCW

Headon, (Nicky) Topper 1956(?)-... **CLC 30**

Heaney, Seamus (Justin)
1939- ...... **CLC 5, 7, 14, 25, 37, 74, 91;**
DAB; DAM POET
See also CA 85-88; CANR 25, 48;
CDBLB 1960 to Present; DLB 40;
DLBY 95; MTCW

Hearn, (Patricio) Lafcadio (Tessima Carlos)
1850-1904 ....**TCLC 9**
See also CA 105; DLB 12, 78

Hearne, Vicki 1946-............... **CLC 56**
See also CA 139

Hearon, Shelby 1931-............. **CLC 63**
See also AITN 2; CA 25-28R; CANR 18,
48

Heat-Moon, William Least......... **CLC 29**
See also Trogdon, William (Lewis)
See also AAYA 9

Hebbel, Friedrich
1813-1863 .... **NCLC 43; DAM DRAM**
See also DLB 129

Hebert, Anne
1916- .... CLC 4, 13, 29; DAC;
DAM MST, POET
See also CA 85-88; DLB 68; MTCW

Hecht, Anthony (Evan)
1923- ...... CLC 8, 13, 19; DAM POET
See also CA 9-12R; CANR 6; DLB 5, 169

Hecht, Ben 1894-1964 .... CLC 8
See also CA 85-88; DLB 7, 9, 25, 26, 28, 86

Hedayat, Sadeq 1903-1951....... TCLC 21
See also CA 120

Hegel, Georg Wilhelm Friedrich
1770-1831 .... NCLC 46
See also DLB 90

Heidegger, Martin 1889-1976 ...... CLC 24
See also CA 81-84; 65-68; CANR 34;
MTCW

Heidenstam, (Carl Gustaf) Verner von
1859-1940 .... TCLC 5
See also CA 104

Heifner, Jack 1946- .... CLC 11
See also CA 105; CANR 47

Heijermans, Herman 1864-1924 ... TCLC 24
See also CA 123

Heilbrun, Carolyn G(old) 1926-..... CLC 25
See also CA 45-48; CANR 1, 28

Heine, Heinrich 1797-1856 .... NCLC 4, 54
See also DLB 90

Heinemann, Larry (Curtiss) 1944- .. CLC 50
See also CA 110; CAAS 21; CANR 31;
DLBD 9; INT CANR-31

Heiney, Donald (William) 1921-1993
See Harris, MacDonald
See also CA 1-4R; 142; CANR 3

Heinlein, Robert A(nson)
1907-1988 ...... CLC 1, 3, 8, 14, 26, 55;
DAM POP
See also AAYA 17; CA 1-4R; 125;
CANR 1, 20, 53; DLB 8; JRDA;
MAICYA; MTCW; SATA 9, 69;
SATA-Obit 56

Helforth, John
See Doolittle, Hilda

Hellenhofferu, Vojtech Kapristian z
See Hasek, Jaroslav (Matej Frantisek)

Heller, Joseph
1923- .... CLC 1, 3, 5, 8, 11, 36, 63; DA;
DAB; DAC; DAM MST, NOV, POP;
WLC
See also AITN 1; CA 5-8R; CABS 1;
CANR 8, 42; DLB 2, 28; DLBY 80;
INT CANR-8; MTCW

Hellman, Lillian (Florence)
1906-1984 ...... CLC 2, 4, 8, 14, 18, 34,
44, 52; DAM DRAM; DC 1
See also AITN 1, 2; CA 13-16R; 112;
CANR 33; DLB 7; DLBY 84; MTCW

Helprin, Mark
1947- .... CLC 7, 10, 22, 32;
DAM NOV, POP
See also CA 81-84; CANR 47; DLBY 85;
MTCW

Helvetius, Claude-Adrien
1715-1771 .... LC 26

Helyar, Jane Penelope Josephine 1933-
See Poole, Josephine
See also CA 21-24R; CANR 10, 26;
SATA 82

Hemans, Felicia 1793-1835 ...... NCLC 29
See also DLB 96

Hemingway, Ernest (Miller)
1899-1961 .... CLC 1, 3, 6, 8, 10, 13, 19,
30, 34, 39, 41, 44, 50, 61, 80; DA; DAB;
DAC; DAM MST, NOV; SSC 25; WLC
See also AAYA 19; CA 77-80; CANR 34;
CDALB 1917-1929; DLB 4, 9, 102;
DLBD 1; DLBY 81, 87; MTCW

Hempel, Amy 1951- .... CLC 39
See also CA 118; 137

Henderson, F. C.
See Mencken, H(enry) L(ouis)

Henderson, Sylvia
See Ashton-Warner, Sylvia (Constance)

Henley, Beth .... CLC 23; DC 6
See also Henley, Elizabeth Becker
See also CABS 3; DLBY 86

Henley, Elizabeth Becker 1952-
See Henley, Beth
See also CA 107; CANR 32; DAM DRAM,
MST; MTCW

Henley, William Ernest
1849-1903 .... TCLC 8
See also CA 105; DLB 19

Hennissart, Martha
See Lathen, Emma
See also CA 85-88

Henry, O. .... TCLC 1, 19; SSC 5; WLC
See also Porter, William Sydney

Henry, Patrick 1736-1799 .... LC 25

Henryson, Robert 1430(?)-1506(?).... LC 20
See also DLB 146

Henry VIII 1491-1547 .... LC 10

Henschke, Alfred
See Klabund

Hentoff, Nat(han Irving) 1925- ..... CLC 26
See also AAYA 4; CA 1-4R; CAAS 6;
CANR 5, 25; CLR 1; INT CANR-25;
JRDA; MAICYA; SATA 42, 69;
SATA-Brief 27

Heppenstall, (John) Rayner
1911-1981 .... CLC 10
See also CA 1-4R; 103; CANR 29

Heraclitus
c. 540B.C.-c. 450B.C........ CMLC 22
See also DLB 176

Herbert, Frank (Patrick)
1920-1986 ...... CLC 12, 23, 35, 44, 85;
DAM POP
See also CA 53-56; 118; CANR 5, 43;
DLB 8; INT CANR-5; MTCW; SATA 9,
37; SATA-Obit 47

Herbert, George
1593-1633 .... LC 24; DAB;
DAM POET; PC 4
See also CDBLB Before 1660; DLB 126

Herbert, Zbigniew
1924- .... CLC 9, 43; DAM POET
See also CA 89-92; CANR 36; MTCW

Herbst, Josephine (Frey)
1897-1969 .... CLC 34
See also CA 5-8R; 25-28R; DLB 9

Hergesheimer, Joseph
1880-1954 .... TCLC 11
See also CA 109; DLB 102, 9

Herlihy, James Leo 1927-1993 ...... CLC 6
See also CA 1-4R; 143; CANR 2

Hermogenes fl. c. 175- .... CMLC 6

Hernandez, Jose 1834-1886...... NCLC 17

Herodotus c. 484B.C.-429B.C..... CMLC 17
See also DLB 176

Herrick, Robert
1591-1674 ..... LC 13; DA; DAB; DAC;
DAM MST, POP; PC 9
See also DLB 126

Herring, Guilles
See Somerville, Edith

Herriot, James
1916-1995 .... CLC 12; DAM POP
See also Wight, James Alfred
See also AAYA 1; CA 148; CANR 40;
SATA 86

Herrmann, Dorothy 1941-......... CLC 44
See also CA 107

Herrmann, Taffy
See Herrmann, Dorothy

Hersey, John (Richard)
1914-1993 .... CLC 1, 2, 7, 9, 40, 81, 97;
DAM POP
See also CA 17-20R; 140; CANR 33;
DLB 6; MTCW; SATA 25;
SATA-Obit 76

Herzen, Aleksandr Ivanovich
1812-1870 .... NCLC 10

Herzl, Theodor 1860-1904........ TCLC 36

Herzog, Werner 1942- .... CLC 16
See also CA 89-92

Hesiod c. 8th cent. B.C.- .... CMLC 5
See also DLB 176

Hesse, Hermann
1877-1962 .... CLC 1, 2, 3, 6, 11, 17, 25,
69; DA; DAB; DAC; DAM MST, NOV;
SSC 9; WLC
See also CA 17-18; CAP 2; DLB 66;
MTCW; SATA 50

Hewes, Cady
See De Voto, Bernard (Augustine)

Heyen, William 1940- .... CLC 13, 18
See also CA 33-36R; CAAS 9; DLB 5

Heyerdahl, Thor 1914-............ CLC 26
See also CA 5-8R; CANR 5, 22; MTCW;
SATA 2, 52

Heym, Georg (Theodor Franz Arthur)
1887-1912 .... TCLC 9
See also CA 106

Heym, Stefan 1913- .... CLC 41
See also CA 9-12R; CANR 4; DLB 69

Heyse, Paul (Johann Ludwig von)
1830-1914 .... TCLC 8
See also CA 104; DLB 129

Heyward, (Edwin) DuBose
1885-1940 .... TCLC 59
See also CA 108; DLB 7, 9, 45; SATA 21

Hughes, Richard (Arthur Warren)
1900-1976 . . . . . **CLC 1, 11; DAM NOV**
See also CA 5-8R; 65-68; CANR 4;
DLB 15, 161; MTCW; SATA 8;
SATA-Obit 25

Hughes, Ted
1930- . . . . **CLC 2, 4, 9, 14, 37; DAB;**
DAC; PC 7
See also Hughes, Edward James
See also CA 1-4R; CANR 1, 33; CLR 3;
DLB 40, 161; MAICYA; MTCW;
SATA 49; SATA-Brief 27

Hugo, Richard F(ranklin)
1923-1982 . . . . **CLC 6, 18, 32;**
DAM POET
See also CA 49-52; 108; CANR 3; DLB 5

Hugo, Victor (Marie)
1802-1885 . . . . **NCLC 3, 10, 21; DA;**
DAB; DAC; DAM DRAM, MST, NOV,
POET; PC 17; WLC
See also DLB 119; SATA 47

Huidobro, Vicente
See Huidobro Fernandez, Vicente Garcia

Huidobro Fernandez, Vicente Garcia
1893-1948 . . . . **TCLC 31**
See also CA 131; HW

Hulme, Keri 1947- . . . . **CLC 39**
See also CA 125; INT 125

Hulme, T(homas) E(rnest)
1883-1917 . . . . **TCLC 21**
See also CA 117; DLB 19

Hume, David 1711-1776 . . . . **LC 7**
See also DLB 104

Humphrey, William 1924- . . . . **CLC 45**
See also CA 77-80; DLB 6

Humphreys, Emyr Owen 1919- . . . . . **CLC 47**
See also CA 5-8R; CANR 3, 24; DLB 15

Humphreys, Josephine 1945- . . . . **CLC 34, 57**
See also CA 121; 127; INT 127

Huneker, James Gibbons
1857-1921 . . . . **TCLC 65**
See also DLB 71

Hungerford, Pixie
See Brinsmead, H(esba) F(ay)

Hunt, E(verette) Howard, (Jr.)
1918- . . . . **CLC 3**
See also AITN 1; CA 45-48; CANR 2, 47

Hunt, Kyle
See Creasey, John

Hunt, (James Henry) Leigh
1784-1859 . . . . . . **NCLC 1; DAM POET**

Hunt, Marsha 1946- . . . . **CLC 70**
See also BW 2; CA 143

Hunt, Violet 1866-1942 . . . . **TCLC 53**
See also DLB 162

Hunter, E. Waldo
See Sturgeon, Theodore (Hamilton)

Hunter, Evan
1926- . . . . **CLC 11, 31; DAM POP**
See also CA 5-8R; CANR 5, 38; DLBY 82;
INT CANR-5; MTCW; SATA 25

Hunter, Kristin (Eggleston) 1931- . . . **CLC 35**
See also AITN 1; BW 1; CA 13-16R;
CANR 13; CLR 3; DLB 33;
INT CANR-13; MAICYA; SAAS 10;
SATA 12

Hunter, Mollie 1922- . . . . **CLC 21**
See also McIlwraith, Maureen Mollie
Hunter
See also AAYA 13; CANR 37; CLR 25;
DLB 161; JRDA; MAICYA; SAAS 7;
SATA 54

Hunter, Robert (?)-1734 . . . . **LC 7**

Hurston, Zora Neale
1903-1960 . . . . **CLC 7, 30, 61; BLC; DA;**
DAC; DAM MST, MULT, NOV; SSC 4
See also AAYA 15; BW 1; CA 85-88;
DLB 51, 86; MTCW

Huston, John (Marcellus)
1906-1987 . . . . **CLC 20**
See also CA 73-76; 123; CANR 34; DLB 26

Hustvedt, Siri 1955- . . . . **CLC 76**
See also CA 137

Hutten, Ulrich von 1488-1523 . . . . **LC 16**

Huxley, Aldous (Leonard)
1894-1963 . . . . . **CLC 1, 3, 4, 5, 8, 11, 18,**
35, 79; DA; DAB; DAC; DAM MST,
NOV; WLC
See also AAYA 11; CA 85-88; CANR 44;
CDBLB 1914-1945; DLB 36, 100, 162;
MTCW; SATA 63

Huysmans, Charles Marie Georges
1848-1907
See Huysmans, Joris-Karl
See also CA 104

Huysmans, Joris-Karl . . . . **TCLC 7, 69**
See also Huysmans, Charles Marie Georges
See also DLB 123

Hwang, David Henry
1957- . . . . **CLC 55; DAM DRAM; DC 4**
See also CA 127; 132; INT 132

Hyde, Anthony 1946- . . . . **CLC 42**
See also CA 136

Hyde, Margaret O(ldroyd) 1917- . . . **CLC 21**
See also CA 1-4R; CANR 1, 36; CLR 23;
JRDA; MAICYA; SAAS 8; SATA 1, 42,
76

Hynes, James 1956(?)- . . . . **CLC 65**

Ian, Janis 1951- . . . . **CLC 21**
See also CA 105

Ibanez, Vicente Blasco
See Blasco Ibanez, Vicente

Ibarguengoitia, Jorge 1928-1983 . . . . **CLC 37**
See also CA 124; 113; HW

Ibsen, Henrik (Johan)
1828-1906 . . . . **TCLC 2, 8, 16, 37, 52;**
DA; DAB; DAC; DAM DRAM, MST;
DC 2; WLC
See also CA 104; 141

Ibuse Masuji 1898-1993 . . . . **CLC 22**
See also CA 127; 141

Ichikawa, Kon 1915- . . . . **CLC 20**
See also CA 121

Idle, Eric 1943- . . . . **CLC 21**
See also Monty Python
See also CA 116; CANR 35

Ignatow, David 1914- . . . . . . **CLC 4, 7, 14, 40**
See also CA 9-12R; CAAS 3; CANR 31, 57;
DLB 5

Ihimaera, Witi 1944- . . . . **CLC 46**
See also CA 77-80

Ilf, Ilya . . . . **TCLC 21**
See also Fainzilberg, Ilya Arnoldovich

Illyes, Gyula 1902-1983 . . . . **PC 16**
See also CA 114; 109

Immermann, Karl (Lebrecht)
1796-1840 . . . . **NCLC 4, 49**
See also DLB 133

Inclan, Ramon (Maria) del Valle
See Valle-Inclan, Ramon (Maria) del

Infante, G(uillermo) Cabrera
See Cabrera Infante, G(uillermo)

Ingalls, Rachel (Holmes) 1940- . . . . . **CLC 42**
See also CA 123; 127

Ingamells, Rex 1913-1955 . . . . **TCLC 35**

Inge, William (Motter)
1913-1973 . . **CLC 1, 8, 19; DAM DRAM**
See also CA 9-12R; CDALB 1941-1968;
DLB 7; MTCW

Ingelow, Jean 1820-1897 . . . . **NCLC 39**
See also DLB 35, 163; SATA 33

Ingram, Willis J.
See Harris, Mark

Innaurato, Albert (F.) 1948(?)- . . **CLC 21, 60**
See also CA 115; 122; INT 122

Innes, Michael
See Stewart, J(ohn) I(nnes) M(ackintosh)

Ionesco, Eugene
1909-1994 . . . . **CLC 1, 4, 6, 9, 11, 15, 41,**
86; DA; DAB; DAC; DAM DRAM,
MST; WLC
See also CA 9-12R; 144; CANR 55;
MTCW; SATA 7; SATA-Obit 79

Iqbal, Muhammad 1873-1938 . . . . . **TCLC 28**

Ireland, Patrick
See O'Doherty, Brian

Iron, Ralph
See Schreiner, Olive (Emilie Albertina)

Irving, John (Winslow)
1942- . . . . . **CLC 13, 23, 38; DAM NOV,**
POP
See also AAYA 8; BEST 89:3; CA 25-28R;
CANR 28; DLB 6; DLBY 82; MTCW

Irving, Washington
1783-1859 . . . . . **NCLC 2, 19; DA; DAB;**
DAM MST; SSC 2; WLC
See also CDALB 1640-1865; DLB 3, 11, 30,
59, 73, 74; YABC 2

Irwin, P. K.
See Page, P(atricia) K(athleen)

Isaacs, Susan 1943- . . . **CLC 32; DAM POP**
See also BEST 89:1; CA 89-92; CANR 20,
41; INT CANR-20; MTCW

Isherwood, Christopher (William Bradshaw)
1904-1986 . . . . **CLC 1, 9, 11, 14, 44;**
DAM DRAM, NOV
See also CA 13-16R; 117; CANR 35;
DLB 15; DLBY 86; MTCW

Jimenez Mantecon, Juan
    See Jimenez (Mantecon), Juan Ramon

Joel, Billy . . . . CLC 26
    See also Joel, William Martin

Joel, William Martin   1949-
    See Joel, Billy
    See also CA 108

John of the Cross, St.   1542-1591 . . . . LC 18

Johnson, B(ryan) S(tanley William)
    1933-1973 . . . . CLC 6, 9
    See also CA 9-12R; 53-56; CANR 9;
    DLB 14, 40

Johnson, Benj. F. of Boo
    See Riley, James Whitcomb

Johnson, Benjamin F. of Boo
    See Riley, James Whitcomb

Johnson, Charles (Richard)
    1948- . . . . CLC 7, 51, 65; BLC;
                                              DAM MULT
    See also BW 2; CA 116; CAAS 18;
    CANR 42; DLB 33

Johnson, Denis   1949- . . . . CLC 52
    See also CA 117; 121; DLB 120

Johnson, Diane   1934- . . . . CLC 5, 13, 48
    See also CA 41-44R; CANR 17, 40;
    DLBY 80; INT CANR-17; MTCW

Johnson, Eyvind (Olof Verner)
    1900-1976 . . . . CLC 14
    See also CA 73-76; 69-72; CANR 34

Johnson, J. R.
    See James, C(yril) L(ionel) R(obert)

Johnson, James Weldon
    1871-1938 . . . . TCLC 3, 19; BLC;
                                       DAM MULT, POET
    See also BW 1; CA 104; 125;
    CDALB 1917-1929; CLR 32; DLB 51;
    MTCW; SATA 31

Johnson, Joyce   1935- . . . . CLC 58
    See also CA 125; 129

Johnson, Lionel (Pigot)
    1867-1902 . . . . TCLC 19
    See also CA 117; DLB 19

Johnson, Mel
    See Malzberg, Barry N(athaniel)

Johnson, Pamela Hansford
    1912-1981 . . . . CLC 1, 7, 27
    See also CA 1-4R; 104; CANR 2, 28;
    DLB 15; MTCW

Johnson, Robert   1911(?)-1938 . . . . . TCLC 69

Johnson, Samuel
    1709-1784 . . . . . LC 15; DA; DAB; DAC;
                                       DAM MST; WLC
    See also CDBLB 1660-1789; DLB 39, 95,
    104, 142

Johnson, Uwe
    1934-1984 . . . . CLC 5, 10, 15, 40
    See also CA 1-4R; 112; CANR 1, 39;
    DLB 75; MTCW

Johnston, George (Benson)   1913- . . . CLC 51
    See also CA 1-4R; CANR 5, 20; DLB 88

Johnston, Jennifer   1930- . . . . CLC 7
    See also CA 85-88; DLB 14

Jolley, (Monica) Elizabeth
    1923- . . . . CLC 46; SSC 19
    See also CA 127; CAAS 13

Jones, Arthur Llewellyn   1863-1947
    See Machen, Arthur
    See also CA 104

Jones, D(ouglas) G(ordon)   1929- . . . . CLC 10
    See also CA 29-32R; CANR 13; DLB 53

Jones, David (Michael)
    1895-1974 . . . . CLC 2, 4, 7, 13, 42
    See also CA 9-12R; 53-56; CANR 28;
    CDBLB 1945-1960; DLB 20, 100; MTCW

Jones, David Robert   1947-
    See Bowie, David
    See also CA 103

Jones, Diana Wynne   1934- . . . . CLC 26
    See also AAYA 12; CA 49-52; CANR 4,
    26, 56; CLR 23; DLB 161; JRDA;
    MAICYA; SAAS 7; SATA 9, 70

Jones, Edward P.   1950- . . . . CLC 76
    See also BW 2; CA 142

Jones, Gayl
    1949- . . . . CLC 6, 9; BLC; DAM MULT
    See also BW 2; CA 77-80; CANR 27;
    DLB 33; MTCW

Jones, James   1921-1977 . . . . CLC 1, 3, 10, 39
    See also AITN 1, 2; CA 1-4R; 69-72;
    CANR 6; DLB 2, 143; MTCW

Jones, John J.
    See Lovecraft, H(oward) P(hillips)

Jones, LeRoi . . . . CLC 1, 2, 3, 5, 10, 14
    See also Baraka, Amiri

Jones, Louis B. . . . . CLC 65
    See also CA 141

Jones, Madison (Percy, Jr.)   1925- . . . CLC 4
    See also CA 13-16R; CAAS 11; CANR 7,
    54; DLB 152

Jones, Mervyn   1922- . . . . CLC 10, 52
    See also CA 45-48; CAAS 5; CANR 1;
    MTCW

Jones, Mick   1956(?)- . . . . CLC 30

Jones, Nettie (Pearl)   1941- . . . . CLC 34
    See also BW 2; CA 137; CAAS 20

Jones, Preston   1936-1979 . . . . CLC 10
    See also CA 73-76; 89-92; DLB 7

Jones, Robert F(rancis)   1934- . . . . . . CLC 7
    See also CA 49-52; CANR 2

Jones, Rod   1953- . . . . CLC 50
    See also CA 128

Jones, Terence Graham Parry
    1942- . . . . CLC 21
    See also Jones, Terry; Monty Python
    See also CA 112; 116; CANR 35; INT 116

Jones, Terry
    See Jones, Terence Graham Parry
    See also SATA 67; SATA-Brief 51

Jones, Thom   1945(?)- . . . . CLC 81

Jong, Erica
    1942- . . . . CLC 4, 6, 8, 18, 83;
                                       DAM NOV, POP
    See also AITN 1; BEST 90:2; CA 73-76;
    CANR 26, 52; DLB 2, 5, 28, 152;
    INT CANR-26; MTCW

Jonson, Ben(jamin)
    1572(?)-1637 . . . . . . LC 6, 33; DA; DAB;
                              DAC; DAM DRAM, MST, POET;
                                         DC 4; PC 17; WLC
    See also CDBLB Before 1660; DLB 62, 121

Jordan, June
    1936- . . . . . CLC 5, 11, 23; DAM MULT,
                                                   POET
    See also AAYA 2; BW 2; CA 33-36R;
    CANR 25; CLR 10; DLB 38; MAICYA;
    MTCW; SATA 4

Jordan, Pat(rick M.)   1941- . . . . CLC 37
    See also CA 33-36R

Jorgensen, Ivar
    See Ellison, Harlan (Jay)

Jorgenson, Ivar
    See Silverberg, Robert

Josephus, Flavius   c. 37-100 . . . . . . CMLC 13

Josipovici, Gabriel   1940- . . . . CLC 6, 43
    See also CA 37-40R; CAAS 8; CANR 47;
    DLB 14

Joubert, Joseph   1754-1824 . . . . NCLC 9

Jouve, Pierre Jean   1887-1976 . . . . . . CLC 47
    See also CA 65-68

Joyce, James (Augustine Aloysius)
    1882-1941 . . . . TCLC 3, 8, 16, 35, 52;
                              DA; DAB; DAC; DAM MST, NOV,
                                       POET; SSC 3; WLC
    See also CA 104; 126; CDBLB 1914-1945;
    DLB 10, 19, 36, 162; MTCW

Jozsef, Attila   1905-1937 . . . . TCLC 22
    See also CA 116

Juana Ines de la Cruz   1651(?)-1695 . . . LC 5

Judd, Cyril
    See Kornbluth, C(yril) M.; Pohl, Frederik

Julian of Norwich   1342(?)-1416(?) . . . . LC 6
    See also DLB 146

Juniper, Alex
    See Hospital, Janette Turner

Junius
    See Luxemburg, Rosa

Just, Ward (Swift)   1935- . . . . CLC 4, 27
    See also CA 25-28R; CANR 32;
    INT CANR-32

Justice, Donald (Rodney)
    1925- . . . . CLC 6, 19; DAM POET
    See also CA 5-8R; CANR 26, 54;
    DLBY 83; INT CANR-26

Juvenal   c. 55-c. 127 . . . . CMLC 8

Juvenis
    See Bourne, Randolph S(illiman)

Kacew, Romain   1914-1980
    See Gary, Romain
    See also CA 108; 102

Kadare, Ismail   1936- . . . . CLC 52

Kadohata, Cynthia . . . . CLC 59
    See also CA 140

Kafka, Franz
    1883-1924 . . . . TCLC 2, 6, 13, 29, 47, 53;
                              DA; DAB; DAC; DAM MST, NOV;
                                         SSC 5; WLC
    See also CA 105; 126; DLB 81; MTCW

Kahanovitsch, Pinkhes
    See Der Nister

Kahn, Roger   1927- . . . . CLC 30
    See also CA 25-28R; CANR 44; DLB 171;
    SATA 37

Kain, Saul
    See Sassoon, Siegfried (Lorraine)

Kaiser, Georg 1878-1945 . . . . **TCLC 9**
See also CA 106; DLB 124

Kaletski, Alexander 1946- . . . . **CLC 39**
See also CA 118; 143

Kalidasa fl. c. 400- . . . . **CMLC 9**

Kallman, Chester (Simon)
1921-1975 . . . . **CLC 2**
See also CA 45-48; 53-56; CANR 3

Kaminsky, Melvin 1926-
See Brooks, Mel
See also CA 65-68; CANR 16

Kaminsky, Stuart M(elvin) 1934- . . . **CLC 59**
See also CA 73-76; CANR 29, 53

Kane, Francis
See Robbins, Harold

Kane, Paul
See Simon, Paul (Frederick)

Kane, Wilson
See Bloch, Robert (Albert)

Kanin, Garson 1912- . . . . **CLC 22**
See also AITN 1; CA 5-8R; CANR 7;
DLB 7

Kaniuk, Yoram 1930- . . . . **CLC 19**
See also CA 134

Kant, Immanuel 1724-1804 . . . . . . **NCLC 27**
See also DLB 94

Kantor, MacKinlay 1904-1977 . . . . . . **CLC 7**
See also CA 61-64; 73-76; DLB 9, 102

Kaplan, David Michael 1946- . . . . . . **CLC 50**

Kaplan, James 1951- . . . . **CLC 59**
See also CA 135

Karageorge, Michael
See Anderson, Poul (William)

Karamzin, Nikolai Mikhailovich
1766-1826 . . . . **NCLC 3**
See also DLB 150

Karapanou, Margarita 1946- . . . . **CLC 13**
See also CA 101

Karinthy, Frigyes 1887-1938 . . . . . . **TCLC 47**

Karl, Frederick R(obert) 1927- . . . . . **CLC 34**
See also CA 5-8R; CANR 3, 44

Kastel, Warren
See Silverberg, Robert

Kataev, Evgeny Petrovich 1903-1942
See Petrov, Evgeny
See also CA 120

Kataphusin
See Ruskin, John

Katz, Steve 1935- . . . . **CLC 47**
See also CA 25-28R; CAAS 14; CANR 12;
DLBY 83

Kauffman, Janet 1945- . . . . **CLC 42**
See also CA 117; CANR 43; DLBY 86

Kaufman, Bob (Garnell)
1925-1986 . . . . **CLC 49**
See also BW 1; CA 41-44R; 118; CANR 22;
DLB 16, 41

Kaufman, George S.
1889-1961 . . . . . . **CLC 38; DAM DRAM**
See also CA 108; 93-96; DLB 7; INT 108

Kaufman, Sue . . . . **CLC 3, 8**
See also Barondess, Sue K(aufman)

Kavafis, Konstantinos Petrou 1863-1933
See Cavafy, C(onstantine) P(eter)
See also CA 104

Kavan, Anna 1901-1968 . . . . . . **CLC 5, 13, 82**
See also CA 5-8R; CANR 6, 57; MTCW

Kavanagh, Dan
See Barnes, Julian (Patrick)

Kavanagh, Patrick (Joseph)
1904-1967 . . . . **CLC 22**
See also CA 123; 25-28R; DLB 15, 20;
MTCW

Kawabata, Yasunari
1899-1972 . . . . **CLC 2, 5, 9, 18;
DAM MULT; SSC 17**
See also CA 93-96; 33-36R

Kaye, M(ary) M(argaret) 1909- . . . . . **CLC 28**
See also CA 89-92; CANR 24; MTCW;
SATA 62

Kaye, Mollie
See Kaye, M(ary) M(argaret)

Kaye-Smith, Sheila 1887-1956 . . . . . **TCLC 20**
See also CA 118; DLB 36

Kaymor, Patrice Maguilene
See Senghor, Leopold Sedar

Kazan, Elia 1909- . . . . **CLC 6, 16, 63**
See also CA 21-24R; CANR 32

Kazantzakis, Nikos
1883(?)-1957 . . . . **TCLC 2, 5, 33**
See also CA 105; 132; MTCW

Kazin, Alfred 1915- . . . . **CLC 34, 38**
See also CA 1-4R; CAAS 7; CANR 1, 45;
DLB 67

Keane, Mary Nesta (Skrine) 1904-1996
See Keane, Molly
See also CA 108; 114; 151

Keane, Molly . . . . **CLC 31**
See also Keane, Mary Nesta (Skrine)
See also INT 114

Keates, Jonathan 19(?)- . . . . **CLC 34**

Keaton, Buster 1895-1966 . . . . **CLC 20**

Keats, John
1795-1821 . . . . **NCLC 8; DA; DAB;
DAC; DAM MST, POET; PC 1; WLC**
See also CDBLB 1789-1832; DLB 96, 110

Keene, Donald 1922- . . . . **CLC 34**
See also CA 1-4R; CANR 5

Keillor, Garrison . . . . **CLC 40**
See also Keillor, Gary (Edward)
See also AAYA 2; BEST 89:3; DLBY 87;
SATA 58

Keillor, Gary (Edward) 1942-
See Keillor, Garrison
See also CA 111; 117; CANR 36;
DAM POP; MTCW

Keith, Michael
See Hubbard, L(afayette) Ron(ald)

Keller, Gottfried 1819-1890 . . . . **NCLC 2**
See also DLB 129

Kellerman, Jonathan
1949- . . . . **CLC 44; DAM POP**
See also BEST 90:1; CA 106; CANR 29, 51;
INT CANR-29

Kelley, William Melvin 1937- . . . . . . **CLC 22**
See also BW 1; CA 77-80; CANR 27;
DLB 33

Kellogg, Marjorie 1922- . . . . **CLC 2**
See also CA 81-84

Kellow, Kathleen
See Hibbert, Eleanor Alice Burford

Kelly, M(ilton) T(erry) 1947- . . . . . . **CLC 55**
See also CA 97-100; CAAS 22; CANR 19,
43

Kelman, James 1946- . . . . **CLC 58, 86**
See also CA 148

Kemal, Yashar 1923- . . . . **CLC 14, 29**
See also CA 89-92; CANR 44

Kemble, Fanny 1809-1893 . . . . **NCLC 18**
See also DLB 32

Kemelman, Harry 1908-1996 . . . . **CLC 2**
See also AITN 1; CA 9-12R; 155; CANR 6;
DLB 28

Kempe, Margery 1373(?)-1440(?) . . . . . **LC 6**
See also DLB 146

Kempis, Thomas a 1380-1471 . . . . **LC 11**

Kendall, Henry 1839-1882 . . . . **NCLC 12**

Keneally, Thomas (Michael)
1935- . . . . . . **CLC 5, 8, 10, 14, 19, 27, 43;
DAM NOV**
See also CA 85-88; CANR 10, 50; MTCW

Kennedy, Adrienne (Lita)
1931- . . . . . **CLC 66; BLC; DAM MULT;
DC 5**
See also BW 2; CA 103; CAAS 20; CABS 3;
CANR 26, 53; DLB 38

Kennedy, John Pendleton
1795-1870 . . . . **NCLC 2**
See also DLB 3

Kennedy, Joseph Charles 1929-
See Kennedy, X. J.
See also CA 1-4R; CANR 4, 30, 40;
SATA 14, 86

Kennedy, William
1928- . . . **CLC 6, 28, 34, 53; DAM NOV**
See also AAYA 1; CA 85-88; CANR 14,
31; DLB 143; DLBY 85; INT CANR-31;
MTCW; SATA 57

Kennedy, X. J. . . . . **CLC 8, 42**
See also Kennedy, Joseph Charles
See also CAAS 9; CLR 27; DLB 5;
SAAS 22

Kenny, Maurice (Francis)
1929- . . . . **CLC 87; DAM MULT**
See also CA 144; CAAS 22; DLB 175;
NNAL

Kent, Kelvin
See Kuttner, Henry

Kenton, Maxwell
See Southern, Terry

Kenyon, Robert O.
See Kuttner, Henry

Kerouac, Jack . . . . . **CLC 1, 2, 3, 5, 14, 29, 61**
See also Kerouac, Jean-Louis Lebris de
See also CDALB 1941-1968; DLB 2, 16;
DLBD 3; DLBY 95

Kerouac, Jean-Louis Lebris de 1922-1969
See Kerouac, Jack
See also AITN 1; CA 5-8R; 25-28R;
CANR 26, 54; DA; DAB; DAC;
DAM MST, NOV, POET, POP; MTCW;
WLC

Kerr, Jean 1923- . . . . **CLC 22**
See also CA 5-8R; CANR 7; INT CANR-7

Kerr, M. E. . . . . **CLC 12, 35**
See also Meaker, Marijane (Agnes)
See also AAYA 2; CLR 29; SAAS 1

Kerr, Robert . . . . **CLC 55**

Kerrigan, (Thomas) Anthony
1918- . . . . **CLC 4, 6**
See also CA 49-52; CAAS 11; CANR 4

Kerry, Lois
See Duncan, Lois

Kesey, Ken (Elton)
1935- . . . . . . **CLC 1, 3, 6, 11, 46, 64; DA;
DAB; DAC; DAM MST, NOV, POP;
WLC**
See also CA 1-4R; CANR 22, 38;
CDALB 1968-1988; DLB 2, 16; MTCW;
SATA 66

Kesselring, Joseph (Otto)
1902-1967 . . . . . **CLC 45; DAM DRAM,
MST**
See also CA 150

Kessler, Jascha (Frederick) 1929- . . . . **CLC 4**
See also CA 17-20R; CANR 8, 48

Kettelkamp, Larry (Dale) 1933- . . . . **CLC 12**
See also CA 29-32R; CANR 16; SAAS 3;
SATA 2

Key, Ellen 1849-1926 . . . . **TCLC 65**

Keyber, Conny
See Fielding, Henry

Keyes, Daniel
1927- . . . . **CLC 80; DA; DAC;
DAM MST, NOV**
See also CA 17-20R; CANR 10, 26, 54;
SATA 37

Keynes, John Maynard
1883-1946 . . . . **TCLC 64**
See also CA 114; DLBD 10

Khanshendel, Chiron
See Rose, Wendy

Khayyam, Omar
1048-1131 . . . . **CMLC 11; DAM POET;
PC 8**

Kherdian, David 1931- . . . . **CLC 6, 9**
See also CA 21-24R; CAAS 2; CANR 39;
CLR 24; JRDA; MAICYA; SATA 16, 74

Khlebnikov, Velimir . . . . **TCLC 20**
See also Khlebnikov, Viktor Vladimirovich

Khlebnikov, Viktor Vladimirovich 1885-1922
See Khlebnikov, Velimir
See also CA 117

Khodasevich, Vladislav (Felitsianovich)
1886-1939 . . . . **TCLC 15**
See also CA 115

Kielland, Alexander Lange
1849-1906 . . . . **TCLC 5**
See also CA 104

Kiely, Benedict 1919- . . . . **CLC 23, 43**
See also CA 1-4R; CANR 2; DLB 15

Kienzle, William X(avier)
1928- . . . . **CLC 25; DAM POP**
See also CA 93-96; CAAS 1; CANR 9, 31;
INT CANR-31; MTCW

Kierkegaard, Soren 1813-1855. . . . **NCLC 34**

Killens, John Oliver 1916-1987. . . . . **CLC 10**
See also BW 2; CA 77-80; 123; CAAS 2;
CANR 26; DLB 33

Killigrew, Anne 1660-1685. . . . . **LC 4**
See also DLB 131

Kim
See Simenon, Georges (Jacques Christian)

Kincaid, Jamaica
1949- . . . . **CLC 43, 68; BLC;
DAM MULT, NOV**
See also AAYA 13; BW 2; CA 125;
CANR 47; DLB 157

King, Francis (Henry)
1923- . . . . **CLC 8, 53; DAM NOV**
See also CA 1-4R; CANR 1, 33; DLB 15,
139; MTCW

King, Martin Luther, Jr.
1929-1968 . . . . **CLC 83; BLC; DA; DAB;
DAC; DAM MST, MULT**
See also BW 2; CA 25-28; CANR 27, 44;
CAP 2; MTCW; SATA 14

King, Stephen (Edwin)
1947- . . . . **CLC 12, 26, 37, 61;
DAM NOV, POP; SSC 17**
See also AAYA 1, 17; BEST 90:1;
CA 61-64; CANR 1, 30, 52; DLB 143;
DLBY 80; JRDA; MTCW; SATA 9, 55

King, Steve
See King, Stephen (Edwin)

King, Thomas
1943- . . . . . . **CLC 89; DAC; DAM MULT**
See also CA 144; DLB 175; NNAL

Kingman, Lee. . . . . **CLC 17**
See also Natti, (Mary) Lee
See also SAAS 3; SATA 1, 67

Kingsley, Charles 1819-1875 . . . . . **NCLC 35**
See also DLB 21, 32, 163; YABC 2

Kingsley, Sidney 1906-1995. . . . . . . **CLC 44**
See also CA 85-88; 147; DLB 7

Kingsolver, Barbara
1955- . . . . **CLC 55, 81; DAM POP**
See also AAYA 15; CA 129; 134; INT 134

Kingston, Maxine (Ting Ting) Hong
1940- . . . . **CLC 12, 19, 58; DAM MULT,
NOV**
See also AAYA 8; CA 69-72; CANR 13,
38; DLB 173; DLBY 80; INT CANR-13;
MTCW; SATA 53

Kinnell, Galway
1927- . . . . **CLC 1, 2, 3, 5, 13, 29**
See also CA 9-12R; CANR 10, 34; DLB 5;
DLBY 87; INT CANR-34; MTCW

Kinsella, Thomas 1928- . . . . **CLC 4, 19**
See also CA 17-20R; CANR 15; DLB 27;
MTCW

Kinsella, W(illiam) P(atrick)
1935- . . . . **CLC 27, 43; DAC;
DAM NOV, POP**
See also AAYA 7; CA 97-100; CAAS 7;
CANR 21, 35; INT CANR-21; MTCW

Kipling, (Joseph) Rudyard
1865-1936 . . . . . . **TCLC 8, 17; DA; DAB;
DAC; DAM MST, POET; PC 3; SSC 5;
WLC**
See also CA 105; 120; CANR 33;
CDBLB 1890-1914; CLR 39; DLB 19, 34,
141, 156; MAICYA; MTCW; YABC 2

Kirkup, James 1918- . . . . **CLC 1**
See also CA 1-4R; CAAS 4; CANR 2;
DLB 27; SATA 12

Kirkwood, James 1930(?)-1989 . . . . . . **CLC 9**
See also AITN 2; CA 1-4R; 128; CANR 6,
40

Kirshner, Sidney
See Kingsley, Sidney

Kis, Danilo 1935-1989 . . . . **CLC 57**
See also CA 109; 118; 129; MTCW

Kivi, Aleksis 1834-1872 . . . . **NCLC 30**

Kizer, Carolyn (Ashley)
1925- . . . . . **CLC 15, 39, 80; DAM POET**
See also CA 65-68; CAAS 5; CANR 24;
DLB 5, 169

Klabund 1890-1928. . . . . **TCLC 44**
See also DLB 66

Klappert, Peter 1942- . . . . **CLC 57**
See also CA 33-36R; DLB 5

Klein, A(braham) M(oses)
1909-1972 . . . . **CLC 19; DAB; DAC;
DAM MST**
See also CA 101; 37-40R; DLB 68

Klein, Norma 1938-1989 . . . . **CLC 30**
See also AAYA 2; CA 41-44R; 128;
CANR 15, 37; CLR 2, 19;
INT CANR-15; JRDA; MAICYA;
SAAS 1; SATA 7, 57

Klein, T(heodore) E(ibon) D(onald)
1947- . . . . **CLC 34**
See also CA 119; CANR 44

Kleist, Heinrich von
1777-1811 . . . . **NCLC 2, 37;
DAM DRAM; SSC 22**
See also DLB 90

Klima, Ivan 1931- . . . . . **CLC 56; DAM NOV**
See also CA 25-28R; CANR 17, 50

Klimentov, Andrei Platonovich 1899-1951
See Platonov, Andrei
See also CA 108

Klinger, Friedrich Maximilian von
1752-1831 . . . . **NCLC 1**
See also DLB 94

Klopstock, Friedrich Gottlieb
1724-1803 . . . . **NCLC 11**
See also DLB 97

Knapp, Caroline 1959- . . . . **CLC 99**
See also CA 154

Knebel, Fletcher 1911-1993. . . . . **CLC 14**
See also AITN 1; CA 1-4R; 140; CAAS 3;
CANR 1, 36; SATA 36; SATA-Obit 75

Knickerbocker, Diedrich
See Irving, Washington

Knight, Etheridge
1931-1991 . . . . **CLC 40; BLC;
DAM POET; PC 14**
See also BW 1; CA 21-24R; 133; CANR 23;
DLB 41

Knight, Sarah Kemble 1666-1727 . . . . . **LC 7**
See also DLB 24

Knister, Raymond 1899-1932. . . . . . **TCLC 56**
See also DLB 68

Kyprianos, Iossif
See Samarakis, Antonis

La Bruyere, Jean de 1645-1696...... **LC 17**

Lacan, Jacques (Marie Emile)
1901-1981 .... **CLC 75**
See also CA 121; 104

Laclos, Pierre Ambroise Francois Choderlos
de 1741-1803 .... **NCLC 4**

La Colere, Francois
See Aragon, Louis

Lacolere, Francois
See Aragon, Louis

La Deshabilleuse
See Simenon, Georges (Jacques Christian)

Lady Gregory
See Gregory, Isabella Augusta (Persse)

Lady of Quality, A
See Bagnold, Enid

La Fayette, Marie (Madelaine Pioche de la
Vergne Comtes 1634-1693....... **LC 2**

Lafayette, Rene
See Hubbard, L(afayette) Ron(ald)

Laforgue, Jules
1860-1887 .... **NCLC 5, 53; PC 14;**
SSC 20

Lagerkvist, Paer (Fabian)
1891-1974 .... **CLC 7, 10, 13, 54;**
DAM DRAM, NOV
See also Lagerkvist, Par
See also CA 85-88; 49-52; MTCW

Lagerkvist, Par .... **SSC 12**
See also Lagerkvist, Paer (Fabian)

Lagerloef, Selma (Ottiliana Lovisa)
1858-1940 .... **TCLC 4, 36**
See also Lagerlof, Selma (Ottiliana Lovisa)
See also CA 108; SATA 15

Lagerlof, Selma (Ottiliana Lovisa)
See Lagerloef, Selma (Ottiliana Lovisa)
See also CLR 7; SATA 15

La Guma, (Justin) Alex(ander)
1925-1985 .... **CLC 19; DAM NOV**
See also BW 1; CA 49-52; 118; CANR 25;
DLB 117; MTCW

Laidlaw, A. K.
See Grieve, C(hristopher) M(urray)

Lainez, Manuel Mujica
See Mujica Lainez, Manuel
See also HW

Laing, R(onald) D(avid)
1927-1989 .... **CLC 95**
See also CA 107; 129; CANR 34; MTCW

Lamartine, Alphonse (Marie Louis Prat) de
1790-1869 ..... **NCLC 11; DAM POET;**
PC 16

Lamb, Charles
1775-1834 ...... **NCLC 10; DA; DAB;**
DAC; DAM MST; WLC
See also CDBLB 1789-1832; DLB 93, 107,
163; SATA 17

Lamb, Lady Caroline 1785-1828.. **NCLC 38**
See also DLB 116

Lamming, George (William)
1927- .... **CLC 2, 4, 66; BLC;**
DAM MULT
See also BW 2; CA 85-88; CANR 26;
DLB 125; MTCW

L'Amour, Louis (Dearborn)
1908-1988 .... **CLC 25, 55; DAM NOV,**
POP
See also AAYA 16; AITN 2; BEST 89:2;
CA 1-4R; 125; CANR 3, 25, 40;
DLBY 80; MTCW

Lampedusa, Giuseppe (Tomasi) di
1896-1957 .... **TCLC 13**
See also Tomasi di Lampedusa, Giuseppe
See also DLB 177

Lampman, Archibald 1861-1899 .. **NCLC 25**
See also DLB 92

Lancaster, Bruce 1896-1963....... **CLC 36**
See also CA 9-10; CAP 1; SATA 9

Lanchester, John.................. **CLC 99**

Landau, Mark Alexandrovich
See Aldanov, Mark (Alexandrovich)

Landau-Aldanov, Mark Alexandrovich
See Aldanov, Mark (Alexandrovich)

Landis, Jerry
See Simon, Paul (Frederick)

Landis, John 1950-............... **CLC 26**
See also CA 112; 122

Landolfi, Tommaso 1908-1979... **CLC 11, 49**
See also CA 127; 117; DLB 177

Landon, Letitia Elizabeth
1802-1838 .... **NCLC 15**
See also DLB 96

Landor, Walter Savage
1775-1864 .... **NCLC 14**
See also DLB 93, 107

Landwirth, Heinz 1927-
See Lind, Jakov
See also CA 9-12R; CANR 7

Lane, Patrick
1939- .... **CLC 25; DAM POET**
See also CA 97-100; CANR 54; DLB 53;
INT 97-100

Lang, Andrew 1844-1912........ **TCLC 16**
See also CA 114; 137; DLB 98, 141;
MAICYA; SATA 16

Lang, Fritz 1890-1976 .... **CLC 20**
See also CA 77-80; 69-72; CANR 30

Lange, John
See Crichton, (John) Michael

Langer, Elinor 1939- .... **CLC 34**
See also CA 121

Langland, William
1330(?)-1400(?) ...... **LC 19; DA; DAB;**
DAC; DAM MST, POET
See also DLB 146

Langstaff, Launcelot
See Irving, Washington

Lanier, Sidney
1842-1881 ...... **NCLC 6; DAM POET**
See also DLB 64; DLBD 13; MAICYA;
SATA 18

Lanyer, Aemilia 1569-1645 ..... **LC 10, 30**
See also DLB 121

Lao Tzu .... **CMLC 7**

Lapine, James (Elliot) 1949-....... **CLC 39**
See also CA 123; 130; CANR 54; INT 130

Larbaud, Valery (Nicolas)
1881-1957 .... **TCLC 9**
See also CA 106; 152

Lardner, Ring
See Lardner, Ring(gold) W(ilmer)

Lardner, Ring W., Jr.
See Lardner, Ring(gold) W(ilmer)

Lardner, Ring(gold) W(ilmer)
1885-1933 .... **TCLC 2, 14**
See also CA 104; 131; CDALB 1917-1929;
DLB 11, 25, 86; MTCW

Laredo, Betty
See Codrescu, Andrei

Larkin, Maia
See Wojciechowska, Maia (Teresa)

Larkin, Philip (Arthur)
1922-1985 .... **CLC 3, 5, 8, 9, 13, 18, 33,**
39, 64; DAB; DAM MST, POET
See also CA 5-8R; 117; CANR 24;
CDBLB 1960 to Present; DLB 27;
MTCW

Larra (y Sanchez de Castro), Mariano Jose de
1809-1837 .... **NCLC 17**

Larsen, Eric 1941- .... **CLC 55**
See also CA 132

Larsen, Nella
1891-1964 .... **CLC 37; BLC;**
DAM MULT
See also BW 1; CA 125; DLB 51

Larson, Charles R(aymond) 1938-... **CLC 31**
See also CA 53-56; CANR 4

Larson, Jonathan 1961(?)-1996..... **CLC 99**

Las Casas, Bartolome de 1474-1566.. **LC 31**

Lasker-Schueler, Else 1869-1945 .. **TCLC 57**
See also DLB 66, 124

Latham, Jean Lee 1902-........... **CLC 12**
See also AITN 1; CA 5-8R; CANR 7;
MAICYA; SATA 2, 68

Latham, Mavis
See Clark, Mavis Thorpe

Lathen, Emma.................... **CLC 2**
See also Hennissart, Martha; Latsis, Mary
J(ane)

Lathrop, Francis
See Leiber, Fritz (Reuter, Jr.)

Latsis, Mary J(ane)
See Lathen, Emma
See also CA 85-88

Lattimore, Richmond (Alexander)
1906-1984 .... **CLC 3**
See also CA 1-4R; 112; CANR 1

Laughlin, James 1914-............ **CLC 49**
See also CA 21-24R; CAAS 22; CANR 9,
47; DLB 48

Laurence, (Jean) Margaret (Wemyss)
1926-1987 .... **CLC 3, 6, 13, 50, 62;**
DAC; DAM MST; SSC 7
See also CA 5-8R; 121; CANR 33; DLB 53;
MTCW; SATA-Obit 50

Laurent, Antoine 1952- .... **CLC 50**

Lauscher, Hermann
See Hesse, Hermann

Lautreamont, Comte de
  1846-1870 . . . . NCLC 12; SSC 14

Laverty, Donald
  See Blish, James (Benjamin)

Lavin, Mary
  1912-1996 . . . . . . CLC 4, 18, 99; SSC 4
  See also CA 9-12R; 151; CANR 33;
    DLB 15; MTCW

Lavond, Paul Dennis
  See Kornbluth, C(yril) M.; Pohl, Frederik

Lawler, Raymond Evenor 1922- . . . . CLC 58
  See also CA 103

Lawrence, D(avid) H(erbert Richards)
  1885-1930 . . . . TCLC 2, 9, 16, 33, 48, 61;
          DA; DAB; DAC; DAM MST, NOV,
          POET; SSC 4, 19; WLC
  See also CA 104; 121; CDBLB 1914-1945;
    DLB 10, 19, 36, 98, 162; MTCW

Lawrence, T(homas) E(dward)
  1888-1935 . . . . TCLC 18
  See also Dale, Colin
  See also CA 115

Lawrence of Arabia
  See Lawrence, T(homas) E(dward)

Lawson, Henry (Archibald Hertzberg)
  1867-1922 . . . . TCLC 27; SSC 18
  See also CA 120

Lawton, Dennis
  See Faust, Frederick (Schiller)

Laxness, Halldor . . . . CLC 25
  See also Gudjonsson, Halldor Kiljan

Layamon fl. c. 1200- . . . . CMLC 10
  See also DLB 146

Laye, Camara
  1928-1980 . . . . CLC 4, 38; BLC;
                              DAM MULT
  See also BW 1; CA 85-88; 97-100;
    CANR 25; MTCW

Layton, Irving (Peter)
  1912- . . . . CLC 2, 15; DAC; DAM MST,
                              POET
  See also CA 1-4R; CANR 2, 33, 43;
    DLB 88; MTCW

Lazarus, Emma 1849-1887 . . . . NCLC 8

Lazarus, Felix
  See Cable, George Washington

Lazarus, Henry
  See Slavitt, David R(ytman)

Lea, Joan
  See Neufeld, John (Arthur)

Leacock, Stephen (Butler)
  1869-1944 . . TCLC 2; DAC; DAM MST
  See also CA 104; 141; DLB 92

Lear, Edward 1812-1888 . . . . NCLC 3
  See also CLR 1; DLB 32, 163, 166;
    MAICYA; SATA 18

Lear, Norman (Milton) 1922- . . . . . . CLC 12
  See also CA 73-76

Leavis, F(rank) R(aymond)
  1895-1978 . . . . CLC 24
  See also CA 21-24R; 77-80; CANR 44;
    MTCW

Leavitt, David 1961- . . . CLC 34; DAM POP
  See also CA 116; 122; CANR 50; DLB 130;
    INT 122

Leblanc, Maurice (Marie Emile)
  1864-1941 . . . . TCLC 49
  See also CA 110

Lebowitz, Fran(ces Ann)
  1951(?)- . . . . CLC 11, 36
  See also CA 81-84; CANR 14;
    INT CANR-14; MTCW

Lebrecht, Peter
  See Tieck, (Johann) Ludwig

le Carre, John . . . . CLC 3, 5, 9, 15, 28
  See also Cornwell, David (John Moore)
  See also BEST 89:4; CDBLB 1960 to
    Present; DLB 87

Le Clezio, J(ean) M(arie) G(ustave)
  1940- . . . . CLC 31
  See also CA 116; 128; DLB 83

Leconte de Lisle, Charles-Marie-Rene
  1818-1894 . . . . NCLC 29

Le Coq, Monsieur
  See Simenon, Georges (Jacques Christian)

Leduc, Violette 1907-1972 . . . . CLC 22
  See also CA 13-14; 33-36R; CAP 1

Ledwidge, Francis 1887(?)-1917 . . . TCLC 23
  See also CA 123; DLB 20

Lee, Andrea
  1953- . . . . . CLC 36; BLC; DAM MULT
  See also BW 1; CA 125

Lee, Andrew
  See Auchincloss, Louis (Stanton)

Lee, Chang-rae 1965- . . . . CLC 91
  See also CA 148

Lee, Don L. CLC 2
  See also Madhubuti, Haki R.

Lee, George W(ashington)
  1894-1976 . . . . CLC 52; BLC;
                              DAM MULT
  See also BW 1; CA 125; DLB 51

Lee, (Nelle) Harper
  1926- . . . . CLC 12, 60; DA; DAB; DAC;
                  DAM MST, NOV; WLC
  See also AAYA 13; CA 13-16R; CANR 51;
    CDALB 1941-1968; DLB 6; MTCW;
    SATA 11

Lee, Helen Elaine 1959(?)- . . . . CLC 86
  See also CA 148

Lee, Julian
  See Latham, Jean Lee

Lee, Larry
  See Lee, Lawrence

Lee, Laurie
  1914- . . . . CLC 90; DAB; DAM POP
  See also CA 77-80; CANR 33; DLB 27;
    MTCW

Lee, Lawrence 1941-1990 . . . . CLC 34
  See also CA 131; CANR 43

Lee, Manfred B(ennington)
  1905-1971 . . . . CLC 11
  See also Queen, Ellery
  See also CA 1-4R; 29-32R; CANR 2;
    DLB 137

Lee, Stan 1922- . . . . CLC 17
  See also AAYA 5; CA 108; 111; INT 111

Lee, Tanith 1947- . . . . CLC 46
  See also AAYA 15; CA 37-40R; CANR 53;
    SATA 8, 88

Lee, Vernon . . . . TCLC 5
  See also Paget, Violet
  See also DLB 57, 153, 156, 174

Lee, William
  See Burroughs, William S(eward)

Lee, Willy
  See Burroughs, William S(eward)

Lee-Hamilton, Eugene (Jacob)
  1845-1907 . . . . TCLC 22
  See also CA 117

Leet, Judith 1935- . . . . CLC 11

Le Fanu, Joseph Sheridan
  1814-1873 . . . . NCLC 9, 58; DAM POP;
                              SSC 14
  See also DLB 21, 70, 159

Leffland, Ella 1931- . . . . CLC 19
  See also CA 29-32R; CANR 35; DLBY 84;
    INT CANR-35; SATA 65

Leger, Alexis
  See Leger, (Marie-Rene Auguste) Alexis
    Saint-Leger

Leger, (Marie-Rene Auguste) Alexis
    Saint-Leger
  1887-1975 . . . . CLC 11; DAM POET
  See also Perse, St.-John
  See also CA 13-16R; 61-64; CANR 43;
    MTCW

Leger, Saintleger
  See Leger, (Marie-Rene Auguste) Alexis
    Saint-Leger

Le Guin, Ursula K(roeber)
  1929- . . . . . . CLC 8, 13, 22, 45, 71; DAB;
          DAC; DAM MST, POP; SSC 12
  See also AAYA 9; AITN 1; CA 21-24R;
    CANR 9, 32, 52; CDALB 1968-1988;
    CLR 3, 28; DLB 8, 52; INT CANR-32;
    JRDA; MAICYA; MTCW; SATA 4, 52

Lehmann, Rosamond (Nina)
  1901-1990 . . . . CLC 5
  See also CA 77-80; 131; CANR 8; DLB 15

Leiber, Fritz (Reuter, Jr.)
  1910-1992 . . . . CLC 25
  See also CA 45-48; 139; CANR 2, 40;
    DLB 8; MTCW; SATA 45;
    SATA-Obit 73

Leibniz, Gottfried Wilhelm von
  1646-1716 . . . . LC 35
  See also DLB 168

Leimbach, Martha 1963-
  See Leimbach, Marti
  See also CA 130

Leimbach, Marti . . . . CLC 65
  See also Leimbach, Martha

Leino, Eino . . . . TCLC 24
  See also Loennbohm, Armas Eino Leopold

Leiris, Michel (Julien) 1901-1990 . . . CLC 61
  See also CA 119; 128; 132

Leithauser, Brad 1953- . . . . CLC 27
  See also CA 107; CANR 27; DLB 120

Lelchuk, Alan 1938- . . . . CLC 5
  See also CA 45-48; CAAS 20; CANR 1

Lem, Stanislaw 1921- . . . . CLC 8, 15, 40
  See also CA 105; CAAS 1; CANR 32;
    MTCW

Lemann, Nancy 1956-............ **CLC 39**
See also CA 118; 136

Lemonnier, (Antoine Louis) Camille
1844-1913 .... **TCLC 22**
See also CA 121

Lenau, Nikolaus 1802-1850...... **NCLC 16**

L'Engle, Madeleine (Camp Franklin)
1918- .... **CLC 12; DAM POP**
See also AAYA 1; AITN 2; CA 1-4R;
CANR 3, 21, 39; CLR 1, 14; DLB 52;
JRDA; MAICYA; MTCW; SAAS 15;
SATA 1, 27, 75

Lengyel, Jozsef 1896-1975......... **CLC 7**
See also CA 85-88; 57-60

Lenin 1870-1924
See Lenin, V. I.
See also CA 121

Lenin, V. I. .... **TCLC 67**
See also Lenin

Lennon, John (Ono)
1940-1980 .... **CLC 12, 35**
See also CA 102

Lennox, Charlotte Ramsay
1729(?)-1804 .... **NCLC 23**
See also DLB 39

Lentricchia, Frank (Jr.) 1940-...... **CLC 34**
See also CA 25-28R; CANR 19

Lenz, Siegfried 1926-............ **CLC 27**
See also CA 89-92; DLB 75

Leonard, Elmore (John, Jr.)
1925- ...... **CLC 28, 34, 71; DAM POP**
See also AITN 1; BEST 89:1, 90:4;
CA 81-84; CANR 12, 28, 53; DLB 173;
INT CANR-28; MTCW

Leonard, Hugh.................... **CLC 19**
See also Byrne, John Keyes
See also DLB 13

Leonov, Leonid (Maximovich)
1899-1994 .... **CLC 92; DAM NOV**
See also CA 129; MTCW

Leopardi, (Conte) Giacomo
1798-1837 .... **NCLC 22**

Le Reveler
See Artaud, Antonin (Marie Joseph)

Lerman, Eleanor 1952-............. **CLC 9**
See also CA 85-88

Lerman, Rhoda 1936-............. **CLC 56**
See also CA 49-52

Lermontov, Mikhail Yuryevich
1814-1841 .... **NCLC 47**

Leroux, Gaston 1868-1927....... **TCLC 25**
See also CA 108; 136; SATA 65

Lesage, Alain-Rene 1668-1747...... **LC 28**

Leskov, Nikolai (Semyonovich)
1831-1895 .... **NCLC 25**

Lessing, Doris (May)
1919-.... **CLC 1, 2, 3, 6, 10, 15, 22, 40,**
94; DA; DAB; DAC; DAM MST, NOV;
SSC 6
See also CA 9-12R; CAAS 14; CANR 33,
54; CDBLB 1960 to Present; DLB 15,
139; DLBY 85; MTCW

Lessing, Gotthold Ephraim
1729-1781 .... **LC 8**
See also DLB 97

Lester, Richard 1932-............ **CLC 20**

Lever, Charles (James)
1806-1872 .... **NCLC 23**
See also DLB 21

Leverson, Ada 1865(?)-1936(?) .... **TCLC 18**
See also Elaine
See also CA 117; DLB 153

Levertov, Denise
1923- ...... **CLC 1, 2, 3, 5, 8, 15, 28, 66;**
DAM POET; PC 11
See also CA 1-4R; CAAS 19; CANR 3, 29,
50; DLB 5, 165; INT CANR-29; MTCW

Levi, Jonathan.................... **CLC 76**

Levi, Peter (Chad Tigar) 1931-..... **CLC 41**
See also CA 5-8R; CANR 34; DLB 40

Levi, Primo
1919-1987 .... **CLC 37, 50; SSC 12**
See also CA 13-16R; 122; CANR 12, 33;
DLB 177; MTCW

Levin, Ira 1929- ..... **CLC 3, 6; DAM POP**
See also CA 21-24R; CANR 17, 44;
MTCW; SATA 66

Levin, Meyer
1905-1981 .... **CLC 7; DAM POP**
See also AITN 1; CA 9-12R; 104;
CANR 15; DLB 9, 28; DLBY 81;
SATA 21; SATA-Obit 27

Levine, Norman 1924-............ **CLC 54**
See also CA 73-76; CAAS 23; CANR 14;
DLB 88

Levine, Philip
1928- .... **CLC 2, 4, 5, 9, 14, 33;**
DAM POET
See also CA 9-12R; CANR 9, 37, 52;
DLB 5

Levinson, Deirdre 1931-.......... **CLC 49**
See also CA 73-76

Levi-Strauss, Claude 1908- .... **CLC 38**
See also CA 1-4R; CANR 6, 32, 57; MTCW

Levitin, Sonia (Wolff) 1934- .... **CLC 17**
See also AAYA 13; CA 29-32R; CANR 14,
32; JRDA; MAICYA; SAAS 2; SATA 4,
68

Levon, O. U.
See Kesey, Ken (Elton)

Levy, Amy 1861-1889.......... **NCLC 59**
See also DLB 156

Lewes, George Henry
1817-1878 .... **NCLC 25**
See also DLB 55, 144

Lewis, Alun 1915-1944............ **TCLC 3**
See also CA 104; DLB 20, 162

Lewis, C. Day
See Day Lewis, C(ecil)

Lewis, C(live) S(taples)
1898-1963 ..... **CLC 1, 3, 6, 14, 27; DA;**
DAB; DAC; DAM MST, NOV, POP;
WLC
See also AAYA 3; CA 81-84; CANR 33;
CDBLB 1945-1960; CLR 3, 27; DLB 15,
100, 160; JRDA; MAICYA; MTCW;
SATA 13

Lewis, Janet 1899-............... **CLC 41**
See also Winters, Janet Lewis
See also CA 9-12R; CANR 29; CAP 1;
DLBY 87

Lewis, Matthew Gregory
1775-1818 .... **NCLC 11**
See also DLB 39, 158

Lewis, (Harry) Sinclair
1885-1951 ..... **TCLC 4, 13, 23, 39; DA;**
DAB; DAC; DAM MST, NOV; WLC
See also CA 104; 133; CDALB 1917-1929;
DLB 9, 102; DLBD 1; MTCW

Lewis, (Percy) Wyndham
1884(?)-1957.............. **TCLC 2, 9**
See also CA 104; DLB 15

Lewisohn, Ludwig 1883-1955...... **TCLC 19**
See also CA 107; DLB 4, 9, 28, 102

Leyner, Mark 1956-............. **CLC 92**
See also CA 110; CANR 28, 53

Lezama Lima, Jose
1910-1976 .... **CLC 4, 10; DAM MULT**
See also CA 77-80; DLB 113; HW

L'Heureux, John (Clarke) 1934-.... **CLC 52**
See also CA 13-16R; CANR 23, 45

Liddell, C. H.
See Kuttner, Henry

Lie, Jonas (Lauritz Idemil)
1833-1908(?) .... **TCLC 5**
See also CA 115

Lieber, Joel 1937-1971............. **CLC 6**
See also CA 73-76; 29-32R

Lieber, Stanley Martin
See Lee, Stan

Lieberman, Laurence (James)
1935- .... **CLC 4, 36**
See also CA 17-20R; CANR 8, 36

Lieksman, Anders
See Haavikko, Paavo Juhani

Li Fei-kan 1904-
See Pa Chin
See also CA 105

Lifton, Robert Jay 1926-.......... **CLC 67**
See also CA 17-20R; CANR 27;
INT CANR-27; SATA 66

Lightfoot, Gordon 1938-.......... **CLC 26**
See also CA 109

Lightman, Alan P. 1948- .... **CLC 81**
See also CA 141

Ligotti, Thomas (Robert)
1953- .... **CLC 44; SSC 16**
See also CA 123; CANR 49

Li Ho 791-817.................... **PC 13**

Liliencron, (Friedrich Adolf Axel) Detlev von
1844-1909 .... **TCLC 18**
See also CA 117

Lilly, William 1602-1681.......... **LC 27**

Lima, Jose Lezama
See Lezama Lima, Jose

Lima Barreto, Afonso Henrique de
1881-1922 .... **TCLC 23**
See also CA 117

Limonov, Edward 1944-.......... **CLC 67**
See also CA 137

Lin, Frank
See Atherton, Gertrude (Franklin Horn)

Lincoln, Abraham 1809-1865..... **NCLC 18**

Lowry, (Clarence) Malcolm
1909-1957 .... **TCLC 6, 40**
See also CA 105; 131; CDBLB 1945-1960;
DLB 15; MTCW

Lowry, Mina Gertrude 1882-1966
See Loy, Mina
See also CA 113

Loxsmith, John
See Brunner, John (Kilian Houston)

Loy, Mina .... **CLC 28; DAM POET; PC 16**
See also Lowry, Mina Gertrude
See also DLB 4, 54

Loyson-Bridet
See Schwob, (Mayer Andre) Marcel

Lucas, Craig 1951- .... **CLC 64**
See also CA 137

Lucas, George 1944- .... **CLC 16**
See also AAYA 1; CA 77-80; CANR 30;
SATA 56

Lucas, Hans
See Godard, Jean-Luc

Lucas, Victoria
See Plath, Sylvia

Ludlam, Charles 1943-1987 ..... **CLC 46, 50**
See also CA 85-88; 122

Ludlum, Robert
1927- .... **CLC 22, 43; DAM NOV, POP**
See also AAYA 10; BEST 89:1, 90:3;
CA 33-36R; CANR 25, 41; DLBY 82;
MTCW

Ludwig, Ken .... **CLC 60**

Ludwig, Otto 1813-1865 .... **NCLC 4**
See also DLB 129

Lugones, Leopoldo 1874-1938 ..... **TCLC 15**
See also CA 116; 131; HW

Lu Hsun 1881-1936 ...... **TCLC 3; SSC 20**
See also Shu-Jen, Chou

Lukacs, George .... **CLC 24**
See also Lukacs, Gyorgy (Szegeny von)

Lukacs, Gyorgy (Szegeny von) 1885-1971
See Lukacs, George
See also CA 101; 29-32R

Luke, Peter (Ambrose Cyprian)
1919-1995 .... **CLC 38**
See also CA 81-84; 147; DLB 13

Lunar, Dennis
See Mungo, Raymond

Lurie, Alison 1926- .... **CLC 4, 5, 18, 39**
See also CA 1-4R; CANR 2, 17, 50; DLB 2;
MTCW; SATA 46

Lustig, Arnost 1926- .... **CLC 56**
See also AAYA 3; CA 69-72; CANR 47;
SATA 56

Luther, Martin 1483-1546 .... **LC 9, 37**

Luxemburg, Rosa 1870(?)-1919 .... **TCLC 63**
See also CA 118

Luzi, Mario 1914- .... **CLC 13**
See also CA 61-64; CANR 9; DLB 128

Lyly, John 1554(?)-1606 .... **DC 7**
See also DAM DRAM; DLB 62, 167

L'Ymagier
See Gourmont, Remy (-Marie-Charles) de

Lynch, B. Suarez
See Bioy Casares, Adolfo; Borges, Jorge
Luis

Lynch, David (K.) 1946- .... **CLC 66**
See also CA 124; 129

Lynch, James
See Andreyev, Leonid (Nikolaevich)

Lynch Davis, B.
See Bioy Casares, Adolfo; Borges, Jorge
Luis

Lyndsay, Sir David 1490-1555 ...... **LC 20**

Lynn, Kenneth S(chuyler) 1923- .... **CLC 50**
See also CA 1-4R; CANR 3, 27

Lynx
See West, Rebecca

Lyons, Marcus
See Blish, James (Benjamin)

Lyre, Pinchbeck
See Sassoon, Siegfried (Lorraine)

Lytle, Andrew (Nelson) 1902-1995 .. **CLC 22**
See also CA 9-12R; 150; DLB 6; DLBY 95

Lyttelton, George 1709-1773 .... **LC 10**

Maas, Peter 1929- .... **CLC 29**
See also CA 93-96; INT 93-96

Macaulay, Rose 1881-1958 ..... **TCLC 7, 44**
See also CA 104; DLB 36

Macaulay, Thomas Babington
1800-1859 .... **NCLC 42**
See also CDBLB 1832-1890; DLB 32, 55

MacBeth, George (Mann)
1932-1992 .... **CLC 2, 5, 9**
See also CA 25-28R; 136; DLB 40; MTCW;
SATA 4; SATA-Obit 70

MacCaig, Norman (Alexander)
1910- ..... **CLC 36; DAB; DAM POET**
See also CA 9-12R; CANR 3, 34; DLB 27

MacCarthy, (Sir Charles Otto) Desmond
1877-1952 .... **TCLC 36**

MacDiarmid, Hugh
.... **CLC 2, 4, 11, 19, 63; PC 9**
See also Grieve, C(hristopher) M(urray)
See also CDBLB 1945-1960; DLB 20

MacDonald, Anson
See Heinlein, Robert A(nson)

Macdonald, Cynthia 1928- ...... **CLC 13, 19**
See also CA 49-52; CANR 4, 44; DLB 105

MacDonald, George 1824-1905 ..... **TCLC 9**
See also CA 106; 137; DLB 18, 163;
MAICYA; SATA 33

Macdonald, John
See Millar, Kenneth

MacDonald, John D(ann)
1916-1986 .... **CLC 3, 27, 44;**
DAM NOV, POP
See also CA 1-4R; 121; CANR 1, 19;
DLB 8; DLBY 86; MTCW

Macdonald, John Ross
See Millar, Kenneth

Macdonald, Ross ..... **CLC 1, 2, 3, 14, 34, 41**
See also Millar, Kenneth
See also DLBD 6

MacDougal, John
See Blish, James (Benjamin)

MacEwen, Gwendolyn (Margaret)
1941-1987 .... **CLC 13, 55**
See also CA 9-12R; 124; CANR 7, 22;
DLB 53; SATA 50; SATA-Obit 55

Macha, Karel Hynek 1810-1846 .. **NCLC 46**

Machado (y Ruiz), Antonio
1875-1939 .... **TCLC 3**
See also CA 104; DLB 108

Machado de Assis, Joaquim Maria
1839-1908 ..... **TCLC 10; BLC; SSC 24**
See also CA 107; 153

Machen, Arthur .... **TCLC 4; SSC 20**
See also Jones, Arthur Llewellyn
See also DLB 36, 156

Machiavelli, Niccolo
1469-1527 .... **LC 8, 36; DA; DAB;**
DAC; DAM MST

MacInnes, Colin 1914-1976 ...... **CLC 4, 23**
See also CA 69-72; 65-68; CANR 21;
DLB 14; MTCW

MacInnes, Helen (Clark)
1907-1985 ..... **CLC 27, 39; DAM POP**
See also CA 1-4R; 117; CANR 1, 28;
DLB 87; MTCW; SATA 22;
SATA-Obit 44

Mackay, Mary 1855-1924
See Corelli, Marie
See also CA 118

Mackenzie, Compton (Edward Montague)
1883-1972 .... **CLC 18**
See also CA 21-22; 37-40R; CAP 2;
DLB 34, 100

Mackenzie, Henry 1745-1831 .... **NCLC 41**
See also DLB 39

Mackintosh, Elizabeth 1896(?)-1952
See Tey, Josephine
See also CA 110

MacLaren, James
See Grieve, C(hristopher) M(urray)

Mac Laverty, Bernard 1942- .... **CLC 31**
See also CA 116; 118; CANR 43; INT 118

MacLean, Alistair (Stuart)
1922-1987 .... **CLC 3, 13, 50, 63;**
DAM POP
See also CA 57-60; 121; CANR 28; MTCW;
SATA 23; SATA-Obit 50

Maclean, Norman (Fitzroy)
1902-1990 .... **CLC 78; DAM POP;**
SSC 13
See also CA 102; 132; CANR 49

MacLeish, Archibald
1892-1982 .... **CLC 3, 8, 14, 68;**
DAM POET
See also CA 9-12R; 106; CANR 33; DLB 4,
7, 45; DLBY 82; MTCW

MacLennan, (John) Hugh
1907-1990 .... **CLC 2, 14, 92; DAC;**
DAM MST
See also CA 5-8R; 142; CANR 33; DLB 68;
MTCW

MacLeod, Alistair
1936- ...... **CLC 56; DAC; DAM MST**
See also CA 123; DLB 60

Marat, Jean Paul 1743-1793 .... **LC 10**

Marcel, Gabriel Honore
  1889-1973 .... **CLC 15**
  See also CA 102; 45-48; MTCW

Marchbanks, Samuel
  See Davies, (William) Robertson

Marchi, Giacomo
  See Bassani, Giorgio

Margulies, Donald................ **CLC 76**

Marie de France c. 12th cent. -.... **CMLC 8**

Marie de l'Incarnation 1599-1672.... **LC 10**

Marier, Captain Victor
  See Griffith, D(avid Lewelyn) W(ark)

Mariner, Scott
  See Pohl, Frederik

Marinetti, Filippo Tommaso
  1876-1944 .... **TCLC 10**
  See also CA 107; DLB 114

Marivaux, Pierre Carlet de Chamblain de
  1688-1763 .... **LC 4; DC 7**

Markandaya, Kamala .... **CLC 8, 38**
  See also Taylor, Kamala (Purnaiya)

Markfield, Wallace 1926-.......... **CLC 8**
  See also CA 69-72; CAAS 3; DLB 2, 28

Markham, Edwin 1852-1940 ...... **TCLC 47**
  See also DLB 54

Markham, Robert
  See Amis, Kingsley (William)

Marks, J
  See Highwater, Jamake (Mamake)

Marks-Highwater, J
  See Highwater, Jamake (Mamake)

Markson, David M(errill) 1927-.... **CLC 67**
  See also CA 49-52; CANR 1

Marley, Bob..................... **CLC 17**
  See also Marley, Robert Nesta

Marley, Robert Nesta 1945-1981
  See Marley, Bob
  See also CA 107; 103

Marlowe, Christopher
  1564-1593 ..... **LC 22; DA; DAB; DAC;**
        DAM DRAM, MST; DC 1; WLC
  See also CDBLB Before 1660; DLB 62

Marlowe, Stephen 1928-
  See Queen, Ellery
  See also CA 13-16R; CANR 6, 55

Marmontel, Jean-Francois
  1723-1799 .... **LC 2**

Marquand, John P(hillips)
  1893-1960 .... **CLC 2, 10**
  See also CA 85-88; DLB 9, 102

Marques, Rene
  1919-1979 ..... **CLC 96; DAM MULT;**
        HLC
  See also CA 97-100; 85-88; DLB 113; HW

Marquez, Gabriel (Jose) Garcia
  See Garcia Marquez, Gabriel (Jose)

Marquis, Don(ald Robert Perry)
  1878-1937 .... **TCLC 7**
  See also CA 104; DLB 11, 25

Marric, J. J.
  See Creasey, John

Marrow, Bernard
  See Moore, Brian

Marryat, Frederick 1792-1848 .... **NCLC 3**
  See also DLB 21, 163

Marsden, James
  See Creasey, John

Marsh, (Edith) Ngaio
  1899-1982 ...... **CLC 7, 53; DAM POP**
  See also CA 9-12R; CANR 6; DLB 77;
  MTCW

Marshall, Garry 1934-............ **CLC 17**
  See also AAYA 3; CA 111; SATA 60

Marshall, Paule
  1929- .... **CLC 27, 72; BLC;**
        DAM MULT; SSC 3
  See also BW 2; CA 77-80; CANR 25;
  DLB 157; MTCW

Marsten, Richard
  See Hunter, Evan

Marston, John
  1576-1634 .... **LC 33; DAM DRAM**
  See also DLB 58, 172

Martha, Henry
  See Harris, Mark

Martial c. 40-c. 104 .... **PC 10**

Martin, Ken
  See Hubbard, L(afayette) Ron(ald)

Martin, Richard
  See Creasey, John

Martin, Steve 1945-.............. **CLC 30**
  See also CA 97-100; CANR 30; MTCW

Martin, Valerie 1948-............ **CLC 89**
  See also BEST 90:2; CA 85-88; CANR 49

Martin, Violet Florence
  1862-1915 .... **TCLC 51**

Martin, Webber
  See Silverberg, Robert

Martindale, Patrick Victor
  See White, Patrick (Victor Martindale)

Martin du Gard, Roger
  1881-1958 .... **TCLC 24**
  See also CA 118; DLB 65

Martineau, Harriet 1802-1876.... **NCLC 26**
  See also DLB 21, 55, 159, 163, 166;
  YABC 2

Martines, Julia
  See O'Faolain, Julia

Martinez, Jacinto Benavente y
  See Benavente (y Martinez), Jacinto

Martinez Ruiz, Jose 1873-1967
  See Azorin; Ruiz, Jose Martinez
  See also CA 93-96; HW

Martinez Sierra, Gregorio
  1881-1947 .... **TCLC 6**
  See also CA 115

Martinez Sierra, Maria (de la O'LeJarraga)
  1874-1974 .... **TCLC 6**
  See also CA 115

Martinsen, Martin
  See Follett, Ken(neth Martin)

Martinson, Harry (Edmund)
  1904-1978 .... **CLC 14**
  See also CA 77-80; CANR 34

Marut, Ret
  See Traven, B.

Marut, Robert
  See Traven, B.

Marvell, Andrew
  1621-1678 ...... **LC 4; DA; DAB; DAC;**
        DAM MST, POET; PC 10; WLC
  See also CDBLB 1660-1789; DLB 131

Marx, Karl (Heinrich)
  1818-1883 .... **NCLC 17**
  See also DLB 129

Masaoka Shiki................... **TCLC 18**
  See also Masaoka Tsunenori

Masaoka Tsunenori 1867-1902
  See Masaoka Shiki
  See also CA 117

Masefield, John (Edward)
  1878-1967 .... **CLC 11, 47; DAM POET**
  See also CA 19-20; 25-28R; CANR 33;
  CAP 2; CDBLB 1890-1914; DLB 10, 19,
  153, 160; MTCW; SATA 19

Maso, Carole 19(?)- .... **CLC 44**

Mason, Bobbie Ann
  1940- .... **CLC 28, 43, 82; SSC 4**
  See also AAYA 5; CA 53-56; CANR 11,
  31; DLB 173; DLBY 87; INT CANR-31;
  MTCW

Mason, Ernst
  See Pohl, Frederik

Mason, Lee W.
  See Malzberg, Barry N(athaniel)

Mason, Nick 1945-.............. **CLC 35**

Mason, Tally
  See Derleth, August (William)

Mass, William
  See Gibson, William

Masters, Edgar Lee
  1868-1950 ...... **TCLC 2, 25; DA; DAC;**
        DAM MST, POET; PC 1
  See also CA 104; 133; CDALB 1865-1917;
  DLB 54; MTCW

Masters, Hilary 1928-............ **CLC 48**
  See also CA 25-28R; CANR 13, 47

Mastrosimone, William 19(?)-...... **CLC 36**

Mathe, Albert
  See Camus, Albert

Matheson, Richard Burton 1926-... **CLC 37**
  See also CA 97-100; DLB 8, 44; INT 97-100

Mathews, Harry 1930-.......... **CLC 6, 52**
  See also CA 21-24R; CAAS 6; CANR 18,
  40

Mathews, John Joseph
  1894-1979 ...... **CLC 84; DAM MULT**
  See also CA 19-20; 142; CANR 45; CAP 2;
  DLB 175; NNAL

Mathias, Roland (Glyn) 1915-...... **CLC 45**
  See also CA 97-100; CANR 19, 41; DLB 27

Matsuo Basho 1644-1694........... **PC 3**
  See also DAM POET

Mattheson, Rodney
  See Creasey, John

Matthews, Greg 1949-............ **CLC 45**
  See also CA 135

Matthews, William 1942-......... **CLC 40**
See also CA 29-32R; CAAS 18; CANR 12, 57; DLB 5

Matthias, John (Edward) 1941-...... **CLC 9**
See also CA 33-36R; CANR 56

Matthiessen, Peter
1927-........... **CLC 5, 7, 11, 32, 64;**
DAM NOV
See also AAYA 6; BEST 90:4; CA 9-12R;
CANR 21, 50; DLB 6, 173; MTCW;
SATA 27

Maturin, Charles Robert
1780(?)-1824 .... **NCLC 6**

Matute (Ausejo), Ana Maria
1925-....................... **CLC 11**
See also CA 89-92; MTCW

Maugham, W. S.
See Maugham, W(illiam) Somerset

Maugham, W(illiam) Somerset
1874-1965 .... **CLC 1, 11, 15, 67, 93;**
DA; DAB; DAC; DAM DRAM, MST,
NOV; SSC 8; WLC
See also CA 5-8R; 25-28R; CANR 40;
CDBLB 1914-1945; DLB 10, 36, 77, 100,
162; MTCW; SATA 54

Maugham, William Somerset
See Maugham, W(illiam) Somerset

Maupassant, (Henri Rene Albert) Guy de
1850-1893 ..... **NCLC 1, 42; DA; DAB;**
DAC; DAM MST; SSC 1; WLC
See also DLB 123

Maupin, Armistead
1944-............ **CLC 95; DAM POP**
See also CA 125; 130; INT 130

Maurhut, Richard
See Traven, B.

Mauriac, Claude 1914-1996........ **CLC 9**
See also CA 89-92; 152; DLB 83

Mauriac, Francois (Charles)
1885-1970 .... **CLC 4, 9, 56; SSC 24**
See also CA 25-28; CAP 2; DLB 65;
MTCW

Mavor, Osborne Henry 1888-1951
See Bridie, James
See also CA 104

Maxwell, William (Keepers, Jr.)
1908-....................... **CLC 19**
See also CA 93-96; CANR 54; DLBY 80;
INT 93-96

May, Elaine 1932-............... **CLC 16**
See also CA 124; 142; DLB 44

Mayakovski, Vladimir (Vladimirovich)
1893-1930 .... **TCLC 4, 18**
See also CA 104

Mayhew, Henry 1812-1887 ...... **NCLC 31**
See also DLB 18, 55

Mayle, Peter 1939(?)-............. **CLC 89**
See also CA 139

Maynard, Joyce 1953-............ **CLC 23**
See also CA 111; 129

Mayne, William (James Carter)
1928-....................... **CLC 12**
See also AAYA 20; CA 9-12R; CANR 37;
CLR 25; JRDA; MAICYA; SAAS 11;
SATA 6, 68

Mayo, Jim
See L'Amour, Louis (Dearborn)

Maysles, Albert 1926-............ **CLC 16**
See also CA 29-32R

Maysles, David 1932-............. **CLC 16**

Mazer, Norma Fox 1931- .... **CLC 26**
See also AAYA 5; CA 69-72; CANR 12,
32; CLR 23; JRDA; MAICYA; SAAS 1;
SATA 24, 67

Mazzini, Guiseppe 1805-1872 .... **NCLC 34**

McAuley, James Phillip
1917-1976 .... **CLC 45**
See also CA 97-100

McBain, Ed
See Hunter, Evan

McBrien, William Augustine
1930-....................... **CLC 44**
See also CA 107

McCaffrey, Anne (Inez)
1926-...... **CLC 17; DAM NOV, POP**
See also AAYA 6; AITN 2; BEST 89:2;
CA 25-28R; CANR 15, 35, 55; DLB 8;
JRDA; MAICYA; MTCW; SAAS 11;
SATA 8, 70

McCall, Nathan 1955(?)-.......... **CLC 86**
See also CA 146

McCann, Arthur
See Campbell, John W(ood, Jr.)

McCann, Edson
See Pohl, Frederik

McCarthy, Charles, Jr. 1933-
See McCarthy, Cormac
See also CANR 42; DAM POP

McCarthy, Cormac 1933-..... **CLC 4, 57, 59**
See also McCarthy, Charles, Jr.
See also DLB 6, 143

McCarthy, Mary (Therese)
1912-1989 ...... **CLC 1, 3, 5, 14, 24, 39,**
59; SSC 24
See also CA 5-8R; 129; CANR 16, 50;
DLB 2; DLBY 81; INT CANR-16;
MTCW

McCartney, (James) Paul
1942-..................... **CLC 12, 35**
See also CA 146

McCauley, Stephen (D.) 1955- ..... **CLC 50**
See also CA 141

McClure, Michael (Thomas)
1932-..................... **CLC 6, 10**
See also CA 21-24R; CANR 17, 46;
DLB 16

McCorkle, Jill (Collins) 1958-...... **CLC 51**
See also CA 121; DLBY 87

McCourt, James 1941-............. **CLC 5**
See also CA 57-60

McCoy, Horace (Stanley)
1897-1955 .... **TCLC 28**
See also CA 108; 155; DLB 9

McCrae, John 1872-1918........ **TCLC 12**
See also CA 109; DLB 92

McCreigh, James
See Pohl, Frederik

McCullers, (Lula) Carson (Smith)
1917-1967 .... **CLC 1, 4, 10, 12, 48, 100;**
DA; DAB; DAC; DAM MST, NOV;
SSC 24; WLC
See also CA 5-8R; 25-28R; CABS 1, 3;
CANR 18; CDALB 1941-1968; DLB 2, 7,
173; MTCW; SATA 27

McCulloch, John Tyler
See Burroughs, Edgar Rice

McCullough, Colleen
1938(?)- .... **CLC 27; DAM NOV, POP**
See also CA 81-84; CANR 17, 46; MTCW

McDermott, Alice 1953- .... **CLC 90**
See also CA 109; CANR 40

McElroy, Joseph 1930- .... **CLC 5, 47**
See also CA 17-20R

McEwan, Ian (Russell)
1948-......... **CLC 13, 66; DAM NOV**
See also BEST 90:4; CA 61-64; CANR 14,
41; DLB 14; MTCW

McFadden, David 1940-........... **CLC 48**
See also CA 104; DLB 60; INT 104

McFarland, Dennis 1950- .... **CLC 65**

McGahern, John
1934-.......... **CLC 5, 9, 48; SSC 17**
See also CA 17-20R; CANR 29; DLB 14;
MTCW

McGinley, Patrick (Anthony)
1937-....................... **CLC 41**
See also CA 120; 127; CANR 56; INT 127

McGinley, Phyllis 1905-1978 ...... **CLC 14**
See also CA 9-12R; 77-80; CANR 19;
DLB 11, 48; SATA 2, 44; SATA-Obit 24

McGinniss, Joe 1942-............. **CLC 32**
See also AITN 2; BEST 89:2; CA 25-28R;
CANR 26; INT CANR-26

McGivern, Maureen Daly
See Daly, Maureen

McGrath, Patrick 1950-........... **CLC 55**
See also CA 136

McGrath, Thomas (Matthew)
1916-1990 .... **CLC 28, 59; DAM POET**
See also CA 9-12R; 132; CANR 6, 33;
MTCW; SATA 41; SATA-Obit 66

McGuane, Thomas (Francis III)
1939-............... **CLC 3, 7, 18, 45**
See also AITN 2; CA 49-52; CANR 5, 24,
49; DLB 2; DLBY 80; INT CANR-24;
MTCW

McGuckian, Medbh
1950-.......... **CLC 48; DAM POET**
See also CA 143; DLB 40

McHale, Tom 1942(?)-1982....... **CLC 3, 5**
See also AITN 1; CA 77-80; 106

McIlvanney, William 1936-........ **CLC 42**
See also CA 25-28R; DLB 14

McIlwraith, Maureen Mollie Hunter
See Hunter, Mollie
See also SATA 2

McInerney, Jay
1955-............ **CLC 34; DAM POP**
See also AAYA 18; CA 116; 123;
CANR 45; INT 123

McIntyre, Vonda N(eel) 1948- ..... **CLC 18**
See also CA 81-84; CANR 17, 34; MTCW

Miles, Josephine (Louise)
1911-1985 . . . . **CLC 1, 2, 14, 34, 39;**
DAM POET
See also CA 1-4R; 116; CANR 2, 55;
DLB 48

Militant
See Sandburg, Carl (August)

Mill, John Stuart 1806-1873 . . **NCLC 11, 58**
See also CDBLB 1832-1890; DLB 55

Millar, Kenneth
1915-1983 . . . . **CLC 14; DAM POP**
See also Macdonald, Ross
See also CA 9-12R; 110; CANR 16; DLB 2;
DLBD 6; DLBY 83; MTCW

Millay, E. Vincent
See Millay, Edna St. Vincent

Millay, Edna St. Vincent
1892-1950 . . . . . . **TCLC 4, 49; DA; DAB;**
DAC; DAM MST, POET; PC 6
See also CA 104; 130; CDALB 1917-1929;
DLB 45; MTCW

Miller, Arthur
1915- . . . . **CLC 1, 2, 6, 10, 15, 26, 47, 78;**
DA; DAB; DAC; DAM DRAM, MST;
DC 1; WLC
See also AAYA 15; AITN 1; CA 1-4R;
CABS 3; CANR 2, 30, 54;
CDALB 1941-1968; DLB 7; MTCW

Miller, Henry (Valentine)
1891-1980 . . . . **CLC 1, 2, 4, 9, 14, 43, 84;**
DA; DAB; DAC; DAM MST, NOV;
WLC
See also CA 9-12R; 97-100; CANR 33;
CDALB 1929-1941; DLB 4, 9; DLBY 80;
MTCW

Miller, Jason 1939(?)- . . . . **CLC 2**
See also AITN 1; CA 73-76; DLB 7

Miller, Sue 1943- . . . . . **CLC 44; DAM POP**
See also BEST 90:3; CA 139; DLB 143

Miller, Walter M(ichael, Jr.)
1923- . . . . **CLC 4, 30**
See also CA 85-88; DLB 8

Millett, Kate 1934- . . . . **CLC 67**
See also AITN 1; CA 73-76; CANR 32, 53;
MTCW

Millhauser, Steven 1943- . . . . **CLC 21, 54**
See also CA 110; 111; DLB 2; INT 111

Millin, Sarah Gertrude 1889-1968 . . **CLC 49**
See also CA 102; 93-96

Milne, A(lan) A(lexander)
1882-1956 . . . . **TCLC 6; DAB; DAC;**
DAM MST
See also CA 104; 133; CLR 1, 26; DLB 10,
77, 100, 160; MAICYA; MTCW;
YABC 1

Milner, Ron(ald)
1938- . . . . . **CLC 56; BLC; DAM MULT**
See also AITN 1; BW 1; CA 73-76;
CANR 24; DLB 38; MTCW

Milosz, Czeslaw
1911- . . . . **CLC 5, 11, 22, 31, 56, 82;**
DAM MST, POET; PC 8
See also CA 81-84; CANR 23, 51; MTCW

Milton, John
1608-1674 . . . . . . **LC 9; DA; DAB; DAC;**
DAM MST, POET; WLC
See also CDBLB 1660-1789; DLB 131, 151

Min, Anchee 1957- . . . . **CLC 86**
See also CA 146

Minehaha, Cornelius
See Wedekind, (Benjamin) Frank(lin)

Miner, Valerie 1947- . . . . **CLC 40**
See also CA 97-100

Minimo, Duca
See D'Annunzio, Gabriele

Minot, Susan 1956- . . . . **CLC 44**
See also CA 134

Minus, Ed 1938- . . . . **CLC 39**

Miranda, Javier
See Bioy Casares, Adolfo

Mirbeau, Octave 1848-1917 . . . . . . **TCLC 55**
See also DLB 123

Miro (Ferrer), Gabriel (Francisco Victor)
1879-1930 . . . . **TCLC 5**
See also CA 104

Mishima, Yukio
. . . . **CLC 2, 4, 6, 9, 27; DC 1; SSC 4**
See also Hiraoka, Kimitake

Mistral, Frederic 1830-1914 . . . . . . **TCLC 51**
See also CA 122

Mistral, Gabriela . . . . **TCLC 2; HLC**
See also Godoy Alcayaga, Lucila

Mistry, Rohinton 1952- . . . . . . **CLC 71; DAC**
See also CA 141

Mitchell, Clyde
See Ellison, Harlan (Jay); Silverberg, Robert

Mitchell, James Leslie 1901-1935
See Gibbon, Lewis Grassic
See also CA 104; DLB 15

Mitchell, Joni 1943- . . . . **CLC 12**
See also CA 112

Mitchell, Joseph (Quincy)
1908-1996 . . . . **CLC 98**
See also CA 77-80; 152

Mitchell, Margaret (Munnerlyn)
1900-1949 . . . . . . **TCLC 11; DAM NOV,**
POP
See also CA 109; 125; CANR 55; DLB 9;
MTCW

Mitchell, Peggy
See Mitchell, Margaret (Munnerlyn)

Mitchell, S(ilas) Weir 1829-1914 . . **TCLC 36**

Mitchell, W(illiam) O(rmond)
1914- . . . . . . **CLC 25; DAC; DAM MST**
See also CA 77-80; CANR 15, 43; DLB 88

Mitford, Mary Russell 1787-1855 . . **NCLC 4**
See also DLB 110, 116

Mitford, Nancy 1904-1973 . . . . **CLC 44**
See also CA 9-12R

Miyamoto, Yuriko 1899-1951 . . . . . **TCLC 37**

Mo, Timothy (Peter) 1950(?)- . . . . . . **CLC 46**
See also CA 117; MTCW

Modarressi, Taghi (M.) 1931- . . . . . . **CLC 44**
See also CA 121; 134; INT 134

Modiano, Patrick (Jean) 1945- . . . . . **CLC 18**
See also CA 85-88; CANR 17, 40; DLB 83

Moerck, Paal
See Roelvaag, O(le) E(dvart)

Mofolo, Thomas (Mokopu)
1875(?)-1948 . . . . **TCLC 22; BLC;**
DAM MULT
See also CA 121; 153

Mohr, Nicholasa
1935- . . . . . **CLC 12; DAM MULT; HLC**
See also AAYA 8; CA 49-52; CANR 1, 32;
CLR 22; DLB 145; HW; JRDA; SAAS 8;
SATA 8

Mojtabai, A(nn) G(race)
1938- . . . . **CLC 5, 9, 15, 29**
See also CA 85-88

Moliere
1622-1673 . . . . . **LC 28; DA; DAB; DAC;**
DAM DRAM, MST; WLC

Molin, Charles
See Mayne, William (James Carter)

Molnar, Ferenc
1878-1952 . . . . . **TCLC 20; DAM DRAM**
See also CA 109; 153

Momaday, N(avarre) Scott
1934- . . . . . **CLC 2, 19, 85, 95; DA; DAB;**
DAC; DAM MST, MULT, NOV, POP
See also AAYA 11; CA 25-28R; CANR 14,
34; DLB 143, 175; INT CANR-14;
MTCW; NNAL; SATA 48;
SATA-Brief 30

Monette, Paul 1945-1995 . . . . **CLC 82**
See also CA 139; 147

Monroe, Harriet 1860-1936 . . . . **TCLC 12**
See also CA 109; DLB 54, 91

Monroe, Lyle
See Heinlein, Robert A(nson)

Montagu, Elizabeth 1917- . . . . **NCLC 7**
See also CA 9-12R

Montagu, Mary (Pierrepont) Wortley
1689-1762 . . . . **LC 9; PC 16**
See also DLB 95, 101

Montagu, W. H.
See Coleridge, Samuel Taylor

Montague, John (Patrick)
1929- . . . . **CLC 13, 46**
See also CA 9-12R; CANR 9; DLB 40;
MTCW

Montaigne, Michel (Eyquem) de
1533-1592 . . . . . . **LC 8; DA; DAB; DAC;**
DAM MST; WLC

Montale, Eugenio
1896-1981 . . . . **CLC 7, 9, 18; PC 13**
See also CA 17-20R; 104; CANR 30;
DLB 114; MTCW

Montesquieu, Charles-Louis de Secondat
1689-1755 . . . . **LC 7**

Montgomery, (Robert) Bruce 1921-1978
See Crispin, Edmund
See also CA 104

Montgomery, L(ucy) M(aud)
1874-1942 . . . . **TCLC 51; DAC;**
DAM MST
See also AAYA 12; CA 108; 137; CLR 8;
DLB 92; DLBD 14; JRDA; MAICYA;
YABC 1

Montgomery, Marion H., Jr. 1925- . . **CLC 7**
See also AITN 1; CA 1-4R; CANR 3, 48;
DLB 6

Montgomery, Max
See Davenport, Guy (Mattison, Jr.)

Montherlant, Henry (Milon) de
1896-1972 .... CLC 8, 19; DAM DRAM
See also CA 85-88; 37-40R; DLB 72,
MTCW

Monty Python
See Chapman, Graham; Cleese, John
(Marwood); Gilliam, Terry (Vance); Idle,
Eric; Jones, Terence Graham Parry; Palin,
Michael (Edward)
See also AAYA 7

Moodie, Susanna (Strickland)
1803-1885 .... NCLC 14
See also DLB 99

Mooney, Edward 1951-
See Mooney, Ted
See also CA 130

Mooney, Ted .... CLC 25
See also Mooney, Edward

Moorcock, Michael (John)
1939- .... CLC 5, 27, 58
See also CA 45-48; CAAS 5; CANR 2, 17,
38; DLB 14; MTCW

Moore, Brian
1921- ...... CLC 1, 3, 5, 7, 8, 19, 32, 90;
DAB; DAC; DAM MST
See also CA 1-4R; CANR 1, 25, 42; MTCW

Moore, Edward
See Muir, Edwin

Moore, George Augustus
1852-1933 .... TCLC 7; SSC 19
See also CA 104; DLB 10, 18, 57, 135

Moore, Lorrie .... CLC 39, 45, 68
See also Moore, Marie Lorena

Moore, Marianne (Craig)
1887-1972 .... CLC 1, 2, 4, 8, 10, 13, 19,
47; DA; DAB; DAC; DAM MST, POET;
PC 4
See also CA 1-4R; 33-36R; CANR 3;
CDALB 1929-1941; DLB 45; DLBD 7;
MTCW; SATA 20

Moore, Marie Lorena 1957-
See Moore, Lorrie
See also CA 116; CANR 39

Moore, Thomas 1779-1852 .... NCLC 6
See also DLB 96, 144

Morand, Paul 1888-1976 .. CLC 41; SSC 22
See also CA 69-72; DLB 65

Morante, Elsa 1918-1985 .... CLC 8, 47
See also CA 85-88; 117; CANR 35;
DLB 177; MTCW

Moravia, Alberto
1907-1990 .... CLC 2, 7, 11, 27, 46
See also Pincherle, Alberto
See also DLB 177

More, Hannah 1745-1833 .... NCLC 27
See also DLB 107, 109, 116, 158

More, Henry 1614-1687............. LC 9
See also DLB 126

More, Sir Thomas 1478-1535 .... LC 10, 32

Moreas, Jean .... TCLC 18
See also Papadiamantopoulos, Johannes

Morgan, Berry 1919- .... CLC 6
See also CA 49-52; DLB 6

Morgan, Claire
See Highsmith, (Mary) Patricia

Morgan, Edwin (George) 1920-..... CLC 31
See also CA 5-8R; CANR 3, 43; DLB 27

Morgan, (George) Frederick
1922- .... CLC 23
See also CA 17-20R; CANR 21

Morgan, Harriet
See Mencken, H(enry) L(ouis)

Morgan, Jane
See Cooper, James Fenimore

Morgan, Janet 1945- .... CLC 39
See also CA 65-68

Morgan, Lady 1776(?)-1859...... NCLC 29
See also DLB 116, 158

Morgan, Robin 1941-............. CLC 2
See also CA 69-72; CANR 29; MTCW;
SATA 80

Morgan, Scott
See Kuttner, Henry

Morgan, Seth 1949(?)-1990 .... CLC 65
See also CA 132

Morgenstern, Christian
1871-1914 .... TCLC 8
See also CA 105

Morgenstern, S.
See Goldman, William (W.)

Moricz, Zsigmond 1879-1942 ..... TCLC 33

Morike, Eduard (Friedrich)
1804-1875 .... NCLC 10
See also DLB 133

Mori Ogai .... TCLC 14
See also Mori Rintaro

Mori Rintaro 1862-1922
See Mori Ogai
See also CA 110

Moritz, Karl Philipp 1756-1793 ...... LC 2
See also DLB 94

Morland, Peter Henry
See Faust, Frederick (Schiller)

Morren, Theophil
See Hofmannsthal, Hugo von

Morris, Bill 1952-................ CLC 76

Morris, Julian
See West, Morris L(anglo)

Morris, Steveland Judkins 1950(?)-
See Wonder, Stevie
See also CA 111

Morris, William 1834-1896 .... NCLC 4
See also CDBLB 1832-1890; DLB 18, 35,
57, 156

Morris, Wright 1910-... CLC 1, 3, 7, 18, 37
See also CA 9-12R; CANR 21; DLB 2;
DLBY 81; MTCW

Morrison, Chloe Anthony Wofford
See Morrison, Toni

Morrison, James Douglas 1943-1971
See Morrison, Jim
See also CA 73-76; CANR 40

Morrison, Jim .... CLC 17
See also Morrison, James Douglas

Morrison, Toni
1931- .... CLC 4, 10, 22, 55, 81, 87;
BLC; DA; DAB; DAC; DAM MST,
MULT, NOV, POP
See also AAYA 1; BW 2; CA 29-32R;
CANR 27, 42; CDALB 1968-1988;
DLB 6, 33, 143; DLBY 81; MTCW;
SATA 57

Morrison, Van 1945- .... CLC 21
See also CA 116

Morrissy, Mary 1958- .... CLC 99

Mortimer, John (Clifford)
1923- ...... CLC 28, 43; DAM DRAM,
POP
See also CA 13-16R; CANR 21;
CDBLB 1960 to Present; DLB 13;
INT CANR-21; MTCW

Mortimer, Penelope (Ruth) 1918-.... CLC 5
See also CA 57-60; CANR 45

Morton, Anthony
See Creasey, John

Mosher, Howard Frank 1943-...... CLC 62
See also CA 139

Mosley, Nicholas 1923-........ CLC 43, 70
See also CA 69-72; CANR 41; DLB 14

Mosley, Walter
1952- ..... CLC 97; DAM MULT, POP
See also AAYA 17; BW 2; CA 142;
CANR 57

Moss, Howard
1922-1987 .... CLC 7, 14, 45, 50;
DAM POET
See also CA 1-4R; 123; CANR 1, 44;
DLB 5

Mossgiel, Rab
See Burns, Robert

Motion, Andrew (Peter) 1952-...... CLC 47
See also CA 146; DLB 40

Motley, Willard (Francis)
1909-1965 .... CLC 18
See also BW 1; CA 117; 106; DLB 76, 143

Motoori, Norinaga 1730-1801 .... NCLC 45

Mott, Michael (Charles Alston)
1930- .... CLC 15, 34
See also CA 5-8R; CAAS 7; CANR 7, 29

Mountain Wolf Woman
1884-1960 .... CLC 92
See also CA 144; NNAL

Moure, Erin 1955- .... CLC 88
See also CA 113; DLB 60

Mowat, Farley (McGill)
1921- ...... CLC 26; DAC; DAM MST
See also AAYA 1; CA 1-4R; CANR 4, 24,
42; CLR 20; DLB 68; INT CANR-24;
JRDA; MAICYA; MTCW; SATA 3, 55

Moyers, Bill 1934-................ CLC 74
See also AITN 2; CA 61-64; CANR 31, 52

Mphahlele, Es'kia
See Mphahlele, Ezekiel
See also DLB 125

Mphahlele, Ezekiel
1919- ..... CLC 25; BLC; DAM MULT
See also Mphahlele, Es'kia
See also BW 2; CA 81-84; CANR 26

Mqhayi, S(amuel) E(dward) K(rune Loliwe)
   1875-1945 . . . . TCLC 25; BLC;
                                          DAM MULT
   See also CA 153

Mrozek, Slawomir 1930- . . . . CLC 3, 13
   See also CA 13-16R; CAAS 10; CANR 29;
   MTCW

Mrs. Belloc-Lowndes
   See Lowndes, Marie Adelaide (Belloc)

Mtwa, Percy (?)- . . . . CLC 47

Mueller, Lisel 1924- . . . . CLC 13, 51
   See also CA 93-96; DLB 105

Muir, Edwin 1887-1959 . . . . TCLC 2
   See also CA 104; DLB 20, 100

Muir, John 1838-1914 . . . . TCLC 28

Mujica Lainez, Manuel
   1910-1984 . . . . CLC 31
   See also Lainez, Manuel Mujica
   See also CA 81-84; 112; CANR 32; HW

Mukherjee, Bharati
   1940- . . . . CLC 53; DAM NOV
   See also BEST 89:2; CA 107; CANR 45;
   DLB 60; MTCW

Muldoon, Paul
   1951- . . . . CLC 32, 72; DAM POET
   See also CA 113; 129; CANR 52; DLB 40;
   INT 129

Mulisch, Harry 1927- . . . . CLC 42
   See also CA 9-12R; CANR 6, 26, 56

Mull, Martin 1943- . . . . CLC 17
   See also CA 105

Mulock, Dinah Maria
   See Craik, Dinah Maria (Mulock)

Munford, Robert 1737(?)-1783 . . . . LC 5
   See also DLB 31

Mungo, Raymond 1946- . . . . CLC 72
   See also CA 49-52; CANR 2

Munro, Alice
   1931- . . . . . . CLC 6, 10, 19, 50, 95; DAC;
                          DAM MST, NOV; SSC 3
   See also AITN 2; CA 33-36R; CANR 33,
   53; DLB 53; MTCW; SATA 29

Munro, H(ector) H(ugh) 1870-1916
   See Saki
   See also CA 104; 130; CDBLB 1890-1914;
   DA; DAB; DAC; DAM MST, NOV;
   DLB 34, 162; MTCW; WLC

Murasaki, Lady . . . . CMLC 1

Murdoch, (Jean) Iris
   1919- . . . . . CLC 1, 2, 3, 4, 6, 8, 11, 15,
           22, 31, 51; DAB; DAC; DAM MST,
                                                NOV
   See also CA 13-16R; CANR 8, 43;
   CDBLB 1960 to Present; DLB 14;
   INT CANR-8; MTCW

Murfree, Mary Noailles
   1850-1922 . . . . SSC 22
   See also CA 122; DLB 12, 74

Murnau, Friedrich Wilhelm
   See Plumpe, Friedrich Wilhelm

Murphy, Richard 1927- . . . . CLC 41
   See also CA 29-32R; DLB 40

Murphy, Sylvia 1937- . . . . CLC 34
   See also CA 121

Murphy, Thomas (Bernard) 1935- . . . CLC 51
   See also CA 101

Murray, Albert L. 1916- . . . . CLC 73
   See also BW 2; CA 49-52; CANR 26, 52;
   DLB 38

Murray, Les(lie) A(llan)
   1938- . . . . CLC 40; DAM POET
   See also CA 21-24R; CANR 11, 27, 56

Murry, J. Middleton
   See Murry, John Middleton

Murry, John Middleton
   1889-1957 . . . . TCLC 16
   See also CA 118; DLB 149

Musgrave, Susan 1951- . . . . CLC 13, 54
   See also CA 69-72; CANR 45

Musil, Robert (Edler von)
   1880-1942 . . . . TCLC 12, 68; SSC 18
   See also CA 109; CANR 55; DLB 81, 124

Muske, Carol 1945- . . . . CLC 90
   See also Muske-Dukes, Carol (Anne)

Muske-Dukes, Carol (Anne) 1945-
   See Muske, Carol
   See also CA 65-68; CANR 32

Musset, (Louis Charles) Alfred de
   1810-1857 . . . . NCLC 7

My Brother's Brother
   See Chekhov, Anton (Pavlovich)

Myers, L. H. 1881-1944 . . . . TCLC 59
   See also DLB 15

Myers, Walter Dean
   1937- . . . . . CLC 35; BLC; DAM MULT,
                                                NOV
   See also AAYA 4; BW 2; CA 33-36R;
   CANR 20, 42; CLR 4, 16, 35; DLB 33;
   INT CANR-20; JRDA; MAICYA;
   SAAS 2; SATA 41, 71; SATA-Brief 27

Myers, Walter M.
   See Myers, Walter Dean

Myles, Symon
   See Follett, Ken(neth Martin)

Nabokov, Vladimir (Vladimirovich)
   1899-1977 . . . . . CLC 1, 2, 3, 6, 8, 11, 15,
          23, 44, 46, 64; DA; DAB; DAC;
          DAM MST, NOV; SSC 11; WLC
   See also CA 5-8R; 69-72; CANR 20;
   CDALB 1941-1968; DLB 2; DLBD 3;
   DLBY 80, 91; MTCW

Nagai Kafu . . . . TCLC 51
   See also Nagai Sokichi

Nagai Sokichi 1879-1959
   See Nagai Kafu
   See also CA 117

Nagy, Laszlo 1925-1978 . . . . CLC 7
   See also CA 129; 112

Naipaul, Shiva(dhar Srinivasa)
   1945-1985 . . . . . CLC 32, 39; DAM NOV
   See also CA 110; 112; 116; CANR 33;
   DLB 157; DLBY 85; MTCW

Naipaul, V(idiadhar) S(urajprasad)
   1932- . . . . CLC 4, 7, 9, 13, 18, 37; DAB;
                       DAC; DAM MST, NOV
   See also CA 1-4R; CANR 1, 33, 51;
   CDBLB 1960 to Present; DLB 125;
   DLBY 85; MTCW

Nakos, Lilika 1899(?)- . . . . CLC 29

Narayan, R(asipuram) K(rishnaswami)
   1906- . . . . . . CLC 7, 28, 47; DAM NOV;
                                             SSC 25
   See also CA 81-84; CANR 33; MTCW;
   SATA 62

Nash, (Frediric) Ogden
   1902-1971 . . . . CLC 23; DAM POET
   See also CA 13-14; 29-32R; CANR 34;
   CAP 1; DLB 11; MAICYA; MTCW;
   SATA 2, 46

Nathan, Daniel
   See Dannay, Frederic

Nathan, George Jean 1882-1958 . . . TCLC 18
   See also Hatteras, Owen
   See also CA 114; DLB 137

Natsume, Kinnosuke 1867-1916
   See Natsume, Soseki
   See also CA 104

Natsume, Soseki . . . . TCLC 2, 10
   See also Natsume, Kinnosuke

Natti, (Mary) Lee 1919-
   See Kingman, Lee
   See also CA 5-8R; CANR 2

Naylor, Gloria
   1950- . . . . . CLC 28, 52; BLC; DA; DAC;
                       DAM MST, MULT, NOV, POP
   See also AAYA 6; BW 2; CA 107;
   CANR 27, 51; DLB 173; MTCW

Neihardt, John Gneisenau
   1881-1973 . . . . CLC 32
   See also CA 13-14; CAP 1; DLB 9, 54

Nekrasov, Nikolai Alekseevich
   1821-1878 . . . . NCLC 11

Nelligan, Emile 1879-1941 . . . . TCLC 14
   See also CA 114; DLB 92

Nelson, Willie 1933- . . . . CLC 17
   See also CA 107

Nemerov, Howard (Stanley)
   1920-1991 . . . . CLC 2, 6, 9, 36;
                                          DAM POET
   See also CA 1-4R; 134; CABS 2; CANR 1,
   27, 53; DLB 5, 6; DLBY 83;
   INT CANR-27; MTCW

Neruda, Pablo
   1904-1973 . . . . . CLC 1, 2, 5, 7, 9, 28, 62;
          DA; DAB; DAC; DAM MST, MULT,
                       POET; HLC; PC 4; WLC
   See also CA 19-20; 45-48; CAP 2; HW;
   MTCW

Nerval, Gerard de
   1808-1855 . . . . . NCLC 1; PC 13; SSC 18

Nervo, (Jose) Amado (Ruiz de)
   1870-1919 . . . . TCLC 11
   See also CA 109; 131; HW

Nessi, Pio Baroja y
   See Baroja (y Nessi), Pio

Nestroy, Johann 1801-1862 . . . . . . NCLC 42
   See also DLB 133

Neufeld, John (Arthur) 1938- . . . . . . CLC 17
   See also AAYA 11; CA 25-28R; CANR 11,
   37, 56; MAICYA; SAAS 3; SATA 6, 81

Neville, Emily Cheney 1919- . . . . CLC 12
   See also CA 5-8R; CANR 3, 37; JRDA;
   MAICYA; SAAS 2; SATA 1

Oskison, John Milton
1874-1947 . . . . . **TCLC 35; DAM MULT**
See also CA 144; DLB 175; NNAL

Ossoli, Sarah Margaret (Fuller marchesa d')
1810-1850
See Fuller, Margaret
See also SATA 25

Ostrovsky, Alexander
1823-1886 . . . . **NCLC 30, 57**

Otero, Blas de 1916-1979 . . . . **CLC 11**
See also CA 89-92; DLB 134

Otto, Whitney 1955- . . . . **CLC 70**
See also CA 140

Ouida . . . . **TCLC 43**
See also De La Ramee, (Marie) Louise
See also DLB 18, 156

Ousmane, Sembene 1923- . . . . **CLC 66; BLC**
See also BW 1; CA 117; 125; MTCW

Ovid
43B.C.-18(?) . . . **CMLC 7; DAM POET;**
PC 2

Owen, Hugh
See Faust, Frederick (Schiller)

Owen, Wilfred (Edward Salter)
1893-1918 . . . . . . **TCLC 5, 27; DA; DAB;**
DAC; DAM MST, POET; WLC
See also CA 104; 141; CDBLB 1914-1945;
DLB 20

Owens, Rochelle 1936- . . . . **CLC 8**
See also CA 17-20R; CAAS 2; CANR 39

Oz, Amos
1939- . . . . **CLC 5, 8, 11, 27, 33, 54;**
DAM NOV
See also CA 53-56; CANR 27, 47; MTCW

Ozick, Cynthia
1928- . . . . **CLC 3, 7, 28, 62; DAM NOV,**
POP; SSC 15
See also BEST 90:1; CA 17-20R; CANR 23;
DLB 28, 152; DLBY 82; INT CANR-23;
MTCW

Ozu, Yasujiro 1903-1963 . . . . **CLC 16**
See also CA 112

Pacheco, C.
See Pessoa, Fernando (Antonio Nogueira)

Pa Chin . . . . **CLC 18**
See also Li Fei-kan

Pack, Robert 1929- . . . . **CLC 13**
See also CA 1-4R; CANR 3, 44; DLB 5

Padgett, Lewis
See Kuttner, Henry

Padilla (Lorenzo), Heberto 1932- . . . **CLC 38**
See also AITN 1; CA 123; 131; HW

Page, Jimmy 1944- . . . . **CLC 12**

Page, Louise 1955- . . . . **CLC 40**
See also CA 140

Page, P(atricia) K(athleen)
1916- . . . . **CLC 7, 18; DAC; DAM MST;**
PC 12
See also CA 53-56; CANR 4, 22; DLB 68;
MTCW

Page, Thomas Nelson 1853-1922 . . . . **SSC 23**
See also CA 118; DLB 12, 78; DLBD 13

Paget, Violet 1856-1935
See Lee, Vernon
See also CA 104

Paget-Lowe, Henry
See Lovecraft, H(oward) P(hillips)

Paglia, Camille (Anna) 1947- . . . . . . **CLC 68**
See also CA 140

Paige, Richard
See Koontz, Dean R(ay)

Pakenham, Antonia
See Fraser, (Lady) Antonia (Pakenham)

Palamas, Kostes 1859-1943 . . . . **TCLC 5**
See also CA 105

Palazzeschi, Aldo 1885-1974 . . . . **CLC 11**
See also CA 89-92; 53-56; DLB 114

Paley, Grace
1922- . . . . **CLC 4, 6, 37; DAM POP;**
SSC 8
See also CA 25-28R; CANR 13, 46;
DLB 28; INT CANR-13; MTCW

Palin, Michael (Edward) 1943- . . . . . **CLC 21**
See also Monty Python
See also CA 107; CANR 35; SATA 67

Palliser, Charles 1947- . . . . **CLC 65**
See also CA 136

Palma, Ricardo 1833-1919 . . . . **TCLC 29**

Pancake, Breece Dexter 1952-1979
See Pancake, Breece D'J
See also CA 123; 109

Pancake, Breece D'J . . . . **CLC 29**
See also Pancake, Breece Dexter
See also DLB 130

Panko, Rudy
See Gogol, Nikolai (Vasilyevich)

Papadiamantis, Alexandros
1851-1911 . . . . **TCLC 29**

Papadiamantopoulos, Johannes 1856-1910
See Moreas, Jean
See also CA 117

Papini, Giovanni 1881-1956 . . . . **TCLC 22**
See also CA 121

Paracelsus 1493-1541 . . . . **LC 14**

Parasol, Peter
See Stevens, Wallace

Pareto, Vilfredo 1848-1923 . . . . **TCLC 69**

Parfenie, Maria
See Codrescu, Andrei

Parini, Jay (Lee) 1948- . . . . **CLC 54**
See also CA 97-100; CAAS 16; CANR 32

Park, Jordan
See Kornbluth, C(yril) M.; Pohl, Frederik

Parker, Bert
See Ellison, Harlan (Jay)

Parker, Dorothy (Rothschild)
1893-1967 . . . . **CLC 15, 68;**
DAM POET; SSC 2
See also CA 19-20; 25-28R; CAP 2;
DLB 11, 45, 86; MTCW

Parker, Robert B(rown)
1932- . . . . **CLC 27; DAM NOV, POP**
See also BEST 89:4; CA 49-52; CANR 1,
26, 52; INT CANR-26; MTCW

Parkin, Frank 1940- . . . . **CLC 43**
See also CA 147

Parkman, Francis, Jr.
1823-1893 . . . . **NCLC 12**
See also DLB 1, 30

Parks, Gordon (Alexander Buchanan)
1912- . . . **CLC 1, 16; BLC; DAM MULT**
See also AITN 2; BW 2; CA 41-44R;
CANR 26; DLB 33; SATA 8

Parmenides
c. 515B.C.-c. 450B.C. . . . . **CMLC 22**
See also DLB 176

Parnell, Thomas 1679-1718 . . . . **LC 3**
See also DLB 94

Parra, Nicanor
1914- . . . . . . **CLC 2; DAM MULT; HLC**
See also CA 85-88; CANR 32; HW; MTCW

Parrish, Mary Frances
See Fisher, M(ary) F(rances) K(ennedy)

Parson
See Coleridge, Samuel Taylor

Parson Lot
See Kingsley, Charles

Partridge, Anthony
See Oppenheim, E(dward) Phillips

Pascal, Blaise 1623-1662 . . . . **LC 35**

Pascoli, Giovanni 1855-1912 . . . . . . **TCLC 45**

Pasolini, Pier Paolo
1922-1975 . . . . **CLC 20, 37; PC 17**
See also CA 93-96; 61-64; DLB 128, 177;
MTCW

Pasquini
See Silone, Ignazio

Pastan, Linda (Olenik)
1932- . . . . **CLC 27; DAM POET**
See also CA 61-64; CANR 18, 40; DLB 5

Pasternak, Boris (Leonidovich)
1890-1960 . . . . . . **CLC 7, 10, 18, 63; DA;**
DAB; DAC; DAM MST, NOV, POET;
PC 6; WLC
See also CA 127; 116; MTCW

Patchen, Kenneth
1911-1972 . . . **CLC 1, 2, 18; DAM POET**
See also CA 1-4R; 33-36R; CANR 3, 35;
DLB 16, 48; MTCW

Pater, Walter (Horatio)
1839-1894 . . . . **NCLC 7**
See also CDBLB 1832-1890; DLB 57, 156

Paterson, A(ndrew) B(arton)
1864-1941 . . . . **TCLC 32**
See also CA 155

Paterson, Katherine (Womeldorf)
1932- . . . . **CLC 12, 30**
See also AAYA 1; CA 21-24R; CANR 28;
CLR 7; DLB 52; JRDA; MAICYA;
MTCW; SATA 13, 53, 92

Patmore, Coventry Kersey Dighton
1823-1896 . . . . **NCLC 9**
See also DLB 35, 98

Paton, Alan (Stewart)
1903-1988 . . . . . . **CLC 4, 10, 25, 55; DA;**
DAB; DAC; DAM MST, NOV; WLC
See also CA 13-16; 125; CANR 22; CAP 1;
MTCW; SATA 11; SATA-Obit 56

Paton Walsh, Gillian 1937-
See Walsh, Jill Paton
See also CANR 38; JRDA; MAICYA;
SAAS 3; SATA 4, 72

Paulding, James Kirke 1778-1860 . . **NCLC 2**
See also DLB 3, 59, 74

Pinckney, Darryl 1953- . . . . CLC 76
See also BW 2; CA 143

Pindar 518B.C.-446B.C. . . . . CMLC 12
See also DLB 176

Pineda, Cecile 1942- . . . . CLC 39
See also CA 118

Pinero, Arthur Wing
1855-1934 . . . . . TCLC 32; DAM DRAM
See also CA 110; 153; DLB 10

Pinero, Miguel (Antonio Gomez)
1946-1988 . . . . CLC 4, 55
See also CA 61-64; 125; CANR 29; HW

Pinget, Robert 1919- . . . . CLC 7, 13, 37
See also CA 85-88; DLB 83

Pink Floyd
See Barrett, (Roger) Syd; Gilmour, David;
Mason, Nick; Waters, Roger; Wright,
Rick

Pinkney, Edward 1802-1828 . . . . . NCLC 31

Pinkwater, Daniel Manus 1941- . . . . CLC 35
See also Pinkwater, Manus
See also AAYA 1; CA 29-32R; CANR 12,
38; CLR 4; JRDA; MAICYA; SAAS 3;
SATA 46, 76

Pinkwater, Manus
See Pinkwater, Daniel Manus
See also SATA 8

Pinsky, Robert
1940- . . CLC 9, 19, 38, 94; DAM POET
See also CA 29-32R; CAAS 4; DLBY 82

Pinta, Harold
See Pinter, Harold

Pinter, Harold
1930- . . . . . CLC 1, 3, 6, 9, 11, 15, 27, 58,
73; DA; DAB; DAC; DAM DRAM,
MST; WLC
See also CA 5-8R; CANR 33; CDBLB 1960
to Present; DLB 13; MTCW

Piozzi, Hester Lynch (Thrale)
1741-1821 . . . . NCLC 57
See also DLB 104, 142

Pirandello, Luigi
1867-1936 . . . . . . TCLC 4, 29; DA; DAB;
DAC; DAM DRAM, MST; DC 5;
SSC 22; WLC
See also CA 104; 153

Pirsig, Robert M(aynard)
1928- . . . . CLC 4, 6, 73; DAM POP
See also CA 53-56; CANR 42; MTCW;
SATA 39

Pisarev, Dmitry Ivanovich
1840-1868 . . . . NCLC 25

Pix, Mary (Griffith) 1666-1709 . . . . LC 8
See also DLB 80

Pixerecourt, Guilbert de
1773-1844 . . . . NCLC 39

Plaidy, Jean
See Hibbert, Eleanor Alice Burford

Planche, James Robinson
1796-1880 . . . . NCLC 42

Plant, Robert 1948- . . . . CLC 12

Plante, David (Robert)
1940- . . . . CLC 7, 23, 38; DAM NOV
See also CA 37-40R; CANR 12, 36;
DLBY 83; INT CANR-12; MTCW

Plath, Sylvia
1932-1963 . . . . . CLC 1, 2, 3, 5, 9, 11, 14,
17, 50, 51, 62; DA; DAB; DAC;
DAM MST, POET; PC 1; WLC
See also AAYA 13; CA 19-20; CANR 34;
CAP 2; CDALB 1941-1968; DLB 5, 6,
152; MTCW

Plato
428(?)B.C.-348(?)B.C. . . . . CMLC 8; DA;
DAB; DAC; DAM MST
See also DLB 176

Platonov, Andrei . . . . TCLC 14
See also Klimentov, Andrei Platonovich

Platt, Kin 1911- . . . . CLC 26
See also AAYA 11; CA 17-20R; CANR 11;
JRDA; SAAS 17; SATA 21, 86

Plautus c. 251B.C.-184B.C. . . . . DC 6

Plick et Plock
See Simenon, Georges (Jacques Christian)

Plimpton, George (Ames) 1927- . . . . . CLC 36
See also AITN 1; CA 21-24R; CANR 32;
MTCW; SATA 10

Plomer, William Charles Franklin
1903-1973 . . . . CLC 4, 8
See also CA 21-22; CANR 34; CAP 2;
DLB 20, 162; MTCW; SATA 24

Plowman, Piers
See Kavanagh, Patrick (Joseph)

Plum, J.
See Wodehouse, P(elham) G(renville)

Plumly, Stanley (Ross) 1939- . . . . . . CLC 33
See also CA 108; 110; DLB 5; INT 110

Plumpe, Friedrich Wilhelm
1888-1931 . . . . TCLC 53
See also CA 112

Poe, Edgar Allan
1809-1849 . . . . NCLC 1, 16, 55; DA;
DAB; DAC; DAM MST, POET; PC 1;
SSC 1, 22; WLC
See also AAYA 14; CDALB 1640-1865;
DLB 3, 59, 73, 74; SATA 23

Poet of Titchfield Street, The
See Pound, Ezra (Weston Loomis)

Pohl, Frederik 1919- . . . . . CLC 18; SSC 25
See also CA 61-64; CAAS 1; CANR 11, 37;
DLB 8; INT CANR-11; MTCW;
SATA 24

Poirier, Louis 1910-
See Gracq, Julien
See also CA 122; 126

Poitier, Sidney 1927- . . . . CLC 26
See also BW 1; CA 117

Polanski, Roman 1933- . . . . CLC 16
See also CA 77-80

Poliakoff, Stephen 1952- . . . . CLC 38
See also CA 106; DLB 13

Police, The
See Copeland, Stewart (Armstrong);
Summers, Andrew James; Sumner,
Gordon Matthew

Polidori, John William
1795-1821 . . . . NCLC 51
See also DLB 116

Pollitt, Katha 1949- . . . . CLC 28
See also CA 120; 122; MTCW

Pollock, (Mary) Sharon
1936- . . . . . CLC 50; DAC; DAM DRAM,
MST
See also CA 141; DLB 60

Polo, Marco 1254-1324 . . . . CMLC 15

Polonsky, Abraham (Lincoln)
1910- . . . . CLC 92
See also CA 104; DLB 26; INT 104

Polybius c. 200B.C.-c. 118B.C. . . . . CMLC 17
See also DLB 176

Pomerance, Bernard
1940- . . . . CLC 13; DAM DRAM
See also CA 101; CANR 49

Ponge, Francis (Jean Gaston Alfred)
1899-1988 . . . . . CLC 6, 18; DAM POET
See also CA 85-88; 126; CANR 40

Pontoppidan, Henrik 1857-1943 . . . TCLC 29

Poole, Josephine . . . . CLC 17
See also Helyar, Jane Penelope Josephine
See also SAAS 2; SATA 5

Popa, Vasko 1922-1991 . . . . CLC 19
See also CA 112; 148

Pope, Alexander
1688-1744 . . . . . . LC 3; DA; DAB; DAC;
DAM MST, POET; WLC
See also CDBLB 1660-1789; DLB 95, 101

Porter, Connie (Rose) 1959(?)- . . . . . CLC 70
See also BW 2; CA 142; SATA 81

Porter, Gene(va Grace) Stratton
1863(?)-1924 . . . . TCLC 21
See also CA 112

Porter, Katherine Anne
1890-1980 . . . . . . CLC 1, 3, 7, 10, 13, 15,
27; DA; DAB; DAC; DAM MST, NOV;
SSC 4
See also AITN 2; CA 1-4R; 101; CANR 1;
DLB 4, 9, 102; DLBD 12; DLBY 80;
MTCW; SATA 39; SATA-Obit 23

Porter, Peter (Neville Frederick)
1929- . . . . CLC 5, 13, 33
See also CA 85-88; DLB 40

Porter, William Sydney 1862-1910
See Henry, O.
See also CA 104; 131; CDALB 1865-1917;
DA; DAB; DAC; DAM MST; DLB 12,
78, 79; MTCW; YABC 2

Portillo (y Pacheco), Jose Lopez
See Lopez Portillo (y Pacheco), Jose

Post, Melville Davisson
1869-1930 . . . . TCLC 39
See also CA 110

Potok, Chaim
1929- . . . . CLC 2, 7, 14, 26; DAM NOV
See also AAYA 15; AITN 1, 2; CA 17-20R;
CANR 19, 35; DLB 28, 152;
INT CANR-19; MTCW; SATA 33

Potter, Beatrice
See Webb, (Martha) Beatrice (Potter)
See also MAICYA

Potter, Dennis (Christopher George)
1935-1994 . . . . CLC 58, 86
See also CA 107; 145; CANR 33; MTCW

Pound, Ezra (Weston Loomis)
1885-1972 ...... **CLC 1, 2, 3, 4, 5, 7, 10, 13, 18, 34, 48, 50; DA; DAB; DAC; DAM MST, POET; PC 4; WLC**
See also CA 5-8R; 37-40R; CANR 40; CDALB 1917-1929; DLB 4, 45, 63; MTCW

Povod, Reinaldo 1959-1994 .... **CLC 44**
See also CA 136; 146

Powell, Adam Clayton, Jr.
1908-1972 .... **CLC 89; BLC; DAM MULT**
See also BW 1; CA 102; 33-36R

Powell, Anthony (Dymoke)
1905- .... **CLC 1, 3, 7, 9, 10, 31**
See also CA 1-4R; CANR 1, 32; CDBLB 1945-1960; DLB 15; MTCW

Powell, Dawn 1897-1965 .... **CLC 66**
See also CA 5-8R

Powell, Padgett 1952-............ **CLC 34**
See also CA 126

Power, Susan..................... **CLC 91**

Powers, J(ames) F(arl)
1917- .... **CLC 1, 4, 8, 57; SSC 4**
See also CA 1-4R; CANR 2; DLB 130; MTCW

Powers, John J(ames) 1945-
See Powers, John R.
See also CA 69-72

Powers, John R................... **CLC 66**
See also Powers, John J(ames)

Powers, Richard (S.) 1957- .... **CLC 93**
See also CA 148

Pownall, David 1938-............. **CLC 10**
See also CA 89-92; CAAS 18; CANR 49; DLB 14

Powys, John Cowper
1872-1963 .... **CLC 7, 9, 15, 46**
See also CA 85-88; DLB 15; MTCW

Powys, T(heodore) F(rancis)
1875-1953 .... **TCLC 9**
See also CA 106; DLB 36, 162

Prager, Emily 1952-............. **CLC 56**

Pratt, E(dwin) J(ohn)
1883(?)-1964 .... **CLC 19; DAC; DAM POET**
See also CA 141; 93-96; DLB 92

Premchand..................... **TCLC 21**
See also Srivastava, Dhanpat Rai

Preussler, Otfried 1923-........... **CLC 17**
See also CA 77-80; SATA 24

Prevert, Jacques (Henri Marie)
1900-1977 .... **CLC 15**
See also CA 77-80; 69-72; CANR 29; MTCW; SATA-Obit 30

Prevost, Abbe (Antoine Francois)
1697-1763 .... **LC 1**

Price, (Edward) Reynolds
1933- .... **CLC 3, 6, 13, 43, 50, 63; DAM NOV; SSC 22**
See also CA 1-4R; CANR 1, 37, 57; DLB 2; INT CANR-37

Price, Richard 1949- .... **CLC 6, 12**
See also CA 49-52; CANR 3; DLBY 81

Prichard, Katharine Susannah
1883-1969 .... **CLC 46**
See also CA 11-12; CANR 33; CAP 1; MTCW; SATA 66

Priestley, J(ohn) B(oynton)
1894-1984 .... **CLC 2, 5, 9, 34; DAM DRAM, NOV**
See also CA 9-12R; 113; CANR 33; CDBLB 1914-1945; DLB 10, 34, 77, 100, 139; DLBY 84; MTCW

Prince 1958(?)-................... **CLC 35**

Prince, F(rank) T(empleton) 1912-.. **CLC 22**
See also CA 101; CANR 43; DLB 20

Prince Kropotkin
See Kropotkin, Peter (Alekseevich)

Prior, Matthew 1664-1721.......... **LC 4**
See also DLB 95

Pritchard, William H(arrison)
1932-...................... **CLC 34**
See also CA 65-68; CANR 23; DLB 111

Pritchett, V(ictor) S(awdon)
1900- .... **CLC 5, 13, 15, 41; DAM NOV; SSC 14**
See also CA 61-64; CANR 31; DLB 15, 139; MTCW

Private 19022
See Manning, Frederic

Probst, Mark 1925- .... **CLC 59**
See also CA 130

Prokosch, Frederic 1908-1989.... **CLC 4, 48**
See also CA 73-76; 128; DLB 48

Prophet, The
See Dreiser, Theodore (Herman Albert)

Prose, Francine 1947-............. **CLC 45**
See also CA 109; 112; CANR 46

Proudhon
See Cunha, Euclides (Rodrigues Pimenta) da

Proulx, E. Annie 1935- .... **CLC 81**

Proust, (Valentin-Louis-George-Eugene-) Marcel
1871-1922 .... **TCLC 7, 13, 33; DA; DAB; DAC; DAM MST, NOV; WLC**
See also CA 104; 120; DLB 65; MTCW

Prowler, Harley
See Masters, Edgar Lee

Prus, Boleslaw 1845-1912 .... **TCLC 48**

Pryor, Richard (Franklin Lenox Thomas)
1940-....................... **CLC 26**
See also CA 122

Przybyszewski, Stanislaw
1868-1927 .... **TCLC 36**
See also DLB 66

Pteleon
See Grieve, C(hristopher) M(urray)
See also DAM POET

Puckett, Lute
See Masters, Edgar Lee

Puig, Manuel
1932-1990 .... **CLC 3, 5, 10, 28, 65; DAM MULT; HLC**
See also CA 45-48; CANR 2, 32; DLB 113; HW; MTCW

Purdy, Al(fred Wellington)
1918- .... **CLC 3, 6, 14, 50; DAC; DAM MST, POET**
See also CA 81-84; CAAS 17; CANR 42; DLB 88

Purdy, James (Amos)
1923- .... **CLC 2, 4, 10, 28, 52**
See also CA 33-36R; CAAS 1; CANR 19, 51; DLB 2; INT CANR-19; MTCW

Pure, Simon
See Swinnerton, Frank Arthur

Pushkin, Alexander (Sergeyevich)
1799-1837 ..... **NCLC 3, 27; DA; DAB; DAC; DAM DRAM, MST, POET; PC 10; WLC**
See also SATA 61

P'u Sung-ling 1640-1715 .... **LC 3**

Putnam, Arthur Lee
See Alger, Horatio, Jr.

Puzo, Mario
1920- ..... **CLC 1, 2, 6, 36; DAM NOV, POP**
See also CA 65-68; CANR 4, 42; DLB 6; MTCW

Pygge, Edward
See Barnes, Julian (Patrick)

Pym, Barbara (Mary Crampton)
1913-1980 .... **CLC 13, 19, 37**
See also CA 13-14; 97-100; CANR 13, 34; CAP 1; DLB 14; DLBY 87; MTCW

Pynchon, Thomas (Ruggles, Jr.)
1937- ..... **CLC 2, 3, 6, 9, 11, 18, 33, 62, 72; DA; DAB; DAC; DAM MST, NOV, POP; SSC 14; WLC**
See also BEST 90:2; CA 17-20R; CANR 22, 46; DLB 2, 173; MTCW

Pythagoras
c. 570B.C.-c. 500B.C......... **CMLC 22**
See also DLB 176

Qian Zhongshu
See Ch'ien Chung-shu

Qroll
See Dagerman, Stig (Halvard)

Quarrington, Paul (Lewis) 1953-.... **CLC 65**
See also CA 129

Quasimodo, Salvatore 1901-1968 ... **CLC 10**
See also CA 13-16; 25-28R; CAP 1; DLB 114; MTCW

Quay, Stephen 1947- .... **CLC 95**

Quay, The Brothers
See Quay, Stephen; Quay, Timothy

Quay, Timothy 1947-............. **CLC 95**

Queen, Ellery.................. **CLC 3, 11**
See also Dannay, Frederic; Davidson, Avram; Lee, Manfred B(ennington); Marlowe, Stephen; Sturgeon, Theodore (Hamilton); Vance, John Holbrook

Queen, Ellery, Jr.
See Dannay, Frederic; Lee, Manfred B(ennington)

Queneau, Raymond
1903-1976 .... **CLC 2, 5, 10, 42**
See also CA 77-80; 69-72; CANR 32; DLB 72; MTCW

Quevedo, Francisco de 1580-1645.... **LC 23**

Quiller-Couch, Arthur Thomas
        1863-1944 . . . . **TCLC 53**
    See also CA 118; DLB 135, 153

Quin, Ann (Marie) 1936-1973 . . . . **CLC 6**
    See also CA 9-12R; 45-48; DLB 14

Quinn, Martin
    See Smith, Martin Cruz

Quinn, Peter 1947- . . . . **CLC 91**

Quinn, Simon
    See Smith, Martin Cruz

Quiroga, Horacio (Sylvestre)
        1878-1937 . . . . . **TCLC 20; DAM MULT;**
                                                                        HLC
    See also CA 117; 131; HW; MTCW

Quoirez, Francoise 1935- . . . . **CLC 9**
    See also Sagan, Francoise
    See also CA 49-52; CANR 6, 39; MTCW

Raabe, Wilhelm 1831-1910 . . . . **TCLC 45**
    See also DLB 129

Rabe, David (William)
        1940- . . . . . . **CLC 4, 8, 33; DAM DRAM**
    See also CA 85-88; CABS 3; DLB 7

Rabelais, Francois
        1483-1553 . . . . . . **LC 5; DA; DAB; DAC;**
                                                        DAM MST; WLC

Rabinovitch, Sholem 1859-1916
    See Aleichem, Sholom
    See also CA 104

Rachilde 1860-1953 . . . . **TCLC 67**
    See also DLB 123

Racine, Jean
        1639-1699 . . . . **LC 28; DAB; DAM MST**

Radcliffe, Ann (Ward)
        1764-1823 . . . . **NCLC 6, 55**
    See also DLB 39

Radiguet, Raymond 1903-1923 . . . . **TCLC 29**
    See also DLB 65

Radnoti, Miklos 1909-1944 . . . . **TCLC 16**
    See also CA 118

Rado, James 1939- . . . . **CLC 17**
    See also CA 105

Radvanyi, Netty 1900-1983
    See Seghers, Anna
    See also CA 85-88; 110

Rae, Ben
    See Griffiths, Trevor

Raeburn, John (Hay) 1941- . . . . **CLC 34**
    See also CA 57-60

Ragni, Gerome 1942-1991 . . . . **CLC 17**
    See also CA 105; 134

Rahv, Philip 1908-1973 . . . . **CLC 24**
    See also Greenberg, Ivan
    See also DLB 137

Raine, Craig 1944- . . . . **CLC 32**
    See also CA 108; CANR 29, 51; DLB 40

Raine, Kathleen (Jessie) 1908- . . . **CLC 7, 45**
    See also CA 85-88; CANR 46; DLB 20;
        MTCW

Rainis, Janis 1865-1929 . . . . **TCLC 29**

Rakosi, Carl . . . . **CLC 47**
    See also Rawley, Callman
    See also CAAS 5

Raleigh, Richard
    See Lovecraft, H(oward) P(hillips)

Raleigh, Sir Walter 1554(?)-1618 . . . . **LC 31**
    See also CDBLB Before 1660; DLB 172

Rallentando, H. P.
    See Sayers, Dorothy L(eigh)

Ramal, Walter
    See de la Mare, Walter (John)

Ramon, Juan
    See Jimenez (Mantecon), Juan Ramon

Ramos, Graciliano 1892-1953 . . . . . **TCLC 32**

Rampersad, Arnold 1941- . . . . **CLC 44**
    See also BW 2; CA 127; 133; DLB 111;
        INT 133

Rampling, Anne
    See Rice, Anne

Ramsay, Allan 1684(?)-1758 . . . . **LC 29**
    See also DLB 95

Ramuz, Charles-Ferdinand
        1878-1947 . . . . **TCLC 33**

Rand, Ayn
        1905-1982 . . . . . . **CLC 3, 30, 44, 79; DA;**
            DAC; DAM MST, NOV, POP; WLC
    See also AAYA 10; CA 13-16R; 105;
        CANR 27; MTCW

Randall, Dudley (Felker)
        1914- . . . . . . **CLC 1; BLC; DAM MULT**
    See also BW 1; CA 25-28R; CANR 23;
        DLB 41

Randall, Robert
    See Silverberg, Robert

Ranger, Ken
    See Creasey, John

Ransom, John Crowe
        1888-1974 . . . . **CLC 2, 4, 5, 11, 24;**
                                                                    DAM POET
    See also CA 5-8R; 49-52; CANR 6, 34;
        DLB 45, 63; MTCW

Rao, Raja 1909- . . . **CLC 25, 56; DAM NOV**
    See also CA 73-76; CANR 51; MTCW

Raphael, Frederic (Michael)
        1931- . . . . **CLC 2, 14**
    See also CA 1-4R; CANR 1; DLB 14

Ratcliffe, James P.
    See Mencken, H(enry) L(ouis)

Rathbone, Julian 1935- . . . . **CLC 41**
    See also CA 101; CANR 34

Rattigan, Terence (Mervyn)
        1911-1977 . . . . **CLC 7; DAM DRAM**
    See also CA 85-88; 73-76;
        CDBLB 1945-1960; DLB 13; MTCW

Ratushinskaya, Irina 1954- . . . . **CLC 54**
    See also CA 129

Raven, Simon (Arthur Noel)
        1927- . . . . **CLC 14**
    See also CA 81-84

Rawley, Callman 1903-
    See Rakosi, Carl
    See also CA 21-24R; CANR 12, 32

Rawlings, Marjorie Kinnan
        1896-1953 . . . . **TCLC 4**
    See also AAYA 20; CA 104; 137; DLB 9,
        22, 102; JRDA; MAICYA; YABC 1

Ray, Satyajit
        1921-1992 . . . **CLC 16, 76; DAM MULT**
    See also CA 114; 137

Read, Herbert Edward 1893-1968 . . . . **CLC 4**
    See also CA 85-88; 25-28R; DLB 20, 149

Read, Piers Paul 1941- . . . . . . **CLC 4, 10, 25**
    See also CA 21-24R; CANR 38; DLB 14;
        SATA 21

Reade, Charles 1814-1884 . . . . **NCLC 2**
    See also DLB 21

Reade, Hamish
    See Gray, Simon (James Holliday)

Reading, Peter 1946- . . . . **CLC 47**
    See also CA 103; CANR 46; DLB 40

Reaney, James
        1926- . . . . . . **CLC 13; DAC; DAM MST**
    See also CA 41-44R; CAAS 15; CANR 42;
        DLB 68; SATA 43

Rebreanu, Liviu 1885-1944 . . . . **TCLC 28**

Rechy, John (Francisco)
        1934- . . . . **CLC 1, 7, 14, 18;**
                                                            DAM MULT; HLC
    See also CA 5-8R; CAAS 4; CANR 6, 32;
        DLB 122; DLBY 82; HW; INT CANR-6

Redcam, Tom 1870-1933 . . . . **TCLC 25**

Reddin, Keith . . . . **CLC 67**

Redgrove, Peter (William)
        1932- . . . . **CLC 6, 41**
    See also CA 1-4R; CANR 3, 39; DLB 40

Redmon, Anne . . . . **CLC 22**
    See also Nightingale, Anne Redmon
    See also DLBY 86

Reed, Eliot
    See Ambler, Eric

Reed, Ishmael
        1938- . . . . **CLC 2, 3, 5, 6, 13, 32, 60;**
                                                        BLC; DAM MULT
    See also BW 2; CA 21-24R; CANR 25, 48;
        DLB 2, 5, 33, 169; DLBD 8; MTCW

Reed, John (Silas) 1887-1920 . . . . . . **TCLC 9**
    See also CA 106

Reed, Lou . . . . **CLC 21**
    See also Firbank, Louis

Reeve, Clara 1729-1807 . . . . **NCLC 19**
    See also DLB 39

Reich, Wilhelm 1897-1957 . . . . **TCLC 57**

Reid, Christopher (John) 1949- . . . . . **CLC 33**
    See also CA 140; DLB 40

Reid, Desmond
    See Moorcock, Michael (John)

Reid Banks, Lynne 1929-
    See Banks, Lynne Reid
    See also CA 1-4R; CANR 6, 22, 38;
        CLR 24; JRDA; MAICYA; SATA 22, 75

Reilly, William K.
    See Creasey, John

Reiner, Max
    See Caldwell, (Janet Miriam) Taylor
        (Holland)

Reis, Ricardo
    See Pessoa, Fernando (Antonio Nogueira)

Remarque, Erich Maria
        1898-1970 . . . . **CLC 21; DA; DAB; DAC;**
                                                        DAM MST, NOV
    See also CA 77-80; 29-32R; DLB 56;
        MTCW

Robbins, Thomas Eugene   1936-
See Robbins, Tom
See also CA 81-84; CANR 29; DAM NOV,
POP; MTCW

Robbins, Tom. . . . . **CLC 9, 32, 64**
See also Robbins, Thomas Eugene
See also BEST 90:3; DLBY 80

Robbins, Trina   1938-. . . . . **CLC 21**
See also CA 128

Roberts, Charles G(eorge) D(ouglas)
1860-1943 . . . . **TCLC 8**
See also CA 105; CLR 33; DLB 92;
SATA 88; SATA-Brief 29

Roberts, Elizabeth Madox
1886-1941 . . . . **TCLC 68**
See also CA 111; DLB 9, 54, 102;
SATA 33; SATA-Brief 27

Roberts, Kate   1891-1985 . . . . **CLC 15**
See also CA 107; 116

Roberts, Keith (John Kingston)
1935- . . . . **CLC 14**
See also CA 25-28R; CANR 46

Roberts, Kenneth (Lewis)
1885-1957 . . . . **TCLC 23**
See also CA 109; DLB 9

Roberts, Michele (B.)   1949-. . . . . **CLC 48**
See also CA 115

Robertson, Ellis
See Ellison, Harlan (Jay); Silverberg, Robert

Robertson, Thomas William
1829-1871 . . . . **NCLC 35; DAM DRAM**

Robinson, Edwin Arlington
1869-1935 . . . . **TCLC 5; DA; DAC;
DAM MST, POET; PC 1**
See also CA 104; 133; CDALB 1865-1917;
DLB 54; MTCW

Robinson, Henry Crabb
1775-1867 . . . . **NCLC 15**
See also DLB 107

Robinson, Jill   1936-. . . . . **CLC 10**
See also CA 102; INT 102

Robinson, Kim Stanley   1952- . . . . . . **CLC 34**
See also CA 126

Robinson, Lloyd
See Silverberg, Robert

Robinson, Marilynne   1944-. . . . . **CLC 25**
See also CA 116

Robinson, Smokey. . . . . **CLC 21**
See also Robinson, William, Jr.

Robinson, William, Jr.   1940-
See Robinson, Smokey
See also CA 116

Robison, Mary   1949-. . . . . **CLC 42, 98**
See also CA 113; 116; DLB 130; INT 116

Rod, Edouard   1857-1910 . . . . **TCLC 52**

Roddenberry, Eugene Wesley   1921-1991
See Roddenberry, Gene
See also CA 110; 135; CANR 37; SATA 45;
SATA-Obit 69

Roddenberry, Gene. . . . . **CLC 17**
See also Roddenberry, Eugene Wesley
See also AAYA 5; SATA-Obit 69

Rodgers, Mary   1931-. . . . . **CLC 12**
See also CA 49-52; CANR 8, 55; CLR 20;
INT CANR-8; JRDA; MAICYA;
SATA 8

Rodgers, W(illiam) R(obert)
1909-1969 . . . . **CLC 7**
See also CA 85-88; DLB 20

Rodman, Eric
See Silverberg, Robert

Rodman, Howard   1920(?)-1985 . . . . . **CLC 65**
See also CA 118

Rodman, Maia
See Wojciechowska, Maia (Teresa)

Rodriguez, Claudio   1934-. . . . . **CLC 10**
See also DLB 134

Roelvaag, O(le) E(dvart)
1876-1931 . . . . **TCLC 17**
See also CA 117; DLB 9

Roethke, Theodore (Huebner)
1908-1963 . . . . . . **CLC 1, 3, 8, 11, 19, 46;
DAM POET; PC 15**
See also CA 81-84; CABS 2;
CDALB 1941-1968; DLB 5; MTCW

Rogers, Thomas Hunton   1927- . . . . . **CLC 57**
See also CA 89-92; INT 89-92

Rogers, Will(iam Penn Adair)
1879-1935 . . . . . . **TCLC 8; DAM MULT**
See also CA 105; 144; DLB 11; NNAL

Rogin, Gilbert   1929-. . . . . **CLC 18**
See also CA 65-68; CANR 15

Rohan, Koda . . . . **TCLC 22**
See also Koda Shigeyuki

Rohmer, Eric. **CLC 16**
See also Scherer, Jean-Marie Maurice

Rohmer, Sax . . . . **TCLC 28**
See also Ward, Arthur Henry Sarsfield
See also DLB 70

Roiphe, Anne (Richardson)
1935- . . . . **CLC 3, 9**
See also CA 89-92; CANR 45; DLBY 80;
INT 89-92

Rojas, Fernando de   1465-1541 . . . . . . **LC 23**

**Rolfe, Frederick (William Serafino Austin
Lewis Mary)**   1860-1913. . . . . . **TCLC 12**
See also CA 107; DLB 34, 156

Rolland, Romain   1866-1944. . . . . . . **TCLC 23**
See also CA 118; DLB 65

Rolle, Richard   c. 1300-c. 1349 . . . **CMLC 21**
See also DLB 146

Rolvaag, O(le) E(dvart)
See Roelvaag, O(le) E(dvart)

Romain Arnaud, Saint
See Aragon, Louis

Romains, Jules   1885-1972 . . . . **CLC 7**
See also CA 85-88; CANR 34; DLB 65;
MTCW

Romero, Jose Ruben   1890-1952 . . . **TCLC 14**
See also CA 114; 131; HW

Ronsard, Pierre de
1524-1585 . . . . **LC 6; PC 11**

Rooke, Leon
1934- . . . . **CLC 25, 34; DAM POP**
See also CA 25-28R; CANR 23, 53

Roosevelt, Theodore   1858-1919. . . . **TCLC 69**
See also CA 115; DLB 47

Roper, William   1498-1578 . . . . **LC 10**

Roquelaure, A. N.
See Rice, Anne

Rosa, Joao Guimaraes   1908-1967. . . **CLC 23**
See also CA 89-92; DLB 113

Rose, Wendy
1948- . . . . **CLC 85; DAM MULT; PC 13**
See also CA 53-56; CANR 5, 51; DLB 175;
NNAL; SATA 12

Rosen, Richard (Dean)   1949-. . . . . . . **CLC 39**
See also CA 77-80; INT CANR-30

Rosenberg, Isaac   1890-1918. . . . . . **TCLC 12**
See also CA 107; DLB 20

Rosenblatt, Joe . . . . **CLC 15**
See also Rosenblatt, Joseph

Rosenblatt, Joseph   1933-
See Rosenblatt, Joe
See also CA 89-92; INT 89-92

Rosenfeld, Samuel   1896-1963
See Tzara, Tristan
See also CA 89-92

Rosenstock, Sami
See Tzara, Tristan

Rosenstock, Samuel
See Tzara, Tristan

Rosenthal, M(acha) L(ouis)
1917-1996 . . . . **CLC 28**
See also CA 1-4R; 152; CAAS 6; CANR 4,
51; DLB 5; SATA 59

Ross, Barnaby
See Dannay, Frederic

Ross, Bernard L.
See Follett, Ken(neth Martin)

Ross, J. H.
See Lawrence, T(homas) E(dward)

Ross, Martin
See Martin, Violet Florence
See also DLB 135

Ross, (James) Sinclair
1908- . . . . . . **CLC 13; DAC; DAM MST;
SSC 24**
See also CA 73-76; DLB 88

Rossetti, Christina (Georgina)
1830-1894 . . . . . **NCLC 2, 50; DA; DAB;
DAC; DAM MST, POET; PC 7; WLC**
See also DLB 35, 163; MAICYA; SATA 20

Rossetti, Dante Gabriel
1828-1882 . . . . **NCLC 4; DA; DAB;
DAC; DAM MST, POET; WLC**
See also CDBLB 1832-1890; DLB 35

Rossner, Judith (Perelman)
1935- . . . . **CLC 6, 9, 29**
See also AITN 2; BEST 90:3; CA 17-20R;
CANR 18, 51; DLB 6; INT CANR-18;
MTCW

Rostand, Edmond (Eugene Alexis)
1868-1918 . . . . . . **TCLC 6, 37; DA; DAB;
DAC; DAM DRAM, MST**
See also CA 104; 126; MTCW

Roth, Henry   1906-1995 . . . . **CLC 2, 6, 11**
See also CA 11-12; 149; CANR 38; CAP 1;
DLB 28; MTCW

Salinas, Luis Omar
  1937- ..... **CLC 90; DAM MULT; HLC**
  See also CA 131; DLB 82; HW

Salinas (y Serrano), Pedro
  1891(?)-1951 .... **TCLC 17**
  See also CA 117; DLB 134

Salinger, J(erome) D(avid)
  1919- ...... **CLC 1, 3, 8, 12, 55, 56; DA;**
    DAB; DAC; DAM MST, NOV, POP;
    SSC 2; WLC
  See also AAYA 2; CA 5-8R;
    CDALB 1941-1968; CLR 18; DLB 2, 102,
    173; MAICYA; MTCW; SATA 67

Salisbury, John
  See Caute, David

Salter, James 1925- .... **CLC 7, 52, 59**
  See also CA 73-76; DLB 130

Saltus, Edgar (Everton)
  1855-1921 .... **TCLC 8**
  See also CA 105

Saltykov, Mikhail Evgrafovich
  1826-1889 .... **NCLC 16**

Samarakis, Antonis 1919- .... **CLC 5**
  See also CA 25-28R; CAAS 16; CANR 36

Sanchez, Florencio 1875-1910 ..... **TCLC 37**
  See also CA 153; HW

Sanchez, Luis Rafael 1936- .... **CLC 23**
  See also CA 128; DLB 145; HW

Sanchez, Sonia
  1934- ...... **CLC 5; BLC; DAM MULT;**
    PC 9
  See also BW 2; CA 33-36R; CANR 24, 49;
    CLR 18; DLB 41; DLBD 8; MAICYA;
    MTCW; SATA 22

Sand, George
  1804-1876 .... **NCLC 2, 42, 57; DA;**
    DAB; DAC; DAM MST, NOV; WLC
  See also DLB 119

Sandburg, Carl (August)
  1878-1967 .... **CLC 1, 4, 10, 15, 35; DA;**
    DAB; DAC; DAM MST, POET; PC 2;
    WLC
  See also CA 5-8R; 25-28R; CANR 35;
    CDALB 1865-1917; DLB 17, 54;
    MAICYA; MTCW; SATA 8

Sandburg, Charles
  See Sandburg, Carl (August)

Sandburg, Charles A.
  See Sandburg, Carl (August)

Sanders, (James) Ed(ward) 1939- ... **CLC 53**
  See also CA 13-16R; CAAS 21; CANR 13,
    44; DLB 16

Sanders, Lawrence
  1920- .... **CLC 41; DAM POP**
  See also BEST 89:4; CA 81-84; CANR 33;
    MTCW

Sanders, Noah
  See Blount, Roy (Alton), Jr.

Sanders, Winston P.
  See Anderson, Poul (William)

Sandoz, Mari(e Susette)
  1896-1966 .... **CLC 28**
  See also CA 1-4R; 25-28R; CANR 17;
    DLB 9; MTCW; SATA 5

Saner, Reg(inald Anthony) 1931- .... **CLC 9**
  See also CA 65-68

Sannazaro, Jacopo 1456(?)-1530 ...... **LC 8**

Sansom, William
  1912-1976 ...... **CLC 2, 6; DAM NOV;**
    SSC 21
  See also CA 5-8R; 65-68; CANR 42;
    DLB 139; MTCW

Santayana, George 1863-1952 ..... **TCLC 40**
  See also CA 115; DLB 54, 71; DLBD 13

Santiago, Danny .... **CLC 33**
  See also James, Daniel (Lewis)
  See also DLB 122

Santmyer, Helen Hoover
  1895-1986 .... **CLC 33**
  See also CA 1-4R; 118; CANR 15, 33;
    DLBY 84; MTCW

Santos, Bienvenido N(uqui)
  1911-1996 ...... **CLC 22; DAM MULT**
  See also CA 101; 151; CANR 19, 46

Sapper .... **TCLC 44**
  See also McNeile, Herman Cyril

Sapphire 1950- .... **CLC 99**

Sappho
  fl. 6th cent. B.C.- .... **CMLC 3;**
    DAM POET; PC 5
  See also DLB 176

Sarduy, Severo 1937-1993 .... **CLC 6, 97**
  See also CA 89-92; 142; DLB 113; HW

Sargeson, Frank 1903-1982 .... **CLC 31**
  See also CA 25-28R; 106; CANR 38

Sarmiento, Felix Ruben Garcia
  See Dario, Ruben

Saroyan, William
  1908-1981 ..... **CLC 1, 8, 10, 29, 34, 56;**
    DA; DAB; DAC; DAM DRAM, MST,
    NOV; SSC 21; WLC
  See also CA 5-8R; 103; CANR 30; DLB 7,
    9, 86; DLBY 81; MTCW; SATA 23;
    SATA-Obit 24

Sarraute, Nathalie
  1900- .... **CLC 1, 2, 4, 8, 10, 31, 80**
  See also CA 9-12R; CANR 23; DLB 83;
    MTCW

Sarton, (Eleanor) May
  1912-1995 .... **CLC 4, 14, 49, 91;**
    DAM POET
  See also CA 1-4R; 149; CANR 1, 34, 55;
    DLB 48; DLBY 81; INT CANR-34;
    MTCW; SATA 36; SATA-Obit 86

Sartre, Jean-Paul
  1905-1980 .... **CLC 1, 4, 7, 9, 13, 18, 24,**
    44, 50, 52; DA; DAB; DAC;
    DAM DRAM, MST, NOV; DC 3; WLC
  See also CA 9-12R; 97-100; CANR 21;
    DLB 72; MTCW

Sassoon, Siegfried (Lorraine)
  1886-1967 .... **CLC 36; DAB;**
    DAM MST, NOV, POET; PC 12
  See also CA 104; 25-28R; CANR 36;
    DLB 20; MTCW

Satterfield, Charles
  See Pohl, Frederik

Saul, John (W. III)
  1942- ...... **CLC 46; DAM NOV, POP**
  See also AAYA 10; BEST 90:4; CA 81-84;
    CANR 16, 40

Saunders, Caleb
  See Heinlein, Robert A(nson)

Saura (Atares), Carlos 1932- .... **CLC 20**
  See also CA 114; 131; HW

Sauser-Hall, Frederic 1887-1961.... **CLC 18**
  See also Cendrars, Blaise
  See also CA 102; 93-96; CANR 36; MTCW

Saussure, Ferdinand de
  1857-1913 .... **TCLC 49**

Savage, Catharine
  See Brosman, Catharine Savage

Savage, Thomas 1915- .... **CLC 40**
  See also CA 126; 132; CAAS 15; INT 132

Savan, Glenn 19(?)- .... **CLC 50**

Sayers, Dorothy L(eigh)
  1893-1957 ..... **TCLC 2, 15; DAM POP**
  See also CA 104; 119; CDBLB 1914-1945;
    DLB 10, 36, 77, 100; MTCW

Sayers, Valerie 1952- .... **CLC 50**
  See also CA 134

Sayles, John (Thomas)
  1950- .... **CLC 7, 10, 14**
  See also CA 57-60; CANR 41; DLB 44

Scammell, Michael 1935- .... **CLC 34**
  See also CA 156

Scannell, Vernon 1922- .... **CLC 49**
  See also CA 5-8R; CANR 8, 24, 57;
    DLB 27; SATA 59

Scarlett, Susan
  See Streatfeild, (Mary) Noel

Schaeffer, Susan Fromberg
  1941- .... **CLC 6, 11, 22**
  See also CA 49-52; CANR 18; DLB 28;
    MTCW; SATA 22

Schary, Jill
  See Robinson, Jill

Schell, Jonathan 1943- .... **CLC 35**
  See also CA 73-76; CANR 12

Schelling, Friedrich Wilhelm Joseph von
  1775-1854 .... **NCLC 30**
  See also DLB 90

Schendel, Arthur van 1874-1946 ... **TCLC 56**

Scherer, Jean-Marie Maurice 1920-
  See Rohmer, Eric
  See also CA 110

Schevill, James (Erwin) 1920- .... **CLC 7**
  See also CA 5-8R; CAAS 12

Schiller, Friedrich
  1759-1805 .... **NCLC 39; DAM DRAM**
  See also DLB 94

Schisgal, Murray (Joseph) 1926- ..... **CLC 6**
  See also CA 21-24R; CANR 48

Schlee, Ann 1934- .... **CLC 35**
  See also CA 101; CANR 29; SATA 44;
    SATA-Brief 36

Schlegel, August Wilhelm von
  1767-1845 .... **NCLC 15**
  See also DLB 94

Schlegel, Friedrich 1772-1829 .... **NCLC 45**
  See also DLB 90

Schlegel, Johann Elias (von)
  1719(?)-1749 .... **LC 5**

Schlesinger, Arthur M(eier), Jr.
1917- .... CLC 84
See also AITN 1; CA 1-4R; CANR 1, 28;
DLB 17; INT CANR-28; MTCW;
SATA 61

Schmidt, Arno (Otto) 1914-1979.... CLC 56
See also CA 128; 109; DLB 69

Schmitz, Aron Hector 1861-1928
See Svevo, Italo
See also CA 104; 122; MTCW

Schnackenberg, Gjertrud 1953-..... CLC 40
See also CA 116; DLB 120

Schneider, Leonard Alfred 1925-1966
See Bruce, Lenny
See also CA 89-92

Schnitzler, Arthur
1862-1931 .... TCLC 4; SSC 15
See also CA 104; DLB 81, 118

Schopenhauer, Arthur
1788-1860 .... NCLC 51
See also DLB 90

Schor, Sandra (M.) 1932(?)-1990 ... CLC 65
See also CA 132

Schorer, Mark 1908-1977 .... CLC 9
See also CA 5-8R; 73-76; CANR 7;
DLB 103

Schrader, Paul (Joseph) 1946-...... CLC 26
See also CA 37-40R; CANR 41; DLB 44

Schreiner, Olive (Emilie Albertina)
1855-1920 .... TCLC 9
See also CA 105; DLB 18, 156

Schulberg, Budd (Wilson)
1914- .... CLC 7, 48
See also CA 25-28R; CANR 19; DLB 6, 26,
28; DLBY 81

Schulz, Bruno
1892-1942 .... TCLC 5, 51; SSC 13
See also CA 115; 123

Schulz, Charles M(onroe) 1922- .... CLC 12
See also CA 9-12R; CANR 6;
INT CANR-6; SATA 10

Schumacher, E(rnst) F(riedrich)
1911-1977 .... CLC 80
See also CA 81-84; 73-76; CANR 34

Schuyler, James Marcus
1923-1991 ..... CLC 5, 23; DAM POET
See also CA 101; 134; DLB 5, 169; INT 101

Schwartz, Delmore (David)
1913-1966 ... CLC 2, 4, 10, 45, 87; PC 8
See also CA 17-18; 25-28R; CANR 35;
CAP 2; DLB 28, 48; MTCW

Schwartz, Ernst
See Ozu, Yasujiro

Schwartz, John Burnham 1965- .... CLC 59
See also CA 132

Schwartz, Lynne Sharon 1939-..... CLC 31
See also CA 103; CANR 44

Schwartz, Muriel A.
See Eliot, T(homas) S(tearns)

Schwarz-Bart, Andre 1928-....... CLC 2, 4
See also CA 89-92

Schwarz-Bart, Simone 1938-........ CLC 7
See also BW 2; CA 97-100

Schwob, (Mayer Andre) Marcel
1867-1905 .... TCLC 20
See also CA 117; DLB 123

Sciascia, Leonardo
1921-1989 .... CLC 8, 9, 41
See also CA 85-88; 130; CANR 35;
DLB 177; MTCW

Scoppettone, Sandra 1936-........ CLC 26
See also AAYA 11; CA 5-8R; CANR 41;
SATA 9, 92

Scorsese, Martin 1942- .... CLC 20, 89
See also CA 110; 114; CANR 46

Scotland, Jay
See Jakes, John (William)

Scott, Duncan Campbell
1862-1947 .... TCLC 6; DAC
See also CA 104; 153; DLB 92

Scott, Evelyn 1893-1963.......... CLC 43
See also CA 104; 112; DLB 9, 48

Scott, F(rancis) R(eginald)
1899-1985 .... CLC 22
See also CA 101; 114; DLB 88; INT 101

Scott, Frank
See Scott, F(rancis) R(eginald)

Scott, Joanna 1960- .... CLC 50
See also CA 126; CANR 53

Scott, Paul (Mark) 1920-1978.... CLC 9, 60
See also CA 81-84; 77-80; CANR 33;
DLB 14; MTCW

Scott, Walter
1771-1832 .... NCLC 15; DA; DAB;
DAC; DAM MST, NOV, POET; PC 13;
WLC
See also CDBLB 1789-1832; DLB 93, 107,
116, 144, 159; YABC 2

Scribe, (Augustin) Eugene
1791-1861 .... NCLC 16; DAM DRAM;
DC 5

Scrum, R.
See Crumb, R(obert)

Scudery, Madeleine de 1607-1701..... LC 2

Scum
See Crumb, R(obert)

Scumbag, Little Bobby
See Crumb, R(obert)

Seabrook, John
See Hubbard, L(afayette) Ron(ald)

Sealy, I. Allan 1951- .... CLC 55

Search, Alexander
See Pessoa, Fernando (Antonio Nogueira)

Sebastian, Lee
See Silverberg, Robert

Sebastian Owl
See Thompson, Hunter S(tockton)

Sebestyen, Ouida 1924-........... CLC 30
See also AAYA 8; CA 107; CANR 40;
CLR 17; JRDA; MAICYA; SAAS 10;
SATA 39

Secundus, H. Scriblerus
See Fielding, Henry

Sedges, John
See Buck, Pearl S(ydenstricker)

Sedgwick, Catharine Maria
1789-1867 .... NCLC 19
See also DLB 1, 74

Seelye, John 1931-................ CLC 7

Seferiades, Giorgos Stylianou 1900-1971
See Seferis, George
See also CA 5-8R; 33-36R; CANR 5, 36;
MTCW

Seferis, George .... CLC 5, 11
See also Seferiades, Giorgos Stylianou

Segal, Erich (Wolf)
1937- .... CLC 3, 10; DAM POP
See also BEST 89:1; CA 25-28R; CANR 20,
36; DLBY 86; INT CANR-20; MTCW

Seger, Bob 1945-................. CLC 35

Seghers, Anna .... CLC 7
See also Radvanyi, Netty
See also DLB 69

Seidel, Frederick (Lewis) 1936-..... CLC 18
See also CA 13-16R; CANR 8; DLBY 84

Seifert, Jaroslav
1901-1986 .... CLC 34, 44, 93
See also CA 127; MTCW

Sei Shonagon c. 966-1017(?) ...... CMLC 6

Selby, Hubert, Jr.
1928- .... CLC 1, 2, 4, 8; SSC 20
See also CA 13-16R; CANR 33; DLB 2

Selzer, Richard 1928-............. CLC 74
See also CA 65-68; CANR 14

Sembene, Ousmane
See Ousmane, Sembene

Senancour, Etienne Pivert de
1770-1846 .... NCLC 16
See also DLB 119

Sender, Ramon (Jose)
1902-1982 .. CLC 8; DAM MULT; HLC
See also CA 5-8R; 105; CANR 8; HW;
MTCW

Seneca, Lucius Annaeus
4B.C.-65....... CMLC 6; DAM DRAM;
DC 5

Senghor, Leopold Sedar
1906- ..... CLC 54; BLC; DAM MULT,
POET
See also BW 2; CA 116; 125; CANR 47;
MTCW

Serling, (Edward) Rod(man)
1924-1975 .... CLC 30
See also AAYA 14; AITN 1; CA 65-68;
57-60; DLB 26

Serna, Ramon Gomez de la
See Gomez de la Serna, Ramon

Serpieres
See Guillevic, (Eugene)

Service, Robert
See Service, Robert W(illiam)
See also DAB; DLB 92

Service, Robert W(illiam)
1874(?)-1958 ...... TCLC 15; DA; DAC;
DAM MST, POET; WLC
See also Service, Robert
See also CA 115; 140; SATA 20

Seth, Vikram
1952- . . . . CLC 43, 90; DAM MULT
See also CA 121; 127; CANR 50; DLB 120;
INT 127

Seton, Cynthia Propper
1926-1982 . . . . CLC 27
See also CA 5-8R; 108; CANR 7

Seton, Ernest (Evan) Thompson
1860-1946 . . . . TCLC 31
See also CA 109; DLB 92; DLBD 13;
JRDA; SATA 18

Seton-Thompson, Ernest
See Seton, Ernest (Evan) Thompson

Settle, Mary Lee 1918- . . . . CLC 19, 61
See also CA 89-92; CAAS 1; CANR 44;
DLB 6; INT 89-92

Seuphor, Michel
See Arp, Jean

Sevigne, Marie (de Rabutin-Chantal) Marquise
de 1626-1696 . . . . LC 11

Sexton, Anne (Harvey)
1928-1974 . . . . CLC 2, 4, 6, 8, 10, 15, 53;
DA; DAB; DAC; DAM MST, POET;
PC 2; WLC
See also CA 1-4R; 53-56; CABS 2;
CANR 3, 36; CDALB 1941-1968; DLB 5,
169; MTCW; SATA 10

Shaara, Michael (Joseph, Jr.)
1929-1988 . . . . CLC 15; DAM POP
See also AITN 1; CA 102; 125; CANR 52;
DLBY 83

Shackleton, C. C.
See Aldiss, Brian W(ilson)

Shacochis, Bob . . . . CLC 39
See also Shacochis, Robert G.

Shacochis, Robert G. 1951-
See Shacochis, Bob
See also CA 119; 124; INT 124

Shaffer, Anthony (Joshua)
1926- . . . . CLC 19; DAM DRAM
See also CA 110; 116; DLB 13

Shaffer, Peter (Levin)
1926- . . . . . . CLC 5, 14, 18, 37, 60; DAB;
DAM DRAM, MST; DC 7
See also CA 25-28R; CANR 25, 47;
CDBLB 1960 to Present; DLB 13;
MTCW

Shakey, Bernard
See Young, Neil

Shalamov, Varlam (Tikhonovich)
1907(?)-1982 . . . . CLC 18
See also CA 129; 105

Shamlu, Ahmad 1925- . . . . CLC 10

Shammas, Anton 1951- . . . . CLC 55

Shange, Ntozake
1948- . . . . CLC 8, 25, 38, 74; BLC;
DAM DRAM, MULT; DC 3
See also AAYA 9; BW 2; CA 85-88;
CABS 3; CANR 27, 48; DLB 38; MTCW

Shanley, John Patrick 1950- . . . . CLC 75
See also CA 128; 133

Shapcott, Thomas W(illiam) 1935- . . CLC 38
See also CA 69-72; CANR 49

Shapiro, Jane . . . . CLC 76

Shapiro, Karl (Jay) 1913- . . CLC 4, 8, 15, 53
See also CA 1-4R; CAAS 6; CANR 1, 36;
DLB 48; MTCW

Sharp, William 1855-1905 . . . . TCLC 39
See also DLB 156

Sharpe, Thomas Ridley 1928-
See Sharpe, Tom
See also CA 114; 122; INT 122

Sharpe, Tom . . . . CLC 36
See also Sharpe, Thomas Ridley
See also DLB 14

Shaw, Bernard . . . . TCLC 45
See also Shaw, George Bernard
See also BW 1

Shaw, G. Bernard
See Shaw, George Bernard

Shaw, George Bernard
1856-1950 . . . TCLC 3, 9, 21; DA; DAB;
DAC; DAM DRAM, MST; WLC
See also Shaw, Bernard
See also CA 104; 128; CDBLB 1914-1945;
DLB 10, 57; MTCW

Shaw, Henry Wheeler
1818-1885 . . . . NCLC 15
See also DLB 11

Shaw, Irwin
1913-1984 . . . . CLC 7, 23, 34;
DAM DRAM, POP
See also AITN 1; CA 13-16R; 112;
CANR 21; CDALB 1941-1968; DLB 6,
102; DLBY 84; MTCW

Shaw, Robert 1927-1978 . . . . CLC 5
See also AITN 1; CA 1-4R; 81-84;
CANR 4; DLB 13, 14

Shaw, T. E.
See Lawrence, T(homas) E(dward)

Shawn, Wallace 1943- . . . . CLC 41
See also CA 112

Shea, Lisa 1953- . . . . CLC 86
See also CA 147

Sheed, Wilfrid (John Joseph)
1930- . . . . CLC 2, 4, 10, 53
See also CA 65-68; CANR 30; DLB 6;
MTCW

Sheldon, Alice Hastings Bradley
1915(?)-1987
See Tiptree, James, Jr.
See also CA 108; 122; CANR 34; INT 108;
MTCW

Sheldon, John
See Bloch, Robert (Albert)

Shelley, Mary Wollstonecraft (Godwin)
1797-1851 . . . . NCLC 14, 59; DA; DAB;
DAC; DAM MST, NOV; WLC
See also AAYA 20; CDBLB 1789-1832;
DLB 110, 116, 159; SATA 29

Shelley, Percy Bysshe
1792-1822 . . . . NCLC 18; DA; DAB;
DAC; DAM MST, POET; PC 14; WLC
See also CDBLB 1789-1832; DLB 96, 110,
158

Shepard, Jim 1956- . . . . CLC 36
See also CA 137; SATA 90

Shepard, Lucius 1947- . . . . CLC 34
See also CA 128; 141

Shepard, Sam
1943- . . . . CLC 4, 6, 17, 34, 41, 44;
DAM DRAM; DC 5
See also AAYA 1; CA 69-72; CABS 3;
CANR 22; DLB 7; MTCW

Shepherd, Michael
See Ludlum, Robert

Sherburne, Zoa (Morin) 1912- . . . . . . CLC 30
See also AAYA 13; CA 1-4R; CANR 3, 37;
MAICYA; SAAS 18; SATA 3

Sheridan, Frances 1724-1766 . . . . LC 7
See also DLB 39, 84

Sheridan, Richard Brinsley
1751-1816 . . . . NCLC 5; DA; DAB;
DAC; DAM DRAM, MST; DC 1; WLC
See also CDBLB 1660-1789; DLB 89

Sherman, Jonathan Marc . . . . CLC 55

Sherman, Martin 1941(?)- . . . . CLC 19
See also CA 116; 123

Sherwin, Judith Johnson 1936- . . . CLC 7, 15
See also CA 25-28R; CANR 34

Sherwood, Frances 1940- . . . . CLC 81
See also CA 146

Sherwood, Robert E(mmet)
1896-1955 . . . . . . TCLC 3; DAM DRAM
See also CA 104; 153; DLB 7, 26

Shestov, Lev 1866-1938 . . . . TCLC 56

Shevchenko, Taras 1814-1861 . . . . NCLC 54

Shiel, M(atthew) P(hipps)
1865-1947 . . . . TCLC 8
See also CA 106; DLB 153

Shields, Carol 1935- . . . . CLC 91; DAC
See also CA 81-84; CANR 51

Shields, David 1956- . . . . CLC 97
See also CA 124; CANR 48

Shiga, Naoya 1883-1971 . . . CLC 33; SSC 23
See also CA 101; 33-36R

Shilts, Randy 1951-1994 . . . . CLC 85
See also AAYA 19; CA 115; 127; 144;
CANR 45; INT 127

Shimazaki, Haruki 1872-1943
See Shimazaki Toson
See also CA 105; 134

Shimazaki Toson . . . . TCLC 5
See also Shimazaki, Haruki

Sholokhov, Mikhail (Aleksandrovich)
1905-1984 . . . . CLC 7, 15
See also CA 101; 112; MTCW;
SATA-Obit 36

Shone, Patric
See Hanley, James

Shreve, Susan Richards 1939- . . . . . . CLC 23
See also CA 49-52; CAAS 5; CANR 5, 38;
MAICYA; SATA 46; SATA-Brief 41

Shue, Larry
1946-1985 . . . . . . CLC 52; DAM DRAM
See also CA 145; 117

Shu-Jen, Chou 1881-1936
See Lu Hsun
See also CA 104

Shulman, Alix Kates 1932- . . . . . . CLC 2, 10
See also CA 29-32R; CANR 43; SATA 7

Shuster, Joe 1914- . . . . CLC 21

Slaughter, Carolyn 1946-......... **CLC 56**
See also CA 85-88

Slaughter, Frank G(ill) 1908- ...... **CLC 29**
See also AITN 2; CA 5-8R; CANR 5;
INT CANR-5

Slavitt, David R(ytman) 1935-.... **CLC 5, 14**
See also CA 21-24R; CAAS 3; CANR 41;
DLB 5, 6

Slesinger, Tess 1905-1945 .... **TCLC 10**
See also CA 107; DLB 102

Slessor, Kenneth 1901-1971....... **CLC 14**
See also CA 102; 89-92

Slowacki, Juliusz 1809-1849 ..... **NCLC 15**

Smart, Christopher
1722-1771 ... **LC 3; DAM POET; PC 13**
See also DLB 109

Smart, Elizabeth 1913-1986....... **CLC 54**
See also CA 81-84; 118; DLB 88

Smiley, Jane (Graves)
1949- .... **CLC 53, 76; DAM POP**
See also CA 104; CANR 30, 50;
INT CANR-30

Smith, A(rthur) J(ames) M(arshall)
1902-1980 .... **CLC 15; DAC**
See also CA 1-4R; 102; CANR 4; DLB 88

Smith, Adam 1723-1790........... **LC 36**
See also DLB 104

Smith, Alexander 1829-1867 ..... **NCLC 59**
See also DLB 32, 55

Smith, Anna Deavere 1950-........ **CLC 86**
See also CA 133

Smith, Betty (Wehner) 1896-1972... **CLC 19**
See also CA 5-8R; 33-36R; DLBY 82;
SATA 6

Smith, Charlotte (Turner)
1749-1806 .... **NCLC 23**
See also DLB 39, 109

Smith, Clark Ashton 1893-1961 .... **CLC 43**
See also CA 143

Smith, Dave................... **CLC 22, 42**
See also Smith, David (Jeddie)
See also CAAS 7; DLB 5

Smith, David (Jeddie) 1942-
See Smith, Dave
See also CA 49-52; CANR 1; DAM POET

Smith, Florence Margaret 1902-1971
See Smith, Stevie
See also CA 17-18; 29-32R; CANR 35;
CAP 2; DAM POET; MTCW

Smith, Iain Crichton 1928- .... **CLC 64**
See also CA 21-24R; DLB 40, 139

Smith, John 1580(?)-1631 .... **LC 9**

Smith, Johnston
See Crane, Stephen (Townley)

Smith, Joseph, Jr. 1805-1844 .... **NCLC 53**

Smith, Lee 1944-.............. **CLC 25, 73**
See also CA 114; 119; CANR 46; DLB 143;
DLBY 83; INT 119

Smith, Martin
See Smith, Martin Cruz

Smith, Martin Cruz
1942- ..... **CLC 25; DAM MULT, POP**
See also BEST 89:4; CA 85-88; CANR 6,
23, 43; INT CANR-23; NNAL

Smith, Mary-Ann Tirone 1944-..... **CLC 39**
See also CA 118; 136

Smith, Patti 1946- .... **CLC 12**
See also CA 93-96

Smith, Pauline (Urmson)
1882-1959 .... **TCLC 25**

Smith, Rosamond
See Oates, Joyce Carol

Smith, Sheila Kaye
See Kaye-Smith, Sheila

Smith, Stevie .... **CLC 3, 8, 25, 44; PC 12**
See also Smith, Florence Margaret
See also DLB 20

Smith, Wilbur (Addison) 1933-..... **CLC 33**
See also CA 13-16R; CANR 7, 46; MTCW

Smith, William Jay 1918- .... **CLC 6**
See also CA 5-8R; CANR 44; DLB 5;
MAICYA; SAAS 22; SATA 2, 68

Smith, Woodrow Wilson
See Kuttner, Henry

Smolenskin, Peretz 1842-1885.... **NCLC 30**

Smollett, Tobias (George) 1721-1771 .. **LC 2**
See also CDBLB 1660-1789; DLB 39, 104

Snodgrass, W(illiam) D(e Witt)
1926- .... **CLC 2, 6, 10, 18, 68;
DAM POET**
See also CA 1-4R; CANR 6, 36; DLB 5;
MTCW

Snow, C(harles) P(ercy)
1905-1980 ...... **CLC 1, 4, 6, 9, 13, 19;
DAM NOV**
See also CA 5-8R; 101; CANR 28;
CDBLB 1945-1960; DLB 15, 77; MTCW

Snow, Frances Compton
See Adams, Henry (Brooks)

Snyder, Gary (Sherman)
1930- .. **CLC 1, 2, 5, 9, 32; DAM POET**
See also CA 17-20R; CANR 30; DLB 5, 16,
165

Snyder, Zilpha Keatley 1927-...... **CLC 17**
See also AAYA 15; CA 9-12R; CANR 38;
CLR 31; JRDA; MAICYA; SAAS 2;
SATA 1, 28, 75

Soares, Bernardo
See Pessoa, Fernando (Antonio Nogueira)

Sobh, A.
See Shamlu, Ahmad

Sobol, Joshua.................... **CLC 60**

Soderberg, Hjalmar 1869-1941 .... **TCLC 39**

Sodergran, Edith (Irene)
See Soedergran, Edith (Irene)

Soedergran, Edith (Irene)
1892-1923 .... **TCLC 31**

Softly, Edgar
See Lovecraft, H(oward) P(hillips)

Softly, Edward
See Lovecraft, H(oward) P(hillips)

Sokolov, Raymond 1941-........... **CLC 7**
See also CA 85-88

Solo, Jay
See Ellison, Harlan (Jay)

Sologub, Fyodor .... **TCLC 9**
See also Teternikov, Fyodor Kuzmich

Solomons, Ikey Esquir
See Thackeray, William Makepeace

Solomos, Dionysios 1798-1857 ... **NCLC 15**

Solwoska, Mara
See French, Marilyn

Solzhenitsyn, Aleksandr I(sayevich)
1918- ...... **CLC 1, 2, 4, 7, 9, 10, 18, 26,
34, 78; DA; DAB; DAC; DAM MST,
NOV; WLC**
See also AITN 1; CA 69-72; CANR 40;
MTCW

Somers, Jane
See Lessing, Doris (May)

Somerville, Edith 1858-1949 ...... **TCLC 51**
See also DLB 135

Somerville & Ross
See Martin, Violet Florence; Somerville,
Edith

Sommer, Scott 1951- .... **CLC 25**
See also CA 106

Sondheim, Stephen (Joshua)
1930- .... **CLC 30, 39; DAM DRAM**
See also AAYA 11; CA 103; CANR 47

Sontag, Susan
1933- .... **CLC 1, 2, 10, 13, 31;
DAM POP**
See also CA 17-20R; CANR 25, 51; DLB 2,
67; MTCW

Sophocles
496(?)B.C.-406(?)B.C..... **CMLC 2; DA;
DAB; DAC; DAM DRAM, MST; DC 1**
See also DLB 176

Sordello 1189-1269............. **CMLC 15**

Sorel, Julia
See Drexler, Rosalyn

Sorrentino, Gilbert
1929- .... **CLC 3, 7, 14, 22, 40**
See also CA 77-80; CANR 14, 33; DLB 5,
173; DLBY 80; INT CANR-14

Soto, Gary
1952- .... **CLC 32, 80; DAM MULT;
HLC**
See also AAYA 10; CA 119; 125;
CANR 50; CLR 38; DLB 82; HW;
INT 125; JRDA; SATA 80

Soupault, Philippe 1897-1990 ...... **CLC 68**
See also CA 116; 147; 131

Souster, (Holmes) Raymond
1921- ... **CLC 5, 14; DAC; DAM POET**
See also CA 13-16R; CAAS 14; CANR 13,
29, 53; DLB 88; SATA 63

Southern, Terry 1924(?)-1995 .... **CLC 7**
See also CA 1-4R; 150; CANR 1, 55;
DLB 2

Southey, Robert 1774-1843 .... **NCLC 8**
See also DLB 93, 107, 142; SATA 54

Southworth, Emma Dorothy Eliza Nevitte
1819-1899 .... **NCLC 26**

Souza, Ernest
See Scott, Evelyn

Sterne, Laurence
1713-1768 . . . . . . **LC 2; DA; DAB; DAC;
DAM MST, NOV; WLC**
See also CDBLB 1660-1789; DLB 39

Sternheim, (William Adolf) Carl
1878-1942 . . . . **TCLC 8**
See also CA 105; DLB 56, 118

Stevens, Mark 1951- . . . . **CLC 34**
See also CA 122

Stevens, Wallace
1879-1955 . . . . **TCLC 3, 12, 45; DA;
DAB; DAC; DAM MST, POET; PC 6;
WLC**
See also CA 104; 124; CDALB 1929-1941;
DLB 54; MTCW

Stevenson, Anne (Katharine)
1933- . . . . **CLC 7, 33**
See also CA 17-20R; CAAS 9; CANR 9, 33;
DLB 40; MTCW

Stevenson, Robert Louis (Balfour)
1850-1894 . . . . . **NCLC 5, 14; DA; DAB;
DAC; DAM MST, NOV; SSC 11; WLC**
See also CDBLB 1890-1914; CLR 10, 11;
DLB 18, 57, 141, 156, 174; DLBD 13;
JRDA; MAICYA; YABC 2

Stewart, J(ohn) I(nnes) M(ackintosh)
1906-1994 . . . . **CLC 7, 14, 32**
See also CA 85-88; 147; CAAS 3;
CANR 47; MTCW

Stewart, Mary (Florence Elinor)
1916- . . . . **CLC 7, 35; DAB**
See also CA 1-4R; CANR 1; SATA 12

Stewart, Mary Rainbow
See Stewart, Mary (Florence Elinor)

Stifle, June
See Campbell, Maria

Stifter, Adalbert 1805-1868 . . . . . . **NCLC 41**
See also DLB 133

Still, James 1906- . . . . **CLC 49**
See also CA 65-68; CAAS 17; CANR 10,
26; DLB 9; SATA 29

Sting
See Sumner, Gordon Matthew

Stirling, Arthur
See Sinclair, Upton (Beall)

Stitt, Milan 1941- . . . . **CLC 29**
See also CA 69-72

Stockton, Francis Richard 1834-1902
See Stockton, Frank R.
See also CA 108; 137; MAICYA; SATA 44

Stockton, Frank R. . . . . **TCLC 47**
See also Stockton, Francis Richard
See also DLB 42, 74; DLBD 13;
SATA-Brief 32

Stoddard, Charles
See Kuttner, Henry

Stoker, Abraham 1847-1912
See Stoker, Bram
See also CA 105; DA; DAC; DAM MST,
NOV; SATA 29

Stoker, Bram
1847-1912 . . . . **TCLC 8; DAB; WLC**
See also Stoker, Abraham
See also CA 150; CDBLB 1890-1914;
DLB 36, 70

Stolz, Mary (Slattery) 1920- . . . . **CLC 12**
See also AAYA 8; AITN 1; CA 5-8R;
CANR 13, 41; JRDA; MAICYA;
SAAS 3; SATA 10, 71

Stone, Irving
1903-1989 . . . . **CLC 7; DAM POP**
See also AITN 1; CA 1-4R; 129; CAAS 3;
CANR 1, 23; INT CANR-23; MTCW;
SATA 3; SATA-Obit 64

Stone, Oliver (William) 1946- . . . . . . **CLC 73**
See also AAYA 15; CA 110; CANR 55

Stone, Robert (Anthony)
1937- . . . . **CLC 5, 23, 42**
See also CA 85-88; CANR 23; DLB 152;
INT CANR-23; MTCW

Stone, Zachary
See Follett, Ken(neth Martin)

Stoppard, Tom
1937- . . . . . . **CLC 1, 3, 4, 5, 8, 15, 29, 34,
63, 91; DA; DAB; DAC; DAM DRAM,
MST; DC 6; WLC**
See also CA 81-84; CANR 39;
CDBLB 1960 to Present; DLB 13;
DLBY 85; MTCW

Storey, David (Malcolm)
1933- . . . . . **CLC 2, 4, 5, 8; DAM DRAM**
See also CA 81-84; CANR 36; DLB 13, 14;
MTCW

Storm, Hyemeyohsts
1935- . . . . **CLC 3; DAM MULT**
See also CA 81-84; CANR 45; NNAL

Storm, (Hans) Theodor (Woldsen)
1817-1888 . . . . **NCLC 1**

Storni, Alfonsina
1892-1938 . . . . . **TCLC 5; DAM MULT;
HLC**
See also CA 104; 131; HW

Stout, Rex (Todhunter) 1886-1975 . . . **CLC 3**
See also AITN 2; CA 61-64

Stow, (Julian) Randolph 1935- . . **CLC 23, 48**
See also CA 13-16R; CANR 33; MTCW

Stowe, Harriet (Elizabeth) Beecher
1811-1896 . . . . . **NCLC 3, 50; DA; DAB;
DAC; DAM MST, NOV; WLC**
See also CDALB 1865-1917; DLB 1, 12, 42,
74; JRDA; MAICYA; YABC 1

Strachey, (Giles) Lytton
1880-1932 . . . . **TCLC 12**
See also CA 110; DLB 149; DLBD 10

Strand, Mark
1934- . . **CLC 6, 18, 41, 71; DAM POET**
See also CA 21-24R; CANR 40; DLB 5;
SATA 41

Straub, Peter (Francis)
1943- . . . . **CLC 28; DAM POP**
See also BEST 89:1; CA 85-88; CANR 28;
DLBY 84; MTCW

Strauss, Botho 1944- . . . . **CLC 22**
See also DLB 124

Streatfeild, (Mary) Noel
1895(?)-1986 . . . . **CLC 21**
See also CA 81-84; 120; CANR 31;
CLR 17; DLB 160; MAICYA; SATA 20;
SATA-Obit 48

Stribling, T(homas) S(igismund)
1881-1965 . . . . **CLC 23**
See also CA 107; DLB 9

Strindberg, (Johan) August
1849-1912 . . . . . . **TCLC 1, 8, 21, 47; DA;
DAB; DAC; DAM DRAM, MST; WLC**
See also CA 104; 135

Stringer, Arthur 1874-1950 . . . . **TCLC 37**
See also DLB 92

Stringer, David
See Roberts, Keith (John Kingston)

Strugatskii, Arkadii (Natanovich)
1925-1991 . . . . **CLC 27**
See also CA 106; 135

Strugatskii, Boris (Natanovich)
1933- . . . . **CLC 27**
See also CA 106

Strummer, Joe 1953(?)- . . . . **CLC 30**

Stuart, Don A.
See Campbell, John W(ood, Jr.)

Stuart, Ian
See MacLean, Alistair (Stuart)

Stuart, Jesse (Hilton)
1906-1984 . . . . **CLC 1, 8, 11, 14, 34**
See also CA 5-8R; 112; CANR 31; DLB 9,
48, 102; DLBY 84; SATA 2;
SATA-Obit 36

Sturgeon, Theodore (Hamilton)
1918-1985 . . . . **CLC 22, 39**
See also Queen, Ellery
See also CA 81-84; 116; CANR 32; DLB 8;
DLBY 85; MTCW

Sturges, Preston 1898-1959 . . . . **TCLC 48**
See also CA 114; 149; DLB 26

Styron, William
1925- . . . . **CLC 1, 3, 5, 11, 15, 60;
DAM NOV, POP; SSC 25**
See also BEST 90:4; CA 5-8R; CANR 6, 33;
CDALB 1968-1988; DLB 2, 143;
DLBY 80; INT CANR-6; MTCW

Suarez Lynch, B.
See Bioy Casares, Adolfo; Borges, Jorge
Luis

Su Chien 1884-1918
See Su Man-shu
See also CA 123

Suckow, Ruth 1892-1960 . . . . **SSC 18**
See also CA 113; DLB 9, 102

Sudermann, Hermann 1857-1928 . . **TCLC 15**
See also CA 107; DLB 118

Sue, Eugene 1804-1857 . . . . **NCLC 1**
See also DLB 119

Sueskind, Patrick 1949- . . . . **CLC 44**
See also Suskind, Patrick

Sukenick, Ronald 1932- . . . . . **CLC 3, 4, 6, 48**
See also CA 25-28R; CAAS 8; CANR 32;
DLB 173; DLBY 81

Suknaski, Andrew 1942- . . . . **CLC 19**
See also CA 101; DLB 53

Sullivan, Vernon
See Vian, Boris

Sully Prudhomme 1839-1907 . . . . . . **TCLC 31**

Su Man-shu . . . . **TCLC 24**
See also Su Chien

Tolson, M. B.
See Tolson, Melvin B(eaunorus)

Tolson, Melvin B(eaunorus)
1898(?)-1966 . . . . **CLC 36; BLC;**
DAM MULT, POET
See also BW 1; CA 124; 89-92; DLB 48, 76

Tolstoi, Aleksei Nikolaevich
See Tolstoy, Alexey Nikolaevich

Tolstoy, Alexey Nikolaevich
1882-1945 . . . . **TCLC 18**
See also CA 107

Tolstoy, Count Leo
See Tolstoy, Leo (Nikolaevich)

Tolstoy, Leo (Nikolaevich)
1828-1910 . . . . . **TCLC 4, 11, 17, 28, 44;**
DA; DAB; DAC; DAM MST, NOV;
SSC 9; WLC
See also CA 104; 123; SATA 26

Tomasi di Lampedusa, Giuseppe 1896-1957
See Lampedusa, Giuseppe (Tomasi) di
See also CA 111

Tomlin, Lily . . . . **CLC 17**
See also Tomlin, Mary Jean

Tomlin, Mary Jean 1939(?)-
See Tomlin, Lily
See also CA 117

Tomlinson, (Alfred) Charles
1927- . . . . **CLC 2, 4, 6, 13, 45;**
DAM POET; PC 17
See also CA 5-8R; CANR 33; DLB 40

Tonson, Jacob
See Bennett, (Enoch) Arnold

Toole, John Kennedy
1937-1969 . . . . **CLC 19, 64**
See also CA 104; DLBY 81

Toomer, Jean
1894-1967 . . . . . . **CLC 1, 4, 13, 22; BLC;**
DAM MULT; PC 7; SSC 1
See also BW 1; CA 85-88;
CDALB 1917-1929; DLB 45, 51; MTCW

Torley, Luke
See Blish, James (Benjamin)

Tornimparte, Alessandra
See Ginzburg, Natalia

Torre, Raoul della
See Mencken, H(enry) L(ouis)

Torrey, E(dwin) Fuller 1937- . . . . **CLC 34**
See also CA 119

Torsvan, Ben Traven
See Traven, B.

Torsvan, Benno Traven
See Traven, B.

Torsvan, Berick Traven
See Traven, B.

Torsvan, Berwick Traven
See Traven, B.

Torsvan, Bruno Traven
See Traven, B.

Torsvan, Traven
See Traven, B.

Tournier, Michel (Edouard)
1924- . . . . **CLC 6, 23, 36, 95**
See also CA 49-52; CANR 3, 36; DLB 83;
MTCW; SATA 23

Tournimparte, Alessandra
See Ginzburg, Natalia

Towers, Ivar
See Kornbluth, C(yril) M.

Towne, Robert (Burton) 1936(?)- . . . . **CLC 87**
See also CA 108; DLB 44

Townsend, Sue 1946- . . **CLC 61; DAB; DAC**
See also CA 119; 127; INT 127; MTCW;
SATA 55; SATA-Brief 48

Townshend, Peter (Dennis Blandford)
1945- . . . . **CLC 17, 42**
See also CA 107

Tozzi, Federigo 1883-1920 . . . . **TCLC 31**

Traill, Catharine Parr
1802-1899 . . . . **NCLC 31**
See also DLB 99

Trakl, Georg 1887-1914 . . . . **TCLC 5**
See also CA 104

Transtroemer, Tomas (Goesta)
1931- . . . . **CLC 52, 65; DAM POET**
See also CA 117; 129; CAAS 17

Transtromer, Tomas Gosta
See Transtroemer, Tomas (Goesta)

Traven, B. (?)-1969 . . . . **CLC 8, 11**
See also CA 19-20; 25-28R; CAP 2; DLB 9,
56; MTCW

Treitel, Jonathan 1959- . . . . **CLC 70**

Tremain, Rose 1943- . . . . **CLC 42**
See also CA 97-100; CANR 44; DLB 14

Tremblay, Michel
1942- . . . . . . **CLC 29; DAC; DAM MST**
See also CA 116; 128; DLB 60; MTCW

Trevanian . . . . **CLC 29**
See also Whitaker, Rod(ney)

Trevor, Glen
See Hilton, James

Trevor, William
1928- . . . . . **CLC 7, 9, 14, 25, 71; SSC 21**
See also Cox, William Trevor
See also DLB 14, 139

Trifonov, Yuri (Valentinovich)
1925-1981 . . . . **CLC 45**
See also CA 126; 103; MTCW

Trilling, Lionel 1905-1975 . . . . **CLC 9, 11, 24**
See also CA 9-12R; 61-64; CANR 10;
DLB 28, 63; INT CANR-10; MTCW

Trimball, W. H.
See Mencken, H(enry) L(ouis)

Tristan
See Gomez de la Serna, Ramon

Tristram
See Housman, A(lfred) E(dward)

Trogdon, William (Lewis) 1939-
See Heat-Moon, William Least
See also CA 115; 119; CANR 47; INT 119

Trollope, Anthony
1815-1882 . . . . . **NCLC 6, 33; DA; DAB;**
DAC; DAM MST, NOV; WLC
See also CDBLB 1832-1890; DLB 21, 57,
159; SATA 22

Trollope, Frances 1779-1863 . . . . . **NCLC 30**
See also DLB 21, 166

Trotsky, Leon 1879-1940 . . . . **TCLC 22**
See also CA 118

Trotter (Cockburn), Catharine
1679-1749 . . . . **LC 8**
See also DLB 84

Trout, Kilgore
See Farmer, Philip Jose

Trow, George W. S. 1943- . . . . **CLC 52**
See also CA 126

Troyat, Henri 1911- . . . . **CLC 23**
See also CA 45-48; CANR 2, 33; MTCW

Trudeau, G(arretson) B(eekman) 1948-
See Trudeau, Garry B.
See also CA 81-84; CANR 31; SATA 35

Trudeau, Garry B. . . . . **CLC 12**
See also Trudeau, G(arretson) B(eekman)
See also AAYA 10; AITN 2

Truffaut, Francois 1932-1984 . . . . . . **CLC 20**
See also CA 81-84; 113; CANR 34

Trumbo, Dalton 1905-1976 . . . . **CLC 19**
See also CA 21-24R; 69-72; CANR 10;
DLB 26

Trumbull, John 1750-1831 . . . . . . **NCLC 30**
See also DLB 31

Trundlett, Helen B.
See Eliot, T(homas) S(tearns)

Tryon, Thomas
1926-1991 . . . . . . **CLC 3, 11; DAM POP**
See also AITN 1; CA 29-32R; 135;
CANR 32; MTCW

Tryon, Tom
See Tryon, Thomas

Ts'ao Hsueh-ch'in 1715(?)-1763 . . . . . . **LC 1**

Tsushima, Shuji 1909-1948
See Dazai, Osamu
See also CA 107

Tsvetaeva (Efron), Marina (Ivanovna)
1892-1941 . . . . **TCLC 7, 35; PC 14**
See also CA 104; 128; MTCW

Tuck, Lily 1938- . . . . **CLC 70**
See also CA 139

Tu Fu 712-770 . . . . **PC 9**
See also DAM MULT

Tunis, John R(oberts) 1889-1975 . . . **CLC 12**
See also CA 61-64; DLB 22, 171; JRDA;
MAICYA; SATA 37; SATA-Brief 30

Tuohy, Frank . . . . **CLC 37**
See also Tuohy, John Francis
See also DLB 14, 139

Tuohy, John Francis 1925-
See Tuohy, Frank
See also CA 5-8R; CANR 3, 47

Turco, Lewis (Putnam) 1934- . . . **CLC 11, 63**
See also CA 13-16R; CAAS 22; CANR 24,
51; DLBY 84

Turgenev, Ivan
1818-1883 . . . . **NCLC 21; DA; DAB;**
DAC; DAM MST, NOV; DC 7; SSC 7;
WLC

Turgot, Anne-Robert-Jacques
1727-1781 . . . . **LC 26**

Turner, Frederick 1943- . . . . **CLC 48**
See also CA 73-76; CAAS 10; CANR 12,
30, 56; DLB 40

Tutu, Desmond M(pilo)
1931- ..... **CLC 80; BLC; DAM MULT**
See also BW 1; CA 125

Tutuola, Amos
1920- .... **CLC 5, 14, 29; BLC;**
DAM MULT
See also BW 2; CA 9-12R; CANR 27;
DLB 125; MTCW

Twain, Mark
..... **TCLC 6, 12, 19, 36, 48, 59; SSC 6;**
WLC
See also Clemens, Samuel Langhorne
See also AAYA 20; DLB 11, 12, 23, 64, 74

Tyler, Anne
1941- .... **CLC 7, 11, 18, 28, 44, 59;**
DAM NOV, POP
See also AAYA 18; BEST 89:1; CA 9-12R;
CANR 11, 33, 53; DLB 6, 143; DLBY 82;
MTCW; SATA 7, 90

Tyler, Royall 1757-1826 .... **NCLC 3**
See also DLB 37

Tynan, Katharine 1861-1931 .... **TCLC 3**
See also CA 104; DLB 153

Tyutchev, Fyodor 1803-1873 ..... **NCLC 34**

Tzara, Tristan
1896-1963 .... **CLC 47; DAM POET**
See also Rosenfeld, Samuel; Rosenstock,
Sami; Rosenstock, Samuel
See also CA 153

Uhry, Alfred
1936- ..... **CLC 55; DAM DRAM, POP**
See also CA 127; 133; INT 133

Ulf, Haerved
See Strindberg, (Johan) August

Ulf, Harved
See Strindberg, (Johan) August

Ulibarri, Sabine R(eyes)
1919- .... **CLC 83; DAM MULT**
See also CA 131; DLB 82; HW

Unamuno (y Jugo), Miguel de
1864-1936 ... **TCLC 2, 9; DAM MULT,**
NOV; HLC; SSC 11
See also CA 104; 131; DLB 108; HW;
MTCW

Undercliffe, Errol
See Campbell, (John) Ramsey

Underwood, Miles
See Glassco, John

Undset, Sigrid
1882-1949 .... **TCLC 3; DA; DAB;**
DAC; DAM MST, NOV; WLC
See also CA 104; 129; MTCW

Ungaretti, Giuseppe
1888-1970 .... **CLC 7, 11, 15**
See also CA 19-20; 25-28R; CAP 2;
DLB 114

Unger, Douglas 1952- .... **CLC 34**
See also CA 130

Unsworth, Barry (Forster) 1930- .... **CLC 76**
See also CA 25-28R; CANR 30, 54

Updike, John (Hoyer)
1932- ...... **CLC 1, 2, 3, 5, 7, 9, 13, 15,**
23, 34, 43, 70; DA; DAB; DAC;
DAM MST, NOV, POET, POP;
SSC 13; WLC
See also CA 1-4R; CABS 1; CANR 4, 33,
51; CDALB 1968-1988; DLB 2, 5, 143;
DLBD 3; DLBY 80, 82; MTCW

Upshaw, Margaret Mitchell
See Mitchell, Margaret (Munnerlyn)

Upton, Mark
See Sanders, Lawrence

Urdang, Constance (Henriette)
1922- .... **CLC 47**
See also CA 21-24R; CANR 9, 24

Uriel, Henry
See Faust, Frederick (Schiller)

Uris, Leon (Marcus)
1924- .... **CLC 7, 32; DAM NOV, POP**
See also AITN 1, 2; BEST 89:2; CA 1-4R;
CANR 1, 40; MTCW; SATA 49

Urmuz
See Codrescu, Andrei

Urquhart, Jane 1949- .... **CLC 90; DAC**
See also CA 113; CANR 32

Ustinov, Peter (Alexander) 1921- .... **CLC 1**
See also AITN 1; CA 13-16R; CANR 25,
51; DLB 13

Vaculik, Ludvik 1926- .... **CLC 7**
See also CA 53-56

Valdez, Luis (Miguel)
1940- ..... **CLC 84; DAM MULT; HLC**
See also CA 101; CANR 32; DLB 122; HW

Valenzuela, Luisa
1938- ... **CLC 31; DAM MULT; SSC 14**
See also CA 101; CANR 32; DLB 113; HW

Valera y Alcala-Galiano, Juan
1824-1905 .... **TCLC 10**
See also CA 106

Valery, (Ambroise) Paul (Toussaint Jules)
1871-1945 .... **TCLC 4, 15;**
DAM POET; PC 9
See also CA 104; 122; MTCW

Valle-Inclan, Ramon (Maria) del
1866-1936 ..... **TCLC 5; DAM MULT;**
HLC
See also CA 106; 153; DLB 134

Vallejo, Antonio Buero
See Buero Vallejo, Antonio

Vallejo, Cesar (Abraham)
1892-1938 .... **TCLC 3, 56;**
DAM MULT; HLC
See also CA 105; 153; HW

Vallette, Marguerite Eymery
See Rachilde

Valle Y Pena, Ramon del
See Valle-Inclan, Ramon (Maria) del

Van Ash, Cay 1918- .... **CLC 34**

Vanbrugh, Sir John
1664-1726 .... **LC 21; DAM DRAM**
See also DLB 80

Van Campen, Karl
See Campbell, John W(ood, Jr.)

Vance, Gerald
See Silverberg, Robert

Vance, Jack .... **CLC 35**
See also Vance, John Holbrook
See also DLB 8

Vance, John Holbrook 1916-
See Queen, Ellery; Vance, Jack
See also CA 29-32R; CANR 17; MTCW

Van Den Bogarde, Derek Jules Gaspard Ulric
Niven 1921-
See Bogarde, Dirk
See also CA 77-80

Vandenburgh, Jane .... **CLC 59**

Vanderhaeghe, Guy 1951- .... **CLC 41**
See also CA 113

van der Post, Laurens (Jan)
1906-1996 .... **CLC 5**
See also CA 5-8R; 155; CANR 35

van de Wetering, Janwillem 1931- .. **CLC 47**
See also CA 49-52; CANR 4

Van Dine, S. S. .... **TCLC 23**
See also Wright, Willard Huntington

Van Doren, Carl (Clinton)
1885-1950 .... **TCLC 18**
See also CA 111

Van Doren, Mark 1894-1972 ..... **CLC 6, 10**
See also CA 1-4R; 37-40R; CANR 3;
DLB 45; MTCW

Van Druten, John (William)
1901-1957 .... **TCLC 2**
See also CA 104; DLB 10

Van Duyn, Mona (Jane)
1921- .... **CLC 3, 7, 63; DAM POET**
See also CA 9-12R; CANR 7, 38; DLB 5

Van Dyne, Edith
See Baum, L(yman) Frank

van Itallie, Jean-Claude 1936- .... **CLC 3**
See also CA 45-48; CAAS 2; CANR 1, 48;
DLB 7

van Ostaijen, Paul 1896-1928 ..... **TCLC 33**

Van Peebles, Melvin
1932- .... **CLC 2, 20; DAM MULT**
See also BW 2; CA 85-88; CANR 27

Vansittart, Peter 1920- .... **CLC 42**
See also CA 1-4R; CANR 3, 49

Van Vechten, Carl 1880-1964 ...... **CLC 33**
See also CA 89-92; DLB 4, 9, 51

Van Vogt, A(lfred) E(lton) 1912- ..... **CLC 1**
See also CA 21-24R; CANR 28; DLB 8;
SATA 14

Varda, Agnes 1928- .... **CLC 16**
See also CA 116; 122

Vargas Llosa, (Jorge) Mario (Pedro)
1936- .... **CLC 3, 6, 9, 10, 15, 31, 42, 85;**
DA; DAB; DAC; DAM MST, MULT,
NOV; HLC
See also CA 73-76; CANR 18, 32, 42;
DLB 145; HW; MTCW

Vasiliu, Gheorghe 1881-1957
See Bacovia, George
See also CA 123

Vassa, Gustavus
See Equiano, Olaudah

Vassilikos, Vassilis 1933- .... **CLC 4, 8**
See also CA 81-84

Vaughan, Henry 1621-1695 . . . . **LC 27**
See also DLB 131

Vaughn, Stephanie . . . . **CLC 62**

Vazov, Ivan (Minchov)
1850-1921 . . . . **TCLC 25**
See also CA 121; DLB 147

Veblen, Thorstein (Bunde)
1857-1929 . . . . **TCLC 31**
See also CA 115

Vega, Lope de 1562-1635 . . . . **LC 23**

Venison, Alfred
See Pound, Ezra (Weston Loomis)

Verdi, Marie de
See Mencken, H(enry) L(ouis)

Verdu, Matilde
See Cela, Camilo Jose

Verga, Giovanni (Carmelo)
1840-1922 . . . . **TCLC 3; SSC 21**
See also CA 104; 123

Vergil
70B.C.-19B.C. . . . . . **CMLC 9; DA; DAB;
DAC; DAM MST, POET; PC 12**

Verhaeren, Emile (Adolphe Gustave)
1855-1916 . . . . **TCLC 12**
See also CA 109

Verlaine, Paul (Marie)
1844-1896 . . . . **NCLC 2, 51;
DAM POET; PC 2**

Verne, Jules (Gabriel)
1828-1905 . . . . **TCLC 6, 52**
See also AAYA 16; CA 110; 131; DLB 123;
JRDA; MAICYA; SATA 21

Very, Jones 1813-1880 . . . . **NCLC 9**
See also DLB 1

Vesaas, Tarjei 1897-1970 . . . . **CLC 48**
See also CA 29-32R

Vialis, Gaston
See Simenon, Georges (Jacques Christian)

Vian, Boris 1920-1959 . . . . **TCLC 9**
See also CA 106; DLB 72

Viaud, (Louis Marie) Julien 1850-1923
See Loti, Pierre
See also CA 107

Vicar, Henry
See Felsen, Henry Gregor

Vicker, Angus
See Felsen, Henry Gregor

Vidal, Gore
1925- . . . . . **CLC 2, 4, 6, 8, 10, 22, 33, 72;
DAM NOV, POP**
See also AITN 1; BEST 90:2; CA 5-8R;
CANR 13, 45; DLB 6, 152;
INT CANR-13; MTCW

Viereck, Peter (Robert Edwin)
1916- . . . . **CLC 4**
See also CA 1-4R; CANR 1, 47; DLB 5

Vigny, Alfred (Victor) de
1797-1863 . . . . . . **NCLC 7; DAM POET**
See also DLB 119

Vilakazi, Benedict Wallet
1906-1947 . . . . **TCLC 37**

**Villiers de l'Isle Adam, Jean Marie Mathias
Philippe Auguste Comte**
1838-1889 . . . . **NCLC 3; SSC 14**
See also DLB 123

Villon, Francois 1431-1463(?) . . . . **PC 13**

Vinci, Leonardo da 1452-1519 . . . . . . **LC 12**

Vine, Barbara . . . . **CLC 50**
See also Rendell, Ruth (Barbara)
See also BEST 90:4

Vinge, Joan D(ennison)
1948- . . . . **CLC 30; SSC 24**
See also CA 93-96; SATA 36

Violis, G.
See Simenon, Georges (Jacques Christian)

Visconti, Luchino 1906-1976 . . . . **CLC 16**
See also CA 81-84; 65-68; CANR 39

Vittorini, Elio 1908-1966 . . . . . **CLC 6, 9, 14**
See also CA 133; 25-28R

Vizinczey, Stephen 1933- . . . . **CLC 40**
See also CA 128; INT 128

Vliet, R(ussell) G(ordon)
1929-1984 . . . . **CLC 22**
See also CA 37-40R; 112; CANR 18

Vogau, Boris Andreyevich 1894-1937(?)
See Pilnyak, Boris
See also CA 123

Vogel, Paula A(nne) 1951- . . . . **CLC 76**
See also CA 108

Voight, Ellen Bryant 1943- . . . . **CLC 54**
See also CA 69-72; CANR 11, 29, 55;
DLB 120

Voigt, Cynthia 1942- . . . . **CLC 30**
See also AAYA 3; CA 106; CANR 18, 37,
40; CLR 13; INT CANR-18; JRDA;
MAICYA; SATA 48, 79; SATA-Brief 33

Voinovich, Vladimir (Nikolaevich)
1932- . . . . **CLC 10, 49**
See also CA 81-84; CAAS 12; CANR 33;
MTCW

Vollmann, William T.
1959- . . . . . . **CLC 89; DAM NOV, POP**
See also CA 134

Voloshinov, V. N.
See Bakhtin, Mikhail Mikhailovich

Voltaire
1694-1778 . . . . . **LC 14; DA; DAB; DAC;
DAM DRAM, MST; SSC 12; WLC**

von Daeniken, Erich 1935- . . . . **CLC 30**
See also AITN 1; CA 37-40R; CANR 17,
44

von Daniken, Erich
See von Daeniken, Erich

von Heidenstam, (Carl Gustaf) Verner
See Heidenstam, (Carl Gustaf) Verner von

von Heyse, Paul (Johann Ludwig)
See Heyse, Paul (Johann Ludwig von)

von Hofmannsthal, Hugo
See Hofmannsthal, Hugo von

von Horvath, Odon
See Horvath, Oedoen von

von Horvath, Oedoen
See Horvath, Oedoen von

von Liliencron, (Friedrich Adolf Axel) Detlev
See Liliencron, (Friedrich Adolf Axel)
Detlev von

Vonnegut, Kurt, Jr.
1922- . . . . . . **CLC 1, 2, 3, 4, 5, 8, 12, 22,
40, 60; DA; DAB; DAC; DAM MST,
NOV, POP; SSC 8; WLC**
See also AAYA 6; AITN 1; BEST 90:4;
CA 1-4R; CANR 1, 25, 49;
CDALB 1968-1988; DLB 2, 8, 152;
DLBD 3; DLBY 80; MTCW

Von Rachen, Kurt
See Hubbard, L(afayette) Ron(ald)

von Rezzori (d'Arezzo), Gregor
See Rezzori (d'Arezzo), Gregor von

von Sternberg, Josef
See Sternberg, Josef von

Vorster, Gordon 1924- . . . . **CLC 34**
See also CA 133

Vosce, Trudie
See Ozick, Cynthia

Voznesensky, Andrei (Andreievich)
1933- . . . . . . **CLC 1, 15, 57; DAM POET**
See also CA 89-92; CANR 37; MTCW

Waddington, Miriam 1917- . . . . **CLC 28**
See also CA 21-24R; CANR 12, 30;
DLB 68

Wagman, Fredrica 1937- . . . . **CLC 7**
See also CA 97-100; INT 97-100

Wagner, Richard 1813-1883 . . . . **NCLC 9**
See also DLB 129

Wagner-Martin, Linda 1936- . . . . **CLC 50**

Wagoner, David (Russell)
1926- . . . . **CLC 3, 5, 15**
See also CA 1-4R; CAAS 3; CANR 2;
DLB 5; SATA 14

Wah, Fred(erick James) 1939- . . . . . . **CLC 44**
See also CA 107; 141; DLB 60

Wahloo, Per 1926-1975 . . . . **CLC 7**
See also CA 61-64

Wahloo, Peter
See Wahloo, Per

Wain, John (Barrington)
1925-1994 . . . . **CLC 2, 11, 15, 46**
See also CA 5-8R; 145; CAAS 4; CANR 23,
54; CDBLB 1960 to Present; DLB 15, 27,
139, 155; MTCW

Wajda, Andrzej 1926- . . . . **CLC 16**
See also CA 102

Wakefield, Dan 1932- . . . . **CLC 7**
See also CA 21-24R; CAAS 7

Wakoski, Diane
1937- . . . . **CLC 2, 4, 7, 9, 11, 40;
DAM POET; PC 15**
See also CA 13-16R; CAAS 1; CANR 9;
DLB 5; INT CANR-9

Wakoski-Sherbell, Diane
See Wakoski, Diane

Walcott, Derek (Alton)
1930- . . . . **CLC 2, 4, 9, 14, 25, 42, 67, 76;
BLC; DAB; DAC; DAM MST, MULT,
POET; DC 7**
See also BW 2; CA 89-92; CANR 26, 47;
DLB 117; DLBY 81; MTCW

Waldman, Anne 1945- . . . . CLC 7
See also CA 37-40R; CAAS 17; CANR 34;
DLB 16

Waldo, E. Hunter
See Sturgeon, Theodore (Hamilton)

Waldo, Edward Hamilton
See Sturgeon, Theodore (Hamilton)

Walker, Alice (Malsenior)
1944- . . . . CLC 5, 6, 9, 19, 27, 46, 58;
BLC; DA; DAB; DAC; DAM MST,
MULT, NOV, POET, POP; SSC 5
See also AAYA 3; BEST 89:4; BW 2;
CA 37-40R; CANR 9, 27, 49;
CDALB 1968-1988; DLB 6, 33, 143;
INT CANR-27; MTCW; SATA 31

Walker, David Harry 1911-1992 . . . . CLC 14
See also CA 1-4R; 137; CANR 1; SATA 8;
SATA-Obit 71

Walker, Edward Joseph 1934-
See Walker, Ted
See also CA 21-24R; CANR 12, 28, 53

Walker, George F.
1947- . . . . CLC 44, 61; DAB; DAC;
DAM MST
See also CA 103; CANR 21, 43; DLB 60

Walker, Joseph A.
1935- . . . . CLC 19; DAM DRAM, MST
See also BW 1; CA 89-92; CANR 26;
DLB 38

Walker, Margaret (Abigail)
1915- . . . . CLC 1, 6; BLC; DAM MULT
See also BW 2; CA 73-76; CANR 26, 54;
DLB 76, 152; MTCW

Walker, Ted . . . . CLC 13
See also Walker, Edward Joseph
See also DLB 40

Wallace, David Foster 1962- . . . . CLC 50
See also CA 132

Wallace, Dexter
See Masters, Edgar Lee

Wallace, (Richard Horatio) Edgar
1875-1932 . . . . TCLC 57
See also CA 115; DLB 70

Wallace, Irving
1916-1990 . . . . . CLC 7, 13; DAM NOV,
POP
See also AITN 1; CA 1-4R; 132; CAAS 1;
CANR 1, 27; INT CANR-27; MTCW

Wallant, Edward Lewis
1926-1962 . . . . CLC 5, 10
See also CA 1-4R; CANR 22; DLB 2, 28,
143; MTCW

Walley, Byron
See Card, Orson Scott

Walpole, Horace 1717-1797 . . . . LC 2
See also DLB 39, 104

Walpole, Hugh (Seymour)
1884-1941 . . . . TCLC 5
See also CA 104; DLB 34

Walser, Martin 1927- . . . . CLC 27
See also CA 57-60; CANR 8, 46; DLB 75,
124

Walser, Robert
1878-1956 . . . . TCLC 18; SSC 20
See also CA 118; DLB 66

Walsh, Jill Paton . . . . CLC 35
See also Paton Walsh, Gillian
See also AAYA 11; CLR 2; DLB 161;
SAAS 3

Walter, Villiam Christian
See Andersen, Hans Christian

Wambaugh, Joseph (Aloysius, Jr.)
1937- . . . . CLC 3, 18; DAM NOV, POP
See also AITN 1; BEST 89:3; CA 33-36R;
CANR 42; DLB 6; DLBY 83; MTCW

Ward, Arthur Henry Sarsfield 1883-1959
See Rohmer, Sax
See also CA 108

Ward, Douglas Turner 1930- . . . . CLC 19
See also BW 1; CA 81-84; CANR 27;
DLB 7, 38

Ward, Mary Augusta
See Ward, Mrs. Humphry

Ward, Mrs. Humphry
1851-1920 . . . . TCLC 55
See also DLB 18

Ward, Peter
See Faust, Frederick (Schiller)

Warhol, Andy 1928(?)-1987 . . . . CLC 20
See also AAYA 12; BEST 89:4; CA 89-92;
121; CANR 34

Warner, Francis (Robert le Plastrier)
1937- . . . . CLC 14
See also CA 53-56; CANR 11

Warner, Marina 1946- . . . . CLC 59
See also CA 65-68; CANR 21, 55

Warner, Rex (Ernest) 1905-1986 . . . . CLC 45
See also CA 89-92; 119; DLB 15

Warner, Susan (Bogert)
1819-1885 . . . . NCLC 31
See also DLB 3, 42

Warner, Sylvia (Constance) Ashton
See Ashton-Warner, Sylvia (Constance)

Warner, Sylvia Townsend
1893-1978 . . . . CLC 7, 19; SSC 23
See also CA 61-64; 77-80; CANR 16;
DLB 34, 139; MTCW

Warren, Mercy Otis 1728-1814 . . . NCLC 13
See also DLB 31

Warren, Robert Penn
1905-1989 . . . . CLC 1, 4, 6, 8, 10, 13, 18,
39, 53, 59; DA; DAB; DAC; DAM MST,
NOV, POET; SSC 4; WLC
See also AITN 1; CA 13-16R; 129;
CANR 10, 47; CDALB 1968-1988;
DLB 2, 48, 152; DLBY 80, 89;
INT CANR-10; MTCW; SATA 46;
SATA-Obit 63

Warshofsky, Isaac
See Singer, Isaac Bashevis

Warton, Thomas
1728-1790 . . . . LC 15; DAM POET
See also DLB 104, 109

Waruk, Kona
See Harris, (Theodore) Wilson

Warung, Price 1855-1911 . . . . TCLC 45

Warwick, Jarvis
See Garner, Hugh

Washington, Alex
See Harris, Mark

Washington, Booker T(aliaferro)
1856-1915 . . . . TCLC 10; BLC;
DAM MULT
See also BW 1; CA 114; 125; SATA 28

Washington, George 1732-1799 . . . . . . LC 25
See also DLB 31

Wassermann, (Karl) Jakob
1873-1934 . . . . TCLC 6
See also CA 104; DLB 66

Wasserstein, Wendy
1950- . . . . CLC 32, 59, 90;
DAM DRAM; DC 4
See also CA 121; 129; CABS 3; CANR 53;
INT 129

Waterhouse, Keith (Spencer)
1929- . . . . CLC 47
See also CA 5-8R; CANR 38; DLB 13, 15;
MTCW

Waters, Frank (Joseph)
1902-1995 . . . . CLC 88
See also CA 5-8R; 149; CAAS 13; CANR 3,
18; DLBY 86

Waters, Roger 1944- . . . . CLC 35

Watkins, Frances Ellen
See Harper, Frances Ellen Watkins

Watkins, Gerrold
See Malzberg, Barry N(athaniel)

Watkins, Gloria 1955(?)-
See hooks, bell
See also BW 2; CA 143

Watkins, Paul 1964- . . . . CLC 55
See also CA 132

Watkins, Vernon Phillips
1906-1967 . . . . CLC 43
See also CA 9-10; 25-28R; CAP 1; DLB 20

Watson, Irving S.
See Mencken, H(enry) L(ouis)

Watson, John H.
See Farmer, Philip Jose

Watson, Richard F.
See Silverberg, Robert

Waugh, Auberon (Alexander) 1939- . . CLC 7
See also CA 45-48; CANR 6, 22; DLB 14

Waugh, Evelyn (Arthur St. John)
1903-1966 . . . . . . CLC 1, 3, 8, 13, 19, 27,
44; DA; DAB; DAC; DAM MST, NOV,
POP; WLC
See also CA 85-88; 25-28R; CANR 22;
CDBLB 1914-1945; DLB 15, 162; MTCW

Waugh, Harriet 1944- . . . . CLC 6
See also CA 85-88; CANR 22

Ways, C. R.
See Blount, Roy (Alton), Jr.

Waystaff, Simon
See Swift, Jonathan

Webb, (Martha) Beatrice (Potter)
1858-1943 . . . . TCLC 22
See also Potter, Beatrice
See also CA 117

Webb, Charles (Richard) 1939- . . . . . . CLC 7
See also CA 25-28R

Webb, James H(enry), Jr. 1946- . . . . CLC 22
See also CA 81-84

Webb, Mary (Gladys Meredith)
1881-1927 .... **TCLC 24**
See also CA 123; DLB 34

Webb, Mrs. Sidney
See Webb, (Martha) Beatrice (Potter)

Webb, Phyllis 1927-.............. **CLC 18**
See also CA 104; CANR 23; DLB 53

Webb, Sidney (James)
1859-1947 .... **TCLC 22**
See also CA 117

Webber, Andrew Lloyd............. **CLC 21**
See also Lloyd Webber, Andrew

Weber, Lenora Mattingly
1895-1971 .... **CLC 12**
See also CA 19-20; 29-32R; CAP 1;
SATA 2; SATA-Obit 26

Weber, Max 1864-1920 .... **TCLC 69**
See also CA 109

Webster, John
1579(?)-1634(?) ...... **LC 33; DA; DAB;**
DAC; DAM DRAM, MST; DC 2; WLC
See also CDBLB Before 1660; DLB 58

Webster, Noah 1758-1843 .... **NCLC 30**

Wedekind, (Benjamin) Frank(lin)
1864-1918 ...... **TCLC 7; DAM DRAM**
See also CA 104; 153; DLB 118

Weidman, Jerome 1913-............ **CLC 7**
See also AITN 2; CA 1-4R; CANR 1;
DLB 28

Weil, Simone (Adolphine)
1909-1943 .... **TCLC 23**
See also CA 117

Weinstein, Nathan
See West, Nathanael

Weinstein, Nathan von Wallenstein
See West, Nathanael

Weir, Peter (Lindsay) 1944- .... **CLC 20**
See also CA 113; 123

Weiss, Peter (Ulrich)
1916-1982 .... **CLC 3, 15, 51;**
DAM DRAM
See also CA 45-48; 106; CANR 3; DLB 69,
124

Weiss, Theodore (Russell)
1916- .... **CLC 3, 8, 14**
See also CA 9-12R; CAAS 2; CANR 46;
DLB 5

Welch, (Maurice) Denton
1915-1948 .... **TCLC 22**
See also CA 121; 148

Welch, James
1940- ..... **CLC 6, 14, 52; DAM MULT,**
POP
See also CA 85-88; CANR 42; DLB 175;
NNAL

Weldon, Fay
1933- .... **CLC 6, 9, 11, 19, 36, 59;**
DAM POP
See also CA 21-24R; CANR 16, 46;
CDBLB 1960 to Present; DLB 14;
INT CANR-16; MTCW

Wellek, Rene 1903-1995.......... **CLC 28**
See also CA 5-8R; 150; CAAS 7; CANR 8;
DLB 63; INT CANR-8

Weller, Michael 1942- .... **CLC 10, 53**
See also CA 85-88

Weller, Paul 1958-.............. **CLC 26**

Wellershoff, Dieter 1925-........ **CLC 46**
See also CA 89-92; CANR 16, 37

Welles, (George) Orson
1915-1985 .... **CLC 20, 80**
See also CA 93-96; 117

Wellman, Mac 1945- .... **CLC 65**

Wellman, Manly Wade 1903-1986 .. **CLC 49**
See also CA 1-4R; 118; CANR 6, 16, 44;
SATA 6; SATA-Obit 47

Wells, Carolyn 1869(?)-1942 ..... **TCLC 35**
See also CA 113; DLB 11

Wells, H(erbert) G(eorge)
1866-1946 ...... **TCLC 6, 12, 19; DA;**
DAB; DAC; DAM MST, NOV; SSC 6;
WLC
See also AAYA 18; CA 110; 121;
CDBLB 1914-1945; DLB 34, 70, 156;
MTCW; SATA 20

Wells, Rosemary 1943-............ **CLC 12**
See also AAYA 13; CA 85-88; CANR 48;
CLR 16; MAICYA; SAAS 1; SATA 18,
69

Welty, Eudora
1909- ...... **CLC 1, 2, 5, 14, 22, 33; DA;**
DAB; DAC; DAM MST, NOV; SSC 1;
WLC
See also CA 9-12R; CABS 1; CANR 32;
CDALB 1941-1968; DLB 2, 102, 143;
DLBD 12; DLBY 87; MTCW

Wen I-to 1899-1946 .... **TCLC 28**

Wentworth, Robert
See Hamilton, Edmond

Werfel, Franz (V.) 1890-1945 ...... **TCLC 8**
See also CA 104; DLB 81, 124

Wergeland, Henrik Arnold
1808-1845 .... **NCLC 5**

Wersba, Barbara 1932-............ **CLC 30**
See also AAYA 2; CA 29-32R; CANR 16,
38; CLR 3; DLB 52; JRDA; MAICYA;
SAAS 2; SATA 1, 58

Wertmueller, Lina 1928- .... **CLC 16**
See also CA 97-100; CANR 39

Wescott, Glenway 1901-1987....... **CLC 13**
See also CA 13-16R; 121; CANR 23;
DLB 4, 9, 102

Wesker, Arnold
1932- .... **CLC 3, 5, 42; DAB;**
DAM DRAM
See also CA 1-4R; CAAS 7; CANR 1, 33;
CDBLB 1960 to Present; DLB 13;
MTCW

Wesley, Richard (Errol) 1945-....... **CLC 7**
See also BW 1; CA 57-60; CANR 27;
DLB 38

Wessel, Johan Herman 1742-1785 .... **LC 7**

West, Anthony (Panther)
1914-1987 .... **CLC 50**
See also CA 45-48; 124; CANR 3, 19;
DLB 15

West, C. P.
See Wodehouse, P(elham) G(renville)

West, (Mary) Jessamyn
1902-1984 .... **CLC 7, 17**
See also CA 9-12R; 112; CANR 27; DLB 6;
DLBY 84; MTCW; SATA-Obit 37

West, Morris L(anglo) 1916-..... **CLC 6, 33**
See also CA 5-8R; CANR 24, 49; MTCW

West, Nathanael
1903-1940 .... **TCLC 1, 14, 44; SSC 16**
See also CA 104; 125; CDALB 1929-1941;
DLB 4, 9, 28; MTCW

West, Owen
See Koontz, Dean R(ay)

West, Paul 1930- .... **CLC 7, 14, 96**
See also CA 13-16R; CAAS 7; CANR 22,
53; DLB 14; INT CANR-22

West, Rebecca 1892-1983 .. **CLC 7, 9, 31, 50**
See also CA 5-8R; 109; CANR 19; DLB 36;
DLBY 83; MTCW

Westall, Robert (Atkinson)
1929-1993 .... **CLC 17**
See also AAYA 12; CA 69-72; 141;
CANR 18; CLR 13; JRDA; MAICYA;
SAAS 2; SATA 23, 69; SATA-Obit 75

Westlake, Donald E(dwin)
1933- .... **CLC 7, 33; DAM POP**
See also CA 17-20R; CAAS 13; CANR 16,
44; INT CANR-16

Westmacott, Mary
See Christie, Agatha (Mary Clarissa)

Weston, Allen
See Norton, Andre

Wetcheek, J. L.
See Feuchtwanger, Lion

Wetering, Janwillem van de
See van de Wetering, Janwillem

Wetherell, Elizabeth
See Warner, Susan (Bogert)

Whale, James 1889-1957......... **TCLC 63**

Whalen, Philip 1923- .... **CLC 6, 29**
See also CA 9-12R; CANR 5, 39; DLB 16

Wharton, Edith (Newbold Jones)
1862-1937 ...... **TCLC 3, 9, 27, 53; DA;**
DAB; DAC; DAM MST, NOV; SSC 6;
WLC
See also CA 104; 132; CDALB 1865-1917;
DLB 4, 9, 12, 78; DLBD 13; MTCW

Wharton, James
See Mencken, H(enry) L(ouis)

Wharton, William (a pseudonym)
.... **CLC 18, 37**
See also CA 93-96; DLBY 80; INT 93-96

Wheatley (Peters), Phillis
1754(?)-1784 .... **LC 3; BLC; DA; DAC;**
DAM MST, MULT, POET; PC 3; WLC
See also CDALB 1640-1865; DLB 31, 50

Wheelock, John Hall 1886-1978.... **CLC 14**
See also CA 13-16R; 77-80; CANR 14;
DLB 45

White, E(lwyn) B(rooks)
1899-1985 .. **CLC 10, 34, 39; DAM POP**
See also AITN 2; CA 13-16R; 116;
CANR 16, 37; CLR 1, 21; DLB 11, 22;
MAICYA; MTCW; SATA 2, 29;
SATA-Obit 44

White, Edmund (Valentine III)
1940- .... **CLC 27; DAM POP**
See also AAYA 7; CA 45-48; CANR 3, 19,
36; MTCW

White, Patrick (Victor Martindale)
1912-1990 .. **CLC 3, 4, 5, 7, 9, 18, 65, 69**
See also CA 81-84; 132; CANR 43; MTCW

White, Phyllis Dorothy James 1920-
See James, P. D.
See also CA 21-24R; CANR 17, 43;
DAM POP; MTCW

White, T(erence) H(anbury)
1906-1964 .... **CLC 30**
See also CA 73-76; CANR 37; DLB 160;
JRDA; MAICYA; SATA 12

White, Terence de Vere
1912-1994 .... **CLC 49**
See also CA 49-52; 145; CANR 3

White, Walter F(rancis)
1893-1955 .... **TCLC 15**
See also White, Walter
See also BW 1; CA 115; 124; DLB 51

White, William Hale 1831-1913
See Rutherford, Mark
See also CA 121

Whitehead, E(dward) A(nthony)
1933- .... **CLC 5**
See also CA 65-68

Whitemore, Hugh (John) 1936- ..... **CLC 37**
See also CA 132; INT 132

Whitman, Sarah Helen (Power)
1803-1878 .... **NCLC 19**
See also DLB 1

Whitman, Walt(er)
1819-1892 ..... **NCLC 4, 31; DA; DAB;**
DAC; DAM MST, POET; PC 3; WLC
See also CDALB 1640-1865; DLB 3, 64;
SATA 20

Whitney, Phyllis A(yame)
1903- .... **CLC 42; DAM POP**
See also AITN 2; BEST 90:3; CA 1-4R;
CANR 3, 25, 38; JRDA; MAICYA;
SATA 1, 30

Whittemore, (Edward) Reed (Jr.)
1919- .... **CLC 4**
See also CA 9-12R; CAAS 8; CANR 4;
DLB 5

Whittier, John Greenleaf
1807-1892 .... **NCLC 8, 59**
See also DLB 1

Whittlebot, Hernia
See Coward, Noel (Peirce)

Wicker, Thomas Grey 1926-
See Wicker, Tom
See also CA 65-68; CANR 21, 46

Wicker, Tom .... **CLC 7**
See also Wicker, Thomas Grey

Wideman, John Edgar
1941- .... **CLC 5, 34, 36, 67; BLC;**
DAM MULT
See also BW 2; CA 85-88; CANR 14, 42;
DLB 33, 143

Wiebe, Rudy (Henry)
1934- .... **CLC 6, 11, 14; DAC;**
DAM MST
See also CA 37-40R; CANR 42; DLB 60

Wieland, Christoph Martin
1733-1813 .... **NCLC 17**
See also DLB 97

Wiene, Robert 1881-1938 .... **TCLC 56**

Wieners, John 1934- .... **CLC 7**
See also CA 13-16R; DLB 16

Wiesel, Elie(zer)
1928- ...... **CLC 3, 5, 11, 37; DA; DAB;**
DAC; DAM MST, NOV
See also AAYA 7; AITN 1; CA 5-8R;
CAAS 4; CANR 8, 40; DLB 83;
DLBY 87; INT CANR-8; MTCW;
SATA 56

Wiggins, Marianne 1947- .... **CLC 57**
See also BEST 89:3; CA 130

Wight, James Alfred 1916-
See Herriot, James
See also CA 77-80; SATA 55;
SATA-Brief 44

Wilbur, Richard (Purdy)
1921- ... **CLC 3, 6, 9, 14, 53; DA; DAB;**
DAC; DAM MST, POET
See also CA 1-4R; CABS 2; CANR 2, 29;
DLB 5, 169; INT CANR-29; MTCW;
SATA 9

Wild, Peter 1940- .... **CLC 14**
See also CA 37-40R; DLB 5

Wilde, Oscar (Fingal O'Flahertie Wills)
1854(?)-1900 .... **TCLC 1, 8, 23, 41; DA;**
DAB; DAC; DAM DRAM, MST, NOV;
SSC 11; WLC
See also CA 104; 119; CDBLB 1890-1914;
DLB 10, 19, 34, 57, 141, 156; SATA 24

Wilder, Billy .... **CLC 20**
See also Wilder, Samuel
See also DLB 26

Wilder, Samuel 1906-
See Wilder, Billy
See also CA 89-92

Wilder, Thornton (Niven)
1897-1975 ...... **CLC 1, 5, 6, 10, 15, 35,**
82; DA; DAB; DAC; DAM DRAM,
MST, NOV; DC 1; WLC
See also AITN 2; CA 13-16R; 61-64;
CANR 40; DLB 4, 7, 9; MTCW

Wilding, Michael 1942- .... **CLC 73**
See also CA 104; CANR 24, 49

Wiley, Richard 1944- .... **CLC 44**
See also CA 121; 129

Wilhelm, Kate .... **CLC 7**
See also Wilhelm, Katie Gertrude
See also AAYA 20; CAAS 5; DLB 8;
INT CANR-17

Wilhelm, Katie Gertrude 1928-
See Wilhelm, Kate
See also CA 37-40R; CANR 17, 36; MTCW

Wilkins, Mary
See Freeman, Mary Eleanor Wilkins

Willard, Nancy 1936- .... **CLC 7, 37**
See also CA 89-92; CANR 10, 39; CLR 5;
DLB 5, 52; MAICYA; MTCW;
SATA 37, 71; SATA-Brief 30

Williams, C(harles) K(enneth)
1936- .... **CLC 33, 56; DAM POET**
See also CA 37-40R; CAAS 26; CANR 57;
DLB 5

Williams, Charles
See Collier, James L(incoln)

Williams, Charles (Walter Stansby)
1886-1945 .... **TCLC 1, 11**
See also CA 104; DLB 100, 153

Williams, (George) Emlyn
1905-1987 ...... **CLC 15; DAM DRAM**
See also CA 104; 123; CANR 36; DLB 10,
77; MTCW

Williams, Hugo 1942- .... **CLC 42**
See also CA 17-20R; CANR 45; DLB 40

Williams, J. Walker
See Wodehouse, P(elham) G(renville)

Williams, John A(lfred)
1925- ... **CLC 5, 13; BLC; DAM MULT**
See also BW 2; CA 53-56; CAAS 3;
CANR 6, 26, 51; DLB 2, 33;
INT CANR-6

Williams, Jonathan (Chamberlain)
1929- .... **CLC 13**
See also CA 9-12R; CAAS 12; CANR 8;
DLB 5

Williams, Joy 1944- .... **CLC 31**
See also CA 41-44R; CANR 22, 48

Williams, Norman 1952- .... **CLC 39**
See also CA 118

Williams, Sherley Anne
1944- ..... **CLC 89; BLC; DAM MULT,**
POET
See also BW 2; CA 73-76; CANR 25;
DLB 41; INT CANR-25; SATA 78

Williams, Shirley
See Williams, Sherley Anne

Williams, Tennessee
1911-1983 ..... **CLC 1, 2, 5, 7, 8, 11, 15,**
19, 30, 39, 45, 71; DA; DAB; DAC;
DAM DRAM, MST; DC 4; WLC
See also AITN 1, 2; CA 5-8R; 108;
CABS 3; CANR 31; CDALB 1941-1968;
DLB 7; DLBD 4; DLBY 83; MTCW

Williams, Thomas (Alonzo)
1926-1990 .... **CLC 14**
See also CA 1-4R; 132; CANR 2

Williams, William C.
See Williams, William Carlos

Williams, William Carlos
1883-1963 .... **CLC 1, 2, 5, 9, 13, 22, 42,**
67; DA; DAB; DAC; DAM MST, POET;
PC 7
See also CA 89-92; CANR 34;
CDALB 1917-1929; DLB 4, 16, 54, 86;
MTCW

Williamson, David (Keith) 1942- .... **CLC 56**
See also CA 103; CANR 41

Williamson, Ellen Douglas 1905-1984
See Douglas, Ellen
See also CA 17-20R; 114; CANR 39

Williamson, Jack .... **CLC 29**
See also Williamson, John Stewart
See also CAAS 8; DLB 8

Williamson, John Stewart 1908-
See Williamson, Jack
See also CA 17-20R; CANR 23

Willie, Frederick
See Lovecraft, H(oward) P(hillips)

Willingham, Calder (Baynard, Jr.)
1922-1995 .... CLC **5, 51**
See also CA 5-8R; 147; CANR 3; DLB 2,
44; MTCW

Willis, Charles
See Clarke, Arthur C(harles)

Willy
See Colette, (Sidonie-Gabrielle)

Willy, Colette
See Colette, (Sidonie-Gabrielle)

Wilson, A(ndrew) N(orman) 1950- .. CLC **33**
See also CA 112; 122; DLB 14, 155

Wilson, Angus (Frank Johnstone)
1913-1991 .. CLC **2, 3, 5, 25, 34; SSC 21**
See also CA 5-8R; 134; CANR 21; DLB 15,
139, 155; MTCW

Wilson, August
1945- .... CLC **39, 50, 63; BLC; DA;**
DAB; DAC; DAM DRAM, MST,
MULT; DC 2
See also AAYA 16; BW 2; CA 115; 122;
CANR 42, 54; MTCW

Wilson, Brian 1942- .... CLC **12**

Wilson, Colin 1931- .... CLC **3, 14**
See also CA 1-4R; CAAS 5; CANR 1, 22,
33; DLB 14; MTCW

Wilson, Dirk
See Pohl, Frederik

Wilson, Edmund
1895-1972 .... CLC **1, 2, 3, 8, 24**
See also CA 1-4R; 37-40R; CANR 1, 46;
DLB 63; MTCW

Wilson, Ethel Davis (Bryant)
1888(?)-1980 .... CLC **13; DAC;**
DAM POET
See also CA 102; DLB 68; MTCW

Wilson, John 1785-1854......... NCLC **5**

Wilson, John (Anthony) Burgess 1917-1993
See Burgess, Anthony
See also CA 1-4R; 143; CANR 2, 46; DAC;
DAM NOV; MTCW

Wilson, Lanford
1937- ..... CLC **7, 14, 36; DAM DRAM**
See also CA 17-20R; CABS 3; CANR 45;
DLB 7

Wilson, Robert M. 1944-........ CLC **7, 9**
See also CA 49-52; CANR 2, 41; MTCW

Wilson, Robert McLiam 1964- ..... CLC **59**
See also CA 132

Wilson, Sloan 1920-.............. CLC **32**
See also CA 1-4R; CANR 1, 44

Wilson, Snoo 1948-.............. CLC **33**
See also CA 69-72

Wilson, William S(mith) 1932- ..... CLC **49**
See also CA 81-84

Winchilsea, Anne (Kingsmill) Finch Counte
1661-1720 .... LC **3**

Windham, Basil
See Wodehouse, P(elham) G(renville)

Wingrove, David (John) 1954-...... CLC **68**
See also CA 133

Winters, Janet Lewis .... CLC **41**
See also Lewis, Janet
See also DLBY 87

Winters, (Arthur) Yvor
1900-1968 .... CLC **4, 8, 32**
See also CA 11-12; 25-28R; CAP 1;
DLB 48; MTCW

Winterson, Jeanette
1959- .... CLC **64; DAM POP**
See also CA 136

Winthrop, John 1588-1649......... LC **31**
See also DLB 24, 30

Wiseman, Frederick 1930-........ CLC **20**

Wister, Owen 1860-1938 .... TCLC **21**
See also CA 108; DLB 9, 78; SATA 62

Witkacy
See Witkiewicz, Stanislaw Ignacy

Witkiewicz, Stanislaw Ignacy
1885-1939 .... TCLC **8**
See also CA 105

Wittgenstein, Ludwig (Josef Johann)
1889-1951 .... TCLC **59**
See also CA 113

Wittig, Monique 1935(?)-........ CLC **22**
See also CA 116; 135; DLB 83

Wittlin, Jozef 1896-1976 .... CLC **25**
See also CA 49-52; 65-68; CANR 3

Wodehouse, P(elham) G(renville)
1881-1975 ... CLC **1, 2, 5, 10, 22; DAB;**
DAC; DAM NOV; SSC 2
See also AITN 2; CA 45-48; 57-60;
CANR 3, 33; CDBLB 1914-1945;
DLB 34, 162; MTCW; SATA 22

Woiwode, L.
See Woiwode, Larry (Alfred)

Woiwode, Larry (Alfred) 1941-... CLC **6, 10**
See also CA 73-76; CANR 16; DLB 6;
INT CANR-16

Wojciechowska, Maia (Teresa)
1927- .... CLC **26**
See also AAYA 8; CA 9-12R; CANR 4, 41;
CLR 1; JRDA; MAICYA; SAAS 1;
SATA 1, 28, 83

Wolf, Christa 1929- .... CLC **14, 29, 58**
See also CA 85-88; CANR 45; DLB 75;
MTCW

Wolfe, Gene (Rodman)
1931- .... CLC **25; DAM POP**
See also CA 57-60; CAAS 9; CANR 6, 32;
DLB 8

Wolfe, George C. 1954-........... CLC **49**
See also CA 149

Wolfe, Thomas (Clayton)
1900-1938 ..... TCLC **4, 13, 29, 61; DA;**
DAB; DAC; DAM MST, NOV; WLC
See also CA 104; 132; CDALB 1929-1941;
DLB 9, 102; DLBD 2; DLBY 85; MTCW

Wolfe, Thomas Kennerly, Jr. 1931-
See Wolfe, Tom
See also CA 13-16R; CANR 9, 33;
DAM POP; INT CANR-9; MTCW

Wolfe, Tom .... CLC **1, 2, 9, 15, 35, 51**
See also Wolfe, Thomas Kennerly, Jr.
See also AAYA 8; AITN 2; BEST 89:1;
DLB 152

Wolff, Geoffrey (Ansell) 1937- ..... CLC **41**
See also CA 29-32R; CANR 29, 43

Wolff, Sonia
See Levitin, Sonia (Wolff)

Wolff, Tobias (Jonathan Ansell)
1945- .... CLC **39, 64**
See also AAYA 16; BEST 90:2; CA 114;
117; CAAS 22; CANR 54; DLB 130;
INT 117

Wolfram von Eschenbach
c. 1170-c. 1220 .... CMLC **5**
See also DLB 138

Wolitzer, Hilma 1930-............ CLC **17**
See also CA 65-68; CANR 18, 40;
INT CANR-18; SATA 31

Wollstonecraft, Mary 1759-1797...... LC **5**
See also CDBLB 1789-1832; DLB 39, 104,
158

Wonder, Stevie .... CLC **12**
See also Morris, Steveland Judkins

Wong, Jade Snow 1922-........... CLC **17**
See also CA 109

Woodcott, Keith
See Brunner, John (Kilian Houston)

Woodruff, Robert W.
See Mencken, H(enry) L(ouis)

Woolf, (Adeline) Virginia
1882-1941 .... TCLC **1, 5, 20, 43, 56;**
DA; DAB; DAC; DAM MST, NOV;
SSC 7; WLC
See also CA 104; 130; CDBLB 1914-1945;
DLB 36, 100, 162; DLBD 10; MTCW

Woollcott, Alexander (Humphreys)
1887-1943 .... TCLC **5**
See also CA 105; DLB 29

Woolrich, Cornell 1903-1968....... CLC **77**
See also Hopley-Woolrich, Cornell George

Wordsworth, Dorothy
1771-1855 .... NCLC **25**
See also DLB 107

Wordsworth, William
1770-1850 .... NCLC **12, 38; DA; DAB;**
DAC; DAM MST, POET; PC 4; WLC
See also CDBLB 1789-1832; DLB 93, 107

Wouk, Herman
1915- .. CLC **1, 9, 38; DAM NOV, POP**
See also CA 5-8R; CANR 6, 33; DLBY 82;
INT CANR-6; MTCW

Wright, Charles (Penzel, Jr.)
1935- .... CLC **6, 13, 28**
See also CA 29-32R; CAAS 7; CANR 23,
36; DLB 165; DLBY 82; MTCW

Wright, Charles Stevenson
1932- .... CLC **49; BLC 3;**
DAM MULT, POET
See also BW 1; CA 9-12R; CANR 26;
DLB 33

Wright, Jack R.
See Harris, Mark

Wright, James (Arlington)
1927-1980 .... CLC **3, 5, 10, 28;**
DAM POET
See also AITN 2; CA 49-52; 97-100;
CANR 4, 34; DLB 5, 169; MTCW

Wright, Judith (Arandell)
1915- .... CLC **11, 53; PC 14**
See also CA 13-16R; CANR 31; MTCW;
SATA 14

Zuckmayer, Carl 1896-1977........ **CLC 18**
  See also CA 69-72; DLB 56, 124

Zuk, Georges
  See Skelton, Robin

Zukofsky, Louis
    1904-1978 .... **CLC 1, 2, 4, 7, 11, 18;**
                  DAM POET; PC 11
  See also CA 9-12R; 77-80; CANR 39;
    DLB 5, 165; MTCW

Zweig, Paul 1935-1984........ **CLC 34, 42**
  See also CA 85-88; 113

Zweig, Stefan 1881-1942 .... **TCLC 17**
  See also CA 112; DLB 81, 118

Zwingli, Huldreich 1484-1531....... **LC 37**

Cumulative Nationality Index

ALGERIAN
Camus, Albert **2**

AMERICAN
Baldwin, James (Arthur) **1**
Baraka, Amiri **6**
Brown, William Wells **1**
Bullins, Ed **6**
Chase, Mary (Coyle) **1**
Childress, Alice **4**
Chin, Frank (Chew Jr.) **7**
Fuller, Charles (H. Jr.) **1**
Gray, Spalding **7**
Hansberry, Lorraine (Vivian) **2**
Hellman, Lillian (Florence) **1**
Henley, Beth **6**
Hughes, (James) Langston **3**
Hwang, David Henry **4**
Kennedy, Adrienne (Lita) **5**
Mamet, David (Alan) **4**
Mann, Emily **7**
Miller, Arthur **1**
Odets, Clifford **6**
Shange, Ntozake **3**
Shepard, Sam **5**
Sheridan, Richard Brinsley **1**
Wasserstein, Wendy **4**
Wilder, Thornton (Niven) **1**
Williams, Tennessee **4**
Wilson, August **2**
Zindel, Paul **5**

AUSTRIAN
Hofmannsthal, Hugo von **4**

BARBADIAN
Kennedy, Adrienne (Lita) **5**

CZECH
Capek, Karel **1**
Havel, Vaclav **6**

ENGLISH
Beaumont, Francis **6**
Behn, Aphra **4**
Churchill, Caryl **5**
Congreve, William **2**
Dryden, John **3**
Fletcher, John **6**
Jonson, Ben(jamin) **4**
Kyd, Thomas **3**
Lyly, John **7**
Marlowe, Christopher **1**
Middleton, Thomas **5**
Orton, Joe **3**
Shaffer, Peter (Levin) **7**
Stoppard, Tom **6**
Webster, John **2**

FRENCH
Beaumarchais, Pierre-Augustin Caron de **4**
Camus, Albert **2**
Dumas, Alexandre **1**
Marivaux, Pierre Carlet de Chamblain de **7**
Sartre, Jean-Paul **3**
Scribe, (Augustin) Eugene **5**

GERMAN
Brecht, Bertolt **3**

GREEK
Aristophanes **2**
Euripides **4**
Menander **3**
Sophocles **1**

IRISH
Synge, (Edmund) J(ohn) M(illington) **2**

ITALIAN
Pirandello, Luigi **5**

JAPANESE
Mishima, Yukio **1**
Zeami **7**

NIGERIAN
Clark, John Pepper **5**
Soyinka, Wole **2**

NORWEGIAN
Ibsen, Henrik (Johan) **2**

ROMAN
Seneca, Lucius Annaeus **5**
Terence **7**

RUSSIAN
Gogol, Nikolai (Vasilyevich) **1**
Turgenev, Ivan **7**

SOUTH AFRICAN
Fugard, (Harold) Athol **3**

SPANISH
Calderon de la Barca, Pedro **3**
Garcia Lorca, Federico **2**

ST. LUCIAN
Walcott, Derek (Alton) **7**

DC Cumulative Title Index

Title Index